Completely Queer

COMPLETELY QUEER

THE GAY AND LESBIAN ENCYCLOPEDIA

STEVE HOGAN AND LEE HUDSON

HENRY HOLT AND COMPANY
NEW YORK

Henry Holt and Company, Inc./*Publishers since 1866*
115 West 18th Street/New York, New York 10011

Henry Holt® is a registered trademark of Henry Holt
and Company, Inc.

Published in Canada by Fitzhenry & Whiteside Ltd.,
195 Allstate Parkway, Markham, Ontario L3R 4T8.

Library of Congress Cataloging-in-Publication Data
Hogan, Steve.
Completely queer : the Gay and Lesbian encyclopedia /
by Steve Hogan and Lee Hudson.
p. cm.
Includes bibliographical references and index.
ISBN 0-8050-3629-6 (alk. paper)
1. Gays—Encyclopedias. 2. Gay men—Encyclopedias.
3. Lesbians—Encyclopedias. I. Hudson, Lee.
II. Title. III. Series.
HQ75.H63 1998
305.9′0664—dc20 96-22676

Henry Holt books are available for special promotions
and premiums. For details contact: Director, Special Markets.

First Edition 1998
Designed by Brian Mulligan

Printed in the United States of America
All first editions are printed on acid-free paper. ∞

10 9 8 7 6 5 4 3 2 1

To those who first
took the risk of remembering:
the grassroots lesbian
and gay archives
and oral history projects.

CONTENTS

ACKNOWLEDGMENTS

First, we respectfully acknowledge the hundreds of lesbian, gay, bisexual, and heterosexual scholars who have illuminated gay and lesbian life, transforming it from a "twilight world" to one visible enough to be surveyed in an encyclopedia. And we, like those scholars, in turn owe an inestimable debt to community lesbian and gay archives and oral history projects. Knowing that a people's history is fundamental to their sense of dignity and humanity, these community archives preserved books, documents, oral histories, and ephemera at a time when most mainstream libraries and archives dismissed them. The Lesbian Herstory Archives was an especially valuable resource for this volume.

We also thank the many activists, scholars, writers, and artists who answered questions and guided us to sources of information, especially J. C. Barone, Terry Boggis, Mimi Bolin, Pat Colley, Honey Lee Cottrell, Diana Davies, John DeSantis, Charles Diago, Katy Doran, Allen Ellenzweig, Nancy Falconer, Barbara Gittings, Paula Grant, Stephen Greco, Pam Haller, Barbara Hopson, Stephen Hunt, Sara Karon, Jonathan Ned Katz, Gregory King, Zan Knudson, Marie Kuda, Kay Tobin Lahusen, the staff of *Lambda Book Report*, Jennifer Lee, Stefan Lynch, Sheila McLaughlin, Lou Messina, Stephen O. Murray, Queen Alison Murray, Lillian Negron, Catherine Odette, Connie Panzarino, Jane Rule, Boden Sandstrom, Matt Sartwell, Judith Schwarz, Barbara Smith, Benjamin Stilp, Polly Thistlethwaite, Ginny Vida, Lisa Vogel, Sloan Wiesen, and Fran Winant.

Morgan Gwenwald and Saskia Scheffer, the encyclopedia's photographic researchers, respectively made major contributions to the finished work, as did Brenda Currin, our primary research assistant. In addition, Gary Newman, and Ron Mandelbaum of Photofest provided invaluable assistance in finding photos and illustrations.

For her crucial insights and unflagging support and love throughout this project, Lee Hudson thanks Joan Nestle. Without Nancy Dyer, Alex Fraser, Erik Harrington, Steve MacDougall, and Susan Waggoner, Steve Hogan would never have completed his part of this sometimes exasperating project.

We also wish to express our gratitude to Patty Otis Abel, Charles Busch, Adrian Danzig, Anne Downes, Robert Downes, Candice Dunn, Cambrea Ezell, Stephen Frommer, Robyn Goodman, Anne-Marie Hedge, Doris Hogan, John Hogan, Stephen Holden, Richard L. Hudson, Ritsu Katsumata, Irina Aleksandrovna Kronrod, James Lecesne, Pierre-Jude Légaré, Armistead Maupin, Ann Jackson Nakano, Serena Nanda, Robin Romeo, Rebecca Reed Shanor, Masa Shibusawa, Payton Silver, Stafford Smith, Jay Sullivan, Boris Thomas, Vivian Ubell, Phyllis Wells, Beverly Whitaker-Long, and Peter Wright.

And finally, we thank our literary agent, Bob Markel; our editors Mary Kay Linge, Ken Wright, Kevin Ohe, and Darcy Tromanhauser; and our gifted, invariably accurate copy editor, Trent Duffy.

After all this help and support, any errors that remain in the encyclopedia are the authors' own.

Illustration Credits

The Advocate: page 325
Prinny Alavi: page 93
AP Wide World Photos: page 185, 486
Archive Photos: page 65, 327, 465
Alison Bechdel: page 147
JEB (Joan E. Biren): pages 8, 17 (top), 47, 87, 225, 233, 258, 266, 393 (top), 402
Paul Cadmus: page 115
J. C. Collins: page 116
Honey Lee Cottrell: page 219
Tee A. Corinne: pages 24, 43, 153, 187, 255, 334, 429
Diana Davies, the NewYork Public Library: pages 240, 346, 351, 477
Diane DiMassa: page 147
Betty Fairbank: page 482
Susan Fleishmann: page 415
Courtesy of Barney Frank: page 224
Courtesy of Fox: page 594
Robert Giard: page 509
Courtesy of the Estate of Duncan Grant: page 520
Paula Grant: page 369
Ann Grifalcone, courtesy of the Literary Estate of May Swenson: page 529
Jim Gruber: page 383
Morgan Gwenwald: pages 17 (bottom), 36, 42, 79, 108, 129, 135, 145, 195, 253, 268, 273, 332, 345, 362, 381, 408, 420, 491, 508, 587
William Jacobellis: page 232
Courtesy of the Kinsey Institute: pages 303, 373, 578
Kathryn Kirk: pages 237, 238
Carolina Kroon: pages 71 (bottom), 170, 186, 360, 492, 522
Kay Tobin Lahusen: pages 16, 31, 96, 230, 322, 481, 537 (top)
Bettye Lane: pages 104, 234, 485
Courtesy of the Lesbian Herstory Archives: pages 66, 173, 280, 339, 340, 422, 433, 446 (bottom), 461, 503, 527, 539; the Mabel Hampton Collection, 112, 113 (Taylor); the Bubbles Kent Collection, 70, 241; Irene Kloepfer Collection, 396
Library of Congress: page 216
Joan Marcus: page 335
Andrea Natalie: page 504
National Portrait Gallery: page 263
Serena Nanda: page 517
Carol L. Newsom: page 411
Esther Newton Collection: page 215
New York Public Library Picture Collection: pages 11, 33, 45, 82, 84, 94, 102, 122, 123, 133, 141, 161 (bottom), 164, 168, 182, 202, 227, 262, 270, 281, 283, 285, 386, 390, 471, 480, 493, 495, 510, 520, 535, 541, 554, 558, 561, 573, 576, 581, 596
Alvin Orloff: page 192
Photofest: pages 7, 20, 26, 38, 71 (top), 73, 127, 156, 190, 206, 208, 209, 218, 248, 265, 286, 287, 288, 289, 293, 311, 313, 316 (Photographer: Michael O'Neill), 333 (Photographer: Gene Bagnato), 353, 372, 384, 397, 401, 403, 416, 432, 514, 515, 518, 532, 537 (bottom), 540, 562, 569, 589
The Christopher Rage Collection: pages 159, 242, 393 (bottom), 445, 502
Courtesy of the San Francisco Gay and Lesbian Historical Society: 326 (Photographer: Walter Blumoff;
Saskia Scheffer: pages 5, 158, 160, 410, 450 (top and bottom), 470, 497, 524, 545
Pearl Schwartz, Courtesy of the Literary Estate of May Swenson: page 90
Staten Island Historical Society: page 51
Jay Sullivan: page 247
Tom of Finland Foundation: pages 76, 139, 161 (top), 507, 544
Courtesy of Lisa Vogel: page 392
Randy Wicker Collection: page 575
Courtesy of Rex Wockner: 584
Women of Achievement: page 80

Every effort has been made to trace the copyright holders of material reproduced in this book. The authors and publisher request that any copyright holder not listed here contact the publisher so that due acknowledgment may appear in subsequent editions.

Introduction

They were regular in being gay, they learned little things that are things in being gay, they learned many little things that are things in being gay, they were gay every day, they were regular, they were gay, they were gay the same length of time every day, they were gay, they were quite regularly gay.

from Gertrude Stein's "Miss Furr and Miss Skeene" (1922)

Who are gay people? Where have we been in history? And most important, What might we be for?

Harry Hay (c. 1950)

"They asked me if I was homosexual or heterosexual, and I said, 'Baby, I'm just sexual.' "

from Irving Wallace's The Seven Minutes *(1971)*

Homosexuality has been around at least as long as heterosexuality. "Faggots" and "dykes," in hundreds of vernacular equivalents, have probably existed since whenever people first started categorizing themselves by sexual tastes. "Femmes" and "butches" and other rebels against gender have an even longer history. But "gays and lesbians" are comparative newborns, as much a 20th-century phenomenon as rock stars and baby boomers.

Completely Queer: The Gay and Lesbian Encyclopedia is a concise guide to that phenomenon. It is not an encyclopedia of "homosexuality," a word so broad in meaning it can refer to forms of plant reproduction as well as behavior common among the "straight" inmates of prisons. Rather, it is an attempt, in the original meaning of the word "encyclopedia," to *encircle* the learning amassed to date on a group of men and women who have chosen, mostly in the West and mostly in the last three decades of the 20th century, to think of themselves as gay and lesbian.

The main focus of *Completely Queer* is the multifaceted international subculture self-identified lesbians and gay men have cultivated and refined in the second half of the 20th century. Nevertheless, as Harry Hay asserted when he began elaborating a mission statement for what would become the Mattachine Society, the question of where today's lesbians and gay men come from is an important one. Essentialists believe that something similar to a modern gay and lesbian identity may have come into existence with prehistoric shamans and proud amazon warriors. Constructionists more modestly look back to premodern all-women communities and men's cruising subcultures, both documented in Europe as early as the Middle Ages. In *Completely Queer*, we have tried to steer a compromise course by summarizing what is now known about a wide range of historical communities that seem analogous, if not ancestral, to the current gay and lesbian subculture. We have also included biographical information on a number of people, ranging from Sappho to William Shakespeare, who may or may not have been lesbian or gay in the sense those words have today, but who are important to contemporary gay men and lesbians by virtue of having been claimed as ancestors. And we have made a special effort to cite the grandparents of today's subcultures, people like Edward Carpenter and Renée Vivien, who pioneered ways of thinking about and enacting their sexual identities that have since become common for millions of men and women.

Similarly, since gay and lesbian subcultures have matured almost entirely in developed, North American, Western European, or English-speaking countries, most of the topics and people covered by *Completely Queer* reflect a Western bias. At the same time, we have tried to define and explore the frontiers of gay and lesbian life via overviews of still nascent movements in Africa, Asia, Eastern Europe, the Pacific Islands, and Latin America. And, while focusing on the West, we have sought to convey the diversity of the subcultures in existence today—as well as the still more definition-confounding diversity of individual "gay and lesbian" identities. As Gertrude Stein knew, Helen Furr was not the only one who "learned very many little ways to use in being gay." Even in 1922, "Very many were telling about using other ways in being gay."

Selection and Sources

In 1950, all the famous "known" homosexuals in the world could have gathered in one very small bar—and easily brought along with them all the widely available English-language reference works on "homosexuals" and "homosexuality." Less than five decades later, there are "out" celebrities in virtually every area of politics, entertainment, and the arts, and it would take the world's largest archive to house every English-language gay and lesbian book and periodical printed since Stonewall. Given the dizzying task of surveying all these people and all this information in a single printable volume, we found it impossible not to make decisions many readers may find subjective, arbitrary, and even, in some cases, ill-informed. Pleading guilty to all the above, we list here the objectives we set for ourselves in deciding who and what to include as an article in the A to Z section of (the perhaps unconscionably named) *Completely Queer*:

- balance between lesbian and gay male interests;
- integration, wherever possible, of the two (gay male and lesbian) points of view; contrast, where not;
- comprehensive coverage of the most influential early movement leaders and organizations;
- extensive coverage of pre-Stonewall groups and notables who laid the groundwork for later developments;
- representative coverage of important post-Stonewall groups and celebrities, with emphasis on individuals who have voluntarily come out;
- global coverage of the state of gay and lesbian life, with separate entries on 25 major countries;
- selective coverage of issues, concepts, and historical periods important to an understanding of gay and lesbian subcultures;
- complete coverage of all large and several small religious groups and their positions on same-sex eroticism.

Finally, we wish to emphasize that our selection reflects not only the dauntingly wide range of accessible lesbian and gay scholarship but also, in some areas, its omissions. To date, for example, no scholarly work has comprehensively covered post-Stonewall U.S. gay and lesbian rights movement activities outside the East and West coasts.

HOW TO USE THIS ENCYCLOPEDIA

Look for Major Subjects and Prominent Individuals in the Alphabetized Entry Section

In addition to articles on about 600 topics and persons, the A to Z section of *Completely Queer* also contains cross-references for alternative names ("Ellerman, Annie Winifred; see BRYHER"), countries for which substantive information is included in a regional entry ("Ghana, see AFRICA, SUB-SAHARAN,"), and suggestions for locating information on some topics not treated in separate articles ("Gyms, see BODY-BUILDING; SPORT").

Refer to Other Articles for More Information on Words in Small Capitals

Within the text of the articles and chronology entries, the first mention of subjects and persons for which *Completely Queer* offers separate articles is generally printed in SMALL CAPITALS. Dates included in the Chronology also appear in **bold**. Related articles and chronology events not mentioned in the body of the entries are cross-referenced at the end of the articles. (Occasionally, *incidental* mentions of another article's subject in an article's text are not cross-referenced.)

Use the Reading Lists to Find More In-Depth Information

Most of the articles conclude with a brief list of sources readers may consult for more information on the topic covered. Often, one or more of these sources will provide a comprehensive bibliography on the featured subject. Where we had a choice, we have given precedence to works that relate the person or topic treated in the article to a lesbian or gay context. We have also tried to cite easily available works—books and articles recently published in English, usually in the United States.

See the Chronology for Relevant Events and Developments

Extensively cross-referenced, the Chronology serves as a companion to the articles, providing dates of important events and developments in the prehistory as well as the history of modern gay and lesbian subcultures.

Further Information on Sources

Due to space considerations, sources of information have generally not been cited. Researchers wishing to learn the source(s) of a fact or event included in *Completely Queer* are welcome to e-mail queries to the authors at Shoganink@aol.com or Leehudson@juno.com.

Completely Queer

A

Abbott, Berenice

(1898–1991)

U.S. photographer. An Ohio native, Abbott was raised by her mother after her parents' divorce. In 1918, she moved to New York City to become a sculptor and fell in with a bohemian Greenwich Village crowd that included DJUNA BARNES, Man Ray, and Marcel Duchamp. In 1921, she moved to Paris and, except for a stay in Berlin, lived there until 1929. She worked at a variety of jobs, most often as an artist's model, but had reached the verge of starvation when Ray hired her as his assistant in 1923. She learned photography quickly and in 1926 opened her own studio. Besides promoting her own photographs, she was also credited with rediscovering and popularizing the work of Eugène Atget.

Well-acquainted with most of the lesbian émigré set and their friends, Abbott proceeded to photograph many of them, creating some of the most memorable portraits to survive from the era. Unlike the dictatorial Ray, Abbott let her subjects relax, then shot them in revealingly natural poses. Reviewing her first show in 1927, JANET FLANNER wrote: "Stolidly, as if almost accidentally, she arrives at a posturing of her subject so that mind and matter are clothed and balanced against a sensitive plate." Abbott's subjects included Barnes, SYLVIA BEACH, JEAN COCTEAU, ANDRÉ GIDE, James Joyce, Marie Laurencin, Claude McKay, and Barnes's lover, Thelma Wood. (Barnes later wrote: "I gave Berenice the extra E in her name, and she gave me Thelma. I don't know who made out better.")

Considered a renegade by her male peers, she faded from the public eye for several decades following her return to New York, but remained active, teaching and compiling two massive photo documentaries, *Changing New York* and *Route 1*. In 1958, she began a series of imaginative science photographs, which reestablished her as a leading photographer. She spent her later years living and working in Maine.

✧ H. O'Neal, *Berenice Abbott: Sixty Years of Photography* (1982).

Abbott, Sidney A.

(1937–)

U.S. activist, writer. Raised on and near military bases, Abbott grew up a studious child encouraged by an intellectually curious mother and grandmother. She attended Smith College and the University of New Mexico, earned an M.S. in urban planning at Columbia University, and worked in publishing in New York City.

In 1970, she and her then lover, BARBARA LOVE, were among the first feminist activists to join the nascent GAY LIBERATION movement. Intent on forging alliances among women, they organized a consciousness-raising "supergroup" that inspired 21 other similar groups. As Abbott commented more than two decades later, "these groups changed the way lesbians thought about themselves." Besides participating in the formation of RADICALESBIANS, she and Love published *Sappho Was a Right-On Woman: A Liberated View of Lesbianism* in 1972. One of the first books to articulate the intrinsic connections as well as the tensions between the women's and the gay/lesbian movements and to document the early years of LESBIAN FEMINISM, *Sappho* was still in print two and a half decades later.

Abbott served as a coordinator for the first National Sexuality and Lesbianism Task Force of the NATIONAL ORGANIZATION FOR WOMEN and was a founding member of the board of directors of the NATIONAL GAY (later: AND LESBIAN) TASK FORCE. She was also the first openly lesbian member of a New York City community board.

✧ Sidney Abbott, "Lesbians and the Women's Movement," in *Our Right to Love,* edited by Ginny Vida (1978).

Abū Nuwās

(Abū Nuwās al-Hasan ibn Hānī' al-Hakamī, c. 755–c. 815)

Arab poet. One of the most lauded and influential poets in Arabic, Abū Nuwās spent most of his life in Baghdad at the beginning of the Abbāsid caliphate (749–1258). He is said to have been the submissive sex partner of his teacher, the master poet Waliba ibn al-Hubab; until the end of his life, when he became deeply religious, he reveled in the practice of PEDERASTY, only rarely evincing interest in women and slightly older young men. He helped establish love poetry written to boys as a genre of Arabic literature, penning verse of exquisite beauty as well as ribald satires on topics ranging from the joys of drunkenness to the ludicrousness, in his view, of lesbianism. His popularity and eminence are often cited as evidence that, despite the prohibitions of ISLAM, Arab culture has been relatively tolerant of same-sex love, at least when it is confined to men making use of younger men and boys. Like his patron, the caliph Harun al-Rashid, he appears as a character in *A Thousand and One Nights.*

✧ *The Genius of Arab Civilization,* edited by J. R. Hayt (1983).

Ackerley, J. R.

(Joseph "Joe" Randolph Ackerley; 1896–1967)

English writer, editor. Ackerley came from what he thought was a typical English upper-class background. Then, at 33, he discovered that his recently deceased father had led a double life, supporting another household and several half siblings Ackerley knew nothing about. Further investigation led him to suspect his father had once been kept by a German count. Ackerley melded his inquiries with his own self-examination in the posthumously published *My Father and Myself* (1968), a book most critics consider his finest achievement.

Ackerley first began to think of himself as "homo" in 1917 while interned as a prisoner of war. For the rest of his life, he was one of the least closeted men in England. He dealt openly with sexual themes in his writing as early as 1925, when his play, *The Prisoners of War,* was produced in London (with a brief Broadway run in 1935). Later, as editor (1935–1959) of the influential BBC publication *The Listener,* he championed the work of W. H. AUDEN and CHRISTOPHER ISHERWOOD and once wrote a letter to *The Guardian* protesting the trials of 20 Welshmen for "indecency between males" (see **1942**).

Despite masculine good looks and decades

of cruising the working-class men who most attracted him, Ackerley never found what he called the "Ideal Friend," although he succeeded in introducing his close friend E. M. FORSTER to the London policeman who became Forster's lifelong lover. In later years, Ackerley relinquished his quest and settled down with a dog named Queenie. Queenie inspired two popular books, *My Dog Tulip* (1956) and *We Think the World of You* (1960). Both have been dramatized for TELEVISION with gay subplots. Ackerley also wrote *Hindoo Holiday* (1932), a comic journal of his and Forster's experiences at the court of a boy-loving maharaja. His *Letters from Japan* (1960) include descriptions of encounters with young men in Tokyo.

✧ Peter Parker, *Ackerley: A Life of J. R. Ackerley* (1989).

Activism

Practice of—or belief in—vigorous engagement in the fight for or against a political, social, or cultural matter of controversy. The words "activism" and "activist" first appeared in European languages in a political sense in the years preceding World War I. Since then—and especially since the 1960s—they have come to describe a level of commitment to resolving controversial issues that goes beyond simply voting in elections or contributing money to organizations and that includes participation in demonstrations, canvassing, lobbying, encouraging boycotts, civil disobedience, etc.

Although the men and women who campaigned for gay and lesbian civil rights in GERMANY beginning in the late 19th century are sometimes called activists, their tactics, which included petition drives and public meetings, were less confrontational than those associated with today's militants. Modern lesbian and gay activism began in the U.S. in the 1960s with actions pioneered by FRANK KAMENY, RANDY WICKER, BARBARA GITTINGS, and other movement leaders. It spread around the world and peaked in the early 1970s after the STONEWALL Uprising and the formation of groups such as the GAY LIBERATION FRONT, GAY ACTIVISTS AL-

New York City lesbian rights and AIDS activist Alexis Danzig is arrested at a demonstration in front of St. Patrick's Cathedral.

LIANCE, and RADICALESBIANS. Activism resurfaced in the late eighties in the U.S., the UNITED KINGDOM, and other countries in response to the spread of AIDS and the rise of conservative, antilesbian and -gay religious and political movements.

➤ Also see ASSIMILATIONISM/CONFRONTATIONALISM; DIRECT ACTION.

- Toby Marotta, *The Politics of Homosexuality* (1981).
- John D'Emilio, *Sexual Politics, Sexual Communities: The Making of a Homosexual Minority in the United States, 1940–1970* (1983).
- Barry D. Adam, *The Rise of a Gay and Lesbian Movement* (rev. ed., 1995).

Actors/Acting

No one knows if actors are more likely to be gay, lesbian, or bisexual than other people, but few would disagree that the world of THEATER (as opposed to HOLLYWOOD and TELEVISION) has been friendlier toward all varieties of nonconformists than most professional fields. Acting has been associated with same-sex love in the West since Roman times and in the East since at least the time of the *hwarang* (see KOREA), 2,000 years ago.

There are several possible reasons for this having been the case. Show business in general and acting in particular have been considered less than respectable professions in many cultures, so they were perhaps more accepting environments for nonconformists. In Japan, for example, the government at one time actually used the Japanese counting word for animals, *hiki,* to tally up the population of actors. In addition, acting was often associated with prostitution, and sex workers of all sexual orientations have as a matter of course been less judgmental of sexual "deviation." And finally, since most modern societies (and many premodern cultures) have conflated gender nonconformity with homosexuality, the prevalence of gay, lesbian, and bisexual actors may support what QUEER THEORY considers the "performative" nature of GENDER: the idea that gender "identity" is actually nothing more than a "role" one learns to play in the course of growing up and taking part in social interaction. If this is in fact true, actors may simply be more skilled at experimenting with roles not sanctioned by the rest of society.

Paradoxically, the increased status of actors in the 20th century—when screen stars began to supplant politicians and military leaders as role models and public idols—has probably made it more difficult for performers to flaunt societal norms. Increasingly, fans enjoyed the fantasy that their favorite stars, especially those who played romantic leads, were in real life similar to the characters they played. Public fascination with stars fueled the growth of a media machine devoted to publicizing actors' private lives. As a result, especially in Hollywood, actors' CLOSETS became more and more constricted: when the media could be manipulated easily by Hollywood publicists, it was possible for bisexual, gay, and lesbian actors like Montgomery Clift, James Dean, Greta Garbo, Cary Grant, and Randolph Scott to lead double lives. Hollywood insiders winked at their offscreen indiscretions as long as the public accepted the heterosexual fantasies they were fed. As the media grew less manageable, however, unconventional sex lives became more of a liability. By the 1990s, few closeted actors would dare live together, as Cary Grant and Randolph Scott did in the 1940s, or be seen in gay bars, as James Dean was in the 1950s. For many actors, the advent of OUTING provided impetus to burrow even deeper into the closet—or to deny that a closet existed: in

A few well-known actors, like Rupert Everett, have been out their entire careers.

1994, Richard Gere and Cindy Crawford paid more than $100,000 for a full-page ad in *The Times* of London stating that they were both heterosexual.

There is some evidence that, even in an age of increasing lesbian and gay visibility, coming out adversely affects an actor's career. As late as 1995, a Gallup poll commissioned by *Entertainment Weekly* found that 29 percent of Americans would be "less interested" in seeing their favorite actor perform in a movie or TV show if they learned that he or she was "gay" (66 percent claimed such a revelation would not change their opinion). Not coincidentally, the magazine article that accompanied the poll reported that for every lesbian or gay Hollywood celebrity who agreed to speak on the record, "dozens" asked that their name not be mentioned.

On the other hand, character actors, who have always enjoyed more freedom in Hollywood, are less likely to be penalized for coming out. This is perhaps why the first well-known openly gay star to play a gay character in films, HARVEY FIERSTEIN, was a comedic rather than a romantic lead. It remains to be seen whether other actors who have come out—such as Mitchell Anderson, Amanda Bearse (see **9/21/1993**), Dan Butler, Ellen DeGeneres, and Cherry Jones—will enjoy careers as successful as if they had remained in the closet.

In the English-speaking world, actors in the UNITED KINGDOM have been the most open about their sexuality: Rupert Everett, John Gielgud, Alec McCowen, and IAN McKELLEN are just a few of the British performers who have come out publicly. Among women, Miriam Margolyes led the way in 1979 when she told an interviewer that she was "deliberately unmarried" and suggested the reporter add, "An evil leer played about her lips, and there was a twinkle in her eye."

- ✧ "The Gay '90s: Entertainment Comes Out of the Closet. A Special Report," *Entertainment Weekly* (September 8, 1995).
- ✧ Alan Frutkin, "Out in Prime Time," *The Advocate* (May 14, 1996).

ACT UP (AIDS Coalition to Unleash Power)

DIRECT ACTION group formed on **March 14, 1987,** in New York City by LARRY KRAMER and several hundred other activists to fight for a more effective response to the AIDS epidemic from government and business. ACT UP employed a radically democratic decision-by-consensus meeting style and an antihierarchical organizational structure reminiscent of 1960s COUNTERCULTURE groups. Although its official motto was "United in anger and committed to direct action to end the AIDS crisis," members also used the PINK TRIANGLE with the slogan "Silence = Death" as the group's emblem.

Hailed as a return to the ACTIVISM of the GAY LIBERATION era, ACT UP galvanized the energies of the gay and lesbian communities, channeling the anger and frustration that had built as the epidemic spread unchecked into dramatic public demonstrations (see **3/24/1987**; **10/11/1988**; **12/10/1989**). By the end of 1988, ACT UP had surfaced in Dallas, Los Angeles, Philadelphia, San Francisco, and other cities across the country. Canadians organized the similarly focused AIDS Action Now! in 1988, and an ACT UP group was formed in London in early 1989.

ACT UP scored an early success in 1988, when the U.S. Food and Drug Administration agreed to streamline and accelerate its drug approval process. Other developments that were largely the result of AIDS activism initiated by ACT UP included agreements reached with some drug manufacturers to lower the price of AIDS medications, the beginning of public awareness of AIDS cases among lesbians, and the 1993 Centers for Disease Control decision to broaden its definition of AIDS to include diseases such as PID (pelvic inflammatory disease) that primarily affect women.

One unintended result of the successes of ACT UP was that many of its most prominent leaders across the U.S. were recruited into less radical organizations and bureaucratic positions. In the mid-1990s, attendance at ACT UP meetings dwindled, its leadership decimated by AIDS-related deaths but also split by a lack of consensus on AIDS treatment issues. In the Bay Area, for example, ACT UP Golden Gate continued to apply pressure to

One of ACT UP's most publicized—and most effective—demonstrations was staged at the Food and Drug Administration building in Rockville, Maryland, on October 11, 1988.

drug manufacturers to research new treatments while ACT UP San Francisco cast doubt on the efficacy of conventional AIDS drugs, advocating alternative treatments not sold by drug companies.

Issues addressed by ACT UP groups in the mid-1990s included care and shelter for the homeless and the IMMIGRATION status of HIV-positive individuals.

➤ Also see LESBIAN AVENGERS; QUEER NATION.

Addams, Jane

(1860–1935)

U. S. social reformer, feminist, peace activist, writer. Born into a locally prominent Cedarville, Illinois, family, Addams grew up in an atmosphere of elegance, sophistication, and social assurance. She completed college and briefly studied medicine until poor health forced her to leave school. In the 1880s, she traveled extensively with her "devoted companion" (see ROMANTIC FRIENDSHIPS), Ellen Gates Starr, a former classmate at the Rockford (Illinois) Female Seminary. While in England, Addams and Starr discovered *settlement houses,* homes located in city slums where social workers "settled" to provide services to the surrounding community.

In 1889, Addams and Starr founded Hull House in Chicago. By 1900, Hull House was a hub of political, educational, and social activity, drawing over two thousand visitors a week. Its success brought Addams widespread renown and helped launch a nationwide settlement house movement.

Addams published four major books about the ethical and sociological effects of industrialization on immigrants and the working poor, in addition to two books chronicling Hull House. A leading feminist and suffragette, she called attention to poverty, adverse working conditions, and prostitution among poor urban women. Beyond addressing specific problems, she fought for a radically transformed social order in which women and men and people of all races and nationalities would be fully equal and all would be guaranteed economic security.

Addams called herself a "Tolstoyan anarchist." Like Leo Tolstoy, she was an unequivocal pacifist. She vehemently opposed U.S. involvement in World War I, helping found the American Union Against Militarism (and, in 1920, its offshoot, the AMERICAN CIVIL LIBERTIES UNION). She also headed the Woman's Peace Party, and, later, published the controversial *Peace and Bread in Time of War* (1922). Her efforts were recognized with a Nobel Peace Prize in 1931.

Historian Blanche Wiesen Cook has written about the network of women, including LILLIAN D. WALD, who supported Addams. Among them were the two women with whom she had her most intimate relationships, Starr and Mary Rozet Smith. Smith, who shared Addams's life for 40 years, has been described as a "spouse surrogate." Addams herself seems to have considered their bond a marriage. As she wrote Smith in 1902: "You must know, dear, how I long for you all the time and especially during the last three weeks. There is reason in the habit of married folks keeping together." When they traveled, Addams always wired ahead to order a large double bed for their hotel room. Besides being a colleague on the board of Hull House and one of its benefactors, Smith gave Addams the affection and support she needed to pursue her social and political missions.

✧ Allen F. Davis, *The Life and Legend of Jane Addams* (1973).

✧ Blanche Wiesen Cook, *Women and Support Networks* (1979).

Addiction/Recovery

In the 1970s, few people were surprised when the first scientific studies on alcohol and drug use among lesbians and gay men reported higher rates of alcoholism and addiction than in the general population. Experts attributed these higher rates to the stresses of being gay or lesbian in a society characterized by HETEROSEXISM as well as to the importance of BARS in lesbian and gay social life.

Later, however, social scientists criticized these early studies for recruiting a disproportionate number of respondents from among people who frequented bars. In 1989, a study using a larger, more broadly based sample (3,400 participants) found that the most notable difference between lesbians/gay men and heterosexuals was that there were fewer alcohol and drug *abstainers* among gay and lesbian adults than in the population at large. The number of "problem drinkers" and drug "abusers" among lesbians and gay men is still a matter of dispute, but it is certainly not as high as once believed. In addition, several studies have shown a sharp decrease in alcohol and drug use among gay men since the early 1980s. A study conducted by J. Martin and others found, for example, that use of amphetamines, barbiturates, hallucinogens, and inhalant nitrites among a group of gay men in New York fell 80 percent between 1981 and 1987. Experts attribute this trend to fear of AIDS as well as changing social mores.

Whatever its frequency, alcohol and drug abuse among lesbians and gay men continues to be a major concern of community health activists. Beginning in the 1960s, gay men and lesbians began forming their own 12-step groups such as Alcoholics Anonymous (AA). By **April 1974**, when the national board of AA agreed to allow "gay" meetings to be listed in their directory, there were at least 16 across the country. In 1976, San Francisco was the site of the first gay and lesbian AA Living Sober conference; since then, similar conferences, attended by as many as five thousand people, have been held annually in large cities in the U.S. and CANADA. In 1981, a special International Advisory Council for Homosexual Men and Women in Alcoholics Anonymous was formed in Washington, D.C. The council works with professionals and publishes a worldwide directory listing several hundred gay- and lesbian-identified groups.

Today, thanks in large part to the growth of lesbian and gay COMMUNITY CENTERS and SWITCHBOARDS, every large North American urban area has a wide range of gay- and lesbian-identified 12-step programs as well as therapists and special programs to help people in recovery. In 1996, for example, the New York City Lesbian and Gay Community Services Center hosted almost 80 meetings a week for 17 different 12-step programs. New Yorkers also had access to free individual and group counseling for addictive-compulsive disorders through the center's Project Connect, which in 1995 launched a smoking cessation program whose success underscored one of the most important reasons health activists believe addiction and recovery programs are often most effective in a comfortably "queer" setting. As Dr. Barbara Warren, director of mental health and social services at the center, commented, announcing the continuation of the quit-smoking program in 1996: "We provide an environment that is supportive of gay, lesbian, bisexual, and transgender persons. People feel free to discuss stressful issues such as relationships, HIV, HOMOPHOBIA, GENDER identity, and other related topics that may contribute to their continued addiction."

✧ Sheppard B. Kominars, *Accepting Ourselves: The 12-Step Journey of Recovery from Addiction for Gay Men and Lesbians* (1989).

- J. Martin, L. Dean, M. Garcia, and W. Hall, "The Impact of AIDS on a Gay Community: Changes in Sexual Behavior, Substance Abuse, and Mental Health," *American Journal of Community Psychology* (vol. 17, no. 3, 1989).
- *Psychological Perspectives on Lesbian and Gay Male Experiences,* edited by Linda D. Garnets and Douglas C. Kimmel (1993).
- *Lesbian, Gay, and Bisexual Identities over the Lifespan: Psychological Perspectives,* edited by Anthony R. D'Augelli and Charlotte J. Patterson (1995).
- Thomas S. Weinberg, *Gay Men, Drinking, and Alcoholism* (1995).

Adoption, see CHILDREN.

Advertising

The most closeted form of public communications, at least in its mass-market manifestations, advertising has always had a complex relationship with lesbians and gay men. The model who posed as the Arrow Collar Man in the early 20th century, one of advertising's legendary icons and a prototype of the all-American male, was Charles Beach, the lover of J. C. Leyendecker, the artist who created the highly successful illustrations for the ads. Many other lesbians and gay men have worked as advertising art directors, copywriters, or account executives, including MALCOLM BOYD, PAUL CADMUS, HART CRANE, RICHARD HALL, GEORGE PLATT LYNES, SHELLY ROBERTS, and TOM OF FINLAND. Not coincidentally, the New York Advertising and Communications Network, established in 1983, quickly became one of the largest and most active gay and lesbian organizations in the city, with over 900 members in 1996.

On the other hand, advertising is in many ways the most conservative mass medium. As late as the 1940s, an advertising billboard with the headline "Give a Ham" was considered a daring—even risqué (because it punned on the word "damn")—creative breakthrough. Advertising has been much slower than other media to feature openly gay and lesbian characters and spokespersons, and the industry has at times allied itself with conservative, antigay and -lesbian groups: for instance, advertisers pulled commercials from a **November 1989** episode of *Thirtysomething* on ABC in which two men were shown in bed together, costing the show about $500,000 in revenues. Not until 25 years after STONEWALL did a major advertiser, the furniture chain Ikea, introduce a TV commercial that included a gay couple. In its 30-second spot, which ran in selected markets in 1994, two attractive middle-aged gay men discuss their new dining room set, comment-

Gay and lesbian icons have been a part of advertising since at least the first decades of the 20th century.

ing that a table that comes with an extra leaf means "staying together—commitment."

Ikea was one of very few advertisers willing to advertise to lesbians and gay men in a straight environment. Many other companies, beginning with Absolut vodka in 1979, have bought ad space in gay and lesbian publications, or served as sponsors of events that appeal directly to lesbians and gay men. These, with a few exceptions (such as Saab and AT&T), have been in a limited number of advertising categories that are thought to have a built-in, and potentially profitable, gay and lesbian audience—chiefly liquor, bottled waters, cigarettes, and fashion.

HOMOEROTICISM, nevertheless, is commonly believed to be a powerful component of advertising imagery. One early example is the 1960s Marlboro Man, who became an icon for a generation of gay men (see CLONES), but the most frequently cited homoerotic advertising "breakthrough" in the U.S. is a 1980 Calvin Klein campaign that used a shirtless male model to advertise the designer's new line of jeans. Two years later, gigantic billboards and print ads spotlighted Bruce Weber's photography of a handsome Brazilian pole vaulter named Tom Hintnaus wearing Calvin Klein underwear. Although the success of these campaigns inspired a host of other American advertisers to feature beefcake in their advertising, most denied that they were aiming their sell at gay men. As Klein himself stated: "We do not try to appeal to gays. We try to appeal, period."

Further evidence of the reluctance of advertisers to be perceived as making a pitch to a lesbian and gay audience is provided by British scholar Gregory Woods, who analyzed several dozen mail-order fashion catalogs, supposedly a gay-friendly environment, and found that most advertisers go to great lengths to "heterosexualize" their homoerotic images to avoid "the slightest whiff of deviancy."

Besides the 1994 Ikea commercial, acknowledged lesbian and gay breakthroughs in American advertising include a trio of 1995 print ads: a magazine ad for the clothing brand Diesel with two "sailors" (bodybuilders and then-lovers Rod and Bob Jackson-Paris) kissing passionately in one corner of a busy dock scene; a nationally placed ad for Tanqueray that showed a gay bar with caricatures of gay men, "lipstick lesbians," and a drag queen of color described as "rather burly for a glamour girl"; and MELISSA ETHERIDGE's antifur ad in which she posed nude with her lover, filmmaker Julie Cypher.

Some advertisers outside the U.S. have been more adventurous. In 1991, in AUSTRALIA, Toyota broadened its image of a "family car" (as the headline proclaimed) with an ad portraying two men and their two dogs loading up in front of their upscale suburban home. And at the end of **1993**, the Dutch government published advertising brochures to encourage lesbians and gay men in the country's navy to be open about their sexuality, in the belief that uncloseted service personnel would be happier and more productive in their jobs.

Among gay and lesbian groups and companies, the Homophile Action League of Philadelphia was perhaps the first to appropriate an advertising strategy for movement aims. In the early 1970s, the organization launched a citywide sticker and poster campaign with a headline that read: "The person standing next to you may be a homosexual. Why isn't he free?" In October 1995, Do Tell, Inc., a lesbian-owned firm based in Pennsylvania, debuted a "Rainbow" credit card, complete with TV commercials featuring MARTINA NAVRATILOVA.

✧ Grant Lukenbill, *Untold Millions: Positioning Your Business for the Gay and Lesbian Consumer Revolution* (1995).

✧ Gregory Woods, "We're Here, We're Queer and We're Not Going Catalogue Shopping," in *A Queer Romance: Lesbians, Gay Men and Popular Culture,* edited by Paul Burston and Colin Richardson (1995).

Advocate, The

Major American gay and lesbian newsmagazine, first published in August 1967 (issue dated September 1967). *The Advocate* evolved out of a newsletter edited for PRIDE (Personal Rights in Defense and Education), a Los Angeles–based HOMOPHILE organization formed in May 1966 to fight police harassment. In 1967, writer and PRIDE member Dick Michaels (PSEUDONYM of Richard Mitch) envisioned a local publication with a substantial circulation that would report "what gay people needed to know about what was happening in their world." Michaels joined with his lover, Bill Rand (pseudonym of Bill Rau), and Sam Winston, an artist who chaired the PRIDE publications committee, to produce a 12-page newspaper they called *The Los Angeles Advocate.* The first edition of 500 copies was furtively printed after hours in the basement of ABC-TV's L.A. office. It sold for 25 cents in area bars.

Michaels, Rand, and Winston bought the publication rights from PRIDE for $1 in February 1968, a few months before the organization officially disbanded. By March 1970, circulation was over 5,000 and the publication, now typeset, boasted 32 pages of articles, editorials, reviews, cartoons, and advertisements. Writer and activist JIM KEPNER had joined the staff, and the paper was well positioned to become the first nationally distributed publication of the fast-breaking GAY LIBERATION era. "Los Angeles" was dropped from the paper's name, and in April 1970, *The Advocate,* then subtitled "The Newspaper of America's Homophile Community," converted from monthly to biweekly editions.

In 1975, *The Advocate* was bought by David B. Goodstein, a wealthy and controversial gay entrepreneur who maintained control of the publication until his death in 1985. Goodstein moved the editorial offices to the San Francisco area and converted the paper into a less political, more commercial tabloid. JOHN PRESTON served as editor and Dennis Forbes as artist-editor. That same year, Robert I. McQueen took over as editor in chief, and Niles Merton was named publisher. McQueen's decade-long tenure saw *The Advocate* emerge as the unofficial "gay journal of record," the source other national publications were most likely to quote when they wanted a gay point of view.

In 1984, *The Advocate* returned to Southern California and was once again reformatted, this time as a glossy-covered newsmagazine. In the decade that followed, editors in chief Lenny Giteck, Stuart Kellogg, Richard Rouilard, and Jeff Yarbrough in turn sought to enliven, diversify, and update the magazine. Sam Watters became publisher in 1992. The same year, *The Advocate* converted to an all-glossy format and spun its unabashedly prurient "pink pages" into a separate publication.

Controversy has attended nearly every issue of *The Advocate.* It was criticized for its lack of coverage of lesbians and people of color in the 1970s (the word "lesbian" was not added to the cover until 1990), its late response to the AIDS crisis in the 1980s, its position against OUTING in the early 1990s—and its decision to out Pentagon spokesman Pete Williams in 1992.

The Advocate has been the leading gay and lesbian newsmagazine since its founding.

Despite the problems it has had representing the many gay and lesbian viewpoints throughout its history, no other publication has provided better or more comprehensive coverage of gay and lesbian community growth and social development.

At one time or another, almost every prominent lesbian and gay man in the U.S. has written for or been written about in *The Advocate.* PAT CALIFIA, RICHARD HALL, and RANDY SHILTS are among the many writers whose careers have been advanced by the publication.

✧ *Long Road to Freedom: The Advocate History of the Gay and Lesbian Movement,* edited by Mark Thompson (1994).

Afghanistan, see CENTRAL ASIA.

Africa, Sub-Saharan

All same-sex relations illegal in Angola, Cape Verde, Ethiopia, Ghana, Malawi, Namibia, Togo, and Zaire, with penalties varying from a fine to three years' imprisonment. Only male-male relations illegal in Kenya, Mozambique, Nigeria, Tanzania, Uganda, Zambia, and Zimbabwe, with penalties ranging up to five years' imprisonment.

No relevant laws for consenting adults in Benin, Botswana, Burkina Faso, Cameroon, Central African Republic, Chad, Congo, Côte d'Ivoire, Equatorial Guinea, Gabon, Lesotho, Liberia, Madagascar, Senegal, SOUTH AFRICA, *and Swaziland. In Burkina Faso,* AGE OF CONSENT *higher for same-sex (21) than for heterosexual (13) relations.*

No official information forthcoming from the governments of Burundi, Djibouti, Eritrea, The Gambia, Guinea, Guinea-Bissau, Mali, Mauritania, Niger, Rwanda, São Tomé and Principé, Sierra Leone, and Somalia.

Visible, active organizations and developed social scene in South Africa and Zimbabwe. Informal groups reported in Botswana, Ghana, Nigeria, and Uganda.

With the exception of South Africa and Zimbabwe, sub-Saharan Africa remains largely apart from the international gay and lesbian rights movement. Yet many of the peoples of Africa have long and rich traditions of same-sex relations as well as relationships. If recent developments in South Africa are any indication, other Africans may be ready to create unique contemporary lesbian and gay subcultures when social and political forces permit them.

The history of same-sex relations in Africa is obscured by a host of factors, including the almost ungraspable diversity of cultures on the continent, the lingering effects of colonialism, and the fact that most reports have been written by non-Africans. Popular traditions, as preserved in oral histories and folklore, are often contradictory. The Azande, for example, a people who once ruled much of central Africa, told European anthropologists that heterosexual marriage was obligatory in their society, but that men often had sex with other men, especially when serving in the military. Women, however, were said to receive a severe beating or even the death penalty if caught having same-sex relations. Nevertheless, (male) informants said, sex between women was quite common, in folk stories as well as in real life.

Information for most other African peoples is even less conclusive. Until recently, most non-African missionaries and anthropologists wrote nothing about homosexuality in Africa—not surprising, considering how little was published about the emerging lesbian and gay subcultures in their native countries—and African commentators have tended to deny its existence in their native cultures. Nevertheless, surviving records suggest patterns of same-sex relations that conform to those studied in other parts of the world. These include male-male relationships among segregated military groups, such as Zulu warriors who were required to shun relations with women for years on end. Some warriors, including Shaka, the legendary Zulu king, are said to have shown a clear preference for men or boys even when sex with women was permitted. Somewhat more common were peoples who permitted or even encouraged premarital same-sex relations, usually in the form of mutual masturbation. Anthropologists have also reported at least a dozen types of BERDACHE-like options among groups of Africans.

One type of same-sex relationship that seems to have been more common in Africa than elsewhere is marriage between two women. Although the form varied from place to place, "woman marriages" were generally considered economic unions, often related to trading networks created by African women. Among Bantu speakers, childless widows sometimes married younger women, who were then expected to produce heirs to the family fortune. Many contemporary Africans deny that these marriages were sexual; others point to them as an acceptable option open to women who were attracted to other women.

By the time African nations began to achieve independence in the 1950s and 1960s, most of these traditional patterns of sexuality had faded away (although a traditional female-female marriage was ruled legal by a judge in Swaziland in 1992). As part of the social, political, and technological developments that convulsed and, in many cases, destroyed cultures all over the continent, Christian and Muslim missionaries had converted millions from relatively sex-positive religions to belief systems that forbade same-sex relations. Smaller but equally influential numbers of Africans had adopted Marxism in one form or another and were deeply influenced by theorists such as the Martinique-born Frantz Fanon, who asserted that homosexuality was an alien perversion forced on Africans (and their descendants in the New World) by white oppressors. Whatever their political persuasion, African leaders from Jomo Kenyatta to Winnie Mandela to Robert Mugabe (see **8/1/1995**) have expressed hostility toward lesbians and gay men.

Outside of a few big cities and resort areas popular with non-Africans, very few Africans identify themselves as gay or lesbian in the sense these words have acquired in industrialized countries. Marriage is compulsory virtually everywhere; desperate poverty makes social experimentation impractical for most women and men, who remain dependent on traditional family systems for survival. Open sexual and gender nonconformity means risking derision, ostracism, and even, in countries such as Ghana, imprisonment and torture. Very discreet same-sex contacts, nonetheless, are often tolerated, especially if they in no way disrupt conventional family life. An intriguing indication of what may someday emerge from the African CLOSET came at a presentation on lesbianism at a U.N. conference on women held in Nairobi in 1985. Silvia Borren, one of the founders of the International Lesbian Information Service, which sponsored the presentation, reported that every time someone objected that lesbianism didn't exist in Kenya, a group of Kenyan women would call out, "Yes it does! Yes it does!"

The INTERNATIONAL LESBIAN AND GAY ASSOCIATION has received reports of nascent gay and lesbian organizations in Ghana (Gay Liberation Group, 1990), Nigeria (Gentlemen Alliance, 1989), Uganda (Good Samaritan Project, 1992), and Zimbabwe (Gay and Lesbian Association of Zimbabwe, 1990).

➤ Also see ARAB WORLD; SOUTH AFRICA.

✧ *The Third Pink Book: A Global View of Lesbian and Gay Liberation and Oppression,* edited by Aart Hendriks, Rob Tielman, and Evert van der Veen (1993).

✧ Lars Eighner, "Black Ganymede" and "A Brief Cross-Cultural Survey," in his *Gay Cosmos* (1995).

African-Americans

Throughout the 20th century, African-Americans have played a pivotal role in shaping every aspect of the international gay and lesbian SUBCULTURES from ART, LITERATURE, and MUSIC to political ACTIVISM. At the same time, black gay men and lesbians have also created unique subcultures of their own, ones that have survived despite, and occasionally triumphed over, both HOMOPHOBIA in African-American society and racism in the gay and lesbian communities.

African-American activists like Ernestine Eckstein (left) have played major roles in the gay and lesbian rights movement since the first demonstrations, such as this one at the White House in 1965.

Today, black lesbians, bisexuals, and gay men are organized in hundreds of political and social groups across the United States. Pioneering organizations like the Third World Gay Revolution (1971), Salsa Soul Sisters (1974; later AFRICAN ANCESTRAL LESBIANS UNITED FOR SOCIETAL CHANGE), National Coalition of Black Lesbians and Gays (1978), Black and White Men Together (1980; later, Men of All Colors Together and People of All Colors Together), the African-American Lesbian and Gay Alliance (1986), Gay Men of African Descent (1986), and Black Gay and Lesbian

Gloria and Charmaine, Baltimore, 1979.

Leadership Forum (1989) have fostered the growth of more specialized groups ranging from Brothers in Leather (1994) to Bisexual Womyn of Colour (1994).

Still, despite the proliferation of black gay and lesbian "safe spaces," many black lesbians and gay men would second writer Bruce Morrow's feeling, expressed in a 1994 *New York Times* essay: "My life usually feels like I'm balancing on a thin wire strung across the city."

History

Historians and anthropologists have begun to uncover homoerotic traditions in AFRICA, but it remains unclear to what extent these traditions were translated to North America in the days of the slave trade. As with Americans of European descent, the first body of documented evidence of same-sex desire among African-Americans comes in the form of court and prison records. Historian JONATHAN NED KATZ reports that a government document dating from 1880 shows that more black men (32) were incarcerated for "crimes against nature" than white men (31) across the United States, despite their making up less than 15 percent of the total population at the time. (That black men and women continue to suffer disproportionately from American homophobia is suggested by MILITARY discharge rates for homosexuality.)

Along with Greenwich Village, Harlem was in the 1920s the site of the first multifaceted American gay and lesbian subcultures (see HARLEM RENAISSANCE). While white gay men like CARL VAN VECHTEN flocked to the lively Harlem clubs of the era, gay BATHHOUSES and BARS in other parts of New York—and in most other American cities—remained off-limits to people of color. As a result, black lesbians and gay men formed their own friendship networks, meeting sometimes in clubs in black

Sergeant Perry Watkins achieved national prominence when he brought suit against the army in 1981 to fight his discharge on grounds of homosexuality.

neighborhoods but more often through parties thrown at private homes.

Long after "whites only" signs were taken down in the South, many gay and lesbian discos, bars, and bathhouses continued to discriminate against black customers, either through quota systems or outright refusal of entry. These discriminatory door policies were among the catalysts to the formation of groups like Salsa Soul Sisters and Black and White Men Together.

Black men and women were among the early members of groups like ONE, INC., the MATTACHINE, and DAUGHTERS OF BILITIS, but after STONEWALL, many people of color felt marginalized by groups such as GAY ACTIVISTS ALLIANCE and in response founded their own organizations.

A distinctive factor of black lesbian and gay life has been that a higher percentage of African-American lesbians and gay men live outside gay and lesbian GHETTOS than their white counterparts. Their contributions to the lesbian and gay subcultures, on the other hand, have been disproportionately large, beginning with the writers, musicians, performers, and artists of the Harlem Renaissance, extending through JAMES BALDWIN and SAMUEL R. DELANY, and continuing through the renaissance of African-American gay and lesbian creativity of the past decades, just a few of whose representatives include ESSEX HEMPHILL, AUDRE LORDE, and MARLON RIGGS.

✧ *In the Life: A Black Gay Anthology,* edited by Joseph Beam (1986).

✧ *Critical Essays: Gay and Lesbian Writers of Color,* edited by Emmanuel S. Nelson (1988).

✧ *Brother to Brother: New Writings by Black Gay Men,* edited by Essex Hemphill (1991).

African Ancestral Lesbians United for Societal Change (formerly Salsa Soul Sisters)

Oldest organization of AFRICAN-AMERICAN lesbians in the U.S., established by Rev. Dolores Jackson with Harriet Austin, Sonia Bailey, Luvenia Pinson, and others in New York City in 1974. One of Jackson's primary objectives was to provide black and Latina lesbians with an alternative to lesbian and gay BARS, many of which at the time either had racist door policies or were Mafia-controlled, or both. The organization, which met weekly, sponsored political, social, and cultural events for the African-American and Latina lesbian community. The organization's first newsletter described its mission: "We came into being because there was no other organization that we know of in the New York area, existing for or dealing with the serious needs of third world gay women."

✧ Candice Boyce, "In Their Own Words," in *The Question of Equality: Lesbian and Gay Politics in America Since Stonewall,* edited by David Deitcher (1995).

Age of Consent

Age at which law codes deem individuals either permissible sex partners for others who have reached sexual majority, or legally responsible for their own sex acts. Through most of legal history, "age of consent" has referred to the age at which persons might marry, generally fixed at or shortly after the average age of puberty. In the early 19th century, it was legal for children as young as 10 to marry in many parts of the U.S. The so-called purity movements of the second half of the 19th century played a strong role in changing cultural attitudes toward youth, extending the idea of childhood "innocence" into adolescence. By 1900, most American states and European countries had raised the age of consent to between 14 and 18 and legislated severe penalties for adults who had sexual relations with minors.

As same-sex relations have been decriminalized in much of the world, age of consent has become one of the most hotly contested issues addressed by lesbian and gay activists. The UNITED KINGDOM, for example, has maintained a higher age of consent for male-male sex than for sex between male-female or female-female partners in the belief, as expressed in parliamentary debates, that young men are especially vulnerable to being "converted" by older gay men. As a result, an English 18-year-old man may legally have sex with a 16-year-old girl, but can be imprisoned for having sex with a 17-year-old boy. The NETHERLANDS and FRANCE are two examples of countries in which activists, after years of protests, obtained legislation revoking discriminatory ages of consent. Today, typical ages of consent range from 14 in most parts of JAPAN to 15 or 16 in much of Europe to 18 in most of the United States.

✧ *The Third Pink Book: A Global View of Lesbian and Gay Liberation and Oppression,* edited by Aart Hendriks, Rob Tielman, and Evert van der Veen (1993).

✧ David Smith and Colin Richardson, "18: Thanks for Nothing!," *Gay Times* (March 1994).

Aging

Despite its universality, aging remains one of the least discussed, least studied, and, probably as a result, least celebrated aspects of gay and lesbian lives. Nevertheless, a few relevant sociological and psychological studies as well as testimony from increasingly vocal elders indicate that growing older as a lesbian or gay man is a much more positive phenomenon than is commonly thought.

The vast majority of research on adult development has been linked in some way to traditional notions of the heterosexual nuclear family. Studies of middle-aged women, for example, have tended to focus on the departure of children from the home, return to the workforce, etc. In addition, researchers conducting long-term studies began to ask questions about sexual orientation only in the mid-1970s. In the absence of facts, fictional representations like the pathetic old Aschenbach in Thomas Mann's *Death in Venice* helped establish stereotypes of older gay men and lesbians as desperately lonely individuals completely cut off from friends and family, not to mention sex and romance. Such gay male slang as "troll," applied sometimes to men who were barely past 30, and humor ("I'm 40—that's 280 in dog years, dead and buried in gay years") served only to reinforce these stereotypes.

There is no question that ageism is rampant in the SUBCULTURE, especially among gay men. Many clubs have top age limits, and older gay men can be made to feel, if not unwelcome, then invisible in many parts of the gay GHETTO. This prejudice notwithstanding, several studies have shown that older gay men actually tend on average to be better adjusted and more satisfied with their lives than young gay men.

Ageism is exacerbated by a generation gap unique to the gay and lesbian subcultures. Sociologists note enormous attitudinal, even cultural, differences among the three main gay and lesbian "cohorts" active today: men and women who reached sexual maturity before STONEWALL, those who came OUT during the "liberated" 1970s, and those who have come of age since the advent of AIDS in the early 1980s. Representatives of these three cohorts are sometimes divided even in the ways they describe themselves—"HOMOSEXUAL," "GAY" or "LESBIAN," "QUEER."

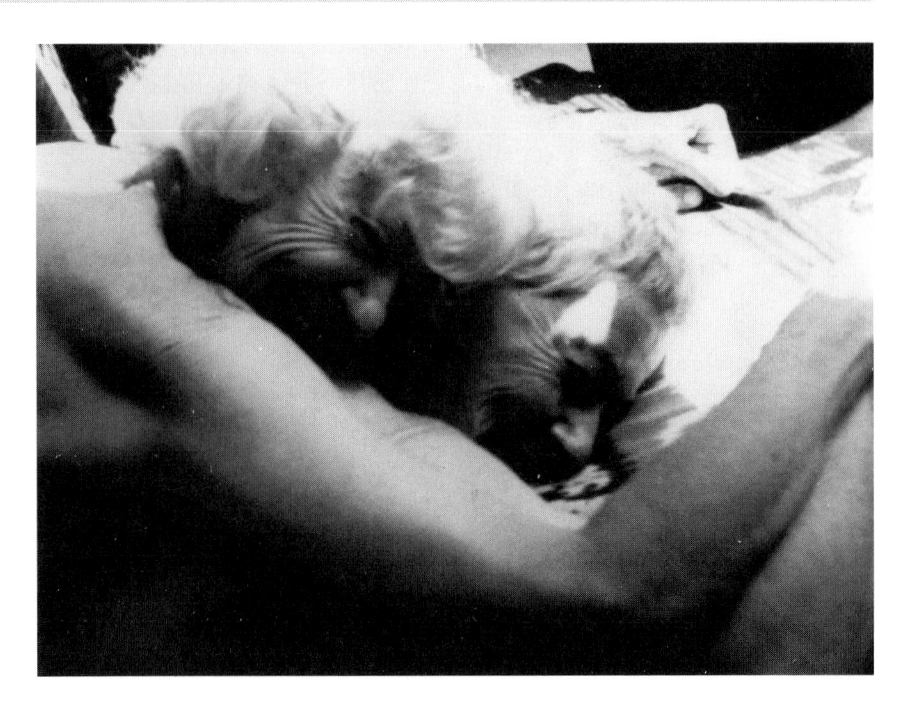

Timeless sensuality: Frances Lorraine and Sally Binford in Barbara Hammer's Nitrate Kisses (1992).

Activism

On November 2, 1977, Chris Almvig and others founded Senior Action in a Gay Environment (SAGE). Based in New York City, where it provides a wide range of social and support services, SAGE was the first nationwide advocacy agency for aging lesbians and gay men. SAGE has inspired others to form social service organizations in a number of cities, including Gay and Lesbian Outreach to Elders (GLOE, San Francisco), Project Rainbow (Los Angeles), and Metropolitan Retirees (Washington, D.C.). Besides providing educational and recreational services and outreach to homebound seniors, all these programs also work to fight ageism and to raise the visibility of older gay men and lesbians in the community and in the media.

After several years of organizing annual conferences, Shevy Healey and others founded Old Lesbians Organizing for Change (OLOC) in San Francisco in 1989. OLOC militantly embraces the word "old" while fighting special programs that isolate seniors. "I'm not the least bit interested in a Home for Old Dykes," Healey has said, "but I am very interested in intergenerational, intercultural housing for all dykes. My dream is not of a segregated old age."

Friendship, Romance, Sex

Most observers believe that lesbians are less likely than gay men to perceive aging as a negative, anxiety-producing phenomenon. In many parts of the U.S., women have actually developed special "croning" ceremonies to celebrate a woman's entry into old age (usually at her fifty-sixth birthday). Still, some lesbians experience isolation and loneliness as they grow older. To attempt to solve this problem, Christine Burton, a successful businesswoman living in Carmel, New York, began publishing *Golden Threads,* a quarterly magazine, in 1985; it helps lesbians over 50 connect with one another for friendship or romance. The publication now has subscribers all over the world and also sponsors annual Golden Threads festivals where hundreds of older lesbians gather. Burton, *Golden Threads,* and the festival were the subject of a documentary (1996) made by Karen Eaton, Lucy Winer (*Silent Pioneers*), and Frances Reid (*The Times of Harvey Milk*). In lesbian culture, JUNE ARNOLD's novel *Sister Gin* (1975), which featured a sexy octogenarian, and BARBARA HAMMER's film *Nitrate Kisses* (1992) were two of the earliest works to explore the erotic potential of older women.

Perhaps even more revolutionary, considering the gerontophobia thought to be rampant in the gay male world, is the Chiron Rising movement founded by Pat Colley and his partner, Bruce Vaughan, on April 1, 1986, with an informal newsletter addressed to older gay male acquaintances and friends. The newsletter led to a full-scale magazine, *Chiron Rising,* and quarterly *Chiron Classics* complete with PERSONAL ADS, homoerotic short stories, and nude photography of lusty gay seniors and the men who love them. *Chiron Rising*'s monthly circulation topped 10,000 in 1995. Through their Swan Production Company, Colley and Vaughan have also produced popular erotic videos featuring some of the same older men, including *Centaur* (1986), *Triplex* (1987), and *Quadriplex* (1992), and Colley has published a groundbreaking collection of short stories, *Quincunx* (1993), that eroticize older men in a range of genres, including semiautobiographical romances and SCIENCE FICTION fantasies. Chiron Rising had its first all-male convention in 1991. More than 5,000 older men and their admirers attended the 1996 convention in San Diego, California.

Chiron Rising, a movement and a publication that celebrates the eroticism of mature men, challenges Michel Foucault's dictum that the 20th century brought next to nothing new to the world of sex.

- *Psychological Perspectives on Lesbian and Gay Male Experiences,* edited by Linda D. Garnets and Douglas C. Kimmel (1993).

- *Lesbian, Gay, and Bisexual Identities over the Lifespan: Psychological Perspectives,* edited by Anthony R. D'Augelli and Charlotte J. Patterson (1995).

AIDS

Acronym for "acquired immunodeficiency syndrome," an immune system disorder that as of 1996 had been diagnosed in more than 250,000 gay and bisexual men and an estimated 8,000 lesbians in the U.S., and in more than 5 million people around the world. First noticed in the early 1980s (see **7/2/1981**) and officially named on **July 27, 1982**, AIDS has had dramatic effects on virtually every aspect of gay and lesbian life.

Strictly defined, AIDS is a multifaceted *syndrome* rather than one identifiable disease. As of

1996, the U.S. Centers for Disease Control definition for AIDS is based on the presence of one or more of a variety of conditions and diseases, including a CD4 (or T-helper cell) lymphocyte count of less than 200, or infections such as *Pneumocystis carinii* pneumonia (PCP), cancers, and wasting syndrome.

The vast majority of the world's scientists believe that AIDS is caused by the human immunodeficiency virus, more commonly called HIV. Exactly how HIV infection wears the immune system down and results in AIDS is not known.

Several forms of HIV have been identified but the two thought most relevant to the AIDS epidemic are HIV1 (most common in the United States) and HIV2 (more common in some parts of Africa). HIV is a *retrovirus:* unlike most organisms, which convert genetically coded deoxyribonucleic acid (DNA) into ribonucleic acid (RNA), HIV works in reverse, transcribing the RNA contained in the virus's core into DNA, which is in turn inserted into the host cell's stock of DNA. Enormous numbers of new viral particles are then created in the cell and later released, moving on to invade other cells.

HIV infection results in the body secreting antibodies that usually show up in tests within a few weeks of exposure (although, in some cases, not until as long as six months later). When test results show the presence of antibodies, people are said to have *seroconverted,* i.e., converted from HIV-negative (no antibodies) to HIV-positive (antibodies present). Many (perhaps most) people who exhibit HIV infection eventually develop one or more of the conditions that are defined as AIDS. In the first decade of the epidemic, medical authorities believed HIV infection was a certain death sentence, but large numbers of HIV-positive persons have survived in perfect health more than fifteen years after seroconverting, forcing doctors and the media to begin to question the inevitability of full-blown AIDS and subsequent death. In addition, the development of new treatment regimens has led to more optimistic prognoses for even larger numbers of HIV-positive persons.

Currently, 1 out of every 93 American men aged 27 to 39 is HIV-positive, and AIDS is the most frequent cause of death in this age group. Researchers report that a large number of these men became infected as teenagers.

Community Response

A catastrophe of profound proportions, the AIDS epidemic has had an immeasurable effect on gay and lesbian identity, politics, sexual practices, social life, and cultural expression.

By the 1990s, more than 600 AIDS-related service organizations had been formed across the U.S. The first such organizations, New York City's Gay Men's Health Crisis (see **1/12/1982**) and San Francisco's Kaposi's Sarcoma Foundation, were joined by dozens of other groups across the country—including AIDS Project Los Angeles (APLA), the California-based Shanti Project, and the Minority AIDS Project—as awareness of the epidemic spread. Besides offering counseling and assistance to persons with HIV and AIDS (often by assigning specially trained volunteer "buddies"), many of these organizations launched programs to research and promote SAFE(R) SEX education.

On the political front, GAY AND LESBIAN RIGHTS MOVEMENT activists waged a long and bitter struggle to win adequate government funding to battle the epidemic. Public awareness of AIDS increased dramatically when ROCK HUDSON succumbed to the disease. Although fear of AIDS was blamed for a resurgence in antigay and -lesbian prejudice, the epidemic also galvanized the community to unprecedented levels of political activity, including the return to DIRECT ACTION strategies exemplified by new groups like ACT UP.

An unforeseen consequence of the epidemic was a renewed spirit of cooperation between lesbians and gay men. Although the number of lesbians diagnosed with AIDS remained only a fraction of the count among gay men, lesbians were quick to come to the support of gay men and made major contributions to both the social service and political sides of the struggle against AIDS.

Among gay men, AIDS helped unify the community; at the same time, however, it had the divisive effect of creating two new "classes" of gay men based on their HIV status, the "positive" and the "negative." Although by the 1990s, gay men were beginning to realize that positive test results were not the certain death sentence they were once believed to be, seroconversion was still the source of enormous pain and stress. As a result, a major part of the gay and lesbian response to AIDS has been the development of counseling programs to support HIV-positive individuals.

Cultural Response

One of the consequences of the decimation of a generation of gay men due to AIDS was an outpouring of art dealing with the disease. Jeffrey Hagedorn's one-man, one-act play *One,* which premiered in Chicago in August 1983, was probably the first theatrical work to deal with AIDS. That same year, ARMISTEAD MAUPIN included a character with AIDS in his *Tales of the City* series in the *San Francisco Chronicle.* By the late 1980s, AIDS was a commonplace theme in LITERATURE, drama, and even MUSIC: John Corigliano's Symphony No. 1 is one of the most frequently performed pieces composed in response to AIDS. Donald Briggs and Loren Linnard premiered the first opera to deal with AIDS in San Francisco in May 1989. New York City Opera debuted an unsuccessful production of *La Traviata* in 1991 in which Violetta dies in an AIDS ward. Probably the most critically acclaimed work to deal with AIDS before 1995 was TONY KUSHNER's two-part epic drama *Angels in America.*

HOLLYWOOD, although as affected by AIDS-related deaths within the FILM and TELEVISION industry as any other area of the performing arts, was late in acknowledging the epidemic. Before *Philadelphia* (1993), the only movies that dealt with AIDS as a major theme were independent productions like Arthur J. Bressan Jr.'s *Buddies* (1985), Bill Sherwood's *Parting Glances* (1986), and director Norman René and writer Craig Lucas's *Longtime Companion* (1990). After *An Early Frost* (1985), AIDS was occasionally the theme of made-for-TV movies and, somewhat more often, part of the plotline of daytime and evening dramas.

➤Also see HEALTH, LESBIAN; KRAMER, LARRY; MONETTE, PAUL; NAMES PROJECT; SEX; SHILTS, RANDY; WOJNAROWICZ, DAVID.

✧ Randy Shilts, *And the Band Played On: Politics, People, and the AIDS Epidemic* (1987).

✧ *The Social Impact of AIDS in the United States,* edited by A. R. Jonsen and J. Stryker (1993).

✧ Rob Baker, *The Art of AIDS: From Stigma to Conscience* (1994).

✧ *Lesbian, Gay, and Bisexual Identities over the Lifespan: Psychological Perspectives,* edited by Anthony R. D'Augelli and Charlotte J. Patterson (1995).

Albee, Edward

(1928–)

U.S. playwright. The adopted son of a wealthy show-business family, Albee settled in Greenwich Village in the 1950s to pursue a writing career. In 1958, he completed *The Zoo Story*, a one-act play about a suicidally depressed young man that premiered the next year in Berlin and then opened off-Broadway. After several off-Broadway successes, his play *Who's Afraid of Virginia Woolf?* was one of the hits of the 1962–1963 Broadway season. Other plays include the Pulitzer Prize–winning *A Delicate Balance* (1966) and *Three Tall Women* (1994).

Early in his career, several heterosexual critics accused Albee of subversively developing gay themes with faux-heterosexual characters (see **11/5/1961**). Some gay critics have castigated him for *not* exploring gay themes or, paradoxically, for what John M. Clum calls "the far from gay homosexuality" underlying his allegedly glum artistic vision. His best-known play has been at the center of this controversy: Albee has repeatedly denied that George and Martha, the combative main characters of *Who's Afraid of Virginia Woolf?*, are a gay couple in disguise. In 1984, he successfully blocked an all-male production of the play.

Albee has objected to these criticisms, asserting that he is openly, proudly gay but that he opposes "ghettoization," and that an artist's understanding of the human condition is not confined by sexuality. He also points to *Finding the Sun* (1982), his one-act play about two unhappily married gay men; numerous gay characters in his other works; and his dramatic adaptations of novels by JAMES PURDY and CARSON MCCULLERS.

✧ Kaier Curtin, *"We Can Always Call Them Bulgarians": The Emergence of Lesbians and Gay Men on the American Stage* (1987).

Edward Albee: A Collection of Critical Essays, edited by C. W. E. Bigsby (1987).

John M. Clum, *Acting Gay: Male Homosexuality in Modern Drama* (1992).

Alcoholism, see ADDICTION/RECOVERY.

Allen, Paula Gunn
(1939–)

U.S. writer, educator. Allen grew up in a small New Mexico town near two different NATIVE AMERICAN reservations, and of all the eclectic influences on her childhood—which included Scottish and Lebanese ancestry, Presbyterian and Jewish grandparents, and a Catholic education—her mother's Sioux and Laguna Pueblo heritage left the deepest impressions. After college, an M.F.A. in creative writing, marriage, motherhood, and divorce, she published a book of poetry, *The Blind Lion*, in 1974 and completed a Ph.D. in American studies in 1975. She has since taught at several universities and published a novel, seven books of poetry, and a number of works of nonfiction.

Allen was one of the first scholars to research and write about "two-spirited" (see

Paula Gunn Allen.

BERDACHE) Native American women and their relationship to a tradition in which, as she wrote, "the American Indians were clearly aware of the power that woman possessed." *Hwame, Koshkalak, and the Rest: Lesbians in American Indian Cultures* (1981) and *The Sacred Hoop: Recovering the Feminine in American Indian Traditions* (1986) broke long-standing taboos in Native American studies and laid a foundation for a deeper understanding of traditional Indian concepts of GENDER and sexuality. Her novel in progress, *Raven's Road,* is probably the first whose main character is an openly lesbian (or gay) Native American.

✧ Elizabeth I. Hanson, *Paula Gunn Allen* (1990).

Allison, Dorothy E.

(1949–)

U.S. writer. Born into a working-class Greenville, South Carolina, family, Allison discovered her talent for storytelling as a child desperately seeking escape from the sexual abuse and beatings she suffered from her stepfather. By adolescence, she was writing short lesbian romances, one of which she made the mistake of showing to the girl on whom its heroine was based. Stung by the ridicule of her classmates, she continued writing but made a ceremony of periodically burning her stories.

Allison published her first book of poetry, *The Women Who Hate Me,* in 1983 (expanded edition, 1991) and reached a broad audience with her first collection of short stories, *Trash* (1988). Like her best-selling novel, *Bastard Out of Carolina* (1992), *Trash* unflinchingly detailed the multifaceted miseries of southern "white trash" life. Although many readers assumed *Bastard* was autobiographical, Allison told *The New York Times* in 1992 that "it would have been a lot meaner" if it were.

After the mainstream success of *Bastard,* Allison returned to gay and lesbian publishing with *Skin* (1993), a collection of essays, mostly on sex-related topics. In 1995, she published a book of short stories she has described as her most autobiographical, *Two or Three Things I Know for Sure.*

Critics have praised Allison for the fiercely lyric honesty of her work and for the compelling power of her writer's voice. She often describes writing as if it were a lifeline: "The story becomes the thing needed," she writes in *Two or Three Things,* whose title comes from this passage: "Two or three things I know for sure and one of them is what it means to have no loved version of your life but the one you make."

Allison has also been a prominent prosex partisan of the lesbian SEX WARS. She lives in San Francisco with her lover, Alix, and their son, Wolf.

Allston, Washington

(1779–1843)

Pioneering American painter. Born into a wealthy South Carolina plantation family, Allston attended Harvard, then spent two seven-year periods in London studying, painting, and acquainting himself with leading intellectuals of the time, including Samuel Taylor Coleridge, whose portrait he painted, and Washington Irving. Although Allston married twice, art historian Phoebe Lloyd has brought to light documents which suggest that he fled London in 1818, amid intensified persecution of "sodomites" (see **1810**), to escape blackmailers. Back in the Boston area, Allston painted a few more of the romantic landscapes that had won him acclaim in England and the U.S. (including *Moonlit Landscape,* 1819), but increasingly focused on religious subjects in an attempt, Lloyd believes, to resolve the painful conflict of his attraction to other men. In his later years, Allston was best known for never finishing paintings, including several prestigious commissions.

✧ Phoebe Lloyd, "Washington Allston: American Martyr?," *Art in America* (March 1984).

Almodóvar, Pedro

(1951–)

Spanish filmmaker. Born in the La Mancha region, Almodóvar began his own quixotic quest for fame and fortune by fleeing his conservative hometown for Madrid in the late 1960s. While supporting himself with a job at the national phone company, he wrote a scandal-packed "autobiography" of a fictitious porn star he called Patty Diphusa (a pun on *patidifusa,* "flabbergasted"), acted with an avant-garde theater company, and performed in his own CROSS-DRESSING punk band. His cinematic career began with Super-8 experiments, followed by a 1980 feature, *Pepi, Luci, Bom.* Though lacking the hypertechnicolor, haute-couture gloss of his later work, this first film established kink, camp, and black humor as Almodóvar trademarks.

Antonio Banderas in a scene from Almodóvar's Law of Desire.

Almodóvar, who has resisted being identified as a "gay" filmmaker, describes his own sexuality as fluid and spontaneous, open to change. Not surprisingly, his films include gay men who fall in love with women (*Labyrinth of Passion,* 1982), straight men who fall in love with men (*Matador,* 1986), as well as unexpected cross-dressing and TRANSSEXUAL scenarios (*Law of Desire,* 1987; *High Heels,* 1991; *Kika,* 1993; etc.). Equally resistant to political correctness, he has used murder, incest, bondage, and rape to satirize everything from bourgeois respectability to Spanish popular culture and exploitative TV journalism. Despite—or perhaps because of—continuing controversy, he is the most commercially successful director in the history of Spanish cinema.

✧ Pedro Almodóvar, *Patty Diphusa and Other Writings* (1991).

✧ Paul Julian Smith, *Desire Unlimited: The Cinema of Pedro Almodóvar* (1994).

Alther, Lisa

(née Lisa Reed; 1944–)

U.S. writer. Born and raised in eastern Tennessee, she attended Wellesley College, married painter Richard Alther, and had a daughter. Alther's fiction has exemplified her real-life fascination with the changing boundaries and definitions of a woman's sexuality. She told *Out* magazine: "When I was married, I was straight, but now that I am with a woman, I feel that I am a lesbian. I hope that I am with her five years from now, but if I'm not, I don't know what I might be. I might be a real estate agent!"

Alther's most popular novel, *Kinflicks* (1975), features a young woman who leaves Tennessee to attend "Worthley" College.

There, she meets a radical lesbian and is lured away to a commune in Vermont for a time before rejecting lesbian SEPARATISM and trying to find happiness in heterosexual marriage. *Other Women* (1984) delves into the past and present psyche of a woman in therapy. *Bedrock* (1990) portrays the late-20th-century equivalent of a ROMANTIC FRIENDSHIP. *Five Minutes in Heaven* (1995) explores polymorphously "queer" pairings, including sex between lesbians and gay men.

✧ Sarah Pettit, "Her Blue Heaven," *Out* (June 1995).

Altman, Dennis

(1943–)

Australian writer, theorist, activist, educator. A Sydney-born Fulbright scholar, Altman earned a master's degree in political science from Cornell. He returned to the U.S. for an extended visit the summer after the STONEWALL Uprising, met and worked with leading gay activists on both coasts, and even participated in an attempted ZAP on New York City Mayor John V. Lindsay. Back in AUSTRALIA, he published *Homosexual: Oppression and Liberation* (1971), now considered the definitive account of the ideas that shaped the GAY LIBERATION era. Synthesizing deviance theory, Marxism, and the Reichian rhetoric of the sexual revolution, he wrote, "As long as society is based on competitiveness and sexual repression, there will be a need to demarcate it into categories, to maintain socially induced repressions by stigmatizing heavily all those who fall outside the norm." Like many others at the time, he hoped for a day when the right to individualized sexual expression would be so accepted that the very category of "gay" would cease to have meaning.

In a pessimistic vein, Altman warned that commercialization threatened the sexual revolution and that sexual desirability could become just another capitalist commodity. He expanded on this theme in *Coming Out in the Seventies* (1979), observing a new spirit of accommodationism among once radical movement leaders. Gay men, he observed, were increasingly "self-assertive" and "unapologetic," but they had also become "consumerist" and only potentially political.

In *The Homosexualization of America, the Americanization of the Homosexual* (1982), Altman chronicled the emergence of a distinctive gay lifestyle and its repercussions, negative as well as positive, in the U.S. and abroad. He was among the first to describe evolving gay social groupings as alternative "families."

AIDS in the Mind of America (1986; British edition entitled *AIDS and the New Puritanism*) was an early account of the American response to AIDS, both in the gay community and the nation at large, and a perceptive prophecy of the rebirth of lesbian and gay ACTIVISM that was to occur in the latter years of the decade.

Although Altman is perhaps best known for his trenchant analyses of gay and lesbian life in the U.S., he has also reported on developments in Europe, particularly in FRANCE, and has been a prominent member of the INTERNATIONAL LESBIAN AND GAY ASSOCIATION.

A Melbourne resident, he is probably Australia's best-known and most often quoted gay activist. His first novel, *The Comfort of Men* (1993), was described by Robert Dessaix in the introduction to his anthology, *Australian Gay and Lesbian Writing* (1993), as Australia's first "full-length, more or less traditional novel focusing on homosexuality."

Amazons

Legendary women warriors of antiquity; by extension, any fiercely independent women-identified women. Many ancient historians and geographers, including Herodotus and Diodorus Siculus, wrote of formidable all-female armies led by warrior queens in distant lands, usually around the Black Sea or in northwest Africa. Amazons make several appearances in Greek and Roman mythology, and *Amazonomachy* (battling amazons) was one of the most common themes in classical Greek art, depicted in some 800 surviving artifacts. These facts have led some theorists to speculate that the amazon legends preserve a memory of matriarchal or even gynecocratic times. Most historians, however, think it is more likely that the amazon legends grew out of contacts with cultures in which women had a higher social position than among the stridently patriarchal Greeks. Evidence for this theory comes from Scythian and Sarmatian graves north of the Black Sea, where women were sometimes buried in full battle gear.

Some feminist historians, notably Eva Keuls, have suggested that the Greeks used Amazon legends to keep men vigilant against the threat of female power. Whether or not this is true, Greek amazon lore tended to be markedly misogynist. Even the word "amazon" was thought to mean "breastless," based on the fanciful belief that a woman would have to remove at least one breast to draw a bowstring quickly and accurately. Amazons, some writers claimed, lopped or burned off their right breast—although they were never pictured in Greek art with anything but well-formed breasts. Most often, in fact, they were shown being stabbed through a breast by a Greek hero.

In Homer, amazons are invariably referred to as *antianeirai,* literally "anti-male" but commonly translated as "a match for men." Amazons were usually thought to live in an all-female society, venturing out from time to time to get pregnant and then killing or giving away any male babies that resulted.

Amazons loved hunting and arduous exercise. Besides bows and arrows, their favorite weapon was a two-headed ax called a LABRYS. Some amazons, according to JUDY GRAHN, dressed in red leather. They often had two queens, one to lead in battle, the other to rule the homeland. Northwest African ("Libyan") amazons, sometimes associated with Atlantis, were said to have conquered and ruled vast areas of the Mediterranean world. Many cities, including SAPPHO's hometown of Mytilene, were believed to have been founded by amazons.

Amazons became part of the iconography of lesbian feminism.

Whatever their origin, the amazon legends became a part of Roman and medieval European folklore. Almost every ruling European queen was at one time or another (flatteringly) called an amazon. Writers from Christine de Pizan to WILLIAM SHAKESPEARE included amazon characters in their works. For centuries, whenever Europeans encountered a group of armed women, they immediately dubbed them "amazons." (The Amazon River, California, and PAT CALIFIA's pseudonymous surname are all derived from stories told by Spanish colonizers of New World women warriors led by a fearsome queen named Califia.)

In the early 20th century, amazons became associated with lesbians when NATALIE BARNEY began calling herself "*une amazone.*" Half a century was to go by before the association became widespread. In 1969, MONIQUE WITTIG presaged an onslaught of lesbian amazon imagery and symbolism with the publication of *Les Guérillères.* In the 1970s, lesbian feminists and separatists popularized "amazon" as a forceful synonym for lesbian, as in the *Amazon Quarterly* (1972–1975), *Lesbian Separatism: An Amazon Analysis*, and *Amazon Poetry* (edited by Elly Bulkin and JOAN LARKIN, 1975). Many writers, including MARION ZIMMER BRADLEY, have also created fictitious amazon characters.

➤ Also see BERDACHE; LESBIAN FEMINISM; SEPARATISM.

- Donald J. Sobol, *The Amazons of Greek Mythology* (1972).
- Eva C. Keuls, *The Reign of the Phallus: Sexual Politics in Ancient Athens* (1985).
- Christine Downing, *Myths and Mysteries of Same-Sex Love* (1991).
- Jessica A. Salmonson, *The Encyclopedia of Amazons: Women Warriors from Antiquity to the Modern Age* (1991).

American Civil Liberties Union (ACLU)

Organization founded in 1920 by JANE ADDAMS, Roger Baldwin, Norman Thomas, and others to safeguard and ensure the basic human rights laid out in the U.S. Constitution. For over four decades after its founding, the ACLU refused to challenge SODOMY statutes because, in its leaders' opinion, homosexuality was not a form of "belief" or "speech" protected by the Constitution. On **January 7, 1957**, the ACLU board of directors reaffirmed this position and stated explicitly that it also did not consider federal security restrictions on gay men and lesbians unconstitutional.

In the late 1950s, FRANK KAMENY and other activists targeted local branches of the ACLU to advance the HOMOPHILE cause. By 1964, ACLU branches in Washington, D.C., New York City, and Southern California had reconsidered the union's position and begun to offer support on local cases. Together, these local branches lobbied other affiliates and succeeded in persuading that year's national convention to pass a resolution opposing government interference in the sex lives of consenting adults. After two years of consideration, the national board, encouraged by a 1965 Supreme Court decision that found Connecticut's anticontraception law unconstitutional on grounds of the right to privacy, confirmed the 1964 resolution and committed the union to a campaign against sodomy legislation and discriminatory practices.

In the late 1960s, the ACLU launched a multitargeted attack on behalf of lesbians and gay men, which included the first major study of arrests and prosecutions of gay men in California, legal assistance for persons caught in BAR and BATHHOUSE raids, and actions against discriminatory civil service restrictions. Since 1979, the ACLU has had a special Project on Lesbian and Gay Rights. The union remains active in virtually every area of gay and lesbian civil rights concerns.

➤ Also see GAY AND LESBIAN RIGHTS MOVEMENT; NATIONAL GAY AND LESBIAN TASK FORCE.

- John D'Emilio, *Sexual Politics, Sexual Communities: The Making of a Homosexual Minority in the United States, 1940–1970* (1983).
- *Lesbians, Gay Men, and the Law,* edited by William B. Rubenstein (1993).

American Indians, see NATIVE AMERICANS.

American Library Association (ALA)

First U.S. professional organization to sanction a gay and lesbian group (1970). In 1969, the ALA instituted the Social Responsibilities Round Table to "address issues previously neglected" by library science. The next year, Janet Cooper and Israel Fishman met at ALA's annual conference in Detroit and decided to seek approval and funding via the Round Table for a "Task Force on Gay Liberation." At the 1971 ALA conference in Dallas, this task force launched an array of special programs and presentations, including a "gay bibliography," the first gay book AWARDS and even an attention-getting "hug-a-homosexual" kissing booth. In response, the ALA became one of the first professional organizations in the world to pass a resolution in support of gay and lesbian rights.

From 1972 through 1986, BARBARA GITTINGS coordinated activities for the task force (which changed its name to the Gay Task Force in 1975, the Gay and Lesbian Task Force in 1987, and the Gay, Lesbian, and Bisexual Task Force in 1994), supported by Jack Baker, Kay (Tobin) Lahusen, Frances Hanckel, and other activists. The group's achievements include extensive surveys on relevant library holdings and influential recommendations for improvement; promotion of the words "GAY" and "LESBIAN" in place of "HOMOSEXUAL"; employment and benefit rights advocacy for lesbian and gay librarians; critiques of mainstream reference books; and—perhaps most important, since so many young people first seek information on same-sex relations at libraries—reforms of the Library of Congress classification system to include subject headings for "gays" and "lesbians" as classes of persons and to delete "see also sexual perversion" from catalog listings.

➤ Also see ARCHIVES AND LIBRARIES; LITERATURE.

- Barbara Gittings, *Gays in Library Land: The Gay and Lesbian Task Force of the American Library Association: The First Sixteen Years* (1990).

American Psychiatric Association (APA)

Major professional organization in its field, founded in 1844. The APA had no official position on homosexuality in its first century of existence. Its members' views, however, as expressed in papers presented at its conferences and articles published in the *American Journal of Psychiatry,* seem to have evolved from Freud-influenced tolerance in the 1920s and 1930s to a belief that homosexuality was a serious disorder requiring aggressive treatment.

Reflecting the growing prestige of PSYCHOLOGY in the years after World War II, the American Medical Association decided that the APA should take over the task of classifying "illnesses" thought to be mental disorders. Under the supervision of the U.S. Public Health Service, a group of experts worked to put together a new classification system, and in **1952** the APA published the first *Diagnostic and Statistical Manual, Mental Disorders (DSM-I).* "Homosexuality" appeared in this edition under "sociopathic" personality disturbances, which meant that lesbians and gay men were "ill primarily in terms of society and of con-

"Doctor H. Anonymous" (John Fryer) testifies with Barbara Gittings and Frank Kameny against the APA's stance on homosexuality.

formity with the prevailing cultural milieu." In the next edition, *DSM-II* (1968), homosexuality was moved to "non-psychotic mental disorders," a category that included sadistic sexual assault.

These classifications not only influenced psychoanalysis, but also had a broad impact on laws, in particular on SODOMY and IMMIGRATION regulations. As a result, the APA became a target of some of the earliest ZAPS (see **5/14/1970**) staged as part of the GAY LIBERATION era. Beginning in 1971, activists, including BARBARA GITTINGS, Ron Gold, FRANK KAMENY, and Dr. Charles Silverstein, made a series of presentations to the group, culminating in a decision by the APA board of trustees on **December 15, 1973**, to remove "homosexuality" from the *DSM*.

In a referendum the following year, 53 percent of the responding psychiatrists confirmed the board's decision. For the 37 percent who opposed it, the board had included a loophole: patients who were unhappy about their sexuality could be treated under the classification of "sexual disturbance disorder" (from 1980 through 1986, "ego-dystonic homosexuality").

Today, the APA is in general gay- and lesbian-friendly, although the issue of whether a lesbian or gay man can be an effective psychoanalyst continues to be controversial among more conservative psychoanalysts. Even before the 1973 decision, some 200 APA members had joined together in a secret group they called the GAY-PA. In 1975, they came OUT and formed an open caucus, which after several name changes is today the Association of Lesbian and Gay Psychiatrists. The APA also has a Committee on Gay and Lesbian Concerns.

✧ Ronald Bayer, *Homosexuality and American Psychiatry: The Politics of Diagnosis* (1981).

Amnesty International (AI)

Worldwide volunteer organization of more than 1 million members founded in 1961 to fight and prevent governmental abuse of human rights. The organization's primary mission is to combat torture and capital punishment in all circumstances and to work to free prisoners of conscience. In 1979, AI explicitly confirmed that individuals imprisoned for advocating gay and lesbian rights would be considered prisoners of conscience. In **September 1991**, after considerable debate, an international conference of the organization resolved to mandate activism on behalf of all persons imprisoned for consensual same-sex acts between adults or simply on account of their sexual orientation. Since this decision, the organization has documented "gross violations of human rights against lesbians and gay men" in more than a dozen countries. In recent years, AI has begun to study and consider other gay and lesbian human rights concerns, such as discrimination in the statutory AGE OF CONSENT and prejudicial use of a defendant's sexual orientation in court cases.

➤ Also see INTERNATIONAL LESBIAN AND GAY ASSOCIATION.

✧ *Breaking the Silence: Human Rights Violations Based on Sexual Orientation* (Amnesty International USA report, 1994).

Amsterdam, see NETHERLANDS.

Anderson, Margaret C.
(1886–1973)

U.S. editor/publisher, critic, memoirist. Born into a cultured, well-to-do Indianapolis family, she attended college in Ohio, then moved to Chicago in search of intellectual and social stimulation. In 1914, she started *The Little Review,* a magazine that, her friend JANET FLANNER said, "shattered complacent literary customs, aroused curiosity, and became a kind of monthly cult among its devotees." In 1916, Anderson met Jane Heap (1887–1964), a brilliantly outspoken, CROSS-DRESSING writer and painter, and Heap soon left DJUNA BARNES for Anderson and *The Little Review.* Under Heap's guidance, *The Little Review* championed experimentalism in all the arts, publishing works by Ezra Pound (who was for several years the magazine's influential though contentious foreign editor), H.D., HART CRANE, T. S. Eliot, and, most famously, James Joyce. Joyce's *Ulysses* was serialized in the magazine, leading to a court case in which Heap and Anderson were found guilty of obscenity and fined $100. Especially in its early years, the magazine was also a mouthpiece for Anderson's radical politics. Its **March 1915** issue contained Anderson's impassioned critique of a lecture given by EDITH ELLIS. Anderson's article is probably the first defense of same-sex love published by an American lesbian.

Anderson and Heap joined the flourishing Paris lesbian émigré community in 1923 and published their magazine from Europe as a quarterly through 1929. In its last decade, the magazine promoted important work by, among others, BRYHER, JEAN COCTEAU, GERTRUDE STEIN, photographer BERENICE ABBOTT, and the Dadaists.

After 1929, Anderson led an increasingly secluded life, although she corresponded extensively and wrote three volumes of memoirs, and one novel, *Forbidden Fires* (published posthumously in 1996). She and former opera star Georgette Leblanc were lovers from 1923 until Leblanc's death in 1940. After LeBlanc's death, Anderson shared her life for nearly 14 years with Dorothy Caruso, widow of the tenor Enrico Caruso.

Anderson's relationships and *The Little Review* are the subjects of Wendy Weinberg's 30-minute film, *Beyond Imagining* (1994).

Androgyny

Term that combines the Greek words for "man" (*andros*) and "woman" (*gyne*) to describe behavior, mannerisms, speech styles, modes of dress, grooming, etc., that are considered both masculine and feminine, or neither masculine nor feminine, or that invert conventional GENDER expectations. Although androgyny can describe physical characteristics, it is generally kept distinct from *hermaphroditism,* which means having both male and female sex organs.

Romaine Brooks's portrait of Peter (A Young English Girl) (1923–1924) was an early lesbian expression of androgyny.

Androgyny is an especially slippery concept since it is based on a conflation, confusion, or rejection of expected notions of gender, which in turn are unfixed and constantly changing. One example is hair length. In the BIBLE, Samson's long hair is a sign of his "masculine" strength and power. If he had journeyed a little to the southwest, he would have encountered Egyptian women who shaved their heads bald to accentuate their "feminine" purity. Yet both hairstyles would probably be considered androgynous in a contemporary American context.

Closely related to CROSS-DRESSING, androgyny has been viewed in many cultures throughout history as an innate characteristic of men and women erotically attracted to persons of their own sex. Contemporary social historians emphasize, however, that homosexuality and gender nonconformity are two distinct phenomena: androgyny has at times been mandated by heterosexuals, as in CHINA during the Cultural Revolution; and HOMOEROTICISM has often been rooted not in a rejection but rather in an exaggeration of gender difference, as in the 1970s gay male CLONE look.

An increasing number of lesbians and gay men, especially artists and writers, have consciously used androgyny to underscore what QUEER THEORY treats as the "performative" nature of gender—the idea that all gender "roles" are part of a complex performance scripted and rehearsed by social and cultural forces.

✧ Marjorie Garber, *Vested Interests: Cross-Dressing and Cultural Anxiety* (1993).

Anger, Kenneth

(Kenneth Wilbur Anglemyer; 1927–)

U.S. filmmaker, writer. Born in Santa Monica, California, Anger literally attended Hollywood High and figuratively nurtured himself on American movie mythology. He made his first short film, *Fireworks* (1947), at the age of 19 while his parents were away for a weekend. Characteristically surreal, *Fireworks,* as VITO RUSSO wrote, is a film in which "Anger dared to film one of his own wet dreams," a boy's violent encounter with a group of hunky sailors. Although restrained by today's standards, it was one of the first films to feature overt HOMOEROTICISM and as such was subjected to police prosecution until 1959, when the California Supreme Court failed to find it obscene.

Fireworks earned Anger an invitation from JEAN COCTEAU to work with him in FRANCE. Although nothing came of their collaboration,

Anger remained in France in the 1950s and made several more avant-garde shorts.

Back in the U.S., Anger filmed *Scorpio Rising* (1963), provocatively combining imagery from 1950s motorcycle gang pictures, biblical epics, and the emerging gay leather scene (see S/M). Legend has it that Anger was sued by the American Nazi Party for "defaming" the swastika in his film.

Anger's "underground" movies were a major influence on independent filmmakers, but he is probably best known for his tell-all *Hollywood Babylon* chronicles (the first of which was published in France in 1960 but not in the U.S. until publisher Jann Wenner's 1975 edition; *II*, 1984), which were among the first widely read books to acknowledge the existence of (albeit closeted) gay men and lesbians in HOLLYWOOD.

✧ Bill Landis, *Anger: The Unauthorized Biography of Kenneth Anger* (1995).

Anglican Communion

Thirty-five self-governing churches, with more than 70 million members in more than 160 countries, including the EPISCOPAL CHURCH in the U.S., that share the faith and beliefs of the Church of England, the oldest and largest denomination to derive from Henry VIII's break with the ROMAN CATHOLIC CHURCH in 1534. Although traditionally opposed to all extramarital sex acts, Anglican church leaders were nevertheless among the first to call for legal tolerance of same-sex relations. In **March 1954**, an English church body recommended the decriminalization of sex between consenting male adults (female-female acts were never criminalized in England). Most churches in the Communion have continued to view same-sex acts as a moral failing, but many congregations have welcomed lesbian and gay parishioners. The most controversial issue everywhere in the world has been whether or not to allow the ordination of openly gay and lesbian deacons and priests. In 1991, the English House of Bishops urged "homophile clergy and ordinands not to enter into sexually active relationships." In 1994, the DIRECT ACTION group OUTRAGE! launched a campaign of OUTING British bishops; this led to a public announcement the next year by the bishop of London, David Hope, that his sexuality was "ambiguous" although he had always led a "single, celibate life." On March 16, 1995, the Archbishop of Canterbury told the press: "We reject homophobia in any form. Homosexuals must be treated as people made in the image and likeness of God." He joined with the 35 other Anglican primates to recommend a Communion-wide discussion "to face the questions about sexuality with honesty and integrity, avoiding unnecessary confrontation and polarization."

Anthropology

Study of the origin, organization, culture, and social relations of human beings. Cultural, or social, anthropology is the branch of the science that has been most involved in the study of same-sex eroticism, although it was not until 1970 that the American Anthropological Association (AAA) followed Clark Taylor's suggestion and officially recognized the importance of such studies. Since then, and especially since the 1980s, an ever increasing number of anthropologists have focused on same-sex relations as an object of research.

Anthropology emerged as an independent, established academic field around the beginning of the 20th century. True to the intellectual climate of their time—as well as their European and North American cultural backgrounds—most early-20th-century anthropologists viewed homosexuality as an individual "problem" or "deviation" that lay within the realm of PSYCHOLOGY or SOCIOLOGY rather than anthropology. On the relatively rare occasions when an anthropologist mentioned same-sex practices, he or she often betrayed cultural blinders: one, for example, referred to the male homosexual practices mandated by many Australian aboriginal cultures as "sexual abnormalities" and "perversions," even though they were the accepted norm among these peoples.

Although scholarly writers from the late 18th century on had left an enormous variety of accounts of same-sex practices in various parts of the world, no discrete anthropological "theory" of homosexuality was developed. Cross-cultural comparisons were generally left to lay anthropologists such as EDWARD CARPENTER. The roles of BERDACHES in NATIVE AMERICAN cultures were among the first subjects related to same-sex eroticism to receive serious anthropological study. RUTH BENEDICT and MARGARET MEAD both contributed pioneering works in this area and helped convince other anthropologists that such studies were worthwhile.

As late as April 1966, however, anthropologist David Sonnenschein, writing in *Anthropological Quarterly,* felt obliged in an article entitled "Homosexuality as a Subject of Anthropological Inquiry" to make "a simple plea for research," lamenting that "anthropologists have ignored homosexuality in Western societies and, what is worse, have barely taken note of it as it manifests itself in primitive groups."

After STONEWALL—and the AAA's official acknowledgment of the importance of studies of same-sex eroticism in cultures the following year—the field began to change dramatically. The AAA held a symposium called "Homosexuality in Cross-cultural Perspective" in 1974 in Mexico City, and the Anthropological Research Group on Homosexuality (renamed the Society of Lesbian and Gay Anthropologists in 1987) was formed in the same decade.

The first—and until the mid-1980s the only—anthropological study to focus solely on women was D. G. Wolf's *The Lesbian Community,* published in 1979. Since then, other anthropologists, such as Evelyn Blackwood, have looked at same-sex erotic behavior in other cultures, arriving at positions that sometimes run counter to the assumption—common in LESBIAN AND GAY STUDIES—of the universality of COMPULSORY HETEROSEXUALITY. As Blackwood writes, "In contrast to this analysis, the history of sexual relations is not one of total heterosexual dominance. The construction of sexuality in many non-class societies validated variant sexual behavior for women."

Other groundbreaking anthropological publications related to gay and lesbian studies include Walter L. Williams's work on "sexual diversity in American Indian culture" and a collection on *Latin American Male Homosexualities* (1995) overseen by Stephen O. Murray.

- *The Many Faces of Homosexuality: Anthropological Approaches to Homosexual Behavior,* edited by Evelyn Blackwood (1986).
- *Gay Culture in America: Essays from the Field,* edited by Gilbert Herdt (1992).
- Walter L. Williams, *The Spirit and the Flesh: Sexual Diversity in American Indian Culture* (1993).
- *Third Sex, Third Gender: Beyond Sexual Dimorphism in Culture and History,* edited by Gilbert Herdt (1994).
- *Out in the Field: Reflections of Lesbian and Gay Anthropologists,* edited by Ellen Lewin and William L. Leap (1996).

Antinous, see HADRIAN AND ANTINOUS.

Anzaldúa, Gloria (Evangelina)

(1942–)

U.S. writer, editor, teacher. Anzaldúa grew up in rural South Texas. After her father died when she was 15, her family survived by working in the fields in Texas and Arkansas. Anzaldúa persisted in her studies and became one of the first rural Chicanos (not to mention Chicanas) to go to college. She went on to earn a master's degree in English and education from the University of Texas at Austin and spent almost two years teaching migrant workers' children. She moved to California in the late 1970s to pursue Chicano and feminist studies and began lecturing at San Francisco State in 1979.

By the time Anzaldúa met CHERRÍE MORAGA in the late 1970s, both women had grown angry and frustrated by their experiences in the predominantly Anglo feminist community. Determined "to examine incidents of intolerance, prejudice and denial of differences within the feminist movement [and] create a definition that expands what 'feminist' means to us," they coedited *This Bridge Called My Back: Writings by Radical Women of Color* (1981). Along with two other books on women of color published that year by Kitchen Table Press, their anthology, as SARAH SCHULMAN noted in *Womanews* in February 1982, succeeded in making "race, racism, and racial identity . . . the most widely and heatedly debated concerns in the radical women's movement."

Gloria Anzaldúa.

In addition to raising the visibility of women of color, *This Bridge Called My Back* helped launch an unprecedented surge of Chicana writing, a movement Anzaldúa enriched with *Borderlands/La Frontera: The New Mestiza* (1987), an unclassifiable collection of prose and poetry that some critics have called a "cultural autobiography." As the words "borderlands" and "*mestiza*" suggest, Anzaldúa's book delineates the convergence of influences that are part of her heritage yet transcends them to forge a new (anti-)identity that is quintessentially "queer," a word she began using several years before it came into vogue. She asserts that "the mestizo and the queer exist at this time and point on the evolutionary continuum for a purpose" because both "are a blending that proves that all blood is intricately woven together, and that we are spawned out of similar souls."

Anzaldúa has also edited another anthology, *Making Face, Making Soul/Haciendo Caras: Creative and Critical Perspectives by Women of Color* (1990), and published an experimental short story cycle, *Prieta* (1994).

Arab World

All same-sex relations illegal in Algeria, Bahrain, Jordan, Kuwait, Lebanon, Libya, Morocco, Oman, Qatar, Saudi Arabia, Sudan, Syria, Tunisia, United Arab Emirates, and Yemen, with penalties ranging from a fine and six months' imprisonment to capital punishment.

No relevant laws for consenting adults in Egypt and Iraq.

Informal support groups in Alexandria and Cairo.

Of all the world's regions, the Arab nations have remained the most isolated from the modern international gay and lesbian rights movement. Despite a centuries-old tradition of HOMOEROTICISM in poetry and a widespread tolerance of CIRCUMSTANTIAL HOMOSEXUALITY, especially among unmarried young men, very few Arabs identify themselves as "lesbian" or "gay" in the international sense of these words.

The rise of Islamic fundamentalism has led to greater hostility toward all forms of same-sex eroticism and, in many countries, the reimposition of *shari'a* (Islamic law), which not only severely penalizes same-sex relations but also keeps women out of public life and thus reduces their chances of meeting one another.

The Gay and Lesbian Arabic Society, founded in the U.S. in 1988, is a support network for lesbians and gay men of Arab descent.

➤ Also see ABŪ NUWĀS; CENTRAL ASIA; ISLAM.

✧ *The Third Pink Book: A Global View of Lesbian and Gay Liberation and Oppression,* edited by Aart Hendriks, Rob Tielman, and Evert van der Veen (1993).

Araki, Gregg

(1959–)

U.S. filmmaker. Born in Santa Barbara, California, Araki earned an M.F.A. in film from U.C. Santa Barbara in 1984. He worked as a music critic for *L.A. Weekly* and made his first widely released feature in 1987. He has continued to write, direct, and shoot his films on budgets as low as $5,000.

Most critics consider Araki one of the leading auteurs of 1990s "queer cinema," but his movies transcend—some would say transgress—political orthodoxy. His characters—gay, lesbian, bisexual, and straight—seem to live in the same desolate, despairing California neighborhoods as DENNIS COOPER's men and boys, but his plots are lightened with absurdist touches that help viewers empathize with the moral ambiguities of his films. In his movies and in interviews, Araki is as critical of the ways gay people treat themselves and one another as he is of homophobia. Consequently, as he told *Genre* magazine, his "harshest criticism" has come from gay journalists.

Araki's features include the self-explanatory *Three Bewildered People in the Night* (1987); *The Long Weekend (o' Despair)* (1989), in which two men and a woman attempt to sort out their respective relationships; *The Living End* (1992), a dark romance about two HIV-positive men, one of whom can't stop expressing himself with a gun; and *Totally F***ed Up* (1994) and *Doom Generation* (1995), the first two films in a projected trilogy about gay and straight youth.

✧ Daryl Chin, "Girlfriend in a Coma: Notes on the Films of Gregg Araki," in *Queer Looks,* edited by Martha Gever, John Greyson, and Pratibha Parmar (1993).

Archives and Libraries

According to the Lesbian and Gay Archives Roundtable of the Society of American Archivists, there were 121 archives and special library collections devoted to lesbian and gay studies in 35 American states as of 1996. That same year, Canada had 15 such collections in 7 different provinces. The largest collection of books and materials relating to sexuality is held

Araki's Living End unleashed HIV-positive desperadoes on a generally apathetic California. Lead actors Mike Dytri and Craig Gilmore.

by the Kinsey Institute for Sex Research at Indiana University in Bloomington. The most extensive community-based collections are the International Gay and Lesbian Archive in Los Angeles (begun by JIM KEPNER in 1943, opened to the general public in 1979, housed in the University of California as of 1996), the Canadian Gay Archives (founded in Toronto by the publishers of the now defunct newspaper *The Body Politic*), and the LESBIAN HERSTORY ARCHIVES (founded in 1974 in New York).

MAGNUS HIRSCHFELD began the first gay and lesbian library and archive in 1897 as part of the Scientific Humanitarian Committee, which became the Berlin Institute of Sexual Research in 1919. When the Nazis set fire to the collection in a public ceremony on MAY 6, 1933, the institute held more than 20,000 books and a sizable picture and manuscript collection. Some of the remains found their way into the Kinsey Institute collection.

Brenda Marston of Cornell University was the first academic archivist to aggressively acquire lesbian archival material in an academic setting. Her pioneering efforts made Cornell the first academic institution to offer a gay and lesbian archival collection.

Classification

The Library of Congress classification system did not include a subject heading for "homosexuality" until 1946. "Lesbianism" followed in 1954. Both subject headings were accompanied by "see also sexual perversion" until 1972. As lesbian librarian and archivist Polly Thistlethwaite reported in her study of American classification practices, "It was not until 1976 that the Library of Congress denoted 'lesbians' and 'homosexuals, male' as classes of persons, and 'gay' was only sanctioned as a subject heading in 1987, the same year *The New York Times* sanctioned it for use by reporters in writing copy." Thistlethwaite and others credit leadership in changing national and local cataloging practice to Sanford Berman of the Hennepin County Public Library in Minnesota as well as the efforts of the AMERICAN LIBRARY ASSOCIATION's Gay and Lesbian Task Force.

✧ James A. Fraser and Harold A. Averill, *Organizing an Archives: The Canadian Gay Archives Experience* (1983).

Arenas, Reinaldo

(1943–1990)

Cuban writer. Arenas grew up in poverty so bitter he ate dirt as a young child to stave off hunger. He committed himself wholeheartedly to Fidel Castro's revolution (1956–1959) but soon grew to loathe the repressive policies of the new regime, in particular its persecution of gay men and lesbians (see **1960**). After publishing one novel in 1967, he was blacklisted by the government and forced to smuggle his manuscripts abroad, where they received awards and critical acclaim.

In Miami and New York after his 1980 escape (see **4/14/1980**), Arenas at first celebrated his hard-won freedom in his public appearances and publications. As the years passed, however, he grew increasingly critical of the Cuban émigré community as well as of American gay men—whom he found less attractive as sexual partners than the straight-identified men he had courted in Cuba. "Everything here is so regulated," he wrote in his memoir, "that groups and societies have been created in which it is very difficult for a homosexual to find a man, that is, the real object of his desire."

After Arenas was diagnosed with AIDS in 1987, he worked obsessively to complete several works he considered his most important statements as a writer. Racked by fevers, he was also tortured by the prospect of aging. In his autobiography, he described entering a public rest room and being ignored by the men who gathered there in search of sex: "I no longer existed. I was not young anymore. Right then and there I thought that the best thing for me was to die."

Arenas's work is filled with references to gay and lesbian life in CUBA. Of particular interest are: *Arturo, la Estrella Mas Brillante* (1984; English translation: *The Brightest Star,* included in *Old Rosa: A Novel in Two Stories,* 1989), a harrowing yet darkly humorous tale, loosely based on a real-life story, of a young man in a Cuban concentration camp who devises a cabaret act in an attempt to survive the sexual abuse of the camp guards and the sadistic cruelty of the *locas* ("queens") imprisoned with him; and *Antes que Anochezca* (1992; English translation: *Before Night Falls,* 1993), completed shortly before Arenas's suicide in 1990, an autobiographical catalog of the appalling conditions of Cuban life as well as a kind of "greatest hits" rundown of dozens of Arenas's estimated 10,000 sexual encounters.

Argentina

No laws against same-sex relations between consenting adults, but laws against "incitement to sex" and "offenses against morality" are sometimes used to arrest and jail openly gay men and lesbians. Developed social scene and rights organizations in Buenos Aires and a few other cities.

Argentinians endured some of the most brutal campaigns of official and unofficial persecution of lesbians and gay men anywhere in the 20th century, yet Buenos Aires emerged in the 1990s as the gay capital of South America, with vocal rights organizations and a lively gay and lesbian media presence, in addition to an array of clubs, cafés, and CRUISING areas. Activists continue to struggle against a particularly conservative ROMAN CATHOLIC CHURCH, a traditional reverence for machismo, and the rigid GENDER boundaries typical of much of LATIN AMERICA, but there are signs of change. In July 1995, for example, the country was in an uproar over a revelation by gay activist Carlos Jaureguí that at least two of the *muy macho* members of the 22-man national soccer squad were gay.

Other gay, lesbian, and bisexual Argentinians of note include activists Ilse Fiskóva-Kornreich and Alejandra Sarda; and writers Carlos Arcidiácono, Carlos Correas, Alejandra Pizarnik (1936–1972; poet and author of one of the first explicitly lesbian-themed vampire novellas, *La Condesa Sangrienta* [1971; English translation: *The Bloody Countess,* 1986]), MANUEL PUIG, and the renowned children's author María Elena Walsh.

History

Scholars, including Daniel Bao and Jorge Salessi, have documented a well-developed gay male SUBCULTURE in all classes of Buenos Aires society by the first years of the 20th century. At about the same time, Argentinian doctors began to write scholarly articles warning that "inverted" (masculinized) schoolmistresses and tough working-class women were corrupting increasing numbers of young women. Salessi's research suggests that most Argentinians at the time equated homosexuality with gender nonconformity.

Public awareness of homosexuality increased in the 1940s, when newspapers reported a series of scandals, including one involving "orgies" in a military high school for young men. In the 1950s, successive governments launched draconian campaigns against "immorality" that included mass raids against gay BARS and cruising areas and, at one point, the closing of public rest rooms throughout Buenos Aires. Gay men and lesbians, however, continued to form social networks and to gather discreetly in bars and cafés into the 1970s.

The group Nuevo Mundo, formed in 1969, is considered the first gay rights organization in Latin America, but it was not until the formation of the Frente de Liberación Homosexual (FLH) in 1973 that activists achieved visibility, staging demonstrations and ZAPS for the first time in Argentinian history. FLH remained active until **March 24, 1976**, when a military coup brought about a right-wing dictatorship and drove activists underground.

According to Jaureguí, some 400 gay men were "disappeared"—kidnapped, barbarically tortured, and executed—while the regime was in power. Encouraged by Roman Catholic church leaders, the dictatorship raided and closed gay bars, arresting as many as 1,400 men in a particularly brutal 1978 campaign that took place on the eve of the World Cup soccer tournament in Buenos Aires. In 1982 and 1983, the last two years of the dictatorship, paramilitary groups assassinated a number of gay men working in the arts. Less visible, lesbians were not explicitly targeted by the regime, but overtly BUTCH women were frequently detained by police, beaten, and raped.

Gay and lesbian activists resurfaced in April 1984 to form the Communidad Homosexual Argentina (CHA) in the wake of mass arrests at a gay disco in Bueno Aires. CHA later founded its own nationally distributed publication. Argentinian women began publishing *Cuaderno de Existencia Lesbiana* ("Notebook of

Lesbian Existence") in 1987 and formed small lesbian feminist discussion groups later in the decade.

CHA was denied official recognition in an appeal to the Argentinian High Court in 1990, but the national government officially reversed its previously negative position on gay and lesbian rights in 1991, and extended recognition to CHA in 1992, but only after oppression in the country had gained international attention when an Argentinian, José Inaudi, became the first gay person to be given asylum in CANADA on grounds of persecution in his native country. On **July 3, 1992**, several hundred lesbians and gay men staged the first PRIDE CELEBRATION in Buenos Aires.

A lesbian archive, Escrito en el Cuerpo (Written on the Body) was formed in 1995, while groups like Lesbianas a la Vista (Lesbians in Sight) worked to achieve increased visibility with actions that included slogan-bearing kite launchings in city parks.

✧ Daniel Bao, "Invertidos Sexuales, Tortilleras, and Maricas Machos: The Construction of Homosexuality in Buenos Aires, Argentina, 1900–1950," in *If You Seduce a Straight Person, Can You Make Them Gay: Issues in Biological Essentialism Versus Social Constructionism in Gay and Lesbian Identities,* edited by John P. DeCecco and John P. Elia (1993).

✧ Ilse Fuskóva-Kornreich and Dafna Argov, "Lesbian Activism in Argentina: A Recent but Very Powerful Phenomenon" in *The Third Pink Book: A Global View of Lesbian and Gay Liberation and Oppression,* edited by Aart Hendriks, Rob Tielman, and Evert van der Veen (1993).

✧ Jorge Salessi, "The Argentine Dissemination of Homosexuality, 1890–1914," in *Entiendes?: Queer Readings, Hispanic Writings,* edited by Emilie L. Bergmann and Paul J. Smith (1995).

Armenia, see CENTRAL ASIA.

Arnold, June

(née June Davis; 1926–1982)

U.S. author, publisher. Born in South Carolina and raised in Houston, Arnold's southern roots and sense of humor were as apparent in her writing as her commitment to lesbian power and independence. Arnold returned to Texas after studying at Vassar College, earned degrees at Rice University, got married, had four children, and divorced. She then moved with her children to Greenwich Village and wrote her first novel, *Applesauce.*

Published by McGraw-Hill in 1967, *Applesauce* debuted several years in advance of its intended lesbian feminist audience. When it was rediscovered in 1977, critics compared its GENDER-confounding main character and structural experimentalism to VIRGINIA WOOLF's *Orlando.* In the meantime, Arnold and her lover, attorney Parke Bowman, had moved to Vermont and in 1972 founded Daughters Inc., a press that gave literary expression to—and began to build a readership for—the radically new lesbian cultural vision Arnold and others were pioneering.

1973 saw Daughters' publication of RITA MAE BROWN's best-selling *Rubyfruit Jungle* and Arnold's *The Cook and the Carpenter* (published under the PSEUDONYM Carpenter), a novel featuring gender-neutral characters pronominalized as "na" (s/he) and "nam" (her/him). In 1975, Arnold electrified readers with *Sister Gin,* which included an even more revolutionary creation: a sensuous and sexual love affair between fifty-something Su and octogenarian Mamie Carter. *Sister Gin,* Arnold's most popular work, also treats class and race issues, as well as alcoholism, obesity, and mother-daughter relationships, ending with a call for lesbians to come "in" rather than OUT and find a haven in what she had previously described as "one untouchable safe sea of women."

In addition to her work for Daughters, Arnold championed feminist PUBLISHING and her belief that "women's art is politics, the means to change women's minds" via a highly influential Women in Print conference held in Nebraska in 1976.

- ✧ June Arnold, "Lesbians and Literature" and "Lesbian Fiction: A Dialogue," *Sinister Wisdom* (Fall 1976).
- ✧ Marie Kuda, "June Arnold," in *Gay and Lesbian Literature,* edited by Sharon Malinowski (1994).

Art

Lesbians and, especially, gay men have long been so associated with the fine arts that "artistic" was once a common euphemism for "homosexual." Just as genius and madness are often thought to be closely related, artistic talent is associated with individual eccentricity in both the Western and Eastern traditions. As a result, careers in the arts have often afforded gay men and lesbians a level of tolerance available almost nowhere else in their cultures. More often than not, however, critics and historians have tended to ignore or even aggressively deny the existence of same-sex relations in artists' lives, not to mention the presence of homoerotic themes in their work. In extreme cases, blatantly homoerotic art, such as the ceramic erotica created by Moche artists in present-day Peru (see **c. 200 B.C.**), has been either destroyed or hidden in the storerooms of museums.

The rise of GAY AND LESBIAN STUDIES has encouraged critics and historians to explore what relationship, if any, an artist's sexuality has to his or her work. Artists like MICHELANGELO have been reclaimed by some as "gay" artists, by others as creative ancestors who bequeathed homoerotic legacies that stimulated and inspired later, consciously gay and lesbian artists.

Still, lesbian and gay artists and theorists dispute not only the definition of "gay and lesbian art," but its very existence. Some contend

Paul Cadmus with his painting *What I Believe* (1947–1948) at the groundbreaking Center Show in New York City in 1989.

Female homoeroticism by and for women: Tee Corinne's solarized Yantras of Woman Love #56 (1982).

that art is universal, that there is only art created by lesbians and gay men, and no such thing as a unique gay or lesbian sensibility. Most, however, would agree with Emmanuel Cooper, a pioneering historian of gay and lesbian art, that "the homosexual artist's response is governed by concerns which heterosexuals do not have," and, furthermore, that even "when artists who are homosexual are denied the means to express their sexuality, their art itself may become that means, even if this demands changing or subverting art."

Gay and Lesbian Content in Art

The most universally agreed upon definition of "gay and lesbian art" is that it is art created by lesbians or gay men that communicates or comments on aspects of gay or lesbian lives, especially their sexual or romantic lives. By this definition, lesbian artists like ROSA BONHEUR, who was most famous for her paintings of horses, did not create "lesbian art."

Before STONEWALL, appreciation of gay and lesbian themes in art usually demanded special knowledge on the part of the viewer or at least the ability to decode subtle indications of homoerotic intent. An extreme example of this is MARSDEN HARTLEY's *Portrait of a German Officer* (1914), a memorial to his love for Karl von Freyburg, a German lieutenant who was killed in the early days of WORLD WAR I. A collection of flags, insignia, and other military artifacts associated with his lover, the painting also includes the initials "Kv.F" and the number "24" (von Freyburg's age at his death). Other artists of the period, such as ROMAINE BROOKS, portrayed the sexual and GENDER identities of their subjects in less arcane ways, usually through their posturing or clothing. In the background of PAUL CADMUS's *Sailors and Floosies* (1938), a young man in slightly dandified civilian garb makes conversation with a sailor; that the scene represents an attempted pickup is communicated by the young man's red tie, which signaled his homosexuality to knowing New Yorkers of the 1930s as clearly as a PINK TRIANGLE would today. More blatantly homoerotic art, such as CHARLES DEMUTH'S paintings of BATHHOUSES and BEACHES or GEORGE PLATT LYNES'S photographic nudes, were hidden away from the general public in private collections.

By the 1960s, a few prominent artists, such as DAVID HOCKNEY, were OUT both to their public and in their creative work. And gay and lesbian magazines, both serious and pornographic, had provided a forum since the 1950s for a number of popular artists like TOM OF FINLAND to take homoerotic themes to new levels of explicitness.

Lesbian Art

Most contemporary lesbian art is rooted in the explosion of "women's art" that was a part of 1970s feminism. Through LESBIAN FEMINISM, it began to carve out a distinctively lesbian sphere in the late 1970s, when *Heresies: A Feminist Publication on Art and Politics* devoted a special issue in 1977 to "Lesbian Art and Artists," and when "A Lesbian Show" (1978) and "The Great American Lesbian Art Show" (see **8/1979**) were presented in New York City and Los Angeles respectively. Among the first openly lesbian artists to gain prominence were TEE CORINNE, Harmony Hammond, and the photographer JOAN E. "JEB" BIREN.

By the 1980s, these women had been joined by innovative performance artists (see THEATER) like Holly Hughes and Marga Gomez. The decade also saw the emergence of lesbian PORNOGRAPHY in the wake of the stormy SEX WARS.

AIDS and Queer Art

Two major shows evidenced the scope and diversity of gay and lesbian art in the U.S. two decades after Stonewall: the 1989 "Center Show" at the New York Lesbian and Gay Community Services Center, which featured work by more than 50 artists, ranging from Cadmus to KEITH HARING; and "In a Different Light," a show mounted in 1995 at the University of California at Berkeley, with dozens of artists as diverse in their chosen media as in their sexual self-identification. Both shows evidenced the impact of AIDS on the gay and lesbian art scene, in the number of artists who had died of AIDS-related causes as well as in the passionate protests of artists like DAVID WOJNAROWICZ. "In a Different Light" in particular demonstrated the trend toward "queering" art that curator Nayland Blake characterized as "an attitude that is aggressive and anti-assimilationist." The possibilities of queer art were manifest in the titles of the nine different groups of works exhibited: Void, Self, Drag, Other, Couple, Family, Orgy, World, Utopia.

➤ Also see specific individual artists; COMICS/CARTOONS; FILM AND VIDEO, GAY, LESBIAN, AND QUEER; HOMOEROTICISM; PHOTOGRAPHY.

✧ Emmanuel Cooper, *The Sexual Perspective: Homosexuality and Art in the Last 100 Years in the West* (2d ed., 1994).

✧ *In a Different Light: Visual Culture, Sexual Identity, Queer Practice,* edited by Nayland Blake, Lawrence Rinder, and Amy Scholder (1995).

✧ Jewelle L. Gomez, "Lesbians in the Arts" in *The New Our Right to Love: A Lesbian Resource Book,* edited by Ginny Vida (1996).

Arzner, Dorothy

(1900–1979)

American film director. Growing up in Hollywood, Arzner waited on many of the pioneers of the U.S. film industry at her father's café. After serving as an ambulance driver in WORLD WAR I, studying medicine and working briefly at a newspaper, she got a job at a studio and rose over three years from stenographer to script clerk to film editor. The originality and power of her editing helped persuade Paramount to sign her as director of *Fashions for Women* (1927), and she was later assigned the studio's first talkie, *The Wild Party* (1929), during the filming of which she devised the first boom, attaching a microphone to a fishing pole suspended over Clara Bow's head. Arzner directed 17 feature FILMS between 1927 and 1943, produced WAC training films during World War II, then taught film at UCLA.

Arzner is often cited as the "only woman director" in HOLLYWOOD during this period. While this is not strictly true, she was by all accounts the most successful. As such, she was early on "rediscovered" by feminist film critics, who tended to downplay or ignore her lesbianism. It took Judith Mayne's work beginning in the late 1980s to reclaim her as a lesbian visionary.

According to VITO RUSSO, Hollywood insiders felt Arzner's obvious lesbianism gained her acceptance as "one of the boys." Though discreet about her private life, Arzner's tailored suits, men's ties, and unconventionally short hair showed she cared little about dispelling rumors. Gossips linked her romantically with some of the women she helped launch to stardom, but she focused her attentions on choreographer Marion Morgan, with whom she shared a four-decade relationship. Her films favored capable, self-reliant heroines, played by stars like Claudette Colbert, Rosalind Russell, and Joan Crawford. Her most memorable movies include: *The Wild Party* (1929), a schoolgirl comedy many viewers find playfully homoerotic; *Christopher Strong* (1933), with Katharine Hepburn as a dashing AMELIA EARHART type; and *Dance, Girl, Dance* (1940), starring Maureen O'Hara and Lucille Ball as dancers pitted against the world of burlesque.

A studio publicity shot of Arzner directing in 1927.

✧ Judith Mayne, *Directed by Dorothy Arzner* (1995).

Asian-Americans and Pacific Islanders

Boasting heritages shared by almost half the population of the planet, Americans of Asian and Pacific Island (API) ancestry—7 million people, according to the 1990 U.S. census (growing to an estimated 20 million by 2020)—are an extraordinarily diverse mix of individuals. Non-Asian Canadians and Americans tend nonetheless to group them together, and as a result lesbians and gay men whose ancestors came from cultures as distinct as Tibet and Samoa often find that they have more in common with one another than their grandparents would ever have suspected.

Homosexuality is a taboo topic among many API groups, especially Asian-American peoples. When discussed, it is often considered something that occurs only among white people, a view tacitly supported by most published and broadcast reports on Asian-American communities. As Cantonese-American writer Russell Leong writes, "the myth of Asian-Americans as a homogeneous, heterosexual 'model minority' population has worked against exploration into the varied nature of our sexual drives and gendered diversity."

Achieving visibility within the larger lesbian and gay SUBCULTURES has been equally difficult. Even when their existence is acknowledged, many API lesbians and gay men report that they have to fight limiting racial/sexual stereotypes, ranging from the passive "geisha" to the evil "dragon lady." Richard Fung, a videomaker and activist of Chinese ancestry but a fourth-generation Trinidadian and a long-term Toronto resident, reports that potential sex partners often believe that men of Japanese origin tend to be identified with "strength, virility, perhaps a certain kinkiness," while men of Chinese ancestry are associated with a softer, more yielding sexuality. As a result, one of his friends, frustrated by always being asked where he is from—and immediately stereotyped—responds with a question: "Where would you like me to be from?"

Fung has also written about the racist stereotypes he finds predominant in gay male pornographic representations of Asian and Asian-American men—although, as the title of his influential essay, "Looking for My Penis," suggests, his and other Asian-Americans' biggest criticism of gay male porn is their *lack* of representation.

In recent years, an increasing number of gay and lesbian API commentators, including writers Justin Chin and Margaret Mihee Choe, have expanded this debate to challenge another stereotype: the expectation that API lesbians and gay men will seek sexual partners outside their respective racial and ethnic groups. As poet Indigo Chih-Lien Som writes, "Just once before I die I want someone to make love to me in Cantonese." For API men, the availability of a glossy erotic international publication, *OG* (*Oriental Guys: Presenting a Positive Image of Asian Men*), has encouraged many to take greater pride and interest in the diverse attractions of their fellows, who have been underrepresented in conventional gay skin magazines.

Lesbians and gay men of API ancestry include activist Melinda Paras; comic book artist Fish; Olympic diver GREG LOUGANIS; filmmaker Arthur Dong; supermodel Jenny Shimizu; and writers Angel Abcede, Willyce Kim, Barbara Noda, Dwight Okita, KITTY TSUI, Norman Wong, and Merle Woo.

Activism and Communications

One of the founding members of DAUGHTERS OF BILITIS was a Filipina. Other Asian-Americans, including writer and former NATIONAL GAY AND LESBIAN TASK FORCE director Urvashi Vaid and Oregon activist Scot Nakagawa, have been prominent participants in the GAY AND LESBIAN RIGHTS MOVEMENT. Nevertheless, many lesbian and gay Asian-Americans have long felt as marginalized within the gay and lesbian rights movement as within Asian-American communities.

The first U.S. group to address this issue was the Lesbian and Gay Asian Collective, organized during the first National Third World Lesbian and Gay Conference (see **10/12/1979**). Days after the collective's formation, one of its organizers, Michiyo Cornell, addressed the first March on Washington (see **10/14/1979**), demanding "that you white lesbians and gay men begin to think of how you repress and oppress your Asian-

Asian-American activists participated in the first March on Washington in 1979.

American lesbian and gay sisters and brothers."

In the 1980s, activists founded a number of local, national, and international organizations for Asian and Pacific Islander lesbians and gay men, including the Asian/Pacific Lesbian (later: and Bisexual) Network (1988), the Gay Asian Pacific Alliance (1988), and the Asian Lesbian Network (1989). The first national meeting of lesbian and gay API activists in the U.S., themed "Breaking the Silence: Beginning the Dialogue," was held in North Hollywood, California, in 1987. In later years, especially in the 1990s, multinational API organizations gave rise to a host of nationality-specific support groups, such as the Filipino group Kamal sa Lusog, organized in New York City in 1992.

Because API groups are most active on the West and East Coasts, publications and, beginning in the 1990s, on-line services have been crucial to the development of a continent-wide sense of API solidarity. Notable collections of API gay and lesbian writing have ranged from the first anthology, *Aiiieeeee!* (1974), to special issues of magazines, such as *The APA Journal*'s Spring/Summer 1993 issue, "Witness Aloud." Most API groups also issue newsletters, and many have begun computer network home pages and bulletin boards, thus extending their reach to once isolated API men and women across North America.

✧ Richard Fung, "Looking for My Penis: The Eroticized Asian in Gay Video Porn," in *How Do I Look?: Queer Film and*

Video, edited by Bad Object-Choices (1991).

✧ *Asian-American Sexualities: Dimensions of the Gay and Lesbian Experience,* edited by Russell Leong (1996).

Assimilationism/Confrontationalism

Two strategies for determining the goals and methods of the GAY AND LESBIAN RIGHTS MOVEMENT. They are usually seen as polar opposites, although there is often overlap between the two. In theory, *assimilationists* work for social *acceptance* by minimizing the differences between straight and gay/lesbian individuals and promoting the benefits of all living together in harmony; *confrontationalists* (more commonly called militants or radicals), on the other hand, work for social *change,* demanding that society learn to accommodate gay and lesbian nonconformity. In the words of common movement slogans, assimilationists assert, "We Are Everywhere" already, and it is to everyone's advantage to accept that fact; confrontationalists defiantly counter with: "We're Here. We're Queer. Get Used to It."

The conflict between the two strategies dates back at least as far as the early days of the German HOMOPHILE emancipation movement. The MATTACHINE Society, however, was the site of the first full-fledged battle between the two camps: in 1953, cautious, assimilationist homophiles wrenched control of the organization from Marxist-inspired confrontationalists like HARRY HAY (see **4/11/1953** and **5/23–24/1953**). Similar disagreements created controversy in the 1960s within the DAUGHTERS OF BILITIS and local chapters of the Mattachine. Believing in the effectiveness of assimilationism, organizers of the first public demonstrations (see **9/19/1964** and **7/4/1965**) insisted that lesbians wear skirts and gay men jackets and ties; just a few years later, GAY LIBERATION FRONT (GLF) activists, without a skirt or necktie in sight, took to the streets to hand out confrontational fliers that read, "Do You Think Homosexuals Are Revolting? You Bet Your Sweet Ass We Are."

DONALD WEBSTER CORY, once called the Father of the Homophile Movement, provides extreme examples of both positions. In **1951**, he wrote that homosexuals were by nature champions of freedom because of the "inherent lack of assimilability that is the greatest historic value of homosexuality." In the late 1950s, however, he began urging lesbians and gay men to seek psychiatric treatment so that they could "fit in" with society, get married, have families, and work toward "acceptance of heterosexual life."

Much of the history of the gay and lesbian rights movement is marked by assimilationist/confrontationalist pairs of individuals or organizations. Recent examples include: Sir IAN MCKELLEN's Stonewall Group (see **5/1989**) and Peter Tatchell's OUTRAGE! in the UNITED KINGDOM; the LOG CABIN Republicans and "queer" activism, exemplified by groups like QUEER NATION and LESBIAN AVENGERS; and Andrew Sullivan's *Virtually Normal* and Urvashi Vaid's *Virtual Equality,* both published in 1995.

Sometimes one of the two strategies has dominated the movement, virtually eclipsing the other. In the year after the STONEWALL Uprising, for example, both the GLF and GAY ACTIVISTS ALLIANCE (GAA) advocated confrontationalist stances. A major difference between these two groups was one of scope: GLF had a broad agenda of revolutionary social change that included issues of race and class; GAA limited its mission to gay-related issues.

SEPARATISM, the belief that the movement's goals can only be achieved in a discrete society, has at times been a third strategy for gay men and, especially, lesbians.

- Toby Marotta, *The Politics of Homosexuality* (1981).
- Barry D. Adam, *The Rise of a Gay and Lesbian Movement* (rev. ed., 1995).

Association of Lesbian and Gay Psychiatrists,

see AMERICAN PSYCHIATRIC ASSOCIATION.

Astrology

System of prognostication and character analysis based on the positions and movements of celestial bodies. The progenitor of astronomy, astrology was a complex, centuries-old science by the time the Greeks adopted it from the Babylonians in the 6th century B.C. and began to codify it in a form similar to modern astrology. Reflecting the cultures in which it developed, traditional astrology made no moral distinctions between same- and different-sex desire. Astrologers instead believed that zodiacal combinations—(male) Mars and (female) Venus in certain relations, for example—produced same-sex desire as well as varying GENDER identities, and that these desires and identities were as "natural" as any other. Unusually intense heterosexual feelings, according to some astrologers, were the result of peculiar combinations of Mars and Venus at the time of a person's birth.

Astrology was suppressed by the early Christians but survived among Muslims to be reintroduced to Christian Europe during the Renaissance. MICHELANGELO, among others, seems to have believed that his attraction to other men was ordained by the stars.

Belief in astrology among lesbians and gay men has remained strong despite the attempts of modern science to discredit it and the HETEROSEXISM of many astrological practitioners. Contemporary astrologers, including Michael Jay, have used astrology to address specifically gay and lesbian concerns. Some lesbian and gay thinkers, most notably CAMILLE PAGLIA, believe astrology contains unique psychological insights. Paglia calls it the "oldest organized art form of sexual personae."

- Michael Jay, *Gay Love Signs* (1980).

Auden, W. H.

(Wystan Hugh Auden, 1907–1973)

Anglo-American poet. Born into an upper-middle-class York family, Auden studied at Oxford and lived in GERMANY in 1928 and 1929. In the 1930s, he and his friends CHRISTOPHER ISHERWOOD (with whom he wrote three plays), Cecil Day-Lewis, Louis MacNiece, and Stephen Spender were widely considered Britain's most promising young writers. Like many young intellectuals of the era, Auden was attracted by socialism and worked briefly as a broadcast announcer for the Republican government in SPAIN. Other travels included a trip to Iceland with MacNeice in 1936, a tour of CHINA with Isherwood in 1938, and a subsequent visit to the United States. He decided to immigrate to the U.S. in 1939, partly because he was outraged by British Prime Minister Neville Chamberlain's attempts to placate Nazi Germany but also because he had come to find English intellectual life overly confining. After becoming an American citizen in 1946, he spent most of the remainder of his life outside England, first in New York and later mainly at his home in Austria.

Auden married Thomas Mann's daughter Erika in 1935 to help her get an exit visa out of Nazi Germany. Although the marriage was purely a formality, they remained close friends until her death. Auden's most important relationship was with Chester Kallman (1921–1975), whom he met in the spring of 1939 shortly after arriving in New York. Kallman, also a poet, collaborated with Auden on six librettos, including one for Igor Stravinsky's *The Rake's Progress* (1951). The two remained a couple until Auden's death, although both had sexual and romantic attachments with other men. Several biographers have speculated that Auden's return to the ANGLICAN COMMUNION in the 1940s was in part a response to the pain of Kallman's infidelities.

Auden resisted being characterized as a "gay poet," although he once remarked, "I had no trouble after I learned that I was queer." During his lifetime, most of Auden's associates and his more knowledgeable readers knew he was gay, although blatant HOMOEROTICISM was never a feature of the work published under his own name. Gay and lesbian readers, however, have strongly identified with the sentiments expressed in many of his poems, such as "Lullaby" (1937), which critic Claude J. Summers has called "perhaps the greatest love poem of the century" and which begins with the lines: "Lay your sleeping head, my love, / Human on my faithless arm. . . ."

Other gay and lesbian associations include Auden's sexually explicit poems written in German in the 1920s; "Pleasure Island," his 1948 poem about life on FIRE ISLAND; his choice of ADRIENNE RICH to receive the Yale Younger Poets award in 1951; and *Markings* (1964), his translation of DAG HAMMARSKJÖLD's writings.

Auden's most unique contribution to gay male culture, however, is perhaps "A Day for a Lay" (c. 1948), a poem not included in Auden's collected work. In an anonymously published version, it was once confiscated in a bookstore raid by New York City police. "A Day for a Lay" details the process of picking up and performing oral sex on a muscular 24-year-old mechanic called Bud in 34 brilliantly evocative, *abab*-rhymed stanzas.

- W. H. Auden, "A Day for a Lay," in *Gay Roots: Twenty Years of Gay Sunshine,* edited by Winston Leyland (1991).
- Claude J. Summers, "American Auden," in *Columbia History of American Poetry,* edited by Jay Parini (1993).
- Richard Davenport-Hines, *Auden* (1996).

Austen, Alice

(née Elizabeth Alice Munn, 1866–1952)

U.S. photographer. Alice's English father deserted his family shortly after her birth, and her mother changed their last name to her maiden name, Austen, and moved back to Clear Comfort, her family's Staten Island (N. Y.) home, where Alice grew up a TOMBOY. She received a camera from a seafaring uncle at the age of ten and became an accomplished photographer by her late teens. Over the next five decades, she took some 9,000 photographs, documenting working-class life on the Eastern Seaboard as well as the lives led by herself and her friends, many of whom were typical of the vigorously independent "New Women" of the era.

Austen's crisp, sharply focused photos depict a world in which middle-class women were free to devote themselves to sports, playfully experiment with CROSS-DRESSING, and even develop intimate relationships with one another. Some of her most intriguing portraits were of close friends like Violet Ward, who helped popularize the crossbar-free "girls'" bicycle and published *Bicycling for Ladies* (1896) with Austen's photos as illustrations. Austen's photos of a young, high-spirited Ward affectionately posed with her equally attractive female lover contradict the stereotype of BOSTON MARRIAGES as unions of desiccated spinsters.

Austen's own life provides evidence of growing suspicion and disapproval of women's

Alice Austen and Gertrude Tate at their Staten Island home in 1944. They would be evicted the following year.

ROMANTIC FRIENDSHIPS. In 1899, Austen began a relationship with Gertrude Tate, a teacher and dance instructor five years her junior. It was not until 1917, however, when Tate was in her mid-40s, that she was able to circumvent her family's objections to her "wrong devotion" and move into Clear Comfort to live with Austen.

Austen lost her fortune in the 1929 stock market crash. She and Tate struggled desperately to make ends meet but were finally evicted from Clear Comfort in 1945. Five years later, the two women were too sick and poor to continue living together in an apartment they had rented. Tate went to live with a sister. Austen was forced into the Staten Island poorhouse. Shortly before her death, art historian Oliver Jensen discovered her photo plates at the Staten Island Historical Society (where about 3,500 of them remain), and enough money was raised from selling the publication rights to allow her to move into a nursing home.

- ✧ Oliver Jensen, *The Revolt of American Women* (1952).
- ✧ Ann Novotny, "Alice Austen's World," *Heresies* (vol. 1, no. 3, 1977).

Australia

No laws against consensual same-sex relations between adults (except in Tasmania, where the law has been contested). Higher AGE OF CONSENT *for male-male sex acts in all states and territories except Queensland, South Australia, and Victoria. No discrimination in the* MILITARY. *Federal rights protection, and local protection and domestic partnership benefits in most states and many cities.* IMMIGRATION *rights for same-sex partners. Well-developed social and cultural scenes in all large cities except Darwin. Active political groups at the national, state, and local levels.*

Since the 1960s, when male-male sex was illegal in every Australian state and there was not a single lesbian or gay rights organization, Australia has transformed itself into one of the most hospitable and well-developed gay and lesbian environments in the world. In 1986, the Australian Human Rights and Equal Opportunity Commission began to investigate complaints of discrimination based on sexual orientation in employment, and Australia became in the 1990s one of the few countries in the world to allow same-sex partners the right to immigrate (under a category of "relationships of emotional interdependency," which can apply to nonsexual, nonromantic relationships as well). The government has also granted asylum to lesbians and gay men who face persecution in their home countries due to their sexual orientation. And as of 1992,

Australian law protects people with HIV from discrimination.

Australia's best-known gay and lesbian attraction is Sydney's annual Mardi Gras celebration, which draws almost a million people from all over the world.

History

Same-sex relationships were reported to be scandalously common among the convicts who formed the bulk of Australia's first settlers. For decades, men vastly outnumbered women in Australia, especially in the sparsely settled interior sections of the country, and a tradition of "mateship" developed that had much in common with ROMANTIC FRIENDSHIPS.

Lesbians and gay men had begun to develop a recognizable SUBCULTURE by the beginning of the 20th century. In 1965, Reuters called Bayswater Road in Sydney "a street of homosexuals, with bright-fronted shops and gay window displays, bars and plush hotels."

Australia's first lesbian and gay rights organizations emerged in the early 1970s (see **1/1970**; **7/1970**). On **September 19, 1970**, John Ware and Christabel Poll, founders of the Campaign Against Moral Persecution, Inc. (CAMP, Inc.), were the first Australians to come OUT in a public forum, the newspaper *The Australian.* GAY LIBERATION groups formed around the same time, and a gay magazine, *Camp Ink,* was begun in Sydney in 1970.

In 1972, New South Wales became the first Australian state to decriminalize consensual same-sex acts. Other successes, such as the removal of homosexuality from the official list of mental disorders by the nation's College of Psychiatrists (see **2/1974**), followed, but the next major turning point came in **July 1978** when police harassment of a Sydney gay PRIDE CELEBRATION (which led to the tradition of the city's gay and lesbian Mardi Gras) provoked large-scale demonstrations and served to revitalize and strengthen the gay and lesbian rights movement.

✧ Robert French, *Camping by a Billabong* (1993).

Australian Gay and Lesbian English

beat	cruising area
camp/kamp [dated]	gay
lunch	crotch
poofter	(effeminate) gay man

Austria

No laws against same-sex relations between consenting male partners over 18 or female partners over 14 (the AGE OF CONSENT *for heterosexual relations), but prohibitions, largely unenforced, against "advocacy" of homosexuality by individuals and "favoring homosexual lewdness" by organized groups. Social scene and active political groups in Vienna and a few other large cities.*

Gay and lesbian Austrians lead relatively comfortable lives despite the ambivalence of the country's official policies on homosexuality. A national group, Homosexuelle Initiative, founded in Vienna in 1979, works for lesbian and gay rights and publishes the quarterly *Lambda-Nachrichten,* even though "advocacy" of homosexuality is technically illegal in Austria. One example of the odd legal status of gay men and lesbians in Austria is that the government itself has extended an official press subsidy to *Lambda-Nachrichten* since 1987, while continuing to use the laws to ban gay and lesbian PORNOGRAPHY and even SAFE(R) SEX literature. Austria has also granted asylum to gay male refugees from persecution. At the local level, the Vienna City Council provided assistance when lesbian and gay Austrians opened Rosa Lila Villa, a gay and lesbian COMMUNITY CENTER, in 1982.

Most lesbian and gay Austrians remain so invisible that even heterosexual writers have commented on the dearth of famous Austrian queers. Rare exceptions include (perhaps) the composer Franz Schubert (1797–1828; see MUSIC); Colonel Alfred Redl (1864–1913), an Austro-Hungarian double agent whose treasonous behavior led both to his forced suicide (see **5/25/1913**) and, some historians believe, a hardening all over the world of the suspicion that homosexuals posed security risks; Aimée Duc (PSEUDONYM of Minna Wettstein-Adelt; 1867–?), author of *Sind Es Frauen?* (**1901**, "Are These Women?"), one of the first positive novels about a group of lesbians and their love relationships; and the philosopher Ludwig Wittgenstein (1889–1951).

History

In 1787, Austria became one of the first countries in Europe to abolish capital punishment, which had been the punishment for male-male SODOMY under laws inherited from the Holy Roman Empire. The punishment for sodomy remained life imprisonment with hard labor until **1852**, when a new penal code reduced sentences for men at the same time it criminalized sexual relations between women, previously unmentioned in Austrian law.

A gay and lesbian SUBCULTURE was flourishing in Vienna by the end of the 19th century, despite police surveillance and the efforts of sexologists like RICHARD VON KRAFFT-EBING, who spent his most productive years in Austria, to persuade medical and judicial authorities that homosexuality was a pathological condition. In the early 1900s, psychiatrists Otto Weininger and Sigmund Freud published important papers on BISEXUALITY and sexual development that profoundly affected 20th century concepts of homosexuality, both in PSYCHOLOGY and in popular culture.

Along with GERMANY, Austria was the site of the world's first HOMOPHILE emancipation movement. Engineer Joseph Nicoladoni and psychoanalyst Wilhelm Stekel established a branch of MAGNUS HIRSCHFELD's reform-minded Scientific Humanitarian Committee in Vienna in 1906.

Tolerance of lesbians and gay men decreased in the grim years following Austria's defeat in WORLD WAR I and the country's subsequent loss of empire. On **February 4, 1923**, Nazi youths attacked a Vienna homophile gathering attended by Hirschfeld, fired into the crowd, and wounded dozens of participants. After 1938, when Germany annexed Austria, a large but still uncertain number of Austrian gay men became victims of the NAZI PERSECUTION of homosexuality. Several surviving German government documents of the period indicate that Nazi jurists ordered Austrian courts to toughen interpretations of the laws related to male-male sex acts. At the same time, several Nazi jurists wrote admiringly of the Austrian prohibition of female-female sex acts (which were not criminalized in Germany), and recommended the adoption of similar measures for the entire Reich.

Despite strong opposition from ROMAN CATHOLIC CHURCH groups, Austria decriminalized same-sex relations on **July 1, 1971**, but left a higher age of consent for male-male sex. The country also instituted the above-mentioned prohibitions against advocacy of homosexuality. The Constitutional Court rejected arguments against the unequal age of consent in March 1988. Although the court has yet to rule on the laws prohibiting advocacy of homosexuality, there are no reports in recent years of government prosecutions based on these laws.

Awards

Although it might not seem particularly noteworthy for a group of people with interests and passions in common to present each other with awards, the first awards given by lesbians and gay men to one another marked a kind of revolution. After decades when "the love that dare not speak its name" (a phrase coined by OSCAR WILDE's lover Alfred Douglas) had become a clichéd synonym for homosexuality, many gay men and lesbians marveled when authors not only spoke their names but were also pleased to accept awards that connected them with the previously taboo topic.

The first such awards were presented by the AMERICAN LIBRARY ASSOCIATION's "Task Force on Gay Liberation" in 1971. Since 1971, awards programs have been instituted in dozens of areas of gay and lesbian life.

American Library Association's Gay, Lesbian, and Bisexual Book Award

1971 ISABEL MILLER, *Patience and Sarah*
1972 Peter Fisher, *The Gay Mystique*
DEL MARTIN and PHYLLIS LYON, *Lesbian/Woman*
1973 no award
1974 JEANNETTE FOSTER, *Sex Variant Women in Literature: A Historical and Quantitative Survey*
1975 JONATHAN NED KATZ, ed., *Homosexuality: Lesbians and Gay Men in Society, History, and Literature*
1976 no award
1977 HOWARD BROWN, *Familiar Faces, Hidden Lives: The Story of Homosexual Men in America Today*
1978 Ginny Vida, ed., *Our Right to Love: A Lesbian Resource Book*
1979 Betty Fairchild and Nancy Hayward, *Now That You Know: What Every Parent Should Know About Homosexuality*
1980 Winston Leyland, ed., *Now the Volcano: An Anthology of Latin American Gay Literature*
1981 JOHN BOSWELL, *Christianity, Social Tolerance, and Homosexuality: Gay People in Western Europe from the Beginning of the Christian Era to the Fourteenth Century*
1982 LILLIAN FADERMAN, *Surpassing the Love of Men: Romantic Friendship and Love Between Women from the Renaissance to the Present*
J. R. Roberts, *Black Lesbians: An Annotated Bibliography*
VITO RUSSO, *The Celluloid Closet: Homosexuality in the Movies*
1983 no award
1984 JOHN D'EMILIO, *Sexual Politics, Sexual Communities: The Making of a Homosexual Minority in the United States, 1940–1970*
1985 JUDY GRAHN, *Another Mother Tongue: Gay Words, Gay Worlds*
1986 Cinty Patton, *Sex and Germs: The Politics of AIDS*
1987 Walter Williams, *The Spirit and the Flesh: Sexual Diversity in American Indian Culture*
1988 JOAN NESTLE, *A Restricted Country*

RANDY SHILTS, *And the Band Played On: Politics, People, and the AIDS Epidemic*

1989 Andrew Hollinghurst, *The Swimming-Pool Library*
SARAH SCHULMAN, *After Delores*

1990 Nonfiction: Neil Miller, *In Search of Gay America: Women and Men in a Time of Change*
Literature: DAVID B. FEINBERG, *Eighty-Sixed*
Exceptional Achievement: ARMISTEAD MAUPIN, *Tales of the City* series

1991 Nonfiction: Wayne Dynes, ed., *The Encyclopedia of Homosexuality*
Literature: MINNIE BRUCE PRATT, *Crime Against Nature*

1992 Nonfiction: LILLIAN FADERMAN, *Odd Girls and Twilight Lovers: A History of Lesbian Life in Twentieth-Century America*
Literature: PAUL MONETTE, *Halfway Home*

1993 Nonfiction: Eric Marcus, *Making History: The Struggle for Gay and Lesbian Equal Rights, 1945–1990*
Literature: ESSEX HEMPHILL, *Ceremonies: Prose and Poetry*

1994 Nonfiction: Phyllis Burke, *Family Values: Two Moms and Their Son*
Literature: Leslie Feinberg, *Stone Butch Blues*

1995 Nonfiction (tie): DOROTHY ALLISON, *Skin: Talking About Sex, Class and Literature;* Phillip Sherman and Samuel Bernstein, *Uncommon Heroes: A Celebration of Heroes and Role Models for Gay and Lesbian Americans*
Literature: Marion Dane Bauer, ed., *Am I Blue? Coming Out from the Silence*

1996 Nonfiction: Urvashi Vaid, *Virtual Equality: The Mainstreaming of Gay and Lesbian Liberation*
Literature: Jim Grimsley, *Dream Boy*

Lambda Literary Awards

1988

AIDS	PAUL MONETTE, *Borrowed Time*
Debut	Madelyn Arnold, *Bird-Eyes;* Alan Hollinghurst, *The Swimming-Pool Library*
Editor's Choice	KAREN THOMPSON and Julie Andrzejewski, *Why Can't Sharon Kowalski Come Home?*
Fiction	DOROTHY ALLISON, *Trash;* EDMUND WHITE, *The Beautiful Room Is Empty*
Mystery/Science Fiction	Antoinette Azolakov, *Skiptrace;* Michael Nava, *Goldenboy*
Nonfiction	Sarah Hoagland, *Lesbian Ethics;* PAUL MONETTE, *Borrowed Time*
Poetry	Carl Morse and JOAN LARKIN, eds., *Gay and Lesbian Poetry in Our Time*
Publisher's Service Award	Sasha Alyson
Small Press	DOROTHY ALLISON, *Trash;* Michael Nava, *Goldenboy;* Almad-al Tifashi, *The Delight of Hearts*

1989

AIDS	LARRY KRAMER, *Reports from the Holocaust*
Anthologies	TEE CORINNE, ed., *Intricate Passions;* MARTIN BAUML DUBERMAN, Martha Vicinus, and George Chauncey Jr., eds., *Hidden from History: Reclaiming the Gay and Lesbian Past;* Christian McEwen and Sue O'Sullivan, eds., *Out the Other Side*
Children's/Young Adult:	MaryKate Jordan, *Losing Uncle Tim*
Debut	Patricia Roth Schwartz, *The Names of the Moons of Mars;* John Weir, *The Irreversible Decline of Eddie Socket*
Editor's Choice	Rebecca Mark, ed., *Lifting Belly* by GERTRUDE STEIN
Fiction	Nisa Donnelly, *The Bar Stories;* DAVID B. FEINBERG, *Eighty-Sixed*
Humor	Robert Triptow, ed., *Gay Comics*
Mystery	KATHERINE V. FORREST, *The Beverly Malibu;* Mark Richard Zubro, *Simple Suburban Murder*
Nonfiction	JUDY GRAHN, ed., *Really Reading Gertrude Stein;* Neil Miller, *In Search of Gay America*
Poetry	Michael Klein, ed., *Poets for Life*
Publisher's Service Award	Carol Seajay, *Feminist Bookstore News*
Science Fiction/Fantasy	Jeffrey N. McMahan, *Somewhere in the Night;* Jessica Amanda Salmonson, ed., *What Did Miss Darrington See?*
Small Press	Larry Mitchell, *My Life as a Mole*

1990

AIDS	Elizabeth Osbourn, ed., *The Way We Live Now*
Anthologies	JOAN NESTLE and Naomi Holoch, eds., *Women on Women;* George Stambolian, ed., *Men on Men 3*
Debut	Cherry Muhanji, *Her;* Lev Raphael, *Dancing on Tisha B'av*
Editor's Choice	Wayne Dynes, ed., *The Encyclopedia of Homosexuality*
Fiction	Allen Barnett, *The Body and Its Dangers;* Paula Martinac, *Out of Time*
Humor	ALISON BECHDEL, *New, Improved Dykes to Watch Out For*
Mystery	Lauren Wright Douglas, *Ninth Life;* Michael Nava, *Howtown;* BARBARA WILSON, *Gaudí Afternoon*
Nonfiction	Allan Bérubé, *Coming Out Under Fire;* Bonnie Zimmerman, *The Safe Sea of Women*
Poetry	MARILYN HACKER, *Going Back to the River;* Michael Lassell, *Decade Dance*
Publisher's Service Award	Phil Wilkie and Greg Baysans, *The James White Review*
Science Fiction/Fantasy	Gael Baudino, *Gossamer Axe;* To Johnson, *Secret Matter;* Mercedes Lackey, *Magic's Price*
Small Press	GLORIA ANZALDÚA, *Making Face, Making Soul;* Louise Rafkin, ed., *Different Mothers;* Michael Wilhoite, *Daddy's Roommate*

1991

Anthologies	ESSEX HEMPHILL, ed., *Brother to Brother;* Carla Trujillo, ed., *Chicana Lesbians: The Girls Our Mothers Warned Us About*
Children's/Young Adult	Johnny Valentine, *The Duke Who Outlawed Jelly Beans*
Editor's Choice	LILLIAN FADERMAN, *Odd Girls and Twilight Lovers: A History of Lesbian Life in Twentieth-Century America*
Fiction	Blanche McCrary Boyd, *The Revolution of Little Girls;* JEWELLE GOMEZ, *The Gilda Stories;* Harlan Greene, *What the Dead Remember*
Humor	Joe Keenan, *Putting On the Ritz*
Mystery	JOSEPH HANSEN, *A Country of Old Men;* KATHERINE V. FORREST, *Murder Tradition*
Nonfiction	Sandra Butler and Barbara Rosenblum, *Cancer in Two Voices;* Will Roscoe, *The Zuni Man-Woman*
Poetry	ADRIENNE RICH, *Atlas of the Difficult World: Poems 1988–1991;* ASSOTTO SAINT, ed., *The Road Before Us: 100 Black Gay Poets*
Publisher's Service Award	BARBARA GRIER and Donna McBride, Naiad Press
Science Fiction/Fantasy	JEWELLE GOMEZ, *The Gilda Stories;* Frank M. Robinson, *The Dark Beyond the Stars*
Small Press	Winston Leyland, ed., *Gay Roots: Twenty Years of Gay Sunshine*

1992

Anthologies	JOHN PRESTON, ed., *A Member of the Family;* JOAN NESTLE, ed., *The Persistent Desire*
Children's/Young Adult	Penny Raife Durant, *When Heroes Die*
Editor's Choice	Richard Mohr, *Gay Ideas*
Fiction	Judith Katz, *Running Fiercely Toward a High Thin Sound;* RANDALL KENAN, *Let the Dead Bury the Dead*
Humor	ALISON BECHDEL, *Dykes to Watch Out For (The Sequel)*
Mystery	Jaye Maiman, *Crazy for Loving;* Michael Nava, *The Hidden Law;* Elizabeth Pincus, *Bit Tango*
Nonfiction	Blanche Wiesen Cook, *Eleanor Roosevelt;* PAUL MONETTE, *Becoming a Man*
Poetry	Edward Field, *Counting Myself Lucky;* AUDRE LORDE, *Undersong*
Publisher's Service Award	CRAIG RODWELL, Oscar Wilde Memorial Bookstore
Science Fiction/Fantasy	Nicola Griffith, *Ammonlite;* Maureen F. McHugh *China Mountain Zhang*

1993

Anthologies	Henry Abelove, Michele Aina Barale, and David Halperin, eds., *Lesbian and Gay Studies Reader*
Biography/Autobiography	Josyanne Savigneau, *Marguerite Yourcenar;* EDMUND WHITE, *Genet*
Children's/Young Adult	Hilary Mullins, *The Cat Came Back*
Drama	TONY KUSHNER, *Angels in America: Millennium Approaches*
Editors' Choice	Coleman Dowell, *A Star Bright Lie*
Fiction	JEANETTE WINTERSON, *Written on the Body;* JOSEPH HANSEN, *Living Upstairs*
Humor	ALISON BECHDEL, *Spawn of Dykes to Watch Out For*
Lesbian/Gay Studies	ELIZABETH KENNEDY and MADELINE DAVIS, *Boots of Leather, Slippers of Gold;* RANDY SHILTS, *Conduct Unbecoming*
Mystery	Mary Wings, *Divine Victim;* Steven Saylor, *Catilina's Riddle*
Poetry	AUDRE LORDE, *The Marvelous Arithmetics of Distance;* James Schuyler, *Collected Poems;* Michael Klein, *1990*
Publisher's Service Award	Michael Denneny
Science Fiction/Fantasy	Starhawk, *The 5th Sacred Thing*
Small Press Book Award (tie)	Leslie Feinberg, *Stone Butch Blues;* B. Michael Hunter, managing editor, *Sojourner*

1994

Anthologies/Fiction	LILLIAN FADERMAN, ed., *Chloe Plus Olivia*
Anthologies/Nonfiction	JOAN NESTLE and JOHN PRESTON, eds., *Sister and Brother*

Biography/Autobiography	Renate Stendahl, *Gertrude Stein in Words and Pictures;* Abraham Verghese, *My Own Country*
Children's/Young Adult	Marion Dane Bauer, ed., *Am I Blue? Coming Out from the Silence*
Drama	TONY KUSHNER, *Angels in America, Part 2: Perestroika*
Editor's Choice	Mab Segrest, *Traitor to the Race*
Fiction	Rebecca Brown, *Gifts of the Body;* Alan Hollinghurst, *The Folding Star*
Gay/Lesbian Studies	DOROTHY ALLISON, *Skin: Talking About Sex, Class and Literature;* George Chauncey, *Gay New York*
Humor	Ellen Galford, *The Dyke and the Dybbuk*
Mystery	John Berendt, *Midnight in the Garden of Good and Evil;* Ellen Hart, *Small Sacrifice*
Photography/Visual Arts	Nancy Andrews, *Family*
Poetry	Thom Gunn, *Collected Poems;* MARILYN HACKER, *Winter Numbers*
Publisher's Service Award	BARBARA SMITH, Kitchen Table Press
Science Fiction/Fantasy	Melissa Scott, *Trouble and Her Friends*
Small Press	Kiss & Tell, *Her Tongue on My Theory*

1995

Anthologies/Fiction	E. J. Levy, ed., *Tasting Life Twice*
Anthologies/Nonfiction	Claude J. Summers, ed., *Gay and Lesbian Literary Heritage*
Biography/Autobiography	Erica Fischer, *Aimee and Jaguar;* Lyle Leverich, *Tom: The Unknown Tennessee Williams*
Children's/Young Adult	JACQUELINE WOODSON, *From the Notebooks of Melanin Sun*
Drama	TONY KUSHNER, *Thinking About the Longstanding Problems of Virtue and Happiness (Slavs!);* Guinevere Turner and Rose Troche, *Go Fish*
Editor's Choice	PAT CALIFIA and Janine Fuller, introductions, *Forbidden Passages;* Janine Fuller and Stuart Blackley, *Restricted Entry*
Fiction	Michael Cunningham, *Flesh and Blood;* JACQUELINE WOODSON, *Autobiography of a Family Photo*
Gay/Lesbian Studies	Joseph Carrier, *De Los Otros;* Karla Jay, ed., *Dyke Life*
Humor	Ellen Orleans, *The Butches of Madison County*
Lambda Literary Foundation Pioneer Award	L. Page "Deacon" Maccubbin
Mystery	J. M. Redmann, *Intersection of Law and Desire;* R. D. Zimmerman, *Closet*
Photography/Visual Arts	Andrea Weiss, *Paris Was a Woman*
Poetry	Mark Doty, *Atlantis;* ADRIENNE RICH, *Dark Fields of the Republic*
Publisher's Service Award	Nancy Bereano, Firebrand Press

Science Fiction/Fantasy	Nicola Griffith, *Slow River;* Melissa Scott, *Shadow Man*
Small Press	Liz Kotz and EILEEN MYLES, eds., *The New Fuck You*
Spirituality	Brian Bouldrey, ed., *Wrestling with the Angel*

Publishing Triangle Awards

The Publishing Triangle, a professional organization of lesbians and gay men in book publishing, has presented its Bill Whitehead Award for Lifetime Achievement in Gay and Lesbian Literature annually since 1989 in memory of the pioneering gay editor. The Ferro-Grumley Awards, made possible by the estates of novelists and lovers Robert Ferro and Michael Grumley, are administered by Stephen Greco and are given to two works of fiction a year (one by a man, one by a woman). The Ferro-Grumley Awards joined the Publishing Triangle ceremony in 1994, as did the Robert Chesley Playwriting Awards, named for the playwright. The Chesley Awards are administered by playwright Victor Bumbalo for the Robert Chesley Foundation. The Gregory Kolovakos Award is named after the writer, journalist, and cofounder of GAY AND LESBIAN ALLIANCE AGAINST DEFAMATION.

1989 Whitehead Award: EDMUND WHITE

1990 Whitehead Award: AUDRE LORDE
Ferro-Grumley Awards: DENNIS COOPER, *Closer;* Ruthann Robson, *Eye of the Hurricane*

1991 Whitehead Award: James Purdy
Ferro-Grumley Awards: Allen Barnett, *The Body and Its Dangers;* Cherry Muhanji, *Her*

1992 Whitehead Award: ADRIENNE RICH
Ferro-Grumley Awards: Blanche McCrary Boyd, *The Revolution of Little Girls;* MELVIN DIXON, *Vanishing Rooms*

1993 Whitehead Award: SAMUEL R. DELANY
Ferro-Grumley Awards: DOROTHY ALLISON, *Bastard Out of Carolina;* RANDALL KENAN, *Let the Dead Bury Their Dead*
Kolovakos Award: Herve Guibert, *To the Friend Who Did Not Save My Life*

1994 Whitehead Award: JUDY GRAHN
Ferro-Grumley Awards: John Berendt, *Midnight in the Garden of Good and Evil* [nonfiction]; JEANETTE WINTERSON, *Written on the Body*
Chesley Awards: Lisa Kron; lifetime achievement, Doric Wilson
Kolovakos Award: Thom Gunn, *The Man with Night Sweats*

1995 Whitehead Award: JONATHAN NED KATZ
Ferro-Grumley Awards: Heather Lewis, *House Rules;* Mark Merlis, *American Studies*

Chesley Award: Victor Lodato

1996 Whitehead Award: JOAN NESTLE

Ferro-Grumley Awards: FELICE PICANO, *Like People in History;* SARAH SCHULMAN, *Rat Bohemia*

Chesley Awards: Susan Miller; lifetime achievement, ROBERT PATRICK

Sappho Award of Distinction

This honor is presented by the Astraea National Lesbian Action Foundation, a multiracial, multiclass organization that was founded in 1977, becoming the first national lesbian foundation. The organization makes grants and awards to community organizations and individuals to support lesbian leadership, activism, and creativity.

1991 AUDRE LORDE
1992 GLORIA ANZALDÚA
1993 ADRIENNE RICH
1994 JOAN NESTLE
1995 CHRYSTOS
1996 CHRYSTOS

Azerbaijan, see CENTRAL ASIA.

B

Bacon, Francis

(1909–1992)

Irish-born painter. The son of a Dublin horse trainer, Bacon ran away to London when his family discovered he was having sex with the grooms in his father's stable. He taught himself how to paint with help from his lover, the Australian painter Roy de Maistre, and in 1944, after a decade of adventures on the Continent and a brief career as a furniture and rug designer, burst upon London's art scene with an exhibition that included his triptych, *Three Studies,* figures for the base of a crucifixion. In the decades that followed, Bacon gained widespread recognition as one of the most important painters of the 20th century.

Like most of his subsequent work, *Three Studies* features male figures deconstructed to look as if they have exploded from within or are in the process of decaying. Critics have seen the influence of Picasso as well as MICHELANGELO in his disturbing depictions of violence, evil, and disintegration, although his most famous paintings were sinister takes on Velázquez and Rembrandt. Bacon's sexuality was always a given in his painting, but he rejected conventional HOMOEROTICISM as absolutely as he spurned comfortable aesthetics.

Away from the studio, Bacon was a rowdy eccentric given to haunting bars with his face powdered pink and his hair lacquered with boot polish. His private life inspired some of his most memorable works, such as *Triptych August 1972,* which recalls the messy death by drug overdose of his lover George Dyer. His provocative belief that an artist "can't be more horrible than life itself" prefigured a transgressive vein of queer culture that has been more evident in literature (see DENNIS COOPER; MONIQUE WITTIG) than in the visual arts. Hardly an exponent of "gay pride," Bacon instead advocated the courage to, as he once said, "believe in an ordered chaos."

✧ Daniel Farson, *The Gilded Gutter Life of Francis Bacon* (1995).

Baha'i

Religious faith founded in 1863 by Mirza Husayn Ali Nuri (called Baha' Ullah, "Glory of God," 1817–1892), with about 5 million adherents around the world, many in AFRICA. An outgrowth of Shia ISLAM in Iran, Baha'ism holds that God has sent a series of prophets, including Jesus and Muhammad, and that all religions are essentially one. Stressing the unity of all peoples, it advocates a single world government and universal sexual and racial equality. As such, it has appealed to many lesbians and gay men. Although Baha'i headquarters in Haifa, Israel, has never issued an official statement on same-sex relations, some Baha'i leaders have advised gay men and lesbians to seek medical treatment.

Baker, S. Josephine

(Sara Josephine "Jo" Baker; 1873–1945)

U.S. physician, public health reformer. The TOMBOY daughter of a Poughkeepsie, New York, lawyer who died of typhoid fever when she was 16, Baker managed to attend college and become an M.D. (1898) largely thanks to the support of her Vassar College–educated mother, who managed to fund Baker's education despite the family's straitened circumstances. Baker studied with Dr. Emily Blackwell (1826–1910) and Blackwell's companion and colleague, Dr. Elizabeth Cushier, at the Women's Medical College of the New York Infirmary for Women and Children, a medical school established by Blackwell and her sister Elizabeth in 1868. After completing an internship in Boston, Baker began to build a pediatrics practice in New York City while working for the municipal health department as a medical inspector.

Baker's autobiography *Fighting for Life* (1939) describes the antagonism that women doctors faced in the first decades of the 20th century, as well as the appalling health problems she encountered in New York City slums. Finding "dying baby after dying baby," she in 1908 established the municipal Division of Child Hygiene, the first such public agency in the world. Male doctors, who at first refused to work with her, eventually yielded to her visionary persistence, and she succeeded in instituting programs that more than halved the city's infant mortality rate, saving an estimated 82,000 children's lives between 1908 and 1923, when she retired from the health department. Besides teaching, writing extensively, and serving on state and federal commissions, Baker also represented the U.S. on children's health issues at the League of Nations.

As was the case with JANE ADDAMS, Helen Hull, and a number of other, less famous women reformers of her era, Baker's most important personal attachments were to devoted women friends and colleagues. These included Dr. Florence Laighton, with whom she lived and set up her private medical practice, and, beginning in the 1920s, a lover, Australian-born novelist and fellow HETERODOXY member I.A.R. Wylie (Ida Alexa Ross Wylie, 1885–1959). Baker and Wylie left New York City to live in Princeton, New Jersey, in the 1930s. There they were joined by another respected physician, Dr. Louise Pearce (1855–1959), famous for her work treating African sleeping sickness. The three women later moved to a farm in Belle Mead, New Jersey, and continued "living," as Wylie described their Princeton days in her autobiography, *My Life with George* (1940), "amicably and gaily together."

✧ Judith Schwarz, *Radical Feminists of Heterodoxy: Greenwich Village 1912–1940* (rev. ed., 1986).

Baldwin, James [Arthur]

(1924–1987)

U.S. writer. The son of Emma Berdis Jones, he received his last name from his minister stepfather, David Baldwin. Raised in Harlem with eight younger siblings, he grew up in a strict religious household he described as "a Southern community displaced into the streets of New York." At the age of 14, he became a minister and began preaching at Pentecostal churches. He performed defense work during World War II, began publishing articles in prestigious publications, won fellowships, and left the U.S. in 1948 for France, where he spent most of the rest of his life. He received that country's highest honor, investment as a Commander of the Legion of Honor, a year before he died of stomach cancer.

The preeminent AFRICAN-AMERICAN intellectual of his time, Baldwin wrote 17 books of

James Baldwin, c. 1950.

prose, essays, plays, and poetry that had a profound influence on the development of a contemporary American identity.

Baldwin attributed his facility with language, his obsessive curiosity, and his insatiable reading to his mother's influence. His first novel, *Go Tell It on the Mountain* (1953), framed an account of growing up in Harlem in a context characteristic of his writing—a concern for the rights of America's oppressed and a compassionate search for human dignity amid the frustration and rage of blacks fighting for justice.

Baldwin fell in love with Lucien Happersberger in 1949. Happersberger took Baldwin to a family chalet in the Swiss Alps to recover from a debilitating illness and complete his first novel. Happersberger was to marry several times but, as Baldwin later confided, he remained the love of Baldwin's life.

His male love story, *Giovanni's Room* (1956), was one of the first novels to deal openly with homosexuality through its main characters. Rejecting the advice of his agent that he burn the manuscript, Baldwin managed to publish the work in both the U.S. and the U.K. It wasn't, however, the first time he had considered the subject in print. In an early essay, "Preservation of Innocence" (1949), not included in *Notes of a Native Son* (1955), he took on the charge that homosexuality was "unnatural" when he questioned just how "a phenomenon as old as mankind" could possibly be considered unnatural. Baldwin viewed the social fear of homosexuality ("a terror of flesh") in the context of a fear of sex in general, the complexities of gender, and each individual's pursuit of genuine love and passion. He noted that *Giovanni's Room* is not really about homosexuality (just as *Go Tell It on the Mountain* is not about a church): "It's about what happens to you if you're afraid to love anybody."

In addition to his writing, Baldwin was a popular public speaker on race relations and civil rights, although (along with BAYARD RUSTIN) he was not asked to play a visible role in historic events such as the 1963 March on Washington because movement organizers regarded his homosexuality as a liability.

When he told the editor of *Black Scholar,* "I love men but I'm not a homosexual," he rejected the simplifications of identity that labels confer—what he elsewhere termed "tampering with the insides of a stranger." Later, in his 1984 interview with gay journalist Richard Goldstein, Baldwin discussed the difficulty he experienced coming to terms with his sexual preference ("It is difficult to be despised"). He resisted use of the term "gay" because, he believed, it put the discussion in the language of the oppressor and suggested "you have to prove your right to be here. . . . I have nothing to prove. The world also belongs to me."

- *James Baldwin: The Legacy,* edited by Quincy Troupe (1989).
- Randall Kenan, *James Baldwin* (1994).

Bangladesh, see SOUTH ASIA.

Bannon, Ann

(née Ann Weldy; later used stepfather's name, Thayer; 1932–)

U.S. writer of PULP FICTION, educator. Raised in Joliet, Illinois, she married soon after graduating from college and had two daughters. She later earned a Ph.D. in linguistics from Stanford and currently holds a deanship at California State University at Sacramento.

From 1957 through 1962, Bannon published five novels that were among the best-read and most influential depictions of urban lesbian life before STONEWALL. Although she began writing her first lesbian-themed novel while still in college after reading Vin Packer's (PSEUDONYM of Ann Aldrich) *Spring Fire* and RADCLYFFE HALL'S THE WELL OF LONELINESS, she later acknowledged that at the time she had no "intellectual or emotional connection" to lesbian life apart from observation of two roommates.

Bannon's own "isolation and ignorance" were reflected in her first novel, *Odd Girl Out* (1957), as was the emotional dilemma she faced. Which of the routes taken by the two femme "nice girls" of the novel should she follow? Beth's into marriage? Or Laura's to Greenwich Village? Bannon eventually did both. She drew her pen name from a list of her husband's sales customers after he forbade her to use his last name. She was pleased that Bannon contained her first name.

Divorced and living in California, Bannon published five more popular novels: *I Am a Woman* (1959), *Women in the Shadows* (1959), *Journey to a Woman* (1960), *The Marriage* (1960; peripherally lesbian), and *Beebo Brinker* (1962). (All except *The Marriage* were reissued by Naiad Press in 1983.)

Bannon's novels vividly captured the emotional conflicts, social repression, and insecurity of lesbian life in the 1950s and 1960s at the same time that they introduced readers around the world to the Greenwich Village bar scene. Many of her characters evolve over several novels; the choices they make reflect both the harsh realities and romantic possibilities of the time. Among the most memorable of Ban-

Bannon's "boyishly appealing" lesbian pulp heroine, Beebo Brinker.

non's women is swaggering butch Beebo Brinker, a character who seduced the author herself: "I, like many readers, fell in love with one of my characters, and because of her, the books became known as the 'Beebo Brinker' series." Beebo's meeting with Laura is a now classic account of BUTCH/FEMME sexual tension. Noting that the "cloud of criticism" which long enveloped butch-femme relationships has largely dissipated, Bannon contends: "Butch women are exciting women. Their power, the sexual excitement—there's a lot of romance and mystery. Butches are exciting. Beebo is one of them."

✧ "Ann Bannon: The Mystery Solved!" *Gay Community News* (January 8, 1983).

✧ "As Her Hand Crept Slowly up Her Thigh: Ann Bannon and the Politics of Pulp," *Social Text* (Fall/Winter 1989).

✧ "Ann Bannon: The Queen of Lesbian Pulp Talks," *Girl Friends* (July 1994).

Baptists

Evangelical Protestant Christian denomination with more than 30 million members around the world. The first Baptists separated from the Church of England in the early 17th century. Advocates of fundamentalist interpretations of the BIBLE, Baptists tend to be among the most conservative Christians on matters of sexuality.

Congregations are self-governing, but are linked by associations such as the Southern Baptist Convention, the largest Protestant denomination in the U.S. and the most conservative of the major Baptist groups: slavery, believed to be condoned by the Bible, was not repudiated by the Southern Baptists until 1995. On **June 16, 1988**, Southern Baptist Convention delegates passed a resolution that called homosexuality a "manifestation of a depraved nature" and blamed AIDS on gay men.

American Baptists, a smaller, less conservative group, are open to gay and lesbian membership, but are opposed to the ordination of openly lesbian or gay candidates. They have also denied official recognition to American Baptists Concerned, an educational and support group for lesbian and gay church members founded in 1972.

Barnes, Djuna

(1892–1982)

U.S. writer, journalist, illustrator. Born in Cornwall-on-Hudson, New York, Barnes spent her early years on a Long Island farm in a polygamous home, educated by a feminist, almost incestuously free-loving grandmother. "Djuna," bestowed on her by a father who gave all his dozen-odd children unusual names, meant "light of the moon."

In 1909, her father arranged a short-lived marriage for her with his second wife's brother. After another brief relationship with a man, she moved to New York City, attended the Pratt Institute (1911–1912), studied with the Art Students League (1915), and began writing stories for newspapers and, later, popular magazines under PSEUDONYMS ranging from Lydia Steptoe to Gunga Duhl, the Pen Performer. Barnes's eventful early years inspired the semiautobiographical best-seller *Ryder* (1928).

Barnes lived in Paris and England from 1920 until 1940. Her first decade abroad was overshadowed by a troubled eight-year relationship with the handsome Kansas-born silverpoint artist and sculptor Thelma Ellen Wood (1901–1970), who left photographer BERENICE ABBOTT for Barnes in about 1922. Barnes later wrote: "The only time I was a doormat was to Thelma, and then I was a damned good doormat." In her poetic, stylistically innovative novel *Nightwood* (1936), Barnes used the pain and anger she experienced in the wake of their relationship to create a work of fiction that is now considered a lesbian literary classic. Wood appears in the intense psychological novel as Robin Vote, the unfaithful indiscriminate lover whose rejection underscores Barnes's belief in the futility of desire. Years later, Wood wrote Barnes that reading *Nightwood* made her feel as if "a truck had hit her."

In addition to writing plays, essays, satirical sketches, and poetry, and illustrating books and drawing portraits, Barnes privately printed the *Ladies Almanack* (1928) "by a Lady of Fashion," a witty, highly original chronicle of the foibles of the most celebrated Parisiennes of the era.

Barnes's last years were spent in ill health and self-enforced solitude broken only by a rare friendship, such as the one she enjoyed with DAG HAMMARSKJÖLD. She was also desperately poor until the 1970s, when some of her books were reissued and she sold her papers to the University of Maryland in 1972.

Although Barnes is reported to have had affairs with other women besides Wood, she ended her life protesting that she was not a lesbian: she "just loved Thelma." BERTHA HARRIS nevertheless celebrated her work as "practically the only available expression of lesbian culture we have in the modern western world" since Sappho. JANET FLANNER felt Barnes was "the most important woman writer we had in Paris." Other lesbian writers, including MONIQUE WITTIG, have mined her work for insights into the construction of GENDER and the nature of sexuality.

✧ *Silence and Power: A Reevaluation of Djuna Barnes,* edited by Mary Lynn Broe (1991).

✧ Monique Wittig, *The Straight Mind and Other Essays* (1992).

✧ Phillip Herring, *Djuna: The Life and Work of Djuna Barnes* (1995).

Some of the Ladies of Ladies Almanack

Laura Barney	"Sister"
NATALIE BARNEY	Dame Evangeline Musset
ROMAINE BROOKS	Cynic Sal
Ilse Baroness Deslandes	"One dear old Countess"
JANET FLANNER and Solita Solano	Nip and tuck
Mimi Franchetti	Senorita Fly-About
RADCLYFFE HALL	Lady Tilly-Tweed-in-Blood
Mina Loy	Patience Scalpel
Esther Murphy	Bounding Bess
UNA TROUBRIDGE	Lady Buck & Balk
DOLLY WILDE	Doll Furious

Barney, Natalie [Clifford]

(1876–1972)

U.S.-born writer. Sometimes called "the wild girl from Cincinnati," Barney was actually born in Dayton, Ohio, the oldest daughter of the painter Alice Pike and railway-coach heir Albert Clifford Barney. She summarized her education in an often quoted quip: "My only books were women's looks."

From the beginning, her love affairs were not only the stuff of legends but the subject of literature. Visiting Paris with her mother in 1899, she seduced the era's most famous courtesan, Liane de Pougy. Two years later, de Pougy thrilled Paris with *Idylle Saphique,* a novel based on her affair with the 22-year-old American. Back in the U.S., Barney also wrote about de Pougy, leading to press reports of a "Sappho in Washington" (where she and her family were living) and Barney's flight with her mother to take up permanent residence in Paris.

Meanwhile, on a famous night in a room filled with lilies, Barney seduced the second major love of her life, RENÉE VIVIEN. Together, inspired by SAPPHO, they dreamed of founding a colony of women poets at Mytilene on Sappho's isle of Lesbos. Although both their relationship and their plans for Mytilene ultimately led nowhere, Barney did create the most lavish salon in Paris at her 300-year-old home on the rue Jacob. Over the course of five decades, her guests included DJUNA BARNES, TRUMAN CAPOTE, COLETTE, JANET FLANNER, RADCLYFFE HALL, Ernest Hemingway, Ezra Pound, MARCEL PROUST, and William Carlos Williams—not to mention Mata Hari and Greta Garbo. So important was Barney's home as a literary salon that James Joyce personally delivered the first printed copies of *Ulysses* there in 1922, but, as SYLVIA BEACH noted, it was best known for its celebrated lesbians: "Paris ones and those only passing through town."

Barney cut an unusual figure not only in conservative Washington, D.C., but also in Paris, as shown here c. 1905.

A millionaire heiress, Barney was as renowned for her generosity with friends as her political small-mindedness. Although part Jewish on her mother's side, she was given to voicing anti-Semitic sentiments and, under the influence of Pound, admired Mussolini's brand of fascism. She spent World War II in comfortable exile in Italy.

Barney wrote nearly two dozen books, mostly in French, including a novel, plays, poems, memoirs, and collections of letters and epigrams. During her lifetime, she called herself the "AMAZON of letters," but, partly because her books were not widely available in English until long after her death (and then only a small portion of her work), she is remembered mainly as the inspiration for thinly disguised characters in the works of de Pougy, Vivien, Barnes, Hall, and others. In 1928, Sylvia Beach affirmed, "Yes, you are the heroine in all the outstanding books this season." Barney more than fulfilled the directive of her mentor, the French symbolist Rémy de Gourmont, to "write with one's life."

Also written with her life was a manifesto of lesbian adventure and sexual abandon. Barney's relationship with the painter ROMAINE BROOKS endured nearly 50 years after their meeting in 1915, but, scorning bourgeois notions of fidelity, she also had literally hundreds of intense but shorter-lived affairs with other women, including Barnes, Lily de Clermont-Tonnerre, Colette, Lucie Delarue-Mardue, Eva Palmer, and DOLLY WILDE. Brooks bore up under the onslaught of rivals until the last years of her life, when Barney, at the age of 88, met a married woman named Janice Lahovary on a park bench. Lahovary left her husband and sons to care for Barney, and Brooks, despite Barney's pleading, broke with her once and for all.

- ✧ George Wickes, *The Amazon of Letters: The Life and Loves of Natalie Barney* (1976).
- ✧ Karla Jay, *The Amazon and the Page: Natalie Clifford Barney and Renée Vivien* (1988).

Bars

Centers of gay and lesbian social life in much of the world. Some lesbian and gay guidebooks estimate that there may be as many as 10,000 gay and lesbian bars worldwide. Bars vary widely, from multilevel complexes in Chicago to intimate nightspots in Tokyo that seat fewer than five customers.

Although some activists attacked the gay and lesbian bar scene as early as the founding of the DAUGHTERS OF BILITIS in the mid-1950s, bars have in many places been the only signs of a community. Today, especially in rural areas and smaller towns, bars continue to serve this purpose, often drawing customers from a wide area. In larger cities, gay and lesbian bars tend to be fairly specialized according to age, race, taste in music, and sexual interests, so communities that develop there are more focused.

Although documentation survives of taverns frequented by "sodomites" in Italy in the Middle Ages, perhaps the first modern gay bars were the "molly houses" of 18th-century En-

Waitresses at Howdy's, a New York City bar popular with lesbians, c. 1945.

The film adaptation of The Boys in the Band (1970) provided a glimpse of what Hollywood publicists described as the "underworld-like atmosphere of a gay bar."

gland. They were also one of the first sites of resistance against LAW enforcement (see **1725**). By the beginning of the 20th century, most large cities had at least one bar or café known for its gay and, increasingly in places like Paris and Berlin, lesbian clientele.

Gay and lesbian bars reemerged in the United States after Prohibition but were increasingly subject to police raids, which, combined with laws in many states that forbade the serving of liquor to "sexual deviants," led to most bars being operated under the auspices of

New York City's Meow Mix, a mid-1990s trendsetter.

organized crime. Perhaps the most famous example of such a bar is the STONEWALL Inn.

The 1970s marked the zenith of gay male bars in the United States. After AIDS, both drinking and bar attendance fell off, and today large American cities generally have fewer bars catering to gay men than in the past. Lesbian bars and nightclubs, on the other hand, after a period of decreasing unpopularity—bar owner and activist RIKKI STREICHER commented in 1991, "By and large, women are no longer going to bars that represent lesbians. They're just going where they want to go"—made a comeback in the 1990s and became chic even for straight-identified clientele.

➤ Also see **1810**; **1936**; **1940**.

Bashing, see HATE CRIME.

Bates, Katharine Lee
(1859–1929)

U.S. poet, educator, writer of "America the Beautiful." Bates attended Wellesley College, where she later became head of the English department. In 1890, she and Katharine Coman, a professor of history and political economy, began a love relationship that lasted until Coman's death 25 years later.

Both women were successful in and out of academia. Besides authoring six books on social, economic, and historical topics, Coman organized Wellesley's department of economics, helped found settlement houses, and worked on behalf of immigrants and African-American freehold farmers. Bates wrote six volumes of poetry, textbooks, children's fiction, and travel books. "America the Beautiful," inspired by the view from Pikes Peak of the "purple" Rockies and nearby "fruited plains," was published and set to a previously composed melody in 1895. The song's popularity incited massive petition drives to make it the national anthem, but in 1931 Congress rejected Bates's celebration of natural beauty and call for "brotherhood" in favor of the battle imagery of "The Star-Spangled Banner."

Bates and Coman are representative of the intimate female relationships that flourished at women's colleges during the period. Their friends included other academic couples, such as Vida Scudder and Florence Converse, Margaret Sherwood and Martha Shackford, Jeannette Marks and Mary Emma Woolley.

Bates expressed her grief at Coman's death in a memorial book of 47 sonnets called *Yellow Clover: A Book of Remembrance,* privately published after her own death, in 1929. Bates and Coman had exchanged yellow clover as a symbol of "Love's letter to be glad about / Like sunshine when it came!"

✧ Dorothy Burgess, *Dream and Deed: The Story of Katharine Lee Bates* (1952).

✧ Judith Schwarz, "Yellow Clover: Katharine Lee Bates and Katharine Coman, *Frontiers* (vol. 4, 1979).

Baths/Bathhouses

Facilities originally intended for personal hygiene that also accommodated CRUISING and that, by the 1950s in the U.S., began to cater almost exclusively to men in search of on-premise sex with other men. Bathhouses generally offer steam rooms and saunas in addition to lockers and a warren of cot-appointed cubicles. Some provide more elaborate facilities, such as swimming pools, gyms, massage rooms, snack bars, TV rooms, and sun decks. Through the 1980s—until the advent of AIDS awareness and stricter health regulations—many also featured dimly lit "orgy rooms" and large communal "bunkrooms." In 1994, *Steam,* a quarterly journal "intended for gay and bisexual men with an interest in public and semipublic sex," listed 65 bathhouses in the U.S. and 28 in

Perry King (seated at left) and Doug Higgins (seated at right) relax at the baths, then at the height of their popularity, in a scene from A Different Story (1978).

CANADA. (In comparison, there were over 160 baths in the U.S. alone in 1982.) Although facilities vary widely, gay-friendly baths and "saunas" have remained more common in the rest of the world, especially in Western Europe and LATIN AMERICA.

History

At least as far back as Roman times, public baths were a convenient sexual meeting ground. Diaries and pornographic fiction indicate that some of the sex-segregated Turkish baths that became popular in Europe in the 19th century were known as places where men—and according to some reports, women—could form sexual liaisons.

Indoor public bathhouses spread across the United States after the People's Baths was successfully launched in New York City in 1891. More elaborate, privately operated Russian and Turkish baths opened at about the same time. By **February 21, 1903**, at least one of these, the Ariston in midtown Manhattan, had become so notorious for male-male sex that it was raided by police. Somewhat later, CHARLES DEMUTH began to depict the homoerotic ambience of New York baths in paintings like *Turkish Bath* (see **1918**).

Historian George Chauncey notes that there were two types of "gay" bathhouses during this period. The first was open to both straight-identified men and gay men who wanted to "service" them; the second discouraged straight patronage, "creating an environment in which homosexual activity was encouraged and safeguarded."

As more homes acquired private baths, most bathhouses in American cities closed by the beginning of WORLD WAR II. The few that remained came to rely increasingly on gay male patronage, especially at night. Police raids were infrequent but always a possibility. As a result, patrons usually took men they met elsewhere for sex. It was not until the 1950s that on-premise sex became the norm.

After STONEWALL, new, lavishly appointed bathhouses, some with as many as ten floors of rooms, opened in every large American and Canadian city. By 1973, Club Baths, a national chain, had almost 500,000 card-carrying members. An entire sexual subculture evolved around gay baths, one that the French theorist GUY HOCQUENGHEM praised as close to "primary sexual communism." Writer Arthur Bell described his discovery of the baths when he was a 17-year-old visiting New York from Montreal as representing "freedom to me—a place where I could have sex without plodding through the required conversation of the bar, where points are given for social status and artistic tastes and deducted . . . for staying in the wrong borough."

One of the most interesting accounts of the 1970s bathhouse scene was recorded by

RITA MAE BROWN, who disguised herself as a man to invade the all-male enclave of the New York Club Baths. Brown's male drag—a mustache, stuffed briefs, and the unusual attire of a bathrobe (most bath patrons dispensed with all clothing except a plain white towel wrapped around the waist)—allowed her to cruise the premises without anyone suspecting she was a woman. A "man" in a gay man's world for the first and only time in her life, Brown was struck by the speed and casualness with which gay men made sexual decisions; the utter seriousness and lack of conversation (some baths actually had signs in the orgy rooms reading "No Talking Allowed"); the almost paradoxical combination of sexual tension and aggression-free security; and the democratizing effect of being judged solely by physical attributes, with no recourse to displays of wealth, status, or intelligence. She speculated that an all-female bathhouse would "be less competitive than the gay men's baths, more laughter would ring in the saunas, and you'd touch not only to fuck but just to touch," but concluded wishfully: "Like men we should have choices: long-term relationships, the baths, short-term relationships." (In fact, some entrepreneurs tried to launch all-female bath nights in New York and San Francisco but failed to attract lesbians in large enough numbers to keep them in operation.)

Even in the 1970s, some gay men were as resistant to bathhouse chic as lesbians. A few gay critics maintained that the popularity of the baths led to epidemics of gonorrhea, syphilis, and an assortment of previously rare intestinal afflictions, including amebiasis (the incidence of which increased by 7,000 percent among gay men between 1974 and 1981). Later, the gay and lesbian communities were split by a stormy debate over whether to close bathhouses as a means of fighting the spread of AIDS (see **4/9/1984**; **11/1985**; **11/17/1985**).

➤ Also see SEX; SEX WARS.

Beach, Sylvia

(Nancy Woodbridge Beach; 1887–1962)

U.S.-born bookshop owner, publisher, writer, translator. Beach changed her name to Sylvia in honor of her Presbyterian minister father, Sylvester. She began living in Paris while still an adolescent and, after a stint with the Red Cross in Serbia, settled permanently in the city after WORLD WAR II. Soon after arriving, she began a 38-year relationship with Adrienne Monnier (1892–1955), the owner of an elite French-language bookshop.

Monnier, a former schoolteacher and literary secretary, helped Beach found Shakespeare and Company in November 1919. The first American lending library and bookshop in Paris, Shakespeare became a center of Left Bank expatriate life. T. S. Eliot called Beach's and Monnier's shops "the Franco-Anglo-American literary world of Paris." Loyal customers included DJUNA BARNES, JANET FLANNER, Ernest Hemingway, Ezra Pound, and GERTRUDE STEIN. For the writer BRYHER (who provided considerable financial support), however, the shop's appeal "was Sylvia herself . . . waiting to help us and be our guide. She found us printers, translators, and rooms."

In 1922, Beach solicited subscriptions to finance the printing of James Joyce's banned *Ulysses,* eleven years before it could be published in the U.S.

Besides championing experimental writers, Beach and Monnier edited literary reviews and translated Eliot, WALT WHITMAN, and others into French. A feminist, a socialist, and a frequent guest at NATALIE BARNEY's fabled salon, Beach remained nonetheless what Monnier called a "flower of the parsonage," almost puritanically discreet about their sexual relationship. When she chose to abandon discretion—and described Barney's lesbian demimonde in her memoirs, for example—her editor suppressed the controversial passage.

In 1936, Monnier left Beach for a brief affair with photographer Gisèle Freund. Although Monnier and Beach never lived together again, they remained close friends until Monnier, stricken with a debilitating illness, committed suicide in 1955.

- ✧ Sylvia Beach, *Shakespeare and Company* (1959).
- ✧ Noel Riley Fitch, *Sylvia Beach and the Lost Generation* (1983).
- ✧ Andrea Weiss, *Paris Was a Woman: Portraits from the Left Bank* (1995).

Beaches

As early as 1918, the *American Journal of Urology and Sexology* noted that beaches served as a meeting place for male prostitutes and their customers. Around the same time, the painter CHARLES DEMUTH depicted burly, megaphallic sailors urinating exhibitionistically on a beach somewhere near New York City. From these and other indications, including evidence drawn from memoirs, beaches seem to have been well established in the U.S. and Europe as male CRUISING venues by the 1920s. Later, as SUBCULTURES grew in large cities, they also became one of the earliest places where lesbians and gay men could develop a sense of being part of a larger community.

According to anthropologist Esther Newton, beaches were a type of retreat that afforded a public place where gay men and lesbians "could socialize and assemble without constant fear of hostile straight society." This meant that lesbians and gay men tended to gather on somewhat more isolated, less convenient stretches of beach than straight beachgoers. Even today, "gay and lesbian" sections of public beaches are usually farther from parking lots and public transportation than beaches frequented by straight families.

By WORLD WAR II, some beaches, such as those north of Santa Monica, California, and on FIRE ISLAND had become well-known gathering places for both lesbians and gay men. In the years after the war, when HARRY HAY was trying to drum up support for the establishment of the organization that later became the MATTACHINE, he went directly to Los Angeles area beaches popular with gay men and lesbians. At the time, when there was as yet no gay and lesbian press, and gay and lesbian GHETTOS were only beginning to form, beaches were one of the few places he knew he could find large numbers of potential sympathizers.

JOAN NESTLE has written about the importance of the gay and lesbian beach she frequented in the early 1960s—the Riis Park beach in Brooklyn, New York—in the development of her lesbian identity: "This tired beach, filled with the children of the boroughs, was my first free place where I could face the ocean that claimed me as its daughter and kiss in blazing sunlight the salt-tinged lips of the woman I loved." For Nestle and others, beaches provided a chance to "drink in the spectacle of Lesbian and gay men's sensuality."

According to *Steam* magazine, there are today as many as 200 beaches around the world well-known to be frequented by gay men. Many of these same beaches also accommodate lesbians, or adjoin stretches of shore popular with women.

Bears

Called a "new macho image" by the authors of *The New Joy of Gay Sex* (1992), bears evolved out of the mid-1980 "daddy" craze to become

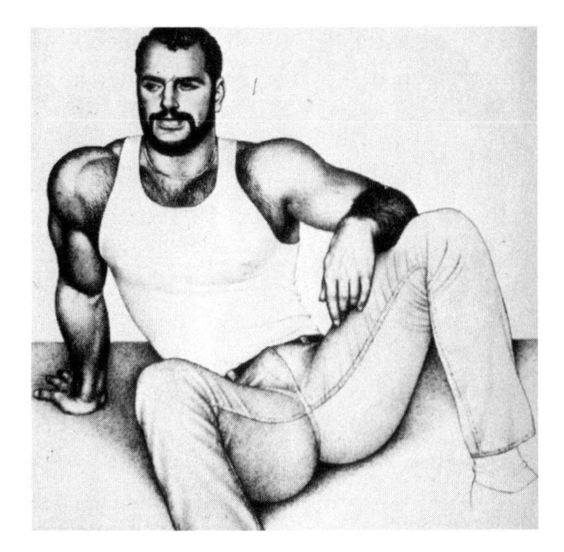

The bear phenomenon grew out of popular post-Stonewall "new macho images" like this one created by Tom of Finland in 1980.

an established part of the gay male landscape. Bears are defined as "natural," often bearded, almost always hairy, husky, gently masculine gay men, usually over (at least) 30. A reaction to a culture that generally idolizes and idealizes youth, the bear phenomenon has given rise to newsletters, a magazine, Internet sites, and groups all across the United States. Bears tend to wear "country" clothes and project an image of he-man (but not overly macho) hominess.

Beat Generation

A loosely knit group of writers who became prominent in the 1950s. Although the nucleus of this group—WILLIAM BURROUGHS, ALLEN GINSBERG, and Jack Kerouac—formed in 1944, the term did not enter public parlance until Ginsberg's 1955 reading of "Howl" in San Francisco, at the Six Gallery, a North Beach artists' cooperative, and didn't become widely known until the publication of Kerouac's novel *On the Road* (1957). As a literary and social movement, "beat" has been variously interpreted as: being *beat*en down in an oppressive and depressive world; a spiritual *beat*itude or inspirational insight; and a musical *beat* linked to jazz. These associations coalesced in poems like Ginsberg's "Howl," which rejected the materialism and conformity of American society, sought transcendence in Eastern mysticism and drugs, and celebrated sexual freedom with jazz-influenced lyricism.

Many of the writers associated with the Beat Generation were gay or bisexual, including Ginsberg, Kerouac, Burroughs, ROBERT DUNCAN, Jack Spicer, and Robin Blaser. Gay, straight, or bisexual, the beats—and the "beatniks" who gathered around them—championed a sexual freedom that scandalized and titillated the straitlaced American society of the fifties. Although the beats were often ridiculed in the press and popular culture of the period, the attention paid them helped publicize the existence of sexual SUBCULTURES in places like San Francisco and Greenwich Village. Even those who could not or would not move to these subcultural meccas were able to take pride and a newfound sense of identity in the status the beats conferred on the outcast.

Gay and lesbian historians have also seen the influence of the beats in the philosophy of social ACTIVISM embraced by later gay and lesbian leaders. In addition, the beats pointed the way to reclaiming earlier traditions created by writers like WALT WHITMAN, HART CRANE, and FEDERICO GARCÍA LORCA, whose gay identities had been obscured in posthumous criticism.

✧ Bruce Cook, *The Beat Generation* (1971).

✧ John Tytell, *Naked Angels* (1976).

✧ John D'Emilio, *Sexual Politics, Sexual Communities: The Making of a Homosexual Minority in the United States, 1940–1970* (1983).

Bechdel, Alison
(1960–)

U.S. cartoonist. Born in Lock Haven, Pennsylvania, Bechdel began drawing as a child. Unlike the cartoons that have made her famous, her early caricatures were all of men and boys, a reflection, she later realized, of both the privileged status of males and the lack of strong, desirable images of women. After coming OUT in her junior year at Oberlin College and moving to New York City, she began including pictures of "crazy lesbians" in letters to friends, who urged her to publish her cartoons. "Dykes to Watch Out For" first appeared in the New York City feminist newspaper *Womanews* in 1983. By 1996, the strip was a regular feature in more than 45 lesbian, gay, feminist, and alternative publications in the U.S., CANADA, GERMANY, and the UNITED KINGDOM. Bechdel has also published an annual calendar and six best-selling books, two of which have won Lambda LITERARY AWARDS.

Satiric, critical, but always affectionate, "Dykes to Watch Out For" addresses a wide range of issues, usually political ones, that engage a group of closely knit women friends in the course of their daily lives. Bechdel sees the strip as "utopian" because "it's a much more cohesive community than I've ever found." Yet, as fellow cartoonist Kris Kovick has commented: "It's believable—it really is our community. We see ourselves mirrored in it."

Bechdel describes the emergence of lesbian culture as a volcano, underground for eons and now erupting: "What I try to do with my cartoons is document culture, but what is also happening is that I'm taking part in *creating* the culture."

✧ Alison Bechdel and Kris Kovick, "Confabulation," *Hot Wire* (September 1990).

✧ Katie Brown, "An Interview with Alison Bechdel," in *Dyke Strippers: Lesbian Cartoonists A to Z,* edited by Roz Warren (1995).

Behn, Aphra
(1640–1689)

English writer. Of uncertain parentage, Behn was probably born in Kent but spent most of her youth in the then Dutch colony of Surinam. The surname by which she is known came from a Dutch merchant she is thought to have married in 1664. After his death in 1665, she journeyed to Antwerp to work as a spy for King Charles II, but was never paid for her efforts. Destitute after her return to England, she was in 1668 thrown into a debtor's prison, an experience that strengthened her resolve to achieve financial independence. According to VITA SACKVILLE-WEST and VIRGINIA WOOLF, she subsequently became the first English woman to earn a living from writing.

Also the first—and, during her lifetime, the only—English woman playwright, Behn succeeded in mounting at least 20 dramas and bawdy comedies at London theaters, earning renown as the Incomparable Astrea (the name she had used during her career in espionage). When she was in her 40s, she published a serial, called *Love Letters Between a Nobleman and His Sister* (1682–1685), that is now considered the first English-language novel. Her most popular novel, *Oronooko or The Royal Slave* (1688), appeared the year before her death. She is most remembered today, however, for her playfully erotic—often homoerotic—poems, which include daring descriptions of everything from incest to impotence.

Contemporaries gossiped about Behn's affairs with men as well as her close friendship with John Hoyle, who was famous for his dalliances with other men. If her poetry is any indication, Behn also had same-sex romances, although she used her gift for wordplay to keep generations of readers guessing whether genital intimacy was a part of her relationships with the friends she referred to in a poem as "My Cabal." In "To the Fair Clarinda, Who Made Love to Me, Imagined More than Woman," for example, she argues that since Clarinda combines the charms of both a man and a woman, she is more powerfully attractive than a mere man could ever be. Yet the attraction is also nobler and more innocent because "no sure Crime with thee we can commit / or if we shou'd—thy Form excuses it."

Behn is buried in Westminster Abbey.

✧ Vita Sackville-West, *Aphra Behn: The Incomparable Astrea* (1927).

✧ Virginia Woolf, *A Room of One's Own* (1929).

✧ Arlene Stiebel, "Not Since Sappho: The Erotic in Poems of Katherine Philips and Aphra Behn," in *Homosexuality in Renaissance and Enlightenment England,* edited by Claude J. Summers (1992).

Belgium

No laws against same-sex relations between consenting adults over 16. Well-developed social and cultural scene and political groups in Brussels, Antwerp, Ghent, and Liège.

Belgium's reputation for being more conservative than neighboring countries is reflected in its comparatively less visible lesbian and gay SUBCULTURE. Gay and lesbian social life in Belgium is centered less on cafés and bars than on dances and parties sponsored by dozens of groups around the country. Brussels also has a biannual PRIDE CELEBRATION and march.

Belgian-born men and women who have explored lesbian and gay themes in the arts include Chantal Akerman, Eric de Kuyper, Tom Lanoye, and MARGUERITE YOURCENAR.

History

The territory that was to become the kingdom of Belgium after 1830 was the site of two Western European firsts: the earliest documented execution for SODOMY (the burning at the stake of a knifemaker named John in Ghent on **September 28, 1292**) and the first known case of a woman being tried for sodomy (**1391**). Historians are divided on the question of whether the frequency of same-sex eroticism rose when Belgians crowded into northern Europe's first urban commercial centers or whether civil authorities were simply more likely to regulate public sex than their rural neighbors. Some have speculated that these cases evidence the development of subcultures based on erotic affinities, a phenomenon not documented in most of Europe until much later.

On a slightly more positive note, Belgium was one of the first countries to end *public* executions of sodomites. After 1795, all same-sex acts were decriminalized with the imposition of the French penal code (see **9/25/1791**) and remained unpenalized in subsequent legal codes.

A gay and lesbian subculture developed in cities like Brussels by the second half of the 19th century, but political ACTIVISM did not surface in Belgium until the 1960s. A HOMOPHILE organization modeled on the Dutch COC (see the NETHERLANDS) was established in Antwerp in **1965**, and GAY LIBERATION groups formed on university campuses in the early 1970s. An umbrella organization for Dutch-speaking groups, the Federatie Werkgroepen Homofilie (FWH), began in 1975, joined later by a similar Fédération des Groupes Homosexuelles (FGH) for French speakers. Among their accomplishments were legislation approving a universal AGE OF CONSENT of 16 on June 8, 1985, and the ending of discrimination in the MILITARY in 1986.

Bellas, Bruce, see BRUCE OF LOS ANGELES.

Ben, Lisa

(Edith Eyde; 1921–)

U.S. editor of VICE VERSA, the first U.S. periodical for lesbians; science fiction writer; singer. Born and raised on a fruit ranch in northern California, Eyde was forced by her father to give up the violin and attend business school instead. In the mid-1940s, she moved to Los Angeles, where she met other lesbians and became part of the burgeoning postwar SUBCULTURE. While working as a secretary in a movie studio, she began to write and edit an anonymous monthly publication because, as she wrote, "we don't have any gay magazines, and I think we should." From June 1947 to February 1948, Eyde published nine issues of *Vice Versa,* which she called "America's Gayest Magazine." She typed two carbon sets of six copies of each issue in her office, then distributed the twelve finished copies at no charge via her network of friends, instructing them to "pass it on."

Lisa Ben, pioneering journalist and editor, as well as "the first gay folk singer."

In the fifties, Eyde wrote articles for THE LADDER under the name "Lisa Ben" (an anagram for lesbian) after the editor rejected her first PSEUDONYM, Ima Spinster. Pursuing her childhood interest in music, she traded in a dishwasher for a guitar and began performing parodies of popular songs ("I'm going to sit right down and write my butch a letter") at local clubs. In 1960 the Los Angeles chapter of DAUGHTERS OF BILITIS, of which she was a member, released a recording of her lesbian renditions of "Frankie and Johnny" and "Cruising down the Avenue," billing her as "the first gay folk singer."

- Leland Moss, "Lisa Ben," *Gaysweek* (January 23, 1978).
- Eric Marcus, *Making History: The Struggle for Gay and Lesbian Equal Rights, 1945–1990* (1992).
- Rodger Streitmatter, *Unspeakable: The Rise of the Gay and Lesbian Press in America* (1995).

Benedict, Ruth

(née Ruth Fulton; pseudonym as poet: Anne Singleton; 1887–1948)

Influential American anthropologist. Born in New York City but raised on her family's upstate farm, she grew up haunted by what she described as the "primal scene" of her mother sobbing over her father's coffin and her mother's unending "cult of grief." After graduating from Vassar, she traveled to Europe and later married Stanley Benedict. Although they did not officially separate until 1930, their marriage devolved into a formality within two years. In her poetry and journals, Benedict criticized conventional marriages and expressed her need for "a great love," a sense of personal validation, and an understanding of her own sexuality. She read widely among philosophers and feminists and wrote poetry and a book on Mary Wollstonecraft before returning to school and discovering ANTHROPOLOGY. Supported by mentors who figured among the founders of modern anthropology—Elsie Clews Parsons, Franz Boas, and Edward Sapir—she completed her dissertation in 1923 and began teaching at Columbia University.

A 1923 journal entry reveals that Benedict was seeking "a companion in harness." By that time, she had already had several love affairs with women and met MARGARET MEAD, a Columbia student almost 15 years her junior. "In harness" intellectually, emotionally, and, for a period, sexually, the two women profoundly influenced each other's work over the next 25 years. Mead's poem "New Year" is a tribute to their tender and supportive relationship, as is her memorial to Benedict, *An Anthropologist at Work*.

Ruth Benedict.

Benedict's cross-cultural studies, most notably her pivotal work, *Patterns of Culture* (1934), were among the first to argue that culture, not heredity, played a dominant role in forming individual personalities. Observing NATIVE AMERICAN societies as well as peoples in Europe and Asia, she advanced a theory of "cultural relativity," asserting that society, not BIOLOGY or nature, created the categories "normal" and "abnormal," and that these categories, though powerful, are both arbitrary and malleable. She believed that labeling a type of person "unnatural"—as medicine and society had labeled homosexuals—could lead to neurosis and even madness: "The adjustments that society demands of [homosexuals] would strain any man's vitality."

Benedict's affirmation of her own "misfit" status as a lesbian was a major influence both on the direction of her work and the conclusions she reached. Living at a time when there was no political movement to join, she instead sought to change the intellectual climate of society. She was optimistic that "social engineering" could free individuals for happier, more productive lives. To this end, she contributed to fighting anti-Semitism and, especially in the 1940s, racism. Her widely read *Race: Science and Politics* (1940) attacked time-honored, pseudoscientific notions of innate "racial characteristics," including the linkage of race with IQ.

Benedict found a "perfect companion" in research chemist Natalie Raymond, with whom she shared an apartment overlooking Central Park in the 1930s. By the early 1940s, she had separated from Raymond and begun living with psychologist Ruth Valentine. Valentine and Margaret Mead were with Benedict when she died of angina at the age of 61.

➤ Also see BERDACHE; CONSTRUCTIONISM VS. ESSENTIALISM.

✧ Margaret Mead, *An Anthropologist at Work* (1959).

✧ Margaret M. Caffrey, *Ruth Benedict: Stranger in the Land* (1989).

Bentham, Jeremy

(1748–1832)

English philosopher, founder of utilitarianism. Bentham believed that people were ruled by "two sovereign masters, pain and pleasure," and that an ideal legal and social system would be based on a "hedonic calculus" of the two: i.e., the goodness or badness of an action can be judged by how much happiness it gives how many people. One of the most influential thinkers of his time, Bentham had a profound effect on the evolution of law codes and constitutions in Europe and the Americas.

Between 1774 and 1824, Bentham wrote more than 500 pages on what he called "paederasty" or "Attic" love, sometimes explicitly defining these as sex between adult men. Historian Louis Crompton has analyzed these writings and considers them the first modern treatment of the subject. In addition to attempting to write a history of male-male love, Bentham argued from his theory of utilitarianism that it had "beneficial effects." He condemned contemporary persecution of "sodomites" as forms of "cruelty and intolerance." Furthermore, almost two centuries before the word was coined, he tried to explain the origins of HOMOPHOBIA.

Bentham apparently felt these writings were too controversial to share with the public: they remained unpublished and virtually unstudied until a partial text was issued in 1931. Crompton's 1985 study was the first comprehensive examination of these writings.

✧ Louis Crompton, *Byron and Greek Love: Homophobia in Nineteenth-Century England* (1985).

Bentley, Gladys

(1907–1960)

U.S. singer, lyricist. Bentley fled Pennsylvania at the age of 16 to join the HARLEM RENAISSANCE and come OUT as a "bulldagger" (BUTCH lesbian). She supported herself at first by singing at rent parties and "buffet flats," then graduated to speakeasies and nightclubs. By the late 1920s, she was as famous for her glamorous girlfriends and tailor-made white tuxedos as for her powerfully throaty voice and hilariously obscene parodies of show tunes and blues standards. She headlined at Harry Hansberry's notorious Clam House, a speakeasy on Harlem's 133rd Street "Jungle Alley" frequented by black and white celebrities as well as lesbians and gay men, and, later, at the Ubangi Club, backed by a chorus of female impersonators.

Bentley projected an image that was literally bigger than life: memoirists described her as weighing almost 400 pounds, although photographs show she was actually closer to 250. She was blatant about her attraction to women, performing at lesbian bars including Mona's in San Francisco and titillating the nation in the 1940s by telling gossip columnists that she had married a white woman in Atlantic City.

As attitudes toward homosexuality hardened in the 1940s, Bentley was harassed by Los Angeles police for wearing men's clothes and ridiculed or ignored by the press. In 1952, an *Ebony* article entitled "I Am a Woman Again" recounted her regret over her previous life, her hormone "cure" for homosexuality, and her recent marriage, this time to a man. She died of influenza at the age of 52, shortly before she was to be ordained a minister in an evangelical church.

✧ Eric Garber, "Gladys Bentley: The Bulldagger Who Sang the Blues," *Out/look* (Spring 1988).

Berdache

Term used by historians and social scientists for a person, especially a NATIVE AMERICAN, who is viewed by others in the society as having a GENDER role and identity different from those commonly associated with his or her biological sex.

Because "berdache" was derived via French from a Persian word referring to a young male sex slave, many activists find the term pejorative and prefer using specific Native American words, like the Dakota *wingkta* or Navajo *na'adleeh,* or "two-spirit," a reference to the common belief that berdaches possessed both female and male spirits. Some anthropologists, including Walter L. Williams, reserve "berdache" to describe biological males, preferring "AMAZON" for biological females. In addition, some purists object to the use of "berdache" to refer to persons other than Native Americans. In practice, however, "berdache" is often used indiscriminately as a way of distinguishing persons who live in societies—found in AFRICA, the PACIFIC ISLANDS, Siberia, and elsewhere—that recognize and, by extension, legitimize gender nonconformity, from similar persons in cultures that view such people as rare anomalies. In other words, some writers will refer to a Tahitian *mahu* as a kind of "berdache," but few would use the term to describe a Danish TRANSSEXUAL or an American PASSING woman.

Anthropologists have observed (male) berdaches in 133 North American societies and (female) amazons in almost half that number. Berdaches varied widely from one people to another, but they most commonly: wore all or most of the items of clothing associated with the opposite sex; performed the social and economic functions of the opposite sex; were inspired to change their gender role by a message from the spirits communicated in a dream or a sacred ceremony; and generally, but not always, had sexual relations with "conventional" members of their own biological sex.

We'wha of the Zuñi was the most famous berdache of the 19th century.

Berdaches also frequently took wives or husbands of their own sex.

Berdaches were treated with respect by most Native American peoples. In some groups, they were revered as shamans or healers. Some documentation exists for amazons who became leading warriors (see **c. 1835**). The first Europeans to write about American berdaches were French and Spanish missionaries in the 17th century. Unused to such people in their own societies, most Europeans and, later, Americans and Canadians, conflated them with "sodomites" or, in some cases, mistakenly believed male berdaches to be biological females. Historian Rudi C. Bleys hypothesizes that the European "discovery" of berdaches may have been a contributing factor in the association, common in the West by the end of the 18th century, of same-sex eroticism with cross-gender social behavior.

Perhaps the most famous berdache was We'wha (1849–1896), a Zuñi *lhamana* whom anthropologist Matilda Stevenson accompanied to Washington, D.C., in the 1880s. We'wha, taken to be an "Indian princess," charmed Washington society and was even presented to President Grover Cleveland on June 23, 1886. No one present was aware that We'wha was a biological male.

When missionaries or government officials discovered berdaches and amazons in the late 19th century, they often forced them to change their mode of dress and manner of life to conform to American and Canadian gender expectations. Many are reported to have committed suicide rather than do so. A few resisters were discovered and written about by RUTH BENEDICT and other anthropologists in the 20th century, but it was not until the 1970s that a revival of Native American traditions and GAY LIBERATION combined to bring large numbers of amazons and berdaches out of the CLOSET.

✧ Walter Williams, *The Spirit and the Flesh: Sexual Diversity in American Indian Culture* (1993).

✧ Rudi C. Bleys, *The Geography of Perversion: Male to Male Sexual Behavior Outside the West and the Ethnographic Imagination, 1750–1918* (1996).

Berlin, see GERMANY.

Bias Crime, see HATE CRIME.

Bible, The

Sacred scriptures of JUDAISM and, including the New Testament, CHRISTIANITY that, depending on interpretation, are generally held to contain the following negative references to same-sex eroticism: Genesis 19:4–11; Leviticus 18:22, 20:13; Deuteronomy 23:17–18; Judges 19:22; Romans 1:26–27; I Corinthians 6:9; I Timothy 1:10; II Peter 2:6; and Jude 7–8. CROSS-DRESSING, either by women or men, is also condemned as an "abomination" in Deuteronomy 22:5. In addition, the Bible includes several positive accounts of relationships—such as those between David and Jonathan (I and II Samuel), Ruth and Naomi (Ruth), and even Jesus and John (John 13:23; 21:20)—that some readers have interpreted as homoerotic.

The exact makeup of the Bible differs among religions, but there is even greater dispute among Jews and Christians alike over how the Bible should be interpreted and how literally its proscriptions, including those that seem to condemn same-sex eroticism, should be observed. As gay and lesbian theologians point out, many biblical directives are ignored by the most fundamentalist Christians: the Bible condones slavery (Leviticus 25:44–45; I Timothy 6:1–2; etc.), commands wives to "submit" themselves to their husbands "in

Not openly mentioned in the Old Testament, lesbians have laid claim to biblical heroines like Ruth and Naomi.

every thing" (Ephesians 5:22–24), advocates the death penalty for children who "curse" their parents (Leviticus 20:9), and sentences male-female couples to "be cut off from among their people" if they have sex while the woman is menstruating (Leviticus 20:18).

Behind the issue of how literally Jews and Christians should follow the dictates of the Bible lies the equally contentious question of how to translate the Hebrew and Greek words of the original texts. Deuteronomy 23:17–18 contains, for example, the Hebrew word "*qadhesh,*" which the translators of the King James Version of the Bible interpreted as "sodomite" but which most modern scholars believe referred to a temple servant, male or female, who had sex with worshipers as part of fertility cults common among the peoples who lived near the ancient Hebrews. (The original implication of the word "sodomite," never used with its present meaning in the Bible, has also been disputed by scholars such as JOHN BOSWELL—see SODOM AND GOMORRAH.) Thus, the passage may not be meant to condemn all who engage in same-sex relations, only those who do so as part of an idolatrous cult. Similarly, in the New Testament, some scholars believe that Paul meant only to condemn the "effete" (and not the "effeminate" as the King James Version translates) and men who subjected others to abusive anal intercourse (and not all "homosexuals" as the Living Bible asserts) in I Corinthians 6:9.

Romans 1:26 is the only verse in the Bible that most commentators think refers to same-sex eroticism between women, although even

Despite its prohibitions, the Bible has inspired homoerotic fantasies. Here David triumphs over the strong man Goliath.

this passage is vaguely worded, attacking women "who did change the natural use into that which is against nature."

Whatever the original meaning of these passages, there is no doubt, however, that by the early Christian era, almost all Jewish and Christian commentators believed that the Bible condemned same-sex love, and this belief has continued to influence legal and judicial proceedings as late as the *Bowers v. Hardwick* decision (see **6/30/1986**).

➤ Also see **c. 450 B.C.**

- ✧ Daniel A. Helminiak, *What the Bible Really Says About Homosexuality* (1994).
- ✧ Raymond-Jean Frontain, "The Bible," in *The Gay and Lesbian Literary Heritage: A Reader's Companion to the Writers and Their Works, from Antiquity to the Present,* edited by Claude J. Summers (1995).

Biology

One of the paradoxes of gay and lesbian consciousness in the 1990s is that scholars active in LESBIAN AND GAY STUDIES and the persons they purport to study generally have two very different conceptions of homosexuality and its origins. The vast majority of scholars in lesbian and gay studies today work from the hypothesis that homosexuality is a modern Western "social construction" (see CONSTRUCTIONISM VS. ESSENTIALISM), while an almost equally large majority of nonacademic lesbians and gay men, as consistently demonstrated in opinion surveys, believe that homosexuality is inborn. Support for the latter position has come from a number of scientific studies, chiefly by biologists.

In 1991, gay scientist Simon LeVay studied the brains of 35 men, most of whom had died of AIDS, and 6 women, and found that a section of the hypothalamus was smaller in gay-identified men (and women) than in straight men. The following year, University of California researchers Roger Gorski and Laura S. Allen looked at the anterior commissure of the brains of 109 men, 34 of whom were gay, and found it *larger* in gay men than in straight men. In 1994, Canadian researchers (led by Sandra Witelson of McMaster University) surveyed yet another part of the brain, the corpus callosum, and determined that it was 13 percent *thicker* in gay men. Later that year, another group of Canadians, this time at the University of Western Ontario, examined the fingerprints of 66 gay men and 182 heterosexual men and found that 30 percent of the gay men studied had more ridges on their left hand than their right, compared with only 14 percent of the straight men. If confirmed by other researchers, this last result overrides the "chicken/egg" objections raised against the brain studies—that brain differences in gay men might result from environmental factors in gay male lives rather than be the source of the potential for same-sex desire—because fingerprints are known to be largely set for life by genetic factors at 16 weeks after conception.

None of these studies looked for differences between lesbians and straight women, but lesbians have been the focus of twin studies (research that compares data from fraternal and/or identical twins with data from singlet siblings). According to LeVay and fellow researcher Dean H. Hamer, a National Cancer Institute geneticist, data pooled from six different twin studies show that 50 percent of identical twins of lesbians also self-identify as lesbians, compared with 16 percent of fraternal twin sisters and 13 percent of singlet sisters. The same number (13 percent) of singlet brothers of gay men also self-identify as gay, but a slightly higher percentage of gay male identical and fraternal twins report the same sexual self-identification: 57 percent and 24 percent, respectively. These studies have led some geneticists to speculate that homosexuality—or a potential to be homosexual—is at least partly inherited.

Clues to how one group of gay men may have inherited a potential for homosexuality came from genetic research conducted by a team led by Hamer and reported in 1993. Focusing on 40 families in which two brothers were gay, Hamer's team examined the brothers' X chromosomes and found that 33 of the 40 pairs of brothers shared a marker at the tip of the X chromosome, the Xq28 region. In comparison, a control group of 314 pairs of brothers drawn from the general population showed only random distribution (about 50 percent) of the marker. Although press reports hailed the discovery of the "gay gene," the Xq28 area actually contains several hundred genes, any one of which may be a factor in determining sexuality. Furthermore, 6 pairs of gay brothers did not share the same marker, suggesting that for them at least the Xq28 area had nothing to do with their sexuality.

Since the X chromosome is inherited from one's mother, Hamer's team took the Xq28 research a step further and analyzed the extended maternal and paternal families of gay men. Again, they found a statistically significant higher likelihood of maternal uncles and cousins who were gay also having the same Xq28 marker. No correlation was found among paternal relatives.

Geneticists emphasize that no one gene or combination of genes is likely to determine an adult's sexuality in the comparatively straightforward way that genes determine eye or hair color. If such a gene (or combination of genes) existed, there would be a 100 percent correlation in the sexualities of identical twins, which is clearly not the case. Rather, there may be a genetic *predisposition* toward a particular sexuality that then is influenced by unknown factors after conception.

Nevertheless, some activists worry that a study conclusively proving that the potential for homosexuality is genetically transmitted will lead to people aborting potentially gay and lesbian babies—or finding ways of biologically engineering heterosexuality. Others, including a spokesperson for the NATIONAL GAY AND LESBIAN TASK FORCE speaking in 1994, believe that such findings may help lesbians and gay men overcome HOMOPHOBIA because they would prove that "homosexuality is a naturally occurring and common variation among humans."

➤ Also see SOCIOBIOLOGY; ZOOLOGY.

✧ Simon LeVay, *The Sexual Brain* (1993).

✧ *Sex, Cells, and Same-Sex Desire: The Biology of Sexual Preference,* edited by John P. De Cecco and David Allen Parker (1995).

✧ Chandler Burr, *A Separate Creation: The Search for the Biological Origins of Sexual Orientation* (1996).

Biphobia

Dislike or suspicion of bisexuals and BISEXUALITY. Coined by bisexual activists after the example of "HOMOPHOBIA," biphobia refers as much to disapproving attitudes among nonbisexual lesbians and gay men as it does to prejudices held by heterosexuals. These attitudes include: "Bisexuals are unable or unwilling to make a satisfying commitment to one person"; "Bisexuals find it difficult to love and lust after the same person"; and "Bisexuality is only a phase people go through on their way to a 'full-fledged' gay or lesbian identity." Perhaps the most common biphobic attitude is the belief that "true" bisexuality is an impossibility. In a survey THE ADVOCATE conducted of its male readers in 1994, 33 percent of the respondents did not believe in the existence of bisexuality. In society at large, biphobia manifests itself in the fear that bisexuals are a conduit for the spread of AIDS to heterosexuals.

The pervasiveness of biphobia was one of the major reasons bisexuals began to organize their own advocacy groups in the late 1970s.

✧ *Bisexuality: A Reader and Sourcebook,* edited by Thomas Geller (1990).

Biren, Joan E.

("JEB"; 1944–)

U.S. photographer, activist. Born and raised in Washington, D.C., JEB attended Mount Holyoke College and did graduate work in political science at Oxford for three years. Back in the U.S., she worked in the civil rights, antiwar, and women's movements. From 1971 to 1972, she was a founding member of the FURIES, an influential lesbian-feminist political collective. After it disbanded, she studied political science and broadcast communications at the American University.

While part of the Furies, JEB realized that she had grown, as she later explained, "unhappy with being a verbal person." She set about training herself as a photographer by taking a correspondence course, working in a camera store, and taking pictures for a small-town newspaper and a photographers' trade association. By 1975, she had established herself as a full-time freelance photographer and had begun to put together an unmatched documentary record of the first decade of the post-STONEWALL era.

Many of her most memorable images, ranging from shots of political actions to depictions of women hard at work on the MICHIGAN WOMYN'S MUSIC FESTIVAL, were collected in *Eye to Eye: Portraits of Lesbians* (1979), which

JEB, self-portrait.

she published with financial assistance from the lesbian community. The first book of its kind, *Eye to Eye* was hailed as a breakthrough in lesbian visibility.

JEB widened her focus beyond still photography in the 1980s, compiling documentary slide shows, publishing another book of portraits of lesbians (*Making a Way: Lesbians Out Front,* 1987), and creating an ever increasing variety of images for periodicals, music packaging, postcards, calendars, and posters. She was also the video producer for the **April 25, 1993**, March on Washington, overseeing simultaneous big-screen projection and worldwide satellite broadcasts, and later making *A Simple Matter of Justice,* the official videotape of the march.

✧ Denise Sudell, "Portraits of Lesbians," *Gay News* (1979).

✧ Heidi Laudon, "A New Way of Seeing Ourselves," *Body Politic* (May 1981).

Birtha, Becky

(1948–)

U.S. writer. Birtha was introduced to the AFRICAN-AMERICAN literary heritage by her mother, a children's librarian in Hampton, Virginia. Named after her great-grandmother, who was born a slave, Birtha is also mindful of her Irish, Cherokee, and Choctaw roots, contributing to the emergence of a uniquely diversified lesbian LITERATURE by making, as she described the experience of the protagonist of her short story "Ice Palace," "all her colors leap into focus."

Birtha majored in children's studies and earned an M.F.A. in creative writing at the State University of New York at Buffalo. She came OUT in 1976, later served on the editorial board of the Lesbian-Feminist Study Clearinghouse, and published her first book of short stories, *For Nights Like This One: Stories of Loving Women,* in 1983. In addition to fiction and nonfiction contributions to a number of anthologies, she has also written *Lover's Choice* (1987), a second short story collection (which contains "Ice Palace"), and a book of poetry, *The Forbidden Poems* (1991). Her work has been praised for its humor, directness, frequent elements of surprise, and, especially, her daring in taking on controversial issues like interracial relationships, rape, and incest.

Birtha lives in Philadelphia with her adopted daughter, Tasha Alfrieda.

✧ Rebecca Mark, "Becky Birtha," in *Contemporary Lesbian Writers of the United States,* edited by Sandra Pollack and Denise D. Knight (1993).

Bisexuality

As it is most commonly understood, bisexuality is the potential for sexual attraction to both men and women. Bisexual activists, however, reject attempts to define "bisexuals," describing themselves instead as people who are attracted to *individuals* rather than to persons of a particular GENDER or biological sex.

Since Freud, many people have come to believe that human beings begin their lives in a state of *polymorphous perversity*—that is, with a desire (libido) for sexual pleasure that does not distinguish the object of desire by biological sex or gender. Freud himself was never satisfied with his explanations of how human beings were able to suppress desire for one sex and, in their conscious mind at least, feel attraction only for the other. Many other thinkers—most notably JONATHAN NED KATZ, Jeffrey Weeks, and MICHEL FOUCAULT, but also GORE VIDAL, and LILLIAN FADERMAN—have asserted that society and culture artificially create the categories of "homosexuality" and "heterosexuality."

Speaking for many, Faderman wrote: "I truly believe that bisexuality is the natural human condition." But this and similar contentions are controversial in some quarters because they seem to imply that "monosexuals"—as bisexual activists call exclusively gay, lesbian, or straight individuals—exhibit an *un*natural condition. Yet there is no question that many cultures throughout history, including Western European culture in the Middle Ages, believed that all sexually mature persons were capable of having sex with both women and men, even when same-sex relations were considered a sin "against nature." Some cultures have actually made having sex with both men and women compulsory (see CIRCUMSTANTIAL HOMOSEXUALITY) or at least socially advantageous (see GREECE); many others, including contemporary JAPAN and LATIN AMER-

ICA, have tolerated discreet same-sex relations (especially between men) provided participants follow the dictates of COMPULSORY HETEROSEXUALITY—i.e., marry and attempt to procreate.

All these facts lead most sexologists to distinguish between bisexual *behavior* and bisexual *desire,* considering the latter a better indication of a bisexual *orientation* than the former. Looked at as a behavior, bisexuality is common: according to the KINSEY REPORTS, 33 percent of adult men and 11 percent of adult women had sex to orgasm with members of both sexes—although a 1994 University of Chicago study reported figures of less than half the Kinsey incidence for both women and men. Defined solely as desire, bisexuality may be as common as 50 percent (Kinsey), or as rare as 1.5 percent among women and virtually nonexistent among men. The last figures come from studies conducted at the National Institutes of Health by geneticists Dean H. Hamer, hypothesizer of a "gay gene" (see BIOLOGY), and lesbian scientist Angela Pattatucci. Hamer and Pattatucci designed a study that focused on feelings of sexual and romantic attraction—rather than behavior—as expressed by interviewees. In 1996, they reported that, according to the specifications of their study, men not only were seldom significantly attracted to both sexes, they also almost never exhibited signs of a change in sexual orientation over time. Women, on the other hand, were a little more likely to change orientations over the course of adult life—although Pattatucci noted that women whose desires qualified them as bisexual were statistically no less stable in this orientation than their lesbian or straight counterparts.

Pattatucci also speculated that the variation between men and women in rates of bisexuality may be the result of a (perhaps cultural) GENDER difference. Men, she believes, are more "bimodal," likely to think in either/or, yes/no terms, while women are much more likely to consider contributing factors, and to answer "it depends" when queried on matters as complex as sexuality.

Activism

Many bisexuals contributed to the actions and achievements of the GAY LIBERATION era in the early 1970s. In the mid-1970s, bisexuals began to seek greater visibility for themselves, leading to the first era of so-called "bisexual chic"—as it was hailed in the U.S. media—around 1974. (Short-lived periods of chicdom were proclaimed by newsmagazines again in 1987, 1990, and 1995.) Bisexual Forum was formed in New York City in 1975 and continued to be active through 1983. Other affinity groups included the San Francisco Bisexual Center (1976–1984) and Bi-Ways Chicago (1978–1983).

In the second half of the 1980s, bisexual activism was revitalized as bisexuals found themselves increasingly vilified as "conduits" of AIDS from the gay community to the supposedly HIV-free heterosexual population. At the same time, queer activism, which opposed the imposition of cut-and-dried sexual labels, encouraged many gay men and, especially, lesbians to come OUT as bisexuals, both in their private lives and in publications like the quarterly *Anything That Moves.*

By the 1990s, bisexual activists had gained a measure of recognition in the lesbian and gay communities, as evidenced by a worldwide trend toward adding "and bisexual" to the names of queer organizations and events such as PRIDE CELEBRATIONS. The 1990s also saw the proliferation of ever more specialized organizations, such as the New York–based Bisexual Womyn of Colour, which aimed to provide members a "safe space" to explore and develop their own unique identities.

➤ Also see BIPHOBIA; GAY AND LESBIAN RIGHTS MOVEMENT; LESBIAN, POLITICAL.

- ✧ *Bi Any Other Name: Bisexual People Speak Out,* edited by Loraine Hutchins and Lani Kaahumanu (1991).
- ✧ Amanda Udis-Kessler, "Identity/Politics: Historical Sources of the Bisexual Movement," in *Queer Studies: A Lesbian, Gay, Bisexual, and Transgendered Anthology* (1996).

Bishop, Elizabeth
(1911–1979)

American poet. Born in Worcester, Massachusetts, Bishop was raised by relatives in Nova Scotia after her father died and her mother was committed to a mental institution. She attended boarding schools and Vassar and lived most of her adult life "in exile": outside of New York City and the American literary scene, which she found discomforting. Bishop spent nearly 20 years in Brazil with her lover, Lota de Macedo Soares. Later, back in the U.S., she shared her life with Alice Methfessel.

Although comfortable with both traditional and free structures, Bishop was loath to express rhetorical or confessional impulses in her poetry. Clues to her political views and personal intimacies are hidden within perceptively rendered objects, generalities, and places. When she was less discreet, as in "Rooster," "One Art," "In the Waiting Room," or "The Shampoo" (a love poem between two women), her revelations generally went unnoticed.

She was open about being a lesbian with friends, who included BEAUFORD DELANEY, JAMES MERRILL, and MAY SWENSON, but she was pessimistic about society's ever accepting same-sex relationships. She once told RICHARD HOWARD that she believed in "closets, closets and more closets!" She hated being characterized as a "woman poet" and refused to allow her work to be part of "segregated" anthologies, even when asked by writers she admired, such as ADRIENNE RICH. Her insistence on personal privacy led her to consider W. H. AUDEN as ultimately more courageous than the very public ALLEN GINSBERG.

Left to right: May Swenson, Beauford Delaney, and Elizabeth Bishop at Yaddo in 1950.

Bishop's major writings include *North and South—A Cold Spring* (Pulitzer Prize, 1956), *Complete Poems* (National Book Award, 1970), and *Geography III* (National Book Critics' Circle Award, 1977).

- ✧ Brett C. Millier, *Elizabeth Bishop: Life and the Memory of It* (1993).
- ✧ *One Art: The Letters of Elizabeth Bishop,* edited by Robert Giroux (1994).
- ✧ Gary Fountain and Peter Brazeau, *Remembering Elizabeth Bishop: An Oral Biography* (1993).

Black Triangle, see PINK TRIANGLE.

Bloomsbury

Group of English writers and artists who associated with one another from about 1904. Many in the Bloomsbury group were bisexual, gay, or lesbian, including the painter Duncan Grant (1885–1978), economist John Maynard Keynes (1883–1946), writer Lytton Strachey (1880–1932), and VIRGINIA WOOLF. Their friends and lovers included Dora Carrington (1893–1932), E. M. FORSTER, and VITA SACKVILLE-WEST.

The group first assembled in a decaying, bohemian section of London called Bloomsbury at 46 Gordon Square, the home to which the Stephen siblings—Vanessa [Bell], Thoby, Virginia [Woolf], and Adrian—moved after their father's death. The Stephens formed the nucleus of the group with Thoby's friends from his Cambridge days: art critic Clive Bell, Grant, Keynes, Strachey, and journalist/politician Leonard Woolf. Strachey, famous for his irreverent wit, set the tone for the group's lively Thursday evening gatherings, which some biographers consider the sequel to meetings of the Apostles, a secret *conversazione* society several of the men had joined while at Cambridge. The raison d'être of the Apostles was absolute freedom of speech—and undiluted candor. To Strachey, that meant discussing sex, especially sex with other men, a topic the Bloomsbury set picked up with gusto.

"The word bugger was never far from our lips," Virginia Woolf later wrote. "We discussed copulation with the same excitement and openness that we discussed the good of nature."

"Sex talk," as Woolf called it, was only one of the ways the friends defied convention. Over the years, they launched a series of assaults on the manners, morals, and aesthetics that had overshadowed their Victorian youths. Roger Fry (1866–1934), who joined the group in 1910, championed "Manet and the Post-Impressionists" in a controversial show in 1912. Strachey introduced a fresh—and widely imitated—genre of biography with his wittily iconoclastic *Eminent Victorians* (1918) and *Queen Victoria* (1921). His brother James translated Sigmund Freud into English for the first time. Virginia Woolf pioneered modernism in the novel and helped establish feminist literary criticism. And in a completely different arena, Keynes developed new theories that revolutionized the relationship between government and economics.

The love lives of the Bloomsbury group were equally innovative—and QUEER in every sense of the word. Grant, for example, had a love affair with his cousin Strachey while still at Cambridge, then successively paired off with Keynes, Vanessa Bell (with whom he shared a home and a studio most of his life), and David "Bunny" Garnett, a writer who later married Grant and Bell's daughter, Angelica. Strachey, who was possibly the most promiscuous of the group, failed to form a sexual relationship with the painter Dora Carrington in 1915 but maintained with her a passionate friendship so important to both of them that she committed suicide shortly after he died of stomach cancer at the age of 52. Carrington, who thought of herself as a sexual "hybrid," fell in love with both men and women, including Strachey's sister Julia, who was in turn married to sculptor Stephen Tomlin (1901–1937), who was also bisexual and may also have been in love with Lytton. (Carrington's affairs with women were not included in the 1995 film *Carrington,* which focused on her relationship with Strachey). Carrington, when she wasn't involved with other women, sometimes shared male lovers with Strachey.

The love affairs of the Bloomsbury group were complex, multidirectional, and seemingly devoid of possessiveness. Their marriages, though not sexually passionate, persisted: no one divorced. Keynes had a happy (although unpopular with his Bloomsbury friends) marriage with ballerina Lydia Lopokova.

D. H. Lawrence (1885–1930) led public criticism of the group: "Men lovers of men, they give me a sense of corruption, almost of putrescence. . . . It is abominable." Within the group Vanessa Bell's daughter, Angelica (1918–), wrote in *Deceived with Kindness* (1994) of the deep unhappiness that had resulted from her discovering that her father was not Bell but her mother's lover Grant and that her husband had been at one time her father's lover.

On a more positive note, Strachey articulated a position against the shame of his era, and saw meaningful same-sex relationships as possible and equivalent to heterosexual ones. In a letter to Keynes, Strachey wrote, "I believe our time will come about 100 years hence, when preparations will have been made, and compromises too, so that, at the publication of our letters, everyone will be finally converted."

✧ David Chura, "Bloomsbury: A Gay Perspective," in *Gay Roots: Twenty Years of Gay Sunshine,* edited by Winston Leyland (1991).

Bodybuilding

Regimen of weight lifting to enhance the appearance of musculature popular among gay men and, increasingly, lesbians.

In July 1989, Bob Paris, a former Mr. Universe, "married" Rod Jackson, and together they became the first gay couple on the cover of a sports magazine (the next month's issue of the British *Bodypower*). Earlier, when Paris came out in the muscle magazine *Ironman,* he had given the ultramasculine world of bodybuilding its first openly gay face.

Culturally, muscles are more than body power—they are GENDER power. Muscles *mean* masculinity in a society that enforces many gender-based restraints on the body, including its representation, production, reproduction, and even maintenance. Women bodybuilders challenge some of those restrictions by recasting the "feminine" away from the passive and weak into a control and definition of their bodies.

Gay male bodybuilders also challenge gender assumptions when they reverse the stereotype of the effeminate sissy. As symbols of masculinity, muscles are attractive to gay men in real life and fantasy because they reflect their interest in masculine appearance and contact. From Duncan Grant to TOM OF FINLAND, the muscular athlete has been seen as a homoerotic example of "human art." Brian Pronger describes this as "*paradoxical* masculinity"—the forces that constitute the "jock" as traditionally masculine are the same forces that make him so attractive to gay men.

Despite their challenges to gender, both heterosexual and homosexual female and male bodybuilders ultimately echo traditional gender images of the body. For instance, although controversial within the sport, the women who win bodybuilding competitions are typically those with more build than bulk and more feminine "aesthetics" in posing, symmetry, and presentation. While individual judges can vary, gay and lesbian competitions (such as the physique event in the GAY GAMES) follow the direction of the international standards. The ongoing dispute over interpreting those rules for women is dramatically illustrated in the film *Pumping Iron II: The Women* (1984): International Federation of Bodybuilding officials placed the audience's favorite (and most muscular) Bev Francis eighth, while awarding the title to a woman who "set the standard of femininity." Throughout, the film poses the question: Can a woman still be a woman if she looks like a man?

Since the early 1970s, both gymnastics and bodybuilding have become tremendously popular among women. Historian Susan Cahn sees contradictory images between the two with gymnastics representing "young girl" cuteness and bodybuilding representing a "masculine posture." Women have been competing worldwide in the latter sport only since 1980 and their participation is not accepted in all countries. For example, not until 1994 did the International Federation of Bodybuilding sanction a women's event at the Ibero-America Body-building Championship, the competition for Spanish- and Portuguese-speaking countries.

The internationally celebrated 19th-century strong man Eugene Sandow is considered the first popular bodybuilding model for men. Sociologist Michael Messner finds the interest in athletics that sprang up in gay male communities in the 1970s and 1980s mirrored by the rapid growth of bodybuilding among young urban gay men. Lou Messina, a bodybuilder and openly gay competition judge, describes himself as a baby boomer who was drawn to bodybuilding to accentuate his masculinity. At gyms, gay men have found an alternative to the BARS for social contacts, especially in the era of AIDS.

Bodybuilders report feelings of an inner and outer strength and beauty, simple physical pleasure and empowerment. For professional bodybuilders, an economic and commercial component is also present. Muscular bodies sell products. Bodybuilders are an important part of fashion and product marketing in general. Publishers know that putting a muscled body on the cover of a publication will sell copies.

While most serious gay and lesbian bodybuilders are members of mainstream associations for competitive purposes and some see no need for separate community groups, gay and lesbian organizations do exist. These include the Arcadia Bodybuilding Society in San Francisco and the North American Bodybuilding Judges Guild, a gay and lesbian group of bodybuilding officials based in Seattle.

✧ Brian Pronger, *The Arena of Masculinity: Sports, Homosexuality and the Meaning of Sex* (1990).

✧ *Sport, Men, and the Gender Order: Critical Feminist Perspectives,* edited by Michael A. Messner and D. F. Sabo (1990).

✧ Michael A. Messner, *Power at Play: Sports and the Problem of Masculinity* (1992).

✧ Anne Balsamo, "Feminist Bodybuilding," and Christine Anne Holmlund, "Visible Difference and Flex Appeal: The Body, Sex, Sexuality, and Race in the *Pumping Iron* Films," in *Women, Sport, and Culture,* edited by Susan Birrell and Cheryl L. Cole (1994).

✧ Susan K. Cahn, *Coming On Strong: Gender and Sexuality in Twentieth-Century Women's Sport* (1994).

✧ Calvin Sims, "Argentine Women Break Social Barriers to Pump Iron," *New York Times* (December 20, 1995).

Bond, Pat

(1925–1990)

U.S. actress, comic, activist. Born and raised in Chicago, Bond was a child member of the Goodman Theater Jack and Jill Players, which performed on a weekly radio program called *Let's Pretend*. As a teenager she moved with her family to Davenport, Iowa, and attended a Catholic women's college for two years, an experience Bond described as "a finishing school where they finished me." After studying theater at the University of Iowa, she enlisted in the U.S. Army medical corps in 1945 in an attempt "to forget" an unrequited love but had her service career cut short when she was one of 500 servicewomen discharged during a lesbian "witch-hunt" in Tokyo. She moved to San Francisco, became the Bay Area's best-known openly lesbian comic and began running a lesbian club called Bond Street while touring the U.S. and Canada extensively in the 1980s. She also founded the New York chapter of the Eulenspiegel Society, "the only aboveground S&M group in the world."

Bond's one-woman shows included *Conversations with Pat Bond, Conversations with Lorena Hickok, Mädchen in Uniform,* and *Gertie, Gertie, Gertie, Stein Is Back, Back, Back,* the last of which was the subject of a documentary sponsored by Maryland Public Television.

Bond appeared with 25 other gay men and lesbians in the Mariposa Film Group's groundbreaking documentary *Word Is Out* (1977). Remembering the thunderous applause that greeted the performers when they appeared onstage at the San Francisco opening, Bond commented, "It was the first time in my life that I've been vindicated as a human being."

Rosa Bonheur in her youth.

Bonheur, Rosa

(Marie-Rosalie Bonheur; 1822–1899)

French painter. Adherents of the libertarian social philosophy of Claude de Saint Simon, her bohemian parents made sure she received as comprehensive an education as her brother. Her father taught her to paint, and she began exhibiting at official salons while still a teenager. By the 1850s, she had won international acclaim for the vigor and immediacy of her paintings of animals, such as *The Horse Fair* (1853–1855), which Queen Victoria asked to have exhibited in Windsor Castle. In 1865, when she became the first woman to receive the cross of the Legion of Honor, the Empress

Eugénie was said to remark, "Genius has no sex."

Bonheur was famous for her "emancipated" eccentricities: she smoked cigarettes, refused to ride sidesaddle and, with the permission of the Paris Prefect's office, wore trousers on her field trips to slaughterhouses and horse fairs. Her considerable earnings allowed her to buy a chateau, which she shared with her lifelong companion, an amateur inventor named Nathalie Micas, as well as a pet lioness, two mustangs (presents from Buffalo Bill Cody), and assorted yaks and gazelles. After Micas's death in 1889, she formed a passionate relationship with an American artist, Anna Klumpke (1856–1942), whom she described as her "wife." Klumpke, who also wrote a posthumous biography of the artist, inherited her entire estate. The three women's ashes are buried together in Père Lachaise Cemetery in Paris.

LILLIAN FADERMAN has suggested that Bonheur "had little feminist consciousness" and that she mimicked heterosexual models in her relationships. In fact, Bonheur considered ANDROGYNY not only a human ideal but also divine: Christ's wounds, she believed, represented a mystical analogy to female genitalia. She was supportive of other ambitious women and, most unusual in the 19th century, left evidence that she considered herself a lesbian, writing MAGNUS HIRSCHFELD that she belonged to what Hirschfeld called the "third sex."

✧ Dore Ashton and Denise Broume Hare, *Rosa Bonheur: A Life and Legend* (1981).

Bookstores

In addition to selling books and periodicals, gay and lesbian—and feminist/women's—bookstores have traditionally served as informal community centers, offering everything from space for bulletin boards to tourist information to legal and medical referrals. Many also provide space for meetings, performances, and readings. In 1996, there were more than 140 lesbian and gay bookstores and about 100 women's/feminist bookstores in the U.S. CANADA, with about 10 percent of the population of the U.S., has only 4 gay or lesbian bookstores, mainly because Canadian bookstore owners incur the added business expense of having to do frequent battle with the country's customs authorities.

When Craig Rodwell opened the Oscar Wilde Memorial Bookshop in New York's Greenwich Village on **November 24, 1967**, it was the first nonpornographic gay or lesbian bookstore in North America, possibly the world. After the STONEWALL Uprising, several others opened in large cities across the continent, including Glad Day (Toronto, 1970), Giovanni's Room (Philadelphia, 1973), Lambda Rising (Washington, D.C., 1974), and A Different Light (Los Angeles, 1979).

Women's bookstores played a pivotal role in the LESBIAN LAND and SEPARATISM movements as well as in the spread of women's MUSIC and the development of women's small arts and crafts businesses. Two of the earliest were ICI (Information Center Inc.), A Woman's Place in Oakland, California, and the Amazon Bookstore in Minneapolis, both founded in 1971. The Amazon Bookstore is one of fewer than 10 feminist bookstores that have remained in continuous operation since the 1970s. Many, such as the Bona Dea Women's Bookstore in Anchorage, one of the best-stocked and most active in the U.S. before its closing in November 1995, have been "squeezed out with the advent of superstores," according to Carol Seajay, publisher of *Feminist Bookstore News*. These superstores are increasingly among the more than 500 general-

Craig Rodwell's Oscar Wilde Memorial Bookshop was the first nonpornographic openly gay bookstore in the U.S.

interest bookstores in the U.S. that now have special "gay and lesbian" sections.

➤ Also see PUBLISHING.

Boston Marriage

Term used in late-19th-century America to describe a passionate long-term relationship between mostly upper-class, generally feminist women who usually lived together. Whether or not such a relationship was sometimes sexual is a matter of controversy in LESBIAN AND GAY STUDIES, but the term—like "love of kindred spirits," "sentimental friendship," ROMANTIC FRIENDSHIP, and other near synonyms—implies it was not.

Forerunners of the 20th-century "women-identified women," women who formed Boston marriages focused their emotional energies on other women. They were thus true to one contemporary definition of "LESBIAN" without meeting the requirements of those who consider same-sex eroticism a prerequisite for a lesbian identity.

The term, which was familiar to readers of Henry James (e.g., *The Bostonians,* 1886), predates widespread usage of the word "lesbian." ELSA GIDLOW's autobiography provides an informative mention of the term as it was used by Gidlow's lover, Tommy (Violet Winifred Leslie Henry-Anderson), in the 1920s: "It was from Tommy I first heard the term 'Boston marriage,' as applied to households where two women lived together in life affinity."

More recently, the term has returned as a synonym for lesbian *mariages blancs,* committed relationships that are no longer—or never were—sexual.

✧ Lillian Faderman, *Surpassing the Love of Men: Romantic Friendship and Love Between Women from the Renaissance to the Present* (1981).

✧ Esther Rothblum and Kathleen A. Brehony, *Boston Marriages* (1993).

Boswell, John [Eastburn]

(1947–1994)

U.S. historian. Born in Boston, Boswell studied at the College of William and Mary and Harvard. He joined the Yale history department in 1975 and was chairman of the department from 1990 to 1992. After early work on Islamic Spain, Boswell published his path-breaking *Christianity, Social Tolerance, and Homosexuality* (1980; American Book Award for History, 1981), arguing against what he called "the common idea that religious belief—Christian or other—has been the cause of intolerance in regard to gay people." Boswell's thesis, that the hostility of CHRISTIANITY toward same-sex relations became serious only after the 12th century, was hailed as "revolutionary" by most reviewers, but his usage of the word "GAY" for everyone from Plato to Edward II landed him in the thick of the then emerging CONSTRUCTIONISM VS. ESSENTIALISM battle. Boswell rejected the constructionists' charges in numerous articles and interviews, insisting that they were a matter of semantic misunderstanding. He remained nonetheless identified as the most prominent critic of constructionism.

In 1987, Boswell helped found the Lesbian and Gay Studies Center at Yale. In 1994, he published his long researched, almost equally inflammatory *Same-Sex Unions in Premodern Europe.*

Through much of his career, a smaller debate centered on his being a practicing Catholic. He once responded: "I believe probably as much of the Church's official teaching as the Pope does . . . but we interpret it very differently."

Boswell's work was as controversial as it was erudite, resulting from years of research in 17 different languages. Entire articles were written to assail a point he had made in a single formidable footnote. The high standards of scholarship he set for himself helped bring LESBIAN AND GAY STUDIES to the attention of a broader academic audience, out of what some have called the "ivory CLOSET."

Boswell died of complications of AIDS on December 25, 1994.

➤ Also see SAME-SEX UNIONS.

✧ John Boswell, "Concepts, Experience, and Sexuality," in *Forms of Desire: Sexual Orientation and the Social Constructionist Controversy,* edited by Edward Stein (1992).

✧ Lawrence D. Mass, "Sexual Categories, Sexual Universals: A Conversation with John Boswell," in *Dialogues of the Sexual Revolution, Volume II: Homosexuality as Behavior and Identity* (1990).

Boyd, Malcolm

(1923–)

U.S. theologian, writer, editor, activist. Born in New York City, Boyd studied at the University of Arizona, the Divinity School of the Pacific, and Oxford University. Boyd worked in ADVERTISING before deciding to become a priest of the EPISCOPAL CHURCH. He became nationally famous with his inspirational best-seller *Are You Running with Me, Jesus?* (1965). Long a civil rights and antiwar activist, he came OUT in 1976 and has since devoted himself to a wide range of gay- and lesbian-related issues.

Boyd has written more than twenty works of fiction and nonfiction, including *Gay Priest: An Inner Journey* (1987), as well as five plays and numerous articles. His lover since the late 1980s is editor, writer, and spiritual activist Mark Thompson.

Bradley, Marion Zimmer

(née Marion Zimmer 1930–)

U.S. writer. The prolific Bradley has published more than 50 books of SCIENCE FICTION, fantasy, romance, gothic fiction, short stories, and poetry, including lesbian PULP FICTION in the 1960s under the PSEUDONYMS Lee Chapman, John Dexter, Miriam Gardner, and Morgan Ives. Growing up in an abusive family on a run-down farm in upstate New York during the Depression, Bradley early on developed an "outcast" identity. Health problems and lack of money prevented her from pursuing a career in opera. She turned instead to writing, publishing her first science fiction story in 1954.

In the 1950s, Bradley met BARBARA GRIER, who in turn introduced her to the DAUGHTERS OF BILITIS (DOB). She wrote book reviews for THE LADDER and collaborated with Grier on DOB bibliographies published to supplement JEANNETTE FOSTER's pioneering work on "sex variant" women in literature. Her involvement with the HOMOPHILE movement also included contributions to *The* MATTACHINE *Review* and, in the 1960s under a male pseudonym, writing advice and astrology columns for a gay publication. She also pseudonymously published six lesbian romances, ranging from *I Am a Lesbian* (1962) to *No Adam for Eve* (1966).

By the 1970s, Bradley had become estranged from moderate as well as radical lesbian politics. She objected in particular to the demands of some proponents of lesbian SEPARATISM that men and even male children be completely excluded from lesbian lives. At the same time, her novels and short stories continued to explore themes of lesbian and gay concern in imaginative and innovative ways. In particular, her extensive Darkover series, which has achieved cult status among science fiction fans, contrasts the polymorphously gendered world of the Darkovans with that of the comparatively straight Terrans. Her work has always been notable for its strong, independent women and its insistence on the right of individuals to make choices unfettered by GENDER roles. She has published a "mainstream" gay novel about 1940s circus performers called *The Catch Trap* (written in 1959, but not published until 1979).

Bradley is also the author of the best-selling Arthurian novel *The Mists of Avalon* (1982), as well as *The Firebrand* (1987). She has married and divorced twice (once to a gay man, Walter Breen) and has three biological and several foster children. After many years of providing private and pastoral counseling at the Gay Pacific Center, she and Breen were ordained in the Eastern Orthodox priesthood by gay Bishop Mikhail Itkin in 1980.

- Rosemarie Arbur, *Marion Zimmer Bradley* (1985).
- *Lesbian Texts and Contexts: Radical Revisions,* edited by Karla Jay and Joanne Glasgow (1990–1992).

Brand, Adolf

(1874–1945)

German editor, publisher, activist. After a brief career as a teacher, Brand decided to devote himself full-time to anarchist and HOMOPHILE pursuits. He founded, edited, and published *Der Eigene* ("One's Own" or "The Special"), considered the first gay male periodical, from **1896** through 1931, and formed the Gemeinschaft der Eigenen (Community of [Those Who Are] Their Own Persons) in 1903. Both the magazine and the organization were in part inspired by the anarchist writings of the philosopher Max Stirner, who advocated individual self-determination and the rejection of religious, political, or ideological authority.

Along with fellow theorists Bernard Friedlander and John Mackay, Brand represented an ideology of same-sex love that stood in sharp contrast to the emancipationism of MAGNUS HIRSCHFELD. Heaping ridicule on Hirschfeld's "third sex" concept of homosexuality, they saw love between men—especially love between men and boys—as the ultimate expression of masculinity. In their writings, they praised PEDERASTY and attempted to create a nationalistic German variety of "Greek love."

Brand, who was married, is noted as an example of the erratic nature of the Nazi persecution of homosexuality. Although the Nazis confiscated his archives and prevented him from carrying on his organizational activities, he was never arrested or charged with any violations of the German legal code. Shortly before the end of World War II, he and his wife died when their home was hit by an Allied bomb.

➤ Also see NAZI PERSECUTION.

✧ *Homosexuality and Male Bonding in Pre-Nazi Germany,* edited by Harry Oosterhuis and Hubert Kennedy (1991).

Brant, Beth

(Degonwadonti; 1941–)

U.S. writer, editor, archivist, activist. Brant was born in Detroit, Michigan, into a working-class Mohawk of the Bay of Quinte family. She married at 17 and has three daughters and three grandchildren.

At the age of 40, Brant was driving one day through Seneca land when a bald eagle landed in a tree and communicated, she recounts, "a message to write."

"When one is a Native lesbian," she has also written, giving another explanation for her compulsion to write, "the desire to connect all becomes an urgent longing. Faced with HOMOPHOBIA from our own communities, faced with racism and homophobia from the outsiders who hold semblances of power over us, we feel that desire to connect in a primal way."

In 1983, Brant assembled *A Gathering of Spirit: A Collection by North American Indian Women* (first published as a double edition of the magazine *Sinister Wisdom* in 1983–1984; reprinted in book form, 1988), the first anthology of Native writing edited by a NATIVE AMERICAN. The internationally successful anthology included works by a number of women who have written on lesbian themes, including PAULA GUNN ALLEN, CHRYSTOS, Janice Gould, Mary Moran, Vickie Sears, and Midnight Sun.

Brant's later short fiction, published in *Mohawk Trail* (1985) and *Food and Spirits* (1991), ranges from bawdy lesbian takes on traditional stories ("Coyote Learns a New Trick") to heartbreaking tales of loss, past and present ("A Long Story"). "Being a Native lesbian," she writes, "is like living in the eye of the hurricane—terrible, beautiful, filled with sounds and silences, the music of life-affirmation and the disharmony of life-despising. To balance, to create in this midst is a gift of honor and respect."

Brant and her lover, Denise Dorsz, have co-founded a library and archive on Native American women.

✧ Beth Brant, "Giveaway: Native Lesbian Writers" *Signs* (Summer 1993).

Brazil

No laws against consensual same-sex relations between adults over 18 except for soldiers in the MILITARY. *Antidiscrimination protection in the states of Sergipe and Mato Grosso and in more than 70 municipalities. Well-developed social scene and active rights groups in the state of Bahia, Rio de Janeiro, and São Paulo.*

The lives and identities of Brazilian queers are as diverse as the country itself, ranging from backcountry BERDACHES and internationally renowned CROSS-DRESSING sex workers to sophisticated urbanites virtually indistinguishable from lesbians and gay men in Western Europe or North America. NATIVE AMERICAN, African, and Portuguese-Catholic constructions (see CONSTRUCTIONISM VS. ESSENTIALISM) of sexuality have competed and mingled in the country since the 16th century, when it was colonized by the Portuguese. For most of the population, however, only men who take the passive role in anal intercourse are considered *bichas* (faggots); insertors retain their "macho" status. Lesbians, who have their own rights groups and social facilities in large cities, are nonetheless much less visible than gay men.

Even before STONEWALL and the emergence of GAY LIBERATION in other parts of the world, visitors from abroad were struck by the vivacity and comparative openness of gay and lesbian life in Brazil, especially in Rio de Janeiro. Paradoxically, gay and lesbian activists have achieved significant legal gains since the 1980s at the same time that HATE CRIME has reached epidemic proportions: between 1985 and 1995, some 1,000 gay men and more than 30 lesbians were murdered; many others were brutally attacked. Only a handful of the attackers have been brought to justice.

According to activist and scholar Luiz Mott, the Brazilian gay and lesbian rights movement consists of about 40 groups but "no more than 200 engaged militants—in a country in which millions engage in homosexuality." Mott also asserts that "if a Brazilian is discreetly gay or lesbian or is aggressively transvestite, s/he won't suffer too much discrimination." Nevertheless, "there are no gay parades or openly gay politicians, intellectuals, or artists."

History

Portuguese colonists relayed reports of berdaches, both male and female, back to their homeland as they explored Brazil in the 16th century. Some historians believe that the Amazon River got its name from the fierce women-loving female warriors the Portuguese encountered there.

More than 5 million African slaves were brought to Brazil during almost four centuries of Portuguese rule. With them came African religions that flourished in the New World, and continue to this day to offer both men and women a variety of opportunities for popularly sanctioned same-sex eroticism.

The Portuguese also brought the INQUISITION to Brazil, but despite more than 300 denunciations for SODOMY, there is no record of anyone being burned at the stake for the offense.

Same-sex relations between women were made illegal by the Inquisition in **1646**, but extensive documentation of lesbianism in Brazil does not appear until almost two centuries later and then not in a court case, but in the correspondence of the Empress Leopoldina with her English lady-in-waiting and lover, Maria Graham.

Adolfo Caminha's classic novel, Bom-Crioulo, published in 1895, was a frank depiction of the star-crossed relationship of a black sailor and a 15-year-old white cabin boy.

Same-sex acts were decriminalized in 1823, when the country adopted laws influenced by the Napoleonic Code (see **1810**). Later in the century, the comparative tolerance of contemporary Brazilian attitudes toward homosexuality was evidenced by the publication of Adolfo Caminha's *Bom-Crioulo* (see **1895**), one of the first novels in the world to treat a male-male love affair sympathetically. Around the same time, however, Brazilian doctors were beginning to publish studies of homosexuality influenced by then current European theories of sexual pathology.

The first signs of gay liberation in Brazil were the founding of a gay journal, *O Lampão* in **April 1978** (also see **8/1978**) and the founding of a rights group, Somos (We Are) in São Paulo in **February 1979.** Two national congresses followed later in 1979 and in 1980, drawing representatives from 22 newly organized groups, but the movement foundered in the mid-1980s despite legal recognition from the national government.

✧ *Latin American Male Homosexualities,* edited by Stephen O. Murray (1995).

Bright, Susie

(pseudonym: Susie Sexpert; 1956–)

U.S. writer, editor. From a conventional middle-class background and a relatively staid initiation to lesbian life in the 1970s, Bright burst upon the American sex scene in the early 1980s as a partisan in the lesbian SEX WARS, ready to challenge lesbian biases against everything from strippers to S/M. As she later reported, "When I came out, I didn't even get that you were a lesbian for sexual reasons. It was almost like another political challenge."

In 1984 in San Francisco, Bright helped launch the iconoclastic erotic publication *On Our Backs* (a playfully unsubtle reference to the ur-feminist *Off Our Backs*). Under Bright's direction, *On Our Backs* set a world record for circulation figures for a lesbian magazine, providing evidence that, as SARAH SCHULMAN claims in *My American History* (1994), "the 'sex radicals' won control of the lesbian community."

Bright has also edited anthologies of erotic writings and published widely as "Susie Sexpert," a sexual advisor for men and women of diverse sexual orientations.

Britain, see UNITED KINGDOM.

Broadway, see THEATER.

Bronski Beat, see SOMERVILLE, JIMMY.

Bronski, Michael

(1945–)

U.S. writer, critic, cultural historian, activist. A Boston native, Bronski threw himself into the GAY LIBERATION movement in the late 1960s. Besides participating in numerous movement activities, he provided critical essays and articles on sexuality for a number of gay and lesbian publications ranging from serious political newspapers to "skin" magazines. He drew on his broad experience of the SUBCULTURE to publish his first book, the pioneering *Culture Clash: The Making of a Gay Sensibility,* in 1984. One of the first and most often quoted overviews of the rapidly evolving gay male subculture, *Culture Clash* traced the development of a "gay sensibility" from WALT WHITMAN to the onset of AIDS. Bronski characterized the "gay sensibility" as "progressive, liberating, visionary." He linked "unrestrained sexual passion" with cultural and artistic creativity and opposed gay and lesbian assimilationism (see ASSIMILATIONISM/CONFRONTATIONALISM).

Bronski has continued to publish articles on topics ranging from S/M to SPIRITUALITY in dozens of gay, lesbian, and mainstream periodicals and anthologies, including *Flashpoint* (1996), a provocatively selected compilation of "gay male sexual writing" that reflected many of the changes that had occurred in the gay male subculture since the publication of *Culture Clash.* The poet Walta Borawski was Bronski's lover from the mid-1970s until Borawski's death from complications of AIDS in 1995.

Brooks, Romaine

(née Beatrice Romaine Mary Goddard; 1874–1970)

U.S. painter. The daughter of wealthy, notoriously eccentric American expatriates, she managed to escape a miserable family life in her 20s, studying ART and MUSIC and marrying a gay man, John Ellington Brooks, to help secure her inheritance. Based in Paris after 1905, she made a name for herself as a painter and was awarded the French Legion of Honor for her portraits and her patriotic propaganda paintings completed during WORLD WAR I. During this period, she was also part of a triangle with Italian poet Gabriele D'Annunzio and the dancer Ida Rubinstein, whom she portrayed nude in one of her best-known paintings, *Le Trajet* ("The Crossing," 1911). At the age of 40, she and NATALIE BARNEY formed a relationship that endured through Barney's passionate affairs with other women for over five decades.

Brooks was strongly influenced by the aesthetic movement but ultimately developed a style that was independent of contemporary art trends. Her most important contributions to lesbian culture were the eerily evocative portraits she painted of the writers and artists associated with Barney's Paris salon, including Barney herself, Lily de Clermont-Tonnerre (Elisabeth de Gramont), and UNA TROUBRIDGE. Like Barney, Brooks also inspired a number of fictionalized characters in novels, such as

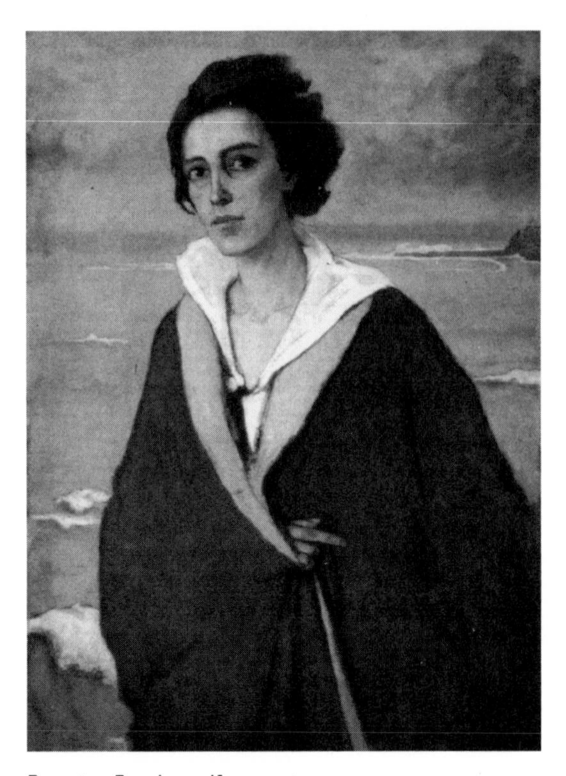

Romaine Brooks, self-portrait.

Olympia Leigh in Compton Mackenzie's *Extraordinary Women* (1928) and Venetia Ford in RADCLYFFE HALL's *The Forge* (1924). The National Museum of American Art in Washington, D.C., has the largest collection of her paintings.

✧ Adelyne Dohme Breeskin, *Romaine Brooks* (1986).

Broughton, James

(1913–)

U.S. filmmaker, poet, playwright, teacher. Born into a well-to-do San Francisco family, Broughton was sent at the age of nine to a military academy at the insistence of his stepfather, who was appalled that the boy wanted to be a ballerina. At the academy, Broughton formed his first romantic and sexual attachments with boys and began to write poetry and plays inspired by these passions. When he was fifteen, his mother read a letter he had written to a young lover (whom he recalled as "Littlejohn" in *The Androgyne Journal,* 1977), and Broughton was abruptly withdrawn from the academy and kept home to attend a local public high school, where he could be kept under close surveillance.

Studying at Stanford University, Broughton had a brief but intense affair with HARRY HAY in 1931. Three years later, he dropped out of college to hitchhike to New York and work in the merchant marine, where he became close friends on his first voyage with Emil Opffer, who had been HART CRANE's lover. Opffer later introduced him to magazine editors, and Broughton began a career as a freelance writer.

Back in San Francisco after World War II, Broughton emerged as one of the city's leading experimental filmmakers with *Mother's Day* (1948) and other critically acclaimed avant-garde shorts, such as *Loony Tom, the Happy Lover* (1951) and *The Pleasure Garden* (1953). Self-described as "androgynous" (in preference to the word "bisexual"), Broughton married twice (his first wife was the film critic Pauline Kael) and had two children, but continued to have long-term relationships with men, including Kermit Sheets, with whom he founded the Centaur Press and who helped him produce plays and films in addition to acting in films like *Loony Tom.*

Broughton left filmmaking in 1958 to concentrate on the theater and teaching, but in 1967 the Royal Film Archive of Belgium commissioned him to make a new film. The result was *The Bed* (1968), a 20-minute film he called "a celebration of the polymorphous possibilities of the life of a bed."

At the age of 61, Broughton became the lover of Joel Singer, a 26-year-old Canadian student, and began to explore HOMOEROTICISM more openly in his poetry and in films such as *Hermes Bird* (1979), a close-up look at Singer's penis erecting in 10, slow-motion minutes, with a voice-over by Broughton; and *Devotions* (1983), a gay counterpart to his earlier *The Bed* and one of eight films he and Singer collaborated on.

In his work and in interviews, Broughton proclaims ANDROGYNY as "the true image of the soul," defining it as "not an amorphous freakhood located between male and female" but rather "a concept of wholeness, a guide to experiencing the full range of yang and yin."

- "James Broughton Interviewed by Robert Peters," in *Gay Sunshine Interviews, Volume Two,* edited by Winston Leyland (1982).
- "James Broughton: Gaiety of Soul," in *Gay Soul: Interviews and Photographs by Mark Thompson* (1995).

Broumas, Olga
(1949–)

Greek-born U.S. poet, translator, educator. Born in Syros, GREECE, Broumas came to the U.S. in 1959 and spent two years in Washington, D.C., where her father was posted as a NATO aide. She returned to the U.S. in 1969 as a Fulbright scholar, and studied architecture at the University of Pennsylvania. She later earned an M.F.A. in creative writing and helped shape a women's studies program at the University of Oregon. She has since taught at universities in addition to codeveloping two women's fine arts programs that incorporate techniques drawn from her practice as a bodywork therapist.

Broumas's first book of poetry published in the U.S., *Caritas* (1976), comprised five openly lesbian "womanly songs of praise." Her second U.S. book, *Beginning with O* (1977), was chosen by poet and critic Stanley Kunitz for the prestigious Yale Younger Poets award. Kunitz praised Broumas's "wild avowals, unabashed eroticism," while lesbian critics hailed its political power as well as its sensual lyricism. Like SAPPHO, Broumas's poetry combines concrete, physical imagery with arrestingly direct, colloquial language. Her Greek heritage is also reflected in her imaginative use of mythology.

Broumas has published one Greek and seven English books of poetry, including two in collaboration: *Black Holes, Black Stockings* (1985) with Jane Miller, and *Sappho's Gymnasium* (1995) with T Begley. She has also translated three books of poetry and essays by 1979 Nobel Laureate Odysseus Elytis, whom Broumas calls "the second great Lesbian."

Brown, Howard

(1924–1975)

U.S. physician, health administrator, activist. Brown was born in Peoria, Illinois, and attended Hiram College in Ohio. After completing medical school, he pursued a career in health care from the 1940s. By the time he was appointed New York City's first commissioner of health and its health services administrator on June 3, 1966, he had already earned a national reputation for his success in establishing model neighborhood health care centers in economically disadvantaged areas across the country.

In 1968, Brown learned that *The New York Times* was considering publishing an exposé by columnist Drew Pearson of homosexual commissioners in Mayor John V. Lindsay's administration. Fearful of being one of those named, he resigned from his position. The article was never published.

STONEWALL and the activities of GAY ACTIVISTS ALLIANCE (GAA) led Brown to question the compromises he had made as a successful but closeted gay man. As he later told THE ADVOCATE, "The gay freedom fighters redefined my sense of shame at being a homosexual into a sense of rage that society could do this to me

Howard Brown announces the founding of the National Gay Task Force on October 15, 1973, at a press conference in New York City. With him (left to right) are: Martin Duberman, Ron Gold, Barbara Gittings, Frank Kameny, Bruce Voeller, and Nath Rockhill.

and so many of the people I loved." After suffering a heart attack in June 1972, he, along with three activists (Dr. Henry Messer, MARTIN DUBERMAN, and Dr. Bruce Voeller), began to discuss how he could maximize the public impact of coming OUT. On October 3, 1973, Brown proclaimed his homosexuality and spoke of the problems gay doctors face in an address to 600 physicians attending a symposium on human sexuality. Notified in advance via a GAA news release, the media were present in force. News of his announcement had already appeared on the front page of *The New York Times* that morning. Historians consider Brown the most "respectable" American to come out willingly in the two years following novelist MERLE MILLER's precedent-setting revelation in an article he wrote for the *Times* (see **1/17/1971**).

Brown went on to become a founder and cochair of the NATIONAL GAY (later: AND LESBIAN) TASK FORCE and a member of the board of directors of the Lambda Foundation and of the Institute for Human Identity.

✧ Howard Brown, *Familiar Faces, Hidden Lives: The Story of Homosexual Men in America Today* (1976).

Brown, Rita Mae

(1944–)

U.S. activist, novelist, poet, screen and teleplay writer. In her 1972 essay calling for political lesbian identity and action, "The Shape of Things to Come," Brown described herself when she said: "You will be part of that surge forward and you will leave your fingerprints on the shape of things to come."

Born in Hanover, Pennsylvania, she was adopted by her natural mother's cousin. The working-class family later moved to Fort Lauderdale, Florida. Brown attended the University of Florida in Gainesville until she was expelled for her civil rights activism. She hitchhiked to New York City and went on to earn a B.A. from New York University in 1968 and a certificate in cinematography from the School of Visual Arts. While at NYU, she cofounded the Student Homophile League. With JUNE ARNOLD and others she established a women's center and was a member of the radical feminist group the Redstockings and the NATIONAL ORGANIZATION FOR WOMEN (NOW), serving as NOW's national administrative coordinator and publisher of their New York newsletter. Disillusioned by NOW's HOMOPHOBIA and refusal to address lesbian issues, Brown resigned in 1970 and shifted her attention to recruiting women from the GAY LIBERATION FRONT into RADICALESBIANS. She wrote for *Rat,* New York City's first women's liberation newspaper, published an early book of poems, *The Hand That Cradles the Rock* (1971); coauthored the pivotal "WOMAN-IDENTIFIED WOMAN" statement; and participated in its public release by the LAVENDER MENACE. After moving to Washington, D.C., she was part of the influential FURIES separatist collective and earned her Ph.D. from the Institute for Policy Studies in 1973, the year *Rubyfruit Jungle,* her semiautobiographical lesbian classic, was published. Her advance from Daughters, Inc., was $1,000.

Rubyfruit Jungle has sold millions of copies to crossover readers. Considered perhaps the earliest lesbian comedic novel, it delighted readers with its humor, its eroticism, and its groundbreaking depiction of a proud picaresque heroine who considers homosexuality perfectly normal.

Brown resists the label "lesbian writer," considering the purpose of art to be about connection, not the divisions labels create. Inspired by sources ranging from Aristophanes to Alice Walker, she has written more than a dozen novels as well as several mysteries with her cat,

Sneaky Pie. The novels frequently feature class and gender struggles and challenges to social convention. The book Brown once said she likes least is *Sudden Death* (1983) because it wasn't really hers. She honored a wish from dying friend and Boston sportswriter Judy Lacy to "write that book I'm always talking about." Critical of the tennis world, many readers had speculated it fictionalized her former relationship with MARTINA NAVRATILOVA.

Many of Brown's early influential essays are collected in *A Plain Brown Rapper* (1976). She has taught creative writing, written a writing manual (*Starting from Scratch,* 1988), and received Emmy nominations for *The Long Hot Summer* (Best Mini-Series, 1985) and "I Love Liberty" (Best Variety Show, 1982). She coauthored the lesbian-themed television movie, *My Two Loves* (1986), and narrated the landmark film *Before Stonewall* (1985). In addition to breeding horses (her "touchstone"), she remains active in lesbian and gay issues, notably those related to queer YOUTH, from her farm in Charlottesville, Virginia.

✧ Jonathan Dollimore, "The Dominant and the Deviants," *Critical Quarterly* (vol. 28, no. 1/2, Spring/Summer 1986).

✧ Shane Snowdon, "A Conversation with Rita Mae Brown," *Sojourner* (May 1986).

✧ Louise Kawada, "Liberating Laughter: Comedic Form in Novels," in *Sexual Practice, Textual Theory,* edited by Susan J. Wolfe and Julia Penelope (1993).

Bruce of Los Angeles

(pseudonym of Bruce Bellas; 1907–1974)

U.S. photographer, filmmaker, publisher. Bellas began photographing male models for bodybuilding entrepreneur and publisher Joe Weider in the 1940s. In the 1950s, as "Bruce of Los Angeles," he also started selling photos directly to collectors and through his and others' PHYSIQUE MAGAZINES. One of the more artistically gifted physique photographers, he was known for his highly crafted studio shots of bodybuilders in posing straps and models costumed as sailors or cowboys. Unlike most physique photographers, he also took "on location" photos, documenting rodeos, the 1950s Muscle Beach scene, and Mardi Gras drag shows in New Orleans.

His photos continued to appear in magazines through the 1960s. Allen Ellenzweig credits him with influencing later photographers like ROBERT MAPPLETHORPE and Herb Ritts. His somewhat surreal, typically 1950s use of color is also reflected in the art of Pierre et Gilles. In the 1990s, his work was rediscovered as part of a critical reassessment of physique PHOTOGRAPHY.

✧ Allen Ellenzweig, *The Homoerotic Photograph: Male Images from Durieu/Delacroix to Mapplethorpe* (1992).

✧ F. Valentine Hooven, III, *Beefcake: The Muscle Magazines of America, 1950–1970* (1995).

Bryher

(pseudonym of Annie Winifred Ellerman; 1894–1983)

English writer. Born into one of the British Empire's wealthiest families, she was an unconventional, rebellious child who refused to be "like other girls." As an adult, she used the name Bryher, taken from one of the Scilly Islands, which she had visited as a girl.

In her memoir *The Heart to Artemis* (1963), Bryher described her first meeting with H.D. (Hilda Doolittle) on July 17, 1918, as "the moment that I had longed for during seven interminable years." Bryher had already memorized H.D.'s book of poems *Sea Garden* (1916), because it "made her aware of herself" and had grown even more interested in the mysterious

"H.D." when she learned that she was an American woman. As a suffragette and an heiress who yearned in vain to run her family's business, Bryher loved America because it was the country where "girls had jobs."

Bryher and H.D. settled in Europe and spent most of the next four decades in Switzerland. Beginning with the novel *Development* (1920), Bryher published more than a dozen works of fiction, poetry, and nonfiction. She founded and coedited the first avant-garde FILM periodical in English, *Close-up,* and helped found *Psychoanalytic Review,* a publication credited with bringing psychological analysis to Britain.

To gain control of her inheritance, she made a marriage of convenience with the bisexual American writer Robert McAlmon in 1921. She later married a lover of H.D.'s, partly to keep up appearances for all three members of the ménage but also to negotiate her lifelong desire to be male and to support H.D. and H.D.'s daughter, Frances Perdita, whom she adopted. "The essential," she once wrote, "is to know what you want."

Bryher was known for her generosity. She gave BERENICE ABBOTT her first camera and helped support SYLVIA BEACH and Shakespeare and Company, her bookstore, and, after GERTRUDE STEIN's death, ALICE B. TOKLAS. She also helped more than 100 Jews escape Nazi GERMANY through SWITZERLAND.

✧ Susan Stanford Friedman, *Penelope's Web: Gender, Modernity, H.D.'s Fiction* (1990).

✧ Renee R. Curry, "Bryher," *Gay and Lesbian Literature,* edited by Sharon Malinowski (1994).

Buddhism

Religion and philosophy based on the teachings of Siddhārtha Gautama (c. 563–c. 483 B.C.), the Buddha (Sanskrit for "enlightened" or "awakened one"). Although many varieties of Buddhism have arisen in the last two and a half millennia, most of the more than 300 million Buddhists around the world share beliefs that include commitment to a "middle way" that avoids extremes of either self-sacrifice or self-indulgence in the quest for enlightenment; recognition of *karma,* the principle that all conscious thoughts, words, and deeds have a positive or negative consequence depending on whether they are good or bad; emphasis on self-purification; and compassion for all living creatures.

Although Buddhist attitudes toward sexual nonconformity have varied greatly from country to country, era to era, and sect to sect, Buddhists have generally not considered sexual pleasure more or less immoral than other kinds of physical enjoyment. And unlike most forms of CHRISTIANITY, ISLAM, and JUDAISM, mainstream Buddhism makes little distinction between same-sex and different-sex eroticism. For these reasons, Buddhism is sometimes singled out as the world's only "sex-positive" religion. The reality, however, is much more complex. Tantric Buddhism, for example, refined sexual intercourse (usually short of orgasm) as a means of attaining enlightenment yet strongly condemned masturbation and same-sex eroticism because they did not involve the union of female and male elements sought by the sect. Some modern Buddhists, including several groups in JAPAN, have been as negative toward "gay lifestyles" as their Christian counterparts. Even in countries like THAILAND, where Buddhism is credited with contributing to an exceptionally high level of tolerance for same-sex eroticism, this tolerance extends only to physical acts; same-sex relationships that might disturb the COMPULSORY HETEROSEXUALITY of Thai society are frowned upon. Other predominantly Buddhist countries, such as Cambodia and Myanmar

(Burma), are described by the INTERNATIONAL LESBIAN AND GAY ASSOCIATION as "very hostile" toward homosexuality.

Nevertheless, wherever Buddhism has spread—from northern India to Sri Lanka, SOUTHEAST ASIA, CHINA, KOREA, Japan, and beyond—it has had and, in many cases, continues to have, associations with same-sex eroticism. Erotic same-sex relationships were popularly believed to be common among Buddhist monks and nuns in China and Japan. In addition, Taoist and Buddhist "vegetarian halls" were traditionally one of the few refuges for Chinese women who refuse to marry. Many of these women had lesbian relationships in the halls.

Outside Asia, Buddhism has attracted EDWARD CARPENTER, ALLEN GINSBERG, and many other less famous lesbians and gay men. Most Buddhist groups in the U.S., CANADA, and Europe have welcomed gay men and lesbians, and there are several support and social groups for gay and lesbian Buddhists, including the non-denominational Buddhist Association. The U.S. branch of Soka Gakkai International voted to sanction SAME-SEX UNIONS in April 1995.

✧ John Stevens, *Lust for Enlightenment: Buddhism and Sex* (1990).

Bunch, Charlotte

(1944–)

U.S. political organizer, writer. In her introduction to her collection of nearly 20 years of essays and speeches (*Passionate Politics,* 1987), Bunch identifies 1963 as the birthdate of her political activism and a lifelong commitment to community organizing, progressive movements, and feminist issues worldwide. She is recognized as a founder and leading thinker in the women's movement and LESBIAN FEMINISM.

The third of four children, Bunch was born in Artesia, New Mexico, to supportive middle-class professional parents who encouraged her independence (and who once claimed the title of New Mexico's Methodist Family of the Year). Her education included a degree in history and political science from Duke University in North Carolina and a long-term alliance with the Institute for Policy Studies, a progressive think tank in Washington, D.C. Married for four years, Bunch divorced and came OUT in 1971. Encountering considerable HOMOPHOBIA in the feminist movement, she joined with RITA MAE BROWN and ten other women to form the lesbian feminist collective, the FURIES.

The Furies fostered a lesbian-feminist political analysis articulated in their newspaper between 1972 and 1973. Bunch and other Furies urged their readers to see the innerconnection between lesbianism and feminism. As political theory, lesbian feminism opposes HETEROSEXISM and the institutional and ideological reinforcement it provides for male supremacy. Later, with Nancy Myron, Bunch edited three collections of those essays: *Women Remembered*

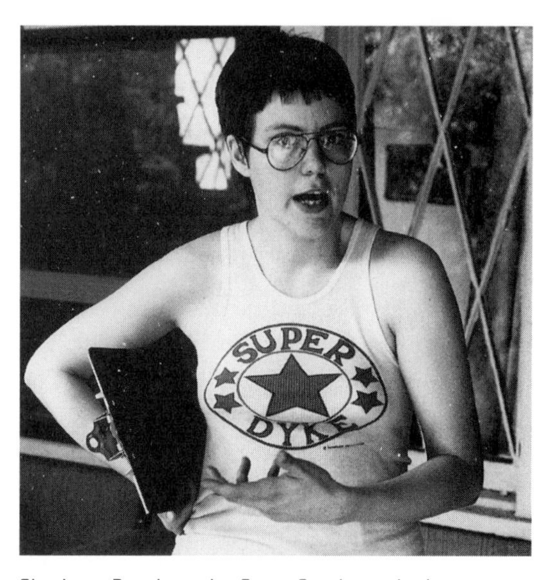

Charlotte Bunch at the Great Southeast Lesbian Conference in Atlanta, 1975.

(1974), *Class and Feminism* (1974), and *Lesbianism and the Women's Movement* (1975).

In 1973, Bunch cofounded *Quest: A Feminist Quarterly.* The following year, Bunch joined the first board of directors for the NATIONAL GAY (later: AND LESBIAN) TASK FORCE (NGTF). With Frances Doughty of NGTF, she negotiated a groundbreaking pro-lesbian-rights plank in the Plan of Action at the National Women's Conference in 1977. She also edited *Learning Our Way* (with Sandra Pollack, 1983), a book on feminist education, and *International Feminism: Networking Against Female Sexual Slavery* (with Kathleen Barry, 1984).

Currently, Bunch runs Interfem Consultants and holds the Laurie Chair in Women's Studies at Douglass College, Rutgers University. Her later work emphasizes feminism in the third world.

✧ Charlotte Bunch, "Lesbian Feminist Theory," in *Our Right to Love,* edited by Ginny Vida (1978).

✧ Charlotte Bunch, *Passionate Politics, Essays 1968–1986: Feminist Theory in Action* (1987).

Burke, Glenn

(1952–1995)

U.S. athlete, outfielder for the Los Angeles Dodgers (1976–1978) and the Oakland A's (1978–1980), first professional baseball player to come OUT. Perhaps most famous for having invented the sports ritual of the "high five," Burke was born and raised in Oakland, California, in a family of eight children. Before making his way into the major leagues, Burke was drafted in 1972 and played on Dodger farm teams at a time when the stress of standing out as an AFRICAN-AMERICAN in overwhelmingly white small towns intensified the pressures of living a closeted life in the macho world of professional baseball.

The highlight of Burke's career with the Dodgers was his participation in the 1977 World Series. His Dodgers career was complicated by his friendship with Dodgers manager Tommy Lasorda's openly gay son, Tommy Lasorda Jr. On May 16, 1978, Burke was traded from the Dodgers to the A's, but the tensions of concealing his sexuality amid growing rumors continued to mount. He was released from the A's by manager Billy Martin at the

end of the 1980 season. No other team picked him up, although he was only 27 and had a batting average of .237. Burke subsequently came out in an article in *Inside Sports* in 1982.

"I had finally gotten to the point," Burke later stated, "where it was more important to be myself than a baseball player." Burke said he longed for the day when it would be easier for young gays to go into sports. He was active for a time in Black and White Men Together, a gay community organization.

After leaving the sports world, Burke struggled with drug abuse, severe injuries from a 1987 auto accident, and AIDS. He was imprisoned for grand theft and possession of drugs in 1991. His health failing, he moved to his sister Lutha's home in Oakland in 1994. He died of complications from AIDS on May 30, 1995.

- Michael J. Smith, "The Double Life of a Gay Dodger," *Inside Sports* (October 1982).
- Jennifer Frey, "A Boy of Summer's Long, Chilly Winter," *New York Times* (October 18, 1994).

Burroughs, William Seward

(1914–1997)

U.S. writer, actor. In 1929, Burroughs's family received $200,000 for the stock they held in the company his grandfather, the inventor of the adding machine, had founded, leaving them comfortably well off but not remarkably wealthy during the Depression. After majoring in English literature at Harvard University, Burroughs briefly studied medicine at the University of Vienna. In 1938, he married a Jewish woman, Ilse Klapper, so she could obtain a U.S. visa and escape being deported from Yugoslavia back to Nazi GERMANY. (Klapper and Burroughs, who never lived together, were divorced in 1945.) Back in the U.S., Burroughs worked at his family's gift shop, an ADVERTISING agency, a detective firm, and as an insect exterminator before settling in New York City in 1943. There, Burroughs, ALLEN GINSBERG, and Jack Kerouac became friends and, in 1945, roommates. Together they began to experiment with drugs and unconventional writing styles, both of which would later be identified with the BEAT GENERATION.

Burroughs had affairs with women as well as men (including Ginsberg), but his only serious heterosexual relationship was with Joan Vollmer, a Columbia University journalism student. Vollmer and Burroughs had a son, William Jr., and lived together in New York, Texas, Algiers, and Mexico City. The couple's frequent scrapes with the law climaxed at a drinking party in Mexico City on September 6, 1951, when they performed a "William Tell act" for the assembled guests. Burroughs missed, killing Vollmer with a bullet through the brain.

Addicted to heroin through 1957, Burroughs wrote sporadically and published *Junky: Confessions of an Unredeemed Drug Addict* in 1953 under the PSEUDONYM William Lee (his mother's maiden name). Drugs and addiction also provided the impetus for *Naked Lunch* (published as *The Naked Lunch* in Paris in 1959), a fragmented, paranoically surreal work of fiction that *The New York Times* called "not a novel but a booty brought back from a nightmare." Among a host of controversial sections, *Naked Lunch* contained two violent, explicitly rendered orgies, one of which featured boys of assorted nationalities and races. The book was subjected to several obscenity trials and at first (before its publication by Grove Press in 1962) failed to reach a wide audience.

According to Barry Miles, his biographer, "sexuality finally becomes the central metaphor in Burroughs's work, replacing drug addiction," with *The Wild Boys* (1971), which revolves around a war set in the near future between the U.S. Army and an all-male gang of young outlaws. Sexuality is also at the center of *Cities of the Red Night* (1981), a multilayered novel about a viral plague many critics have compared to AIDS.

EDMUND WHITE has cited *Naked Lunch* as one of the few books with homoerotic content available to him in the 1960s, yet Burroughs's unique blend of pop culture and hallucinatory horror has had a more discernible impact on heterosexual writers, filmmakers, and musicians than on gay or lesbian artists. His unromantic brand of HOMOEROTICISM ("The point of sexual relations between men is nothing that we could call love, but rather what we might call *recognition*") has nonetheless influenced writers of so-called transgressive fiction, such as DENNIS COOPER.

- Barry Miles, *William Burroughs: El Hombre Invisible* (1993).
- Edmund White, "This Is Not a Mammal: A Visit with William Burroughs," in *The Burning Library* (1994).

Butch/Fem(me)

Terms used to contrast two complex ranges of sexual-emotional identity and self-presentation: a "butch" dresses and acts in ways generally considered "masculine"; a "femme" displays "feminine" codes of dress and manner. ("Ki-ki," pronounced with two long *i*s, is the traditional term for a woman who is indeterminately butch or fem.) JOAN NESTLE, who helped restore respectability to the terms in the early 1980s, cautions that, just as concepts of "masculinity" and "femininity" vary widely over time and from culture to culture, "Butch-fem is not a monolithic social-sexual category. Within its general outline, class, race, and region give rise to style variations."

Today, "butch/fem" is almost exclusively a term of lesbian discourse, but "butch" and "fem(me)" were also commonly used before STONEWALL to describe the role variations frequently observed in gay male relationships of the time. HARRY HAY told biographer Stuart Timmons that butch-fem gay male couples were the norm in Southern California in the early 1950s. At parties, he reported, the butch would invariably wear a suit; his fem lover appeared in a de rigueur flowered Hawaiian shirt.

Among both women and men, the most common criticism of the butch-fem couple has been their seeming assumption of heterosexual roles. Although butch-fem codes both derive and differ from heterosexual models, the fact that both partners are women, or men, fundamentally distinguishes the sexual attraction from a heterosexual one. Lesbian gender theorist Judith Butler considers that this erotic attraction between lesbian butch and fem lies not in their PASSING as male or female but in their reshaped masculine and feminine identities, citing the fem who states that she "likes her boys to be girls." Also, when the butch-fem roles are seen as parodies of heterosexual norms, it perpetuates the assumption that conventional gender roles are the preferred "natural" ones against which butch-fem roles are measured. Instead, butch-fem challenges the experience of GENDER and its connection to biological sex. Likewise, lesbian theorist Gayle Rubin sees these lesbian butch-fem identities as distinct "categories of lesbian gender," as does Nestle, who emphasizes the uniqueness of the erotic elements in butch-fem relationships, maintaining that they boast "their own rituals of courtship, seduction, and offers of mutual protection."

Oral histories, such as those compiled by pioneering ethnohistorians ELIZABETH KENNEDY and MADELINE DAVIS in a Buffalo, New York, working-class lesbian community, establish the appearance of the butch-fem concept in the

Butch/femme in 1950s New Orleans: (left to right) Doris "Big Daddy" King, Stacey "Stormy" Lawrence, and Doris Luden.

1920s and its prevalence in the 1930s. The terminology, however, differed from community to community: AFRICAN-AMERICANS, for example, favored "stud" or "bulldagger" for "butch," "my lady" or "my family" for "femme," and "stud and her lady" to describe the resulting couple. In the Philippines, "TOMBOY" and "LESBIAN" are still commonly used in lieu of "butch" and "fem."

From the mid-1800s until the appearance of the second of the KINSEY REPORTS, *Sexual Behavior in the Human Female* (1953), sexologists promoted the allegedly "masculinized" butch as *the* female homosexual by emphasizing gender nonconformity as the identifying feature of the lesbian, rather than her sexual desires for a female partner. Since fems generally exhibited no discernable behavioral differences, they were either overlooked in studies or considered the passive prey of "mannishly" aggressive butches. As Kennedy and Davis point out, however, few women in places like Buffalo or Harlem had access to these scholarly medical reports. On their own, women drew from the masculine and feminine symbols around them and developed new gender strategies to understand themselves and to establish practicable sexual identities. Mixing and matching elements of CROSS-DRESSING, fashion codes, and gender play, they created identities, "ways of loving" (in Nestle's words), and, eventually, communities so strong that butch-fem relationships remained the norm even in the 1950s, when lesbianism was increasingly defined as a sexual orientation rather than a gender anomaly.

Davis and Kennedy find in them an "authentic lesbian lifestyle," a courageous statement of a "sexual and emotional accomplishment that did not include men," and the development of solidarity, consciousness, and "prepolitical" resistance. It was a critical cultural step of community building and personal validation toward the claiming of public space that made the GAY LIBERATION politics of the late 1960s possible.

From the fem perspective, lesbian feminist theorist Amber Hollibaugh has noted, "I think the reason butch-femme stuff got hidden within lesbian feminism is because people are profoundly afraid of questions of power in bed." Fem women were dismissed by feminists as oppressed women and by lesbian feminists as passing as straight. Fems became "obvious" lesbians only when they were with butches.

The butch-fem community was, Nestle observes, "the first publicly visible lesbian community"—and thus the most outcast. Some lesbian activists in the 1950s and in the 1960s found their very visibility encumbering to assimilation and acceptance by society. Lesbian feminists in the 1970s saw in butch-fem the reemergence of oppressive gender roles and later in the 1980s echoed charges of patriarchal sexuality from members of the antipornography movement. However, the 1980s also fostered the sex-positive movement, which affirmed the erotic elements of butch-fem relationships. In the 1990s butch-fem is seen as an erotic choice, a performance, and a lesbian-specific challenge to the norms of gender. There has been a rediscovery, a celebration, and even a commercialization of butch-fem roles and identity. Butch-fem informs some philosophical and historical areas in LESBIAN AND GAY STUDIES while in the gay and lesbian community there are contact and support groups and publications for the butch-fem lesbian.

Mary Jane Butler, a close friend of Mabel Hampton, in Harlem, c. 1930.

A 1995 ADVOCATE survey reported that 29 percent of the respondents considered their lesbian love relationships a "butch-femme pairing"; 17 percent "femme-femme"; 8 percent "butch-butch"; 32 percent "neutral"; and 14 percent a match between a butch or femme "while the other was neither."

- *The Persistent Desire, A Femme-Butch Reader,* edited by Joan Nestle (1992).
- Elizabeth Lopovsky Kennedy and Madeline D. Davis, *Boots of Leather, Slippers of Gold: The History of a Lesbian Community* (1994).
- Biddy Martin, "Sexualities Without Genders and Other Utopias," *Diacritics* (Summer/Fall 1994).
- Janet Lever, "Lesbian Sex Survey," *The Advocate* (August 22, 1995).

Butler, Lady Eleanor, see LLANGOLLEN, LADIES OF.

Button, Dick

(Richard Totten Button; 1929–)

U.S. figure skating star, Olympic gold medalist in 1948 and 1952. Born and raised in Englewood, New Jersey, Button became in 1948 the first and only man to capture the Olympic, World, European, North American, and U.S. championships in a single year. After he retired from active competition, he became a TV sports commentator.

On July 5, 1978, a gang of "fag bashers" invaded the Central Park Ramble, a well-known New York City CRUISING area. Armed with baseball bats, the bashers attacked Button and five other men, leaving Button and four others seriously injured. Six assailants were apprehended, four of whom were later convicted of assault (the other two were too young to be indicted). In part because of Button's celebrity status, the attack was widely reported in the national news media, helping to draw attention to the prevalence of antigay HATE CRIME and the way it is dealt with by LAW enforcement agencies.

Byron, Lord

(George Gordon Noel Byron; 1788–1824)

English poet. As an adult, Byron had sex with women, including his half sister, and with assorted English, French, Albanian, and Greek boys and young men. During his school days, he also formed ROMANTIC FRIENDSHIPS. One, in particular, with John Edleston, inspired the poem "To Thyrsa" and was compared by Byron in a letter to a woman friend to that of the LADIES OF LLANGOLLEN. Hounded by rumors alluding to incest as well as SODOMY, he fled to the Continent and settled in Venice. He burned his autobiography, *My Life and Adventures.*

Byron's last affair was with Lukas, a 15-year-old Greek boy; he memorialized it in "On This Day I Complete My Thirty Sixth Year." A still later poem, "Love and Death," not published until 1887, claimed that, though Lukas did not requite his love, the poet had no choice but "to strongly—wrongly—vainly—love thee still."

After Byron's death, an unknown poet wrote *Don Leon* (see **8/1833**), revising it several times before its first publication in the 1850s. *Don Leon* purports to be by Byron himself, but it includes details of many events that occurred after his death. It is one of the earliest protests against the harsh antisodomy laws of the period.

- Louis Crompton, *Byron and Greek Love: Homophobia in Nineteenth-Century England* (1985).
- Terry Castle, *The Apparitional Lesbian* (1993).

C

Cadmus, Paul

(1904–)

U.S. artist. The child of artists, Cadmus left high school at the age of 15 to study ART at the National Academy of Design. After graduating with honors in 1926, he worked for several years in ADVERTISING. In 1931, he and his friend Jared French traveled to Europe together and settled in a Majorcan fishing village. There, French encouraged Cadmus to sketch and paint in the style of the old masters, but by their return to the U.S. at the end of 1933, Cadmus had evolved a sensuous realism that was uniquely his own.

In **1934**, Cadmus achieved national notoriety overnight when his painting *The Fleet's In!,* commissioned as part of the Public Works of Art Project, was pulled from a Corcoran Gallery exhibit for allegedly "defaming" American sailors. Like several of his paintings of the 1930s, *The Fleet's In!* featured well-built men in various stages of drunkenness being courted by a horde of feral women and, a little to the side, an overgroomed man in a telltale red tie. Like CHARLES DEMUTH, Cadmus memorialized the ways gay men found sex at a time when there were no gay GHETTOS to cruise. Unlike Demuth, Cadmus exhibited his paintings to the public.

Cadmus's HOMOEROTICISM is even more apparent in his paintings completed after WORLD WAR II, which include romanticized male

The Haircut (1986): Cadmus (seated) with his model and lover of three decades, Jon Andersson.

nudes in FIRE ISLAND settings; beautiful young male couples (*The Bath,* 1951); and his masterpiece, *What I Believe* (1947–1948), painted in response to his friend E. M. FORSTER's call for "tolerance, good temper, and sympathy." In *What I Believe,* Cadmus, Forster, and dozens of other naked men and women sun at the shore, bravely, perhaps defiantly, oblivious of the apocalyptic forces massing in the background.

Cadmus's later work also includes three decades of drawings and paintings of his model and lover, the cabaret singer Jon Andersson.

✧ Lincoln Kirstein, *Paul Cadmus* (1992).

✧ Emmanuel Cooper, *The Sexual Perspective: Homosexuality and Art in the Last One Hundred Years in the West* (rev. ed., 1994).

Califia, Pat

(1954–)

U.S. author, journalist, activist, sex educator. Born in Corpus Christi, Texas, Califia grew up in a working-class MORMON family. She came OUT as a 17-year-old freshman at the University of Utah and changed her last name to Califia after a legendary AMAZON queen. After leaving school, she moved to California and worked as a volunteer at the San Francisco Sex Information Switchboard. In 1978, she cofounded Samois, a lesbian feminist S/M group. Beginning in 1979, she served as a writer, editorial staffer, and columnist with THE ADVOCATE while publishing more than a dozen books, erotic short stories, poetry, and nearly 100 articles and essays in the U.S. and abroad.

Califia was a central figure in the lesbian SEX WARS. Her popular sex manual *Sapphistry: The Book of Lesbian Sexuality* (1980; revised edition, 1988) established her as not only an authority on lesbian sex practices but also an advocate for the then emerging lesbian S/M community. In 1982, she once again challenged "currently accepted politics" as one of the writers of *Coming to Power,* a collection of essays, graphics, and fiction about lesbian S/M. Often savaged in the intense political battle that ensued, Califia responded with her own diverse collection of erotic fiction, *Macho Sluts* (1988). As the title suggests, Califia leavens her provocative demands for an expanded definition of "dyke passion" with a sly sense of humor, but she has remained relentless in her criticism of lesbians and other feminists who oppose PORNOGRAPHY. In a variety of media, Califia has insisted on tolerance of sexual minorities, no matter how unpopular, most recently in *Sex Changes: The Politics of Transgenderism* (1997). She has also been a leader in promoting safe yet creative sex practices among gay men as well as among lesbians.

✧ Pat Califia, "A Personal View of the History of the Lesbian S/M Community

Pat Califia.

and Movement in San Francisco," in *Coming to Power,* edited by Samois (1982).

- Pat Califia, *Public Sex: The Culture of Radical Sex* (1994).

Camp

A modern "sensibility" or "stylization," according to culture critic Susan Sontag, who aroused popular interest in the concept with an influential 1964 essay entitled "Notes on Camp." Since camp by its very nature transforms the serious into the frivolous, Sontag cautioned that camp is likely to be *produced* if one becomes too solemn in defining and analyzing it.

In his slang dictionary *The Queen's Vernacular: A Gay Lexicon* (1972), Bruce Rodgers traces camp to the 16th-century theatrical word "camping," meaning "young men wearing the costume of women in a play." This usage possibly came from *campagne,* the French word for "countryside," where "strolling mime troops entertained" in medieval times (see MATTACHINE for a related gay etymology). In the UNITED KINGDOM and AUSTRALIA, "camp" or "kamp" predated the words "QUEER" and "GAY" as adjectives used to describe men thought to be attracted to other men.

Gay historian George Chauncey (*Gay New York,* 1994) found "camp" serving as the most distinctive and characteristic gay male cultural style in the U.S. as early as the 1920s, when the expression "You are a camp!" was a way of complimenting a witty gay man. Chauncey describes camp as a "cultural strategy" rooted in the conscious experience of deviance. Reduced by society from male to female status, obvious "fairies" used camp as a kind of compensatory behavior, dramatizing (and humorizing) the ironies of the conventionally "masculine" or "feminine" and demonstrating the artificiality of "natural" social roles. Camp thus allowed gay men to disarm the very categories of gender and sexuality that marginalized them.

Observing camp as it manifested itself in the 1950s and 1960s, Sontag considered "love of the unnatural: of artifice and exaggeration" the essence of camp. She defined "pure camp" as a naïve and unintentional seriousness that fails, a delicate balance between parody and self-parody. Because there is good taste even in bad taste, the ultimate camp statement, according to Sontag, is "It's good because it's awful." She placed old Flash Gordon comics, Tiffany lamps, and stag movies viewed without lust in the "canon of camp." Although she has been criticized for editing homosexuality out of camp, she conceded, "While it's not true that camp taste *is* homosexual taste, there is no doubt a peculiar affinity and overlap."

Far from viewing camp as having a gay "overlap," lesbian anthropologist Esther Newton's pioneering study of (mostly pre-STONEWALL) female impersonators contended that the campy queen was the "best-defined role figure in homosexual life," camp itself was "one of the most striking features of homosexual culture," and camp style was representative of "all that is most unique in the homosexual subculture."

Newton saw camp as one way gay men coped with their perilous social situation. Practitioners of camp made incongruity (usually between masculinity and femininity) their subject matter, theatricality their style, and humor their strategy. The result was sometimes an aggressively self-affirming gay identity. As one of her interviewees declared: "A camp is a flip person who has declared emotional freedom. She is going to say to the world, 'I'm queer.' "

Camp humor could—and can—also be a mock heroic response to a threatening situation. Perhaps the most famous example of this is the impromptu chorus line that faced off against the helmeted, club-wielding police and performed a full kick routine the first night of the Stonewall Uprising.

Lesbian Camp?

Some feminists have seen camp as a form of misogyny, a combination of antiwoman mimicry and self-mockery that actually furthers the oppression of both women and gay men. Ethnohistorians MADELINE DAVIS and ELIZABETH KENNEDY counter this critique by examining camp in the context of individual and communal strategies of resistance. Intrigued by the high development of camp in the 20th-century gay male SUBCULTURE and its almost complete absence in the pre-Stonewall lesbian community, they hypothesized that the physical struggles faced by butch women did not lend themselves to camp, and that GENDER roles seem to have been more forcefully directive for working-class lesbians than for gay men. As a result, "the queen's camp was key in building a gay-male consciousness while the butch's aggressive protection shaped the formation of lesbian consciousness."

If, as Kennedy and Davis suggest, camp was alien to pre-Stonewall BUTCH/FEMME lesbians, it has nonetheless emerged as an important element in later, more playful interpretations of the butch/femme aesthetic, especially in performances by lesbian drag kings. In addition, as critics including Sue-Ellen Case, Andrea Weiss, and Z. Isiling Nataf have noted, lesbians have increasingly made use of the distancing potential of camp to commandeer pleasure from forms of entertainment, ranging from lesbian vampire movies to 1970s black exploitation films, that would otherwise be seen as misogynistic and lesbophobic.

Contemporary Camp

Although camp may at times seem apolitical, overly aesthetic, even silly, it has served, in the opinion of arts critic Moe Meyer, as a way of creating a gay identity through "the production of queer social visibility." Meyer insists that "Camp" with a capital *C* is "solely queer"; heterosexual and/or pop culture appropriations are always derivative—camp with a lowercase *c*. Camp has further evolved as an activist strategy of "queer parody" for groups like ACT UP, LESBIAN AVENGERS, QUEER NATION, and the RADICAL FAERIES as well as for individuals like Chicago mayoral candidate and drag queen Joan Jett Blakk, who in 1991 promised her electorate that she would "put the camp back into campaign."

✧ Susan Sontag, "Notes on Camp," in *Against Interpretation* (1964).

✧ Esther Newton, *Mother Camp: Female Impersonators in America* (1972).

✧ Jack Babuscio, "Camp and the Gay Sensibility," in *Gays and Film,* edited by Richard Dyer (1977).

✧ Philip Core, *Camp: The Lie That Tells the Truth* (1984).

✧ Andrea Weiss, "The Vampire Lovers," in *Lesbian Words,* edited by Randy Turoff (1995).

✧ Z. Isiling Nataf, "Black Lesbian Spectatorship and Pleasure in Popular Cinema," in *A Queer Romance: Lesbians, Gay Men and Popular Culture,* edited by Paul Burston and Colin Richardson (1995).

Canada

No laws against consensual same-sex relations for persons over 14, with the exception of anal intercourse, for which the AGE OF CONSENT *is 18. Broad legal protection against discrimination under the country's Charter of Rights. Specific protection against discrimination based on sexual orientation in British Columbia, Manitoba, Nova Scotia, Ontario, Quebec, and the Yukon. Well-developed social and cultural scenes, active political organizations, especially in Montreal, Ottawa, Toronto, and Vancouver.*

Gay and lesbian life in Canada is a cluster of paradoxes further complicated by the size and diversity of the country. More gay men and lesbians have been arrested on sex-related charges in Canada since 1969 than in any other English- or French-speaking country—despite the fact that 1969 was the year the Canadian government technically decriminalized private sexual acts between two consenting adults over 21. Lesbians and gay men are free to join the MILITARY; most are protected from discrimination in the workplace and in housing; thousands of couples enjoy liberal DOMESTIC PARTNERSHIP benefits; yet censorship restrictions on imported literature are so severe that only four lesbian and gay BOOKSTORES have managed to survive in the entire country—and these only through costly and Kafkaesque legal battles. Canadians also have the distinction of being the only people in the developed world who are officially forbidden to purchase copies of the partly homoerotic *Greek Anthology,* a staple of studies of the classics since the 10th century.

With the exception of a few groups like the National Lesbian Forum (founded in 1987) and the Canadian Human Rights Campaign (founded in 1995), most Canadian gay and lesbian rights organizations have been active only at the local or provincial level.

Notable bisexual, lesbian, and gay Canadians include actor/comedian Scott Thompson; artist Attila Richard Lukacz; filmmakers Denys Arcand, John Greyson, and Bruce LaBruce; historian and sociologist Barry D. Adam; singer K. D. LANG; and writers Marie-Claire Blais, Thomson Highway, JANE RULE, Makeda Silvera, Michel Tremblay, and Ian Young.

History

In the 17th century, French missionaries based in Quebec were among the first to report on the phenomenon of BERDACHES among indigenous North American peoples. Missionaries and Canadian government officials later worked to suppress the berdache traditions, and they disappeared or went underground until the late 20th century.

In Quebec, French officials prosecuted men on SODOMY charges on at least two occasions (1648 and 1691), although there is no record of anyone being sentenced to death for the crime. Canada followed British legal precedents through the 20th century, until decriminalizing consensual same-sex acts between men in private on **May 15, 1969**. Same-sex relations between women were never illegal in Canada.

Canada's first HOMOPHILE magazine was *Two* (inspired by the American ONE magazine), which was first issued in **1964** by Kamp Publishing Company in Toronto. The country's first homophile organization, Association for Social Knowledge (ASK), was founded in Vancouver in **April 1964**. Despite these developments and a public debate over decriminalization of homosexuality after the appearance in the UNITED KINGDOM of the WOLFENDEN REPORT, lesbians and gay men were almost invisible in the country until after STONEWALL and the spread of GAY LIBERATION to Toronto, Vancouver, and other large cities and to university campuses.

The first effort to mobilize gay men and lesbians at the national level was the National Gay Rights Coalition/Coalition Nationale pour les Droits des Homosexuels, formed in 1975. Widespread ACTIVISM came later, however, and was stimulated not by organization leaders but by anger at the attempts of police in Montreal, Toronto, and elsewhere to repress the growing network of BATHHOUSES and gay and lesbian BARS. Activists protested raids beginning on **May 14, 1976**, in Montreal launched by local police to "clean up" the city in preparation for the upcoming Olympic Games. But the largest demonstrations occurred in the wake of a brutal raid on Toronto bathhouses, in which a record 286 men were arrested on **February 5, 1981**. At midnight on Friday, **February 6, 1981**, some 3,000 demonstrators took to the streets of downtown Toronto shouting, "Enough is enough" and "No more shit." Finding themselves blocked by police barricades, the demonstrators made a dash for the Ontario Parliament building, almost succeeding in breaking into the building before the police arrived. This "night of rage," popularly remembered as "Canada's Stonewall," revitalized rights organizations like the Right to Privacy Committee (which had been formed in 1978) and inspired Toronto's first (now annual) Lesbian and Gay Pride Day the following summer.

Another important factor in the building of a Canadian gay and lesbian consciousness was the country's internationally renowned gay and lesbian newspaper, *The Body Politic.* From its first issue in November 1971 to its demise in January 1987, *The Body Politic* was one of the most influential and controversial publications in the gay and lesbian world. Yet it was also one of the most oppressed, suffering police raids on **December 30, 1977**, and **May 12, 1982**, and eventually folding as a result of mounting legal defense bills. The Canadian Gay Archives, begun by *The Body Politic* in 1973, continues in operation.

Despite continued oppression by police, local government, and Canada Customs, lesbian and gay Canadians made important advances in the 1980s. By the end of the decade, there were lesbian and gay rights organizations active in every province except Prince Edward Island, Quebec's parliament had become the first government body in North America to extend domestic partnership benefits to same-sex couples (**12/18/1982**), and Vancouver M.P. Svend J. Robinson had come OUT on national television (see **2/29/1988**).

➤ Also see **February 27, 1992**.

✧ Gary Kinsman, *The Regulation of Desire: Sexuality in Canada* (1987).

✧ Line Chamberland, "Remembering Lesbian Bars: Montreal, 1955–1975," in *Gay Studies from the French Cultures: Voices from France, Belgium, Brazil, Canada, and the Netherlands,* edited by Rommel Mendès-Leite and Pierre-Olivier de Busscher (1993).

✧ Barry D. Adam, "Winning Rights and Freedoms in Canada," in *The Third Pink Book: A Global View of Lesbian and Gay Liberation and Oppression,* edited by Aart Hendriks, Rob Tielman, and Evert van der Veen (1993).

✧ *Forbidden Passages: Writings Banned in Canada,* introductions by Pat Califia and Janine Fuller (1995).

✧ Donald W. McLeod, *Lesbian and Gay Liberation in Canada: A Selected Annotated Chronology, 1964–1975* (1996).

Capote, Truman

(Truman Streckfus Persons, 1924–1984)

U.S. novelist, journalist, socialite. Born in New Orleans but raised mostly in Alabama (by eccentric relatives who later became memorable characters in his writing), Capote dropped out of high school in the 1940s and began publishing short stories in *The New Yorker* and other magazines. His first novel, *Other Voices, Other Rooms* (1948), brought him international critical acclaim, which grew with *Breakfast at Tiffany's* (1958) and peaked with the reception given his trend-setting "nonfiction novel" *In Cold Blood* (1966): this last book was so successful that *Esquire* called 1966 the "year of Capote." As famous for his jet-set connections as his writing, his social life also peaked that year with his highly publicized Black and White Ball, a gala for several hundred very select guests at the Plaza Hotel in New York City. Capote later alienated almost all his socialite friends by publishing excerpts of a never finished novel, *Answered Prayers,* in *Esquire* in 1975 and 1976, in which he revealed scandalous secrets friends had confided in him in much the same way he had used murderers' confessions to construct *In Cold Blood.* A self-confessed alcoholic and drug addict, Capote and his work deteriorated over the next decade, and he died in Los Angeles shortly before his 60th birthday.

OUT virtually from the beginning of his career, Capote was—along with LIBERACE, GORE VIDAL, and Tennessee Williams—one of the best-known "known homosexuals" in the U.S. in the 1960s. The (deeply closeted) bisexual writer John Cheever described him in a 1959 journal entry as "a conspicuous male coquette" who seemed "to excite more curiosity than intolerance." Others, while appreciating his wit and the brilliance of his early prose, cringed at his public manner, believing he reinforced the stereotype of the gay man as "bitchy queen" and, especially in his later years, "tragic homosexual." Gerald Clarke's biography paints a more complex portrait of Capote's homosexuality and its relationship to his life and work. Jay Presson Allen's hit Broadway play *Tru* (1990) was based on Capote's life.

- Lawrence Grobel, *Conversations with Capote* (1985).
- Gerald Clarke, *Capote: A Biography* (1988).

Caribbean

No laws against same-sex relations between consenting adults in the Dominican Republic and U.S., French, Dutch, and British territories. All same-sex relations illegal in Trinidad and Tobago, with penalties up to life imprisonment. Male-male relations illegal in the Bahamas, Barbados, Grenada, Jamaica, and Saint Lucia, with penalties ranging up to 20 years' imprisonment. Small social and political groups in the Dominican Republic.

Although closeted homosexuality is to a certain extent tolerated, open lesbians and gay men face a tremendous amount of hostility in many areas of the Caribbean. Just one example is a Trinidad and Tobago law that makes it illegal for lesbians or gay men to enter the country. Even more disturbingly, homophobic messages have been delivered by some of the region's leading pop stars, such as the Jamaican ragga singer Buju Banton, whose "Boom, Bye, Bye" (1992) urged listeners to shoot and kill ("boom, bye, bye") a "batty boy" (gay man). French- and Spanish-influenced cultures are somewhat more tolerant, although even on these islands very few men or women self-identify as "GAY" or "LESBIAN" in the international sense of those words.

Jamaican-born writer and publisher Makeda Silvera believes Caribbean hostility toward lesbians and gay men is rooted in the particularly strong influence of the BIBLE in the Caribbean tradition. In colonial times, the Bible provided slaves with the chance to attain literacy—through stories of strength and hope as well as Old Testament condemnations of homosexuality. Colonial economics also made it almost as important for slaves to *re*produce as to produce for their masters; and even after emancipation, strict adherence to GENDER roles was mandatory for social mobility and acceptance.

In spite of this unfriendly climate, a rich literature has developed based on Caribbean gay ("sodomite") and lesbian (or "man royal," as a lesbian is called on some English-speaking islands) traditions. Gay and lesbian writers with roots in the Caribbean include Dionne Brand, MICHELLE CLIFF, filmmaker and critic Richard Fung, Greg Henry, Sharon Lim-Hing, AUDRE LORDE, and Silvera. In addition, Caribbean carnivals and other cultural rituals often feature elements of CROSS-DRESSING and even transsexuality. Lesbians and gay men of Caribbean origin have also been a major force in the creation of North American and British groups like Zami and Lesbians of Colour.

➤ Also see CUBA; HAITI; LATIN AMERICA.

✧ Makeda Silvera, "Man Royals and Sodomites: Some Thoughts on the Invisibility of Afro-Caribbean Lesbians," in *Piece of My Heart: A Lesbian of Colour Anthology* (1991).

✧ Tracey Skelton, " 'Boom, Bye, Bye': Jamaican Ragga and Gay Resistance," in *Mapping Desire: Geographies of Sexualities,* edited by David Bell and Gill Valentine (1995).

Carpenter, Edward
(1844–1929)

English writer, sociopolitical theorist. The son of an upper-middle-class Anglican clergyman, Carpenter was himself ordained a priest and served as a curate at Cambridge until, finding himself increasingly attracted to feminism, socialism, and other men, he renounced his ordination in 1874. By this time, he had already discovered the homoerotic sculpture of Florence and the poetry of WALT WHITMAN.

After corresponding with Whitman, he visited the poet in America in 1877 and 1883 and began to synthesize his own Whitmanesque erotic, political, and aesthetic vision in a long poem called *Towards Democracy.* He went on to develop the utopian and feminist aspects of his philosophy even more explicitly in *Love's Coming of Age* (1896), a work that marked his public debut as a leader of the sexual emancipation movement. Published the same year as OSCAR WILDE's trial, the book coincidentally contained an unapologetic defense of "the love that dare not speak its name."

Carpenter was one of the first to assert that same-sex love was not only natural and wholesome, it actually made a positive contribution to society. Even more radically, he believed that gay men (and by implication,

Edward Carpenter, 1905.

lesbians) "are superior to the normal men in this respect—in respect of their love-feeling," because, he asserted, persons capable of what he called "homogenic" love combined positive qualities of both sexes. As sexual "intermediaries," they could act not only as "interpreters of men and women to each other" but also as a bridge to a more spiritually advanced, more harmonious future. He rejected the "civilization" he saw around him, advocating instead an advance in individual awareness within a context of "cosmic consciousness."

His own life provided a model. Carpenter lived outside Sheffield on a farm, where he worked at market gardening and sandal making. One day in 1891, he met a young working-class man named George Merrill on a train. The two men were deeply drawn to each other and remained lovers until Merrill's death, a year before Carpenter's. Their relationship shocked Carpenter's acquaintances as much because of the class difference between the two men as because of their both being men. Some of Carpenter's friends drifted away when he and Merrill began living together, but others, such as E. M. FORSTER and HAVELOCK ELLIS's lesbian wife, Edith, were drawn to the couple. Their relationship was one of the inspirations of Forster's posthumously published novel *Maurice.*

In 1902, Carpenter published the first major English-language collection of writings on homoerotic themes, *Iolaus: An Anthology of Friendship.* His most influential book, *Intermediate Types Among Primitive Folk,* followed in 1914.

Carpenter's writings fell into obscurity for several decades before being rediscovered by the BEAT GENERATION in the 1960s and American and British activists and theorists in the 1970s. More recently, his work has influenced JUDY GRAHN, HARRY HAY, and Hay's RADICAL FAERIES and other proponents of alternative lesbian and gay SPIRITUALITIES.

In his own time, Carpenter was a major influence on Forster, who wrote in his "Terminal Note" to *Maurice,* "He was a socialist who ignored industrialism and a simple-lifer with an independent income and a Whitmannic poet whose nobility exceeded his strength and, finally, he was a believer in the Love of Comrades, whom he sometimes called Uranians."

✧ Chushichi Tsuzuki, *Edward Carpenter, 1844–1929: Prophet of Human Fellowship* (1980).

Carson, Rachel [Louise]

(1907–1964)

U.S. naturalist, writer. Carson grew up in rural Pennsylvania, studied ZOOLOGY at Johns Hopkins, and worked as a marine biologist for the Fish and Wildlife Service in Washington, D.C. She wrote four best-sellers, including *The Sea Around Us* (1951), before publishing the phenomenally influential *Silent Spring* (1962). A founding text of the international environmental movement, *Silent Spring* was the first book to communicate the dangers of pesticides to a broad public.

In the early 1950s, Carson became friends with Dorothy Murdoch Freeman (1898–1978), an administrator for the Massachusetts Department of Agricultural Services. Carson built a summer home in Maine near the house Freeman shared with her husband and son, and the two women spoke on the phone or wrote each other almost daily from 1952 until Carson's death of cancer in 1964.

In a carefully annotated collection of their surviving correspondence, Freeman's granddaughter Martha struggles in her introduction to define Carson and Freeman's intense relationship. She reveals that Carson and Freeman marked their letters with one of three codes:

"sharing," which includes letters containing important autobiographical statements about Carson's research and writing; "apple," denoting passionate letters for private reading; and "the strong box," letters meant to be destroyed immediately after reading.

Both women realized their relationship might be described as lesbian. Shortly before Carson's death, Freeman begged her to destroy the "strong box" letters, reminding Carson of the publicity given journalist Dorothy Thompson and *Mädchen in Uniform* author Christa Winsloe's relationship when Syracuse University received their love letters in the early 1960s. Carson and Freeman are reported to have burned hundreds of "strong box" letters.

✧ *Always, Rachel: The Letters of Rachel Carson and Dorothy Freeman, 1952–1964,* edited by Martha Freeman (1995).

Cartoons, see COMICS AND CARTOONS.

Cather, Willa

(Born Wilella; called herself William or Billy Cather into college; 1873–1947)

U.S. writer. Born in Virginia, Cather moved with her family to Red Cloud, Nebraska, when she was 11 and launched a now legendary four-year GENDER rebellion as the rough-and-ready "William" Cather Jr., complete with male attire, crew cut, and a convincingly bass voice. Cather traded trousers for a skirt when she entered college, but classmates still remarked on her "masculine personality."

In 1891, Cather switched from pre-med to LITERATURE and began writing for campus and local publications. After college, she supported herself by working as a journalist and editor in Lincoln, Nebraska, and in Pittsburgh and New York before completing her first novel, *Alexander's Bridge,* in 1912. Popular and critical success followed, and she published a total of 19 books in a variety of genres, most notably novels, including *O Pioneers!* (1913), *My Ántonia* (1918), the Pulitzer Prize–winning *One of Ours* (1922), *Death Comes for the Archbishop* (1927), and the autobiographical *The Song of the Lark* (1915).

Willa Cather, 1895.

Her writings explore the power of the land and the complex, passionate relationships of those who dwell on it. She often used Nebraska and Western pioneer farm settings to frame vividly crafted characters, including memorably strong women. Cather was also concerned with the role of creativity in her characters' lives. Fittingly, she herself experimented with unusual narrative structures and voices.

Before her death, Cather took pains to destroy as much of her personal correspondence as she could lay her hands on, and it is likely that she would have fought any attempt to consider her writing in a lesbian context. Clues to her sense of personal identity, however, survive in letters written while in college to Louise Pound in which she laments her "unnatural" attraction and love for the young woman. Some biographers and critics now acknowledge her lesbianism and explore its impact on her writing, and historians cite her reticence as evidence of the dramatic increase in societal awareness and disapproval of lesbianism in the 1890s, contrasting her discomfort with the acceptance given previously to ROMANTIC FRIENDSHIPS between women, such as the BOSTON MARRIAGE enjoyed by Cather's mentor and friend SARAH ORNE JEWETT. Besides Pound, Cather appears to have been in love with Isabelle McClung in Pittsburgh and Edith Lewis, with whom she lived nearly 40 years in New York.

✧ Sharon O'Brien, *Willa Cather* (1987).

Cavafy, Constantine

(Konstantínos Pétrou Kaváfis, 1863–1933)

Egyptian-born Greek poet. The youngest son of a once wealthy Greek merchant family, Cavafy spent his youth in Alexandria, London, and Constantinople. He moved back to Alexandria in 1885 and worked at low-paying civil service jobs until retiring in 1922. Fluent in several languages, he chose to write poetry in demotic (modern spoken) Greek, evoking Hellenistic and Byzantine themes and, especially after he turned 40, fleeting encounters with handsome young men.

Although his work was not made widely available until an authorized collection of 154 poems was issued two years after his death, he was nonetheless honored in his lifetime as Alexandria's leading literary celebrity and one of the most important Greek-language poets of the 20th century. E. M. FORSTER became a friend (and perhaps a lover) and subsequently introduced Cavafy to British readers in a journal article published in 1923. Most English-language readers, however, did not discover him until after 1951, when John Mavrogordato's translation of the authorized collected poems was published. Cavafy's best known poems are probably "The City," "Ithaca," and "Waiting for the Barbarians."

About 50 poems, including some of the roughly 100 not included in the authorized collection, are relevant to his love of men. His homoerotic poems share the melancholy, irony, and, often, the historical settings of the rest of his work. They are confessional to the extent that they portray a man much like Cavafy, someone who thirsts for other men but, for reasons never explained, fails to find requited, enduring love. Paradoxically deep beneath their simple, straightforward language, his poems have influenced many other gay and lesbian writers including W. H. AUDEN, JAMES MERRILL, and MARGUERITE YOURCENAR (who translated his poems into French besides writing about him). Gay artists such as DAVID HOCKNEY and Duane Michals have also drawn inspiration from his work.

✧ Robert Liddell, *Cavafy: A Critical Biography* (1974).

✧ Peter Bien, "Cavafy's Homosexuality and His Reputation Outside Greece," *Journal of Modern Greek Studies* (vol. 8, no. 2, October 1990, 110–17).

✧ Peter G. Christensen, "C. P. Cavafy," in *The Gay and Lesbian Literary Heritage* (1995).

Central America, see LATIN AMERICA.

Central Asia

All same-sex relations illegal in Afghanistan and Iran, with punishment ranging from 100 lashes of the whip to beheading or stoning to death. Male-male anal intercourse illegal in Armenia, Azerbaijan, Georgia, Kazakhstan, Kyrgyzstan, Tajikistan, Turkmenistan, and Uzbekistan, with penalties ranging from three to eight years' imprisonment.

Most Central Asians are Muslim (see ISLAM), except in Armenia and Georgia, where Christians (see ORTHODOX EASTERN CHURCHES) are in the majority (in the other parts of the former USSR, there are also large numbers of Christian Russian immigrants). As a result, attitudes to same-sex eroticism are similar to those in the modern ARAB WORLD, especially since the rise of Islamic fundamentalism in the region in recent years. There is no gay and lesbian rights movement in any Central Asian country, although Iranians living in exile in London and other parts of the world have formed a gay and lesbian support group called HOMAN. Since the official reinstitution of *shari'a* (Islamic religious law) in Iran on August 25, 1982, and in Afghanistan in the 1990s, the world press has periodically reported instances of persecution, including public executions, of lesbians and gay men (see **1/1/1990**). In addition, women have lost the right to work outside the home in large areas of Afghanistan and face severe restrictions in much of the rest of the region, making it difficult, if not impossible, for most women to achieve the kind of economic independence that would facilitate a long-term same-sex relationship.

History

Central Asia was the birthplace of Zoroastrianism, a Persian belief system many religious historians consider the most homophobic of all religions. Zoroastrianism, which dates back to the 6th century B.C., saw the world as a battleground between sharply opposing forces of good and evil spirits. Individuals who had same-sex relations were automatically assumed to be allies of the evil spirits and thus, in theory at least, were to be killed on sight. Some religious historians believe that Zoroastrianism influenced the Jewish authors of the Laws of Leviticus (see BIBLE).

Despite these proscriptions, man-boy PEDERASTY and sexual/romantic relationships among women confined in harems were reported to be common during the two millennia when much of the region was conquered and ruled in turn by Greeks, Romans, Arabs, and Turks. Many of the most respected Persian and Afghani poets, from the 13th-century Sa'di of Shīrāz to Iradj Mirza (1874–1926), wrote verse in praise of the love of boys, which was often considered a more respectable sexual outlet than resorting to female prostitutes. As in many Arab countries, discreet CIRCUMSTANTIAL HOMOSEXUALITY was widely tolerated, especially among unmarried young men.

In the 20th century, every country in the region codified laws proscribing SODOMY. In Afghanistan, for example, the Penal Code of 1925 made sodomy punishable by death. Azerbaijan, Georgia, Turkmenistan, and Uzbekistan were the only Soviet republics to retain prerevolutionary laws against male-male sex in the period between **December 21, 1917**, and **March 7, 1934**, when same-sex relations were decriminalized in the rest of the USSR. Western-style bars and discos opened in large Iranian cities in the 1970s, but most openly gay and lesbian Iranians fled the country or retreated back into the CLOSET after the establishment of the Ayatollah Khomeini's regime in 1979.

AMNESTY INTERNATIONAL has protested rights abuses against gay men and lesbians in Iran and Uzbekistan.

➤ Also see RUSSIA.

✧ *The Third Pink Book: A Global View of Lesbian and Gay Liberation and Oppression,* edited by Aart Hendriks, Rob Tielman, and Evert van der Veen (1993).

✧ *Breaking the Silence: Human Rights Violations Based on Sexual Orientation,* Amnesty International USA report (1994).

Cernuda, Luis

(Luis Cernuda y Bidón, 1902–1963)

Spanish-born poet, critic. Born and educated in Seville, he studied law before deciding to pursue a career in LITERATURE. Along with FEDERICO GARCÍA LORCA, who may have been his lover for a time, Cernuda was one of the iconoclastic, antibourgeois poets who became famous in SPAIN as the Generation of '27.

Cernuda was the first widely read Spanish-language poet to express HOMOEROTICISM openly and positively. As the title of his 1936 collection of poems—*La Realidad y el Deseo* ("Reality and Desire")—suggests, one of his most important themes was the conflict between the repressive society he lived in and his own solitary, unsatisfied longings. His early work is marked by surreal imagery; in "Sailors Are the Wings of Love" (in *The Forbidden Pleasures,* 1931), he writes: "love is blond, just like their eyes." As he grew older, he wrote with a bittersweet directness, as in "Farewell" (in *The Chimera's Wasteland,* 1956): "Boys / who never were my life's companions / goodbye."

After fleeing the Spanish Civil War in the late 1930s, Cernuda supported himself with odd jobs and translations, living in England, the U.S., and, for the last decade of his life, Mexico City, where he died in November 1963. Until the 1970s, most critics chose to ignore the homoerotic content of his work, emphasizing instead that he was known as a difficult, unhappy loner. He has since come to be recognized as a major 20th-century Spanish-language poet.

✧ Salvador Jiménez-Fajardo, *The Word and the Mirror: Critical Essays on the Poetry of Luis Cernuda* (1989).

Jane Chambers.

Chambers, [Carolyn] Jane

(1937–1983)

U.S. playwright, novelist, screenwriter. Born in South Carolina, Chambers was raised in Florida by her mother and grandmother after her parents' divorce and the departure of her sexually abusive father and uncle. She began writing radio scripts while still a teenager and wanted to study directing and playwriting. Her college, however, like most colleges in the 1950s, reserved directing and playwriting classes for male students, so she left school in 1956 to study acting at the Pasadena Playhouse. She spent most of the rest of her life in the Northeast, mainly in New York City and Greenport, New York, working in television and, eventually, writing and producing several of the first positive plays about lesbians.

In 1974, New York City's Playwrights Horizons produced Chambers's *A Late Snow.* The first lesbian-positive play to reach a wide audience, *A Late Snow* explored a college professor's relationships with four other women gathered at her lakeside cabin during a snowstorm. The publicity the play received cost Chambers her writing job on the CBS soap opera *Search for Tomorrow.*

In 1980, The Glines (producer John Glines's pioneering gay theatrical company, where Chambers served as playwright-in-residence) presented *Last Summer at Bluefish Cove,* the story of a dying woman's last stay at a lesbian resort and her breakthrough play. Five years in preparation, *Bluefish Cove* established Chambers's reputation not only as the most popular openly lesbian playwright but also as a writer able to address life-and-death issues with humor and humanity.

With *Kudzu* (1981), Chambers began to integrate gay and straight characters in her work. She confided to friends that she planned to exemplify a world of harmonious lesbian and straight coexistence by climaxing her seven-play sequence, *The Georgia Tapestry,* with a play featuring characters of unidentified sexuality.

In 1981, Chambers was diagnosed with brain cancer—coincidentally, the same disease Lil, the main character in *Last Summer at Bluefish Cove,* had suffered. Chambers wrote that Lil's reactions to her illness had been "honest and real." Her own memorial service ("Warrior at Rest") included a reading of Lil's goodbye speech.

In addition to 16 plays, she also wrote screenplays, poetry, and two novels, *The Burning* (1978) and *Chasin' Jason* (1987). Her many awards included a Eugene O'Neill fellowship, a DramaLogue Critics Circle award, a Villager Downtown Theatre award, and a Fund for Human Dignity award. She was one of the founders of the New Jersey Women's Political Caucus (1971) and was active in the Long Island East End Gay Organization (EEGO). Mindful of the difficulties she had experienced breaking into the theater, she helped establish the Women's Interart Theater (1972) and participated in an American Theatre Association "Action for Women" (1976) that investigated employment discrimination against women playwrights and directors.

She shared most of her adult life with Beth Allen, who was also her manager.

✧ Emily Sisley, "Playwright Jane Chambers: The Long Road to *Last Summer at Bluefish Cove,*" *The Advocate* (November 13, 1980).

✧ Claire Coss, "On Jane Chambers: An Interview with Beth Allen and Jere Jacob," *Heresies* 17 (1984).

Children

Lesbians and gay men have always had children, but it was not until the 1970s that large numbers of gay men and, especially, lesbians decided to raise children outside traditional heterosexual marriages. By the 1980s, the gay and lesbian media were heralding a "lesbian baby boom" and, in the 1990s, as gay men increasingly became fathers, a generalized "gayby boom."

According to a 1993 survey conducted by Yankelovitch Partners Inc., U.S. lesbians are almost as likely to be mothers as straight women (67 percent and 72 percent respectively). About 27 percent of U.S. gay men are reported to be fathers (as opposed to 60 percent of straight men). How many lesbians and gay men have custody of their children is not known, but, according to the same survey, 15 percent of gay male and 32 percent of lesbian households included children among their members.

Many more would like to have children. In the Boston area alone, for example, the Fenway Community Health Center reported 2,400 calls from lesbian and gay parents and prospective parents just in 1994.

Lesbian and gay parents have had to pro-

Wayne Steinman (left), 1996 president of Gay and Lesbian Parents Coalition International, with partner Sal Iaculla and daughter Hope.

ceed cautiously due to the alleged (and false—see PEDOPHILIA) connection of homosexuality with sexual abuse of children, as well as the widespread (and equally unfounded) suspicion that gay men and lesbians actively "recruit" young people. Even more serious, in some cases, has been the fact that same-sex relations remain illegal in more than 20 states, making lesbians and gay men de facto "criminals" and thus, as Sharon Bottoms discovered in Virginia in 1993 when she was denied custody of her two-year-old son, "unfit" to be parents.

Several studies have shown that children raised by gay or lesbian parents are no more likely to be gay or lesbian themselves than children raised by straight parents. Ironically, the publicity given these surveys can make it difficult for the minority of children who *do* grow up to be lesbian or gay. As some members of Children of Lesbians and Gays Everywhere (COLAGE) report, gay and lesbian parents sometimes feel they have "failed" as parents if their children do not turn out straight.

Adoption

An ever increasing number of lesbians and gay men in the U.S. adopt children. Outside of Florida, Nebraska, and New Hampshire, no laws bar a gay man or lesbian from adopting a child as a single parent; however, some courts may deny adoptions based on allegations of an "inappropriate environment" or even, as in a 1995 decision in Virginia, the belief that growing up in a gay household would place an insupportable "burden" on the child.

Adopting a child as a same-sex couple—or becoming the adoptive parent of a lover's child—is more problematic. The supreme courts of Massachusetts, Vermont, and New York and lower courts in 11 other states and the District of Columbia have ruled that unmarried couples have the right to adopt children. Practices vary in other jurisdictions, with some family courts consistently refusing to allow lesbian or gay male couples to adopt and others, such as in California, authorizing a limited "coparent" status for a second parent.

Despite decreasing legal barriers, would-be adopters face long waits at state and county agencies in the U.S. and even longer waiting lists in Western Europe and CANADA, where fewer children are put up for adoption. In the NETHERLANDS, for example, only about 40 children are available for adoption each year. As a result, many lesbians and gay men go abroad to adopt, make private arrangements with birth mothers, or choose to adopt older or disabled children.

In some places, such as New York City and

San Francisco, government agencies attempt whenever possible to place gay and lesbian teenagers with gay and lesbian foster parents. In the UNITED KINGDOM, the Albert Kennedy Trust, founded in Manchester and named after a gay runaway who killed himself, also works to place gay and lesbian teenagers in homes where their sexuality will be supported.

Support Services

Lesbians began providing counseling on artificial insemination and adoption procedures in the 1970s through women's centers in the U.S. and abroad. One of the first support organizations was the Lesbian Mothers' National Defense Fund (now Lavender Families, based in Seattle), founded by 12 lesbians in Eatonville, Washington, in 1974. Responding to the need for a wider range of family support services, lesbian and gay families founded Center Kids as a project of the New York Lesbian and Gay Community Service Center in 1988. The project grew from an informal social network of 99 gay and lesbian families to a multifaceted program serving more than 1,500 families in the New York metropolitan area in the mid-1990s. Since 1988, a number of other similar programs have been founded at COMMUNITY CENTERS and health centers throughout North America. Most groups are affiliated with the Washington, D.C.–based Gay and Lesbian Parents Coalition International.

➤ Also see DOMESTIC PARTNERSHIP; LAW; MARRIAGE; YOUTH, GAY AND LESBIAN.

- April Martin, *The Lesbian and Gay Parenting Handbook: Creating and Raising Our Families* (1993).
- Laura Benkov, *Reinventing the Family: The Emerging Story of Lesbian and Gay Parents* (1994).
- Terry Boggis, "Lesbian Parenting 1994," in *The New Our Right to Love: A Lesbian Resource Book,* edited by Ginny Vida (1996).

Chile, see LATIN AMERICA.

China

No laws against same-sex relations, but gay men and lesbians are sometimes prosecuted for "hooliganism." Informal support groups in some large mainland cities. Developed social scene and nascent rights organizations in Hong Kong and Taiwan.

"Gay and lesbian" identities (in the international sense of the words) have only begun to emerge among the more than 1 billion people who live in China. Historians have uncovered unique constructions (see CONSTRUCTIONISM VS. ESSENTIALISM) of homosexuality and BISEXUALITY in premodern China, but two tumultuous centuries of Chinese history have cut most people off from traditional sexualities. Today, many Chinese in both Communist and non-Communist parts of the Chinese culture sphere consider homosexuality a Western import, despite China's rich literary tradition of homoerotica. As a result, even in places such as Taiwan or Hong Kong, where there is a developed bar scene and lesbian and gay Chinese-language publications are widely available, many of the most common gay and lesbian slang words are borrowings from English. In 1994, the first guide for gay men published in Taiwan included a chronology of gay and lesbian history that began with SAPPHO and continued through the STONEWALL Uprising without a single reference to anyone or anything Chinese. In fact, the guide's first mention of a Chinese event was the 1986 release in Taiwan of a movie version of novelist Pai Hsien-Yung's bleak depiction of Taiwanese gay life, *Niedz* (literally, "Son of a Whore"; English translation: *Crystal Boys,* 1990).

Still, the appearance of the guide was itself a sign that lesbians and gay men in many parts of the Chinese-speaking world are beginning to forge their own SUBCULTURES. Another indication was the formation four years earlier (see **2/23/1990**), also in Taiwan, of the first organization for Chinese lesbians in Asia.

The cover of the first book published in Taiwan (in 1995) on the gay rights movement.

History

Premodern China had a richly documented tradition of same-sex love. HOMOEROTICISM in Chinese poetry goes back at least as far as the Zhou (Chou) dynasty (see **c. 700 B.C.**). As early as **c. 500 B.C.**, a courtier called Mizi Xia became famous enough as the lover of a duke to be alluded to in later books as the type of a man-loving man. References to love between women date back to the Han Dynasty (see **c. 200**), an era when almost all the emperors had young male favorites in addition to wives (see **A.D. 1**).

References to same-sex eroticism were common in the following centuries (see **c. 275; 960**), and eventually become even more frequent with the development of fiction written in the vernacular in the late 16th century. Although these stories include some characters who seem close to what modern Westerners would call "exclusively homosexual," the most common attitude at the time seems to have been that virtually any adult male had the potential to be attracted to a beautiful boy. Male prostitutes as young as 20 years old were considered by some writers to be long past their prime.

Accounts of same-sex relations between women were also a feature of erotic novels in the Ming and early Qing (Ch'ing) dynasties, but as in the West, they were usually contrived to titillate male fantasies. More significantly, feminist scholars have recently begun to research and analyze letters that generations of educated Chinese women wrote to other women in a special coded form of Chinese characters apparently devised to conceal same-sex relationships similar to Western ROMANTIC FRIENDSHIPS.

The Qing Emperor Kangxi was known to be intolerant of same-sex eroticism, especially when his second son, the heir apparent, indulged in it. In **1697**, he had three of his son's servants executed when he learned that they and his son had been having sex with young men. The Emperor's antipathy to same-sex eroticism, unusual in premodern China, perhaps reflected his comparatively puritanical Manchu heritage, or, as historian Vivien W. Ng suggests in an analysis of later instances of oppression, was symptomatic of the Qing government's insistence on strictly defined GENDER roles. In **1740**, the Qing government enacted the first law forbidding consensual SODOMY between adults. The statute, however, was rarely enforced.

Around the middle of the 19th century, economic developments made it possible for women to support themselves independently of their families by working in the booming silk spinning industry. Many women, especially in southern China, participated in a "marriage resistance movement," formalizing bonds with each other and living apart from their families. The movement, which disintegrated in the turmoil caused by the Japanese invasion of China in the late 1930s, had more than 100,000 women at its peak, many of whom formed long-term sexual relationships with each other. Some couples were even able to adopt female children.

The 19th century also saw the first persecution of homosexuality per se in China. Hung Xiuquan (Hsiu-ch'üan), inspired by his reading of the BIBLE to believe that he was Christ's unacknowledged Chinese brother, began a political and religious movement that led to the Taiping Rebellion (1850–1865), a bloody civil war during which tens of millions perished. Hung's interpretation of CHRISTIANITY was in most ways idiosyncratic, but it was orthodox in its condemnation of sodomy. Hung is recorded to have ordered an untold number of obvious "sodomites" massacred in the territories his forces occupied.

Although homosexuality was most commonly associated with actors and prostitutes (female as well as male), China remained a fairly permissive society until the advent of communism. In the late 1940s and early 1950s, government officials arrested and "rehabilitated" sex workers, closed gay- and lesbian-friendly bars, and launched an unofficial but nonetheless harsh campaign to eradicate "decadent Western" homosexuality from the country. Oppression intensified again during the Cultural Revolution (1966–1976), when thousands of lesbians and gay men were publicly humiliated, tortured, exiled to the countryside, driven to commit suicide, and, in many instances, executed.

The 1990s saw moves toward greater tolerance of homosexuality throughout most of Chinese-speaking Asia. In 1991, Hong Kong repealed its British-influenced laws against consensual sex between men. In **April 1992**, the Chinese Ministry of Public Security ordered the release of two lesbians who had been imprisoned for two weeks on charges of "unruly behavior" simply for living together, and the ministry announced that there was no legal basis for forbidding lesbians from cohabiting. In **November 1992**, the national government reported that same-sex acts were no longer considered an offense against "social order." Still, lesbian and gay Chinese on the mainland remain extremely isolated from one another. In the 1990s, the most vocal rights organization was Chinese Rainbow, which cofounder Gary Wu describes as "a wide network of individuals, both homosexual and heterosexual, involved in working with and for the gay community." Chinese Rainbow had about 20 members in 1995.

✧ Vivien W. Ng, "Homosexuality and the State in Late Imperial China," in *Hidden from History: Reclaiming the Gay and Lesbian Past,* edited by Martin Bauml Duberman, Martha Vicinus, and George Chauncey Jr. (1989).

- ✧ Bret Hinsch, *Passions of the Cut Sleeve: The Male Homosexual Tradition in China* (1990).
- ✧ Giovanni Vitiello, "Chinese Literature," in *The Gay and Lesbian Literary Heritage: A Reader's Companion to the Writers and Their Works, from Antiquity to the Present,* edited by Claude J. Summers (1995).

Choruses and Bands

Begun in the 1970s, the U.S. and Canadian lesbian and gay chorus and band movement has grown to include 128 choruses (41 mixed, 62 men's, 25 women's) and 24 marching and symphonic bands, many with accompanying brigades of baton twirlers. A fixture of PRIDE CELEBRATIONS and fund-raising events, gay and lesbian musical groups embrace more than 6,500 members across North America and reach an estimated 500,000 people each year in concerts and many hundreds of thousands more through marches and other outdoor celebrations.

Many of the women's bands and musical groups that formed in the early 1970s had close connections with LESBIAN FEMINISM, but the San Francisco Freedom Day Marching Band and Twirling Corps, founded in 1977, is believed to be the first explicitly *gay and lesbian* group of its kind. Jon Sims established the first Gay Men's Chorus in San Francisco in 1978. Within a decade, 55 choruses were giving regular performances everywhere from San Diego to Halifax, Nova Scotia.

Although many groups are still segregated by sex, the trend since the mid-1980s has been for lesbians and gay men to join together in forming choruses and bands. Most groups are affiliated with either the Gay and Lesbian Chorus Association (GALA), established in 1980, or the Lesbian and Gay Bands of America, established in 1982.

Christianity

Religion based on the teachings of Jesus Christ, with almost 2 billion adherents worldwide. Divided into dozens of major—and hundreds of minor—denominations, Christianity encompasses an enormous range of doctrines and policies on sex and sexuality. Of the four largest world religions (see BUDDHISM, HINDUISM, ISLAM), however, Christianity is distinguished by a comparatively negative view of

Love "beyond all reckoning": despite age-old prohibitions against eroticism, Christian lore includes paired saints like the martyred Saints Boris and Gleb, popular since the 11th century in the Russian Orthodox tradition.

sexual pleasure in general and same-sex eroticism in particular. The only one of these four religions whose founder is believed to have remained a lifelong celibate, Christianity has also been the least affirmative of all forms of extramarital sexuality.

According to a 1993 *Time* magazine poll, homosexuality was considered "morally wrong" by 53 percent of Americans (the same percentage as reported in 1978)—evidence of the persistence of traditional Christian attitudes in American society.

Christian opposition to same-sex eroticism is based on interpretations of the BIBLE that emerged over the first millennium of the Christian era and became more or less fixed by the time of Thomas Aquinas (see **1252**). Homosexuality was viewed as "against nature" since it did not lead to procreation.

Today, there is a split between "fundamentalist" and "mainstream" congregations, with a further split between those mainstream congregations such as QUAKERS, who profess full equality but stop short of allowing lesbians and gay men to be ordained, and faiths such as the ROMAN CATHOLIC CHURCH that condemn homosexuality but call for some degree of compassion.

Many caucuses and support groups work to advocate change. The Catholic group Dignity was the earliest (1969). Recent decades have also seen the emergence of gay-founded Christian churches such as the METROPOLITAN COMMUNITY CHURCH, established in 1968.

➤ Also see entries on specific denominations.

Christian Science

(Church of Christ, Scientist)

Religion begun in 1866 by Mary Baker Eddy (1821–1910) based on her interpretations of Christ's words and deeds and principles of "divine healing" derived therefrom. In the 19th century, Eddy's advocacy of equal rights for women was as radical a departure from mainstream Christian sects as her belief in a "Father-Mother God" who transcended GENDER. Less radical was her assertion that "chastity is the cement of civilization and progress." Eddy apparently never made any public statements about same-sex relations, but church leaders have interpreted "chastity" as precluding them and advised gay men and lesbians to "heal" their sexuality. Church employees suspected of being lesbian or gay have been dismissed on several occasions, drawing protests from members and, as in 1982, when the "Mother Church" in Boston fired two gay employees, setting off public demonstrations. In 1994, the church's Committee on Publication issued *Some Thoughts on Homosexuality,* reasserting "homosexuality to be inconsistent with basic Christian teachings" and citing "testimonies of healing written by individuals who have found healing from homosexuality."

Church activists established Gay People in Christian Science in the 1970s and, later, the Christian Science Group.

Many well-known lesbians and gay men have had Christian Science upbringings, including Kay Tobin Lahusen and Craig Rodwell, who modeled the Oscar Wilde Memorial Bookshop, the world's first gay bookstore, on Christian Science "reading rooms" (see **11/24/1967**). Rodwell also called his pioneering gay lib newsletter, started in **February 1968**, *Hymnal,* an echo of the Christian Science Hymnal used as part of the Church's services.

Chrystos

(1946–)

U.S. writer, activist, artist. Chrystos has described her early years in San Francisco as "liv-

Chrystos, 1961.

ing on many razors of contradictions." She was born to a Menominee father and a mother who had emigrated from Lithuania and Alsace-Lorraine; raised among AFRICAN-AMERICANS, Latins, Asians, and whites; and initiated into adulthood via sexual abuse, jail, mental institutions, substance abuse, and prostitution. She credits writing with "saving" her life from the age of nine and describes the force behind her work as "wanting to make it clear that this is our land, and we have survived incredible genocide of every variety, and we continue to be the sacred keepers of this earth."

An "urban Indian," as she calls herself, using a government term for a NATIVE AMERICAN not born on a reservation, she grew up conscious of the pain Anglo culture had inflicted on her father. By the time she began exploring the city's working-class BAR scene at the age of 19, she thought of herself as so multiple an outcast that coming OUT was not "a very traumatic experience for me because my whole life has been traumatic, and being gay is the one good thing that's ever happened to me."

Nevertheless, she has expressed anger at the insensitivities of the overwhelmingly white lesbian and gay movement, accusing it of extending a "basket empty with promises" in her poem "Gay American Indians March on Washington, D.C." In *Not Vanishing* she attacks white condescension: "Don't admire what you perceive as our stoicism or spirituality—work for our lives to continue in our own Ways. Despite the books which still appear, even in radical bookstores, we are not Vanishing Americans."

Although she is one of the most popular Native writers, she resists being called a "voice" or "spiritual leader" of her people. She instead works for a deeper understanding of the ways colonialism, genocide, class, and GENDER oppression contribute to hunger, forced sterilization, substance abuse, radiation poisoning, land theft, and harassment from both "tribal" and federal authorities.

Widely anthologized, Chrystos has also published a play and five collections of her writing, including *Not Vanishing* (1988), *Dream On* (1991), and *In Her I Am* (1993). Her later work lustily evokes the BUTCH-FEMME and S/M sexual cultures, challenging the sex phobia she believes remains a part of both the First Nations and lesbian communities. *Fugitive Colors* (1995) was a winner of the 1994 Audre Lorde International Poetry Competition.

✧ Ruth Baetz, *Lesbian Crossroads: Personal Stories of Lesbian Struggles and Triumphs* (1980).

✧ Barbara Dale May, "Chrystos," in *Contemporary Lesbian Writers of the United States,* edited by Sandra Pollack and Denise D. Knight (1993).

✧ Cyd Ybarra, "How Writing Saved a Life: A Conversation with Chrystos," *Sojourner* (November 1995).

Circuit, see DANCING, SOCIAL.

Circumstantial Homosexuality

Also called "situational homosexuality." Sexual relations between individuals of the same sex motivated by reasons other than mutual desire or affection. Terms like "circumstantial" and "situational homosexuality" were coined by anthropologists and sociologists to distinguish a wide range of same-sex relations from what most people would consider "lesbian" or "gay" sex—i.e., eroticism between people who self-identify as "gay" or "lesbian." The distinction, which many social historians consider a 20th-century phenomenon (see CONSTRUCTIONISM VS. ESSENTIALISM), has become a key component in the development of a contemporary international lesbian and gay consciousness.

One of the most common examples of circumstantial homosexuality is sex in PRISONS. Most prisoners who have sex with each other, even those who do so willingly, use same-sex intercourse as a substitute for heterosexual relations. According to some studies, as few as 5 percent (or as many as 15 percent, according to others), think of themselves as "gay," "lesbian," or "bisexual," and most resume a heterosexual sex life after they are released.

Other examples of circumstantial homosexuality include erotic play between boys and between girls in sex-segregated schools and sexual practices—especially common among unmarried young men—in societies such as the ARAB WORLD where premarital intermingling of the sexes is virtually prohibited.

Some "straight-identified" men and women also indulge in circumstantial homosexuality for economic reasons. Examples include some male and female sex workers as well as "gay for pay" performers in all-male PORNOGRAPHY.

Ritual Homosexuality

Anthropologists have documented a number of societies in which same-sex relations are compulsory at certain times in persons' lives. One of the most famous examples is the practice of the Sambia, a New Guinea people who believe that boys require the semen of adult males to mature into potent adult males themselves. In theory, all Sambian boys perform oral sex on unmarried young adult males over a period lasting from puberty to their initiation into adulthood, when they in turn become the recipients of oral sex. Once married a few years later, Sambian men are expected to cease all same-sex erotic contact. In fact, however, anthropologists have found that a small percentage of Sambian boys refuse to engage in oral sex with men and that a similar number continue to have furtive same-sex relations even after they are married.

Same-sex eroticism has also been a part of initiation ceremonies and religious rites in some cultures (see **c. 600 B.C.**; **c. 40 B.C.**).

✧ Gilbert H. Herdt, *Ritualized Homosexuality in Melanesia* (1984).

✧ *The Many Faces of Homosexuality: Anthropological Approaches to Homosexual Behavior,* edited by Evelyn Blackwood (1986).

Clarke, Cheryl

(1947–)

U.S. poet, critic, essayist, and activist. Born and raised in Washington, D.C., in a lower-middle-class family that valued education and self-sufficiency, Clark graduated from Howard University and immersed herself in the writings of JAMES BALDWIN, Zora Neale Hurston, Gwendolyn Brooks, AUDRE LORDE, and other AFRICAN-AMERICAN writers. She later entered a graduate English program at Rutgers University in New Jersey and stayed to serve in an administrative capacity.

Following her dramatic staging of the first of her four collections of poetry, *Narratives: Poems in the Tradition of Black Women* (1982), she described her work as "resistance against the destructive, dishonest, stereotyped images projected of black people, particularly black women, particularly women who are lesbians." Clarke has written landmark essays on HOMOPHOBIA in the African-American community. She expresses the rage and hurt experienced by those who, like herself, are members of both communities.

Clarke served on the editorial collective of the lesbian feminist journal *Conditions,* and she has written on the power of sexuality in light of historical implications of the erotic for African-American women and her own growth from a suppressed sexuality to embracing a sexual politics of lesbianism in her poetry.

In a biographical note for her contribution to BARBARA SMITH's collection *Home Girls* (1983), Clark stated: "I count the support and encouragement of women as my primary motivation for writing."

✧ Cheryl Clarke, "The Everyday Life of Black Lesbian Sexuality," in *Inversions: Writings by Dykes, Queers, and Lesbians,* edited by Betsy Warland (1991).

Clarke, Helen Archibald
(1860–1926), and
Porter, Charlotte Endymion
(Helen Charlotte Porter; 1857–1942)

U.S. editors, writers. Both Pennsylvania natives, the two women met in Philadelphia around 1883 after Clarke submitted an article on Shakespeare's use of music to *Shakespeariana,* a publication Porter edited. Sharing a love of Browning as well as of Shakespeare, they became lifelong companions, exchanging rings and living together until Clarke's death in 1926.

In 1889, they founded *Poet Lore* and moved to Boston to manage its publication. "Devoted to Shakespeare, Browning, and the comparative study of literature," *Poet Lore* was through the 1920s one of the most influential "little magazines" in the U.S. Clarke and Porter stopped editing the publication in 1903, but they continued to make frequent contributions under the pen name "H.A.C" (Helen and Charlotte). Besides leading a Browning "movement," they eventually broadened the scope of the publication to include a wide range of international authors.

Porter and Clarke were open about their relationship. In 1910, Porter published *Lips of Music,* a collection of love lyrics inspired by SAPPHO that included verse previously published under a masculine pseudonym, Robert Iphys Everett. She was also the founding president of what was later called the Drama League of America. Clarke was the founder of the American Music Society.

✧ Melvin H. Bernstein, "The Early Years of *Poet Lore,* 1889–1929," *Poet Lore* (Spring 1966).

Clergy, see RELIGIOUS ORDERS.

Cliff, Michelle
(1946–)

Jamaican-born novelist, editor, educator. Cliff has described herself as a "light-skinned colonial girlchild . . . halfway between Africa and England, patriot and expatriate, white and Black." Shortly after her birth, her middle-class family, called "red" to signify a degree of whiteness, moved to New York City for seven years before returning to the West Indies. Later Cliff went back to New York to study European history at Wagner College. She wrote her dissertation on the Italian Renaissance at the Warburg Institute in London.

Cliff has worked in publishing as a copy and production editor and, with life partner ADRIENNE RICH, edited the revolutionary lesbian feminist cultural journal *Sinister Wisdom* (1981–1983). She later became Allen K. Smith Professor of English language and literature at Trinity College, living alternately in Connecticut and California.

Cliff edited LILLIAN SMITH's antiracist writings, *The Winner Names the Age* (1978), before publishing five books of her own writing, including *Claiming an Identity They Taught Me to Despise* (1980), the celebrated novel *Abeng* (1984), and its sequel, *No Telephone to Heaven* (1987). Often blending prose and poetry as well as her native patois and standard English, Cliff explores her identity as a woman of color, a woman, and a lesbian. She writes as a "Jamaica white," reclaiming her West Indian history, including its African roots, to recover the powerful "past bleached from our minds," and memories of individuals like Nanny, a Coromantyn guerrilla fighter from the Windward Maroons, naked but for a necklace of white men's teeth.

In the powerful "If I Could Write This in Fire, I Would Write This in Fire" she expresses her outrage through a litany of brutal abuses toward Africans and her observations as one caught on the margins PASSING (Cliff says "hiding") as white and heterosexual. Cliff describes it as "hiding" from her sources and her survival—"I and Jamaica is who I am."

While some West Indian feminists debate whether Cliff's novels are part of Afrocentric Caribbean discourse, since she as a white creole woman embodies both first and third world sensibilities, critic Belinda Edmondson points out that Cliff is well situated to explore race and GENDER and expose the connections between black history/identity, latent feminism, and revolutionary social consciousness.

✧ Beth Hodges, "An Interview with Michelle Cliff," *Gay Community News* (February 7, 1981).

✧ Belinda Edmondson, "Race, Privilege, and the Politics of (Re)Writing History: An Analysis of the Novels of Michelle Cliff," *Callaloo* (vol. 16, no. 1, 1993, 180–91).

Clinton, Kate

(1951–)

U.S. comedian, writer. Born and raised in Syracuse, New York, Clinton worked as a high school English teacher and began emceeing at women's MUSIC festivals before turning to COMEDY full-time in 1981. Performing for lesbian groups, at clubs, and frequently for major gay and lesbian events—in addition to scoring an off-Broadway hit with her show *Out Is In* (1994)—Clinton has refined a comedic repertory that irreverently takes on the SUBCULTURE, religion (she calls herself a "recovering Catholic"), politicians (the "ethically challenged"), and current events (she dubbed the U.S. MILITARY's don't ask, don't tell policy "a screen door to the closet").

One of the first openly gay or lesbian comics to appear on TELEVISION, Clinton sees lesbian comedy as "humor activism." Women, she says, "have been laughing together for survival for years."

Clinton and activist Urvashi Vaid became lovers in 1988. The two women made PROVINCETOWN their base after 1992. Clinton later began writing for Rosie O'Donnell's TV talk show.

✧ Roz Warren, "Kate Clinton," in *Revolutionary Laughter: The World of Women Comics* (1995).

In 1980, Tom of Finland captured three subtle variations on the clone look.

Clones

Usually pejorative term for gay men, and sometimes lesbians, who slavishly conform to a particular style to the point of being almost indistinguishable from others affecting the same look. "Clone" remains a current term in expressions such as "Chelsea clone" (which refers to the residents of New York City's gayest neighborhood and, from the early 1990s, fairly or unfairly, conjured up an image of a mindless gym addict).

The term was originally used to describe gay men who adopted a style popular from about 1974 through the mid-1980s, the stereotypical components of which were a mustache, a flannel shirt, and tight button-fly jeans, all ideally accentuated by well-developed muscles and a masculine carriage. More than simply a "look," the clone defined an era for gay men. As sociologist Martin P. Levine has written, "gay media, arts, and pornography promoted clones as the first post-Stonewall form of homosexual life. Clones came to symbolize the liberated gay man."

Clones also came to symbolize *belonging.* After recounting his experiences growing up as a misfit in a straight world, DAVID B. FEINBERG concluded his explanation of "Why I Always Wanted to Be a Clone" in his autobiographical novel, *Eighty-Sixed* (1989), with the confession: "Invisibility is what I sought. I've always wanted to be exactly like everyone else. I wanted to blend into a crowd of clones and disappear."

The clone phenomenon started in the gay GHETTOS of San Francisco and New York City but spread quickly all around the world. Rooted in masculine symbols associated with traditional American images of masculinity, the clone look had leather, Western, and military variations. Marking a dramatic break from the hippie styles and the longer-haired, softer fashions then current among straight men, the clone look was a kind of proclamation that from now on, gay men were first and foremost *men,* no matter how often they had been denigrated as effeminate "pansies" in the past.

Some observers found the masculinity of the clone contrived to the point of being off-putting. Many gay men, however, would have agreed with French writer Renaud Camus when he expressed his preference for these "fake butch types" in his 1981 sexual travelogue *Tricks:* "The real ones are a pain in the ass. I like guys who look very male, physically, but who are actually very sweet and nice, and not aggressive at all."

As Camus's comment suggests, clones were for many gay men the ultimate sex symbol of the 1970s. This made them a revolutionary development in the history of gay male HOMOEROTICISM. After decades of idealizing "trade" (sexually available but straight-identified men, usually young and working-class), as exemplified in homoerotic paintings and photographs of sailors and the like, gay men for the first time came to see *themselves* as the most attractive objects of desire. By the end of the clone era, gay male sexuality had been so transformed that even the word "trade" had largely disappeared from gay male slang.

Always criticized in some quarters of the gay and lesbian world (see, for example, the RADICAL FAERIES), the clone phenomenon was excoriated by many commentators with the onset of AIDS, which some blamed on the promiscuity and extensive drug use that were usually part of the clone lifestyle. "Many clones either became sick or died of AIDS," Levine notes. "In fact, more than half the sample of three intensely studied cliques died. The rest were in varying stages of infection and illness. Only a handful tested negative for the HIV antibody."

- Martin P. Levine, "The Life and Death of Gay Clones," in *Gay Culture in America,* edited by Gilbert Herdt (1992).
- Ian Young, *The Stonewall Experiment: A Gay Psychohistory* (1995).

Closet

Term used to describe a state of conscious overt, tacit, or implicit denial of being primarily attracted to one's own sex, as in the expressions "in the closet," "out of the closet," "closet case," "closeted," etc. Historian George Chauncey has found no evidence in American HOMOPHILE publications or lesbian PULP FICTION that "closet" was ever used in a gay or lesbian context before the 1960s. Before STONEWALL, most lesbians and gay men seem to have thought of themselves as "secret" or "open" about their sexuality or as leading or not leading a "double life."

Since Stonewall, however, the "closet" has become one of the most widely used metaphors for the evolution—or nonevolution—of a gay or lesbian consciousness. Most lesbians and gay men experience not one but, rather, a series of closets: one can be "out of the closet" with friends but not family, at home but not at work, in private but not on a public stage, or even everywhere except when surrounded by people who look like queer bashers. Most commonly, people remain in the closet out of fear of negative social, economic, or professional consequences (but see **8/4/1995**).

➤ Also see OUT; OUTING; PASSING.

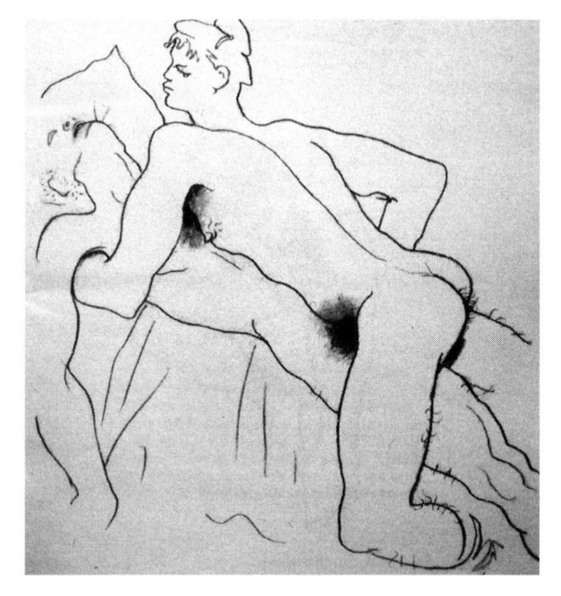

Never ascribed to him in his lifetime, Cocteau's erotic drawings appeared in some published versions of his autobiographical Le Livre Blanc.

Cocteau, Jean

(1889–1963)

French writer, filmmaker, artist. Born to an aristocratic mother and a stockbroker father who died when he was 10, Cocteau ran away from school at 17 after a boy he had been in love with died. In Marseilles, he discovered opium, Turkish BATHS, and sexually available sailors; he then returned to Paris to become the lover of a distinguished actor and man about town, and a close friend and colleague of many gay men and lesbians, including SERGEI DIAGHILEV, GEORGE PLATT LYNES, ANDRÉ GIDE, and JEAN GENET.

For much of his life, his lover and constant companion was Jean Marais, whom he described as an "Antinous sprung from the people" and who became one of the most popular leading men in French cinema of the 1940s and 1950s.

Cocteau worked in virtually every imaginable medium, scoring successes in theater, movies, ballet, poetry, fashion, art, and even interior design. He was elected to the Académie Française in 1955.

He once asserted the importance of knowing "how far one can go too far." Although few believed he was heterosexual, he was deeply closeted in public appearances—despite writing, "I don't want to be tolerated. That offends my love of love and of liberty." He secretly published, however, *Le Livre Blanc* ("The White Book") in 1928, an autobiographical—and often pornographic—account of his affairs with fellow schoolboys and young working-class men.

Exuberantly outgoing, Cocteau met and charmed everyone and was famous for having the wit and *esprit* of a character in a French farce. His last lover was Eduard Dermit, whom he adopted. As he wrote in *Le Livre Blanc,* "Love is to be reinvented."

✧ Arthur King Peters, *Jean Cocteau and His World: An Illustrated Biography* (1986).

Colette (left) performs with Missy, c. 1895.

Colette

(Sidonie Gabrielle Colette; 1873–1954)

French writer. Colette grew up in the country, nurtured by her mother, Sido (Adele-Eugenie-Sidonie), whom she idolized. At the age of 20 she moved to Paris to marry Henry "Willy" Gauthier-Villars. Willy discovered her notebooks of schoolgirl memories, locked her in a room, and forced her to convert them into novels with "a little spice," which he then published under his own name in the best-selling *Claudine* series. Colette later regretted publishing them, feeling they were too close to fact and were guilty of "a thoughtlessness in hurting others." Scholar Elaine Marks says of the series: "In 1900, for the first time since SAPPHO, the narrator Claudine in *Claudine à l'École* looks at another woman as an object of pleasure and without any excuses describes her pleasure. A great revolution had begun."

After twelve difficult years, Colette and Willy separated and Colette began a six-year relationship with "Missy" (Mathilde de Morny, known after her brief marriage as the Marquise de Belboeuf). Missy dressed like a man and was well-known in Paris lesbian circles as "Monsieur Belboeuf."

From about the same time, Colette also became one of NATALIE BARNEY's great loves (Barney appeared as "Flossie" in the *Claudine* series). Colette worked as a bawdy music hall dancer and mime—a career she initiated at a party in Barney's garden. Missy occasionally performed with her as "Yssim," and in 1907, the two women scandalized the Moulin Rouge with "Egyptian Dream," in which Colette, playing a mummy, rose out of a sarcophagus to fall in love with a cross-dressed scholar (Missy/Yssim). Colette seductively peeled off her bandages, danced nearly nude, and nearly provoked a riot when she and Missy joined in a passionate kiss. The Paris police commissioner banned the 15-minute performance.

Colette's largely autobiographical novels are famous for lush characters who prefer passion to goodness. Her writing drew from her fondness and identification with animals (especially cats), nature, and the mysteries and magic of physical love. In *The Pure and the Impure* (1941) she reflected upon the ambiguities of gender and sexual orientation and included groundbreaking sketches of Paris lesbians including Missy (called "La Chevaliere") and RENÉE VIVIEN ("Amalia X"), as well as the 18th-century LADIES OF LLANGOLLEN. Originally titled *Ces Plaisirs* ("These Pleasures"), the sketches were serialized in 1930 in the Paris weekly *Gringoire* until the Christmas Day issue, when the editors abruptly broke the controversial series off in midsentence with the one-word comment *"FIN"* ("the end"). The remaining five installments appeared as part of its publication in book form in 1932. The retitled 1941 edition was published with an introduction by JANET FLANNER. Colette once commented that *The Pure and the Impure* "will perhaps be recognized one day as my best book."

Writing of Colette's pleasure in the natural world, lesbian author and critic JANE RULE observes: "One of the qualities she admired in certain lesbian relationships was the ability of women not only to enjoy the ecstasy of orgasm but to cultivate a more diffused and warm sensuality." In a letter to UNA TROUBRIDGE, RADCLYFFE HALL's lover, Colette explained why she disagreed with THE WELL OF LONELINESS's conception of abnormality: for her, "an abnormal man or woman should never feel abnormal; quite the contrary." Rule also feels, however, that Colette did not believe that women could sustain isolation from men, needing them at least for whipping boys or models.

Although much celebrated—she received the Grand Cross of the Legion of Honor and was named president of the famed Goncourt Academy—Colette remained controversial even in death: condemning her remarriages and scandalous affairs, the Catholic Church refused to allow a cross to be raised over her grave, and no priest was present when she became the first woman honored with a French state funeral.

✧ Jane Rule, *Lesbian Images* (1975).

✧ Elaine Marks, "Lesbian Intertextuality," in *Homosexualities and French Literature: Cultural Contexts/Critical Texts,* edited by George Stambolian and Elaine Marks (1979).

✧ Herbert Lottman, *Colette: A Life* (1991).

Colombia, see LATIN AMERICA.

Coman, Katherine, see BATES, KATHERINE LEE.

Combahee River Collective

AFRICAN-AMERICAN feminist (later, lesbian feminist) group that began meeting in 1974. Initially associated with the Boston-based National Black Feminists Organization, the collective embraced black feminism as "the logical political movement to combat the manifold and simultaneous oppressions that all women of color face." In April 1977, the group issued the influential "Combahee River Collective Statement," committing members to "struggling against racial, sexual, heterosexual, and class oppression . . . based upon the fact that the major systems of oppression are interlocking." This statement of black feminist theory and practice was written by BARBARA SMITH, Beverly Smith, and Demita Frazier in response to a request for a submission to Zillah Eisenstein's anthology, *Capitalistic Patriarchy and the Case for Socialist Feminism*. It was extensively reprinted and circulated, notably at the 1985 U.N. women's conference in Nairobi, Kenya. Barbara Smith writes that the statement marks "the first time in the race's history that Black women refused to hide their sexual orientations in exchange for 'permission' to participate in political struggle."

Besides recording the beginnings of contemporary black feminism, the statement outlined a nonhierarchical structure for the group and a dedication to an ongoing struggle for social revolution. It opposed SEPARATISM, stressing the importance of an inclusive lesbian stance and the need for a broad study of economic and sexual politics. It also addressed the issue of racism within the white women's movement.

The collective, whose work involved hundreds of women, began as a support group, evolved into a political action group, and ended up a study group. One of its most notable achievements was a political action in 1979 that brought together third world and feminist communities to demand more police action and media attention after 12 black women had been murdered in quick succession in Boston. In the course of the action the collective circulated over 30,000 pamphlets in English and Spanish to address this crisis and the larger problem of widespread violence against black women.

The collective was named after the South Carolina site of Harriet Tubman's 1863 guerrilla action to free more than 750 slaves, perhaps the only American military campaign planned and led by a woman.

- ✧ Combahee River Collective, "Twelve Black Women: Why Did They Die?," in *Fight Back: Feminist Resistance to Male Violence,* edited by Frederique Delacoste and Felice Newman (1981).
- ✧ "The Combahee River Collective Statement," in *Home Girls,* edited by Barbara Smith (1983).

Comedy

Since at least the spread of CAMP, one of the gay and lesbian SUBCULTURE's most representative and expressive communications media. Although wit and humor have been associated with gay men and lesbians since OSCAR WILDE, mainstream stand-up comedy remained an almost entirely straight (or closeted) realm until the 1990s. Then, in a series of groundbreaking firsts, lesbian and gay comics began to appear at top comedy clubs across the U.S., on public TELEVISION (KATE CLINTON, KQED's *Comedy Tonight,* 1991), cable shows (Frank Maya, MTV's *Half-Hour Comedy Special,* 1992), and finally on major network programming like *The Arsenio Hall Show* (Lea Delaria, March 1993) and *The Tonight Show* (Bob Smith, July 1994). In the meantime, Comedy Central had earned the highest ratings in its history with the first all-gay and -lesbian comedy special, "Out There" (December 1993). And a year later, in July 1994, Smith and Suzanne Westenhoefer became the first gay and lesbian comics to play solo half-hour specials with back-to-back editions of HBO's *One Night Stand*.

Behind all these "overnight successes" were almost two decades of comedy performances that went virtually unnoticed by straight audiences. One of the first gay or lesbian comics to gain a measure of visibility was Robin Tyler, who joined with Patty Harrison to pioneer feminist comedy in the 1970s. Tyler performed solo on the Showtime cable network as early as 1979 (making her probably the first openly lesbian or gay performer to appear on national U.S. television).

Many of the lesbian comics who are well-known today debuted as emcees at women's MUSIC festivals and other lesbian-friendly events. By the 1980s, comics like Clinton were popular enough to perform entire 45-minute sets at festivals rather than simply filling in between music acts, and local bars and groups began to book lesbian comics on a regular basis.

Gay men had the advantage over lesbians of a better-developed THEATER scene in which they could practice their craft. But because of the time-honored tradition of featuring drag queens as emcees at gay clubs and events, they had comparatively few venues to try stand-up as an OUT comic.

Both lesbians and gay men profited from regularly scheduled "gay comedy nights" at clubs like Ron Lanza and Donald Montwill's Valencia Rose and, later, Josie's Cabaret and Juice Joint, both in San Francisco, which premiered comics like Tom Ammiano, Delaria, and Marga Gomez.

Many lesbians as well as gay men, including Maya and Gomez, developed comic skills giving performance pieces. Emmett Foster toured the U.S. with *Emmett: A One-Mormon Show* in the mid-1980s. Funny Gay Males (Jaffe Cohen, Danny McWilliams, Bob Smith) opened a show off-Broadway in 1989 that ran for two years. And some, like Karen Williams, who performed at mostly black clubs before coming out as one of the few black lesbian comics in the 1980s, garnered experience in alternative corners of the world of comedy.

Wherever they began their careers, it took great courage for performers like Suzy Berger, Maya (who was the first openly gay performer at Caroline's Comedy Club, a major New York City venue), Smith, and Westenhoefer to openly test lesbian and gay humor at straight clubs. Stand-up audiences may not be any more homophobic than fans of other forms of entertainment, but they tend to be much more vociferous in voicing their dislikes. "Bombing" in a stand-up club, where hecklers abound, is a particularly humiliating experience. Still, some gay and lesbian comics actually prefer to play to mostly straight audiences—although Westenhoefer, who is one of them, calls them her "version of S/M."

With a growing assortment of venues and ever larger audiences, lesbian and gay comedy has become increasingly diversified in terms of subject matter as well as styles, ranging from Sara Cytron and writer/partner Harriet Malinowitz's Jewish butch shtick and Carmelita Tropicana's Latina femme comedy to Delaria's bawdy takes on sex ("Q: What do you call it when you masturbate? A: I call it the end of the day"). Pomo African Homos, who premiered at Josie's in San Francisco in 1991, bring a unique brand of black gay male humor to their performance pieces. And Steve Moore

Left to right: Sara Cytron, Kate Clinton, and Lea Delaria, three leading lesbian comics, in 1993.

ventured into completely unexplored territory when he came out as the first openly HIV-positive comedian in the early 1990s.

According to *New York Times* television critic John J. O'Connor, gay and lesbian comics have "a knack of turning the conventional on its head," which may make comedy "a great medium for social change," as Clinton calls it. Viewing stand-up as "playing with power," Williams believes that "when we laugh, we can open up to the issues and begin to work on them."

✧ *Out, Loud, and Laughing,* edited by Charles Flowers (1995).

✧ *Revolutionary Laughter: The World of Women Comics,* edited by Roz Warren (1995).

Comics and Cartoons

Popular artistic and literary media that have played an important role in elaborating and portraying the development of distinctive gay and lesbian SUBCULTURES. Beyond their value as entertainment, lesbian and gay comic strips serve much the same function for their readers that American TELEVISION situation comedies provide for the culture at large. Because, until recently, there were almost no lesbian or gay characters in U.S. television programs—and even less discussion of issues of concern to gay men and lesbians—comics and cartoons have been one of the few ways lesbians and gay men could learn what's in, what's out, and what's being talked—and laughed—about in everyday queer lives. Together with the gay and lesbian press (where they have been a prominent feature), comics have helped build communal identities by inviting readers to recognize themselves and their friends in the strips while making them aware of emerging issues and trends.

History

Cartoonish humor was part of the appeal of the art of TOM OF FINLAND as early as the late 1950s, and the artist's pornographic comic books starring the randy Kake were the first to reach large numbers of gay men all over the world. But according to Rodger Streitmatter, author of *Unspeakable: The Rise of the Gay and Lesbian Press in America,* no gay or lesbian publication featured a regular comic strip until *Drum* magazine, founded in 1966, began featuring A. Jay's (PSEUDONYM of Al Shapiro) "Harry Chess: The Man from A.U.N.T.I.E." Inspired by the spy novels, movies, and TV programs that were popular in the 1960s, Chess was, like James Bond, hirsute, muscular, and never more than a plot twist away from an erotic encounter; unlike Bond, he and his partner, Mickey Muscle, operated in a recognizably gay world populated with characters like Big Bennie the lesbian bartender and limned with CAMP signage like "The Toilet Seat Health Food Bar: Fresh Fruits, Plucky Seafood, Exotic Juices."

The popularity of "Harry Chess" inspired other publications to begin their own humorously erotic strips. At the end of the 1960s, THE ADVOCATE weighed in with Joe Johnson's queenly "Miss Thing" and, a little later, Johnson's king-size "Big Dick." Diametrically opposed, Thing and Dick were, according to cartoonist Gerard Donelan, "both stereotypes, but put them together and you've got every fairy there is."

The advent of GAY LIBERATION persuaded *The Advocate* to banish the newly unfashionable Miss Thing from its pages at the same time that it inspired an explosion of gay comic strip superheroes in local and regional publications. Typical was "Lavender Kid," who appeared in *Gay Flames* (a publication founded by GAY LIBERATION FRONT members in New York City in September 1970). Lavender Kid promoted resistance to oppression as well as promiscuity by rescuing (and invariably seducing) victims of HOMOPHOBIA.

Heterosexual cartoonist Trina Robbins introduced a lesbian main character in *Wimmen's Comix #1* (1972) with her strip, "Sandy Comes Out." Feeling Sandy lacked authenticity, lesbian writer Mary Wings responded with her own visions of lesbian life with *Come Out Comix,* published later in 1972. Four years passed before another lesbian cartoonist, Roberta Gregory, reached a national audience with *Dynamite Damsels* (1976).

The 1970s were also the golden age of "underground comics." Many of these were overtly homophobic and misogynist, but gay and lesbian cartoonists credit them with helping to break taboos and build a larger market for unconventional comics. Through the decade, gay and lesbian comic strips and cartoons appeared mostly in local, regional, and national lesbian and gay publications.

Howard Cruse, whose "Barefootz" was one of the first strips to touch on gay themes in a "mainstream" environment, edited the first four issues of the landmark eleven issue series, *Gay Comix,* beginning in 1980. In 1983,

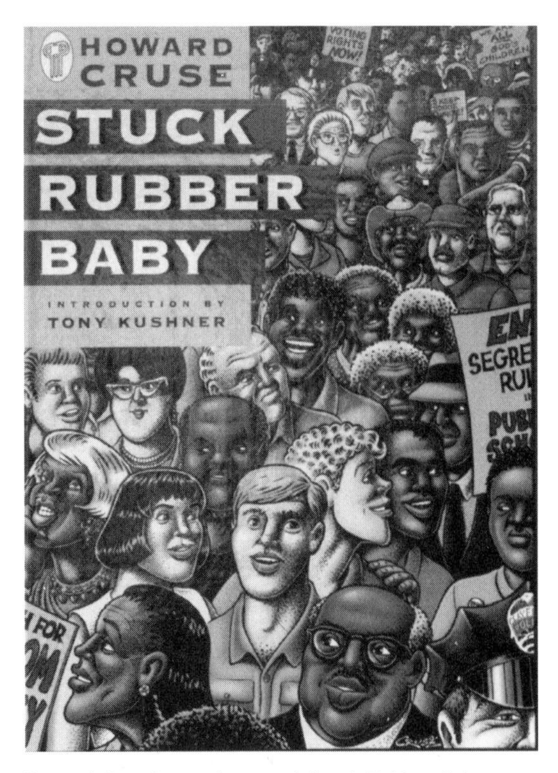

Howard Cruse's graphic novel Stuck Rubber Baby (1995) took gay male comics to a new level of sophistication.

Alison Bechdel began populating the world of comics with "Dykes to Watch Out For" in 1983.

Cruse also introduced the highly influential "Wendel," featuring the writer Wendel Trupstock, one of the first fully developed nonstereotypical gay male comic strip characters. "Wendel" marked a trend toward depicting "real" people in everyday situations; it has since been joined by Tim Barela's West Hollywood couple, Leonard and Larry, and ALISON BECHDEL's "Dykes to Watch Out For."

Although popular male cartoonists (such as Bruce Billings, Rick Campbell, Donelan, Jerry Mills, and many others) outnumbered lesbian artists at the beginning of the 1980s, women came into their own in the late 1980s and, in some ways, surpassed gay men in number and range of syndication. A particularly varied group, popular lesbian cartoonists in the 1990s included Jennifer Camper, Diane DiMassa ("Hothead Paisan"), Fish, Kris Kovick, Andrea Natalie ("Stonewall Riots"), and Noreen Stevens ("The Chosen Family").

Mainstream Comics

Many lesbians and gay men report that comic books like *Batman* and *Wonder Woman* were a rich source of homoerotic fantasies in their childhoods. Overt sexuality of any kind, however, is rare in mainstream comic books produced for children, so many lesbians were surprised when Marvel Comics hinted at woman-loving bonding with its *Sisterhood of Steel* team of martial artists in the late 1970s. Marvel went even further in March 1992, when Canadian superhero Northstar defiantly announced: "Do not presume to lecture me on the hardships homosexuals must bear. No one knows them better than I. For while I am not inclined to discuss my sexuality with people for whom it is none of their business—I am gay!"

Blasting taboos: Diane DiMassa's Hothead Paisan.

Captain Maggie Sawyer of D.C. Comics' Metropolitan Special Crimes Unit.

Although not as explicitly out as Northstar, DC Comics' Metropolis Special Crime Unit Captain Maggie Sawyer was seen by many as a pioneering lesbian role model in her four-issue miniseries published in late 1994.

In newspapers, Andy Lippincott made comic strip history when he came OUT in Garry Trudeau's "Doonesbury" on **February 10, 1976**. More controversial, however, was teenager Lawrence Poirier's coming out in Lynn Johnston's "For Better or for Worse" on **March 22, 1993**.

✧ *Gay Comics,* edited and introduced by Robert Triptow (1989).

✧ *Dyke Strippers: Lesbian Cartoonists A to Z,* edited by Roz Warren (1995).

Coming Out, see OUT.

Community Centers

As of 1996, the gay and lesbian communities had access to special social-service facilities in about 70 locations in the United States and CANADA, ranging from small- and medium-scale resource centers to wide-ranging community services centers with full-time staffs and multimillion-dollar budgets. The SOCIETY FOR INDIVIDUAL RIGHTS opened the first gay community center in the United States in San Francisco in **April 1966**; Canada's first was the Association for Social Knowledge's center in Vancouver, founded on **December 31, 1966**. Sixty-five gay and lesbian community centers across the country joined together in October 1995 to form the National Association of Lesbian and Gay Community Centers. One of the association's aims was to develop new centers in small cities and towns.

Although a few centers specialize in services for women or bisexual, lesbian, and gay YOUTH, most welcome people of all ages across a wide spectrum of "QUEER" identities. Community centers are supported by donations, subscriptions, bequests, corporate sponsorships, and, for some programs, public moneys: the City of West Hollywood, for example, helps fund programs at the Los Angeles Gay and Lesbian Community Services Center, where approximately 80 percent of the $11 million budget comes from government sources.

The Lesbian and Gay Community Services Center in New York City, which *The New York Times* once called "a kind of social and political Grand Central Terminal for gay men and lesbians," is in a former public schoolhouse over 150 years old. Though neither the first nor the oldest, the New York facility claims to be the "largest lesbian and gay community-based organization" in the United States.

Compulsory Heterosexuality

Term popularized in an influential essay written by ADRIENNE RICH in 1979 to designate the complex forces that compel women to lead heterosexual lives. By critiquing compulsory HETEROSEXUALITY as a multifaceted system based on male supremacy over women, Rich hoped to "encourage heterosexual feminists to examine heterosexuality as a political institution which disempowers women—and to change it."

In a foreword added in 1982, Rich wrote that the essay was originally "written in part to challenge the erasure of lesbian existence from so much of scholarly feminist literature," referring to the pervasive presumption of heterosexuality that has kept lesbianism nearly invisible.

The term has come to be used more generally to describe cultural and social practices that coerce men as well as women into believing—and behaving—as if heterosexuality were the only conceivable sexuality.

➤ Also see LESBIAN CONTINUUM.

✧ Adrienne Rich, "Compulsory Heterosexuality and Lesbian Existence," in *The Lesbian and Gay Studies Reader,* edited by Henry Abelove, Michèle Aina Barale, and David M. Halperin (1993).

Confrontationalism, see ASSIMILATIONISM/CONFRONTATIONALISM.

Constructionism vs. Essentialism

Also "social constructionism vs. biological essentialism," opposing points of view on the nature of sexuality and GENDER and their relationship to society and culture. In their purest—and most extreme—forms, essentialism is the belief that sexual orientations are naturally occurring phenomena with an existence (or *essence*) independent of time, place, and social forces; constructionism holds that sociocultural forces impose artificial systems (constructs or *constructions*) of sexuality on people, and that these systems differ radically across time and space. JUDY GRAHN, a leading lesbian author and a radical essentialist, writes: "Gay culture is old, extremely old, and it is continuous. I have found that Gay culture has its traditionalists, its core group, that it is worldwide, and that it has tribal and spiritual roots." In contrast, David M. Halperin, a professor of literature and an equally radical constructionist, speculates that "it may well be that homosexuality properly speaking has no history of its own outside the West or much before the beginning of [the 20th] century."

Halperin's "properly speaking" points to one of the confusing and frustrating elements of the debate between constructionists and essentialists, an element also implied in the name of the most important international conference on the issue, "Homosexuality, Which Homosexuality?," held at the Free University of Amsterdam **December 15–18, 1987**. Depending on the context, the word "homosexuality" may refer to an isolated behavior, a tendency, a psychomedical condition (Halperin's usage), an identity, or, as Grahn defines it, "a way of being." This semantic confusion can obscure the debate to the point that scholars often end up seeming to disagree with each other while actually saying the same thing: Grahn would no doubt be 100 percent in agreement with Halperin that homosexuality is only about a century old if he defined it as a "theory of sexual deviance elaborated by 19th- and 20th-century psychologists."

Paradoxically, this semantic confusion has also resulted in one of the most productive outcomes of the debate. Today, scholars are much more careful than they were in the past to consider the context of sexual behavior and to be wary of surface similarities. To use one well-studied example, most scholars now agree that the most important factor in the ancient Greek "construction" of sexuality was the social status rather than the biological sex of the participants. In ancient GREECE, "normal" sexuality embraced any behavior in which an adult (male) citizen played what the Greeks considered the dominant role (insertion) with someone of lower status, who could be a woman, a male or female slave, or a boy. Other behaviors, such as a male citizen prostituting himself to a foreigner or letting a male slave be the insertor, were condemned or, such as in the case of sex between women, barely worth considering. Recognition of this construction helps clarify, for example, the radical difference between the prosecution of Timarchus (see **346 B.C.**) and the trial of OSCAR WILDE (see **5/25/1895**). Both, in a sense, were accused of "homosexuality" with social inferiors, yet their alleged "crimes"—and the attitudes of their prosecutors—were dramatically different.

Nevertheless, all of this begs the question that is at the root of the constructionism/essentialism debate: Are the categories "GAY," "LESBIAN," "bisexual," and "straight" *natural* (biological, genetic, or spiritual) or *artificial* (social, cultural, or ideological)? Essentialists would say that just because the Greeks did not classify people as homo- or heterosexual does not mean that the categories did not exist—any more than the fact that they knew nothing of blood types means that they were all one type. Constructionists would counter that saying that Plato and SAPPHO were gay is as absurdly anachronistic as calling Hercules a Chippendale's hunk.

For nonacademics, the debate has broad political and cultural ramifications, calling into question, for example, the relevance of modern, Western lesbian and gay identities to non-Western cultures, and even the very future—and value—of those identities in the West. If, as constructionists suggest, one's sense of sexual identity is imposed by sociocultural forces, new "regimes" of sexuality are likely to emerge as those forces evolve.

Although constructionist perspectives dominate LESBIAN AND GAY STUDIES and QUEER THEORY, most scholars have come to recognize the limitations of both points of view. John P. De Cecco and John P. Elia, both scholars of human sexuality, criticize essentialism for reducing human sexuality to a "biological mechanism" and constructionism for portraying "the individual as an empty organism that is filled and shaped by culture and society and is devoid of consciousness and intention." They instead propose an alternative perspective "that views sexual and gender expression as a product of complementary biological, personal, and cultural influences."

Background

Throughout the 19th century, writers like HEINRICH HOESSLI, KARL HEINRICH ULRICHS, and JOHN ADDINGTON SYMONDS sought to discredit their societies' condemnation of HOMOEROTICISM by arguing that many of the most respected luminaries of the past had indulged in it, and that it had been a positive feature of advanced cultures, most notably that of ancient Greece. By the end of the century, even medical researchers who thought that homoeroticism was a sign of "degeneracy" were mostly in agreement that "homosexuality" (as it had come to be called—see **5/6/1868**) was an age-old phenomenon that occurred more or less frequently in virtually all societies. At the same time, the definition of homosexuality was complicated by a growing tendency to link it—or even conflate it—with gender nonconformity. An enormous body of writing, pro and con, became available on the subject and gave rise to a multitude of popular "constructions" of homosexuality, the most prestigious of which were so-called medical models that sought to explain homosexuality as "caused" by biological or psychological processes.

British sociologist Mary McIntosh is generally credited with being the first to question the scientific validity of classifying or "labeling" people as homosexual or heterosexual. In an influential 1968 article entitled "The Homosexual Role," she asserted that "social labeling of persons as deviant" functions as "a mechanism of social control" by providing "a clear-cut, publicized and recognizable threshold between permissible and impermissible behaviour" and by working "to segregate the deviants from others." Thus, "the creation of a specialized, despised and punished role of homosexuality keeps the bulk of society pure in rather the same way that the similar treatment of some kinds of criminals helps keep the rest of society law-abiding."

McIntosh's article, published in English, coincidentally echoed many of the same ideas that were then emerging in French in the writings of MICHEL FOUCAULT. Foucault, however, later went a step further and actually gave a year, 1870 (based on the publication, actually in **1869**, of Dr. Karl von Westphal's article on "contrary sexual feeling"), when this social role first emerged. In a now famous passage in *History of Sexuality* (**1976**), Foucault declared: "As defined by the ancient civil or canonical codes, sodomy was a category of forbidden acts; their perpetrator was nothing more than a juridical subject of them. The nineteenth-century homosexual became a personage, a past, a case history. . . . Sodomy had been a temporary aberration; the homosexual was now a species."

Foucault's *History of Sexuality* was first published in English in the U.S. in November 1978. Much more typical of gay and lesbian publication trends at the time was Arthur Evans's *Witchcraft and the Gay Counterculture,* also published in 1978. Evans's book was only the latest in an onslaught of fundamentally "essentialist" books, including JONATHAN NED KATZ's *Gay American History* (1976), that foraged through the distant past in search of "gay" roots. The popularity of these books set the stage for an often vituperative confrontation when British historian and theorist Jeffrey Weeks and many others began to advance contrary, social constructionist views similar to McIntosh's and Foucault's.

In the 1980s, constructionism came to dominate lesbian and gay studies. As Celia Kitzinger observes, "Both sides of the debate were named by the social constructionists, and 'essentialist' quickly became a term of abuse, with scholars so labeled eager to defend themselves against the charge." The result was a continuum of constructionist ideas, from the inarguable observation that modern homosexuality has characteristics unique to modern times to an almost metaphysical questioning of the very knowability of sex and gender ("the very idea of scientific progress," according to psychologist Ken Gergen, "is a literary achievement"). In between were attempts such as sociologist David F. Greenberg's and anthropologist/sociologist Stephen O. Murray's to categorize and compare different constructions of sexuality through history and around the world.

Some gay and lesbian intellectuals, like philosopher Richard D. Mohr, have vociferously objected to constructionism and argued that it is out of touch with the realities of lesbian and gay life. And, as Kitzinger points out, "most of psychology retains a strong commitment to essentialism," an observation that is equally valid for BIOLOGY. These objections aside, the main result of the constructionism vs. essentialism debate has been less the stifling of essentialist voices than the proliferation of approaches to lesbian and gay studies witnessed by the ever widening scope of the field.

➤ Also see ANTHROPOLOGY; BISEXUALITY; BOSWELL, JOHN; GAY; LESBIAN; PSYCHOLOGY; and SOCIOLOGY.

✧ David F. Greenberg, *The Construction of Homosexuality* (1988).

✧ David M. Halperin, *One Hundred Years of Homosexuality* (1990).

✧ Judy Grahn, *Another Mother Tongue: Gay Words, Gay Worlds* (1990).

✧ *Forms of Desire: Sexual Orientation and the Social Constructionist Controversy,* edited by Edward Stein (1992).

✧ Richard D. Mohr, *Gay Ideas: Outing and Other Controversies* (1992).

✧ *If You Seduce a Straight Person, Can You Make Them Gay?: Issues in Biological Essentialism versus Social Constructionism in Gay and Lesbian Identities,* edited by John P. De Cecco and John P. Elia (1993).

✧ Celia Kitzinger, "Social Constructionism: Implications for Lesbian and Gay Psychology," in *Lesbian, Gay, and Bisexual Identities over the Lifespan: Psychological Perspectives,* edited by Anthony R. D'Augelli and Charlotte J. Patterson (1995).

Cooper, Dennis

(1953–)

U.S. writer. A Pasadena native, Cooper creates characters uniquely acclimatized to the postmodern wastelands of greater Los Angeles. Disturbingly casual, almost comically disengaged, his gay male characters matter-of-factly smell, taste, torture, murder, and disembowel one another in quest not of sadistic pleasure or even of cheap thrills but, rather, of "information"—as Dennis in *Frisk* calls the feces sample he requests from a callboy. Although some characters (such as Ziggy in *Try,* who has been adopted by two gay fathers) have been the objects of sexual aggression as children, Cooper is less interested in explaining what turns his characters into masochists, sadists, or voyeurs than in exploring what they learn—and cannot learn—from the carnage they crave. Ultimately, his work is about the insatiable need to know in an unknowable world and the impossibility of connecting to another person when one's own sense of self is fragmented beyond repair.

One of the leading gay innovators of transgressive fiction, Cooper has a growing cult following, especially among young gay and lesbian readers. He issued his first works of poetry as chapbooks in the 1970s, published with FELICE PICANO's SeaHorse Press during the same decade, and owned and directed *Little Caesar* magazine (1976–1978) and its press (1978–1982). After several years in New York and an extended stay in Europe, Cooper settled in Venice, California, where he runs a creative writing center. His published works include the novels *Safe* (1984) and *Closer* (1989); the collections of poems and short prose *The Tenderness of Wolves* (1982) and *Wrong* (1988); and a book of poetry, *Idols* (1979). In 1995, a film version of *Frisk* appeared.

✧ Edmund White, "The Lost Boys," *Times Literary Supplement* (April 1989).

Corelli, Marie

(pseudonym of Mary Mackay; 1855–1924)

English romantic novelist. Mackay seems to have intentionally cultivated confusion about her early life, even retailing a self-manufactured "baby in a basket on a doorstep" legend.

She was probably the illegitimate daughter of a London couple who remained unmarried until she was nine. There is no reason to doubt her assertion that "as a child, I was one of the most solitary ever born."

She changed her name to Marie Corelli to pursue a career as a pianist but, encouraged by George Meredith, began earning a living for herself and her father by writing instead. Working spiritualism, mythology, and scientific phenomena as well as personal problems into her romantic fiction, she reigned as the world's best-selling writer for 30 years. Typical of her 34 published works, half of which were best-sellers, was *The Treasures of Heaven* (1906), which sold 100,000 copies on its first day in print. She appealed to readers as diverse as Queen Victoria and OSCAR WILDE.

Corelli was a prickly personality by all accounts. She insisted on celebrity treatment in Stratford-upon-Avon, where from 1876 until her death she lived with her companion, Bertha Vyver. Their ROMANTIC FRIENDSHIP seems to have been more obviously intimate than most: they would spend entire evenings out in public with their arms around each other. Corelli wore a ring given to her by Vyver (whom she called "Adrian" or "my man Friday") and commissioned a bas-relief of a heart over their fireplace with their initials and the inscription *"Amor Vincit."*

✧ Brian Masters, *Now Barabbas Was a Rotter: The Extraordinary Life of Marie Corelli* (1978).

Corinne, Tee A.

(1943–)

U.S. artist, writer, editor, educator. A Florida native, Corinne was educated in her home state and at the Pratt Institute (M.F.A., 1968) in New York. In the 1970s, she moved to California and worked at the San Francisco Sex

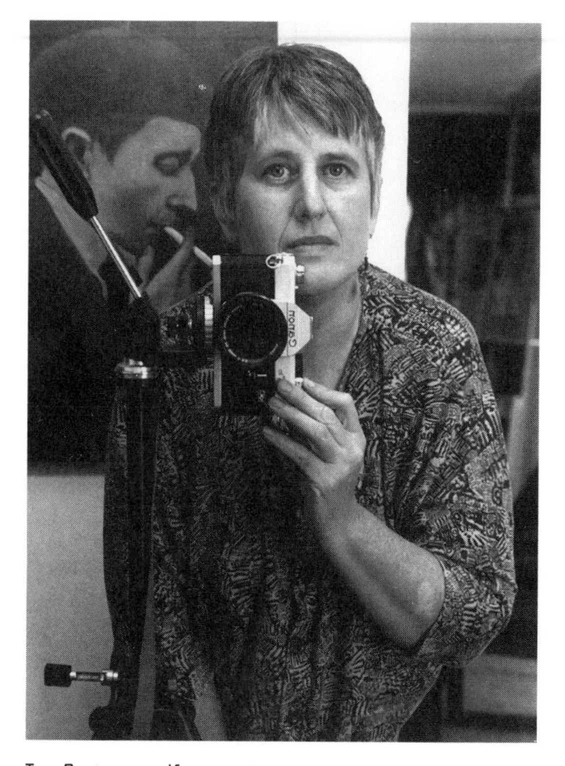

Tee Corinne, self-portrait.

Information Switchboard, a unique hotline established to give nonjudgmental answers to any and all questions about sex. While working there, Corinne, photographer Honey Lee Cottrell (her lover at the time and a frequent collaborator in the decades since), and Oscar-nominated director Ann Hershey made the first lesbian sex education FILM, *We Are Ourselves.*

In the mid-1970s, years before the lesbian SEX WARS, Corinne emerged as a prominent advocate of lesbian HOMOEROTICISM in the fine arts. She published the revolutionary drawings in the *Cunt Coloring Book* in 1975, contributed 16 color studies of female genitalia to Cottrell's *I Am My Lover* (an innovative masturbation manual), and toured the country giving a slide lecture entitled "Lesbian Sexual Imagery in the Fine Arts," which was perhaps the first such presentation that was both prosex and proactively lesbian. In 1977, she created a best-selling lesbian erotic poster, a copy of the cover she had done for the third issue of the journal *Sinister Wisdom*. In **August 1979**, she was one of the exhibitors at "The Great American Lesbian Art Show." In 1981, she co-founded, with her lover at the time, novelist Lee Lynch, and others, *Blatant Image/A Magazine of Feminist Photography*. And in 1982, she debuted a one-woman collection of erotica which was later published with Jacqueline Lapidus as *Yantras of Womanlove: Diagrams of Energy*.

Corinne's work is noted (and sometimes disparaged) for its lush romanticism, but she has also been a pioneer in celebrating the sensuality of fat, old, disabled, and, as she calls them, "old-gay" BUTCH women. She is probably best known for her mastery of manipulating photographic techniques like solarization, a process she began using partly to safeguard her models' privacy but also to make her images "look the way sex feels, very magical and mysterious." She has also pointed out that no publication would accept her *un*solarized lesbian erotica until 1984.

In 1984, Corinne's short story "The Drainage Ditch" (published under the PSEUDONYM Giselle Commons in Lonnie Barbach's *Pleasures: Women Write Erotica*) launched a second career as a writer and editor of lesbian erotica. One of her most notable achievements in print was the Lambda Literary AWARD–winning anthology *Intricate Passions: A Collection of Erotic Short Fiction* (1989).

Corinne is one of the most visible and accessible lesbian artists in the world. Her work can be seen on the covers of more than 50 Naiad publications, in PAT CALIFIA's landmark *Sapphistry: The Book of Lesbian Sexuality* (1980), and in prints, collections, and exhibitions of her imaginative portraits of literally hundreds of lesbian writers, activists, and fictional heroines.

✧ *Nothing but the Girl: The Blatant Lesbian Image*, edited by Susie Bright and Jill Posener (1996).

Cory, Donald Webster

(pseudonym of Edward Sagarin; 1913–1986)

U.S. writer, sociologist. Born in Schenectady, New York, "Cory" began having sex with boys as an adolescent but learned that there were other people who actually preferred their own sex only when a teacher told him about "inverts" during his senior year in high school. Self-characterized as short, "hunchbacked," and Jewish, he managed through psychoanalysis to find contentment both as a gay man and as a husband and father: he believed that only "maladjusted homosexuals" refused to get married.

In the 1940s, his observations of the National Association for the Advancement of Colored People (NAACP) and reading of Gunnar Myrdal's influential book on racial issues, *An American Dilemma* (1944), inspired him to conceive of gay people as a persecuted "minority," an idea never before articulated in print, at least in the U.S. Like racism and anti-Semitism, he believed, prejudice against gay people was rooted in ignorance and misunderstanding. To advance his views, he began corresponding with HARRY HAY and Chuck Rowland in the late 1940s and in **1951** published *The Homosexual in America* under the PSEUDONYM Donald Webster Cory ("Cory" and "Don" from ANDRÉ GIDE's essay *Corydon*, "Webster" after the American orator and politician).

A manifesto as well as a memoir of his 25 years' experience of same-sex love, *The Homosexual in America* was the first widely read book to reveal the geography, mores, and vernacular of the postwar gay SUBCULTURE. It saw six printings through 1956 (although a New York court ordered its publisher, Greenberg, never to issue another book on homosexuality). Historians stress its introduction of the "minority" concept and its call for gay men to "rise up and demand" their rights. Its most notable short-term effect, however, was to increase public awareness of gay life.

Through the 1950s, Cory was hailed as a hero of the HOMOPHILE movement. He gave speeches to MATTACHINE groups, started the mail-order Cory Book Service to make publications on homosexuality more widely available, and served as an editor for ONE magazine and, in the early 1960s, as a board member of the New York Mattachine Society. He also published *The Homosexual and His Society: A View from Within* (with John P. LeRoy, 1963) and the highly sensational but relatively sympathetic *The Lesbian in America* (1964).

His activism notwithstanding, Cory gradually but drastically revised his views on homosexuality. As early as 1954, he began comparing homosexuality not to an ethnic identity but to alcoholism—an innate, incurable problem that needed to be controlled so that gay men and lesbians could fit into heterosexual society as responsible citizens. In a 1964 speech to a DAUGHTERS OF BILITIS convention, he blasted homophile activists for their "defensive, neurotic, disturbed denial" that homosexuality was a disease. Lesbians and gay men, he later wrote, were "frequently borderline psychotics."

As more and more people in the homophile movement rejected the disease model of homosexuality, Cory found himself shunted to the sidelines. In 1965, FRANK KAMENY wrote that he was "no longer the vigorous Father of the Homophile Movement . . . but the senile Grandfather." The following year, Cory emerged as the Wicked Stepfather: to earn a Ph.D. in sociology at New York University he submitted a thesis that was a scathing attack on the New York Mattachine Society.

Cory, who worked in the cosmetics and fragrance industry from 1939 to 1961, pursued a career in academic life from the early 1960s. Using his real name, Edward Sagarin, he taught at the City College of New York and continued to publish antigay articles in sociology journals through the 1970s.

✧ Edward Sagarin, *Structure and Ideology in an Association of Deviants* (1966).

✧ Toby Marotta, *The Politics of Homosexuality* (1981).

Costa Rica, see LATIN AMERICA.

Counterculture

Subculture that emerged in Western countries in the mid-1960s and greatly influenced the character and course of GAY LIBERATION. Its values and mores ran *counter* to those of mainstream society: participants emphasized pleasure over the work ethic, self-exploration over materialistic ambition, mutual understanding ("relating") and pacifism over confrontation, and sexual liberation and communal living over traditional "family values."

Unlike the New Left, the 1960s political movement with which it had strong links, the counterculture was more a lifestyle than an ideology. Many of those who embraced the counterculture "dropped out" of mainstream society to become what the media called "hippies" or what counterculturists themselves tended to call "freaks." Although New Leftists and counterculturists alike voiced opposition to racism, sexism, and puritanism, both groups tended to blame these problems on the business and political leaders (the "establishment") who ran society. Their HOMOPHOBIA, however, could be remarkably similar to the establishment's. Drug guru Timothy Leary, for example, recommended LSD in a 1966 *Playboy* interview as a "cure" for the "perversion" of homosexuality.

As a result of confrontations between the (mostly white, straight) men who dominated the counterculture and those who felt ignored or slighted by them, the counterculture became increasingly fractured. AFRICAN-AMERICANS, feminists, and eventually gay men and lesbians independently developed their own distinctive versions of the counterculture.

➤ Also see GAY LIBERATION FRONT; LESBIAN FEMINISM.

- Toby Marotta, *The Politics of Homosexuality* (1981).
- Dennis Altman, *Homosexual: Oppression and Liberation* (1971; reissue, 1993).

Coward, Noël

(1899–1973)

English playwright, lyricist, performer. Born into a show business family, Coward began acting as a child. In the 1920s, he became one of the most acclaimed writers of sophisticated comedies and witty lyrics in the English-speaking world, with major hits that included *Hay Fever* (1925), *Private Lives* (1930), and *Design for Living* (1932).

Offstage, Coward embodied the arch but charming, sexually ambiguous personalities of his most famous male characters. An intimate of everyone from Humphrey Bogart to the Queen Mother, his gayness, though an open secret, was always discreet and unprovocative. Over the years, especially after he launched a second career as a cabaret performer in the 1950s, he came to epitomize the post–OSCAR WILDE, pre-STONEWALL gay socialite, a "homosexual gentleman" so amusing that it would

Left to right, Alfred Lunt, Noël Coward, and Lynn Fontanne cavort in a scene from Coward's Design for Living.

have been in bad taste to pass moral judgment on his "private lives."

Despite having written songs like "Mad About the Boy" (1932), Coward seems to have believed that his public was unsure about his sexuality. Writing in his diary in 1955, he lamented that after his death there would be "books proving conclusively that I was homosexual and books proving equally conclusively that I was not." To date, no writer has attempted the latter task.

✧ Cole Lesley, *Remembered Laughter* (1976).

Crane, [Harold] Hart
(1899–1932)

U.S. poet. Crane's troubled relationships with his cold, businesslike father and his unstable, demanding mother have been cited by some biographers as keys to understanding the difficulties not only of his adult life but also of his poetry: some critics believe he purposely wrote in an opaque style to conceal his HOMOEROTICISM from his parents as well as the uninitiated general reading public. Crane himself explained his evocative but mystifying imagery as the triumph of the "logic of metaphor" over "so-called pure logic."

Crane published his first poems in Greenwich Village literary magazines in 1916 and moved back and forth between New York and his native Ohio over the next decade. He struggled to make ends meet with subsidies from his family and income from a variety of jobs, most frequently in ADVERTISING, before publishing two books of poems, *White Buildings* (1926) and *The Bridge* (1930), that helped earn him a Guggenheim fellowship. He also traveled to California, Europe, MEXICO, KEY WEST, and other parts of the CARIBBEAN. Everywhere he went, he became as famous for his riotous drinking as for his poetry.

Crane had his first sexual experiences with men while still a teenager. His adult sex life, revealed in detail in his private papers and the memoirs of acquaintances, has become almost legendary. Like many gay men of his era, Crane was sexually obsessed with sailors. He had extended relationships with a few of them, including Emil Opffer, a handsome blond Danish sea captain who inspired six poems Crane entitled "Voyages" (1921–1926). Crane wrote a friend that he and Opffer had achieved "indestructibility . . . where flesh became transformed through intensity of response to counter-response, where sex was beaten out, where a purity of joy was reached that included tears."

During a stay in Mexico in 1932, Crane turned from the pursuit of local young men to Peggy Cowley, the soon-to-be ex-wife of his friend Malcolm Cowley, and began his first heterosexual affair. Traveling back to the U.S. by sea, the lovers quarreled and Crane threw himself into a drinking binge that led to his getting badly beaten by sailors he had attempted to seduce. Shortly before noon the next day, he appeared on deck, removed his jacket, and matter-of-factly jumped into the ocean.

For several decades after Crane's suicide, biographers and critics either passed over his homosexuality or entombed him as yet another "doomed homosexual." One biographer, John Unterecker, actually lauded his affairs with men as examples of "Platonic love." As late as 1993, a major gay reference book described him as sexually frustrated and "lonely most of his life," ignoring the evidence in his published correspondence of deep friendships and practically daily sexual encounters. More recently, Thomas E. Yingling and others have suggested that his life and work provide testimony of the emergence of a conscious, if tragic, homosexual identity. They point out that his first published poem, "C 33" (1916), takes its title from OSCAR WILDE's prison cell number and that his work constantly shows an awareness of WALT WHITMAN and Whitman's "love of comrades." Hailing him as, after Whitman, the second great gay American poet, they have reinterpreted his poems in light of his homosexuality, which Yingling believes was "socially and psychically designed as an unlivable existence."

Perhaps Crane himself best captured his dilemma and his artistic response in the first lines of "C 33": "He has woven rose-vines / about the empty heart of night. . . ."

➤ Also see HARTLEY, MARSDEN.

✧ John Unterecker, *Voyager: A Life of Hart Crane* (1969).

✧ Thomas E. Yingling, *Hart Crane and the Homosexual Text: New Thresholds, New Anatomies* (1990).

Crisp, Quentin

(Denis Crisp, 1908–)

English writer, actor, wit. The man who reconstructed himself as "one of the stately homòs of England" was born in Surrey, educated on scholarship at a public school, and briefly studied journalism in London before resigning himself to the realization that "his great gift was for unpopularity." Living with his parents, Crisp ventured out into London's West End, where he met kindred spirits and began to have an active, sometimes even lucrative, sex life. "The men of the twenties," he later wrote, "searched themselves for vestiges of effeminacy as though for lice," but Crisp opted instead for henna, mascara, lipstick, and nail polish, becoming "not merely a self-confessed homosexual, but a self-evident one." As a result, he was ridiculed, insulted, and, not infrequently, physically assaulted.

Transgender activist and writer Leslie Feinberg (seated at left) interviews Quentin Crisp.

With the 1968 publication and 1975 TELEVISION adaptation of his memoir, *The Naked Civil Servant* (a reference to a brief career as a nude model for art classes), Crisp became the most "self-evident" gay man in England. A PBS broadcast in 1976 extended his celebrity to the U.S., and he eagerly expatriated himself to the country whose uniformed "bundles for Britain" he had so enjoyed during WORLD WAR II ("Never in the history of sex was so much offered to so many by so few"). Sometimes vilified by British gay men for projecting the "wrong image," Crisp found a kind of acceptance, even veneration, in New York City, despite his aversion to politics and the occasional contretemps, as when he once dismissed AIDS as a "fashionable disaster." He has made frequent public appearances, written several other books, worked as a film critic for *Christopher Street* and reigned as Queen Elizabeth I in the 1992 film version of VIRGINIA WOOLF's *Orlando.* In 1987, the singer Sting paid tribute to Crisp with "Englishman in New York," a song whose refrain runs: "Be yourself, no matter what they say."

Cross-Dressing

Term coined by EDWARD CARPENTER for the practice of women dressing as men or men dressing as women. "Transvestism," a word coined by MAGNUS HIRSCHFELD from the Latin roots for "cross" and "dressing," has much the same meaning but has come to convey negative nuances due to its association with PSYCHOLOGY. Forms of cross-dressing related to lesbian and gay traditions include drag, costuming oneself as a member of the other biological sex (usually) for theatrical or humorous effect; PASSING, disguising oneself to live in society as a man (if a woman) or a woman (if a man); and GENDER-bending, mixing "male" and "female" styles or physical characteristics (such as a bra worn over a hairy chest) to demonstrate the arbitrary nature of "femininity" and "masculinity."

People have probably cross-dressed ever since the first group of human beings decided that men and women should dress differently. Of the hundreds of reasons that someone might want to wear the other sex's clothes—from curiosity to envy—only a few have anything to do with same-sex eroticism, and historians of sexuality emphasize that in many cultures and eras the two were not linked. Even today, one common form of cross-dressing—wearing the clothes of the other sex to become sexually aroused—is usually associated

Unlike heterosexual cross-dressing, which usually has an element of erotic fetishism, gay male cross-dressing may "bend" or "blend" gender signals.

with heterosexual males. Many of the most famous cross-dressers in history—such as Edward Hyde, Viscount Cornbury, a colonial governor of New York and New Jersey; the 18th-century spy Chevalier d'Eon; or even Joan of Arc—left no record of being attracted to their own sex. In some cultures, cross-dressing was thought to have a spiritual significance; by cross-dressing, one transcended the confines of one's own biological sex and was thus better qualified to communicate with the spirit world. This "pagan" practice is probably why there is a proscription against cross-dressing in the BIBLE and why it was associated with heresy (but not sexual deviance) in the early Middle Ages.

In a large number of cultures, however, homosexuality has come to be associated with gender nonconformity and, as a result, cross-dressing. As "third sex" theories of homosexuality became common in the late 19th century (see KARL HEINRICH ULRICHS and MAGNUS HIRSCHFELD), stereotypes of effeminate "fairies" and "mannish lesbians" predominated, at least in popular representations of gay men and lesbians. Much of the history of gay and lesbian life in the 20th century has been about resisting, accommodating, or subverting these stereotypes.

✧ Marjorie Garber, *Vested Interests: Cross-Dressing and Cultural Anxiety* (1993).

Cruising

Scouting sexual partners. A late-fifth-century (c. 420 B.C.) play by Theopompus, surviving only in a fragment, has Mount Lykabettus, a hill on the outskirts of Athens, say: "Beside me, young men [*meirakion*—i.e., in their early 20s] too far advanced in years give themselves to their coevals." There may have been brothels there, or else this may be the first evidence of an outdoor Central Park Ramble–style cruising ground.

In the Middle Ages and the Renaissance, the streets near or the porches of churches served as gay cruising areas. The porch of Santa Maria Mater Domini, a church in Venice, was a popular gay gathering place in the 15th century. According to court records

Drag kings strut their stuff in the "It's Just a Drag" march in New York City.

Tom of Finland envisioned this cruising scene in 1968.

made during a wave of persecution in 18th-century Holland (see **1730**), men seeking sex with other men knew that certain areas of Dutch cities were gathering places for similarly minded men and boys. Among these were the most public areas—streets and back alleys near town halls, cathedrals, and markets—as well as clandestine meeting spots, such as beneath certain bridges. Public toilets or urinating spots such as fences were reported as meeting spots in other places.

London's Moorfields in the 18th century had an area called Sodomites' Walk because it was such an active cruising ground. Police hired agents provocateurs to entrap men who cruised there, a practice that continued through the early 19th century.

In WORLD WAR II—as reported by sources as diverse as GORE VIDAL and TOM OF FINLAND—the concentration of men in uniform in large cities led to the highest density and frequency of cruising opportunities in history.

WALT WHITMAN, for his part, memorialized the communicative element of cruising as "the talk of the turning eyeballs."

Cruz, Sor Juana Inés de la

(Juana Inés de Asbaje; 1651–1695)

Mexican poet. Probably illegitimate, young Juana astounded her mother and, later, the viceroy's court in Mexico City with her remarkable aptitude for everything from Latin to geometry. At the age of 16, she took vows as Sor (Sister) Juana Inés de la Cruz. As a nun she was free to study the more than 4,000 books she collected in her cell and to write poems and plays that earned her a reputation in Europe and Spanish America as one of the greatest lyric poets of the age. In her work as in her

Sor Juana Inés de la Cruz.

life, she acknowledged being "*en dos partes dividida* (divided in two parts)," torn between passion and reason, sensuality and religious devotion. Contemporaries gossiped about her liaisons with other nuns and the viceroy's wife, but it was her audaciously brilliant verse that proved her undoing. In 1691, Archbishop Aguiar y Seixas, a notorious puritan and misogynist, ordered her silenced and stripped of her books, writing utensils, and musical instruments. She died four years later, at the age of 43, while attending victims of a plague.

Sor Juana's sexuality has been a matter of controversy for centuries. Critics such as Octavio Paz have asserted that the homoerotic elements in her work are simply literary conventions, while contemporary Mexican lesbian writers claim her as their foremother. (El Clóset de Sor Juana, for example, is a major Mexican lesbian advocacy group.) No one, however, disputes her genius, nor her status as one of the first European-Americans to honor what she called the "*mágicas infusiones* (magical infusions)" of NATIVE AMERICAN cultures.

Cuba

No laws against consensual same-sex relations between adults unless they give "public scandal," which is punishable by prison sentences of up to 12 months. Nascent rights organization and wide-ranging social scene in Havana.

In 1986, Cuban exile Armando Valladares wrote, "There have been few examples of repression of homosexuals in history as virulent as in Cuba." Two years later, an INTERNATIONAL LESBIAN AND GAY ASSOCIATION document stated that the mere "public expression of homosexuality" was punishable by prison sentences of up to 20 years. These and a host of other accounts by Cubans and non-Cubans alike have given Cuba a worldwide reputation for HOMOPHOBIA and repression.

The reality of gay and lesbian life in Cuba, according to Ian Lumsden and other recent visitors, is more complicated. While it is a fact that thousands of gay men and an unknown number of lesbians were incarcerated in the 1960s and 1970s, lesbian and gay Cubans in the 1990s are more constrained by economic factors than by official actions. Although they have access to a varied assortment of CRUISING areas and entertainments (ranging from gay- and lesbian-themed movies, plays, and even television programs to privately organized Saturday-night queer "fiestas"), severe overcrowding makes privacy—let alone an apartment in which lovers can live together—hard to come by. Ironically, the earlier oppressive policies of the government may have been a factor in galvanizing a stronger sense of a shared *entendido* (literally, "understood"), or "gay," identity than in most of the rest of LATIN AMERICA.

Despite several decades of Communist rule, traditional Latin American GENDER codes—machismo for men and subservient *marianismo* (emulation of the Virgin Mary) for women—are still strong in Cuba. Yet observers note a higher degree of tolerance for nonconformity in Cuba, especially among younger, better educated urbanites. And HATE CRIME, which has reached tragic proportions in much of the rest of Latin America, is said to be almost unknown in Cuba.

Celebrated lesbians, gay men, and bisexuals of Cuban origin include musicians Amaury Pérez, Xiomara Laugart, and the internationally popular Pablo Milanés, who released Cuba's first gay protest song, "El Pecado Original" ("Original Sin"), in 1994; and writers Magaly Alabau, REINALDO ARENAS, Achy Obejas, Virgilio Piñera, Severo Sarduy, and René Vasquez Diaz.

History
Little is known about the Carib Indians who inhabited Cuba before the island was conquered by Spain in the 16th century, but some missionaries left shocked reports of "sodomitical" practices among them. On at least one occasion, Spanish colonists castrated offenders and forced them to eat their own testicles. Later, the Spanish INQUISITION is recorded to have prosecuted 18 "effeminate" men in a trial held in Havana's Plaza de Armas.

In the 18th and 19th centuries, Cuba developed into one of the leading producers of sugar, importing huge numbers of African slaves and, later, indentured Chinese workers to work in the fields. Field-workers were mostly men: male slaves outnumbered female slaves two to one; fewer than 1 percent of Chinese immigrants were female. As a result, both groups acquired a reputation for same-sex relations, and homosexuality acquired the additional stigma of being associated with slavery.

In the 20th century, Havana became an internationally notorious playground, famous as much for the ready availability of all varieties of sex as for its balmy climate and colorful nightlife. Nevertheless, discontent with the decadence and corruption of the old regime was widespread. After Fidel Castro's successful revolution in 1959, most Cubans supported the government's campaign to "clean up" the country.

Persecution of gay men and lesbians began with Operación P (see **1960**) against prostitutes, pimps, and "pederasts"; it was expanded in the following years with the incarceration of thousands of "known" and suspected gay men and lesbians in labor camps. At the same time, the government launched a massive purge of gay and lesbian intellectuals and artists from government-supported institutions. In 1971, the government formalized this policy with the issue of a new labor code that made it illegal for "known homosexuals" to pursue careers in education, sports, and medicine (restrictions that, although largely unenforced, remain on the books today).

Tens of thousands of lesbians and gay men were among the Cubans who fled the country, most notably at the time of the Mariel exodus (see **4/14/1980**). In exile, writers like Arenas publicized the plight of gay men and lesbians in Cuba, and the country became the focus of protests by international gay and lesbian rights organizations.

Partly as a result of criticism from abroad but more probably part of a generalized relaxation of censorship and government restrictions in Cuba, official repression of lesbians and gay people substantially decreased in the late 1980s and early 1990s. The government began to allow openly homoerotic productions of plays like FEDERICO GARCÍA LORCA's *El Público* and the release of sympathetic films like *Fresa y Chocolate* (1993, *Strawberry and Chocolate*), as well as access to gay and lesbian books and films from abroad.

One sign of improvement was the formation of the Gay and Lesbian Association of Cuba, which issued a manifesto on July 28, 1994, and called for an annual celebration of the date as the Gay Pride Day of Cuba.

✧ Ian Lumsden, *Machos, Maricones, and Gays: Cuba and Homosexuality* (1996).

Cullen, Countee

(Countee Leroy Porter; 1903–1946)

U.S. writer. Raised by his grandmother and brought to Harlem at the age of nine, he was unofficially adopted by a locally prominent pastor, Frederick A. Cullen, after his grandmother died, and began using Cullen as his last name after 1920. A brilliant student, Cullen graduated Phi Beta Kappa from New York University and earned an M.A. in LITERATURE from Harvard in 1926.

Countee Cullen, c. 1920.

While still an undergraduate, Cullen published several poems in prestigious publications like *Harper's* and a first book of poetry, *Color* (1925), which won him acclaim as the "poet laureate" of the HARLEM RENAISSANCE. His most famous line was also one of his earliest: "Yet do I marvel at this curious thing: To make a poet black, and bid him sing!" ("Yet Do I Marvel," 1923). The line, critics note, frames an issue that pervades discussion of the poet, beginning with a statement Cullen gave a reporter in 1924: "I am going to be *poet* and not *Negro poet*."

In his poetry, Cullen endeavored to work contemporary AFRICAN-AMERICAN themes within traditional, often Keatsian poetics. As a result, readers and critics have divided between admiring the accessibility of his writing and finding it strained. His subsequent poetry collections, *Copper Sun* (1927), and *The Black Christ and Other Poems* (1929), whose title poem was an epic about lynching, were as successful as his first. However, a satirical novel, *One Way to Heaven* (1932), and two children's books went almost unnoticed by critics and the reading public alike.

Cullen seems to have acknowledged his gayness at an early age. His mentor, ALAIN LOCKE, introduced him to the HOMOPHILE writings of EDWARD CARPENTER, and remembered Cullen as being moved and inspired by Carpenter's work. He had an intimate friendship from his school days with Harold Jackman, his best man at his wedding with Yolande Du Bois, the daughter of W.E.B. Du Bois, the legendary intellectual and cofounder of the National Negro Committee (the forerunner of the National Association for the Advancement of Colored People). They married in a ceremony with 16 bridesmaids and over 6,000 guests, but neither groom nor bride was interested in the other; their marriage was probably never consummated. Cullen and Jackman went to Paris a few months after the wedding.

Besides writing, Cullen taught French and other subjects in New York City public schools. JAMES BALDWIN was one of his students.

✧ Amitai F. Avi-Ram, "The Unreadable Black Body: 'Conventional' Poetic Form in the Harlem Renaissance," *Genders* (vol. 7, 1990).

✧ Alden Reimonenq, "Countee Cullen's Uranian 'Soul Windows,' " *The Journal of Homosexuality* (vol. 26 no. 2/3, Fall 1993).

"Cures," see PSYCHOLOGY.

Cushman, Charlotte, and "the White, Marmorean Flock"

(1816–1876)

U.S. actress and a group of Rome-based U.S. artists whom she supported. "Born a tomboy" (according to the first sentence of her memoirs) in Boston, Cushman pursued a career in opera before turning to the THEATER and establishing herself as the leading American actress of her era. Although she was most acclaimed for her Lady Macbeth, she also drew praise for her performances in male roles, which included Romeo and Hamlet.

Cushman had already formed what her friend Elizabeth Barrett Browning called a "female marriage" by the time she established a base for herself in Rome in 1852. In the following years, she became the center of a circle of "emancipated" American women artists, mostly sculptors, whom the writer Henry James described as "the white, marmorean flock." Among them was Emma Stebbins (1815–1882), a New York–born artist who journeyed to Rome to study sculpture at the age of 41 and formed a relationship with Cushman that endured until the actress's death 19 years later. Stebbins earned several important commissions, the most lastingly famous of which is probably her *Angel of the Waters* (c. 1862), sculpted for the Bethesda Pool in New York City's Central Park. (The sculpture figures in the last scene of TONY KUSHNER's epic *Angels in America*.) Stebbins also wrote a biography of Cushman.

Another artist associated with Cushman was Mary Edmonia Lewis (1843–c.1900), a Boston-trained sculptor of Chippewa and AFRICAN-AMERICAN descent who earned her passage to Rome by creating a medallion of Colonel Robert Gould Shaw, the white commander of a famed African-American combat unit in the Civil War. Her work, most of which has been lost, often reflected both aspects of her African- and NATIVE AMERICAN heritage: *Forever Free* (1867), a tribute to the Emancipation Proclamation, and *The Old Indian Arrowmaker and His Daughter* (c. 1872) were two of her most popular sculptures. Little is known about Lewis's life after her return to the U.S. to exhibit at the Philadelphia Exposition of 1876.

Harriet Hosmer (1830–1908), the artist who introduced Lewis into Cushman's circle, also became famous as a sculptor. She scandalized polite society by galloping horseback through the streets of Rome dressed in "mannish" clothes. Of all the "marmorean flock," her work was the most blatantly feminist. *Xenobia in Chains* (1859), a seven-foot statue of the AMAZON-like Queen of Palmyra, was her most popular work. Its colossal size so impressed viewers that the London *Art Journal* denied the sculpture could have been accomplished by a woman.

Cushman extended hospitality and, sometimes, financial support to these and other émigré artists. Stebbins wrote that "for all her life long, her friendships were of the nature of passions." Uncertain whether or not these "passions"—and the other intimate relationships the women in her circle formed with one another—were consciously sexual, LILLIAN FADERMAN points to them as examples of 19th-century ROMANTIC FRIENDSHIPS.

✧ Emma Stebbins, *Charlotte Cushman: Her Letters and Memories of Her Life* (1879).

✧ Lillian Faderman, *Surpassing the Love of Men: Romantic Friendship and Love Between Women from the Renaissance to the Present* (1981).

✧ Nancy G. Heller, *Women Artists: An Illustrated History* (1987).

✧ Emmanuel Cooper, *The Sexual Perspective: Homosexuality and Art in the Last One Hundred Years in the West* (rev. ed., 1994).

Cyberspace, see DIGITAL QUEERS; QRD.

Czechoslovakia/Czech Republic, see EASTERN EUROPE.

D

Daly, Mary
(1928–)

U.S. theologian, philosopher, feminist theorist, educator, writer. Born in Schenectady, New York, Daly studied at St. Mary's College at the University of Notre Dame and in Fribourg, Switzerland, earning doctorates in philosophy and theology. In 1968, armed with "a great sense of pride, anger, and hope," she took on the ROMAN CATHOLIC CHURCH, accusing it in *The Church and the Second Sex* not simply of the sexism she found part of the Christian tradition but of outright hostility toward women. By 1973, when she published *Beyond God the Father: Toward a Philosophy of Women's Liberation,* she had evolved from "radical Catholic to postchristian feminist," and become a leader in a movement that urged women to "graduate" from traditional CHRISTIANITY and JUDAISM. Believing that "if God in 'his' heaven is a father ruling 'his' people, then it is in the 'nature' of things and according to divine plan and the order of the universe that society be male-dominated," Daly at first attempted to degender the concept of God, but later, with the 1978 publication of *Gyn/Ecology: The Metaethics of Radical Feminism,* concluded that there was "no way to remove male/masculine imagery from *God.*" She instead chose "to write/speak gynomorphically because *God* represents the necrophilia of patriarchy, whereas *Goddess* affirms the life-loving be-ing of women and nature."

Along with spiritual transformation, Daly's *Gyn/Ecology* and *Pure Lust* (1984) called for a linguistic revolution that would empower women to appropriate the "right to name" from the "phallocracy," and claim—or reclaim—words like "hag," "crone," "crone/ology," "harpy," "spinster," "virago," and "lust."

Convinced that language both shapes and limits consciousness, Daly asserts that "the liberation of language is rooted in the liberation of ourselves." In *Webster's First New Intergalactic Wickedary of the English Language* (with Jane Caputi, 1987), she defines "gyn/ecology" as "knowledge enabling Crones to expose connections among institutions, ideologies, and atrocities."

The author of eight books, Daly, as lesbian philosopher Claudia Card notes, has had a "global" impact on LESBIAN FEMINISM and the development of lesbian and gay SPIRITUALITIES. She teaches at Boston College.

➤ Also see WICCA.

- Marilyn Fry, "Famous Lust Words," *Women's Review of Books* (August 1984).
- Madeline M. Kunin, "On Political Courage, Witches, and History," *Ms* (November 1987).

✧ Wanda Warren Berry, "Feminist Theology: The 'Verbing' of Ultimate/Intimate Reality in Mary Daly," *Ultimate Reality and Meaning* (vol. 11, September 1988).

Dance

Art and profession popularly associated since the early years of the 20th century with gay men and, to a lesser extent, lesbians. As late as the 1980s, aficionados of dance tended to get defensive when the subject of the gay and lesbian presence in dance came up in interviews and articles. Many followed the lead of Emma (Anne Bancroft) in the movie *The Turning Point* (1977) in claiming that the queer dancer was a dated stereotype and that red-blooded heterosexuals like Mikhail Baryshnikov heralded a new trend in dance. In the 1990s, however, the sexuality of dancers became largely a nonissue: more and more dancers and choreographers came OUT with no apparent adverse effect on their careers—and without being rejected by their fans (large numbers of whom were gay or lesbian themselves).

Today, open HOMOEROTICISM is an increasingly common element in modern dance choreography. At least two companies—Les Ballets Trockadero de Monte Carlo and the St. Petersburg Men's Ballet—have put a queer spin on the classics with tutu-clad men on pointe. Dance stars like Paul Taylor and Robert La Fosse have discussed their sexuality candidly in autobiographies. And BILL T. JONES smashed one of the last taboos by making AIDS and its impact on dancers a conspicuous part of the discourse of modern dance.

Lesbian dancers and choreographers have yet to achieve the visibility of their gay male counterparts, but all-female companies have begun to build audiences at lesbian arts festivals and venues for avant-garde performance pieces.

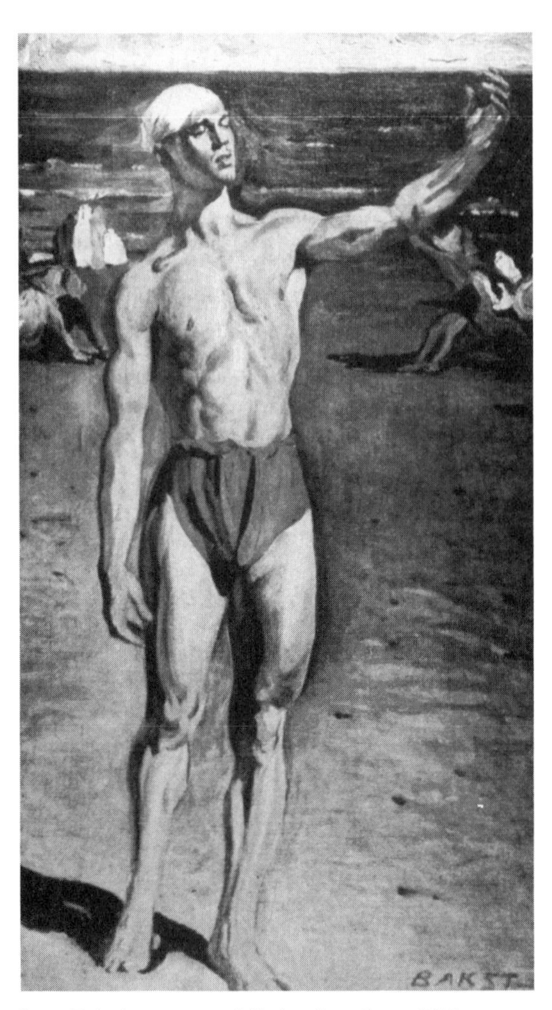

Leon Bakst's portrait of Vaslav Nijinsky, c. 1909.

History

MARGARET MEAD and other anthropologists have pointed out that in almost all societies male-dominated occupations have been seen as more prestigious than female-dominated ones, and that occupations—such as weaving and sewing, elementary school teaching, and clerical work—have actually lost prestige when they became associated with women. Something similar happened to dance in the West at about the time of the French Revolution. Previously, when men had danced even the women's roles in ballet, it was so prestigious an avocation that Louis XIV (reigned 1643–1715) enjoyed performing for his subjects: his sobriquet "The Sun King" came from his dancing the role of a sun god at the age of 15, but he also performed at least once costumed as a milkmaid. JAPAN provides a similar, non-Western example: the two most prestigious forms of traditional dance, courtly *bunraku* and *noh* drama, are even today an all-male realm.

Abandoned by elite males for reasons not well understood, Western European ballet gradually became an almost exclusively female preserve, to the point that male roles were often performed by women in the 19th century. At least one of the most innovative dancers of the 18th century, Marie Sallé (c. 1707–1756), was rumored to have had female lovers, but 19th-century stars, even when they danced as men, were considered purely heterosexual fantasy figures. Outside Russia and Denmark, men were little more than props on the ballet stage.

All this began to change dramatically around the year 1900. Modern dance, pioneered by the lesbian Loie Fuller (1862–1928), the bisexual Isadora Duncan, and, a little later, a number of mostly heterosexual women, assailed conventional notions of femininity, liberating women and men from the fossilized GENDER strictures of classical ballet. Meanwhile, classical ballet itself had emerged as a mature, respected art form with the arrival in Western Europe and North America of SERGEI DIAGHILEV's Ballets Russes.

These developments elevated the status of dance and its choreographers while leaving male dancers in an ambiguous, sexually suspect position. The prodigious athleticism of dancers like Vaslav Nijinsky (1890–1950) notwithstanding, dance remained associated in the public mind with "feminine" grace and sensitivity. Throughout the 20th century men pursuing a career in dance were stereotyped as "pansies." Perhaps the earliest attempt to attack this stereotype head-on was the All-Male Dancers Group, established by Ted Shawn (1891–1972) in the U.S. in 1933. The bisexual Shawn had—with his wife, Ruth St. Denis—founded the Denishawn schools (the first in Los Angeles in 1915), which are today credited with establishing modern dance as an important American art form. Touring the U.S. from 1933 to 1940, Shawn's male dancers, many of whom were trained athletes, endeavored to persuade Americans that dancing could be as masculine as playing football or basketball—dribbling and basket-shooting moves were in fact choreographed into some of Shawn's manly dance creations.

By the 1950s, modern dance choreographers like Merce Cunningham (whose life partner and collaborator was the composer John Cage) and Alwin Nikolais and his lover Murray Louis were taking another tack. Cunningham and Nikolais—who "abhorred the idea of male and female as opposed, as if we were all walking around in heat"—transcended gender typing by creating abstract, unisex choreography. In the 1960s, women choreographers like Anna Halprin and Meredith Monk further weakened gender stereotypes by choreographing conventionally "masculine" movements for women.

Early examples of open homoeroticism in dance include ballet scenes in Benjamin Britten's opera *Death in Venice* (choreographed by Sir Frederick Ashton in 1973) and the Joffrey Ballet's *The Relativity of Icarus* (choreographed by Robert Arpino in 1974), both cited by *New York Times* critic Clive Barnes in a landmark 1974 article on "Homosexuality in Dance." Although the 1970s were still an era when the sexuality of even relatively uncloseted dancers and choreographers was almost never mentioned in print, gay and lesbian dance professionals found themselves under less pressure to hide their private lives from the public.

➤ Also see ART; MUSIC.

- ✧ Judith Lynne Hanna, "Patterns of Dominance: Men, Women, and Homosexuality in Dance," *The Drama Review* (vol. 31, no. 1, Spring 1987).
- ✧ Sarah Schulman, "Letter to Jennifer Dunning," in *My American History: Lesbian and Gay Life During the Reagan/Bush Years* (1994).

Dancing, Social

Activity once officially prohibited for same-sex couples in many countries that is now a mainstay of gay and lesbian social life. Tantamount to a public display of affection, same-sex social dancing was long what queer theorists call a "site of contention," behavior considered so shocking even in supposedly tolerant places like Paris (see **2/1/1949**) that it was against the law.

Widespread fear of the erotic potential of same-sex dancing may have actually affected the evolution of modern dance steps. Argentinian gay historians claim that the tango originated as a way for *gauchos* (who lived in areas where there were few women) to dance together that was more macho than a waltz or a polka. Writer Midge Decter believes the modern custom of dancing without touching was "a borrowing from the homosexuals" that originated in the line dances popular among gay men and lesbians in the 1950s and early 1960s as a means of circumventing prohibitions against same-sex ballroom dancing.

Despite prohibitions, same-sex dancing at drag balls, in the dark backrooms of BARS, and at private parties flourished long before STONEWALL and the proliferation in the 1970s of public gay and lesbian dance parties and discos. After Stonewall, however, many lesbians and gay men began to see social dancing not simply as a pastime but also as a powerful means of building a sense of communal gay and lesbian identity. In Chicago, for example, the GAY LIBERATION movement was launched with a series of dances for lesbians and gay

men in 1970. Later that year, a RADICALESBIANS publication cited the first all-women's GAY LIBERATION FRONT dances (see **4/1970**) in New York City as pivotal events in the development of LESBIAN FEMINISM.

Disco

"Discothèque" originated in Western Europe in the early 1960s as a term for a small dance club that featured recorded music in place of a dance band, but *disco* as a musical genre was an AFRICAN-AMERICAN creation refined and popularized by disc jockeys (DJs) at underground clubs for black gay men in the late 1960s. Disco began to cross over to predominantly white gay male clubs as early as 1969, when Ted Drach and Tiger Curtis transformed the Cherry Grove Sea Shack (see FIRE ISLAND) into the prototype of the 1970s disco: a DJ booth, lighting coordinated to the music, and speakers blasting nonstop, wall-to-wall sound. The format had become common enough by 1973 for *Billboard* magazine to note it as a new trend in dance music. Soon, it was so pervasive in the gay male SUBCULTURE that THE ADVOCATE proclaimed 1975 "The Year of Disco." Dance clubs became the social and cultural centers of gay male life, and dancing the cement that held the gay male community together. In *The Joy of Gay Sex* (1977), EDMUND WHITE and Dr. Charles Silverstein hailed "big, spacious, luxurious discos as proof . . . of the emergence of gays from their closets." The biggest problem facing gay discos, they added, was "how to keep straights from moving in and elbowing out the original gay clientele."

House

The fact that disco originated in black gay clubs did not stop white entrepreneurs from instituting racist door policies at many gay clubs (see, for example, **8/7/1981**). Music historian Tony Cummings marks 1972 as the first year black and white gay men mixed on the dance floor, but even then integrated dance clubs remained the exception. As a result, many African-Americans and LATINOS patronized alternative discos like the Paradise Garage in New York City and the Warehouse in Chicago.

The Warehouse opened in Chicago in 1977 as an after-hours dance club accommodating as many as 5,000 mostly black gay and lesbian patrons between midnight Saturday and the following Sunday afternoon. Soon after its opening, DJ Frankie Knuckles invented "house" music by mixing records to emphasize complex percussive cross-rhythms and accelerating the mix to at least 120 beats per minute. From Chicago, house spread to other clubs, gay and straight, in Europe as well as in the U.S., evolving in Detroit into "techno-house" and inspiring massive dance gatherings in London that came to be called "raves."

The popularity of these new forms of dance music had the added effect of making DJs like Knuckles, Junior Vasquez, and Susan Morabito—all openly gay or lesbian—stars in their own right, with international followings among both queer and straight clubgoers.

The Circuit

AIDS spelled the end of disco as the most prominent symbol of gay male community. As thousands of men sickened and died, club attendance slumped, and many discos closed their doors. At the same time, some clubs began making their facilities available for special AIDS benefits modeled after the theme parties that had grown popular at discos in the late 1970s and early 1980s. Out of these special events, typical of which was the New York City "Black Party" held annually the weekend before the spring solstice, grew the now worldwide "Circuit." Since the late 1980s, the Circuit has expanded to encompass several dozen major parties lasting as long as 18 hours and attracting enough participants to transform an entire city, according to the magazine *Circuit Noize,* into "an instant gay ghetto full of hot men who are behaving as queer as they care to be." Although the Circuit now includes parties in CANADA, Europe, and AUSTRALIA as well as throughout the U.S., it is everywhere a remarkably homogeneous, mostly male, overwhelmingly white phenomenon. The largest Circuit event is the Sydney Gay and Lesbian Mardi Gras Party, which admits 20,000 circuit fans for 12 hours of dancing punctuated by five lavish live shows.

Lesbian and Queer Clubs

Most gay and lesbian historians view women's MUSIC festivals as the lesbian equivalent in the 1970s of the male-dominated Disco Era. But in the 1990s, lesbians increasingly came to be seen as the trendsetters in gay and lesbian social dancing, thanks as much to the popularity of "grrrl" bands like Tribe 8 as to the proliferation of innovative, fast-changing clubs like San Francisco's G-Spot and Muffdive, Houston's The Ranch, and New York City's Clit Club and Meow Mix, all offering attractions (apart from dancing) as provocatively diverse as the club patrons themselves.

➤ Also see SYLVESTER.

✧ Anthony Thomas, "The House the Kids Built: The Gay Black Imprint on American Dance Music," in *Out in Culture: Gay, Lesbian, and Queer Essays on Popular Culture,* edited by Corey K. Creekmur and Alexander Doty (1995).

✧ Frank DeCaro, "Full Circuit: A Brief History of Party Time," *Genre* (April 1996).

Daughters of Bilitis (DOB)

First lesbian membership organization in the U.S., DOB was founded by four couples in San Francisco on **September 21, 1955** (first meeting held on October 19, 1955; incorporated in the State of California in January 1957), to provide personal support and social contacts for individual lesbians and to advance the status and understanding of lesbianism in society at large. Other DOB chapters were established in New York City in 1958 and later in Boston, Chicago, Cleveland, Denver, Detroit, Los Angeles, New Orleans, Philadelphia, Portland (OR), Reno, Rhode Island, and San Diego, as well as in Melbourne, AUSTRALIA.

The eight founders, most of whose names remain confidential, included DEL MARTIN and PHYLLIS LYON. Four of the women were blue-collar and four white-collar; one was Filipina and one Chicana. DOB's founders and later leaders were, according to lesbian historians, primarily semiprofessional women seeking a social alternative to the BAR scene. The founders were initially unaware of MATTACHINE and ONE, INC., the other early U.S. HOMOPHILE organizations. DOB's first president was Helen Sandoz.

The organization's name came from Pierre Louÿs's fictional work, *The Songs of Bilitis* (published in French in 1894 and in English in 1933). Dedicated to "the young daughters of future society," Louÿs's prose poems relate the tale of Bilitis, a fictitious student of SAPPHO, Bilitis's 10-year love affair with a woman named Mnasidice, and her later years as a courtesan in Cyprus. The name "Daughters of Bilitis" thus encoded a subtle lesbian reference while suggesting a Greek poetry appreciation group to the uninitiated. It also echoed the names of heterosexual women's groups such as the Daughters of the American Revolution or the Daughters of the Nile. Similarly encoded, the DOB emblem and motto were a *d* and a *b*

The January 1957 cover of The Ladder featured a graphic explanation of the publication's title. The triangular DOB emblem and motto, "Qui vive," appear in the lower right corner.

inset inside a triangle above the words "Qui vive" ("Who lives" or "Who goes there?" in French), which, in the once common English expression "on the *qui vive,*" means being alert to danger.

The early members of DOB had good reason to exercise caution. In later discussions, DOB's founders pointed to U.S. government purges of lesbians and gay men and frequent police raids on bars to explain the fear and isolation of lesbians in the 1950s. The founders' initial objective was to create a safe, supportive environment in which women could come OUT, meet other lesbians, and begin to form a community. Public advocacy of social change would come later.

Members typically protected themselves by using PSEUDONYMS or first names only. Fear of being identified publicly as a lesbian severely restricted membership building and outreach.

DOB activities included "gab 'n' java" discussion groups in private homes, picnics, encounter sessions, public forums, and research projects. As the homophile movement spread, DOB sometimes joined in social, religious, and political activities with other female, male, and mixed groups, such as the Mattachine Society or the Council on Religion and the Homosexual. In the 1960s, some DOB members went public with lectures, interviews in the press and on radio and TELEVISION, and appearances before college classes.

In **October 1956**, DOB began publication of THE LADDER, a monthly journal that provided lesbians with information and links with others across the country. DOB also sponsored the first national lesbian convention in San Francisco in **May 1960**, probably the earliest public gathering in the U.S. to focus exclusively on lesbianism.

As in the other American homophile groups, a conflict arose early on within DOB between members who wanted the organization to become a vocal advocate for social change and those who simply wanted a supportive social club. This conflict led to the splintering off of members into two other secret California lesbian clubs, Quatrefoil and Hale Aikane. By the mid-1960s, many lesbian activists criticized DOB for its low profile, moderate stance, and carefully measured challenges to conventional assumptions about the mental health, legal status, and morality of homosexuality, accusing the organization of encouraging conformity to societal norms.

Other aspects of DOB were also controversial, including the content and philosophy of *The Ladder* and even the name of the organization itself. Open discussion of sex was considered taboo until 1968, 13 years after DOB's founding, when the National Sex Forum was founded in San Francisco. The issue that finally caused the national organization to dissolve, however, was the role of "radical feminism" in the lesbian rights movement: In 1970, *Ladder* editor BARBARA GRIER and national DOB president Rita Laporte, both activist feminists, learned that they were likely to lose editorial control of *The Ladder* at that year's biennial convention. In response, they absented themselves from the convention, moved production of the magazine to Reno, Nevada, and took the organization's mailing list. The convention delegates believed they lacked the financial resources to pursue an interstate legal battle and, without a membership list, felt they had no

This four-part statement of purpose was routinely printed inside the front cover of the Daughters of Bilitis's *The Ladder* until 1970:

A Women's Organization for the Purpose of Promoting the Integration of the Homosexual into Society by:

(1) Education of the variant, with particular emphasis on the psychological, physiological and sociological aspects, to enable her to understand herself and make her adjustment to society in all its social, civic and economic implications—this to be accomplished by establishing and maintaining as complete a library as possible of both fiction and non-fiction literature on the sex deviant theme; by sponsoring public discussions on pertinent subjects to be conducted by leading members of the legal, psychiatric, religious and other professions; by advocating a mode of behavior and dress acceptable to society.

(2) Education of the public at large through acceptance first of the individual, leading to an eventual breakdown of erroneous taboos and prejudices; through public discussion meetings aforementioned; through dissemination of educational literature on the homosexual theme.

(3) Participation in research projects by duly authorized and responsible psychologists, sociologists and other such experts directed towards further knowledge of the homosexual.

(4) Investigation of the penal code as it pertains to the homosexual, proposal of changes to provide an equitable handling of cases involving this minority group, and promotion of these changes through due process of law in the state legislatures.

choice but to disband the national organization. *The Ladder* continued until 1972 as an independent publication.

✧ Del Martin and Phyllis Lyon, *Lesbian Women* (1972).

✧ Interview with Del Martin and Phyllis Lyon in *Our Right to Love,* edited by Ginny Vida (1978).

✧ Jonathan Ned Katz, *Gay American History,* interview with Barbara Gittings (1992).

✧ Eric Marcus, *Making History: The Struggle for Gay and Lesbian Equal Rights, 1945–1990* (1992).

Davis, Madeline D.
(1940–)

U.S. activist, historian, librarian, musician. Born and raised in Buffalo, New York, Davis became active in the gay and lesbian rights movement in the fall of 1969, when Buffalo's first lesbian and gay COMMUNITY CENTER opened on the site of a gay BAR that had been raided by police. In March 1970, she joined the MATTACHINE Society of the Niagara Frontier (MSNF), a group that had formed at the center following a speech by pioneering activist FRANK KAMENY. The next year, inspired by her "experience on the real, public firing line" as a participant in the first gay and lesbian rights march in the New York state capital, Albany, she wrote the anthem "Stonewall Nation," considered the first gay rights song in the U.S. On **July 12, 1972**, as president of MSNF, she and JIM FOSTER addressed the Democratic National Convention, becoming the first openly gay or lesbian delegates to address a national political-party meeting.

In addition to her activism, Davis has won renown for groundbreaking contributions to LESBIAN AND GAY STUDIES. In 1972, she co-developed and taught the first course on lesbianism in the U.S. In 1978, she and ELIZABETH KENNEDY, among others, founded the Buffalo Women's Oral History Project and began to compile the most comprehensive account of a lesbian community ever attempted. The result was the landmark *Boots of Leather, Slippers of Gold: The History of a Lesbian Community* (1993). Davis and Kennedy also gave public presentations and helped create a local ARCHIVE.

Davis is a member of Buffalo's lesbian repertory Hag Theatre and the founder of the Spiderwoman coven (see WICCA). In 1995, Davis and Wendy Smiley became the first lesbian couple to have a marriage ceremony performed by a rabbi at a major Reform (JUDAISM) temple in Buffalo.

Delaney, Beauford
(1901–1979)

U.S. painter. Born and raised in Knoxville, Tennessee, the son of a minister and a nurse, Delaney had a happy childhood in what he described as the "Negro south." After studying art at the Massachusetts Normal School, he moved to Harlem in 1929 and then to Greenwich Village. In 1953 he stopped in Paris on his way to Rome and stayed for the remainder of his life. He was much admired by the French for his singing in the cafés of the city.

In 1940, Delaney and JAMES BALDWIN met and began a lifelong friendship. Baldwin described his first meeting with Delaney in the introduction to *The Price of the Ticket* (1985) as a rite of passage. He considered Delaney the most important influence of his life, his "spiritual father." As a gay man, artist, and celebrator of AFRICAN-AMERICAN culture, Delaney served as Baldwin's role model and mentor. Biographer David Leeming wrote that Delaney taught Baldwin "to react to life as an artist." He also introduced Baldwin to jazz and the blues.

At one time, Baldwin planned a novel based on Delaney's life; he wanted to call it *A Higher Place.*

Delaney's paintings appeared in major exhibitions in the U.S. and abroad. His portraits of Baldwin, W.E.B. Du Bois, Marian Anderson, Duke Ellington, and many other African-Americans are considered classics.

✧ David Leeming, *James Baldwin* (1994).

Delany, Samuel R.
(1942–)

U.S. writer, literary theorist, educator. Born and raised in Harlem, Delany began concocting elaborate homoerotic "masturbation fantasies" ("full of kings and warriors, leather armor, slaves, swords and brocade") at the age of ten—and was dispatched to a psychotherapist when his mother discovered the notebook in which he recorded his imaginings.

Delany was most interested in the sciences as a child, but he was also, in spite of struggles with dyslexia, an artistic prodigy, completing his first novels and a violin concerto while still in his teens. In 1961, at the age of 19, he married MARILYN HACKER, who was then 18 and pregnant by Delany. Although the pregnancy ended in a miscarriage (and Hacker knew Delany was primarily attracted to men), they stayed together for several years and had a daughter before separating and, in 1980, formally divorcing. Delany's first published novel, *The Jewels of Aptor* (1962), was in part inspired by Hacker's disgust at the shallow, unflattering characterizations of women in the books she labored over as an editorial assistant at Ace Books. A relatively conventional SCIENCE FICTION novel compared to Delany's later work, *The Jewels of Aptor* nonetheless presaged the complex re-visions of GENDER that are a characteristic of his better-known stories.

Delany won his second and third Nebula Awards from the Science Fiction Writers of America with two gender-bending tales, the novel *The Einstein Intersection* (1967), which includes an exploration of a people divided into three biological sexes, and the short story "Aye, and Gomorrah" (also 1967), in which genetically altered astronaut "spacers" have no sex or gender at all. "Aye, and Gomorrah" also featured "frelks," decadent outer-space outcasts who admit to a "perverted" lust for the spacers and inhabit an unsavory shadow world reminiscent of the clandestine gay and lesbian SUBCULTURES of the period.

Overt HOMOEROTICISM—as well as adventurous experimentation with language and form—surfaced in Delany's work with the publication of the best-selling *Dhalgren* in 1975, and further evolved in his four-volume Nevèrÿon series (1979–1987), which included graphic S/M and, in *Flight from Nevèrÿon,* a treatment of the AIDS epidemic. Another novel from this period (not part of the Nevèrÿon series) *Stars in My Pocket like Grains of Sand* (1984), revolved around a love affair between two men in the distant future.

In addition to fiction and works of literary criticism, Delany has authored a series of unusually explicit memoirs, beginning with *The Motion of Light in Water: Sex and Science Fiction Writing in the East Village, 1957–1965* (1988). In these memoirs as well as in journal articles and addresses to lesbian and gay groups, Delany has emerged as a vigorous advocate of sexual openness. "The advent of AIDS," he told the Fifth Annual Lesbian and Gay Conference on Gay Studies in 1991, "made absolutely imperative an inflated level of sexual honesty."

✧ Samuel R. Delany, "Aversion/Perversion/Diversion," in *Negotiating Lesbian and Gay Subjects,* edited by Monica Dorenkamp and Richard Henke (1995).

✧ Earl Jackson Jr., "Imagining It Otherwise: Alternative Sexualities in the Fictions of Samuel R. Delany," in *Strategies of Deviance: Studies in Gay Male Representation* (1995).

D'Emilio, John

(1948–)

U.S. historian. Born and raised in New York City, D'Emilio attended Columbia University and earned a Ph.D. in 1982. He was a founding member of the Gay Academic Union in 1973 and published his first book, *The Civil Rights Struggle: Leaders in Profile,* in 1979.

When D'Emilio decided to do his doctoral thesis on the early years of the GAY AND LESBIAN RIGHTS MOVEMENT, most gay men and lesbians—and even gay and lesbian historians—had only the sketchiest, most anecdotal idea of the organizations and events that had preceded STONEWALL and the GAY LIBERATION era. D'Emilio's meticulously documented history, published as *Sexual Politics, Sexual Communities: The Making of a Homosexual Minority in the United States, 1940–1970* in 1983, not only laid a foundation for all subsequent research in the field, it also provided interpretive analyses of mid-20th-century lesbian and gay history that are today considered practically canonical.

Addressing a broader historical issue, D'Emilio's 1979–1980 lectures, later adapted and published as *Capitalism and Gay Identity,* developed the idea that capitalism made lesbian and gay identities possible by freeing individuals from the economic control of families and by fostering the development of sexualities disengaged from procreation.

In addition to coauthoring *Intimate Matters: A History of Sexuality in America* (1988) with Estelle Freedman, D'Emilio has also written a widely published article entitled "Gay Politics and Community in San Francisco Since World War II" (1989) and *Making Trouble: Essays on Gay History, Politics, and the University* (1992).

D'Emilio taught U.S. and gay history at the University of North Carolina at Greensboro from 1983 until taking a policy position at the NATIONAL GAY AND LESBIAN TASK FORCE in the 1990s.

➤ Also see CONSTRUCTIONISM VS. ESSENTIALISM.

Deming, Barbara

(1917–1984)

U.S. peace activist, poet, essayist, and journalist. Born in New York City, Deming began writing poetry, including lesbian love poems, in her teen years. Her first love, at 17, Norma Millay, sister of Edna St. Vincent Millay, was formative and positive. But, as she later told her mother, she learned to feel shame for her lesbianism "all too soon," and this sense of shame oppressed her writing.

Judith McDaniel, a lesbian poet, critic, and the executor of Deming's estate, notes that in the mid-1930s Deming had no publishing outlet, no audience for her lesbian poems to develop "the faculty of self-evaluation" important for her artistic growth. McDaniel discovered that at one point, Deming returned to dozens of these poems and penciled in "omit" in the upper-right-hand corner. Deming's friend, author and activist Grace Paley, believed that Deming's attention to the "other" led her "inexorably to the shadowed lives of women and finally to the unknown humiliated lesbian, herself." Ultimately, however, this awareness compelled her to openly challenge her comrades to recognize the oppression of the lesbian class, perhaps no more powerfully than in her essay "A New Spirit Moves Among Us."

Like other lesbians and gay men, Deming was an important part of the peace and civil rights movements in the 1960s through the

1980s. She was imprisoned in 1963 in Birmingham, Alabama, for walking half a block with a sign around her neck that read "All Men Are Brothers"; two decades later she was one of 54 women jailed following a march through upstate New York to the Seneca Women's Base Peace Camp near the missile base in Romulus. From her experiences in prison came her most compelling writing, through which she reflected on dehumanizing institutionalization and her staunch hope for social change through nonviolence.

In addition to the posthumously published collection *Prisons That Could Not Hold*, Deming was the author of six books, including *We Are All Part of One Another: A Barbara Deming Reader* and *A Humming Under My Feet*.

Deming was living in the Florida Keys with the writer and painter Jane Gapen and a close community of women when she died of ovarian cancer.

✧ Judith McDaniel, "Taking Risks, Becoming a Writer as a Lesbian," in *Inversions: Writings by Dykes, Queers and Lesbians*, edited by Betsy Warland (1991).

Demuth, Charles
(1883–1935)

U.S. painter. Demuth studied at the Pennsylvania Academy of Fine Arts and in Paris, where he was particularly influenced by the work of Paul Cézanne but also drew inspiration from his friend, the iconoclastic artist Marcel Duchamp, and—through visits to the salon of GERTRUDE STEIN—the Cubists. In 1921, he returned to his hometown, Lancaster, Pennsylvania, as he told a friend, "to speak for vice"—a quote on which art critic Jonathan Weinberg based the title of his book on Demuth, Demuth's close friend MARSDEN HARTLEY, and "the first American avant-garde." Diagnosed with diabetes in 1920, Demuth spent the last years of his life in increasingly poor health.

In his lifetime, Demuth was best known as a leader of the so-called Precisionist movement, which depicted urban and industrial scenes in a clean-cut, decorative manner. But his varied output also included watercolors that are perhaps the first explicit depictions by an American painter of gay male life. Demuth's homoerotic work ranged from *Turkish Bath* (1915), one of a series of sexually charged paintings he set in a BATHHOUSE popular with gay men of the era (probably the Lafayette Baths in New York City), to the daringly pornographic *Three Sailors on the Beach* (1930), in which one well-endowed, erect man seeks to interest another in oral sex while a third strips in the background. As the title of another painting, *On "That" Street* (1932), suggests, Demuth documented the existence of CRUISING areas for gay men at a time they could be only obliquely described in print. His work also captures the particular HOMOEROTICISM of his times, when, for many gay men, hypermasculine sailors had replaced the androgynous boys of earlier times as the idealized objects of sexual desire. Although Demuth never exhibited his homoerotic work during his lifetime, he is thought to have shared the paintings with his close friends. He willed his unsold watercolors and home to one of them, Robert Locher, another Lancaster native, who may also have been his lover.

✧ Jonathan Weinberg, *Speaking for Vice: Homosexuality in the Art of Charles Demuth, Marsden Hartley, and the First American Avant-Garde* (1993).

Denmark, see SCANDINAVIA.

Detective Fiction

A particularly hospitable genre for gay and lesbian writers, detective fiction provides an ideal environment to explore the "mysteries" of gay and lesbian life in a way legions of fans find particularly entertaining. Lesbian writers in particular have made detective fiction a forum for the discussion and scrutiny of political and social issues, ranging from alcoholism to GENDER-bending and PORNOGRAPHY to prostitution.

Gay and lesbian characters were long a part of "mainstream" detective fiction, but as pioneering gay mystery writer JOSEPH HANSEN wrote in *Twentieth Century Crime and Mystery Writers* (1985), "Homosexuals have been treated shabbily in detective fiction—vilified, pitied, at best patronized. . . . When I sat down to write *Fadeout* in 1967 I wanted to write a good, compelling whodunit, but I also wanted to right some wrongs."

Some writers, such as SARAH SCHULMAN (*After Delores*) and MONIQUE WITTIG (*Les Guérillères*) have incorporated elements of detective and suspense fiction into "serious" experimental novels. More commonly, however, gay and lesbian writers have not so much innovated as replicated detective fiction, generating almost all the varieties of the mainstream genre but with a lesbian and gay sensibility and, of course, a gay or lesbian detective character. Since the 1970s, gay and lesbian "cosies," "hard-boiled" tales, and occult and comic approaches have mirrored the varied styles within the mainstream genre.

But lesbian and gay mystery series also have features that distinguish them from their mainstream counterparts. Many chart a character's progress OUT of the CLOSET and toward an acceptance of his or her gayness. RICHARD HALL's *Butterscotch Prince* (1975), in which a black detective character searches for his lover's killer and deals with his own internalized HOMOPHOBIA and changing sense of identity in the process, was perhaps the first in this category.

Once out, detectives have to contend with the problems of finding and keeping a lover, fidelity issues, career conflicts, disagreement with intimates over how out they should come, and, sometimes, the death of loved ones, either by violence or from AIDS-related illnesses. In addition, almost all lesbian and gay mysteries deal in some way with HETEROSEXISM and homophobia. Some of the more innovative novels in the genre, such as those by BARBARA WILSON, have used mystery plots to "investigate" issues of particular import for the gay and lesbian communities, including the 1980s SEX WARS, leather and S/M, OUTING, sex workers, and parenting.

Through the 1980s, lesbian mysteries tended to take place in an all-lesbian world, or at least a world devoid of gay men. Perhaps as a reflection of revitalized links between lesbians and gay men, KATHERINE FORREST and a few other prominent writers in the genre have in the 1990s consciously tried to incorporate gay male characters.

Unique conventions have arisen in the genre. Lesbian detectives most often have straight male partners. Gay male detectives almost always work alone, often drawing on their wide circle of gay male contacts for information and support. What characters eat and when is an important part of the story, especially in lesbian mysteries (Mabel Maney has parodied this feature in her Nancy Clue and Cherry Aimless mysteries). Both men and women probably have sex with suspects and witnesses more often than their heterosexual counterparts.

➤ Also see HIGHSMITH, PATRICIA.

Author	Series Protagonist(s)	Setting(s)
Nathan Aldyne	Daniel Valentine (social worker turned bartender) and Clarisse Lovelace (real estate agent turned law student)	Boston; Provincetown
Kate Allen	Alison Kaine (police officer)	Denver
Nikki Baker	Virginia Kelly (investment advisor)	Chicago; Provincetown
George Baxt	Pharaoh Love (homicide detective)	New York City
Rose Beecham	Amanda Valentine (homicide detective)	New Zealand
Stan Cutler	Mark Bradley (writer)	Hollywood
Diane Davidson	Tori Underwood (homicide detective)	Southern California
Lauren Wright Douglas	Caitlin Reece (private investigator)	Vancouver Island, British Columbia
Sarah Dreher	Stoner McTavish (travel agent)	Boston; Maine; the Old West
Stella Duffy	Saz Martin (private investigator)	London
Tony Fenelly	Matt Sinclair (dealer in faux antiques)	New Orleans
KATHERINE FORREST	Kate Delafield (homicide detective)	Los Angeles
Lisa Haddock	Carmen Ramirez (newspaper editor)	"Frontier City," Oklahoma
JOSEPH HANSEN	Dave Brandstetter (insurance investigator)	Southern California
Ellen Hart	Jane Lawless (restaurant owner)	Twin Cities, Minnesota
Steve Johnson	Doug Orlando (homicide detective)	Brooklyn
Phyllis Knight	Lil Ritchie (private investigator)	Maine and other U.S. locales
Randye Lordon	Sidney Sloane (private investigator)	Upper West Side, New York City
Frances Lucas	Diana Mendoza (lawyer, scriptwriter)	Los Angeles
Vicki P. McConnell	Nyla Wade (journalist)	Colorado; Oregon
Val McDermid	Lindsay Gordon (journalist)	England; Scotland
Claire McNab	Carol Ashton (detective inspector)	Sydney, Australia
Jaye Maiman	Robin Miller (private investigator)	San Francisco; New York City; Poconos
Mabel Maney	Cherrie Aimless (nurse) and Nancy Clue ("girl detective")	San Francisco; "River Depths," Illinois
Jackie Manthorne	Harriet "Harry" Hubbley (physical education instructor)	Provincetown; Montreal; Nova Scotia
Jane Meyerding	Brigid Donovan (ex-nun, carpenter)	Maine
Grant Michaels	Stanislav "Vannos" Kraychic (hairdresser)	Boston

Penny Mickelbury	Gianna Maglione (HATE CRIME detective) and Mimi Patterson (investigative reporter)	Washington, D.C.
Michael Nava	Henry Rios (criminal defense attorney)	California
Elizabeth Pincus	Nell Fury (private investigator)	San Francisco
J. M. Redmann	Michele "Micky" Knight (private investigator)	New Orleans
Sandra Scoppetone	Lauren Laurano (private investigator)	Greenwich Village, New York City
Richard Stevenson	Donald Strachey (private investigator)	Albany, New York
SAMUEL M. STEWARD	GERTRUDE STEIN (writer) and ALICE B. TOKLAS (private secretary)	Paris
Penny Sumner	Victoria "Tor" Cross (private investigator)	England
Jean Taylor	Maggie Garrett (private investigator)	San Francisco
Larry Townsend	Bruce MacLeod (therapist)	West Hollywood and Beverly Hills, California
Pat Welch	Helen Black (private investigator)	Berkeley, California
BARBARA WILSON	Pam Nilsen (print shop cooperative member)	Seattle
	Cassandra Reilly (translator, world traveler)	Exotic European locales
Mary Wings	Emma Victor (publicist)	Boston; California
Kieran York	Royce Madison (sheriff's deputy)	"Timber City," Colorado
R. D. Zimmerman	Todd Mills (TV newscaster)	Minneapolis
Mark Richard Zubro	Tom Mason (high school English teacher) and Scott Carpenter (major league pitcher)	Chicago
	Paul Turner (homicide detective)	Chicago

Elsie De Wolfe, a fashion leader, in 1895.

De Wolfe, Elsie
(1865–1950), and
Marbury, Elisabeth
(1856–1933)

U.S. actress, interior decorator, socialite, and her companion of more than two decades, a theatrical agent and politician. Both De Wolfe and Marbury came from good families, but Marbury's had the advantage of great wealth and high status in 19th-century New York City society. De Wolfe pursued a career on Broadway but drew more acclaim for her impeccable taste in clothes than for her lackluster performances. Marbury, a few years older than De Wolfe, epitomized the independent "new woman" of the period, shunning fashion and prospective (male) suitors, while establishing herself as the world's most powerful theatrical agent, with clients who included OSCAR WILDE and offices in Europe as well as in New York. The two women became friends in 1886 and rented a house together in 1892.

From the beginning, the relationship of the "Bachelors," as their friends called them, titillated New York society, but Marbury's wealth and De Wolfe's taste silenced the gossips—at least in their presence. Backed by Marbury, De Wolfe left the THEATER in 1896 and launched a second career as an interior decorator. If not the first interior decorator in the world, as she later claimed, she was certainly the most famous and influential. Biographers now credit her with transforming the American home, replacing Victorian clutter with, as she wrote in her best-selling *The House in Good Taste* (1913), "plenty of optimism and white paint." The era's leading tastemaker, not only did she popularize beige and cream-colored paints and simpler furnishings, she also promoted her own inventions, which included everything from large pillows with arms for reading in bed to built-in switches that turned on all the lamps in a room as well as ceiling lights.

As De Wolfe became nationally famous for her design savvy, Marbury extended her influence from theater to relief work in WORLD WAR I and politics. After helping elect Al Smith as governor of New York, she was chosen to serve as the national committeewoman from New York for several terms beginning in 1920. That same year, Marbury, De Wolfe, and a contingent of their unmarried women friends (who included fellow socialites Anne Morgan and Anne Vanderbilt) moved simultaneously to then squalid Sutton Place. According to *Gossip* magazine, a local scandal sheet, the gentrifying "Amazons" excited "an avalanche of controversy of a racy variety" in large part because of the wealthy women's efforts to assist and entertain "the less fortunate but talented young ladies in whom they are intensely interested."

De Wolfe surprised Marbury in 1926 by suddenly deciding to marry Sir Charles Mendl, a British career diplomat (who was also rumored to be attracted mainly to his own sex). The two women reconciled after De Wolfe assured her that the union was purely a marriage of convenience and remained intimate until Marbury's death at the age of 76. De Wolfe remained one of Europe's most famous hostesses until her own death 17 years later at the age of 85. Her last words were: "They can't do this to me. I don't want to go."

✧ Jane S. Smith, *Elsie De Wolfe: A Life in the High Style* (1982).

✧ Nina Campbell and Caroline Seebohm, *Elsie De Wolfe: A Decorative Life* (1992).

Diaghilev, Sergei Pavlovich
(1872–1929)

Russian impresario, critic. From a provincial, middle-class background, Diaghilev settled in St. Petersburg in 1890 armed with a first-rate education and the growing realization that his greatest talent lay in his ability to promote others. In the late 1890s, he cofounded a cultural organization and an extraordinarily influential journal (1898–1904), both called *Mir Iskusstva* ("World of Art"), and began organizing art exhibits, first of progressive foreign painters, then of Russian artists in Paris as well as in RUSSIA. As "World of Art" suggested, Diaghilev envisioned a new movement that would embrace all the arts. After promoting concerts and opera performances, he turned to ballet, first producing new works and later founding his own company, the Ballets Russes.

Despite the company's name (Russian Ballets), Diaghilev's dancers never performed in Russia. Instead, beginning in 1909, they dazzled—and sometimes scandalized—Western European audiences with seasons that debuted masterpieces like Igor Stravinsky's *Firebird* (1910), *Petrushka* (1911), and *The Rite of Spring* (1913), and Claude Debussy's *Afternoon of a Faun* (1912). A master of creating collaborative teams, Diaghilev revolutionized DANCE staging, effectively founding modern ballet.

Diaghilev's attractions and attachments to men were well-known. Most of his friends believed that he and his cousin, Dmitri (Dima) Filosofov, were lovers in the 1890s. Living and working in libertine, artistic circles, Diaghilev never worried much about what others might think: he once made a point of walking arm-in-arm down a crowded street with the then disgraced OSCAR WILDE.

His most famous romance was with his brilliant protégé, the legendary dancer (and, after 1912, innovative choreographer) Vaslav Nijinsky (1890–1950). Nijinsky later claimed that from their first meeting, he "hated" Diaghilev but "pretended because I knew that my mother and I were starving." By all accounts, Diaghilev was a jealous and hot-tempered lover, and he was enraged when Nijinsky married a Hungarian countess, Romola de Pulsky, in 1913. The men later reconciled, but Nijinsky had already begun a decline into schizophrenia that lasted the rest of his life.

Diaghilev also worked with a number of gay artists, including JEAN COCTEAU and composer François Poulenc, whose ballet *Les Biches* he produced in 1924.

Diaghilev sickened and died suddenly while on holiday in Venice. His tomb there remains a place of pilgrimage for ballet lovers.

- ✧ *Diaghilev: Creator of the Ballets Russes—Art, Music, Dance,* edited by Ann Kodicek (1996).

Dickinson, Emily
(1830–1886)

U.S. poet. Born into a prominent Amherst, Massachusetts, family, Dickinson studied at the Amherst Academy and for a year at the Mount Holyoke Female Seminary. After a conventionally social youth, she gradually cut herself off from society, living alone with her younger sister Lavinia and a servant and, in her last years, not even allowing her doctor to be in the same room with her. Throughout her adult life, however, she maintained intimate relationships with both women and men via an extensive correspondence. Although only 8 of her 1,776 poems were published during her lifetime, many others were sent to her correspondents, who recognized and appreciated her originality if not always her genius.

One of her correspondents, the critic Thomas Wentworth Higginson (who is most remembered for advising Dickinson in 1862 not to publish her "remarkable, though odd" poems but who was better known in the 19th century for his savage attacks on WALT WHITMAN and OSCAR WILDE), "corrected" and published a selection of 115 of Dickinson's poems in 1890, four years after her death. The poems caused a sensation, and, over the next six decades, as more of her poems and letters saw print, Dickinson was acclaimed, second only to Whitman, as the greatest and most influential American poet of the 19th century.

Dozens of theories have been proposed to explain Dickinson's stubborn self-seclusion and the despair apparent in so much of her poetry. Until the 1950s, most biographers conjectured a tragic love for one or more of the important men in her life, virtually ignoring her equally passionate—and more extensively documented—relationships with women. In 1951, Rebecca Patterson sought to explain what she called *The Riddle of Emily Dickinson* by suggesting that Dickinson had never recovered from a love affair with Kate Scott Anthon, a beautiful widow Dickinson met in 1859 and with whom she spent at least one night alone. Critics reviled Patterson for suggesting Dickinson was a lesbian, but it has become a commonplace of subsequent scholarship to ascribe HOMOEROTICISM or at least bisexual tendencies to her poems and letters, especially those addressed to her friend and sister-in-law Susan Gilbert Dickinson.

Not surprisingly, considering the era in which she lived, Dickinson never wrote explicitly about her sexual desires, nor is it clear that the words "Sapphist" or "LESBIAN" would have meant anything to her. The power of her work lies in the profoundly original ways she could, as ADRIENNE RICH writes, "retranslate her own unorthodox, subversive, sometimes volcanic propensities into a dialect called metaphor: her native language. 'Tell the Truth—but tell it Slant.' " A number of recent writers, from Rich to Martha Nell Smith and CAMILLE PAGLIA, have reexamined Dickinson's "native language" and found complexities of emotional expression and GENDER identification that escaped earlier critics.

On another front, Dickinson's correspondence has been a catalyst in the debate over 19th-century women's ROMANTIC FRIENDSHIPS. LILLIAN FADERMAN's pivotal study, *Surpassing the Love of Men* (1981), was stimulated by her discovery of Dickinson's "love poems and letters to Sue Gilbert" and her hypothesis that their friendship was not "a lesbian relationship as such relationships have been lived through much of our century."

✧ Lillian Faderman, "Emily Dickinson's Letters to Sue Gilbert," *Massachusetts Review* (vol. 18, Summer 1977).

✧ Adrienne Rich, "Vesuvius at Home: The Power of Emily Dickinson," in *On Lies, Secrets and Silence: Selected Prose, 1966–1978* (1979).

✧ Camille Paglia, *Sexual Personae: Art and Decadence from Nefertiti to Emily Dickinson* (1990).

✧ Martha Nell Smith, *Rowing in Eden: Rereading Emily Dickinson* (1992).

Didrikson, Babe

(Mildred Ella Didrikson Zaharias; 1911–1956)

U.S. athlete. Born in Port Arthur, Texas, she was the sixth of seven children. Her father, a carpenter, and her mother, a former skiing and ice skating champion, had emigrated from Norway before her birth. The congenitally athletic Didrikson was first called "Baby," then "Babe" from the Norwegian *baden* ("baby"). Typically self-mythologizing, she later claimed that it came from childhood teammates considering her their "Babe" (Ruth).

Considered one of the 20th century's greatest athletes, Didrikson's contributions to women's competitive athletics were unprecedented, with 364 first-place medals in track and field alone. Over the course of her career, she also won championships in basketball, baseball, boxing, swimming, diving, horseback riding, shooting, fencing, tennis, golf, and billiards. At the 1932 Olympics, she entered three events (the limit for women) and won two gold medals and in the high jump a gold-silver medal (the only one awarded in Olympic history), because the judges ruled her style (the "Western roll") illegal.

Didrikson received the Associated Press Woman Athlete of the Year award six times, and she was named Woman Athlete of the Half Century in 1950. She dominated amateur and professional women's golf for 18 years, winning all major titles, including the first British Women's Amateur Championship (1947). In 1949, she joined with five other women to found the Ladies Professional Golf Association. Didrikson died of colon cancer two years after her third U.S. Women's Open win in 1954.

Babe Didrikson (left) and protégée Betty Dodd shoot a practice round at the Tampa Women's Open, 1955.

Although Didrikson married professional wrestler George Zaharias in 1938, many fans and colleagues suspected that Didrikson had lesbian affairs, including a long-term relationship with fellow golfer Betty Dodd. She was also one of the first famous women athletes to have her "femininity," GENDER identity, and even her estrogen level called into question. More significantly, her extraordinary combination of coordination, strength, and competitiveness inspired generations of women athletes to defy convention and redefine female athletic "norms."

- ✧ Betty Hicks, "Babe Didrikson Zaharias," *Women Sports* (November/December 1975).
- ✧ Victoria A. Brownworth, "Locker-Room Lockout: Dyke Bashing in American Sports," *The Advocate* (June 4, 1991).
- ✧ Susan E. Cayleff, *Babe: The Life and Legend of Babe Didrikson Zaharias* (1995).

Digital Queers (DQ)

Group of computer professionals founded by Tom Rielly and Karen Wickre in 1991 to help lesbian and gay organizations make more effective use of cybernetics and cyberspace. Based in San Francisco, with offices in Boston, Los Angeles, and Atlanta, and members across the country, DQ has worked with organizations ranging from the NATIONAL GAY AND LESBIAN TASK FORCE to Parents, Family, and Friends of Lesbians and Gays (PFLAG). Besides providing expert guidance, DQ promotes computer industry philanthropy to lesbian and gay causes. Rielly told THE ADVOCATE in 1995 that he wanted DQ to help create a "queer global village."

- ✧ Sam Gallegos, "Gay Guerillas in Cyberspace," *The Advocate* (February 7, 1995).

Direct Action

Term used to describe highly confrontational protest tactics and the groups that advocate them. Nineteenth-century labor unionists,

Lesbian Avengers eat fire at a massive demonstration in Washington, D.C., in March 1990.

abolitionists, temperance advocates, and suffragettes pioneered "direct actions" that ranged from strikes to Carry Nation–style bar smash-ups. In the early 1970s, lesbian and gay activists renewed the tradition of direct action protests in the form of ZAPS. Direct action tactics resurfaced in the late 1980s and early 1990s with the formation of groups such as ACT UP, QUEER NATION, LESBIAN AVENGERS, and, in Great Britain, OUTRAGE!

Notable actions included: the **October 13, 1987**, demonstration on the steps of the U.S. Supreme Court in which more than 600 protesters were arrested; a **December 10, 1989**, protest that drew 5,000 angry demonstrators to St. Patrick's Cathedral in New York City; the **April 24, 1993**, permitless nighttime march in Washington, D.C., in which some 20,000 Lesbian Avengers, including some fire-eaters, converged on the White House.

➤ Also see ASSIMILATIONISM/CONFRONTATIONALISM.

Disabled Lesbians and Gay Men

All disabled persons face formidable psychological, economic, environmental, sexual, and spiritual challenges. Many are additionally marginalized by racism, ageism, and class prejudice. Disabled lesbians and gay men describe still further complications: a twofold struggle for a self-accepting identity that demands they come OUT both as gay or lesbian *and* as disabled. And once out, they often have difficulty finding nonhomophobic personal care attendants—not to mention access to gay and lesbian social life.

Some disabilities pose special problems when considered in a lesbian and gay context. Many blind gay men and lesbians are in the unique position of having to ask straight people to obtain information on lesbian and gay groups and activities, since bulletin boards, posters, and local publications are seldom available in braille. Deaf gay people often report they know less about their family members than if they could hear, and thus find it harder to predict whether or not their families will reject them if they come out. In addition, the heightened body consciousness and "lookism" that almost everyone experiences as part of the lesbian and gay SUBCULTURES have an exacerbated effect on disabled gay men and lesbians, making some feel even more insecure in gay and lesbian circles than in the straight world.

That virtually everyone benefits when the disabled make gains is demonstrated by a term disabled people have coined to replace "able-bodied": "TAB," or *temporarily* able-bodied. The term serves as a reminder that "disabled" eventually describes almost everyone who lives long enough. Yet as Canadian writer and activist Gerald Hannon points out, TABs, gay

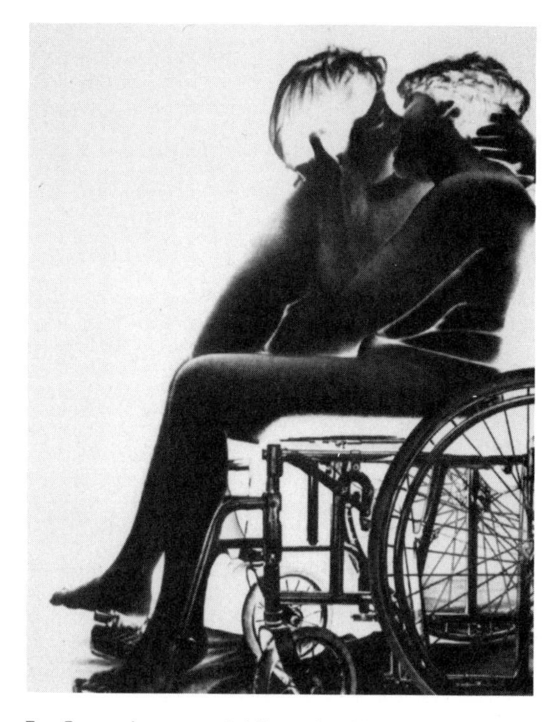

Tee Corinne's vision of differently abled eroticism.

and straight alike, "are still some way from seeing that to be handicapped means simply to be human in a slightly different way."

Activism

Alliances with disabled persons have long been a part of gay and lesbian ACTIVISM but were perhaps most evident in the extended campaign in support of SHARON KOWALSKI. The Kowalski case also built awareness among lesbians and gay men of the unique difficulties they face as members of generally nontraditional family structures when confronting disabilities.

Early disabled gay and lesbian organizational efforts included the formation in New York City of groups like Disabled Lesbian Alliance (1978) by Connie Panzarino, Janet Pearl, Roz Richter, Rose Resto, and Lynn Shoenfeld; Gay and Lesbian Blind (1979) by Raul Lugo; and in Chicago, the Lambda Resource Center for the Blind (LRC, 1979) by John Feldman, Terry Gorman, and Stephen Hunt. The first group to provide lesbian and gay blind people with books, LRC also produced a special magazine that featured gay and lesbian history, culture, travel, book reviews, and personal ads. In the early 1980s, a group of women led by Marj Schneider began offering braille and recorded versions of feminist and lesbian publications through the Minneapolis-based Womyn's Braille Press. Important publications have included *A Disabled Gays Guide* (1981), written in the UNITED KINGDOM, and beginning in the summer of 1988, *Dykes, Disability, and Stuff,* a newsletter edited by Catherine Odette and Sara Karon in Madison, Wisconsin, to provide a forum for lesbians to write on a wide variety of topics important to the disabled.

These and other community institutions have proliferated in the U.S. and abroad. Deaf gay and lesbian groups, for example, are now active in 19 states and 13 countries, and a multinational European Deaf Lesbian and Gay Conference held its first meeting in Paris in December 1992.

Culture

One of the earliest and most visible indications of a disabled presence in the lesbian and gay communities was the movement to provide sign language interpreters at women's MUSIC festivals and other events, a campaign pioneered by National Theatre of the Deaf actor Timothy Near, who began signing her sister HOLLY NEAR's performances in the 1970s. Unaware of Near's initiative, Susan Freundlich independently began to sign women's music concerts in 1976 after "realizing the women's movement had been very closed to deaf women, to disabled women in general." The group SWEET HONEY IN THE ROCK took signing another step forward in 1980 by making interpreter Shirley Childress Johnson part of their ensemble, rather than placing her off to the side.

A number of literary anthologies and magazines have also evidenced the development of a unique disabled lesbian and gay culture. Embarking on what he called "the voyage of self-empowerment," deaf gay writer Raymond Luczak edited the pioneering *Eyes of Desire: A Deaf Gay and Lesbian Reader* in 1993. Early disabled women's collections included *With the Power of Each Breath* (1985), edited by Susan Browne, Debra Connors, and Nanci Stern, and *With Wings* (1987), edited by Marsha Saxton and Florence Howe.

AIDS as a Disability

Opinions vary as to whether alliances between the lesbian and gay disabled and the larger community have been strengthened because of

AIDS. Boston lesbian disabled activist Carrie Dearborn observes that "many people who have been disabled in one way or another by AIDS are still reluctant to identify themselves as disabled." Persons with AIDS have nonetheless benefited from disabled activism. As of 1990, they were protected from many forms of discrimination by being included in the groundbreaking Americans with Disabilities Act.

- Gerald Hannon, "No Sorrow, No Pity; The Gay Disabled," in *Flaunting It: A Decade of Gay Journalism from The Body Politic,* edited by Ed Jackson and Stan Persky (1982).
- *The Blind, the Deaf, and the Physically Handicapped with Alternative Sexual Orientation,* edited by Gays for Equality and the Council on Homosexuality and Religion (1984).
- Connie Panzarino, *The Me in the Mirror* (1994).

Disciples of Christ

Protestant denomination, formally known as the Christian Church, founded in the early 19th century by Alexander Campbell and his father, Thomas. The million-plus Disciples of Christ believe that individual interpretation of the BIBLE is the sole basis of faith. In 1977, however, the church issued a "Study Packet on Homosexuality and the Church" that cited biblical sources to affirm heterosexuality as the only legitimate form of sexual expression. The Gay, Lesbian and Affirming Disciples Alliance was established in 1979 to provide education and support for both the laity and the clergy.

Disco, see SOCIAL DANCING.

Divine

(Harris Glenn Milstead; 1945–1988)

U.S. performer. To his grandmother's dismay, Glenn began CROSS-DRESSING as a child growing up in Baltimore. By the time he appeared in his first movie, his friend JOHN WATERS's 8-mm *Roman Candles* (1966), he had reconsecrated himself as the flamboyant "Divine," a 300-pound contender for the title of "The Most Beautiful Woman in the World." Along with Waters, Divine innovated a déclassé variation on CAMP and drag that was so aggressively (and hilariously) repellent, it was paradoxically almost inoffensive. After several other starring roles in Waters's films, including *Mondo Trasho* (1970), and appearances in San Francisco revues, Divine became internationally famous as Babs Johnson in *Pink Flamingos* (1972), earning the title of "the filthiest person alive" by eating dog feces on film.

Divine went on to make records and to perform in plays, TELEVISION programs, and other FILMS, even occasionally playing male roles, such as a gangster in *Trouble in Mind* (1985). Firmly established as one of the most famous gay male icons of his day, he died of a heart attack just as he reached the brink of stardom with a wider audience after his performance in the "mainstream" hit *Hairspray* (1988).

Dixon, Melvin

(1950–1992)

U.S. writer, translator, critic. Born and raised in Connecticut, Dixon attended Wesleyan University and earned an M.A. and a Ph.D. from Brown University. He taught English at Williams College from 1976 until 1980 and then at Queens College of the City University of New York until his death from complications of AIDS.

Dixon published his first book of poetry, *Climbing Montmartre,* in 1974. Two other

Two of Divine's original looks.

books of poetry, works of criticism, a major translation (*The Collected Poems of Léopold Sédar Senghor,* 1991), and several widely anthologized stories followed, but at his death Dixon had received his greatest acclaim for his two novels: *Trouble the Water* (1983), a southern gothic tale of a Harvard professor's fateful return to his grandmother's North Carolina home; and *Vanishing Rooms* (1991), which probes the psychologically complex reactions of a black man whose white lover has been killed by queer bashers, a black woman to whom he turns for comfort, and a sexually ambivalent white man who was one of the queer bashers.

✧ Melvin Dixon interviewed by Clarence Bard Cole, *Christopher Street* (vol. 14, no. 1, 1991).

Dobkin, Alix

(1940–)

U.S. folksinger, songwriter, women's MUSIC pioneer. Dobkin was born in New York City but grew up in Kansas City and Philadelphia, the daughter of Jewish Communist parents who were as musical as they were leftist. Besides her father, who sang folk songs, and her mother, who played the piano and taught her that "nothing unites people in the moment like music," other early influences included Woody Guthrie, Pete Seeger, Balkan musician Ethel Raim, and Broadway musicals. After earning a B.F.A. in painting at Temple University, she returned to New York to pursue a career as a folksinger, making the Gaslight Café in Greenwich Village her base. Married and the mother of a daughter, Adrian, she met Lisa Diamond Cowan, fell in love, and came OUT in 1972.

In 1973, Dobkin and flautist Kay Gardner teamed up as Lavender Jane (named after fugitive radical feminist Jane Alpert, who had publicly condemned the sexism of male leftists), later adding Pat Moschetta (Patches Attom) on bass guitar. That same year, the group released and distributed (under Dobkin and Gardner's own label, Women's Wax Works) *Lavender Jane Loves Women,* the first album produced, engineered, and performed entirely by lesbians. Still popular more than two decades later (not only in the U.S. but also abroad: Irish activist Joni Crone has noted its influence on the women who began organizing a lesbian movement in IRELAND in 1978), the album features songs inspired by Dobkin's experiences in consciousness-raising sessions, which were a driving force of LESBIAN FEMINISM. Dobkin describes the songs as political statements "that we love each other, are powerful together, have a space where we can just be who we are, live in harmony with the creatures, the land and with each other—all ages, races, classes, cultures."

After 1975, Dobkin continued performing around the world as a solo artist. Her sixth album, *Love and Politics* (1992), was a 30-year retrospective of her songs and arrangements as well as a memoir of the events in her life that inspired them. Rejoicing in an identity as a "professional lesbian," Dobkin affirms an all-encompassing "commitment to international lesbian culture—I can't even imagine what my life would be like any more without it."

✧ Alix Dobkin, *Adventures in Women's Music* (1979).

✧ Toni Armstrong Jr., "A Mother-Daughter Conversation: Alix Dobkin and Adrian Hood," *Hot Wire* (May 1989).

Dodson, Betty [Ann]

(1929–)

U.S. artist, writer, sex educator. Born in Wichita, Kansas, the only daughter of four children, Dodson left college after one year to study art at the National Academy of Design and the Art Students League in New York City. After further study in Paris and the end of a seven-year marriage, she took advantage of the 1960s group sex scene to get the education in sex she felt she—and other women—were lacking.

In the 1970s, Dodson emerged as a pioneering voice for sex-positive feminism, promoting sex workshops and publishing *Liberating Masturbation* in 1974. She opened a body sex studio in her home in 1973 to provide physical and sexual consciousness raising for feminists viewing masturbation and sex awareness as "a meditation on self-love." To counter the negative body image, body shame, and repressions about sex and pleasure that women faced, she recommended "an intense love affair with yourself."

An early voice of sex liberation, Dodson views sexual repression as a socially enforced vehicle for keeping women in place. A bisexual, she has endorsed all forms of sexuality—including "self-sexuality"—as a total sex life. She views masturbation as a fundamental way to break the social bonds and fight the repression, fear, guilt, and misunderstanding of the antisexual social system.

Liberating Masturbation, her contribution to feminism, which was reissued in 1996 as *Sex for One,* remains a classic. Her one-woman shows of female genitalia art are reminiscent of the work of TEE CORINNE or Marilyn Gayle. She received a Ph.D. in sexology in 1992 and produces sexuality workshop videos.

Artist Alvin Orloff hit on one of the problems of domestic partnership in this 1991 cartoon.

Domestic Partnership

Government or corporate recognition of a special relationship or expanded family unit between two unmarried people living together. As of 1997, more than 400 U.S. companies offer some benefits to domestic partners. Although domestic partnerships also cover unmarried heterosexual couples, they have become strongly identified with the GAY AND LESBIAN RIGHTS MOVEMENT. Benefits vary widely but may include visiting rights in hospitals and jails, the right to assume or share an apartment lease, and health benefits for partners of employees working in firms or civil service jobs that recognize domestic partnerships.

Some airlines, such as American Airlines, have special bereavement rates for domestic partners and allow partners to use each other's frequent flyer miles.

On **December 18, 1982**, the Quebec parliament became the first North American legislative body to authorize domestic partner benefits for same-sex couples. On **December 5, 1984**, Berkeley, California, was the first city in the U.S. to extend spousal benefits to the domestic partners of city employees.

Same-sex MARRIAGE advocates caution that domestic partnerships fall far short of conventional wedlock in terms of the rights and privileges they offer. Objections from other quarters include artist Alvin Orloff's montage in which he warns: "Poets beware: Nothing rhymes with domestic partner."

Domestic Violence

Among gay men and lesbians, sometimes called "lover battery" or "partner battering." Lesbian activists often use the term "lesbian battering" to shift the focus of attention from the usual site of occurrence ("domestic") to the persons involved and their troubled relationship.

Domestic violence is commonly defined as a pattern (rather than isolated acts) of violent and coercive behaviors used to dominate and control a partner. It includes damage to property and threats of bodily harm as well as acts of assault and battery. Once established, the pattern of violence is unlikely to cease. Experts are pessimistic about the chances for changing a batterer's behavior and strongly recommend that battered partners cut off all contact with batterers before the violence escalates to even more tragic proportions.

The extent and frequency of domestic violence among lesbians and gay men is still a matter of speculation. Even among heterosexual couples, most domestic violence goes unreported; it is thought that an even higher proportion of gay men and lesbians keep lover battery hidden. Reasons for this reluctance to come forward include fear of public exposure of their sexual orientation, expectations of HOMOPHOBIA in social welfare and LAW enforcement institutions, and shame at being the victim of a person of their own sex. The U.S. government offers almost no relevant data—although, according to Bureau of Justice Statistics reports, 95 percent of the victims of domestic violence are women. Within the gay and lesbian communities, the problem has only recently begun to be addressed. Two major collections of articles on gay and lesbian perspectives in PSYCHOLOGY, published in 1993 and 1995, contain no mention of domestic violence.

Domestic violence has been a thorny issue in the gay and lesbian communities for several reasons. One is the political mandate to project a consistently positive, even utopian public image of lesbian and gay sisterhood/brotherhood, egalitarian relationships, and law-abiding nonviolence; this leads some battered partners, especially lesbians, to hide the problem even from their friends, out of the specious concern that they will be perceived as "letting down" the gay and lesbian cause. Another is reluctance to rekindle the homosexuality-as-sickness theories that dominated public discourse before the GAY LIBERATION era. (In fact, one of the first times the U.S. mass media discussed lesbianism came on **January 26, 1892**, when newspapers headlined the sensational "love murder" of Freda Ward by Alice Mitchell. Subsequent reports linked violence and "perverted love.") In the past, some have blamed gay and lesbian battering on S/M or BUTCH-FEMME relationships or attributed it to the effects of drugs and alcohol, racism, or internalized homophobia. Studies have found, however, that the causes are complex and individual.

One of the first organized attempts to address the problem was the Lesbian Task Force formed in 1978 in response to U.S. Commission on Civil Rights and National Coalition Against Domestic Violence (NCADV) hearings on the abuse of women. Overcoming resistance to a specifically lesbian workshop, the NCADV Lesbian Task Force called for further discussion and study of key issues, which included deciding the kinds of services to be offered, developing ways of making programs accountable to the lesbian community, and studying whether or not it was possible to change batterer behavior. Barbara Hart, a leader in the movement, further observed that lesbians must stop viewing battered lesbians as "weak sisters," and instead accept their leadership and develop ways of holding batterers accountable for their behavior.

Gay men have lagged behind lesbians—who have begun providing shelters and advocacy/intercession programs for battered partners—in addressing the problem of domestic violence, although special hotlines and support groups have been established in a few large cities. Both communities have benefited from the efforts of the New York–based Anti-Violence Project, which in 1987 established the Seeking Non-violent Alternatives Program (SNAP) to assist battered partners. In 1995, SNAP launched a pilot project to seek ways of working with batterers to change their behavior.

When lover battery leads to legal actions, attorneys have found it difficult to get juries to construe same-sex battering as domestic violence. As a result, they often have these cases tried in another context. The first lesbian to use a battered woman defense was Annette Green, who in 1988 shot her lover, Ivonne

Julio, at their home in Palm Beach County, Florida. Although initially unsuccessful, the defense was seen as largely responsible for the reduction of Green's conviction from second-degree murder to manslaughter in a retrial and for her early release from PRISON in 1991.

➤ Also see DOMESTIC PARTNERSHIP; MARRIAGE.

- ✧ *Naming the Violence: Speaking Out About Lesbian Battering,* edited by Kerry Lobel (1986).
- ✧ David Island and Patrick Letellier, *Men Who Beat the Men Who Love Them* (1991).
- ✧ Joelle Taylor and Tracey Chandler, *Lesbians Talk Violent Relationships* (1995).
- ✧ Claudia Card, *Lesbian Choices* (1995).

Dooley, Dr. Tom

(Thomas Anthony Dooley III; 1927–1961)

U.S. doctor, humanitarian, writer. A St. Louis native, Dooley grew up in a devout Catholic family and attended the University of Notre Dame. As a navy doctor, he supervised a medical assistance program for more than 600,000 refugees fleeing from North Vietnam to the south in 1954. After his discharge in 1956, Dooley established a network of hospitals and clinics in Southeast Asia to serve the rural poor. He described his experiences in several best-sellers, including *Deliver Us from Evil* (1956). Considered America's answer to Albert Schweitzer, Dooley was named the seventh most-admired man in the U.S. in a 1959 Gallup poll. He was proposed as a candidate for sainthood after his death, from cancer, at the age of 34.

In 1993, RANDY SHILTS revealed a well-kept secret: Lieutenant Dr. Tom Dooley had been dishonorably discharged from the MILITARY for his homosexuality. Following an anonymous tip, the navy had launched an elaborate six-week investigation that included bugging private phones and monitoring Dooley's personal contacts during a lecture tour organized to promote *Deliver Us from Evil.*

In 1995, Cliff Anchor, Dooley's lover, visited Notre Dame, where a statue honoring Dooley stands, in the midst of an administrative struggle over recognition of a campus gay and lesbian organization. Anchor spoke with the president emeritus of the college and later commented: "I felt that he understood that Dooley was the greater hero for having withstood all this bigotry and turning out as he did."

- ✧ Randy Shilts, *Conduct Unbecoming: Gays and Lesbians in the U.S. Military* (1993).

Doolittle, Hilda, see H.D.

Drag, see CROSS-DRESSING.

Drug Abuse/Drugs, see ADDICTION/RECOVERY.

Duberman, Martin Bauml

(1930–)

U.S. historian, playwright, educator, founder of the Manhattan-based Center for Lesbian and Gay Studies (CLAGS), the first institute of its kind in the U.S. Duberman grew up in New York City and suburban Westchester. He toured with a summer stock company at the age of 17, but decided to study history instead of acting when he entered Yale University the following year. He received his Ph.D from Harvard University in 1957, and taught at Yale and Princeton University in the 1960s. In 1971, he was named Distinguished Professor of History at Herbert H. Lehman College, City University of New York (CUNY). He established CLAGS at CUNY's Graduate Center in 1991.

Martin Bauml Duberman (right) with Jonathan Ned Katz.

Duberman has published 16 books in addition to authoring more than a dozen plays. His first play, *In White America* (produced on Broadway in 1963), documented two centuries of AFRICAN-AMERICAN life, and, along with an award-winning biography, *Charles Francis Adams, 1807–1886* (1963), earned him a reputation as an historian who could engage the general public as persuasively as his academic peers.

Duberman's academic and theatrical achievements stood in sharp contrast to the stagnation of his private life. In the first of his memoirs, *Cures: A Gay Man's Odyssey* (1991), Duberman describes more than two tortured decades of struggle with his sexuality, culminating in his leaving psychotherapy and coming OUT in print in 1972 with the publication of *Black Mountain: An Exploration in Community.*

Once out, Duberman quickly established himself as a leading intellectual and activist in the then nascent field of LESBIAN AND GAY STUDIES. Besides publishing influential articles on a wide range of topics, he was a founding member of LAMBDA LEGAL DEFENSE AND EDUCATION FUND and the NATIONAL GAY (later: AND LESBIAN) TASK FORCE, as well as the Gay Academic Union (see **11/23/1973**). In 1989, he was one of the editors of *Hidden from History: Reclaiming the Gay and Lesbian Past;* in 1991, many of his most important essays were collected in *About Time: Exploring the Gay Past;* and in 1993, he published *Stonewall,* the first book-length account of the STONEWALL Uprising.

Along with his scholarly achievements in lesbian and gay studies, Duberman has also begun to record his own wide-ranging experiences as a gay man, beginning with *Cures* and continuing with *Midlife Queer: Autobiography of a Decade, 1971–1981* (1996).

Duncan, Robert

(1919–1988)

U.S. writer. Duncan grew up in a somewhat unconventional family that adhered to a form of theosophism. One of his first sexual experiences, at the age of 17, was with a young drifter he met in a park near his home. After the two boys had reached orgasm, the drifter put on brass knuckles and proceeded to pummel Duncan so severely he required plastic surgery. Duncan later learned that the young man was a psychopath who had already killed at least two other boys. Undaunted, Duncan continued to explore his sexuality while a student at the University of California at Berkeley, and afterward in Venice, Italy, and New York City.

In **August 1944**, Duncan, a published poet with a growing audience, became the first American man to come OUT in a public forum, an essay written for the journal *Politics*. Duncan's essay, entitled "The Homosexual in Society," included the then startling assertion that homosexuals were a persecuted minority, not unlike Jews or blacks, yet condemned the "cult of homosexual superiority" he believed was embodied in CAMP as "a tone and a vocabulary that is loaded with contempt for the human." In place of a specifically homosexual rights movement, he advocated an all-encompassing "devotion to human freedom, toward the liberation of human love, human conflicts, human aspirations."

Back in Berkeley after WORLD WAR II, Duncan became one of the leaders—along with his lover, the painter Jess Collins, and fellow poets Jack Spicer and Kenneth Rexroth—of what came to be known as the Berkeley–San Francisco Renaissance. In the mid-1950s, he taught at Black Mountain College in North Carolina.

Despite his left-wing politics and sexual openness—and sometimes unconventional behavior, as when he gave poetry readings in the nude—Duncan was widely acclaimed as one of the leading poets of his generation. His most popular work was *Bending the Bow* (1968). Many of his poems express the need for men to search "for a joining that is not easy" ("Sonnet 1," in *Roots and Branches,* 1964).

✧ Steve Abbott and Aaron Shurin, "Robert Duncan," in *Gay Sunshine Interviews, Volume Two,* edited by Winston Leyland (1982).

Dworkin, Andrea

(1946–)

U.S. antipornography activist, writer. Dworkin grew up on a street in Camden, New Jersey, where WALT WHITMAN once lived. While studying at Bennington College, she was arrested for taking part in a protest against the Vietnam War and jailed for four days. After her release, she spoke and wrote widely about the sexual abuse she had suffered at the hands of PRISON authorities and her fear of the "rampant" lesbianism among her fellow inmates. She later apologized in print for the latter remarks, but she insisted that the prisoners had behaved "like men—macho, brutish, threatening." After years of thought on sexism, its origins and its consequences, she published *Woman Hating: A Radical Look at Sexuality* in 1974, calling for "a political action where revolution is the goal."

Dworkin subsequently elaborated her call for a lesbian feminist revolution in a series of speeches, articles, and a book, but by the 1980s she was most famous for her activism against PORNOGRAPHY. With legal scholar Catharine MacKinnon she advanced the idea that pornography was a form of discrimination that deprived women of their civil rights. The U.S. Supreme Court found legislation based on their positions unconstitutional in 1986, but Dworkin continued to press for new civil laws, in spite of opposition from prosex lesbian activists like PAT CALIFIA, who wrote: "While trumpeting against the evils of S/M and pornography, Dworkin is trying to distract us as she tamps a gag in our mouths."

Dworkin has also written several autobiographical novels, including *Ice and Fire* and *Mercy*.

➤ Also see **February 27, 1992**.

✧ Andrea Dworkin, "A Letter to M," in *Lavender Culture,* edited by Karla Jay and Allen Young (1978; reissue, 1994).

✧ Andrea Dworkin, *Letters from a War Zone* (1989).

✧ Pat Califia, *Public Sex: The Culture of Radical Sex* (1994).

Dykewomon, Elana

(Elana Nachman; 1949–)

U.S. writer, activist, printer. Her father was a lawyer, her mother a library researcher who reportedly once lost a job for smuggling arms to Israel. Elana attempted suicide as an adolescent and was forced to undergo treatment she later described as "psychiatric assault." After receiving a B.F.A. in creative writing from the California Institute of Art, she published her first book, *Riverfinger Women* (1974), a nontraditional novel that chronicles a woman's resistance to and escape from cruelly exploitative heterosexual relationships and her assertion of a heroic lesbian identity.

Reflecting her evolving commitment to lesbian SEPARATISM and a desire to escape a long male-dominated Hasidic tradition, she published her second book, a collection of stories and poems entitled *They Will Know Me by My Teeth* (1976), marked "womyn-only," as "Elana Dykewoman" and her third book, *Fragments from Lesbos* (1981), a collection of poems "for lesbians only," with her surname respelled "Dykewomon." In 1980, she issued statements throughout the lesbian press protesting the inclusion of her work in an anthology published by a company (Harper and Row) owned and operated by men. In 1987, she became editor of the lesbian journal *Sinister Wisdom.* While some of her ultimatums have evolved with time, Dykewomon continues to write for lesbians, protect lesbian communication networks, and encourage mutual support to build an economic and cultural base. Her novel *Beyond the Pale* appeared in 1997.

Dykewomon's widely published articles and essays have attacked sociocultural attitudes toward fat women ("Traveling Fat") and sought to forge a positive Jewish/lesbian identity ("The Fourth Daughter's 400 Questions"). With her lover, Dolphin Waletzky, she prints and distributes "the work of lesbians to lesbians."

✧ Elana Dykewomon, "To the Lesbian and Women's Presses," *Inciter* (August 1980).

✧ Anna Livia, "Elana Dykewomon," in *Contemporary Lesbian Writers of the United States,* edited by Sandra Pollack and Denise D. Knight (1993).

E

Eakins, Thomas

(1844–1916)

U.S. artist. Except for four years' study in Paris in the 1860s, Eakins spent his life in and around Philadelphia. Famous for his portraiture during his lifetime, he is today considered a founder of American realism.

From 1873, Eakins taught at the Pennsylvania Academy of Fine Arts. Then, in 1886, he was forced to resign after he ripped a male model's loincloth off during a life class, as he later said, "to demonstrate an anatomical point." Eakins since has been canonized by historians as a martyr in the struggle for artistic freedom, but letters that surfaced in the 1980s reveal that the "loincloth incident" was only part of why he was dismissed. Eakins, apparently, had removed his own clothes on several occasions and pressured students, male and female, into shedding theirs.

Eakins left behind hundreds of carefully posed nude photos. Some were photo studies for paintings such as *The Swimming Hole* (1883). Others reflect the late-19th-century fascination with exploring classical themes in PHOTOGRAPHY. Like the Greeks (and JOHANN JOACHIM WINCKELMANN), Eakins saw the male body as the ideal. His legacy to homoerotic photography is the way he translated this ideal into a Whitmanesque vision of "comradely" play.

There is no evidence that Eakins ever acted on the HOMOEROTICISM apparent in his work. He had intimate friendships with the sculptor Samuel Murray, a younger student with whom he shared a studio, and WALT WHITMAN, whom he painted and photographed from 1887 to 1892. He was married from 1884 until his death to Susan MacDowell, a selflessly devoted former student and a painter in her own right.

- William Innes Homer, *Thomas Eakins: His Life and Art* (1992).
- Allen Ellenzweig, *The Homoerotic Photograph* (1992).
- Adam Gopnik, "Eakins in the Wilderness," *The New Yorker* (December 26, 1994).

Earhart, Amelia

(Amelia Mary Earhart Putnam; 1897–1937?)

U.S. aviator, social worker, writer. Earhart's Atchison, Kansas, parents let her wear bloomers and play with footballs as a child and generally supported her lifelong defiance of convention. Although less than enthusiastic when Earhart left social work for aviation, her mother, the first woman to reach the 14,000-foot summit of Pikes Peak, applauded her daughter's first transatlantic venture by wiring: "We are not worrying. Wish I were with you. Good luck and cheerio."

Beginning in 1928, Earhart embarked on a career of aviation firsts. She was the first woman to fly the Atlantic Ocean solo (1932), receive the U.S. government's Distinguished Flying Cross, make a transcontinental nonstop flight, fly an autogiro, and be inducted into the Aviation Hall of Fame. She was also the first aviator, male or female, to fly solo from Hawaii to California and to fly nonstop from Mexico City to Newark. In 1929, she and her close friend Ruth Nichols helped found the Ninety-Nines, an international organization of women pilots (today it has more than ten thousand members).

On July 2, 1937, Earhart and navigator Fred Noonan were on the last leg of an unprecedented round-the-Equator flight when they vanished in the South Pacific. No one has ever satisfactorily accounted for their disappearance.

Although there is no evidence that Earhart had sexual relationships with other women, her TOMBOY youth, masculine dress, competitiveness, adventurous spirit, outspoken advocacy of feminism, and insistence on self-fulfillment have made her an icon for generations of lesbians. As CAMILLE PAGLIA, who became obsessed with Earhart while still in high school, has written, "She provided a role model when there was none." Principled and controversial, Earhart once accused a chapter of the Daughters of the American Revolution of glorifying war, adding, "You really all ought to be drafted." When she married publisher George Putnam in 1931, she presented him with a contract that stated her reluctance to marry, neither offered nor demanded fidelity, and exacted a "cruel promise" that they would reassess their marriage in a year. This unconventional contract, many biographers conclude, suggests that the marriage served pragmatic rather than romantic purposes for both Earhart and Putnam, who acted as her promoter and agent.

Whatever Earhart's sexuality was, few lesbians can help but sigh when reading the admiring profile she wrote of her friend Nichols: "Even in the air she is apt to be garbed in her favorite color, which happens to be purple, and she owns a specially made purple leather flying suit and helmet."

- Amelia Earhart, *The Fun of It* (1932).
- Jean L. Backus, *Letters from Amelia: An Intimate Portrait* (1982).
- Nancy Shore, *Amelia Earhart* (1987).

Eastern Europe

No laws against consensual same-sex relations between adults in Albania, Bulgaria, Croatia, the Czech Republic, Estonia, Hungary, Latvia, Lithuania, Montenegro, Poland, Slovakia, Slovenia, and Ukraine. Higher AGE OF CONSENT *for same-sex relations as opposed to different-sex relations in Bulgaria and Croatia.*

All male-male sex acts illegal in Bosnia-Herzegovina, Macedonia, and Serbia (including Kosovo), with penalties of up to one year's imprisonment. Male-male anal intercourse illegal in Belarus and Moldova.

All same-sex relations resulting in "public scandal" illegal in Romania, with penalties of up to five years' imprisonment.

Active rights movement, developing social and cultural scenes in the Czech Republic, Estonia, Hungary, Latvia, Lithuania, Poland, Slovakia, and Slovenia. Small rights organizations, informal social networks in Albania, Bulgaria, Croatia, Ukraine, and Yugoslavia.

Although the word "homosexual" was coined by a Hungarian (writing in German—see **5/6/1868**), gay and lesbian Eastern Europeans have lagged behind the rest of Europe in developing a distinctive identity and SUBCULTURE. Change has come rapidly, however, since the collapse of the Iron Curtain, and today lesbian and gay organizations all over Eastern Europe are linked with one another and the rest of the world. Gay and lesbian SWITCHBOARDS, publications, and even radio broadcasts have sprung up everywhere from Latvia to Slovenia, and cities like Budapest, Cracow, Prague, and Warsaw have become popular destinations for lesbian and gay tourists from more developed countries. Although Romania is almost alone in continuing official persecution of lesbian and gay activities—AMNESTY INTERNATIONAL reported arrests, torture, and imprisonment of dozens of gay men and lesbians in the country through the mid-1990s—unofficial hostility is widespread, and Western-style "queer-bashing" is on the rise throughout the region. The ROMAN CATHOLIC CHURCH, ORTHODOX EASTERN CHURCHES, and the Evangelical Lutheran Church in Latvia are just a few of the religious groups that have actively fought the development of a lesbian and gay rights movement.

History

At the beginning of the 20th century, sex between men was illegal in all the countries that now form Eastern Europe; sex between women was also a crime in Austrian and Hungarian territories. Poland decriminalized same-sex relations in 1932.

Same-sex relations were decriminalized by the Communist Hungarian government in 1962, and Budapest had at least one fairly well-known gay bar for at least 20 years before the fall of communism. Lesbian and gay characters and concerns were a part of some films and novels in Hungary as early as 1982, when the semiautobiographical novel of a well-known writer, Erzsebet Galgoczi, was made into the movie *Another Way* by director Karoly Makk. Set against the backdrop of the 1956 revolt, the film gives a good idea of what life was like for lesbians under the old regime.

In 1988, Hungary was also the first country in Eastern Europe to extend official recognition to a gay and lesbian organization, Homeros Lambda. The group fell apart due to internal disputes within a few years, but a large-circulation gay magazine *Mások* ("Another") remains in print, despite sporadic police harassment. Some small organizations have been formed in Hungary's larger cities, and Budapest today has an active bar scene, supplemented by private lesbian and gay networks.

Change came later to other Eastern European countries. A rights movement began in **February 1990** in Czechoslovakia and, building on mostly underground efforts of the 1980s, about the same time in Poland. After the breakup of the Soviet Union, groups began to organize in the Baltic countries, and contacts between Eastern and Western European gay and lesbian groups became common.

➤ Also see CENTRAL ASIA; RUSSIA.

✧ Keith Hale, *In the Land of Alexander: Gay Travels with History and Politics, in Hungary, Yugoslavia, Turkey, and Greece* (1990).

✧ *The Third Pink Book: A Global View of Lesbian and Gay Liberation and Oppression,* edited by Aart Hendriks, Rob Tielman, and Evert van der Veen (1993).

✧ *Breaking the Silence: Human Rights Violations Based on Sexual Orientation,* Amnesty International USA report (1994).

Effeminacy, see GENDER.

Ellerman, Annie Winifred, see BRYHER.

Havelock Ellis.

Ellis, Henry Havelock
(1859–1939), and

Ellis, Edith Lees
(1856–1916)

English writer, sex researcher; his wife, a writer and lecturer. As a young adult, Ellis became fascinated by the then emerging study of sexuality. He studied medicine but supported himself by writing reviews and essays on a variety of social issues. His first books advanced views influenced by contemporary socialism that included the emancipation of women and a rejection of Victorian prudery in favor of "science."

Ellis met Edith Lees, then working as a secretary, through his socialist friends, and they married in 1891—although most biographers doubt their marriage was ever consummated. Partly influenced by her husband's studies, which included a published analysis of her own sexual development, Edith came to embrace a lesbian identity, had a number of passionate relationships with women (as well as close friendships with gay men such as EDWARD CARPENTER), and became one of the first public, if cautious, proponents of lesbian rights, lecturing in England and the U.S. (see **2/4/1915**) and publishing papers in defense of "abnormality." Her husband, on the other hand, who acknowledged a sexual fetish for what he dubbed urolognia (watching women urinate), was apparently uninterested in affairs of any kind. Some commentators, including British historian and theorist Jeffrey Weeks, believe that consciousness of his own sexual oddity helped him empathize with other sexual nonconformists.

In the early 1890s, Ellis began corresponding with JOHN ADDINGTON SYMONDS, and the two men decided to collaborate on a book on same-sex relations that would combine Symonds's historical and cultural studies with Havelock's critique of current medical and psychological theories. Havelock completed the book after Symonds's death in 1893.

Sexual Inversion was first published in a German translation (as *Das Kontrare Geschlechtsgefühl*) in 1896. The first English edition, published in 1897, was bought out by Symonds's heirs to prevent the reading public from learning of his involvement with the book. A second English edition, published without Symonds's name, came out later that year, but was effectively banned when the police arrested George Bredborough, the secretary of an allegedly radical organization called the Legitimation League, for selling the book, which the indictment called "a certain lewd wicked bawdy scandalous and obscene libel." Bredborough pleaded guilty, and Ellis resolved not to publish *Sexual Inversion* or any of the subsequent volumes of what became the seven-volume *Studies in the Psychology of Sex* (1897–1928) in the UNITED KINGDOM. He instead issued them in the U.S., where his books were read with interest, especially by medical and psychological specialists.

Weeks sees Ellis less as an innovative thinker than as someone who synthesized the thinking of others working in England and on the

Continent. These ideas included the assertion that most cases of homosexuality were not evidence of "degeneration," but were rather harmless anomalies, and that the social and psychological "disorders" commonly associated with homosexuality were actually caused by social oppression.

Despite their sexual incompatibility, the Ellises remained close until the last few years of Edith's life, when she suffered a series of collapses that led to her being institutionalized.

➤ Also see HALL, RADCLYFFE.

- Jeffrey Weeks and Sheila Rowbotham, *Socialism and the New Life: The Personal and Sexual Politics of Edward Carpenter and Havelock Ellis* (1977).
- Phyllis Grosskurth, *Havelock Ellis: A Biography* (1984).

Empress Court, see CROSS-DRESSING.

England, see UNITED KINGDOM.

Episcopal Church

Branch of the ANGLICAN COMMUNION officially established in the U.S. in 1789, with more than 2.4 million members. The Church has traditionally tolerated a wide range of believers within its membership. As a result, policies on homosexuality vary radically from one diocese to another. As early as 1968, a group of Episcopalian priests in the New York area issued a statement urging that same-sex relations be considered "morally neutral." On **January 10, 1977**, the year after the Church first allowed women to be ordained as priests, Bishop Paul Moore Jr. of New York City ordained Ellen Marie Barrett; she thus became the first openly lesbian cleric of any major religious organization in the United States.

In some Episcopal dioceses, however, more conservative bishops have protested these actions and even accused gay- and lesbian-friendly bishops of heresy. On August 24, 1994, a meeting of Episcopal bishops in Indianapolis issued an ambivalent "study document" that both affirmed the responsibility of the Church to "respond pastorally" to the needs of lesbian and gay church members and appended a statement from a conservative faction describing same-sex relations as a "denial of God's plan."

The controversy came to a head in 1995, when ten Episcopalian bishops formally charged Bishop Walter C. Righter, retired Episcopal bishop of Iowa, with heresy for having ordained a noncelibate gay man, Barry Stopfel, as a deacon while Righter was serving as bishop of Newark, New Jersey. On **May 15, 1996**, a Church court made up of eight bishops ruled in Righter's favor, issuing a majority opinion that "there is no core doctrine prohibiting the ordination of a noncelibate, homosexual person living in a faithful and committed sexual relationship with a person of the same sex." But as evidenced by the careful wording of the opinion—and two dissenting statements from three of the court's bishops—the moral status of same-sex relations remained an issue of contention for the church. Meanwhile, however, Stopfel, the openly gay deacon whose ordination was the subject of the trial, had been ordained as a priest and assigned to a parish in Maplewood, New Jersey, where he lived openly with his companion, Will Leckie. Stopfel noted that his parish grew from 350 to 400 members during the time the heresy trial was in the news.

Integrity, a "justice ministry" for gay and lesbian Episcopalians, was established in 1974.

Erotica, see HOMOEROTICISM; PORNOGRAPHY.

Essentialism, see CONSTRUCTIONISM VS. ESSENTIALISM.

Etheridge, Melissa

(1961–)

U.S. rock star. Born in Leavenworth, Kansas, Etheridge had her first intimate relationship with a woman, her "best friend," while still in high school, but discovered she "wasn't alone" only after moving to Boston to study at the Berklee College of Music. After coming OUT to her father (whose response was a simple, accepting "Is that all?"), she relocated to Long Beach, California, and began performing in local lesbian bars, including the Que Sera Sera, where in 1986 she was discovered and signed by Island Records founder Chris Blackwood.

The most popular of a new breed of forceful women rockers, Etheridge's appeal transcends gender and sexual orientation. After coming out to the world in January 1993 at the Triangle Ball, a gay and lesbian celebration of Bill Clinton's presidential inauguration, she went on to release a fourth album, *Yes I Am,* which went platinum and won a second Grammy.

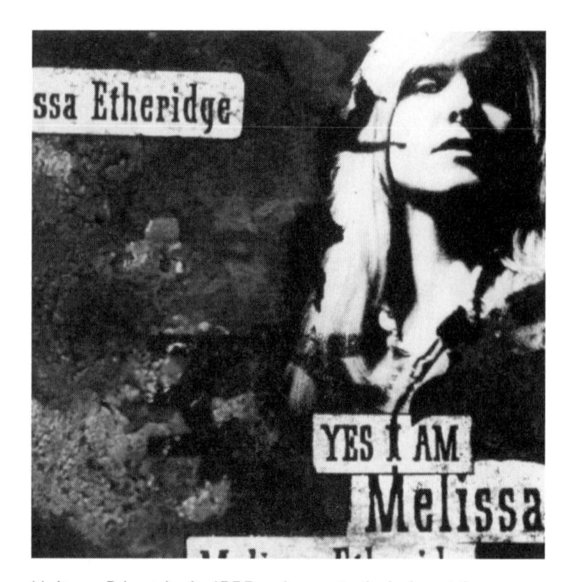

Melissa Etheridge's 1993 release included a title song that (coincidentally?) asserted, "Yes I Am."

Etheridge met filmmaker Julie Cypher in 1988 while working on a video, and the two women gradually became lovers over the next two years. Although Etheridge eschews "role model" status, she and Cypher were by the mid-1990s the most photographed—and arguably the most celebrated—gay or lesbian couple in the world.

F

Faderman, Lillian

(1940–)

U.S. writer, historian, educator. A native of the Bronx, New York, Faderman began to explore the gay and lesbian SUBCULTURE as a teenager living in Los Angeles in the 1950s. Early on she found herself frustrated by the paucity of "real literature" written by and for lesbians. About her education at the Universities of California at Berkeley and Los Angeles, she once remarked: "In 1967, I received a Ph.D. in English without the slightest notion that lesbian literature had a rich history and that many of the writers I admired had contributed to that history."

Faderman's first major contribution to LESBIAN AND GAY STUDIES was *Surpassing the Love of Men: Romantic Friendships and Love Between Women from the Renaissance to the Present* (1981), a groundbreaking analysis of the nature of women's relationships before the development of consciously lesbian identities. She further advanced her exploration of this theme with *Scotch Verdict: Miss Pirie and Miss Woods v. Dame Cumming Gordon* (1983), examining the social context and theoretical implications of a scandal involving two boarding school mistresses (see **1812**). In 1991, she brought her analysis into the present with the landmark *Odd Girls and Twilight Lovers: A History of Lesbian Life in Twentieth-Century America.*

Faderman has also edited *Chloe Plus Olivia* (1994), a literary anthology of lesbian writers over the past four centuries that tracks the changing sense of what constitutes "lesbian literature." Less well known but also influential was her early work on *Lesbian-Feminism in Turn-of-the-Century Germany* (1980) with Brigitte Eriksson.

An outspoken proponent of social constructionism (see CONSTRUCTIONISM VS. ESSENTIALISM), Faderman views a lesbian or gay orientation as a (potentially positive) *choice* as opposed to a biologically or psychologically mandated identity. Writing in THE ADVOCATE in 1995, she further asserted that BISEXUALITY "is the natural human condition."

Faderman is a professor of English and Lesbian Studies at California State University, Fresno, where she lives with partner Phyllis Irwin and son Aurom.

➤ Also see ROMANTIC FRIENDSHIPS.

Fassbinder, Rainer Werner

(1946–1982)

German filmmaker, actor. Born and raised in Bavaria, Fassbinder and other actors formed the Anti-Teater theater troupe in Munich in 1968. He turned to feature FILMS in 1969 and soon won international recognition as the leading auteur of the New German Cinema. He wrote and directed almost 60 film and TV productions, besides acting in his and others' films.

Dieter Schidor's documentary The Wizard of Babylon (1982) includes an interview with Rainer Werner Fassbinder completed a few hours before his death. Here, from left to right, Franco Nero, Schidor, Fassbinder, Brad Davis, and Andy Warhol pose on the set of Querelle.

Fassbinder had sex with both women and men but identified himself and his artistic point of view as "gay," a sensibility most apparent in his sardonic wit and blend of CAMP with melodrama but also perceptible in his empathy with losers and society's victims. The two most important loves of his life were El Hedi Ben Salem and Armin Maier, both of whom committed suicide after stormy relationships with Fassbinder. Fassbinder himself died of a drug and alcohol overdose at the age of 36.

Even his fans were put off by at least some elements of his work. *New York Times* critic Vincent Canby, a longtime supporter, wrote of one of his films that its "only redeeming feature is genius." Never afraid to offend, Fassbinder was the first German director to make gay and lesbian themes a prominent part of his work, most notably in *The Bitter Tears of Petra von Kant* (1972), a lurid look at a lesbian triangle; *Fox and His Friends* (1975), in which a lower-class lottery winner shares his fortune with his upper-class lover; *In a Year of Thirteen Moons* (1978), about a transsexual rejected by the man she has become a woman for; and the homoerotic *Querelle* (1982), based on JEAN GENET's novel *Querelle de Brest.*

✧ Robert Katz, *Life Is Colder Than Death: The Life and Times of Rainer Werner Fassbinder* (1987).

Feinberg, David B.

(1956–1994)

U.S. writer, AIDS activist. Feinberg grew up in Massachusetts and attended the Massachusetts Institute of Technology. He came OUT shortly after graduating from college while living in Los Angeles. He moved to New York City in the late 1970s, joined a gay writers' group, and earned an M.A. from New York University in 1981.

In 1989, Feinberg published the first volume of what he called his "trilogy of terror," the novel *Eighty-Sixed*. Like the linked short stories in *Spontaneous Combustion* (1991) and the essays collected in *Queer and Loathing: Rants and Raves of a Raging AIDS Clone* (1995), *Eighty-Sixed* by turns celebrates and savages the Manhattan gay SUBCULTURE and its response to AIDS. Unlike his other books, *Eighty-Sixed* also critiques pre-AIDS manners and mores. The first half of the novel, "1980: Ancient History," is a kind of downscale sequel to LARRY KRAMER's saga of A-list *Faggots* (1978). The second half, "1986: Learning How to Cry," draws the main character, B. J. Rosenthal, inexorably into the "age of anxiety."

Feinberg's widely published stories and essays were almost unanimously praised in mainstream media for their acid humor and unflinching frankness. Some gay critics were disturbed by Feinberg's polemics on gay life and politics, but most agreed with FELICE PICANO, who wrote that Feinberg's essays on the "multiple and manifold distortions of reality brought about by the disease [AIDS]" reached "new levels of weirdness, cynicism, humor and even art."

Feinberg died of complications of AIDS shortly before his 38th birthday.

✧ Felice Picano, "Humor from the Horror," *Lambda Book Report* (January/February 1995).

✧ Jim Marks, "Generation Gap," *Harvard Gay and Lesbian Review* (Winter 1995).

Fem(me), see BUTCH/FEM(ME).

Female impersonators, see CROSS-DRESSING.

Feminism, see LESBIAN FEMINISM.

Femininity, see GENDER.

Fiction, see DETECTIVE FICTION LITERATURE, and SCIENCE FICTION.

Field, Michael

(Katharine Harris Bradley; 1846–1914. Edith Emma Cooper; 1862–1913)

English writing team. The daughters of wealthy Birmingham manufacturer and merchant families, they both were allowed to direct their own studies, although Bradley, who was Cooper's aunt and 16 years older, mentored Cooper's girlhood education. Both women became leaders in the women's suffrage movement while studying classics and linguistics at University College, Bristol.

Their "spiritual partnership" began with *The New Minnesinger* (1875), poems published under the pseudonyms "Arran and Isla Leigh." Almost a decade later, "Michael Field" debuted as the author of a play, *Callirrhoe* (1884). Eight books of lyric poetry, another play, and over two dozen tragic poetic dramas followed. Besides the subject of love, their work explored feminist themes while celebrating self-sacrifice and joie de vivre. Their popularity fluctuated, but Robert Browning, George Meredith, and W. B. Yeats remained constant supporters.

One of their first poems announced, "My love and I took hands and swore, / Against the world, to be / Poets and lovers evermore. . . ." For their advocacy of women's rights—and their own relationship—to be taken seriously, however, they felt they had to use a male pseudonym. They selected "Michael" because they admired William Michael Rossetti; "Field" was an old nickname of Cooper's. In private,

Cooper was "Henry" and Bradley was "Michael."

Writing to HAVELOCK ELLIS, Bradley characterized their collaboration as a "perfect mosaic: we cross and interlace like a company of dancing summer flies." They described themselves as "closer married" than the Brownings. Some of the love poetry they wrote to each other can be found in *Underneath the Bough* (1893) and *Mystic Trees* (1913).

- Mary Sturgeon, *Michael Field* (1922).
- Chris White, " 'Poets and Lovers Evermore': Interpreting Female Love in the Poetry and Journals of Michael Field," *Textual Practice* (vol. 4, no. 2, Summer 1990).

Fierstein, Harvey
(1954–)

U.S. playwright, actor. Born and raised in Brooklyn, Fierstein came OUT to his parents at the age of 13 and had his first job performing in drag three years later, acting in Andy Warhol's off-off-Broadway play *Pork* (1971). By the time he graduated with a B.F.A. from the Pratt Institute in 1973, he had already written and performed in two of his own drag-themed plays and went on to produce a third before writing and presenting the plays that became *Torch Song Trilogy* in 1981. *Torch Song* told the story of Arnold Beckoff, a drag queen whose search for love leads to relationships with a bisexual man, Ed, and a gay man, Alan. Despite featuring unfashionable BUTCH-FEMME relationships at the height of the macho CLONE era—not to mention what some critics found an overly heterosexual vision of coupled bliss, complete with a child—*Torch Song* was immensely popular: its Broadway incarnation ran for more than 1,000 performances and earned Fierstein Tony Awards for Best Actor and Best Play. Fierstein summarized the play's message in

Harvey Fierstein (seated) with Susan Edwards in a scene from the Broadway production of *Torch Song Trilogy*.

1983, when he told *Newsweek* that "gay liberation should not be a license to be a perpetual adolescent. If you deny yourself commitment then what can you do with your life?"

Fierstein won a third Tony for his book for the hit musical comedy *La Cage aux Folles* (1983). In 1987, he tackled AIDS with *Safe Sex,* three one-act plays, one of which was broadcast on HBO as *Tidy Evenings* (1989). He also wrote the screenplay for the 1995 FILM *Dr. Jekyll and Ms. Hyde.*

The most successful and most frequently cast openly gay male ACTOR in U.S. entertainment, Fierstein's credits include the gay brother in *Mrs. Doubtfire* (1993) and the voice of a secretary in *The Simpsons.*

Film and Video, Gay, Lesbian, and Queer

Kinetic visual media—usually directed by lesbian, gay, or bisexual filmmakers—with an explicitly gay, lesbian, or queer theme. As with all ART, queerness is very much in the mind of the beholder. No critic has managed to fix a clear-cut boundary between "gay and lesbian" and "straight" film and video. Gay filmmakers like TODD HAYNES release (more or less) straight films like *Safe* (1995); a movie as ostensibly devoid of sex, sexuality, and even romance as *The Wizard of Oz* (1939) had such a strong appeal for gay and lesbian audiences that "friend of Dorothy" became synonymous with queer. As a result, an enormous number of films and videos are considered gay or lesbian, and an even larger number, queer. One particularly comprehensive guide lists more than 3,000 movies and videos from 36 countries on close to 50 themes, ranging from AFRICAN-AMERICANS to "woman/girl love." About 30 gay or lesbian feature films—and several hundred short films and videos—were released in the U.S. in 1995.

"Honey" in Lizzie Borden's politically charged science fiction film, Born in Flames (1983).

Since STONEWALL, the proliferation of gay and lesbian film festivals and, perhaps even more significantly, the popularity of VCRs have combined to multiply the potential viewing audience for lesbian and gay films and videos, new and old. The longest-running annual gay and lesbian film festival is Frameline's San Francisco International Lesbian and Gay Film Festival, which began with a program of Super-8 shorts on **February 9, 1977**.

Pre-Stonewall Features

On one level, the genealogy of gay and lesbian film and video is easy to outline: although hundreds, perhaps thousands, of movies had at least one character, usually less than positive, who appears gay or lesbian to present-day audiences, only a few dozen films made before Stonewall had overtly gay or lesbian major themes. On another level, many other movies contain subtexts that generations of lesbians and gay men have claimed for themselves. An example of this, although almost too overt to call a "subtext," survives from one of the earliest experimental films made at the Thomas Edison Studio: *The Gay Brothers* (1895), in which two men dance a waltz together.

The oldest surviving feature with an openly homoerotic theme is Swedish director Mauritz Stiller's *The Wings* (1916), a tragic tale of a man's obsession for a youth based on Danish novelist Herman Bang's *Mikaël* (1906). The first movie (and almost the last until the 1960s) to make its main theme a plea for social tolerance of adult gay men and lesbians was probably Richard Oswald's *Anders als die Andern* ("Different from the Others"—see **5/24/1919**), produced by (and featuring) MAGNUS HIRSCHFELD. The release of *Anders als die Andern* may also mark the first time an ACTOR widely known to have sexual relationships with men, Conrad Veidt, played a gay man on film. Except for a fragmentary 30-minute version found in Ukraine in 1976, all known copies of the film and its 1927 remake were destroyed during the NAZI PERSECUTION.

Another German film, *Pandora's Box* (1929), contained the first full-fledged lesbian character: tuxedo-clad, cigar-smoking Countess Anna Geschwitz (Alice Roberts), depicted as both fiercely possessive and nobly self-sacrificing in her unconsummated love for the amoral Lulu (Louise Brooks). Leontine Sagan's *Mädchen in Uniform* (1931), based on Christa Winsloe's play about a girl at a Prussian boarding school, was not only the first sympathetic treatment of lesbian love, it was also one of the first movies directed, produced, and scripted by women. All explicit homoerotic references were censored when the film was released in the U.S. in 1932, so that most viewers would have found the main character's love for her teacher no more shocking than an "innocent" schoolgirl crush. Also censored was the response of her teacher (and love interest) to the school principal's condemnation of same-sex love: "What you call sins, Principal, I call the great spirit of love, which has thousands of forms."

Many American movies from the period contain playful or derisive depictions of gay or lesbian characters and situations (especially CROSS-DRESSING), but, apart from a few curiosities like silent film star Alla Nazimova's all-lesbian/gay, all-CAMP tribute to OSCAR WILDE, *Salome* (1922), U.S. censorship restrictions (see **4/1/1930**; **7/1/1934**) made it impossible to release an overtly pro-gay or -lesbian film until the 1960s.

Art Films

From the 1930s through the early 1960s—the decades film historian VITO RUSSO calls "the invisible years"—overt HOMOEROTICISM was banned from popular film entertainment, but it occasionally surfaced in avant-garde art films, such as JEAN COCTEAU's *Blood of a Poet* (1930) or Kenneth McPherson's *Borderline* (1930), which explored sexual and racial tensions through the relationships of its characters (played by BRYHER, H.D., Paul Robeson, and Robeson's wife, Eslanda). Much more explicit representations of gay male desire emerged in the late 1940s with the underground films of KENNETH ANGER and in 1950 with JEAN GENET's lyrically pornographic PRISON elegy, *Un Chant d'Amour.*

The audience for these films, which were most frequently shown at "art houses" that also screened high-quality European features not widely released in the U.S., was small compared with the millions who flocked to mainstream movies, but it was influential and cosmopolitan. The International Confederation of Art Houses, established in Paris in 1955, linked several hundred cinemas in 20 countries. Yet even these theaters were subject to police raids as late as the 1970s, and art film critics seldom acknowledged the importance of homoeroticism in the genre. As the editors of *Queer Looks: Perspectives on Lesbian and Gay Film and Video* (1993) note, "avant-garde canons" have "disproportionately featured lesbian and gay artists yet disconcertingly bent over backwards to erase this sexual fact." Sometimes, as in the films of avant-garde master JAMES BROUGHTON, whose most homoerotic films were made beginning in the late 1970s, this was as much the result of self-censorship as of outside pressure.

In the 1960s, as mainstream cinema began once again to take up lesbian and gay themes, art films became even more daring and explicit. Jack Smith's camp classic, *Flaming Creatures* (1962), which was confiscated at its New York City premiere and ruled obscene in criminal court, and several equally controversial features made by Anger presaged Andy Warhol's experimental, frequently homoerotic films (made between 1963 and 1968) as well as those of his protégé, Paul Morrissey.

The underground films of the 1960s also reflected the influence of a genre that would later evolve into post-Stonewall gay male PORNOGRAPHY. "Physique" films—the first of which, bodybuilder Richard Fontaine's *Days of Greek Gods* (1948), actually predated the golden age of PHYSIQUE MAGAZINES—had become increasingly available thanks to the marketing efforts of BOB MIZER and others.

Meanwhile, in Europe, same-sex eroticism between women and/or between men began to surface in the work of major auteurs like Ingmar Bergman (*Persona,* 1966), PIER PAOLO PASOLINI (*Teorema,* 1968), Luchino Visconti (*The Damned,* 1969; *Death in Venice,* 1971), Bernardo Bertolucci (*The Conformist,* 1970), and RAINER WERNER FASSBINDER (*Beware a Holy Whore,* 1970).

After Stonewall: Divergent Trends

Gay and lesbian film evolved in several, sometimes interconnected directions in the 1970s and 1980s. Some directors, such as JOHN WATERS and Richard Benner (*Outrageous!,* 1977, starring Canadian female impersonator Craig Russell), blended camp comedy with relatively conventional narrative structures. ROSA VON PRAUNHEIM and DEREK JARMAN built on the art film tradition with features that appealed to smaller, more sophisticated audiences. And BARBARA HAMMER, among others, insisted that only a "change in film form" could be compatible with the fundamental social and political changes sought by GAY LIBERATION and LESBIAN FEMINISM. As Hammer said, "radical content deserves radical form." She and other pioneering lesbian filmmakers like Jan Oxenberg created experimental films that challenged conventional film aesthetics in an attempt, as Andrea Weiss elaborates, "to control and define lesbian representation in terms other than those offered by the dominant media." Reflecting the influence of 1970s lesbian SEPARATISM, many of these films were shown only to all-women audiences.

Film Theory

Feminist film theory of the 1970s also had a major effect on the content as well as the style of films, especially those made by and for lesbians. In 1975, feminist film critic Laura Mulvey published a much discussed article entitled "Visual Pleasure and Narrative Cinema" in which she argued that mainstream cinema was dominated by the male "gaze" (a look that has the effect of objectifying the person viewed—see QUEER THEORY) in three ways: (1) through the "eye" of the camera, generally operated by men; (2) in the way films are edited, most often, according to Mulvey, so that men look and women are looked at; (3) via the look of the "spectator" (audience member) who is forced by (1) and (2) to watch the film from a male perspective. In a later article, Mulvey hypothesized that the only way women could derive pleasure from male-dominated cinema was to adopt a male point of view, a process she called "visual transvestism." Women, she believed, had to pretend to be men to enjoy conventional films.

Mulvey's articles were extremely controversial, especially among lesbian critics, who saw themselves as ignored by the theory: lesbians, presumably, did not have to pretend to be men to enjoy an eroticized film depiction of a woman. They also pointed out that a few mainstream directors, such as DOROTHY ARZNER, had in fact been women (and lesbians). But the consensus was that lesbian filmmakers were in the unique position of having *no* film tradition to build on, freeing innovators like Hammer, Oxenberg, Chantal Akerman, Yvonne Ranier, Monika Treut, and Ulrike Ottinger to make radical breaks with film conventions—even art film conventions—in their attempts to translate lesbian experience to the screen.

Documentaries

The 1970s saw the arrival of the first lesbian- and gay-themed documentaries. One of the earliest to have significant gay content was *A Bigger Splash* (1974), a look at the artist DAVID HOCKNEY. The Mariposa Film Group's *Word Is Out* broke new ground in 1977 by recording the experiences of a diverse collection of 26 lesbians and gay men. GUY HOCQUENGHEM'S *Race d'Ep* (retitled in English as *Homosexual Century*) was perhaps the first gay historical documentary.

Gay and lesbian documentary filmmaking has been especially strong in Western Europe and CANADA, where government funding is sometimes easier to obtain than in the U.S. In the UNITED KINGDOM, Channel 4, an alternative TELEVISION network established in 1982, pioneered a national gay and lesbian TV newsmagazine format with *Out on Tuesday* (1989–1990) and *Out* (1991–1992). In both Europe and the U.S., filmmakers like ISAAC JULIEN, PRATIBHA PARMAR, and MARLON RIGGS have made effective use of documentaries to achieve a higher level of visibility for black and Asian lesbians and gay men.

New Queer Cinema and Old-fashioned Movie Entertainment

By the 1990s, gay and lesbian film and video was growing ever more diverse in style as well as content, ranging from the avant-garde protest videos of the Testing the Limits Collective (formed in 1987) and the ACT UP–affiliated DIVA TV (Damned Interfering Video Activists, from 1989) to the almost "mainstream" *Desert Hearts* (1986), which SARAH SCHULMAN called "the first lesbian feature in the history of the world made with lesbian money for a lesbian audience." In between were an array of features, like Sheila McLaughlin's *She Must Be Seeing Things* (1988) and Todd Haynes's *Poison* (1991), that provided viewing satisfaction for movie fans and academic film theorists alike. As for the genre that critics came to call "new queer cinema"—which included work by GREGG ARAKI, Bruce LaBruce (*Super 8-1/2* 1994), Rose Troche (*Go Fish,* 1994), GUS VAN SANT, and many other directors—these films had little more in common than an in-your-face cinematic stance.

True to the gay and lesbian art film heritage, many film and video makers continue to reject mainstream movie conventions. Lesbian filmmaker Cecilia Dougherty, just to name one example, filmed *Coal Miner's Granddaughter* (1991), a feature-length coming-out story, with a Fisher-Price toy camera. Yet perhaps the most discussed film trend of the 1990s was the unprecedented increase in production of gay- and lesbian-themed features for wide release.

➤ Also see ACTORS/ACTING; HOLLYWOOD.

✧ Parker Tyler, *Screening the Sexes: Homosexuality in the Movies* (1972).

✧ Vito Russo, *The Celluloid Closet: Homosexuality in the Movies* (rev. ed., 1987).

- *Queer Looks: Perspectives on Lesbian and Gay Film and Video,* edited by Martha Gever, John Greyson, and Pratibha Parmar (1993).
- Sarah Schulman, "What Is the Role of Gay Film Festivals," in *My American History: Lesbian and Gay Life During the Reagan/Bush Years* (1994).
- *Out in Culture: Gay, Lesbian, and Queer Essays on Popular Culture,* edited by Corey K. Creekmur and Alexander Doty (1995).
- Raymond Murray, *Images in the Dark: An Encyclopedia of Gay and Lesbian Film and Video* (rev. ed., 1996).

Finland

No laws against same-sex relations between consenting adults, but AGE OF CONSENT *is 18, two years higher than for heterosexual relations. Some discriminatory legislation as well as a degree of rights protection. Developed social scene and political groups in Helsinki, Tampere, and Turku.*

Traditionally more conservative than its Scandinavian neighbors, Finland has lagged behind most of Western Europe both in rights protection and the development of an open, multifaceted gay and lesbian SUBCULTURE. Although there had long been public cruising areas and cafés known to be frequented by lesbians and gay men in Helsinki, the first bona fide gay BARS did not open until the late 1950s, and almost all lesbian and gay Finns remained discreetly CLOSETed through the 1960s. Same-sex relations were decriminalized in 1971, but the penal code was simultaneously amended to mandate a six-month to four-year sentence for anyone who "publicly encourages unchastity between persons of the same sex."

In 1981, gay and lesbian Finns founded a national rights organization, Sexuaalinen Tasavertaisuus (SETA), which mobilized demonstrations against the 1971 amendment. Twenty protesters who were arrested were released without being charged.

Despite the amendment, SETA now has offices throughout the country, and gay and lesbian publications, foreign and Finnish, are widely available. Antigay and -lesbian discrimination in the MILITARY is officially forbidden, and some social benefits have been extended to gay and lesbian couples in DOMESTIC PARTNERSHIPS. Finnish activists continued to campaign in the 1990s to obtain adoption and MARRIAGE rights for same-sex couples and a nondiscriminatory age of consent.

Firbank, Ronald

(Arthur Annesley Ronald Firbank; 1886–1926)

English writer. The son of a knighted, immensely wealthy member of Parliament, Firbank was a sickly nine-year-old when OSCAR WILDE's career as English aesthete and wit laureate ended in ignominy. A decade later, Firbank launched himself as an equally outrageous though less publicly scandalous writer by self-publishing a pamphlet containing a fairy tale and a novella. Between 1905 and the beginning of World War I, he studied for six terms at Cambridge, converted to Catholicism, traveled extensively, and frequented London's bohemian cafés and salons. When war came, he secluded himself in Oxford and wrote four novels in five years, beginning with *Vainglory* (1915). He continued writing and publishing in the 1920s until chronic illness and heavy drinking led to his death at the age of 40.

Firbank's eight novels and two plays take place in "a Nirvana," as critic Ernest Jones wrote in 1951, "in which homosexuals are the ultimate chic and in which almost everybody turns out to be at least bisexual." Typical is *Val-*

mouth (1919), a novel inspired by a trip to HAITI, in which a group of colorfully queer centenarians pursue romantic and erotic adventures at a utopian resort directed by a black masseuse named Mrs. Yajñavalkya. In addition to exotic black characters and a host of outrageous aesthetes, Firbank packed his comic novels with queer nuns and priests, the most famous of whom, Cardinal Pirelli (*Concerning the Eccentricities of Cardinal Pirelli,* 1926), collapses and dies in the course of chasing a beautiful choirboy around a church.

In private life, Firbank fashioned himself into a character every bit as outlandish as his literary creations. He painted his nails carmine, wrote his novels on lavender postcards, and claimed to live on nothing but flower petals and champagne. Although as OUT as anyone in his era could be, he had no major relationships, preferring, as he put it, to "buy companionship." He once wrote his friend and supporter CARL VAN VECHTEN: "I am a *spinster* sir, & by God's grace, intend to remain one."

The British literary establishment refused to take his work seriously in his lifetime, but critics have since acknowledged his contributions to modernism. He was one of the first writers to leave the task of plot construction to the reader, and he pioneered the technique, now as common in movies as in novels, of opening a scene with a non-sequitur series of quotes, creating the effect of walking briskly through a chatty cocktail party. Gay and lesbian critics like Brigid Brophy and JEANNETTE HOWARD FOSTER, who relished his "delightful absurdities," have noted his influence on dozens of more widely read writers, ranging from Evelyn Waugh to JAMES PURDY.

✧ Brigid Brophy, *Prancing Novelist: A Defense of Fiction in the Form of a Critical Biography in Praise of Ronald Firbank* (1973).

Fire Island

New York State barrier island south of Long Island, site of Cherry Grove and Fire Island Pines. A 32-mile-long sliver of sandy beaches and low dunes, "Fire Island" became a code term for queer liberation in the late 1930s, even though only two of its seventeen communities have sizable lesbian and gay populations.

Cherry Grove has been called "America's first gay and lesbian town" by anthropologist and historian Esther Newton. From 1986 to 1993, Newton interviewed past and current residents of the community and traced its history from the first hotel (which began as a restaurant in 1869) through the town's emergence as a safe haven for gay men and lesbians in the 1940s to its present status as an internationally renowned lesbian and gay resort.

Even before the island became a lesbian and gay refuge, it figured in the writings of WALT WHITMAN, who wrote that the shores of the Great South Bay were "woven all through" his *Leaves of Grass.* OSCAR WILDE enjoyed a stay at the Perkinson Hotel in Cherry Grove in 1882. By the 1920s and 1930s, Broadway and Greenwich Village "artistic types" were renting rooms, but it was especially after Cherry Grove was devastated by a hurricane on September 21, 1938, that Long Islanders, badly in need of money to pay for rebuilding, began renting their summer cottages to better-heeled New Yorkers, an ever increasing number of whom were gay or lesbian.

The lesbian and gay summer population burgeoned in the years following World War II. Visitors included PAUL CADMUS, JANET FLANNER, CHRISTOPHER ISHERWOOD, TENNESSEE WILLIAMS, and W. H. AUDEN, who immortalized both the merriment and the alcoholic excesses of "this outpost where nothing is wicked / But to be sorry or sick" in his poem "Pleasure

Cherry Grove was already a gay and lesbian port of call in the late 1940s.

Island" (1948). Less famous gay and lesbian residents developed rich traditions of CAMP theatricals and elaborate theme parties, while all had the chance to learn the vocabulary and fashion mandates of the emerging SUBCULTURE.

Fire Island was a haven where gay men and lesbians felt free to be themselves, but it was not without reminders of the mainland. Police raids on the "Bushes" or "Meat Rack," wooded areas popular for public sex, escalated through the 1960s until New York MATTACHINE president Dick Leitsch began a barrage of protests and legal challenges that resulted in police ignoring the island sex scene after the summer of 1968.

Fire Island Pines, one mile east of Cherry Grove, was founded in the 1950s by nongay developers but by the late 1960s had become a predominantly gay, mostly affluent white male community, at a time when Cherry Grove was beginning to become more lesbian and more ethnically varied. Just as Cherry Grove had helped to propagate camp in the 1950s, the Pines played a pivotal role in popularizing the CLONE aesthetic of the 1970s and the no-bulk-barred "buff" look of the late 1980s (see BODYBUILDING). Its 500-odd homes and 1½-mile-long beach have been settings in dozens of novels, including ANDREW HOLLERAN's *Dancer from the Dance,* EDMUND WHITE's *Forgetting Elena,* LARRY KRAMER's *Faggots,* and FELICE PICANO's *Like People in History.*

Popular historians have credited Fire Island with the first gay disco and even the beginnings of modern no-touch social dancing. Tragically, it has also figured prominently in the history of the AIDS epidemic. As the first, and still one of the few, places in the world dominated by lesbians and gay men, Cherry Grove and Fire Island Pines remain, summer after summer, the towns where the best and worst of the international gay and lesbian subculture have their time in the sun.

✧ Esther Newton, *Cherry Grove, Fire Island: Sixty Years in America's First Gay and Lesbian Town* (1993).

Flanner, Janet [Tyler]

(pseudonym: Genêt; 1892–1978)

U.S. journalist, essayist, translator. Born and raised the daughter of progressive Indianapolis QUAKERS (her father founded a settlement house for AFRICAN-AMERICANS after Booker T. Washington, who had been denied accommodations at local hotels, stayed with the Flanners), Flanner studied at the University of Chicago and wrote art and film criticism for the *Indianapolis Star.* She married William Lane Rehm in 1918 and moved with him to Greenwich Village. By the time they divorced amicably in 1926, Flanner had become aware of her "lesbic approach to all life" and was already living with writer Solita Solano (Sarah Wilkinson) in Paris. She and Solano were later caricatured as the feisty journalists Nip and Tuck in DJUNA BARNES's *Ladies Almanack* (1928). For much of her life, Flanner had concurrent long-term relationships with Solano, Noel Haskins Murphy, and Natalia Danesi Murray, each of whom lived in a different country. After Flanner's death, Murray edited and annotated four decades of their correspondence in *Darlinghissima: Letters to a Friend* (1985). In addition to providing insights into the social and intellectual currents of their times, the letters also document the mutually supportive communities Flanner and the women in her life developed for themselves.

Janet Flanner.

Flanner became *The New Yorker*'s Paris correspondent in 1925. Her innovative "Letter from Paris" essays, which ran through September 1975, never overtly broached the topic of lesbianism, but they often spotlighted the activities of women, including her friends SYLVIA BEACH and NATALIE BARNEY, whose salon she frequented. The letters were later republished in three collections.

The New Yorker originally had a policy that writers use PSEUDONYMS, and Harold Ross, the founding editor, christened Flanner "Genêt" for reasons she never ascertained. Writing under a pseudonym suited Flanner, who took pains to conceal her complicated private life. She once told a musician friend: "The trick is never to say 'I.' You're safer with 'one' or 'it.' 'I' is like a fortissimo. It's too loud." BERENICE ABBOTT photographed Genêt dressed in a black velvet jacket and striped silk trousers—with a double set of masks wrapped around a top hat. Flanner's own choice of a pseudonym for some of her profiles was "Hippolyta," after the legendary queen of the AMAZONS.

In addition to profiles of noteworthy individuals (including her friend MARGARET ANDERSON), Flanner wrote a novel, *The Cubical City* (1926), and translated some of COLETTE's writings.

✧ Brenda Wineapple, *Genêt: A Biography of Janet Flanner* (1989).

Forrest, Katherine V.

(Katherine Virginia Forrest; 1939–)

Canadian-born writer, editor. Born in Windsor, Ontario, Forrest studied at Wayne State University and UCLA. After graduating, she worked at a variety of jobs before establishing herself as an editor and popular writer. She has spent most of her adult life in the Los Angeles and San Francisco areas.

In the space of two years, Forrest published three novels that were so successful they established new lesbian literary conventions in three different genres. Her first novel, *Curious Wine* (1983), an erotic romance, sold more than 100,000 copies. After RADCLYFFE HALL's THE WELL OF LONELINESS, it is probably the most widely read lesbian novel of all time. (In 1994, it also became the first lesbian—and the second gay/ lesbian—novel to be recorded on audiotape.) *Daughters of a Coral Dawn* (1984) transported readers to the planet Maternas, a lesbian SCIENCE FICTION utopia ruled by the inimitable Megan. And *Amateur City* (1984) ushered in a new wave of lesbian DETECTIVE FICTION with the introduction of Forrest's most popular heroine, LAPD investigator Kate Delafield.

Besides succeeding as ingeniously plotted police procedurals, Forrest's Lambda Literary AWARD-winning Delafield mysteries have allowed her to probe facets of gay and lesbian life that range from the CLOSET and McCarthyism (see MCCARTHY ERA) to coming OUT and the communities that form around lesbian BARS. In 1996, a movie adaptation of *Murder at the Nightwood Bar* was planned by filmmaker Tim Hunter with Mary-Louise Parker playing the Lesbian Nation's favorite cop.

Flashpoint (1994), set in California in the early 1990s, was Forrest's first political thriller. Forrest has also coedited, with BARBARA GRIER, three genre-defining lesbian anthologies: *The Erotic Naiad* (1992), *The Romantic Naiad* (1993), and *The Mysterious Naiad* (1994).

✧ Nancy Boutilier, "Breathing the Rarified Air of Freedom," *Lambda Book Report* (January/February 1995).

Forster, E. M.

(Edward Morgan Forster; 1879–1970)

English writer, critic. Forster began publishing sketches and essays while attending King's College, Cambridge (where he was also named a Fellow late in life). While at Cambridge, he fell in love with at least one male classmate and became a member of the Apostles (many of whom were gay—see BLOOMSBURY). His first published work of fiction, "Albergo Empedocle," which appeared in the little-read magazine *Temple Bar* in 1903, tells the story of a young man who travels to GREECE with his fiancée and becomes convinced that he lived in Ancient Greece and not only "loved very differently" but "loved better too." Gradually the young man loses touch with his surroundings and ends up a virtual vegetable in an asylum.

Like his fictional hero, Forster also traveled to Greece, but with his mother, with whom he lived for years and who was part of his reason for staying in the CLOSET. In private, however, he wrote erotic short stories after 1910, some of which were published after his death in *The Life to Come and Other Stories* (1972). Forster's close friend, J. R. ACKERLEY, citing ANDRÉ GIDE's courageous self-disclosure (see **1926**), urged Forster on several occasions to be more open about his sexuality. Forster, according to Ackerley, would always reply: "But Gide hasn't got a mother!"

The sensuality of the Mediterranean—and the threat it posed to the ordered respectability of English life—is a theme in several of Forster's novels, including his first, *Where Angels Fear to Tread* (1905), and especially his third, *A Room with a View* (1908). Forster, however, ultimately found the inspiration that propelled him to affirm his sexuality back home in the

James Wilby (left) and Rupert Graves starred in the 1987 film adaptation of E. M. Forster's Maurice.

English countryside. Visiting EDWARD CARPENTER in 1913, Forster was deeply impressed by Carpenter's loving relationship with his working-class "comrade," George Merrill. One day, Merrill "touched" him, "gently and just above the buttocks." At that exact moment, Forster later wrote, he "conceived" his only openly homoerotic novel. *Maurice* tells the story of a young man much like Forster, his abortive attraction to a fellow Cambridge student, and, eventually, his successful relationship with a lower-class gamekeeper, Alec. When Forster completed *Maurice* "without a hitch" in 1914, he wrote across the top of the manuscript: "Publishable but is it worth it?" He decided it was not, and *Maurice* was not published until 1971, the year after his death.

Despite triumphs like *Howards End* (1910), Forster stopped writing novels after publishing *A Passage to India* (1924), commonly considered his masterpiece. ("Sex got in the way," he later said.) He remained a prominent public figure and critic. His humanism and lifelong commitment to protecting civil liberties (which included a vocal defense of RADCLYFFE HALL'S THE WELL OF LONELINESS) deeply influenced a generation of more openly gay writers and artists, including W. H. AUDEN, CHRISTOPHER ISHERWOOD, and PAUL CADMUS.

Behind the scenes, Forster found the handsome working-class man of his dreams in a masculine, married policeman, Bob Buckingham, whom Ackerley introduced to him. In 1960, writing a "Terminal Note" for the as-yet unpublished *Maurice,* Forster avowed: "I was determined that in fiction anyway two men should fall in love and remain in it for the ever and ever that fiction allows." If Forster and Buckingham did not, as he wrote of Maurice and Alec, "still roam the greenwood," they did at least remain happily together for over four decades: Buckingham's wife came to accept their friendship, and Forster died in Buckingham's house in Coventry.

✧ P. N. Furbank, *E. M. Forster: A Life* (1978).

✧ Claude J. Summers, *E. M. Forster* (1983).

Foster, Jeannette Howard

(pseudonyms: Hilary Farr, Jan Addison, Abigail Sanford; 1895–1981)

U.S. librarian, scholar, writer, translator. Of the generation that, as she put it, "concealed our gayness as if it were syphilis," Foster revealed little about her background out of fear of "violating the privacy" of those intimate with her.

"I can say, however," she wrote, "that I have been deeply attached to a number of women from the time I was four, and six of these affairs had physical expression."

Born in Oak Park, Illinois, Foster studied literature and earned a Ph.D. in library science. While she was serving on her college's student council, the group voted without discussion to expel two young women for spending time together behind locked doors. Haunted by this "morals case," she began reading everything she could find on the psychology of sex. Three decades of study later, she published what has been called the "bible of lesbian literature."

Sex Variant Women in Literature (1956) was the first book to cull Western literature for references to "variant women," which in Foster's definition included bisexuals and cross-dressers. (She reserved the term "lesbian" for "variant women" who had explicitly erotic relations with other women.) The 324 works surveyed, which include dozens of books never translated into English, range from Greek writings and the BIBLE to 1950s PULP FICTION.

Sex Variant Women remains one of the most important resources in LESBIAN AND GAY STUDIES. BARBARA GRIER, who sought Foster out in Kansas City in 1956 after learning about the book and who, along with BARBARA GITTINGS, was instrumental in getting it reprinted in 1975 and 1983, believes there still exists "no substitute for its in-depth analysis of the genre."

Jeannette Howard Foster.

Foster researched *Sex Variant Women* while working as a teacher and librarian at a number of colleges and universities. She sometimes took jobs just to gain access to the closed collections where controversial books tended to be kept, often uncataloged.

Difficult as it was to research, *Sex Variant Women* was even more of a challenge to publish. Her first editor at Rutgers University Press died, and his successor rejected the manuscript because of its subject matter. Since no other publisher would buy it, she was forced to publish with Vantage Press at her own expense. Vantage rearranged the text without her permission, then withheld royalties as payment for restoring it. Later, Vantage sold the rights for a British edition (1958) without telling her or paying her anything. The only money she earned from those editions was $240 from a dealer who bought 2,400 unbound, unfolded sheets.

She worked as a librarian for the Kinsey Institute and, later, for the President's Advisory Committee on Education.

Foster is credited with "rediscovering" NATALIE BARNEY, ROMAINE BROOKS, and RENÉE VIVIEN and with translating Vivien's *Une Femme M'Apparut* into English (*A Woman Appeared to Me,* 1976). She was also a personal friend of JANET FLANNER, MAY SARTON, and many other lesbian writers. She contributed articles to THE LADDER in the 1960s. Her poetry appears in *Two Women: The Poetry of Jeannette Foster and Valerie Taylor* (1976).

When *Sex Variant Women* won the AMERICAN LIBRARY ASSOCIATION's third annual Gay Book Award in 1974, Foster expressed her delight that "my long respected ALA is willing to admit the existence—and even honor it—of Gaiety!"

✧ Karla Jay, "The X-Rated Bibliographer," in *Lavender Culture*, edited by Karla Jay and Allen Young (revised edition, 1994).

✧ Marie Kuda, "Jeannette Howard Foster," in *Gay and Lesbian Literature,* edited by Sharon Malinowski (1994).

Foster, Jim

(James M. Foster; 1935–1990)

U.S. activist. A Long Island native, Foster studied English at Brown University. He was drafted immediately after graduating and served in the Military Intelligence Command. On July 15, 1959, the army expelled him on grounds of homosexuality. He would later point to his dishonorable discharge as the event that sparked his career of activism.

Foster cofounded the SOCIETY FOR INDIVIDUAL RIGHTS (SIR) in San Francisco in **September 1964** and served as one of the most visible officers of the organization into the 1970s. In 1971, he converted SIR's political action committee into the Alice B. Toklas Memorial Democratic Club and in 1973 became treasurer of the California Democratic Committee. San Francisco Mayor George Moscone named him and lesbian activist Jo Daly to the mayoral appointment committee in 1976, and he later served as a member of the San Francisco Health Commission.

On **July 12, 1972**, Foster made history as the first openly gay person to address a major national political gathering, delivering a 10-minute speech at the Democratic National Convention and then yielding the podium to MADELINE DAVIS of the MATTACHINE Society of the Niagara Frontier (Buffalo, N.Y.). In their addresses, both Foster and Davis emphasized their pride in representing, along with three alternate delegates (Renee Cafiero, Danece Covello, Lowell Williams), the gay and lesbian community. CBS broadcast their speeches live, and NBC devoted two minutes of its evening news program to an interview with Foster in which he protested discrimination against gay people.

On January 29, 1985, Foster joined fellow San Francisco Health Commission officers in rejecting the arguments of a group seeking to keep the city's BATHHOUSES open. In *And the Band Played On* (1987), RANDY SHILTS noted that Larry Ludwig, Foster's lover of 12 years, had died of complications of AIDS just 30 hours before the hearing.

Foucault, Michel

(Paul-Michel Foucault; 1926–1984)

French philosopher, sociocultural historian. The son and grandson of medical doctors, Foucault rebelled against family tradition and pursued a career as a philosopher after an education at elite public and Jesuit schools and the prestigious École Normale Supérieure.

While in university, Foucault attempted suicide and was sent to see a psychiatrist. The psychiatrist's efforts to "treat" Foucault's homosexuality both stimulated his interest in PSYCHOLOGY and left him suspicious of its "scientific" impartiality. Through the 1950s, while teaching in Sweden, Poland, and Germany, Foucault continued to research and contemplate the foundations of psychology. In 1961, he published *Folie et Déraison* (abridged English translation, *Madness and Civilization: A History of Insanity in the Age of Reason,* 1965), analyzing the origins and social consequences of psychology as well as laying the groundwork for his subsequent writings on medicine (*The Birth of the Clinic: An Archaeology of Medical Perception,* 1963; English translation, 1973) and on PRISONS (*Discipline and Punish: The Birth of the Prison,* 1975; English translation, 1977).

The idea at the heart of all these books—and most of his other writings—is an extension of the maxim "Knowledge is power." For Foucault, who was skeptical of the existence of absolute truth—especially when it came to human beings—there could be no such thing as knowledge *without* power because force, either physical or intellectual, was required to make people accept "knowledge" as "truth." Foucault believed that Western social sciences had imposed artificial constructions, or "regimes," of knowledge by which certain kinds of behavior—and by extension, certain types of people—were labeled as "sick," "insane," "criminal," or simply "abnormal" so that the rest could by exclusion be considered "healthy," "sane," "law-abiding," or "normal." Along with creating categories of abnormality, social scientists also developed institutions (prisons, clinics, insane asylums, etc.) where those labeled as abnormal could be set apart from other people and studied intensively. Foucault further maintained that these regimes of knowledge were particularly effective because they were eventually internalized: people came to police themselves by accepting the constructions as "scientific" reality.

Although all Foucault's books and articles have had an impact on LESBIAN AND GAY STUDIES, his most influential contributions to the field were three of his last books, published between 1976 and 1984 in French (1978 and 1986 in English) and collected as *The History of Sexuality.* In these books, Foucault compared what he called the *scientia sexualis*—the enormous body of 19th- and 20th-century Western texts on sex that he believed had resulted in the invention of a concept of "sexuality" and the subsequently widespread conviction that sexuality is a profoundly important part of a person's "nature"—with Greek and Roman conceptions of the body and sex. One of the major outcomes of the modern "discourse" on sex and sexuality, he asserted, was that SODOMY, which previously had been "a category of forbidden acts," was replaced by the "psychological, psychiatric, medical category of homosexuality"; and the sodomite, "a temporary aberration," mutated into the "homosexual . . . a personage, a past, a case history . . . a species." In other words, whereas before sodomy had been seen as a sin that, like theft, anyone could conceivably commit, it now became only a symptom of a condition, homosexuality, that characterized a type of person, the homosexual.

Foucault's argument cast doubt on the value of uncovering and asserting a gay "identity" since, according to Foucault, this identity was in large part an artificial construction of social scientists. As a result, some activists accused Foucault of undermining the lesbian and gay rights movement. Foucault countered that *resistance* also played an integral role in shaping identities, and that it was imperative to fight for the right not only to choose and express one's sexuality but also "to go a step further" and create "new forms of life" and "new forms of pleasure."

One of the "new forms of pleasure" that Foucault acclaimed was gay and lesbian S/M, which he discovered after 1975 during stays in San Francisco and New York City. Foucault viewed S/M as a "creative enterprise," the invention of "new possibilities of pleasure with strange parts of the body."

Although the particulars of Foucault's arguments have been disputed by gay, lesbian, and straight historians—and many have criticized him for virtually ignoring women in his writings on sexuality—his theories nonetheless had an enormous impact on a generation of lesbian and gay intellectuals.

Foucault was more or less closeted in French public life, but he was open about his sexuality with friends. For more than two decades he was in what he described as a "state of passion" with Daniel Defert, a philosophy student and later sociology professor ten years his junior. Together with Defert, he played a prominent role in a variety of political actions, in particular the movement for prison reform.

Foucault died of AIDS-related complications at the age of 57. It is not clear whether Foucault knew he had AIDS: he apparently never discussed it with his friends or even with Defert, and his family told the press he had died of a "nervous illness." He appears as Muzil in Hervé Guibert's semiautobiographical novel, *To the Friend Who Did Not Save My Life* (1990; English translation, 1991).

➤ Also see CONSTRUCTIONISM VS. ESSENTIALISM; QUEER THEORY.

- ✧ Bob Gallagher and Alexander Wilson, "Sex and the Politics of Identity: An Interview with Michel Foucault," in *Gay Spirit: Myth and Meaning,* edited by Mark Thompson (1987).
- ✧ James Miller, *The Passion of Michel Foucault* (1993).
- ✧ David Halperin, *Saint = Foucault* (1995).

France

No laws against same-sex relations for consenting adults over 15. Broad rights protections in employment and the MILITARY. *Well-developed social and cultural scenes throughout the country. Active political organizations.*

Lesbia, France's leading publication for women, is part of a thriving gay and lesbian subculture.

Gay and lesbian life in France is, not surprisingly, uniquely French. Along with GERMANY and the English-speaking countries, France has the richest and most varied 20th-century lesbian and gay subcultures in the world. Today, the country is also one of the most progressive in terms of rights protections for gay men and lesbians. Although some French lesbian and gay activists complain that they lack the visibility attained by their counterparts in a few other countries, they nonetheless have access to gay and lesbian support groups and social activities throughout the country. In addition, the French as a people are considered somewhat more tolerant of homosexuality than most other Europeans: According to surveys, only 24 percent object to lesbians or gay men as neighbors, compared with 34 percent of Germans and 31 percent of the British.

Dozens of French artists, filmmakers, intellectuals, and writers are among the most celebrated people in the gay and lesbian subculture. Just a few include ROSA BONHEUR, JEAN COCTEAU, COLETTE, MICHEL FOUCAULT, YVES NAVARRE, and MARGUERITE YOURCENAR.

History

Little is known about the sex lives of the Celts who lived in the territory that later became France, although some Greek and Roman writers mentioned instances of same-sex eroticism (see **c. 40 B.C.**). As in the rest of Europe, the first clear-cut references to same-sex relations come from Church documents (see **1212**, **1252**) and laws (see **c. 1270**). In **1323**, one of the most interesting accounts was recorded in the form of detailed court records for the prosecution of a Franciscan subdeacon, Arnold of Verniolle, on charges of SODOMY and heresy.

Throughout the Middle Ages and the Renaissance, French men and women were prosecuted—and sometimes burned at the stake—on charges of sodomy and CROSS-DRESSING. By the early 18th century, police in Paris had begun to keep lists of suspected "pederasts," recording 20,000 in **1725** and 40,000 in 1783. Around the same time, Enlightenment thinkers like Voltaire and the Italian Cesare Beccaria began to question the right of governments to intervene in the private sex lives of citizens. Even before the French Revolution, when all consensual adult sex acts were decriminalized (see **9/25/1791**), French authorities had stopped executing people who had committed no crime other than sodomy (see **7/1750**; **1783**).

In the 19th century, France was paradoxically both a country of refuge for people fleeing oppression based on sodomy laws in their own country and a place where popular hostility toward "sodomites" and "sapphists" was on the rise (see **7/20/1845**). Nevertheless, French writers of the period, from Honoré de Balzac and Charles Baudelaire to PAUL VERLAINE, pioneered new representations of HOMOEROTICISM, and Paris became one of the centers of the nascent international gay and lesbian SUBCULTURE, boasting everything from a lesbian restaurant (see **1889**) to Turkish BATHS patronized by gay men from all over the world.

Probably because same-sex relations were not illegal in France, a distinctly French HOMOPHILE emancipation movement developed much later than in Germany. Gay, lesbian, and bisexual artists and writers, like Cocteau, Colette, ANDRÉ GIDE, and MARCEL PROUST, were well integrated in the intellectual life of the country, and Paris attracted large numbers of famous gay and lesbian émigrés (see NATALIE BARNEY, GERTRUDE STEIN, etc.) throughout the century, but a "gay rights" movement did not begin until the late 1960s. Social historians note a sharp divide between the libertine, permissive attitudes of the Parisian elites and the restrictive CLOSET of the rest of French society. For ordinary lesbians and gay men, life in the provinces was as constricted as in most other parts of the Western world.

After **May 1968**, French activists like GUY HOCQUENGHEM formulated a uniquely French concept of GAY LIBERATION that was more Marxist and less connected to notions of "gay pride" than its American variant. Radical groups like the Front Homosexuel d'Action Révolutionnaire formed and inspired similar organizations in BELGIUM and ITALY.

Since the 1970s, French lesbian and gay life has been characterized by two major developments. On one side, political activists have fought with conservative forces within French society to repeal restrictive and pejorative legislation (see **7/30/1960**), to achieve an equal AGE OF CONSENT, and to seek new rights such as *certificats de concubinage* (DOMESTIC PARTNERSHIP registrations). On the other, lesbians and gay men have developed a richly varied social and cultural network, with publications such as *Lesbia* and *Gai Pied* (see **2/1979**), radio broadcasts, and special-interest groups all over the country. The French also led the way into queer cyberspace via the national Minitel system, introduced in 1982, and hundreds of "chat lines" that connect thousands of lesbians and gay men all over the country.

In 1985, France became, after Norway (see SCANDINAVIA), the second country in the world to enact legal protections against discrimination based on sexual orientation.

✧ Antony Copley, *Sexual Moralities in France, 1780–1980: New Ideas on the Family, Divorce and Homosexuality* (1989).

✧ Christopher Robinson, *Scandal in the Ink: Male and Female Homosexuality in Twentieth-Century French Literature* (1995).

Frank, Barney
(1940–)

Barney Frank.

U.S. Democratic politician, first congressman to come OUT voluntarily. Born and raised in Bayonne, New Jersey, Frank studied and later taught political science at Harvard. In 1972, after working as an assistant to Boston mayor Kevin White and U.S. Congressman Michael Harrington, he was elected to serve in the Massachusetts House of Representatives from a heavily gay Beacon Hill and Back Bay district in Boston. In 1973 and 1974, he (unsuccessfully) introduced a series of bills to decriminalize same-sex acts and extend civil rights protections to lesbians and gay men. He was elected to the U.S. House of Representatives in 1980 and has been repeatedly reelected, with majorities as high as 70 percent. Known for his wit and keen strategic skills, Frank emerged as one of the most visible and vocal leaders of the liberal opposition after the 1994 congressional elections put conservative Republicans in control of the House and Senate.

On **May 30, 1987**, the *Boston Globe* published an interview in which Frank confirmed that he was gay. He was the second congressman to come out while in office (see GERRY STUDDS). Reaction from both constituents and the press was generally favorable, although his image was marred by a scandal that surfaced in 1989 involving a male prostitute, Steven Gobie, whom Frank had employed between 1985 and 1987. Conservative critics alleged that Gobie, who had been trying to sell his story to the media for at least two years, had operated a sex business out of Frank's home. Frank called for a House ethics panel investigation, which led to the House formally reprimanding him in 1990.

Frank played a leading role in the 1993 debate on discrimination against gay men and lesbians in the MILITARY. His initial support of the "don't ask, don't tell" compromise was criticized by many lesbian and gay activists. Two years later, he was back in the national news when House majority whip Dick Armey (R–Tex.) referred to him as "Barney Fag" in a press conference on **January 27, 1995**.

Frank fought for a number of gay and lesbian civil rights bills, but, next to the inclusion of people with HIV and AIDS in fair-housing legislation, perhaps his most historic achievement has been the acceptance he gained in Washington for himself and his relationship with his lover, mortgage banker Herb Moses, whom he began dating in August 1987. Frank and Moses are thought to be the first male couple to dance together at a White House event (a reception later that year, during the Reagan administration). Moses has also been invited to White House receptions for congressional "spouses."

Freud, Sigmund, see PSYCHOLOGY.

Furies, The

Washington, D.C., women's collective and the name of the influential lesbian-feminist publication it produced. Furies members included Ginny Berson, JOAN E. BIREN (JEB), RITA MAE BROWN, CHARLOTTE BUNCH, Sharon Deevey, Helaine Harris, Susan Hathaway, Nancy Myron, Tasha Peterson, Coletta Reid, Lee Schwing, and Jennifer Woodul. The cover story of the first issue of their newspaper, also called *The Furies,* which appeared in January 1972, explained why the group had named itself after the vengeful, serpent-haired Furies of Greek mythology: "We call our paper *The Furies* because we are also angry . . . because we are oppressed by male supremacy . . . fucked

The Furies at work putting out a mailing in 1972.

over all our lives by a system which is based on the domination of men over women . . . and which defines male as good and female as only as good as the man you are with."

Confrontational, disruptive, and chauvinistically lesbian, the Furies were considered the "outlaws" of the heated debates between feminists and lesbian feminists that characterized this era. They defined lesbianism as a political choice (see LESBIAN, POLITICAL) rather than a sexual preference, asserting that every woman must "come out as a woman-identified-woman or be subjected to male supremacy in all of its economic, personal, and political implications." Their radical articulations of feminist theory attracted a wide readership, although most non-lesbian feminists resisted the erotic limitations of their call for universal SEPARATISM.

The Furies lived together as a collective in two houses, convening in consciousness-raising sessions in which they clashed on issues of class, race, and age as well as differences over heterosexuality and children. The group dissolved in April 1972, one year after its founding. The publication continued until the summer of 1973.

➤ Also see LESBIAN FEMINISM.

✧ *Lesbianism and the Women's Movement*, edited by Nancy Myron and Charlotte Bunch (1975).

✧ Alice Echols, *Daring to Be Bad: Radical Feminism in America, 1967–1975* (1989).

G

Ganymede

In Greek mythology, a beautiful shepherd boy abducted by Zeus and flown to Olympus to serve as cupbearer to the gods. Ganymede was said to have lived in Phrygia (in modern-day western Turkey), and the myth probably originated in Asia Minor. In its oldest surviving form, the myth casts Ganymede as a handsome young man whom Zeus rapes and takes to Olympus, where he replaces (or, in some versions, supplements) the goddess Hebe as divine cupbearer. Over time, the myth changed: Zeus was said to have disguised himself as an eagle, and Ganymede grew younger, becoming a prepubescent boy in most versions.

Early Greek representations of Ganymede depicted him as a young man, in contrast to later images, in which he became progressively younger.

Even in ancient times, Ganymede and Hebe were cited as symbols of what were considered the two most attractive objects of male sexual desire, beautiful youths and (young) women. At least one anonymous medieval poet continued this tradition, pitting Ganymede and Hebe in a hotly contested debate over which form of love was superior. In the Renaissance, artists depicted Ganymede as even younger than before and sometimes treated him as a nonsexual symbol of divine love. In one of MICHELANGELO's drawings, he is almost indistinguishable from a cherub.

Of uncertain etymology (variously explained as "enjoying intelligence" and "joyful genitals"), "Ganymede" is the source, via Etruscan and Latin, of the word "catamite" (a usually pejorative term for a boy or young man who provides sexual services for older men). In the 1990s, some lesbian and gay groups in Slovakia were named Ganymedes.

✧ James M. Saslow, *Ganymede in the Renaissance: Homosexuality in Art and Society* (1986).

García Lorca, Federico
(1898–1936)

Spanish poet, dramatist. The son of upper-class Andalusian landowners, García Lorca spent his teens in Granada, a city that would figure in much of his poetry. His writing career began with a book of essays (1918), a play (1920), and a first book of poetry (1921). In 1919, he moved to Madrid to study and became part of a group of young intellectuals who included Luis Buñuel, LUIS CERNUDA, and Salvador Dalí. An infatuation for Dalí was unrequited, but they remained close friends until the late 1920s, when Buñuel succeeded in alienating Dalí and Lorca from each other. (Prone to paranoia, Lorca thought the title of Buñuel and Dalí's famous 1928 film, *Un Chien Andalou*—"An Andalusian Dog"—was a reference to him.) That same year, Lorca's most popular work, *Romancero Gitano* (*Gypsy Ballads*), earned him acclaim as SPAIN's beloved "gypsy poet," an identity he loathed. That same year, a relationship with a young sculptor, Emilio Aladrén Perojo, came to a bitter end, leaving him "full of despair . . . listless and crippled." In deep depression, feeling misunderstood by his public, Lorca set off for New York to study English at Columbia University from June 1929 to March 1930.

Lorca was appalled by the crowds, industrial squalor, and pervasive racism he found in the city—as is clear from his letters and a posthumously published book of poetry, *Poeta en Nueva York* (*Poet in New York,* 1940). "Besides black art," he wrote, "there is only automation and mechanization." One of the highlights of his stay was being shown around Harlem by HARLEM RENAISSANCE writer Nella Larsen. Lorca also briefly met HART CRANE.

Poeta en Nueva York includes "Ode to Walt Whitman" (privately printed in Mexico in 1933), which extends his theme of urban corruption. Lorca addresses WHITMAN with epithets that include "beautiful old man," "lover of bodies beneath rough cloth," "virile beauty," and "Macho," and then expresses his outrage that *maricas* ("fairies") claim Whitman as one of them. In the poem, he contrasts screaming queens (whom he detests) with the closeted (with whom he sympathizes). He has nothing against "the boy who dresses as a bride / in the darkness of the wardrobe / nor against the solitary men in casinos / who drink prostitution's water." On the other hand, he considers the blatant and effeminate *maricas* an offense to the memory of Whitman, calling them "mothers of mud." In his final stanza, he tells Whitman to "Sleep on, nothing remains."

In the 1930s, Lorca turned to the THEATER, writing plays that included *Bodas de Sangre* (*Blood Wedding,* 1933) and *La Casa de Bernarda Alba* (*The House of Bernarda Alba,* 1936). An explicitly gay play, *The Public,* was not performed until the 1980s.

At the beginning of the Spanish Civil War, Lorca left Madrid for what he thought would be the relative safety of Granada. On August 16, 1936, he was arrested, held for two days, tortured, and shot by Nationalist partisans. Exactly why they singled him out remains unclear, but there is some indication that his homosexuality infuriated his captors as much as his leftist views: According to his biographer, Ian Gibson, one of the assassins boasted that he had shot "two bullets into his arse for being a queer."

Mention of Lorca's homosexuality remained taboo in Spain and rare elsewhere until Paul Binding and Angel Sahuquillo's pioneering critical works in the mid-1980s.

✧ Paul Binding, *Lorca: The Gay Imagination* (1985).

✧ Ian Gibson, *Federico García Lorca: A Life* (1989).

Gay

Term used to describe a person who feels sexual desire exclusively or predominantly for persons of her or his own sex; and more broadly, objects, places, and abstract concepts identified with such persons (e.g., a "gay book," "gay resort," "gay humor").

The word "gay" has been linked with sex and romance ever since it surfaced in Provençal as *gai* in the 13th century, when its primary meaning of "merry" was already associated with troubadors who sang of courtly and, sometimes (see c. **1200**), same-sex love. The word was probably derived from the Frankish *wahi,* meaning "lively" or "boiling," rather than, as some have suggested, the earth goddess Gaia. Over the centuries, as *"gaya"* in Catalonian, *"gai"* in French, and "gay" in English, the word was often used in contexts that implied relaxed or even nonexistent moral scruples. "Gay Paree" and "gay divorcée" are two examples of this usage that have survived until today.

By the 19th century, "gay" was also commonly associated with (female heterosexual) prostitution. Like "molly," which was originally slang for a female prostitute, "gay" may have been extended to describe male transvestites who often frequented the same neighborhoods (the "gay" quarters).

In the first few decades of the 20th century, after "HOMOSEXUAL" had begun to spread via medical writings, "gaycat" was used in U.S. hobo slang to refer to young male novices who sometimes formed protective, often sexual, alliances with older, more experienced tramps, and "gay boy" had similarly suggestive connotations in AUSTRALIA. About this time, some English speakers began to use "gay" as a playful, double-entendre code word. An early example of this usage in print is GERTRUDE STEIN's characteristically repetitive language in her short story "Miss Furr and Miss Skeene" (1922): "They were quite regularly gay there, Helen Furr and Georgine Skeene, they were regularly gay there when they were gay. They were very regularly gay."

By World War II, New Yorkers were using "gay" as a less nuanced alternative to "fairy," "pansy," and "QUEER." In the 1938 film *Bringing Up Baby,* Cary Grant exclaims, "I've just gone gay—all of a sudden" to explain why he is wearing a fur-trimmed nightgown. VITO RUSSO has pointed out that this line was adlibbed and thus is an indication that people in Hollywood, at least in Grant's circles, were already familiar with the slang connotations of the word.

The term did not become widely familiar to the general public, however, until the 1960s. In the 1940s, LISA BEN could discreetly call her lesbian friends "gay gals" and her publication, VICE VERSA, "America's gayest magazine," knowing that most heterosexuals would not grasp the full implication of the word. Similarly, DONALD WEBSTER CORY wrote in 1951 that it was such an insiders' term that "an advertisement for a roommate can actually ask for a gay youth, but could not possibly call for a homosexual." Mass-media attestations of "gay" in today's sense began in the 1950s, although purists such as the editors of *The New York Times* resisted "gay" until much later (see **6/15/1987**), and many writers, ignoring the word's history, attacked the "new" usage as a corruption of a useful, "innocent" adjective.

Once out of the CLOSET, "gay" quickly supplanted the medical-sounding and less specific "homosexual" in all but the most pedantic contexts. The usage of "gay" as the preferred term for both men and women, however, was short-lived. Early in the 1970s, many lesbians remarked that "gay" and "gays" were most often used in ways that excluded or ignored women. The word "LESBIAN" became favored by a majority of women, although 34 percent of women responding to a 1995 ADVOCATE survey preferred to be called "gay women."

Most writers, conscious of the CONSTRUCTIONISM VS. ESSENTIALISM controversy, are careful to use "gay" (and to a slightly lesser degree, "lesbian") only in era-, culture-, and situation-specific contexts. By this definition, "gay" people are not simply persons who experience same-sex desire but, rather, those who also associate themselves with the international gay and lesbian SUBCULTURE that emerged in the 20th century.

Gay Activists Alliance (GAA)

Influential gay and lesbian rights group founded **December 21, 1969**, by Arthur Bell, Arthur Evans, Kay Tobin Lahusen, MARTY ROBINSON, and Jim Owles, among others. As opposed to the GAY LIBERATION FRONT (GLF), from which most of the original members came, GAA limited its mission to gay and lesbian issues including legislation, electoral politics, police harassment, and media defamation. It also was much more formal than the COUNTERCULTURE-based GLF, using Robert's Rules of Order in its meetings and featuring a conventional organizational structure. GAA was nonetheless a radical DIRECT ACTION group and in the early 1970s launched the majority of ZAPS that characterized the era. GAA also opened the Firehouse, one of the first COMMUNITY CENTERS in the United States. The organization lasted until the late 1970s in New York, when it gave way to still more tightly organized groups like NATIONAL GAY [later: and LESBIAN] TASK FORCE, although groups inspired by GAA in other parts of the country had a longer life.

Even in its heyday, GAA was criticized by activists, especially feminists and AFRICAN-AMERICANS, for being dominated by white

Among the early Gay Activists Alliance leaders were Arthur Bell (seated at center), Arthur Evans (left), Kay Tobin (standing at center), and (right) Marty Robinson and Tom Doerr.

males. Lesbian Feminist Liberation emerged as a separate group.

GAA leaders included Pete Fisher, Ron Gold, Arnie Kantrowitz, Joe Kennedy, Dinah Robertson, Nath Rockhill, Marc Ruben, Ginny Vida, and Rich Wandel.

✧ Donn Teal, *The Gay Militants: How Gay Liberation Began in America, 1969–1971* (1971).

✧ Toby Marotta, *The Politics of Homosexuality* (1981).

Gay and Lesbian Alliance Against Defamation (GLAAD)

U.S. national cultural advocacy organization founded in 1985 "to fight the defamation of lesbians and gays and their enforced invisibility in the popular culture." GLAAD works through public education campaigns, letter-writing drives, and media seminars to fight HOMOPHOBIA and discrimination based on sexual orientation or identity in all forms of mass media, public arts funding, education, and reference works. It also publishes a media guide and holds annual dinners to bestow its Media Awards. The group relies on persuasion rather than coercion or legal actions. Its four national offices are located in Washington, D.C. (administration), New York City (news media), Los Angeles (entertainment media), and Portland, Oregon (field office). GLAAD also has 7 local chapters and 45 "outposts" across the country.

Gay and lesbian media activism began with a GAY ACTIVISTS ALLIANCE sit-in at *Harper's* magazine on **October 27, 1970**. Also in the 1970s, activist Ginny Vida launched a broader campaign against HETEROSEXISM while serving as media director for the NATIONAL GAY [later: AND LESBIAN] TASK FORCE. Later, provoked by sensational media coverage of ROCK HUDSON's struggle with AIDS and an editorial in *Christopher Street* magazine calling for media reform, a group of writers and journalists, including Greg Kolovakos, VITO RUSSO, Arnie Kantrowitz, and Darrell Yates Rist, formed GLAAD in New York City after a meeting held on **November 17, 1985**. The group appointed its first executive director, Craig J. Davidson, in June 1987.

Although GLAAD is best known for its protests against defamation and stereotypical portrayals of lesbians and gay men, it also works to foster increased queer visibility. In response to charges that its original emphasis on promoting a "positive image" did not reflect community diversity, GLAAD board members later amended the group's mission statement to promote "fair, accurate, and inclusive" portrayals rather than exclusively positive ones.

GLAAD actions have had a major impact on TELEVISION programming, news coverage, and other aspects of popular culture. Successes include comedian Bob Hope's apology and agreement to make a public service announcement denouncing violence against gay men and lesbians after he had used the word "fag" on *The Tonight Show;* pundit Andy Rooney's temporary suspension following antigay remarks on CBS; revisions and new lesbian- and gay-inclusive entries in a number of reference works, ranging from *The American Sign Language Dictionary* to *MicroSoft's Spell Check;* and acceptance of listings for gay/lesbian organizations in local yellow pages.

✧ Marshall K. Kirk and Erastes Pill, "Waging Peace," *Christopher Street* (no. 33, 1985).

✧ Craig J. Davidson and Michael G. Valentini, "Cultural Advocacy: A Non-Legal Approach to Fighting Defamation of Lesbians and Gays," *Law and Sexuality* (vol. 2, 1992).

Gay and Lesbian Rights Movement, U.S.

American lesbians and gay men began to organize a movement much later than their counterparts in GERMANY and a few other countries in northern Europe. Except for HENRY GERBER's abortive Society for Human Rights (see **12/10/1924**), the first known groups were formed in the late 1940s and then only with extreme caution.

HARRY HAY, a founder and theorist of the MATTACHINE Society, is often called the "Father of the Gay and Lesbian Rights Movement." The Mattachine was the first group to attract large numbers of gay men (and smaller numbers of lesbians) and the first to launch public protests against police harassment (see **2/1952**). After a brief period of ACTIVISM, however, Mattachine leaders, fearful of the harsh repression that characterized the MCCARTHY ERA, retreated to a more cautious "HOMOPHILE" strategy of banding together for mutual support and seeking to advance social tolerance and "understanding" of homosexuality rather than pursuing radical change. DAUGHTERS OF BILITIS, the first lesbian homophile group (founded **9/21/1955**), followed a similar strategy through the 1950s.

In the early 1960s, more radical leaders like FRANK KAMENY launched the first concerted campaigns to achieve gay and lesbian rights in employment and the MILITARY (see **9/19/1964**). Kameny was also instrumental in uniting activists from different parts of the United States into a concerted national movement, forming ECHO (East Coast Homophile Organizations) in **January 1963** and NACHO (North American Conference of Homophile Organizations) on **August 12, 1968**.

As a result of the activism of Kameny and others in the 1960s, a firm foundation was already in place for a full-fledged GAY LIBERATION movement to erupt after the STONEWALL Uprising. Many lesbians and gay men—especially on the West Coast (see **1/5/1967**)—had rejected the almost apologetic tone of 1950s homophile activities and were ready to come out publicly in support of Kameny's then radical 1966 slogan, "Gay is good."

In the early 1970s, hundreds of rights groups, social service organizations, political clubs, and special interest organizations formed all over the U.S., and gay men and lesbians began to achieve an unprecedented level of visibility. SUBCULTURES and GHETTOS sprang up from coast to coast; publications flourished; state after state repealed SODOMY legislation; and lesbians and gay men achieved a series of notable "firsts," from the first favorable mass-media representations to the first progay speech at a national political conven-

In 1963, the gay male rights movement was centered on Mattachine Society offices in a few large cities.

By 1979, the year of the first March on Washington, the movement drew hundreds of thousands of supporters.

tion (see **7/12/1972**) and the first openly gay elected officials and judges (see **4/1/1974**; **11/5/1974**; **12/9/1974**).

For most lesbians and gay men, however, the 1970s were less a time of political activism than a period in which they could explore previously repressed gay and lesbian identities. Many lesbians sought this identity via SEPARATISM or the women's liberation movement. Gay men, in contrast, flocked to BARS, discos, and BATHHOUSES: by far the largest gay membership organization of the period was the Club Baths, which had almost 500,000 card carriers by 1973.

Gay liberation activism subsided in the mid-1970s. Later in the decade, a conservative backlash, which included numerous incidents of arson against gay and lesbian clubs and institutions as well as the "Save the Children" campaign of Anita Bryant (see **1/18/1977**), helped reignite the movement, leading to record attendance at gay pride demonstrations (see **6/26/1977**) and a renewed spirit of cooperation between lesbians and gay men.

The advent of AIDS in the early 1980s again transformed the movement, although it was not until later in the decade that groups such as ACT UP were formed. Confronted with an ever growing religious-right movement and

WE ARE
EVERYWHERE
STOP
ARCH
GAY
14

Slogans

Gay and lesbian activists have used slogans since the early days of the homophile movement. Many seem to have arisen spontaneously in several places at once, so accurate attributions are not always possible.

Pre-Stonewall

Per scientiam ad justitiam ("Justice through knowledge").

MAGNUS HIRSCHFELD

Gay is good.

Frank Kameny, approved as slogan at NACHO in 1966

Glad to be gay.

Los Angeles activists, late 1960s (later the title of a Tom Robinson song)

Stonewall Era: 1969–1970

Gay power to the gay people

GAY LIBERATION FRONT (GLF)

How dare you assume I'm heterosexual?

GLF/GAY ACTIVISTS ALLIANCE (GAA)

Out of the closets and into the streets.

GLF/GAA

Lesbians ignite!

GLF/GAA

1970s

We are everywhere.

U.S. activists

Better blatant than latent.
A day without human rights is like a day without sunshine.
Promote homosexuality.

Anti-Anita Bryant campaign

1980s

Give up the guilt.

Sisters of Perpetual Indulgence, San Francisco (see **1/10/1980**)

Queers bash back.

UNITED KINGDOM activists

Silence = Death.

ACT UP and other AIDS activists

1990s

We're here. We're queer. Get used to it.

QUEER NATION

We're here. We're queer. We're (not) going shopping.

Queer Nation, San Francisco

Dyke + Fag = Queer.

U.K. activists

Recruit Recruit Recruit

LESBIAN AVENGERS

frustrated by the slow pace of change, a new generation of activists took to the streets as part of groups like QUEER NATION and LESBIAN AVENGERS.

In the 1990s, the gay and lesbian rights movement was diverse and multidirectional. In addition to civil rights and AIDS activism, it was characterized by a renewed campaign to obtain equal rights in the military and, especially later in the decade, the pursuit of DOMESTIC PARTNERSHIP and MARRIAGE benefits.

➤ Also see ASSIMILATIONISM/CONFRONTATIONALISM; DIRECT ACTION; HUMAN RIGHTS CAMPAIGN; LAMBDA LEGAL DEFENSE AND EDUCATION FUND; LAW; LESBIAN FEMINISM; NATIONAL GAY AND LESBIAN TASK FORCE; ZAPS.

Gay Games

International gay and lesbian athletic event held every four years. Originally called the Gay Olympics, the Gay Games were instituted, in the words of their founder, Olympic athlete Dr. TOM WADDELL, "to enhance the dignity, pride and self-respect of lesbians and gay men everywhere." Fostering national and international amateur sports competition, the Gay Games are based upon affirmative principles of inclusion—"personal best" rather than adversarial exclusion—and a philosophy of sports that emphasizes friendship, spiritual growth, and health. Open to all, they are also conceived as a form of communication, a means of promoting understanding in the nongay world by increasing lesbian and gay visibility. For many gay men and lesbians, the games also offer the only HOMOPHOBIA-free environment in which they can compete.

The Gay Games are a not-for-profit event financed by contributions, registration fees, and ticket sales. They are directed by the Federation of Gay Games.

History

Tom Waddell and Mark Brown came up with the idea for the games in 1980 at a San Francisco Cable Car Awards ceremony at which Waddell was acclaimed Outstanding Athlete. Together with other Bay Area athletes, the two men founded San Francisco Arts and Athletics (SFAA), which organized and oversaw the games until July 1989.

In 1982, the year of the first games, the U.S. Olympic Committee secured a court order preventing SFAA from using the word "Olympics." Later, in *SFAA and Thomas F. Waddell v. U.S. Olympic Committee* (1987), the U.S. Supreme Court ruled 5–4 that, based on the Amateur Sports Act of 1978, the U.S. Olympic Committee had exclusive rights to the word "Olympics" for public identification and promotion in the U.S. Since the word had been around for centuries, some legal authorities viewed this ruling as discriminatory. They pointed out that other uses of the word, including Special Olympics, Police Olympics, Senior Olympics, K-9 Olympics, and even Rat Olympics, had gone unchallenged by the committee. (Since the decision, relations with the committee, which seated its first openly lesbian member in the 1990s, have improved greatly: the committee now lists the games in its annual directory of sports events and assists games organizers in obtaining entry visas for athletes from abroad.)

Despite the controversy, the first Gay Games, held in San Francisco on **August 28–September 5, 1982**, were an unqualified success, attracting more than 50,000 people from countries all over the world. Each successive event has seen large-scale growth and increased public attention. The fourth Gay Games, held in New York in 1994, attracted more participants than the previous Winter Olympics.

Federation of Gay Games

International governing board of the Gay Games. The federation was founded in July

Women's figure skating competition, 1994 Gay Games.

Men's figure skating competition, 1994 Gay Games.

1989 under the direction of RIKKI STREICHER (legendary San Francisco founding proprietor of Maud's, "the world's oldest lesbian bar") and other community activists, as an outgrowth of the more local San Francisco Arts and Athletics organization, which had run the games since 1981.

Considered the official voice of the Gay Games, the federation preserves and promotes the games, determines site selection, and ensures adherence to the original principles of the games (participation rather than winning and inclusion over exclusion). The all-volunteer board is made up of about 50 athletic and cultural leaders from around the world. Since 1989, the federation has established the Gay Games Archives, instituted an international outreach program, and set up an endowment fund for the long-term financial security of the games. The federation also publishes a newsletter and awards the Tom Waddell Sports Cup.

✧ Roy M. Coe, *A Sense of Pride: The Story of Gay Games II* (1986).

Gay Holocaust, see NAZI PERSECUTION.

Gay Liberation

A New Left countercultural movement whose aims were first articulated by the GAY LIBERATION FRONT in New York City in July 1969. In contrast to the more cautious HOMOPHILE movements of the 1950s and 1960s as well as to the more narrowly focused groups that followed, the gay liberation movement sought nothing less than a radical transformation of society at large through fundamental changes in social and individual "consciousness." In effect, this meant a true revolution that would

Gay Games I
August 28–September 5, 1982—San Francisco
"Challenge '82"
1,300 participants; 179 cities; 12 nations; 14 events
50,000 in attendance

Gay Games II
August 9–17, 1986—San Francisco
"Triumph in '86"
3,482 participants; 259 cities; 16 nations; 17 events
75,000 in attendance

Gay Games III
August 4–11, 1990—Vancouver
"Celebration '90"
7,300 participants; 30 nations; 26 events
200,000 in attendance

Gay Games IV
June 18–25, 1994—New York City
"Unity '94"
15,000 participants; 44 nations; 31 events
500,000 in attendance

Gay Games V
scheduled for August 1–8, 1998—Amsterdam
"Friendship '98"

abolish existing sexual institutions, redefine sex roles, and create new social relations based on "sisterhood, cooperation, human love and uninhibited sexuality."

➤ Also see COUNTERCULTURE; GAY AND LESBIAN RIGHTS MOVEMENT, U.S.

✧ Dennis Altman, *Homosexual: Oppression and Liberation* (1971; reissue, 1993).

Gay Liberation Front (GLF)

A militant New Left gay and lesbian organization formed in New York City in the month following the STONEWALL Uprising. The first group to articulate the ideas of GAY LIBERATION, GLF was so named in part to echo Vietnam's (Marxist) National Liberation Front but also to suggest an all-embracing movement—or front—that other groups could participate in rather than a single, exclusive organization.

GLF emerged over the course of a series of meetings beginning on **July 9, 1969**, at which militant activists gained ascendency over the more cautious HOMOPHILE veterans of the MATTACHINE Society of New York. By **July 31, 1969**, the group had officially agreed on its name (which is said to have been first suggested by Martha Shelley) and a statement of purpose, which first appeared in the community paper *Rat* on August 12, 1969. It was later reprinted in the first issue of *Come Out!,* a newspaper "by and for the Gay Community," published by an open collective of GLF members on **November 14, 1969**.

Over the next year, the GLF concept spread rapidly over the radical activist network, and numerous GLFs began on college campuses and in cities in the U.S., CANADA,

Gay Liberation Front meetings had the feel of a counterculture gathering.

and Europe. Lesbians in the New York group early on formed a separate caucus called GLF Women, as much in response to problems they encountered working with GLF men as to signal their dual allegiance to women's and gay liberation. Most caucus members later merged into other women's groups like RADICALESBIANS.

By the end of 1970, GLF had dissolved. Former members and historians point to a number of factors that contributed to its collapse: a lack of structure; antagonism toward people who subscribed to "traditional gay ways," such as CROSS-DRESSING and BUTCH-FEMME; and an ideological dogmatism that tied the group to other varieties of cultural reform (such as the peace and ecology movements and the fights to end racism, classism, and sexism)—thus, in the opinion of many, diffusing the movement's effectiveness.

Defections had actually already begun in late 1969, spurred by the dissatisfactions of several GLF leaders who wanted an organization single-mindedly devoted to the pursuit of gay and lesbian civil rights. The constitution of GAY ACTIVISTS ALLIANCE was approved with this focus on **December 21, 1969**.

Early leaders included Ron Ballard, Ellen Bedoz (PSEUDONYM of Ellen Shumsky), Michael Brown, Jim Fouratt, Lois Hart, Jerry Hoose, Bob Ketzener, Bob Kohler, Leo Martello, Jim Owles, Charles Pitts, MARTY ROBINSON, Martha Shelley, Bill Weaver, Pete Wilson, and Allen Young.

- ✧ Donn Teal, *The Gay Militants: How Gay Liberation Began in America, 1969–1971* (1971).
- ✧ Toby Marotta, *The Politics of Homosexuality* (1981).

Gay Men's Health Crisis (GMHC, Inc.),

see AIDS.

Gay Studies,

see LESBIAN AND GAY STUDIES.

Gearhart, Sally Miller

(1931–)

U.S. activist, educator, writer. Born in rural Virginia, Gearhart was raised by her divorced mother, an executive secretary, and her grandmother, a schoolteacher. She and her first lover, Lakey, met while they were attending Sweet Briar College and continued their relationship while Gearhart pursued graduate studies. Later Lakey, under pressure from her family, reluctantly got married (with a distraught Gearhart as a bridesmaid), and the two women parted, never to see each other again. Although she was hurt and angry at the time, Gearhart later wrote that Lakey had been the agent of her "greatest self-discovery" and that the legacy of their relationship was the strength to make it through the "dark closet years" of the 1950s and early 1960s.

After completing her doctorate at the University of Illinois, Gearhart taught communication arts at colleges in Texas and the Midwest. She relocated to San Francisco in 1968 and joined the GAY AND LESBIAN RIGHTS MOVEMENT. In 1970, she and Jack Stokes were named to the San Francisco Family Services Administration, making history as the first openly lesbian and gay persons to be hired by the city. Over the next decade, Gearhart gained national visibility for her campaign efforts on behalf of HARVEY MILK and for her leadership in the movement to defeat Proposition 6 (see **11/7/1978**), an initiative that would have banned gay or lesbian teachers from California public schools.

Gearhart is also well-known for her writings on SPIRITUALITY, which include *Loving Women/Loving Men: Gay Liberation and the Church* (with William Johnson, 1974), and her contributions to LESBIAN FEMINISM, the most enduringly popular of which is her now classic fictional account of a woman's utopia, *The Wanderground: Stories of the Hill Women* (1978).

Gearhart appeared in two landmark documentaries, *Word Is Out* (1977) and *The Times of Harvey Milk* (1984).

✧ Sally Miller Gearhart, "Notes from a Recovering Activist," *Sojourner* (vol. 21, no. 1, September 1995).

✧ Dana R. Shugar, *Separatism and Women's Community* (1995).

✧ Sally Miller Gearhart, "First Love at Sweet Briar," in *The New Our Right to Love: A Lesbian Resource Book*, edited by Ginny Vida (1996).

Gender

Usually defined in LESBIAN AND GAY STUDIES as the psychological counterpart of biological sex: one may identify oneself as biologically female but claim a "male" gender, or vice versa. QUEER THEORY, on the other hand, views gender as an artificial social or cultural "construction" (see CONSTRUCTIONISM VS. ESSENTIALISM) or a "performance" one learns as part of developing an individual identity. This concept was anticipated as early as the mid-19th century by thinkers such as KARL HEINRICH UL-

Gender reinterpreted: popular 1930s New York City male impersonator "Blackie."

RICHS, who wrote that "urnings [gay men] play the male just as an actress plays a man on stage." In popular usage, the boundaries between *sex* and *gender* tend to blur (as in "same-gender" relationships, which could technically describe a heterosexual union, such as a relationship between a female-identified biological male and a biologically and psychologically female-identified woman).

Some theorists, like sexologist John Money, distinguish between interior gender *identity* and exterior gender *role.* In other words, one may feel like a man inside but be forced to behave as a woman to achieve social acceptance.

Anthropologists have found societies in which people appear to believe in more than two genders. Some NATIVE AMERICAN peoples, for example, traditionally thought of BERDACHES as neither male nor female but as members of their own distinct gender. Writer and scientist Martine Rothblatt, who describes herself as a "transperson," has advanced the hypothesis that there are at least as many possible genders as there are shades of color and that people should be free to select a unique gender identity and change it at will.

For lesbians and gay men, concepts of gender are important because of the tendency in many cultures, including modern Western civilization, to conflate gender and sexual nonconformity. Some scientists, such as biologist Simon LeVay, believe that *all* lesbians and gay men experience to some degree a sense of not conforming entirely to the gender identity socially mandated by their biological sex. LeVay asserts that lesbians and gay men almost universally experience "a childhood history of mild gender nonconformity, perhaps, an unusual profile of cognitive skills, or a preference for a sex-atypical role in sexual intercourse." Most queer theorists, however, would disagree with LeVay. They would instead assert that since gender itself is an artificial construction,

Gender exaggerated: hypermasculinity as expressed by porn star Piper.

a sense of gender nonconformity is also only a consequence of cultural attitudes. Similarly, many less scholarly gay men and lesbians insist that the fact that they are attracted to members of their own sex has nothing to do with their gender identity. Marshall Kirk and Hunter Madsen, the authors of *After the Ball: How America Will Conquer Its Fear and Hatred of Gays in the 90s* (1989), group gay men in two categories: "R" (for regular) and "Q" (for queer); the latter includes "queens," leathermen, "Bruce Weber hyperboys," and other gay men who, they say, find "manliness . . . troublesome" and feel it "must be deflated by burlesque."

The fact that there is heated disagreement even among gay men and lesbians over issues of gender and whether or not gender and sexual nonconformity are—or should be—connected is one sign of the extraordinary power concepts of gender wield in everyday life. In response, many lesbian and gay performers, writers, artists, and filmmakers have sought to defuse or "de-naturalize" (rid of its supposed naturalness) this power by demonstrating, often humorously, how arbitrary gender expectations can be. Examples of gay and lesbian strategies against gender include "gender-bending" and "gender-blending" (startling representations of gender, such as a hairy man in drag or a mustachioed woman smoking a cigar).

Theorist Judith Butler, among others, has suggested that biological sex itself is a construction. She has attempted to de-naturalize the belief in two sexes by looking at how different groups of people distinguish "male" from "female."

Gender identity is further complicated by ethnic, class, and racial diversity. AFRICAN-AMERICANS, ASIAN-AMERICANS, and almost all other distinguishable groups have their own unique heritages of gender identities that in many cases are different again from stereotypical expectations. For example, a Chinese-American lesbian who identifies herself as "butch" (see BUTCH/FEM(ME)) might feel that cooking is a part of her butch identity because in her culture, cooking is a masculine avocation.

Finally, gender identity changes over time. Just one example of how gender assumptions can change is the colors of clothes worn by American babies. In the early 20th century, baby boys wore pink (a variation of "aggressive" red) and baby girls wore "soothing," feminine blue.

➤ Also see ANDROGYNY; CROSS-DRESSING; TRANSSEXUALS.

✧ Marshall Kirk and Hunter Madsen, *After the Ball: How America Will Conquer Its Fear and Hatred of Gays in the 90s* (1989).

✧ Judith Butler, *Gender Trouble: Feminism and the Subversion of Identity* (1990).

✧ *Third Sex, Third Gender: Beyond Sexual Dimorphism in Culture and History,* edited by Gilbert Herdt (1994).

✧ Martine Rothblatt, *The Apartheid of Sex: A Manifesto on the Freedom of Gender* (1995).

✧ Simon LeVay and Elisabeth Nonas, *City of Friends: A Portrait of Gay and Lesbian Community in America* (1995).

Genet, Jean

(1910–1986)

French writer. Illegitimate, Genet grew up on the streets and in reform school, selling drugs and his body, picking pockets, and begging. He deserted from the French Foreign Legion in 1930 and spent time in Spanish and French PRISONS. In jail, he began writing brutal, homoerotically poetic works such as *Our Lady of the Flowers* (1944), *Miracle of the Rose* (1946), and *Querelle de Brest* (1947).

In 1948, he was sentenced to life imprisonment as a habitual criminal. Only the testimony of JEAN COCTEAU, Jean-Paul Sartre, and other major intellectuals that he was a genius got him a reprieve. Sartre later helped to make him an even more popular and acclaimed writer by promoting him in *Saint Genet: Actor and Martyr* (1952).

Genet went on to write theatrical pieces that included CROSS-DRESSING themes like *The Maids* (1947) and *The Blacks* (1958). He refused to involve himself with gay causes, but was a fervent supporter of people he considered outlaws, such as the Black Panthers, the Palestine Liberation Organization, and the German terrorist Baader-Meinhof gang.

✧ Edmund White, *Jean Genet* (1993).

Genetics, see BIOLOGY; SOCIOBIOLOGY.

Georgia, see CENTRAL ASIA.

Gerber, Henry

(pseudonym: Parisex; 1892–1972)

German-born U.S. writer, editor, founder of first American gay rights organization. Born and raised in Bavaria, Gerber immigrated to the U.S. as a young man and then returned to GERMANY after WORLD WAR I as part of the U.S. Army occupation forces. There Gerber discovered the German HOMOPHILE movement and resolved to found a similar movement in the U.S. On **December 10, 1924**, he and six other men received a charter from the State of Illinois for a Society for Human Rights, the earliest known homophile organization in the U.S. Gerber also edited two issues of a publication called *Friendship and Freedom* for the organization. Early in 1925, the wife of one of the founders reported the group, and the Chicago police arrested Gerber on an obscenity charge. By the time the charge was dismissed in court, Gerber had used up his savings paying for his defense. A few weeks later, he was fired from his post office job for "conduct unbecoming a postal worker."

Gerber continued to write and translate articles in support of gay rights for the next three decades, including stories for a mimeographed newsletter called *The Chanticleer* in the 1930s and homophile publications beginning in the 1950s, and to send protest letters to mainstream magazines. As early as the 1930s, he sometimes signed his letters and articles with his real name instead of using a number or a PSEUDONYM, the usual practice for gay men and lesbians at the time. After leaving Chicago, he lived most of his life in New York City and Washington and was a member of both city's MATTACHINE Society chapters. Although Gerber probably never realized it, his Chicago group was part of the inspiration for the Mattachine: HARRY HAY, a Mattachine founder, had learned about the Society for Human Rights from a lover who had years before had an affair with one of its members. Gay and lesbian historians cite Gerber as a visionary and pioneer who anticipated strategies others would use with more success.

✧ Jonathan Ned Katz, *Gay and Lesbian Almanac: A New Documentary* (1983).

✧ Jonathan Ned Katz, *Gay American History: Lesbians and Gay Men in the U.S.A.* (1992).

A mass-market German magazine asks, "Do gays live better?," claiming: "They can dance better. They have the coolest clothes. They know the most interesting women."

Germany

No laws against same-sex relations between women over 14 and between men over 18. Thriving social and cultural scene in cities, major university towns, and some resorts. Small but vocal national and local rights organizations.

Although Germans were the first to develop a HOMOPHILE rights movement, and German cities like Berlin have been centers of a lively gay and lesbian SUBCULTURE since the 19th century, the contemporary German lesbian and gay rights movement has lagged behind those of neighboring countries like Denmark (see SCANDINAVIA) and the NETHERLANDS. The INTERNATIONAL LESBIAN AND GAY ASSOCIATION rates German society as "moderately tolerant" of gay men and lesbians, citing a 1992 survey in which 34 percent of the Germans polled said they would "object to homosexuals as neighbors" (compared with 31 percent in the UNITED KINGDOM and 24 percent in FRANCE). Violence against lesbians and gay men has been on the rise since 1990, especially in the formerly Communist eastern portion of the country. The AIDS epidemic, however, has been less severe in Germany than in the U.S. or France, and German lesbians and gay men enjoy one of the most developed networks of social and cultural resources in the world.

Contemporary lesbian, gay, and bisexual Germans of note include: filmmakers Lothar Lambert, Ulrike Ottinger, Werner Schroetter, Monika Treut, and ROSA VON PRAUNHEIM; Holocaust historian Dr. Klaus Müller; photographer Wilfried Forster; and writers Detlev Meyer, Napoleon Seyfarth, and Marlene Stenten.

History

Except for some homoerotic poetry, evidence of same-sex desire is largely absent from the LITERATURE, histories, and even the legal records of German-speaking peoples until **1531**, when Martin Luther attacked Roman Catholic RELIGIOUS ORDERS as hotbeds of SODOMY. Coincidentally, sexual relations between men and between women were made a capital crime the following year (see **1532**) in the Holy Roman Empire, which included most of the territory that would later become Germany.

Persecutions of witchcraft (see WICCA), which some historians believe was linked to same-sex eroticism, were particularly virulent in German-speaking areas through the late 17th century. An unknown number of men, and in a few cases women, were also executed on charges of sodomy or CROSS-DRESSING before the end of the 18th century, when records of nascent sexual subcultures (see **1782** and **1791**) begin to appear.

In the 19th century, German-speaking intellectuals took the lead in two areas critical to the development of a modern gay and lesbian consciousness. On one hand, theorists and activists like KARL HEINRICH ULRICHS, MAGNUS HIRSCHFELD, and ADOLF BRAND began a "homophile emancipation" movement that worked for repeal of Paragraph 175 (united Germany's antisodomy legislation—see **1871**) and, at the same time, instituted the first openly gay and lesbian publications and rights organizations. On the other, doctors and psychologists like Sigmund Freud and BARON RICHARD VON KRAFFT-EBING devised medical theories of "homosexuality" (a term that was first coined in the late 1860s by KÁROLY MÁRIA KERTBENY, a Hungarian-born doctor writing in German) that had a profound influence on 20th-century conceptions of lesbians and gay men.

Also in the second half of the 19th century, Berlin and other large German cities became the centers of increasingly developed gay and lesbian subcultures, complete with transvestite balls, well-known CRUISING areas, and bohemian cafés.

In 1907, the Eulenburg Scandal filled the newspapers with accounts of an alleged "homosexual clique" surrounding the Kaiser. The scandal marked not only the first mass-media reports on gay men and lesbians; it was also the first time the words "homosexual" and "homosexuality" came into common parlance in any country.

By the 1920s, Berlin boasted the world's most open and best-developed gay and lesbian subculture. Scholars gathered at Hirschfeld's Institute of Sexual Research (opened on **7/1/1919**), and gay men and lesbians from all over Europe flocked to the city's 300 gay BARS and cafés, a tenth of which catered mostly to lesbians. Slickly produced gay and lesbian magazines were sold on newsstands throughout the city, and there was even a THEATER group that specialized in gay plays.

The rise of Nazism in 1933 brought the end of tolerance. One of Hitler's first official acts was to ban PORNOGRAPHY (interpreted to include all gay and lesbian publications) and homophile organizations. Two months later, Nazi youth gangs attacked Hirschfeld's Institute of Sexual Research and burned its priceless collection of books and photographs in a public ceremony viewed in newsreel reports by millions around the world. Large-scale persecution began in 1934: thousands of gay male Germans were arrested, tortured, and sent to concentration camps from which few returned. Although Nazi law never criminalized sex between women, a large number of the most prominent lesbians were Jewish, socialist, or both. Many fled Germany to escape arrest; many others perished in concentration camps.

Gay and lesbian life resurfaced after WORLD WAR II, but it was not to recover its prewar vibrancy until the 1970s. Sex between men remained a criminal offense until 1969 in West Germany, and gay bars and cruising areas were subject to sporadic police raids. In Soviet-controlled East Berlin, the Communist government closed all gay bars and banned lesbians and gay men from Party membership, government employment, and teaching positions.

In 1970, the West Berlin premiere of Rosa von Praunheim's film *It's Not the Homosexual Who Is Perverse but the Society in Which He Lives* set the stage for the birth of Germany's GAY LIBERATION movement. Groups were formed at universities throughout the country at the same time that less political Germans opened American-style bars and BATHHOUSES in major cities.

In 1975, when the East German government decriminalized all consensual sex acts for persons 14 or older, a few gay and lesbian bars opened in East Berlin, mostly concentrated around Alexanderplatz, and a small gay and lesbian organization formed as part of an officially sanctioned LUTHERAN CHURCH group. Although the East German secret police, the Stasi, kept close watch on all suspected lesbians and gay men, East Berlin was still the most tolerant city in Communist Europe. The government even permitted same-sex couples to apply for housing together.

As the capital of a reunited Germany, Berlin once again became a major international center of gay and lesbian culture, politics, and social life. In 1989, Germany's first public office devoted to lesbian and gay concerns opened in Berlin. Called the Referat für Gleichgeschlectliche Lebensweisen (Center for Homosexual Lifestyles), the state-level office works to eliminate discrimination and to promote understanding of gay men and lesbians.

➤ Also see NAZI PERSECUTION.

✧ James D. Steakley, *The Homosexual Emancipation Movement in Germany* (1975).

Ghettoes—and the pride celebrations that take place in them—provide gay men and lesbians with public spaces where they can be themselves most openly.

✧ *Gay Voices from East Germany,* edited by Jürgen Lemke (1991).

Ghana, see AFRICA, SUB-SAHARAN.

Ghettos, Gay and Lesbian

Cities, towns, or, especially, urban neighborhoods where gay men and lesbians are numerous enough to dominate social, cultural, and economic activities.

Geographers distinguish ghettos from the gay and lesbian entertainment centers that have arisen in cities like London and Tokyo. Conventionally, ghettos are places where lesbians and gay men not only play but also live and, often, work. Another kind of ghetto is the predominantly lesbian residential community, which may or may not include overtly lesbian commercial establishments.

Most gay and lesbian ghettos evolved out of traditionally libertine parts of towns, such as the French Quarter in New Orleans, or areas where artists and political radicals gathered, such as Greenwich Village in New York City.

Gentrification is often associated with gay ghettos. Perhaps the earliest example of this is New York's Sutton Place, which was converted in the early 20th century from a grimy industrial area to a chic place to live by lesbians led by ELSIE DE WOLFE AND ELISABETH MARBURY.

Often dominated by white male "guppies," ghettos are not always friendly to women or to men of color. In response, these groups have increasingly moved to places like Jackson Heights and Park Slope in New York City and Northampton in Massachusetts. One group of women, most of whom were lesbians, defied the gay cliché "we're not in Kansas anymore" to found Womontown in Kansas City, Kansas, in 1990.

Belying the expression "safety in numbers," statistics show HATE CRIME to be most common in ghettos.

➤ Also see SUBCULTURE.

✧ *The Margins of the City: Gay Men's Urban Lives,* edited by Stephen Whittle (1994).

✧ *Mapping Desire: Geographies of Sexualities,* edited by David Bell and Gill Valentine (1995).

Gide, André

(1869–1951)

French writer, one of the first prominent persons to come OUT. After a strict Protestant upbringing in Paris, it was not until Gide experienced the sexual ambivalence of the ARAB WORLD that he began to allow himself to consider being sexually attracted to young men. In 1895, he ran into OSCAR WILDE and Lord Alfred Douglas at a hotel in Algiers and, at Wilde's urging, had his first sexual experience with a man, a young musician.

Gide's struggles with his sexuality and with

James Dean and Louis Jourdan (standing) starred in a 1954 Broadway adaptation of André Gide's The Immoralist.

the double life he led—he married in 1895—are the background of early novels like *The Immoralist* (1902). Too severely honest with himself to remain closeted, he wrote a defense of PEDERASTY in *Corydon* and *Si le Grain ne Meurt (If It Dies . . .)*, both written in 1924, coming out to the French public—to the outrage of his friends—when the latter book was issued by a major press in 1926. He remained a prominent literary personage, however, and became the first openly gay man to receive a Nobel Prize (for LITERATURE, in 1947).

Although remembered as a hero, many of Gide's views on homosexuality would outrage modern gay men and lesbians as much as they did his heterosexual contemporaries. Gide scorned effeminacy, strongly advocated pederasty, and actually criticized men who were attracted to other adult men.

✧ Christopher Robinson, *Scandal in the Ink: Male and Female Homosexuality in Twentieth-Century French Literature* (1995).

Gidlow, Elsa

(Elfie Gidlow; 1898–1986)

Anglo-Canadian-American poet and philosopher, among the first whose writings were explicitly lesbian. Born in England, she moved with her parents to Quebec at the age of six and then settled permanently in the San Francisco area in the early 1920s. Largely self-educated, Gidlow lived off her editing and journalism. Her writings include *On a Grey Thread,* a book of explicitly lesbian love poetry published in 1923, seven other books of poetry, a drama in verse, an autobiography, and a collection of essays. She founded Druid Heights, a Bay Area publishing house and support center for women artists, and cofounded, in 1962, the Society for Comparative Philosophy. In the 1960s, she became a member of DAUGHTERS OF BILITIS. In 1975, at the age of 77, she was featured in the landmark Mariposa Film Group book (and later documentary) *Word Is Out: Stories of Some of Our Lives.* Also that year, she published a highly influential essay entitled "Ask No Man Pardon: The Philosophical Significance of Being Lesbian."

Passionate yet in command of a powerful inner stillness, Gidlow wrote proudly and boldly of her love for other women and of the unique contributions she felt lesbians made to the world. Her lyrical writings are redolent of what she described as "a magic that haunted dreams." Reinforced by friendships with people like Alan Watts, she brought a Zen-influenced philosophy to the mission of building a lesbian feminist community. In 1981, accepting a Lesbian Rights Award from the Southern California Women for Understanding and the International Gay and Lesbian Archives, she recalled the lonely struggle of her early years and expressed her hope that the growth of a lesbian community would not separate its members from society but rather "live as another sort of flower in the garden of humankind."

✧ Elsa Gidlow, *Elsa, I Come with My Songs: The Autobiography of Elsa Gidlow* (1986).

Gilgamesh

Sumerian epic that is considered the oldest surviving literary narrative. A man named Gilgamesh ruled the Mesopotamian city of Uruk around 2700 B.C. Over the next millennium, Sumerian and Babylonian poets wrote numerous, conflicting accounts of his life, fragments of which survive. Today's standard version is based on 7th century B.C. Assyrian cuneiform tablets found at Nineveh in the 19th century.

Modern interpretations of Gilgamesh, such as this contemporary Arabic version, have tended to play down the homoerotic implications of the story.

Most scholars interpret the Gilgamesh epic as an allegory of the development and value of civilization. At the beginning of the tale, Gilgamesh, who is described as two-thirds god and one-third man, has been ravishing the young men and women of Uruk. In response to the people's complaints, the gods decide to give him a friend, a "wild man" they call Enkidu, and cause both men to dream in symbolic, erotic terms of the relationship they are destined to have with each other. When they finally meet, they fight savagely but end up embracing and vowing comradeship. Gilgamesh becomes a wise and capable ruler, and together the two men triumph over one fearsome adversary after another. In the end, however, the gods become angry over Gilgamesh's arrogance, which includes rejecting Ishtar, the goddess of love, and decide to punish Gilgamesh by causing Enkidu to sicken and die. Mad with grief, Gilgamesh sets off to find the secret of eternal life but returns to Uruk unsuccessful and begins recording his story on the towering walls of the city.

Although the epic contains no explicit description of sex between the two men, their friendship is cast in homoerotic terms, which are reinforced in some versions by puns of a sexual nature. Once joined, Gilgamesh and Enkidu reject the love of women, devoting themselves wholeheartedly to each other and becoming noble and heroic in the process.

Scholars dispute what, if anything, the epic tells us about same-sex eroticism three or four thousand years ago, but it seems clear that the ancient Mesopotamians at least recognized the positive potential of loving bonds between men.

✧ David M. Halperin, "Heroes and Their Pals," in *One Hundred Years of Homosexuality and Other Essays on Greek Love* (1990).

✧ *Homosexuality in the Ancient World,* edited by Wayne R. Dynes and Stephen Donaldson (1992).

Ginsberg, Allen

(1926–1997)

U.S. poet, teacher. Ginsberg grew up in Paterson, New Jersey, the son of a high school teacher and a mother who was in mental hospitals during much of his youth. He began studying at Columbia University in 1943 but was expelled after he was discovered in bed with fellow BEAT GENERATION leader-to-be Jack Kerouac. After years of travel—and a brief stay in a mental hospital in 1948 to avoid a prison sentence for transporting stolen goods—Ginsberg, inspired by his readings of William Blake and WALT WHITMAN, began writing poetry in earnest.

In **October 1955**, he debuted his long poem *Howl* at riotous public readings in San Francisco. *Howl,* which openly celebrated the joys of rough gay male sex, led to an obscenity trial (which the San Francisco police lost) and established Ginsberg as the poet laureate of his generation. Ginsberg changed the direction of American poetry with his open and spontaneous literary forms, explored in more than two dozen books, as well as his revolutionary themes.

Ginsberg was active on both coasts in the early GAY AND LESBIAN RIGHTS MOVEMENT. In 1959, he published a love poem to Neal Cassady in the *The Mattachine Review* and later attended meetings of the San Francisco chapter of the MATTACHINE Society. On the East Coast, Ginsberg was in the early 1960s a board member of the New York League for Sexual Freedom, the group that organized the first public demonstrations in the U.S. in favor of gay and lesbian rights (see **9/19/1964**). He appeared on the second night of the STONEWALL Uprising, proclaimed "Gay is good!," and announced his readiness to lead a group "om" chant should further violence arise. He later met with police to protest entrapment and harassment. On **July 12, 1972**, he appeared on national TELEVISION along with the first openly gay representatives to the Democratic National Convention.

Ginsberg continued writing important poetry and taking part in a variety of political movements. Until his death, he lived simply on New York City's Lower East Side, donating most of his earnings to the Naropa Institute's Jack Kerouac School of Disembodied Poetics. He was also a defender of the North American Man-Boy Love Association (NAMBLA; see PEDOPHILIA). Writer Peter Orlovsky was his lover for 18 years.

✧ Jane Kramer, *Allen Ginsberg in America* (1969).

✧ Allen Young, "Allen Ginsberg," in *Gay Sunshine Interviews, Volume One,* edited by Winston Leyland (1978).

✧ Michael Schumacher, *Dharma Lion: A Biography of Allen Ginsberg* (1992).

Gittings, Barbara [Brooks]

(1932–)

U.S. activist, editor, librarian/bibliographer. Born in Vienna, Austria, where her father was posted with the U.S. Foreign Service, Gittings moved to Wilmington, Delaware, with her family in the early 1940s and to Philadelphia in 1951. She received a traditional Catholic education before, at her insistence, transferring to public school and studying for one year at Northwestern University.

Her college realization that she was a lesbian sent her to the library where she found demoralizing entries under "deviance," "perversion," "pathology," and "abnormality," in addition to reports of "scientific" studies of body part measurements that attempted to define the group characteristics of homosexuals.

At the invitation of DEL MARTIN and PHYLLIS LYON, Gittings founded the first East Coast chapter of the DAUGHTERS OF BILITIS (DOB) in New York City on **September 20, 1958**. Fewer than a dozen women responded to her call "for all women in the New York area who are interested in forming a chapter of the DOB" to gather at the Sixth Avenue loft offices of the local MATTACHINE chapter. She served as president of the New York group until 1961.

In 1959, she began editing a newsletter for the New York chapter, and in 1963 was named editor of THE LADDER, the national publication of DOB. Among her innovations were the addition of the words "A Lesbian Review" and photos of lesbians on the publication's cover—both considered provocative at the time, since the word "lesbian" was not even a part of the DOB's statement of purpose—and the inclusion of personal interviews and positive accounts of coming OUT called "Living Propaganda." Her militancy, advocacy of openness, and support for public protests led to her removal by the national DOB board in 1966.

In the 1960s, Gittings joined with FRANK KAMENY and his Washington, D.C., chapter of the Mattachine to fight U.S. government employment discrimination against gay men and lesbians. She participated in the first gay and lesbian picket lines at the White House, the Pentagon, the Civil Service Commission, and the State Department in 1965. She was also a part of the annual Independence Day picket line conducted at Independence Hall in Philadelphia from 1965 through 1969.

Remembering the frustration she had experienced trying to research lesbianism in her college library, Gittings served as coordinator of the Task Force on Gay Liberation of the AMERICAN LIBRARY ASSOCIATION, a member of the organization's Social Responsibilities Round Table, and editor of its "Gay Bibliography" and other reading lists from 1971 through 1986. "Maybe today someone seventeen looking in those libraries will find right away what I couldn't find," she later commented, hoping that young lesbians and gay men would now have access to "reinforcement and a positive view of gay love and the gay world."

With six other women (including BARBARA LOVE and Lilli Vincenz), she was part of a breakthrough all-lesbian panel that appeared on David Susskind's nationally televised show in 1971 to discuss the direction of gay liberation.

On another important front, she was one of the activists in the confrontation with the AMERICAN PSYCHIATRIC ASSOCIATION (APA) that led on **December 15, 1973**, to the removal of "homosexuality" from the organization's list of psychiatric disorders. She coordinated gay and lesbian exhibits at APA conventions in 1972, 1976, and 1978.

In 1993, she joined the board of the Delaware Valley Legacy Fund. She is also on the advisory board of the Philadelphia Lesbian and Gay Task Force. Her life partner, whom she met at a DOB picnic in 1961, is writer, photographer, and fellow activist Kay Tobin Lahusen.

Gittings describes her early awareness of her sexuality as a personal struggle for a positive self-image rather than a drive to effect social change. As she came to the realization, however, that the "problems" of homosexuality derived from society rather than from individuals, she embraced public education as an effective way of advancing lesbian and gay liberation, opening CLOSET doors, nurturing a positive lesbian and gay identity, and changing the attitudes of society.

✧ Eric Marcus, *Making History: The Struggle for Gay and Lesbian Equal Rights, 1945–1990* (1992).

GLOE, see AGING.

Gloeden, Baron Wilhelm von
(1856–1931)

German photographer. A Prussian aristocrat, Gloeden was diagnosed with tuberculosis while in art school and advised by doctors to move to a warmer climate. He settled in Taormina, Sicily, at the age of 23 and remained there the rest of his life.

Already an amateur photographer, he took up PHOTOGRAPHY in earnest to support himself in 1888 after his stepfather's involvement in a financial scandal resulted in his family's losing their fortune. By 1900, Gloeden had made his own small fortune off his best-selling postcards of Mediterranean landscapes, carefully posed scenes of peasant life, and painterly, pseudo-classical photos of nude or scantily clad Sicilian boys (infrequently posed with girls or older men). He became one of the most renowned photographers in Europe and was visited by royalty, millionaires, and celebrities, including Edward VII, Alexander Graham Bell, and OSCAR WILDE.

The reaction of Gloeden's contemporaries to his male nudes is of as much interest to historians of sexuality as the photos themselves: they were praised as "art" and judged so "an-

Gloeden took homoerotic icons like this photo, inspired by Hippolyte-Jean Flandrin's *Jeune Homme Nu Assis au Bord de la Mer* ("*Young Male Nude Seated by the Sea*," 1835–1836).

thropologically" significant that they were published in *National Geographic* magazine. A select group of cognoscenti, however, appreciated Gloeden's HOMOEROTICISM. His photos were featured in the "Uranian" magazine *Artist* and ADOLF BRAND's *Der Eigene* (see **1896**) and directly supplied to wealthy collectors like Friedrich Krupp.

Gloeden got along well with the residents of Taormina, despite his penchant for late-night romps with local youths. He made donations to the community and set up a fund for his models. One of them, Pancrazio "Il Moro" Bucini, grew up to become his companion, business manager, and heir to Gloeden's 7,000 negatives.

Bucini lived to see attitudes change as Europeans became more aware of homosexuality: Italian Fascists seized and destroyed much of Gloeden's work in 1939, and Bucini stood trial on obscenity charges in 1942. Although he was acquitted, it was not until the 1970s that Gloeden's homoerotic photos became widely available again.

Gloeden has influenced the work of many contemporary gay male artists, including the Italian photographer Tony Patrioli's more blatantly prurient photos of Sicilian youths. Roger Peyrefitte's novel *Les Amours Singulières* (1949) is based on Gloeden's life.

✧ Allen Ellenzweig, *The Homoerotic Photograph: Male Images from Durieu/Delacroix to Mapplethorpe* (1992).

✧ Robert Aldrich, *The Seduction of the Mediterranean: Writing, Art and Homosexual Fantasy* (1993).

Gomez, Jewelle L.
(1948–)

U.S. writer, activist. Born in Boston, Gomez was raised by a supportive extended family, including her parents, grandparents, a step-

Jewelle Gomez.

mother, and her maternal great-grandmother, who fostered a strong sense of history and the importance of social activism. After attending Northeastern University and earning an M.S. from the Columbia School of Journalism, she worked on public television productions (including *Say Brother,* a pioneering weekly program in Boston devoted to AFRICAN-AMERICAN topics) and on off-Broadway shows in New York City. She served as director of the New York State Council on the Arts literature program from 1989, before moving to San Francisco in 1993. Her life partner is Diane Sabin.

Experienced in the 1960s black nationalist and antiwar movements, Gomez became a lesbian activist in the 1970s. She was a founding board member of the GAY AND LESBIAN ALLIANCE AGAINST DEFAMATION, a contributing editor to feminist and lesbian publications like *Conditions* and *Belles Lettres,* and an outspoken proponent of sex-positive campaigns such as the Feminist Anti-Censorship Taskforce.

Gomez's early books of poetry, *The Lipstick Papers* (1980) and *Flamingoes and Bears* (1987), were acclaimed for their lyricism, sensuousness, and sensitivity to historical and cultural themes. She reached a much broader audience with her Lambda AWARD–winning *The Gilda Stories: A Novel* (1991). The first African-American lesbian vampire, Gilda journeys from 1850 to 2050, transcending not only time and place but literary genres as well. In other writings, Gomez has advocated speculative fiction as a way of revealing the ordinary through the extraordinary or, as she puts it, "heavy ideas" through a form that is often considered "lightweight." She believes it is an especially important creative vehicle for black lesbians because of its capacity for creating a vision of "life as it might be" independent of harsh realities. Gomez has collected many of her essays in *Forty-three Septembers* (1993).

- Linda L. Nelson, "Jewelle L. Gomez," in *Contemporary Lesbian Writers of the United States,* edited by Sandra Pollack and Denise D. Knight (1993).
- Jewelle Gomez, "Speculative Fiction and Black Lesbians," *Signs* (Summer 1993).

Gorris, Marleen

(1948–)

Dutch filmmaker. One of six children raised Protestant in a small, overwhelmingly Catholic village in the NETHERLANDS, Gorris left home at the age of 17 to study drama, English, and documentary filmmaking at Dutch, British, and French schools. Inspired by a news article about a woman caught shoplifting, she wrote her first screenplay in the hope that Chantal Akerman, a Belgian-born lesbian filmmaker with a reputation for handling provocative subject matter in innovative ways, would direct the FILM. Akerman refused but persuaded Gorris to make the film herself. The result was the award-winning *A Question of Silence* (1982), a controversial account of three unrelated women who kill and sexually mutilate a male shopkeeper. The *Los Angeles Times* called the film "an inflammatory, subversive (in the best sense of the word) black comedy."

A Question of Silence was the first of a radical feminist trilogy that continued with *Broken Mirrors* (1984), about S/M and an Amsterdam brothel, and climaxed with *The Last Island* (1990), a suspense-packed thriller in which five men (including two unfavorably portrayed gay characters) and two women battle one another on a desert island.

Gorris's fourth film, the Oscar-winning *Antonia's Line* (1995), marked the debut of her first fully developed lesbian character, the adult daughter of the eponymous Antonia, as well as a lighter, more optimistic comic style. Antonia returns to her native village after 20 years in the big city and becomes house mother and ringleader to a colorful group of local eccentrics.

Like Akerman, Gorris rejects the role of lesbian spokesperson, insisting that she is a director "who *happens* to make feminist films and who *happens* to be gay." She prefers to be recognized for her visions of antipatriarchal communities "in which mutual support enables everyone to live life as it comes."

- Howard Feinstein, "Hook, *Line,* and Thinker," *Out* (February 1996).
- Ingrid Abramovitch, "Chronicling Women Free of Men," *The New York Times* (February 18, 1996).

Grahn, Judy

(Judith Rae Grahn; 1940–)

U.S. writer, cultural theorist, activist. Born in Chicago, Grahn grew up in a poor New Mex-

Judy Grahn.

ico desert town that she later described as a "wasteland of human relationships and social rigidity." She began writing at an early age and by 12 was submitting poems for publication under the PSEUDONYM Amelia Silver. After her first relationship with a woman ended in a forced separation, she joined the Air Force but was discharged as part of a lesbian witch-hunt.

Before her first visit to a gay BAR at the age of 21, Grahn saw herself as "a nice white Protestant girl with a tomboy nature who had once had a secret and very loving Lesbian relationship with another nice girl who was attending college to become a teacher." In the 1960s, she actively participated in the gay and civil rights movements, demonstrating with the MATTACHINE Society in front of the White House (see **5/29/1965**) and publishing her first poems in THE LADDER. In 1964, she published an article (as "Carol Silver") in *Sexology Magazine* arguing against the idea, then current, that most lesbians were "sick." The next year, she satirized the so-called medical model of lesbianism with one of her most popular poems, "The Psychoanalysis of Edward the Dyke."

After nearly dying from misdiagnosed cat scratch fever and encephalitis, Grahn rededicated herself to achieving her artistic and spiritual goals. Unable to get her openly lesbian work published, she and artist Wendy Cadden, her lover for 14 years, began a mimeographing operation in 1969 that became one of the first lesbian presses, the Oakland-based Women's Press Collective. The collective printed 60,000 copies of books by nearly 200 women before merging with Diana Press in the late 1970s. During this time, Grahn also helped found the first lesbian/feminist separatist collective, the Gay Women's Liberation Group, and the first women's bookstore in the U.S., A Woman's Place.

Grahn is probably best known for *The Common Woman,* self-published in 1969, although she has cited her protest poem, "A Woman Is Talking to Death" (1973), as "the most articulated in poetry I could be." An immediate hit, mimeographed copies of *The Common Woman* were passed hand to hand across the country and around the world. The seven portrait poems, which served as the model for Ntozake Shange's *For Colored Girls Who Have Considered Suicide When the Rainbow Is Enuf,* were set to music and presented by performance artists. The title and selected passages appeared on posters and T-shirts and inspired the names of magazines, bookstores, and coffee shops. The poems were finally published in book form in 1978.

Grahn emerged as an influential philosopher and spiritual theorist with the publication of *Another Mother Tongue: Gay Words, Gay Worlds* in 1979 (expanded edition, 1984). *Another Mother Tongue* weaves the story of—and a tribute to—her late first lover, Yvonne, with a wide-ranging exploration of myths, stereotypes, anthropological lore, and etymologies that together suggest the age-old "parameters and characteristics of homosexual culture." The book concludes with Grahn's vision of the role gay culture can play in society today. Her *Blood, Bread, and Roses: How Menstruation Changed the World* (1994) uses a similar approach to explore women's contributions to world culture.

One of the most influential and beloved writers in American gay and lesbian LITERATURE, Grahn has also contributed groundbreaking works of literary criticism on writers ranging from EMILY DICKINSON and GERTRUDE STEIN to PAULA GUNN ALLEN and OLGA BROUMAS. In 1984, she cofounded a Gay and Lesbian Studies Program at the New College of California.

- Judy Grahn, *The Highest Apple: Sappho and the Lesbian Poetic Tradition* (1985).
- Judy Grahn, "The Common Woman—A Map of Seven Poems," in *Inversions: Writing by Dykes, Queers, and Lesbians,* edited by Betsy Warland (1991).
- Felice Picano, "Feminine/Masculine: An Interview with Judy Grahn," *Playguy* (June 1995).

Great Britain, see UNITED KINGDOM.

Greece

No laws against consensual same-sex relations between persons 15 years of age or older, although gay men are barred from service in the navy. Social scene and political organizations in large cities.

"Greek love" has been a euphemism for love between men for centuries, but a contemporary gay and lesbian rights movement was late in arriving in the country many gay men and lesbians consider almost their homeland. Helped by the country's need to comply with the European Union's high standards of human and civil rights, gay and lesbian activists have begun to win a greater level of visibility—and a lower level of official harassment—in large Greek cities like Athens. Police raids on gay BARS have largely ceased, and an openly gay and lesbian press has emerged as a force in building a SUBCULTURE.

Ancient Greece

HOMOEROTICISM was a major feature of ancient Greek art, poetry, and even SPORT, and same-sex relations were an accepted part of ancient Greek life, although in a "construction" very different from modern gay and lesbian conceptions of sexuality.

The Greeks looked at sex in hierarchical terms. Adult male citizens, the only people with rights and power, were in most respects free to take their pleasure with whomever they chose—slaves, women, younger men—as long as they: (1) respected others' "property" rights (i.e., did not seduce other people's slaves, or citizens' wives and daughters); (2) scrupulously avoided *receptive* anal or oral intercourse; and (3) fulfilled their societal obligations, which included marriage and the conception of (male) heirs.

In Athens especially, PEDERASTY, considered vital to the education of young male citizens-to-be, was practically a social duty, but Greek "man-boy love" also had characteristics most people would find odd today: boys, for example, were expected to resist the advances of older men, relenting only after a long and involved courtship and then only to allow the older man "intracrural" (between the thighs) intercourse. In addition, it was considered shameful for the boy to derive sexual pleasure from his mating with older men. The sexuality of women, most of whom were secluded from society in special sections of homes, was largely ignored. SAPPHO provides a rare surviving hint of what woman-woman love was like in ancient Greece.

Much of what the Greeks wrote about same-sex love (and depicted in art found on vases) probably reflected social ideals. Just as some contemporary Americans idealize traditional notions of the family and marriage as a lifelong, heterosexual institution, yet in practice divorce at higher rates than any other nationality, the ancient Greeks did not always remain faithful to their own idealized social codes. Some records survive of men who continued to have sexual, romantic relationships with each other into adulthood and of male citizens who played the receptive role in anal intercourse. Similarly, modern scholars suspect that in private some boys did actually enjoy sex with adult men.

Although Greek political power declined after the 4th century B.C., Greek culture and, to a certain extent, Greek attitudes toward homoeroticism spread throughout the Mediterranean region over the next centuries. Novels written in Greek in the first centuries of the first millennium often featured subplots centered on same-sex romances between men; other Greek writings provide rare accounts of "tribades" (lesbians; see **c. 160**). At the same time, Greek and "Hellenized" non-Greek thinkers like Philo (see **c. 40**) began to take positions against homoeroticism that would later strongly influence CHRISTIANITY.

Byzantine Empire

The last centuries of the Roman Empire saw a gradual shift toward repression of same-sex eroticism, especially when it involved "passive" or effeminate men (see **249**; **342**; **390**). In the Byzantine Empire, as the eastern portion of the Roman Empire came to be called, laws against SODOMY became increasingly strict (see **533**), although many historians believe these laws were seldom enforced except against political enemies of those in power. In particular, the reign of Justinian I (ruled 527–565) and his consort, Theodora, was notable for several gruesome prosecutions of political enemies based on their allegedly having committed sodomy. In one such case, two prominent bishops, Isaiah of Rhodes and Alexander of Diospolis, were accused of sodomy and brought to Constaninople to be tortured. Alexander was castrated and dragged naked through the streets of the city.

Over the next centuries, before Greece became part of the Ottoman Empire (see TURKEY), evidence for same-sex relations comes mainly from court gossip and accounts of life in sex-segregated monasteries and convents. One intriguing incident was the Emperor Michael III's SAME-SEX UNION with a handsome young courtier (who later murdered him and usurped the throne) in **866**.

Modern Greece

Historians of sexuality believe that contemporary Greek attitudes toward same-sex eroticism are more the product of the long Ottoman rule of Greece (from 1453 to 1821) than of any lingering effects of ancient Greek culture. JOHANN JOACHIM WINCKELMANN, LORD BYRON, NATALIE BARNEY, and RENÉE VIVIEN—as well as Greeks like CONSTANTINE CAVAFY and OLGA BROUMAS—are just a few of the intellectuals who have encouraged a revival of interest in Greek homoerotic traditions over the past few centuries.

✧ K. J. Dover, *Greek Homosexuality* (1978).

- Eva Cantarella, *Pandora's Daughters: The Role and Status of Women in Greek and Roman Antiquity* (1987).
- Keith Hale, *In the Land of Alexander: Gay Travels with History and Politics, in Hungary, Yugoslavia, Turkey, and Greece* (1990).
- *Before Sexuality: The Construction of Erotic Experience in the Ancient Greek World,* edited by David M. Halperin, John J. Winkler, and Froma I. Zeitlin (1990).

Grier, Barbara G.

(pseudonyms: Gene Damon, etc.; 1933–)

U.S. activist, editor, publisher, writer, bibliographer. Born into a working-class Cincinnati family, Grier came OUT to her mother at the age of 12, at which time she renamed herself "Gene Damon" (from the German for "demon") and began a lifelong study of the lesbian in LITERATURE. Educated in Kansas City, Kansas, she went to work after high school to help support her sisters and divorced mother, finding employment in a variety of clerical jobs while beginning her writing, editing, and publishing careers. After a long relationship with librarian Helen L. Bennett, she met Donna J. McBride, head of several departments at the Kansas City, Missouri, Public Library. The two women have been together since 1972.

Active in the HOMOPHILE movement from 1956, she helped arrange for the first national meeting of the National Conference of Homophile Organizations (NACHO, 1966), but she was most effective in building awareness of lesbian literature. Her reviews of lesbian and gay publications appeared in the column "Lesbiana" (her term for the genre of lesbian literature) in THE LADDER (1957–1972) and "Reader at Large" in *Tangents* (1965–1970). She served as fiction and poetry editor of *The Ladder* from 1966 to 1967, editor from 1968 through its separation from DAUGHTERS OF BILITIS in 1970, and publisher until its demise in 1972. Inspired by JEANNETTE FOSTER, Grier compiled and published extensive bibliographies, *The Lesbian in Literature* (1967, 1975, 1981), and other collections of reviews, essays, and articles from *The Ladder.*

In 1973, Grier, McBride, and legal professionals Anyda Marchant (PSEUDONYM: Sarah Aldridge) and Muriel Crawford formed the Naiad Press, building a distribution network

Barbara Grier (left) with lover Donna McBride, 1979.

from the original *Ladder* mailing list. Their first book, Sarah Aldridge's *Latecomer,* was published in 1974. Best-sellers such as *Desert of the Heart* and *Outlander* by JANE RULE, Sheila Ortiz Taylor's *Faultline,* and mysteries from KATHERINE V. FORREST have helped make Naiad the largest and most successful lesbian press in the world.

Literature can provide a crucial point of identity and connection for a woman coming out, Grier believes, and beyond that, coming out is itself an urgent moral obligation: "It is the closet that is our sin and shame."

Grier has published widely under her own name and under pseudonyms that include Gene Damon, Marilyn Barrow, Gladys Casey, Irene Fiske, Vern Niven, Lennox Strang, and Lennox Strong.

✧ Barbara Grier, "Neither Profit nor Salvation," *Sinister Wisdom* (vol. 5, Winter 1978).

✧ Barbara Grier, "The Garden Variety Lesbian," in *The Coming Out Stories,* edited by Susan J. Wolfe and Julia Penelope Stanley (1980).

✧ Jim Kepner, "Barbara Grier," in *Gay and Lesbian Literature* (1994).

Griffin, Susan

(1943–)

U.S. essayist, playwright, poet. Born into a family of conservative Los Angeles Republicans, Griffin was nine when her parents divorced. She was sent to live with her maternal grandparents for two years, and her sister Joanna (who also grew up to be a lesbian) went with an aunt 600 miles away. She spent the remainder of her youth moving from one close relative's home to another before going to San Francisco State University to study English and creative writing. After graduating with honors, she taught in the Bay Area and worked on the staff of *American Radical* magazine.

In her twenties, Griffin was married for four years and had a daughter. Later, her experiences as a single mother and as a participant in the civil rights and peace movements came together in her writing as well as in her evolving feminist convictions. "I could no longer separate any part of myself from my political consciousness," she later explained.

At about the same time, she began to come to terms with her lesbianism, acknowledging that tensions between herself and her already OUT sister—as well as her family's disapproval of her sister—had contributed to her censoring her own feelings to the point of being afraid to use the word "lesbian." In 1976, sitting on a Modern Language Association panel discussing lesbians and LITERATURE, she framed her personal coming out process in the context of an emerging lesbian culture, observing that lesbians "are a community of those coming to speech from silence."

Griffin has published twelve books of poetry and prose and three plays, including *Voices* (1975), which won an Emmy Award. Her best-known work is probably *Women and Nature: The Roaring Inside Her* (1978). Blending science, SPIRITUALITY, and feminism, *Women and Nature* contends that men seek to dominate and control nature through women because they associate women with natural creative and destructive forces. A similar perspective informs Griffin's *Pornography and Silence: Culture's Revenge Against Nature* (1981), one of the most influential texts of the women's anti-PORNOGRAPHY movement.

Griffin has also won acclaim for the power and originality of her books and articles on the environment and on 20th-century inhumanity (*A Chorus of Stones: The Private Life of War,* 1992). She has received many awards, including, in 1990, the MacArthur Foundation Grant for Peace and International Cooperation.

- ✧ "Lesbians and Literature," *Sinister Wisdom* (vol. 1, issue 2, Fall 1976).
- ✧ Susan Griffin, *Made from This Earth: Selections from Her Writings, 1967–1982* (1982).

Grimké, Angelina Weld
(1880–1958)

U.S. poet. The daughter of Archibald Grimké, a prominent Boston lawyer and AFRICAN-AMERICAN rights activist, she was named after her white great aunt, a famous abolitionist. Ironically, that Angelina Grimké dedicated herself to the cause of reform while her brother John owned slaves, and fathered Archibald by one of them.

After an education in elite schools, where she was often the only black student in the class, Grimké began teaching in Washington, D.C., and writing drama, short fiction, and poetry. She took an early retirement in 1926 and moved to Brooklyn, New York, after her father's death in 1930.

Grimké's lyric poetry, which she began publishing at the age of 11, was included in HARLEM RENAISSANCE collections such as ALAIN LOCKE's epoch-making *The New Negro* (1925). Despite her privileged, sheltered background, she was deeply affected by racism. Her first major work, the play *Rachel* (1916; published, 1920), dramatizes the protagonist's desire never to bring children into a racist world. *Rachel* was sponsored by the National Association for the Advancement of Colored People (NAACP) in response to the racist 1915 film *The Birth of a Nation.* The NAACP considered the play "the first attempt to use the stage for race propaganda."

Years after her death, Grimké was rediscovered as an important lesbian poet. Her story serves as a tragic answer to the question critic and activist Gloria T. Hull has posed: "What did it mean to be a Black Lesbian/poet in America at the beginning of the twentieth century?" Hull and others have examined Grimké's love poetry, much of it never published, and found evidence of isolation, despair, and self-abnegation. Although not completely silenced, Grimké was never able to publish her most intensely felt work, her poems to and about other women. In one, entitled "Caprichosa," she wrote: "If I might taste but once, just once / The dew / Upon her lips."

One relationship with a woman has been documented. Grimké was involved with a school friend, Mamie Burrill, from 1896 to 1903. The two young women's letters reveal Mamie wanting to "like an angel bending o'er you breathe into your ear, 'I love you.' " Grimké, who asked Mamie to be her wife, once wrote: "Oh Mamie if you only knew how my heart overflows with love for you and how it yearns and pants for one glimpse of your lovely face."

- ✧ Gloria T. Hull, " 'Under the Days': The Buried Life and Poetry of Angelina Weld Grimké," in *Conditions: Five* (1979).
- ✧ Gloria T. Hull, *Color, Sex, and Poetry: Three Women Writers of the Harlem Renaissance* (1987).
- ✧ Phyllis Wood, "Angelina Weld Grimké," in *Epic Lives: One Hundred Black Women Who Made a Difference,* edited by Jessie Carney Smith (1993).

Gyms, see BODYBUILDING; SPORT.

H

Hacker, Marilyn

(1942–)

U.S. poet, editor, educator. Born an only child in the Bronx, New York, Hacker's early passions for reading and writing were encouraged by her mother, an elementary school teacher, and her father, an industrial chemist. At the age of 18, she married SAMUEL R. DELANY (and had a daughter, Iva, with him before finally separating in 1974). After graduating from New York University with a degree in French and studying with the Art Students League, she worked as an editor in New York and San Francisco and moved to London in 1970. On a business trip to Paris that same year, she fell in love with the city's "rhythms of life," and today divides her time between homes in New York and Paris.

Hacker has published ten acclaimed volumes of poetry, including *Presentation Piece* (1974; Lamont Poetry Selection of the Academy of American Poets and the National Book Award). *Selected Poems 1965–1990* (1996; Poet's Prize) included many of the poems she published since coming OUT in 1976. Her *Winter Numbers* (1995) won a Lambda Literary Award.

Commenting on Hacker's ability to meld street-tough language with formal rhyme and meter schemes, critic Suzanne Gardinier lauds Hacker's "Houdini panache" for audacious escapes from the "net of form into sense and music and revelation." Hacker has explained that she uses rhyme and meter "not to contain the anarchy, but to communicate it." Her poems have explored themes ranging from her identity as a Jew and her struggle with breast cancer to what she calls the "subtle colorations of relationships between women, erotic or not."

Hacker's life partner is Karyn London, a medical professional who was one of the owners of Womanbooks, an important early feminist bookstore in New York City.

✧ Lawrence Joseph, "A Formal Life: Marilyn Hacker's Deep Structure," *Voice Literary Supplement* (February 1995).

✧ Suzanne Gardinier, "An Interview with Marilyn Hacker," *Associated Writing Programs Chronicle* (vol. 28, no. 5, March/April 1996).

Hadrian

(Publius Aelius Hadrianus; 76–138) and Antinous (c. 110–130)

Roman emperor and his most famous lover. Edward Gibbon described Hadrian as "by turns, an excellent prince, a ridiculous sophist, and a jealous tyrant"; most historians consider his reign, remarkable for its relative peacefulness and the quantity and quality of its public works, more or less the apogee of the ROMAN EMPIRE.

Hadrian.

Hadrian was married to the grandniece of his predecessor, Trajan, but his primary sexual and romantic interests were for young men—most notably, Antinous, a famously handsome Greek boy from Asia Minor. Their love affair was probably the best-known real-life romance in antiquity, mostly because of its tragic end. Just as Antinous was on the verge of adult manhood, he drowned in the Nile. No one has satisfactorily explained his death. Some historians, including Royston Lambert, have suggested that he drowned himself as a kind of religious sacrifice for Hadrian's benefit. Whatever the circumstances, Hadrian was inconsolable. He had Antinous deified, and then commissioned coins, monuments, and even a city (Antinoöpolis) in his honor. The cult of the "god" Antinous survived in some cities until Christian officials suppressed it in the fourth century.

MARGUERITE YOURCENAR's *Memoirs of Hadrian* (1951) is a vividly imagined first-person account of Hadrian's life.

✧ Royston Lambert, *Beloved and God: The Story of Hadrian and Antinous* (1988).

Haiti

No laws against same-sex relations between adults over 18.

Although same-sex relations have not been illegal in Haiti since French colonial times (see **9/25/1791**), neither the cultural nor the political aspects of the contemporary gay and lesbian movement have had an appreciable impact. At the same time, anthropological studies have reported that Haitians tend to be more tolerant of GENDER nonconformity than Spanish-speaking Latin Americans.

The advent of AIDS focused attention on gay male sex tourism in Haiti during the 1970s. Although some, including RANDY SHILTS, suggested this was one of the ways AIDS was transmitted into the U.S., others such as Canadian poet and essayist Ian Young felt such theories smacked of racism.

➤ Also see SAINT, ASSOTTO.

Hall, Radclyffe

(Marguerite Antonia Radclyffe-Hall, "John"; 1880–1943)

English novelist, poet. Hall was born on the eve of her parents' separation. She was educated primarily at home and at day schools and took courses at King's College, Cambridge. Tensions between her and her Philadelphia-born mother, Marie Jane Diehl, led to her leaving home when she turned 21 and living on her own off the multimillion-pound inheritance she had received from her grandfather, a physician and spa entrepreneur.

Hall's first relationship was with "Ladye" Mabel Veronica Batten, an older married woman who shared Hall's talents for music. During their relationship, which lasted from 1908 until Ladye's death in 1916, Hall turned from writing poetry to prose, converted (with

Ladye) to Catholicism, and met other lesbians, like Winnaretta Singer (daughter of the sewing machine manufacturer, she married a gay man to become the Princesse de Polignac), composer ETHEL SMYTH, and suffragette Emmeline Pankhurst.

Hall became involved with Ladye's cousin, UNA TROUBRIDGE, six months before Ladye's death. Guilt over her infidelity tortured Hall throughout her life. She held seances to conjure Ladye and dedicated her last five novels to "Our Three Selves," a reference to herself, Una, and Ladye, the three of whom were buried together in Highgate Cemetery in London. Late in life, Hall was in turn unfaithful to Troubridge with Evguenia Souline, a young White Russian nurse she had hired to care for Una. Troubridge destroyed Souline's letters to Hall after Hall's death, but 600 love letters from Hall to Souline dated from 1934 through 1939 have survived.

Of Hall's eight novels, her fifth, THE WELL OF LONELINESS (1928), was by far her most famous, although she felt *The Master of the House* (1932) was her strongest.

An essentialist before the term existed (see CONSTRUCTIONALISM VS. ESSENTIALISM), Hall believed her lesbianism a biological fact of nature. She considered herself a "true invert," a man in a woman's body. Widely read in the psychology of her time, she was most influenced by RICHARD VON KRAFFT-EBING and HAVELOCK ELLIS (who wrote the sympathetic introductory "commentary" to *The Well of Loneliness*). She flirted with the women's suffrage movement, but—perhaps because of her identification with men—never committed herself to feminism, although she supported women-centered reform in divorce and prostitution. Her conservatism was also evident in her class prejudice and anti-Semitism.

Radclyffe Hall, 1932.

The notoriety of *The Well of Loneliness* made Hall a spokesperson for the cause of the "invert."

No other novel has figured so prominently in lesbian lives around the world as *The Well of Loneliness.* Although some lesbians have criticized the book's BUTCH-FEMME characterizations and its bleak, self-sacrificial ending, for decades it was the only widely available challenge to what Hall termed the "conspiracy of silence" surrounding lesbians.

Hall was well acquainted with a number of women in European and North American lesbian communities. Her American friends included writer and suffragette Ida A. R. Wylie and her lover and fellow HETERODOXY member Dr. M. JOSEPHINE BAKER, a physician and director of the New York City Division of Child Hygiene. In Paris, Hall and Troubridge were friends of NATALIE BARNEY, ROMAINE BROOKS, COLETTE, and many others.

✧ Michael Baker, *Our Three Selves: The Life of Radclyffe Hall* (1985).

✧ Lovat Dickson, *Radclyffe Hall at the Well of Loneliness: A Sapphic Chronicle* (1975).

Hall, Richard W.

(Richard Hirshfeld; 1926–1992)

U.S. writer. Born into a New York City Jewish family, he moved as a child to Westchester

County, where his mother had him baptized an Episcopalian and changed the family name to Hall. After service in WORLD WAR II, study at Harvard, jobs in ADVERTISING and public relations, and earning an M.A. in English education from New York University, he turned full-time to writing and PUBLISHING. As THE ADVOCATE's book editor from 1976 until 1982, he was widely praised for helping raise the standards of gay and lesbian literary criticism. He was the first openly gay critic elected to the National Book Critics Circle.

His debut novel, *The Butterscotch Prince* (1975; revised edition, 1983) was a pioneering work of gay DETECTIVE FICTION. His short stories—collected in *Couplings* (1981), *Letter from a Great Uncle* (1985), and *Fidelities* (1992)—addressed an imaginative range of themes, from the surrealities of life ("Backwards," included in the first *Men on Men* anthology, 1986) to AIDS ("The Jilting of Tim Weatherall," which critic Claude J. Summers thinks "may be his most powerful story"). He also wrote three successful plays and a second, semiautobiographical novel, *Family Fiction* (1991).

A widely published and highly influential essayist, Hall wrote a series of articles on Henry James that played a decisive role in persuading critics, including Leon Edel, to acknowledge James's attraction to other men. His essay "Gay Fiction Comes Home" ran on the front page of *The New York Times Book Review* in June 1988, signaling a new level of recognition for gay authors.

Arthur Marceau was his lover from the 1970s until Marceau's death in 1989. Three years later, Hall died in Manhattan of AIDS-related complications.

✧ Jim Marks, "The Dilemmas of Richard Hall," *Lambda Book Report* (September/October 1992).

✧ Claude J. Summers, "Richard Hall," in *Contemporary Gay American Novelists*, edited by Emmanuel S. Nelson (1993).

Hammarskjöld, Dag
(1905–1961)

Swedish diplomat, writer. The son of a prime minister, he was an official in the Swedish finance and foreign ministries before heading his country's delegation to the United Nations from 1951 to 1953. He served as secretary-general of the U.N. from 1953 until his death on a mission to the Congo (Zaire) in a plane crash in present-day Zambia. As secretary-general he established the first U.N. emergency force and greatly expanded the organization's role as international peacemaker. He was posthumously awarded the Nobel Peace Prize (1961).

Close friends and colleagues knew that Hammarskjöld was gay despite his—and later biographers'—denials. After his death, a collection of his prose pieces and poetry was published as *Vägmärken* (1963; translated by W. H. AUDEN and Leif Sjöberg as *Markings*, 1964). In these writings, Hammarskjöld emerges as a deeply religious man determined to sublimate himself and his desires for a greater good. Many passages seem to express the pain of being a closeted public figure, such as: "Pray that your loneliness may spur you into something to live for, great enough to die for."

✧ *Dag Hammarsköld Revisited*, edited by Robert S. Jordan (1983).

Hammer, Barbara
(1939–)

U.S. filmmaker. A Hollywood, California, native, Hammer has lived and worked most of her adult life in the Bay Area. She began experimenting with 8-mm FILM in the late 1960s and made her first 16-mm short, *A Gay Day*,

Salena and J. C. Barone, lovers in Barbara Hammer's Nitrate Kisses.

in 1973. Her four-minute film, *Dyketactics* (1974), is probably the first explicit film about lesbian sexuality made by a lesbian; it also established her as the first openly lesbian filmmaker to reach a wide audience.

She made more than 70 short films in the 1970s and 1980s, exploring topics ranging from modern-day AMAZONS (*Superdykes,* 1975) to the rise and fall of romance (*Double Strength,* 1978), relationships (*Women I Love,* 1979) to abstract meditations on nature (*Pond and Waterfall,* 1982), and old age (*Dream Age,* 1979) to death (*Vital Signs,* 1991). *Nitrate Kisses* (1992), her first full-length film, juxtaposed scenes of startlingly original sensuality with commentary on WILLA CATHER and films from the 1930s, underscoring the need to preserve lesbian and gay history. *Out in South Africa* (1994) documented Hammer's encounters in that country at a turning point in its history.

A teacher and theorist as well as a consummate artist, Hammer was among the first to advance the belief that "radical content deserves radical form": i.e., lesbians must forsake artistic traditions developed in heterosexual- and male-dominated cultures to invent their own unique, necessarily experimental art forms.

✧ Barbara Hammer, "The Politics of Abstraction," in *Queer Looks: Perspectives on Lesbian and Gay Film and Video,* edited by Martha Gever, John Greyson, and Pratibha Parmar (1993).

Hampton, Mabel

(1902–1989)

U.S. entertainer, activist, domestic worker. Orphaned at birth in Winston-Salem, North Carolina, Hampton was raised by her grandmother and aunt until her grandmother died when she was seven, precipitating a series of moves and traumatic experiences that included being sexually abused by an uncle and a year's stay in a reformatory on a false charge of prostitution.

Mabel Hampton, 1977.

In the 1920s, a job singing and dancing in a Coney Island show led to star turns in all-black productions at the Garden of Joy and the Lafayette Theater in Harlem. There she moved "in the life," meeting other lesbian and bisexual HARLEM RENAISSANCE entertainers like GLADYS BENTLEY, ALBERTA HUNTER, Moms Mabley, BESSIE SMITH, and ETHEL WATERS, frequenting A'lelia Walker's salon, and attending the era's legendary drag balls. In the 1930s, jobs for black performers grew scarce, and she went to work as a cleaning woman for the next four decades.

In 1932, Hampton met Lillian Foster (1906–1978), a dry cleaning presser from Norfolk, Virginia, and the two women formed a relationship that lasted until Foster's death.

Through the 1960s, Hampton was the central figure of a black lesbian community that flourished in the Bronx. She was a devoted member of the Eastern Star, a women's Masonic organization, and studied with the Rosicrucians.

Over the years, she built a personal library that reflected her passions for metaphysics, AFRICAN-AMERICAN history, and lesbian culture. In 1974, she began working with the LESBIAN HERSTORY ARCHIVES to be, as she said, "a part of going on." She had been a close friend and lesbian role model for JOAN NESTLE, one of the archive founders, since 1950, when Nestle's working mother hired her to help care for her then ten-year-old daughter.

Hampton appears in the films *Silent Pioneers* (1984) and *Before Stonewall* (1985). These and other sources document the inspiration she provided for younger lesbians, who relished her resilient spirit and joie de vivre. In 1984, she addressed New York's annual Gay/Lesbian Pride Rally with the words: "I, Mabel Hampton, have been a lesbian all my life, for 82 years, and I am proud of myself and my people. I would like all my people to be free in this country and all over the world, my gay people and my black people."

- Joan Nestle, "Surviving and More: An Interview with Mabel Hampton," *Sinister Wisdom* (no. 10, Summer 1979).
- Mabel Hampton, "I Didn't Go Back There Anymore: Mabel Hampton Talks about the South," *Feminary* (vol. 10, no. 2, 1979).
- Joan Nestle, "I Lift My Eyes to the Hill: The Life of Mabel Hampton as Told by a White Woman," in *Transforming the Categories: A CLAGS Reader,* edited by Martin Duberman (forthcoming).

Hansberry, Lorraine

(1930–1965)

U.S. writer, activist. The daughter of a wealthy Chicago businessman and civil rights activist, she moved to New York City in 1950 and worked as a writer at *Freedom,* Paul Robeson's newspaper. In 1953, she married Robert Nemiroff, who remained a close friend and collaborator after their separation in 1957. Her award-winning play, *A Raisin in the Sun* (1959), whose title was a quote from one of LANGSTON HUGHES's poems, was the first by an AFRICAN-AMERICAN woman to be produced on Broadway and a major stimulus of the 1960s African-American THEATER movement.

Active in the civil rights movement her entire life, Hansberry began to identify herself as a feminist and a lesbian in the 1950s. She contributed at least two long letters to THE LADDER (published under the initials "L.H.N." and "L.N." in May and August 1957, respectively), in which she applauded the growing West Coast HOMOPHILE movement and speculated that "homosexual persecution and condemnation" were rooted in "a philosophically active anti-feminist dogma" as well as "social ignorance." She opposed SEPARATISM but recognized the need for women's organizations and publications. As biographer Diana Marre notes, Hansberry linked "the struggle for gay rights, rights for people of color, and rights for women long before such terms as *homophobia* and *feminism* had come into the vernacular." She was one of the first members of the New York chapter of DAUGHTERS OF BILITIS (see **9/20/1958**) and also sent letters to ONE MAGAZINE.

Hansberry's play *The Sign in Sidney Brustein's Window* (1964) included a sympathetically depicted gay male character. At the time of her death (from cancer, at the age of 34), she was working on *Les Blancs,* a play that included a gay couple.

- Lorraine Hansberry, *To Be Young, Gifted and Black: Lorraine Hansberry in Her Own Words* (1969).
- Diana Marre, "Lorraine Hansberry," in *Notable Black American Women,* edited by Jessie Carney Smith (1992).

Hansen, Joseph

(pseudonyms: Rose Brock, James Colton; 1923–)

U.S. writer. Hansen began writing as a teenager growing up in Altadena, California. He met his first lover, Robert Ben Ali, while studying at Pasadena City College. In 1943, he met, fell in love with, and married Jane Bancroft. They had a daughter, Barbara. Struggling to support himself as a writer, Hansen also found time to join the editorial staff of ONE MAGAZINE, and, in 1965, *One*'s influential offshoot, *Tangents.*

He issued his first overtly gay book in 1964

under the PSEUDONYM James Colton and in 1970 pioneered the genre of gay and lesbian DETECTIVE FICTION with *Fadeout,* the first Dave Brandstetter novel. Brandstetter, a nonstereotypical gay man, works as an insurance investigator in Southern California. Besides featuring one of the first positive (and macho) gay detective characters, the Brandstetter novels and stories also reflect the changing California gay scene—from the eruption of GAY LIBERATION–style ACTIVISM (*Troublemaker,* 1975) to the onset of AIDS (*Early Graves,* 1987). On a personal level, Brandstetter meets and loses lovers, adjusts to an increasingly diverse social landscape (*Obedience,* 1988), and explores the frontiers of old age (*A Country of Old Men: The Last Dave Brandstetter Mystery,* 1991).

A unique—and sometimes controversial—voice, Hansen calls himself a "homosexual writer" rather than a "gay writer" in protest of the effeminate characterizations of gay men he finds in others' work. He also wrote *Lassie* scripts and romance novels (published under the pseudonym Rose Brock) and has earned acclaim for nonmystery novels such as *A Smile in His Lifetime* (1981) and *Living Upstairs* (1993).

✧ "Joseph Hansen," in *Colloquium on Crime: Eleven Renowned Mystery Writers Discuss Their Work,* edited by Robin W. Winks (1986).

Haring, Keith

(1958–1990)

U.S. artist. Born in Kutztown, Pennsylvania, Haring moved to New York City in 1978 to study at the School of Visual Arts. Inspired by the graffiti that at the time blanketed the city's subway system, he launched his own graffiti art campaign in 1981 with cartoonlike images chalked on the black paper that covered unused advertising boards in stations. Months be-

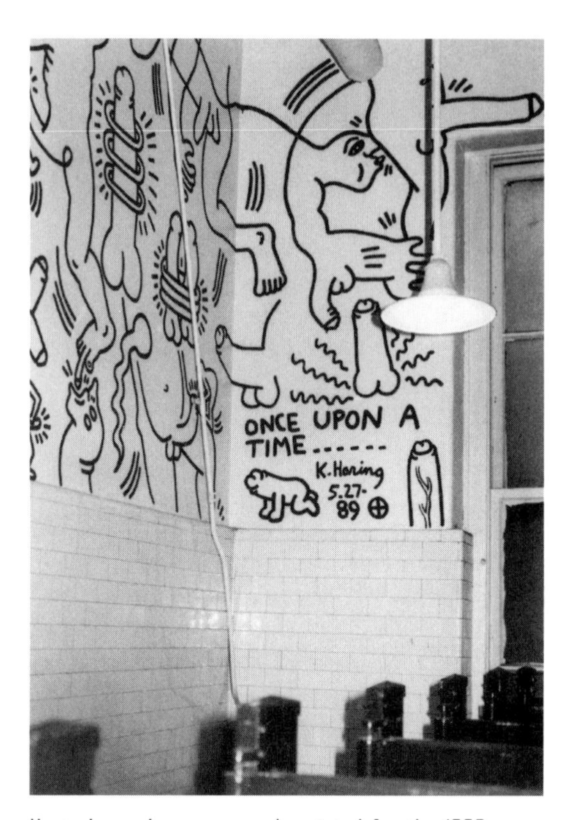

Haring's men's room mural, painted for the 1989 Center Show at the New York Lesbian and Gay Community Services Center.

fore anyone knew his name, subway riders began to recognize his distinctive graphics: writhing stick figures, creeping babies, and eight-legged barking alligator/dogs, surrounded and interconnected with zigzagging, hypnotically pulsating lines.

Although Haring was occasionally arrested for "criminal mischief," most New Yorkers loved his imaginative graffiti. By 1984, when art historian Henry Geldzahler lauded the artist's work as "a tuneful celebration of urban commonality," Haring had become one of the most famous downtown artists. In the 1980s, he presented 42 one-man exhibits all over the world and was commissioned to do paintings, wall sculptures, murals, and constructions for venues ranging from trendy discos and department stores to children's hospitals. In 1986, he opened the Pop Shop in New York's SoHo district to market posters, T-shirts, toys, and a host of other objects imprinted with his art. Criticized for commercialism, Haring responded: "My shop is an extension of what I was doing in the subway stations, breaking down the barriers between high and low ART."

According to friends, Haring plunged into the backroom BAR scene as soon as he moved to New York but resisted the prevailing gay fashion of the time: he is said to have stenciled "CLONES Go Home" all over the East Village. Committed to the fight against apartheid and other political movements throughout his career, he became a prominent AIDS activist in the late 1980s, contributing paintings like *Ignorance = Fear, Silence = Death* (1989) to support ACT UP. He also painted an enigmatic, blatantly pornographic men's room mural for the 1989 Center Show at the New York Lesbian and Gay Community Services Center, which he entitled *Once Upon a Time.*

Haring died of complications of AIDS on February 16, 1990.

✧ John Gruen, *Keith Haring: The Authorized Biography* (1991).

✧ *Keith Haring: Journals* (1996).

Harlem Renaissance

AFRICAN-AMERICAN cultural movement that flourished in the 1920s. First called the "New Negro Renaissance" by Howard University intellectual ALAIN LOCKE, the Harlem Renaissance emerged after World War I when an extraordinary collection of writers, musicians, artists, and socialites converged on Harlem, a district in New York City (roughly, between 114th Street and 155th Street in northern Manhattan). Originally a white middle-class neighborhood, Harlem became integrated after landlords began renting to nonwhites in 1905. In the next decade, a depressed real estate market made the area affordable for African-Americans at a time when job shortages and an epidemic of lynching in the South drove southern blacks to move north in unprecedented numbers.

Many, perhaps a majority, of the most famous and accomplished people associated with the Harlem Renaissance were bisexual, gay, or lesbian. Writers included COUNTEE CULLEN, ANGELINA WELD GRIMKÉ, LANGSTON HUGHES, Locke, Richard Bruce Nugent (see **1926**), and Wallace Thurman. Singers, dancers, and musicians ranged from MA RAINEY and BESSIE SMITH to MABEL HAMPTON. If the Harlem Renaissance was largely scripted by gay men, it was played to a lesbian soundtrack (see **6/1928**; **1930**).

Less famous African-Americans achieved another accomplishment: the formation of the first multifaceted American gay and lesbian SUBCULTURE. Social life ranged from *buffet flats* (apartments offering everything from cheap lodging to gambling, bootleg alcohol, and even live sex shows) to enormous drag balls ("spectacles of color," as Hughes called them) at Rockland Palace and the Savoy Ballroom, which accommodated 4,000 people.

With the exception of ETHEL WATERS, most of the entertainers associated with the Harlem Renaissance went into decline in the 1930s with the onset of the Depression. Black gay and lesbian life shifted back into private homes and social networks. It was not until the 1970s that scholars and the general public began to acknowledge the influence of the lesbians and gay men who largely defined the Harlem Renaissance.

✧ Gloria T. Hull, *Color, Sex, and Poetry: Three Women Writers of the Harlem Renaissance* (1987).

Gladys Bentley was one of the prominent men and women who gave the Harlem Renaissance a distinctively gay and lesbian flavor.

✧ George Chauncey, *Gay New York: Gender, Urban Culture, and the Making of the Gay Male World, 1890–1940* (1994).

✧ Steven Watson, *The Harlem Renaissance: Hub of African-American Culture, 1920–1930* (1995).

Harris, Bertha

(1937–)

U.S. writer, editor. In the introduction to the 1993 reprint of her novel *Lover* (1976), Harris cites the "alternate existence" of her father's vaudeville career as one of the influences that later shaped the comic surrealities of her fiction. As a "lonely, anxious, skinny child" growing up in Fayetteville, North Carolina, she accompanied her father to state asylums and homes for the deaf and blind and learned what it was like "to tap dance for people who cannot hear and do soft shoe for people who cannot see and both for people who are certain . . . they were Satan and the Holy Ghost, or a plate of fried chicken, or President Harry S. Truman. . . ."

Harris attended the Women's College of the University of North Carolina (now the University of North Carolina at Greensboro), which she has described as a "hotbed of lesbianism." She moved to New York City in 1959, married briefly, had a daughter, then returned to school in North Carolina and wrote her first novel, the semiautobiographical *Catching Saradove* (1969), in partial fulfillment of an M.F.A.

In 1973, she contributed "The More Profound Nationality of Their Lesbianism: Lesbian Society in Paris in the 1920s" to the anthology *Amazon Expedition,* protesting the disappearance of lesbians from literary history. In the article, Harris recalled a college teacher introducing GERTRUDE STEIN as "Hemingway's teacher" and confessed not only to a longing to have been part of the elite lesbian Paris demimonde of the 1920s but also to leaving sweetheart roses in DJUNA BARNES's Greenwich Village mailbox.

Harris's darkly comic *Confessions of Cherubino* (1972) and wildly imaginative *Lover* have been praised as innovative new forms of the novel unique to a contemporary lesbian consciousness. Harris also wrote *The Joy of Lesbian Sex* (1977) with Emily Sisley, taught in the women's studies program at Richmond College, City University of New York, and worked as an editor at Daughters, Inc. (see JUNE ARNOLD).

✧ Bertha Harris, "Introduction," in *Lover* (1993).

Hart, Pearl M.

(Pearl Minnie Harchovsky; 1890–1974)

U.S. attorney, activist. Born in Michigan, Hart was the daughter of a rabbi, who, like her mother, had emigrated from Russia to the U.S. She was admitted to the Illinois bar in 1914, and in the 1930s was the first woman to be named a public defender in Morals Court (later called Women's Court), where she became a legal activist for prostitutes. "When I went into that court," she later noted, "none of the women had defense attorneys and 90 percent of the accused were found guilty. When I left four years later, the statistics were reversed, and 90 percent went free." Hart ran unsuccessfully for chief justice of the Municipal Court in 1948.

In addition to earning a reputation as an expert on women's legal issues and on juvenile LAW, Hart received national attention in the 1950s when she represented immigrants investigated by the U.S. House Un-American Activities Committee (see MCCARTHY ERA). Perhaps the first lesbian to argue a case before the U.S. Supreme Court, Hart was, according to historian MARIE KUDA, one of four women Eleanor Roosevelt considered qualified to be President of the United States.

Discreet about her sexuality in public, Hart shared her private life with Blossom O'Bryan, an actress. O'Bryan later became involved with a prominent female physician, and the three women lived together until O'Bryan's death. Hart worked with MATTACHINE Chicago and was active in the defense of gay men harassed by the police. She was a founding member of Mattachine Midwest in 1965, and of DAUGHTERS OF BILITIS Chicago in 1961. In her 80s, Hart joined her former student, attorney and lesbian activist Renee Hanover, to create the Women's Law Center, which assisted women in cases that included lesbian custody battles. The Gerber-Hart Library, founded in Chicago in 1981, was named in her (and HENRY GERBER's) honor.

✧ Marie Kuda, "Chicago's Gay and Lesbian History: From Prairie Settlement to World War II," *Outlines* (June 1994).

Hartley, Marsden

(1877–1943)

U.S. painter, poet. Hartley moved from symbolic, nonrepresentative paintings influenced by the work of artists he saw during his travels in Europe to (after 1920) realistic paintings of people and places in Maine, where he was born and lived most of his life. One of his symbolic paintings was created to mourn the loss of a young German lover, Karl von Freyburg, who was killed in battle in 1914 (see ART). In Maine, he painted local French-Canadian sailors, leaving some of the first unambiguously masculine imagery in homoerotic art.

Hartley was connected with WALT WHITMAN's "comrade" Peter Doyle, as well as GERTRUDE STEIN, CHARLES DEMUTH, DJUNA BARNES, and, notably, HART CRANE. In 1933, Hartley, who had become friends with Crane in Mexico, painted *Eight Bells Folly, Memorial for Hart Crane* to commemorate the poet's suicide.

✧ Jonathan Weinberg, *Speaking for Vice: Homosexuality in the Art of Charles Demuth, Marsden Hartley, and the First American Avant-Garde* (1993).

Hate Crime

Violent actions against a person or property motivated by hostility toward a particular race, religion, ethnicity, or sexual orientation. Characterized as "terrorism" by sociologist Carole Sheffield, hate crimes affect not only their victims but also the communities to which the victims belong. As of 1997, 17 states had passed laws that included sexual orientation as part of the language defining hate crime. Some cities and states have also instituted special programs to train police and other investigative units.

Most hate crimes are committed by individuals acting alone, although some are instigated by organized groups like the Ku Klux Klan or skinheads. National and local studies of hate crime, such as those conducted by the National Institute of Justice, the FBI Uniform Crime Reports, and the National Crime Surveys, indicate that lesbians and gay men are the group most likely to be the targets of hate violence in the U.S. HIV-related violence makes up 10 to 15 percent of these crimes.

Awareness of the problem of hate crimes against lesbians and gay men increased in 1984, when the NATIONAL GAY AND LESBIAN TASK FORCE released the results of the first national study on antigay violence, a survey of more than 2,000 gay men and lesbians in eight U.S. cities. Nearly all (94 percent) had experienced some form of verbal, physical, or property-related abuse; 83 percent feared suffering it in the future. Annual documentation has shown that hate-motivated violence against lesbians and gay men has continued to increase. In addition there has been an increase in the average number of offenders participating per hate incident and in the number of crimes committed by young offenders. Gay men and lesbians are more likely than other groups not to report the crime: some sources believe as much as 90 percent of all antigay crime goes unreported.

Other findings have emerged. Crimes against lesbians are complicated by sexism, and those against gay men and lesbians of color, by racism. The risk of violence is almost twice as high for lesbians and gay men of color as for whites. When homocides occur, they are characterized by what police call "overkill"—especially brutal violence—and are solved only 51 percent of the time. Hate crime homicide victims are on average older than other homicide victims. While gay men seem to incur violence in gay-identified areas, lesbians are more often victimized in nongay settings or at home. Hate crime on campuses is also rising.

Rape of lesbians poses unique problems: few lesbian-specific services are available, and investigation and prosecution is often complicated by bias against lesbians in the police, justice, and health care systems.

✧ Gary David Comstock, *Violence Against Lesbians and Gay Men* (1991).

✧ *Hate Crimes: Confronting Violence Against Lesbians and Gay Men,* edited by Gregory M. Herek and Kevin T. Berrill (1992).

✧ Carole Sheffield, "Hate Violence," in *Race, Class, and Gender in the United States,* edited by Raula S. Rothenberg (1992).

Hate Crime Statistics Act

A bill passed by the 101st Congress and signed by President George Bush on **April 23, 1990**, as Public Law 101-275. The act, which required the Department of Justice to collect and publish statistics for five years on crimes motivated by prejudice based on race, religion, ethnic origin, or sexual orientation, was the first to provide any federal recognition of gay and lesbian people. Passage was assisted by the Coalition on Hate Crimes, 60 different civil, religious, ethnic, peace, and gay/lesbian rights groups.

The exclusion of women's rights groups from that coalition was controversial, as was the refusal of legislators to make "sex"—specifically hatred or prejudice against women—a consideration in drafting the final version of the law.

Hay, Harry

(Henry Hay, 1912–)

English-born U.S. activist, spiritual leader, founder of the MATTACHINE Society. Hay's father worked as a mining manager, and his family moved frequently when Harry was a young child. The Hays eventually settled in Southern California and Hay grew up there, attending high school in Los Angeles and studying drama at Stanford University. He became involved with leftist THEATER productions and joined the Communist Party in 1934. Already sexually active with men since his teenage days, Hay told his fellow Communists about his attraction to other men in 1938. They asked him to restrain himself and strongly suggested that he get married. Hay took their advice and married Anna Platky later that year, but continued having affairs with men on the side.

By the late 1940s, Hay was increasingly eager to become a HOMOPHILE activist. After several false starts, he managed to find other men who were interested in the cause and organized the first meeting, on **November 11, 1950**, of the society that came to be called, at his recommendation, the Mattachine. Although the group flourished, Hay's Communist background led to his leadership being repudiated by conservative Mattachine members, and he broke his ties with the organization (see **2/1953**; **4/11/1953**).

Disillusioned with the movement, Hay spent much of the next three decades studying NATIVE AMERICAN culture while maintaining connections with ONE, INC., and fellow activists such as JIM KEPNER. At a One gathering in 1963, he met a kindred spirit in scientist and inventor John Burnside. The two men became lovers and the core (perhaps the only) members of a group Hay called the Circle of Loving Companions. The "circle" participated in most of the major homophile demonstrations in California in the 1960s and, beginning at the end of the decade, the first GAY LIBERATION actions in Los Angeles. In May 1970, Hay and Burnside resettled in Santa Fe, New Mexico, where they worked with local activists to block the construction of a canal that would

Harry Hay (right) with lover John Burnside, 1995.

have drawn water off the Rio Grande. In 1976, they joined Lambdas de New Mexico, one of the state's first gay and lesbian groups, to fight HATE CRIME.

Hay resurfaced in the late 1970s to serve as the spiritual godfather of the RADICAL FAERIES. Although he later broke with the group, he remained a kind of shaman to thousands of gay men the world over, a guru who had devoted his life to answering the questions he asked in an article published in *RFD* in 1975: "The Gays—Who Are We? Where Do We Come From? What Are We For?" Ever at the heart of controversy, he was stopped by police and almost arrested in 1986 when he attempted to march in the Los Angeles Gay Pride Day Parade with a sign reading "NAMBLA Walks with Me" in defiance of the organizers' banning of the group (see PEDOPHILIA). Recalling his affair at the age of 14 with a 24-year-old named Matt, Hay confessed to "having molested an adult when I was a child until I found out what I needed to know."

- Stuart Timmons, *The Trouble with Harry Hay: Founder of the Modern Gay Movement* (1990).
- Harry Hay, *Radically Gay: Gay Liberation in the Words of Its Founder,* edited by Will Roscoe (1996).

Hayes, Bruce
(1963–)

U.S. swimmer, Olympic medalist. Born and raised in Texas, Hayes won the 200-meter freestyle at the World University Games and three gold medals at the Pan Am Games, both held in 1983. He went on to win a gold medal and help set a world record as the anchor swimmer in the 800-meter freestyle relay at the 1984 Summer Olympics in Los Angeles.

Hayes came OUT to his family and friends in 1987 after graduating from Northwestern University's School of Journalism. He became the first Olympic swimmer to come out to the general public at the Vancouver GAY GAMES III in 1990, where he won six gold medals. He later credited the games with having changed his life.

A vice president in a public relations firm, Hays remains an active supporter of the games and other gay and lesbian athletic activities.

- Erik Brady, "The Credo: Don't Ask, Don't Tell," *USA Today* (June 24, 1993).
- "In the Pink: Gay Games Are Opening Closets as Well as Doors," *New York Times* (August 8, 1993).
- Allen St. John, "Faster, Stronger, Queerer," *Village Voice* (June 21, 1994).

Haynes, Todd
(1961–)

U.S. filmmaker. A California native, Haynes started making movies as a child and continued experimenting with the medium while studying art and semiotics at Brown University. Important early influences on his work included RAINER WERNER FASSBINDER and Alfred Hitchcock.

Haynes first attracted attention in the late 1980s with the underground cult hit, *Superstar: The Karen Carpenter Story,* which used dolls to relate the pop singer's life story. *Assassins* (1987) looked at the relationship between PAUL VERLAINE AND ARTHUR RIMBAUD. *Poison* (Sundance Grand Jury Prize, 1991), his first feature, intercuts three different stories, each with its own filmic style: a documentarylike account of a boy who has murdered his father, a 1950s sci-fi tale of a scientist who isolates the human sex drive, and a tensely erotic re-creation of situations and characters inspired by JEAN GENET.

Adamantly independent, Haynes is one of the few openly gay directors who also make "straight" features. Some gay and lesbian viewers see the influence of a detached, "gay" sensibility even in these FILMS, which include *Safe*, a wickedly subtle satire about a Southern Californian housewife who discovers she is allergic to her life.

H.D.

(Hilda Doolittle; 1886–1961)

U.S. poet, novelist, translator. Born in Bethlehem, Pennsylvania, the only daughter of a professor and a teacher, she studied at private schools, attended Bryn Mawr College for a little over a year, then returned home to study the classics and write poetry after failing her college English class. She was already engaged to the soon-to-be-famous poet Ezra Pound, a neighbor boy she had met in 1901, when she fell in love with Frances Josepha Gregg in 1910. An intense emotional tug-of-war ensued, in the wake of which she traveled to Europe with Gregg and Gregg's mother.

In England, she began writing modernist poems that critics considered perfect examples of the precise, concrete representations and fresh, direct language of imagism. Pound, who remained a close friend, dubbed her "H.D. Imagiste," and her first book of poems, *Sea Garden* (1916), was published under that name. In addition to nearly a dozen volumes of poetry spanning five decades, H.D. published novels, plays, children's fiction, and translations of Greek classics.

H.D. had important relationships with both men and women. Sigmund Freud, who analyzed her in Vienna in the 1930s, considered her an "all but extinct" example of a complete bisexual. After an unsuccessful marriage to writer Richard Aldington and an affair that left her pregnant and desperately ill, the poet BRYHER came to her rescue and formed a relationship with her that was to last four decades. Bryher remained passionately devoted to H.D. and H.D.'s daughter, Frances Perdita, through her own marriages of convenience and H.D.'s "girl loves" and heterosexual affairs.

H.D. made her troubled relationships with men the subject of many of her poems, especially those published in the 1920s. Her intimacies with Gregg, Bryher, and other women were the theme of three largely confessional novels on whose title pages she wrote, "Destroy": *HERmione* (written 1927; published 1981), *Paint It Today* (written 1921; published 1992), and *Asphodel* (written 1921–1922; published, 1992). These novels illuminate her rejection of traditional concepts of GENDER and express her lesbianism as a yearning for equality, support, inspiration, and even salvation. Her later poems attack misogyny and seek healing in a feminist goddess mythology that anticipates the work of many later poets, including ROBERT DUNCAN, JUDY GRAHN, and Muriel Rukeyser.

Today considered one of the most important writers of the 20th century, H.D. was the first woman to receive the American Academy of Arts and Letters poetry award (1960).

- Susan Stanford Friedman, *Penelope's Web: Gender, Modernity, H.D.'s Fiction* (1990).
- Cassandra Laity, "Lesbian Romanticism: H.D.'s Fictional Representations of Frances Gregg and Bryher," introduction to H.D.'s *Paint It Today* (1992).

Health, Lesbian

Lesbians have greatly suffered from limited physical and mental health care services because of the stigmatized status of homosexuals in society. Researchers may disagree about the adequate representation of lesbians in clinical studies, but they agree that the results of these studies are poorly understood and rarely incorporated into a general understanding of women's health. In addition, providers often fail to create a trusting relationship with their lesbian patients, who can be reluctant to use the health care system, fearing discrimination, negative attitudes, and even sexual assault.

These concerns are well founded. Health educator and researcher Elizabeth Rankow reports that in a 1982 study of California medical personnel, 40 percent expressed discomfort treating lesbians, and over 40 percent would not make referrals to a lesbian colleague. Further, a majority of nurse educators surveyed in 1988 considered lesbianism an "unnatural expression of human sexuality," and a 1994 survey conducted among the membership of the American Association of Physicians for Human Rights found that an alarming majority had witnessed antigay bias and substandard care to gay and lesbian patients. So, although lesbians know coming OUT to their doctors could enhance their odds for appropriate care, more than 65 percent do not.

Lesbian physician H. Joan Waitkevicz, cofounder (1973) of St. Mark's Women's Health Collective, has summarized lesbian medical issues as: access to care, pregnancy, violence, substance abuse, sexual practices and sexually transmitted diseases, and cancer—especially breast cancer. Health educator Risa Denenberg found similar concerns in her research. She further emphasized that many lesbians have unhealthy coping mechanisms, health beliefs, and other attitudes that contribute to their increased risk of disease. Other research with lesbians should consider stress and autoimmune illness and woman-to-woman transmission of sexually transmitted diseases, including HIV infection. The latter is an area where lesbians were excluded from research, clinical care, and prevention efforts early in the AIDS epidemic; when panelist Dr. Anke Ehrhardt at the 1990 National Conference on Women and HIV Infection in Washington, D.C., was asked about the actual incidence of woman-to-woman transmission, she ruefully replied, "Since we are doing no research on this issue, we will hardly find out how rare it really is." All of these areas require lesbian-specific applications of medical research and practice and as Waitkevicz notes, political and health ACTIVISM.

Awareness of gay and lesbian health concerns has consistently been a part of community organizing, informal networks, and formal meetings like the Annual National Lesbian and Gay Health Conference, which celebrated its 18th year in 1996.

The AIDS epidemic has further influenced activists to maximize the potential for community health organizing and care delivery. Spurred by participation in the fight against AIDS, areas of lesbian health activism include recruitment and retention of lesbians in clinical health studies and women's health surveys, health fairs, clinics, and other outreach efforts, and campaigns to ensure representation of lesbian issues at public health policy-making forums, professional medical organizations, and publications.

✧ Lyon Martin Women's Health Services, *Lesbian Health Care Information, Research, and Reports, 1993* (1993).

✧ Risa Denenberg, "Report on Lesbian Health" (National Gay and Lesbian Task Force Policy Institute, 1994).

✧ Elizabeth J. Rankow, "Lesbian Health Issues for the Primary Care Provider," *The Journal of Family Practice* (vol. 40, no. 5, May 1995).

✧ H. Joan Waitkevicz, M.D., "Lesbian Health Issues," in *The New Our Right to Love: A Lesbian Resource Book,* edited by Ginny Vida (1996).

Heap, Jane, see ANDERSON, MARGARET C.

Hemphill, Essex

(1957–1995)

U.S. poet, editor, essayist. Born in Chicago, Hemphill grew up in southeast Washington, D.C. He cofounded the *Nethula Journal of Contemporary Literature* and published two chapbooks, *Earth Life* (1985) and *Conditions* (1986), before coming to the attention of a broader audience as one of the contributors to *In the Life* (1986), Joseph Beam's pioneering anthology of black gay male writers. After Beam's death in 1988, Hemphill edited and contributed to the sequel Beam had planned, *Brother to Brother* (1991). The following year, he published a wide-ranging collection of his own work, *Ceremonies: Prose and Poetry* (1992). His poetry also figured prominently in two FILMS by MARLON RIGGS, *Tongues Untied* (1989), in which Hemphill also appeared, and *Black Is, Black Ain't* (1995), as well as in ISAAC JULIEN's groundbreaking *Looking for Langston* (1989).

As in his poem "For My Own Protection," which begins with the lines "I want to start / an organization / to save my life," Hemphill's work confronted the minefield of hostile forces arrayed against black gay men both from within and without the black and gay communities. He protested what he called the "white-washing" of black gay lives as well as the racial stereotypes and sexual objectification he found in the work of gay-identified artists like ROBERT MAPPLETHORPE, asserting, as in his essay "Does Your Mama Know About Me?" (reprinted in *Ceremonies*), that, for black gay men, "our only sure guarantee of survival is that which we construct from our own self-determination."

Essex Hemphill (right) and Marlon Riggs, in Riggs's groundbreaking documentary Tongues Untied (1989).

He died of AIDS-related complications in Philadelphia in November 1995.

Heterodoxy

Influential New York City club for "free-willed" women, both lesbian and straight. Founded by Marie Jenney Howe in 1912, Heterodoxy met biweekly in Greenwich Village until 1940. Members gathered for luncheons, meetings, and spirited discussions of social and political issues, in the course of which they formed one of the earliest documented women's support networks. Variously described as the "women of the future" and "women who did things and did them openly," Heterodoxy members were considered individualistic, unruly, and willful by contemporaries. Many of the 120 known members were active in labor, suffrage, and peace movements.

Heterodoxy distinguished itself from other women's groups of its time by the diversity of its members, as well as by not being founded because of a belief or interest common to them. The group has remained of compelling interest to women's historians primarily as an early example of women forming a personal and political community, but also because of the light its history sheds on what society and individuals considered "unorthodox" for women.

Among the well-known straight or bisexual members of Heterodoxy were Agnes de Mille,

Crystal Eastman, Charlotte Perkins Gilman, Susan Glaspell, Fannie Hurst, Grace Nail Johnson, and Fola La Follette. The members known to be lesbian included Katharine Anthony, Helen Arthur, Dr. S. JOSEPHINE BAKER, Myran Louise Grant, Helen Hull, Elisabeth Irwin, Paula Jakobi, Mary Margaret McBride, Ida A. R. Wylie, Rose Young, and perhaps as many as 24 others.

✧ Judith Schwarz, *Radical Feminists of Heterodoxy* (1986).

✧ Nancy Cott, *The Grounding of Modern Feminism* (1987).

Heterosexism

Overt or tacit bias against lesbians, gay men, or bisexuals based on a belief in the superiority or, sometimes, the omnipresence of HETEROSEXUALITY. Heterosexism is a broader term than HOMOPHOBIA in that it need not imply the fear and loathing the latter term suggests. It can describe seemingly benign overstatements, such as "She'd drive any man wild" or "He's every woman's dream husband." More seriously, heterosexism is often characteristic of the workplace, MILITARY regulations, visitor policies at hospitals and other institutions, and IMMIGRATION laws.

➤ Also see COMPULSORY HETEROSEXUALITY.

✧ Gregory M. Herek, "Psychological Heterosexism in the United States," in *Lesbian, Gay, and Bisexual Identities over the Lifespan: Psychological Perspectives,* edited by Anthony R. D'Augelli and Charlotte J. Patterson (1995).

Heterosexuality

Broadly defined, female-to-male or male-to-female sexual desire and/or sexual behavior; more specifically, a marked preference on the part of a male for sex with a female, or on the part of a female for sex with a male.

GORE VIDAL has called heterosexuality "a weird concept of recent origins but terrible consequences." Historians of sexuality believe that there was no abstract concept exactly equivalent to the modern notion of "heterosexuality" before the late 19th century. The word "heterosexuality" itself was not widely used in the U.S. with its now current meaning until the 1920s. Previously, it had most commonly signified either a strong sexual attraction for both males and females (KÁROLY MÁRIA KERTBENY's original meaning) or "abnormal" desire involving a person of the "opposite" sex (as, for example, when RICHARD VON KRAFFT-EBING used it to qualify certain types of "fetishists").

Linguists and historians agree that the word "heterosexuality" evolved to serve as a convenient counterpart to the word "homosexuality." Whether or not either was a meaningful, generally comprehensible *concept* before the 19th century is a matter of great dispute. Social historians from MICHEL FOUCAULT to JONATHAN NED KATZ have theorized that the very concept of *sexuality* is a recent invention, that prior to the 19th century people thought in terms of sex *acts,* rather than in terms of a psychological potential or predisposition for particular kinds of sex, and that these acts were characterized, depending on the era and culture, as pleasurable/nonpleasurable, honorable/shameful, sinful/permissible, etc. Foucault, sociologist Mary McIntosh, and others have asserted that the hetero/homo distinction is a tool of social control, a way of regimenting society by constructing "normal" and "abnormal" sexual categories and then force-fitting people into one or the other. Taking a different tack, Katz has pointed out that Judeo-Christian cultures traditionally categorized sex as "natural" or "unnatural" based not on the biological sex of the participants but rather on whether or not the acts they indulged in could lead to procreation. Katz believes that the hetero/homo distinction arose with Sigmund Freud's "discovery" of the sex "drive," or "libido," and his assertion that its primary motivation is pleasure, not procreation. (Freud was at a loss to explain "exclusive sexual interest," homosexual or heterosexual.) Katz theorizes that the idea of a "normal" heterosexual libido came along at a time when Westerners needed to justify nonprocreative female/male sex. With Freud, Katz writes, "we experience the historic shift from the late-Victorian procreation ethic to the modern 'pleasure principle.' "

On another front, beginning in the early 1970s, many lesbian feminist thinkers—including the RADICALESBIANS, CHARLOTTE BUNCH, Gayle Rubin, and ADRIENNE RICH—critiqued heterosexuality as a psychosocial system whose primary function was to give men power over women. This idea has seen further development in QUEER THEORY.

➤ Also see BISEXUALITY; COMPULSORY HETEROSEXUALITY; CONSTRUCTIONISM VS. ESSENTIALISM; GENDER; LESBIAN FEMINISM.

✧ Mary McIntosh, "The Homosexual Role," in *Forms of Desire: Sexual Orientation and the Social Constructionist Controversy,* edited by Edward Stein (1990).

✧ Jonathan Ned Katz, *The Invention of Heterosexuality* (1995).

Hetrick-Martin Institute, see YOUTH, GAY AND LESBIAN.

Hickok, [Alice] Lorena

("Hick"; 1893–1968)

U.S. journalist, author. Born in Wisconsin but raised in South Dakota, she had an unhappy childhood and grew to despise her abusive parents. Armed with some college education, she stormed the male-dominated world of journalism, working for papers in the Midwest and New York before becoming one of the first women to have a byline with the Associated Press.

Her 20-year career as a nationally syndicated reporter was cut short when her close friendship with Eleanor Roosevelt led to suspicions that she was no longer objective in her writing. In 1933, she was hired as chief investigator for Harry L. Hopkins, director of the Federal Emergency Relief Administration. Her detailed, insightful reports were also read by President Franklin Roosevelt. After 1936, she did promotional work for the 1939 World's Fair and the Democratic National Committee. She also wrote six biographies for young readers, including *The Story of Helen Keller* (1958) and two about Eleanor Roosevelt.

Hickok's considerable accomplishments have been overshadowed by her 30-year friendship with Eleanor Roosevelt, whom she called "E.R." The more than 3,000 letters they wrote to each other, some of which were destroyed by Hickok and her sister, evidence a physically intimate relationship. "I wish I could lie down beside you tonight and take you in my arms," wrote the First Lady. From "Hick": "I remember . . . the feeling of that soft spot just northeast of the corner of your mouth against my lips. I wonder what we'll do when we meet—what we'll say. Well, I'm rather proud of us, aren't you? I think we've done rather well."

Other women in Hickok's life included Ella Morse (Dickinson) and, from 1942, Marion Janet Harron, a U.S. tax court judge. Hickok placed Harron's love letters with the E.R. correspondence she left for the FDR Library.

✧ Blanche Wiesen Cook, *Eleanor Roosevelt. Volume One: 1884–1933* (1992).

Highsmith, Patricia

(Mary Patricia Plangman; 1921–1995)

U.S. writer. Her parents, who were both commercial artists, were divorced by the time she was born in Fort Worth, Texas, and she spent her first years with her maternal grandmother (who taught her how to read at the age of three). She moved to New York when she was six to live with her mother and stepfather, whose name she used and who later officially adopted her. She became a successful freelance writer after attending Barnard College, where she edited the school's literary magazine.

By the time she published the landmark lesbian romance *The Price of Salt* (1952), under the PSEUDONYM Claire Morgan, Highsmith was already known to the reading public as the author of the celebrated psychological suspense novel *Strangers on a Train* (1949), which Alfred Hitchcock filmed in 1951. *The Price of Salt* took lesbian PULP FICTION to a new level of literacy, besides being perhaps the first American gay or lesbian novel to have a positive ending. As Highsmith wrote in an afterword to a 1984 Naiad reprint of the novel, the two lovers "actually came out alive at the end and with a fair amount of hope for a happy future." Its hardback edition received "serious and respectable reviews," Highsmith recalled, and "was a landslide in paperback, when the advertising was by word of mouth." The author was deluged with letters from lesbian and gay readers thanking her for the optimistic ending and for dealing with real-life issues like coming OUT and child custody disputes.

Highsmith had discovered the shadow world of gay and lesbian BARS in New York in the 1940s. She lived with pulp novelist Ann Aldrich in Bucks County, Pennsylvania, in the late 1950s but spent most of her adult life in Europe, finally settling in Switzerland.

Highsmith wrote 20 crime novels, including five featuring the "Talented" and "Mysterious" Mr. Tom Ripley, and several collections of short crime fiction. Subtle male HOMOEROTICISM is a feature of much of her work, but she did not focus on gay/lesbian themes again until her last book, *Small g: A Summer Idyll* (1995). Critics and fans alike have been most struck by the amorality of her stories, in which wrongdoing often goes unpunished and readers find themselves empathizing with the wrongdoers. Film and tele-

Published under a pseudonym as a pulp novel, Patricia Highsmith's The Price of Salt was one of the first positive representations of lesbian love.

vision productions of her work continue to widen her audience.

Highsmith guarded her privacy, although she was proud of the important place *The Price of Salt* held in lesbian fiction. When BARBARA GRIER coaxed her into using her own name on the 1984 reissue, Highsmith wrote: "I am happy to think that it gave several thousand lonely and frightened people something to hang onto."

✧ Joan Dupont, "The Poet of Apprehension: Patricia Highsmith's Furtive Generosities," *Village Voice* (May 30, 1995).

✧ Brooks Peters, "Stranger than Fiction," *Out* (June 1995).

Hinduism

Western term for a wide variety of religious beliefs that have developed in India since ancient times. More than 500 million people around the world consider themselves Hindus although the religion has no unified hierarchy, organization, or creed. Most Hindus stress *dharma,* the right way of living, over dogma, in the belief that a life properly lived can liberate a person from the cycle of reincarnation or transmigration.

Hindu attitudes toward sex, sexuality, and gender vary widely. The Hindu pantheon and the Vedas (ancient texts most Hindus consider sacred) contain many examples of transsexual gods/goddesses. Many modern Hindus, however, consider homosexuality a foreign phenomenon, derived either from ISLAM or the modern West, and thus condemn Hindu lesbians and gay men as traitors to their native tradition.

➤ Also see SOUTH ASIA.

Shiva is only one of the androgynous, gender-confounding gods and goddesses of traditional Hinduism.

Hirschfeld, Dr. Magnus

(1868–1935)

German sex researcher, pioneering activist. Hirschfeld studied philology and philosophy before deciding on a career in medicine. Through his practice he became increasingly aware of the social oppression suffered by people who had what the medical discourse of the time called "contrary" sexualities. He read widely on the subject and in 1896 published *Sappho und Sokrates* ("Sappho and Socrates") under the PSEUDONYM Th. Ramien, arguing that same-sex love should be accepted as part of a range of human sexuality. On **May 14, 1897**, he founded the Scientific Humanitarian Committee to fight for the repeal of Paragraph 175, the German law punishing male SODOMY, and to help men prosecuted or blackmailed because of the law. The committee, based in Berlin, was the first public organization of its kind in the world.

Hirschfeld's campaign for legal reform failed (see **1/13/1898**; **3/18/1922**) and his committee never attracted more than 1,500 members, but he was much more successful in other endeavors. Believing that scientific research and education would lead to society accepting gay men and lesbians, he wrote almost 200 articles, pamphlets, and books, including *Homosexuality in Men and Women* (1918–1920), a groundbreaking study over 1,000 pages long. From **1899** until 1923, he published the *Jahrbuch für Sexuelle Zwischenstufen* ("Yearbook for Sexual Intermediate Types"), an annual compendium of scholarly articles and bibliographies related to the study of male and female homosexuality. He also launched the first major sex survey (see **1903**), founded the legendary Institute of Sexual Research (see **7/1/1919**), and on **May 24, 1919** premiered *Anders als die Andern* ("Different from the Others"), the first sympathetic FILM portrayal of adult gay men.

Hirschfeld believed that homosexuality derived from inborn biological factors that also affected male and female psychological characteristics—i.e., GENDER—and resulted in a "third" or "intermediate sex." This theory was opposed by most medical authorities of the time, who had come to believe that homosexuality was usually an acquired "deviation" from "normal" sexuality. It was also a point of contention for other German activists, such as ADOLF BRAND, who were repelled by the equation of same-sex desire with gender nonconformity.

Hirschfeld enjoyed widespread celebrity—as well as notoriety. He was physically attacked by right-wing thugs on several occasions—once, in 1921, almost fatally. His gay opponents nicknamed him "Tante [Aunt] Magnesia" and gossiped about his penchant for CROSS-DRESSING and alleged foot fetish. Friends and enemies alike questioned his fund-raising tactics, which sometimes came suspiciously close to extortion. Nevertheless, he is remembered as a founding father of the gay and lesbian rights movement.

Hirschfeld was traveling abroad when the Nazis came to power in 1933 and destroyed most of his life's work (see **5/6/1933**). He moved to Nice and began to rebuild a replica of the institute, but, his health broken, he died two years later, on his 67th birthday. In 1983, a Magnus Hirschfeld Society was founded in Berlin to promote the reestablishment and continuation of the work Hirschfeld pioneered. James D. Steakley and Manfred Herzer, both pioneering historians of German gay culture, were among the founding members.

➤ Also see GERMANY.

- ✧ *The Writings of Dr. Magnus Hirschfeld: A Bibliography,* edited by J. D. Steakley (1985).
- ✧ Charlotte Wolff, *Magnus Hirschfeld: A Portrait of a Pioneer in Sexology* (1986).

Hispanic-Americans, see LATINOS.

HIV, see AIDS.

Hockney, David
(1937–)

English artist. From a working-class north English background, Hockney studied in London at the Royal College of Art from 1959 to 1962. Taught by his father, as he later related, "not to care what the neighbors think," he was not only OUT at school, he made his gayness the theme of his best-known work of the period, which included oils inspired by WALT WHITMAN. Enthralled by the PHYSIQUE MAGAZINES and iconography of the U.S., he traveled to New York in 1961 and later used his experiences there as the subject of a one-man show, "Rake's Progress" (1963). In 1964, he moved to California and began developing the sun-drenched "swimming pool" pictures that made him as famous in the U.S. as in Europe.

Since the 1960s, Hockney has traveled widely, lived in Paris as well as California, and created in a variety of media, from stage and opera sets to photomontages and computer art. In his work—as in his public statements against censorship and repressive legislation—his gayness has remained a given, never presented as more than one of the traits that make Hockney Hockney. In 1974, a semibiographical British TELEVISION documentary, *A Bigger Splash,* explored his breakup and subsequent friendship with California artist Peter Schlesinger. He has also written a candid autobiography, *David Hockney: My Early Years* (1977).

The accessibility of Hockney's work and its popularity with a mass audience are sometimes cited by critics as reasons to consider Hockney an "artist who is gay" rather than a "gay artist." Nevertheless, many gay men and lesbians find more of their own experiences reflected in his straightforward, light-drenched imagery than in the darker visions of more confrontational gay artists.

✧ Peter Webb, *Portrait of David Hockney* (1988).

Hocquenghem, Guy

(1946–1988)

French writer, theorist, activist, filmmaker. Born and raised in the Paris area, Hocquenghem took part in the **May 1968** demonstrations and became involved with the fledgling French GAY LIBERATION movement (see **3/10/1971**). In 1972, he published *Le Désir Homosexuel* (*Homosexual Desire,* 1978), the first of three books on homosexuality and the origins of HOMOPHOBIA that greatly influenced the course of Western European gay liberation. Drawing on Marxism and French

Always out, David Hockney (left) spoke frankly about his troubled relationship with lover and model Peter Schlesinger (right) in A Bigger Splash, Jack Hazan's 1974 documentary.

psychoanalytic theory, Hocquenghem's complex critique centered on his concept of the "privatized anus" as both an example and a metaphor of the ways capitalism created an artificial distinction between good (productive, heterosexual) and bad (nonproductive, homosexual) desire. Capitalism, according to Hocquenghem, glorified and socialized the power of the phallus while degrading the nonprocreative anus, rendering it private and shameful. Hocquenghem believed that empowering the anus, transforming it into a "desiring machine," defied and endangered the established social order—thus, casual, anonymous anal sex was potentially revolutionary.

Although Hocquenghem advocated an anti-assimilationist stance (see ASSIMILATIONISM/CONFRONTATIONALISM), he also rejected the idea of a gay "identity." In this respect, he and other like-minded European gay leaders differed significantly from most of their U.S. counterparts in the 1970s.

Hocquenghem was expelled from the Communist Party for his homosexuality, but he remained a Marxist. He taught philosophy at the University of Paris, wrote for the left-wing daily *Libération* and *Gai Pied* (see **2/1979**) and spoke frequently on Fréquence Gai, the French gay radio station, and French TELEVISION. Besides advocating gay and lesbian rights, he also contested racism against blacks and Arabs. In 1979, he and Lionel Soukaz produced one of the first major documentaries on gay history, *Race d'Ep* (retitled in English as *Homosexual Century*).

Hocquenghem also published short stories and, in the 1980s, four novels that reflected the gnosticism and epicureanism he embraced in his last years. He died of complications of AIDS at the age of 42.

✧ Jeffrey Weeks, *Against Nature: Essays on History, Sexuality, and Identity* (1991).

Hoessli, Heinrich

(1784–1864)

Swiss writer. A milliner by profession—with a lucrative interior design business on the side—Hoessli married, had two sons, and ran a successful business until retiring in 1851. In about 1820, he decided to research and write a history and defense of same-sex love. In **1836**, he published the first volume of *Eros: Die Männerliebe der Griechen* ("Eros: The Love Between Men of the Greeks") in his hometown of Glarus. The second volume was published in Bern, since Glarus authorities objected to the work, two years later.

As its subtitle explained, *Eros* recounted the "history, education, literature and legislation" of love between men in Hoessli's time, in Islamic cultures and, especially, in Ancient GREECE. *Eros* was not only one of the first books to protest the persecution of man- and boy-loving men, it also included an extensive list of famous devotees of same-sex love. Hoessli died before a third volume could be published.

Although *Eros* had a very limited distribution, it influenced KARL HEINRICH ULRICHS and other 19th-century German activists.

✧ *Documents of the Homosexual Rights Movement in Germany, 1836–1927* (1975).

Holleran, Andrew

(pseudonym of Eric Gerber; 1943–)

U.S. writer. Holleran was born in Aruba and educated at prep schools and Harvard. He had his first brush with gay BARS and sex while serving in the MILITARY in GERMANY in the mid-1960s. After studying at the University of Iowa Writers' Workshop (where he met fellow VIOLET QUILL member Robert Ferro), he moved to New York City in 1971.

Holleran's first novel, *Dancer from the Dance,* appeared in 1978, a breakthrough year for gay male writers that also saw the successful publication of LARRY KRAMER's *Faggots* and EDMUND WHITE's *Nocturnes for the King of Naples.* Of the three, *Dancer* earned the most praise from both straight and gay reviewers, and it remains one of the most widely read novels of the era. Originally entitled "Letters from an American Faggot" (before Holleran's publisher convinced him to use a line from W. B. Yeats instead), *Dancer* both satirized and romanticized the aimlessly frenzied promiscuity of its Manhattan and FIRE ISLAND heroes, who are, as the doomed Malone says, "completely free and that's the horror."

Holleran's second novel, *Nights in Aruba* (1983), told the story of a gay man not unlike Holleran, who grows up in Aruba and comes OUT in Germany and Manhattan but remains closeted with his family in Florida. By the end of *Nights in Aruba,* a number of the narrator's friends and acquaintances "were dying of bizarre cancers."

The complex effects of AIDS on himself and the SUBCULTURE have, along with aging, been the main focus of Holleran's writing since the mid-1980s. His essays were collected in *Ground Zero* (1988) and published regularly in *Christopher Street.* In 1996, he published *The Beauty of Men,* a novel fellow writer Michael Carroll calls "a logical, and unrelentingly realistic, next installment in Holleran's continuing coverage of the post-Stonewall generation of gays in America." The novel describes the dreary Florida MIDLIFE of an ex-New Yorker "facing," as Holleran writes, "the Void."

✧ Michael Carroll, "The Return of a Novelist," *The Harvard Gay and Lesbian Review* (Summer 1996).

Hollywood

Defined by Ephraim Katz, author of a major film encyclopedia, as a "state of mind" and a "dream shared by millions," "Hollywood" is shorthand for the mainstream American movie industry—in contrast to independent and foreign cinema—as well as the communities of people who earn their livelihood from that industry. Although only a fraction of the gay and lesbian actors who are among Hollywood's best-known citizens are OUT, an ever increasing number of producers, directors, screenwriters, creative personnel, and agents have emerged from the CLOSET. Many of them have joined influential groups like Hollywood Supports, cofounded in 1991 by entertainment industry moguls Barry Diller and Sid Sheinberg to fight AIDS and HOMOPHOBIA in the workplace, and Out There, a Hollywood-based political advocacy organization cofounded by executive producer Bruce Cohen and senior production executive Nina Jacobsen in 1995 that within a year boasted a membership of about 500 lesbians and gay men. Also notable was entertainment mogul and Dreamworks SKG president David Geffen, whose foundation had contributed more than $35 million to AIDS-related and civil rights causes.

The greater visibility of lesbians and gay men in Hollywood has not, however, resulted in a corresponding increase in gay and lesbian content in Hollywood movies. Writer ARMISTEAD MAUPIN and director Tanya Wexler, among many who have had dealings with Hollywood, have noted that lesbian and gay studio executives are often more uncomfortable with queer content than their straight counterparts. And, as *Entertainment Weekly* magazine noted in 1996, "some critics complain that Hollywood remains skittish about gay films that don't fall into two relatively safe categories—cross-dressing minstrel shows or AIDS dramas." Several Hollywood films in these "safe" categories—including *Philadelphia* (1993), *To Wong Foo, Thanks for Everything, Julie Newmar* (1995), and *The Birdcage* (1996)—had

1930s denial: "Bachelor housemates" Cary Grant and Randolph Scott pose by their pool in this studio publicity shot.

scored impressive grosses at the box office by the mid-1990s; more adventurous screen treatments of lesbian and gay life continued to come not from major Hollywood studios but rather from independent producers and distributors. Many of the most successful of these were made by openly lesbian or gay filmmakers: Donna Deitch's *Desert Hearts* (1986), Bill Sherwood's *Parting Glances* (1986), GUS VAN SANT's *My Own Private Idaho* (1991), Rose Troche's *Go Fish* (1994), Maria Maggenti's *The Incredibly True Adventures of Two Girls in Love* (1995), and writer Paul Rudnick and director Christopher Ashley's *Jeffrey* (1995). A number of others were produced outside the U.S.: *My Beautiful Laundrette* (UNITED KINGDOM, 1986), *Maurice* (U.K., 1987), *The Wedding Banquet* (Taiwan, 1993), and *The Adventures of Priscilla, Queen of the Desert* (AUSTRALIA, 1994).

The conservative nature of Hollywood is demonstrated by two movies that were both hailed as "breakthroughs" when they were released: *Making Love* (1982) and *Philadelphia*. Both featured popular straight actors in the leading gay male roles; both were scripted by openly gay writers (Barry Sandler and Ron Nyswaner, respectively); both were judged tame but relatively positive by gay and lesbian audiences. Although *Making Love* dared show two men kissing, a decade later director Jonathan Demme decided to cut a male kissing scene from Nyswaner's *Philadelphia* script because he feared it would alienate straight viewers.

On the other hand, Hollywood movies have increasingly featured gay and lesbian characters, especially in supporting roles. A 1992 advertisement in *Variety* listed 92 well-known movie actors who had played lesbian

Ambiguous glamour: Marlene Dietrich (seated, dressed as Leda) and friend Elizabeth Allan at a party at Basil Rathbone's.

Audrey Hepburn (left) and Shirley MacLaine starred in The Children's Hour, one of the first Hollywood treatments of lesbianism.

or gay roles. (However, the ad, which was in support of a movie version of PATRICIA NELL WARREN's *The Front Runner,* ironically demonstrated the difficulty of getting major studio support for films whose main theme is gay or lesbian: the best-selling novel remained unfilmed more than two decades after its publication.) Thanks in large part to the efforts of groups like the GAY AND LESBIAN ALLIANCE AGAINST DEFAMATION and media activists like Michelangelo Signorile, these roles are more and more likely to be positive—or at least not blatantly heterosexist.

➤ Also see ACTORS/ACTING; ARZNER, DOROTHY; FILM AND VIDEO, GAY, LESBIAN, AND QUEER; HUDSON, ROCK; MUSIC; RUSSO, VITO; TELEVISION.

✧ Vito Russo, *The Celluloid Closet: Homosexuality in the Movies* (rev. ed., 1987).

✧ Andrea Weiss, *Vampires and Violets: Lesbians in Film* (1992).

✧ Boze Hadleigh, *Hollywood Lesbians* (1994).

✧ Raymond Murray, *Images in the Dark: An Encyclopedia of Gay and Lesbian Film and Video* (rev. ed., 1996).

✧ "Out in Hollywood," *Out* (March 1996).

✧ A. J. Jacobs, "Are Gay Movies Still in the Closet?," *Entertainment Weekly* (no. 339, August 9, 1996).

Holocaust, see NAZI PERSECUTION.

The cast of the 1970 Hollywood film adaptation of The Boys in the Band.

Homoeroticism

Expression of sexual attraction to a person or persons of one's own biological sex. A rarer term, "homoaffectionality," is sometimes used to distinguish expressions of nonerotic emotional attraction from those inspired by sexual desire. Although "homoeroticism" derives from Greek roots meaning "sexual desire for the same," it is hardly ever purely narcissistic. Some theorists believe that homoeroticism is in fact imbued with unique power because, more commonly than (hetero)eroticism, it can simultaneously be desire *for* another, desire to be *like* another, and identification *with* another. In practice, much homoeroticism actually accentuates differences in age, race, physical characteristics, GENDER identity, sex roles, power, status, and the like.

Homoeroticism in ART and LITERATURE has a long and distinguished history in the West (see **c. 2600 B.C.**; **c. 2500 B.C.**; etc.) and the East (see **c. 700 B.C.**), as well as in pre-Columbian America (see **c. 200 B.C.**). Although it never completely disappeared from cultural representations, by the 19th century it was most common in underground art and literature or in guises subtle and ambiguous enough to get by censors. As late as the mid-1970s, male homoeroticism remained so exotic a concept for mainstream Americans that the gay male narrator of PATRICIA NELL WARREN's *The Front Runner* had to explain that he saw his young lover's legs much as a straight man might appreciate Raquel Welch's. Female "homoerotica" was by contrast comparatively common, but as SUSIE BRIGHT notes, typically "understood to be a picture imagined, taken, and appreciated by men." With the explosive growth in gay and lesbian SUBCULTURES since STONEWALL has come an increasingly widespread awareness of both lesbian and gay male homoeroticism as well as a trend toward adapting it to creative uses in mass-market ADVERTISING, FILM, and TELEVISION.

➤ Also see PHOTOGRAPHY; PORNOGRAPHY; SEX; SEX WARS, LESBIAN.

- ✧ Jonathan Dollimore, *Sexual Dissidence: Augustine to Wilde, Freud to Foucault* (1991).
- ✧ Emmanuel Cooper, *The Sexual Perspective: Homosexuality and Art in the Last 100 Years in the West* (2nd ed., 1994).
- ✧ *Nothing but the Girl: The Blatant Lesbian Image,* edited by Susie Bright and Jill Posener (1996).

Homophile

Term popularized in the 1950s and 1960s as an alternative to the word "HOMOSEXUAL"; now used to distinguish the GAY AND LESBIAN RIGHTS MOVEMENT before STONEWALL, and to characterize the organizations of that era and their comparatively more cautious political strategies.

"Homophile," along with "similisexual," was one of many words coined in the late 19th and early 20th centuries out of dissatisfaction with "homosexual." After World War II, activists in Western Europe and the U.S. began to use "homophile" to promote understanding and tolerance of homosexuality. Since *phile* was from a Greek root meaning "love," they reasoned, "homophile" suggested same-sex romance and relationships and was less blatantly erotic and hence less provocative than "homosexual." For the closeted, it also had the advantage of vagueness: as in "Anglophile," you didn't have to be one to like them.

"Homophile" fell into disuse in the late 1960s as growing openness about sexual matters in the U.S. and Europe began to make the word "homosexual" more acceptable in public discourse and the word "GAY" became the preferred term among both lesbians and gay men.

➤ Also see ASSIMILATIONISM/CONFRONTATIONALISM.

Homophobia

As defined by psychologist George Weinberg, who popularized the term through his book *Society and the Healthy Homosexual* (1972), "the dread of being in close quarters with homosexuals" or, more generally, "revulsion toward homosexuals." Today, however, homophobia is generally thought of as an unreasonable fear or hatred of homosexuality, especially in others but also in oneself (internalized homophobia). Like the word "HOMOSEXUAL," homophobia is technically nongendered; however, some writers use the word "lesbophobia" for specifically antilesbian manifestations of homophobia.

Some people have come to prefer the term "HETEROSEXISM" to describe the negative attitudes and biases associated with homophobia, reserving the latter term for extreme manifestations of abhorrence of gay men and lesbians, but homophobia is still the word most commonly used to describe rational fears ("gay people are changing society") as well as irrational ones ("they convert young people to their perverted lifestyle").

The extent of homophobia in American society is open to speculation. According to a Yankelovich Monitor study, about 41 percent of Americans surveyed in 1993 "would prefer not to be around gay people." This number, however, was down from more than 50 percent in 1979. In contrast, some 62 percent of Americans were found to be in favor of job

Famous Homophobes: A Sampling

Anita Bryant

Ex-beauty queen and orange juice spokesperson, leader of early "family values" campaign (see **1/18/1977**) in defense of which she liked to remark:

> "If homosexuality were the normal way, God would have made Adam and Bruce."

Pat Buchanan

Television commentator and conservative Republican politician:

> "We cannot worship the false god of gay rights. To put that kind of relationship on the same level as marriage is a moral lie."

William F. Buckley

Political commentator, editor, and author, to GORE VIDAL on live television in 1968:

> "Now, listen, you queer. Stop calling me a crypto-Nazi or I'll sock you in your goddam face."

Eldridge Cleaver

Former Black Panther leader, in his autobiographical manifesto *Soul on Ice* (1968):

> "Homosexuality is a sickness, just as are baby-rape or wanting to become president of General Motors."

Jesse Helms

U.S. senator (R-N.C.) and conservative leader, condemning a March on Washington (see **10/10/1987**):

> "We have to call a spade a spade and a perverted human being a perverted human being."

Robert Mugabe

President of Zimbabwe, who, in a speech given at the opening of a human rights book fair in Harare on **August 1, 1995**, expressed his opinion of "sodomists and sexual perverts":

> "I don't believe they have any rights at all. I hope the time never comes when we want to reverse nature and men bear children."

Nancy Reagan

Former First Lady, speaking to the *Boston Globe* on March 31, 1981:

> "It is appalling to see parades in San Francisco and elsewhere proclaiming 'gay pride' and all that. What in the world do they have to be proud of?"

Byron White

U.S. Supreme Court Justice, writing in *Bowers v. Hardwick* opinion (see **6/30/1986**):

> "It is obvious that neither of these formulations [based on due process] would extend a fundamental right to homosexuals to engage in acts of consensual sodomy. Proscriptions against that conduct have ancient roots."

rights protection for lesbians and gay men in a *New York Times*/CBS poll taken in 1994.

The most extreme example of homophobia is HATE CRIME directed at lesbians and gay men.

Origins

Psychologists and sociologists have advanced several theories to explain homophobia. One of the most common is that homophobia is simply part of a generalized fear of sexuality (erotophobia). Another theory dates back to Sigmund Freud and his belief that people are born pansexual and "progress" via a complicated process to a more limited sexuality: according to this theory, homophobes are people who are disturbed and frightened by their suppressed but still latent homosexual feelings and project their negative feelings onto others. A third, more recent theory holds that homophobia is a mechanism for enforcing rigid GENDER distinctions: gay men and lesbians are perceived as people who disturb traditional gender roles and the social system they support, and are thus dangerous. This last theory is also one of the more common explanations for internalized homophobia: lesbians and gay men come to hate themselves for not being "woman enough" or "man enough" to meet society's expectations.

As writers like ESSEX HEMPHILL have pointed out, both the origins and the nature of homophobia differ depending on racial, ethnic, and class backgrounds. Hemphill critiqued the homophobic writings of psychiatrist Dr. Frances Cress Welsing (who once wrote: "Black psychiatrists must understand that whites may condone homosexuality for themselves, but we as Blacks must see it as a strategy for destroying Black people that must be countered") as reflecting "a disturbing need for a convenient 'other' to vent anger against, to blame, to disparage, to denigrate."

- ✧ Essex Hemphill, "If Freud Had Been a Neurotic Colored Woman: Reading Dr. Frances Cress Welsing," in *Ceremonies: Prose and Poetry* (1992).
- ✧ *Psychological Perspectives on Lesbian and Gay Male Experiences,* edited by Linda D. Garnets and Douglas C. Kimmel (1993).

Homosexual

Term coined by KÁROLY MÁRIA KERTBENY c. 1868 to describe a person who feels sexual desire exclusively or primarily for persons of his or her own sex. The oldest surviving attestation of the word is from a draft of a letter written in German by Kertbeny to the "Uranian" (gay) rights activist KARL HEINRICH ULRICHS on **May 6, 1868**.

"Homo" is from the Greek word for "same" (as in *homo*geneous), not, as is sometimes suggested, the Latin word *homo* (meaning person, as in *Homo sapiens*). In 1963, the British Broadcasting Company's Pronunciation Unit actually directed all employees to pronounce "homosexual" with a short *o,* so that its first syllable would rhyme with "Tom" rather than "tome," as a way of reminding listeners that homosexual meant "same-sex" and not "man sex."

Because "sexual," on the other hand, is derived from a Latin root, purists have objected for over a century that the word is a "barbaric" hybrid of Greek and Latin. Nevertheless, the completely Latin version, "similisexual," has never caught on.

"Homosexual" was first widely used in Germany at the kaiser's court in 1907 in reports of an espionage scandal that involved, according to the press, a "homosexual clique." Linguists believe it supplanted "variant," "deviant," "Uranian," etc., because it had a handy opposite, "heterosexual," and half-opposite, "bisexual," and because it came along with an abstract noun, "homosexuality," that facilitated discussions of the subject.

Since the 1970s, "homosexual" has been increasingly displaced by terms such as "GAY," "LESBIAN," "same-sex," and "QUEER," both because it has an overly formal feel for most everyday contexts and because of its long association with HETEROSEXISM in medical, psychological, and political discourse.

Peter McEnery appeared as a doomed gay man in the 1961 British film Victim, the first English-language movie to use the word "homosexual."

Homosociality, see ROMANTIC FRIENDSHIPS.

Hong Kong, see CHINA.

Hooker, Dr. Evelyn

(1908–1996)

U.S. psychologist. Hooker earned her Ph.D. in psychology from Johns Hopkins in 1932. She had settled into a teaching and research position at UCLA when she became friends in the mid-1940s with one of her former students, a gay man named Sammy, and his lover, George. Sammy introduced her to the Californian gay SUBCULTURE and then challenged her to do psychological research on gay men. In 1953, she obtained a grant from the National Institute of Mental Health and began giving "projective personality tests" (including the Rorschach test) to 30 gay and 30 straight men. Her findings, evaluated by three independent experts, dramatically contradicted the then current position of American PSYCHOLOGY that homosexuality was a form of "mental illness": there was no appreciable difference between the two groups in terms of psychological adjustment or "psychopathology."

Hooker presented her findings at several psychological association meetings from 1954 to 1956 and published a report on her study in the premiere issue of *The* MATTACHINE *Review* (**1/1955**). Although her peers were slow to take notice, her research eventually influenced psychiatrists like Dr. Judd Marmor to revise his views on homosexuality, making possible the December 15, 1975, AMERICAN PSYCHIATRIC ASSOCIATION (APA) vote that eliminated homosexuality from the APA's list of psychological disorders.

Hooker spent decades fighting for gay and lesbian civil rights. She was appointed by President Lyndon B. Johnson to chair a task force on homosexuality that recommended the decriminalization of private sex acts between consenting adults on **October 2, 1969**.

✧ Eric Marcus, *Making History: The Struggle for Gay and Lesbian Equal Rights, 1945–1990* (1992).

Housman, A. E.

(Alfred Edward Housman; 1859–1936)

English poet, classical scholar. He studied at Oxford, wrote scholarly articles while working in the London Patent Office, and then began an academic career in 1892, becoming professor of Latin at Trinity College, Cambridge, in 1911. He published his most famous book of poems, *A Shropshire Lad,* in 1896 and the best-selling *Last Poems* in 1922. His melodious, hauntingly wistful poems were among the most beloved and most quoted of his era.

Most of Housman's contemporaries identified his evocations of doomed youth and unrequited love with their own personal losses, especially the tragedies of WORLD WAR I. Behind the poems—and more overtly in his posthumously published *More Poems* (1936) and *Additional Poems* (1937)—were protests against the persecution of people like OSCAR WILDE (who was a friend of his brother, Laurence, and to whom he sent an autographed copy of *A Shropshire Lad*).

Like many other upper-class English men of his era, Housman led a careful, discreet life at home but found sexual satisfaction during frequent sojourns in France and Italy, where same-sex relations were legal. In 1900, he met a 23-year-old gondolier in Venice and returned for summer trysts with him, later supporting him during a serious illness. He is also said to have pursued soldiers and other sexually available men at brothels and Turkish BATHS in Paris.

✧ Richard P. Graves, *A. E. Housman: The Scholar-Poet* (1980).

Howard, Richard

(1929–)

U.S. poet, translator, critic, educator. A Cleveland, Ohio, native, Howard grew up in an enormous house with an excellent library. He learned to read when he was three and by the age of four had decided to be a writer. After attending the progressive Park School, he continued his studies at Columbia University and the Sorbonne. In Paris, he met many of the French intellectuals whose writings he would later translate, including semiotician and critic Roland Barthes, JEAN COCTEAU, JEAN GENET, and ANDRÉ GIDE. Based in the U.S. after the late 1950s, he earned a reputation over the next decades as a brilliant poet, translator, and critic—three professions whose essence he describes as "getting out of the way of voices, letting the voices speak through me and for me." He was active in the early conferences of the Gay Academic Union (see **11/23/1973**), and was for many years the lover of Sanford Friedman, whose novel

Totempole (1965) was one of the first positive portrayals of a gay man's coming to terms with his sexuality. In addition to publishing ten books of poetry, two major works of criticism, and serving as poetry editor of the *Paris Review,* Howard has taught at Yale and, as University Professor of English, at the University of Houston.

Howard began writing poetry in the mid-1950s while working as a lexicographer, and published his first book of poems, *Quantities,* in 1962. He and critics alike have noted the influence of his friend W. H. AUDEN, especially on Howard's early work. His Pulitzer Prize–winning *Untitled Subjects* (1969) was a collection of 15 monologues voiced by characters of the past, some real, some imagined. He continued to use monologues and, with *Two-Part Inventions* (1974), dialogues to explore a wide variety of personae, including WALT WHITMAN and OSCAR WILDE, whose legendary 1882 meeting he re-created in "Wildflowers." His later books have increasingly featured contemporary themes, as in "Man Who Beat Up Homosexuals Reported to Have AIDS Virus" (*Like Most Revelations,* 1994).

Howard has also translated more than 150 books from French into English, ranging from the poetry of Charles Baudelaire to the war memoirs of Charles de Gaulle. Among his translations are landmark texts by gay authors like Barthes, novelist Renaud Camus (*Tricks,* or "25 sexual encounters," 1979; English translation, 1981), MICHEL FOUCAULT, and, as a long-term project in the 1990s, MARCEL PROUST.

✧ Claude J. Summers and Ted-Larry Pebworth, "We Join the Fathers: Time and the Maturing of Richard Howard," *Contemporary Poetry: A Journal of Criticism* (vol. 3, no. 4, 1978).

✧ David Bergman, *Gaiety Transfigured: Gay Self-Representation in American Literature* (1991).

Hudson, Rock

(Born Roy Scherer Jr., adopted as Roy Fitzgerald; 1925–1985)

U.S. screen star, the first major celebrity to acknowledge having AIDS. Hudson spent his childhood in the suburbs of Chicago. After military service during WORLD WAR II, he moved to Los Angeles and worked as a truck driver until he was discovered by Henry Willson, a gay talent agent who also launched Troy Donahue and Tab Hunter. Acting lessons and small parts led to his first leading role, in *Magnificent Obsession* (1954), and by the late 1950s he was one of the most popular stars in the world.

Tall, dark, and handsome, Hudson was the epitome of everything the public sought in a

Rock Hudson's screen image, as here with Piper Laurie in the 1953 film The Golden Blade, belied his private life.

romantic male movie star. Behind the scenes, however, Hudson had numerous affairs with men, including, allegedly, LIBERACE. To squelch rumors, he was married to his secretary for three years in the 1950s, but he stayed sexually active with men throughout his life.

On **July 25, 1985**, a spokesperson for Hudson acknowledged reports that the actor was suffering from AIDS. The publicity given his illness had an enormous impact on building awareness of AIDS and in galvanizing public support of efforts to fight the disease. Before his death on October 2, 1985, Hudson made important contributions to several major fundraising efforts.

Years before the public revelation of his sexuality, Hudson was a figure of gay folklore, one of numerous Hollywood stars widely rumored to be gay or lesbian. He and actor/singer Jim Nabors were (falsely) alleged to have joined in a secret marriage, and ARMISTEAD MAUPIN included a thinly disguised character modeled on Hudson in his *Tales of the City* novels. Nevertheless, most Americans were shocked to learn he was gay. Some commentators believe that the publicity surrounding his gayness challenged commonly held stereotypes; others point to a reactionary reassessment of his film career to refit it to those same stereotypes.

- ✧ Rock Hudson and Sara Davidson, *Rock Hudson: His Story* (1986).
- ✧ Randy Shilts, *And the Band Played On: Politics, People, and the AIDS Epidemic* (1987).

Hughes, Langston

(James Mercer Langston Hughes; 1902–1967)

U.S. poet. Impoverished when his father left his mother shortly after his birth, Hughes grew up in Kansas, working from earliest youth to

Isaac Julien called his 1989 documentary exploration of the roots of African-American homoeroticism Looking for Langston.

help support himself and his mother. After studying for two years at Columbia University, Hughes worked his way on board ships to Europe and AFRICA, then returned to the U.S. to finish his studies.

With the publication of his first book of poems, *Weary Blues* (1926), Hughes earned a reputation as one of the finest poets of the HARLEM RENAISSANCE. He continued to write and publish a remarkable variety of works until his death in 1967.

Hughes's sexuality is a matter of dispute. Although it is known that he had sex with a man (a sailor) on at least one occasion, he was considered asexual—or at least not interested in sex with men or women—by his gay male contemporaries, who included fellow Harlem Renaissance intellectuals ALAIN LOCKE, COUNTEE CULLEN, and Richard Bruce Nugent. Many readers find examples of HOMOEROTICISM in his work as well as protests against the oppression of gay people, such as "Café: 3 A.M." (see **1951**). ISAAC JULIEN's film *Looking for Langston* was in part inspired by the enigma of Hughes's sexuality. One sign of the controversy that has attended linking Hughes with AFRICAN-AMERICAN gay male culture is that the Hughes estate refused Julien permission to use Hughes's poems as part of the voice-over of the film.

✧ Essex Hemphill, "*Looking for Langston:* An Interview with Isaac Julien," in *Brother to Brother,* edited by Essex Hemphill (1991).

✧ Gregory Woods, "Gay Re-readings of the Harlem Renaissance Poets," *Journal of Homosexuality* (Fall 1994).

Hujar, Peter

(1934–1987)

U.S. photographer. Hujar started working as a photo assistant in his late teens. After two extended trips to ITALY in the late 1950s and early 1960s, he opened his own New York studio in 1967. In 1975, he moved to a loft in Soho. In the late 1970s and 1980s, he exhibited infrequently at Samuel Hardison's Robert Samuel Gallery in Greenwich Village.

Even before he moved his studio downtown, Hujar focused on people, famous (Warhol star *Candy Darling on Her Deathbed,* 1974) and obscure (*The Shareef Twins,* 1985), who were part of New York's avant garde or were most at home in the clubs and streets on its fringes. Anticommercial to the point of alienating critics as well as potential dealers, he eschewed glamorized sexuality even in his male nudes, which he most often shot backdropped against the walls of his bare studio. Some of his most memorable images are of friends and lovers, including DAVID WOJNAROWICZ.

✧ Allen Ellenzweig, *The Homoerotic Photograph: Male Images from Durieu/Delacroix to Mapplethorpe* (1992).

Human Rights Campaign (HRC)

Largest national gay and lesbian political organization in the U.S. Founded on October 1980, the Human Rights Campaign Fund (HRCF—"Fund" was dropped from the organization's name in 1995) was the first national gay and lesbian political action committee (PAC). The Gay Rights National Lobby, founded in 1976, merged with HRCF in December 1985. By the 1990s, HRCF had grown to become one of the nation's 50 largest PACs.

Besides supporting lesbian- and gay-friendly candidates to the U.S. House and Senate, HRC lobbies Congress and the federal government on relevant civil rights, health, and safety issues. It also monitors and fights antigay initiatives at the state level and sponsors a variety of public education programs and campaigns, including National Coming Out Day

(October 11). HRC had more than 80,000 members and a staff of 40 in 1997.

Humor, see CAMP; COMEDY.

Hungary, see EASTERN EUROPE.

Hunter, Alberta

(1895–1984)

U.S. singer, nurse. Hunter had a rich and varied performance career that included nightclubs, radio, Broadway musicals, and recordings.

Like most other blueswomen of the 1920s, Hunter was born into poverty (in Memphis, Tennessee), received little formal education, and no formal musical training. She talked a teacher headed for Chicago into taking her along and was soon singing in nightclubs for $10 a week. Not knowing one note from another, she was helped along by the pimps and prostitutes she sang for at the nightclub Dago Frank's. Soon she became known as "the South Side's Sweetheart."

After a brief marriage in 1927, she was vacationing in Europe when she was invited by Oscar Hammerstein II and Jerome Kern to audition for *Show Boat.* She got the part of Queenie and performed with Paul Robeson. In the early 1930s in Paris, she replaced Josephine Baker as the top cabaret star and went on to perform in the international vaudeville circuit and on world tours with the first black USO unit. She quit singing abruptly when her mother died in 1954, and began a 20-year career as a nurse. In 1977, she enjoyed a resounding comeback.

Dismissing any connection between her own experiences and her trademark "heartbreak songs," such as "A Good Man Is Hard to Find," she commented: "I never did have the blues about no man in my entire life!" Biographer Frank C. Taylor notes: "Alberta was a lesbian [but] she grew up in an era that did not permit discussion of sexuality, much less acceptance of homosexuality. The subject matter remained one she refused to discuss."

✧ Sally Placksin, *American Women in Jazz: 1900 to the Present* (1982).

✧ Linda Dahl, *Stormy Weather: The Music and Lives of a Century of Jazzwomen* (1984).

✧ Frank C. Taylor, with Gerald Cook, *Alberta Hunter: A Celebration in Blues* (1987).

Iceland, see SCANDINAVIA.

Immigration

Several countries, including the United States (1952–1990) and CANADA (1952–1977), have officially barred all gay and lesbian foreigners from entry at some point in the 20th century. Today, however, except for Trinidad and Tobago (see CARIBBEAN) and a few, relatively isolated instances of harassment at borders (in particular, the U.S./Canada border), the most important immigration-related issues for lesbians and gay men are not entry or naturalization but rather asylum for victims of persecution, and residence permission for partners of gay and lesbian citizens. Denmark, Norway, and Sweden (see SCANDINAVIA), AUSTRALIA, AUSTRIA, BELGIUM, FINLAND, GERMANY, the NETHERLANDS, the UNITED KINGDOM, and the U.S. are among the countries that have given asylum to gay or lesbian refugees from persecution from some 35 countries, including ARGENTINA, CUBA, Iran (see CENTRAL ASIA), and TURKEY. Countries that allow the partner of a gay or lesbian resident to immigrate include Australia, Denmark, Hungary (see EASTERN EUROPE), the Netherlands, NEW ZEALAND, Norway, and Sweden.

A related issue has been the free passage of people with AIDS and HIV-positive individuals. Several countries, including CHINA and RUSSIA, require foreign applicants for long-term residence to test free of HIV, but the U.S. remains the only country that officially bars all foreign visitors with HIV.

➤ Also see **June 27, 1952**; **1967**; **September 8, 1983**; **October 27, 1990**.

✧ *The Third Pink Book: A Global View of Lesbian and Gay Liberation and Oppression,* edited by Aart Hendriks, Rob Tielman, and Evert van der Veen (1993).

India, see SOUTH ASIA.

Indonesia, see SOUTHEAST ASIA.

Inquisition, The

Roman Catholic tribunal formed in 1231 by Pope Gregory IX to prosecute heresy. The use of torture to obtain confessions was authorized by Pope Innocent IV in 1252. The Spanish Inquisition, begun in 1478, and the Portuguese Inquisition, authorized in 1562, were independent of the papal Inquisition and in general harsher in their methods and punishments. In all forms of the Inquisition, persons found guilty were turned over to secular authorities to be punished. Penalties ranged from imprisonment and confiscation of property to burning at the stake.

The Church did not at first consider same-sex SODOMY a "heresy" in itself, but it was often associated with heretics, since it was thought that anyone despicable enough to commit heresy would probably not be above committing other infamies ranging from treason to bestiality. In time, heresy and sodomy became so linked in the public imagination that one word for heretic in medieval French, *bougre* (from *bulgarus,* "Bulgarian," a reference to the country where the Bogomil heresy originated in the 10th century), evolved into the English word "bugger," roughly synonymous with "sodomite." Only in **1451**, however, did Pope Nicholas V authorize the papal Inquisition to investigate cases solely involving sodomy.

The Spanish Inquisition was established initially to investigate Jews and Moors suspected of being insincere in their conversions to Christianity. In 1524, the Spanish Inquisition received permission to begin investigating cases of sodomy, which was already subject to some of the harshest civil laws in Europe (see **1497**). Indeed, in some cities, such as Seville, sodomy remained solely under the jurisdiction of the civil authorities. In others, such as Valencia and Barcelona, it was prosecuted by the local Holy Office. Estimates of the number of Spanish sodomites prosecuted and punished vary widely, from several hundred to tens of thousands.

The Portuguese Inquisition was more lenient in its prosecution of sodomites. Brazilian historian Luiz Mott has calculated that of 4,419 men denounced for sodomy between 1587 and 1794, only 408 went to trial and only 30 were actually burned at the stake.

➤ Also see ROMAN CATHOLIC CHURCH; WICCA.

✧ *The Pursuit of Sodomy: Male Homosexuality in Renaissance and Enlightenment Europe,* edited by Kent Gerard and Gert Hekma (1989).

International Lesbian and Gay Association (ILGA)

Loose federation of over 400 gay, lesbian, and bisexual groups from more than 50 countries on every continent. ILGA's primary mission is to facilitate contacts among lesbian and gay groups around the world and to provide information on the legal and social status of gay men, lesbians, and bisexuals in every country, including those in which no rights movement exists. ILGA has an Information Secretariat headquartered in Brussels and independently appointed activist arms, which have included the International Gay and Lesbian Human Rights Commission (IGLHRC), based in San Francisco, and OCCUR, based in JAPAN. In addition to publishing newsletters, reports, and the *Pink Book* (see below), ILGA sponsors frequent regional and international meetings and conferences. Due to the widely varied ideologies of its members (and the organization's constitutional requirement that all decisions be approved by an 80 percent majority), ILGA advocates few specific policies apart from a broad support of basic civil rights for gay men and lesbians.

ILGA grew out of a meeting held on **August 8, 1978**, in Coventry, England, attended by 30 men representing 17 organizations from 14 mostly European countries. Although no women attended this first meeting, the International Gay Association (IGA), as it was then called, saw itself as an international advocacy organization for both lesbians and gay men. In 1986, reflecting the ever increasing involvement of women's and lesbian groups, the organization officially changed its name to the International Lesbian and Gay Association (ILGA). Similarly, ILGA evolved in the 1980s from a primarily European and Australian/New Zealand organization to include more representatives from the U.S. and

CANADA, and, later, South America, Asia, and AFRICA.

In 1985, the organization published its first *Pink Book,* a collection of articles on the international gay and lesbian rights movement and the most comprehensive country-by-country summary of the legal and social status of lesbians and gay men. The three editions of the *Pink Book* (1985, 1988, 1993) have covered 88, 124, and 202 countries respectively.

Despite its loose, sometimes chaotic structure, ILGA has won successes on several fronts. It was instrumental in persuading AMNESTY INTERNATIONAL to make gay and lesbian rights abuses part of its agenda (see **9/1991**) and the World Health Organization to drop "homosexuality" from its list of sicknesses (see **1/1/1993**). It has also presented influential studies and reports to the European Union.

ILGA has been less successful at the U.N. After years of lobbying, ILGA became in **July 1993**, the first and only gay or lesbian group to join the more than 1,500 groups that have nongovernmental organization (NGO) representative status at the U.N. Later that year, U.S. Senator Jesse Helms (R-N.C.) amended the U.S. bill authorizing U.N. financing to prohibit support of U.N. bodies that grant official status to "any organization which promotes, condones or seeks the legalization of PEDOPHILIA." In response, ILGA expelled several groups, including the North American Man-Boy Love Association, in June 1994. Several ILGA groups in Europe, however, chiefly organizations that advocate lower AGE OF CONSENT laws, protested ILGA's action, and, later that year, the organization told the U.N. that it could not vouch that none of its 400-plus member groups condoned pedophilia. As a result—again largely due to pressure exerted on American U.N. representatives by Senator Helms—the U.N. suspended ILGA's NGO status on **September 16, 1994**.

✧ *The Third Pink Book: A Global View of Lesbian and Gay Liberation and Oppression,* edited by Aart Vendriks, Rob Tielman, and Evert van der Veen (1993).

Iran, see CENTRAL ASIA.

Ireland

In the Republic of Ireland, no laws against consensual same-sex relations for adults 17 and older. Extensive legislation protecting lesbians and gay men from discrimination in the workplace, the MILITARY, *and elsewhere. Limited social scene in Dublin; organizations and support services in Dublin, Cork, Galway, Limerick, and Waterford.*

Gay and lesbian life in Ireland remains more closeted than in most other Western European countries. Although the level of overt hostility, as indicated by HATE CRIME statistics, is low compared with many other countries, and Irish lesbians and gay men have gained some of the most comprehensive rights protections anywhere, they also continue to face unique problems—in particular what activist Kieran Rose calls "the stranglehold that the Catholic Church has over education, health and some community/youth services in Ireland."

The Gay and Lesbian Equality Network, founded in 1988, is Ireland's largest advocacy group. Openly gay and lesbian Irish celebrities include writers Emma Donoghue, Mary Dorcey, and Desmond Hogan; musician Zrazy; and parliamentary leader David Norns.

History

Ancient Greek and Roman writers wrote of the prevalence of PEDERASTY among Celtic warriors and described sacred sexual rituals among Celtic women. These practices may have spread to Ireland when the Celts invaded in the 2nd century B.C. The earliest references to same-sex eroticism by Irish writers are in penitentials (see **700**) dating from the 6th century. Regulation and punishment of same-sex acts remained under the purview of the ROMAN CATHOLIC CHURCH until the 17th century, when the Irish House of Commons made "buggery" punishable by hanging (see **11/11/1634**). Same-sex relations between women were never against the law in Ireland.

Except for court records and an occasional poem, the Irish remained silent on lesbian and gay life until fairly recently. In **1732**, William King published *The Toast,* a vicious poetic satire on a group of Dublin women he accused of having "lesbian loves." Later in the century, two Irishwomen eloped to Wales to become the celebrated LADIES OF LLANGOLLEN. The 19th century saw the birth in Dublin of the most famous Irish gay man of all, OSCAR WILDE.

The penalty for same-sex relations between men was reduced to a prison sentence after 1861. Prosecutions multiplied in the mid-20th century: from 1962 to 1974, there were almost 600 court cases. In the early 1970s, David Norris and others formed the Irish Gay Rights Movement (IRGM), which began offering a SWITCHBOARD in 1974. That same year, Norris and other activists successfully campaigned to end police enforcement of SODOMY laws.

Meanwhile, Irish lesbians had begun to play a prominent role in early feminist organizations such as Irishwomen United (formed in 1975). Beginning in 1978, activists like Joni Crone organized women's dances, discussion groups, a lesbian switchboard, and conferences, out of which grew Liberation for Irish Lesbians (1978–1985). Crone later helped achieve a new level of awareness of lesbianism in Ireland when, in 1980, she became the first open lesbian to appear on Irish TELEVISION.

In the late 1970s, IRGM was succeeded by the National Gay Federation, which opened the Hirschfeld Centre in Dublin to provide social, cultural, educational, and counseling facilities and to serve as a political hub. In 1987, Norris won election to the Upper House of the Irish parliament. On **October 26, 1988**, he persuaded the European Court of Human Rights to rule Irish sodomy laws in violation of the European Charter of Human Rights. On **June 30, 1993**, the Irish parliament decriminalized same-sex relations for consenting adults and set a universal AGE OF CONSENT. Even before 1993, parliament had extended a wide range of equal rights protections to gay men and lesbians.

➤ For Northern Ireland (Ulster), also see UNITED KINGDOM.

✧ David Norris, "The Development of the Gay Movement in Ireland: A Personal and Political Memoir," in *The Third Pink Book: A Global View of Lesbian and Gay Liberation and Oppression,* edited by Aart Hendriks, Rob Tielman, and Evert van der Veen (1993).

✧ *Quare Fellas: New Irish Gay Writing,* edited by Brian Finnegan (1994).

✧ *Lesbian and Gay Visions of Ireland,* edited by Íde O'Carroll and Eoin Collins (1995).

Isherwood, Christopher

(1904–1986)

British-born writer, based in the U.S. from 1939. The son of an army officer killed in WORLD WAR I, Isherwood received a typically upper-class education that included study at Cambridge University. While still in prep

Christopher Isherwood, c. 1940, photographed by George Platt Lynes.

school, he met W. H. AUDEN; when the two met again in 1925, they remained friends their entire lives. Although Auden and Isherwood were not lovers, they had a sporadic sexual relationship beginning in the mid-1920s, and the two men influenced each other profoundly. Isherwood first came to the attention of the public in the 1930s as the coauthor, with Auden, of three plays, but he achieved more lasting recognition for his semiautobiographical stories, published in three books in the late 1930s, about life in Berlin during the era when the Nazis came to power. Isherwood's *Berlin Stories,* among the first in English to convey the flavor of the city's gay and lesbian SUBCULTURE, later served as the basis for the play (1952) and film (1955) *I Am a Camera,* and the musical (1966) and film (1972) *Cabaret.*

A pacifist and increasingly committed to the study of Hindu Vedanta, Isherwood spent WORLD WAR II in the United States, working to help refugees in the Philadelphia area and later settling in California to write and deepen his knowledge of the Vedanta.

In 1953, Isherwood became lovers with an 18-year-old American artist, Don Bachardy, and the two men remained devoted to each other, living together until Isherwood's death at the age of 82.

In 1964, Isherwood published *A Single Man,* a groundbreaking novel that describes an ordinary day in the life of an unprecedentedly ordinary gay man. Critics have hailed *A Single Man* as one of the first novels to "deproblematize" homosexuality. Frankly autobiographical works such as *Christopher and His Kind* (1976) followed, solidifying Isherwood's position as a gay male mentor and spokesperson.

✧ Claude J. Summers, *Christopher Isherwood* (1980).

Islam

Religious faith based on the teachings of the Prophet Muhammad. Islam is defined by believers as "surrendering" (*islam,* in Arabic) to the will of Allah, the one and only God. A Muslim (literally, "one who surrenders") serves Allah through prayer and submission to the guidance of divine law or *shari'a.* Divine law is in turn based on the Koran (Qur'ān), the revealed writings of the Prophet Muhammad, and the Hadith, sayings of the Prophet recorded by his followers. In theory, divine law is absolute and eternal; in practice, different schools of Islam interpret some aspects of divine law in contradictory ways.

The Koran contains three overt references to homosexuality, all alluding to the destruction of the Cities of the Plain (see SODOM AND GOMORRAH) for sins that included men "lusting after men." Although same-sex fornication is described as a "great sin," the Koran does not specify how believers are to treat transgressors.

The Hadith, on the other hand, explicitly calls for punishments ranging from 80 strokes of the lash to stoning to death.

Despite the harsh language of the Hadith, Islam has tolerated homosexuality through much of its history and in many regions where it is the dominant religion. Islamic mystics (Sufis) have even used erotic attraction between males as a metaphor for the relationship of a believer to Allah. And some believers conceive of heaven as a sexual paradise complete with ever virginal girls and handsome boys.

An explanation for this paradox lies in unique features of Islamic belief. Muslims view the pleasures of the world, including sex, as part of Allah's munificence. At the same time, believers must preserve a social order decreed by Allah. Universal marriage—and the inviolability of the family—are the cornerstones of this order. Sexual activities outside of marriage are thus proscribed because they endanger the social order.

In most schools of Islam, same-sex relations are considered simply a subset of adultery. Like extramarital sex between a man and a woman, homosexuality poses the greatest threat to the social order when it is public. As long as one is discreet, most Muslims are willing to look the other way. This is one reason that harem lesbianism is believed to be widespread.

The level of tolerance of homosexuality also depends in large part on the local culture underlying Islam. In AFRICA, for example, Swahili Muslim women have preserved a homoerotic subculture that is probably centuries old. Here, a society in which women have a higher status than in most of the Islamic world condones and encourages lesbian relationships between independent wealthy older women and young, usually poor women.

➤ Also see ARAB WORLD; NATION OF ISLAM.

✧ *Sexuality and Eroticism Among Males in Moslem Societies,* edited by Arno Schmitt and Jehoeda Sofer (1992).

✧ Warren J. Blumenfeld and Diane Raymond, *Looking at Gay and Lesbian Life* (1993).

Israel

No laws against consensual same-sex relations between adults. Broad antidiscrimination protections, including in the MILITARY, *encoded in law. Active social and cultural scene in large cities. National political organizations.*

Israel is today one of the few countries in the world that guarantees gay and lesbian rights against discrimination in employment and elsewhere. Nevertheless, the influence of Orthodox JUDAISM remains strong. Most Israeli lesbians and gay men remain cautiously closeted, and an open lesbian and gay SUBCULTURE began to develop only after the late 1980s. A Gay Pride Week was celebrated for the first time in June 1989, a year after the Knesset decriminalized same-sex relations between men (same-sex relations between women had never been illegal in Israel). Discrimination against lesbians and gay men in employment was made illegal in 1992. Military restrictions were lifted by a special order of the Israeli Defense Forces in 1993, although commanding officers are still required to report the presence of openly lesbian and gay soldiers and to have special security checks run on them. Since 1994, a series of Israeli Supreme Court decisions have established the rights of gay men and lesbians to several types of DOMESTIC PARTNERSHIP benefits. Activists have been less successful in child custody battles, which are in large part decided by religious tribunals. Political groups include the Society for the Protection of Personal Rights, founded in Haifa in 1976, and Community for Lesbian Feminists, founded in 1977.

- ✧ *Lesbiot: Israeli Lesbians Talk About Sexuality, Feminism, Judaism and Their Lives,* edited by Tracy Moore (1995).

Italy

No laws against consensual same-sex relations between persons over 14, although "public decency" laws and allegations of "corruption of minors" are sometimes used to prosecute same-sex acts. Active social and cultural scene, especially in the northern part of the country. Active national political organizations. Antidiscrimination laws and DOMESTIC PARTNERSHIP *provisions in some cities.*

Photographer Tiziano Bedin reclaims the century-old tradition of "Mediterranean" homoeroticism.

Gay and lesbian life remains less visible in Italy than in most of Europe, due as much to the power of the ROMAN CATHOLIC CHURCH as the all-pervasive influence of the Italian family. The comfort level for lesbians and gay men varies greatly from city to city, even within the generally more tolerant northern part of the country. The leading Italian gay and lesbian rights movement organization is Arci Gay Arci Lesbica, a federation of groups with headquarters in Bologna. Turin has a large, well-established gay and lesbian ARCHIVE. Publications include *Babilonia* and *Quir.*

Italians like LEONARDO DA VINCI and MICHELANGELO have had a major influence on the development of gay and lesbian cultural traditions. Twentieth-century gay, lesbian, and bisexual Italians of note include filmmakers PIER PAOLO PASOLINI, Luchino Visconti, and Franco Zeffirelli; and writers Aldo Busi, Dacia Maraini, Sandro Penna, Umberto Saba, and Pier Vittorio Tondelli.

History

In the late Middle Ages and early Renaissance, Italian cities like Florence were so well-known for same-sex eroticism, especially among young men, that *Florenzer* (Florentine) became a common German word for "sodomite." Although SODOMY was a crime in most Italian city-states and extremely severe punishments are recorded on some law books, in practice the majority of offenders seem to have gotten off by paying fines (see **1432**; **1514**). In at least two cases, young Florentines actually protested these fines (see **1497**; **1512**). Together with contemporary accounts, such as Dante's list of Florentine sodomites in his *Inferno,* these documented incidents have led historians to assume that a kind of "sodomite subculture" existed in Italy as early as the beginning of the 14th century.

Throughout the Renaissance and perhaps even later, Italy was one of the few places in Western Europe where same-sex eroticism, especially between men and youths, was widely tolerated as long as it remained relatively discreet. Fewer records of homoeroticism survive from the 17th and 18th centuries, but there is some evidence that authorities were increasingly reluctant to impose capital punishment for sodomy. In 1764, the Italian jurist and writer Cesare Beccaria was one of the first to defend what he called "Attic love" and to recommend that it be decriminalized.

Even before a unified Italy had officially decriminalized consensual same-sex acts among adults in **1889**, the country was well-known as a haven for gay and lesbian expatriates like the BARON WILHELM VON GLOEDEN. Lesbians were said to gather in Florence and Capri, and gay men from all over Western Europe and the United States found a greater degree of tolerance throughout Italy than in their own countries. Many began to take advantage of what came to be called the "Mediterranean" model of homosexuality: the social attitude that same-sex relations are permissible for men, especially for young men and boys, as a form of sexual release when women are not available. "Mediterraneans" were said to be particularly tolerant of men who were "active" (i.e., insertors) rather than "passive" (i.e., insertees). An entire body of homoerotic art and literature, much of it written by English and German visitors, evolved in praise of supposedly hot-blooded "Mediterranean" men and the sexual and romantic adventures such social attitudes made possible.

As in the rest of Western Europe, lesbian relationships are well attested among upper-class women and intellectuals in Italy since at least the Renaissance. Scholars including Judith Brown have also researched HOMOEROTICISM in Renaissance RELIGIOUS ORDERS in Italy. And Italian lesbian historians have found evidence of lower-class "BUTCH" women who transgressed social norms and managed to lead unconventional lives, even in extremely conservative areas of the country such as Calabria.

Social tolerance of all kinds of social deviation lessened during the Fascist era. Some gay men were arrested and exiled to remote islands, but nothing like the NAZI PERSECUTION of gay men occurred in Italy.

GAY LIBERATION came to Italy in 1971 with the formation of FUORI (the Italian word for "out," also an acronym of Fronte Unitario Omosessuale Rivoluzzionario Italiano), one of whose founders, Mario Mieli (1953–1983), was also a leading Western European gay theorist. FUORI launched ZAPS against targets such as psychiatrists intent on "treating" homosexuality and began a tradition of gay and lesbian visibility in radical Italian politics. Lesbian groups, such as Collegamento Tra Lesbiche Italiane (Italian Lesbian Link), were formed later in the decade.

Despite the existence of BARS, dance clubs, and BATHS in cities like Milan and Turin, a full-fledged gay and lesbian SUBCULTURE has been slower to come to Italy, especially southern Italy, than many other Western countries. Lesbian activists like Rosanna Fiocchetto complain of the lack of a developed community and the marginalization openly lesbian women face in Italian society. One sign of the increasing prominence of lesbians in the Italian rights movement was the 1994 decision of the sixth national congress of Italy's largest gay and lesbian rights organization to change the group's name from Arci Gay to Arci Gay Arci Lesbica.

- Mario Mieli, *Homosexuality and Liberation: Elements of a Gay Critique,* translated by David Fernbach (1980).
- Judith C. Brown, *Immodest Acts: The Life of a Lesbian Nun in Renaissance Italy* (1986).
- Rosanna Fiocchetto, "Italy," *Feminist Review* (no. 34, Spring 1990).
- Robert Aldrich, *The Seduction of the Mediterranean: Writing, Art and Homosexual Fantasy* (1993).

J

Jamaica, see CARIBBEAN.

James, Alice

(1848–1892)

U.S. writer. The youngest and only girl of five children, she was best known during her life as the invalid younger sister of psychologist William and novelist Henry James. Contemporary scholars have rediscovered the literary legacy she left in her diary and letters and used them to explore a world in which women had limited opportunities for self-expression. In her writings, James emerges as an exceptionally intelligent woman caught between family pressure to be as "extraordinary" as her brilliant father and brothers and societal constraints that urged a life of feminine domesticity. Her letters describe the GENDER conflicts she suffered as a result, as well as her "neurasthenia," "hysteria," and other recurring, debilitating afflictions for which no organic cause was ever found.

When she was almost 30, James became intimate with Katharine Loring (1849–1943), whom she described as "a most wonderful being. She has all the mere brute superiority which distinguishes man from woman combined with all the distinctively feminine virtues. There is nothing she cannot do from hewing wood and drawing water to driving run-away horses and educating all the women in North America." Loring, active in educational and library associations, had cofounded the Society to Encourage Studies at Home with Anna Ticknor and the Saturday Morning Club of Boston with Julia Ward Howe.

James and Loring's relationship and its "peculiar intense and interesting affections" were part of what inspired the sexually nuanced BOSTON MARRIAGE in Henry James's novel *The Bostonians.* In 1891, the two women acquired a house together, and James wrote her brother William: "This year has been the happiest I have ever known, surrounded by such affection and devotion, but I won't enter into details, as I see the blush mantle the elderly cheek of my scribe." Shortly thereafter, Alice's lifelong wish for an identifiable illness—one she was not responsible for—was perversely fulfilled: she was diagnosed with breast cancer. As her health failed, she dictated her last diary entries to Loring, who privately printed four copies of the small volume after her death.

✧ Jean Strouse, *Alice James* (1980).

Japan

Same-sex relations not mentioned in law. AGE OF CONSENT *from 14 to 17, depending on local laws. Well-developed gay male, and to a lesser extent, lesbian social and cultural scene in Tokyo, Osaka, and other large cities. Small but visible rights movement.*

After ancient GREECE, Japan probably has the richest premodern heritage of same-sex eroticism of any country. Yet many Japanese have come to believe, despite overwhelming evidence to the contrary, that their culture has always been conservative in matters of sexuality. In 1994, Dr. Yuichi Shiokawa, the chairman of the organizing committee for the International AIDS Conference, blamed the spread of AIDS in Japan on "American-style morals." Asked to elaborate, he responded: "I meant to say that traditionally Japanese had sex only with a spouse and that because of Americanization sexual conduct is much freer."

Tokyo has more BARS catering to gay men than Amsterdam, New York City, and San Francisco combined, and the 1990s have seen the development of a vibrant Japanese lesbian rights movement, centered around such groups as Regumi Studio in Tokyo and the nationwide Kokusai Bian Renmei (International Lesbians United). Nevertheless, life continues to be difficult for gay- and lesbian-identified Japanese. Although there are no legal restrictions on same-sex eroticism, gay spokespersons such as Shigenobu Sakuragi, one of the writers who contributed to *Yoku Wakaru Gei Raifu Handobukku* ("In-Depth Gay Life Handbook," 1994), note that parents, relatives, companies, and a concern for "proper appearances" combine to be as constraining as laws are in other countries.

The Japanese continue to consider the international gay and lesbian subculture as "entertainment" rather than a serious political movement, as suggested by this 1994 guide to "gay presents."

PUBLISHING is one area in which Japanese gay life is particularly rich. A huge number of American and European books with gay and lesbian content—in addition to Japanese-written novels, guidebooks, and books of essays—are translated and sold in Japan. Gay men have access to a uniquely varied selection of magazines, including (since 1982) perhaps the only gay male magazine that spotlights men who weigh more than 90 kilos (198 lbs.), with a special emphasis on middle-aged men, reflecting the age-graded relationships that are a feature of Japanese gay male life. Since May 1995, Japanese women have been able to purchase *Phryne,* the first nationally distributed lesbian/bisexual magazine.

History

HOMOEROTICISM makes an appearance quite literally at the dawn of Japanese prehistory. To lure the Sun Goddess Amaterasu out of the cave in which she had in anger hidden herself (taking all the world's sunlight with her), a lesser goddess, Ama-no-Uzume (Heavenly Alarming Female), assembled the other gods and goddesses at the mouth of the cave and

Takeo Nakahara (left) and Takehiro Murata in Murata's Okoge (1992).

proceeded to perform an outrageously brazen striptease. When Amaterasu stuck her head out to get a look for herself, her light was captured in a sacred mirror, and she was forced out of the cave. Amaterasu went on to become the ancestress of the Japanese imperial family.

Despite this and a few other early homoerotic legends (see **720**), Japanese tradition holds that the practice of same-sex love was imported along with BUDDHISM from CHINA in **806** by the monk Kukai. In the centuries that followed, graphic accounts of sexual affairs between Buddhist monks and *chigo* (young boys) eventually became common in literature (see **1254**) and scroll art.

Because Buddhist monasteries had close ties to the samurai warriors who wielded power over Japan after the 12th century, the monastic heritage of man-boy love is thought to have influenced the development of a similar tradition among samurai. Historical records of the next six centuries casually document the fact that the majority of *daimyo* (warlords) and *shogun* (supreme commanders) who ruled Japan during the period had relationships with boys or young men (see, for example, **1582**) as well as with women. In at least one instance (see **1542**), a powerful *daimyo* formally contracted a kind of SAME-SEX UNION with his beloved, who later became one of his top generals.

The first Christian missionaries to Japan (see **1549**; **1596**) were horrified by the Japanese acceptance of same-sex relations. More surprisingly, considering the relatively low status of Japanese women in the 20th century, they also commented on how much more independent and better educated Japanese women were compared with Western women at the time. Yet few records of erotic attachments between women have survived, other than erotic tales (probably told to amuse males) about intrigues and entanglements in the harems of warlords, stories that have given rise to the Japanese equivalent of Western women's prison movies.

One of the earliest accounts of a same-sex attachment between women outside convents or a samurai household appeared in a story published by Ihara Saikaku in **1686**. Saikaku, a leading writer of the era, also published *The Great Mirror of Male Love* (see **1687**), a classic account of love between men that evidences the spread of same-sex relations from the samurai class to the lively, more diverse urban cultures that came to typify the Tokugawa era (1603–1868).

The Tokugawa era was a golden age of homoeroticism, in some ways unequaled anywhere else in the world before or since. Unlike previous periods in Japanese history, same-sex relationships are attested among all classes, at least in large Japanese cities. Viewed from a modern perspective, the Tokugawa era concept of "normal" sexuality seems to have been similar to what would today be considered BISEXUALITY, but with remarkably "queer" permutations. There were special words to describe men who were *not* attracted to one or the other sex; the average man was expected to find both sexes attractive. *Onnagata*—male kabuki actors who specialized in playing female roles (see **1652**)—were fashion leaders and sex symbols for men and women alike. Some brothels specialized in female prostitutes dressed and groomed to look like boy prostitutes or even (conventionally masculine) adult men. Male prostitutes representing the entire spectrum of possible GENDER expressions were available for women as well as men. And, perhaps most unusual, an entire section of the Edo (present-day Tokyo) pleasure quarter of Yoshiwara was reserved for female prostitutes who catered exclusively to women clients.

Some moralists were appalled by the popularity of ANDROGYNY and the alleged promiscuity of their fellow citizens. The Tokugawa government, which kept most forms of commercial sex safely isolated in special districts located away from city centers, repeatedly imposed censorship restrictions on LITERATURE and THEATER. Nonetheless, most imaginable forms of sexuality found expression in the ARTS that flourished in the period, which ranged from kabuki drama to woodblock-print PORNOGRAPHY by top artists like Kitagawa Utamaro (see **c. 1785**), and also included beautifully crafted double-ended dildos (*tagaigata,* or "mutual shapes"), which were openly marketed to female couples.

Throughout this period, Japan maintained itself in rigid isolation from the rest of the world. When the country was finally opened to the West in the mid-19th century—and especially after the end of the shogunate in 1868—government officials hastened to rid the country of a wide range of practices, such as mixed bathing and the use of gigantic phalluses in religious ceremonies, that were deemed "primitive" and "shameful" in the supposedly more advanced West. In **May 1873**, the government actually went so far as to make consensual same-sex relations illegal (with a penalty of 90 days' imprisonment). Although there is no record of the law ever having been enforced (and it was quietly repealed in **1883**), the homoerotic practices and art forms of the previous centuries disappeared from public life, replaced by concepts of sexuality strongly influenced by the Western "medical model" espoused by sexologists like RICHARD VON KRAFFT-EBING.

Several theories have been put forth to explain this radical change. Historian Gary P. Leupp, for example, believes: "No transition in sexual attitudes and behavior better illustrates the social-constructionist thesis" (see CONSTRUCTIONISM VS. ESSENTIALISM).

COMPULSORY HETEROSEXUALITY continued to characterize Japanese life throughout the 20th century, although oppression of homosexuality never became as severe as in many countries in the West. Men, for the most part, were free to pursue sex and even relationships with other men as long as they kept them hidden and conformed to societal obligations to marry and have children. An underground gay male subculture, described by YUKIO MISHIMA and others, persisted, but for the most part Japanese homoeroticism was so submerged that many Japanese came to believe it did not exist in their country. A discreet but immense underground male SUBCULTURE made up of bars, BATHHOUSES, CRUISING areas, and even magazines (see **9/1971**) developed during the last half of the 20th century; starting in the 1970s organizations and social facilities for Japanese lesbians followed. Nevertheless, GAY LIBERATION and a concerted lesbian and gay rights movement were slow to take root in Japan. The formation of advocacy groups like OCCUR (in 1986), the country's first PRIDE CELEBRATION (see **8/1994**), and the development of vocal, self-assertive lesbian social and cultural organizations are among the signs of change in the last years of the 20th century.

- ✧ Tsuneo Watanabe and Jun'ichi Iwata, *The Love of the Samurai: A Thousand Years of Japanese Homosexuality* (1989).
- ✧ Ihara Saikaku, *The Great Mirror of Male Love,* translated by Paul Schalow (1990).
- ✧ *Yoku Wakaru Gei Raifu Handobukku,* edited by Takarajima Gay Staff (1994).
- ✧ Gary P. Leupp, *Male Colors: The Construction of Homosexuality in Tokugawa Japan* (1995).
- ✧ Sachiko Ishino and Naeko Wakabayashi, "Japan," in *Unspoken Rules: Sexual Orientation and Women's Human Rights,* edited by Rachel Rosenbloom (1996).

Jarman, Derek
(1942–1994)

English filmmaker, artist, writer, activist. Jarman grew up on Royal Air Force bases. After attending public school and university, he studied ART at the Slade and began designing stage productions in the mid-1960s. About that time, he came OUT and threw himself into rounds of anonymous sex, which he celebrated in paintings, poetry, and FILM, as well as in prose writings such as: "Sexuality is a diversity. Every orgasm brings its own liberty."

After art-directing Ken Russell's *The Devils* (1971), Jarman began filming experimental Super-8 shorts. From his first feature, *Sebastiane* (1976), in which he made the saint of the title

A climactic scene from Derek Jarman's Sebastiane (1976).

the unresponsive love object of the Emperor Diocletian, his work was marked by both HOMOEROTICISM and disregard for the box office: *Sebastiane,* for example, had a Latin soundtrack. Over the next 15 years, he refined his film style with CAMP grace notes (such as Elisabeth Welch's rendition of "Stormy Weather" in his reworking of *The Tempest,* 1978) and increasingly interwove confessional, autobiographical reveries, sometimes delivered on camera.

Jarman's first film to address AIDS was *The Angelic Conversation* (1985), an abstract evocation of SHAKESPEARE's sonnets. He was himself diagnosed as HIV-positive in 1986 while making *The Last of England* (1987) and was one of the first celebrities to publicize his HIV status. Long a vocal activist for sexual freedom, he became one of the UNITED KINGDOM's most visible supporters of DIRECT ACTION groups such as OUTRAGE!, some of whose members appeared in his 1991 film, *Edward II.*

Before becoming almost completely blind in 1993, Jarman painted a series of angrily graphic canvases attacking HOMOPHOBIA and society's response to AIDS. He also published his third and fourth works of largely autobiographical prose: *Modern Nature* (1991) and *At Your Own Risk: A Saint's Testament* (1992). His last film, *Blue* (1993), projected a blue screen with voice-over readings from his journals.

Universally recognized as a prophet of queer cinema, Jarman was canonized by the Sisters of Perpetual Indulgence (see **1/10/1980**) as St. Derek of Dungeness of the Order of Celluloid Knights before his death from complications of AIDS on February 19, 1994.

Jewel Box Revue

U.S. touring troupe of female (and one male) impersonators active from 1939 to 1973. Probably the first such troupe to be integrated, the Jewel Box Revue featured AFRICAN-AMERICAN, LATINO, NATIVE AMERICAN, and white performers.

Initially produced by lovers Doc Benner and Danny Brown at a Miami club called the Jewel Box, the revue was conceived to "bring back female impersonation as a true art" at a time when drag shows were increasingly under siege from municipal ordinances against CROSS-DRESSING. After 1942, the troupe also toured programs of song, dance, and theatrical sketches, performing everywhere from private homes to the Apollo Theater in Harlem. In 1946, Fred Coleman and Frank Reid hired them to open the Garden of Allah, one of America's first gay-owned cabarets, in Seattle, Washington.

Advertised as "all boy plus one girl," the revue was emceed for 14 years by the now legendary Stormé DeLarverié in drag: the audience did not discover that Stormé was the "one girl" until the "surprise" number near the show's close. Lesbian filmmaker Michelle Parkerson released a documentary FILM about DeLarverié called *Stormé: The Lady of the Jewel Box* in 1987.

✧ Elizabeth Dorbaugh, "Sliding Scales," in *Crossing the Stage: Controversies on Cross-Dressing,* edited by Lesley Ferris (1993).

✧ Roger Simpson and Don Paulson, *An Evening at the Garden of Allah* (1996).

Jewett, [Theodora] Sarah Orne

(1849–1909)

American novelist, poet, and short story writer. Born in South Berwick, Maine, Jewett was praised for the "local color" she evoked in her gently humorous accounts of life in this seaport region. Jewett published three novels and nine collections of short stories, earning the most lasting acclaim for *Deephaven* (1877) and *The Country of the Pointed Firs* (1896).

Among her unpublished verse are love poems evidently written to women. Coupled with her early diaries, these verse fragments challenge the received image of Jewett as a "passionless spinster," implying a lesbian emotional orientation that casts a fresh light on her writing.

Jewett shared her life for nearly 30 years with friend and, later, companion Annie Adams Fields (1834–1915), former wife of publisher James T. Fields. Their relationship has been characterized by lesbian and gay historians as a quintessential BOSTON MARRIAGE. Jewett's letters to Fields were suppressed and edited by her family and later scholars to remove intimate endearments. Critics suggest that Henry James drew on Jewett and Fields, among others, to create the characters of Olive Chancellor and Verena Tarrant in *The Bostonians.* Jewett left her own description of a Boston marriage in her story "Martha's Lady" (1896).

In her later years, Jewett developed a mentoring relationship with WILLA CATHER, encouraging her to strengthen her writing with female, not male, characters.

✧ Josephine Donovan, *Sarah Orne Jewett* (1980).

✧ Lillian Faderman, *Surpassing the Love of Men: Romantic Friendships and Love Between Women from the Renaissance to the Present* (1981).

Johnston, Jill

(1929–)

British-born U.S. journalist, author, critic. Born in London to an unmarried mother and a father she never knew, Johnston calls herself a "paper daughter," meaning that her life was hers to invent. After college, she married, had a son and daughter, divorced, went on and off welfare, worked as a critic for *ArtNews* and was hospitalized for what she called "breakthroughs" (instead of breakdowns). In 1970, she came OUT in her *Village Voice* column "Knowing Who You Are."

Lesbian Nation (1973), a term she first used in her 1971 Dance Journal column, chronicles her "slouching toward consciousness." In the collection, which included many of her 1970–1972 *Village Voice* columns, she envisioned a safe Lesbian Nation in which proud women would live independently of men in supportive tribal communities. Although Johnston distinguished herself from lesbian SEPARATISM, believing that a lesbian identity included sexual involvement, she emphasized the political identification exemplified by women-identified women committed to themselves and other women. *Lesbian Nation* established Johnston as an influential voice of early LESBIAN FEMINISM, but it was not popular with everyone. Shortly after its release, Johnston wryly told an audience, "My biggest mistake was calling my book *Lesbian Nation.* I will call my future books *My Father America.*"

From the 1950s, Johnston was an enthusiastic voice for new DANCE, painting, and sculpture, championing artistic innovators like Merce Cunningham, Yvonne Rainer, and Andy Warhol. As a critic, she evolved a highly personal life-in-art style evident in her three volumes of autobiography and five essay collections on ART, performance, and LITERATURE.

In 1993, Johnston revised her earlier opinion on monogamy, moved to Denmark, and married her partner Ingrid Nyeboe.

✧ Chris Chase, "jilljohnstonjilljohnstonjill-johnstonjilljohnston," *Ms.* (November 1973).

✧ Nancy and Alice, "Jill Johnston," *Lesbian Tide* (July 1973).

Jones, Bill T.

(William Tass Jones; 1952–)

U.S. dancer, choreographer. Born in Florida the tenth of twelve children of migrant farmworkers, Jones moved with his family to other parts of the South before settling in 1959 in Wayland, New York, a small, almost completely white village in the state's Finger Lakes region. A precocious student, Jones was also a talented athlete, and was on the track team at the State University of New York at Binghamton when, at the age of 19, he met Arnie Zane, a 22-year-old dancer and choreographer. Zane, who was the first man Jones had sex with, became his lover and collaborator for the next 17 years, steering Jones into the world of DANCE and cofounding the Bill T. Jones/Arnie Zane Dance Company in 1982. Together, Jones and Zane developed a postmodern approach to dance influenced by feminist choreographer and filmmaker Yvonne Rainer as well as the avant-garde performance ART of the period. Zane and Jones were both diagnosed as HIV-positive in 1985. Zane died from AIDS-related complications in 1988.

After years of struggling to support himself and his company, working at odd jobs that once included laundering adult diapers for a hospital, Jones began to attain international renown during an extraordinarily successful tour of France in 1990. Among the works he debuted that year was *Last Supper at Uncle Tom's Cabin/The Promised Land,* which Jones has described as beginning with a remembrance of slavery, continuing with an exploration of "the things that separate people," and culminating with a call for unity and an "ultimate vision of freedom": his company joined by up to 50 fat, thin, old, middle-aged, and young nondancers from the local community, all naked together on stage.

Beginning in 1992, Jones conducted a nationwide series of "survival workshops" with people who had been diagnosed with multiple sclerosis, cancer, AIDS, and other life-threatening diseases. Out of these workshops he created *Still/Here,* a combination of video, music, speech, and dance which premiered in Lyons, France, on September 14, 1994. The first part,

Bill T. Jones.

Still, communicates the shock of receiving a medical death sentence; *Here* explores the experience of living—and surviving—in the face of death.

When *Still/Here* had its New York premiere in December 1994 at the Brooklyn Academy of Music, Jones found himself at the center of an art world controversy. Writing in the December 22 issue of *The New Yorker,* dance critic Arlene Croce announced her refusal to review the piece because she considered it "victim art" and thus aesthetically "indiscussable" and "beyond criticism." A number of intellectuals, including writer Joyce Carol Oates, came forward to defend Jones and praise his work in the debate that ensued. The controversy also had the effect of stimulating a more open discussion of the predicament of HIV-positive dancers, many of whom were less fortunate than Jones, who remained completely healthy more than a decade after testing HIV-positive.

Noted for his verbal eloquence as well as his often provocative opinions, Jones emerged in the mid-1990s as a spokesperson for artistic innovation and a proponent of an unabashedly AFRICAN-AMERICAN, vehemently prosex vision of HOMOEROTICISM.

✧ Larry Kaplan, "Bill T. Jones on Top," *Poz* (vol. 1, no. 1. June/July 1994).

✧ Henry Louis Gates Jr., "The Body Politic," *The New Yorker* (November 28, 1994).

✧ Bill T. Jones, *Last Night on Earth* (1995).

Jones, Cleve

(1954–)

Political activist and founder of the NAMES PROJECT. Brought up as a QUAKER in Phoenix, Arizona, Jones left his home state while still a student to work as an intern for San Francisco Supervisor HARVEY MILK. After Milk was assassinated, Jones served as a legislative consultant to Art Agnos, the California State assemblyman who later was elected mayor of San Francisco. Jones was one of the first gay activists to engage in the struggle against AIDS.

The idea for the Names Project came to him the night of November 27, 1985. At Jones's suggestion, protesters attending a candlelight AIDS vigil outside a U.S. government building had brought pieces of paper and cardboard inscribed with the names of loved ones who had died of AIDS. When he saw the building's façade covered with names, Jones imagined a quilt that would commemorate those who had died as well as remind people of the traditional American ideal of ordinary people working together to solve problems. He completed the first quilt piece on February 20, 1987, in memory of Marvin Feldman, a friend of 14 years who had died of AIDS four months earlier.

Jones is well-known in San Francisco as an accomplished community leader, but as he himself has said, "The Quilt is the best thing I've ever done."

✧ Randy Shilts, *And the Band Played On: Politics, People, and the AIDS Epidemic* (1987).

✧ Cindy Ruskin, *The Quilt: Stories from the Names Project* (1988).

Jordan, June

(1936–)

U.S. writer, activist, journalist, educator. The daughter of Jamaican immigrants, she grew up in the Bedford-Stuyvesant section of Brooklyn, New York. She began writing poems at the age of seven and later studied LITERATURE and architecture. In "For My American Family" (*Technical Difficulties,* 1992), she describes her childhood as a time of hope and racial affirmation and her international neighborhood as a shaping force in her lifelong dedication to justice, self-determination, and social responsibility. She married a white man while studying at Barnard College, had a son, and later divorced.

Known primarily as a poet, Jordan published 20 works, which also included novels, plays, musicals, and critically acclaimed essays. Besides teaching AFRICAN-AMERICAN studies at the University of California, Berkeley, she is a political columnist for *The Progressive* and a popular speaker and reader.

In the belief that "freedom is indivisible," Jordan equates sexual oppression with racial and ethnic oppression. She compares staying in the CLOSET to assimilation; both, in her view, are "suicidal" and impossible to do partially or intermittently. She considers her BISEXUALITY as having all the complexities of an interracial or multiracial identity, advocating a "New Politics of Sexuality" that is true to the heart as well as the "honest human body."

In 1986, Ku Klux Klan members stormed the Seven Stages Theatre in Atlanta before the first performance of Jordan's *Bang Bang uber Alles,* a musical drama that urges women and men of different races, religions, classes, and sexual orientations to unite against a single enemy more threatening than their differences: the Klan. Threatening to return if the show was not canceled, the Klan at length departed the theater. The production ran for five weeks.

✧ Pratibha Parmar, "Black Feminism: The Politics of Articulation," in *Identity, Community, Culture, Difference,* edited by Jonathan Rutherford (1990).

✧ June Jordan, *Technical Difficulties* (1992).

Juana Inés de la Cruz, Sor, see CRUZ, SOR JUANA INÉS DE LA.

Judaism

Religion of the Jewish people, with almost 4.5 million adherents in the United States and more than 14 million worldwide as of 1996. Judaism encompasses Orthodox, Conservative, Reform, and Reconstructionist movements, each with its own policies and practices related to homosexuality. There are also several million secular (nonreligious) Jews.

The Torah ("Law"), elaborated in the first five books of the BIBLE and other time-honored writings, promotes sex solely as a means of procreating within marriage. Among its 248 positive and 365 negative mitzvot ("commandments") are strict injunctions not only against all forms of sex, such as masturbation and coitus interruptus, that do not lead to procreation, but also against behaviors, such as CROSS-DRESSING, that blur the distinction between male and female. Historians believe that many of these commandments, which also include regulations on diet, hygiene, and even agricultural methods, evolved out of the desire of the ancient Hebrews—as well as their descendants living in exile—to keep themselves distinct from neighboring peoples. In modern times, Jews have interpreted this body of law in different ways. Reform and Conservative Jews have generally stressed the "spirit" or ethical content of the Law over strict adherence to its minutiae, while Orthodox Jews have continued to honor the "letter" of the Law as well as its spirit.

Interpreted literally, the Torah is most negative toward sex between men, which merited the death penalty. Sex between women, while also proscribed, was considered less serious because it did not involve the "waste" of semen (it was judged merely "obscene").

Little attention was paid to homosexuality among religious Jews until the 1970s. Many Jews have taken the comparative lack of writing on the subject as evidence of the rarity of same-sex relations among Jews, an argument contemporary lesbian and gay activists dispute. Through the 1970s, most religious Jews continued to view homosexuality as opposed to the Jewish tradition, although many also voiced the opinion that homosexuality was a kind of "illness" and as such deserved a degree of social tolerance. This attitude was reflected in public statements such as a resolution passed in 1972 by the San Francisco Board of Rabbis, representing all three major Jewish movements (Conservative, Orthodox, and Reform), that called for the decriminalization of all consensual, private, adult sex acts.

Beginning in the early 1970s, gay and lesbian Jews began to organize to gain greater acceptance within the Jewish community. In 1972, a small group of gay men and lesbians met at the METROPOLITAN COMMUNITY CHURCH in Los Angeles and founded the first "gay outreach" synagogue, Beth Chayim Chadashim (BCC). BCC was granted membership in the Reform movement's Union of American Hebrew Congregations in 1973.

By 1976, when the First International Conference of Gay and Lesbian Jews met in Washington, D.C., almost a dozen gay and lesbian synagogues or groups had been established in the United States, CANADA, and Europe, including London's Jewish Gay Group (1973), New York City's Congregation Beth Simchat Torah (1973), Toronto's Ha Mishpacha, and Montreal's Naches.

Multinational groups played a pivotal role in stimulating the beginnings of a gay and lesbian rights movement in ISRAEL. In 1979, when the International Conference of Gay and Lesbian Jews was held in Israel for the first time, conference participants joined with Israeli lesbians and gay men to stage the country's first gay and lesbian rights demonstration, a march in Tel Aviv's Independence Park. The event also inspired the first Israeli TELEVISION broadcast to address the lesbian and gay rights movement.

Also in 1979, Allen B. Bennett became the first openly gay spiritual leader to be hired by a synagogue when San Francisco's Sha'ar Zahav engaged him as its first rabbi. The first lesbian hire was Janet Ross Marder, chosen to serve as a rabbi at Congregation Beth Simchat Torah in Manhattan in 1983.

In the mid-1990s, there were about forty "gay and lesbian outreach" synagogues around the world, three of which are recognized as members of the Union of American Hebrew Congregations. The World Congress of Gay and Lesbian Jewish Organizations, formally established in 1980 and based in New York City, acts as a liaison for Jewish groups within the lesbian and gay communities.

✧ *Homosexuality and Religion,* edited by Richard Hasbany (1989).

Julien, Isaac

(1960–)

English filmmaker, artist. Julien studied painting and exhibited in London before turning to FILM as a founding member, along with Maureen Blackwood, Robert Crusz, and Nadine Marsh Edwards, of Britain's pioneering Sankofa Collective. He contributed to *Framed Youth* (1984), an award-winning documentary about British gay and lesbian YOUTH; worked on Sankofa's first feature, *Gary's Diary* (1987); and subsequently earned international critical acclaim as the director of the documentary *Looking for Langston* (1988) and the feature *Young Soul Rebels* (1991). Julien has emerged as an acute observer of British culture and its treatment of black people (*Black and White in Colour,* 1992) as well as gay and lesbian issues, such as in *A Darker Side of Black* (1993), which addresses HOMOPHOBIA in black popular music with a special focus on the historical elements of antigay sentiment in Jamaica. He also served as the senior producer on the multipart *A Question of Equality* (shown on American public television in 1995), the first full-scale documentary history of the American GAY AND LESBIAN RIGHTS MOVEMENT.

✧ "The Last 'Special Issue' on Race," *Screen* (vol. 29, no. 4, Autumn 1988; issue editors Kobena Mercer and Isaac Julien).

K

Kameny, Frank

(Franklin Edward Kameny; 1925–)

U.S. astronomer, pioneering gay activist and theorist. A New York City native, Kameny entered college at the age of 15 but left to serve in the U.S. MILITARY during WORLD WAR II. After the war, he returned to his studies, receiving a Ph.D. in astronomy at Harvard in 1956. In 1957, he was fired from his job as an astronomer with the U.S. Army Map Service for alleged homosexuality: he had been arrested the previous year on a "lewd conduct" charge. Unlike most of the thousands of lesbians and gay men who were dismissed from government employment in the 1950s, Kameny decided to fight back. Penniless, unable to get a security clearance for a job in his field, Kameny continued waging battle until March 1961, when the Supreme Court declined to review his case.

That same year, Kameny decided to try a different strategy. Joining with Jack Nichols and others, he formed an independent chapter of the MATTACHINE Society in Washington, D.C. The organization, which held its first meeting on **November 15, 1961**, billed itself as a "civil-liberties, social-action organization dedicated to improving the status of the homosexual citizen through a vigorous program of action." Unlike other HOMOPHILE organizations, which generally attempted to elude government scrutiny, Kameny's group actively sought contact with public officials. The group even mailed its sporadically issued newsletter, *The Gazette,* directly to a long list of government figures, including J. Edgar Hoover.

If Kameny was not the first homophile leader to advocate militancy, he was certainly the most prominent and by far the most influential. He gave the movement a political dimension by placing legal reform at the center of a bold drive for civil rights. In contrast to other gay and lesbian organizers, who sought to "educate the homophile," Kameny believed in educating—and changing—straight society.

In **January 1963**, Kameny was instrumental in forming ECHO (East Coast Homophile Organizations), a coalition of Kameny's group, the New York chapters of DAUGHTERS OF BILITIS and the Mattachine, and the Janus Society of Philadelphia; they united to "explore ways of closer intergroup cooperation." In 1965, Kameny led the attack against the idea, then prevalent among homosexuals as well as heterosexuals, that homosexuality was somehow unhealthy, issuing a statement first adopted by the Washington Mattachine that read, in part: "In the continuing absence of valid scientific evidence to the contrary, homosexuality per se cannot properly be considered a sickness, illness, disturbance, disorder, or pathology of any kind nor a symptom of any of these, but must be considered as a preference, orientation, or propensity, not different in kind from heterosexuality and fully on par with it." Kameny shifted the blame for the "problem" of homosexuality away from homosexuals and onto social prejudice.

He also challenged the presumption that homosexuality is immoral. His 1966 slogan, "Gay is good," officially adopted at the 1968 North American Conference of Homophile Organizations (NACHO, see **8/12–17/1968**), emphasized the need for gay pride and self-esteem. In May 1971, he led a ZAP of the AMERICAN PSYCHIATRIC ASSOCIATION's annual meeting, grabbing the microphone to harangue psychiatrists, whom he characterized as victimizers of gay people.

Also in 1971, Kameny became the first openly gay person to run for Congress. Assisted by a contingent of volunteers from GAY ACTIVISTS ALLIANCE, he secured the requisite number of nominating signatures the weekend before the deadline for filing. Although he lost the election, placing fourth among six candidates, he ran a credible campaign and succeeded in raising awareness of gay issues on both the local and national fronts. His campaign also led to the formation of the locally influential Gay and Lesbian Activists Alliance and the Gertrude Stein Democratic Club.

Kameny's persistence, intelligence, and leadership skills had an impact on virtually every facet of the gay rights movement, including the fight for equal MARRIAGE rights, nondiscrimination in the military, and the repeal of antisolicitation statutes and SODOMY laws. He took on the Pentagon, government officialdom, psychiatrists, lawyers, the media, and even the AMERICAN CIVIL LIBERTIES UNION. He organized pickets, wrote and circulated radically defiant pamphlets ("How to Handle a Federal Interrogation," "What to Do If You Are Arrested"), pressured government agency officials into granting him policy review meetings, encouraged the creation of legal test cases, and spearheaded gay and lesbian involvement in the electoral process.

Kameny authored numerous influential legal briefs and articles for professional publications. He was a founder and board member of the NATIONAL GAY [later: AND LESBIAN] TASK FORCE and the Gay Rights National Lobby and in 1975 was the first openly gay person to re-

Frank Kameny takes time out from his campaign for public office to speak to Rosalyn Regelson's course on homosexuality at New York University.

ceive a mayoral appointment in Washington, D.C.

On **July 3, 1975**, the battle he had set out to fight almost 20 years earlier was partially won. On that day, the U.S. Civil Service Commission issued a press release stating that homosexuals would no longer be excluded from government employment. Another 20 years later, on **August 4, 1995**, President Bill Clinton announced that federal employers would henceforth be barred from denying security clearances on the basis of sexual orientation. Kameny told *The New York Times,* "The Government has gone beyond simply ceasing to be a hostile and vicious adversary and has now become an ally."

✧ Kay Tobin and Randy Wicker, *The Gay Crusaders* (1972).

✧ John D'Emilio, *Sexual Politics, Sexual Communities: The Making of a Homosexual Minority in the United States, 1940–1970* (1983).

✧ Eric Marcus, *Making History: The Struggle for Gay and Lesbian Equal Rights, 1945–1990* (1992).

✧ *Out for Office: Campaigning in the Gay Nineties,* edited by Kathleen DeBold (1994).

Katz, Jonathan Ned

(1938–)

U.S. historian, writer, editor. Katz grew up in Greenwich Village and attended several different colleges before beginning work as a textile designer in 1960. In the 1960s, he also wrote radio documentaries, including a dramatization of an 1851 fugitive slave uprising, which he later expanded into the book *Resistance at Christiana* (1974).

In 1970, Katz began to get involved with the GAY ACTIVISTS ALLIANCE (GAA) and came, after a long struggle in therapy, to accept—even, as he later wrote, "embrace"—his feelings for other men. In 1972, the same year he left the design field, he presented *Coming Out!,* about "Gay Life and Liberation in the U.S.A.," to electrified audiences at the GAA Firehouse. *Coming Out!* was hailed as the first successful, overtly political gay play. In 1973, he was one of the founders of the Gay Academic Union. In 1976, after years of research, he published *Gay American History,* a meticulously annotated collection of documents and interviews covering three centuries of American life.

Katz told THE ADVOCATE in 1976 that one of his reasons for writing the book was his fear that each successive generation "would think they were the first gay people on earth." By 1983, however, when he published his second nonfiction collection, *Gay/Lesbian Almanac,* he was an outspoken adherent of the constructionist belief that successive generations can and do remake their sense of themselves and their "ways of loving" (see CONSTRUCTIONALISM VS. ESSENTIALISM). In 1995, he expanded on this idea in *The Invention of Heterosexuality,* postulating that HETEROSEXUALITY was constructed in opposition to HOMOSEXUALITY to justify nonprocreative male-female sex.

Katz also directed the 69-volume Arno Press reprint project, *Homosexuality: Lesbians and Gay Men in Society, History and Literature* (1975).

Kenan, Randall

(1963–)

U.S. writer. Born in Brooklyn, New York, Kenan grew up in a small North Carolina town. After graduating from the University of North Carolina in 1985, he worked in PUBLISHING for four years before turning to lecturing and writing full-time. He lives in New York City.

A modern "fabulist," as Henry Louis Gates Jr., has called him, Kenan introduced the inhabitants of the fictional town of Tims Creek, North Carolina, in his first novel, *A Visitation of Spirits* (1989). In *Let the Dead Bury Their Dead and Other Stories* (1992, Lambda Literary AWARD), Kenan illuminated more of the rich/poor, black/white, past/present/future Tims Creek cosmos with bold flashes of magical realism, hetero- and HOMOEROTICISM, and a virtuoso stylistic range that runs from folklore to annotated oral history.

Kenan has also written a biography of JAMES BALDWIN (1994), a writer he calls "practically my only role model," for MARTIN DUBERMAN's Chelsea House series of books for young adults on gay and lesbian lives.

Kennedy, Elizabeth Lapovsky

(1939–)

U.S. ethnohistorian, activist, educator. Born and raised in New York City, Kennedy earned a B.A. in philosophy from Smith College and graduate degrees in ANTHROPOLOGY from the University of New Mexico and Oxford University. She did field studies among the Waunan Indians in Colombia, and participated in the antiwar, civil rights, and feminist movements before coming OUT in 1976 and moving with her partner, pioneering lesbian activist Bobbi Prebis, to Buffalo, New York. There Kennedy began teaching at the State University of New York and building a women's studies program.

In 1978, Kennedy and MADELINE DAVIS, among others, founded the Buffalo Women's Oral History Project and began an in-depth study of Buffalo's working-class lesbian community. The findings of the 14-year project were published as *Boots of Leather, Slippers of Gold: The History of a Lesbian Community* in 1993. Hailed as setting new standards for gay and lesbian community history scholarship, the book won an American Sociological Association award, a Lambda Literary AWARD, and the Ruth Benedict Award of the Society of Lesbian and Gay Anthropologists. Kennedy followed up the book with a study of the life of Julia Boyer Reinstein, an upper-class Buffalo lesbian who, according to Kennedy, "relied upon discretion to build an active lesbian life as contrasted with working class women's commitment to announcing their lesbianism."

Kenric

British lesbian organization. In **1963**, Diana Chapman, Esmé Langley, and three other British women founded the Minorities Research Group in London to provide social and educational opportunities for lesbians. In **1964**, the group shifted its focus and began publishing the country's first lesbian magazine, *Arena Three.* Many members still wanted discreet opportunities to socialize, however, so in 1965 an organization similar to the American DAUGHTERS OF BILITIS was founded by a group of women that included Cynthia Reid. Named after the *Ken*sington and *Ric*hmond districts, where most of the original members lived, Kenric brought isolated, usually closeted lesbians together in private homes and clubs. Although not as large as other, more politically militant British lesbian groups, Kenric maintains chapters throughout the country. *Arena Three* ceased publication in 1971.

Kenya, see AFRICA, SUB-SAHARAN.

Kepner, Jim

(1923–)

U.S. writer, archivist, activist. A Texas native, he was found under an oleander bush when he was about seven months old and was adopted. Kepner moved to San Francisco in 1942, ready to come OUT and immerse himself in the city's dynamic, if still closeted, social scene. A voracious reader, he began in 1942 to amass a col-

Jim Kepner.

lection of gay and lesbian books, documents and visual material that later became the International Gay and Lesbian Archives (see ARCHIVES AND LIBRARIES), the largest such collection in the world.

Supporting himself through a variety of odd jobs, Kepner was from 1952 a leading participant and one of the most published writers of both the MATTACHINE Society and ONE INC./MAGAZINE. He also taught a variety of courses through One's gay studies program. He later served as an early staff member of THE ADVOCATE. In addition to publishing perhaps the first gay or lesbian SCIENCE FICTION "fanzine," Kepner has compiled *Becoming a People: A 4,000 Year Gay and Lesbian Chronology* and has written more than 1,600 widely published articles. Well-known among gay and lesbian scholars for his prodigious memory, Kepner contributed crucial insights and information on early gay and lesbian ACTIVISM to the work of pioneering historians such as JOHN D'EMILIO and JONATHAN NED KATZ.

✧ Eric Marcus, *Making History: The Struggle for Gay and Lesbian Equal Rights, 1945–1990* (1992).

Kertbeny, Károly Mária

(Karol Maria Benkert; 1824–1882)

Hungarian-German writer, translator, originator of the words "HOMOSEXUAL" and "heterosexual." Born and reared in Vienna, he officially changed his last name, Benkert, to its ancestral, aristocratic Hungarian form in 1847. A letter written in German by Kertbeny to the Prussian "Uranian" (gay) rights activist KARL HEINRICH ULRICHS on **May 6, 1868**, contains the oldest documented use of "homosexual" and "heterosexual" (in German: *homosexuel* and *heterosexuel*), although by "heterosexual" he meant what is now called "bisexual." In 1869, Kertbeny anonymously published two pamphlets in Berlin arguing that the state had no right to interfere with private sexual behavior. In other writings, he stated that he himself was "normalsexual"—i.e., heterosexual. Kertbeny died in Budapest, probably of syphilis.

✧ Manfred Herzer, "Kertbeny and the Nameless Love," *Journal of Homosexuality* (vol. 12, 1985).

Key West

Florida city located on an island about 90 miles southwest of Miami that has attracted large numbers of gay and lesbian vacationers since the 1960s. The southernmost city in the continental U.S., Key West was established as a fishing center and naval station. It became a popular resort after the construction of the Overseas Highway in 1938 made it easily accessible from the mainland.

Early visitors included Winslow Homer, who found inspiration during a stay in Key West for one of his most famous homoerotic paintings, *The Gulf Stream* (1899). In the late

1940s and 1950s, a number of artists and writers, including TENNESSEE WILLIAMS, gathered on the island.

By the 1960s, the gay and lesbian presence had become much more apparent, but even today, Key West remains, unlike FIRE ISLAND, a predominantly heterosexual resort: only about 25 percent of the year-round population and a similar percentage of visitors are lesbian or gay. As a result, the social scene is somewhat less visible than in other popular gay and lesbian vacation destinations. One of the most visited tourist attractions is the home of the notoriously homophobic Ernest Hemingway, while the house Tennessee Williams lived in remains unmemorialized. Over the years, there have been infrequent outbreaks of HATE CRIME against lesbians and gay men. In 1995, local religious groups refused to allow the local branch of the METROPOLITAN COMMUNITY CHURCH to take part in a Christmas parade.

Despite these incidents, Key West maintains a reputation as a haven of tolerance. In 1983, the city elected one of the country's first openly gay mayors, Richard A. Heyman. The Key West Business Guild, formed in 1978 by local business leaders to promote lesbian and gay tourism, numbered almost 400 members in 1996. Annual events of gay and lesbian interest include the now traditional Fantasy Fest, Women in Paradise (started in 1986), and the Gay Arts Festival (begun in 1992). Canadian writer Marie-Claire Blais and JAMES MERRILL are just two of the many gay and lesbian celebrities who have lived for long periods in Key West since the 1970s.

Kight, Morris
(1919–)

U.S. activist, health worker. Kight grew up in a small Texas town so conservative he was once arrested for serving a black family at a diner where he worked as a teenager. Years of civil rights, health advocacy, and antiwar ACTIVISM followed, including a campaign of protests against manufacturers of napalm and herbicides used in the Vietnam War.

Morris Kight, Don Kilhefner (standing), and John Vincent Platania on the steps of the Los Angeles Gay Community Services Center, 1971.

Kight settled in Los Angeles in 1959 and, though closeted, became acquainted with HARRY HAY and other pioneering gay activists. The STONEWALL Uprising inspired him to come OUT and put his wide-ranging activist experience to work for the Los Angeles GAY LIBERATION FRONT, which he helped launch in December 1969. In 1972, Kight, Don Kilhefner, and John Vincent Platania were among the founders of the Los Angeles Gay Community Services Center, whose unprecedented range of health and social programs served as a model for similar facilities across the U.S. (see COMMUNITY CENTERS). Kight was later one of the leaders of the successful fight against the antigay and -lesbian Briggs initiative (see **11/7/1978**).

In addition to decades of activism, Kight is also credited with coining or popularizing terms that include "physically challenged" and "people of color." Kight's 3,000-piece collection of gay and lesbian ART is now housed as the Morris Kight Collection at the University of Southern California in the ONE Institute facility.

King, Billie Jean

(née Billie Jean Moffitt; 1943–)

U.S. athlete, professional tennis player, coach. Born in Long Beach, California, King started playing tennis at the age of 11. She was world-class from the first year of her career (1960), when at the age of 17 she earned ranking among the top-ten players in the U.S. Over the next two decades, in both singles and mixed doubles competition, she won a record 20 Wimbledon championships as well as 13 U.S. Open titles. The first woman athlete to earn $100,000 in a single season (1971), she stayed in

Billie Jean King at Wimbledon, 1962.

the top ten for 17 years and was inducted into the International Tennis Hall of Fame. King has been a leader in the struggle for increased prestige, television coverage, and prize money for women's tennis and a pioneer on behalf of open tennis, team tennis, the Women's Tennis Association, and the Women's Sports Foundation, which she helped organize. Her victory in a singles match over Bobby Riggs (televised as the "battle of the sexes") in 1973 underscored her role as a feminist symbol.

In 1981, King was forced OUT when Marilyn Barnett brought a palimony suit against her based on their relationship from 1972 to 1976. King, who had been married since 1965, initially denied not only the relationship but also her BISEXUALITY. Then, in a statement broadcast nationally two days later, she admitted to having been involved with Barnett and apologized for her "mistake." The statement and her apology were taken as an affront to lesbians. Later, however, King claimed that by the word "mistake" she was referring to adultery.

The publicity given the suit and King's statement led to increased, largely unfavorable public scrutiny of lesbianism in SPORTS. Fans of women's sports worried about the scandal's effect on commercial sponsorship of women's events. King, in fact, lost lucrative endorsement fees after her public statement. Barnett's suit was dismissed in 1982. King has been a vocal supporter of the GAY GAMES.

✧ Billie Jean King, *Billie Jean* (1982).

✧ Billie Jean King with Cynthia Starr, *We Have Come a Long Way* (1988).

Kinsey Reports

Popular names for *Sexual Behavior in the Human Male* (1948) and *Sexual Behavior in the Human Female* (1953), based on studies directed by Alfred Charles Kinsey (1894–1956), cofounder of the Institute for Sex Research at Indiana University. The reports, among whose revelations was the prevalence of same-sex erotic behavior, sent shock waves through American society. His biographer, Wardell B. Pomeroy, described the controversy that resulted "as one of the most violent and widespread storms since Darwin."

Kinsey, a highly accomplished zoologist, realized while teaching a course on marriage at Indiana University in 1938 that there were almost no reliable data available on human sexual behavior, so he began collecting his own. By the end of 1939, he had completed interviews with hundreds of American men and women across the country.

Sexual Behavior in the Human Male, published almost a decade later, was an exhaustively wide-ranging study of male sexuality, but its findings on same-sex behavior were among the most discussed—and the most inspiring to early activists such as HARRY HAY. Kinsey found that 37 percent of the men interviewed had had at least one same-sex experience to the point of orgasm. About 10 percent were more or less exclusively "homosexual" for at least three years of their lives; 4 percent were judged exclusively "homosexual" their entire lives. The 1953 report found comparable although lower figures for women: respectively, 13 percent (to orgasm), 6 percent, and 2 percent. Among Kinsey's other findings was that the frequency of same-sex behavior appeared to be about the same for the five generations studied.

The Kinsey Reports and the Rockefeller Foundation, which had funded the research, were lambasted by clergymen and conservatives in Congress. Social scientists found fault with some of his selection techniques and other aspects of his methodology. For gay men and lesbians, however, the reports were among the most encouraging books ever published and had effects even Kinsey could not have imagined. In *Another Mother Tongue,* for example, JUDY GRAHN revealed that she learned to masturbate while reading the report.

Subsequent researchers have come up with somewhat lower estimates of the frequency of same-sex behavior, although the "10 percent" statistic, often misinterpreted, has become an established part of folk knowledge of sexuality. Despite criticism, as the largest and most detailed surveys of their kind, the Kinsey Reports have remained an important source of data for sexologists.

Kinsey was also a pioneer in collecting homoerotica, including the PHOTOGRAPHY of GEORGE PLATT LYNES and specially made films on S/M, some starring SAMUEL STEWARD. The Kinsey Institute retains what is probably the world's largest collection of homoerotic art, photographs, and film.

✧ Wardell B. Pomeroy, *Dr. Kinsey and the Institute for Sex Research* (1972).

Klepfisz, Irena

(1941–)

Polish-born U.S. writer, educator, activist. Born a Jew during the Nazi occupation of Poland, Klepfisz lost her father in the Warsaw Ghetto uprising and immigrated with her mother to New York City at the age of eight. She began writing in her teens, earned an M.A. and a Ph.D. from the University of Chicago, and moved back to the East Coast to teach English, Yiddish, and women's studies in New York and Vermont. In 1976, Klepfisz, Elly Bulkin, Jan Clausen, and Rima Shore formed a collective to launch *Conditions,* a feminist and lesbian magazine that Klepfisz edited until 1981. Beginning with *Periods of Stress* (1975), she has also published several books of poetry in addition to essays, a play, and a handbook for Jewish women on the Israeli/Palestinian conflict.

Klepfisz has embraced a Jewish lesbian identity, adding: "And I—to my life's joy—am a poet." Attacking Jewish HOMOPHOBIA as well as gay and lesbian anti-Semitism, she reminds both communities of their similar heritages of oppression and resistance.

Klepfisz also preserves Yiddish culture in her writing, which sometimes intersperses Yiddish passages, a technique influenced by GLORIA ANZALDÚA's strategic multilingualism. In addition, she has fought for recognition of the contributions of women to the Jewish and, specifically, Yiddish cultural traditions.

Some of Klepfisz's most powerful writing is rooted in her experience as a child survivor of the Holocaust. She has compared the fear of oppression that keeps lesbians and gay men closeted to the "death of the spirit" suffered by Jews who "passed" as Gentiles.

✧ Irena Klepfisz, "Forging a Woman's Link in 'di goldene keyt': Some Possibilities for Jewish American Poetry," in *Inversions: Writings by Dykes, Queers, and Lesbians,* edited by Betsy Warland (1991).

✧ Ellen Stone, "Darkness Is the Incubator," *Bridges: A Journal for Jewish Feminists and Our Friends* (vol. 2, no. 1, Spring 1991).

Knudson, R. R. "Zan"

(Ruth Rozanne Knudson; 1932–)

U.S. writer. Born in Washington, D.C., into a large MORMON family, Knudson met MAY SWENSON, who had a similar background, in 1967 while teaching at Purdue University, where Swenson was visiting poet-in-residence. Knudson resigned her position at the end of the year and moved with Swenson to New York. The two women lived together in and near the city until Swenson's death in 1989.

Beginning with *Zanballer* (1972), Knudson has written nearly a dozen novels for young adults often featuring her alter ego, a vigorously athletic heroine named Zan who successfully competes in SPORTS ranging from football to weight training. Although not explicitly lesbian, Zan and many of Knudson's other female characters wage war on confiningly "feminine" GENDER roles, assailing and conquering traditionally male arenas of achievement. In *Zanbanger* (1977), for example, Zan goes to court to win a slot on a boys' team. And, unlike many other characters in fiction for young women, Zan triumphs by making spectacular athletic gains rather than "winning" the boyfriend of her dreams.

"Playing sport," writes Knudson, "is like singing with your body." Her anthology, *Sports Poetry* (1971), further celebrates the similarities between sport and poetry, citing both as playful, ritualistic skills that confront reality by seeming to provide a diversion from it.

Knudson is the author of almost 40 books of prose and poetry, including biographies of BABE DIDRIKSON and MARTINA NAVRATILOVA and, with Franco Columbu (a former Mr. Olympia), *Starbodies* (1978), the first weight training manual for women. She has managed Swenson's literary estate since the poet's death, publishing three additional collections of her poetry, and the first of a two-volume biography, *The Wonderful Pen of May Swenson* (1993).

- Pat Griffin, "R. R. Knudson's Sport Fiction: A Feminist Critique," *Arete* (vol 3, no. 1, 1985).

Kopay, David

(1942–)

First major league U.S. athlete to come OUT. The second of four children, Kopay was born into a strict Roman Catholic family in Chicago. He moved with his family to North Hollywood, California, where he attended high school and played football at a nearby Claretian Order junior seminary. From 1964 through 1972, Kopay was a running back for the San Francisco Forty-Niners, Detroit Lions, Washington Redskins, New Orleans Saints, and Green Bay Packers. He continued playing in spite of suffering from Osgood-Schlatter's disease, a chronic knee inflammation.

Kopay came out in a *Washington Star* article that was part of a series on homosexuals in SPORTS. The editor of the *Star* had decided to assign a reporter to investigate the subject after seeing an ADVOCATE query seeking information on gay athletes. After the first article, which included an anonymous interview with Washington Redskins tight end Jerry Smith (see **8/26/1986**), appeared in December 1975, Kopay contacted the *Star* and agreed to be featured in the series. Kopay has written of the impact of his announcement on his life, his family, and others in his best-selling autobiography. The response from other gay people was one of deep gratitude: in letters and in person, hundreds of gay men and lesbians expressed their appreciation that someone in a classically masculine American sport was brave enough to challenge the stereotypes and offer a role model for other gay athletes. His courage probably cost him the coaching future he had hoped for.

- David Kopay and Perry Deane Young, *The David Kopay Story* (1977).
- Eric Marcus, *Making History: The Struggle for Gay and Lesbian Equal Rights, 1945–1990* (1992).

Korea

No laws against same-sex relations in either North or South Korea. Developed social scene and small-scale rights organizations in Seoul and other large South Korean cities.

BARS, BATHHOUSES, and well-known CRUISING areas have been a feature of gay male life in large South Korean cities since the 1970s, but the conservatism of Korean society stood in the way of the development of political organizations—and social facilities for lesbians—until the mid-1990s. South Koreans celebrated their first gay and lesbian PRIDE CELEBRATION in 1994. The government of North Korea, like most other Communist nations, has been hostile to both traditional and modern manifestations of homosexuality.

History

The pre-Buddhist Korean religion mandated CROSS-DRESSING for male shamans (*paksoo*) and, even more commonly, female shamans (*mootang*). Also probably rooted in shamanism were the *hwarang,* beautiful young men who entertained at court until about A.D. 350, when they were transformed into an elite MILITARY corps in which PEDERASTY was thought to flourish.

BUDDHISM and Confucianism, both imported from CHINA, profoundly influenced Korean attitudes toward homosexuality. Buddhism stressed moderation but tended to be relatively tolerant of most forms of sensual pleasure. Sex between men and between women was rumored to be common in Buddhist RELIGIOUS ORDERS. Confucianism, with its emphasis on maintaining an established social order, viewed same-sex relations among men as a threat to the family. Confucianists tended to ignore them among women, convinced that women were so securely bound to their households for survival that love between them could never jeopardize the social structure. Synthesizing Buddhist and Confucian beliefs, Koreans have traditionally been tolerant of same-sex relations as long as they were discreet and did not interfere with marriage and procreation.

In many ways, intolerance has actually increased in the 20th century with the advent of puritanical Marxism in North Korea and the AIDS epidemic in the South. Since the 1980s, South Korean police and health authorities have monitored and tested sex workers for HIV infection, and there are signs that Korean popular culture grew much more negative toward same-sex relations as they became equated in the media with AIDS infection.

Kowalski, Sharon, (1955–), and Thompson, Karen (1955–)

U.S. disabled rights activists, physical education instructors. Reagan Republicans, closeted from their families and at the schools where they studied and taught, Kowalski and Thompson exchanged rings in 1979 and happily shared a home together in St. Cloud, Minnesota, until November 13, 1983. On that day, a drunk driver smashed into a car Kowalski was driving, leaving her four-year-old niece dead and herself a quadriplegic with a brain stem injury so severe that it was years before she could communicate effectively with those around her.

Thompson was constantly at her lover's bedside until Kowalski's father, Donald, named legal guardian, barred her from visiting, despite pleas from the hospital staff that his daughter seemed to make better progress when Thompson was in attendance. An extended, costly legal battle ensued, over the course of which Kowalski was removed to a remote part of the state. The lovers were prevented from seeing each other for over three years.

Thompson gave speeches across the United States to build support for her cause and to raise money to pay more than $225,000 in legal fees. Advocates for the disabled joined with gay and lesbian movement leaders to organize "Free Sharon Kowalski" days, and Thompson, backed by the Minnesota chapter of the AMER-

Finally reunited, Sharon Kowalski (left) and Karen Thompson attend a Gay Pride Rally in 1994.

ICAN CIVIL LIBERTIES UNION, fought on. Finally, after the elder Kowalski's death and over eight years after the accident, Thompson was named Kowalski's legal guardian in **December, 1991**. The ruling was hailed as a major victory by activists for the disabled. In addition, the decision, in which the district court judge stated that "Thompson and Sharon are a family of affinity, which ought to be accorded respect," was the first time in U.S. legal history that an openly gay or lesbian petitioner had been named her or his lover's guardian.

After the ruling, Thompson and Kowalski were reunited in a wheelchair-accessible home Thompson had built while they were separated.

➤ Also see DISABLED LESBIANS AND GAY MEN.

✧ Nan D. Hunter, "Sexual Dissent and the Family: The Sharon Kowalski Case," in *Sex Wars: Sexual Dissent and Political Culture,* edited by Lisa Duggan and Nan D. Hunter (1995).

Krafft-Ebing, Richard von, Baron

(1840–1902)

German neurologist. Born in Mannheim and educated in Prague, Krafft-Ebing was already one of the most respected professors of psychiatry in Europe when he published his study of "sexual psychopathy," *Psychopathia Sexualis,* in **1886**. Although originally intended for a specialized medical readership, it was probably the most widely cited account of sexual "perversion" until the KINSEY REPORTS.

Krafft-Ebing had become interested in the subject of same-sex eroticism from reading KARL HEINRICH ULRICHS in the mid-1860s. Krafft-Ebing collected hundreds of medical and court reports for his book, but his interpretations were little more than a synthesis of theories developed by other 19th-century doctors. He believed that some people were hereditarily "tainted" at birth and thus especially susceptible to "moral degeneracy." More often than not, this took the form of masturbation, which in turn evolved into "masochism" (a term he coined), "sadism" and "exhibitionism" (terms he popularized), and/or different types of "contrary sexual feeling" (usually, but not always, same-sex desire).

Influenced by MAGNUS HIRSCHFELD (whose petition to decriminalize SODOMY he signed), Krafft-Ebing retracted his degeneracy theory in **1901**. By this time, however, educated people all over the world believed it was a fact of modern science that homosexuality was a kind of mental illness. Krafft-Ebing himself attempted to "cure" homosexuality with hypnotherapy, leaving his male patients with the posthypnotic suggestion that they envision women while having sex.

Most of Krafft-Ebing's case studies focused on effeminate men. The 1901 edition of *Psychopathia Sexualis* claimed that there were only 50 "known" cases of lesbianism in the world.

✧ Jeffrey Weeks, " 'The Medical Model,' " in *Coming Out: Homosexual Politics in Britain from the Nineteenth Century to the Present* (rev. ed., 1990).

Kramer, Larry

(1935–)

U.S. writer, AIDS activist. Born into a prosperous Connecticut family, Kramer attended Yale University and later went to work in the entertainment industry. He scripted and produced the 1970 film adaptation of *Women in Love* and wrote the screenplay for the CAMP movie musical remake of *Lost Horizon* (1973) before publishing *Faggots* (1978), a scathing satire of the sexual and social excesses of gay GHETTO life. One of the most widely read—and most savagely criticized—gay novels of all time, *Faggots* outraged many gay men, including several of Kramer's closest friends, who felt they had been unjustly parodied in the novel. Kramer responded by defending *Faggots* as an attack on the "cowardice" of successful gay men who insisted on living sybaritic lives within the ghetto rather than emerging to become "role models for the rest of us" and to make "our contribution to society."

Larry Kramer.

As Ian Young has pointed out in *The Stonewall Experiment: A Gay Psychohistory* (1995), *Faggots* was "Kramer's warning to gay men that 'We're fucking ourselves to death.' " Just a few years later, Kramer's words proved tragically prophetic as increasing numbers of gay men began succumbing to what was later named AIDS. In response, Kramer invited a number of his friends and acquaintances to his apartment on **January 12, 1982**, and, with Nathan Fain, Dr. Lawrence Mass, Paul Popham, EDMUND WHITE, and others, founded Gay Men's Health Crisis (GMHC). Differences with other members led Kramer to resign from GMHC a year later, but he remained America's best-known AIDS activist. His critically acclaimed, semiautobiographical play *The Normal Heart* (1985) captured the contentions and frustrations of the first years of the epidemic. On **March 14, 1987**, he and 300 other activists founded the AIDS Coalition to Unleash Power (ACT UP), which in turn inspired a return to the DIRECT ACTION strategies of the early days of GAY LIBERATION. Kramer's *Reports from the Holocaust: The Making of an AIDS Activist* (1989) recapped his activist career. His 1992 play, *The Destiny of Me,* a sequel to *The Normal Heart* in part inspired by his testing HIV-positive in 1988, also expressed a matured vision of his own experience of homosexuality.

Often called the "angriest gay man in the world," Kramer is as famous for exasperating other activists as he is for his verbal assaults on government leaders and agencies. Some observers, however, believe he has mellowed somewhat since 1992, when he and a former heartthrob, architect David Webster (upon whom Kramer had based one of the unsympathetically portrayed characters in *Faggots*), met again and became lovers.

Kuda, Marie [Jayne]

(1939–)

U.S. activist, writer, critic, publisher, educator. A lifelong Chicagoan, Kuda lived at boarding schools after her parents' divorce and was on her own by her late teens. She earned a B.A. in English and attended law school for two years before settling on a career centered on her major passions, LITERATURE and history.

Kuda, who says she "knew from day one I was gay," had the common experience of turning to the library for information on homosexuality. Finding almost nothing, her response was not so common. She began her own extensive library and slide collection and became a leading chronicler of lesbian and gay life, particularly as it has unfolded in the Midwest. She has presented more than 20 different slide shows, ranging from "Cross-Dressing in the Military, 1600–Forward" to "From the Fire to the Flood: Chicago Gay and Lesbian History," to audiences across the country, organized the first Lesbian Writers Conferences (1974–1978), founded Womanpress (1974), and published *Women Loving Women: A Select and Annotated Bibliography of Women Loving Women in Literature* (1975). She was also the first openly lesbian reviewer for *Booklist* and has been a regular columnist for gay and lesbian publications in Chicago.

Marie Kuda, 1980.

Kuda was an early member of MATTACHINE Midwest and has been one of the most visible openly lesbian members of the local Democratic Party. For her accomplishments, which include serving as a liaison between police and the lesbian/gay communities, she was awarded the Pearl Hart Memorial Plaque and inducted into the City of Chicago Gay and Lesbian Hall of Fame in 1992.

Kuda's lover, Shirley Rissmann, is a weight lifter and advertising production manager.

✧ Tina Carus, "Kuda: Preserving Lesbian and Gay History," *Outlines* (June 27, 1987).

Kushner, Tony

(1956–)

U.S. playwright. Kushner grew up in a liberal Jewish family in the Louisiana bayou town of Lake Charles. After years of resisting his sexuality, "hating being gay," as he has written, he had "happy sex" for the first time with a man at the age of 21. After studying medieval LITERATURE at Columbia University, he adapted French and Yiddish plays and had his own theatrical works produced by regional THEATERS around the U.S. before achieving worldwide renown with his monumental two-part, seven-hour epic *Angels in America: A Gay Fantasia on National Themes.* Successful productions in San Francisco, London, and other cities preceded the premiere of its Pulitzer Prize–winning first part, *Millennium*

A scene from the Broadway production of Tony Kushner's Angels in America.

Approaches, on Broadway in 1992, and its second part, *Perestroika,* in 1993. Both parts won Tony Awards for Best Play.

True to the Webster's definition of a fantasia as "a work in which the author's fancy roves unrestricted," *Angels* was revolutionary not only because of its multifaceted gay content and its unflinching depiction of the ravages of AIDS, but also because it wove these themes—and others ranging from MORMONS and JUDAISM to the MCCARTHY ERA and the fall of communism—into what drama critic John M. Clum calls "the most comprehensive dramatic commentary on the moral, sexual, and spiritual state of America during and since the Reagan revolution."

Widely hailed as the most promising gay American playwright of his generation, Kushner has also explored gay- and lesbian-related themes in other works, including *Slavs: Thinking About the Longstanding Problems of Virtue and Happiness* (1994), which features a pair of highly contrasted lesbian lovers, and *A Dybbuk, or Between Two Worlds* (1995).

✧ John M. Clum, "Dramatic Literature: Contemporary Drama," in *The Gay and Lesbian Literary Heritage,* edited by Claude J. Summers (1995).

✧ Tony Kushner, *Thinking About the Longstanding Problems of Virtue and Happiness: Essays, a Play, Two Poems and a Prayer* (1995).

Kuzmin, Mikhail Alekseyevich

(1872–1936)

Russian writer, composer. Born into an upper-class family in Yaroslav, Kuzmin moved to St. Petersburg in 1885 to complete his education. After studying music under Nikolai Rimsky-Korsakov, he traveled in his twenties to Egypt and ITALY, and returned to St. Petersburg armed with themes for many of his later poems. In the early 1900s, he was part of a star-studded set of intellectuals and became as famous for his singing performances at bohemian gathering spots like the notorious Stray Dog Cabaret as for his poetry and novels. His essay "On Beautiful Clarity" (1910) was considered a manifesto of the Acmeist movement.

Kuzmin's novella, *Wings* (*Krylya*), serialized in 1906 and published in book form the following year, is generally considered RUSSIA's first "gay novel." It tells the story of a boy named Vanya and his conflicted attraction to Shtrup, a sophisticated older man. More than simply a "coming out" tale, however, *Wings* was an extraordinary development in modern gay and lesbian LITERATURE in that its characters viewed same-sex love as a natural phenomenon sanctioned by the prestigious Greek and Roman traditions. The main conflict of the novel is not whether or not Vanya will accept his homosexuality—his acceptance is virtually a given—but rather his struggle to reconcile his passion with his knowledge of Shtrup's carnal transgressions with lusty servants. Vanya's love takes "wings" when he learns to accept the profane as well as the sublime aspects of same-sex passion. The novel also provides fascinating glimpses of the Turkish BATHS and salons in which men in large cities like St. Petersburg and Rome made contact with one another.

Wings was a *succès de scandale,* making Kuzmin probably the first Russian celebrity to come OUT. His sexuality was so widely known that even poems such as his celebrated "Alexandrian Songs," many of which describe a woman's passion for a man, were considered homoerotic. His love affairs, including one with a handsome young dragoon, Vsevolod Knyazaev, have provided material for researchers trying to "construct" the homosexuality of his time. Knyazaev wrote poetry to

Kuzmin and traveled with him, but then fell passionately in love with Olga Glebova-Sudeikina, one of the most famous actresses of the day (whose husband was also a lover of Kuzmin's for a time). Eventually rejected by the actress and on understandably strained terms with Kuzmin, the young man committed suicide in 1913. Later that year, Kuzmin met Yuri Yurkun, an 18-year-old Lithuanian-born writer, and the two men lived together for the remainder of Kuzmin's life.

Kuzmin continued to write prose and poetry and to compose music after the revolutions of 1917. Generally apolitical, Kuzmin was cautiously supportive of the new Communist regime and never openly opposed it. But, as one publishing house and magazine after another were closed by the Bolsheviks, Kuzmin found himself barred from participation in the intellectual life of the new Soviet state and endured years of cold and deprivation. In the 1920s, he eked out a living with translations and by working in Leningrad theaters. He gave his last public poetry reading in 1928, an event contemporaries recalled as the final "gay event" in Communist Russia. His audience was wildly enthusiastic and reportedly showered him with roses. The next year he published one of his masterpieces, "The Trout Breaks the Ice," a cycle of 12 poems in part inspired by his tragic affair with Knyazaev. His health deteriorating, Kuzmin managed to sell his papers to the State Literary Museum in 1933 for the then enormous sum of 25,000 rubles. He died of pneumonia in 1936, two years before his lover Yurkun was arrested and shot in one of Stalin's purges of intellectuals.

Soviet as well as émigré critics long tended to dismiss Kuzmin's contribution to 20th-century Russian literature, reducing him to a footnote in the lives of more enduring figures such as Anna Akhmatova and Aleksandr Blok. It was not until the 1970s that interest in his life and work was revived by scholars in the West.

The first officially registered gay and lesbian organization in Russia was called Krylya (Wings), after his novella. In 1994, his works were published for the first time in Russia, and his countrymen began to read of his contribution to gay and lesbian consciousness as well as his influence on other Russian writers.

✧ Mikhail Alekseyevich Kuzmin, *Wings: Prose and Poetry,* edited and translated by Neil Granoien and Michael Green (1972).

✧ Simon Karlinsky, "Russia's Gay Literature and Culture: The Impact of the October Revolution," in *Hidden from History: Reclaiming the Gay and Lesbian Past,* edited by Martin Bauml Duberman, Martha Vicinus, and George Chauncey Jr. (1989).

Labrys

(Sometimes incorrectly spelled "labyris")

Lesbian symbol: a double-headed ax said to have been used by AMAZONS and also associated with the Greek goddess Artemis, the androgynous huntress whom (as Artemis of Ephesus) Amazons were thought to worship. "Labrys" was borrowed into Greek from a language spoken in Asia Minor, the homeland of Amazons, according to most ancient historians. Often used as a motif in jewelry, the labrys has been a symbol of lesbianism since the early 1970s.

The labrys, shown here as part of Tee Corinne's cover for Margaret Cruikshank's pioneering anthology The Lesbian Path (1981).

Ladder, The

The first U.S. magazine for lesbians, published by the DAUGHTERS OF BILITIS (DOB) from 1956 through 1970, then independently until 1972. DOB began publishing *The Ladder* in San Francisco monthly in October 1956, about a year after the organization was founded. The title was meant to suggest the pursuit of a higher position in society on the part of individual lesbians as well as the lesbian community as a whole. Initially mimeographed in a magazine format, *The Ladder* contained book reviews, original literature, news items ("Cross-Currents"), research reports, political commentary, articles, and letters, all written in an informal style.

The first editor of *The Ladder* was PHYLLIS LYON using the PSEUDONYM Ann Ferguson. The fourth issue, replete with black border, announced that Ann Ferguson had "died." Lyon, who had previously written an article entitled "Your Name Is Safe!" to reassure potential

subscribers, revealed that she had not been using her real name but henceforth would. Other long-term editors included DEL MARTIN, Helen Sanders, BARBARA GITTINGS, and Gene Damon (BARBARA GRIER). Hundreds of women worked on the publication as volunteers.

From March 1964 to August 1968, *The Ladder* was subtitled "A Lesbian Review." It expanded to 48 pages and became a bimonthly with the October/November 1968 issue.

Like other HOMOPHILE publications, *The Ladder* sought to educate its readers about social, literary, legal, and political developments affecting their lives as gay people while providing connections and a sense of community for lesbians around the country. Although it played a central role in the operation of the national organization of DOB, each issue contained the following statement: "*The Ladder* is regarded as a sounding board for various points of view on the homophile and related subjects and does not necessarily reflect the opinion of the organization." Letters and other submissions in fact advanced an extremely wide variety of viewpoints.

Nevertheless, by the early 1970s the feminist political stance of then current editor Gene Damon (Grier) and National DOB President Rita Laporte caused considerable dissension among the DOB leadership. The DOB national board's attempt to reclaim the publication at its July 1970 convention was frustrated, however, when Damon and Laporte failed to appear—and took the organization's subscription and membership lists to Reno, Nevada. Lacking the funds for an interstate legal battle and reminded of the difficulties ONE, INC. had faced in a similar situation, the DOB board decided it had no choice but to dissolve its national structure and release the local chapters. Grier edited and published *The Ladder* as an independent publication until its final, August/September 1972 issue, which was 56 pages long.

Popular interest in the publication remains strong. Rich in theoretical and social foresight, *The Ladder* provided its readers with reflective essays on everything from gay MARRIAGE and gays in the MILITARY to income tax inequities. Subscriptions had reached only 3,800 by the close of publication in 1972, but readership was much larger since most subscribers passed the publication on to other women. Many contributors became familiar in later PUBLISHING efforts, including—besides Lyon, Martin, and Grier—RITA MAE BROWN, JANE RULE, Martha Shelley, and MARION ZIMMER BRADLEY.

A complete reprint of the magazine was published by Arno Press in 1975. Three anthologies from Diana Press capture a cross section of the extensive material printed in *The Ladder.*

- ✧ Phyllis Lyon and Del Martin, *Lesbian/Woman* (1972).
- ✧ *The Lavender Herring: Lesbian Essays from The Ladder,* edited by Barbara Grier and Colette Reid (1976).
- ✧ *The Lesbian's Home Journal: Stories from The Ladder,* edited by Barbara Grier and Colette Reid, with illustrations by Ellen Vogel (1976).
- ✧ *Lesbian Lives: Biographies of Women from The Ladder,* edited by Barbara Grier and Colette Reid (1976).

Ladies of Llangollen, see LLANGOLLEN, LADIES OF.

Lambda λ

Symbol of the gay and lesbian movement; sometimes, especially in the names of organizations and publications, a shorthand term for gay/lesbian/bisexual/queer. The GAY ACTIVISTS ALLIANCE (GAA), acting on the suggestion of graphic artist Tom Doerr, was the first to use the lowercase version of the eleventh letter of the Greek alphabet as a gay emblem. According to GAA literature printed in the summer of 1970, the lambda symbolized "a complete exchange of energy" in chemistry and physics and signified "a commitment among men and women to achieve and defend their human rights as homosexual citizens."

Although the lambda is most commonly used by scientists to mean "wavelength," GAA activists saw it as a symbol of change or kinetic potential. Others have suggested it had connotations of justice among the ancient Greeks or that it simply stands for *l* as in liberation.

GAA used the lambda on its literature, banners, and posters and sold buttons, T-shirts, and Frisbees with the emblem. It later became a popular motif for jewelry. In December 1974, the first International Gay Rights Congress, held in Edinburgh, Scotland, adopted it as the official emblem of the worldwide movement.

Lambda Legal Defense and Education Fund (LLDEF) (Originally, Lambda Legal Defense Fund)

U.S. gay and lesbian legal and political advocacy group founded in 1972, the oldest and largest national organization of its kind. Founded "to advance the rights of gay people and to educate the public at large about discrimination against gay men and lesbians," LLDEF's establishment was in itself a legal victory: A lower court had refused to charter it as a "legal assistance corporation" on the grounds that it was "neither benevolent nor charitable." The group's founders, who included attorney (and later judge) William Thom, won on appeal and incorporated in New York State in October 1973.

LLDEF litigates test cases across the U.S., monitors and researches legal issues, and conducts a wide variety of educational programs. It has assisted gay and lesbian MILITARY service personnel since the mid-1970s, helped overturn more than a dozen state SODOMY laws, and been a leader in civil rights advocacy for people with HIV and/or AIDS.

LLDEF has grown from an entirely volunteer organization to one professionally staffed in three offices (New York, Los Angeles, and Chicago). It retains a volunteer network of more than 400 legal experts across the country who work with its on-staff attorneys. LLDEF also often works with groups like the AMERICAN CIVIL LIBERTIES UNION, the American Public Health Association, the National Conference of Black Lawyers, and the NATIONAL ORGANIZATION FOR WOMEN.

LLDEF was in the news in 1995 and 1996 for its participation in the fight against Colorado's Amendment 2, a voter initiative that forbade state or local governments from prohibiting discrimination against lesbians, gay men, or bisexuals. The U.S. Supreme Court ruled that the initiative was unconstitutional on **May 20, 1996**.

Lambda Literary Awards, see AWARDS.

lang, k. d.

(Kathy Dawn Lang; 1962–)

Canadian pop singer. Born and raised in rural Alberta, lang changed the spelling of her name and moved to Nashville to build a career in country MUSIC in the mid-1980s. Finding both the country format and the country music business too constricting, lang left Nashville to develop a jazz-influenced singing style that proved appealing to a wide audience, including a large lesbian following.

Lang had come OUT to friends and family as a teenager but avoided public discussions of her sexuality out of consideration for her mother, who remained in lang's hometown. In a **June 16, 1992**, cover story in THE ADVOCATE, lang talked about her sexual preference and its relevance—and irrelevance—to her career as a singer. Lang's public affirmation of her sexuality was widely reported as a sign of the American public's increased awareness and acceptance of lesbians.

✧ Victoria Starr, *k. d. lang: All You Get Is Me* (1994).

Larkin, Joan

(née Joan Moffitt; 1939–)

U.S. writer, anthologist. A Boston native, she started writing as a child, studied at Swarthmore College, and earned an M.A. in English from the University of Arizona. After two marriages—and a brief affair with a woman in between—Larkin joined the emerging lesbian feminist literary movement in the early 1970s, forming a writing group with six other poets, including Jan Clausen and IRENA KLEPFISZ, and cofounding Out & Out Books in 1975. That same year, she published a book of poems, *Housework,* and with Elly Bulkin coedited a groundbreaking anthology of lesbian poets, *Amazon Poetry.* She has since published a second collection, *A Long Sound* (1986), and coedited two other landmark anthologies, *Lesbian Poetry* (1981, also with Bulkin) and *Gay and Lesbian Poetry in Our Time* (1988, with Carl Morse). The latter anthology, the first of its kind in the U.S., won a Lambda Literary AWARD in 1989.

Whether writing about the sexual havoc of her youth, her daughter Kate, her alcoholism, or "How the Healing Takes Place" (*A Long Sound*), Larkin makes brutal honesty poetic. "Watch out!" she writes, "fresh pain / is all over this woman" ("Warning"), yet she also knows how to make her readers laugh, as in the almost ribald " 'Vagina' Sonnet." Over the years, she has sharpened her confessional voice until, as Carll Tucker wrote in the *Village Voice,* "her best poems cut like broken glass."

In *A Long Sound,* Larkin marshaled what critic MARILYN HACKER has called the "gained power" of considering her lesbianism a given to confront ADDICTION AND RECOVERY as unflinchingly as other poets take on less stigmatized taboos, like sex and sexuality.

Larkin has also written a play, *The AIDS Passion* (1996).

- ✧ Elly Bulkin, "Poetry and Recovery: An Interview with Joan Larkin," *Ikon* (2d series, vol. 8, 1987–1988).
- ✧ Cynthia Wertheimer, "Joan Larkin," in *Contemporary Lesbian Writers of the United States,* edited by Sandra Pollock and Denise Knight (1993).

Latin America

Sex between men illegal in Chile, Ecuador, and Guyana, with penalties ranging from 8 months' to 10 years' imprisonment or even life imprisonment (in Guyana for "buggery"). Anal intercourse illegal in Nicaragua, with a penalty of up to 8 years' imprisonment, or, for persons who work with young people, up to 20 years' imprisonment. Laws against public, "scandalous homosexuality" or against public "disorder" used in many countries by local police forces to discourage lesbians and gay men from openly expressing their sexuality.

No laws against same-sex relations between consenting adults in private in Belize, Bolivia, Colombia, Costa Rica, El Salvador, French Guiana, Guatemala, Honduras, Panama, Paraguay, Peru, Suriname, Uruguay, and Venezuela. Social and political organizations in Colombia, Costa Rica, Uruguay, and Venezuela. Informal groups in Chile, Ecuador, Peru, and Suriname.

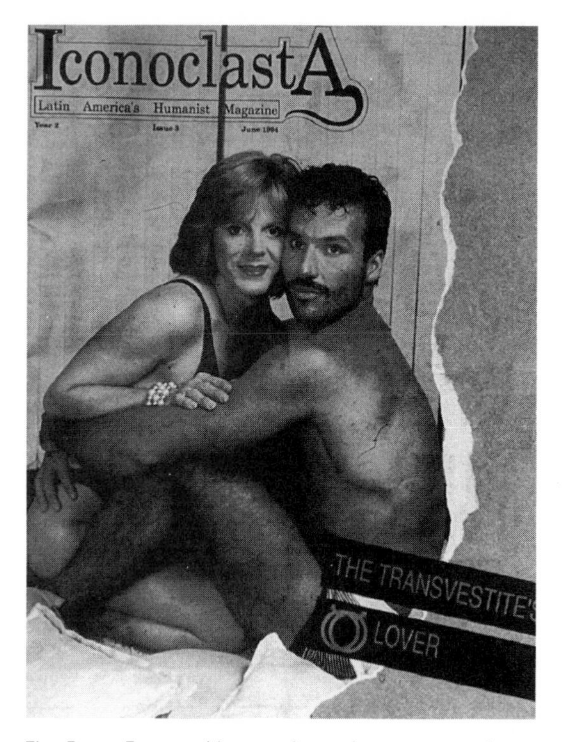

The Costa Rican publication Iconoclasta is part of a growing lesbian and gay rights movement in Latin America.

Contemporary gay and lesbian subcultures have emerged in sophisticated urban areas throughout Latin America, but many (perhaps most) Latin Americans who have same-sex intercourse and even same-sex relationships do not think of themselves as "gay" or "lesbian" in the international sense of these words. In much of the region, sex between "straight"-identified men is considered common and acceptable, especially as a form of sexual release when female sex partners are not easily available (see CIRCUMSTANTIAL HOMOSEXUALITY)—although men known to play the receptive role in anal intercourse risk being stigmatized as "effeminate" *maricones.* Ancient NATIVE AMERICAN conceptions of GENDER and sexuality have also survived in some areas, where "third-gender" BERDACHES remain an accepted and often respected part of community life. The result is that a variety of "constructions" of sexuality (see CONSTRUCTIONISM VS. ESSENTIALISM) flourish simultaneously in Latin America, often in the same locality. Throughout the region, however, the influence of the ROMAN CATHOLIC CHURCH, allied with traditions of *machismo* and *marianismo* (the belief that the Virgin Mary is the ideal role model for women), has complicated and, in some areas, blocked the development of a lesbian and gay rights movement.

Celebrated bisexual, lesbian, or gay Latin Americans include writers REINALDO ARENAS, SOR JUANA INÉS DE LA CRUZ, Sara Levi-Calderón, Sylvia Molloy, MANUEL PUIG, Cristina Peri Rossi, and LUIS ZAPATA.

History

Attitudes toward sexuality among the many peoples who inhabited what is now called Latin America before the arrival of Europeans were probably at least as varied as they are among inhabitants of the region today. The Moche people of present-day Peru, for example, celebrated both same-sex and different-sex eroticism in their highly refined pottery (see **c. 200 B.C.**). The Aztecs and Incas, on the other hand, instituted COMPULSORY HETEROSEXUALITY for all adults and mandated torture and the death penalty for same-sex intercourse (see **1425**; **c. 1475**). Some peoples—including the Mayans and, confusingly, the Aztecs—had rich traditions of homoerotic myths which suggest that ritual homosexuality may have been part of their religious practices.

Reconstructing premodern Latin American sexualities has proved difficult for historians, partly because so much of pre-Columbian culture was destroyed or distorted by European conquerors, but also because the accounts of indigenous sexual practices that have survived—mostly written by military chroniclers and missionaries—are suspect. Ruthless conquistadores like Hernando Cortés claimed that the Aztecs were "all sodomites" and thus not to be pitied. A contemporary, the Spanish Dominican missionary Bartolomé de las Casas, accused him and the other conquistadores of deliberately slandering indigenous peoples to justify enslaving them. Las Casas asserted that same-sex eroticism was virtually unknown among many peoples of the region. A compromise, class-based position arose in accounts of Vasco Núñez de Balboa's massacre of CROSS-DRESSING males on **October 5, 1513**, two days before he "discovered" the Pacific Ocean. Balboa's chroniclers believed that the 40 "sodomites" he fed to his dogs were all native aristocrats. The "innocent" common people, they claimed, abhorred SODOMY so much that they handed over others known to indulge in this "stinking abomination" for Balboa to punish.

During the colonial period, indigenous customs, Roman Catholic teachings, and uniquely Iberian attitudes toward gender and sexuality tended to merge, giving rise to the seemingly uniform but actually complex sense of sexuality apparent in Latin America today. Women led increasingly circumscribed lives that made it difficult for them to form intimate relationships with one another. When they did, as in most other regions of the world at the time, they were largely ignored. Since such relationships did not produce offspring who might lay claim to a family's property and since women, no matter whom they loved, remained under the control of fathers and husbands, they posed no danger to society.

Same-sex relations were decriminalized in the first half of the 19th century throughout most of the region under the influence of the Napoleonic Code (see **1810**). By the turn of the 20th century, most large Latin American cities appear to have had districts where cross-dressed male prostitutes were readily available. Latin American intellectuals, influenced by European medical and psychological writings, began to write about effeminate homosexuality as a pathological condition, and, also around 1900, to decry what they saw as the increasing masculinization of women, particularly those few who were able to support themselves independently of their families. Despite these signs—which some historians believe signal the beginning of gay and lesbian SUBCULTURES—gay- and lesbian-identified activists surfaced in Latin American capitals only after the GAY LIBERATION era had begun in North America and Europe.

Since the 1970s, Latin American lesbians and gay men, especially those living in urban centers, have increasingly allied themselves with others around the world, but increasing awareness of modern gay and lesbian identities has paradoxically led to greater oppression in several countries. In Peru, police have staged violent raids on lesbian BARS (see **October 30, 1986**), and in 1993, President Alberto Fujimori had 117 high-level officials fired on grounds of suspected homosexuality. Paramilitary groups have killed hundreds of transvestites in Colombia. And in Nicaragua, same-sex relations—and the "promotion" of homosexuality—were actually criminalized for the first time in **June 1992**.

➤ Also see ARGENTINA; BRAZIL; CARIBBEAN, THE; CUBA; HAITI; MEXICO.

✧ *Latin American Male Homosexualities,* edited by Stephen O. Murray (1995).

✧ *Unspoken Rules: Sexual Orientation and Women's Human Rights,* edited by Rachel Rosenbloom (1996).

Latinos and Latinas

Also Chicanos/Chicanas, Mexican-Americans, Puerto Ricans, Cuban-Americans, etc. Racially, ethnically, and economically diverse, gay men and lesbians of Hispanic descent nonetheless share a cultural heritage that reflects the influence of the ROMAN CATHOLIC CHURCH and traditional Iberian attitudes toward GENDER roles and sexuality. In addition, many Hispanic-American lesbians and gay men have been deeply influenced by aspects of NATIVE AMERICAN and AFRICAN-AMERICAN traditions.

Since STONEWALL, lesbian and gay Latinos in the United States have mobilized a number of groups to seek greater visibility and to battle racism within both the gay and lesbian communities and society at large. Lesbianas Unidas, founded in Los Angeles in 1980, was the first Latina lesbian organization in the United States. LLEGO (National Latino/a Lesbian and Gay Association, formed in 1987) publishes a newsletter and sponsors national con-

ferences for Latino lesbian and gay activists. It has also been active in the fight against AIDS.

➤ Also see CARIBBEAN; CUBA; LATIN AMERICA; MEXICO.

- ✧ Oliva M. Espin, "Issues of Identity in the Psychology of Latina Lesbians," in *Psychological Perspectives on Lesbian and Gay Male Experiences,* edited by Linda D. Garnets and Douglas C. Kimmel (1993).
- ✧ *Latin American Male Homosexualities,* edited by Stephen O. Murray (1995).
- ✧ Stephen O. Murray, "Mexican-American Homosexuality," in *American Gay* (1996).

Latvia, see EASTERN EUROPE.

Lavender Menace

Term originally used in the late 1960s by NATIONAL ORGANIZATION FOR WOMEN (NOW) founder and first president Betty Friedan to characterize the threat she believed lesbians posed to the credibility of the women's movement. Later, the name of a 1970 RADICALESBIANS/GAY LIBERATION FRONT Women of New York protest action that marked the public debut of LESBIAN FEMINISM.

The rebirth of U.S. feminism in the late 1960s provided the backdrop for both "lavender menace" controversies. As the women's movement gained momentum in some quarters, it was derided elsewhere as a collection of eccentric "bra-burners" and disgruntled "man-haters." Struggling to be taken seriously, Friedan and other movement leaders feared that feminism would be discredited if it were publicly associated with lesbianism. Besides discussing the "lavender menace" among themselves—in public they preferred "lavender herring," since the word "menace" had both racist ("yellow menace") and McCarthyite ("red menace") associations—NOW leaders took steps to distance themselves from lesbians; for example, they omitted the DAUGHTERS OF BILITIS from a list of sponsors in the

Rita Mae Brown (at right) confronts fellow feminists at the Lavender Menace action.

press release announcing the First Congress to Unite Women.

On Friday, **May 1, 1970**, the recently formed Radicalesbians dramatically brought the issue of HOMOPHOBIA in the women's movement to the attention of the 300 women gathered for the Second Congress to Unite Women in New York. When the lights dimmed for a panel discussion, 17 women in lavender T-shirts with "Lavender Menace" stenciled in red leaped onto the stage from the light control booth. Meanwhile in the audience, another 30 "Menaces" unfurled posters with slogans that included: "The Women's Liberation Movement Is a Lesbian Plot —The Lavender Menace" and "Put More Fish in the Sea —The Lavender Herrings." Following the action, conference attendees agreed to discuss the issue of lesbianism in the women's movement in workshops and group sessions held throughout the weekend. The Radicalesbians also distributed their landmark position paper, "WOMAN-IDENTIFIED WOMAN."

As part of the Lavender Menace protest action, the following resolutions were presented to the general planning meeting of the Second Congress to Unite Women. They were later adopted by the Final Assembly.

(1) Be it resolved that Women's Liberation is a lesbian plot.
(2) Resolved that whenever the label lesbian is used against the movement collectively or against women individually, it is to be affirmed, not denied.
(3) In all discussions of birth control, homosexuality must be included as a legitimate method of contraception.
(4) All sex education curricula must include lesbianism as a valid, legitimate form of sexual expression and love.

✧ Donn Teal, *The Gay Militants: How Gay Liberation Began in America, 1969–1971* (1971).

✧ Sidney Abbott and Barbara Love, *Sappho Was a Right-On Woman* (1972).

✧ Alice Echols, *Daring to Be Bad: Radical Feminism in America, 1967–1975* (1989).

Law

Defined as the rules and binding practices that govern the behavior and relationships of individuals in society, law affects virtually every aspect of everyone's life, but its impact has been especially conspicuous in the lives of gay men and lesbians. Some scholars believe that gay and lesbian identities are in large part constructed according to—or in opposition to—a culture's laws. Even at the end of the 20th century, when a majority of the world's population lives in countries where same-sex intercourse between consenting adults has been decriminalized (or was never illegal), laws continue to shape gay and lesbian lives more perceptibly than those of straight-identified individuals. Since no country yet recognizes same-sex MARRIAGE as the exact legal equivalent of heterosexual marriage, lesbian and gay relationships, if they are recognized at all, are subject to different and usually more complex interpretations of laws related to everything from adoption and inheritance to death. A gay male couple in Hempstead, New York, discovered this firsthand in the 1990s, when the town refused their plan to be buried in the same cemetery plot until LAMBDA LEGAL DEFENSE AND EDUCATION FUND lobbied on their behalf. Even celibate lesbians and gay men find themselves treated differently under the law, as in the U.S. MILITARY, where the open expression of a lesbian or gay identity renders service personnel liable to involuntary discharge.

Though complicated and frequently vexatious, the effect of laws related to sexual identities is not always negative. As legal scholar Carl F. Stychin points out, "the law is an arena which demands and warrants social struggle, for despite the frequent failures of the past, it can prove to be (sometimes unintentionally) one mechanism for social/sexual change."

The Criminalization of Same-Sex Eroticism

Throughout history, social taboos and religious beliefs have played at least as important a role as law codes in regulating sexual behavior. Although a host of laws touched on same-sex eroticism, few societies before comparatively modern times regulated it per se. Law codes in premodern CHINA, for example, contained no mention of same-sex eroticism except where it was relevant to the regulation of prostitution (see **c. 1115**). In ancient GREECE and ROME, legislators were almost exclusively concerned with deterring adult males from sexually penetrating freeborn boys (see **594 B.C.**) or, if a citizen, from being sexually penetrated, especially by a slave or a foreign male (see **346 B.C.**; **A.D. 342**). Other forms of sex were left unregulated, although—as in the case of a woman actively seeking sex with another—some instances of same-sex eroticism seem to have incurred harsh condemnations from moralists (see, for example, **c. 120**) despite the fact that they were not illegal.

The legal status of same-sex eroticism in the lands around the Mediterranean changed dramatically toward the end of the Roman Empire. Influenced by Jewish moral teachings (see **c. 450 B.C.**) as well as by the aversion of early CHRISTIANITY toward all forms of eroticism (see **314**) and, in particular, its antipathy to extramarital sex, legislators enacted increasingly harsh edicts that punished at least some instances of sex between men (see **390**; **438**). Similar laws continued in effect in the Byzantine Empire and in the Iberian kingdom of the Visigoths (see **c. 650**). Throughout most of the Mediterranean world, however, the Christian Church and, increasingly, ISLAM, took responsibility for the regulation of sexual behavior. However, surviving records suggest that same-sex eroticism was widely tolerated in the ARAB WORLD and went mostly unpunished among Christians (see, for example, **1051**).

It was not until the 13th century (see **c. 1250**; **1256**; **1260**) that governments in many parts of Western Europe first assumed responsibility for the regulation of sexual behavior. Civil courts, as opposed to church bodies, began to try cases involving same-sex acts and to subject same-sex offenders to increasingly harsh punishments. The first documented sentence of capital punishment for a man convicted of SODOMY was delivered in present-day BELGIUM on **September 28, 1292**. Documents survive to indicate that at least 500 men were executed in Europe and its colonies for the crime over the next five centuries. The actual number of those punished may have been much larger.

In sharp contrast to premodern Europe, many cultures in AFRICA, Asia, and the Americas (see BERDACHE), as well as on the PACIFIC ISLANDS, sanctioned, reverenced, or, in some cases, actually required same-sex relationships (see CIRCUMSTANTIAL HOMOSEXUALITY). Still, as Hindu (see **c. 185 B.C.**), Aztec (see **1425**), Inca (see **c. 1475**), and even Chinese (see **1740**) prohibitions show, intolerance of same-sex eroticism was not exclusively a Western phenomenon.

The Regulation of Lesbianism

Perhaps because so many of the first scholars to study the history of sexuality lived in GER-

MANY or the UNITED KINGDOM, countries in which same-sex eroticism between women was not criminalized, there developed what historian Louis Crompton has called "the myth of lesbian impunity," the idea that sex between women has been traditionally discounted or ignored by (mostly male) legislators and jurists. This in fact happened in the now infamous Woods and Pirie libel suit (see **1812**), in which British jurists found it inconceivable that two middle-class Scottish schoolmistresses could engage in "improper and criminal conduct" with each other. Outside Britain, however, women were not so fortunate. Sex between women was against the law in FRANCE (see **1260**), Aztec MEXICO (see **1425**), BRAZIL (see **1646**), parts of ITALY, colonial America (see **3/1/1656**), the Holy Roman Empire (see **1532**), and elsewhere. Cases of women punished, even executed, for same-sex offenses have been documented in countries that include the NETHERLANDS, SWITZERLAND (see **1568**), and colonial America (see **12/5/1642**; **3/6/1649**).

In numerous other cases, women were arrested and tried for PASSING as men, often after they had married another woman. Researchers have uncovered 119 criminal trials of passing women in the Netherlands alone, and analysis of the sentences given show that those women who had a relationship with another woman were more severely punished than single passing women. All over Western Europe, jurists were particularly affronted by women found guilty of penetrating another with a dildo or, allegedly, an "unnaturally" enlarged clitoris.

In North America, sex acts between women were criminalized in every state before **January 1962** and, between 1954 and **May 15, 1969**, in CANADA as well.

Being vs. Doing: The Outlawing of Gay and Lesbian Identities

Until the end of the 19th century, laws related to sexuality were almost exclusively concerned with outward manifestations of sexual desire. When deemed criminal, same-sex relations were thought of as similar to murder or theft in that they were acts anyone might conceivably commit. Also similar to most other crimes, the mere desire to have same-sex relations was not usually considered punishable if that desire remained unexpressed. Historians of sexuality note a subtle but important distinction between premodern terms like "sodomite" and "tribade" (see **c. 160**; **c. 1600**) and more recent coinages such as "HOMOSEXUAL." The older terms referred to persons known or thought to perform certain acts, while "homosexual" can be applied to someone who merely desires another of his or her own sex—even when he or she is unconscious of this desire (e.g., "latent homosexual"). With the development of modern PSYCHOLOGY and a full-blown concept of "sexuality" in the second half of the 19th century, medical and legal authorities began to concern themselves with the "condition" of homosexuality. The result was that for probably the first time, large numbers of men and women were discriminated against and even prosecuted simply for *being*—or seeming to be—homosexual, whether or not they ever acted on their alleged desires. Examples of legislation and court decisions based on sexuality rather than sex acts include U.S. military discrimination against lesbians and gay men, regulations barring gay men and lesbians from certain professions, and rulings denying lesbians and gay men custody of their children.

The Homosexual Panic Defense

Roughly during the same period that medical and legal authorities began to conceive of homosexuality as a "condition" rather than a behavior, Sigmund Freud and other psychologists came to believe that people were born with a generalized sexuality that became specific and object-oriented in the course of childhood development. This idea gave rise to a notion of latent, or hidden, homosexuality that might manifest itself in unexpected ways even in persons who considered themselves completely heterosexual. Around 1920, Dr. Edward J. Kempf, a U.S. government psychiatrist, coined the term "homosexual panic" to describe the severe anxiety attacks he observed in some men and women when they were forced to live in close quarters with persons of their own sex for an extended period of time. Kempf believed this panic resulted from "the pressure of uncontrollable perverse sexual cravings" stimulated by proximity to members of one's own sex. Within a few years, lawyers began to use Kempf's writings to support a strategy that came to be known as the "homosexual panic defense" to defend clients accused of beating or even killing homosexuals. In its purest form, this defense held that the accused suffered a bout of temporary insanity brought on by being made suddenly aware of his or her own latent homosexuality. The defense was especially effective if it could be proved that the homosexual had made sexual advances. Still occasionally attempted, the homosexual panic defense has received greater scrutiny as a result of the rise of gay and lesbian activism.

➤ Also see entries on individual countries and regions; AGE OF CONSENT; AMERICAN CIVIL LIBERTIES UNION; AMNESTY INTERNATIONAL; CHILDREN; DOMESTIC PARTNERSHIP; GAY AND LESBIAN RIGHTS MOVEMENT, U.S.; IMMIGRATION; INQUISITION, THE; LAW ENFORCEMENT, LESBIANS AND GAY MEN IN; MCCARTHY ERA; NAZI PERSECUTION; PRISON; SAME-SEX UNIONS.

✧ *Lesbians, Gay Men and the Law,* edited by William B. Rubenstein (1993).

✧ Carl F. Stychin, *Law's Desire: Sexuality and the Limits of Justice* (1995).

Law Enforcement, Lesbians and Gay Men in TV

On a recent episode of a popular TV crime series, one police officer casually recommends meetings of GOAL (Gay Officers Action League) to another who thinks she is a lesbian—a far cry from the hot weekend night in June 1969 when police officers made a routine raid on a gay bar called the Stonewall Inn in New York City's Greenwich Village. As the existence of GOAL's chapters attest, some police departments, primarily in urban areas, have made positive inroads into the long tradition of hostility between the police force and the gay and lesbian community. However, even these scattered improvements have come slowly.

Like their MILITARY model, most police departments discourage appointment of openly gay or lesbian officers and harass or remove them if they come out on the job. Since many states retain laws prohibiting SODOMY between consenting adults, homosexuals can be construed as criminals and disqualified. Changes have been forced by individual states' repeal of that legislation, enactment of municipal ordinances or executive orders outlawing discrimination in employment based on sexual orientation, community activism, and even the passage of the federal HATE CRIMES STATISTICS ACT, requiring annual reportage of antigay HATE CRIME. Community meetings, sensitivity dialogues with the police, recruitment campaigns for gay and lesbian officers, openly gay community liaison officers, and revisions of the personality tests and interviews based on stereotyped gender behavior have followed in cities where these changes have occurred.

The experiences of gay and lesbian police officers have only recently been the subject of research. Although they indicate that, as Pedro Velazquez, onetime president of New York City GOAL, has said, "Gay officers share the same concerns as heterosexuals when it comes to law enforcement," the same cannot be said of their working environment.

With the high stakes of disclosure, the gay or lesbian officer soon trades any thrill of "dual identity" for the strain of secrecy in the close quarters of police life. In his research, sociologist and former police lieutenant Stephen Leinen heard stories of an officer finding out, after years of work together, that his (or her) partner was gay (or even a pair of officers discovering both of them were). Leinen discovered these closeted cops often sought more dangerous street work instead of office work rotations to enhance their reputations and credentials as "good cops" and reduce apprehension about coming OUT or being found out. But even top honors in police work can be no comfort, as Los Angeles Police Department Officer Mitchell Grobeson found out. After three and a half years of harassment, in the midst of a robbery, his back-up unit simply didn't show up. The entire watch on duty disregarded the cardinal rule of police work: "Back up your fellow officer."

The police "family" is a complex social dynamic of closely bonded individuals with a culture of rules, internal structures, and communications whose dangerous work and suspicious demeanor isolate them from society. Advancement and even survival requires the officer to be a member in loyal standing for vital group supports. For most gay and lesbian officers this becomes the second "family" they hide from, calling for the ultimate discretion on and off the job.

Gay and lesbian officers also can feel personal tension with the moral charge and pow-

ers given them to define "acceptable" behavior and punish offenders. Both leaders and followers in the police hierarchy share a belief system to justify their actions and preserve a conservative moral order—one that, predictably, excludes homosexuality. Gay cops have been part of raids on gay meeting places.

The transsexual officer presents an additional challenge to gendered social order, particularly if the officer undergoes the sex change while remaining active on the force. One male-to-female transsexual, Lieutenant Janet Aiello of the Hoboken, New Jersey, police force, shares the belief that some people with doubts about their sexual identity are drawn to law enforcement as a façade. A support group formed in July 1994 in Tampa, Florida, Transgendered Officers Protect and Serve, counts several hundred members (although many are transvestites), including some firefighters and soldiers.

Gay Officers Action League (GOAL)
Following Charlie Cochrane's dramatic coming out to support a municipal gay rights ordinance in 1981 at New York City Council hearings, NYPD officers Cochrane and Sam Ciccone founded GOAL in April 1982. Today there are chapters and organizations with a similar structure across the U.S., as well as affiliates in London and Amsterdam. Although a sizable percentage of GOAL members are not out on the job, the organization provides support and contributes to helping officers survive within the force.

✧ Stephen Leinen, *Gay Cops* (1993).

✧ George Chauncey, *Gay New York: Gender, Urban Culture, and the Making of the Gay Male World, 1890–1940* (1994).

✧ Gerry Albarelli, "Interview with a Gay Cop," *Global City Review* (no. 5, Spring 1995).

Leather, see S/M.

Leather Menace

Term coined by anthropologist and activist Gayle Rubin (echoing LAVENDER MENACE) to refer to what she considered an unreasonable fear of and antipathy toward the sexual subcultures of leather and S/M. Part of the lesbian SEX WARS, Rubin's writings and public statements advanced the view that prejudice against these sexual minorities was a form of sexual witch-hunting evolved out of traditional British and American erotophobia. She asserted that anti-S/M activists played into the hands of homophobes and constituted a dangerously divisive force within the lesbian and gay community.

✧ Gayle Rubin, "The Leather Menace: Comments on Politics and S/M," in *Coming to Power,* edited by Samois (1981).

Leavitt, David
(1961–)

U.S. writer. Leavitt grew up in Palo Alto, California, and attended Yale University. In May 1982, a year before he graduated, he published a gay-themed short story, "Territory," in *The New Yorker,* which was later included in his first, critically acclaimed collection, *Family Dancing* (1984). He continued to explore gay themes in the context of middle-class family life in two novels, *The Lost Language of Cranes* (1986; filmed for U.K. TELEVISION in 1992) and *Equal Affections* (1989), that established him as one of the best-known young American novelists. Critics have praised him for his richly developed female characters.

EDMUND WHITE includes Leavitt among writers "who reflect within their work the erotic conservatism of their generation," but his work has at times been controversial. Stephen Spender brought suit against Leavitt for allegedly deriving the plot of *While England Sleeps* (1993), a novel about an English writer and his relationship with a lower-class man, from Spender's memoir *World Within World* (1951). One notable difference between the two was Leavitt's more graphic treatment of sex.

Leavitt also coedited *The Penguin Book of Gay Short Stories* (1993).

Leduc, Violette
(1907–1972)

French writer. An illegitimate, unattractive child, Leduc grew up with a keen sense of shame, once telling her mother: "I was born the bearer of your misfortune." In 1926, she moved to Paris, where she lived, eventually supporting herself as a freelance journalist, until WORLD WAR II. During the war, she returned to her native Normandy and ran a lucrative black-market business, for which she was later arrested and briefly jailed.

Back in Paris, Leduc resumed her exploration of what she ironically called "the paradise of impossible love": a series of obsessive and unrequited infatuations for both men, many of whom were gay, and women, mostly straight. Over her lifetime, they included the gay writer Maurice Sachs, who helped launch her writing career; a husband, Gabriel Mercier, whom she divorced after he returned from military service; Simone de Beauvoir, who alternately supported and tormented her, championing her work but rejecting her advances and humiliating her in public; and JEAN GENET.

Beginning with her first novel, *L'Asphyxie* (1946; English translation: *In the Prison of Her Skin,* 1970), she made her unhappy life the subject of her fiction. *L'Affamée* ("Starved," 1948), for example, recounts her infatuation with de Beauvoir. With *La Bâtarde* (1964; English translation, 1965), her most acclaimed and popular book, she abandoned the pretense of fiction, subtitling it and three subsequent volumes "An Autobiography." A section of an earlier novel (*Ravages,* 1955) detailing lesbian affairs at Leduc's boarding school was at first censored and then published in 1966 as *Thérèse et Isabelle* (English translation, 1967) and adapted to the screen in 1968.

Lesbian and gay critics have reacted ambivalently to Leduc's brilliant but painfully obsessive prose, but many have praised her lyrical candor and celebration of the female body. Scholar Elaine Marks, who views her as an existentialist bridge between the first French-language lesbian writers (such as RENÉE VIVIEN) and 1970s LESBIAN FEMINISM, concludes: "Violette Leduc is indeed the first French writer to take us beyond the SAPPHO model to Sappho's own texts—the lesbian writer writing as lesbian." JANE RULE described Leduc's writing as "the most exact, sensual, emotional, and psy-

Essy Persson and Anne Gael in a scene from the film adaptation of Violette Leduc's Thérèse et Isabelle (1968).

chological record there is of a woman defined and diminished by her sexuality."

✧ Jane Rule, *Lesbian Images* (1975).

✧ Elaine Marks, "Lesbian Intertextuality," in *Homosexualities and French Literature: Cultural Contexts/Critical Texts,* edited by George Stambolian and Elaine Marks (1979).

Lee, Vernon

(pseudonym of Violet Paget; 1856–1935)

French-born English aesthetic theorist, essayist, fiction writer. The daughter of wealthy, educated parents who fostered her interest in the arts, she traveled extensively as a child, learning several languages and completing her first book, *Les Aventures d'une Pièce de Monnaie* ("Adventures of a Coin"), which profiled the owners of a coin from the time of HADRIAN to her own, at the age of 14. Shortly after, she assumed a male PSEUDONYM, maintaining: "No one reads a woman's writing on art or history or aesthetics with anything but unmitigated contempt." She also began wearing men's clothing.

As "Vernon Lee," she published *Studies of the Eighteenth Century in Italy* (1880) and other essays that established her as one of the few women connected with the 19th-century aesthetic movement. She wrote more than 40 books, ranging from trend-setting works on aesthetic theory (*Beauty and Ugliness, and Other Studies in Psychological Aesthetics,* 1912, which brought the German concept of *einfühlung,* or "empathy," into English critical discourse) to equally influential travel writing (*Genius Loci: Notes on Places,* 1899). She also wrote a controversial plea for pacificism, *Satan the Waster* (1920), and a study on the effects of music, *Music and Its Lovers* (1932), which she worked on for more than 25 years, going almost completely deaf before it was published.

Lee was associated with famous male aesthetes like Walter Pater and OSCAR WILDE, but her most important relationships were with women. She had ROMANTIC FRIENDSHIPS with Annie Meyer and writer Mary Robinson before finding what she called "a new love and a new life" in her "Venus," Kit (Clementina) Anstruther-Thomson. Lee paid tribute to their ten-year (1887–1897) relationship, a highly productive time for Lee, by posthumously publishing Anstruther-Thomson's essays, *Art and Man* (1924).

According to her friend ETHEL SMYTH, Lee's personal tragedy was her refusal to acknowledge her lesbian desires. Lee felt obligated to "create a fiction," Smyth wrote, "that these [romantic] friends were merely intellectual necessities." Lee's writings were almost never overtly lesbian, although she did write one play with a cross-dressed heroine (*Ariadne in Mantua,* 1903) and several collections of supernatural, decadence-tinged short fiction (including *Hauntings,* 1890) that have been especially appreciated by gay and lesbian readers.

✧ Peter Gunn, *Vernon Lee: Violet Paget, 1856–1935* (1964).

✧ Phyllis A. Mannocchi, "Vernon Lee and Kit Anstruther-Thomson: A Study of Love and Collaboration Between Romantic Friends," *Women's Studies* (vol. 12, no. 2, 1986).

Lees, Edith, see ELLIS, HAVELOCK.

Le Gallienne, Eva

(1899–1991)

British-born U.S. actress, director, translator, writer. Her father's eccentric belief in an OSCAR WILDE–influenced "New Hedonism" led to an unsettled family life for Eva, her mother, and half sister. Her mother was a Danish journalist who wrote a woman's column under the name "Fru Eva." Le Gallienne later claimed that her mother, who had wanted a boy, named her daughter after her column because she was unable to come up with any other name when a girl was born. For most of her life, she preferred to be known as (Miss) "Le G."

Le G became one of the most popular and critically acclaimed actresses on Broadway beginning in the early 1920s. Over the next 60 years, she acted in or directed almost 150 theatrical productions, besides performing in dozens of FILMS and TELEVISION and radio programs. An idealist, she fought for affordable high-quality THEATER, establishing New York's first repertory group, Civic Repertory Theatre, in 1926. She also taught acting and directing, wrote four books and translated Henrik Ibsen and Hans Christian Andersen. Her many awards included a Tony, an Emmy, and a National Medal of the Arts.

Le G was conscious of her attraction to other women as a child. Although she never denied her lesbianism, she considered it an intensely personal, even embarrassing, subject. One of the most painful episodes in her life came on July 8, 1930, when a *New York Daily News* headline blared, "Bell Divorces Actress Eva Le Gallienne's Shadow." "Shadow," a code word for lesbian lover taken from the play *The Captive* (see **9/29/1926**), referred to actress and socialite Josephine Hutchinson, the wife of Robert Bell, a director, with whom Le G had an extended relationship.

Before and after her lesbianism became a matter of public record, critics accused her, probably unfairly, of being unable to project "feminine" softness or a credible interest in her male costars. Backstage gossips also charged her with favoring other lesbians and "unmasculine" men. Her response, as she advised friend and onetime student MAY SARTON in 1934, was: "The best one can do is be a decent person and realize that lack of understanding always promotes a kind of cruel criticism and censorship. . . . Don't allow that destructive force to spoil something that to you is simple, natural and beautiful."

Besides Hutchinson, her lovers included director Peggy Webster and performers Mercedes de Acosta and Marion "Gun" Evensen.

✧ Robert Schanke, *Shattered Applause: The Lives of Eva Le Gallienne* (1992).

✧ Helen Sheehy, *Eva Le Gallienne* (1996).

Legg, W. Dorr

(William Lambert Dorr Legg; 1905–1994)

U.S. activist, writer, editor, landscape architect. Born in Ann Arbor, Michigan, Legg grew up in a cultured, politically sensitive household and studied piano and landscaping at the University of Michigan.

He had his first relationship with a man during a break from college spent working in Tampa, Florida. After graduating in 1928, Legg moved to New York City, where he was friendly with EVA LE GALLIENNE and Anaïs Nin as well as attendees of HARLEM RENAISSANCE drag balls. Later, after teaching at Oregon State University, he moved to Los Angeles with his lover. There, they met Merton Bird, the AFRICAN-AMERICAN founder and first president of Knights of the Clock (see **6/1950**), a social service group for interracial couples, including gay men and lesbians. Legg was a cofounder and served as secretary/treasurer of the organization. In 1950, he joined the more political MATTACHINE Society and soon became a Guild Member "of the First Order."

On **October 15, 1952**, Legg and six friends, three of whom were also Mattachine members, agreed to begin editing and publishing the country's first openly marketed gay and lesbian periodical under the auspices of ONE, INC. Legg became the first full-time worker for One and probably the first person in the U.S.

to work full-time for a gay or lesbian organization. In 1954, he also arranged for a number of gay men to participate in Dr. EVELYN HOOKER's landmark study.

Following on *One* magazine's success, Legg founded and directed One's Institute for Homophile Studies, which offered an adult education program, a library, ARCHIVES, and, eventually, a graduate school certified by the state of California. The institute also published the *One Institute Quarterly of Homophile Studies* (1958–1968). For Legg, the term "homophile studies" was comprehensive and covered both gay men and lesbians; the field "transcended boundaries through interdisciplinary study and teaching."

Legg authored or edited a number of groundbreaking reference books, including: *Homosexuals Today: A Handbook of Organizations and Publications* (1956, under the PSEUDONYM Marvin Cutler), *Annotated Bibliography of Homosexuality* (1976), and *Homophile Studies in Theory and Practice* (1994). Historian JIM KEPNER called him "one of the towering founding fathers" of the GAY AND LESBIAN RIGHTS MOVEMENT.

His partner of 30 years was John Nojima.

✧ W. Dorr Legg, "Exploring Frontiers: An American Tradition," *New York Folklore* (vol. 19, nos. 1/2, 1993).

Leonardo da Vinci

(1452–1519)

Italian artist, architect, engineer, scientist. The illegitimate son of a peasant girl and a Florentine notary, Leonardo rose from obscurity to become the premier "Renaissance man." In his time, he was also famous for his beauty, physical strength, and personal charm.

As a young man, Leonardo was twice accused (and acquitted) of SODOMY (see **1476**), once with a 17-year-old model/prostitute named Jacopo Saltarelli. He never married, employed handsome young men as assistants, and in his paintings created prototypes of mysteriously beautiful ANDROGYNY that greatly contributed to the development of Western HOMOEROTICISM. Some art historians have even suggested that he made himself the model for his cryptic *Mona Lisa* (c. 1503). For all these reasons, generations of gay men have claimed him as one of their own.

In 1910, Sigmund Freud used a "traumatic" childhood dream recorded in one of Leonardo's notebooks as the starting point of a tortuous essay that sought to explain Leonardo's lack of sexual interest in women as a kind of narcissistic overidentification with his mother. Despite a major mistranslation (a "kite," not a "vulture," had swooped onto the infant Leonardo's mouth—the vulture, in Freud's argument, symbolized forced fellatio), some psychiatrists later attempted to use Freud's "insight" to "treat" homosexuality.

According to James M. Saslow, there is no evidence that Leonardo ever had sex with anyone, male or female. Rather, Leonardo wrote that he was repelled by the very idea of sex—not to mention genitals, which he found "repulsive." Saslow believes that Leonardo's idealized androgynes represent his attempt to sublimate and transcend his conflicting desires.

✧ James M. Saslow, *Ganymede in the Renaissance: Homosexuality in Art and Society* (1986).

Lesbian

Term used to describe: a woman who feels sexual desire exclusively or predominantly for another woman or women; more broadly, objects, places, and abstract concepts identified with such women (e.g., a "lesbian publication," "lesbian café," "lesbian fashion"); still more broadly (see LESBIAN CONTINUUM), a woman whose strongest emotional affinities are for other women.

More than 2,500 years ago, SAPPHO, the first known poet to make love for other women the theme of her writing, put the Aegean island of Lesbos and its inhabitants, the "Lesbians," on the linguistic map by becoming one of the best-loved and most-praised lyric poets of ancient times. At least in part because of the passion of her writing, the ancients liked to believe that the women of Lesbos had unusually strong sex drives for both men and women and were, for some reason, particularly adept at oral sex (one of the Greek verbs for which was *lesbiazein*). As early as **c. 520 B.C.**, however, the poet Anacreon may have used the phrase "girl from Lesbos" to describe a young woman who was more interested in other women than in men (or at least in Anacreon). The more common term for women-loving women in ancient times was "tribade" (from a root meaning "to rub").

Despite the fact that numerous writers had added dramatic heterosexual embellishments to Sappho's life—and, in Christian times, even changed pronoun gender in some translations to suggest male love objects—it was obvious to anyone who could read the original Greek that Sappho was a woman who loved other women. As a result, "sapphist" and "lesbian" vied with "tribade" in European languages for centuries (see **914**; **1732**; **1867**) as a way of describing passion between women and, with the boom in translations and imitations of Sappho's work in the late 19th century, suggested sexual connotations to well-educated Western and Japanese readers by 1900.

Nevertheless, "lesbian" was only one of several terms—such as "Uranian woman" (see KARL HEINRICH ULRICHS), "sexual variant," and "female homosexual"—used by specialists and activists in the 20th century. The mission statement of the DAUGHTERS OF BILITIS, the first lesbian organization in the U.S., for example, addresses "the homosexual" and "the variant" without ever using the word "lesbian."

LISA BEN reports that "gay gal" was the preferred informal term for lesbian in Los Angeles in the late 1940s. The advent of LESBIAN FEMINISM and lesbian SEPARATISM around the time of the STONEWALL Uprising, however, brought a new awareness among lesbians that many people thought only of men when they heard the word "GAY." Although some women actively disliked "lesbian," feeling it made "gay" women sound like cultists, usage of the word became standard in the 1970s and, somewhat later, was fixed in such phrases as "lesbian and gay" and "gay men and lesbians." According to a 1995 ADVOCATE survey, 58 percent of women preferred to be called "lesbian"; 34 percent remained true to "gay" (only 2 percent liked "HOMOSEXUAL").

In contrast to "gay," which is almost always used in contexts that imply at least potential sexuality, "lesbian" has been more inclusively defined by some writers, notably ADRIENNE RICH, as embracing all "women-identified" women. Rich and others have criticized those who view "lesbians" as "female versions of male homosexuality," insisting that the "lesbian experience" is "a profoundly *female* experience, with particular oppressions, meanings and potentialities we cannot comprehend as long as we simply bracket it with other sexually stigmatized existences."

➤ Also see LESBIAN, POLITICAL; QUEER; QUEER THEORY.

✧ Adrienne Rich, "Compulsory Heterosexuality and Lesbian Existence," in *The Lesbian and Gay Studies Reader,* edited by Henry Abelove, Michèle Aina Barale, and David M. Halperin (1993).

Lesbian, Political

Term coined in 1970 to describe a woman-identified woman who calls herself a lesbian out of feminist convictions but does not feel sexual desire for other women. Feminist leader Ti-Grace Atkinson is said to have summarized the concept of political lesbianism at a DAUGHTERS OF BILITIS meeting in June 1970 with the often quoted line: "Feminism is the theory; lesbianism is the practice." (Atkinson later claimed to have said "*a* practice," not "*the* practice.") The concept was further articulated in publications such as *The Furies* (1972–1973).

Since the early 1980s, the concept of political lesbianism has been objected to by activists such as PAT CALIFIA and Gayle Rubin who see it as part of a tendency to downplay the role of sex in lesbian lives. In 1992, Lyndall MacCowan published a critique of political lesbianism in which she charged it with perpetuating "the same old oppression of lesbians on the basis of our sexuality."

➤ Also see FURIES, THE; LESBIAN CONTINUUM; "WOMAN-IDENTIFIED WOMAN."

✧ Lyndall MacCowan, "Recollected History, Renaming Lives: Femme Stigma and the Feminist Seventies and Eighties," in *The Persistent Desire,* edited by Joan Nestle (1992).

Lesbian and Gay Studies

Interdisciplinary scholarship covering a wide range of subjects important to lesbians and gay men, including the history of sexual identities, the development and evolution of a GAY AND LESBIAN RIGHTS MOVEMENT, the formation and analysis of gay and lesbian communities and SUBCULTURES, and the interrelationship of culture and homosexuality.

Although courses in lesbian and gay studies became relatively common in universities in the U.S., Canada, and Western Europe in the last two decades of the 20th century, gay and lesbian scholarship is rooted in the efforts of pioneering researchers, archivists, and writers who for the most part pursued their studies outside academia. Common to many of these pioneers was a belief in what MAGNUS HIRSCHFELD summarized as *"per scientiam ad justitiam,"* or "justice through knowledge." As a result, most of the founders of lesbian and gay studies were, like Hirschfeld, also activists for gay and lesbian rights. Now well established as an academic discipline, lesbian and gay studies as a field has lost some of the passionate militancy that once characterized it. Some writers, including Jeffrey Escoffier, have questioned "whether as an academic discipline it should, or can, exist without structural ties to lesbian and gay political struggles." Others believe that academic respectability makes lesbian and gay studies a potentially powerful agent of change because many more students and academics, straight and gay alike, are today exposed to it than in the past.

Roots and Landmarks

Long before the term "lesbian and gay studies" was coined, individuals like HEINRICH HOESSLI, KARL HEINRICH ULRICHS, JOHN ADDINGTON SYMONDS, and EDWARD CARPENTER began to research the history of same-sex love. Even earlier, an obscure writer in CHINA attempted to document two millenia of what the Chinese called the "love of the cut sleeve" (see **c. 1630**). All these men, living in eras when same-sex love was almost never openly discussed except to condemn it, shared a desire to find historical precedents that would validate their own feelings and prove to society that same-sex love could be a positive phenomenon. Unfortunately, their findings were published in limited editions that, if available at all, were locked in special library collections or, worse—as in the case of Hirschfeld—destroyed (see **5/6/1993**). Until STONEWALL, each generation of lesbians and gay men had to start anew the task of reconstructing a history and a heritage of same-sex love.

More lasting results were achieved after World War II with the efforts of "HOMOPHILE studies" pioneers like DORR LEGG and JIM KEPNER. Legg helped found the ONE Institute in Los Angeles in 1956, the first school to offer graduate level courses and, later, the first to offer an accredited Ph.D. in the subject. Also in the 1950s, JEANNETTE FOSTER published the results of years of research on "sex-variant" women in world LITERATURE.

Despite all these achievements, most of the activists who gave birth to GAY LIBERATION after Stonewall had only the vaguest notions of the history of same-sex love. Although courses in gay studies were instituted at the University of Nebraska as early as 1970, many of the most important lesbian and gay studies projects of this era were achieved by scholars and activists like JONATHAN NED KATZ and VITO RUSSO, working independently—and largely without financial support—outside academia. Meanwhile, a widely varied group of scholars had joined to form the first Gay Academic Union (see **11/23/1973**). And, later in the decade, in the NETHERLANDS, scholars like Gert Hekma and Theo van der Meer helped bring "homostudies" into the Dutch university system.

By the 1980s, a substantial amount of literature relating to lesbian and gay studies had been published, and for the first time the efforts of academic scholars like JOHN BOSWELL, JOHN D'EMILIO, LILLIAN FADERMAN, and Catherine Stimpson were taken seriously. In 1987, Boswell helped found the Lesbian and Gay Studies Center at Yale University. In 1988, the governing board of the City College of San Francisco approved the creation for the fall 1990 semester of the first gay and lesbian studies department in the U.S. Also in the late 1980s, MARTIN DUBERMAN and others began the process of assembling the Center for Lesbian and Gay Studies (CLAGS) at the graduate school of the City University of New York. Formally established in April 1991, CLAGS was the first university research center in the U.S. exclusively dedicated to lesbian and gay studies.

In the 1990s, lesbian and gay studies is a vast and enormously varied field. In addition to the efforts of university-based gay and lesbian scholars, now active in departments ranging from ANTHROPOLOGY and geography to MUSIC and ZOOLOGY, independent scholars continue to make important contributions to the field. At the local and regional levels, an important trend has been the growth of community history projects, often supported by local gay and lesbian ARCHIVES. Another development of long-range significance has been an increased focus on AFRICAN-AMERICAN and NATIVE AMERICAN gay and lesbian traditions.

➤ Also see CONSTRUCTIONISM VS. ESSENTIALISM; QUEER THEORY.

✧ *Lesbian Studies: Present and Future,* edited by Margaret Cruikshank (1982).

✧ *Gay and Lesbian Studies,* edited by Henry L. Minton (1992).

✧ *The Lesbian and Gay Studies Reader,* edited by Henry Abelove, Michèle Aina Barale, and David M. Halperin (1993).

✧ *Tilting the Tower: Lesbians Teaching Queer Subjects,* edited by Linda Garber (1994).

✧ *Negotiating Lesbian and Gay Subjects,* edited by Monica Dorenkamp and Richard Henke (1994).

Lesbian Avengers

DIRECT ACTION group founded in 1992 to "fight for lesbian survival and visibility." SARAH SCHULMAN, Anne-Christine d'Adesky, Marie Honan, Ann MaGuire, Ana Maria Simo, and Maxine Wolfe met in New York City in the spring of 1992 and agreed on the fundamentals of a direct action group they decided to call "Lesbian Avengers." That June, they handed out bright green cards at the city's annual gay PRIDE CELEBRATION with the headline "We want revenge and we want it now! Lesbians! Dykes! Gay women!"

About 50 Avengers held their first public meeting at the New York City Lesbian and Gay Community Services Center on **July 7, 1992**. Less than a year later, the group was able to rally 20,000 women for a nighttime march on the White House (see **4/24/1993**). Chapters formed across the U.S. and in London in 1994.

The Lesbian Avengers distinguished themselves from other similar organizations as much by their sense of humor as by their formidable communications and organizational skills. With members in some 35 chapters in North America and Europe as of 1996, they were one of the most popular direct action groups in the history of the GAY AND LESBIAN RIGHTS MOVEMENT.

✧ Sarah Schulman, *My American History: Lesbian and Gay Life During the Reagan/Bush Years* (1994).

Lesbian Continuum

Term coined by ADRIENNE RICH in 1979 to denote "a range—through each woman's life and throughout history—of woman-identified experience," independent of whether or not "a woman has had or consciously desired genital sexual experience with another woman." Examples included trading networks formed by women in AFRICA, MARRIAGE resistance in CHINA, as well as EMILY DICKINSON and Zora Neale Hurston, for both of whom "women provided the ongoing fascination and sustenance of life."

Two Lesbian Avengers demonstrate their tender side on a New York City street.

Rich contrasted the lesbian continuum with "lesbian existence," which she later defined as "the traces and knowledge of women who have made their primary erotic and emotional choices for women." Asserting that the very existence of lesbianism had most often been denied, ignored, obscured, or subsumed under the category of male homosexuality, she envisaged the lesbian continuum and a political analysis of COMPULSORY HETEROSEXUALITY as ways of approaching "the complex kind of overview needed to undo the power men everywhere wield over women."

Many lesbian scholars have taken issue with Rich's concept. Philosopher Judith Roof, for example, argues that although it promises "power, knowledge, and a challenge to a patriarchal system, or a way out altogether," it actually accomplishes little more than making definitions of sexual orientation meaningless.

✧ Ann Ferguson, Jacqueline Zita, and Kathryn Pyne Addelson, "On 'Compulsory Heterosexuality' and 'Lesbian Existence,' " *Signs* (vol. 7, no. 1, Autumn 1981).

✧ Judith Roof, *A Lure of Knowledge: Lesbian Sexuality and Theory* (1991).

✧ Adrienne Rich, "Compulsory Heterosexuality and Lesbian Existence," in *The Lesbian and Gay Studies Reader,* edited by Henry Abelove, Michèle Aina Barale, and David M. Halperin (1993).

Lesbian Existence, see LESBIAN CONTINUUM.

Lesbian Feminism

A wide-ranging theory connecting lesbianism and feminism. Beyond committing themselves to goals commonly recognized as shared by both the lesbian and feminist movements—self-determination, support for women by women, and revolt against male-controlled institutions—lesbian feminists assert that COMPULSORY HETEROSEXUALITY is the bulwark of male supremacy and hence a common denominator in the oppression of all women. As the influential theorist CHARLOTTE BUNCH wrote, "*No queers* will ever be free as long as sexism persists because male supremacy is at the root of both gay oppression and HOMOPHOBIA . . . *no females* will ever be free to choose to be anything until we are also free to choose to be lesbians."

Lesbian feminism emerged in 1970 as an increasing number of lesbians came to view themselves as marginalized by both heterosexual-dominated feminist groups (see NATIONAL ORGANIZATION FOR WOMEN) and the male-dominated GAY LIBERATION movement. In response, many lesbians confronted heterosexist feminists with protests such as the LAVENDER MENACE action, and distanced themselves from male-chauvinist gay men to devote themselves to lesbian SEPARATISM. At the same time, both heterosexually and homosexually identified feminists began to publish a body of theoretical writings that fostered diverse strains of "lesbian feminism."

Many lesbian feminists have critiqued what they call "heterosexual privilege," a seemingly beneficial but ultimately restrictive socialization that they view as leading heterosexual women to perpetuate their own oppression. Emphasizing feminism as an imperative for lesbians, SIDNEY ABBOTT and BARBARA LOVE wrote in their influential *Sappho Was a Right-On Woman* (1972): "Living without the approval or support of men, Lesbians desperately need women's rights. For Lesbians, independence and responsibility for self are lifelong realities and not merely interim needs between support by father and support by husband."

Before lesbian feminism, most women con-

sidered "lesbianism" synonymous with female homosexuality—i.e., female-female eroticism. Many lesbian feminists, however, sought to broaden the definition of "lesbian" to encompass a "woman-identified woman" exclusively committed to achieving political, social, economic, and emotional solidarity with other women but not necessarily sexually attracted to them. A 1970 epigram usually attributed to feminist activist Ti-Grace Atkinson concisely summarized this concept: "Feminism is the theory; lesbianism is the practice."

Early lesbian feminist writings included Atkinson's "Lesbianism and Feminism," Anne Koedt's "The Myth of the Vaginal Orgasm," articles by Martha Shelley and Rita Mae Brown, and the most influential of all, the Radicalesbians' "Woman-Identified Woman." The spread of lesbian feminism was also promoted by a number of periodicals, such as *Lesbian Tide* (founded by Jeanne Cordova in Los Angeles in 1971), *Amazon* (Milwaukee, 1971), *Lavender Woman* (Chicago, 1971), *Quest* (Washington, D.C., 1973), *The Furies* (Washington, D.C., 1972), *Lesbian Feminist* (New York City, 1973), and *So's Your Old Lady* (Minneapolis, 1973). Important groups included the Furies (1971) and Lesbian Feminist Liberation (1973).

Later theorists sought to locate lesbian sexual desire and erotic relationships within the larger spectrum of female bonding and the development of self-affirming, women-centered communities. Cheryl Clarke summed up the promise of this political vision in her essay, "Lesbianism: An Act of Resistance" (1981): "If radical lesbian-feminism purports an anti-racist, anti-classist, anti-woman-hating vision of bonding as mutual, reciprocal, as infinitely negotiable, as freedom from antiquated gender prescriptions and Lesbian proscriptions, *then all people struggling to transform the character of relationships in this culture have something to learn from lesbians.*"

Beyond its theoretical, political, and cultural contributions, lesbian feminism has had a major impact on every aspect of the women's movement, ranging from the development of a distinctive feminist linguistics and psychology to the fostering of new social services for women.

➤ Also see BUTCH/FEM(ME); LESBIAN; LESBIAN, POLITICAL; LESBIAN CONTINUUM.

✧ *Women Unite! An Anthology of the Canadian Women's Movement* (1972).

✧ *Lesbianism and Feminism,* edited by Charlotte Bunch and Nancy Myron (1975).

✧ Charlotte Bunch, "Lesbian-Feminist Theory," in *Our Right to Love,* edited by Ginny Vida (1978).

✧ Alice Echols, *Daring to Be Bad: Radical Feminism in America, 1967–1975* (1989).

Lesbian Herstory Archives (Lesbian Herstory Educational Foundation, Inc.)

New York City–based institution founded to protect and preserve lesbian culture. The idea for the Archives grew out of a lesbian consciousness-raising group at the Gay Academic Union in 1973. Determined to end the silence that had submerged and obliterated so much lesbian culture over time, the group conceived of an ARCHIVE "in remembrance of the voices we have lost." The first planning committee, whose members included Sahli Cavallero, Deborah Edel, Karla Jay, JOAN NESTLE, Pam Oline, June Rook, and Julia Penelope Stanley, refined the concept of the Archives as a feminist institution over a series of meetings in 1974 and 1975. As set out in the incorporation papers of the Lesbian Herstory Educational Foundation (1980), the Archives is uniquely inclusive, offering access to and accepting materials from any lesbian, not only the famous or published. Funded and staffed by 24 lesbian coordinators, the Archives is also an integral part of the lesbian community and its political struggles.

The Archives opened to the public in 1974 in Nestle and Edel's Manhattan apartment. In 1993, the foundation purchased and renovated a Brooklyn brownstone to house the growing collection. Today the Archives' 10,000-plus books, periodicals, organizational and subject files, photographs, FILM AND VIDEO footage, and special collections including artifacts, posters, buttons, and other memorabilia, constitute the largest and oldest lesbian archive in the world.

Some of the women who have made contributions to the Archives' success are Suzanne Bernard, Paula Grant, Morgan Gwenwald, MABEL HAMPTON, Valerie Itnyre, Joy Rich, Judith Schwarz, Polly Thistlethwaite, Maxine Wolfe, and Lucinda Zoe.

✧ Joan Nestle, "The Will to Remember: The Lesbian Herstory Archives of New York," *Feminist Review* (Spring 1990).

Lesbian Land

A movement that promotes ownership of rural land by and for lesbians, often in the form of trusts, cooperatives, or not-for-profit entities. Inspired in part by the "back to the land" spirit of the 1960s COUNTERCULTURE and especially by the growth of lesbian SEPARATISM, lesbians began acquiring tracts of land on a large scale in the early 1970s. Most sought to use the land as a base for self-sufficient feminist communities devoted to a variety of philosophies and objectives, including partial or total separatism, pacifism, and environmentalism. Land acquisition was seen as an act of political resistance as well as a declaration of lesbian independence.

As the movement grew, workshops were instituted at women's MUSIC festivals and other venues to inform and connect women interested in lesbian land. The periodical *Lesbian Connection* published a "Lesbian Land Directory," and a specialized publication called *Country Women* reached 10,000 subscribers at its peak.

Lesbian land has been put to a wide range

of uses. Some women experienced the land as a place for spiritual healing, a "safe space" defined with vaginal imagery ("cuntry"). Others envisioned a return to agrarian traditions. Still others set out to create seasonal retreats for recreation and education, refuges for emotionally troubled women, and even sanctuaries for "outlaw dykes." Lesbians also launched more focused projects, such as "Lesbians of Color" lands and Eider, a collective farm for DISABLED lesbians in Utah. Almost all were committed to nurturing alternative families.

The restructured social alliances that emerged on lesbian land have made it a particularly fertile arena of controversy, leading to heated debates on how children should be reared; the place of male children, nonlesbians, and TRANSSEXUALS; and the appropriateness of modern conveniences—in addition to issues related to politics, finances, racism, ageism, ableism, privacy, and drug and alcohol use.

In **February 1994**, attempts by Ovett, Mississippi, locals to drive Brenda and Wanda Henson from their feminist Camp Sister Spirit focused national attention on the lesbian land movement. Despite harassment and threats of violence, the two women persisted in developing their 120-acre property, which offered an educational center and a large food bank.

- Sue, Nelly, Dian, Carol and Billie. *Country Lesbians: The Story of the Womanshare Collective* (1976).
- *Maize: A Lesbian Country Magazine* (since 1983).
- *Lesbian Land,* edited by Joyce Cheney (1985).

Lesbian Separatism, see SEPARATISM.

Lesbian Studies, see LESBIAN AND GAY STUDIES.

Liberace

(Wladziu Valentino Liberace; 1919–1987)

U.S. pianist. Of Italian and Polish ancestry, Liberace began studying music as a child growing up in Wisconsin. Encouraged by Ignace Paderewski, he turned to the piano but abandoned the concert stage to play what he called "*Reader's Digest* versions" of familiar classics in nightclubs (originally as "Walter Busterkeys"). In 1940, he relocated to New York and perfected a performance style that combined bravado showmanship, resplendent fur-trimmed, rhinestone-studded, gold lamé costumes, and CAMP fantasy touches like a blazing gilt candelabrum. All this made him perfect for TELEVISION, and in the 1950s he became one of the medium's most popular stars. He was probably the highest-paid pianist in music history.

Liberace's flamboyant stage manner and low-brow approach to classical music earned him adoration in some quarters, ridicule in others. Asked if he was hurt by the jokes sophisticates made at his expense, he liked to say he "cried all the way to the bank." (Tens of millions of dollars in earnings later, he would quip: "You know that bank I used to cry all the way to? Well, now I *own* it!")

Although Liberace successfully brought suit against two publications that had run stories implying he was gay, many contemporaries considered his popularity proof of the naïveté of the older American women who were his biggest fans. Conversely, others felt that no one so "obvious" could really be gay. Whichever, he and his family continued to assert his heterosexuality in the face of widespread rumors, a 1982 palimony suit brought by his chauffeur, and his death due to AIDS-related complications in 1987.

In *The Gay 100,* Paul Russell ranks Liberace number 66, ahead of ALLEN GINSBERG, contending that "in the heart of the repressive

1950s, he managed to bring *gay* into the living rooms of America without ever committing the indiscretion of mentioning it by name."

✧ Scott Thorson with Alex Thorleifson, *Behind the Candelabra: My Life with Liberace* (1988).

✧ Paul Russell, *The Gay 100: A Ranking of the Most Influential Gay Men and Lesbians, Past and Present* (1995).

Lister, Anne

(1791–1840)

English diarist. Raised in Yorkshire, Lister attended boarding school and traveled to Paris as a young woman. Her masculine looks and unladylike enthusiasms for riding and shooting earned her a reputation as a TOMBOY and the nickname "Gentleman Jack." An heiress, she managed her own estate, Shibden Hall, overseeing everything from the farm to the estate's coal mines.

Lister came to the attention of lesbian and gay historians in the mid-1980s after Helena Whitbread discovered her journals and diaries, dated from 1817 through 1840, in a county archive and deciphered them with a key developed by one of Lister's relatives: Lister had devised a code to disguise her writings after the husband of her lover, Marianna Percy Belcombe, intercepted a letter in which Lister fantasized his premature death and her subsequent happy reunion with Marianna.

Lister's writings describe what she called her "oddity" in vividly erotic detail that contradicts the widespread assumptions that women's 19th-century ROMANTIC FRIENDSHIPS were nongenital and that romantic friends were unaware of their "lesbian" orientation: "I love and only love the fairer sex," wrote Lister,

Anne Lister devised a code that allowed her to describe her erotic life in frank detail in her journals.

"and thus, beloved by them in turn, my heart revolts from any other love than theirs."

In 1832, Lister formed a lasting relationship with an heiress named Anne Walker.

- ✧ *I Know My Own Heart: The Diaries of Anne Lister, 1791–1840,* edited by Helena Whitbread (1988).
- ✧ *No Priest but Love: The Journals of Anne Lister, 1824–1826,* edited by Helena Whitbread (1992).
- ✧ Terry Castle, *The Apparitional Lesbian* (1993).

Literature

Because gay men and lesbians are almost always born into families outside of the lesbian and gay SUBCULTURE, the written word has been one of the most important means of transmitting and preserving the gay and lesbian experience. As a result, "literature" is often defined more broadly in a gay and lesbian context than in culture at large. In addition to the *belles lettres* sense of the word, gay and lesbian literature includes nonliterary accounts, often written in the first person, that evidence the existence of HOMOEROTICISM and same-sex bonding in places and at times when positive, open expressions of homosexuality were impossible.

Same-sex love and homoeroticism have been features of literature from its beginnings, both in the Middle East (see **c. 2500 B.C.**) and in CHINA (see **c. 700 B.C.**). In a few cultures, such as that of ancient GREECE and premodern JAPAN, homoerotic themes were much more common in literature than they are today. Specifically "gay and lesbian" literature, however, did not develop until the last half of the 19th century when writers as varied as EDWARD CARPENTER and RENÉE VIVIEN began to publish works that consciously—and positively—asserted a "variant" sexual identity. Although gay and lesbian characters began to appear with increasing frequency in books written by straight as well as lesbian and gay writers in the 20th century, it was not until the 1950s—and, especially, after STONEWALL—that gay and lesbian novels, short stories, poetry, etc., began to be published in quantity.

➤ Also see specific authors and DETECTIVE FICTION; SCIENCE FICTION.

- ✧ Jeannette H. Foster, *Sex Variant Women in Literature* (1985).
- ✧ *Gay and Lesbian Poetry in Our Time: An Anthology,* edited by Carl Morse and Joan Larkin (1988).
- ✧ Bonnie Zimmerman, *The Safe Sea of Women: Lesbian Fiction, 1969–1989* (1990).
- ✧ *Lesbian Criticism: Literary and Cultural Readings,* edited by Sally Munt (1992).
- ✧ *Gay and Lesbian Literature,* edited by Sharon Malinowski (1994).
- ✧ *The Gay and Lesbian Literary Companion,* edited by Sharon Malinowski and Christa Brelin (1995).
- ✧ *The Gay and Lesbian Literary Heritage: A Reader's Companion to the Writers and Their Works, from Antiquity to the Present,* edited by Claude J. Summers (1995).
- ✧ Byrne R. S. Fone, *A Road to Stonewall: Male Homosexuality and Homophobia in English and American Literature, 1750–1969* (1995).

Llangollen, Ladies of

(Lady Eleanor Butler: 1739–1829; Sarah Ponsonby: 1755–1831)

Irish-born women whose ROMANTIC FRIENDSHIP has stimulated two centuries of commentary and speculation. Butler was born into an aristocratic Catholic family and educated at a convent in FRANCE. She met Ponsonby, an upper-class Dublin Protestant 16 years her junior, when the younger woman came to her hometown of Kilkenny to attend boarding school in the late 1760s. Butler became Ponsonby's mentor and confidante, and the two women continued to correspond after Ponsonby left school.

In 1778, Butler and Ponsonby tried to "elope" together, only to be apprehended on the road. Their families later relented, however, and the two women fled, disguised as men. Accompanied by their faithful servant and erstwhile go-between, Mary "Molly the Bruiser" Caryll, they made their way to Llangollen Vale in Wales, where they bought a cottage they called Plas Newydd (New Place).

For the next five decades, they were the "Ladies of Llangollen," internationally renowned for their studious ways, gardening skills, eccentric dress (men's jackets, women's skirts), and, most of all, their success at living happily together without husbands or family. Distinguished guests thronged their cottage, eager to take a firsthand report to friends back home. William Wordsworth lauded them as "sisters in love." King George III rewarded them with an annual stipend in 1787.

Their eminent respectability has led many historians to assume that their friendship, though romantic, was not overtly sexual. LILLIAN FADERMAN called it a "spiritual love" and speculated that since they "had no sexual duty to a husband . . . they were probably happy to be oblivious to their genitals."

Their contemporaries were not so certain: Hester Thrale, a notorious gossip and diarist, called them "damned sapphists" and wrote that women were afraid to spend the night alone with them. ANNE LISTER, who visited them in 1822 (when Butler was in her 80s) and left a detailed account of her own lesbian sex life, also doubted their love was purely platonic: "I feel the infirmity of our nature & hesitate to pronounce such attachments uncemented by something more tender still than friendship." Some writers have even suggested that passages in Butler's diary such as "My beloved and I spent a delightful evening in the shrubbery" (which Butler wrote in the dead of winter) are playfully veiled records of erotic interaction.

- ✧ Lillian Faderman, *Surpassing the Love of Men: Romantic Friendship and Love Between Women from the Renaissance to the Present* (1981).
- ✧ Emma Donoghue, *Passions Between Women: British Lesbian Culture, 1668–1801* (1993).

Locke, Alain LeRoy

(1886–1954)

U.S. professor, essayist, intellectual mentor of the HARLEM RENAISSANCE. Born into a Philadelphia family that was aristocratic even by the standards of the so-called Talented Tenth (the AFRICAN-AMERICAN elite), Locke graduated magna cum laude from Harvard in 1907 and studied at Oxford as the first black Rhodes scholar. A professor of philosophy at Howard University, he mentored several of the most prominent Harlem Renaissance writers, including COUNTEE CULLEN, LANGSTON HUGHES, Richard Bruce Nugent, and Wallace Thurman. In 1925, he compiled and edited the first major collection of writing from what he called the "New Negro Renaissance," first in magazine form, then as the book *The New Negro.* That same year, he was dismissed from his position at Howard University, in part for his advocacy of a black history curriculum. He was later rehired and became one of the university's most influential faculty members. His articles on black culture were published widely throughout his adult life.

Critical appraisal of Locke revolves around three major themes: his influence on the course of the Harlem Renaissance; his flamboyant personal style and scandalously open interest in handsome young men, including Cullen and Hughes; and his self-acknowledged misogyny. Unlike most other Harlem Renaissance leaders, such as W.E.B. Du Bois and Jessie Fauset, Locke championed urban black culture over agrarian stereotypes and the rarefied aspirations of the Talented Tenth. As a gay intellectual, he introduced Cullen and others to the writings of EDWARD CARPENTER, thus helping to link the lively gay, lesbian, and bisexual black SUBCULTURES of the time with European movements. Little is known about his sex life, except that he appears to have been unsuccessful in his pursuit of Hughes.

✧ Steven Watson, *The Harlem Renaissance: Hub of African-American Culture, 1920–1930* (1995).

Log Cabin Federation

Gay and lesbian political organization of Republicans founded in Los Angeles in 1978. Nine Log Cabin clubs joined together in 1990 to form the national Log Cabin Federation. In 1996, Log Cabin clubs had more than 10,000 members in chapters across the U.S.

Since the Log Cabin Federation is not an official Republican National Committee auxiliary organization, it is free to support only the candidates it chooses. Most commonly, Log Cabin backs fiscal conservatives who support lesbian and gay rights.

The group has lobbied for increased funding of AIDS programs and for antidiscrimination policies in the workplace and the MILITARY. Republican reactions to the group have remained mixed (see **8/26/1995**), despite contributions to Republican candidates totaling over $200,000 in 1994.

The Log Cabin Federation is the most prominent group among the "New Gay Right" that emerged in the 1990s, although gay Republican groups go back at least as far as New York City's Stonewall Republicans, founded in 1972. Other right-leaning groups that draw most of their support from gay men and lesbians include the National Coalition for Understanding, founded by conservative leader Marvin Liebman in 1994.

Lorde, Audre

(Audrey Geraldine Lorde; Zami; Gamba Adisa; 1934–1992)
U.S. poet, essayist, librarian, teacher. Born to immigrant parents from Grenada, she described her early years vividly in her autobiography, *Zami: A New Spelling of My Name* (1982), a book she called a "biomythography" and a "bridge and field" between her early sense of self and her maturing identities as a black woman and lesbian. In her essay "Eye to Eye," she credited her mother with giving her the gift of survival. Married to Edwin Ashley Rollins from 1962 to 1972, she had a son, Jonathan, and a daughter, Elizabeth, while working as a librarian and teaching creative writing and LITERATURE. Later, after a lengthy relationship with Frances Louise Clayton, Lorde moved to St. Croix to join partner Gloria I. Joseph.

The author of 17 books, Lorde explored a revolutionary vision of a liberated yet connected society in her writings. Beginning around 1970, when her poem "Martha" was published as part of her collection *Cables to Rage,* her work advanced a black lesbian feminist perspective, whose contradictions and ten-

Audre Lorde.

sions she captured in the title of her 1984 collection of essays, *Sister Outsider.* Yet Lorde always championed a broader "outsider" identity, speaking for and about all who, as she observed about herself, "cannot be categorized." Believing that "I feel, therefore I can be free" and in the "erotic as power," she worked to cast off what she called the "weight of silence" for everyone from lesbian mothers to immigrants and cancer survivors. By the time of her death after fighting cancer for more than 15 years, she had become one of the most widely read and quoted lesbian writers of her generation.

An activist with a diverse, multinational range of concerns, she helped found the Cross Cultural Initiative of Black Women for Minority Rights and Studies in Germany, Sisterhood in Support of Sisters in South Africa, and Women's Coalition of St. Croix. Lorde was also a founder of Kitchen Table: Women of Color Press. Reportedly, the press was born when Lorde said to Barbara Smith, "You know, Barbara, we have to do something about PUBLISHING."

Lorde received the American Book Award in 1989 for *A Burst of Light,* and *From a Land Where Other People Live* was nominated for a National Book Award. Lorde was also named poet laureate of New York State in 1991 and was featured in *Litany for Survival* (1995), a FILM by Michelle Parkerson and Ada Gay Griffin.

✧ Audre Lorde, *Sister Outsider: Essays and Speeches* (1984).

✧ "Audre Lorde" (special section), *Callaloo* (vol. 14, no. 1, 1991).

Louganis, Greg

(Gregory Efthimios Louganis; 1960–)

U.S. athlete, actor. Of Samoan and northern European ancestry, he was reared in San Diego, the second adopted child of Peter and Frances Louganis. Growing up, he struggled with undiagnosed dyslexia, asthma, depression, an overbearing father, and classmates who called him a sissy for his devotion to gymnastics and dancing. Driven by his father, he turned to diving, and competed in his first Olympics at the age of 16.

Louganis was the best diver in the history of the sport. In 1984, he became the first man in 56 years to win Olympic gold medals in both springboard and platform diving, a feat he repeated four years later. He held 29 national crowns and was the only diver to score straight perfect 10s in international competition.

Long rumored to be gay, he found fellow competitors reluctant to room with him as early as the 1976 Olympics. Like MARTINA NAVRATILOVA, he never received the extremely lucrative endorsement contracts typical of an Olympic athlete of his status.

In 1994, he came OUT at the opening ceremonies of the GAY GAMES, declaring: "As an Olympian and a gay man, I'd like to welcome you to the Gay Games." He came out as a person with AIDS on national television in an interview with Barbara Walters on February 24, 1995. The announcement coincided with a controversial revelation in his just published autobiography: After striking his head on the diving board at the 1988 Olympics in Seoul, he neglected to tell the physician who stitched the cut that he was HIV-positive (Louganis then returned to dive in the final round).

Louganis made his off-Broadway debut in *Jeffrey* (1993) playing an HIV-positive chorus boy. Pursuing a new career as an actor, he told fans that he hoped to inspire other HIV-positive people with the message "that life isn't over yet, that HIV and AIDS is not a death sentence."

✧ Greg Louganis, with Eric Marcus, *Breaking the Surface* (1995).

Love, Barbara

(1937–)

U.S. writer, editor, activist. Born in Montclair, New Jersey, Love was an independent, athletic child who was a member of a world-record-breaking swim relay team. After studying at Purdue and Syracuse University, she moved to New York and took a job as an editorial writer for CBS. Later, as president of Foremost Americans Publishing Company, she edited and published *Foremost Women in Communications,* a reference book on women in broadcasting, PUBLISHING, teaching, and other professions.

Love once described her mission as working to make being a lesbian "ordinary." Her activist career began in the women's movement in 1967 and continued after the STONEWALL Uprising, when she was among the leaders of several of the groups out of which LESBIAN FEMINISM was born. She and SIDNEY ABBOTT, then her lover, coauthored the groundbreaking *Sappho Was a Right-On Woman* (1972). She was also a founder of the feminist group Matriarchists and a member of the board of directors of the NATIONAL GAY AND LESBIAN TASK FORCE.

Love's mother needed time to adjust to her daughter's sexual orientation, but in June 1973, she became the only nonlesbian mother to take part in that year's Gay PRIDE CELEBRATION in New York City, carrying a sign that read "Mothers Support Your Lesbian Daughter." "I was so proud of her," Love later commented, "I knew my mother was taking on my fight, my burden and my pain."

✧ Barbara Love, "The Answer Is Matriarchy," in *Our Right to Love,* edited by Ginny Vidu (1978).

Lover Battery, see DOMESTIC VIOLENCE.

Lowell, Amy

(1874–1925)

U.S. poet. One of the Boston Brahmin Lowells, she began writing seriously after meeting the Italian stage legend Eleanora Duse in 1902. Duse inspired many of Lowell's homoerotic poems, including sonnets and longer poems, but the major love of Lowell's life was the divorced actress Ada Dwyer Russell (1863–1952), whom she tenderly called "Dada" or "Peter" (her "rock"). In 1914, after several years of courting Russell, Lowell finally persuaded her to move in for six months to help with publication projects. Russell stayed until Lowell's death 11 years later, inspiring hundreds of Lowell's most celebrated love poems, including "In Excelsis" and the impassioned 43–poem sequence, "Two Speak Together," in *Pictures of the Floating World* (1919).

Lowell's poetry was published in ten volumes, beginning with *A Dome of Many-Coloured Glass* (1912). In 1913, she discovered poems written by "H.D., Imagiste" and journeyed to England to meet their author. The meeting had a profound effect on both poets' lives: Lowell became the undisputed leader of American Imagism (eclipsing Ezra Pound, who subsequently derided the movement as "Amygisme"), and BRYHER was later irresistibly drawn to H.D. by Lowell's revelation in a book of literary criticism that the mysterious poet was both an American and a woman.

In addition to Imagism—poetry distinguished by sharp-hewn word pictures and the direct rhythms of natural speech—Lowell's literary legacy included her vigorous advocacy of American experimental and free-verse poetic forms. Her contributions were recognized with a posthumous Pulitzer Prize for her last collection, *What's O'Clock* (1925).

Lowell poems were most commonly addressed to a "beloved" from a narrator of unspecified gender. That some readers recognized them as lesbian is proven by a biography published by Clement Wood a year after her death. Wood detailed the "masculine" elements of her poetic voice and castigated her as "an impassioned singer of her own desires," adding that her poems were fit only for women "as stand beside her."

Most critics were less direct during her lifetime, although newspaper reporters delighted in mocking descriptions of her obesity, tailored clothes, gruff manners, cigar smoking, and all-round "abnormality." Lowell was sometimes hurt by these articles, but she also took a kind of pride in her eccentricities. Biographer Jean Gould writes that Lowell once likened her slow unwrapping of a cigar to undressing a lady—and then concluded the simile with a seductive suck.

In poor health most of her life, Lowell died of a stroke at the age of 51. As literary executor, Russell's first charge was to burn much of Lowell's personal correspondence, including love letters Lowell had written her.

✧ Jean Gould, *Amy: The World of Amy Lowell and the Imagist Movement* (1975).

Ludlam, Charles

(1943–1987)

U.S. playwright, director, performer. Ludlam fell in love with THEATER as a child playing with puppets and marionettes. At the age of 17, he founded his first theatrical group near his home in Northport, Long Island. After earning a degree in dramatic literature at Hofstra University, he began performing in off-Broadway plays in New York City. In 1967, he broke with Ronald Tavel and John Vaccaro's Play-House of the Ridiculous to found and mastermind his own Ridiculous Theatrical Company. Wanting, as he later confessed, "to commit an outrage," he braved the city's censorship restrictions by writing, directing, and acting in comedies that combined nudity and CROSS-DRESSING, uninhibited expressions of queer sexualities, and his own CAMP philosophy of the ridiculous, which theater critic Don Shewey has described as "an ability to imbue preposterous material with a total artistic commitment." Productions like *Conquest of the Universe or When Queens Collide* (1967) and *Turds in Hell* (1970) attracted a largely gay following, which continued to be Ludlam's core audience as his company became one of off Broadway's most popular attractions.

As early as 1970, Ludlam and his colleague Bill Vehr won an Obie Award for distinguished achievement off-Broadway for their version of *Bluebeard,* but the play—and the role—that brought Ludlam lasting acclaim was *Camille* (1973). In *Camille,* which also won an Obie Award, Ludlam portrayed the doomed heroine with camp panache, managing to move audiences almost to tears one moment and eliciting a house-rocking wave of laughter the next. Other triumphs included *Galas* (1983), an outrageous parody on the cult of the opera diva, and his most widely performed play, *The Mystery of Irma Vep* (1984), a two-actor, multicharactered panoply of 19th-century

Charles Ludlam (left) with Everett Quinton in a scene from Ludlam's play Salammbo.

"penny dreadful" melodramas. The latter play was developed in collaboration with his long-term lover and colleague, the actor Everett Quinton, who continued the work of the Ridiculous Theatre after Ludlam's death from complications of AIDS.

✧ Andrew Holleran, "New York Notebook: Tragic Drag," *Christopher Street* (no. 113, July 1987).

✧ *Ridiculous Theatre, Scourge of Human Folly: Essays and Opinions of Charles Ludlam,* edited by Steven Samuels (1992).

✧ Gregg Bordowitz, "The AIDS Crisis Is Ridiculous," in *Queer Looks: Perspectives on Lesbian and Gay Film and Video,* edited by Martha Gever, John Greyson, and Pratibha Parmar (1993).

Lutheran Churches

Protestant denomination that arose with the writings and teachings of Martin Luther (1483–1546). Doctrine rather than hierarchy unites the more than 70 million Lutherans around the world, so the level of tolerance of same-sex love varies with different congregations. Martin Luther himself condemned same-sex relations as "contrary to nature." While most Lutheran congregations continue to believe that homosexuality is, in the words of a 1970 Lutheran Church in America position statement, "a departure from the heterosexual structure of God's creation," they have also been among the first Christian groups to oppose legal discrimination and societal oppression against lesbians and gay men (see **7/2/1970**). In 1990, however, two churches in San Francisco were suspended from the Evangelical Lutheran Church in America for ordaining lesbians and gay men. Lutherans

Concerned is an advocacy group for gay and lesbian Lutherans in North America.

Lynes, George Platt
(1907–1955)

U.S. photographer. Born in East Orange, New Jersey, and educated at private schools, Lynes was 18 when he made his first trip to Paris, intent on becoming one of the city's celebrated expatriates. Over the next few years, he became friends with many of the era's most famous writers and artists, including JEAN COCTEAU, GERTRUDE STEIN, the gay artist Pavel Tchelitchew, and CARL VAN VECHTEN. In 1927, he turned to PHOTOGRAPHY after abandoning a career as a publisher of avant-garde texts such as Stein's, and he quickly gained renown for his portraiture and Dada-influenced photos. Back in the U.S. in 1931, he established himself as one of New York's most successful commercial photographers, even though he detested the field, preferring to shoot ballet dancers, portraits of his friends, and, increasingly, male nudes.

George Platt Lynes's Fire Island, c. 1950.

After his lover, George Tichenor, died in WORLD WAR II, Lynes sank into a severe depression. He moved to California for three years, living first in Santa Monica and then the Hollywood Hills. Despite working as *Vogue*'s Hollywood photographer, Lynes accumulated enormous debts and decided to move back to New York in an ultimately unsuccessful attempt to regain financial solvency and reestablish himself as a leading commercial photographer.

In the last decade of his life, Lynes published some of his homoerotic photos in the Danish publication *Eos* and the Swiss HOMOPHILE journal *Der Kreis* (see **1933**) under PSEUDONYMS (Robert Orville, Roberto Rolf, etc.). He also sold some 900 prints and negatives to Alfred Kinsey (see KINSEY REPORTS), who believed they contained insights into male homosexuality. The Kinsey Institute for Sexual Research now holds the largest collection of Lynes's photography—Lynes destroyed his remaining fashion and erotic work shortly before his death.

As Lynes's homoerotic work reached a wider audience, critical reception evolved from seeing his male nudes as tragic depictions of, in Jack Woody's words, "individual isolation, sexual conflict and erotic tension" to an acknowledgment of Lynes's positive influence on later photographers such as ROBERT MAPPLETHORPE. Critiquing a major retrospective of Lynes's work in 1993, Kinsey curator James Crump wrote: "As a determinant of Lynes's mode of vision, the male nudes work adversely to a theory of victimization. That is, the images communicate Lynes's celebration and frankness about his own sexuality."

✧ Jack Woody, *George Platt Lynes: Photographs 1931–1955* (1981).

✧ James Crump, *George Platt Lynes: Photographs from the Kinsey Institute* (1993).

Lyon, Phyllis [Ann]

(1924–)

U.S. activist, writer, sex educator, Universal Life Church minister. Born in Tulsa, Oklahoma, Lyon was raised in the San Francisco area and moved into the city in the 1950s. Since 1953, she has shared her life with DEL MARTIN, with whom she helped raise Martin's daughter.

Her lesbian activism began in 1955 when she, Martin, and six other women founded the DAUGHTERS OF BILITIS (DOB), the first lesbian organization in the United States. Lyon was the first editor of DOB's publication, THE LADDER, from its inception in 1956 until 1960. As editor, she initially used the PSEUDONYM Ann Ferguson. In the interests of promoting lesbian visibility and pride, she "killed" Ferguson in a dramatic announcement in the fourth issue and afterward used her real name, a courageous and daring act for the 1950s.

Following the dissolution of the national structure of DOB in 1970, Lyon became increasingly involved with NATIONAL ORGANIZATION FOR WOMEN activities.

In 1968, Lyon began working with the National Sex Forum. In 1976, she received her doctor of education (originally doctor of arts) in human sexuality from the Institute for Advanced Study of Human Sexuality, an institution she has continued to work with in various capacities. She lectures widely on lesbianism, homosexuality, and women's sexuality.

As a sex educator and an expert on sexuality, Lyon was a leader in the movement to bring sexual behavior into lesbian discourse. Among her contributions is the foreword to PAT CALIFIA's groundbreaking book about lesbian sexuality, *Sapphistry,* in which Lyon alluded to her many years' experience counseling lesbians and other women in heralding the arrival of a comprehensive, sex-positive manual for women.

Lyon has coauthored two books with Martin about lesbian life: *Lesbian/Woman* (which won the AMERICAN LIBRARY ASSOCIATION Gay Book Award in 1972) and *Lesbian Love and Liberation* (1973). Both are considered pioneering works for their accounts of lesbian life and their support of freedom of sexual choice. They also offer unique perspectives on activists, organizations, and social influences, both of the past and of that era.

In recent years, Lyon has been active with the Institute for Study of Human Resources, the Gay and Lesbian Historical Society of Northern California, and the Gay/Lesbian Outreach to Elders Advisory Committee. As a community activist, she has served in leadership positions in groups concerned with issues relating to lesbians and other women, public health, health insurance, LAW ENFORCEMENT, and human rights.

As a couple as well as individually, Lyon and Martin have had a profound influence on the gay/lesbian and feminist movements. Not only has Lyon been a member of almost all the major gay and lesbian organizations, she has been a founder or board member of most of them. As a bridge between the HOMOPHILE movement and post-STONEWALL militancy, she and Martin remind contemporary activists that the moderate accommodationist stance of many early leaders resulted from the religious, legal, and psychological standing of homosexuality in the 1950s and early 1960s, evidenced in military and government purges, the witch-hunts of the MCCARTHY ERA, police raids, and what amounted to a blackout in the American media. Long before the advances of the past decades seemed remotely possible, Lyon and Martin recognized that self-acceptance, support networks, and a sense of community were necessary before further positive changes could take place.

✧ Phyllis Lyon and Del Martin, *Lesbian Love and Liberation* (1973).

✧ Phyllis Lyon and Del Martin, *Lesbian/Woman* (rev. ed., 1991).

M

McCarthy Era

Period, roughly between 1950 and 1954 but with long-lasting consequences, of intensified U.S. government scrutiny and persecution of suspected Communists and "sex perverts." The era's name and associated words like "McCarthyite" and "McCarthyism" are references to U.S. Senator Joseph McCarthy (R-Wis.), whose unethical tactics gave rise to many of the worst excesses of the period. The era is most remembered for widespread persecution of Communists, Communist sympathizers, and people who had joined the Communist Party in their youths. Less well-known is the fact that more people lost their jobs as a result of allegations of homosexuality than because of supposed left-wing sympathies.

Since McCarthyite witch-hunts eventually spread from federal agencies and the MILITARY into state and local government and even into private industry—and since many people were given the option by sympathetic supervisors of resigning before being formally charged with "sexual perversion"—it is difficult to arrive at an accurate estimate of the number of lesbians and gay men affected. A few documented statistics suggest the total was enormous: at least 10,000 men and women received "undesirable" discharges from the military on charges of homosexuality in the first half of the 1950s; more than 600 allegedly lesbian and gay federal employees lost their jobs in the first 18 months of the first Eisenhower administration; between 1947 and mid-1950—the years *before* much more stringent screening procedures were implemented—some 1,700 people were denied jobs in federal government based on suspicions of homosexuality. The effect of the often hysterical publicity given "sexual perversion" at the time can also be seen in higher arrest rates for same-sex offenses at the local level (more than 1,000 per year in the District of Columbia in the early 1950s, for example), intensified campaigns of police raids of BARS and CRUISING areas across the country; sweeping witch-hunts that sought to expose underground "homosexual networks" (see **11/2/1955**; **11/24/1955**); and new IMMIGRATION restrictions directed against lesbians and gay men (see **6/27/1952**).

McCarthyism was principally an American phenomenon, but it had its equivalents in CANADA, where the Royal Canadian Mounted Police began to keep extensive records of homosexual activities (see **1952**), and in the UNITED KINGDOM, especially after the May 26, 1951, defection to the Soviet Union of two British diplomats-turned-spies, Guy Burgess (a "known homosexual") and Donald Maclean (considered bisexual). In both countries, lesbians and gay men were increasingly suspected—and persecuted—as "security risks."

➤ Also see TURING, ALAN; **2/28/1950**, **4/1/1950**, **6/14/1950**, **12/15/1950**.

✧ Thomas C. Reeves, *The Life and Times of Joe McCarthy: A Biography* (1982).

✧ John D'Emilio, *Sexual Politics, Sexual Communities: The Making of a Homosexual Minority in the United States, 1940–1970* (1983).

McCullers, Carson

(née Lulu Carson Smith; 1917–1967)

U.S. writer. McCullers spent most of her adult life in New York City, but she set her fiction in stiflingly small southern towns not unlike Columbus, Georgia, where she spent her youth. She married, divorced, and remarried Reeves McCullers, who, like herself, was regarded as bisexual by friends.

Although gossips linked McCullers romantically with everyone from Greta Garbo to Katherine Anne Porter, whom she idolized, and she was friendly with a number of lesbians and gay men, including W. H. AUDEN, LILLIAN SMITH, and TENNESSEE WILLIAMS, her fascination for gay and lesbian readers is largely rooted in the sexually ambivalent loners who populate her southern gothic novels and stories, most notably the deaf-mute Singer (*The Heart Is a Lonely Hunter,* 1940), Captain Penderton (*Reflections in a Golden Eye,* 1941), and the TOMBOYS Mick and Frankie (*The Ballad of the Sad Café,* 1951).

✧ Virginia Spencer Carr, *The Lonely Hunter: A Biography of Carson McCullers* (1975).

McKellen, Sir Ian

(1935–)

English actor, activist. McKellen began performing as a child and studied acting at Cambridge University. Not long after his London stage debut in 1964, Laurence Olivier called him "the greatest young actor in the English language." McKellen earned acclaim as a leading interpreter of SHAKESPEARE as well as in contemporary roles on TELEVISION, beginning in 1966, and in FILM, beginning in 1969.

McKellen played gay and bisexual characters as early as 1966 on radio (Gaveston in Christopher Marlowe's *Edward II,* with another prominent British actor who later came OUT, Alec McCowen, in the title role) and on screen in 1969 (*A Touch of Love*), and actually came out later that year in an interview with a British gay magazine, *Sebastian*. His self-outing went unreported in the general press, however, and he remained discreetly closeted in public—despite his half-joking admission in 1991 that one of the reasons he had become an actor in the first place was "to meet queers." In early 1988, encouraged by his friend ARMISTEAD MAUPIN and impassioned by the movement to defeat Clause 28 (a parliamentary amendment that made it illegal for local authorities in the UNITED KINGDOM to "promote homosexuality"—see **12/8/1987**) he made headlines when he came out in a BBC radio interview. Although Clause 28 was eventually passed (see **5/24/1988**), McKellen established himself as a leading gay activist during the fierce fight against the law. The following year, in **May 1989**, he joined with other prominent activists, including fellow actors Michael Cashman and Pam St. Clement, to establish the Stonewall Group, the country's first major lesbian and gay rights lobbying organization. The group's most visible leader, McKellen fought for measures against AIDS, passage of a proposed Homosexual Equality Bill, and an equal AGE OF CONSENT in the U.K.

Controversy arose in 1991 when McKellen became the first openly gay man to be knighted. DEREK JARMAN publicly attacked him for accepting the knighthood, asserting that such "honors support a dishonorable social structure." In response, an imposing group of self-proclaimed "gay and lesbian artists"—actor/director Simon Callow, Cameron Mackintosh, writer Stephen Fry, film director John Schlesinger, and a dozen others—rallied to McKellen's support with a statement published in the *Guardian* on **January 9, 1991**, that hailed McKellen's knighthood as "a significant event in the history of the British gay movement," and praised him for providing "an inspiration to us all, not only as an artist of extraordinary gifts, but as a public figure of remarkable honesty and dignity."

➤ Also see ACTORS/ACTING.

✧ Paul Russell, "Ian McKellen," in *The Gay 100: A Ranking of the Most Influential Gay Men and Lesbians, Past and Present* (1995).

Malaysia, see SOUTHEAST ASIA.

Male Impersonators, see CROSS-DRESSING; GENDER; PASSING.

Mapplethorpe, Robert
(1946–1989)

U.S. photographer. The third of six children born into a lower-middle-class Catholic family in Queens, New York, Mapplethorpe attended public schools and studied painting and sculpture at the Pratt Institute before moving into Manhattan to live at the bohemian Chelsea Hotel with singer Patti Smith. A resourceful self-promoter, he networked his way into the city's ART scene, first as a collage artist, then as a photographer. With the support of a wealthy lover, art curator Samuel Wagstaff (1921–1987), who bought him a loft and a Hasselblad, Mapplethorpe refined his skills and had established himself as a major new talent by 1977, when he had two simultaneous shows: one "uptown," featuring flowers and portraits, and a second, dominated by homoerotic S/M-themed photos, at the downtown Kitchen exhibition space.

In the decade that followed, Mapplethorpe continued his personal and photographic exploration of the S/M scene while becoming increasingly obsessed with the sexuality of black men. Much of his work from this period was featured in "The Perfect Moment," a show that precipitated the most notorious censorship controversy of the 1980s (see **6/12/1989**), which in turn brought Mapplethorpe, though posthumously, the fame he had always craved.

Some gay writers, including ESSEX HEMPHILL, found Mapplethorpe's black nudes offensive. Henry Louis Gates Jr., on the other hand, speculated that "there may be something salutarily subversive in the way [Mapplethorpe's photography] inserts black bodies into the Western fine-art traditions of the nude—so that, as the black cultural critic Kobena Mercer slyly writes, 'with the tilt of the pelvis, the black man's bum becomes a Brancusi.' " Although biographers have confirmed Hemphill's suspicion that Mapplethorpe was more than ordinarily racist, his work had the positive effect of encouraging black artists, such as BILL T. JONES and British-based African-born photographer Rotimi Fani-Kayode, to pursue their own visions of black HOMOEROTICISM.

Mapplethorpe believed he had successfully hid his homosexuality from his conservative Catholic mother, who died three months after him. His father, a critic he never won over, refused to have Robert's name engraved on the family tombstone.

✧ Kobena Mercer, "Skin Head Sex Thing: Racial Difference and the Homoerotic Imaginary," in *How Do I Look?: Queer Film and Video,* edited by Bad Object-Choices (1991).

✧ Allen Ellenzweig, *The Homoerotic Photograph: Male Images from Durieu/Delacroix to Mapplethorpe* (1992).

✧ Patricia Morrisroe, *Mapplethorpe: A Biography* (1995).

Marbury, Elisabeth, see DE WOLFE, ELSIE.

Marriage

As a goal of the GAY AND LESBIAN RIGHTS MOVEMENT, same-sex marriage is defined as legally indistinguishable from conventional, different-sex marriage. By this definition, no country in the modern world has (as of 1997) granted lesbians and gay men the right to civil marriage. Although the registered partnerships allowed same-sex couples in Denmark (**10/1/1989**), Norway (August 1993), Sweden (January 1995), and Iceland (June 1996) are often called "marriages"—and are equal to heterosexual marriages in matters of property ownership, joint rights to pensions and social benefits, taxation, inheritance, and divorce—they remain distinct from different-sex marriages. Same-sex Scandinavian couples are denied rights to ADOPTION, artificial insemination, and religious wedding ceremonies in state LUTHERAN CHURCHES.

Despite these inequities, the Scandinavian precedents have encouraged gay and lesbian activists in all the developed countries to press for the legal right to same-sex marriage. Many activists, such as Thomas B. Stoddard, believe that equal rights can be achieved only when lesbians and gay men have the same access to marriage as their straight peers.

In the U.S., Hawaii has come closest to allowing same-sex marriages, thanks to a state supreme court decision (see **5/7/1993**). The most dramatic effect of the Hawaii decision, however, was the mobilization by Christian fundamentalists, MORMON, and ROMAN CATHOLIC groups of well-organized campaigns in more than 30 states to bar recognition of same-sex marriages licensed in other states. Utah became the first state to pass such legislation in 1994. By early 1997, 16 states had passed similar laws. On the federal level, President Bill Clinton signed the so-called Defense of Marriage Act on **September 20, 1996**. The act barred gay and lesbian spouses from receiving federal benefits and expressly allowed—perhaps unconstitutionally—states the right to refuse recognition of other states' same-sex marriages.

Same-sex marriages were a part of life in ancient ROME, according to Juvenal and other writers, although historians disagree on whether or not they were recognized by legal authorities. In many NATIVE AMERICAN traditions, BERDACHES also commonly took husbands or wives. In modern times, however, marriage has been considered so inherently heterosexual that LAWS in most states and many countries make no mention of the biological sex of the participants.

Some lesbians and gay men oppose the movement for state-recognized same-sex marriages in the belief that marriage is a heterosexist institution that perpetuates discrimination against individuals who choose to remain single or want to create new forms of relationships. In GERMANY, for example, the Bundesverband Homosexualität objected to another national gay and lesbian group's petition for marriage rights (see **8/19/1992**) and instead called for a debate on whether *different-sex* marriage relationships should continue to have a privileged legislative status. Taking a different tack, some lesbian and gay legal experts have sought ways same-sex couples can obtain the social and financial benefits of marriage without actually taking out a marriage license.

➤ Also see DOMESTIC PARTNERSHIP; SAME-SEX UNIONS.

✧ Thomas B. Stoddard, "Why Gay People Should Seek the Right to Marry," and Paula L. Ettelbrick, "Since When Is Marriage a Path to Liberation?," *Outlook* (no. 6, Fall 1989).

✧ Denis Clifford, Hayden Curry, and Robin Leonard, *A Legal Guide for Lesbian and Gay Couples* (1993).

Martin, Del

(Dorothy L. Martin; 1921–)

U.S. activist, writer. Born in San Francisco, Martin became an avowed feminist at the age of six when she was denied a local *Liberty Magazine* delivery route because she was a girl. Growing up she felt sexually attracted to girlfriends and fantasized getting a sex change operation. Despite this early, gradually increasing awareness of her sexuality, she decided to get married while attending San Francisco State College. She and her husband, James Martin, had one daughter. She has shared her life with PHYLLIS LYON since 1953.

Martin was a reporter, editor, and freelance writer before becoming a pioneering lesbian activist. In 1955, Martin, Lyon, and six other lesbians founded the DAUGHTERS OF BILITIS (DOB), the first national lesbian organization in the U.S. Martin was national president from 1957 to 1960 and editor of DOB's publication, THE LADDER, from 1960 to 1962.

Following the disbanding of DOB's national organization in 1970, Martin became increasingly involved in the activities of the NATIONAL ORGANIZATION FOR WOMEN (NOW), a group she had supported since the 1960s. She was a member of NOW's National Board of Directors from 1973 to 1974 and cochair of NOW's national Task Force on Battered Women and Household Violence from 1975 to 1977.

Martin was among the first lesbians to publicize her dismay at the sexism she found widespread among gay men. In 1970, THE ADVOCATE published an open letter written by Martin with the headline "Good-Bye, My Alienated Brothers," in which she expressed her sorrow and anger at the failure of gay men to integrate the principles of feminism into

Del Martin (right) and Phyllis Lyon.

gay and lesbian liberation. The letter was one of the harbingers of the era of lesbian SEPARATISM.

The importance of Martin's contributions to the lesbian and gay civil rights movement and to feminism is evident in the number of major organizations she helped found. Besides DOB, these include the Council on Religion and the Homosexual (1964), Citizens Alert (1965), San Francisco Women's Centers (1970), Lesbian Mothers Union (1971), the Alice B. Toklas Memorial Democratic Club (1972), the Community Advisory Board of the Center for Special Problems (1973), the Bay Area Women's Coalition (1974), and the Coalition for Justice for Battered Women (1975). Martin has also been a leader in addressing the problems of AGING career women, as well as women's physical and mental health issues and AIDS.

In addition, Martin has worked on a wide range of issues related to LAW enforcement—including helping victims of crimes, developing interfaces with the police, and crime and violence prevention—and shown a deep concern for advancing human rights, particularly freedom of the press, freedom of religion, and abortion rights.

Martin and Lyon have written two books together in which they explore the social, personal, and historical dimensions of lesbianism: *Lesbian/Woman* (which won an AMERICAN LIBRARY ASSOCIATION Gay Book Award in 1972) and *Lesbian Love and Liberation* (1973). *Battered Wives* (1976), a book she wrote alone, reflects her work in the fight against DOMESTIC VIOLENCE and her experiences founding La Casa de las Madres, a shelter for battered women.

In their first years of HOMOPHILE activism, neither Martin nor Lyon could have foreseen the extent of social changes that were to occur from the 1960s through the 1990s. Together and individually, they stand as emblems of the innovative spirit of the homophile movement and of the courageous women and men who laid the foundation for later advances.

- Phyllis Lyon and Del Martin, *Lesbian Love and Liberation* (1973).
- Del Martin, *Battered Wives* (rev. ed., 1981).
- Phyllis Lyon and Del Martin, *Lesbian/Woman* (rev. ed. 1991).

Masculinity, see GENDER.

Mattachine

The first long-standing U.S. organization to advocate gay and lesbian rights. The Mattachine Society (later Foundation) grew out of an informal Saturday afternoon gathering hosted by HARRY HAY on a hillside overlooking his home in the Silver Lake neighborhood of Los Angeles on **November 11, 1950**. Hay had written a prospectus for "a service and welfare organization devoted to the protection and improvement of society's androgynous minority" as early as 1948, but response had been tepid. At the time, all same-sex erotic acts were punishable in California by prison sentences of up to 20 years and/or "cures" at state hospitals like Atascadero and Vacaville, where doctors routinely administered chemical and electroshock "treatments" and sometimes performed castrations on recalcitrant "sex criminals." While the end of WORLD WAR II had drawn large numbers of lesbians and gay men to California's coastal cities, it had also brought the beginning of the Cold War MCCARTHY ERA, a time when the mere suspicion of sexual "perversion" could lead to job dismissals and apartment evictions. It was not until 1950 that Hay was able to find four other men willing to take the considerable risk of organizing to promote gay and lesbian rights.

Founding members of the Mattachine Society (left to right): Harry Hay, Dale Jennings, Rudi Gernreich, Stan Witt, Bob Hull, Chuck Rowland, and Paul Bernard.

The other men were Rudi Gernreich, Hay's lover at the time, a dancer who would become famous in the 1960s as the designer of fashion innovations like the topless swimsuit; Bob Hull and his lover, Chuck Rowland; and Dale Jennings, a writer and former carnival roustabout whose arrest on a sex charge in 1952 was to play a major role in the growth of the Mattachine.

In April 1951, the founding members decided to change the group's name from Society of Fools to the Mattachine Society. The name "Mattachine" was inspired by Hay's research on a secret all-male fraternity dating back to the 15th century. The Matassins in France, Mattaccini in Italy, and Mattachinos in Spain were groups of men who socialized together and performed satirical dances at folk celebrations like the Feast of Fools (the ancestor of today's April Fool's Day).

The Mattachine instituted a dramatic candlelit initiation ceremony during which the members recited a pledge that included the words: "We are resolved that our people shall find equality of security and production in tomorrow's world. We are sworn that no boy or girl, approaching the maelstrom of deviation, need make that crossing alone, afraid and in the dark, ever again."

Some Mattachine meetings attracted as many as 200 people, and groups formed up and down the California coast, from San Diego to the Bay Area. No centralized membership records were kept but participants estimate that at the society's peak between 2,000 and 5,000 people regularly attended meetings.

Behind the enthusiasm for the Mattachine was the group's willingness to take on controversial issues like police entrapment (see **2/1952**; **6/23/1952**). By **February 1953**, some members had begun to fear reprisals against the group as part of the McCarthy era suspicion of "sex perverts." Beginning at a constitutional convention held on **April 11, 1953**, the original founders began to lose control of the Mattachine to more moderate groups. After **May 23–24, 1953**, the Mattachine officially set a low-profile, nonconfrontational course. Less effective as a result, the group's membership and meeting attendance plunged.

In **January 1955**, the group began to publish the *Mattachine Review.* In the years that followed, the publication was the main activity of the national group. At times (see, for example,

12/15/1959), Mattachine officers actively discouraged members from taking an activist approach.

Although the Mattachine was officially disbanded in 1961, local organizations in Chicago, New York City (see **12/1955**), Washington, D.C. (see **11/15/1961**), and other cities continued to call themselves Mattachine societies. In the 1960s, many of these groups pursued a more militant course of activism, paving the way for the GAY LIBERATION movement.

➤ Also see DAUGHTERS OF BILITIS; KAMENY, FRANK; ONE, INC.

✧ John D'Emilio, *Sexual Politics, Sexual Communities: The Making of a Homosexual Minority in the United States, 1940–1970* (1983).

✧ Stuart Timmons, *The Trouble with Harry Hay: Founder of the Modern Gay Movement* (1990).

Maupin, Armistead

(Armistead Jones Maupin Jr.; 1944–)

U.S. writer. Maupin grew up in Raleigh, North Carolina, and graduated from the University of North Carolina at Chapel Hill in 1966. After serving with the navy in Vietnam, he worked in journalism and public relations, moving to San Francisco in 1971.

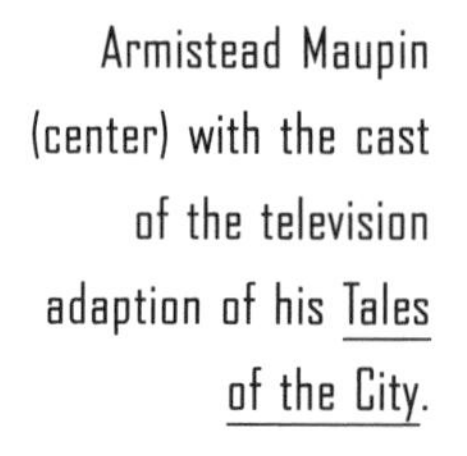

Armistead Maupin (center) with the cast of the television adaption of his Tales of the City.

On **May 24, 1976**, Maupin debuted his *Tales of the City* serial in the pages of the *San Francisco Chronicle.* By 1989, when he published his sixth and last novel-length installment, *Sure of You,* readers all over the world knew more about the gay, lesbian, bisexual, transsexual, and straight residents (and their associates) at 28 Barbary Lane than they knew about their own neighbors. Social history and SUBCULTURE guide, satire, and, ultimately, tragedy, *Tales* probably reached the broadest audience of any gay novels published since STONEWALL. Britain's *Gay Times* uses the word "Maupinesque" to mean much the same thing in a gay context that "Balzacian" conveys in straight LITERATURE.

The success of the series also established Maupin as a popular public speaker on issues that ranged, like his novels, from OUTING to AIDS. He has been an especially vocal and effective proponent of gay and lesbian solidarity and of coming OUT. IAN MCKELLEN is just one of the many people who credit him with inspiring them to leave the CLOSET.

In addition to short stories, writing for the stage, and adapting the first *Tales* for a 1993 TELEVISION production in the UNITED KINGDOM (later broadcast with multiple, Right-fearing disclaimers on American public TV), Maupin wrote a seventh novel, *Maybe the Moon* (1992), about a 31-inch-tall actress trying to make a comeback in Hollywood.

He and his lover, activist Terry Anderson, live in San Francisco.

✧ Barbara Kaplan Bass, "Armistead Maupin," in *Contemporary Gay American Novelists,* edited by Emmanuel Nelson (1993).

Mazer, June [Leah]

(1929–1987)

U.S. activist, archivist. As a tribute to this community worker, lesbian papers at the West Coast Lesbian Collections founded in Oakland, California, in 1981 were named the June Mazer Collection. The collection became the only exclusively lesbian archive in the western U.S. Their mission statement emphasizes that the collection exists "so that every lesbian realizes that she is not alone; so that every lesbian knows she can find herself in every generation."

Mazer was born in Baltimore, Maryland. Following her college and graduate education, she moved to Los Angeles in 1970 to work as a registered occupational therapist. She became active in the gay and lesbian movement in 1976. With her life partner, Bunny MacCulloch, she was a project leader with the AMERICAN CIVIL LIBERTIES UNION of Southern California's Lesbian and Gay Rights Chapter, Connexxus Women's Center/Centro de Mujeres, and the Lesbian Rights Project in San Francisco. As a shaping influence, she was a member of the board of directors for the International Gay and Lesbian Archives and Southern California Women for Understanding. Despite a battle with cancer, when the West Coast Lesbian Collections was near closing, Mazer and MacCulloch moved the materials to Los Angeles and kept the collection intact.

Among her many recognitions, in 1983, Mazer became the first recipient of the Myra Riddell Service Award for her contributions to the Southern California Women for Understanding.

Mead, Margaret

(1901–1978)

U.S. anthropologist, writer. Born in Philadelphia to a mother who was a sociologist and a father who taught economics, Mead attended Barnard College in New York and studied with Franz Boas ("the father of American anthropology") and his assistant, RUTH BENEDICT,

Margaret Mead with a Samoan friend.

whose enthusiasm inspired Mead to pursue a career in the field.

Mead became world famous for her studies of South Sea peoples, especially *Coming of Age in Samoa* (1928), which rejected biological determinism to emphasize the inexorable influence of cultural forces on adolescent development. She later expanded her study (*Growing Up in New Guinea,* 1930), and admonished American parents for what she saw as comparatively inept child-rearing practices. She wrote more than 1,000 articles and 30 books in addition to working as a curator at the American Museum of Natural History in New York City.

After Mead's death, her daughter wrote of her mother's lifelong concurrent relationships with both men and women: "This double pattern must have been satisfying and sustaining, but at the same time it created a kind of isolation, an isolation of secrecy." In the mid-1920s, Mead and Benedict were lovers both before and during Mead's marriage to Gregory Bateson. The relationship affected the two women's perception of what was "normal" in a culture. Conscious of her own nonconformity, Mead later described the "deviant" in positive, validating terms as a person who "demanded a different or improved environment but who rejected the traditional choices" and set up alternate standards. Although their sexual intimacy waned over the course of Mead's serial bisexual relationships, they remained close until Benedict's death in 1948.

Mead was one of the earliest U.S. proponents of BISEXUALITY. Her "Bisexuality: What's It All About?" (1974) characterized bisexuality as potentially creative and innovative and questioned the sociocultural forces that demand people choose between a lifetime of exclusive homosexuality or heterosexuality.

✧ Mary Catherine Bateson, *With a Daughter's Eye: A Memoir of Margaret Mead and Gregory Bateson* (1984).

✧ Jane Howard, *Margaret Mead: A Life* (1984).

Melanesia, see PACIFIC ISLANDS.

Merrill, James
(1926–1995)

U.S. poet. The son of the founder of the brokerage firm of Merrill Lynch, Pierce, Fenner & Smith, his childhood was scarred by his parents' divorce when he was 12 and the subsequent departure of his beloved nanny and governess, a Prussian-English widow who had taught him French and German. He attended the elite Lawrenceville School outside of Princeton, served two years in the MILITARY during WORLD WAR II, and graduated from

Amherst College in 1947. He traveled extensively in the 1950s, then divided his time between homes in Stonington, Connecticut, and GREECE, and, after 1979, Stonington and the home of his lover (whom he had met in 1953), writer and musician David Jackson, in KEY WEST.

Merrill's early poems were privately printed beginning with a volume, *Jim's Book,* published while he was still in high school. He had a play successfully produced and also published *The Seraglio* (1957), a novel loosely based on the events of his youth, before emerging as one of the most promising poets of his generation with the publication of *The Country of a Thousand Years of Peace* (1959) and *Water Street* (1962). Influenced by writers he loved, who included W. H. AUDEN, CONSTANTINE CAVAFY, and MARCEL PROUST, Merrill wrote highly crafted poetry in a style that a 1973 *New York Times* editorial, championing more avant-garde work, disparaged as "literary, private, traditional." Yet by the 1970s, he had become recognized as a poet whose books, as critic Helen Vendler wrote, "readers actively long for," someone who was "writing down your century, your generation, your language, your life."

Never really closeted—"my good fortune," he once wrote, "was to stay in one place while the closet simply disintegrated"—Merrill's love affairs and intimacies with gay and lesbian friends (including, especially, ELIZABETH BISHOP) were important themes in his writing. "Merrill's sexuality," fellow poet J. D. McClatchy wrote, "was like a drop of dye let fall into a glass of water: it is subdued but suffuses everything." His sense of himself as a gay man is especially apparent in his masterwork, three long poems collected as *The Changing Light at Sandover* (1982), a 17,000-line epic that uses Jackson and Merrill's ouija-board probings as a point of departure.

Merrill's last book of poetry, *A Scattering of Salt,* was published two months after his sudden death of a heart attack at the age of 68.

✧ Edmund White, "On Merrill," in *The Burning Library: Essays,* edited by David Bergman (1994).

✧ J. D. McClatchy, "Braving the Elements," *The New Yorker* (March 27, 1996).

Methodism

Christian faith associated with the denominations that grew out of the teachings of John Wesley (1703–1791). The United Methodist Church, whose 8.5 million members make up the largest Methodist group and the second largest Protestant denomination in the U.S., affirmed the "sacred worth" and "human and civil rights" of lesbians and gay men in a statement issued at a quadrennial general conference in 1976. The "practice of homosexuality," however, was declared to be "incompatible with Christian teaching," and official bodies of the church continue to forbid the ordination of "practicing homosexuals." Both these policies were reaffirmed by the Church's general conference in April 1996. Affirmation, founded in 1976, is an advocacy and support group for gay, lesbian, and bisexual Methodists.

Metropolitan Community Churches, The Fellowship of (MCC)

Nondenominational religious group formed by the Reverend Troy Perry, an ordained Pentacostal minister, at a series of meetings beginning in 1967. MCC's first service, attended by 12 people, took place at Perry's home in Los Angeles on **October 6, 1968**. By 1996, MCC had more than 40,000 members and about 300 churches in 16 countries. The Church has welcomed lesbians and gay people of all faiths: the U.S. gay and lesbian movement within JUDAISM in fact began with meetings held at MCC facilities. It is also ac-

Metropolitan Community Church founder the Rev. Troy Perry, in the early 1970s.

tive in AFRICA, especially in Nigeria, where the vast majority of its members do not identify as lesbian or gay.

A Tallahassee, Florida, native and the father of two sons, Perry became an activist for gay rights in the 1960s. After moving to Southern California, divorcing, and serving in the U.S. MILITARY, Perry began to assemble a small congregation of others who believed along with him that one "could be a Christian and a gay person, too!" Besides organizing religious services, which included the first publicized SAME-SEX UNION ceremony on **December 3, 1968**, Perry emerged as one of the most prominent leaders of the GAY LIBERATION movement.

Mew, Charlotte
(1869–1928)

English poet. Born into a middle-class London family, Mew was raised by a stern nurse and educated at home until she was ten. She then attended the Gower Street School, where she became enamored of her lesbian headmistresses, Lucy Harrison and Amy Greener. The two teachers lived together for 30 years in a house Harrison had built largely with her own hands.

Mew's first entry into print was a short story, "Passed," in the prestigious magazine *The Yellow Book* (1894). Other stories, articles, poetry, and a play followed. Although her highly crafted poems were championed by Thomas Hardy and VIRGINIA WOOLF (who once called her "the greatest living poetess"), editors and the reading public were slow to accept them. Publication of a chapbook, *The Farmer's Bride* (1916), and later collections of her work only modestly supplemented her family's diminishing finances, but they did earn her literary and social contacts. A diminutive, short-haired woman who was fond of tailor-made jackets and hand-rolled cigarettes, Mew was famous for her readings and her natural mimic's ability to create the many voices in her poems.

Mew lived with her sister, a gifted painter, in BLOOMSBURY most of her adult life. A year after her sister died of cancer, Mew killed herself by drinking disinfectant.

Mew's poetic themes included the pain of unrequited love, reflecting her own rejection by the writers Ella D'Arcy and May Sinclair. Sinclair added to Mew's pain when she indiscreetly gossiped about "a lesbian poetess, Charlotte M.," who, she alleged, had chased her upstairs and into her bedroom. About her lesbianism Mew wrote: "We are what we are, the spirit afterwards, but first the touch."

✧ Penelope Fitzgerald, *Charlotte Mew and Her Friends* (1984).

Mexican-Americans, see LATINOS AND LATINAS.

Mexico

No laws against same-sex relations, but government and police harassment of individuals and organizations continues to occur. Mexico City and Guadalajara are social, cultural, and political centers for lesbians and gay men.

Same-sex relations between consenting adults were decriminalized in Mexico as early as the 1860s, and gay men have a large, well-developed, and even internationally renowned SUBCULTURE. Nevertheless, gay and lesbian Mexicans lag behind their counterparts in the U.S. and CANADA in terms of social acceptance as well as civil rights. Harassment of activists is routine in many parts of Mexico and, in some cases, leads to extreme violence: in 1992, for example, six gay activists—one of whom, Francisco Estrada Valle, was an internationally recognized AIDS educator and physician—were found bound, gagged, and murdered. Investigations of this and other HATE CRIMES have been lax.

Notable Mexican lesbians, gay men, and bisexuals include activists Patria Jiménez; FILM director Jaime Humberto Hermosillo; writers and theatrical directors Nancy Cardénas and Jesusa Rodríguez; and writer LUIS ZAPATA.

History

Homosexuality was an important motif in the art and religious rituals of the Mayans, Toltecs, Aztecs, and other peoples who dominated the area prior to the arrival of the Spaniards. The Aztecs, for example, worshiped a deity whose male aspect, Xochipili, was associated with sex between men and male prostitution. In private life, however, the Aztecs enforced a rigid code of heterosexual behavior. Men were severely penalized if they did not marry, and women as well as men could receive the death penalty for homosexual relations and transvestism.

Following SPAIN's conquest of the area in the sixteenth century, ROMAN CATHOLIC missionaries, soldiers, and colonists established dominion over the indigenous peoples, and contemporary Spanish LAWS against SODOMY were sporadically enforced. For a brief period, the INQUISITION also prosecuted homosexuals, sometimes handing them over to civil authorities to serve as galley slaves or to be burned at the stake.

By the time Mexico won independence from Spain in 1821, the majority of Mexicans were of mixed indigenous and Spanish ancestry, and their sexual mores reflected this unique blend. As during Aztec times, laws and social pressures discouraged homosexuality, yet, as in Spain, men who played the active role in sex with other men were considered macho and were widely tolerated, while their passive partners were stigmatized as effeminate *maricones.*

During the French occupation of Mexico from 1862 to 1867, Mexicans adopted the Napoleonic Code, which decriminalized sex between consenting adults. Overt homosexuality, however, was widely viewed as an offense against public decency and continued to be prosecuted as such. In one incident in 1901 that attracted widespread press attention, Mexico City police raided a ball and arrested 41 mostly upper-class, cross-dressed men. A few weeks later, police raided a lesbian bar in Santa María.

Despite intermittent police harassment, a gay and lesbian SUBCULTURE began to develop in Mexico's largest cities. BARS and BATHS for men opened as early as the 1930s, and homosexual and bisexual relationships became common in bohemian circles, exemplified by the intellectuals and political activists who surrounded Frida Kahlo and Diego Rivera, two leading Mexican artists of the period.

Inspired by the U.S. GAY LIBERATION groups that sprang up after the STONEWALL Uprising, lesbian and gay Mexicans began to form organizations in the 1970s, including La Frente Homosexual de Acción Revolucionaria, founded in 1978.

Today, gay and lesbian social institutions, publications, and annual PRIDE CELEBRATIONS are a firmly established part of Mexican life. Nevertheless, police and government harassment continues to make sexual openness difficult in many parts of the country.

✧ Asuncion Lavrin, *Sexuality and Marriage in Colonial Latin America* (1982).

✧ Ian Lumsden, *Homosexuality, Society, and the State in Mexico* (1991).

✧ Stephen O. Murray, *Latin American Male Homosexualities* (1995).

✧ Gloria Careaga Pérez and Patria Jiménez, "Mexico," in *Unspoken Rules: Sexual Orientation and Women's Rights,* edited by Rachel Rosenbloom (1996).

✧ Elena M. Martínez, *Lesbian Voices from Latin America: Breaking Ground* (1996).

Michelangelo

(Michelangelo di Lodovico Buonarroti Simoni; 1475–1564)

Italian sculptor, painter, architect, poet. Of respectable Tuscan stock, Michelangelo was 15 when his talents attracted the patronage of the Florentine magnate Lorenzo "The Magnificent" de' Medici. While living in the Medici household, he met many of the luminaries of his time, including the philosopher Marsilio Ficino, whose Renaissance brand of Neoplatonism (reinterpretations of Plato's ideas) strongly influenced Michelangelo's attitudes toward his sexuality as well as his conceptions of the purpose of ART.

According to Ficino, earthly beauty—especially the beauty of young men—was a reflection of the divine ideal, or, as Michelangelo later wrote in a poem: "He who made everything . . . chose the most beautiful to manifest his most exulted properties here [on this earth]." For most of his life, Michelangelo believed that art could in some measure capture and preserve the memory of beauty, but as an old man obsessed with the approach of death, he came to fear that art and his attraction to

Michelangelo Buonarroti.

physical beauty had distracted him from contemplating God, in whom rested his only hope for eternal life.

Except for a few periods spent working in Bologna and Florence (where he completed his *David* in 1504), Michelangelo lived most of his adult life in Rome, employed by Popes Julius II, Leo X, Clement VII, and Paul III. Although his relationships with his patrons were sometimes stormy, he was acclaimed as Il Divino in his lifetime for masterpieces like the Pietà (1500), *The Last Judgment* (1541), and the architectural plans for St. Peter's Basilica. His contemporaries also praised his poetry.

Michelangelo lived during a time of increasingly severe repression of SODOMY (see **11/1/1494**; **1497**; **1512**; **1514**), but he seems to have been more restrained by moral qualms than by fear of prosecution. Despite one of the richest collections of biographical material left by anyone in his era—including 500 letters, several hundred often deeply personal poems, and numerous biographies written by contemporaries—there is no evidence that Michelangelo ever had sex with anyone, male or female. Perhaps as a result, most commentators have glossed over the homoerotic content of his work, or even—as in the case of actor Charlton Heston, who portrayed the artist in the 1965 film *The Agony and the Ecstasy*—adamantly denied the artist's homosexuality. Yet both his art and his poetry evidence a powerful physical and emotional attraction to other men. And, as modern critics like James M. Saslow have pointed out, the fact that he was tortured by guilt over what he called "wicked and depraved desires" suggests that he succumbed to temptation since successfully resisting his desires would not have resulted in actual sin.

A deeply religious man, Michelangelo often portrayed himself as "split into two halves," torn between his love of earthly beauty and his equally passionate love of God. Analogously, his two most important ROMANTIC FRIENDSHIPS were with Tommaso de' Cavalieri, a handsome aristocrat more than 30 years his junior, and Vittoria Colonna, a learned and devout widow with whom he shared his increasingly fervent religious concerns. Neither relationship was sexual, but Michelangelo showered Cavalieri, who was 23 when the two men met in 1532, with passionate sonnets and drawings, including at least one, now lost, of GANYMEDE, while the tone of his correspondence with Colonna remained devout and chastely intellectual. Both friendships lasted for years. Michelangelo was inconsolable after Colonna died in 1547. Cavalieri was present at Michelangelo's death.

Michelangelo left a legacy of male nudes, from infants to old men, unmatched in art until the 20th century. His powerful depictions of the male figure had a lasting impact on the way artists conceive of HOMOEROTICISM. In the 20th century artists as diverse as FRANCIS BACON, the painter Glyn Philpot, British photographer Nicholas Paterson, and TOM OF FINLAND have created homoerotic art that evokes Michelangelo's vision.

In contrast, the homoeroticism of Michelangelo's poetry was obscured for more than 200 years: when Michelangelo the Younger, the artist's grandnephew, extensively revised and published an edition of his great-uncle's poetry in 1623, he changed the gender of pronouns in many of the love poems to suggest they were written to women instead of men, and the original versions did not become available in Italian until 1863. JOHN ADDINGTON SYMONDS made one of the first attempts to reclaim Michelangelo as a hero and originator of homoeroticism by translating his sonnets into English and writing a two-volume biography of the artist, which was privately published in 1893.

✧ James Saslow, *Ganymede and the Renaissance* (1986).

✧ James Saslow, *The Poetry of Michelangelo: An Annotated Translation* (1991).

Michigan Womyn's Music Festival

One of the oldest, largest, and most visible lesbian events in the U.S., the festival is held the second week in August on a square mile of woods and meadows in Hart, Michigan. Nearly 10,000 women attend annually.

Women "festivirgins" and confirmed "festigoers" come from around the world to camp out, listen, and dance to the MUSIC of dozens of established and upcoming performers; attend workshops on political and social topics; take part in craft bazaars and drumming circles; or, as many report, simply find revitalization in a women-only "safe space." The festival is noted for its intergenerational diversity as well as the care organizers take to provide DISABLED women with interpreters, Braille maps, and accessible facilities. Regular performers have included: ALIX DOBKIN, Casselberry-DuPree, Deuce, Ferron, HOLLY NEAR, Rowe, CT and April, Teresa Trull, Linda Tillery, and Edwina Lee Tyler.

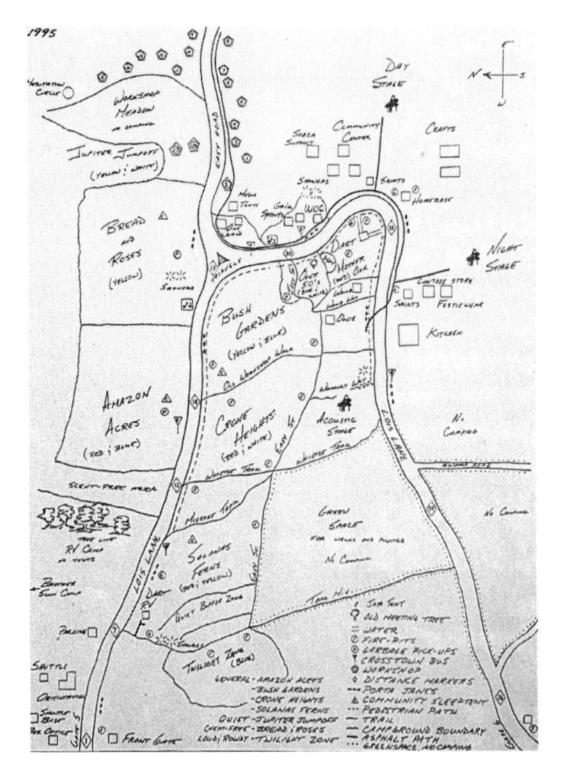

The Michigan Womyn's Music Festival has evolved its own geography.

Begun in 1976 by We Want the Music Collective members Mary Kindig, Kristie Vogel, and Lisa Vogel (the collective disbanded in 1979), the festival has at times been the center of controversies that mirror important issues facing the lesbian community at large, including racism, PORNOGRAPHY, S/M, and whether or not to allow male children at women-only events. In the early 1990s, the organizers' decision to bar male-to-female TRANSSEXUALS was the focus of articles in both the lesbian and mainstream press. In 1994, the festival was the site of a "Transsexual Menace" protest (inspired by the LAVENDER MENACE action). As a result of these disputes, the festival has evolved a more flexible and inclusive brand of lesbian SEPARATISM. Current producer Lisa Vogel defines the festival as a "common meeting ground and an international forum to explore issues and values from all our various communities, and have a very good time while doing it."

Described as surreal, utopian, blissful, and overwhelming, the festival has become a community institution and celebratory symbol of lesbian culture.

✧ Rachel Pepper, "Into the Woods," *Outweek* (September 19, 1990).

✧ Gretchen Phillips and Ricki Anne Wilchins, "Splendor in the Grass," *Village Voice* (September 6, 1994).

Midlife

The least studied phase of gay and lesbian lives, the years between young adulthood (see YOUTH) and old age (see AGING) are probably experienced in more diverse ways by lesbians and gay men than any other period of life. Some women describe them as "the best years of their lives." Some men, exasperated by the obsession with youthfulness in the gay male SUBCULTURE, claim the very words "gay midlife" are an oxymoron. In addition, gay men seem to perceive themselves as aging more rapidly than straight men. One study found that the average gay man believed midlife to begin at the age of 39 while straight men saw themselves as young until 54.

PSYCHOLOGY and SOCIOLOGY have only begun to study the lesbian and gay male experience of midlife, but some generalizations can be made. In one survey conducted by Barbara E. Sang, about half of a group of 110 middle-aged lesbians reported that their sex lives had improved with time. More than 75 percent felt that midlife was the "best period of their life."

For men, the subject of midlife has been complicated by the widespread devastation wrought by AIDS. A number of studies have found surviving middle-aged gay men increasingly isolated as many of their friends succumb to the disease. Other studies, however, have painted a happier picture of gay men. One theory, for example, holds that gay men become happier and more self-sufficient as they grow older because they expend so much time and effort in their youth fighting social disapproval, with the result that their sense of self-worth and their survival mechanisms are more finely honed by the time they reach midlife.

✧ *Psychological Perspectives on Lesbian and Gay Male Experiences,* edited by Linda D. Garnets and Douglas C. Kimmel (1993).

✧ *Lesbian, Gay, and Bisexual Identities over the Lifespan: Psychological Perspectives,* edited by Anthony R. D'Augelli and Charlotte J. Patterson (1995).

Military, The

Major area of contention for lesbian and gay rights activists. Since military groups are almost always segregated by sex and often demand long periods of service with no one but one's fellow soldiers or sailors for companionship, the military is in many ways an environment in which all kinds of same-sex relationships would seem to flourish. Partly because this is indeed the case, many governments and military authorities in modern times have felt obliged to take draconian measures to keep their military forces "safe" from homosexuality.

Few people, however, dispute the fact that gay men and lesbians have always been a part of the military or that their service records have often been outstanding. As early as 1957, the highly confidential Crittenden Report (officially, "Report of the Board Appointed to Prepare and Submit Recommendations to the Secretary of the Navy for the Revision of Policies, Procedures and Directives Dealing with Homosexuals") found that there was "no correlation between homosexuality and either ability or attainments." The report even asserted that "there is some information to indicate that homosexuals are quite good security risks."

The U.S. and the UNITED KINGDOM are among the very few Western nations that still officially bar lesbians and gay men from military service. Most countries, ranging from AUSTRALIA to ISRAEL, that have revoked restrictions, have reported no problems with the new gay- and lesbian-tolerant policies. Few countries, however, have approached the policy of the NETHERLANDS, which actually runs ADVERTISING and promotional campaigns to encourage gay and lesbian service personnel to come OUT, in the belief that uncloseted women and men are happier and thus even more productive members of the military.

✧ Randy Shilts, *Conduct Unbecoming: Lesbians and Gays in the U.S. Military, Vietnam to the Persian Gulf* (1993).

✧ *Homosexuality: Debating the Issues,* edited by Robert M. Baird and M. Katherine Baird (1995).

Milk, Harvey

(1930–1978)

U.S. politician and activist. Born and reared on Long Island, New York, Milk received a dishonorable discharge on grounds of homosexuality from the MILITARY, which prevented him from pursuing a career as a teacher. He worked on Wall Street before moving to San Francisco in 1969 and getting involved in local politics. After two unsuccessful campaigns, Milk was elected to the San Francisco Board of Supervisors on **November 8, 1977**. He was the first openly gay city official in a major American city. Among his accomplishments while in office was the successful passage of the city's first ordinance protecting lesbians and gay men against discrimination in jobs and housing.

On **November 27, 1978**, Milk and Mayor George Moscone were shot to death in their offices at City Hall by Dan White, a former city supervisor and an active opponent of gay and lesbian civil rights. White was charged with first-degree murder but using a defense based on his mind-addling consumption of junk food (derided in the press as the "Twinkie defense"), was found guilty only of manslaughter. He received the maximum sentence of seven years, eight months in prison. The leniency of the verdict sparked widespread protests and a night of rioting in San Francisco. (White left prison in 1984 and committed suicide in 1985.)

A politician who was controversial even among fellow activists, Milk is today remembered both as a martyr of the gay rights movement and a pioneer of the gay and lesbian political strategy of forming coalitions with women's groups and people of color. Milk has been the subject of an award-winning documentary, *The Times of Harvey Milk* (1984), and one of the first gay-themed operas.

✧ Randy Shilts, *The Mayor of Castro Street* (1982).

Miller, Isabel, see ROUTSONG, ALMA.

Miller, Merle
(1919–1986)

U.S. author, editor. Miller was born and raised in Marshalltown, Iowa, the only child of parents who wanted a daughter so badly they dressed him as a girl until the age of four. A devotion to music studies combined with a frail physique, poor eyesight, and inadequate coordination earned him unremitting torment as a "sissy," and the boy made few friends. In high school during the Depression, he discovered that sex could be bought from the hungry young men who drifted through town. Later, while city editor of the University of Iowa newspaper, *The Daily Iowan,* Miller sought to deflect suspicions of his sexual interests by joining in editorial attacks against "queers."

Miller remained closeted through four years in the army, marriage to (and divorce from) Elinor Green, editorial jobs at major publications (*Harper's, Time*), the publication of several well-received novels, and the beginning of his 22-year relationship with David Elliott. Then, on **January 17, 1971**, Miller became one of the first prominent American gay men to come OUT in a public forum: an article in *The New York Times Magazine* entitled "What It Means to Be a Homosexual." Although he received thousands of letters expressing gratitude for his courage in publishing the article, some readers criticized him for writing that he wished he had been straight. In response, he told a GAY ACTIVIST ALLIANCE (GAA) gathering in June that he did not feel being straight was better but that "in this society God knows it's easier." Articles like his were "only the beginning," he said, but "together we're going to change this goddam society."

Miller had also contributed to an earlier GAA action, the *Harper's* ZAP (see **10/27/1970**), by writing a letter in support of the sit-in to *Harper's* staff members. Since Miller had once been editor of the publication, his letter carried both moral and personal weight.

The author of more than a dozen books, including the gay-themed novel *What Happened* (1972), Miller was best known for his masterly oral biographies of Harry S. Truman (1974) and Lyndon B. Johnson (1980).

✧ Merle Miller, *On Being Different: What It Means to Be a Homosexual* (1971).

Millett, Kate

(Katherine Murray Millett; 1934–)

U.S. writer, sculptor, painter, feminist theorist, activist. Born in St. Paul, Minnesota, Millett traces her liberal feminist sensibility to her mother, an Irish immigrant, and her tireless devotion to her three daughters after their father left them. A TOMBOY, Millett struggled against conformity as a student in Catholic schools—and was expelled five times. She credits her stylish Aunt Dorothy with making her an artist, although the same aunt threatened to withdraw tuition support unless she renounced her lesbianism. Their severed relationship became the subject of Millett's memoir *A.D.* (1994).

Millett attended the University of Minnesota and St. Hilda's College in Oxford. She left her first job at the Women's College of the University of North Carolina to begin a career in painting and sculpture in New York and JAPAN. After returning to the U.S., she taught part-time at Barnard while attending Columbia University. Her Ph.D. dissertation, which later served as the basis for her groundbreaking *Sexual Politics* (1970), examined celebrated literary texts to reveal misogny and patriarchal values within.

Millett was an early member of the NATIONAL ORGANIZATION FOR WOMEN (NOW), as well as of Redstockings, LAVENDER MENACE, and RADICALESBIANS. She came OUT as a bisexual at a DAUGHTERS OF BILITIS meeting in New York City on **October 28, 1970**. On December 14 of the same year, *Time* magazine reported that she was a lesbian in a much discussed article that echoed NOW president Betty Friedan's fear that a too obvious lesbian presence would harm the feminist movement. Four days later, feminist leaders held a "Kate Is Great" press conference to show their support of her and the GAY AND LESBIAN RIGHTS MOVEMENT. Millett's personal-political *Flying* (1974) provided one of the first histories of lesbian feminist politics while detailing the trauma of her national OUTING: "There is an enormous psychic rocket effect with coming out," she later reflected, "that does make you so empowered—you've broken that last conceivable barrier . . . there's nothing they can do to you anymore."

Kate Millett.

Her nine published books include *The Prostitution Papers* (1971), which used oral narratives to probe the conflict between feminists and prostitutes, and the autobiographical *Sita* (1977), which tracked the end of a lesbian relationship. In *The Basement* (1979), she wrote of her 14-year obsession with Sylvia Likens, a young woman who was sexually abused, tortured, and murdered by her foster mother and a teen gang. *The Loony-Bin Trip* (1990) discussed her own mental health history as well as the experience of working one summer at the age of 18 in an insane asylum. An accomplished artist, she exhibited at "The Great American Lesbian Art Show" in **August 1979**.

Like most of the other pioneers of GAY LIBERATION, Millett has always asserted that the central issue of the movement was the liberation of all human sexuality. "The more gay liberation, the more sexual possibility," she once observed. "It's really not only sexual. It's the right to fall in love with, experience, be intimate, spend years with, another entire half of the human race." In her own life, Millett has had a 10-year marriage with a man, the artist Fumio Yoshimura, as well as lesbian relationships.

Since 1978, Millett has divided her time between The Farm—an art colony for women she developed on 80 acres in upstate New York—and New York City.

✧ Annette Kolodny, "The Lady's Not for Spurning," *Contemporary Literature* (Autumn 1976).

✧ Arlene Raven and Susan Rennie, "Interview with Kate Millett," *Heresies* (no. 3, 1977).

✧ Bonnie Zimmerman, *The Safe Sea of Women and Lesbian Fiction, 1969–1989* (1990).

Mishima, Yukio

(Kimitake Hiraoka; 1925–1970)

Japanese writer. Born into an upper-class Tokyo family, he was raised largely by his domineering grandmother, Natsu, who discouraged him from playing with other boys and in whose company he learned "women's" Japanese (which employs vocabulary and intonation patterns markedly different from the Japanese spoken by men and boys). A sickly, sensitive child, he nevertheless excelled as a student at the elite Peers' School and the Imperial University of Tokyo. He began writing poems and stories at an early age and had published widely before the success of his second novel, *Confessions of a Mask* (**7/1949**), made him one of the most famous and popular writers in JAPAN.

Largely autobiographical (although he later denied it), *Confessions of a Mask* was the first modern Japanese novel to deal openly with male homosexuality. Mishima showed his broad, even esoteric, knowledge of everyone from RICHARD VON KRAFFT-EBING to JOHANN JOACHIM WINCKELMANN; taken together with another novel, *Forbidden Colors,* which contains a vivid account of the Tokyo gay bar scene of the time, it leaves no doubt about Mishima's sexuality. In Japan, however, critics tended to gloss over the writer's sexuality. His vast read-

Yukio Mishima and cross-dressing actor Miwa Akihiro in a scene from Black Lizard.

ing public thought of him as bisexual, if they thought of his sexuality at all. Married and the father of two children, Mishima was indeed capable of sexual relations with women, yet he was clearly most strongly attracted to men.

His obsession with masculinity led in his 30s to fanatical BODYBUILDING and martial arts training. Later, in his 40s, he even completed MILITARY training and assembled his own paramilitary "Shield Society" (who were posed in loincloths for homoerotic photographs).

On November 25, 1970, Mishima and four cadets from his Shield Society invaded the headquarters of Japan's Self-Defense Forces and addressed troops assembled outside, urging them to revolt, restore the imperial system, and reinstate military sovereignty. After trying in vain to mobilize the troops, Mishima went inside and performed a ritual *seppuku*. His lover, to deliver the coup de grace, beheaded him shortly after the first incision.

Besides publishing some 40 novels, 18 plays, and numerous essays, Mishima also acted on stage and in films.

Mishima remains a paradoxical, enigmatic figure for Japanese and non-Japanese alike. Often portrayed as anti-Western, he was nonetheless extremely cosmopolitan and close to many Westerners. His themes are remarkably similar to WALT WHITMAN's a century earlier: finding modern life sterile and unsatisfying, he sought meaning in the "love of comrades," manly action, and a very Japanese devotion to a hopeless cause—what Ivan Morris has called the "nobility of failure."

✧ Henry Scott Stokes, *The Life and Death of Yukio Mishima* (1974).

✧ Peter Wolfe, *Yukio Mishima* (1989).

Mizer, Bob

(1922–1992)

U.S. photographer, filmmaker, publisher. A former railway employee, Mizer began the Athletic Model Guild (AMG) in his native Los Angeles in **December 1945** to function as a talent scout and modeling agency for male bodybuilders. Mizer honed his own skills as a photographer and began selling photos of his clients via ads in the back pages of men's magazines and, somewhat later, regular promotional mailings to customers across the U.S. In **November 1951**, he had so many of his own

Mizer's Physique Pictorial inspired dozens of imitators in the 1950s and early 1960s.

and other photographers' and artists' prints to advertise that he bound them together in booklet form, creating, almost by accident, the first PHYSIQUE MAGAZINE for gay men, *Physique Pictorial.*

Available by mail and at newstands for 15 cents, *Physique Pictorial* was by 1955 regularly selling more than 40,000 copies an issue. Its success inspired dozens of imitations, but AMG remained the leader. Besides developing offshoot publications, Mizer also began marketing 8-mm shorts with titles like *Aztec Sacrifice, Cruel Stepbrothers,* and *Days of Greek Gods.* CAMP classics, AMG films featured beefy young men barely clad in togas, chaps, Hawaiian wraparounds, or posing pouches (the latter designed, sewed, and lucratively marketed by Mizer's mother from the home they shared).

Mizer decided not to try his hand at the hard-core gay male PORNOGRAPHY that became popular in the 1970s, but AMG photo sets, publications, movies, and videos continued to sell well until the company closed in 1993. Over 6,000 men appeared in AMG photos and films, including the actor Joe Dallesandro, bodybuilder Ed Fury, and porn star Tico Patterson.

Mizer was never directly associated with gay and lesbian ACTIVISM, but his effect on the development of a gay male consciousness was immeasurable. As early as the 1950s, he began urging readers of his publications to demand their rights, join HOMOPHILE organizations, and fight police entrapment and censorship. He himself successfully fought several legal battles (although F. Valentine Hooven III believes he may have served a brief prison sentence in the late 1960s on an unfounded charge of procuring), but his most important legacy is his photography, which both reflected and influenced what contemporary gay men find erotic in other men to a degree never matched by more critically acclaimed high-culture photographers.

- *Physique: A Pictorial History of the Athletic Model Guild,* edited by Winston Leyland (1982).
- F. Valentine Hooven III, *Beefcake: The Muscle Magazines of America, 1950–1970* (1995).

Monette, Paul
(1945–1995)

U.S. writer, AIDS activist. Born in Lawrence, Massachusetts, Monette attended elite New England schools, graduated from Yale in 1967, and began writing poetry while teaching at a prep school outside Boston. Shortly before publishing his first book of poetry, *The Carpenter at the Asylum* (1975), he met Roger Horwitz, an attorney four years his senior of whom Monette later wrote: "How do I speak of the person who was my life's best reason?" The two men moved to Los Angeles in 1977, and Monette turned from poetry to screenplays and novels. Between 1978 and 1982, he published four popular potboilers, three of which featured gay male characters in HOLLYWOOD settings.

The advent of AIDS radicalized Monette, provoking him to write a series of critically acclaimed books beginning with *Borrowed Time: An AIDS Memoir* (1988; Lambda Literary AWARD) and *Love Alone: Eighteen Elegies for Rog* (1988; set to music by Ned Rorem and premiered by the New York City Gay Men's Chorus). Both books centered on Horwitz's struggle with the disease; he died of complications of AIDS in 1986. Later came *Afterlife* (1990), about three gay L.A. widowers; *Halfway Home* (1991), a novel about gay "families," which Monette considered his best book; *Becoming a Man: Half a Life Story* (1992; National

Book Award), memoirs published after Monette was diagnosed with AIDS in December 1991; and *Last Watch of the Night* (1994), a collection of essays on death, AIDS-related politics, and the passions of his life.

After Horwitz's death, Monette was lovers with television executive Stephen Kolzak, who also died of AIDS, and Winston Wilde.

Moraga, Cherríe
(1952–)

U.S. activist, writer, editor. Born and raised in Southern California, the daughter of a Mexican mother and an Anglo father, Moraga has written that she creates from the "oppositions of race" inside her. Her light skin and bicultural education would have allowed her to live as an Anglo, but her affirmation of her lesbianism in 1974 brought a new awareness of herself as a Chicana: she found herself "now darkened by desire" ("Raw Experience"). As she wrote in her poem, "For the Color of My Mother": "I am a white girl gone brown to the blood color of my mother / speaking for her."

Moraga and GLORIA ANZALDÚA coedited the groundbreaking *This Bridge Called My Back: Writings by Radical Women of Color* (1981). In her introduction to the collection, she elaborated on the title: "How can we—this time—not use our bodies to be thrown over a river of tormented history to bridge the gap?" Also in 1981, Moraga wrote (with Amber Hollibaugh) an influential critique of feminism's avoidance of sexuality, "What We're Rollin' Around in Bed With: Sexual Silences in Feminism."

In 1983, she published the acclaimed *Loving in the War Years: Lo Que Nunca Pasó por Sus Labios* ("What Never Passed Her Lips"), the first book of openly lesbian poetry (along with essays) published by a Chicana.

She also coedited the landmark Latina feminist collection *Cuentos: Stories by Latinas* with Alma Gomez and Mariana Romo-Carmona (1983) and has since published five books of prose, essays, poetry, and several much produced plays. She was one of the founders of the Kitchen Table: Women of Color Press and participated in *Just Because of Who We Are* (1986), a film about violence against lesbians (see HATE CRIME).

Moraga views writing as a political act and her lesbianism as "the avenue through which I have learned the most about silence and oppression . . . the most tactile reminder to me that we are not free human beings." She has continued to work for what the gay poet Ricardo Bracho, borrowing an Aztec term, imagined as Queer Aztlan, a "decolonized" sacred space for gay and lesbian Chicanos, but in her later work, she has also embraced what she calls "a much larger community of people" who can "inhabit" and "speak through" her.

Moraga teaches at the University of California, Berkeley. She has a son, Angel Rafael.

- Cherríe Moraga, *The Last Generation* (1993).
- Yvonne Yarbro-Bejarano, "De-constructing the Lesbian Body: Cherríe Moraga's *Loving in the War Years*," in *The Lesbian and Gay Studies Reader*, edited by Henry Abelove, Michèle Aina Barale, and David M. Halperin (1993).
- Tatiana de la Tierra, "Interview with Cherríe Moraga," *Conmocion* (no. 1, 1995).

Mormons

Popular name for the almost 3 million members of the Church of Jesus Christ of Latter-Day Saints, a faith based primarily on the BIBLE, the Book of Mormon, and the revelations of Joseph Smith (1805–1844) and Brigham Young (1801–1877). The Book of Mormon (2 Nephi 13:8–9) condemns persons whose "countenance doth witness against them, and doth declare their sin to be even as Sodom, and they cannot hide it. Wo unto their souls, for they have rewarded evil unto themselves."

Although the early Mormons were themselves persecuted as sexual nonconformists—and driven out of towns and cities for their advocacy of polygamy—the Church is today one of the least tolerant of all religions on matters of sexual nonconformity. Mormons have developed counseling programs and funded "treatments," including shock therapy, for members who admit experiencing same-sex desire. Gay and lesbian Mormons who insist on "practicing" their sexuality—or who publicly affirm it—are excommunicated. The Church has also been a leader and major funding source of the fight against legal recognition of same-sex MARRIAGE in the U.S.

Affirmation, founded in 1977, is a social and support group for lesbian and gay Mormons.

Johnny Mathis was one of the first well-known singers to come out. His announcement had no perceivable effect on his record sales.

Movies, see FILM AND VIDEO, GAY, LESBIAN, AND QUEER; HOLLYWOOD.

Music

Art form that has contributed in a host of ways to the development of distinctive lesbian and gay SUBCULTURES. Although a few people believe along with HARRY HAY that a composer's sexuality can be identified by the musical patterns he or she chooses—in the case of some lesbians, what musicologist Elizabeth Wood calls "sapphonics"—most lesbian and gay musicians would probably agree with Neil Tennant, the openly gay lead singer of the Pet Shop Boys, who told THE ADVOCATE in 1996: "The Pet Shop Boys are not in a group because they're gay. They're in a group because they love making music." Nonetheless, whatever the motivation, an extraordinary number of musicians and composers in virtually every genre of music have been—and continue to be—gay or lesbian.

Before STONEWALL, however, the world of music was at least as closeted as the other arts. Before 1971—when MADELINE DAVIS wrote and recorded GAY LIBERATION's first anthem, "Stonewall Nation"—song lyrics were routinely censored, heterosexualized, or GENDER-neutralized; disagreement exists as to whether songwriters ever intentionally encoded gay or lesbian messages, like "My Heart Belongs to Daddy," written originally from the perspective of a gigolo, Little Richard's "Tutti Frutti" or "Good Golly, Miss Molly," and "Bette Davis Eyes," by Jackie De Shannon and Donna Weiss. Novelist Larry Duplechan considers

The founders of Olivia Records (left to right), Judy Dlugacz, Meg Christian, Ginny Berson, Jennifer Woodul, and Kate Winter.

Elvis Presley's 1957 hit "Jailhouse Rock" the first mention of homosexuality in rock 'n' roll: if the listener didn't know that the slang for "jailhouse sex" was "jailhouse rock," the lyrics "No. 47 said to No. 3, 'You're the cutest jailbird I ever did see' " would have given it away.

Other lyrics that *don't* heterosexually cross-gender with their singer are termed "CVs" (cross-vocals). Music and film journalist Boze Hadleigh considers Jon Terrell's "He Certainly Was Good to Me" (1898) the earliest example of a CV and notes more recent examples including the homoerotic military song "My Buddy" (1922), the original man-to-man love ballad "Wind Beneath My Wings" by Gary Morris, and "Crimson and Clover" by Joan Jett. Lip-syncing in drag shows plays with CV and feigns the cross by aligning the lyric gender with the impersonated gender. Music videos add a visual element that may contradict the literal gender of the lyric, as in Madonna's "Justify My Love," where the lyrics are not CV but the simultaneous video is.

Gay or lesbian parody lyrics sung to the tune of a popular song humorously connect the message directly with a gay/lesbian audience. Perhaps the first to record lesbian parody lyrics was LISA BEN, as in "I'm a *Boy* being a *Girl,*" while Phranc's flattop haircut and grown-up TOMBOY looks twist her rendition of "I Enjoy Being a Girl."

Music also serves as an entertaining part of the BAR culture, providing community connection and identity, and has a similar function in special events such as drag shows and revues. Only recently, however, have gay men and lesbians used music and a music industry to develop a culture and community outside of their immediate social circle. Lesbians have led this effort with the creation of "women's music." Ethnomusicologist Boden Sandstrom finds women's music reflecting social and personal issues, providing a bonding force for communal understanding. In festival format, music displays its unique power to arouse and galvanize its audience.

Elton John is one of the best-known male stars who have (eventually) come out.

Women's Music

In the 1970s, an alternative, largely underground music movement emerged among women active in feminist and lesbian-feminist politics. In styles ranging from acoustic or blues pop to light folk and fusions of jazz and rock, women sought to give expression to their experiences and the ways their lives were evolving as part of the women's movement. As ALIX DOBKIN observed, "Women's music is not a 'sound'; women's music is a consciousness in music."

Not all women's music performers were lesbians, but the genre was most often performed and appreciated in a lesbian environment. Some performers, such as Pam Brandt of the classic 1970s pop group Deadly Nightshade, embraced lesbian SEPARATISM, warning that she could barely "tolerate heterosexual and bisexual women, whether performers or audience."

One of the earliest examples of openly lesbian women's music was Maxine Feldman's "Sappho's Lover Angry Atthis," first performed in 1969 and recorded as "Angry Atthis" in 1971. The song relates Atthis's frustration at not being able to hold Sappho's hand " 'cept under some dimly lit table" and proudly concludes with the statement that she is "no longer afraid of being a lesbian." By 1972 there were groups emerging such as the openly lesbian-feminist Family of Women band (FOW) of Chicago made up of Linda Shear, Joan Capra, Ella Szekely, and Sherry Jenkins; the Chicago and New Haven Women's Liberation Rock Bands and their celebrated *Mountain Moving Day* album; *Virgo Rising*, with many artists contributing traditional folk songs with new feminist lyrics; and *A Few Loving Women*, the first lesbian LP with artists including Margaret Sloan and Jeriann Hilderley (Jeritree). In 1973 Lavender Jane (Alix Dobkin, Kay Gardner, and Pat Moschetta) recorded the wholly lesbian-produced *Lavender Jane Loves Women*. And in 1974, the first National Women's Music Festival was held in Champaign-Urbana, Illinois, under the leadership of Kristin Lems; it was followed by the Amazon Music Festival in Santa Cruz, California, and Womansphere festival in Maryland.

The first generation of women musicians in the 1970s was steeped in the women's liberation movement and created a political/musical consciousness that reached peak popularity within the decade. The early years saw women-identified-women and separatist politics in more traditional folk and pop musical forms with the singers cast as modern-day troubadours creating a safe supportive space for women audiences. While technical and promotional skills were initially scarce, women learned from a few experienced producers and technicians such as Marilyn Ries and Joan Lowe. The groundbreaking Olivia Records was formed in 1973; it was later joined by many other women's labels, including Urana, Redwood, Pleiades, Lima Bean, and Leonarda for classical music. Feminist theory influenced the burgeoning industry and somewhat successfully encouraged noncompetitiveness (no "stars" or groupies), women-only record production and events, and nonprofit sliding-scale economics.

By the mid-1970s, women's music festivals and concert tours were creating audiences, connecting musicians, and feeding a distribution network, leading Alix Dobkin to optimistically report in 1975 that "there was a nationwide demand for lesbian music." By the end of the decade, women's music served vital community needs for political, spiritual, and cultural expression; about 20 recording companies, 45 production companies, and over 24 independent distributors called Women's Independent Labels Distributors (WILD) helped circulate the work of nearly 40 recording artists. Profit margins were slim and fund-raising was required to finance albums, although benefactors like E. Shirley Watt and Joan Gibson often made recordings possible. Early performers included Margie Adams, Meg Christian, Casse Culver, Robin Flower, HOLLY NEAR, Linda Tillery, Willie Tyson, Mary Watkins, and Cris Williamson, whose *The Changer and the Changed* (1975) became the best-selling women's music album.

Distributor Betsy York summed up the 1980s as a time of "outreach, crossover, and integration"; music critic Susan Wilson observed that the types of music, politics, and performers were overwhelming limited, white, and middle-class. Others like Toni L. Armstrong Jr. disagreed, reminding her readers that various styles and musicians of color had always been a part of women's music. During the decade, men entered into production and songwriting and the economics of the industry shifted toward profit. Olivia Records began recording less feminist-identified music on a subsidiary label, Second Wave, and mainstream performers began participating in festivals. Popular artists included Alive!, Tracy Chapman, MELISSA ETHERIDGE, Indigo Girls, Michelle Shocked, SWEET HONEY IN THE ROCK, and Phranc, whose album *I Enjoy Being a Girl* (1989) made her the first openly lesbian singer-songwriter on a major label (Island). Some felt the "authentic" voice of women's music was having an identity crisis.

The many international women's music festivals are cultural events that raise awareness of the social contributions of women and galvanize social and emotional connections. From folk tradition and coffeehouse politics, these festivals grew into large annual events; in addition to the largest, the MICHIGAN WOMYN'S MUSIC FESTIVAL, others include the West Coast Music and Comedy Festival, Sisterspace and Campfest in New Jersey, New England Women's Music Festival in Massachusetts, East Coast Festival, and the Southern Women's Music and Comedy Festival in Georgia. Publications also helped sustain the music scene, such as *Paid My Dues* from Milwaukee; the newsletter *Musica,* edited by Indy Allen; *I Know You Know, Hot Wire, Bay Area Music Magazine;* and, more recently, the 'zine publications and the girl 'zine network.

By the 1990s, a third generation added a mix of feminist and nonfeminist politics, bold punk with sexually ambigious ANDROGYNY, and a wide range of sounds. Cultural critic Arlene Stein said, "If lesbian-feminists of the 1970s fled the restrictions of commercial music to stand outside the dominant culture, today's younger artists are trying to carve out a space for themselves somewhere between the economic constraints of the industry and the imperatives of lesbian identity politics."

Lesbian rockers like Girls in the Nose, Toshi Reagon, and the Famulous Dyketones have existed within women's music but a feminist hard-rock revolution, "Dykecore," began outside that tradition. Such groups include Cunts with Attitude and Tribe 8. As women's music looked less lesbian, Stein found mainstream music looking more lesbian, but without lesbian lyrics. Veteran Alix Dobkin sees connections between women's music and the punk communities, such as the queer-feminist-dyke-punk-women-only band Riot Grrls, begun in Olympia, Washington, in 1991: "We have anger in common, and we have the necessity to create culture for ourselves, because we are not included in mainstream culture."

Michael Callen of the Flirtations, an openly gay-positive a-cappella group formed in 1988, observed that gay male musicians have a way to go: "Our heroic lesbian sisters have created something called women's music, which of course really was lesbian women's music, built an audience, distribution network, recording labels—a cultural phenomenon where women supported women artists. There is absolutely no gay male equivalent of that at all. And I would say that before we talk about crossing over to the mainstream, we have to go through that community building stage."

✧ Joan Nixon and Ginny Berson, "Women's Music," in *Our Right to Love,* edited by Ginny Vida (1978).

✧ Susan Wilson, "The Women's Music Industry," *Equal Times* (September 23, 1979).

✧ Boze Hadleigh, *The Vinyl Closet: Gays in the Music World* (1991).

✧ Arlene Stein, "Androgyny Goes Pop," in *Sisters, Sexperts, Queers: Beyond the Lesbian Nation,* edited by Arlene Stein (1993).

✧ Will Grega, *Gay Music Guide* (1994).

✧ Laura Post, *Backstage Pass: Interviews with Women in Music* (1997).

Myles, Eileen

(1949–)

U.S. poet, performer. A native of Cambridge, Massachussets, Myles had an old-fashioned Catholic primary and secondary education. She graduated from the University of Massachusetts—Boston in 1971 before settling in downtown New York City in 1974. *Chelsea Girls* (1994), a semiautobiographical collection of short stories, evokes her evolution—against a background of drinking, drugs, and stormy affairs—from 1970s quasi-hippiedom to East Village notoriety. She gave her first poetry reading at the club CBGB, edited the poetry magazine *dodgems* from 1977 through 1979, and ran a poetry project from 1984 to 1986. Meanwhile, she gained increasing recognition for her witty, irreverent poems, the first collection of which, *The Irony of the Leash,* was published in 1978. Myles has also written two plays, which were produced at P.S. 122, an avant-garde performance space, and coedited (with Liz Kotz) *The New Fuck You: Adventures in Lesbian Reading,* a collection of the work of 38 emerging and established lesbian writers (and one gay man).

Myles conducted what she called "an openly female presidential campaign," complete with an MTV appearance, in 1992. In addition to performing widely, she teaches poetry at workshops in Manhattan.

✧ Eileen Myles, *Maxfield Parrish: Early and New Poems* (1995).

N

Names Project, The (The AIDS Memorial Quilt)

U.S. not-for-profit organization founded to support a national AIDS memorial and to help local communities fight the disease. Conceived and organized by CLEVE JONES, the San Francisco–based Names Project helps lovers, friends, and families commemorate loved ones who have died of AIDS by creating individualized panels that are sewn together with thousands of others to create a gigantic quilt. Conceptually, the panels are love stories: the design, materials, and decoration selected communicate and pay tribute to an individual life behind the statistics. Seen in part or in its entirety, the Quilt is an almost unbearably powerful testament to the devastation wrought by the disease, but it also serves to inspire and motivate. As Jones described it, "There's promise in a quilt. It's not a shroud or a tombstone. It's so important for people whose greatest enemy is despair." Funds raised by the Names Project are returned to local AIDS organizations working in the communities where the Quilt is displayed.

Each quilt panel is 3 feet by 6 feet. The Names Project provides a workshop in San Francisco where people can work on their quilts. Most, however, are shipped to the workshop where they are stitched together by volunteers into larger sections 12 feet square. On **October 11, 1987**, when it was displayed in Washington, D.C., for the first time (see page 408), the Quilt comprised 1,920 panels, covering a space larger than two football fields. By 1996, it was more than 20 times larger. The Quilt has traveled to more than 30 nations around the world and each year is displayed in about 200 cities. The Names Project has inspired similar efforts in AUSTRALIA, NEW ZEALAND, the UNITED KINGDOM, and other countries.

✧ Cindy Ruskin, *The Quilt: Stories from The Names Project* (1988).

National Gay and Lesbian Task Force (Originally: National Gay Task Force)

U.S. lesbian and gay civil rights advocacy group whose formation was announced in New York City on **October 15, 1973**. The task force, which moved its headquarters to Washington, D.C., and added "and Lesbian" to its name in 1986, has field offices in Boston; Los Angeles; Portland, Oregon; and San Francisco. It had more than 30,000 members in 1996.

The second oldest national gay and lesbian organization (after LAMBDA LEGAL DEFENSE AND EDUCATION FUND), the task force has played a major role in virtually every aspect of the GAY AND LESBIAN RIGHTS MOVEMENT. As the first professional American gay and lesbian political organization with a truly national purview, the task force has fostered a broad range of initia-

By 1987, when the Names Project Quilt was first displayed in Washington, D.C., its nearly 2,000 panels covered the equivalent of more than two football fields.

tives at local and state as well as federal levels, ranging from the Fight the Right Project to the Workplace Initiative Project in support of employment rights for bisexuals, lesbians, and gay men. It has also been active in gay and lesbian HEALTH care issues.

Modeled after the AMERICAN CIVIL LIBERTIES UNION, the task force evolved out of a group called Gay Action founded by GAY ACTIVISTS ALLIANCE leader Bruce Voeller, and was in full operation by 1974. Its founding board members included HOWARD BROWN, MARTIN DUBERMAN, Meryl Friedman, BARBARA GITTINGS, FRANK KAMENY, and Nathalie Rockhill. One of its first successes occurred on **September 27, 1974**, when it persuaded advertisers to withdraw from a TELEVISION program that portrayed a gay male teacher as a rapist (also see **11/24/1974**). Later in the decade, leaders of the task force were the first gay and lesbian rights activists to obtain a meeting at the White House (see **3/26/1977**).

The task force gained strength during periods of intensified right-wing attacks on the gay and lesbian rights movement. In 1977, for example, it was able to back its "We Are Your Children" counterattack against Anita Bryant's "Save the Children" crusade (see **1/18/1977**) with a then unprecedented $1-million fundraising campaign. It has been less successful—and much more controversial—when its leaders have attempted to ally the gay and lesbian rights movement with issues not directly related to bias against lesbians and gay men, as when the task force, then headed by activist Urvashi Vaid, opposed the Gulf War in 1991.

Seeking a broader base of support and improved communications within the communities it represents, the task force underwent extensive reorganization in the 1990s, and began in 1993 to sponsor annual Creating Change conferences, which brought together a large number of the nation's leading gay, lesbian, and bisexual activists.

- Toby Marotta, *The Politics of Homosexuality* (1981).
- Urvashi Vaid, *Virtual Equality: The Mainstreaming of Gay and Lesbian Liberation* (1995).

National Organization for Women (NOW)

Major U.S. feminist group. Founder and first president Betty Friedan rose to national prominence with the publication of her *The Feminine Mystique* (1963), which rejected the commonly held belief that women could find fulfillment only in traditional roles as wife and mother. Although many lesbian activists, including PHYLLIS LYON and DEL MARTIN, were early supporters of the organization, which was founded in 1966, NOW leaders at first refused to express public support of lesbian rights. As RITA MAE BROWN wrote in her letter (published January 1970) explaining her resignation from the New York chapter of NOW, "Lesbian is the one word that can cause the Executive Committee a collective heart attack." By 1970, Brown, Ti-Grace Atkinson, and many other prolesbian members had left NOW, first to join more radical feminist organizations, then to become part of groups advocating LESBIAN FEMINISM.

The LAVENDER MENACE protest action on **May 1, 1970**, marked the beginning of a turnaround in NOW policies. Later that year, KATE MILLETT, NOW's education chair, came OUT as a bisexual. On **September 6, 1971**, the NOW annual convention acknowledged the "oppression of lesbians as a legitimate concern of feminism." And in **February 1973**, the organization declared its proactive support of the lesbian and gay rights movement. Although Friedan responded by attacking lesbians in a *New York Times* op-ed piece (**3/4/1973**), relations between lesbians and NOW leaders have generally been friendly ever since. One sign of how much the organization has changed since its founding was NOW president Patricia Ireland's revelation in a December 1991 ADVOCATE interview that she had a female lover in addition to a (male) husband.

- Sidney Abbott and Barbara Love, *Sappho Was a Right-On Woman* (1972).
- Toby Marotta, *The Politics of Homosexuality* (1981).

Nation of Islam

AFRICAN-AMERICAN nationalist sect founded in Detroit in 1930 and elaborated after 1934 under the leadership of Elijah Muhammad (1897–1975). The Nation of Islam combines teachings derived from ISLAM with a black separatist ideology. As such, its condemnation of gay men and lesbians is based both on interpretations of the Koran and the belief, also voiced by non-Muslim black thinkers like Frantz Fanon and Dr. Frances Cress Welsing (see HOMOPHOBIA), that homosexuality is "the white man's disease." Nation of Islam leader Louis Farrakhan has claimed that membership in his sect can "cure" African-American lesbians and gay men. On at least one occasion, a Nation of Islam spokesperson has recommended that black gay men and lesbians be killed.

➤ Also see **October 16, 1995**.

Native Americans

When Randy Burns (a Paiute), Barbara Cameron (a Lakota), and ten other Native Americans founded Gay American Indians (GAI) in San Francisco in **July 1975**, one of their principal objectives was to let other Native Americans know, as Cameron stated, "that there *are* gay Indians." At the time of GAI's formation, most Native Americans, not to mention most non–Native Americans, had never heard of their centuries-old traditions of accommodation and respect for "two-spirited" BERDACHES and (as the female equivalents of berdaches are sometimes called) amazons.

Today, GAI has more than a thousand members from dozens of tribes living on and off tribal lands across the United States. Although its strongest chapters are still in cities like San Francisco, gay and lesbian Indians report growing acceptance on tribal lands as well, in part because of a nationwide renaissance of Native American religious and cultural traditions that has begun to reverse some of the destructive effects of centuries of European-American domination. GAI has played a part in this renaissance, launching a history project that has documented two-spirited traditions in more than 135 tribes, as well as providing venues where straight, gay, lesbian, and bisexual Indians can come together and attempt to re-create the harmonious extended families that once characterized Native life.

Although Native lesbians and gay men have at times encountered prejudice even within supposedly liberationist gay and lesbian organizations, Native cultural and religious traditions are today studied and revered by large numbers of non-Native gay men and lesbians. In addition, Native writers—including PAULA GUNN ALLEN (Laguna Pueblo/Sioux), BETH BRANT (Mohawk of the Bay of Quinte), CHRYSTOS (Menominee), and Maurice Kenny (Mohawk)—reach audiences that far transcend the 1 percent of U.S. residents who described themselves in the 1990 census as "American Indian, Eskimo, or Aleut." The Native gay and lesbian literary movement, vigorous in CANADA as well as in the U.S., is particularly impressive in light of the fact that Arlene Hirschfelder's *American Indian and Eskimo Authors* (1973) found only a dozen novels published by Indians. Beth Brant's anthology *A Gathering of Spirit: Writing and Art by North American Indian Women* (1983) not only marked the debut of many Native lesbian authors, it was also the very first anthology edited entirely by a Native American. Another breakthrough was scored by Will Roscoe with his collection *Living the Spirit: A Gay American Indian Anthology* (1988).

✧ Paula Gunn Allen, *The Sacred Hoop: Recovering the Feminine in American Indian Traditions* (1986).

✧ Walter L. Williams, *The Spirit and the Flesh: Sexual Diversity in American Indian Culture* (1988).

Navarre, Yves

(1940–1994)

French novelist, playwright, essayist. Navarre worked as an ADVERTISING copywriter until his third published novel, *Les Loukoums* (1973), attracted wide public attention. He won the prestigious Prix Goncourt in 1980 for his novel *Le Jardin d'Acclimation* and an Académie Française prize for lifetime achievement in 1992. Much of Navarre's work is concerned with narcissism, aging, and the complex interplay between cruelty and tenderness in love relationships as well as within families. Critics have noted that gay relationships in Navarre's novels are in general less positively portrayed than heterosexual relationships. Openly gay throughout his public life, Navarre became an activist in the fight against AIDS in the late 1980s, publishing the provocative *Ce Sont Amis Que le Vent Emporte* ("The Wind Is Carrying Away Friends," a pun on the French title of *Gone with the Wind*) in 1992. Navarre committed suicide by drug overdose in 1994.

Navratilova, Martina

(Martina Subertova; 1956–)

Czech-born U.S. tennis star, writer, activist, the first major athlete to come OUT while still active in her or his sport. Born in Prague, Navratilova was on the tennis court by the age of four, following in the footsteps of her grandmother, who was a nationally ranked player. She took part in her first tournament at eight and began competing on the junior circuit at ten. Her stepfather, an economic advisor, adopted her and with her athletic mother, an office worker, guided her early career while serving as government tennis administrators. A younger stepsister, Jana, is also a tournament player.

Martina Navratilova at Wimbledon, 1992.

Conflicts with the Communist government–controlled Czech Tennis Federation contributed to her decision to defect to the U.S. in 1975. She soon emerged as the greatest women's tennis player of all time, winning 167 single and 164 double titles, including 4 at the U.S. Open and an unprecedented 9 at Wimbledon, before her retirement from singles competition in 1994. In the course of her remarkable 24-year career, she set new standards of athleticism, power, and intensity in women's tennis.

Navratilova's relationships with pro golfer Sandra Haynie, basketball pro Nancy Lieberman, writer and lesbian activist RITA MAE BROWN, and businesswoman Judy Nelson (who brought a palimony suit against her in 1991) were so well-known that most people felt she had come out long before her 1991 proclamation on national television. Later, she told a crowd of more than half a million at the 1993 lesbian and gay March on Washington: "I'm convinced that you really do not fully accept yourself as a human being until you're out."

Despite her popularity, Navratilova's sexual openness and aggressive style of play have at times elicited homophobic reactions from the media. Sportswriters even stereotyped her long-standing rivalry with heterosexual friend Chris Evert as a fight between the forces of gender. Her being out also cost her millions of dollars in potential endorsements, a loss she has shrugged off with the statement "Freedom. I left my birth country to get that."

Navratilova has worked as an activist at home in Aspen, Colorado, in the national fight against discrimination in the MILITARY, and, with her good friend and mentor BILLIE JEAN KING, to promote the GAY GAMES. Her writings include the best-selling *Martina: An Autobiography* (with George Vecsey, 1985) and a series of coauthored mystery novels set in a tennis milieu. In 1995, she appeared in television and print ADVERTISING to promote the Rainbow Card, a credit card that directs money to gay and lesbian organizations.

✧ Suzanne Westenhoefer, "The New Martina: An Interview," *The Advocate* (December 12, 1995).

✧ Gilda Zwerman, *Martina Navratilova* (1995).

Nazi Persecution

The intensified oppression of gay men and lesbians that was a feature of National Socialist (Nazi) Party rule of GERMANY (1933–1945) and AUSTRIA (1938–1945), as well as, though less harsh, occupied BELGIUM, FRANCE, and the NETHERLANDS (1940–1945). According to the most reliable estimates, between 10,000 and 15,000 men perished as a result of the persecution; about 50,000 were charged with offenses related to same-sex relations during Nazi rule. German historian Claudia Schoppmann, the leading expert on the Nazi persecution of lesbians, believes that it is impossible to make even a rough estimate of the number of lesbians who died. Since sex between adult women was not against the law in Germany, most lesbians who suffered persecution during the period were prosecuted for other offenses, such as leftist political activities. Some lesbians were also incarcerated for alleged prostitution, and many women suspected of being lesbians suffered especially harsh treatment in Nazi camps.

Like the Nazi genocide of Jews and gypsies, the persecution of gay men was motivated by Adolf Hitler's fanatical belief in the superiority and "racial purity" of the Germans who he believed to be part of the "Aryan race." As Heinrich Himmler, the chief of the SS (Schutzstaffel, or "protective guard," the Nazi police force in charge of enforcing racial-purity policies), stated in a 1936 speech, the Nazis saw homosexuality as "a symptom of racial degeneracy destructive to our race." On the other hand, most German men who engaged in same-sex eroticism were themselves Aryan and even sometimes, as Hitler once averred in a private conversation, "among the best and most masculine natures . . . precisely those whose offspring a people [*Volk*] depended upon." Thus some Nazis believed it was vitally important to seek a "cure" for homosexuality, so that the reproductive potential of these men could be preserved. In the absence of a cure, however, the Nazis agreed that a regime of terror was necessary both to keep gay men from "infecting" others and to dissuade them from acting on their desires.

Nazi party members had begun violent actions against the German HOMOPHILE movement as early as **February 4, 1923**, when they attacked a homophile rally. One of the first measures taken by Hitler after gaining power in Germany (see **2/23–24/1933**) was to ban "pornographic" magazines (which covered all progay and -lesbian publications, no matter how restrained their content) and homophile organizations such as MAGNUS HIRSCHFELD's and ADOLF BRAND's groups. Hirschfeld's Institute of Sexual Research was attacked on **May 6, 1933**, and its valuable books and other archival materials were burned in a public ceremony a few days later. The government also arrested well-known activists like Kurt Hiller, Hirschfeld's assistant. Hiller was sent to a concentration camp for nine months after suffering a near fatal beating at the hands of the SS. He later managed to escape abroad. Hirschfeld, who was on an extended trip abroad when the Nazis took power, settled in France, where he died in 1935.

The Nazi persecution of gay men and lesbians grew increasingly severe through the 1930s, except for a brief respite in deference to world opinion at the time of the Berlin Olympic Games in 1936. Mass arrests began in **October 1934**, the same month the Gestapo formally established the Federal Security Department for Combating Abortion and Homosexuality. On **June 28, 1935**, Paragraph 175, the German law punishing sex between men (see **1871**), was broadened to cover virtually any act, even a mere glance, that courts determined to be "criminally indecent." In the next month, a German court ruled that all acts that offended the "inborn healthy instincts of the German people" could be legally punished. By the end of the decade, a secret directive ordered that offenders who were members of the SS should be sent to concentration camps and then shot "while attempting to escape."

As the numbers of men sentenced for same-sex offenses grew (from 801 in 1932, the year before the Nazis took power, to a high of more than 12,000 men in 1937), offenders were increasingly likely to be transferred from grim prisons to even harsher concentration camps, a policy that was later formalized. Although incarceration in a concentration camp was in effect a death sentence for a majority of gay men, same-sex acts between men were not formally made a capital crime until **February 1, 1942**.

A Gay "Holocaust"?

Although it would seem that the horror of the Nazi persecution of gay men could not be exaggerated, many accounts have in fact inflated the number of men interned in concentration camps and misread the context of the oppression gay men suffered. Gay male Germans were herded into concentration camps along with socialists, habitual criminals, Jehovah's Witnesses, and other "corrupting" influences. Unless they were also Jewish or Romany, they were not sent to extermination camps like Auschwitz.

The peculiarities of the Nazi policy on homosexuality are exemplified by the exemption, at Hitler's explicit orders, of actors, and the fact that in the occupied territories the policy extended only to ethnic Germans (including some residents of Alsace and Lorraine, French territory that the Germans expropriated at the beginning of the war), Austrians, Dutch, and Flemish men. Authorities were told to ignore same-sex behavior among Poles, for example. Since Poles were not Aryan, the Nazis had no interest in protecting the Polish blood lines.

Although the Nazi persecution of homosexuals is probably the best-known 20th-century example of oppression directed against gay men and lesbians, it was by no means the most lethal. It is almost certain that much larger numbers of gay men and lesbians in the USSR (see RUSSIA) perished at the hands of the Soviets. In addition, gay men and lesbians sent to Soviet labor camps during the Stalin era were actually more likely to die of mistreatment than their counterparts in the Nazi camps. Soviet prisoners of the period received even less food and had to endure months of subzero temperatures. Their death rate is thought to have approached 100 percent.

➤ Also see PINK TRIANGLE.

✧ Richard Plant, *The Pink Triangle: The Nazi War Against Homosexuals* (1986).

✧ *Hidden Holocaust? Gay and Lesbian Persecution in Germany 1933–45,* edited by Günter Grau, translated by Patrick Camiller (1995).

✧ Claudia Schoppmann, *Days of Masquerade: Life Stories of Lesbian Women During the Third Reich* (1996).

Near, Holly

(1949–)

U.S. singer-songwriter, activist. Born and raised on her family's sheep farm in Ukiah, California, Near began singing for audiences at the age of seven and grew up yearning for a career in the performing arts. After finishing high school, she studied acting in Los Angeles and won roles in the Broadway musical *Hair,* on TELEVISION, and in FILMS.

In 1971, Near joined Jane Fonda and Donald Sutherland to tour with their "Free the Army" Vietnam War protest show. In 1973, she released her first album, *Hang in There,* on the all-women Redwood Records label she had founded the previous year. Over the next decade, she became a leader of the nascent women's MUSIC movement, performing widely and releasing hit albums like *Imagine My Surprise!* (1978), which is considered her coming OUT statement as well as her most woman-identified album. One of her best-known songs, "Singing for Our Lives," inspired by the assassination of HARVEY MILK, became an anthem of the lesbian and gay rights movement in the 1980s.

Near also became known as an antinuclear and DISABLED rights activist. Influenced by her sister Timothy, a singer and actress who performed with the National Theater of the Deaf, she was one of the first singers to provide sign-language interpreters at concerts.

In her autobiography, *Fire in the Rain . . . Singer in the Storm* (1990), Near revealed: "People who have always thought that I've always been with women will be surprised to hear about my relationships with men." Some of her lesbian fans were disheartened by her coming out as a bisexual; most, however, would agree with Robin Tyler's appraisal of Near as a woman's "cultural giant."

✧ Toni Armstrong Jr., "A Personal Chat with Holly Near," *Hot Wire* (September 1990).

Nestle, Joan

(1940–)

U.S. writer, archivist, educator, activist. Named for her father, Jonas, who died before she was born, Nestle and an older brother were raised by her working-class Jewish mother, Regina Mayer, in the Bronx, New York City. She had her first job at the age of 13 and worked her

Joan Nestle.

way through Queens College, where she later taught as an English professor for 28 years in SEEK (Search for Elevated and Enlightened Knowledge), an educational opportunity program.

In the 1950s, Nestle entered the working-class BAR culture as a young femme and discovered the themes that were to resonate in her writing: memory, history, desire, eroticism, and resistance. Other formative influences included the lingering effects of the MCCARTHY ERA, her participation in the Selma civil rights march, and Jewish Tunisian philosopher Albert Memmi's writings about colonization.

With the advent of GAY LIBERATION, she became a member of GAY ACTIVISTS ALLIANCE and Lesbian Feminist Liberation and was a cofounder of the Gay Academic Union. In 1973, Nestle cofounded the LESBIAN HERSTORY ARCHIVES, stating, "Answering the challenge of exclusion is the work of a lifetime."

Her controversial article "Butch-Fem Relationships: Sexual Courage in the 1950s," published in *Heresies* (1981), initiated a widespread revaluation of the BUTCH-FEM(ME) tradition and, along with her equally controversial erotic writings later, launched her onto the front lines of the lesbian SEX WARS. Nestle's erotica, begun initially as part of her resistance to a chronic illness that kept her "house bound and spirit bound," led to her being called a "pornographer" in some quarters, a "national treasure" in others. Her first collection of stories and political essays, *A Restricted Country* (1987), re-created four decades of a life "worn by the body." As she explained, "All I have are my words and my body, and I will use them to say and picture the truths I know."

Nestle has also compiled a number of important anthologies, including the popular *Women on Women* series (with Naomi Holoch; 1990, 1992, 1996), *The Persistent Desire: A Femme-Butch Reader* (1992), and *Sister and Brother* (with John Preston, 1994). She was the first recipient of the David R. Kessler Award from the Center for Lesbian and Gay Studies at the City University of New York, and has received the AMERICAN LIBRARY ASSOCIATION Gay Book AWARD, the Sappho Award of Distinction from the Astraea Foundation, and four Lambda Book Awards.

✧ Holly Metz, "Interview with Joan Nestle," *American Voice* (no. 21, Winter 1990).

✧ Clare Whatling, "Reading Awry: Joan Nestle and the Recontexualization of Heterosexuality," in *Sexual Sameness: Textual Differences in Lesbian and Gay Writing,* edited by Joseph Bristow (1992).

Netherlands

No laws against consensual same-sex relations for adults; discretionary enforcement of laws against same-sex relations with children. Extensive rights protections. Well-developed social scene and active political organizations.

Surveys have shown that as few as 10 percent of the Dutch oppose gay and lesbian rights, making it one of the most tolerant countries in the world. Nevertheless, Dutch lesbian and gay activists maintain that the country is not quite the queer paradise most people around the world believe it to be. Issues of contention remain, including gay and lesbian rights to adopt CHILDREN, availability of artificial insemination for lesbians, and official state recognition of same-sex MARRIAGE on a par with heterosexual unions.

In other ways, the Netherlands provides freedoms unimaginable in other countries. The Netherlands, for example, is the only country in which PEDOPHILIA and PEDERASTY can be freely researched and discussed. Publications such as *Paidika* are the only journals in the world that offer serious articles on these topics.

Amsterdam is Europe's unofficial gay capital. According to the Dutch government tourist office, about 3,000 of the 25,000 jobs in the Amsterdam tourism industry owed their existence to gay and lesbian tourism as of 1992. Since then the city has actively promoted itself as the Gay Capital, and hundreds of thousands of gay and lesbian visitors, particularly Britons, come to enjoy the city's varied cultural and social attractions each year. One of the most prominent of these is the Homomonument, designed by Karin Daan and constructed in 1987 in the heart of the city. Three interlocking pink granite triangles that commemorate victims of HOMOPHOBIA, the Homomonument has also come to symbolize the struggle against AIDS.

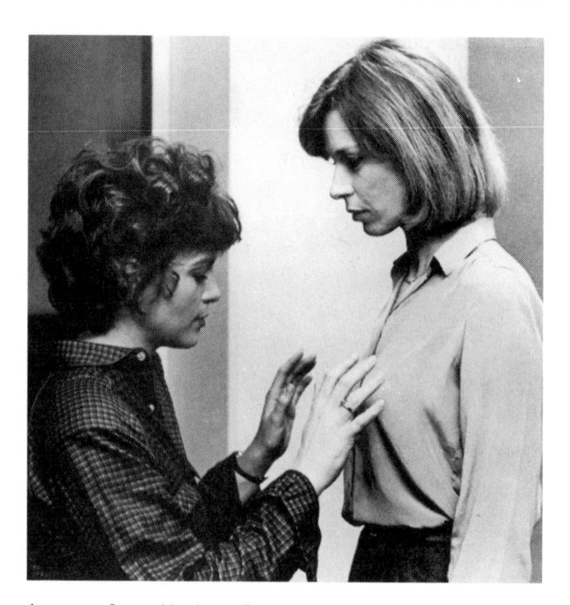

A scene from Marleen Gorris's 1983 Dutch film, A Question of Silence.

History

"Unnatural vice" became a capital crime in the Netherlands in **1532**, but enforcement of the law was relatively lax until the early 18th century, when the country was the site of one of the most savage—and best documented—campaigns against SODOMY. From **1730**, more than 250 men and boys were accused of the crime. About 200 fled into exile to avoid prosecution. Most of the others were tortured to give evidence and subsequently executed (also see **9/1731**). Another wave of persecution later in the 18th century was somewhat less lethal. Consensual sex between adults was officially decriminalized after the country was occupied by French forces between 1795 and 1813. The country continued to follow the Napoleonic Code (see **1810**) after it regained independence but instituted a discriminatory AGE OF CONSENT for same-sex acts in **1911.** This legislation provoked the jurist Jacob Schorer to found a HOMOPHILE organization called the Dutch Scientific Humanitarian

Committee, which he modeled after MAGNUS HIRSCHFELD's pioneering German group.

Despite the existence of a homophile organization, Dutch gay and lesbian life remained much less visible in the first half of the 20th century than in neighboring GERMANY. A group called Levensrecht (Right to Live) was founded in **1939** to promote greater openness, but its activities were suppressed during the German occupation the following year and the subsequent NAZI PERSECUTION of homosexuality. Although the Nazis, encouraged by the ROMAN CATHOLIC CHURCH, criminalized same-sex relations between men (see **7/31/1940**) and attempted to investigate and destroy gay male networks, they received little cooperation from the Dutch police. In a now famous dispatch, a Dutch police chief explained their failure to the Nazis as follows: "The successful combating of homosexuality" requires "experience, investigative skill, and professional zeal. These three conditions are not present in the Netherlands police, however, when it comes to the question of homosexuality." As a result, few Dutch men were arrested. Several gay men, including Willem Arondaus and Sjoerd Bakker, played heroically prominent roles in the Dutch resistance movement against the Nazis.

Homophile advocates resurfaced after World War II to found Cultuur-en OntspanningsCentrum (COC, Culture and Recreation Center) in **1946**. To this day, COC, the world's largest and most developed gay and lesbian organization, continues as the umbrella organization for the Dutch gay and lesbian rights movement, with 30 branches nationwide.

All-male CRUISING venues and a rudimentary BAR subculture are documented for the Netherlands as early as the 18th century and continued to develop discreetly through the 19th century. By the 1960s, large Dutch cities were famous the world over for their well-developed gay male SUBCULTURES. In 1968, a year before STONEWALL, *Newsweek* magazine called Amsterdam a "mecca for homosexuals." Yet DENNIS ALTMAN, visiting the country in the early 1970s, found that "the prevailing social climate is one of tolerance rather than acceptance. Dutch homosexuals, particularly teenagers, are oppressed by the same feelings of guilt and social ostracism as are American or Australian ones." Historians note that the first gay PRIDE CELEBRATION in the Netherlands did not occur until 1977.

Less is known about lesbian life before Stonewall, but scholars speculate that the private women's networks, or "living room culture," first studied in the 1970s began many decades previously. A magazine called *Vriendschap* ("Friendship") provided lesbians a forum for communication in the 1950s. Nevertheless, in 1968, a nationwide survey estimated that 112,000 women who were primarily or strongly attracted to other women were married to men, an indication of the persisting strength of COMPULSORY HETEROSEXUALITY. Lesbian life gradually became more public with the development of special women's cafés and women's nights at gay bars beginning on a large scale in the 1970s.

Also in the 1970s, a split occurred between "lesbian" and "homosexual" women, with the former increasingly drawn to SEPARATISM (see **9/1971**) and the latter advocating cooperation with gay male groups.

Gay and lesbian political successes, which included the end of discrimination in the MILITARY in **1974**, culminated in the Equal Treatment Act, adopted in **February 1993**, which outlawed discrimination based on sexuality. The country has an unequaled record of funding and supporting an enormous range of gay and lesbian organizations and activities, not only in the Netherlands but in other countries as well.

- *Gay Life in Dutch Society,* edited by A. X. van Naerssen (1987).
- "The Netherlands," in *The Pursuit of Sodomy: Male Homosexuality in Renaissance and Enlightenment Europe,* edited by Kent Gerard and Gert Hekma (1989).
- Judith Schuyf, "The Company of Friends and Lovers: Lesbian Communities in the Netherlands," in *Modern Homosexualities: Fragments of Lesbian and Gay Experience,* edited by Ken Plummer (1992).
- Astrid Mattijssen, Mirjam Turksma, and Ineke de Vries, "Netherlands," in *Unspoken Rules: Sexual Orientation and Women's Human Rights,* edited by Rachel Rosenbloom (1996).

New Age Spiritualism, see SPIRITUALITIES, ALTERNATIVE.

New Zealand

No laws against consensual same-sex relations between persons 16 years of age or older. Broad rights protections. Active political organizations and well-developed social scene.

Between **July 9, 1986**, and **July 28, 1993**, New Zealand went from being one of the few countries in the developed world that still criminalized sex between men to become one of only a handful of nations that guarantee equal rights protection for both lesbians and gay men. Today, New Zealand is, at least legally, the most gay- and lesbian-friendly country in the English-speaking world. It also boasts a rich social scene, exemplified by Auckland's Hero Festival, begun in 1991, which offers three weeks of cultural and sport events culminating in a parade and dance party in mid-February.

Prominent lesbian, gay, and bisexual New Zealanders include writer and activist Ngahuia Te Awekotuku; and Tim Barnett and Chris Carter, both of whom have served as members of Parliament.

History

The islands that today make up New Zealand were first settled beginning in about A.D. 800 by Polynesians who came to be called Maoris. Sexually tolerant before the arrival of CHRISTIANITY, the Maoris also are reported to have had less constraining concepts of GENDER than the British colonists who began to arrive in the country in large numbers in the 19th century.

Even after New Zealand became a Dominion in 1907 and an independent country within the British Commonwealth in 1947, the country retained British laws against sex between men (see **1885**). As in the UNITED KINGDOM, sex between women was never criminalized, although lesbian historians have recorded raids of women's BARS into the 1970s, as well as police harassment—especially of BUTCH/FEMME women.

The WOLFENDEN REPORT, released in the U.K. on **September 4, 1957**, inspired gay groups like the Wellington-based Dorian Society to begin a tentative campaign toward law reform as early as 1963. In 1968, the New Zealand Homosexual Law Reform Society petitioned Parliament, only to be ignored by the country's lawmakers. A full-fledged GAY LIBERATION movement began in Auckland, Christchurch, and Wellington in 1972, sparking conferences, demonstrations, and the country's first gay PRIDE CELEBRATION, a march conducted on Auckland's Queen Street that June.

A gay and lesbian rights movement advanced in the late 1970s and early 1980s, although, as in many other countries, conflicts between gay men and lesbians helped foster lesbian SEPARATISM. Increasingly, lesbians formed their own groups and launched their own publications to address issues of particular concern for women. For the most part, however, lesbians and gay men presented a unified front in lobbying Parliament for law reform.

Consensual sex between adult men was finally decriminalized in 1986, despite the concerted efforts of the Coalition of Concerned Citizens, a right-wing group led by the Salvation Army. The coalition presented a petition with 817,000 signatures in protest of reform. Because this number represented more than 25 percent of the total population of the country, including children, most historians believe that the petition contained numerous repetitions and, possibly, even forgeries.

After almost a decade of intensive lobbying, New Zealand amended its Human Rights Commission Act in 1993 to become the seventh country in the world to ban discrimination based on sexual orientation.

✧ Neil Miller, "Australia and New Zealand: The Land They Lost," in *Out in the World: Gay and Lesbian Life from Buenos Aires to Bangkok* (1992).

✧ Julie Glamuzina, *Out Front: Lesbian Political Activity in Aoteroa, 1962 to 1985* (1993).

Nicaragua, see LATIN AMERICA.

Nicolson, Harold, see SACKVILLE-WEST, VITA.

Nigeria, see AFRICA, SUB-SAHARAN.

Nkoli, Simon Tseko

(1957–)

South African activist. Raised in the Johannesburg area by his mother, a maid and later saleswoman, and a devoted stepfather who worked as a chef in a hotel, Nkoli had his first affair with a man at the age of 19. When he came OUT to his mother, she took him to traditional healers in an attempt to "cure" him and then, on his boyfriend's mother's recommendation, sent him to a psychiatrist, who suggested the two men try living together. To do so, in violation of SOUTH AFRICA's apartheid regulations, Nkoli had to register as his (white) boyfriend's servant.

In 1983, he joined the overwhelmingly white male Gay Association of South Africa (GASA). Interested in bringing gay men of color together, he advertised in a black newspaper in August 1983 and organized meetings which led to the formation in May 1984 of the Saturday Group. In September 1984, his involvement with a group associated with the then outlawed African National Congress (ANC) led to his arrest with 21 others on charges that included treason, terrorism, and murder. During his four years in PRISON he was tortured and held in solitary confinement for a year. Nkoli, who was open about his sexuality with his fellow detainees and in court, received considerable support from gay and lesbian activists in Europe, but GASA, his own national organization, refused to help him. GASA was expelled from the INTERNATIONAL LESBIAN AND GAY ASSOCIATION in 1985 as a result.

After his acquittal in 1988, Nkoli founded the Gay and Lesbian Organization of the Witwatersrand, the country's first genuinely multiracial lesbian and gay group. His close ties to the ANC are credited with helping change its antigay positions and influencing its decision to include gay and lesbian rights in the constitutional Bill of Fundamental Rights.

Nkoli has remained one of South Africa's best-known and most effective gay activists. He has campaigned for visibility and understanding in black communities and worked to encourage links between lesbians and gay men. He founded Gay Men's Health Forum in 1992.

✧ *Defiant Desire: Gay and Lesbian Lives in South Africa,* edited by Mark Gevisser and Edwin Cameron (1995).

Noble, Elaine

(1942–)

U.S. politician, activist, educator, health care consultant, the first openly lesbian (or gay) person elected to a statewide public office in the U.S. Born and raised in rural Pennsylvania, Noble came OUT in Boston in the late 1960s while teaching at local universities. She helped produce *Gay Way,* one of the nation's first openly gay and lesbian radio programs, and distinguished herself as an activist for nongay as well as gay community issues before being elected as a Massachusetts state representative on **November 5, 1974**. Noble easily won reelection in November 1976, but lost the Democratic primary for U.S. Senator to Paul Tsongas in 1978.

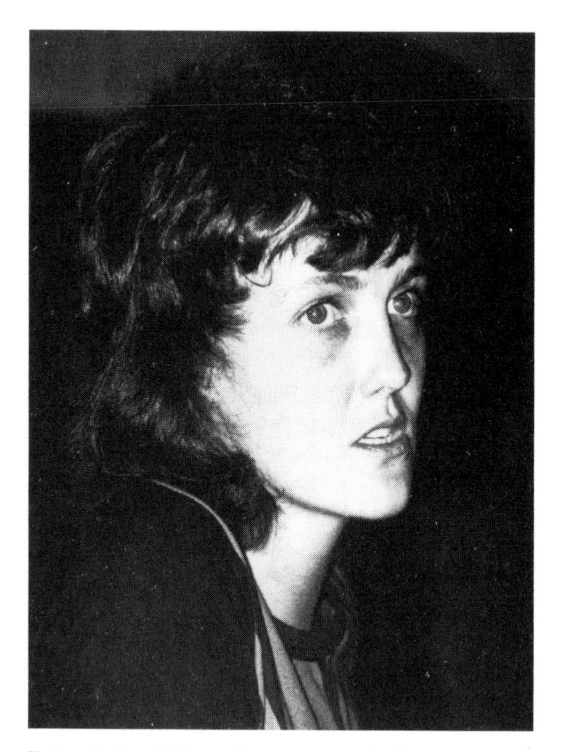

Elaine Noble, 1975, at Sagaris, an early feminist retreat.

As the first prominent openly lesbian politician, Noble is credited with inspiring other uncloseted women, such as Minnesota State Representative Karen Clark, to seek public office. At the same time, she was also among the first to call attention to what she described as the "heavy burden" of being viewed as a representative not simply of one electoral constituency but also of the lesbian and gay communities at large. Besides harassment and death threats based on her lesbianism and support of school integration, Noble also incurred controversy in the separatist lesbian community when she urged participation in electoral POLITICS.

Since leaving public office, Noble has remained active in the lesbian and gay rights movement as a spokesperson and lobbyist. She has also been a leader in the movement to institute ADDICTION treatment centers owned and operated by and for gay men and lesbians.

✧ Reverend Troy D. Perry and Thomas L. P. Swicegood, *Profiles in Gay and Lesbian Courage* (1991).

✧ *Long Road to Freedom: The Advocate History of the Gay and Lesbian Movement,* edited by Mark Thompson (1994).

✧ Elaine Noble, "Chemical Dependency," in *The New Our Right to Love: A Lesbian Resource Book,* edited by Ginny Vida (1996).

Norway, see SCANDINAVIA.

O

O'Hara, Frank

(Francis Russell O'Hara; 1926–1966)

U.S. poet, art critic, and curator. Born in Baltimore, O'Hara grew up in Grafton, Massachusetts, the oldest of three children in an extended Irish-Catholic family that included a sternly traditional father, an alcoholic mother, and several literature-, movie-, and music-loving aunts. Educated by Catholic nuns and brothers, he postponed college to enlist in the Navy in 1944. He later studied music and English at Harvard University and did postgraduate work at the University of Michigan in Ann Arbor. By the time he settled in New York City in 1951, he had already acquired entrée through his friend the poet John Ashberry to a wide-ranging collection of the city's young writers and artists. That same year, he took a job at the Museum of Modern Art gift shop during the Christmas rush, and over the next decade rose to become one of the most influential critics and curators of contemporary art.

O'Hara, who had begun writing seriously while in graduate school, published his first book of poetry, *A City in Winter and Other Poems* in 1952. His latter books of poetry, which included *Lunch Poems* (1964), increasingly evinced his passions for MUSIC, movies, popular culture icons (like Billie Holiday and James Dean) and, especially, ART. In 1958, he and the artist Larry Rivers, with whom O'Hara had an impassioned and sometimes sexual relationship, published *Stones,* a collection of poems and lithographs.

Surrounded by bohemians, O'Hara was unusually open about his sexuality for the conservative 1950s. He loved to regale his friends with accounts of his escapades in pursuit of straight and "straight-appearing" men, adventures that sometimes ended in violence. He was similarly matter-of-fact about his sexuality in his poetry. A few poems explicitly evoke the New York gay CRUISING scenes of his time, as in "Homosexuality," written in the late 1950s: "14th Street is drunken and credulous, / 53rd tries to tremble but is too at rest. / The good love a park and the inept a railroad station." He also described the pathos of the CLOSET, as in "John Button Birthday" (1952): "you find a birthday greeting card with violets / which says 'a perfect friend' and means / 'I love you' but the customer is forced to be / shy. It says less, as all things must."

At the height of his achievements, O'Hara was struck by a dune buggy in a nighttime accident on FIRE ISLAND. His liver weakened by years of excessive drinking, he died a few days later at the age of 40.

✧ Brad Gooch, *City Poet: The Life and Times of Frank O'Hara* (1993).

One, Inc. / One Magazine

HOMOPHILE organization founded on **October 15, 1952**, in Los Angeles to publish a magazine, also called *One,* which was the first national, openly gay or lesbian publication sold publicly in the United States. The founders—Martin Block, Dale Jennings, Dorr Legg, Betty Perdue (under the pseudonym of Geraldine Jackson), Tony Reyes, Chuck Rowland, and Don Slater—were mostly associated with the MATTACHINE Society, and many One, Inc., members remained active in the older organization. One, Inc., core members believed a separate organization could more effectively meet the educational objectives they set out for themselves. "One" came from a passage by Thomas Carlyle: "A mystic bond of brotherhood makes all men one."

The group published the first issue of *One* magazine in **January 1953**. The magazine began with monthly scholarly scientific and historical articles that were nonetheless considered provocative in the 1950s. The Los Angeles postmaster seized copies of *One* in October 1954 and refused to mail it, citing two articles, one on gay marriages and another about lesbians, as "obscene." One, Inc., fought the ruling through appeals brought by attorney Eric Julber until it reached the U.S. Supreme Court, where the lower court rulings were reversed on **January 13, 1958**. The landmark case paved the way for homophile organizations to use the mails and in effect established the right to discuss homosexuality in other than legal, medical, or religious contexts.

A different kind of precedent was set earlier in 1954, when the magazine turned over the entire February issue to its "Feminine Viewpoint" section. This edition, written and edited by women, including Corky Wolf and Jean Corbin, was one of the few issues of *One* that sold out.

By the mid-1950s, One projected a more activist voice than the generally cautious Mattachine. Under the direction of Legg, One, Inc., also began to publish a wide range of books and pamphlets and, beginning in 1956, to sponsor educational programs, lectures, and concerts through the One Institute for Homophile Studies. In turn, the institute pub-

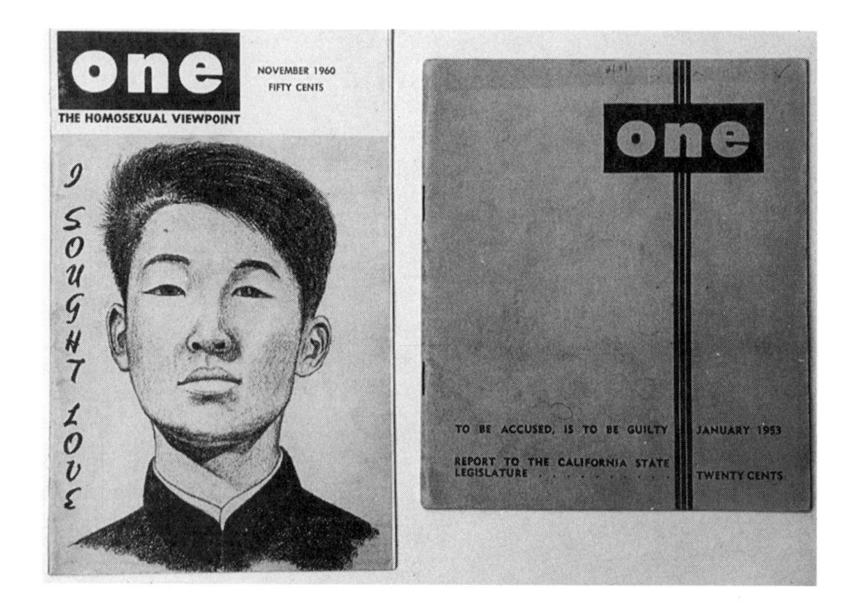

lished the *Journal of Homophile Studies* from 1968 to 1973. It was accredited by the state of California to offer graduate degrees in 1981. The first degree awarded was a Litt. D. (Hon.) to CHRISTOPHER ISHERWOOD in 1982.

In 1965, One suffered a schism due to internal disagreement on how the organization's resources should be allocated. In protest against Legg's emphasis on building a library and on funding academic activities, *One* editor Don Slater departed, taking the magazine's mailing list and continuing to edit and publish *One*. Legg and Slater published two different magazines called *One* from May through October, when a court ordered a settlement in which Legg retained the rights to the name and Slater was able to keep the magazine's office equipment. Slater and writer JOSEPH HANSEN subsequently issued a magazine called *Tangents*, which through 1970 was the most professionally produced and one of the most influential organs of the movement press. Legg's *One* magazine ceased publication in 1967, but One, Inc., continued to issue a wide range of mostly scholarly publications through the 1990s.

✧ John D'Emilio, *Sexual Politics, Sexual Communities: The Making of a Homosexual Minority in the United States, 1940–1970* (1983).

✧ Rodger Streitmatter, *Unspeakable: The Rise of the Gay and Lesbian Press in America* (1995).

Orthodox Eastern Churches

Community of independent but mutually recognized Christian churches, including the Greek and Russian Orthodox Churches, with almost 200 million members. The Orthodox churches developed as the predominant form of CHRISTIANITY in the eastern regions of the Roman Empire and formally split with the ROMAN CATHOLIC CHURCH in 1054.

Persecution of men suspected of having same-sex relations began earlier and was for centuries more virulent in the Orthodox Byzantine Empire than in Western Europe (see **342**; **533**). Much of this persecution, however, was politically motivated and may have had a limited effect on the general population. Folklore suggests that same-sex relationships were common in Orthodox religious orders, and, according to JOHN BOSWELL, the Church may have actually sanctioned SAME-SEX UNIONS. In premodern Russia, same-sex relations were reported to be common by visitors and remained unmentioned in the law books until **1706**.

Some religious historians believe Orthodox Christianity has advocated a gentler, less punishing attitude toward "failings" of the flesh than most Western churches. In fact, the current position of the Orthodox churches on homosexuality is distinguished from that of Roman Catholicism, for example, by an emphasis on "treatment." In 1976, a Greek Orthodox congress declared that "sexual organs . . . are ordained by nature to serve one particular purpose, the procreation of the human kind." It further asserted that "homosexuality should be treated by society as an immoral and dangerous perversion and by religion as a sinful failure" and recommended that lesbians and gay men receive "confidential medical and psychiatric facilities . . . to restore themselves to a self-respecting sexual identity."

Axios, founded in Los Angeles in 1980, is an advocacy group for lesbian and gay Orthodox Christians as well as Byzantine-rite Catholics in the U.S., CANADA, and AUSTRALIA.

➤ Also see **October 21, 1983**.

Ottoman Empire, see TURKEY.

Out

The quality of being openly gay, lesbian, or bisexual. Just as most lesbians and gay men experience not one but a series of CLOSETS, the process of coming "out" usually involves a sequence of self-realizations, decisions, and subsequent declarations to close friends, other lesbians and gay men, family members, colleagues, etc., in an order that varies from one individual to another. Psychologists who have studied the process of coming out find different issues and potential rewards at each stage. Ideally, they note, "new" lesbians and gay men can rely on other, more experienced gay and lesbian mentors for support and encouragement during the process.

Most contemporary gay men and lesbians think of coming—and staying—out as a positive, even praiseworthy objective, but this has not always been the case. Into the 1960s—and even later for some people—lesbians and gay men tended to value discretion in themselves and others. The term "out," in fact, originally referred only to a person's first sexual experience with a member of his or her own sex. A humorous reference to the ceremonious "coming out" balls for traditional debutantes, the term implied that one had been "presented" to lesbian or gay "society." Similarly, it was more common in the days before STONEWALL to speak of a veteran gay man or lesbian "bringing" a neophyte out, rather than a person "coming out" of his or her own volition.

Outing

The practice of publicizing a closeted person's homosexuality. The term "outing" was coined in March 1990 by *Time* magazine to describe a campaign that Michelangelo Signorile and *OutWeek* magazine had launched against closeted Hollywood celebrities and Washington officials. Signorile thought the practice could be better described as "equalizing," since the sex lives of heterosexuals already came under media scrutiny. He believed that gay men and lesbians would achieve equal rights only when all the most powerful among them came out of the closet.

The practice of outing predates the term by at least six centuries. Officials in medieval Florence provided citizens with special boxes for anonymous denunciations of "sodomites." Much more recently, in 1968, an episode of the popular television show *Laugh-In* featured a set with the words "Rock Hudson Is Gay" written on a wall. And in 1988, a "war conference" of leading lesbian and gay activists enthusiastically discussed revealing the sexual orientation of closeted lesbian and gay officials who took stands against the movement. What made Signorile's campaign different was that its aim was not to discredit or discomfit gay men and lesbians but rather to demonstrate how many of the most admired and accomplished people in American society were gay and to try to induce them to lend their prestige to the struggle for equal rights.

A straw poll of 632 gay men and lesbians conducted by the *Washington Blade* in 1990 found that 46 percent of respondents opposed outing, 14 percent favored it, and 34 percent supported it under "limited circumstances."

✧ Larry Gross, *Contested Closets: The Politics and Ethics of Outing* (1993).

✧ Michelangelo Signorile, *Queer in America: Sex, the Media and the Closets of Power* (1993).

OutRage!

U.K. DIRECT ACTION group formed in London on **May 10, 1990**, by Peter Tatchell and others. Like the American QUEER NATION, OutRage! was founded in response to HATE CRIME, in particular the queer-bashing of Michael Boothe, an actor who had been kicked to death. OutRage! updated the confrontational tactics of the GAY LIBERATION era with 1990s media savvy. Actions have included "kiss-ins" (see **2/16/1991**), a lesbian crucifixion at Westminster Cathedral, mock "exorcisms" of the "demons" of HOMOPHOBIA at other Anglican churches, the OUTING of Anglican bishops, "homo promo" drives, mass "queer weddings," and "urban glamour assaults," during which CROSS-DRESSING queers confront London shoppers. Many of Britain's better-known OUT celebrities joined the group, including DEREK JARMAN and JIMMY SOMERVILLE.

Pacific Islands

Sex between men illegal in American Samoa, Cook Islands, Fiji, Guam, Kiribati, Niue, Papua New Guinea, Solomon Islands, Western Samoa, Tonga, and Tuvalu, with penalties ranging from 5 to 14 years' imprisonment. No laws against consensual same-sex relations between adults in French Polynesia, Marshall Islands, Micronesia, New Caledonia, Palau, and Vanuatu. Transgender rights groups in Western and American Samoa and a gay social group in Guam.

Except for the influence of tourists, Pacific Island peoples are mostly isolated from the gay and lesbian rights movements and SUBCULTURES of larger, more developed countries. Much attention, however, has been paid by anthropologists to unique traditions of GENDER concepts and same-sex eroticism in Pacific Island cultures. These include the *mahu* of Tahiti and Hawaii, *fa'afaane* of Samoa, and the *fakaleiti* of Tonga, all biological males who live lives as members of a "third gender," considered neither male nor female. In many of these cultures, such individuals are accorded great respect because it is believed that they are essential to the correct performance of religious ceremonies. On other islands, such as Tonga, they are considered misfits and face harassment from police and hostility from their fellow islanders. Samoan *fa'afaane,* many of whom survive as transvestite sex workers, have organized into groups to demand better treatment and less prejudice.

A completely different construction of sexuality exists in many parts of Melanesia, where some peoples, such as the Sambia, mandate compulsory same-sex relations for adolescent boys in the belief that the semen of adult males is necessary for them to mature to full male potency.

Pacific Island gay and lesbian life has probably always been more varied than anthropological studies would suggest. In the late 18th century, for example, Captain James Cook and other early visitors to the Hawaiian Islands were shocked to find groups of *aikane*—literally, "man-fucking men"—among those close to local kings. *Aikane* appear to have been male-identified adult men who were sexually active with other male-identified adult men, a form of sexual behavior rarely documented even in the West before the 20th century. A similar word, "*moe-aikane,*" is still used today in Hawaii to describe modern gay men.

➤ Also see CIRCUMSTANTIAL HOMOSEXUALITY; NEW ZEALAND.

✧ *Third Sex, Third Gender: Beyond Sexual Dimorphism in Culture and History,* edited by Gilbert Herdt.

✧ Rudi C. Bleys, *Geography of Perversion: Male-to-Male Sexual Behaviour Outside the West and the Ethnographic Imagination, 1750–1918* (1995).

Gay Asian Pacific Alliance is one of the groups that have pressed for increased visibility for gay and lesbian Pacific-Americans.

Paget, Violet, see LEE, VERNON.

Paglia, Camille

(1943–)

U.S. writer, critic, educator. Paglia was raised Catholic in an Italian-American family in Syracuse, New York. She lapsed from the Church in the 1960s, came OUT as a bisexual lesbian, and embraced the then emerging COUNTERCULTURE with an ardor that continues to emanate from almost every page of her writing. While teaching at Bennington College and, later, the University of the Arts in Pennsylvania, she transformed her Ph.D. thesis into the best-selling literary critique and cultural manifesto *Sexual Personae: Art and Decadence from Nefertiti to Emily Dickinson.* Championed by the conservative scholar Harold Bloom, Paglia expounded a controversial theory of the role of biological sex and GENDER in the development of culture. According to Paglia, men create civilization and art in rebellion against—and out of fear of—the forces of nature, especially as embodied by the "chthonian" ("of the earth") procreative powers of women. "Art is form struggling to wake from the nightmare of nature," Paglia argued. More controversial were her statements on the accomplishments, or lack thereof, of women: "If civilization had been left in female hands," Paglia asserted, "we would still be living in grass huts." With notable exceptions like EMILY DICKINSON, Paglia maintained that artistic genius is the domain of men, who are naturally creative: "[Even] male urination really *is* a kind of achievement, an arc of transcendence. A woman merely waters the ground she stands on. Male urination is a form of commentary." In later essays, Paglia singled out the creative contributions of gay men, in particular "queens."

Arguably America's most famous openly bisexual/lesbian intellectual, Paglia has sometimes enraged other lesbians with her provocative writings, which have appeared regularly in THE ADVOCATE, and her public statements. Influential lesbian filmmaker Monika Treut released a FILM featuring her called *Dr. Paglia* in

1992. Her lover, met after a decade of well-publicized sexual frustration, is artist and curator Alison Maddex.

✧ John Gallagher, "Attack of the Fifty-Foot Lesbian," *The Advocate* (October 18, 1994).

Pakistan, see SOUTH ASIA.

Pallone, Dave
(1952–)

U.S. athlete, first professional baseball umpire to come OUT. A Watertown, Massachusetts, native, Pallone moved to the National League as one of eight minor league umpires who joined the majors during a seven-week major league umpire strike in April 1979. On September 21, 1988, the *New York Post* carried an unsubstantiated story alleging his involvement with an underage teen in Saratoga Springs, New York. Other rumors of his being gay and a public altercation with Pete Rose (called the "shoving incident" in the press) led to his being forced to resign by league president A. Bartlett Giamatti on November 30, 1988. Pallone had served 18 years (10 seasons in the National League) as a professional umpire.

As an openly gay man, Pallone has pursued a career as a popular public speaker and author. In his best-selling 1990 autobiography, he discusses his life as a gay man in the world of SPORTS and the need for sports role models for gay and lesbian YOUTH. He urges public figures to come out—"If you're gay, think about removing your mask"—while asserting the need for all gay people, in or out of the public eye, to "have courage and pride and be true to yourself. Let people close to you help you. Let the world see you for who you really are."

✧ Dave Pallone, *Behind the Mask: My Double Life in Baseball* (1990).

Panzarino, Connie
(1947–)

U.S. activist, writer, artist. Panzarino's childhood in her native Brooklyn, New York, was a painful search to diagnose her rare disease, spinal muscular atrophy type III. With support from her father and a grandmother who taught her "love for life and a drive to endure," she graduated from Hofstra University and earned a Masters of Art Therapy from New York University. After discovering her lesbianism, she became a pioneering disability activist within lesbian and gay communities, addressing complex social and personal issues including accessibility, isolation, discrimination, caretaking, independence, privacy, self-image, and sexuality.

In the 1970s, Panzarino established Beechtree Farm in upstate New York, a LESBIAN LAND for disabled lesbians, became a founding member of Disabled Lesbian Alliance in 1978, and co-organized the first Disabled Lesbian Conference in 1981, held at the MICHIGAN WOMYN'S MUSIC FESTIVAL.

After completing her memoir, *The Me in the Mirror* (1994), she wrote two books for children with spinal cord disabilities.

✧ Interview with Connie Panzarino," *Off Our Backs* (May, 1981).

➤ See also DISABLED LESBIANS AND GAY MEN.

Paragraph 175, see GERMANY.

Parenting, see CHILDREN.

Paris, see FRANCE.

Parker, Pat

(née Patricia Cook; 1944–1989)

U.S. poet, activist, educator, women's health care worker. Parker's autobiographical poem "Goat Child" opens with the lines: " 'you were a mistake' / my mother told me." The poem goes on to convey the fierce determination that made her a successful activist and writer who built bridges in and between communities.

Parker grew up outside Houston, Texas, in a Southern Baptist family. After high school she left home for Oakland, California, where she attended college, married and divorced twice (playwright Ed Bullins and Robert Parker), and had two daughters. She worked with the Black Panther Party in the 1960s and was a member of the Black Women's Revolutionary Council and the Lesbian Tide Collective in the 1970s. She shared her life with Marty Dunham.

Pat Parker.

An AFRICAN-AMERICAN lesbian mother from a working-class background, Parker once told her friend JUDY GRAHN: "I'm waiting for the revolution that will let me take all my parts with me." Her five books, which include *Child of Myself* (1972) and *Movement in Black* (1978), feature poems that range from oratories to narratives, all with a strong sense of black culture and history. She chose difficult, even daring themes, including alcoholism, and both recorded and performed her works for audiences across the country. Her signature poem, "Where Will You Be When They Come?," warned gay men and lesbians to unite against the "soul savers" and the "good citizens" crusading against them, but AUDRE LORDE characterized Parker's message as: "*I have survived! I see, and I Speak!*" Parker chose the African symbols for defiance (Aya) and changing one's self (Nkyimkyim) to accompany her collected poems.

Parker was also an activist for improved women's health care and, after her sister was murdered by her husband, against DOMESTIC VIOLENCE.

After her death from breast cancer at the age of 45, friends and admirers established the WIM Publications Memorial Poetry award in her name.

✧ Judy Grahn, "Introduction," in Pat Parker, *Movement in Black* (1978).

✧ Dorothy Allison, "Memorial: Pat Parker," *Outlook* (Fall 1989).

✧ Ayofemi S. Folayan and Stephanie Byrd, "Pat Parker," in *Contemporary Lesbian Writers of the United States,* edited by Sandra Pollack and Denise D. Knight (1993).

Parkhurst, Charlie

(Charlotte Darkey Parkhurst; ?–1879)

U.S. PASSING woman. Orphaned at birth, Parkhurst first donned male clothing to escape an orphanage in Massachusetts. After working in stables until about 1851, she moved to California and settled in Santa Cruz County. She began driving stagecoaches and is reputed to have killed at least one bandit. The advent of the railroad forced her to turn to ranching and lumberjacking. She was nicknamed "One-eyed Charlie" and "Cock-eyed Charlie" after losing her left eye when a horse kicked her.

A memorial in Soquel Village marks the site where Parkhurst voted on November 3, 1868. She is believed to be the first woman to cast a ballot in an American presidential election. At the time, however, no one knew. The discovery after her death that she was a woman came as a surprise even to her business partner, Frank Woodward. She is buried in Watsonville, California.

✧ Jonathan Ned Katz, *Gay American History* (1976).

Parmar, Pratibha

(1955–)

U.K. filmmaker, photographer, activist, writer. Born in Nairobi of Indian ancestry, Parmar and her family were forced by Kenya's Africanization policies to immigrate to England in 1968. She attended school in a working-class London neighborhood where "Paki-bashing" (violence against South Asians) was a constant threat. After university and a year of volunteer work in India, she went to work as a community activist and began making videos and taking photographs of the people she worked with.

As a filmmaker, Parmar has sought to achieve visibility for people and issues never—or hardly ever—portrayed before. She and a number of other artists working in the UNITED KINGDOM aim at "changing the very heart of what constitutes Englishness by recoding it with our diasporan sensibilities." In addition to groundbreaking videos about gay and lesbian South Asians, she has explored the world of DISABLED lesbians and gay men (*Double the Trouble, Twice the Fun,* 1992) and the British response to AIDS (*A Plague on You,* 1987; *Reframing AIDS,* 1988).

Other videos of particular interest to gay and lesbian viewers include: *Flesh and Paper* (1990), on the Indian lesbian poet Suniti Namjoshi; *A Place of Rage* (1991), which features interviews with Angela Davis, JUNE JORDAN, and Alice Walker; *Khush* (1991), a landmark documentary about lesbian and gay South Asians around the world; and *Warrior Marks* (1993), with Alice Walker, a protest against the practice of ritual female "circumcision" (clitoridectomy).

➤ Also see SOUTH ASIA.

✧ "Fighting Back: An Interview with Pratibha Parmar," in *A Lotus of Another Color: An Unfolding of the South Asian Gay and Lesbian Experience,* edited by Rakesh Ratti (1993).

✧ Pratibha Parmar, "That Moment of Emergence," in *Queer Looks: Perspectives on Lesbian and Gay Film and Video,* edited by Martha Gever, John Greyson, and Pratibha Parmar (1993).

Parnok, Sophia Yakovlevna

(1885–1933)

Russian poet, translator, critic. Born into an assimilated upper-middle-class Russian Jewish family in the provincial city of Taganrog, Parnok began writing about her powerful attraction to other girls and women while still a child. Although she was aware of 19th-century French writing that equated lesbianism with decadence, she early on asserted that her own lesbian identity was both innate and potentially positive. She began having affairs with women at the age of 16 and ran away with an actress to Western Europe in 1905. Back in RUSSIA, she briefly married to free herself from her family's influence, then left her husband in 1909 and began supporting herself by writing and translating.

In 1914, Parnok and the poet Marina Tsvetaeva met in Moscow and began a passionate, ultimately unhappy relationship. Parnok's first book, *Poems* (**1916**), published shortly before their breakup, included poems addressed to Tsvetaeva that are probably the first obviously lesbian love poems ever written by a Russian woman. They are also among the first in any language to express lesbian passion without recourse to decadent, Charles Baudelaire–influenced imagery.

Critical reaction to Parnok's *Poems,* though generally positive, was muted on the subject of her overt lesbianism. In the 1920s, when Parnok began publishing poetry inspired by SAPPHO, such as *The Roses of Pieria* (1922) and *The Vine* (1923), critics were more hostile; ultimately, the Soviet literary establishment showed its disapproval by ignoring her. After 1928, she was unable to publish her poetry and supported herself by translating and writing opera libretti and literary criticism. She was written out of Russian literary history after her death of a heart attack in 1933 and not rediscovered by Russian readers until the 1990s.

✧ Diana Lewis Burgin, *Sophia Parnok: The Life and Work of Russia's Sappho* (1994).

Partner Battering, see DOMESTIC VIOLENCE.

Pasolini, Pier Paolo

(1922–1975)

Italian filmmaker, writer. The son of an aristocratic Fascist and his anti-Fascist peasant wife, Pasolini was the embodiment of contradictions. A lifelong Marxist, he was fascinated by CHRISTIANITY. Gentle and well-mannered, he spent years waging vituperative battles in the press and in court. The most famous openly gay Italian intellectual of his era, he refused to publish his most positively homoerotic writing during his lifetime. Repeatedly indicted on obscenity charges, he opposed the sexual revolution, fearful that women's liberation would make young men less sexually available.

Pasolini published his first book of poetry in 1942. After losing his teaching job—and Communist Party membership—when he was caught having sex with teenage boys in 1949, he moved to Rome and supported himself by writing until the 1960s, when he became one of ITALY's best-known and most controversial FILM directors. In 1975, he was knifed, then crushed with his own Alfa Romeo by a street tough he had picked up (or, as some have charged, by political assassins).

In addition to his critically acclaimed poetry, Pasolini's homoerotic work includes: *Teorema* (1968), a film about a young man who seduces an entire family; his film trilogy in praise of supposedly less repressed premodern sexualities, *The Decameron* (1971), *The Canterbury Tales* (1972), and *Arabian Nights* (1974); the film *Salò* (1975), a relentlessly grim tale of degradation, torture, and murder loosely based on the Marquis de Sade's *The 120 Days of Sodom;* and his posthumously published memoirs of his youth, *Amado Mio* and *Atti Impuri* (both 1982).

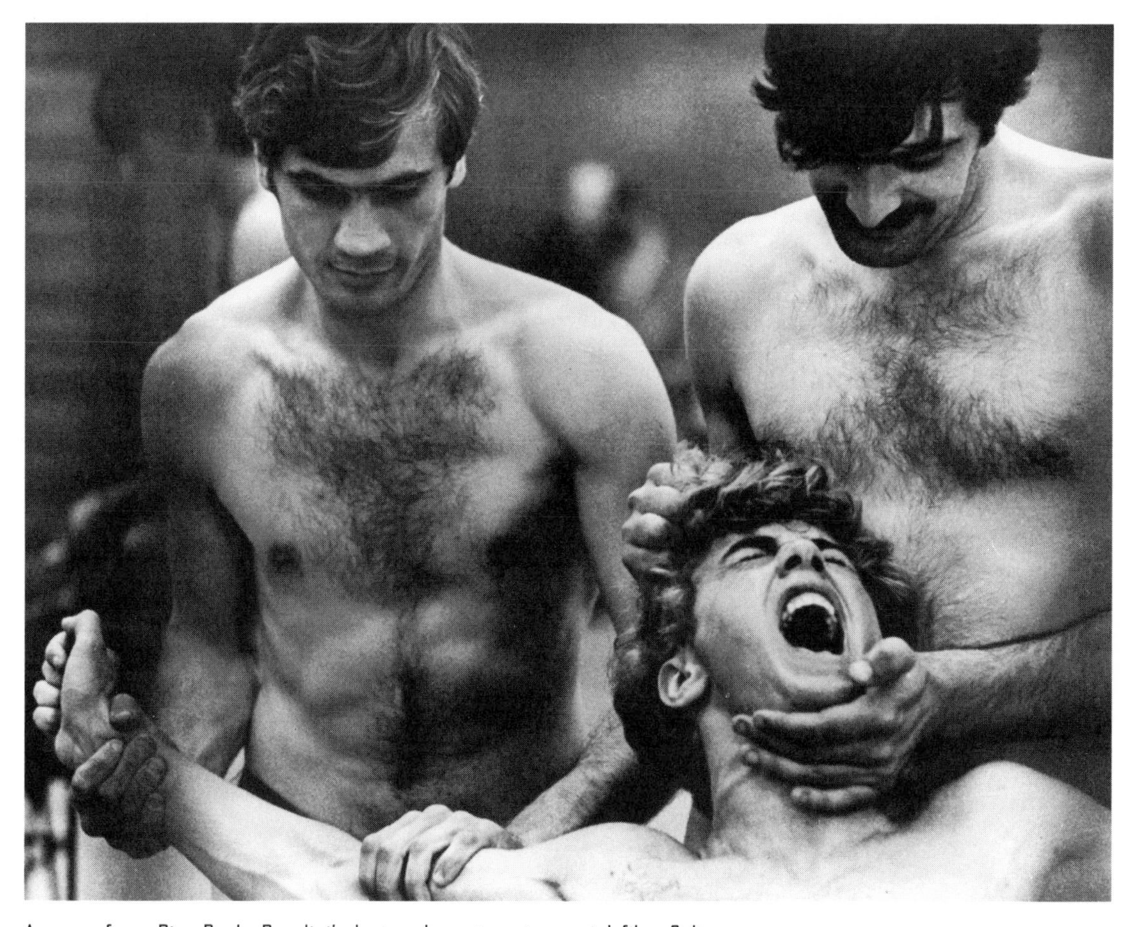

A scene from Pier Paolo Pasolini's last and most controversial film, Salò.

- ✧ Enzo Siciliano, *Pasolini: A Biography,* translated by John Shepley (1982).
- ✧ Naomi Greene, *Pier Paolo Pasolini: Cinema as Heresy* (1990).

Passing

Term describing men or women who succeed in persuading others through their mode of dress and behavior that they are members of the opposite sex, or, if gay or lesbian, straight. Unlike CROSS-DRESSING, a broader term, passing necessarily implies fooling at least some people at least some of the time. Some passing men and women, like CHARLIE PARKHURST and jazz musician Billy Tipton, deceived virtually everyone about their biological sex right up until their deaths.

While it is common for gay men and lesbians to pass in some areas of their life at various times, some researchers distinguish between passing back and forth between social groups, as in the workplace, to a passing that describes a permanent move from an identification with homosexuals to an identification with heterosexuals or to the opposite sex.

Contemporary study suggests that although the "passer" fools outsiders, the pass can be recognized by in-group members. In popular jargon, gay men and lesbians assess their "gaydar," or intuition in spotting passers. However, scholar Amy Robinson observes that this is *more* than intuition. The passing performance is "read" by the in-group member because of their *cultural literacy* as appearance, not truth—in fact, the "pass" *requires* a read by an in-group perceiver, for without it, the pass becomes real.

Passing Women

Passing seems to have been especially common, particularly among women, in the 19th century and early 20th century, when dress, jobs, and social spaces were still strictly segregated by biological sex. Some women passed as men out of necessity, so that they could travel alone, earn a livable wage (without prostituting themselves), or pursue careers, the majority of which were not open to women. Others seem to have simply felt more comfortable living as a man. Men who passed usually did so to have a socially sanctioned MARRIAGE with another man.

Passing women often suffered psychologically and physically from the strain of duplicity, isolation, and the need to avoid medical examinations. Prominent 19th-century New York politician Mary Anderson "Murray Hall" (c. 1850–1901), who passed for over 25 years and married twice, died from breast cancer rather than seek medical attention. As in his

Billy Tipton (1919–1989) at the piano. Tipton, a jazz musician, was a passing woman whose identity was discovered after his death. This album, *Billy Tipton Plays Hi Fi on Piano*, identifies him as "the lad . . . between the pulchritude."

profile of Hall, historian JONATHAN NED KATZ illustrates that a passing woman's wholly restructured life was far more than exchanging one set of costumes for another.

Perhaps because the MILITARY was perceived as a particularly masculine arena of activity, 19th-century readers seem to have been especially fascinated by accounts of passing women who served as soldiers. As early as the American Revolutionary War, Deborah Sampson (see **10/25/1783**) served with distinction in the Massachusetts Regiment. In her study of Civil War soldiers, *An Uncommon Soldier* (1996), Lauren Cook Burgess documents more than 135 women who served in the Union Army (see **1863**).

A trespass of society's GENDER codes, passing has been criminalized and punished severely in many cultures. In the West, the BIBLE (Deuteronomy 22:5) condemns all forms of cross-dressing as an "abomination" worthy of the death penalty. Throughout much of Western European history, men and women who were caught passing as the other sex were in fact executed, as in the documented case of German soldier Catharina Margaretha Linck in 1721.

Although many modern lesbians and gay men identify with historical passing women and men, the degree to which passing coincides with a gay or lesbian identity is a matter of debate among theorists in LESBIAN AND GAY STUDIES, as is the percentage of passing women and men who lived as the opposite sex for erotic reasons. Many contemporary "passing" men and women do not embrace a lesbian or gay identity, preferring instead to call themselves transgendered, TRANSSEXUALS, or members of an intersex.

✧ Jonathan Katz, *Gay American History* (1976).

✧ Allan Bérubé, "Lesbian Masquerade," *Gay Community News* (November 17, 1979).

✧ Rudolf M. Dekker and Lotte C. van de Pol, *The Tradition of Female Transvestism in Early Modern Europe* (1989).

✧ Amy Robinson, "It Takes One to Know One: Passing and Communities of Common Interest," *Critical Inquiry* (vol. 20, Summer 1994).

Passionate Friendships, see ROMANTIC FRIENDSHIPS.

Patrick, Robert

(Robert Patrick O'Connor; 1937–)

U.S. playwright. Raised in the South and Southwest, Patrick moved to New York City in the 1960s and quickly became one of off-off Broadway and off Broadway's most prolific and most popular playwrights. Caffé Cino (see **12/1958**) presented his first produced play, *The Haunted Host* (1964), a comedy about a gay writer attempting to exorcise the memory of a failed love affair. In 1967, he became playwright in residence at Norman Hartman's Old Reliable Tavern Theatre.

By the early 1970s, Patrick's work had been produced at La Mama and in Boston. *Kennedy's Children* (1973), in which five "rejects, nomads, rebels, exiles and outsiders" reminisce about what they were doing the day JFK was assassinated, ran on Broadway and in London, where it later became the first contemporary gay play televised by the British Broadcasting Corporation (1978). London's pioneering Gay Sweatshop also performed two of his plays in its debut season (1975).

Patrick's later, more experimental work built on his trademark CAMP to lampoon the heartlessness and heartbreaks of gay male life. *T-Shirts* (1978) pits a jaded queen against a self-admiring CLONE. *Untold Decades* (1988) unfolds "comedies of gay romance" in seven one-acts that survey gay relationships from before STONEWALL through the advent of AIDS.

In 1994, Patrick published *Temple Slave,* a roman à clef about his jack-of-all-trade days in the service of Caffé Cino.

Pederasty

Most commonly, a sexual relationship between an adult and a minor. Like many sexual terms with a long history (such as SODOMY), "pederasty" has been used in a variety of sometimes confusing ways. Depending on the context, it can mean "homosexuality" in general, "PEDOPHILIA" specifically, or simply "anal intercourse."

Greek for the "[sexual] love of boys," the word was originally coined to describe the practice in ancient GREECE, especially common in Athens, of adult men forming relationships with adolescent boys. Though circumscribed by a host of cultural assumptions—in its ideal form, the boy was supposed to resist the older man's advances and, once conquered, not exhibit signs of sexual enjoyment—pederasty was believed by many Greeks to be a beneficial, even character-building practice. Some writers, including Plato, distinguished between a merely sexual pederastic relationship and one based on mutual spiritual and intellectual enrichment.

Greek pederasty is often compared to the belief among peoples such as the Sambia in New Guinea that boys must have sex with adult men in order to mature into potent males. It is also frequently linked to bonding adult-adolescent relationships in sex-segregated MILITARY units or RELIGIOUS ORDERS. Examples of groups that explicitly or implicitly sanctioned the latter type of pederasty include samurai in JAPAN, *hwarang* in KOREA, Zulu warriors in AFRICA, and many BUDDHIST orders in Asia.

No one has satisfactorily explained why pederastic relationships are so much more common among men than among women. One of the rare female analogies to pederasty is the so-called "mummy-baby" relationship common in Lesotho in which young women and girls form age-differentiated, nurturing, affectionate, often sexual relationships.

Perhaps the reason pederasty is often conflated with homosexuality is that the vast majority of documented references to same-GENDER relations before the 18th century—whether in CHINA, premodern Europe, or the ARAB WORLD—portray adult male attraction to younger men or boys. In many cultures, androgynous, hairless young boys were thought to be satisfactory substitutes for women, especially when sex with women was not possible or advisable. Some men, such as ABŪ NUWĀS and the anonymous 17th-century Italian author of *Alcibiade Fanciullo a Scola,* considered pederasty superior to the love of women; more often, writers asserted the two were virtually interchangeable.

Like the comparative absence of documentation for same-sex relations between women in the historical record, the rarity of references to sexual relationships between adult men has been explained in a variety of ways. Some historians believe they simply did not occur with any frequency until modern times. Others assert that they did but that fear of the consequences of exposure kept them shrouded in secrecy.

Whatever the reason, documented examples of same-sex relations between adult men (and women) began to appear with some frequency in the Renaissance period in Europe and the Tokugawa period (1603–1867) in Japan. By the beginning of the 20th century, they vastly outnumber references to pederasty. Concurrently, Western societies began to look with increasing disapproval on any form of sexual attraction to children, and the fear that gay men and lesbians would "molest" children became one of the major arguments wielded against the nascent sexual rights movement.

In the 20th century, most gay men and lesbians consider homosexuality and pederasty as two distinct phenomena. Mainstream lesbian and gay rights groups have sought to disassociate themselves from pederasty. The mainly male proponents of pederasty have had to form their own groups, such as ADOLF BRAND's Community of the Special in prewar Germany and the North American Man-Boy Love Association (NAMBLA) in the U.S. NAMBLA and other such groups have been banned from many gay PRIDE CELEBRATIONS and from INTERNATIONAL LESBIAN AND GAY ASSOCIATION membership.

➤ Also see AGE OF CONSENT; AGING; CIRCUMSTANTIAL HOMOSEXUALITY; GIDE, ANDRÉ; PEDOPHILIA.

✧ K. J. Dover, *Greek Homosexuality* (1978).

✧ Gilbert Herdt, *Ritualized Homosexuality in Melanesia* (1984).

✧ Judith Gay, " 'Mummies and Babies' and Friends and Lovers in Lesotho," in *The Many Faces of Homosexuality: Anthropological Approaches to Homosexual Behavior,* edited by Evelyn Blackwood (1986).

Pedophilia

Adult sexual attraction to young, usually prepubescent children. To some pedophiles, only the age of a child is a factor in sexual attraction: his or her sex is irrelevant. Others are attracted to girls or boys exclusively. Police records indicate that the vast majority of people arrested for "child molesting" are men attracted to young girls. Nevertheless, since the 19th century, gay men and lesbians have often been unjustly accused of pedophilic tendencies. As a result, most lesbians and gay men have sought to distance themselves from groups such as the North American Man-Boy Love Association (NAMBLA).

Sex with prepubescent children has been taboo in virtually all societies. Today, it remains so controversial that almost no objective scientific studies of pedophilia and its effects have been possible outside of the NETHERLANDS. Proponents argue that noncoercive pedophilia is harmless or even potentially beneficial, as ALLEN GINSBERG called it, "an exchange of nature-bounties." Many people, however, feel that adult sexual interaction with a child is by definition coercive. Sexologist John Money believes that any intrusion on a child's sexuality can be distortive: an adult who punishes a child for masturbating can affect his or her sexual development at least as adversely as one who makes sexual advances.

The issue is further complicated by a lack of consensus on when children reach an age at which they can make responsible sexual decisions.

➤ Also see AGE OF CONSENT; PEDERASTY; PORNOGRAPHY.

✧ John Money, *Gay, Straight, and In-Between: The Sexology of Erotic Orientation* (1988).

✧ Pat Califia, "Feminism, Pedophilia, and Children's Rights," in *Public Sex: The Culture of Radical Sex* (1994).

Periodicals, see PUBLISHING.

Perry, Rev. Troy, see METROPOLITAN COMMUNITY CHURCH.

Persia, see CENTRAL ASIA.

Personal Ads

Brief notices in newspapers, magazines, or online soliciting friendship, sex, and/or a relationship. Historians have documented "personals" for lesbians as far back as 1900, when they began to appear in highly coded form ("my piano needs tuning") in local Dutch publications. Discreetly worded ads placed by gay males have been found in mainstream German and French newspapers before World War I. In their present, often sexually explicit, form, personal advertisements evolved in the U.S. and Europe with the advent of COUNTERCULTURE newspapers and magazines in the mid-1960s. *The Wishing Well* has offered itself as an alternative to THE WELL OF LONELINESS for lesbians since 1974.

In at least two instances, personals have been the subject of legal controversy. In **June 1972,** the British Law Lords ruled the *International Times* "guilty of a conspiracy to corrupt public morals" for publishing "contact adverts" for gay men. And in GREECE in 1991, a court sentenced the editor of *Amphi* to five months in jail because she had *refused* to print ads from straight men seeking lesbians.

Today, gay and lesbian personals appear in a wide variety of publications and computer bulletin boards. They are a major feature and source of revenue for many lesbian and gay newspapers and magazines, and an entire language and protocol has grown up around them.

✧ John Preston and Frederick Brandt, *Classified Affairs: A Gay Man's Guide to the Personal Ads* (1984).

Peru, see Latin America.

Philippines, The

No laws against consensual same-sex relations between adults, although laws against "public immorality" occasionally used to harass lesbians and gay men. Active rights groups and developed cultural and social scene in Manila.

Gay men and lesbians may not have easier lives in the Philippines than in other countries, but they face less HOMOPHOBIA and sexism—or at least less virulent forms of both—than in many parts of the world. *Bakla* (female-identified men) and "TOMBOYS" (male-identified women) have long been a recognized part of cultural, social, and even family life, the former tolerated as hairdressers, houseboys, and the like, the latter stereotyped as security guards. Since STONEWALL, gay and lesbian life has become even more open in the Philippines, although it was not until the advent of international feminism (for women) and the AIDS epidemic (for men) that concerted attempts were made to break free of GENDER-based gay and lesbian stereotypes and to develop a sense of a lesbian and gay community that embraced the entire spectrum of queer identities, from CROSS-DRESSING *bakla* and tomboys to the large numbers of (mostly closeted) lesbians and gay men whose dress and mode of life are conventional. AIDS also had an effect on attitudes toward the CIRCUMSTANTIAL HOMOSEXUALITY common in Philippine life, especially among desperately poor boys and young men who sometimes turn to prostitution for support.

Gay men have their own jargon of Tagalog, called swardspeak. Notable gay Filipinos include internationally acclaimed filmmaker Lino Brocka, playwright and poet Tony Perez, and social scientist and University of the Philippines professor Dr. Michael L. Tan. Many Filipino and Filipina entertainers are also more or less openly gay or lesbian.

History

In the centuries before the Spanish conquest of the Philippines in the mid-16th century, the indigenous inhabitants were grouped in tribes called *balangay,* most of which had, in addition to a chief, a powerful shaman, or *bayaguin* who, like the BERDACHE of NATIVE AMERICAN peoples, was a man who lived and dressed as a woman. Many bayaguin also married and lived with young boys until the boys reached an age when they could be married to a woman. Little is known about same-sex relations among women prior to the Spanish conquest, but ethnographers and traditional legends attest to the existence of AMAZON queens and warriors who may, like the *bayaguin,* have had same-sex marriage–like relationships.

The Spanish conquerors campaigned to destroy the traditional religion, burning, sometimes even crucifying, *bayaguin,* less as punishment for their sexual behavior than for their "pagan" religious function. Although they lost their special status in society, effeminate *bakla* and masculine tomboys became an affectionately tolerated part of life in the Philippines long before the era of GAY LIBERATION. Despite the influence of the ROMAN CATHOLIC CHURCH, Philippine society was in many ways less puritanical than in the West. Perhaps as a result, a politicized gay and lesbian rights movement was slow to form.

In 1988, the Philippine government launched a massive campaign against both heterosexual and same-sex prostitution, live sex shows, and pedophile sex tourism. Many gay bars were raided and closed during the campaign, and several dozen foreign pedophiles were fined and deported. On another front, the powerful Philippine Roman Catholic Church, led by Jaime Cardinal Sin, began a concerted campaign to fight what Sin in a 1994 "letter to parents" called "certain abnormal and perverse relationships and behavior such as homosexuality, lesbianism, incest, sodomy, oral sex, contraception, sterilization, and abortion."

The onset of the AIDS epidemic had the effect of stimulating a new level of gay male consciousness. In the early 1990s, a group of gay men who were regulars at a Manila BAR called the Library Pub formed the Library Foundation, initially as a "socio-civic organization." After 1991, the Library Foundation began to sponsor activities in building awareness of AIDS and providing information on SAFE(R) SEX. Around the same time, in January 1991, ten gay men in Quezon City formed a group they later called Katlo (Tagalog for "third," as in "third sex") as a "community for a gender-sensitive society." More overtly gay and more tied to working-class *bakla* than the Library Foundation, Katlo embraced "many genders" and "many foundations for sexuality." According to sociologist Michael L. Tan, the existence of these groups is one of the factors supporting the development of conscious Filipino gay/*bakla* identities.

By the 1990s, Filipina lesbians in the women's movement had also formed active organizations such as Lesbond, Can't Live in the Closet, and LINK Davao. Despite these groups, lesbian SUBCULTURES and social networks, widespread in rural areas as well as in cities, remained largely invisible to outsiders.

- ✧ Margarita Go Singco-Holmes, *A Different Love: Being Gay in the Philippines* (1993).
- ✧ Jomar Fleras, "Reclaiming Our Historic Rights: Gays and Lesbians in the Philippines," in *The Third Pink Book: A Global View of Lesbian and Gay Liberation and Oppression,* edited by Aart Hendriks, Rob Tielman, and Evert van der Veen (1993).
- ✧ Michael L. Tan, "Tita Aida and Emerging Communities of Gay Men: Two Case Studies from Metro Manila, the Philippines," in *Gays and Lesbians in Asia and the*

Pacific: Social and Human Services, edited by Gerard Sullivan and Lawrence Wai-Teng Leong (1995).

✧ Malu S. Marin, "Philippines," in *Unspoken Rules: Sexual Orientation and Women's Human Rights,* edited by Rachel Rosenbloom (1996).

Photography

One of the youngest of the visual arts, photography has had gay and lesbian associations since its invention in the first half of the 19th century. Besides its potential for homoerotic expression (see, for example, GLOEDEN, BARON WILHELM VON), the development of photography also contributed to documenting the rise of specifically lesbian and gay identities, as in the work of pioneering photographers like ALICE AUSTEN, who was one of thousands of unmarried women photographers active in the U.S. in the last years of the 19th century, and, later, in the work of photographers like BERENICE ABBOTT, who left portraits of prominent lesbian, gay, and bisexual celebrities active in Paris in the 1920s.

Nevertheless, the photographic documentary record of gay and lesbian life remained sparse until the late 20th century. To date, for example, no actual photograph or film of the STONEWALL Uprising has surfaced. In the 1970s, a number of documentary photographers—such as JOAN E. BIREN, Tia Cross, Diana Davies, Robert Girard, KAY TOBIN LAHUSEN, Fred McDarrah, Steve Ziffer, Rich Wandel, Bettye Lane, TEE CORINNE, and Cynthia Macadams—sought to rectify this situation, with the result that today gay and lesbian life is at least as widely photographed as straight life.

➤ Also see ART; FILM AND VIDEO, LESBIAN, GAY, AND QUEER; PORNOGRAPHY; and specific artists.

Physique Magazines

Publications, popular especially in the 1950s and early 1960s, that featured PHOTOGRAPHY and illustrations of scantily clothed males ostensibly as examples of physical development but actually for the entertainment of a growing gay male audience. Most physique photography would not be considered PORNOGRAPHY by today's standards, but in their day, physique magazines were subject to severe postal censorship. By the end of the 1950s, however, physique magazines were arguably the most openly—and self-affirmingly—gay male publications available to a wide American audience. Some publications, according to a leading physique magazine producer, circulated to as many as 60,000 to 70,000 readers by 1958.

Although the audience for physique magazines was made up almost entirely of gay men,

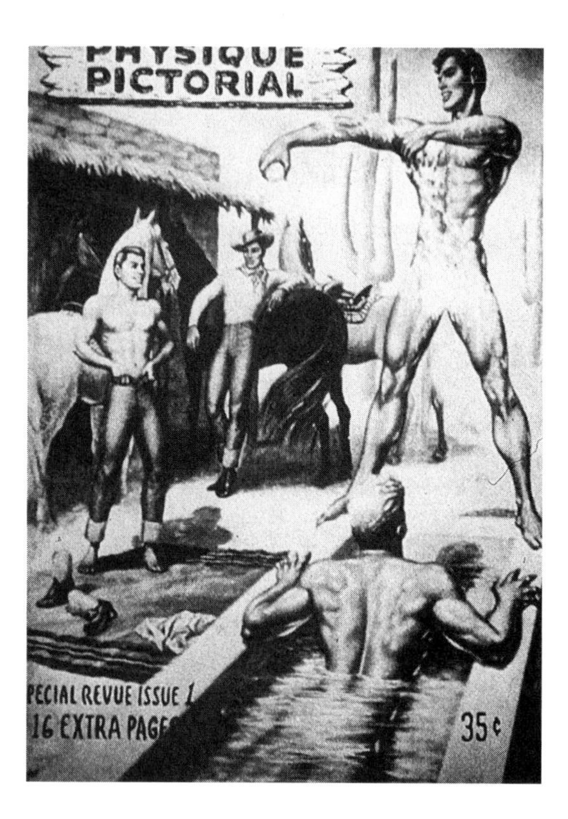

most publishers were careful to "cloak" their scantily clad males in the guise of a "Greek Revival" movement, health promotion, or the athletic ideals of BODYBUILDING. The Greek Revival theme, which played on the multiple nuances of the word *Greek,* was seen in titles like *Adonis, Grecian Guild Pictorial,* and *Young Adonis. Grecian Guild Pictorial* printed a "creed" which began, "I pledge allegiance to my native land," and ended, "I seek a sound body in a sound mind that I may be a complete man; I am a Grecian."

After World War II, photographers such as BOB MIZER and BRUCE OF LOS ANGELES began to market photo sets of nude or scantily clad men by mail order. By 1951, Mizer had produced so many broadsheets advertising his and other photographers' photo sets that he decided to bind them together in magazine form, and *Physique Pictorial* was born.

Through the 1950s, a host of competitors followed. All to one degree or another attempted a camouflage of being just another health/fitness or bodybuilding magazine, similar to those that had been popular in the U.S. since the 1920s. Nonetheless, the publications became increasingly suggestive, using campy double entendres and suggestive poses that few readers would misunderstand.

The degree of nudity permitted by postal censors and local police departments reveals changing standards. In the early 1950s, even body hair (which was also censored in HOLLYWOOD movies until 1952) had to be airbrushed out. Rear views could not reveal the cleft of the buttocks until later in the decade. As late as 1958, the publishers of *Kris* were indicted by the federal Justice Department for "excessive genital delineation."

✧ *Physique: A Pictorial History of the Athletic Model Guild,* edited by Winston Leyland (1982).

✧ F. Valentine Hooven III, *Beefcake: The Muscle Magazines of America, 1950–1970* (1995).

Picano, Felice

(1944–)

U.S. writer. The only member of the VIOLET QUILL who grew up in New York City, Picano was savvy, well read, and bisexually experienced by the time he entered Queens College of the City University of New York and settled in Greenwich Village in the early 1960s. After graduating, he traveled to Europe, then returned to Greenwich Village to begin a career as a writer while he supported himself with jobs in bookstores and the like. He took part in the STONEWALL Uprising and was in the GAY ACTIVISTS ALLIANCE. His first books were "straight" thrillers. With *The Lure,* one of the first gay suspense novels, Picano became a popular gay writer as well.

A committed and constant diarist, Picano has published more than a dozen books, including *Like People in History* (1996), a portrait of four decades of gay life.

Pink Triangle (Rosawinkel)

A badge designed by Nazi concentration camp officials to designate men incarcerated as homosexuals. A three-sided cloth badge sewn onto the left shoulder and right trouser leg of uniforms, the pink triangle was part of an eight-color coding system: yellow for Jews, brown for gypsies, violet for Jehovah's Witnesses, red for political prisoners, blue for émigrés, green for criminals, and black for "antisocial" detainees. The color pink was chosen for male homosexuals as a sign of effeminacy. Prior to the pink triangle, homosexual men were identified by a black dot on their armband, or a yellow band with an *A,* for *Arschficker.* Although sex between women was not against the law in Nazi Germany,

many lesbians were incarcerated as socialists (red triangles), antisocial "perverts" and "prostitutes" (black triangles), and, along with large numbers of gay men, as Jews (two yellow triangles in the form of a Star of David).

In the 1970s, lesbians and gay men began wearing pink triangles as a symbol of pride and solidarity in the face of oppression. For example, in 1975, the emblem was used by a "coalition of conscience" study group within the New York Civil Liberties Union to stress opposition to bigotry while fighting for municipal civil rights legislation. Starting in 1986, AIDS activists plastered New York City with stickers on which pink triangles and the caption *Silence = Death* were printed. ACT UP adopted both the symbol and the slogan in 1987.

Rosawinkel (Pink Triangle) was also the name of a German group that campaigned to get compensation for gay concentration camp survivors. The West German government agreed to the group's demands in 1982, 30 years after compensation had been granted to other persecuted groups.

- Rudiger Lautmann, "The Pink Triangle: The Persecution of Homosexual Males in Concentration Camps in Nazi Germany," in *Historical Perspectives on Homosexuality,* edited by Salvatore J. Licata and Robert P. Petersen (1981).
- Erwin J. Haeberle, "Swastika, Pink Triangle, and Yellow Star: The Destruction of Sexology and the Persecution of Homosexuals in Nazi Germany," in *Hidden from History,* edited by Martin Bauml Duberman, Martha Vicinus, and George Chauncey Jr. (1989).

Poetry, see LITERATURE.

Poland, see EASTERN EUROPE.

Police, see LAW; LAW ENFORCEMENT, GAY MEN AND LESBIANS IN.

Politics, U.S. Electoral

Beginning with the 1972 Democratic National Convention's defeat of Minority Report #8, national political discourse began to include gay and lesbian rights. The vote removed gays and lesbians from the nondiscriminatory plank of the platform despite speeches by the first openly gay convention delegates, JIM FOSTER and MADELINE DAVIS. In the nationally televised commentary, veteran newscaster Walter Cronkite prophetically observed: "So, as 'far out' as the homosexual platform may appear to some tonight—and as serious as it is to others—it may be a portent of things to come." By the 1980 Democratic Convention, the platform plank did include an inclusive nondiscriminatory clause, 77 openly gay and lesbian delegates were present, and political activist Virginia Apuzzo nominated Mel Boozer, an openly gay AFRICAN-AMERICAN delegate from Washington, D.C., for vice president. Electoral politics has been difficult for lesbians and gay men because the visibility and scrutiny of public office requires a personal strength and diplomacy beyond raising campaign funds and being a viable candidate in the face of often hostile social attitudes.

Historically, openly gay people have been outside government at all executive, legislative, and judicial levels, and they have been so victimized by them that their reluctance to seek public office—or believe in it—is not surprising. Before running candidates themselves, early HOMOPHILE organizations volunteered for campaign work and surveyed the attitudes of straight candidates on gay issues. Few gay candidates emerged and fewer still were successful before the 1980s. Campaigns offset stereotypes, energized communities, and guaranteed a public forum and visibility for gay issues. Before there were openly gay elected officials, heterosexual elected officials began appointing gay or lesbian community liaisons, gay and straight. Elliot Blackstone, appointed in 1965 in San Francisco, is considered the first.

Candidates

The first openly gay campaign for public office was José Sarria's bid for the San Francisco Board of Supervisors in 1961. Empress José Sarria, the "Nightingale of Montgomery Street," master of CAMP humor, satirical opera, and parodying torch songs worked at the famous Black Cat BAR. In the early 1950s, he closed his performances with speeches about fighting oppression before leading the audience with linked arms in the song, "God Save Us Nelly Queens." Harassed by the liquor authority and a series of police raids at the bar, he decided to run: "I was trying to prove to my gay audience that I had the right, being as notorious and gay as I was, to run for public office, because people in those days didn't believe you had rights." He pulled nearly 6,000 votes and, as historian JOHN D'EMILIO reports, inspired political organizing that prefigured HARVEY MILK's election to that office 16 years later.

In 1971, Washington, D.C., activist FRANK KAMENY became the next openly gay candidate and the first for the U.S. Congress. While he described the campaign as quixotic, Kameny bused in the GAY ACTIVISTS ALLIANCE to help gather signatures to qualify for the ballot, mounted a full campaign, and ran fourth of six candidates. In 1974, two lesbians became the first openly gay candidates to get *elected*—Kathy Kozachenko to the Ann Arbor, Michigan, City Council (see **4/1/1974**) and ELAINE NOBLE to the Massachusetts House of Representatives (see **11/5/1974**). Although Allan Spear was elected state senator from Minnesota and GERRY STUDDS to the U.S. House of Representatives in 1972, neither was OUT at the time (see **12/9/1974** and **7/18/1983**).

Although others have run successfully since, gay men and lesbians remain one of the most underrepresented groups among political officeholders. Statistics assembled by a national political action committee, the Gay and Lesbian Victory Fund, reveal that of nearly half a million elected U.S. officials in 1994, fewer than 100 are openly gay or lesbian. In the major offices, none of 100 senators are openly gay, only 3 in the 435-member Congress, and only 12 out of 7,461 members of state legislatures. On **August 1, 1996**, a fourth congressman, Republican Jim Kolbe, came out when faced with OUTING after voting against same-sex MARRIAGE.

Organizations

Sarria's campaign inspired the founding of the League for Civil Education by Guy Strait in 1961. Strait's sensationalistic publication, the *LCE News,* according to D'Emilio, became the "first sustained effort to bring the movement into the world of the gay bar." Its extraordinary circulation of 7,000 copies stimulated voter registration and bloc voting by detailing local examples of police abuse. By 1963, candidates were advertising in it.

The Tavern Guild of San Francisco bar owners followed in 1962, its goal to fight closures, police abuse, and extortion. Typically, police raids heated up around election time, so Bill Plath, the guild's founder, responded with voter registration drives, political and legal advice, and a place for candidates to appear. In San Francisco, the Guild supported the formation in 1964 of the SOCIETY FOR INDIVIDUAL RIGHTS. Guild chapters became multifaceted and spread into other cities.

By 1994, the Gay and Lesbian Victory Fund listed 144 political organizations in 39 states, although many more groups later sprang up to address political developments, such as Boycott Colorado's successful fight to remove an anti-gay voter initiative, or the Campaign for Military Service to lift the U.S. Armed Forces ban on homosexuals.

Inspired by EMILY's List (whose slogan is "Early Money Is Like Yeast—it makes dough rise"), the successful national donor network for women candidates founded by lesbian activist Ellen Malcolm in 1985, William Waybourn and Vic Basile formed the Gay and Lesbian Victory Fund in 1991 in time to help Sherry Harris become the nation's first openly lesbian African-American city council member in Seattle, Washington. Other national or international organizations that support elected or appointed officials include the International Network of Lesbian and Gay Officials (founded in 1985), the HUMAN RIGHTS CAMPAIGN, the NATIONAL GAY AND LESBIAN TASK FORCE, and the National Black Gay and Lesbian Leadership Forum.

Political Ideology

Some gay and lesbian activists believe that electoral politics can only achieve assimilation or legitimacy, not real liberation. Seeking deeper changes outside the "gay rights ghetto," radical theorists perceive a failed system with a sexist, capitalist, classist, and racist structure. Its participants, they contend, compromise principle by mainstreaming the issue and themselves. Political access is not political equality, argues progressive activist Urvashi Vaid, former executive director of the National Gay and Lesbian Task Force, but rather "virtual equality," an illusion of power and change.

More politically moderate leaders cannot envision a revolution with motives, structure, or leaders any less flawed than those routinely elected. Since we are governed by the real-life process we seek to change, they contend, improving the system requires a balance of pressure from outside ACTIVISM and inside participation. BARNEY FRANK's insider faith in party politics is clear: "The way to defeat people who would restrict us from enjoying the full rights of American citizens is not to engage in the politics of self-marginalization, but rather to insist on our rights to participate fully in the process by which this society decides important public questions."

Political conservatives urge a tight focus on "gay rights issues," separating them from overarching social issues like welfare, racism, or the economy. Equal treatment and opportunity in the public sphere will come, they believe, with the removal of distinguishing barriers between gay and straight, such as those that deny same-sex marriage, civil rights protection, or inclusion in the MILITARY. Avoiding discussions of sexuality, they frame these issues within widely held values like "fairness" or "privacy."

Party Ideology

A 1960 editorial in the *New York Post* revealed that although the "homosexual issue" rivaled the "Communist issue" in popularity among right-wing Republicans, the best-selling KINSEY REPORTS documenting the prevalence of homosexuality caused the Republican leadership to fear becoming the antihomosexual party. Those fears have apparently dissolved. In 1996, Congressman Barney Frank estimated that when a gay-related issue arises in Congress, Democrat support is 70 to 80 percent while Republican support will rarely reach 15 percent.

Chuck Carpenter, an openly gay member of the Oregon House of Representatives, finds his membership in the Republican Party controversial: "In the gay community, people looked at me for a while as the Jew working for the Nazis." While Carpenter, former U.S. Congressman Steve Gunderson, and others have received support from the LOG CABIN FEDERATION, the organization itself struggles, even having to sue their party to set up an information booth at a state convention.

However contentious, multiple party affiliations have served minority constituencies in leveraging their interests and keeping them on the table when parties change leadership. The presence of openly gay elected Republicans and Republican political organizations has provided representation for the gay men and lesbians who vote Republican, estimated at 34 percent by one exit poll during the 1994 congressional election.

Openly Gay Representation/Identity Politics
Believing the election of more openly gay officials reduces overdependence on "gay friendly" ones, New York Assemblywoman Deborah Glick and Carole Midgen, a member of the San Francisco Board of Supervisors, among others, stress the need for community leaders to place community interests first, change public attitudes, and move from support to advocacy. They echo the early identity politics of Harvey Milk: "It's not enough just to have friends represent us, no matter how good those friends may be. We must give people the chance to judge us by our own leaders, and our own legislators."

Identity politics refers to the creation of a community and/or political agenda based on a person's shared characteristics with others, like race, GENDER, physical ability, sex, or sexual orientation. Since individuals have more than one compelling dimension to their identity (for instance, a disabled Latino father), or some aspects of their identity change, identity politics can lead to tenuous relationships or short-term goals. While often contrasted with a politics of ideas or issues that forge coalitions, another dominant structure in gay and lesbian organizing, identity politics can bring many different people together around powerful characteristics like class and race that often override other less emotional allegiances. Political scientists and activists are divided as to whether that bond is secure and focused enough to create real social change.

- John D'Emilio, *Sexual Politics, Sexual Communities: The Making of a Homosexual Minority in the United States, 1940–1970* (1983).
- *Out for Office: Campaigning in the Gay Nineties,* edited by Kathleen DeBold (1994).
- Andrew Sullivan, *Virtually Normal* (1995).
- Urvashi Vaid, *Virtual Equality: The Mainstreaming of Gay and Lesbian Liberation* (1995).
- Barney Frank, "Time to Think Strategy," *The Harvard Gay and Lesbian Review* (vol. 3, no. 1., Winter 1996).

Polynesia, see PACIFIC ISLANDS.

Ponsonby, Sarah, see LLANGOLLEN, LADIES OF.

Pornography

Visual or verbal works created primarily to stimulate sexual arousal. Some people try to distinguish "erotica" from pornography on the basis of artistic merit or hard-to-define standards of "good" taste; in LESBIAN AND GAY STUDIES, however, the two are practically synonymous. "HOMOEROTICISM," on the other hand, is a broader term that can refer to material which is only incidentally erotic as well as to works created intentionally to arouse lesbians and gay men.

For gay men, pornography represents by far the most developed cultural "artifact" in the anthropological sense of the word. In the

Joe Simmons (Thomas Williams, 1959–1995) broadened the range of erotic portrayals of African-Americans in gay male porn.

United States alone, over $1 billion worth of "all-male" pornographic videos are sold each year. Similarly, sales of nonpornographic magazines like THE ADVOCATE, *Genre,* and *Out* are eclipsed by the number of copies sold each month of more than a dozen nationally distributed monthly magazines featuring erotic fiction and photo features of nude men.

Lesbian pornography (as opposed to pornography featuring female-female sex created for a straight male audience) became common only after the SEX WARS in the 1980s. Even today, it is dwarfed in comparison with gay male pornography.

Although gay men have never had their version of the lesbian Sex Wars, there has always been a contentious divide between pornography and gay male politics. Despite its being blatantly sexual, gay male pornography remains closeted in odd ways. The very word "gay"—not to mention "queer" or "homosexual"—is hardly ever used to market pornography to gay men; videos and fiction are almost always categorized as "male" or "all-male"; an improbable percentage of the characters in both written and video pornography are portrayed as straight. Gay and lesbian scholars—with a few notable exceptions like John R. Burger, Richard Fung, and Thomas Waugh—have virtually ignored the subject. The most important book on the gay and lesbian press in the United States (Rodger Streitmatter's *Un-*

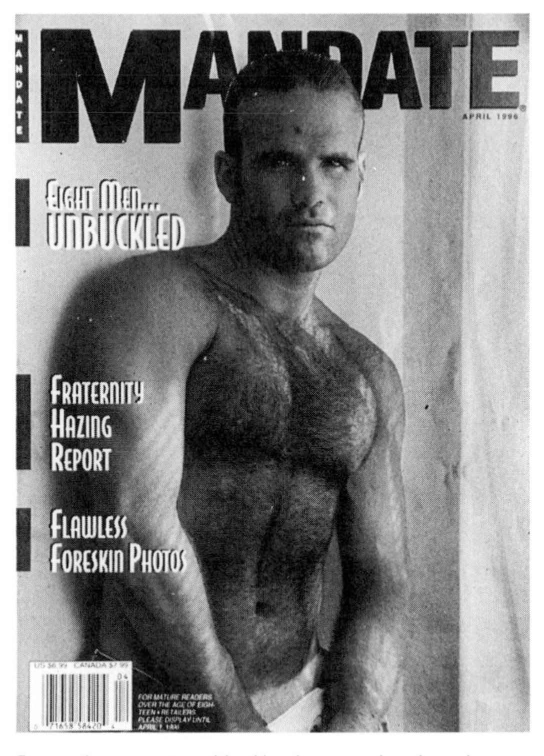

Gay male magazines like Mandate reach a broader audience than non-pornographic periodicals.

The provocatively named On Our Backs was part of a new wave of lesbian erotica that emerged in the mid-1980s.

speakable, 1995) contains not a single mention of *In Touch, Mandate,* or any of the other well-known "skin" magazines. Far more has been written about the supposedly homoerotic content of Alfred Hitchcock's movies than about the thousands of gay male porn films and videos. And, while many "serious" gay writers have written pornography, only a few, such as JOHN PRESTON, JOHN RECHY, and SAMUEL STEWARD, have published it under their own names.

Gay male pornography is at some times even blatantly opposed to the objectives of the GAY AND LESBIAN RIGHTS MOVEMENT, such as freedom from employment discrimination. George Duroy, producer of a phenomenally popular series of videos featuring boyish Eastern European performers, stated in a 1995 *Manshots* interview that "my policy is to don't [*sic*] work with gay boys, and don't employ gay staff," explaining that his straight-identified "boys" would feel uncomfortable around an openly gay man.

✧ John R. Burger, *One-Handed Histories: The Eroto-Politics of Gay Male Video Pornography* (1995).

Porter, Charlotte Endymion, see CLARKE, HELEN ARCHIBALD.

Portugal

No laws against consensual same-sex relations between persons 14 years of age or older. Lesbian and gay groups, social and cultural scene in Lisbon and a few other large cities.

The existence of lavish, well-attended dance clubs in Lisbon and resorts popular with gay men and lesbians from other parts of Europe belies the continued difficulties of leading an openly lesbian or gay life in Portugal. Activists struggle with popular and official attitudes in general more conservative than in neighboring SPAIN. Modern gay and lesbian SUBCULTURES have been slower to develop in the country than in most other parts of Western Europe.

History

Same-sex relations between men had been criminalized for several centuries (see c. **650**) by the time Portugal emerged as an independent kingdom in the 12th century. Subsequent law codes were unusually specific for the Middle Ages, penalizing oral sex, masturbation, and same-sex frottage (rubbing) as well as anal sex and specifically prohibiting sex between women after **1499**. The INQUISITION, on the other hand, was considerably milder in Portugal than in Spain. Among the records left by the Portuguese Inquisition are the first love letters written from one man to another in any modern European language (see **1654**).

The Onania, a much reprinted and revised antimasturbation tract first published in England in 1708, mentions Lisbon as one place female couples had been punished for having sex with each other. Most forms of consensual sex between adults were decriminalized in 1807 when Portugal was conquered by the French (see **9/25/1791**)—and again in the law code of 1852—but police harassment of gay men in public spaces was reported to actually increase in the 19th and 20th centuries.

GAY LIBERATION came to Portugal in the 1970s (see **5/1/1974**), leading to the formation of groups like Gay International Rights (August 1974), a bilingual Portuguese/English newspaper, *The Gay* (April 1977), and links with other groups in Western Europe; nevertheless, gay and lesbian life remained more closeted and less tolerated than in other European countries. Gay historian Julio Gomes noted that by the 1980s, Portugal had at least four BEACHES well-known to be gathering places for lesbians and gay men, at least two of which had been popular since the 1940s.

Pratt, Minnie Bruce
(1946–)

U.S. poet, essayist, educator, activist. Born in Selma, Alabama, Pratt was educated at the Universities of Alabama and North Carolina. She completed graduate work in English LITERATURE after marrying and giving birth to two sons. She came OUT as a lesbian in 1975 and subsequently lost custody of her children after divorcing. She has taught at Shaw University, the Union Institute in Cincinnati, and the University of Maryland.

Pratt joined Susan Ballinger, Helen, Deborah Giddens, Mab Segrest, and Cris South to form the collective Feminary, which published a feminist journal of the same name. "Emphasizing the lesbian vision" with a southern focus, *Feminary* was published from 1978 through 1983. In 1977, the same group also organized WomanWrites, which became an annual writing conference for lesbians. Disappointed that some of her lesbian literary heroines, such as Muriel Rukeyser and LILLIAN SMITH, remained silent about their lesbianism, Pratt vowed to emulate the openness of JUDY GRAHN and AUDRE LORDE, in whose writings she found support and inspiration for her own aesthetic, which she defined as "trying to write poems that hold, in some way, the idea of *lesbian.*"

For *Crime Against Nature* (1990), Pratt won the Academy of American Poets Lamont Poetry Selection in 1989 and the 1991 AMERICAN LIBRARY ASSOCIATION Gay and Lesbian Book AWARD, and she received a Creative Writing Fellowship from the National Endowment for the Arts. Her other publications include *The Sound of One Fork* (1981); *We Say We Love Each Other* (1985); *Rebellion: Essays 1980–1991* (1991); and with Elly Bulkin and BARBARA SMITH, the groundbreaking *Yours in Struggle: Three Feminist Perspectives on Anti-Semitism and Racism* (1984). Her volume of stories *S/He* (1994) describes the struggles and passions of transgender and BUTCH/FEMME relationships and endeavors "to give theory" related to struggles against racism, sexism, classism, and GENDER oppression "flesh and breath."

Pratt shares her life with transgender writer and activist Leslie Feinberg.

✧ Minnie Bruce Pratt, "When the Words Open into Some Not Yet Open Space," in *InVersions: Writings by Dykes, Queers, and Lesbians,* edited by Betsy Warland (1991).

- "Pronouns, Politics, and Femme Practice: An Interview with Minnie Bruce Pratt," in *Fem(me): Histories, Generations, Futures,* edited by Laura Alexandra Harris and Liz Hutchinson Crocker (1997).

Presbyterian Church

Christian faith that grew out of Calvinism (see **1555**) and the Church of Scotland founded by John Knox in 1557. Official Presbyterian positions on homosexuality vary from that of the Free Presbyterian Church of Scotland, which vehemently protested the **July 22, 1980**, decriminalization of male same-sex acts in Scotland, to the somewhat more accommodating attitude of the Presbyterian Church (USA), which lets individual congregations welcome lesbian and gay members but has consistently refused to sanction the ordination of openly gay and lesbian clergy. The Church forced Rev. Jane Spahr, a lesbian activist, to resign a position in Oakland, California, in 1979 and, in 1992, voided a pastoral appointment she had obtained in Rochester, New York. In 1997, a Church convention ruled that all unmarried clergy must remain celibate or face disciplinary action.

Some 75 "More Light" Presbyterian churches welcome lesbians and gay men. Presbyterians for Lesbian and Gay Concerns, an advocacy and support group, was founded in 1974.

Preston, John

(1945–1994)

U.S. writer, editor. Preston grew up in rural Massachusetts, "a big galumphing kid," as he later described himself, "a farm boy, with the wrong accent." Passionately devoted to the civil rights movement from the age of 14, he traveled to Alabama as a freedom rider and tutored students in Chicago slums. He moved to Minneapolis in 1969 and threw himself into GAY LIBERATION activities, founding and directing Gay House, Inc., one of the country's first gay COMMUNITY CENTERS. After serving as editor of THE ADVOCATE in 1975, he settled in Maine in the late 1970s and pursued a career writing and editing for a wide range of straight as well as gay publications.

The author of more than 40 books, Preston's most famous creation was probably *Mr. Benson,* which debuted as a serial in *Drummer,* a gay S/M publication, on May 1, 1979, and was later published in book form. Mr. Benson quickly became known as the world's top topman, a role model and inspiration to S/M activists, lesbian and gay alike. Preston himself preferred the eponymous hero of his seven-volume *Mission of Alex Kane* series (first published between 1984 and 1987; revised editions, 1992 and 1993), in part because Kane, though a macho ex-Marine superhero who comes to the rescue of oppressed gay men, eschewed rigid top/bottom role playing in favor of ad-libbing to suit his mood and the emotional needs of his partners. Preston also published collections of short stories and edited a number of award-winning anthologies, including *A Member of the Family: Gay Men Write About Their Families* (1992) and, with JOAN NESTLE, *Sister and Brother: Lesbians and Gay Men Write About Their Lives Together* (1994).

A fierce advocate of sex and—after the advent of AIDS and the discovery that he himself was HIV-positive—SAFER SEX, Preston told *Honcho* magazine that PORNOGRAPHY "teaches" because it provides "a means to reflect on what's going on sexually. . . . Porn gives us new ways to reflect on what life is like."

- John Preston, *My Life as a Pornographer and Other Indecent Acts* (1993).
- *Looking for Mr. Preston: Interviews, Essays, and Personal Reminiscences of John Preston,* edited by Laura Antoniou (1995).

Pride (Personal Rights in Defense and Education)

Los Angeles HOMOPHILE organization. Founded in May 1966 by activist Steve Ginsberg to fight escalating police harassment, PRIDE drew most of its members from the L.A. "leather and lace" BAR scene. More militant than most homophile groups, PRIDE was one of the first to mobilize public demonstrations against police actions in addition to holding regular meetings and hosting social events. The group formally disbanded in June 1968 in the midst of disagreement among members over how militant the organization should be. Perhaps the most lasting legacy of PRIDE is its newsletter, which became the *Los Angeles Advocate* in August 1967 and later, independent of PRIDE, THE ADVOCATE.

PRIDE's best-known achievement was a demonstration by several hundred people on **January 5, 1967**, called to protest a brutal police raid on the local Black Cat and New Faces BARS on **January 1, 1967**. Although the Black Cat Protest was organized, some historians consider it the Southern California counterpart to the later STONEWALL Uprising.

Pride Celebrations

Marches, rallies, festivals, street fairs, parties, and the like, held annually to promote gay and lesbian visibility, unity, and progress toward equal rights. Reflecting their origin in the first anniversary observances of the STONEWALL Uprising (see **6/28/1969**; **6/28/1970**), the majority of pride celebrations are held in June or July, although increasingly local populations of lesbians and gay men have chosen to commemorate their own versions of Stonewall: in AUSTRALIA, for example, Sydney's Mardi Gras, one of the most lavish and best-attended pride celebrations anywhere, marks the anniversary of a bitter struggle between police and gay/lesbian demonstrators (see **7/1978**).

Europride, a multifaceted celebration hosted by a different European city each year, made its debut in London on June 28, 1992, with about 100,000 people in attendance. San Francisco activist Marsh Levine founded the

International Association of Lesbian/Gay Pride Coordinators, Inc., in 1982 to help communities organize and coordinate their own celebrations. Although the greatest number of pride celebrations are held in the United States and CANADA, they have also become a part of lesbian and gay life in JAPAN, EASTERN EUROPE, and LATIN AMERICA.

Prison

The exact number of persons incarcerated on charges related to same-sex eroticism will probably never be known, but reliable data from a small sampling of countries and time periods suggest the total would be well over 100,000 men and women and perhaps much higher. About 50,000 German men were imprisoned during the NAZI PERSECUTION of homosexuality between 1934 and 1945; British historian and theorist Jeffrey Weeks estimates that in the early 1950s almost 4 percent of prisoners in the UNITED KINGDOM were incarcerated on charges related to homosexuality; as late as 1991, courts in RUSSIA sent 482 men to prison camps on charges of consensual same-sex intercourse—St. Petersburg gay activist Sergei Scherbakov estimates that the average in preceding decades was about 1,000 men a year.

Less visible (and less likely to be apprehended CRUISING in public places), fewer lesbians have served time in prison on sex-related charges. (Yet some have. In 1968, for example, Julie Livermore and Carolyn French unsuccessfully appealed their convictions and sentences of 1½ to 5 years in prison for acts of "gross indecency." Michigan state troopers standing outside their tent at a public campground had claimed they heard the women having sex.) For lesbians, a bigger issue has been the prejudicial effect exposure of their sexuality can have in criminal cases (see LAW).

Homosexuality Behind Bars

Same-sex intercourse in jails and prisons is one of the most common and most studied forms of what social scientists call situational or CIRCUMSTANTIAL HOMOSEXUALITY. Estimates of the number of inmates who take part, willingly or unwillingly, in same-sex relations while serving time in U.S. prisons range from 15 to 86 percent; most experts believe the higher figure is more accurate. The vast majority of inmates who have sex while in prison deny that that they are "gay," "lesbian," or even "bisexual." The minority who identify themselves as gay or lesbian report disproportionate harassment, abuse, violence, and isolation—particularly if they are perceived by guards and other inmates as "obvious," i.e., not conforming to standard GENDER roles.

Female homosexuality behind bars became

a theme of American popular culture in the 1940s and 1950s when movies like *Girls in Chains* (1943) and *Caged* (1950) and much more explicit PULP FICTION novels popularized stereotypes of brutish lesbian wardens and thuggish butch prisoners having their way with innocent young femmes (see BUTCH/FEMME). These stereotypes persist in popular culture despite studies showing that self-identified lesbians are the *least* likely prison population to commit violent acts—and the *most* likely to be victims of prison violence. Studies by criminologist Karlene Faith indicate that most lesbian relationships in prison develop in a context of mutual, noncoercive intimacy.

Depictions of sex in men's prisons—such as *Fortune in Men's Eyes,* Canadian John Herbert's play (1967) and movie (1971)—have tended to recognize the "circumstantial" nature of male-male prison sex. Further recognition came in 1977, when the NATIONAL GAY [later: AND LESBIAN] TASK FORCE succeeded in persuading the federal director of prisons to stop categorizing male-male rape as "homosexual rape" since prison rapes are typically committed by heterosexual men.

Activism

National and international gay and lesbian political organizations have for the most part distanced themselves from prisoner rights issues. Ruthann Robson, a legal scholar and attorney, has argued that lesbian and gay groups ignore prisoners because they fear that association with them will jeopardize the chances of gay men and lesbians assimilating into mainstream society. Exceptions include efforts by the International Gay and Lesbian Human Rights Commission and the INTERNATIONAL LESBIAN AND GAY ASSOCIATION, as well as AIDS-related education and advocacy programs initiated by ACT UP. AMNESTY INTERNATIONAL and the AMERICAN CIVIL LIBERTIES UNION have also developed projects to fight discrimination based on sexual orientation in legal proceedings and imprisonment. On a more local level, Rev. Dolores Jackson of the METROPOLITAN COMMUNITY CHURCH in Brooklyn, New York, developed a long-term ministry for prisoners; and Mike Riegle at the *Gay Community News* in Boston started an innovative writing program.

In the United Kingdom, Lesbians and Gays in Probation, Prisoners' Advice Service, Prison Reform Trust, and Women in Prison have all addressed gay and lesbian prisoner rights issues. These include the legal question of whether a prison cell constitutes a private or public space—an important distinction for men, since male-male sex is legal in the U.K. only if it occurs in private.

Segregation by Sexuality

Since at least the 19th century, many prisons have segregated known gay and lesbian prisoners from other offenders. While this practice has sometimes made prison safer and even resulted in a sense of community for lesbian and gay prisoners, it has also at times actually increased the chances for abuse and discrimination. Some gay and lesbian prisoners have lost visitation rights; others claim their chances for early probation are reduced. Some prisons have used different uniform colors to indicate sexual information; others, like the Los Angeles Sybil Brand Institute, have used a "daddy tank" to separate the butch women from the general population, just as gay men have been placed in a "queen's tank" in New York prisons. Gay and lesbian publications are routinely restricted under bogus concerns, despite the victory of *NGTF v. Carlson,* opening federal prisons to gay and lesbian books and publications.

Lesbians in prison even made history at STONEWALL. In her 1969 memoir, activist FRAN WINANT recalled that incarcerated lesbians, mostly women of color, held in the Women's House of Detention near the Stonewall Inn would call out of the windows to female friends and lovers on the street, defiantly throw objects, and burn bedding. Could it be, she asks, "that the apparently powerless women of the House of D, their bitter gestures striking over and over at the compressed gunpowder of our silence, made the subtle difference that finally lit the explosion of gay liberation at this time and place?" Many of these women were reportedly seen at the windows of the prison holding lit matchbooks during the riot.

- ✧ Barbara Deming, *Prisons That Could Not Hold* (1984).
- ✧ Ruthann Robson, *Lesbian (Out) Law* (1992).
- ✧ Victoria A. Brownworth, "Dykes Behind Bars," *QW* (August 30, 1992).
- ✧ Karlene Faith, *Unruly Women: The Politics of Confinement and Resistance* (1993).
- ✧ Amnesty International USA, *Breaking the Silence: Human Rights Violations Based on Sexual Orientation* (1994).

Proust, Marcel

(1871–1922)

French novelist. The son of a prominent Catholic physician and a cultivated Jewish heiress, Proust had a privileged, sheltered childhood, marred only by attacks of asthma, which worsened as he grew older. After MILITARY service and studies at the Sorbonne, he ascended into the rarefied heights of Parisian society and, somewhat later, began to make a name for himself in the city's literary circles as well, publishing a collection of short stories (*Les Plaisirs et les Jours,* 1896) and writing an autobiographical novel (*Jean Santeuil,* posthumously published in 1952; English translation, 1955). By the 1910s, he was working on his 16-volume magnum opus, *À la Recherche du Temps Perdu* (*In Search of Lost Time* or *Remembrance of Things Past*), which was published in installments between 1913 and 1927. After years of spending most of his days secluded in his cork-lined bedroom, occasionally venturing out late at night, Proust died of pneumonia at the age of 51.

Proust had ROMANTIC FRIENDSHIPS with other men of his class and sexual liaisons with lower-class men, many of whom he met at a brothel he financed. From 1907, he was in love with his chauffeur and then private secretary, Alfred Agostinelli. Proust lavished presents on Agostinelli, who seems not to have been interested in men, and paid for his air pilot training. Proust was ready to surprise Agostinelli with his own airplane when he learned that the younger man had crashed into the Mediterranean on a solo flight.

À la Recherche du Temps Perdu has been acclaimed as the first great "gay" novel and, later, in view of the many different ways the novel can be "read," a seminal "queer" work, but many gay and lesbian readers have been disturbed by Proust's pessimistic and generally negative portrayal of gay and lesbian characters. MONIQUE WITTIG has called the book a "Trojan horse," pointing out that once the novel is well under way, character after character slips OUT until "Proust has succeeded in turning the 'real' world into a homosexual-only world. . . . Everybody ends up being homosexual." Although this is something of an exaggeration, almost all the major characters are either overtly homosexual or, even if ostensibly heterosexual, based on gay and lesbian persons Proust knew. Just one example of the complexities of the characters' sexualities is Albertine, the woman with whom the narrator is obsessed through much of the novel. That Albertine is modeled on Proust's chauffeur Agostinelli is suggested by the present the narrator plans to give Albertine: a Rolls-Royce engraved with the same poem Proust put on the plane he wanted to give Agostinelli.

An extraordinarily complex work, *À la Recherche du Temps Perdu* continues to inspire lesbian and gay readers to craft new interpretations and find new riches hidden within. One of its most significant features, however, is unambiguously stated: Proust's characterization of gay and lesbian people as a "race" apart, similar to the Jews, evidence of the beginning of a consciousness that was to grow much more important through the remainder of the 20th century.

✧ Jarrod Hayes, "Proust in the Tearoom," *PMLA* (vol. 110, no. 5, October 1995).

Provincetown

Cape Cod, Massachusetts, village that has been a popular summer resort and permanent residence for lesbians and gay men since the late 1930s. Local experts estimate that about half the town's 3,700 inhabitants are gay or lesbian, despite its being a difficult place to make a living in the off-season from October through April. Nonetheless, writer Michael Cunningham describes it as "one of the few spots on earth where [people] can be flagrantly queer and, at the same time, pillars of the community."

The landing site where the Pilgrims spent their first winter, Provincetown has been through most of its history a fishing port (and smuggling center). After World War I, it became a popular gathering place for writers, ACTORS, and artists, including lesbians and gay men. Their numbers grew, becoming obvious to most visitors by the 1960s and comfortably OUT in the 1970s.

Although Provincetown is still not as gay or lesbian as FIRE ISLAND's Cherry Grove, it offers a DOMESTIC PARTNERSHIP ordinance and a gay- and lesbian-friendly local government. Many of the most prominent civic leaders, in fact, are gay and lesbian.

Pseudonyms

Lesbians and gay men have been more likely than heterosexuals to use pseudonyms for many reasons, including fear of arrest or of being otherwise persecuted. In the 1950s and 1960s, some HOMOPHILE organizations insisted

Pseudonym	Birth Name
Jan Addison	JEANNETTE HOWARD FOSTER
Warren Adkins	Jack Nichols
Sarah Aldridge	Anyda Marchant
Nathan Aldyne	Michael McDowell and Axel Young
Phil Andros	SAMUEL STEWARD
ANN BANNON	Ann Thayer

Pseudonym	Birth Name
Arthur Bell	Arthur Irving
Ellen Bedoz	Ellen Shumsky
LISA BEN	Edith Eyde
Edgar Box	GORE VIDAL
Rose Brock	JOSEPH HANSEN
BRYHER	Annie Winifred Ellerman
Carpenter	JUNE ARNOLD

Pseudonym	Birth Name
Lee Chapman	MARION ZIMMER BRADLEY
James Colton	JOSEPH HANSEN
Giselle Commons	TEE CORINNE
Florence Conrad	Florence Jaffy
MARIE CORELLI	Mary Mackay
DONALD WEBSTER CORY	Edward Sagarin
F. J. Crowe	JILL JOHNSTON
Marvin Cutler	DORR LEGG
Gene Damon	BARBARA GRIER
John Dexter	MARION ZIMMER BRADLEY
Rey Domini	AUDRE LORDE
Stephen Donaldson	Bob Martin
ELANA DYKEWOMON	Elana Nachman
Alice Eliot	SARAH ORNE JEWETT
Hilary Farr	JEANNETTE HOWARD FOSTER
Ann Ferguson	PHYLLIS LYON
Ronald Forsythe	Donn Teal
Miriam Gardner	MARION ZIMMER BRADLEY
Mary Geller	Mary Wings
Meredith Grey	Marion Glass
Lily Hansen	Lilli Vincenz
Cal Harding	Elver Barker
Morgan Ives	MARION ZIMMER BRADLEY
Geraldine Jackson	Betty Perdue
William (Bill) Lambert	DORR LEGG
Elizabeth Lang	Nancy Dean
VERNON LEE	Violet Paget
Eann MacDonald	HARRY HAY
Artemis March	March Hoffman
Xavier Mayne	Edward I. Stevenson
Maryjane Mecker	Ann Aldrich
Ralph Meeker	Forman Brown
Dick Michaels	Richard Mitch
Isabel Miller	ALMA ROUTSONG
Claire Morgan	PATRICIA HIGHSMITH
Jack Nichols	Warren Adkins
Numa Numantius	KARL HEINRICH ULRICHS
Robert Orville	GEORGE PLATT LYNES
Parisex	HENRY GERBER
Dr. Th. Ramien	MAGNUS HIRSCHFELD
Bill Rand	Bill Rau
MARY RENAULT	Eileen Mary Challans
Roberto Rolf	GEORGE PLATT LYNES
Sagitta	John Henry Mackay
Abigail Sanford	JEANNETTE HOWARD FOSTER
Martha Shelley	Martha Altman*
Carol Silver	JUDY GRAHN
Anne Singleton	RUTH BENEDICT
Lydia Steptoe	DJUNA BARNES
Richard Stevenson	Richard Lipez
Valerie Taylor	Velma Tate
Wykeham Terris	Norman Haire
KAY TOBIN	Kay Lahusen
Aaron Travis	Steven Saylor
Vega	Lloyd Jeffers
RENÉE VIVIEN	Pauline Tarn
Randolfe/Randolphe (RANDY) WICKER	Charlie/Charles Hayden
S. P. Wonder	Elana Nachman
MARGUERITE YOURCENAR	Marguerite de Crayencour

*Legally changed her name to her movement pseudonym.

that members use pseudonyms for all movement business even if they were OUT in other areas of their lives. In addition, many lesbians and some gay men have adopted pseudonyms to protest cultural patriarchy (e.g., ELANA DYKEWOMON; Luke Sissyfag) or to assert a new, heroic identity as a gay man (Phil Andros) or lesbian (PAT CALIFIA).

Psychiatry, see PSYCHOLOGY.

Psychology

The science of mental life and how it relates to human behavior. Modern psychology began to take shape in the late 19th century precisely during the era when modern Western concepts of sexuality were also evolving into a recognizably contemporary form. Many historians of sexuality, such as MICHEL FOUCAULT and JONATHAN NED KATZ, point to this era as a time when psychologists and other theorists played a seminal role in *inventing* concepts of homosexuality and heterosexuality, especially as linked to notions of GENDER identity. Psychology also brought homosexuality into medical discourse and, later, medical "treatment" attempts.

Despite the fact that Sigmund Freud (see **1905**), the father of modern psychology, was never satisfied with his explanations of how exclusive *heterosexuality* developed, many of his followers viewed homosexuality as an aberration and even, later in the 20th century, a mental illness (see AMERICAN PSYCHIATRIC ASSOCIATION). As a result, one of the most important goals of the early GAY AND LESBIAN RIGHTS MOVEMENT in the U.S. (see, for example, **5/14/1970**) was to persuade psychiatrists and psychologists to stop "treating" homosexuality and to recognize it as a healthy adult sexual adaptation.

In the years since STONEWALL, an ever increasing number of gay and lesbian specialists have developed new forms of psychology designed to help lesbians and gay men cope with the particular stresses of gay and lesbian life.

➤ Also see ADDICTION/RECOVERY; ANTHROPOLOGY; SOCIOLOGY.

- *Psychological Perspectives on Lesbian and Gay Male Experiences,* edited by Linda D. Garnets and Douglas C. Kimmel (1993).
- *Lesbian, Gay, and Bisexual Identities over the Lifespan: Psychological Perspectives,* edited by Anthony R. D'Augelli and Charlotte J. Patterson (1995).

Publishing

The most important medium in the development of gay and lesbian SUBCULTURES and a powerful force in the promotion of national

Out emerged in the 1990s as America's highest-circulation gay and lesbian periodical.

and international rights movements, gay and lesbian publishing is today almost as diverse as gay and lesbian life. The medium encompasses a small but influential roster of specialist presses as well as a fast-changing variety of local and national gay and lesbian periodicals, estimated at more than 700 in North America and at least 1,600 around the world. In addition, mainstream publishing, which has always employed large numbers of lesbians and gay men, has become increasingly responsive to gay and lesbian interests and concerns. As late as the early 1980s, sales agents reported widespread resistance to obviously lesbian and gay books on the part of bookstore buyers; a decade later, virtually every major publishing house had issued at least a few titles of particular appeal to lesbians and gay men. Combined with the output of smaller publishers, their entry into the field has resulted in an unprecedented proliferation of lesbian and gay titles in print. Some U.S. BOOKSTORES stock as many as 15,000 gay and lesbian titles; several marketing experts believe more than 20,000 titles will be available in 2000.

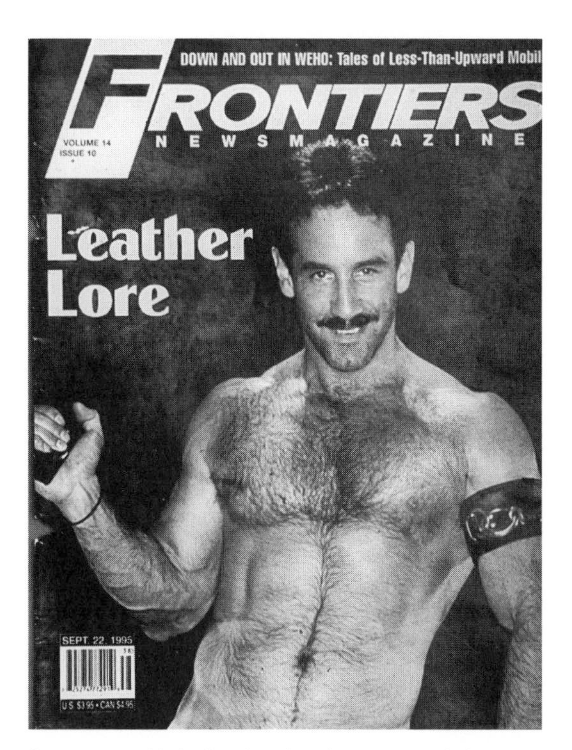

Frontiers, published in Los Angeles, is one of dozens of publications serving local gay and lesbian communities.

From the invention of printing until the second half of the 20th century, most books advocating a positive approach to same-sex eroticism had to be privately published, almost always in extremely limited editions (see, for example, **1836**; **1864**; **1/1895**). Exceptions were virtually all works of LITERATURE. An openly gay and lesbian press was born with the appearance in GERMANY of periodicals for men like ADOLF BRAND's *Der Eigene* in **1896** and MAGNUS HIRSCHFELD's scholarly annual *Jahrbuch für Sexuelle Zwischenstufen* in **1899**. In the 1920s, German lesbians also had access to their own widely distributed periodicals, and some gay publications were circulated in editions of more than 100,000 copies. The onset of the NAZI PERSECUTION in the mid-1930s brought this first flowering of gay and lesbian publishing to an abrupt end. Until the 1950s, the only major gay or lesbian periodical appearing in the world was the Swiss-based *Der Kreis* (see **1933**).

The first gay periodical in the U.S. was probably HENRY GERBER's short-lived *Friendship and Freedom,* published for an organization Gerber founded in Chicago (see **12/10/1924**). More than two decades passed before LISA BEN's Vice Versa, ONE magazine, and THE LADDER helped establish a lasting gay and lesbian press in the U.S., although none of these publications had more than a few thousand subscribers. After STONEWALL, periodicals like THE ADVOCATE achieved national prominence, while local and regional publications burgeoned. Publisher BARBARA GRIER estimates that

The Publishers Behind the Lesbian Publishing Movement

Major Presses	Founders	Years Active
Aunt Lute Book Company*	Joan Pinkvoss Barb Wieser	1982–1986; 1991–
Cleis Press	Frederique Delacoste Felice Newman	1980–
Diana Press	Coletta Reid Kathy Tomyris	1972–1977
Daughters, Inc.	JUNE ARNOLD Parke Bowman	1972–1979
Firebrand Books	Nancy Bereano	1986–
Iowa City Women's Press*		1972–1985
Kitchen Table: Women of Color Press	Hattie Gosset AUDRE LORDE CHERRIE MORAGA BARBARA SMITH, others	1981–
Naiad Press	Muriel Crawford BARBARA GRIER Anyda Marchant Donna McBride	1973–
New Victoria Publishers	Beth Dingman Claudia Lamperti	1976–
Persephone Press	Gloria Greenfield Pat McGloin	1976–1983
Seal Press	Rachel da Silva BARBARA WILSON	1976–
Shameless Hussy Press	Alta	c. 1970
Sheba Feminist Publishers		1980–1992
Sister Vision: Black Women and Women of Colour Press	Makeda Silvera, others	1985–
Spinster's Ink*	Maureen Brady Judith McDaniel Sherry Thomas	1978–1986; 1991–
Spinster's Ink/Aunt Lute Book Company*		1986–
Violet Press	Judy Grepherd FRAN WINANT	1970–1980
Womyn's Braille Press	Marj Schneider, others	1983–1994

*Iowa City Women's Press later became Aunt Lute Book Company in 1982 and merged with Spinster's Ink in 1986 to form Spinster's Ink/Aunt Lute Book Company.

Women's Press Collective	Wendy Cadden Brenda Crider JUDY GRAHN Jane Lawton Anne Leonard Sunny, others	1970–

almost 300 different lesbian periodicals, ranging from mimeographed newsletters to glossy magazines, were published in the U.S. between 1972 and 1990.

In some ways, "gay and lesbian" publishing remains a misnomer, since, with a few exceptions like *The Advocate* and *Out* magazine, both of which currently attempt to appeal to both lesbians and gay men, the market has always been largely segregated by sex. Even book sales are scored on separate male and female best-seller lists that seldom have more than one or two titles in common. Gay male publishing (and to a much lesser extent, since the SEX WARS, lesbian publishing) is further divided by the degree of sexual explicitness allowed in text and photos. Although sales figures for erotic books and magazines dwarf those achieved by less openly prurient gay male publications, few scholars have studied their impact other than to speculate the role they play in building gay male identities in areas otherwise isolated from urban subcultures.

In addition to women's presses (see below), gay and lesbian publishing houses have included Sasha Alyson's Boston-based Alyson Publications, which began as a distribution company before publishing its first book in 1980, and shorter-lived but still influential firms like Crossing Press and SeaHorse Press. In the U.S., many gay and lesbian periodicals are affiliated with the Gay and Lesbian Press Association. Lesbian and gay journalists working for "straight" publications have established the National Gay and Lesbian Journalists' Association. And the Publishing Triangle, which presents a variety of annual AWARDS, is a membership organization dedicated to the promotion of lesbian and gay writing and publishing.

Women's Presses and Lesbian Publishing

As a revitalized feminist movement took shape in the 1960s, a number of women founded presses that specialized in the publication of periodicals and books for, by, and about women. By 1976, when JUNE ARNOLD hosted the first Women in Print conference, some 130 women represented more than 80 presses, publishers, periodicals, and bookstores. Although many "women's" presses were founded or staffed by lesbians and, especially after Stonewall, feminist publications increasingly featured lesbian points of view, it was not until the 1970s and the rise of LESBIAN FEMINISM that strictly "lesbian" publishing began. This new movement nicknamed its adversary "LICE" (Literary-Industrial Corporate Establishment) and signs of its development included MARIE KUDA's Lesbian Writer's Conferences, held annually from 1974 through 1978.

The growth of lesbian-friendly presses in the 1970s made it possible for lesbian fiction, poetry, and nonfiction to be published in book form rather than in small-circulation magazines. Supported by an increase in women's bookstores, which in the 1990s were still responsible for an estimated 75 percent of sales of lesbian-oriented books, these presses made lesbian writing more widely accessible than ever before. Carol Seajay, founder of Feminist Bookstore News, counted 15 women's presses and nine women's bookstores in 1973; some 33 presses and 73 bookstores in 1983; and more than 130 bookstores in 1992. Between 1992 and 1994, 25 new women's bookstores opened in the U.S. and Canada. Sales of lesbian books were estimated at $25 million annually in the mid-1990s. Lesbian-themed books accounted for 40 to 60 percent of total sales in women's bookstores.

Although some writers like SARAH SCHULMAN have alleged that mainstream publishing houses are less receptive to lesbians than to gay men, an increasing number of lesbian writers find themselves faced with a difficult choice between women's presses and mainstream houses. Although mainstream houses sometimes offer higher financial rewards and broader exposure, writers like Jan Clausen, who surveyed 35 fellow lesbian writers, editors, and publishers, believe that many successful lesbian writers stay loyal to women's presses because they "have literally made possible our art, our movement, our lives."

✧ "Lesbian Writing and Publishing," edited by Beth Hodges, *Sinister Wisdom* (special issue, vol. 1, no. 2, 1976).

✧ Carol Seajay, "Twenty Years of Women's Bookstores," *Ms* (July/August, 1992).

✧ Carol Seajay, "The Backlash and the Booklist," *The Women's Review of Books* (vol. 12, no. 3, December 1994).

✧ Rodger Streitmatter, *Unspeakable: The Rise of the Gay and Lesbian Press in America* (1995).

Puig, Manuel

(1932–1990)

Argentinian writer. As a youth growing up in the isolated, provincial town of General Villegas, Puig sought escape from provincial drear in the HOLLYWOOD fantasies he discovered almost daily at his local movie theater. Educated in Buenos Aires, he won a scholarship to study FILM in Rome but later settled in New York City in 1963 to work as a writer after failing to launch a career as a filmmaker. In 1968, he published his first novel, *La Traición de Rita Hayworth* (English translation, 1971: *Betrayed by Rita Hayworth*) in ARGENTINA. The novel won acclaim in French translation and helped establish Puig as one of the most influential writers in LATIN AMERICA.

In addition to thematic elements drawn from popular entertainment, all eight of Puig's novels have at least some characters who appear gay to observant readers, but his most overtly gay—and most successful—novel was *El Beso de la Mujer Araña* (*Kiss of the Spider Woman,* 1976). The story of an imprisoned hairdresser who recounts elaborate movie fantasies to entertain—and eventually seduce—his cellmate, a macho revolutionary, the novel also includes scholarly footnotes written by a fictional Danish doctor. The footnotes, though partially a satire of medical models of homosexuality, also conform to traditional Latin American stereotypes of sex between men, in which a *passivo,* considered not only effeminate but actually a woman trapped in a man's body, seduces and "services" a conventionally masculine *activo.* The footnotes culminate with a call for homosexuals to organize and resist oppression through political activity. One of the best-known gay creative works of all time, *Kiss of the Spider Woman* was successfully dramatized, first as a film (1985) and then a Broadway musical (1993).

Never an activist but open about his sexuality in his private life, Puig, according to writer Jaime Manrique, succumbed to complications of AIDS at the age of 57—although his *New York Times* obituary stated that he had died of cardiac arrest after gallbladder surgery.

✧ Jonathan Tittler, *Manuel Puig* (1993).

✧ Jaime Manrique, "Manuel Puig: The Writer as Diva," *Christopher Street* (no. 203, July 1993).

Pulp Fiction

Cheap, mass-marketed paperback novels published primarily from 1950 to 1966, several hundred of which were lesbian romances. Part of a sex-laden genre sold in supermarkets, drugstores, and bus stations as well as at bookstores and newsstands, most "lesbian" pulp fiction was produced by men to titillate straight male readers. Proportionately few

were written by women. The books were nonetheless a vital source of information for women who otherwise might not even have known the term "lesbian." "Lesbian pulp" was so important in building awareness of the nascent postwar lesbian SUBCULTURE that the LESBIAN HERSTORY ARCHIVES classifies it as "survival literature."

With lurid covers and titles like *Strange Sisters* and *The Dark Side of Venus,* lesbian pulp was formatted to attract curious readers who were just becoming aware of the frequency of same-sex relations thanks to the publication of the KINSEY REPORTS in 1948 and 1953. The genre debuted with Tereska Torres's *Women's Barracks* in 1950, a novel that was singled out for condemnation (although it was judged too pornographic to quote) by the House Subcommittee on Pornographic Affairs in 1952. The number and popularity of lesbian-themed releases continued to increase, however, until the genre peaked in the early 1960s.

Most lesbian pulp was sensationalistic, stylistically limited and highly formulaic, with stereotypical "bad girls" seducing voluptuous young innocents. Writers turned to popular PSYCHOLOGY to explain the characters' lesbianism as the consequence of rape, parental abuse, or other traumas, and editors usually required them to "redeem" their lesbian characters with endings in which the women opted for heterosexual relationships, lost their jobs, or committed suicide. Many lesbian readers, however, were able to read through these conventions.

Emerging during the MCCARTHY ERA, a time of fearful silence for lesbians, the more sympathetically written pulp novels were what JOAN NESTLE calls "conveyors of lesbian culture": they initiated many readers to the language, mores, and social possibilities of lesbian life. BARBARA GRIER believes they actually improved the public image of lesbians by presenting youthful, romantic figures in contemporary settings. Many lesbian writers, including SALLY M. GEARHART, KATE MILLETT, and ALMA ROUTSONG, have discussed the importance of the novels in their own lives. Indeed, pulp authors received hundreds of letters from grateful readers around the world.

Some lesbian pulp novels were published anonymously. Most writers used PSEUDONYMS. Notable authors included: Kay Addams, Ann Aldrich, ANN BANNON, Paula Christian, Claire Morgan (pseudonym for PATRICIA HIGHSMITH), Nancy Morgan, Vin Packer, Jordan Park, Randy Salem, Artemis Smith, and Valerie Taylor.

✧ Gene Damon [Barbara Grier], "The Lesbian Paperback," *Tangents* (June/July 1966).

✧ Roberta Yusba, "Twilight Tales: Lesbian Pulps 1950–1960," *On Our Backs* (Summer 1985).

Purdy, James
(1923–)

U.S. writer. An Ohio native, Purdy moved to Chicago in his teens and studied at the University of Chicago and, later, the University of Puebla in Mexico. After publishing short stories in magazines and teaching at Lawrence College in Wisconsin, he moved abroad and, failing to interest publishers in his work, had editions of his first novel, *63: Dream Palace,* and the collection *Don't Call Me by My Right Name and Other Stories,* privately printed in 1956. Appreciated and supported by British writers like Dame Edith Sitwell and Angus Wilson, he later managed to find publishers, first in the UNITED KINGDOM and later in the U.S. His subsequent work has been acclaimed by many critics and other writers, including GORE VIDAL, who called him "an authentic American genius." Purdy has remained outside both the mainstream as well as the gay and lesbian literary establishments, probably because, as critic Reed Woodhouse hypothesized in 1994, "his fiction fits into none of the usual categories, and worse, seems to mock or disdain those categories."

One of the first American writers to be openly identified as gay, Purdy has published more than 15 novels, numerous short stories, and several plays, almost all of which contain identifiable—if unconventional—gay characters. These range from the eponymous hero of *Malcolm* (1959, adapted by EDWARD ALBEE for a Broadway production in 1965), a young man who has a series of bizarre adventures among the denizens of a surreal demimonde, to the characters in *Garments the Living Wear* (1989), who search for love in a world racked by plague and death. Although wry humor is characteristic of his work, it is also laden with incidents of sudden violence and Gothic tragedy. In *Eustace Chisholm and the Works* (1967), for example, one man's pursuit of another leads to sadistic murder and self-immolation. Among his more light-spirited work, *Out with the Stars* (1992) is a CAMP satire of the events surrounding an opera premiere.

✧ Reed Woodhouse, "James Purdy's Escape from the Wasteland," *The Harvard Gay and Lesbian Review* (Summer 1994).

Q

QRD (Queer Resources Directory)

Pioneering "electronic research library specifically dedicated to sexual minorities," which had been accessed more than 1 million times by the beginning of 1996, making it the most frequently consulted information service of its kind on the World Wide Web. Initially founded by mathematician Ron Buckmire in 1991 to serve as an archive for the DIRECT ACTION group QUEER NATION, QRD's first file went on-line on February 1992 under the direction of David Casti. Operated entirely by volunteers using donated equipment, QRD contains a wide range of news clippings, listings, essays, and graphics. It does not accept erotic artwork or writing.

The success of QRD has inspired similar services in other countries, including AUSTRALIA and NEW ZEALAND.

Quakers

Popular name for the Religious Society of Friends, a Christian sect organized in 1668 by George Fox (1624–1691) in opposition to the established Church of England. Quakers have always had somewhat more lenient views toward same-sex relations than most other Christian groups. From 1682 to 1718, Quaker-dominated Pennsylvania was the only American colony that did not stipulate capital punishment for whites found guilty of SODOMY. (For most of that period, the punishment was hard labor for whites and hanging for blacks.)

In **1945**, Quakers established a center in New York City where young people arrested on same-sex charges could go for assistance and counseling. The Quaker Readjustment Center is believed to be the first social welfare agency for gay men and lesbians in the U.S. And in **1963**, English Quakers were the first major religious group to issue a statement that not only opposed discrimination against lesbians and gay men but fully equated same-sex and heterosexual relations.

Friends for Lesbian and Gay Concerns, an educational and social organization, was established in 1972. Since local Quaker groups are governed by consensus, the level of acceptance varies, but most meetings welcome gay men and lesbians. Quakers are also among the handful of Christian groups that sanction SAME-SEX UNIONS.

Queer

Word used especially since the late 1980s to describe persons (as well as things and concepts associated with them) whose sexual desires or GENDER identity do not conform to socioculturally constructed norms. It has also become a shorthand term for "gay and lesbian" or "gay, lesbian, or bisexual."

Apparently borrowing on the word's original 16th-century meaning of "abnormal,"

American men who were attracted to other men but did not consider themselves effeminate began to use "queer" to distinguish themselves from female-identified "fairies" as early as the 1910s. George Chauncey has traced the evolution of "queer" from this initial, specialized usage to its spread throughout the U.S. and the UNITED KINGDOM as a generalized pejorative term more or less synonymous with HOMOSEXUAL. The word "GAY" began to compete with "queer" in the 1930s, although "gay" apparently lacked the nuance of "male-identified" that "queer" had conveyed. By the late 1940s, many "gay" people, men and women, found "queer" offensive while others preferred it. CHRISTOPHER ISHERWOOD, for example, liked it because "it makes heterosexuals wince."

For similar reasons, some activists readopted the term in the late 1980s, as in the DIRECT ACTION group QUEER NATION. "Queer" came back in vogue as a term that not only expressed nuances of anti-assimilationism, defiance, and pride in nonconformity, but also provided a brief, inclusive, and sometimes usefully vague way of referring to "lesbians, gay men, bisexuals, transvestites, transsexuals, etc." Its reappearance two decades after STONEWALL also gave it a contemporary ring that suited it to descriptions of the tastes, fashions, and lifestyles of "queer youth."

✧ George Chauncey, *Gay New York: Gender, Urban Culture, and the Making of the Gay Male World, 1890–1940* (1994).

✧ William Stewart, *Cassell's Queer Companion: A Dictionary of Lesbian and Gay Life and Culture* (1995).

Queer Nation

DIRECT ACTION group formed in New York City in 1990 by four men, two of whom had been queer-bashed, to fight HOMOPHOBIA and HATE CRIME against lesbians and gay men. Queer Nation mobilized its first public action on **April 28, 1990**, in protest of a pipe bomb attack on Uncle Charlie's, a popular local BAR. Unlike ACT UP, whose militant spirit and radically democratic antiorganizational style the group emulated, Queer Nation embraced a broad agenda of gay- and lesbian-related issues. Its aims were articulated in a manifesto headlined "Queers Read This" that was distributed on **June 24, 1990**, at New York City's annual Gay PRIDE CELEBRATION. With a subhead reading "I Hate Straights," the manifesto urged readers to "Bash Back" and to tell critical straight friends to "go away from me, until *you* change."

The very use of the word "QUEER" signaled an anti-assimilationist stance that by 1990 had come to characterize a new generation of activists. The group popularized the slogan "We're Here. We're Queer. Get Used to It," along with "We're Here. We're Queer. We're Fabulous."

Queer Nation evoked SEPARATISM in its name and its emphasis on creating "safe spaces" for queers. The group also made forays into "heterosexual spaces" to fight COMPULSORY HETEROSEXUALITY in a variety of innovative, media-friendly ways, including "queer-ins" at shopping malls (with the alternative slogan "We're Here. We're Queer. We're Going Shopping"), "kiss-ins" in restaurants and parks, and a much publicized demonstration at the 1992 Academy Award ceremonies.

By the end of 1990, Queer Nation had spread to Boston, Los Angeles, Philadelphia, and other cities across the U.S.

Although Queer Nation had broadly defined goals, it did not advocate a specific ideology. Actions were decided by consensus, a characteristic that some thought led to the group's decline. In 1995, Jonathan Katz, a cofounder of Queer Nation of San Francisco, told *Q San Francisco* that he believed "Queer

Queer Nation protested Cracker Barrel's discriminatory employment policies in a demonstration staged on Wall Street on March 31, 1992.

Nation was involved in a dysfunctional relationship because it tried to shift itself towards the interests of anybody entering in." Disputes arose over the group's protests against the Gulf War and other actions not directly linked to gay or lesbian issues, and Queer Nationals of color accused the groups of being white-dominated. Katz's San Francisco chapter shut down in December 1991, fractured over issues related to BISEXUALITY, GENDER, race, and religion. Groups in some other cities remained active.

➤ Also see ASSIMILATIONISM VS. CONFRONTATIONALISM; LESBIAN AVENGERS; OUTRAGE!; **October 19, 1991**.

✧ Robin Dorman, "The New Activists," *Q San Francisco* (Summer 1995).

Queering the English Language

In her introduction to the revised edition of *Lavender Culture* (1994), Cindy Patton contrasted the gay and lesbian writers of the 1970s with "queer theorists, whose queer prose stylistics and insights we admire, but who don't sound at all like the quotidian 'us.' "

Here is a guide to some of the terms common in queer theory and typical examples of how they are used. Quotations are taken from the writings of leading queer theorists, as well as from other writers who would not call themselves queer theorists but have made contributions to the field.

Agency: freedom to act on desires.
In the 19th century, women may have wanted to have sexual relationships with other women, but most lacked the *agency* to do so.
Bracketed: discounted, passed over as irrelevant.
"Feminist film theory, which has resolutely *bracketed* any discussion of lesbianism or the female homoerotic . . ." (Judith Mayne)
Bricolage: the French word for a makeshift, do-it-yourself repair job, used by writers like Richard Dyer to describe the queer technique of blatantly distorting the original meaning of a (usually negative) text to appropriate it as positive.
Construction: see CONSTRUCTIONISM VS. ESSENTIALISM.
Denaturalize: makes something commonplace or expected seem fantastic, even bizarre.
The primary objective of gender-bending is to denaturalize normative gender identities.
Discourse: anything communicated through words or signs, but especially writings or debates in a specialized area of knowledge.
Foucauldian/Foucaultian: of or relating to MICHEL FOUCAULT and his thought.
Gaze: called by Michel Foucault a "speaking eye"; usually refers to a way of looking that reduces and subordinates the person or thing viewed.
Genealogy: the evolution of a construction.
Constructionists have laid bare the *genealogy* of homosexuality.
Historicity: fact, factuality.
Imbricate: overlap and confuse, often perniciously.
The *imbrication* of transvestitism with homosexuality . . .
Intervene/intervention: the scholarly technique of dissecting an aspect of a concept or construction, often to "queer" it.
Lacanian: of or relating to the theories of the French psychiatrist Jacques Lacan.
Performative/performativity: the idea that some speech is better thought of as an action than as simply a communication. Saying "I'm gay" is *performative* because it is less important for the information it communicates about one's sexuality than for the effect it has on one's status in society and on one's relationships with others.
Phallus: not simply the penis, but the penis as symbol of socioculturally constructed GENDER power—i.e., in most cultures, male dominance.

Privilege: put special emphasis on.
Marxists *privilege* class differences.
Problematize: challenge, make one question or look at something in a new, unexpected way.
The existence of female directors like DOROTHY ARZNER *problematizes* our understanding of HOLLYWOOD's "male gaze."
Recover/recovery: uncover or investigate the evolution or genealogy of a construction.
Reify: treat as a thing or a fact in a way that denies something is actually a socioculturally constructed concept, as to *reify* femininity.
Reverse discourse: Foucauldian term for aggressively coopting and subverting the very terms of oppression, for example, by self-assertively calling oneself a "queer" or a "dyke," or by reveling in a despised identity, such as RONALD FIRBANK's boast that "None but those whose courage is unquestionable can venture to be effeminate."
Site: used as a synonym for situation or instance, as in "*site* of conflict."
Subject: counterintuitively, someone empowered to make someone or something else an object, often linked to "agency."

Queer Resources Directory, see QRD.

Queer Theory

Academic movement especially concerned with issues of GENDER and sexuality. Queer theory first emerged among scholars, most but not all of whom were self-identified as gay, lesbian, or bisexual, in the late 1980s. An even more diffuse phenomenon than LESBIAN AND GAY STUDIES, queer theory is best understood as a methodology rather than a system of abstract principles—a way of *queering* ideas that can be applied to virtually any area of study.

Teresa de Lauretis, professor of the history of consciousness at the University of California, Santa Cruz, probably coined the term when she used it to name an academic conference that convened in February 1990 in Santa Cruz after having participated on October 21, 1989, in another conference entitled "How Do I Look? Queer Film and Video Conference." She later differentiated her usage of the word "QUEER" from QUEER NATION (which she said she had not yet heard about when she named the conference).

Queer theory has roots in postmodernism, as well as in feminist literary, film, and psychoanalytic theory. As the word "queer" suggests, queer theory transcends the categories of "gay" and "lesbian" as well as "bisexual," "transsexual," "transvestite," and other labels applied to sexual nonconformity, opting instead to consider "identity," "sexuality," "gender," "eroticism" and the like as *constructed,* fluid, and unstable constructs that derive what meaning they have from context. Queer theory tends to reject categories in general.

Eve Kosofsky Sedgwick's *Between Men: English Literature and Male Homosexuality* (1985) is often cited as one of the books that helped launch queer theory. Other key works include Judith Butler's *Gender Trouble: Feminism and the Subversion of Identity* (1990), several essays by Teresa de Lauretis, and Jonathan Dollimore's *Sexual Dissidence: Augustine to Wilde, Freud to Foucault* (1991). Many queer theorists have concentrated their studies on FILM AND VIDEO.

- *How Do I Look?: Queer Film and Video,* edited by Bad Object-Choices, (1991).
- *Queering the Pitch: The New Gay and Lesbian Musicology,* edited by Philip Brett, Elizabeth Wood, and Gary C. Thomas (1994).
- *Out in Culture: Gay, Lesbian, and Queer Essays on Popular Culture,* edited by Corey K. Creekmur and Alexander Doty (1995).
- *Queer Studies: A Lesbian, Gay, Bisexual, and Transgender Anthology,* edited by Brett Beemyn, and Mickey Eliason (1996).

Quilt, The, see NAMES PROJECT, THE.

R

Radicalesbians (RL)

U.S. lesbian group organized in New York City in 1970. After failing to persuade the NATIONAL ORGANIZATION FOR WOMEN to address lesbian issues, RITA MAE BROWN resigned from the organization's New York chapter and began consciousness-raising and study groups with women from the GAY LIBERATION FRONT (GLF), The Feminists, Redstockings, and other factions of the radical feminist and gay liberation movements. Six of these women, calling themselves "Radical Lesbians," authored and distributed the influential position paper "WOMAN-IDENTIFIED WOMAN" as part of the LAVENDER MENACE action at the Second Congress to Unite Women in New York City on **May 1, 1970**. Following the action, lesbian women from the gay and women's liberation movements—including SIDNEY ABBOTT, Ellen Bedoz (Shumsky), Suzanne Bevier, Michela Griffo, Lois Hart, March Hoffman (later Artemis March), Arlene Kisner, BARBARA LOVE, and Martha Shelley—joined Brown to form Radicalesbians.

Compared with previous groups, RL advanced a more radical response to the question of how to address the inequities besetting women. They challenged feminists to trust in SEPARATISM as a primary means of achieving self-realization and social validation in both the women's and gay/lesbian movements. Based on the assumption that lesbians did not need men to validate themselves, they saw themselves as the ideal leaders of the women's movement. Furthermore, any woman who was first and foremost a "woman-identified woman" could consider herself a "lesbian." Thus, lesbianism became a political choice rather than simply a form of sexuality (see LESBIAN, POLITICAL).

Several members of the group, including the "big six" who had produced "Woman-Identified Woman," broke off to form GLF's Women's Caucus. FRAN WINANT and Judy Grepperd remained in RL and attempted to lead a collectivist effort that ultimately did not succeed. The group had dissolved by 1971.

- Sidney Abbott and Barbara Love, *Sappho Was a Right-On Woman* (1972).
- Toby Marotta, *The Politics of Homosexuality* (1981).
- Alice Echols, *Daring to Be Bad: Radical Feminism in America, 1967–1975* (1989).

Radical Faeries

Movement (although the founders prefer the word "development," believing movement suggests institutionalization) launched by HARRY HAY, his lover John Burnside, and other gay men at the Labor Day weekend Spiritual Conference for Radical Faeries that convened on **August 31, 1979**. Still devoted to the

Radical Faeries.

1960s COUNTERCULTURE, rebelling against what many felt was the stifling and artificial masculinity of CLONES, the men took their clothes off, danced in "faerie circles," told stories, and held workshops, giving birth to a movement that has since spread around the world. Hay later broke with the group but is still considered its spiritual godfather.

Not formally organized or chartered, Radical Faeries tend to be profeminist and anticonformist. Considered by some to be WICCA for men, the movement is rooted in writings like Arthur Evans's *Witchcraft and the Gay Counterculture* (1978), which rejected the 1970s trend toward assimilationism (see ASSIMILATIONISM VS. CONFRONTATIONALISM) and sought to reclaim ancient "faery" traditions. Although Evans had previously hosted "faerie gatherings," it was Hay, a master phrasemaker, who coined the term Radical Faerie, meaning "radical" in its sense of "root" as well as militant, and "faerie" both as a way of reclaiming the pejorative term "fairy" and as a reference to ancient spiritual traditions.

➤ Also see SPIRITUALITIES, ALTERNATIVE.

✧ Mark Thompson, "This Gay Tribe: A Brief History of Faeries," in *Gay Spirit: Myth and Meaning* (1987).

✧ Stuart Timmons, "Radical Faerie," in *The Trouble with Harry Hay: Founder of the Modern Gay Movement* (1990).

Rainbow Flag

Symbol of the gay and lesbian movement. San Francisco artist Gilbert Baker designed the first rainbow flag for his city's **June 25, 1978**, Gay Freedom Day Parade. The original rainbow flags had eight horizontal bands of equal width, each with a different meaning. From the top down, they were hot pink for sex, red for life, orange for healing, yellow for the sun, green for serenity, turquoise for art, indigo for harmony, and violet for spirit. In 1979, the stripes for sex (hot pink) and art (turquoise) were eliminated and blue was substituted for indigo, leaving the now familiar red-orange-yellow-green-blue-violet-banded flag.

Today, the rainbow flag is a feature of gay PRIDE CELEBRATIONS around the world, and many lesbians and gay men fly it at their homes. Its colorful design has inspired a host of variations, including a seven-striped flag with a black band at the bottom to symbolize the fight against AIDS. The design is also featured on everything from pins to T-shirts. It has been recognized by the International Congress of Flag Makers.

Rainey, Ma

(Gertrude Melissa Nix Pidgett; 1886–1939)

U.S. singer. The daughter of entertainers, she grew up touring the South in minstrel and vaudeville shows. In 1902, she discovered the blues and made them her own, becoming the first of the great, nationally famous blues singers. She married Will Rainey in 1904 and toured with him as the Assassinators of the Blues. She formed her own show a few years after they separated, and continued touring until the Depression forced her retirement in 1933. Between 1923 and 1929, she recorded almost 100 different songs, including "See See Rider Blues" and "Prove It on Me Blues," which contained the lines "Went out last night with a crowd of my friends / They must've been women / 'cause I don't like mens."

Ma Rainey.

Said to have been the woman who introduced BESSIE SMITH to lesbian love, Rainey was one of a number of legendary women singers associated with the HARLEM RENAISSANCE who were known to prefer women over men. In Rainey's case, the affairs were not merely sexual: her nickname, Ma, is said to be a reference to the affection and nurturing she lavished on those around her.

Rechy, John

(1934–)

U.S. writer. The son of a Mexican mother and a Scottish father, Rechy grew up Catholic in El Paso, Texas. After college and military service, he moved to New York and discovered the underground world of male street prostitutes and what he later described as his "ferocious need to hustle." Encouraged by a friend's enthusiastic response to a letter describing a sex-fraught sojourn in New Orleans during Mardi Gras, Rechy spent four years writing the largely autobiographical novel *City of Night*. The book's successful publication in **1963** heralded an era of increasing acceptance of gay sexual openness in LITERATURE—although it was later criticized by some gay commentators for its overwhelmingly bleak portrayals of hustlers and their gay male customers. Rechy, who blamed the negative aspects of gay life on societal oppression, replied that literature dealing with gay themes "must begin with a realistic appraisal of that world. It's not an indictment of the gay world to say that it's a very despairing, lonely world in many respects."

Rechy further explored these themes in *Numbers* (1967), an again largely autobiographical account of a man who sets out to have sex with 30 men in 10 days. Rechy later described his character as "a real existential creature trying to thwart the certain knowledge of doom by collecting and counting sex acts." A "sexual horror story," *Numbers* was one of the first literary treatments of the obsessive promiscuity that many viewed, then and later, as a defining characteristic of gay male life. In three other gay-themed works—*This Day's Death* (1969), about an L.A. police vice raid and its tragic consequences; *The Sexual Outlaw: A Documentary* (1977), subtitled *A Non-Fiction Account, with Commentaries, of Three Days and Nights in the Sexual Underground;* and *Rushes* (1979), a novel about the patrons of a cheerless leather bar—Rechy argued that gay male promiscuity was a revolt against the "life-crushing strictures" of straight society. "The greater the repression, the greater the defiance," Rechy wrote in *The Sexual Outlaw.* "Release the heterosexual pressures on our world—convert the rage—and you release a creative energy to enrich two worlds. Pressurize the homosexual world further, and it may yet set your straight world on fire."

In the 1970s, many writers took up the theme of gay male promiscuity; some (see, for example, GUY HOCQUENGHEM) agreed with Rechy that promiscuity was potentially revolutionary. Rechy, however, distinguished himself as much by his refusal to romanticize the gay sexual underground as by his outspoken—and at times almost paradoxical—denunciations of negative aspects of gay life. One of the first to celebrate gay BODYBUILDING, for example, he also satirized "the new masculinity" or "the new conformity" in *Rushes,* calling it: "as clearly homosexual as drag; contrived, studied. Unreal." A self-proclaimed topman and no stranger to rough sex, he criticized gay S/M as a form of internalized HOMOPHOBIA. He decried gay ageism and the "squalor" of gay sex venues; in 1979, on the eve of AIDS, he warned in an ADVOCATE interview that gay men were "surrendering to death at the age of 35."

Rechy remained passionately—and professionally—devoted to what he called the "sex-hunt" into the 1980s, while continuing to write and to teach FILM and creative writing at the University of Southern California. Although he is probably the best-known gay male LATINO writer in the United States, his gay-themed work reflects little of his Mexican-American heritage (except for surnames such as that of Johnny Rio, the main character in *Numbers*). In contrast, some of his later fiction written in the personae of heterosexual women, in particular the novel *The Miraculous Day of Amalia Gomez* (1991), has centered around Latin women.

- Winston Leyland, *Gay Sunshine Interviews: Volume One* (1978).
- Mitchel Raphael, "Our Man of Babylon—John Rechy: An Interview with the Sexual Outlaw," *Icon* (February 1997).

Religion, see RELIGIOUS ORDERS; SPIRITUALITIES, ALTERNATIVE; specific religions and denominations.

Religious Orders

All major religions have at one time or another harbored leaders who condemned same-sex eroticism. Yet in cultures as different as CHINA and ITALY, religious orders have often been popularly associated with homoerotic opportunity. In particular, sex-segregated religious communities are rivaled only by the MILITARY and PRISON as social settings traditionally thought to promote homosexuality. As early as

423, St. Augustine warned his sister, a nun, that love between women in monastic communities could lead to "shameful" carnal expression. In JAPAN, homosexuality was thought to have been imported from China by Buddhist monks (see **806** and **1254**). Gay and lesbian scholars like JOHN BOSWELL and Judith C. Brown have found extensive documentation of same-sex relations among monks and nuns in Europe in the Middle Ages and the Renaissance. At least one ROMAN CATHOLIC CHURCH council, meeting in **1212**, addressed monastic homoeroticism by ordering that nuns sleep in separate beds and keep a light burning at night. These efforts notwithstanding, no less an authority than Martin Luther claimed that SODOMY remained rampant among Catholic clergy in **1531**.

Today, despite the fact that only a few religious organizations allow openly gay and lesbian applicants to take religious orders—and then often only if they vow to remain celibate—many lesbians and gay men continue to be drawn to the religious life. In one study, a group of Roman Catholic priests, nuns, and brothers told theologian Kevin Gordon, head of a task force set up by the archdiocese of San Francisco, that they estimated 40 to 60 percent of their peers were lesbian or gay. Even if this estimate is inflated, few familiar with clergy members would doubt that they are any *less* likely than persons in other professions to be gay or lesbian. Some people, including 33 percent of the respondents to an *OutLook* magazine survey, believe that lesbians and gay men have a "unique" or "heightened" sense of spirituality which, if true, might explain why so many have taken religious orders. Another reason, especially relevant before the development of accessible gay and lesbian SUBCULTURES, is that the religious life has been in many societies the only alternative to COMPULSORY HETEROSEXUALITY. In particular, women were able to escape marriage and find compatible companionship in Catholic, Orthodox, Anglican, and Buddhist convents. Yet another theory, relevant especially to gay men and lesbians who espouse unconventional GENDER identities, links lesbian and gay vocations to premodern traditions in which shamans were often conceived to be "two-spirited" (i.e., simultaneously embodying male and female spirits).

Many well-known gay men and lesbians have been nuns, monks, ministers, preachers, or priests, including Virginia Apuzzo (activist, former director of the NATIONAL GAY AND LESBIAN TASK FORCE), JAMES BALDWIN (writer), Peter Carey (AIDS activist, writer), Jeanne Cordova (activist, author, publisher), Jim Fouratt (activist, GAY LIBERATION FRONT leader), Hannah Blue Heron (writer), Mary Mendola (writer, producer), Jean O'Leary (activist, former co-director of the National Gay and Lesbian Task Force), and Janice Raymond (educator, philosopher, writer).

➤ Also see BERDACHE; BOYD, MALCOLM; METROPOLITAN COMMUNITY CHURCHES; SPIRITUALITIES, ALTERNATIVE; **7/4/1970**; **6/25/1972**; **1/10/1980**; **5/15/1996**; specific religions and denominations.

✧ John Boswell, *Christianity, Social Tolerance, and Homosexuality: Gay People in Western Europe from the Beginning of the Christian Era to the Fourteenth Century* (1980).

✧ *Homosexuality and the Catholic Church,* edited by Jeannine Gramick (1983).

✧ *Lesbian Nuns: Breaking Silence,* edited by Rosemary Curb and Nancy Manahan (1985).

✧ Judith C. Brown, *Immodest Acts: The Life of a Lesbian Nun in Renaissance Italy* (1986).

- ✧ Christie Balka and Andy Rose, *Twice Blessed: On Being Lesbian, Gay,* and *Jewish* (1989).
- ✧ *Homosexuality and Religion,* edited by Richard Hasbany (1989).
- ✧ Rose Mary Denman, *Let My People In: A Lesbian Minister Tells of Her Struggles to Live Openly and Maintain Her Ministry* (1990).

Renault, Mary

(pseudonym of Eileen Mary Challans; 1905–1983)

British-born South African novelist, nurse. Born and raised in London, she was the child of emotionally distant parents who had longed for a son. Despite the fact that her physician father felt education was wasted on women—and her mother considered female students unfeminine—she earned two degrees at Oxford, made possible by scholarships and supplemental funds from an aunt. Although she had already decided to become a writer, she returned to school to study nursing in 1933. She met her life partner of 48 years, a fellow nurse named Julie Mullard, while training at an infirmary.

Her first novel, *Purposes of Love* (U.S. title: *Promise of Love*), published to considerable acclaim in 1939, explored the possibilities of same-sex love through an openly lesbian (and semiautobiographical) character named Colonna. It also introduced "Mary Renault"—replacing an earlier PSEUDONYM, Martin, she had used in publishing poems, with Renault, after a character in Thomas Otway's 17th-century blank verse drama, *Venice Preserved*. ("Radcliffe," the hospital where she worked, was also considered—until Mullard reminded her of RADCLYFFE HALL.)

Her next four novels continued in a similar vein. *Return to Night* (1947) won a $150,000 MGM prize, allowing her to move to South Africa with Mullard in 1948. Her sixth and last novel set in modern times, *The Charioteer* (1953), debuted the theme of love between men, evoking a soldier's attraction to a former schoolmate convincingly enough to make many readers believe she was actually a gay man. The first major British novel to deal

Mary Renault (right) with lover Julie Mullard.

frankly with same-sex love after World War II, *The Charioteer* was considered so provocative that it was six years before a publisher dared risk obscenity charges and publish it in the U.S.

Starting with *The Last of the Wine* (1956), Renault set her last eight novels in ancient times, a move that not only allowed greater freedom to portray same-sex love but also helped her express her own GENDER persona(e): "I've never been a feminist," she once commented, "simply because all these years my inner persona occupied two sexes too indiscriminately to take part in a sex war." Not surprisingly, one of her most vivid characters is the dual-gendered eunuch Bagoas, the eponymous hero of *The Persian Boy* (1972) who is loved by Alexander the Great.

Renault's best-selling historical novels were acclaimed by critics for their meticulously researched historical detail and rhythmically expressive language. For gay readers, they were practically the only books of their time to present love between men not as a problem but as a part of life.

Renault was largely unaware of her status in gay circles. Ironically, she even objected to the appropriation of the word "GAY." Yet she once tried to enlist the Black Sash, an African civil rights group, in the fight against a Cape Town Parliament proposal to toughen restrictions on gay men. When Black Sash demurred, Renault dispatched her own arguments. Similarly, she wrote *The Spectator* in England to defend homosexuality during the public discussion that followed the WOLFENDEN REPORT.

Before Renault died in 1983, she told her future biographer she wanted to be remembered "as someone who got it right."

✧ David Sweetman, *Mary Renault: A Biography* (1993).

Rich, Adrienne [Cecile]
(1929–)

U.S. poet, essayist, feminist theorist, educator. Rich was born and raised with her younger sister, Cynthia, in Baltimore, Maryland, the daughter of a Jewish (but self-professed "deist") father and a southern Protestant mother. To ensure "a perfectly developing child," her father, a physician and professor, and her mother, an erstwhile pianist and composer, educated Rich at home until she was nine. A year later, she launched her writing career with the publication of *Ariadne: A Play in Three Acts and Poems* (1939). In 1951, she graduated with honors from Radcliffe College and had her first book of poetry, *A Change of World,* "certified," as she describes it, with a foreword by W. H. AUDEN, who also gave it the prestigious Yale Younger Poets award. Since 1966, she has taught in colleges across the U.S.

As early as *A Change of World,* Rich was, as she has written, "coming to terms with her feelings for women" in poems such as "Stepping Backward." She worked for two years (1958–1960) on "Snapshots of a Daughter-in-Law," her first consciously feminist poem, and reflected on her 13-year marriage and experience raising three sons in *Of Woman Born: Motherhood as Experience and Institution* (1976). Her reflections on lesbian motherhood appear throughout the book and, like her poetry after 1963, are more personal, immediate, and less formally controlled. Rich has credited JUDY GRAHN's poem "A Woman Is Talking to Death" for changing her life in 1974.

Rich and her life partner, novelist MICHELLE CLIFF, edited the influential *Sinister Wisdom* from 1981 to 1983. Rich's work, which has been translated into eight languages, ranges over four collections of essays, including *What Is Found There: Notebooks on Poetry and Politics* (1993), and twenty volumes of poetry, including *Dark Fields of the Republic* (1995). Among her numerous awards was a National Book Award in 1973 for *Diving into the Wreck* (1973), the Publishing Triangle's Bill Whitehead Award for lifetime achievement in gay and lesbian literature, and a MacArthur Fellowship.

Rich is recognized as an eloquent and provocative theorist on the politics of sexuality, women's culture, race, and what she calls "life's silences." She has commented: "My poetry had always been a means of surviving, finding out what I thought and what was true for me, one place where I was really honest with myself." She believes poetry can "uncover desires and appetites buried under the accumulating emergencies of our lives. . . ."

➤ Also see COMPULSORY HETEROSEXUALITY; LESBIAN CONTINUUM.

✧ Elly Bulkin, "An Interview with Adrienne Rich," *Conditions One and Two* (1977).

✧ David Trinidad, "Adrienne Rich Charts a Difficult World," *The Advocate* (December 31, 1991).

✧ Barbara C. Gelpi and Albert Gelpi, *Adrienne Rich's Poetry and Prose* (1993).

Riggs, Marlon
(1957–1994)

U.S. filmmaker. Riggs grew up an army brat in Texas, Georgia, and Germany. A graduate of Harvard College in 1978 and the University of California at Berkeley's School of Journalism in 1981, Riggs first rose to prominence as the producer, director, and writer of *Ethnic Notions* (1987), an Emmy Award–winning documentary that explored the effects of AFRICAN-AMERICAN stereotypes. The following year, Riggs was stricken with a near fatal kidney ailment that turned out to be HIV-related. Reviewing the accomplishments of his life, the then 31-year old filmmaker decided it was time to stop, as he described it, "extracting out sexuality" from his work. The result was the groundbreaking documentary *Tongues Untied* (1989), along with ISAAC JULIEN's *Looking for Langston* (1988), the first widely viewed FILM to examine black gay sexuality from a black point of view.

Although *Tongues Untied* met with widespread critical acclaim, it also drew fire from conservative politicians when it was broadcast on American public TELEVISION. In the ensuing controversy, Riggs became one of the best-known and most outspoken black gay male activists. Other important works included *Color Adjustment: Blacks in Prime Time* (1991), an examination of television images of African-Americans; *No Regrets (Non, Je Ne Regrette Rien)* (1993), in which he interviewed HIV-positive African-American men; and *Black Is, Black Ain't* (1995), a wide-ranging look at all the valid ways one can be black, completed by colleagues after his death from complications of AIDS in 1994.

✧ Ron Simmons, "*Tongues Untied:* An Interview with Marlon Riggs," in *Brother to Brother: New Writings by Black Gay Men,* edited by Essex Hemphill (1991).

✧ Kobena Mercer, "Dark and Lovely: Black Gay Men in Independent Film," in *Queer Looks: Perspectives on Lesbian and Gay Film and Video,* edited by Martha Gever, John Greyson, and Pratibha Parmar (1993).

✧ Raymond Murray, *Images in the Dark: An Encyclopedia of Gay and Lesbian Film and Video* (1996).

Rimbaud, Arthur, see VERLAINE, PAUL.

Ritual(ized) Homosexuality, see CIRCUMSTANTIAL HOMOSEXUALITY.

Roberts, Shelly

(née Sheila Rhodes; 1943–)

U.S. writer, humorist, activist. Though born in Chicago, she grew up in Los Angeles and stayed in California through a marriage to B. F. Roberts in 1965 and the birth of a son, Sean, the following year. She had her first affair with a woman in 1971 while visiting Karlsruhe, Germany. Back in Los Angeles, she became active in the women's movement and was named the first vice president in charge of communications for the NATIONAL ORGANIZATION FOR WOMEN in 1973. She published her first book, *What to Do with a Liberated Woman,* in 1977 before moving to New York City in 1978 to work in ADVERTISING. In 1990, several moves later, she settled in south Florida and began writing a humor column for the newsletter of Women in Network, a local lesbian organization. By 1996, the column had evolved into "Roberts' Rules" and was featured in 60 lesbian and gay periodicals and on the Internet, reaching an estimated 1 million readers. Jeni Pacula, copublisher of *Fountain* magazine, cited "Roberts' Rules" as the most widely read column written specifically to a gay and lesbian audience.

A prominent representative of the lesbian humor boom, Roberts has published a number of popular books, including *The Dyke Detector* (1992), *Hey Mom, Guess What! 150 Ways to Tell Your Mother* (1993), and *Roberts' Rules of Lesbian Living* (1996). With equal seriousness, she has been a widely featured speaker at PRIDE CELEBRATIONS and a "guest expert" on more than 400 TELEVISION and radio shows. She was named to the board of governors of the HUMAN RIGHTS CAMPAIGN in 1996.

Robinson, Marty

(1942–1993)

U.S. activist. The son of a doctor, Robinson studied biology at Brooklyn College for three years, came OUT, and moved to Greenwich Village, where he supported himself by working as a carpenter.

Robinson was drawn into gay ACTIVISM on the second night of the STONEWALL Uprising. He joined the MATTACHINE Society of New York and within a matter of weeks was heading the action committee Mattachine had formed in response to the uprising. He first came to prominence when he and Jim Owles

Marty Robinson (left) and lover Tom Doerr in the early 1970s.

walked out of a GAY LIBERATION FRONT meeting and founded GAY ACTIVISTS ALLIANCE (GAA) on **December 21, 1969**. The most visible leader of GAA, he directed a number of important protest actions (see, for example, **6/24/1970**) and appeared on national TELEVISION (see **11/27/1970**) as a spokesperson for the movement. Discouraged by the initial defeat of a proposed gay rights ordinance in New York City (see **1/27/1972**), he withdrew from active participation in the movement in the mid-1970s, but returned a decade later to become one of the few GAY LIBERATION era leaders who was also prominent in AIDS activism.

✧ Kay Tobin and Randy Wicker, *The Gay Crusaders* (1972).

✧ Toby Marotta, *The Politics of Homosexuality* (1981).

Roman Catholic Church

Largest Christian denomination, with more than 1 billion adherents around the world. The official attitude of the Church toward homosexuality—expressed in numerous documents, including Joseph Cardinal Ratzinger's "Letter to the Bishops of the Catholic Church on the Pastoral Care of Homosexual Persons" (see **10/1/1986**)—is that homosexuals are "intrinsically disordered." Ratzinger specified: "Although the particular inclination of the homosexual person is not a sin, it is a more or less strong tendency ordered toward an intrinsic moral evil." The responsibility of the Church is thus to help "homosexual persons" live "a chaste life" and achieve "the abandonment of homosexual activity."

Catholic antipathy to eroticism in general, and same-sex love in particular, dates back to the first centuries of CHRISTIANITY, when early church fathers like Clement of Alexandria, Origen, and John Chrysostom synthesized Judeo-Christian and Hellenistic thinking on sex, rejecting eroticism for asceticism and spirituality. The first penitentials (see **700**), which were a kind of guidebook to the sacrament of penance, included detailed lists of sexual "sins," among which were sex between men and between women. Suggested penances, however, were not much more harsh than for different-sex transgressions. Zealots such as Peter Damian (see **1051**) recommended that the Church root out those who "sinned against nature." Later Thomas Aquinas (see **1252**) refined Church negativity toward homoeroticism, but prosecutions of SODOMY became common only when the emerging states of Western Europe began to institute civil laws on sexual behavior (see **1260**, etc.).

Dignity/USA, the first openly gay and lesbian affinity group of any mainstream denomination, was formed in San Diego in 1969 by Father Pat Nidorf as an advocacy and support group for gay and lesbian Catholics. (In 1982, a group of women, feeling that Dignity was overly male-oriented, formed the Conference for Catholic Lesbians to address the concerns of lesbian Catholics.) Many gay and lesbian Catholics had believed that a rapprochement, similar to those achieved by other Christian denominations, could be achieved, but Ratzinger's 1986 letter signaled the hardening of attitudes within the Church hierarchy. More than 50 Dignity groups were ordered to cease meeting on Church property, and the Church put its support behind campaigns to fight pro-gay and -lesbian legislation.

Dignity today has chapters in the U.S., CANADA, and the NETHERLANDS. Other Catholic gay and lesbian advocacy groups include David et Jonathan, founded in FRANCE in 1972, Acceptance in AUSTRALIA, Ascent in NEW ZEALAND, and Quest in the UNITED KINGDOM.

➤ Also see BOSWELL, JOHN; INQUISITION, THE.

✧ *Homosexuality: Debating the Issues,* edited by Robert M. Baird and M. Katherine Baird (1995).

Roman Empire, see ROME.

Romania, see EASTERN EUROPE.

Romantic Friendships

Also called "passionate friendships"; deeply committed, long-term—often lifelong—same-sex relationships comparable in many respects with idealized male-female love pairings but not necessarily erotic in nature. In gay and lesbian studies, "romantic friendship" is most commonly used to refer to a relationship between two women, but numerous examples also exist of similarly passionate friendships between men.

The scholarly debate on romantic friendships has centered on two related issues: (1) How often were these relationships sexual? (2) What similarities, if any, do they have with modern lesbian and gay relationships?

The topic of romantic friendships has become increasingly contentious, but most scholars agree on the following points: Romantic friendships were common from the Renaissance until roughly the beginning of the 20th century. They were mainly a European and American phenomenon, although similar friendships have been documented in JAPAN and other parts of Asia. They were usually seen by contemporaries as not overtly sexual or—as Goethe described his romantic friendship with Friedrich von Schiller—"unpolluted" by sex.

Contemporaries tended to idealize romantic friendships, often maintaining that they were "purer" than male-female relationships could ever be. Evidence that they sometimes cloaked less than "pure" activities comes from a variety of sources, including the coded diaries of ANNE LISTER.

As people in North America and Europe grew more aware of—or at least more willing to discuss—possibilities for same-sex intimacy at the end of the 19th century, romantic friendships became more suspect. The different experiences of people like SARAH ORNE JEWETT, ALICE AUSTEN, WILLA CATHER, and RACHEL CARSON show how changing social attitudes made romantic friendships increasingly difficult in the 20th century.

➤ Also see BOSTON MARRIAGES.

✧ Lillian Faderman, *Surpassing the Love of Men: Romantic Friendship and Love Between Women from the Renaissance to the Present* (1981).

✧ Eve Kosofsky Sedgwick, *Between Men: English Literature and Male Homosocial Desire* (1985).

✧ Janice G. Raymond, *A Passion for Friends: Toward a Philosophy of Female Affection* (1986).

✧ Emma Donoghue, *Passions Between Women: British Lesbian Culture, 1665–1801* (1993).

Rome (Roman Empire)

Unlike the Greeks, the Romans seldom idealized same-sex eroticism, but they nonetheless indulged in it at least as frequently. In many respects, in fact, the eroticized same-sex SUBCULTURES that existed in Rome are more similar to those that have developed in modern-day America and Europe than to the forms of PEDERASTY that characterized ancient GREECE.

Upper-class Romans were subject to a

Virgil was just one of many Roman writers who wrote homoerotic poems.

form of COMPULSORY HETEROSEXUALITY designed to ensure the continuance of the Roman race and a plentiful supply of citizen soldiers and statesmen. In private life, however, they were often free to explore a wide variety of erotic options, and even though they risked running afoul of Roman laws against adultery, many Romans left records of same-sex relationships. Just a few of the writers who explored homoerotic themes are Catullus (see **c. 55 B.C.**), Virgil (see **c. 30 B.C.**), Petronius (see **c. 60**), Martial (see **c. 85**), and Juvenal (see **c. 120**). Juvenal, most provocatively, wrote of same-sex MARRIAGES, which some historians believe were condoned by the state.

Many emperors, including HADRIAN, were open in expressing their fondness for handsome young men. According to gossip-filled historical accounts, most emperors had sex with both men and women, something Romans seem to have thought was a natural state of affairs. As in Greece, however, it was considered shameful and "soft" (*mollis*) for a free adult man to be the insertee—as opposed to the inserter—in oral or anal intercourse. Yet some men, including Julius Caesar (who was said to have had an affair with the king of Bythinia), did in fact transgress this societal norm and incurred no worse consequences than ridicule.

Upper-class women in Rome were somewhat more independent than in Greece. Some, apparently, were able to form long-term relationships with each other (see **c. 160**).

Although sexual "perversion" is associated with the collapse of the Roman Empire in the popular imagination, historical records show that the empire actually became less tolerant of all forms of sexuality as it went into decline. As Christians became more powerful in the empire, emperors enacted a series of increasingly punitive laws against same-sex eroticism. True to Roman prejudices, they were directed especially toward men who cross-dressed or took a supposedly subordinate role in anal or oral intercourse (see **342**; **390**; **438**).

➤ Also see ITALY.

✧ John Boswell, *Christianity, Social Tolerance, and Homosexuality: Gay People in Western Europe from the Beginning of the Christian Era to the Fourteenth Century* (1980).

✧ Eve Cantarella, *Pandora's Daughters: The Role and Status of Women in Greek and Roman Antiquity* (1987).

Roosevelt, Eleanor, see Hickok, Lorena.

Routsong, Alma

(pseudonym: Isabel Miller, 1924–1996)

U.S. novelist, essayist, editor. Born in Traverse City, Michigan, the daughter of a police officer and a nurse, she interrupted her college studies to serve as a hospital apprentice in the Waves. She married Bruce Brodie in 1947, completed a B.A. in art in 1949, and gave birth to four daughters before divorcing Brodie in 1962.

Routsong's first two novels, *A Gradual Joy* (1954) and *Round Shape* (1959), had no overtly lesbian content. After forming a relationship with a woman in the 1960s, she tried to write about her and her friends' experiences but found herself stymied by a sense that she was "tattling." Then, while visiting a folk art museum in Cooperstown, New York, her lover pointed out a primitive painting of a mermaid (*Mare Maid*) by MARY ANN WILLSON, who, according to the museum, had shared her life in the 1820s with a "farmerette" named "Miss Brundidge." The discovery inspired Routsong to write her most popular novel, *A Place for Us* (later retitled *Patience and Sarah*), a gently romantic, vividly imagined account of the lives of two lovers who settle in New York in the early 19th century.

Unable to find a publisher for the novel, Routsong printed 1,000 copies in 1969 as a "Bleecker Street Press Edition" and peddled them on the streets of Greenwich Village, at DAUGHTERS OF BILITIS (DOB) meetings, and through the DOB publication THE LADDER. Her PSEUDONYM, Isabel Miller, combined an anagram for "lesbia" with her mother's maiden name.

One of the first lesbian-positive historical novels, *A Place for Us* received the first Gay Book Award of the Gay Liberation Task Force division of the Social Responsibilities Round Table of the AMERICAN LIBRARY ASSOCIATION in

Barbara Gittings (left) and Alma Routsong at the American Library Association's first Gay Book Awards ceremony.

June 1971. Some gay and lesbian critics lambasted the novel's anachronistic lesbian feminist consciousness, but most readers, accustomed to "problem" novels in which homosexuality was depicted either as a tragic aberration or a sick perversion, welcomed its positive portrayal of a loving relationship between women. Republished by McGraw-Hill in 1972, *Patience and Sarah* became one of the classics of the post-STONEWALL era.

Routsong joined the GAY LIBERATION movement in 1970 and was an officer in the DOB. Her other works include *The Love of Good Women* (1986), *Side by Side* (1990), and *A Dooryard Full of Flowers* (1993), a collection of short stories, including two parts of a quasi-sequel to *Patience and Sarah*. Routsong died shortly after her last novel, *Laurel,* was published in 1996.

✧ "Alma Routsong: Writing and Publishing *Patience and Sarah,* 'I Felt I Had Found My People,' " in Jonathan Ned Katz, *Gay American History* (1976).

✧ Elizabeth Wavle, "Isabel Miller," in *Contemporary Lesbian Writers of the United States,* edited by Sandra Pollack and Denise D. Knight (1993).

Jane Rule (right) with her lover, Helen Sonthoff, near their home on Galiano Island, British Columbia.

Rule, Jane [Vance]

(1931–)

U.S.-born Canadian writer, critic, teacher. Born in Plainfield, New Jersey, Rule moved often as a child. She studied at Mills College in Oakland, California, and University College in London and taught in Massachusetts before settling with her lover and fellow teacher, Helen Sonthoff, in Vancouver in 1956. She and Sonthoff became Canadian citizens and now live on Galiano Island, British Columbia. For Rule, the change in citizenship was a return to roots: she had been named after a Nova Scotian great-grandmother.

Rule put her teaching career in jeopardy with the publication in 1964 of *Desert of the Heart,* CANADA's first gay- or lesbian-positive novel. By the time a new generation of readers discovered the novel via Donna Deitch's breakthrough "mainstream" film, *Desert Hearts* (1986), Rule was firmly established as one of the most prominent women in the Canadian lesbian movement, despite her uncompromisingly independent, often controversial views on ART and sexual politics. She wrote a column for the Toronto-based newspaper *The Body Politic,* and in 1975 published *Lesbian Images,* profiling 12 preeminent writers ranging from RADCLYFFE HALL to ALMA ROUTSONG and providing the first critical survey of lesbian writing since JEANETTE FOSTER's *Sex Variant Women in Literature* (1956).

Though sometimes labeled a "lesbian

writer," Rule has insisted on a universal vision in her work, concerning herself with gay male and straight characters as well as lesbians and addressing an equally broad range of themes in her seven novels and five collections of short stories and essays. Although she has warned against lesbians and gay men defining themselves too narrowly, she has also written: "W. H. AUDEN said he was a poet only when he was writing a poem. We don't yet have the political freedom to be able to be homosexuals only when we are making love with members of our own sex, but it is that freedom I know I'm working for."

✧ Marie Kuda, "Jane Rule," in *Gay and Lesbian Literature,* edited by Sharon Malowinski (1994).

✧ Jane Rule, "Jane Rule," in *Contemporary Authors Autobiography Series* (vol. 18), edited by Joyce Nakamura (1994).

Russ, Joanna
(1937–)

U.S. novelist, short fiction writer, essayist, and critic. Born in the Bronx, New York, to two secular Jewish schoolteachers, Evarett and Bertha Zinner, Russ garnered high school national science honors and went on to an English degree at Cornell and an M.F.A. in playwriting and dramatic LITERATURE from Yale. She was married briefly and began writing SCIENCE FICTION ("what if" literature, she calls it) while in graduate school. She subsequently taught at schools in New York, Colorado, and Washington before retiring to Arizona, earning a reputation for academic activism on behalf of feminism, civil rights, and gay and lesbian issues. She further elaborated her positions in the collections *How to Suppress Women's Writing* (1983) and *Magic Mommas, Trembling Sisters, Puritans and Perverts: Feminist Essays* (1985).

Her best-known books are the Hugo Award–winning separatist lesbian utopian classic *The Female Man* (1975; reprinted in the Science Fiction Hall of Fame series in 1986), *The Two of Them* (1978), *Extra (Ordinary) People* (1984), and her coming-out novel *On Strike Against God* (1980). She has also published three collections of short stories, children's fiction, and essays.

Critics have praised her intelligence, creativity, and stylistic talents, particularly in her imagery of visionary worlds. *The Female Man* is considered (with MONIQUE WITTIG's *Les Guérillères*) one of the two earliest lesbian and feminist modern utopian texts, and, according to Diane Griffin Crowder, the novel that had "the greatest influence on the development of the genre."

Russ sees hope in change: "One thing I think we must know—that our traditional GENDER roles will not be part of the future, as long as the future is not a second Stone Age."

✧ Joanna Russ, "What Can a Heroine Do? Or Why Women Can't Write," and "The Image of Women in Science Fiction," both in *Images of Women in Fiction: Feminist Perspectives,* edited by Susan Koppelman Cornillon (1972).

✧ Diane Griffin Crowder, "Separatism and Feminist Utopian Fiction," in *Sexual Practice, Textual Theory,* edited by Susan J. Wolfe and Julia Penelope (1993).

Russia

No laws against same-sex relations between adults. Emerging social scene and political groups in Moscow, St. Petersburg, and a few other large cities.

Although Russians suspected of homosexuality are no longer sent to sanatoriums or to Siberian camps, the country is still a difficult place to be openly gay or lesbian. In 1991,

Mikhail Kuzmin, author of Russia's first gay novel.

about the same time gay and lesbian groups were beginning to attract notice in the Russian media, a nationwide survey reported that a majority of Russians thought homosexuals should be killed. The percentage calling for the death penalty declined over the next few years, but even in comparatively sophisticated Moscow, where a mere 31 percent wanted to see homosexuals executed in 1993, the environment was so hostile that gay disco patrons often stayed inside all night rather than risk being queer-bashed outside the club.

Seven decades of Communist rule left Russia and the other republics in the USSR largely isolated, not only from the phenomena that transformed attitudes toward sex and sexuality in capitalist countries but from their own unique heritage of HOMOEROTICISM. Judging from rates of premarital sex, abortion, and divorce, Russians would appear to be as sexually "liberated" as their Western counterparts, but Russian scholars like Igor S. Kon have documented a level of ignorance about sex unimaginable in Western Europe or North America. This ignorance, the legacy of an official prudishness that endured from the time of Stalin through the late 1980s, contributes to a level of HOMOPHOBIA unmatched in the West.

Twentieth-century Russians who have been openly gay, lesbian, or bisexual during at least some part of their lives include activists Yevgeniya Debryanskaya, Roman Kalinin, and Alexander Zaremba; dancers Boris Moiseev and Valery Mikhailovsky; and writers Evgenii Kharitonov (1941–1981), MIKHAIL KUZMIN, SOPHIA PARNOK, and Marina Tsvetaeva.

History

Several of the first Western European visitors to Russia were shocked at how common same-sex relations were, among the peasants as well as Moscow aristocrats. Although both male and female "SODOMY" was considered a sin worthy of capital punishment, Russia was one of the last countries in Europe specifically to criminalize same-sex relations.

Nikolai Mikhailovich Przhevalsky (1839–1888), famous explorer and naturalist, achieved international renown and was well-known for his handsome young protégés who accompanied him on his travels through Siberia, CENTRAL ASIA, and Tibet.

In the 19th century, a Russian SUBCULTURE developed, complete with Turkish BATHS, brothels, and well-known CRUISING grounds. There was at one time a kind of lesbian chic among the bohemian intelligentsia. Kuzmin's *Wings* (1906) was not only the first gay-themed Russian novel; it was also one of the first in any language to transcend the topic of homosexuality as a "problem."

After the Bolshevik Revolution, as the state tightened its control of the presses, a generation of previously open gay men and lesbians emigrated or retreated into the closet. About the same time as the NAZI PERSECUTION, the government began roundups of gay men, sending them to work camps where most died of exhaustion, starvation, or exposure.

CIRCUMSTANTIAL HOMOSEXUALITY among women as well as men is well documented in Siberian camps. Men known to be gay were subjected to gang rapes and horribly persecuted through the 1990s.

A few gay men, such as the film director Sergei Eisenstein, were tolerated by Stalin and later leaders.

✧ Masha Gessen, *The Rights of Lesbians and Gay Men in the Russian Federation: An International Gay and Lesbian Human Rights Commission Report* (1994).

✧ Igor S. Kon, *The Sexual Revolution in Russia: From the Age of the Czars to Today* (1995).

✧ Masha Gessen, "Russia," in *Unspoken Rules: Sexual Orientation and Women's Human Rights,* edited by Rachel Rosenbloom (1996).

✧ *Out of the Blue: Russia's Hidden Gay Literature,* edited by Kevin Moss (1997).

Russo, Vito

(1946–1991)

U.S. film critic, writer, activist. Russo grew up in East Harlem and New Jersey. He began to explore the Greenwich Village and FIRE ISLAND gay scenes while working his way through college and became a vocal and extremely visible member of GAY ACTIVISTS ALLIANCE (GAA) in the early 1970s. Besides writing for GAA, he emceed GAA and related events.

After presenting all-night FILM festivals at the GAA Firehouse in 1971, Russo put together a collection of film clips illustrating movie stereotypes of gay men and lesbians. Audience response at showings around the country inspired six years of research and writing, resulting in the publication by Harper and Row (after 22 publishing houses had

Vito Russo was a well-known activist as well as a movie expert.

turned it down) of *The Celluloid Closet: Homosexuality in the Movies* (1981; revised edition, 1987). Although others, including Parker Tyler, had written important books about gay and lesbian themes in cinema, *The Celluloid Closet* was the first comprehensive popular history of HOLLYWOOD's screen treatment of gay and lesbian characters. It had enormous influence on a generation of critics as well as readers.

Throughout the 1970s and 1980s, Russo wrote articles and conducted interviews for a wide range of publications, reporting on and advocating the emergence of a distinctive gay and lesbian film movement. He also appeared in a number of television and film documentaries, including the 1989 film about THE NAMES PROJECT, *Common Threads: Stories from the Quilt;* its directors, Robert Epstein and Jeffrey Friedman, went on to make a film adaptation of *The Celluloid Closet* (1995).

Rustin, Bayard

(1910–1987)

U.S. civil rights activist, writer. Born in West Chester, Pennsylvania, into a family of nine children, Rustin was raised by his grandparents and his mother, Florence. His grandmother, who was a QUAKER and active in the National Association for the Advancement of Colored People, was an early influence in fostering his dedication to achieving social justice. When the Depression interrupted his college education, Rustin went to New York in 1931 and supported himself by singing in integrated cafés. Meeting Communists who supported racial equality, Rustin joined the Party and helped organize the Young Communist League from 1936 to 1941, but he left when Party officials forbade him to advocate integration in his speeches.

In 1941, Rustin redirected his energies into antiwar activities and the nascent civil rights movement. He organized the New York branch of the Congress of Racial Equality and helped organize a March on Washington movement sponsored by the labor leader A. Philip Randolph. During WORLD WAR II, he was imprisoned for two years as a conscientious objector. In 1947, he spent almost a month on a chain gang in North Carolina as punishment for helping organize the first freedom ride in protest of segregation on buses.

Bayard Rustin (left) with James Baldwin, early 1960s.

As director of Randolph's Committee Against Discrimination in the Armed Forces, he was instrumental in obtaining the 1948 presidential order forbidding racial discrimination in the MILITARY. After being recommended by LILLIAN SMITH, Rustin served from 1955 as Martin Luther King Jr.'s chief political advisor, strategist, and speechwriter, helping King organize all his major civil rights actions, most notably the watershed 1963 March on Washington, where King delivered the "I have a dream" speech.

Through much of his career, Rustin's private life was an issue of contention for other civil rights leaders, including Adam Clayton Powell Jr. and Roy Wilkins, as well as for his political opponents. Earlier Rustin had been arrested on same-sex "morals charges," including a 1953 conviction in Pasadena, California, obtained through police entrapment, which resulted in a 60-day jail sentence. In 1963, shortly before the March on Washington, conservative Strom Thurmond of South Carolina took the floor of the Senate and accused him of being a Communist, a "draft dodger," and a homosexual. Despite widespread news coverage of the speech—and pressure from other civil rights activists to fire Rustin—Randolph and King stayed firm in their support of Rustin.

As director of the A. Philip Randolph Institute from 1964, Rustin was an early advocate of what came to be called "rainbow" politics, a strategic linking of the aims of the GAY AND LESBIAN RIGHTS MOVEMENT with the struggle for racial and economic justice.

Walter Naegle was his companion, colleague, and adopted son in the last years of his life.

✧ Bayard Rustin, *Down the Line* (1971).

✧ Bayard Rustin, *Strategies for Freedom* (1976).

✧ Jervis Anderson, *Bayard Rustin: The Troubles I've Seen* (1997).

S

Sackville-West, Vita
(Victoria Mary Sackville-West; 1892–1962), and
Nicolson, Sir Harold
(1886–1968)

English writers. Both from privileged upper-class backgrounds, Nicolson and Sackville-West met in 1910, married three years later, and had two sons. A career diplomat, Nicolson was one of the authors of the Balfour Declaration (1917) and a representative at the Paris Peace Conference (1919–1920). He retired from government service in 1929 for careers in journalism, broadcasting, and, perhaps most famously, gardening.

Years before they met, Sackville-West and Nicolson recognized that they were primarily attracted to their own respective sexes. Sackville-West once wrote Nicolson that she did not "mind whom you sleep with, as long as I may keep your heart." Unlike Nicolson, however, Sackville-West did not consummate a same-sex relationship until 1918, when she reencountered Violet Keppel, a childhood friend and fellow writer. Their affair continued after Keppel's marriage to Denys Trefusis in 1919 and reached a dramatic climax when the two women "eloped" together in 1920, Sackville-West CROSS-DRESSING as a man she called Julian. Their husbands chartered an airplane and pursued them to France. Sackville-West later wrote a heterosexualized account of the affair in her novel *Challenge* (1924), using the name Julian for the "male" lover. An uncamouflaged version, recorded in a journal, was published by her son Nigel in 1973 as part of his *Portrait of a Marriage,* which also served as the basis for a four-part British TELEVISION production, in 1990.

Sackville-West met VIRGINIA WOOLF in 1922 and the two women formed a close friendship that was at times romantic and probably sexual. Sackville-West's novel *Seducers in Ecuador* (1924) was written for Woolf. Woolf drew inspiration for the title character of her novel *Orlando* (1928) from Sackville-West. Eileen Atkins's play, *Vita and Virginia* (1994), based on the two women's letters, dramatized their 18-year relationship.

Sackville-West had several other long-term relationships with other women. Nicolson, more promiscuous but less amative, has been distinguished by gay biographers for having found his sexual partners among other upper-class men, unlike most aristocrats of his time.

Both were in their lifetimes popular authors of fiction and nonfiction, publishing more than 200 books between them. The secret of their marital success, they told an English radio audience in their program, "Marriage" (1929), was "common values effortlessly accommodating."

✧ Nigel Nicolson, *Portrait of a Marriage* (1973).

✧ Victoria Glendinning, *Vita: The Life of V. Sackville-West* (1983).

✧ *The Black Women's Health Book,* edited by Evelyn C. White (1994).

Sadomasochism, see S/M.

SAGE, see AGING.

Safe(r) Sex

Erotic practices that decrease one's chances of becoming infected with sexually transmitted diseases (STDs), especially HIV (see AIDS). Safe(r) sex covers dozens of sexual practices that vary widely in the degree of risk posed, from completely infection-proof activities like phone sex to possibly risky ones such as anal intercourse with a condom. Since HIV has been found in blood, semen, and vaginal fluid, most safe(r) sex guidelines are formulated to lessen the likelihood of transmitting these fluids from one person to another. Other STDs, such as hepatitis B, herpes, or gonorrhea, can be transmitted in other ways, so they entail a different set of preventative practices.

The word "safer" (rather than "safe") is often used to describe these sexual practices because, as "sexperts" point out, no activity—or inactivity—is entirely devoid of risk: total abstinence from sex may result in health-threatening levels of anxiety for some people. Safe(r) sex is in effect a form of risk management, a highly individual weighing of choices that ideally yields a balance between reasonable caution and sexual satisfaction. For this reason, experts warn that decisions are best made in a state of sobriety. Common sense as well as a multitude of studies suggest that people often take sexual risks under the influence of drugs or alcohol that they regret later.

➤ Also see SEX.

✧ Dr. Charles Silverstein and Felice Picano, *The New Joy of Gay Sex* (1992).

✧ Wendy Caster, *The Lesbian Sex Book* (1993).

Saint, Assotto

(Yves François Lubin; 1957–1994)

Haitian-born U.S. writer, performer, activist. A New York City resident from 1970, he performed with the Martha Graham Dance Company before leaving to found the Metamorphosis Theatre and Xotika, an art-rock dance band, with his lover, composer Jaan Urban (Holmgren). He achieved national prominence in the early 1980s writing and performing in his award-winning multimedia theatrical piece *Risin' to the Love We Need.* Like his later theatrical works, *New Love Song* (1988) and *Nuclear Lovers* (1990), it combined flamboyant drag, incantatory verse, provocative rear projections, and MUSIC composed by Urban to conjure a vision of black gayness powerful enough to overcome the forces arrayed against it.

Saint was also a critically acclaimed and much anthologized poet. His works included *Wishing for Wings* (1995) and *Stations* (1989), a long poem about an interracial relationship. Along with Joseph Beam and ESSEX HEMPHILL, he was a leader in the black gay male poetic renaissance that began with Beam's breakthrough anthology, *In the Life* (1986), and gained momentum with the founding of the Other Countries collective, of which Saint was a charter member. After serving as poetry editor for the group's landmark *Other Countries: Black Gay Voices* (1988), he founded Galiens Press and published two other major anthologies, *The Road Before Us: 100 Gay Black Poets* (1991) and *Here to Dare: 10 Black Gay Poets* (1992). He won the 1990 James Baldwin Award from the Black Gay and Lesbian Leadership Forum and a 1990 fellowship in poetry from the New York Foundation for the Arts.

From left: Essex Hemphill, Craig G. Harris, Assotto Saint, late 1980s.

Saint fought AIDS through his creative work and theatrical street actions, which sometimes resulted in arrest. He was one of five AIDS activists featured in MARLON RIGGS's FILM *No Regrets* (*Non, Je Ne Regrette Rien*) (1993). Black, gay, and HIV-positive, he described himself in his poem "Triple Trouble" as "a black queen / dancing with shadows at high noon / triple trouble that's brutal / chasing America's evil spirits away." He hoped to be remembered as a "fierce black diva."

Same-Sex Unions

Also called "same-sex covenants," weddinglike ceremonies for two women or two men, usually solemnized by a religious rite. JOHN BOSWELL gave the term currency in 1994 with the publication of his *Same-Sex Unions in Premodern Europe.* The book discussed more than 60 different 8th- to 16th-century documents detailing Roman Catholic and Orthodox liturgies for uniting a same-sex couple in "brotherhood" (or, less commonly, "sisterhood"). Although critics agreed that much of the language and many of the aspects of the ceremonies were virtually identical to heterosexual weddings, many insisted that the unions were either of a strictly spiritual nature or were more like a modern "blood brotherhood" than a "gay MARRIAGE." Boswell argued that the unions were often both romantic and sexual and that this was precisely why they were repressed by the Church in the Middle Ages in the West and somewhat later in the East (although the French essayist Montaigne reported hearing about one "some years before" during a stay in Rome in 1578).

The METROPOLITAN COMMUNITY CHURCH began offering lesbian and gay couples same-sex covenant ceremonies shortly after its founding on **October 6, 1968**. QUAKERS, the UNITARIAN UNIVERSALIST ASSOCIATION, and the UNITED CHURCH OF CHRIST are among the handful of mainstream Christian denominations that sanction same-sex unions today. They have also been endorsed by the U.S. Soka Gakkai organization of BUDDHISM and the Reconstructionist Jewish Rabbinical Asso-

ciation, and celebrated at some temples affiliated with Reform JUDAISM and in some dioceses of the EPISCOPAL CHURCH.

Also see ORTHODOX EASTERN CHURCHES; ROMAN CATHOLIC CHURCH.

Samoa, see PACIFIC ISLANDS.

Sapphire

(Ramona Lofton; 1950–)

U.S. writer, performer, and educator. Born the second of four children, near Monterey, California, to MILITARY parents, both veterans of segregated service units in World War II, Sapphire grew up on army bases until her parents' separation when she was 13. After leaving high school at 16, she spent several years on the streets of Los Angeles and read the work of writers from the black power movement. After a pre-med beginning at San Francisco City College, she ran out of funds, dropped out, found the hippie subculture, became "Sapphire," and discovered dancing and the performing arts. She began writing and moved to New York City to study modern DANCE at City College, graduating in 1983. She began focusing on her writing in 1990 and began graduate study soon after, while teaching reading to children in Harlem and the Bronx.

Sapphire's work initially appeared in lesbian journals and collections, including the landmark *Azalea: A Magazine by and for Third World Lesbians* (she later joined their collective) in 1977. The same year, she began Naps, a group that poet and lesbian activist Terri Jewell believed was the first black lesbian performing group in the country, with Aida Mansuer and Irare Sabasu. Sapphire self-published a volume of poems, *Meditations on the Rainbow* (1987), and after her fiction debuted in *Sinister Wisdom* magazine (1987), appeared in the first two volumes of the *Women on Women* lesbian fiction series, edited by Joan Nestle and Naomi Holoch (1991, 1993). The prose and poetry collection *American Dreams* followed in 1994.

Crediting authors Toni Morrison and Alice Walker with making her writing possible, Sapphire examines the issues of race and living as a black American. As an AFRICAN-AMERICAN lesbian feminist, her themes consider sexism and heterosexism, and as a survivor of incest and rape, she explores violence against women.

Sparing the reader little in language, detail, and the horrors of abused lives, she uses her powerful voice and painfully shaped characters to re-create their struggle from bleakness and pain to change, hope, and triumph.

Her first novel, *Push* (1996), tells the story of a teenage girl, Precious, a survivor of incest and other brutalities, and so impressed its mainstream publisher that it became part of a lucrative two-book contract. She didn't write it to pay the rent, she commented, but "to feel this girl's voice. As an artist you have the responsibility."

✧ Terri Jewell, "Sapphire," in *Contemporary Lesbian Writers of the United States,* edited by Denise Knight and Sandra Pollack (1993).

✧ Dinitia Smith, "For the Child Who Rolls with the Punches," *The New York Times* (July 2, 1996).

Sappho

(c.620–c.560 B.C.)

Greek poet. Little is known about the most famous lyrical poet of ancient times, except that she was born on the Aegean isle of Lesbos during a time of civil strife. Later biographers have suggested eight different names for her father, who is not mentioned in her surviving poems, but it is believed that her family was probably aristocratic, that she was exiled for some years to Sicily over a political dispute, and that she returned to Lesbos, where she distinguished herself as a poet and the head of a *thiasos,* a kind of school in which girls studied music, dance, and other arts. She referred to herself as *geraitera,* "somewhat old," in one of her poems, so she probably lived at least into middle age. Although she is known to have written eight volumes of odes, elegies, and hymns, and one volume of epithalamiums (marriage invocations), only one complete ode, four stanzas of a second ode, and some two hundred fragments, including some that are only single words, have been preserved. Most of the fragments come from texts of grammarians quoting her work as examples of Aeolic (a dialect of ancient Greek) usage. Almost all of her surviving verse is love poetry addressed to women.

Like most Greek women of her era, she was probably married off by her family at a young age, but "Kerkylos of Andros," the name of the man reported to be her husband in biographies written hundreds of years after her death, is almost certainly an ancient joke: it translates as "Penis [from the land] of Man."

Generations believed the myth that Sappho jumped off a cliff out of despair over a failed love affair with a ferry boatman.

Like the historian Herodotus—who frequently protests, "I've heard but I don't believe," and then proceeds to relay an unlikely piece of information—Greek and Roman writers seem to have been incapable of passing up a good story. As a result, biographical sketches of Sappho grew over the ages to include dozens of new and imaginative details. Ovid, for example, writing about five centuries after Sappho, claimed that she had thrown herself off a cliff as an old woman in frustration over her unrequited love for a boatman called Phaon.

Despite these heterosexual accretions, ancient writers, who had the advantage over modern critics of knowing her entire opus, seem to be in agreement that her most famous poems were love poems addressed to women and that she felt (and most likely acted upon) a physical attraction for them: if it were a "platonic" love she felt, they would not—as they sometimes did—have criticized it or described it as shameful. The commentaries of these writers are rare sources of information on Greek and Roman attitudes toward women who loved other women—and proof that writers for at least ten centuries recognized Sappho's homoeroticism yet were not too shocked to enjoy the poetry it inspired.

From ancient times, when Plato called her "the Tenth Muse," to today, when with Homer she remains the only Greek poet who is still widely read, almost no one has denied her genius, even if many have tried to gloss over her homoeroticism. Through the centuries, many translators even substituted male pronouns for female in renditions of her work. As late as 1960, an Italian movie called *Saffo—Venere di Lesbo* ("Sappho—Venus of Lesbos") starred Tina Louise as the poet, who, in the movie version, abandons the worship of Aphrodite for a man. The battle to reclaim her as a "LESBIAN" (in the modern sense of the word) has been continually refought by women ranging from NATALIE BARNEY and AMY LOWELL to JUDY GRAHN.

✧ Judy Grahn, *The Highest Apple: Sappho and the Lesbian Poetic Tradition* (1985).

✧ Eve Cantarella, *Pandora's Daughters: The Role and Status of Women in Greek and Roman Antiquity* (1987).

Sarton, [Eleanor] May
(1912–1995)

U.S. writer of more than 40 books (poetry, novels, nonfiction, and children's LITERATURE). Born in Belgium, she moved with her family to the U.S. in 1916. Immediately after high school, she joined a THEATER troupe directed by EVA LE GALLIENNE, who became her lifelong friend. She turned to writing after her own theater company foundered in 1937.

Sarton's poetry and novels attracted a growing and devoted readership, but critical acclaim was slow to follow. Some critics now attribute this to her being a woman and a lesbian. Others point to the difficulty of classifying her within a wider political or literary movement. She wrote to "find out what I'm really feeling," probing relationships between women and, with ever increasing openness, her lesbianism. Her engagingly direct journals, where she "makes myths" of her life, are her most popular works.

Sarton's landmark *Mrs. Stevens Hears the Mermaids Singing* (1965) was one of the first mainstream novels to present a "woman homosexual" character (closely modeled on Sarton herself) positively and nonproblematically. She cites it as her favorite work ("of course that was when I came out"), although its publication led to her losing her teaching job.

Throughout her work, Sarton commands a strong sense of place, illuminating houses, gardens, and seasons through what she calls "the sanctification of the ordinary." With distinctively unsentimental intelligence, she also explores the interiors of emotional and physical life: love ("it opens the door to everything"), solitude ("my last great love"), illness, loss, aging, and death. She hoped to be remembered for "being fully human—if I am."

Sarton shared her life with Judith Matlock for 15 years, until Matlock's death in 1982. She was always a dedicated correspondent, answering massive amounts of mail personally while celebrating the "small shots of courage" the letters delivered.

- ✧ *Conversations with May Sarton,* edited by Peggy Whitman Prenshaw (1991).
- ✧ Sherman, Susan, *Among the Usual Days: Portrait of Sarton* (1994).

Scandinavia

No laws against consensual same-sex relations for persons over 14 in Iceland, 15 in Denmark and Sweden, and 16 in Norway. Broad legal protection against discrimination based on sexual orientation in all countries except Iceland. Well-developed social and cultural scene in large cities. National and local political organizations throughout the region.

As the countries that have come closest to extending legal recognition to gay and lesbian MARRIAGE, Denmark, Norway, and Sweden are, after the NETHERLANDS, commonly considered the most queer-friendly nations in the world. Iceland, a more conservative country, has lagged behind the rest of Scandinavia, but Icelandic lesbians and gay men have also made significant gains in achieving legal and social recognition in recent years. All the Scandinavian countries have active political and social organizations and a well-established gay and lesbian press. Research into popular attitudes has also found Danes, Norwegians, and Swedes to be among the most accepting of homosexuality of all Europeans: for example, a survey conducted in the early 1990s found that only 12 percent of Danes objected to having lesbians or gay men as neighbors, compared with 20 percent in Iceland—but 34 percent in GERMANY.

History

Little evidence remains of same-sex eroticism in pre-Christian Scandinavia except denunciations, in both sagas and the traditional legal system, of free men who allowed themselves to be penetrated in anal intercourse. Like the ancient Greeks and Romans, pre-Christian Scandinavians viewed these men as "soft" and unmanly. With the coming of CHRISTIANITY around the

Sweden's Queen Christina was rumored to be a "tribade."

year 1000, Scandinavians gradually accepted the increasingly common Christian view of all same-sex eroticism as "against nature" and hence sinful. SODOMY, however, was not made a civil crime until 1608 in Sweden and 1683 in Denmark, and almost no records of convictions survive from the era. Scandinavians, moreover, were among the first to end capital punishment (in the second half of the 18th century) for all crimes, including sodomy.

Although a few famous Scandinavians, such as Queen Christina of Sweden (1626–1689), were commonly believed to engage in same-sex eroticism, a distinctive Scandinavian gay and lesbian SUBCULTURE evolved only toward the end of the 19th century, and then only in large cities like Copenhagen and Stockholm. During that period, arrests of men engaging in same-sex relations also increased dramatically. One of the few instances of legal prosecution of lesbians occurred in Sweden in 1943, when several women were arrested and sentenced to up to two years' hard labor in prison.

Despite sporadic oppression, including government harassment reminiscent of the MCCARTHY ERA in the U.S. in the 1950s, Scandinavian countries, especially Denmark, early on acquired a worldwide reputation as being more tolerant of homosexuality than other parts of the world. Same-sex relations were decriminalized in Denmark and Iceland in 1930, Sweden in 1944, and Norway in 1972. National HOMOPHILE groups were founded in Denmark and Norway in 1948, and in Sweden in 1950.

Denmark and, subsequently, Sweden were considered leaders in the so-called sex revolution of the 1960s. Denmark was the first country in the world to liberalize laws restricting PORNOGRAPHY, and became one of the most famous venues for sex-change operations. Gay and lesbian life, however, remained largely invisible until the 1970s and the advent of a GAY LIBERATION movement.

In 1981, Norway became the first country in the world to ban discrimination based on sexual orientation. In the years since, Denmark and Sweden have also instituted wide-ranging rights protections for lesbians and gay men, and all three countries have ended discrimination in the MILITARY. In addition, the Scandinavian countries have led the rest of the world in extending legal recognition to DOMESTIC PARTNERSHIPS. Denmark (**10/1/1989**), Norway (1993), Sweden (1995), and Iceland (1996) have all approved same-sex "registered partnerships," which allow most of the benefits of heterosexual marriage, with the exception of the rights to adoption, artificial insemination, and religious wedding ceremonies in state Lutheran churches. In May 1997, Denmark's bishops voted to allow blessings of partnerships.

➤ Also see FINLAND.

Schulman, Sarah

(1958–)

U.S. writer, activist. As is suggested by much of her fiction, Schulman grew up in New York City, the child of a social worker and a psychiatrist. She became an active lesbian feminist in the 1980s, participated in ACT UP, and co-founded the New York Lesbian and Gay Experimental Film Festival in 1987 and the LESBIAN AVENGERS in 1992. In addition to publishing an enormous number of articles in the mainstream and lesbian/gay press, she has traveled widely and emerged as a leading critic of the tendency of mainstream publishing to reject or marginalize the work of lesbian writers.

Schulman published her first novel, *The Sophie Horowitz Story,* in 1982. Like her subsequent five novels, it combines pathos with offbeat comic relief, and, as critic Sally R. Munt notes, "narrative experimentation with political critique." Schulman's AWARD-winning

Sarah Schulman (standing, center) under arrest at a demonstration in 1995.

After Delores (1988) is a murder mystery—and a provocatively sexual first-person account of a woman's foundering struggle to survive her lover's abrupt and brutal departure. *People in Trouble* (1990) looks at AIDS activism, HOMOPHOBIA, and societal neglect through the experiences of an artist, her husband, and her female lover. Her critically acclaimed *Empathy* (1992) takes on Freudianism and GENDER ambiguity. *Rat Bohemia* (1995), like her other fictional works, explores life on New York's Lower East Side, where Schulman makes her home.

✧ Sally R. Munt, "What Does It Mean to Sing 'Somewhere over the Rainbow . . .' and Release Balloons?: Postmodernism and the Fiction of Sarah Schulman," in her *New Lesbian Criticism: Literary and Cultural Readings* (1992).

✧ Sarah Schulman, *My American History: Lesbian and Gay Life During the Reagan/Bush Years* (1994).

Science Fiction

Rooted in folklore, "tall tales," and age-old mythology, science fiction emerged as a distinct genre of fiction in the 1920s. As "fiction" that by definition was supposed to escape the confines and conventions of everyday life, science fiction would seem an ideal genre for exploring new concepts of GENDER identity and sexual politics, yet most early science fiction writers held fast to negative stereotypes of gay men and lesbians.

The genre began to change with the publication of Theodore Sturgeon's "The World Well Lost" (1953), which featured an androgynous same-gender couple who escape to Earth from a planet daringly suggestive of the repressions of the MCCARTHY ERA. Sturgeon, who continued to explore unconventional gender and sexual models in works such as *Venus Plus X* (1960), opened the way for other writers—including MARION ZIMMER BRADLEY, SAMUEL R. DELANY, Thomas Disch, SALLY GEARHART, Ursula Le Guin, George Nader, Marge Piercy, and JOANNA RUSS—to begin to make even more innovative use of the genre to present provocative concepts of gender, gender relations, and sexuality. At the same time, negative depictions of lesbians and gay men also began to become less common, especially after the 1970s.

Although some science fiction novels continue to feature what critics call "future insulation"—the effect of distancing readers from characters and situations they would find disturbing if depicted as part of contemporary terrestrial life—others have narrowed the gap between science fiction and reality, as in Michael Bishop's *Unicorn Mountain* (1988), which includes a gay man suffering from AIDS. In addition, distinct genres of explicitly gay and lesbian erotic and romantic science fiction have evolved.

Science fiction and fantasy have also had a major impact on many gay and lesbian writers not generally associated with the genre, including WILLIAM BURROUGHS and JEWELLE GOMEZ.

- *Worlds Apart,* edited by Camilla Decarnin, Eric Garber, and Lyn Paleo (1986).
- *Uranian Worlds: A Guide to Alternative Sexuality in Science Fiction, Fantasy, and Horror,* edited by Eric Garber and Lyn Paleo (1990).

Scientology

Church founded in 1952 by L. Ron Hubbard (1911–1986) based on the principles set forth in his *Dianetics: The Modern Science of Mental Health* (1950). In *Dianetics,* Hubbard asserted that "the sexual pervert," defined as including persons prone to "homosexuality, lesbianism, sexual sadism, etc.," is "actually quite physically ill." Although not "culpable for his [*sic*] condition," the pervert is "so extremely dangerous to society that the tolerance of perversion is as thoroughly bad for society as punishment for it." In response, Hubbard developed ways to "handle the problem" that are available to "Operating Thetans" (members) who purchase the Church's courses. Among lesbians and gay men, the Church has become so identified with "curing" those who wish to remain in the CLOSET that Scientology membership, particularly on the part of HOLLYWOOD stars, is often taken almost as "proof" that a celebrity is queer.

Scotland, see UNITED KINGDOM.

Senior Action in a Gay Environment (SAGE), see AGING.

Separatism

Belief in the value of individuals joining together on the basis of a specific, shared identity while excluding persons who do not share that identity. Gay and lesbian separatism has taken an almost indefinably broad variety of forms since the STONEWALL Uprising, from temporary "safe spaces" for special-interest groups to ultraradical lesbian "nations" advocating the total eradication of the Y chromosome. Most commonly, however, lesbian and gay separatism has been a form of identity politics.

JUDY GRAHN, among others, believes that lesbian separatism (a major feature of lesbian and gay life all over the world in the 1970s) was a success, building a power base for women from which they could emerge in the 1980s to lend their strength to the fight against

AIDS, equal rights in the MILITARY, and other causes. She also points out that traditional societies have been overwhelmingly segregated by GENDER. Through history, a large majority of human beings have been socialized in a one-gender environment.

Grahn says elsewhere that the gay movement of the 1970s, with "GAY" taken to mean "gay men" (just as the word "mankind" more often than not means "men"), was in fact a male separatist movement.

Kim Barget, one of the organizers of a separate march for lesbians the week of New York City's PRIDE CELEBRATION in June 1995, described the event to *The New York Times* as "a solidarity march, because lesbians are mostly overlooked in a gay event." Men were welcome to stand and watch on the sidelines.

Lesbian Separatism

Lesbian separatism is a major element of international radical feminist and lesbian theory and politics. It advocates physical, social, emotional, political, economic, and psychological separation from men and institutions operating for the perpetuation of male privilege.

Echoing some sentiments of AFRICAN-AMERICAN, Jewish, and NATIVE AMERICAN nationalists, separatism as an act of resistance and affirmation places women by their choice out of male-dominated culture and society in a struggle against the interrelated oppressions of race, gender, and class. Many separatists emphasize that separatism isn't "no-saying" to men, as much as "yes-saying" to women—in other words, it's less a separation than a connection.

Separatists seek a strong women-centered community to realign power and create a new world and way of living for women. They do not agree on the necessity of a lesbian erotic connection but would likely agree on a woman's fundamental self-determination in various forms. Proponents argue that separatism is a positive goal necessary to examine the nature of oppression apart from the oppressor, foster self-esteem and understanding, build political ideology and pride, and create a strength, unity, and strategy for survival. Others who see separatism as a strategy rather than a goal believe that if alliances with men are to be made, the political force of separatism and its changes must first be realized.

Some would mark the beginnings of organized separatism as the LAVENDER MENACE action in 1970, while others consider that separatism was always implicit in lesbian life. Viewing the relations between men and women as "class warfare," separatists advocate that women create autonomous bases of female social life in the face of, as CHARLOTTE BUNCH has argued, heterosexuality as a political institution in a male-supremacist society.

While meanings of separatism vary widely within the lesbian community, some criticize it for being antisex and elitist, identifying man-hating with political advantage, evading the issues of male supremacy, race, women's privilege, and class, and losing sight of the broader goal of defeating sexism. Others would contend that lesbians by definition are separatists for their lack of dependence upon men; more boldly, as Julia Penelope has argued, separatism is inevitable since even self-realization and political alliances between lesbians and gay men are impossible because of socially polarizing sex-roles and their resultant psychological differences.

Some African-American lesbian writers (including AUDRE LORDE, BARBARA SMITH, and others from the COMBAHEE RIVER COLLECTIVE) distanced themselves in the early 1970s from what they described as the fractionalization, biological determinism, and the race and class privilege of separatism, either as a strategy or as a political analysis. They also questioned separatism's ability to effect real political change. Although they did not speak for all black lesbians (other black lesbians defined themselves as separatists), they did underscore the regularity with which African-American and other women of color were neglected in cultural/political discussions, as if racism and other oppressions would end with the exclusion of men.

Theorist and philosopher Marilyn Fry describes separatist lives as an alternative to assimilation, created by "erotic bonds, economic cooperation, friendship, self-made kin relations, and lesbian/gynocentric cultural production." Further, she describes those lives as creating "webs of female sociality within which women thrive and create themselves far more autonomously than is the norm within patriarchal institutions, and are dramatically less vulnerable to male violence, exploitation, and intellectual/emotional colonization." She emphasizes the need for women to control all access to themselves to realign the power structure between men and women.

Julia Penelope and Sarah Lucia-Hoagland have written extensively about the virtues of separatism as a movement, its ability to create alternative communities, and its place in a lesbian ethics. Their landmark anthology of 87 separatist writings, most written between 1970 and 1984, profiled the complexity of the issue.

Philosopher Claudia Card offers a perspective on the separatist's relationship to the "world." In viewing the presumed "worldless" status of separatist communities, Card considers them rather as another world far better than a life in the CLOSET. Thus, the separatist restructures the lesbian's outlaw status into one that honors and supports a lesbian community within the larger context of society.

In a helpful short history of modern separatism since 1970, Sidney Spinster locates its roots in the community consciousness-raising projects of women's centers, with their array of services from self-defense to rape crisis counseling or more radical political activities. Lesbians typically learned of separatism in writings, in community gatherings, or in the MUSIC of ALIX DOBKIN, Linda Shear of Family of Women band, Sirani Avedis, Flying Lesbians, and others. Dobkin has also written of her understanding of lesbian separatism as "a consciousness, an analysis, and a commitment to the well-being and best interests of women in general and Lesbians in particular."

In her analysis of female friendship, philosopher Jan Raymond considers its personal and political power as "gyn/affection" and finds an advantage in separatism's ability to place women's "care for the world" into their own community, creating a world with roots. JILL JOHNSTON's "dyke separatism" articles were also influential as the genesis of "lesbian nation," a grassroots community of women. Johnston recognized that the meaning of lesbianism was changing from a private identity and behavior to a political identity with a revolutionary vision. As Margaret Sloan-Hunter said: "This is a revolution, not a public relations campaign."

Although many distinctions exist between French-speaking lesbian feminist analysis and American lesbian separatism, a related perspective on "revolutionized language" was popularized by MONIQUE WITTIG in the late 1960s. Its meaning, images, and myths were seen by Wittig as the controlling bastion of male dominance and gender that harbored the central social structures of sexism and HETEROSEXISM. Because of these factors, the language must be changed for self-realization.

In the search for a world other than patriarchy, theologian and philosophy professor MARY DALY in *Gyn/Ecology* also places separatism at a transcendent and inward level of "paring away the layers of false Selves from the Self."

Lesbian separatist utopias appear in the classic writings of Wittig (*Les Guérillères,* 1969), JOANNA RUSS (*The Female Man,* 1975), and SALLY GEARHART (*The Wanderground: Stories of the Hill Women,* 1978). Other writers, such as ELANA DYKEWOMON in *Riverfinger Women* (1974), build women's communities and courageously defiant identities that celebrate a strength and independence in isolation.

Out of the separatist vision came a cultural movement, with lesbian periodicals such as *Dykes and Gorgons* from the Gutter Dyke Collective; *Tribad: A Lesbian Separatist Newsjournal; Dyke* from Liza Cowan and Penny House; Susan Cavin's *Big Apple Dyke News; The Furies; Amazons d'Hier; Lesbiennes d'Aujourd'hui; Green Mountain Dyke News; The Lesbian Insider/Insighter/Inciter; Lunatic Fringe; The Udder Side; Women's Network; The Amazon Nation; The Killer Dyke; Womynlovers Separatists Newsletter;* and *Spectre,* from Ann Arbor, Michigan. Also published were an early handbook on separatism from Seattle, *The Amazon Analysis,* and *The C.L.I.T.* [Collective Lesbian International Terrorists] *Papers.*

Separate spaces such as LESBIAN LAND, storefronts, BOOKSTORES, and women's centers sprang up around the country. Some considered the fullest expression of separatism in the call for a lesbian land that incorporates a communal way of life and economic self-sufficiency, even though others questioned whether such a life could effect real social change.

Since 1976, the MICHIGAN WOMYN'S MUSIC FESTIVAL continues as one of the longest-lasting expressions of lesbian separatism—it now attracts more than 10,000 women a year to its weeklong activities. In some sense the impetus behind women-only events is based on the assumption that women—and lesbians in particular—can freely express themselves only outside the presence of men. In this and other venues, lesbian separatism remains a living force in the national and international lesbian community.

- Charlotte Bunch, "Perseverance Furthers: Separatism and Our Future," and Rita Mae Brown, "Women Who Love Men Hate Them: Male Supremacy Versus Sexism," both in *The Furies* (Fall 1972).
- Estelle Freedman, "Separatism as Strategy: Female Institution Building and American Feminism, 1870–1930," *Feminist Studies* (Fall 1979).
- *For Lesbians Only: A Separatist Anthology,* edited by Sarah Lucia-Hoagland and Julia Penelope (1988).
- Dana R. Shugar, *Separatism and Women's Community* (1995).

Seventh-Day Adventists

Evangelical Christian denomination organized in 1863 with about 750,000 members worldwide. Advocating unusually fundamentalist interpretations of the BIBLE, Adventism considers gay and lesbian sexual practices "obvious perversions of God's original plan." Kinship International works to provide "intellectual, spiritual, and social fellowship" for lesbian and gay Adventists.

Sex

The relationship of sex and sexual attraction to a gay or lesbian identity is not as straightforward as it might seem. One of the reasons that gay and lesbian activists in the 1950s preferred to describe their groups as "HOMOPHILE" was that the word in effect took the "sex" out of "HOMOSEXUAL"; they felt this suggested that gay and lesbian relationships could be based at least as much on the need for affection and companionship as on the desire for sex. Similarly, many advocates of LESBIAN FEMINISM have disputed the definition of "LESBIAN" as a woman who feels sexual desire for other women, extending the meaning of "lesbian" to cover women who make another woman (or other women) the most important person(s) in their lives, whether or not they experience a specifically sexual attraction to other women.

Most self-identified "gay" men and "lesbians" nonetheless experience sexual desire for at least some other members of their biological sex. So important is sex to the identities of some lesbians and gay men that they would assert that feeling sexually attracted predominantly or exclusively to members of their sex is the *only* characteristic that distinguishes them from "heterosexuals."

Porn star Jack Lofton.

However "GAY" or "lesbian" is defined, there are varying levels of comfort among lesbians and gay men when it comes to overt and public sexual displays. Writer and critic Bruce Bawer, among others, has denounced sexual exhibitionism in PRIDE CELEBRATIONS and on the streets of gay/lesbian GHETTOS in the belief that "it is precisely because anti-gay prejudice does exist that some gays, in the interest of self-protection, cling to their sexual identity, and (in some cases) accordingly become preoccupied with sex." If there were no prejudice, Bawer believes, "much of what we think of as the 'gay subculture' would disappear," and gay and lesbian "courtship rituals" would be "comparable" to those of heterosexuals. Among the spokespersons for the opposing point of view is PAT CALIFIA, who advocates open, even public "radical sex," which "means being aware that there is something unsatisfying and dishonest about the way sex is talked about (or hidden) in daily life."

Roles and Role Playing

"Which one's the man?" is a question both lesbian and gay couples have often been asked. Many people who have never experienced same-sex eroticism believe that it must mirror traditional patterns of male-female relations, with one person acting out a dominant "male" role and the other playing the part of a submissive "female." Perhaps as a result of this expectation, some cultures have evolved forms of same-sex eroticism that do in fact cast one participant as the "man" and the other as the "woman." An example of this common in many cultures throughout history is the "active/passive split": the idea, among men at any rate, that the person who does the inserting is more "manly" than the insertee. In ARAB WORLD and so-called Mediterranean traditions, this idea is so powerful that only the insertee role is stigmatized; insertive male-male sex is

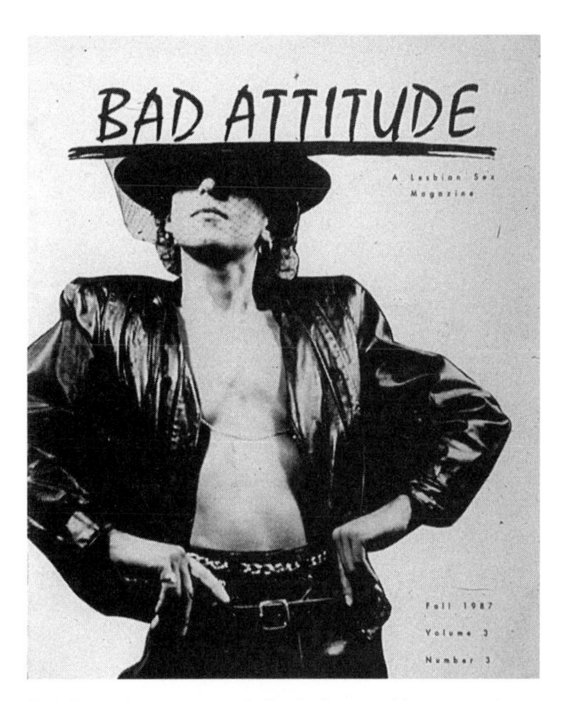

Bad Attitude was one of the lesbian publications that sought to heat up lesbian sex in the 1980s.

sometimes even considered more macho than male-female sex. These cultures also equate the "masculine" role with male status, relegating the "female" role to younger men, slaves, or other social inferiors.

Through the 20th century, new sexual politics evolved among the people who came to be considered "gay" and "lesbian" in North America and Western Europe. Lesbians created BUTCH-FEM(ME) sexual SUBCULTURES that in many ways transgressed "male-female" role playing. Gay men rejected "top" (insertive) and "bottom" (receptive) roles as signifiers of power; most surveys suggested that the majority in fact "swing both ways."

➤ Also see SAFE(R) SEX; PORNOGRAPHY; SEX WARS, LESBIAN

Sex Wars, Lesbian

Heated debates on sexual behaviors, BUTCH/FEMME relationships and role-playing, PORNOGRAPHY, and S/M that began in the late 1970s and raged throughout the lesbian SUBCULTURE in the early and mid-1980s. Complex and multifaceted, the Sex Wars were more than a struggle between "prosex" lesbians and "antipornography" feminists. Relevant to virtually every facet of lesbian life, the issues raised went to the very heart of what determines a lesbian identity.

Cultural historians describe the Sex Wars as a reaction to the highly politicized LESBIAN FEMINISM of the 1970s. As theorist and anthropologist Gayle Rubin has observed, by the late 1970s it had become difficult "to justify lesbianism on grounds other than feminism." In part reacting to psychological and medical distortions of lesbianism, many lesbian feminists embraced the idea that lesbianism was an enlightened political "choice" rather than a sexual "condition." Feminism came to define lesbianism as an act of self-love, a declaration of independence from the woman-oppressing institution of heterosexuality, and a refusal to comply with patriarchal social conditioning. An erotic dimension or actual sexual experience with other women was *not* a prerequisite: any woman could be a "political" lesbian. These positions, coupled with a condemnation of certain sexual practices—especially S/M and butch/femme role playing—as well as virtually all pornography (as by nature "male" and degrading to women), set the stage for the Sex Wars. Lesbian feminism fostered the growth of strong women's communities, but it also, increasingly, made large numbers of lesbians feel excluded. Women who identified as butch/femme or who were committed to exploring S/M, however consensual, became "outlaws," accused of internalizing and promoting misogynism. Some women's BOOKSTORES banned

What constitutes pornography was one of the thorny issues of the lesbian Sex Wars, as depicted here by Andrea Natalie.

"porn" by lesbians; butch/ femme women found themselves ostracized; and S/M activists were literally forbidden entrance to marches, MUSIC festivals, and other cultural events. Even some women's ARCHIVES excluded materials or images of these subcultures.

As the Sex Wars took shape, self-styled sex radicals accused the lesbian feminist community leadership of becoming the "sex police." In response, feminist theorists like Sheila Jeffreys, a founding member of London Women Against Violence, expressed fear and even "shock" at seeing "many lesbians determinedly abandon the egalitarian philosophy that is feminism."

Behind the polemics, Julia Penelope and other cultural historians believe that the sex radicals addressed a vital need for sexual information. While distancing herself from many of their positions, Penelope asserts, "The Lesbian sado-masochists did what no one else seemed willing to do: to take Lesbian sex seriously and to attempt to educate Lesbians about our anatomies, sex techniques, and the importance of talking about what we like and don't like sexually." As lesbians began to discuss sex more openly, new sex therapists emerged, along with self-help books and sexual workshops such as those pioneered by BETTY DODSON, SUSIE BRIGHT, and JoAnn Loulan.

The issues raised in AUDRE LORDE's influential essay "Uses of the Erotic" (1978) were further explored in the prosex writings of PAT CALIFIA, Amber Hollibaugh, CHERRÍE MORAGA, JOAN NESTLE, Esther Newton, Cindy Patton, and Sue O'Sullivan. The year 1984 marked the appearance of lesbian sex/erotica magazines like *On Our Backs,* called by the *Bay Area Reporter* "the single most important event of the decade for lesbians." LUST conferences were held.

One pivotal event was a conference, "The Scholar and the Feminist IX—Toward a Politics of Sexuality," held on April 24, 1982, at Barnard College in New York City. Seven months in preparation, the conference was coordinated by Carole S. Vance, who made it a forum for a wide range of discussions and debates. Cherríe Moraga, a participant, summarized the thrust of the conference with her written comment: "But what of passion? I hunger to ask women. . . ."

Gay men were most noticeable for their nonparticipation in the Sex Wars. One exception was writer and self-acclaimed "pornographer" JOHN PRESTON, who provoked controversy with a December 1981 *Christopher Street* article entitled "Goodbye, Sally Gearhart." In the article, Preston protested lesbian feminist attacks on gay male pornography, promiscuity, and S/M and speculated that "the *maleness* of gay men presents an image many feminists find repulsive."

Perhaps the only consensus among cultural

historians about the Sex Wars is how bitterly divisive they were and how irreconcilable the positions taken were. At the same time, most observers agree that their effect has been to add to the diversity of lesbian lives and lesbian attitudes toward sexuality.

➤ Also see DWORKIN, ANDREA; LESBIAN, POLITICAL; SEX.

✧ *Pleasure and Danger: Exploring Female Sexuality,* edited by Carole S. Vance (1984).

✧ Sheila Jeffreys, *The Sexuality Debates* (1987).

✧ Julia Penelope, *Call Me Lesbian: Lesbian Lives, Lesbian Theory* (1992).

✧ Sheila Jeffreys, *The Lesbian Heresy: A Feminist Perspective on the Lesbian Sexual Revolution* (1993).

✧ Lisa Duggan and Nan D. Hunter, *Sex Wars: Sexual Dissent and Political Culture* (1995).

Shakespeare, William

(1564–1616)

English playwright, poet. By common assent the greatest and one of the most influential writers in the English language, Shakespeare has been "accused" of harboring "unnatural" desires since at least the 18th century, and "claimed" as a gay man as early as the 1830s. Little is known about his private life, however, and no contemporary records remain to suggest he ever had an affair or sex with another man. Many scholars believe that his sonnets addressed to a boy (described by the anonymous author of *Don Leon*—see **8/1833—**as "sonnets to a stripling's praise") were literary exercises, reflecting his era's respect for Greek and Roman homoerotic poets. Others interpret the beginning of Sonnet 144 ("Two loves have I . . . The better angel is a man fair right. / The worser spirit a woman colored ill") as a confession of BISEXUALITY.

In Shakespeare's plays, apparent references to same-sex eroticism include "He's mad that trusts in the tameness of a wolf, a horse's health, a boy's love, or a whore's oath" (*King Lear,* III: 6); Rosalind's adoption of the name GANYMEDE when she disguises herself as a man in *As You Like It;* and the GENDER confusions of Orsino and Viola in *Twelfth Night.* Sonnets judged homoerotic are numbers 20, 29, 35, 36, 53, 55, 57, 60, 67, 87, 94, 104, 110, 116, and 144.

✧ Joseph Pequigney, *Such Is My Love: A Study of Shakespeare's Sonnets* (1985).

✧ Bruce R. Smith, *Homosexual Desire in Shakespeare's England: A Cultural Poetics* (1991).

Shilts, Randy [Martin]

(1951–1994)

U.S. journalist, author. Born in Davenport, Iowa, into a politically conservative Methodist family, Shilts and his three brothers grew up in a suburb of Chicago. He came OUT while attending the University of Oregon, headed the local Gay People's Alliance, and ran (unsuccessfully) for student body president with the slogan "Come Out for Shilts." Despite his high grades and awards, including a 1974 William Randolph Hearst Award for a story about the Empress Court, no publication would hire the openly gay journalist full-time until JOHN PRESTON took him on as a staff writer for THE ADVOCATE in May 1975. After three years at *The Advocate* and several years working in broadcast journalism, Shilts joined the *San Francisco Chronicle* in 1981, becoming, in his words, "the first openly gay news reporter at a mainstream newspaper anywhere in the country."

Before taking the *Chronicle* job, Shilts had finished writing the first of three of the most influential gay-related books of the 20th century: *The Mayor of Castro Street: The Life and Times of Harvey Milk* (1982), a political biography as well as a vivid account of San Francisco politics, gay and straight, and the aftermath of the 1978 assassination of HARVEY MILK.

Shilts was one of the first writers to recognize the seriousness of AIDS. Years of intensive research and reporting resulted in the best-selling *And the Band Played On: Politics, People, and the AIDS Epidemic* (1987), a National Book Award finalist. Before and after the book's publication, Shilts excoriated the Reagan and Bush administrations for inaction in the face of the epidemic and the American public for considering AIDS an irrelevant "gay issue." But he was also vociferous in his criticism of gay men who opposed the closing of BATHS. Although he later expressed disappointment that the book did not "recast the national debate on AIDS," it remains the most incisive account of the first years of the epidemic. Shilts learned that he was HIV-positive the day he turned in the manuscript.

His last book, *Conduct Unbecoming: Lesbians and Gays in the U.S. Military* (1993), chronicled discrimination against gay men and lesbians in the American MILITARY from the Revolutionary War through the 1990s. On a broader level, he conceived of it as his "definitive book on HOMOPHOBIA."

Each of Shilts's books is chronologically structured around vivid cameos of hundreds of individuals, testifying to his belief that "politics are irrelevant unless connected to people's real lives." He combined rigorous journalistic standards with the compelling narrative drive of a suspense novel, creating a Balzacian microcosm of contemporary gay and lesbian life that elucidated complex issues without oversimplifying them. A year before his death from AIDS-related complications, he told an interviewer: "I don't consider myself an activist or an advocacy journalist. I feel that prejudice in our society is born less out of malice than out of ignorance, and that if you just inform people . . . you can do more to erase prejudice than any other kind of action."

Shockley, Ann Allen

(1927–)

U.S. writer, editor, critic, librarian, and author of the first novel to feature an AFRICAN-AMERICAN lesbian as its major character. Born in Louisville, Kentucky, to parents who were social workers, Shockley graduated from Fisk University in 1948 and earned a master's in library science at Western Reserve (now Case Western Reserve University) in 1959. She is divorced from writer William Shockley, with whom she had two children, and teaches and works as an archivist and librarian at Fisk.

In the pioneering annotated bibliography *Black Lesbians* (1981), editor J. R. Roberts credits Shockley with two important breakthroughs: the first sympathetic black lesbian novel (*Loving Her,* 1974) and the first collection of lesbian short stories by a black writer (*The Black and White of It,* 1980). In addition to these literary landmarks, Shockley's articles have also been cited as among the first to raise the issues of African-American lesbian visibility and racism within the lesbian community. She has also addressed HOMOPHOBIA and colorism among African-Americans and, as a librarian, made major bibliographical contributions to both African-American and lesbian studies, including, with Sue P. Chandler, *Living Black American Authors.*

Although popular with readers, Shockley's work has been consistently controversial. *Loving Her* recounts an interracial, interclass love affair, expounding the main character's belief that "you can't confine love to color or object." Her second novel, *Say Jesus and Come to Me* (1982), unites women—black, white, lesbian, straight, Christian, and even sex workers—in a feminist campaign to clean up Nashville. On another front, her story "Family Reunion" contrasts racial integration with the "integration" of a BUTCH daughter into her family.

✧ Rita B. Dandridge, *Ann Allen Shockley: An Annotated Primary and Secondary Bibliography* (1987).

✧ S. Diane Bogus, "The 'Queen B' Figure in Black Literature," in *Lesbian Texts and Contexts: Radical Revisions,* edited by Karla Jay and Joanne Glasgow (1990).

Singapore, see SOUTHEAST ASIA.

SIR, see SOCIETY FOR INDIVIDUAL RIGHTS (SIR).

Slogans, see GAY AND LESBIAN RIGHTS MOVEMENT, U.S.

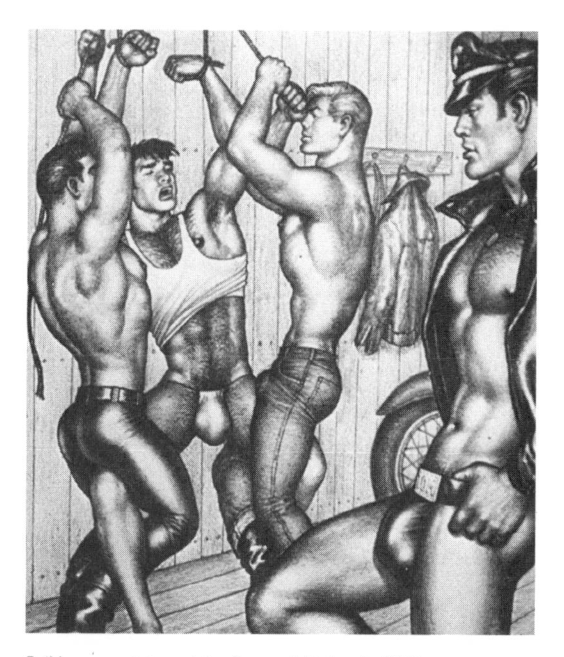

S/M as envisioned by Tom of Finland, 1963.

S/M

Abbreviation—which devotees prefer to the longer, clinical word—for "sadomasochism," perhaps coined by Alfred Kinsey (see KINSEY REPORTS). S/M combines "sadism," the sexual enjoyment of another's pain, humiliation, or powerlessness, and "masochism," the enjoyment of one's own pain, humiliation, or powerlessness. Although S/M is commonly associated with pain, S/M proponents emphasize that it is a form of power play, which demands a complex and emotionally satisfying bond of trust between the dominant "top" (S) and the submissive "bottom" (M). Gay and lesbian S/M activists also stress that serious physical injury is rarely a part of S/M. Participants usually agree upon a signal that the bottom can give to stop activities if things seem to be going beyond the bottom's capacity to enjoy them.

S/M is closely associated with leather, both as a costume and a fetish. Sometimes, however, "leather" is used as a euphemism for S/M, as in Brothers in Leather, an advocacy group for AFRICAN-AMERICAN men founded in New York in 1994. S/M participants also gather in "leather BARS."

JOHN PRESTON described the appeal of S/M as threefold: "intimacy . . . the power of this personal need for connection"; masculine "gender" performance (for women as well as men); and "bonding."

Activities associated with S/M include bondage, verbal abuse, and role playing, as well as piercing, spanking, whipping, asphyxiation, etc. Fans of S/M call non-S/M sex "vanilla."

S/M activists have at times been barred from participation in gay and lesbian public events.

✧ *Leather-folk: Radical Sex, People, Politics, and Practice,* edited by Mark Thompson (1991).

✧ John Preston, "What Happened? An S/M Pioneer Reflects on the Leather World Past and Present," *Out/Look* (Winter 1992).

Small Presses, see PUBLISHING.

Smith, Barbara

(1946–)

U.S. writer, educator, historian, activist, and editor. Smith's pioneering article "Toward a Black Feminist Criticism" (1977) pointed out the scarcity of openly lesbian writings by black women and the culturally coded lesbian relationships in classic black novels. She further confronted the fear held by many AFRICAN-AMERICANS toward black feminists, and especially lesbians.

With her twin sister, Beverly, Smith was raised by a working-class mother, grandmother, great aunts, and aunt in Cleveland. She attended Mount Holyoke College and earned an M.A. from the University of Pittsburgh in 1971. From her family, she learned about the value of education, black feminism, and the struggles that women of color experience. She went on to teach at many universities and hold several arts-in-residence appointments.

Smith sustains Kitchen Table: Women of Color Press, which she helped found with AUDRE LORDE, CHERRÍE MORAGA, Hattie Gosset, and Myrna Bain (among others) in 1981 in New York City. The press is for all women of color, of all nationalities, sexual orientations, classes, and places of origin. Smith believes they have had an impact: "I've seen real

Barbara Smith.

changes since I became a black feminist in 1973 as far as how ready and able people are to deal with these matters. Some of it has to do with the writing we have put out."

In addition to her fiction and many essays, she edited the groundbreaking *Home Girls* (1983), a major collection of writings by and about black feminists; *All the Women Are White, All the Blacks Are Men, but Some of Us Are Brave: Black Women's Studies* (1981); and the earlier celebrated *Conditions: Five, the Black Women's Issue* (1979). Her writings range in focus, including the intersecting oppressions of race, class, sex, and sexual identity; racism and anti-Semitism in the gay and lesbian community; stereotyping; HOMOPHOBIA in the African-American community; the shortage of positive educational material and curriculum presenting sexual identity, sexuality, and sexism; and the need to fight the lies of history that deny the existence and contributions of black lesbians and gays.

Smith has won many awards, including the Anderson Prize Foundation Stonewall Award (1994) and the third David R. Kessler Award (1994) from the Center for Lesbian and Gay Studies at the City University of New York.

Her forthcoming book is *African-American Lesbian and Gay History: An Exploration*. It will examine and reclaim history in the context of the sociological, economic, emotional, and cultural experiences of the black lesbian and gay male heritage.

✧ Terri L. Jewell, "Barbara Smith and Kitchen Table: Women of Color Press," *Hot Wire* (May 1990).

✧ Jewelle Gomez and Barbara Smith, "Talking About It: Homophobia in the Black Community," *Feminist Review* (no. 34, Spring 1990).

Smith, Bessie

(1894–1937)

U.S. singer. A Chattanooga, Tennessee, native, Smith began touring in 1912 with MA RAINEY, who is credited both with mentoring Smith's blues style and introducing her to the joys of sex between women. She signed with Columbia Records in 1923 and promptly scored a major hit with "Down Hearted Blues": it sold almost 800,000 copies in its first six months of release. By the time she debuted Columbia's "race" catalog in 1924, her irrefutable "bellowing voice" (as LANGSTON HUGHES described it) had established her as a major star. More recordings, live performances, and movies followed, until the Depression and Smith's ever more frequent bouts of drinking dampened her career in the early 1930s. Between her recording debut and her death, she received a total of $28,575 from her millions of record sales. Recent biographers have disputed the decades-old charge that her death after a car accident in Clarksdale, Mississippi, was largely due to being denied treatment at a whites-only hospital.

Smith's two marriages were complemented—and sometimes complicated—by affairs with chorines and female fans. Like several other women singers associated with the HARLEM RENAISSANCE, she sang songs that celebrated lesbian lust as "dirty but good, oh yes," as well as lyrics that pretended to find people who were "in the life" odd: "there's two things I don't understand / that's a mannish-actin' woman, and a skippin', twistin', woman-actin' man." Perhaps her greatest contribution to lesbian and gay culture is that, in an era when the CLOSET was so all-pervasive it wasn't even a concept, the "Empress of Jazz," the greatest blues singer ever, sang about it at all.

Bessie Smith.

Smith, Lillian

(1897–1966)

U.S. writer, activist. Smith was the daughter of prosperous southerners who lived in Jasper, Florida, and summered in the north Georgia mountains. After college and studies at the Peabody Conservatory in Baltimore, she was, as she later described herself, "bohemian, arty art, reaching out for everything avant-garde and liberal." She worked as a school MUSIC director in CHINA for three years, then returned to direct her parents' Laurel Falls Camp, the first private camp for girls in Georgia. At the camp, which Smith later bought, she met Paula Snelling, an athletic director, who became her companion for more than 40 years.

In addition to a knowledge of athletics, Snelling had a master's degree in psychology and a deep interest in LITERATURE. She encouraged Smith to turn from music to writing, and together from 1936 to 1946 they edited a "little magazine" called *South Today* (also *Pseudopodia* and *The North Georgia Review*), the first southern journal to publish works by black writers and artists.

Established as a leading southern liberal, Smith built a national reputation with books such as *Strange Fruit* (1944) and *Killers of the Dream* (1949), which explored race relations and the psychological and social devastation wrought by segregation. Of *Strange Fruit,* Richard Wright wrote: "There has never been a more truthful picture of the Southern Negro's desperate plight." Blanche Wiesen Cook credits Smith with making Eleanor Roosevelt aware of the civil rights struggle.

Some of her books were as controversial in the North as in the South. *Strange Fruit* was banned in Boston less than a month after its publication, ostensibly for using the word "fucking," but Smith was also asked to "black out" a description of a rape and an account of a preacher advising interracial marriage. She rejected the edits and subsequently lost a court case over the book.

Her seven books and numerous articles also included work on GENDER roles and Western cultural notions of sexuality. *Strange Fruit* and *One Hour* (1959) addressed gay and lesbian issues in the larger context of sociocultural sexual repression. She likened white Americans' irrational fear of integration to anxieties provoked by same-sex relationships.

Smith relied on Snelling for moral support but also encouraged her to pursue her own objectives, even suggesting that Snelling write about their relationship: "It might be the masterpiece, not my poor little attempts to tell the world how to be good." Smith, who went so far as to burn her letters to Snelling, deeply regretted not being able to be more open herself about her private life, characterizing her reluctance as "my shame about something different and completely good. It has been that shame that has destroyed the keen edge of a pattern of love that was creative and good. Blurring it, dulling it. . . ."

✧ *How Am I to Be Heard? Letters of Lillian Smith,* edited by Margaret Rose Gladney (1993).

Smyth, Dame Ethel
(1858–1944)

English composer, suffragette, memoirist, sports enthusiast. The daughter of a general, Smyth left home in 1877 to study in Leipzig, where she was introduced to Clara Schumann, and PYOTR TCHAIKOVSKY. During an 1882 visit to Florence, Smyth met Henry "Harry" Brewster, a philosopher and writer who became her best friend, collaborator, and, in the 1890s, her companion on extended bicycle tours through Wales and northern ITALY. In the first decades of the 20th century, she rose to prominence in GERMANY, England, and the U.S. as the leading woman composer of the time. Her compositions include Mass in D (1891); *Der Wald* (1902), the first and only opera by a woman to be performed at New York's Metropolitan Opera (1903); and *The Wreckers* (1907), an opera contemporaries considered her masterpiece. A dedicated feminist, she also composed the suffragette anthem "The March of the Women" (1910), which she once conducted from a PRISON cell using a toothbrush as a baton. She was knighted in 1922 and remained for the following two decades a prominent figure in English cultural life, despite increasing deafness.

English conductor Sir Thomas Beecham called Smyth "stubborn, indomitable, unconquerable . . . one of the most remarkable people of her time." Among her remarkable traits was her candor about her sexual and romantic attractions: she came OUT to her friend Brewster in the 1890s and detailed her feelings for women in her nine best-selling books of memoirs. Although no NATALIE BARNEY, she had a lively and well-populated love life. Her great passions (not necessarily requited) included the American-born Winnaretta (Winnie) Singer, the Princesse de Polignac (1865–1943); and, late in life, VIRGINIA WOOLF. She was also a close friend of VERNON LEE and Somerville of SOMERVILLE AND ROSS.

- ✧ Christopher St. John, *Ethel Smyth: A Biography* (1959).
- ✧ Elizabeth Wood, "Lesbian Fugue: Ethel Smyth's Contrapuntal Arts," in *Musicology and Difference: Gender and Sexuality in Music Scholarship,* edited by Ruth A. Solie (1993).

Society for Individual Rights (SIR)

Gay male membership organization founded by Bill Plath, William Beardemphl, JIM FOSTER, and Mark Forrester in San Francisco in **September 1964**. By the 1960s, San Francisco was rivaled only by New York City as the American gay and lesbian capital. Influenced by the anticonformism of the BEAT GENERATION and angry at widespread police harassment, the founders of SIR aimed to mobilize the city's gay population into a social and political force by creating what first president Beardemphl called a "community feeling." JOHN D'EMILIO notes that this is one of the earliest examples of the word "community" in a gay context. According to historian JIM KEPNER, the group broke off from the League for Civil Education (1962), formed by Guy Strait, itself a splinter group of the San Francisco MATTACHINE. Unlike previous HOMOPHILE groups, which positioned themselves outside and above the BAR scene, SIR embraced it and developed its own roster of social activities. Its combination of socializing and comparatively militant political action made it unique among gay organizations of the time.

SIR published a monthly magazine, *Vector,* distributing it to newsstands throughout the city. It opened the first gay community center in the U.S. in **April 1966**, by which time SIR was the largest gay organization in the country, with more than 1,000 members. On the political front, SIR sponsored voter registration drives, candidates' nights, legal suits against bar raids and police entrapment, and demonstrations over issues ranging from discrimination in the MILITARY to the phone company's refusal to list gay organizations.

With the advent of GAY LIBERATION in 1969, SIR was increasingly perceived as cautious, conservative, and assimilationist (see ASSIMILATIONISM/CONFRONTATIONALISM) by many activists, some of whom formed the Committee for Homosexual Freedom in 1969. In 1971, its political action committee became the Alice B. Toklas Memorial Democratic Club organized by Foster.

- ✧ John D'Emilio, *Sexual Politics, Sexual Communities: The Making of a Homosexual Minority in the United States, 1940–1970* (1983).
- ✧ Jim Kepner, *Our Movement Before Stonewall* (1994).

Sociobiology

The study of the role of biological, especially genetic, factors in social behavior and natural selection. Since the 1950s, sociobiologists have sought to explain a phenomenon that seems to contradict Darwin's theory of evolution: if the main imperative of an organism's existence is to ensure the survival of its genes through reproduction, why is there such a high frequency of seemingly antireproductive behavior, such as homosexuality, in human beings? Most scientists have traditionally dismissed this contradiction in the belief that homosexuality results from socialization (nurture) rather than genetic coding (nature). In the 1970s, however, scientists like Edward O. Wilson, James D. Weinrich, and others began to look at a growing body of evidence, including studies of identical twins raised apart from each other, that implicated at least as important a role for biogenetic as for environmental factors in determining sexual orientation. Sociobiologists have sought to reconcile these findings with Darwin's theory of natural selection in several ways, including *kin selection* theory and *heterozygote-advantage* theory.

Kin selection theory, one of the basic tenets of sociobiology, broadens Darwin's definition of reproductive success to include not only one's own offspring but also the offspring of relatives, especially siblings. A lesbian sister, for example, may not have children of her own, but if she increases the survival chances of a niece or nephew, she ensures that as much as half the DNA that would have been passed to a child of her own will survive in the gene pool. Kin selection theory has also been used to explain the BERDACHE phenomenon observed in many societies: GENDER-variant individuals, according to this theory, act as an intermediary between heterosexual males and females, helping them resolve conflicts and thus reproduce more successfully. Another theory holds that gender-variant men and women are apt to be more creative and that their innovations increase their kin's survival chances.

Heterozygote-advantage theory, on the other hand, proposes that sometimes two genes must be combined to create a survival advantage. As proposed by John Kirsch and James Rodman in 1982, this theory hypothesizes that sexuality is determined by two genes, each of which can be either "heterosexual" or "homosexual." Thus, persons with two heterosexual genes or two homosexual genes would be heterosexual or homosexual, respectively; a person with one of each would be bisexual. BISEXUALITY, according to this theory, provides social and reproductive advantages significant enough to keep the "homosexual" genes in the pool.

➤ Also see CONSTRUCTIONISM VS. ESSENTIALISM; ZOOLOGY.

✧ James D. Weinrich, *Sexual Landscapes: Why We Are What We Are, Why We Love Whom We Love* (1987).

✧ Simon LeVay, *The Sexual Brain* (1994).

Sociology

The study of collective behavior, sociology was (like ANTHROPOLOGY, with which it is closely—sometimes almost indistinguishably—related, especially in LESBIAN AND GAY STUDIES) late in giving serious attention to contemporary gay and lesbian SUBCULTURES. The Chicago School of sociology, for example, made a point of studying virtually every identifiable subculture—except the gay subculture. Although University of Chicago students did perform at least one study of the gay community in Chicago some time around 1930, it was never published or presented to others in the field. Gay sociologists like Barry D. Adam, Dennis Magill, and Stephen O. Murray formed the Sociologists' Gay Caucus (later Sociologists' Lesbian and Gay Caucus) in Toronto in 1974, and studies like Laud Humphrey's *Tearoom Trade* (1975) began to be published, leading to a growing body of work that looks at gay and lesbian groups from a sociologist's perspective.

Sociologists like Mary McIntosh, then a professor at Essex University (which has continued to be an important center of gay and lesbian sociological study) in the UNITED KINGDOM, played a formative role in unleashing the CONSTRUCTIONISM VS. ESSENTIALISM debate.

✧ *Modern Homosexualities: Fragments of Lesbian and Gay Experience,* edited by Ken Plummer (1992).

✧ Stephen O. Murray, *American Gay* (1996).

Sodom and Gomorrah

In the BIBLE, the "cities of the plain" destroyed by God because of their wickedness. As described in Genesis, Sodom and Gomorrah were two of five cities located on a plain thought to be near the Dead Sea. In Genesis 18, God tells Abraham that he intends to destroy the cities because "their sin is very grievous." In Genesis 19, two angels arrive in Sodom and are invited home by Lot, apparently the only righteous man in the city. That night the men of Sodom gather outside Lot's house and demand that he hand his guests over to the crowd so that they "may know them." Lot offers his two virginal daughters instead, but the men persist in their demands until they are miraculously blinded. The next morning, urged on by the angels, Lot and his family flee to the neighboring city of Zoar just before Sodom, Gomorrah, and the surrounding plain are destroyed by "brimstone and fire."

Some biblical scholars believe that the Sodomites' wanting to "know" (i.e., gang-rape) the angels, obviously a gross violation of Middle Eastern standards of hospitality, is simply proof of the city's general wickedness and not an indication that the "grievous" sin mentioned in Genesis 18 was sex between men. At least as early as the time of Christ, however, Jewish intellectuals such as Flavius Josephus

A 1963 Italian movie image of the destruction of Sodom and Gomorrah.

and Philo had begun to popularize the idea that it was. Christian thinkers accepted their interpretation, although they tended to conflate the "sin of Sodom"—or "SODOMY"—with a host of other sexual practices they considered "against nature."

The Koran, the sacred text of ISLAM, also includes accounts of the destruction of the cities of the plain without naming them, and one Arabic term for people who engage in same-sex relations can be translated as "the people of Lot."

Starting in the Middle Ages, Sodom's "sister city" Gomorrah was sometimes imagined to have been a hotbed of lesbianism in contrast to its allegedly phallocratic neighbor.

✧ John Boswell, *Christianity, Social Tolerance, and Homosexuality: Gay People in Western Europe from the Beginning of the Christian Era to the Fourteenth Century* (1980).

✧ *Reclaiming Sodom,* edited by Jonathan Goldberg (1994).

Sodomy

Religious and legal term covering a wide range of usually noncoital sexual activities. MICHEL FOUCAULT called sodomy "that utterly confused category" because the term, which dates back to the Middle Ages, has been used to describe so many kinds of sexual behavior, including incest and sex between "man and beast." Depending on the time period and jurisdiction, courts have most commonly judged sodomy to mean: 1) anal intercourse between two men; 2) all male-male sexual activities; 3) all male-male and female-female sexual activities; 4) any sexual activity other than vaginal coitus. To confuse matters further, scholars including JOHN BOSWELL have asserted that biblical mentions of the "sin of SODOM" refer to brazen inhospitality toward strangers.

In the U.S. as of 1996, same-sex sodomy remained a crime in 22 states; heterosexual sodomy, even between a married couple, is illegal in 16 states.

➤ Also see SODOM AND GOMORRAH.

Somerville, Jimmy

(1961–)

Scottish singer, composer. Somerville fled working-class Glasgow for London as much to be a part of the city's gay SUBCULTURE as for its lively pop scene. He, Steve Bronski, and Larry Steinbeck hit the charts in the UNITED KINGDOM in 1984 (and in the U.S. in 1985) as Bronski Beat, the first successful openly all-gay rock band in the world. Their debut album *Age of Consent,* which sold more than a million copies worldwide, featured a PINK TRIANGLE and addressed issues ranging from the controversy suggested by the title to queer-bashing ("Smalltown Boy"), HOMOPHOBIA

Bronski Beat, 1985 (clockwise, from top): Larry Steinbeck, Steve Bronski, Jimmy Somerville.

("Tell Me Why"), and the religious right ("It Ain't Necessarily So").

Also in the 1980s, Somerville became a familiar presence in demonstrations and on TELEVISION talk shows. Disagreement over his politics led to his leaving Bronski Beat and forming the Communards with Richard Coles in 1987. Their single "For a Friend" was one of the first pop hits to address AIDS.

Now a solo artist, Somerville remains one of the most active, visible, and articulate gay celebrities in the U.K. He acted the role of an angel in the film version of VIRGINIA WOOLF's *Orlando* (1992), and his music has been used in numerous gay FILMS, videos, and plays, beginning with *Parting Glances* (1985). He started a film company in 1991 with others, including ISAAC JULIEN.

Somerville and Ross

(Edith Anne Oenone Somerville; 1858–1949. Violet Florence Martin, aka "Martin Ross"; 1862–1915)

Irish collaborative novelists. Second cousins from wealthy Anglo-Irish families, Somerville was born in Cork and Martin in West Galway. Somerville was an accomplished artist before forming a close relationship and literary partnership with Martin in 1886. They published more than two dozen works together, beginning with *An Irish Cousin* (1889), and including their comic masterpiece *Some Experiences of an Irish RM* (1908) and left thousands of letters and 116 volumes of diaries detailing their relationship.

Both women were active in the suffrage movement in Ireland and fought female stereotypes in their writing, as in their best-known novel, *The Real Charlotte* (1894). Somerville was the first woman master of foxhounds (1903) and master of the West Carberry Pack (1912–1919), as well as president of the Munster Women's Franchise League.

Somerville returned to her ART career after Martin's death, but she continued to use their joint name, crediting Somerville's nightly "spiritual" contributions to her work. She was also a close friend and traveling companion of ETHEL SMYTH.

Biographers and several social historians have advanced the idea that their BOSTON MARRIAGE was "innocent" of sexual intimacy, although their letters and diaries make it clear that they considered themselves married. Their devotion to each other and mutual commitment to shared creativity have become legendary.

✧ Maurice Collis, *Somerville and Ross* (1968).

Sor Juana, see CRUZ, SOR JUANA INÉS DE LA.

South Africa

No laws against same-sex relations between consenting adults. Constitutional protection against discrimination on the basis of sexual orientation. Developed social and cultural scene in large cities. Active national and local political organizations.

The first country in the world to make protection against discrimination on the basis of sexual orientation a part of its constitution (Section 8 of the Chapter on Fundamental Rights), South Africa has in the 1990s become one of the most gay-friendly countries in the world—a place where President Nelson Mandela saw fit to call for an end to discrimination against lesbians and gay men in his presidential acceptance speech.

Celebrated gay South Africans include activist SIMON NKOLI and the late writer Koos Prinsloo. Major organizations include the Association for Bisexuals, Gays and Lesbians (ABIGALE) and the National Coalition for Gay and Lesbian Identity, formed in 1995.

History
Same-sex relations between women were never against the law in South Africa, although after 1988 the AGE OF CONSENT for sex between women was set at 19 as opposed to 16 for heterosexual relations. Sex between men, on the other hand, was illegal until the 1990s, but laws were seldom enforced. Beginning in the 1950s, a discreet, underground SUBCULTURE of BARS, carnivals, and, especially for women, sporting clubs began to develop among the white populations of South Africa's major cities.

The first lesbian organization, Lesbians in Love and Compromising Situations, or LILACS, was active in Cape Town from 1983 to 1985. The country's first gay PRIDE CELEBRATION march took place in Johannesburg in 1990. Black lesbian and gay activists joined the movement in large numbers beginning in the early 1990s.

Selema, a Bombay hijra (eunuch).

South America, see LATIN AMERICA.

South Asia

Sex between women and between men illegal in Bangladesh, Bhutan, Nepal, and Pakistan, with penalties ranging from two years' to life imprisonment and the possibility of an additional sentence of a public whipping of 100 lash strokes in Pakistan. Sex between men illegal in India and Sri Lanka, with penalties ranging from ten years' to life imprisonment.

Speaking dozens of mutually unintelligible languages, practicing virtually all variations of the major world religions, and affirming ethnic and political identities sometimes violently in conflict with each other, the over 1 billion citizens of the countries of South Asia have never thought of themselves as one people, yet they are all influenced by many aspects of the same 4,000-year-old cultural tradition. The concept of "South Asian" has evolved largely among the more than 15 million people who trace their ancestry to these countries but now live in AFRICA, the Americas, or Europe, especially in the UNITED KINGDOM. This is also the group that has been most active in forming lesbian and gay South Asian organizations and developing a sense of what it means to be "khush" (gay) for a person of South Asian background.

✧ Rakesh Raffi, *A Lotus of Another Color: An Unfolding of the South Asian Gay and Lesbian Experience* (1993).

Southeast Asia

All same-sex relations illegal in Malaysia and Singapore, with penalties ranging from caning to 20 years' (Malaysia) or life imprisonment (Singapore). No laws against same-sex relations in Indonesia. Legal status unclear in Cambodia, Laos, Myanmar

(Burma), and Vietnam, although arrests have been reported in Burma and Laos. Limited rights protections in Indonesia.

Gay and lesbian identities remain largely a middle- and upper-class phenomenon in Southeast Asia. As a result, many lesbians and gay men immigrate to more hospitable countries. The advent of AIDS has had the unforeseen effect of lessening government opposition to gay male organizing in Singapore and Malaysia, since officials believe discreet gay male groups are an effective means of encouraging SAFER SEX. Lesbian organizing, sometimes in association with feminist groups, has been more limited.

Despite the lack of open lesbian and gay SUBCULTURES in Southeast Asia, HOMOEROTICISM does of course exist. According to a 1996 survey of sexual behavior in Cambodia, for example, about 10 percent of young Cambodian men report having sex with other men.

➤ Also see PHILIPPINES; THAILAND.

South Korea, see KOREA.

A scene from Pedo Almodóvar's Law of Desire.

Spain

No laws against consensual same-sex relations for persons over 12 years old. Some rights protections in some cities and regions. Well-developed social scene and active political organizations, especially in Madrid, Barcelona, and other large cities.

Since Francisco Franco's death in 1975 and the country's subsequent return to democracy, Spanish lesbians and gay men have created one of the most vibrant SUBCULTURES in Western Europe. Popular disapproval of homosexuality is thought to be decreasing, especially in Barcelona and Madrid, where a 1992 study found that only a minority of the population was against gay and lesbian rights.

Active Spanish gay and lesbian organizations include CGB (Gay Collective of Barcelona) and FAGH (Gay Liberation Front of Catalonia), which in 1980 became the first Spanish gay or lesbian organization to receive official government recognition.

Important bisexual, lesbian, and gay Spaniards in the 20th century include filmmakers PEDRO ALMODÓVAR and Eloy de la Iglesia; pop singer and actor Miguel Bosé; and writers LUIS CERNUDA, FEDERICO GARCÍA LORCA, Juan Goytisolo, Marta Portal, and Esther Tusquets.

History

After the fall of the ROMAN EMPIRE, Spain was the first place in Western Europe where harshly repressive laws against SODOMY were instituted. In **c. 650**, the Visigoth rulers of

Iberia made castration the punishment for sex between men. How often this law was enforced is not known, but it was affirmed in **1256**, when Alfonso X of Castile issued *Las Siete Partidas,* one of the first civil law codes in Europe. According to the *Partidas,* the punishment for sodomy was castration—followed by death by stoning.

In **1497**, King Ferdinand and Queen Isabella revised their country's sodomy laws to make confiscation of property and burning at the stake the statutory punishment.

Spanish conquistadores exported their hostility to same-sex eroticism to Spanish colonies in the 16th and 17th centuries. In one particularly gruesome incident recorded in **1513**, Vasco Núñez de Balboa condemned a community of at least 40 CROSS-DRESSING males in present-day Panama to be fed alive to his dogs. Other Spanish authorities and Catholic missionaries are believed to have repressed BERDACHE traditions throughout their American colonies.

Back home, executions of sodomites continued through THE INQUISITION and into the 19th century, when a new penal code in **1822** omitted mention of sodomy. Despite the absence of legal proscriptions, Spain remained an oppressive place to be attracted to one's own sex. García Lorca and other writers have left evidence of the pain they suffered trying to fit into society, which remained overwhelmingly conservative, family dominated, and Roman Catholic.

Bucking international trends, Franco recriminalized sodomy in 1970, giving rise to a small protest movement and the country's first gay magazine, *Aghois* (1972–1973). The pace of GAY LIBERATION intensified after Franco's death in 1975. Sodomy was decriminalized in 1978. Marches and protests followed (see, for example, **6/10/1979**).

Always a popular destination for lesbian and gay tourists, Spanish resorts like Ibiza, Sitges, and the Costa del Sol became more openly gay and lesbian in the 1980s, as did gay and lesbian nightlife and cultural activities in Madrid, Barcelona, and Valencia.

✧ Mili Hernandez, "Spain," in *Unspoken Rules: Sexual Orientation and Women's Human Rights,* edited by Rachel Rosenbloom (1996).

Spiritualities, Alternative

Perhaps because all the major established religions have at one time or another condemned same-sex eroticism, lesbians and gay men have a long and rich association with new religious movements and unconventional spiritualities. The late-19th-century Theosophy movement, for example, included large numbers of women and men now known to have had primary sexual and romantic relationships with persons of their own sex. More confusingly, an equally large number of lesbians and gay men, including RADCLYFFE HALL, left their childhood religion for the ROMAN CATHOLIC CHURCH, an "alternative" spirituality hardly known for its tolerance of HOMOEROTICISM.

As a gay and lesbian consciousness arose in the 20th century, many gay men and lesbians began seeking links with premodern religious traditions that embraced alternative GENDER identities and accepted same-sex relationships. These included NATIVE AMERICAN spiritualities as well as shamanistic traditions rooted in other parts of the world. Beginning in the late 1960s, many women embraced WICCA. And some lesbians, like MARY DALY, rejected traditional concepts of "God" in favor of a Goddess, who, in Daly's words, "affirms the life-loving be-ing of women and nature."

✧ Mark Thompson, *Gay Spirit: Myth and Meaning* (1987).

- Cynthia Eller, *Living in the Lap of the Goddess: The Feminist Spirituality Movement in America* (1995).
- Mark Thompson, *Gay Souls: Finding the Heart of Gay Spirit and Nature with Sixteen Writers, Healers, Teachers, and Visionaries* (1995).

Sport, Gay Men and

While lesbians are routinely assumed to be athletic, gay men rarely are, even by other gay men, as OSCAR WILDE's 19th-century observation reveals: "Football is all very well as a game for rough girls, but it is hardly suitable for delicate boys." For both lesbians and gay men in sport, however, their participation has become more visible in the past two decades.

Sport has inspired much homoerotic art, such as Duncan Grant's Wrestlers.

In his study of GENDER and sport, sociologist Michael Messner considers the contradictory attitudes toward masculinity posed by homosexuality and athletics. The social construction of a masculine identity for sport and a feminine identity for gay men is so strong that the gay athlete often feels estranged. An athletic *gay* man serves as a reminder that gender identity and sexual orientation are not fixed or absolute, and that a correlation of athleticism with masculinity is as false as the correlation of masculinity with sexual attraction to women.

Nonconformity in the conservative gender-determined world of sport is rare, as is even playful gender-bending. Historian Susan Cahn does find "Gorgeous George" Wagner, a wrestler in the 1940s whose CAMP appearance in the ring included satin, silks, and an ermine jockstrap. Although sports reporters felt Wagner discredited wrestling and ridiculed his "pseudo-pswish," they did not question his masculinity. His sex and the masculinity of his sport overcame his cultivated image, which also included permed hair held by gold-plated and sequined "Georgie pins." Cahn found that Wagner's contemporaries felt part of his success was due "to America's fascination with homosexuality."

Wagner's gender play underscores the prevalence of social customs and institutions like dress, adornment, and sport that exaggerate male-female differences to fortify a social definition of gender. Sociologist R. W. Connell has argued that these social practices are necessary because biological or "natural" logic won't sustain gender categories. Sport is not a natural realm where masculinity develops; instead, it is a social institution created by and for men, one that includes considerable HOMOPHOBIA and misogyny to disparage the "feminine" in women and, certainly, in men.

Brian Pronger's research traces the contemporary connection between sports and masculinity to the society and economics of 19th-century Europe and the efforts of Pierre de Coubertin, founder of the modern Olympics. With the symbols of the ancient games, the folk games of the late Middle Ages, and the values of a growing imperial industrial society, sports as we know them took shape.

Other historians find correlations between the development of violent sports and the rise of feminist challenges to gender relations and power distribution. Still others trace the campaign to provide sport instruction for English public school boys to a desire to counter the dominance of female teaching staffs and foster the connection between sport, leadership, and loyalty to authority. With "manly" character-building values of rules, energy, competitive record-setting, initiative, fair play, discipline, cooperation, and team spirit, a sporting ethic was socially embraced that protected and advanced the interests of white upper- and middle-class men.

Although many gay men are also eager, even desperate, to construct the masculine identity sport confers, some have described the sports world as threatening and inappropriate because of its heterosexual "masculine significance" and team dynamics, violence, aggression, and insults. The gender assumptions of sport are highly charged and perhaps the only thing worse than "throwing like a girl" is being beaten by one.

In 1973, the Battle of the Sexes $100,000 tennis challenge match between Bobby Riggs and BILLIE JEAN KING dramatically illustrated the genderized turf of sport. Despite their age difference (at the time King was 29 and Riggs 55), Riggs—the self-described "male chauvinist pig"—was favored to win. Nearly 50 million people watched the televised match and witnessed how the hype preceding the event and descriptions of King's victory tied any advancements in women's sport to social advancements for women in general. Far more than winning the match, Riggs's job was to protect the culturally dominant masculine world of sport from feminine encroachment, and he failed.

While black and LATINO male athletes can find respect and a cultural home in athletics with opportunities for financial and career advancement, they also find themselves symbolically playing out power and racial struggles. Gay AFRICAN-AMERICAN athletes like GLENN BURKE, the first professional baseball player to come OUT, describe substantial additional pressures to prove themselves in light of their race and sexual orientation.

No professional male athlete has come out during his playing career. Some have been outed by AIDS, including Jerry Smith, former Washington Redskins tight end. Other athletes who have come out following their retirement include British skater and Olympic gold medal winner John Curry, football running back DAVID KOPAY, football offensive tackle Roy Simmons, and Olympic diver GREG LOUGANIS.

Since the 1970s, sports clubs have become a visible and important part of the gay male and lesbian community. With the beginning of the GAY GAMES in 1982 a new level of highly visible popular participation was encouraged. Instead of the fearful, tense atmosphere of traditional sport, the gay sport movement encourages alternative values and supportive play.

✧ Brian Pronger, *The Arena of Masculinity: Sports, Homosexuality and the Meaning of Sex* (1990).

✧ *Sport, Men, and the Gender Order: Critical Feminist Perspectives,* edited by Michael A. Messner and D. F. Sabo (1990).

✧ Michael A. Messner, *Power at Play: Sports and the Problem of Masculinity* (1992).

✧ Susan K. Cahn, *Coming on Strong: Gender and Sexuality in Twentieth-Century Women's Sport* (1994).

Sport, Lesbians and

The GAY GAMES did nothing to educate society about the athletic ability of lesbians. It has long been a popular belief that *any* woman who is especially good at—or even simply *interested* in—playing, teaching, officiating, coaching, or writing about sports is likely to be a lesbian. Equally common is the suspicion that women's sports *created* lesbians. No one has statistically proven that lesbians are proportionally more represented in sport than heterosexual women, but few would argue that their presence is felt and their impact substantial.

Despite the growth in women's athletics in the last 60 years, the correlation of masculinity with sport continues to create tension for women, especially for lesbians. Nevertheless, this tension does not prevent lesbians from being attracted to and receiving a unique comfort from athletics. In interviews with lesbian athletes, historian Susan Cahn found that they, like women athletes in general, crave the physical freedoms and personal challenges sports make possible. For lesbians, Cahn noted, sport also creates a site for GENDER innovation or rebellion, a space where restrictive feminine conventions and conformity are not binding. Athletics give lesbians access to social networks, opportunities for female bonding, even a unique culture (e.g., *GirlJock* magazine). The world of sports is an arena where lesbian "jock" behavior is a welcome sign of competence, experience, and a love of the game.

Singer Alix Dobkin has called softball "the single greatest organizing force in lesbian society."

The figure of the "mannish female athlete" appears in psychological literature as early as the 1880s. Lesbianism became even more strongly associated with athletics around the turn of the century, when women were first allowed to play high-energy sports. Physical fitness, medical, and behavioral science experts believed that these sports could "masculinize" women to the point of their acquiring a male sexual appetite and even a "male" attraction to women. By the 1930s, social attitude had shifted slightly: sport was now perceived to be dangerous because it transformed women into "heterosexual failures" no longer attractive to men. This was also when female physical education instructors began to be perceived not as health promoters but as suspect lesbians. After World War II, the fully developed stereotype of the lesbian athlete emerged, sabotaging women's sports to the extent that by the 1950s physical educators felt compelled to enforce dress codes and organize beauty contests and marriage-oriented media events to counter the AMAZON and BUTCH images of women athletes.

In 1966, the International Amateur Athletic Federation began subjecting women athletes to "tests" in which they had to prove their biological sex by parading nude before a panel of gynecologists, a practice quickly replaced by chromatin and drug testing. Many other athletes, including BABE DIDRICKSON and professional softball players Freda and Olympia Savona, had already been subjected to similar "inspections" by the press. They were simply too good to be female.

Some cultural historians feel AFRICAN-AMERICAN athletes have suffered less from HOMOPHOBIA, due not only to black acceptance of active work lives for women and a less restrictive definition of femininity but also to a longstanding African-American denial of black lesbianism. Still, tennis champion Althea Gibson found, after breaking the race barrier, that she also was not immune to speculation about her sexuality as sportswriters routinely described her TOMBOY manner.

Homosexuality in sport is inextricably tied to perceptions of gender difference. Australian power lifter and bodybuilder Bev Francis lost the Miss Olympia title in 1984 because she didn't "look like a woman" according to the International Female Body Building officials. Her "constructed" body was judged too masculine.

Although the heterosexual Francis's deficiency was *looking* too masculine, early-1970s tennis star Richard Raskind "reconstructed" his body and became a TRANSSEXUAL because he *felt* female. Assuming the name Renee Richards after the operation, she clarified the difference between biological sex and an individual's sense of gender when she announced her intention to play tennis in the 1976 U.S. Open in the women's division. She refused to take a chromatin test, won a court challenge on privacy grounds, and succeeded in taking part in the competition, illustrating the ways sport enforces concepts of sex difference, gender, and sex identity along narrow socially constructed lines of what is considered "natural" and permissible. Ultimately, Richards seemed a more acceptable "she" than Francis.

Despite increased visibility in the sports world, lesbianism remains a commercial liability. When a major media commentator charged in 1995 that lesbianism on the professional women's golf tour was hurting sponsorship, a public debate ensued. Stories of "blue dot lesbians" appeared, alleging that some golfers put blue stickers on their lockers as a cue for their hosts on tour to find them dates with women. In the midst of the debate, one sportswriter succinctly summarized the sports identity/gender identity issue in a story titled

"The Key Word Should Be 'Golfer,' Not 'Woman,' 'Heterosexual' or 'Lesbian.' "

Lesbophobia has successfully kept a number of athletes, coaches, and officials in the CLOSET in collegiate as well as professional sports. After BILLIE JEAN KING was outed in a palimony suit, she lost millions in endorsements and financial opportunities. MARTINA NAVRATILOVA became the first professional athlete, male or female, to come out at a high point in her career. She also lost out financially. When Navratilova was congratulated for her courage by an interviewer who suggested many more athletes would surely follow her lead, Navratilova looked over her shoulder and quipped, "I don't see anyone lining up." Recently, professional bicyclist Missy Giove and pro golfer Muffin Spencer-Devlin have come out.

A number of other lesbian athletes have written about lesbians in sport, including Victoria Brownworth, Pat Griffin, Betty Hicks, Michele Kort, Rachel Lurie, Mariah Burton Nelson, Susan Fox Rogers,. and Yvonne Zipter. Their writings explore the feminist interest in redefining the goals and rules of sport and the important cultural position of athletics in the lesbian community for everyone from the legendary dyke gym teacher to softball game enthusiasts to top tennis pros.

✧ *Her Story in Sport: A Historical Anthology of Women in Sports,* edited by Reet Howell (1982).

✧ Susan K. Cahn, *Coming on Strong: Gender and Sexuality in Twentieth-Century Women's Sport* (1994).

✧ *Sportsdykes: Stories from on and off the Field,* edited by Susan Fox Rogers (1994).

✧ *Women, Sport, and Culture,* edited by Susan Birrell and Cheryl L. Cole (1994).

Sri Lanka, see SOUTH ASIA.

Stein, Gertrude
(1874–1946), and
Toklas, Alice B.
(1877–1967)

U.S. writer and her lifelong companion, secretary, and cook. Stein grew up in Oakland, California, and studied psychology with William James at Radcliffe College. In 1897, she entered medical school at Johns Hopkins University for two years, but left to pursue a career as a writer instead. In 1903, she and her brother Leo moved to Paris, and Stein remained based in FRANCE until her death.

Stein had had affairs with at least two women (one of whom, May Bookstaver, inspired a central character in the posthumously published *Q.E.D.,* Stein's only overtly homo-

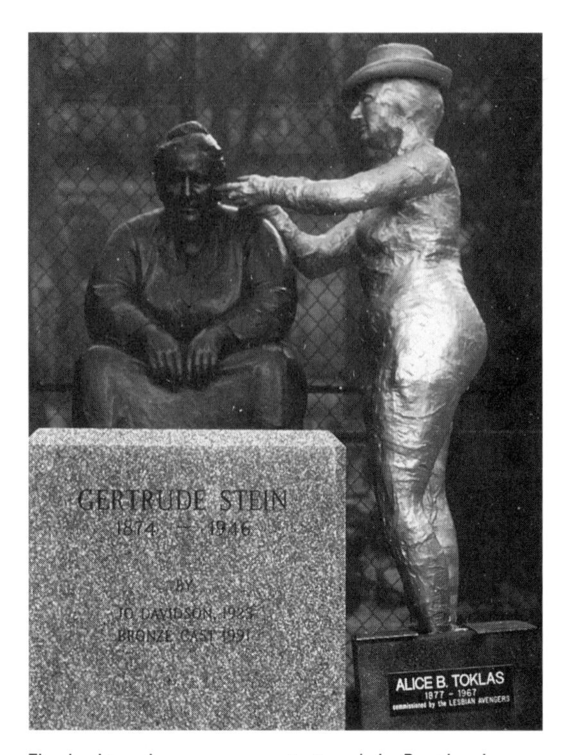

The Lesbian Avengers commissioned Jo Davidson's bronze statue of Alice B. Toklas to join that of Gertrude Stein on Valentine's Day, 1991.

erotic novel) when she met Toklas, a native San Franciscan who had also been involved previously with a woman, in 1907. A few years later, Toklas and Stein moved into an apartment at 27, rue de Fleurus and proceeded to create one of Paris's most star-studded salons, frequented by F. Scott Fitzgerald and Ernest Hemingway as well as gay artists, composers, and writers like GEORGE PLATT LYNES, SAMUEL STEWARD, and Virgil Thomson (with whom Stein collaborated on two operas). She was also well acquainted with the famous expatriate lesbians of her era, in particular SYLVIA BEACH and the women who gathered around NATALIE BARNEY'S rival salon.

One of the best-known intellectuals of her time, Stein came to the attention of a broad public with the successful publication of *The Autobiography of Alice B. Toklas* (1933) and a well-publicized lecture tour of the United States the following year.

Although LILLIAN FADERMAN and others have criticized Stein and Toklas's relationship as heterosexually modeled, with Stein the "man of the house" and Toklas the adoring "little woman," the reality was more complicated. Toklas was probably the first to wholeheartedly agree with Stein's assessment of herself as a "genius" (the only one she knew besides Picasso), and her support encouraged Stein to leap into unknown linguistic and literary terrain. Toklas ran their household, vetted their friends and acquaintances, established a small press, Plain Edition, to publish Stein's work, and managed Stein's career. In return, Stein, if numerous passages in her work are to be taken as autobiographical, lavished love and sensuous affection on Toklas: for example, in the last paragraph of "As a Wife Has a Cow: A Love Story" (1926), the "wife has a cow" (Stein and Toklas's code word for orgasm) a total of eight times.

Soon after Stein's death, critics like Edmund Wilson began to speculate that Stein's style evolved at least in part out of the necessity of concealing the homoerotic content of her work. Her most overtly lesbian writings—*Q.E.D.* (1903; published 1950) and "Lifting Belly" (published 1953), the 60-page ode to the "cow"-filled love life she ("Mount Fatty") and Toklas ("pussy") enjoyed—were not published during her lifetime, but many lesbian and gay readers grasped the import of writings such as "Miss Furr and Miss Skeene" (1922; see "GAY"). Stein could also write movingly about gay men, as in the passage that begins "Sometimes men are kissing" in "Men" (in the collection *Two: Gertrude Stein and Her Brother and Other Early Portraits, 1908–1912;* published 1951); however, she supposedly told Hemingway that "the act male homosexuals commit is ugly and repugnant and afterwards they are disgusted with themselves."

Stein has sometimes been criticized for her male identification. Nevertheless, her last work, the opera (with score by Virgil Thomson) *The Mother of Us All* (1947), is a tribute to the pioneering feminist Susan B. Anthony.

Both Jewish, Stein and Toklas managed to survive the German occupation of France during WORLD WAR II by living quietly at their country home in Bilignin in the Rhône Valley. Toklas, inconsolable after Stein's death of cancer in 1946, continued to live for many years in their painting-filled apartment in Paris. She supervised the publication of special editions of Stein's work and scored literary successes of her own, including an acclaimed culinary memoir, *The Alice B. Toklas Cook Book* (1954), and her memoirs, *What Is Remembered* (1963).

✧ Janet Hobhouse, *Everybody Who Was Anybody: A Biography of Gertrude Stein* (1975).

- Linda Simon, *The Biography of Alice B. Toklas* (1977).
- Judy Grahn, *Really Reading Gertrude Stein: A Selected Anthology with Essays by Judy Grahn* (1989).

Steward, Samuel M.

(pseudonym: Phil Andros; 1909–)

U.S. writer, tattoo artist. Steward grew up in a small town in southeastern Ohio and attended Ohio State University. In high school, he discovered HAVELOCK ELLIS and, as he later told Winston Leyland, "had a dandy time, with the football team, the basketball team, the athletic coach—and many others." In 1930, he privately published a collection of experimental homoerotic sketches, *Pan and the Firebird*. In 1936, he was fired from a teaching job at Washington State University for the (heterosexually) "racy" parts of his first novel, *Angels on the Bough*. Later, bored with his students, he left academia for good in 1952 and opened up a tattoo parlor under the name Phil Sparrow. On the side, he wrote PORNOGRAPHY as Phil Andros ("Man Lover" in Greek).

He started writing letters to famous people, especially gay and lesbian ones, and scored a hit with GERTRUDE STEIN in 1932. A correspondence began and a few years later he went to Europe, where he met ANDRÉ GIDE and Thomas Mann. He even performed oral sex on Lord Alfred Douglas as a sort of pilgrimage to, in Steward's words, "a place OSCAR WILDE's lips had once touched" (although Douglas later told him that he and Wilde had mostly used their hands). He was later one of the informants for the KINSEY REPORTS.

He began publishing his pornographic short stories in the 1960s, reflecting in print some of what TOM OF FINLAND was accomplishing in visual art. Although darker, his work helped establish the masculine stud as a gay icon. Steward wrote an extensive, informative memoir and debuted a DETECTIVE FICTION series with Stein and Toklas as the sleuths in 1985.

He made a comeback with the 1982 republication of *$TUD* by Alyson Publications.

- "Samuel Steward," *Gay Sunshine Interviews, Volume Two,* edited by Winston Leyland (1982).

Stonewall

Tavern and dance BAR at 51–53 Christopher Street in Greenwich Village, New York City, which was the site of a police raid in the early morning hours of **June 28, 1969**, and a subsequent "riot," "rebellion," or "uprising" that continued through the next four days and marked the beginning of GAY LIBERATION in the U.S. Although the disturbance was not the first instance of gay and lesbian resistance to LAW enforcement, it is the most famous and most documented. As a result, "Stonewall" has come to be used to describe a major turning point in the history of any lesbian and gay community's resistance to persecution, as in "CANADA's Stonewall" (see **2/5/1981**) or "AUSTRALIA's Stonewall" (see **7/1978**).

Every detail of the Stonewall Uprising is disputed, from exactly what time it began and who led the resistance to the composition of the crowd that rioted in Sheridan Square outside the tavern. In addition, many rationales are given for exactly why this particular police raid—in an era when raids were commonplace at lesbian and gay bars—inspired resistance, from the fact that there was a full moon to the recent death and funeral of Judy Garland and the astrological explanation that Mars was in retrograde, a bad time for police action.

Most agree, however, that the rebellion began when a police inspector and seven officers arrived at the Stonewall Inn shortly after mid-

Homo Nest Raided, Queen Bees Are Stinging Mad

By JERRY LISKER

She sat there with her legs crossed, the lashes of her mascara-coated eyes beating like the wings of a hummingbird. She was angry. She was so upset she hadn't bothered to shave. A day old stubble was beginning to push through the pancake makeup. She was a he. A queen of Christopher Street.

Last weekend the queens had turned commandos and stood bra strap to bra strap against an invasion of the helmeted Tactical Patrol Force. The elite police squad had shut down one of their private gay clubs, the Stonewall Inn at 57 Christopher St., in the heart of a three-block homosexual community in Greenwich Village.

Queen Power reared its bleached blonde head in revolt. New York City experienced its first homosexual riot.

"We may have lost the battle, sweets, but the war is far from over," lisped an unofficial lady-in-waiting from the court of the Queens.

"We've had all we can take from the Gestapo," the spokesman, or spokeswoman, continued. "We're putting our foot down once and for all." The foot wore a spiked heel.

According to reports, the Stonewall Inn, a two-story structure with a sand painted brick and opaque glass facade, was a mecca for the homosexual element in the village who wanted nothing but a private little place where they could congregate, drink, dance and do whatever little girls do when they get together.

The thick glass shut out the outside world of the street. Inside, the Stonewall bathed in wild, bright psychedelic lights, while the patrons writhed to the sounds of a juke box on a square dance floor surrounded by booths and tables. The bar did a good business and the waiters, or waitresses, were always kept busy, as they snaked their way around the dancing customers to the booths and tables. For nearly two years, peace and tranquility reigned supreme for the Alice in Wonderland clientele.

The Raid Last Friday

Last Friday the privacy of the Stonewall was invaded by police from the First Division. It was a raid. They had a warrant. After two years, police said they had been informed that liquor was being served on the premises. Since the Stonewall was without a license, the place was being closed. It was the law.

All hell broke loose when the police entered the Stonewall. The girls instinctively reached for each other. Others stood frozen, locked in an embrace of fear.

NEWS photo by [illegible]

The Stonewall Inn

Only a handful of police were on hand for the initial landing in the homosexual beachhead. They ushered the patrons out onto Christopher Street, just off Sheridan Square. A crowd had formed in front of the Stonewall and the customers were greeted with cheers of encouragement from the gallery.

The whole proceedings took on the aura of a homosexual Academy Awards Night. The Queens pranced out to the street blowing kisses and waving to the crowd. A beauty of a specimen named Stella wailed uncontrollably while being led to the sidewalk in front of the Stonewall by a cop. She later confessed that she didn't protest the manhandling by the officer, it was just that her hair was in curlers and she was afraid her new beau might be in the crowd and spot her. She didn't want him to see her this way, she wept.

Queen Power

The crowd began to get out of hand, eye witnesses said. Then, without warning, Queen Power exploded with all the fury of a gay atomic bomb. Queens, princesses and ladies-in-waiting began hurling anything they could lay their polished, manicured finger nails on. Bobby pins, compacts, curlers, lipstick tubes and other femme fatale missiles were flying in the direction of the cops. The war was on. The lilies of the valley had become carnivorous jungle plants.

Urged on by cries of "C'mon girls, let's go get'em!," the defenders of Stonewall launched an attack. The cops called for assistance. To the rescue came the Tactical Patrol Force.

Flushed with the excitement of battle, a fellow called Gloria pranced around like Wonder Woman, while several Florence Nightingales administered first aid to the fallen warriors. There were some assorted scratches and bruises, but nothing serious was suffered by these honeys turned Madwomen of Challiot.

Official reports listed four injured policemen with 13 arrests. The War of the Roses lasted about two hours from about midnight to 2 a.m. There was a return bout Wednesday night.

Two veterans recently recalled the battle and issued a warning to the cops. "If they close up all the gay joints in this area there is going to be all out war."

Bruce and Nan

Both said they were refugees from Indiana and had come to New York where they could live together happily ever after. They were in their early 20's. They preferred to be called by their married names, Bruce and Nan.

"I don't like your paper," Nan lisped matter-of-factly. "It's anti-fag and pro-cop."

"I'll bet you didn't see what they did to the Stonewall. Did the pigs tell you that they smashed everything in sight? Did you ask them why they stole money out of the cash register and then smashed it with a sledge hammer? Did you ask them why it took them two years to discover that the Stonewall didn't have a liquor license?"

Bruce nodded in agreement and

(Continued on page M6)

night to issue a warrant charging the tavern with serving liquor without a license.

The patrons were joined by crowds outside, and a melee ensued. A BUTCH lesbian (in some accounts, a young gay man) resisted arrest, and the crowd began tossing cobblestones and coins at the police. The patrons in the paddy wagon escaped, and the police were driven back inside the tavern. Someone threw a torch into the bar and a fire started. The police called for reinforcement. Four officers were injured. By the time the reinforcements arrived, rioting had spread. Transvestites formed a chorus line mocking police. Rioting continued through the night and the rest of the weekend.

Although now enshrined as a gay and lesbian milestone, many contemporaries were shocked and disturbed by the violence and disorder. Although it was several years before the real impact of the incident was understood by many as a milestone in the fight for lesbian and gay rights, within months gay liberation groups were forming across the country.

Marches commemorating Stonewall, which began in 1970, a year after the rebellion, are the origin of the PRIDE CELEBRATIONS now held in many cities every June.

✧ Robert Amsel, "Back to Our Future: A Walk on the Wild Side of Stonewall," *The Advocate* (September 15, 1987).

✧ Martin Bauml Duberman, *Stonewall* (1993).

Streicher, Rikki

(1925–1994)

U.S. activist, businesswoman. From a middle-class Detroit Catholic family, Streicher was in college when she suddenly lost both her parents in an accident in 1944. With nothing to keep her in the Midwest, she set out for Los Angeles with $12 in her pocket.

Later settled in San Francisco, Streicher got

into the food and beverage business. In **April 1966**, she and co-owner Gloria Grant opened Maud's Study, later Maud's, and kept it open 365 days a year until September 9, 1989, making it the longest surviving BAR for lesbians in the U.S. Its name was inspired by Noël Coward: "Maud, there are fairies buried at the bottom of your garden, Maud, you rascal, you. . . ." During its 23 years of operation, Maud's was a center of San Francisco lesbian life, an institution offering everything from dancing to softball teams, as well as a venue for lesbian activists and politicians to raise funds and build awareness of community issues. Paris Poirier featured it in her documentary, *Last Call at Maud's* (1993), as emblematic of the changes in the San Francisco lesbian community from the 1960s to the 1980s.

Streicher also operated the Russian River bars Vieux Carre and Amelia's (named after AMELIA EARHART). Her community activity included leadership roles with the SOCIETY FOR INDIVIDUAL RIGHTS, the Tavern Guild, and the Bay Area Physicians for Human Rights. She was also a co-organizer of the GAY GAMES and cofounder of the Federation of Gay Games. In 1992, she received the Community Service Award from the Gay and Lesbian Historical Society.

In an interview for *Before Stonewall* (1985), the landmark documentary directed by Greta Schiller and Robert Rosenberg, Streicher qualified the importance of the STONEWALL Uprising: "We, I, have been having riots since the forties, and all of a sudden a group of people in New York have a fight and it's supposed to be soul-shaking to the rest of the gay community throughout the world. Ridiculous! . . . Change comes out of hard-working, consistent behavior."

Streicher was survived by Mary Sanger, her lover of 18 years. After her death, the mayor of San Francisco requested all municipal flags be flown at half-mast in her honor.

✧ Ellen Meyers, "In Memory: Rikki Streicher," *Our Stories* (vol. 10, no. 1, 1995; published by the Gay and Lesbian Historical Society of Northern California).

Studds, Gerry [Eastman]

(1937–)

U.S. congressman from Massachusetts (1973–1997). A liberal Democrat, Studds earned loyal support from his Cape Cod constituency, thanks in large part to his successful advocacy on behalf of the local fishing industry.

In 1983, the House Ethics Committee began an investigation of Studds during which he admitted to having had an affair with a 17-year-old House page. Unapologetic, Studds acknowledged his homosexuality in a speech to the House on **July 18, 1983**. In 1984, he was returned to the House, becoming the first openly gay person elected to the U.S. Congress.

In the 1990s, Studds emerged as a leader in the fight for lesbian and gay rights in the U.S. MILITARY. He chose not to run for reelection in 1996.

➤ Also see **July 20, 1983**; **August 15, 1983**.

Subculture

A social group that shares a set of values, customs, artifacts, and a sense of identity which distinguishes the members of the group from society at large. Sociologists are not in agreement over whether contemporary lesbians and gay men constitute a true subculture (or subcultures), nor do historians agree on when a subculture, if it in fact exists, came about. Those who reject the concept point to the diversity of identities among gay men and lesbians and question the degree to which values are shared—and felt to be different from the larger culture's. Most people, however, use the word "subculture" to refer to the customs and material aspects of lesbian and gay lives, which sociologists agree are distinct and well developed.

➤ Also see ANTHROPOLOGY; GHETTOS, GAY AND LESBIAN; SOCIOLOGY.

Sweden, see SCANDINAVIA.

Sweet Honey in the Rock

AFRICAN-AMERICAN women's a cappella singing group based in Washington, D.C. Bernice Johnson Reagon assembled the group out of vocal workshops at the D.C. Black Repertory Company. The original members—Reagon, Louise Robinson, Carol Lynn Maillard, and Mie—gave their debut performance at Howard University on November 23, 1973.

The group was named after the first song they learned, a song Reagon had heard as a child but never sung. According to her minister father, the song derived from a religious parable of a land so rich that honey would flow from a cracked rock. Reagon saw in the image a fitting reflection of the experience and legacy of African-American women.

The group's size and membership has varied over the years. Because of HOLLY NEAR's influence, its members now include a sign language interpreter. The repertory has also broadened to include everything from gospel to rap, folk songs, R&B, ballads, and pieces created in collaboration with dramatic and literary artists.

Social and political commentary on issues that include racism, apartheid, ethnic and class strife, GENDER, and sexuality remains at the heart of the group's musical programming. Lesbian activist Ivy Young lauded them for teaching "a lot of activists about popular culture as politics."

While not all of the singers are lesbian, the group sings "freedom songs" and love songs inspired by the lesbian and gay experience. They committed themselves, according to Reagon, "to celebrate and give comfort to women who were finding strength in spaces with other women." They appeared at the MICHIGAN WOMYN'S MUSIC FESTIVAL in 1990.

The group has released ten albums and presents nearly 100 concerts a year in the U.S. and abroad. In 1988, they received a Grammy Award in the traditional folk music category.

> ✧ Bernice Johnson Reagon and Sweet Honey in the Rock, *We Who Believe in Freedom* (1993).

Swenson, May

(1913–1989)

U.S. author of ten books of poetry and other writings, chancellor of the academy of Amer-

May Swenson (left) and R. R. "Zan" Knudson, 1968.

ican Poets from 1980 to 1989. The oldest of ten children, Swenson was born and raised in a Swedish immigrant Mormon family in Logan, Utah, and still spoke only Swedish as she entered first grade. She spent most of her adult life in and near New York City.

Swenson earned a reputation as one of America's most inventive and skillful poets with witty, thought-provoking writings that probe and celebrate the mysteries of time, Being, and nature. Her work also reflects her fascination with the shape, sound, and evocative quality of language.

She was open and positive about her sexuality in private life, although (like her friend ELIZABETH BISHOP) she resisted being labeled as a "lesbian poet," fearing her sexual orientation would filter perceptions of her poetry. Her submission of "To Confirm a Thing" to the 1975 landmark anthology *Amazon Poetry* (edited by Elly Bulkin and Joan Larkin) was her first to a lesbian publication. The poem had been written nearly 20 years earlier. While often sensuous and erotic, her poetry was rarely rhetorical or openly confessional, with the exception of a few poems like "Zambesi and Ranee" (*A Cage of Spines,* 1958), a description of a lioness and a tigress at the Bronx Zoo that subtly but clearly declaims the social ostracism of lesbians. After a lengthy relationship with Pearl Schwartz, Swenson spent the last 23 years of her life with writer R. R. "ZAN" KNUDSON. *The Love Poems of May Swenson* (1991), selected and republished after Swenson's death, most explicitly reveal Swenson's androgynous and lesbian personae.

- ✧ *Gay and Lesbian Poetry in Our Time: An Anthology,* edited by Carl Morse and Joan Larkin (1988).
- ✧ R. R. Knudson, *The Wonderful Pen of May Swenson* (1993).
- ✧ R. R. Knudson and Suzanne F. Bigelow, *May Swenson: A Poet's Life in Photos* (1997).
- ✧ *Made with Words: The Prose of May Swenson,* edited and with an introduction by Gardner McFall (1997).

Switchboards

In 1997, there were over 120 gay-, lesbian-, and bisexual-related switchboards, helplines, and hotlines in the U.S. and more than 20 similar services in CANADA. Since the late 1960s, the development of community-based switchboards has marked the early stages of an organized gay and lesbian rights movement in countries as different from one another as Estonia and the PHILIPPINES. Although now increasingly replaced by online services, they have remained especially vital services for bisexual, gay, and lesbian YOUTH: a survey conducted in England found that 18 percent of young people begin the process of coming OUT by calling a switchboard. In the 1980s, many switchboards also became important sources of information on AIDS, HIV, and SAFE(R) SEX.

Switchboard services in North America vary widely. Some are little more than automated message centers; others offer on-line counselors trained to cope with everything from questions about BARS to suicide threats. London's highly respected Lesbian and Gay Switchboard, founded in 1974, is the only 24-hour-a-day, seven-day-a-week service of its kind. It also maintains Europe's largest database of gay- and lesbian-related information.

Switzerland

No laws against consensual same-sex relations between adults over 16 years of age or between younger persons not more than 3 years apart in age. Political organizations and active social and cultural scenes throughout the country but especially in Bern,

Geneva, and Zurich. Nondiscrimination policy in the MILITARY.

The Swiss have a reputation for social conservatism, but, compared with several of its neighbors, the country has been a haven of tolerance for lesbians and gay men since the 1930s. Although Swiss gay men and lesbians have not attained specific rights protections, all references to homosexuality were stricken from the law books as of a national referendum conducted on **May 17, 1992**, which was approved by 73 percent of the electorate. Virtually every city and large town has lesbian and gay gathering places, and the Swiss have played host to major multinational gay and lesbian conclaves, ranging from International Gay Ski Week to conventions of gay and lesbian CHORUSES. The country is also a center of German-language gay and lesbian PUBLISHING.

Pink Cross, founded in 1994, is the most prominent national gay and lesbian organization. Celebrated gay and bisexual Swiss include film director Daniel Schmid, and novelists Guido Bachmann and Christoph Geiser.

History

The rise of Calvinism in Geneva in the 16th century resulted in death sentences for SODOMY beginning in **1555**. In at least one case (see **1568**), a woman who had had sexual relations with another woman was executed. Later, however, only sexual conduct between men was criminalized.

On the surface a staid country not known for revolutionary nonconformity, Switzerland has nonetheless been home to a series of publishing events that had enormous impact on the development of a lesbian and gay consciousness all over the world. HEINRICH HOESSLI began publishing his pioneering survey and defense of HOMOEROTICISM in **1836** in the town of Glarus. The Austrian novelist Aimée Duc chronicled the lives and lesbian attachments of university students in Geneva in **1901**. And, perhaps most influential of all, the German-born activist Karl Meier moved publication of *Der Kreis* ("The Circle"), begun the previous year in GERMANY, to Switzerland in 1933. Together with a French edition (called *Le Cercle*) founded in 1943, *Der Kreis* was virtually the only international HOMOPHILE publication through 1967, when it ceased publication.

The Swiss began decriminalizing sex between men at the canton level in 1937. As of **1941**, sex between consenting adult males over 20 became legal throughout the country, but authorities continued to prosecute men who had relations with boys between 16 and 20. As late as the five-year period between 1985 and 1990, at least 500 Swiss men were tried for the offense.

GAY LIBERATION began in Switzerland in the early 1970s, but the movement was marred by a series of failures to bring lesbians and gay men together in the same organizations. AIDS activism emerged as a potent force in the movement in the 1980s, by the end of which Switzerland had the highest per capita rate of AIDS cases in Europe. In the 1990s, after legal victories had given gay men a nondiscriminatory AGE OF CONSENT (as well as legalized male prostitution), lesbians and gay men joined together to pursue social welfare benefits such as legal recognition of same-sex MARRIAGE or DOMESTIC PARTNERSHIPS. A 1994 poll showed that almost 80 percent of the Swiss electorate had no objections to same-sex marriages.

✧ Hans Ineichen, "Swiss Gays: Little Reason to Complain," *Ferrari's Places of Interest* (April 1994–April 1995).

Sylvester in performance.

Sylvester

(Sylvester James Hurd; 1948–1988)

U.S. singer, composer. Born into a middle-class Los Angeles family, Sylvester was guided into a musical career by his grandmother, Julia Morgan, a former blues singer. As the "child wonder of gospel," he began touring the U.S. at the age of eight. Based in San Francisco after 1967, he performed with the GENDER-bending Cockettes in 1970, then embarked on a recording career, alternating between the blues and jazz standards he loved and the dance MUSIC his mass-market fans demanded. At least as popular in Europe as in the U.S., he was the only openly gay disco superstar, and his gold-record composition "You Make Me Feel (Mighty Real)" (1979) is still considered a gay anthem.

ARMISTEAD MAUPIN called Sylvester "one of those few gay celebrities who never renounced his gayness along the ladder of success." Despite pressure from record companies to straighten up his act, he remained a proud spokesperson and role model for ANDROGYNY, blackness, and gay style. He was active in the fight against AIDS and donated much of the $5 million he had earned to AIDS-related causes.

✧ Dominic Lutyens, "Sylvester," *Attitude* (December 1994).

Symonds, John Addington

(1840–1893)

English writer, critic, pioneering activist. The son of a prominent physician, Symonds attended the elite Harrow School and Oxford University. Although he realized in his earliest youth that he was strongly attracted to men, he loathed the coarse "animal lust"—"onanism, mutual masturbation, the sports of naked boys in bed together"—he encountered at Harrow. In 1858, his last year at the school, he denounced his headmaster, Dr. Vaughan, to his father for preaching "purity" while having affairs with the boys under his charge. Vaughan resigned after the elder Symonds threatened to publicize his transgressions. The younger Symonds, whose friends shunned him when they learned what he had done, was never able to resolve the ambivalent remorse he felt in the wake of the episode.

Beginning in childhood, Symonds had a recurring dream that he was in a room surrounded by naked sailors, but it was not until he was 18 that, reading Plato (see **387 B.C.**), he began to acknowledge the implications of his lusting after other men. Around the same time, he had his first relationship, an affair with a younger choirboy he met at Harrow. Although he bowed to his father's advice and broke with the boy, he fell in love with another choirboy, Alfred Brooke, while studying at Oxford. In 1863, after years of worshiping Brooke at a distance and writing reams of anguished love poetry, he traveled to SWITZERLAND to seek treatment for his deteriorating mental and physical health. The following year, in an attempt to "divert [his] passions from the burning channel in which they flowed for Alfred Brooke," he married Catherine North, an Englishwoman he had met in Switzerland. The couple had three daughters, and Symonds avoided entanglements with men for years, channeling his thwarted emotions into poetry—and changing the GENDER of revealing pronouns when his verse was published. Later, he found more satisfaction in furtive but exhilarating encounters with men he met in London parks, and after 1880, when he retired to Switzerland to treat his tuberculosis, he had sexual relationships with a number of Swiss peasants. He was also partial to Venetian gondoliers, especially one named Angelo Fusato, a darkly handsome 24-year-old to whom Symonds gave a gondola and money to help support the Venetian's girlfriend and their children.

On the intellectual front, Symonds struggled to justify and make sense of his sexuality via an extensive correspondence, begun in 1865, with WALT WHITMAN and a series of critical studies of HOMOEROTICISM among the ancient Greeks. Although Symonds idealized "Greek love," his own sexuality was in fact quite different from the edifying love of beautiful boys (see PEDERASTY) espoused by the Greeks. Since his attraction to masculine young working class men seemed closer to Whitman's "love of comrades," Symonds repeatedly pestered Whitman for confirmation that the American poet's concept of "adhesiveness" between men had a physical, i.e., sexual, dimension. Finally, in 1890, Whitman, near death and probably surrounded by curious onlookers, rebuffed him with a letter claiming Symonds had misread him and that he was actually the lusty father of a widely scattered brood of illegitimate children.

In 1883, Symonds published *A Problem in Greek Ethics* in an edition of ten copies "privately printed for the Author's use." Probably the first scholarly work on homosexuality published in the UNITED KINGDOM, the book was not available to a wide reading audience until after Symonds's death, when HAVELOCK ELLIS, who began corresponding and collaborating with Symonds in the early 1890s, made it part of his groundbreaking *Sexual Inversion* (1896 in German; 1897 in English; second edition without acknowledgment of Symonds's contribution due to protests from his heirs).

In addition to his defense of homoeroticism and years of fighting British laws forbidding "gross indecency" between men, Symonds's contributions to the construction of a modern gay identity include an influential biography of MICHELANGELO, in which he was among the first to "reclaim" the homoeroticism of the artist, as well as the first translations into English of Michelangelo's love poetry.

Symonds's revealing memoirs were finally published in 1984.

✧ Phyllis Grosskurth, *The Woeful Victorian: A Biography of John Addington Symonds* (1964).

✧ *The Memoirs of John Addington Symonds: The Secret Homosexual Life of a Leading Nineteenth-Century Man of Letters,* edited by Phyllis Grosskurth (1984).

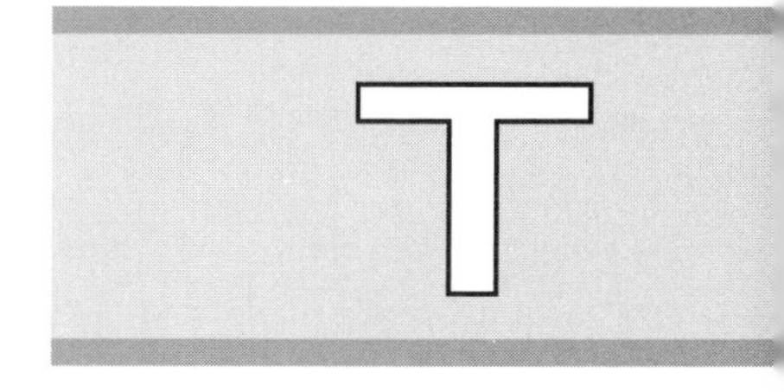

Tahiti, see PACIFIC ISLANDS

Taiwan, see CHINA

Tchaikovsky, Pyotr Ilyich
(1840–1893)

Russian composer. The son of upper-middle-class provincial parents, Tchaikovsky showed signs of extraordinary musical talent as a child but was forced by a practical father to study for a career in the government bureaucracy. After his mother died when he was 14, he turned to composition for solace. He studied at the St. Petersburg Conservatory and then taught there from 1865 until 1878, when a rich widow, Nadezhda von Meck, granted him an allowance that made it possible for him to compose full-time. By the time of his death 15 years later, he had composed six symphonies, four concerti, the fantasy *Romeo and Juliet,* the ballets *Swan Lake* (1876), *Sleeping Beauty* (1889), and *The Nutcracker* (1892), in addition to ten operas, including *Eugene Onegin* (1879) and *The Queen of Spades* (1890).

Based on his own diaries and accounts left by his friends and his older brother Modest (who was also famous for his affairs with men), Tchaikovsky is remembered as a passionate romantic prone to both debilitating, sometimes suicidal, attacks of depression and bursts of manically productive creativity. He had an unsuccessful affair with one woman and a disastrous, short-lived marriage with another. He was deeply, even obsessively, in love with his nephew, Vladimir "Bob" Davydov, to whom he dedicated his masterpiece, the Symphony no. 6 in B Minor (*Pathétique*), but he also had relationships with several other men. He died, probably of cholera, at the age of 53, shortly after the first public performance of the *Pathétique.*

Biographers, gay and straight, have found it difficult to resist portraying Tchaikovsky as either the classic "unappreciated genius" or the epitome of the guilt-ridden "tortured homosexual" (such as in Ken Russell's 1970 film *The Music Lovers,* which was publicized as "the story

Pyotr Ilyich Tchaikovsky.

of a homosexual who married a nymphomaniac!"). Although there are elements of truth in both these characterizations, they are contradicted by a host of less frequently noted facts. A few of his compositions were indeed unpopular with the public, but they were consistently acclaimed by more knowledgeable friends and colleagues, who ranged from Gustav Mahler to ETHEL SMYTH—not to mention the Tsar himself, who granted him a pension in appreciation of his talent. Tchaikovsky no doubt yearned for the stability and respectability of marriage, but his diaries show he nonetheless enjoyed a lively, varied sex life. Moreover, as an increasing number of historians have begun to point out, 19th-century Russia was in many respects more tolerant of same-sex love than most 20th-century societies.

Musicologist Malcolm H. Brown has documented a change in critical appraisal of Tchaikovsky once knowledge of his homosexuality became widespread. Without making direct reference to his sexuality, writers began using words like "hysterical," "effeminate," and "structurally weak" to describe his music.

Meanwhile, in the USSR, Tchaikovsky's sexuality was ignored or even heterosexualized by Soviet writers until 1978, when musicologist Aleksandra Orlova claimed Tchaikovsky had been ordered to commit suicide by a court of honor composed of former schoolmates who were outraged by his having "corrupted" an aristocratic young man. Although experts, including gay historian Simon Karlinsky and author Nina Berberova, have attacked Orlova's contentions as "a web of fantasies," some gay writers have used the story to add pathos to their portrayal of Tchaikovsky as a gay martyr.

✧ Nina Berberova, Malcolm H. Brown, and Simon Karlinsky, "Tchaikovsky's Death Was *Not* a Suicide," *High Fidelity* (August 1981).

Teenagers, see YOUTH, GAY AND LESBIAN.

Television

Entertainment and information medium whose dominance of popular culture makes it a bellwether of the progress of the GAY AND LESBIAN RIGHTS MOVEMENT. The fact that the 1996–97 U.S. television season began with an unprecedented 22 lesbian and gay characters in major network shows was taken as proof of a new, higher level of acceptance of gay men and lesbians among ordinary Americans. Even more dramatic was the April 1997 debut on *Ellen* of the first gay or lesbian leading character to be played by an openly gay actor.

Although many commentators marveled at the sudden visibility of lesbians and gay men on the country's television network programs in the 1990s, American programming has lagged decades behind shows in other countries. In GERMANY, for example, the pioneering gay director ROSA VON PRAUNHEIM premiered documentaries with gay themes on national television as early as 1969. Television in AUSTRALIA and even the UNITED KINGDOM, despite criticism from conservative politicians and tabloids, was even more adventurous. Gay characters appeared on the U.K.'s popular *EastEnders* as early as 1987. By 1996, the show had a total of four major gay male characters.

In the first decades after the invention of the medium, homosexuality was mostly a taboo topic on U.S. television. Stereotypical characters were seldom more than easy targets for humor. With the increasing visibility of gay men and lesbians after STONEWALL, a few programs dared to treat the subject more seriously, although the accent was most often on the tragic aspects of gay lives, such as the loss of children and premature death.

Gay and lesbian media activists worked hard to change the medium's treatment of homosexuality. Comedian and talk show host

Barbara Gittings (far left), Lily Vincenz (third from left), Barbara Love (far right), and others discussed lesbian issues on The David Susskind Show "Women Who Love Women—Seven Lesbians," October 10, 1971.

Johnny Carson was zapped by activists in March 1973 for telling "fag" jokes. Over the years, the situation changed so dramatically that in 1991, British actor Alec McCowen refused to allow *This Is Your Life* to feature him until the producers agreed to mention his relationship with the late actor Geoffrey Burridge.

Major firsts in American television history include: the **July 13, 1984**, Showtime cable telecast of *Brothers,* the first time an American show featured a sympathetic gay recurring character; *An Early Frost* (1985), an Emmy-award production about a gay man with AIDS; and the coming OUT of Ellen Morgan on *Ellen* on April 30, 1997, just after Ellen DeGeneres, who plays the part, came out publicly herself.

➤ Also see ACTORS/ACTING; FILM AND VIDEO, GAY, LESBIAN, AND QUEER.

✧ Keith Howes, *Broadcasting It: An Encyclopedia of Homosexuality on Film, Radio and TV in the U.K., 1923–1993* (1993).

Dan Butler in his role on Frasier.

Thailand

No laws against consensual adult same-sex relations. AGE OF CONSENT *is 18, or 15 with parental permission. Small gay and lesbian organizations and publications. Active gay male bar scene in Bangkok, Chiang Mai, Pattaya, and Phuket.*

The Thais have an international reputation for tolerance of most forms of sexual activity. Same-sex relations have never been against the law, and, in part because of the influence of BUDDHISM, which is practiced by over 90 percent of Thais, sex is viewed as an enjoyable and natural part of life. Nevertheless, very few Thais openly identify themselves as "gay" and even fewer as "lesbian." While sex is not seen as a sin, unconventional relationships can bring on social opprobrium and result in a deep sense of shame for participants. Thai newspapers and magazines frequently titillate readers with gossip about the sex lives of gay and lesbian celebrities, including highly placed government officials. In addition to the fear of mockery, family pressure to marry keeps most lesbians and gay men closeted by Western standards. Traditionally, the most open group has been *kathoey,* male transvestites who take the insertive role in sex. Although tolerated, they have a lower social status than "complete men," who may or may not have sex with them.

Sex tourism, which began in the late 1950s and exploded during the Vietnam War, led to the development of gay BARS offering male prostitutes, many of them in their teens, to foreign tourists. Today, Bangkok has dozens of these but also a small but increasing number of saunas and bars where sex-for-pay is discouraged and where the clientele is mostly Thai. The AIDS crisis has also helped mobilize gay and lesbian Thais to mount safe sex campaigns, which in turn have increased their visibility. One breakthrough was the appearance in the 1990s of an openly gay dance troupe called Purple String, which used traditional Thai dance forms to educate sex workers and gay men about SAFE(R) SEX. A lesbian group, Anjaree, was formed in the late 1980s.

- ✧ Peter A. Jackson, *Dear Uncle Go: Male Homosexuality in Thailand* (1995).
- ✧ Kanokwan Tarowa, "Thailand," in *Unspoken Rules: Sexual Orientation and Women's Human Rights,* edited by Rachel Rosenbloom (1996).

Theater

Theater has typically been literally decades ahead of HOLLYWOOD in its frankness. As early as the 1920s (see **12/19/1922**), openly homosexual themes were treated in dramatic productions despite sometimes dire consequences (see, for example, **3/6/1923**). At the same time, it was not until the development of off Broadway (see **12/1958**) that gay male theater began to become widespread.

Specifically lesbian theater in the U.S.—in the sense of work by, about, and, at least in part, for lesbians—began with experimental work inspired by the women's movement of the 1970s. With only a few exceptions—such as JANE CHAMBERS's landmark play, *Last Summer at Bluefish Cove* (1980)—lesbian theater has remained apart from the commercial theater. Wilhelmina Paulin's *Mom, I'm Gay* (off-off-Broadway, 1988) was, according to *Entertainment Weekly,* the first New York production to center on a black lesbian. New York City's WOW Cafe Theatre, founded by actor and writer Lois Weaver, has helped bring lesbian-themed productions to broader audiences. In addition, a specifically Lesbian Theater Project was formed, also in New York City, in April 1994.

Gay male–themed work, now common in off-Broadway and regional theater productions, has received considerably more attention. Pioneers in the genre include Joe Cino,

At one time, the mere mention of homosexuality on Broadway could land the entire cast in jail.

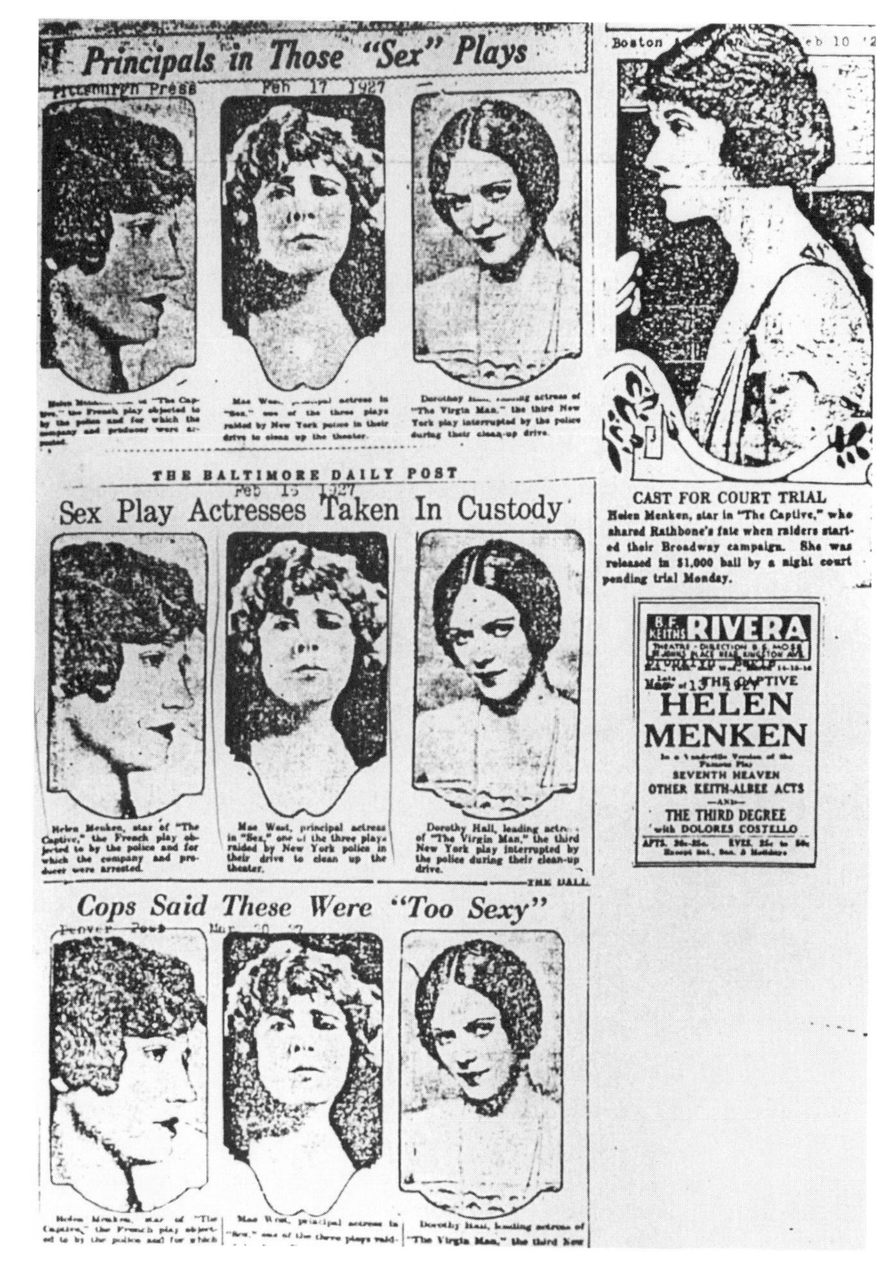
Principals in Those "Sex" Plays

Pittsburgh Press Feb 17 1927

THE BALTIMORE DAILY POST

Sex Play Actresses Taken In Custody

Helen Menken, star of "The Captive," the French play objected to by the police and for which the company and producer were arrested.

Mae West, principal actress in "Sex," one of the three plays raided by New York police in their drive to clean up the theater.

Dorothy Hall, leading actress of "The Virgin Man," the third New York play interrupted by the police during their clean-up drive.

Cops Said These Were "Too Sexy"

CAST FOR COURT TRIAL

Helen Menken, star in "The Captive," who shared Rathbone's fate when raiders started their Broadway campaign. She was released in $1,000 bail by a night court pending trial Monday.

who opened the groundbreaking Caffé Cino in 1958; John Glines, whose New York City–based Glines Theater has been behind many of the most successful gay productions since the 1970s; and CHARLES LUDLAM.

The success of off-Broadway gay plays notwithstanding, the most outstanding theatrical trend of the 20th century has been the gradual integration of gay- and lesbian-themed characters—and entire productions, such as TONY KUSHNER's *Angels in America*—into the repertory of mainstream theater.

Charles Busch (center) in his long-running hit off-Broadway play, Vampire Lesbians of Sodom.

➤ Also see ACTORS/ACTING.

✧ Kaier Curtin, *"We Can Always Call Them Bulgarians": The Emergence of Lesbians and Gay Men on the American Stage* (1987).

✧ Nicholas de Jongh, *Not in Front of the Audience: Homosexuality on Stage* (1992).

✧ *The Actor's Book of Gay and Lesbian Plays,* edited by Eric Lane and Nina Shengold (1995).

"Third Sex," see ULRICHS, KARL HEINRICH.

Thomas, Martha Carey

(1857–1935)

Pioneering U.S. educator, feminist, and social activist. Thomas was born in Baltimore, to a well-known Quaker family. Her physician father was a trustee of Johns Hopkins University and her mother was active in the Woman's Christian Temperance Union. From her TOMBOY childhood, Thomas formed an early understanding of women's struggle for equality and encountered the prevailing prejudices that denied education for women. After harassment at Johns Hopkins, she went abroad with childhood friend Mary Gwinn for graduate education, first to GERMANY and then to Zurich, where she received her summa cum laude doctorate in 1882, the first woman to receive one there. She began her career at Bryn Mawr, the celebrated women's college, in 1884 as the first dean, and later in 1894 as its first woman president. During her 28 years as president, she brought academic rigor into women's education at a time when education was considered unhealthy or biologically impossible for women and finishing schools were the norm. She strove for academic excellence, including faculty screening, demanding admittance exams, graduate programs, required course sequences, and foreign languages.

Thomas and her "first wife," the outstanding educator Gwinn, fictionally appear in GERTRUDE STEIN's early novel *Fernhurst,* written late in 1904 amid the public scandal of Gwinn's triangular relationship with a married faculty member. Unlike in real life, Stein's version keeps the two women together.

Gwinn and Thomas's relationship has been reviewed by lesbian historians for its insights on the changing social perceptions of women's homoerotic ROMANTIC FRIENDSHIPS, especially those developing from "smashes," "raves," or schoolgirl crushes throughout the 19th century between students or a teacher and a student. As the writings of the sexologists RICHARD VON KRAFFT-EBING and HAVELOCK ELLIS gained circulation, naïveté toward these women's pairings gave way to suspicion of inversion or homosexuality, threatening the all-girls school environment. Thomas's journals and letters reveal her lifelong attempts to understand her own sexuality.

After Gwinn married, Mary Elizabeth Garrett (1854–1915) moved into the "deanery" and lived there with Thomas from 1905 until 1915, rekindling campus rumors about their lesbianism. An heiress to the B&O Railroad fortune, Garrett was a philanthropist and, while not an academic, expanded educational opportunities for women. In 1885, she founded, with Thomas and other Baltimore women, the Bryn Mawr School for Girls, a college preparatory school. Garrett also stipulated equal admissions for women to the new medical school at Johns Hopkins in exchange for her generous gifts in 1893. In addition, the women's suffrage movement benefited from her money and social position. She and Thomas worked with many leading suffragists, including Susan B. Anthony, Julia Ward Howe, and Dr. Anna Howard Shaw, and knew influential lesbian educators, including Mary Wooley and Miss Marks, Edith Hamilton and Doris Reid, Vida Dutton Scudder and Florence Converse, and KATHERINE LEE BATES and Katherine Coman. Upon her death in 1915, Garrett left Thomas her estate.

✧ Carroll Smith-Rosenberg, *Disorderly Conduct: Visions of Gender in Victorian America* (1989).

✧ Helen Lefkowitz Horowitz, *The Power and Passion of M. Carey Thomas* (1994).

Thompson, Karen, see KOWALSKI, SHARON.

Tilden, Bill

(William Tatem Tilden II; 1893–1953)

U.S. tennis star, writer. A Philadelphia native, Tilden was one of the best-loved athletes of his time. He dominated tennis during the 1920s despite having his right middle finger amputated at the upper joint in 1922. The first American man to win a Wimbledon singles championship (1920, 1921, 1930; doubles, 1927), he was the number-one-ranked amateur player every year from 1920 through 1929. He turned pro in December 1930 and set an unprecedented 340–147 win/loss record over two decades of competition. He also wrote a nationally syndicated column, tennis books, short stories, a novel, and plays; published and edited *Racquet* magazine; and acted on Broadway, once in a play of his own.

In 1947, Tilden was jailed for 7½ months and ordered to undergo psychiatric treatment for "contributing to the delinquency" of a 14-year-old boy. He was arrested again in 1949 for violating parole and jailed for 10 months. The University of Pennsylvania quietly removed

Bill Tilden.

his picture and trophies from its display collection, but despite the adverse publicity, his fans remained loyal: a 1950 Associated Press poll named him top athlete for the first half of the 20th century by a vote of 310–32.

- Bill Tilden, *My Story: A Champion's Memoirs* (1948).
- Frank Delford, *Big Bill Tilden: The Triumphs and the Tragedy* (1976).

Tobin, Kay

(née Kay Lahusen; 1930–)

U.S. activist, photographer, writer. Born and raised in Ohio by her grandparents, Tobin came to terms with her sexual orientation in high school, despite a CHRISTIAN SCIENCE upbringing and considering herself a puritanical "churchy type." After she left Ohio State University, her first relationship ended traumatically because her lover feared the isolation and stigma of a lesbian life, a situation Tobin resolved to fight. Following her move to Boston in 1956, she began working as a reference librarian for the *Christian Science Monitor.* When she later sought professional help to understand her homosexuality and find other lesbians, the psychiatrist gave her a copy of THE LADDER and directed her to the New York chapter of the DAUGHTERS OF BILITIS (DOB). In 1961, at a DOB picnic in Rhode Island, she met BARBARA GITTINGS, the chapter founder and president, and began their personal and activist life together.

Tobin assisted Gittings with DOB business and contributed writing, PHOTOGRAPHY, and editorial help to *The Ladder.* Her photography included the earliest pickets of the mid-1960s in Washington, D.C., and Philadelphia, activities of the AMERICAN LIBRARY ASSOCIATION's Gay Task Force, and other events through the 1970s. Perhaps the first openly lesbian photographer in the U.S., her photographs provide a unique chronicle of early gay and lesbian ACTIVISM. While living in New York, Tobin worked in Craig Rodwell's landmark Oscar Wilde Memorial Bookshop and became one of the founding members of GAY ACTIVIST ALLIANCE, covering its actions for Lige Clarke and Jack Nichols's important publication *Gay.*

In 1972 she published *The Gay Crusaders* with RANDY WICKER to reflect the new gay militancy in America through a collection of profile-essays of 15 proud gay and lesbian leaders. With echoes of DOB, in 1973, Tobin went on to cofound Gay Women's Alternative in New York City with others, including Marge Barton, Batya Bauman, Vivien Clemons, Jeanne Perry, and Pat Woods (the group is still active), and, with Craig Rodwell, organized Gay People in Christian Science (GPICS) in 1978. After moving to Philadelphia, Tobin remained active with the Homophile Action League and her own gay realtors organization.

- Donn Teal, *The Gay Militants: How Gay Liberation Began in America, 1969–1971* (1971).
- Eric Marcus, *Making History: The Struggle for Gay and Lesbian Equal Rights, 1945–1990* (1992).

Toklas, Alice B., see STEIN, GERTRUDE.

Tomboy

Term usually referring to a young girl who assumes the dress, activities, and manner of a boy. The term is used in a positive, negative, or neutral descriptive manner but typically signals GENDER variance. Tomboys commonly have athletic ability and favor rough outdoor play with boys who share their interests and possess a sense of freedom and independence difficult to find with girl peers. Some psychologists consider tomboyism a form of gender rebellion in which girls, recognizing the socially privileged status of male/masculine, adopt a compensatory status of female/masculine. Once called a "temporary visa to male territory," tomboyism is usually considered "acceptable" in the U.S. until a girl reaches the age of 12 or 13. Tomboy identity can be experienced by girls who develop into either lesbian or heterosexual adults; among lesbians, however, it is commonly linked to an adult BUTCH identity.

Tomboy identities cross racial, ethnic, class, and regional lines with only slight cultural variations. In the Philippines, for example, the English word "tomboy" (or T-bird, *babaeng bakla*—"woman faggot") is used to refer to women who in the U.S. would be called "butch"; "fems" are called "lesbians." As writer Marivic Desquitado explains, "Lesbians are those women who fall in love with tomboys."

Lynne Yamaguchi and Karen Barber note that, according to the *Oxford English Dictionary,* "tom" is cited as a generic term for male at least as early as 1592. By the 17th century, the term was already being used to connote female transgression of gender roles. Later, in 1886, "tomboyade" meant an escapade in the manner of a tomboy. JUDY GRAHN finds "tom" in England as a slang word for lesbian and earlier as a 13th-century "spirit-based" word for a particular British witch accused of having a possessed gray cat named Tomboy. A perceptive early portrait can also be found in *The Autobiography of a Tomboy* (1900) by Jeannette L. Gilder.

Many lesbians remember their "tomboy youths" as a charmed and self-affirming escape from the social imperative of femininity. Athlete BABE DIDRIKSON, despite attempting as an adult to "switch over to being feminine," remained the quintessential tomboy throughout her life. Once, after listing a dozen sports she was adept at, she was asked by an exasperated New York reporter, "Is there anything at all you don't play?" "Yeah," Babe replied, "dolls."

- Marivic R. Desquitado, "A Letter from the Philippines," in *The Persistent Desire: A Femme-Butch Reader,* edited by Joan Nestle (1992).
- *Lesbians and Psychoanalysis: Revolutions in Theory and Practice,* edited by Judith M. Glassgold and Suzanne Iasenza (1995).
- *Tomboys! Tales of Dyke Derring-Do,* edited by Lynne Yamaguchi and Karen Barber (1995).

Tom of Finland

(Touko Laaksonen; 1920–1991)

Finnish artist. The child of two schoolteachers, Laaksonen grew up in a cultured household in a semirural area of southwestern FINLAND. From earliest childhood, he was attracted to the muscular loggers and fieldworkers he saw near his home, as well as virtually any man in a uniform (even bus drivers), and he began drawing them at an early age. In 1939, he moved to Helsinki to study ADVERTISING art. Drafted into the Finnish Army in 1940, he spent the next four years surrounded by men in uniform, including German soldiers whose tight-fitting uniforms and brazen cult of masculinity were a source of inspiration for much of his later art. After the war, he pursued a successful career in advertising while drawing male erotica on the side. In 1957, his work began to appear in gay male magazines like BOB MIZER's *Physique Pictorial,* and he acquired an international reputation as "Tom of Finland," a name Mizer invented. Although his work had to conform to the censorship restrictions of the period, the "Tom of Finland man" was already a fully matured archetype: brash, muscular, macho but good-natured, sexually insatiable.

In the 1960s, as male-oriented photographic PORNOGRAPHY became more prevalent, Laaksonen kept his drawings competitive by creating increasingly more imaginative sexual fantasies and ever more gigantic endowments. His character Kake (pronounced "cake," the word means "BUTCH" in Finnish) starred in dozens of extraordinarily popular novellas that were graphic in every sense of the word. In later years, Laaksonen's work was more varied, although it continued to be marked by mythic proportions, lusty spontaneity, and a uniquely sly sense of humor.

Instantly recognized by millions of people around the world, the Tom of Finland man provided not only sexual entertainment but also a masculine role model for generations of gay boys and men. Historians and archivists of the leather and S/M scenes see his work as one of the major influences on the growth of these sexual SUBCULTURES. Other critics see an even broader impact in the fact that his characters are among the first men in any medium to transcend "top"/"bottom" role adherence and derive pleasure, often in the same sexual encounter, from both "active" and "passive" positions. (Sexual reciprocity has been cited as one of the factors that distinguishes the late-20th-century concept of "gayness" from the typically role-restricted male-male SEX of previous eras. See CONSTRUCTIONISM VS. ESSENTIALISM.) Still others point to his ability to inject affection and emotional bonding into the most extreme sexual situations as a humanizing influence on the gay male subculture.

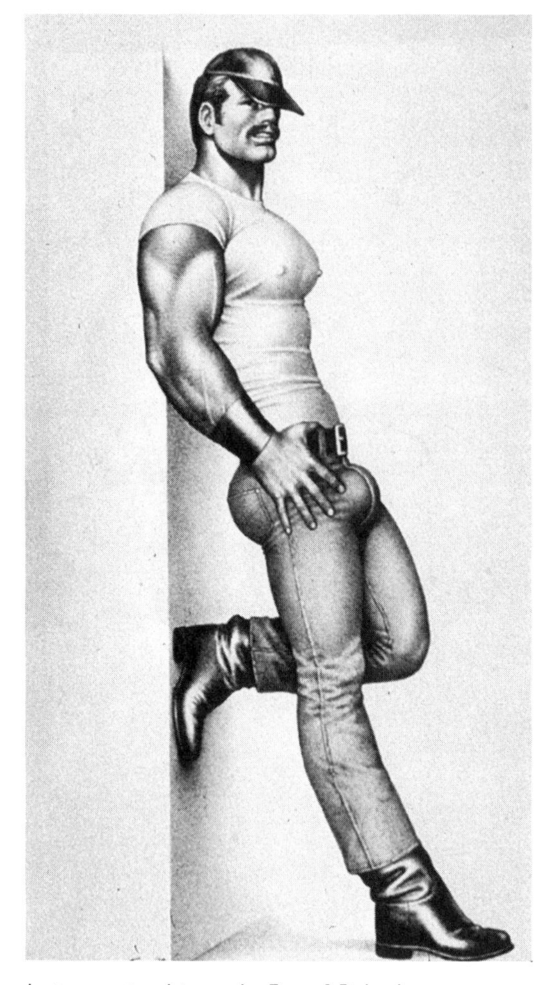

An international icon: the Tom of Finland man.

Perhaps as many as 5,000 different Tom of Finland pictures survive in collections around the world. In 1986, the Tom of Finland Foundation was formed in Los Angeles to preserve and promote his work and to fight piracy, which plagued the artist throughout his career.

- *Tom of Finland Retrospective* (1988).
- *Tom of Finland Retrospective II* (1991).
- F. Valentine Hooven III, *Tom of Finland: His Life and Work* (1993).

Tonga, see PACIFIC ISLANDS.

Transsexuals

Persons whose GENDER identity differs from what is culturally associated with their biological sex at birth. More specifically, persons who have had an operation to change their congenital sex. "Transgendered" is increasingly used to describe persons who assert a gender identity different from their biological sex but choose not to undergo sex reassignment surgery. Transsexual and transgendered activists alike emphasize that their gender identities are not necessarily linked to socially expected sexual orientations: an ever growing number (although still a minority) of post-operative male-to-female (MTF) and female-to-male (FTM) transsexuals become lesbians (MTL) or gay men (FTGM) respectively; a smaller number self-identify as bisexuals. Activists also maintain that, despite common stereotypes, transsexuals and transgendered people do not by definition "hate" the bodies they were born in. Rather, they feel most themselves when their appearance matches the gender identity of the opposite sex.

The first true sex change, a male-to-female reassignment, was accomplished by Dr. Felix Abraham in GERMANY in 1931. The term "transsexual," however, was not coined until 1949, when D. O. Cauldwell used it in an article that appeared in the popular magazine *Sexology*. Widespread awareness of sex reassignment operations began with the publicity given Christine (né George) Jorgensen, an American who traveled to Denmark for surgery in 1951.

More than 30,000 people have undergone sex reassignment surgery. At one time, doctors reported that congenital males were eight times more likely to seek sex reassignment than congenital females, but today most researchers believe the ratio is roughly equivalent, perhaps due to advances in female-to-male surgical techniques. As the surgery has grown more common—and an increasing

The 1990s saw a rise in transgender activism.

number of studies have demonstrated that almost all post-operative transsexuals lead happy, satisfied lives—medical approval for the operation has become much easier to obtain than in the past.

As with sexual orientation and gender identification in general, no one really understands why some people describe themselves as transsexuals or transgendered and others do not. Researchers such as John Money have found no evidence that transsexuals are significantly different from non-transsexuals anatomically, hormonally, or chromosomally; however, a study in 1995 suggested that a predisposition to transsexuality may be genetically coded. Contrary to popular belief, the actions and attitudes of parents also seem to have little connection to the phenomenon.

Transsexuals and transgendered persons report that they face almost as much misunderstanding and hostility from lesbians and gay men as from heterosexuals. In the 1970s, several lesbian feminist critiques described transsexualism as a "final solution" conceived to "neuter" women. Transsexual lesbians have frequently been barred from participation in women's MUSIC festivals. Nevertheless, small-scale studies conducted in the NETHERLANDS indicate that MTLs and FTGMs are as well adjusted as "congenital" lesbians and gay men.

✧ Kate Bornstein, *Gender Outlaw: On Men, Women, and the Rest of Us* (1994).

✧ Vernon A. Rosario II, "Trans (Homo) Sexuality?: Double Inversion, Psychiatric Confusion, and Hetero-Hegemony," in *Queer Studies,* edited by Brett Beemyn and Mickey Eliason (1996).

✧ Leslie Feinberg, *Transgender Warriors* (1996).

Transvestites, see CROSS-DRESSING.

Trinidad and Tobago, see CARIBBEAN.

Troubridge, Una

(née Margot Elena Gertrude Taylor; 1887–1963)

English sculptor, singer, translator. Raised in London, she showed a talent for ART as a young girl and was awarded a scholarship to the Royal College of Art at the age of 13. She soon began receiving commissions and set up her own studio. On the side, she was infatuated with the THEATER, its costumes, and her own theatrical heroine, Sarah Bernhardt.

After her father's death in 1907, she found financial support in a marriage with Ernest Troubridge, a naval officer nearly 25 years her senior. They had one daughter, Andrea Theodosia. In 1913, she found herself blocked artistically, producing little except for a bust of Vaslav Nijinsky, and sought psychological help for depression and marital problems.

Troubridge met RADCLYFFE HALL in 1915. Although Hall was then the lover of her cousin, "Ladye" Mabel Batten, she and Hall fell in love and began an affair, which became a lifelong marriage after Batten's death the following year. She obtained a legal separation from her husband in 1919 and withstood his attempts to gain custody of their daughter.

She stood with Hall through the social and personal attacks that followed in the wake of THE WELL OF LONELINESS (1928). Hall had consulted her before writing the book because she knew Troubridge would "be included in any condemnation." Troubridge was proud to recall her response: "I told her to write what was in her heart, that so far as any effect upon myself was concerned, I was sick to death of ambiguities, and only wished to be known for what I was and to dwell with her in the palace of truth." Troubridge was characteristically supportive although she herself was busy reading manuscripts for publishers, reviewing books for *The Sunday Times,* and translating *La*

Maison de Claudine, COLETTE's first book to appear in English. She even came up with the title *The Well of Loneliness,* which Hall had originally intended to call *Stephen.*

Troubridge stayed in the relationship despite Hall's later affairs, including one with Evguenia Souline that lasted nine years. A convert to Catholicism, Troubridge was once asked how she and Hall handled confession. She replied: "There was nothing to confess."

✧ Richard Ormrod, *Una Troubridge: The Friend of Radclyffe Hall* (1984).

Tsui, Kitty

(Kit Fan Tsui; 1952–)

Hong Kong–born U.S. poet, short story writer, journalist. Raised in Hong Kong and England, Tsui immigrated with her family to San Francisco in 1968. She came OUT in the early 1970s and began working as an activist. Together with Barbara Noda and Z. Wong, she helped build visibility for the ASIAN-AMERICAN community with the publication of *Coming Out: We Are Here in the Asian Community: A Dialogue with Three Asian Women* (1979). She was one of the founders of the Unbound Feet and Unbound Feet Three collectives, edited the collective's poetry anthology in 1981, and later served as coeditor of *New Phoenix Rising: The Asian/Pacific Lesbian Newsletter of the San Francisco Bay Area.* She has since moved to Indianapolis, Indiana. A recovering alcohol and drug abuser turned bodybuilder, she won a bronze medal in physique competition at GAY GAMES II in 1986 and a gold medal at Gay Games III in 1990.

Tsui's poetry and short stories have appeared in a number of publications and anthologies. She has also published collections of her own poetry, *The Words of a Woman Who Breathes Fire* (1983), and erotic prose, *Breathless* (1996). Tsui's most quoted poems use direct, conversational language (including an occasional Cantonese phrase, often quoted from her loving grandmother, Kwan Ying Lin) and everyday situations to construct revealing self-portraits or to forge, in her own image, a Chinese-American lesbian "heritage."

Turing, Alan Mathison

(1912–1954)

English mathematician and cybernetics theorist. Turing excelled in science as a child and had already made groundbreaking contributions to mathematics by the time he graduated from King's College, Cambridge. After earning a Ph.D. at Princeton University, he returned to the UNITED KINGDOM shortly before WORLD WAR II and joined a team working to decode German military communications. A device he helped invent allowed the British to crack codes produced by the German Enigma machines, giving the Allies a decisive intelligence advantage throughout the war.

Turing continued his pioneering work on computer theory and design after the war. His contributions to the Automatic Computing Engine (ACE; 1945–1948) and the Manchester Automatic Digital Machine (MADAM; 1949) as well as his innovative speculations on artificial intelligence have earned him recognition as one of the founders of modern cybernetics. In particular, his conception of a "Universal Turing machine" laid the theoretical foundation for others to design computers as we know them today.

In 1952, Arnold Murray, his 19-year-old boyfriend, helped friends break into and burglarize Turing's home. Turing complained to the police and naïvely affirmed that he and Murray had had a sexual relationship. As a result, he and Murray were both prosecuted and found guilty of "gross indecency." To avoid a PRISON sentence, Turing consented to undergo a year of psychiatric treatment and "organotherapy," a regimen of female hormone injections intended to eradicate his libido. As the months went by, he became impotent, began to develop breasts, reported a loss of mental clarity, and, understandably, grew severely depressed.

Turing recovered from the treatment and was allowed to travel abroad twice in 1953. He began having sexual liaisons with men again but remained despondent. On June 7, 1954, he died after eating an apple that had been injected with potassium cyanide. He was 41.

Andrew Hodges's biography argues that Turing was a victim of relentless persecution by the British security establishment and that his death was a suicide. His life story inspired Hugh Whitemore's play *Breaking the Code* (1986).

✧ Andrew Hodges, *Alan Turing: The Enigma* (1983).

Turkey

No mention of homosexuality in the country's penal code, but prohibitions of "indecency" and "offenses against public morality" frequently used to harass gay men and lesbians, especially rights activists, TRANSSEXUALS, *and other* GENDER *nonconformists. Small but active lesbian and gay male rights groups, and social scene for gay men in Istanbul, Bodrum, and a few other cities.*

Turkish scholar and activist Arslan Yüsgün estimates that there are at least 600,000 gay men and lesbians in Istanbul alone, yet the country lags far behind its neighbors to the west in virtually every aspect of lesbian and gay rights. Progress has been frustrated by a stubbornly repressive police force and the rise of fundamentalist ISLAM as a social and political force. Despite increasingly close economic ties to the liberal democracies of Europe, national and local government officials frequently flaunt international standards of justice and humane treatment with impunity. In July 1993, for example, the governor of Istanbul ordered hotels not to register foreign guests arriving for what was scheduled to be the country's first gay and lesbian PRIDE CELEBRATION. Authorities subsequently apprehended and expelled 28 foreigners who had come to participate in the celebration, and arrested 3 of the organizers of the event. Protests from abroad fell on deaf ears. The celebration never took place.

Although no LAW officially prohibits consensual same-sex intercourse between adults, openly gay men and transvestites are routinely harassed by police and on occasion subjected to imprisonment and torture by authorities. One survey of 223 Turkish gay men found that 61 percent had "experienced humiliating and inhuman police behavior." As a result, most gay men are careful not to attract attention to themselves outside a couple of gay GHETTOS in Istanbul, where many work in the arts or in stereotypical gay professions like hairdressing. Even otherwise privileged gay men face harsh treatment. When Serkan Altan, the teenage son of a famous Turkish chanteuse, came OUT in the early 1990s, he was disowned by his mother, and arrested and physically abused by the police. He subsequently sought asylum in the United States.

Turkish lesbians are even less visible than their male counterparts. Besides being largely isolated from one another, they are often forced into arranged marriages, especially in rural areas. The first lesbian advocacy group, Sisters of Venus, was formed in 1994 by 3 women in Istanbul. It had slightly over 20 members in 1996.

History

European moralists and gay historians alike have long associated traditional Turkey and the Ottoman Empire with rampant homosexuality, yet most of the examples they give—ranging from pre-Islamic shamans who were forbidden from having sex with women to rapes of male captives and special harems for attractive slave boys—are more typical of CIRCUMSTANTIAL HOMOSEXUALITY than anything approaching a modern gay or lesbian identity.

PEDOPHILIA and PEDERASTY flourished during the reigns of a number of Ottoman sultans and among military groups such as the Janissaries. Peoples conquered by the Ottomans have left numerous accounts of mass rapes of boys and young men, and of children as young as 8 being abducted to serve as slaves and to work in brothels. The Ottoman Empire was also famous for its eunuchs, castrated slaves who often rose to positions of considerable power in the court. Lesbian relationships were considered common in the harems, where most women led cloistered lives.

Same-sex desire is also a common motif in traditional Turkish LITERATURE. Sufi poets in particular used homoerotic imagery to symbolize spiritual love.

Closer to modern times, some historians claim that entire sections of 19th-century Constantinople were famous as gathering places for men primarily attracted to boys and other men. In the 20th century, despite increasing police harassment, Istanbul continued to be known for its gay BATHS and brothels.

Efforts to form a Turkish GAY LIBERATION movement were repeatedly thwarted by authorities. A breakthrough occurred in 1986, when Arslan Yüsgün managed to publish the first comprehensive book on homosexuality in Turkey, past and present. Repeatedly reprinted, the book contained the first objective descriptions of gay male life in Turkey, and inspired others to organize for change.

✧ Jale Simsek, "Turkey, A Country with a Long Homosexual History," in *The Second ILGA Pink Book: A Global View of Lesbian and Gay Liberation and Oppression* (1988).

✧ Arslan Yüsgün, "Homosexuality and Police Terror in Turkey," in *If You Seduce a Straight Person, Can You Make Them Gay?: Issues in Biological Essentialism versus Social Constructionism in Gay and Lesbian Identities,* edited by John P. DeCecco and John P. Elia (1993).

✧ Deniz Kilic and Gaye Uncu, "Turkey," in *Unspoken Rules: Sexual Orientation and Women's Human Rights,* edited by Rachel Rosenbloom (1996).

Turkmenistan, see CENTRAL ASIA.

U

Uganda, see AFRICA, SUB-SAHARAN.

Ulrichs, Karl Heinrich

(pseudonym: Numa Numantius; 1825–1895)

German lawyer, writer, activist. Born into a middle-class family in the kingdom of Hanover, Ulrichs studied LAW and worked in civil service before leaving the profession in 1854 to pursue a career as a writer. Exceptionally well read, he began synthesizing a theory to explain his seemingly inborn sexual attraction to other men that combined his knowledge of the classics with his understanding of embryology. By **1862**, he had devised a theory and a new name for what he was: an "Urning" (Uranian), physically male but spiritually female, or as he wrote in Latin, *"anima muliebris virili corpore inclusa"* (a feminine soul confined in a masculine body). Though criticized by later activists, Ulrichs's "third sex" theory, as elaborated in 12 monographs published from **1864** through 1869, was revolutionary: same-sex desire, according to Ulrichs, was neither sinful nor "sick"; rather, it was the result of a process that occurred before birth.

The term was derived from a passage about Aphrodite, the goddess of love, in Plato's *Symposium.* According to Pausanias, one of the symposium guests, there were actually two Aphrodites: one, "not born of woman," the motherless offspring of the god Uranus; and the second, the child of Zeus and the titaness Dione. Of the two, "Uranian" or "heavenly" Aphrodite was the elder and more noble; the second was by extension the "common" Aphrodite, in the sense that she was the goddess of love for "all the people" (*pandemos*). Pausanias asserted that most men, whose loves derived from common Aphrodite, lusted haphazardly after women and boys. A man inspired by Uranian Aphrodite, on the other hand, was not interested in women but instead fell in love only with a boy old enough to show signs of adult intelligence, and then remained nobly devoted to the younger man even after he had grown up.

Embellishing on Pausanias's account, Ulrichs termed a man-loving man an "Urning" (Uranian), a woman-loving woman an "Urningin" (German feminine form of Urning) and different-sex lovers "Dioningen" (male) or "Dioninginnen" (female). Over the years he further elaborated a complex classification system for Uranians of both sexes based on their GENDER characteristics and the gender of the persons to whom they were attracted.

Classical antecedents made these terms much more respectable than "sodomite" or "pederast," both of which Ulrichs detested. He also believed his concept was more scientific: from his studies of embryology, he knew that male and female fetuses were indistinguishable for the first two or three months after conception and that the same preorganic tissue developed into either a clitoris or a penis. Ulrichs believed that the sex drive was independent of the sex organs, that it was contained in one or more psychic "germs," and that sometimes a male germ would end up in a body equipped with female sex organs, or vice versa.

Ulrichs's theories traveled around the world in the second half of the 19th century. Americans were discussing them as early as the 1860s. By the 1880s, variations on the word "Uranian" were appearing in all the Western European languages. His writings stimulated psychiatrists like RICHARD VON KRAFFT-EBING to begin their own scientific investigations of same-sex eroticism, but most ultimately rejected his thinking in favor of disease or degeneration models. Even proponents of same-sex eroticism came to criticize his basic assumption that desire for a woman was "male" and desire for a man "female."

Popular culture, on the other hand, embraced—and sometimes continues to reflect—the theory of a "third sex" (a phrase that had been used at least as early as **1835**) and the idea of a soul or mind of one sex being "trapped" in the body of another.

Ulrichs left Germany in 1880, disturbed that the law code promulgated after German unification (see **1871**) criminalized Uranian love. He spent his last years in Italy.

Some historians, including John Lauritsen and David Thorstad, have called Ulrichs "the grandfather of gay liberation," thanks not so much to his theories as to his being probably the first person in history to come OUT as a political act (see **8/19/1867**).

➤ Also see HIRSCHFELD, MAGNUS.

✧ Hubert Kennedy, *Ulrichs: Life and Works of Karl Heinrich Ulrichs, Pioneer of the Modern Gay Movement* (1987).

Unitarian Universalist Association

Religious denomination professing no creed but noted for its members' devotion to humanitarian and ethical concerns. The present association derives from the 1961 merger of the Universalist Church of America (founded in 1779) and the American Unitarian Association (founded in 1825). It had about 140,000 members in 1997.

Unitarians/Universalists emerged in the 19th century as one of the most liberal religious groups in the Western world. Ralph Waldo Emerson, who championed the early work of WALT WHITMAN, was ordained a Unitarian minister, as was, less auspiciously, Horatio Alger: Alger was charged in 1866 with "unnatural familiarity with boys" while serving as a minister at the Unitarian Church of Brewster, Massachusetts, fled to New York, and began a career as a boys' novelist.

On **July 4, 1970**, the association's General Assembly called for "an end to all discrimination against homosexuals" and recognized the right of lesbians, gay men, and bisexuals to serve as clergy. Unitarians/Universalists for Lesbian and Gay Concerns was established in 1971 to "integrate, educate, and make gay and lesbian influence felt." The association was also the first denomination to establish an official office for gay and lesbian matters.

United Church of Canada

The second largest church and largest Protestant denomination in CANADA, with almost 2 million members in 1997. Since its formal organization in 1925, the United Church has been one of the more progressive Protestant denominations. As early as August 1980, the Church's General Council, meeting in Halifax, Nova Scotia, approved "In God's Image . . . Male and Female," a document that countenanced extramarital sex in some circumstances and recommended that lesbians and gay men be accepted for ordination. In 1981, the Church's Alberta Conference voted in favor of gay and lesbian rights, and the national body followed suit in 1984. The ordination issue, however, remained highly controversial, especially among evangelical church members. When a national convention finally approved ordination of openly lesbian and gay clergy in 1988, about 10 percent of the Church's congregations voted to secede.

United Church of Christ

Ecumenical Protestant denomination founded in 1957 with the merger of the General Council of Congregational Christian Churches with the Evangelical and Reformed Churches. The Church, which had about 1.5 million members in the United States as of 1997, has been one of the most progressive Christian denominations in supporting gay, lesbian, and bisexual rights. The Church was the first in the United States to sponsor the publication of a book of church-related essays by lesbians and gay men (*The Same Sex,* 1969), the first mainstream denomination to ordain an openly gay man (see **6/25/1972**), and, in 1983, the first to rule that a person's sexual orientation should not in itself stand in the way of ordination. By 1990, the Church had also ordained two openly lesbian ministers. Lesbian and gay church members have been critical, however, of residual HOMOPHOBIA in local congregations, where gay and lesbian ministers have had difficulty finding employment.

The United Church Coalition for Lesbian and Gay Concerns, founded in 1972, is a ministry devoted to offering support and advocacy for gay, lesbian, and bisexual church members.

✧ Gary David Comstock, "Aliens in the Promised Land?: Keynote Address for the 1986 National Gathering of the United Church of Christ's Coalition for Lesbian/Gay Concerns," in *Homosexuality and Religion,* edited by Richard Hasbany (1989).

United Kingdom

No laws against consensual same-sex relations for men over 18, women over 16, as long as they are conducted in private, outside the MILITARY, *and with no more than two participants. Prohibitions against local authorities who "promote homosexuality." Well-developed social scene and active rights organizations.*

Although 20th-century British culture is impossible to imagine without the contributions of FRANCIS BACON, E. M. FORSTER, VIRGINIA WOOLF, and dozens of other bisexual, gay, and lesbian celebrities, the United Kingdom remains, in terms of government policies at least, the most homophobic country in Western Europe. Since 1900, tens of thousands of men have been arrested for having sex with each other, a number rivaled only in GERMANY and RUSSIA; the first major lesbian novel, RADCLYFFE HALL'S THE WELL OF LONELINESS, saw its initial banning in England; and as late as 1988, Parliament went against international trends to legislate against the "promotion" of homosexuality. Yet the United Kingdom is today one of the undisputed centers of the international gay and lesbian SUBCULTURE, offering more recreational and cultural opportunities for all varieties of "queers" than any other country except the U.S.

A number of gay and lesbian organizations are active in the United Kingdom, including the Campaign for Homosexual Equality, the Scottish Homosexual Rights Group, the Northern Irish Gay Rights Association, Stonewall, and the DIRECT ACTION group OUTRAGE! Lesbian social groups include KENRIC.

Edward II was deposed and murdered for alleged misdeeds that included being excessively generous to a favorite, Piers Galveston.

History

Male-male "buggery" (anal intercourse) was first criminalized in England in **1533**. The punishment was generally hanging, although some men, such as the Earl of Castlehaven (see **1631**), were beheaded for the crime. Ireland, which was under British rule for centuries until 1922, adopted English SODOMY legislation on **November 11, 1634**, as did the American colonies later in the century.

The British continued prosecuting sodomites vigorously even as their Continental neighbors began to decriminalize same-sex eroticism in the late 18th and early 19th centuries. Despite the prosecutions, gay and lesbian subcultures had begun to develop in London and other cities by the 18th century. Women like the LADIES OF LLANGOLLEN formed ROMANTIC FRIENDSHIPS that in some cases at least were consciously sexual. Men flocked to London's "molly houses" to engage in CROSS-DRESSING, socialize with one another, and at least on one occasion (see **1725**), fight off police harassment.

By the 19th century, London had a well-documented network of "gay bars" (see **1810**), but sodomy remained a dangerous, even fatal activity. Capital punishment for sodomy was abolished and replaced by life imprisonment in **1861** and then reduced to two years' hard labor with the Labouchère Amendment of **1885**. The new legislation, however, also included acts of "gross indecency" in addition to "buggery"—in effect, making it easier to prosecute men on same-sex charges. Among the many men who suffered prosecution under the new law was OSCAR WILDE.

Around the time of Wilde's trial and conviction (see **5/25/1895**), the British public became increasingly aware—and even more intolerant—of the existence of same-sex eroticism. Police harassment and arrests steadily increased, not peaking until the 1950s. In **1952**, for example, 1,686 men were prosecuted on "gross indecency" charges. Some, like ALAN TURING, were ordered to undergo regimens of chemical castration.

Lesbian life in the United Kingdom, less visible because same-sex relations between women were not illegal and because of the Victorian reluctance to view women as sexual (see **1812**), flourished in private social networks from the 18th century on. EDITH ELLIS, ETHYL SMYTH, and Radclyffe Hall were just a few of the women who made it increasingly difficult for Britons to deny the existence of lesbians in their midst.

Although scholars like EDWARD CARPENTER had begun to advocate a gay and lesbian rights movement as early as the late 19th century, serious reform organizations did not form until the 1950s, when Parliament, alarmed by the enormous numbers of men incarcerated each year on same-sex charges, ordered the preparation of the WOLFENDEN REPORT. After almost a decade of debate, private, consensual same-sex relations between men were finally decriminalized in England and Wales on **July 27, 1967**. (Decriminalization was delayed until **July 22, 1980**, for Scotland; **October 25, 1982**, for Northern Ireland.)

Women began to organize in **1963**, when they formed the Minorities Research Group in London. HOMOPHILE groups like Kenric followed in 1965.

GAY LIBERATION spread to the United Kingdom in the months following its emergence in the U.S. The London GAY LIBERATION FRONT was meeting by the fall of 1970. PRIDE CELEBRATIONS began in London, and the city became internationally famous for its clubs and its cultural scene, which included pioneering THEATER groups like the Gay Sweatshop, which began producing gay- and lesbian-themed plays in 1975.

The 1980s saw the rise of an increasingly militant gay and lesbian rights movement all over the United Kingdom (see **11/10/1984**; **10/4/1985**; **11/13/1985**; **1/9/1988**; **2/2/1988**; **1/1989**; etc) in the face of both a conservative backlash and the spread of AIDS.

The Queen's English

American—and international—English has been enriched by dozens of terms that originated as slang among gay and lesbian Britons, including "drag," "queen" (from the Middle English *quean,* meaning "strumpet"), and "(rough) trade." Many terms, however, have never made it across the Atlantic. Some examples are given here.

British	American
contact advert	personal ad
cottage	tearoom
cottaging	cruising/making sexual contact in a tearoom
dandle queen	gay male exhibitionist
muscle Mary	fanatical bodybuilder
naff	tacky
pink pound	lesbian and gay economic power
ponce	pimp or effeminate gay man (pejorative)
pretty policeman	undercover officer who entraps gay men
rent (boy)	male sex worker
snap	makeup, especially when worn by a drag queen
snog	kiss
wank	masturbate

✧ Jeffrey Weeks, *Coming Out: Homosexual Politics in Britain from the Nineteenth Century to the Present* (1990).

✧ Stephen Jeffrey-Poulter, *Peers, Queers and Commons: The Struggle for Gay Law Reform from 1950 to the Present* (1991).

United Nations, see INTERNATIONAL LESBIAN AND GAY ORGANIZATION.

United States of America

No laws as of 1997 against private consensual same-sex relations between adults in 30 states: Alaska, California, Colorado, Connecticut, Delaware, Hawaii, Illinois, Indiana, Iowa, Kentucky,★ Maine, Montana,★ Nebraska, Nevada, New Hampshire, New Jersey, New Mexico, New York,★ North Dakota, Ohio, Oregon, Pennsylvania,★ South Dakota, Tennessee,★ Texas,★ Vermont, Washington, West Virginia, Wisconsin, Wyoming. (The asterisks indicate states in which courts have ruled law[s] barring same-sex relations unconstitutional; in the other states listed, same-sex relations were decriminalized by legislation.)

Laws against at least some forms of private consensual same-sex relations between adults in 20 states (Alabama, Arizona, Arkansas, Florida, Georgia, Idaho, Kansas, Louisiana, Maryland, Massachusetts, Michigan, Minnesota, Mississippi, Missouri, North Carolina, Oklahoma, Rhode Island, South Carolina, Texas, Utah, Virginia) the District of Columbia, Guam, Puerto Rico, and the American Virgin Islands, with maximum punishments ranging from 30 days' imprisonment and/or a fine of $500 (Arizona) to 20 years' imprisonment (Georgia, Massachusetts, Virginia).

Protection against at least some forms of discrimination in about 130 towns, cities, and counties; and in the states of California, Connecticut, Hawaii, Massachusetts, Minnesota, New Jersey, Rhode Island, Vermont, and Wisconsin.

Active rights movement and well-developed social scene in large cities and in several dozen progressive nonurban enclaves, especially college towns.

➤ Also see GAY AND LESBIAN RIGHTS MOVEMENT, U.S.; LAW; POLITICS, U.S. ELECTORAL.

Uranians, see ULRICHS, KARL HEINRICH.

Uzbekistan, see CENTRAL ASIA.

V

Van Sant, Gus

(1953–)

U.S. film- and videomaker. Van Sant began making Super-8 movies as a child and continued experimenting with FILM while studying at the Rhode Island School of Design. After working as a technician in HOLLYWOOD and on TELEVISION commercials in New York, he returned to Portland, Oregon, where his family had moved when he was a teenager, and shot his first feature, *Mala Noche* (1985), on a budget of $25,000. The story of the unrequited attraction of a clerk in a skid-row liquor store for a Mexican teenager, *Mala Noche* established Van Sant's reputation for artistic daring. He won further acclaim—and a wider audience—with *Drugstore Cowboy* (1989), a controversially nonjudgmental look at the lives of a group of 1970s junkies, and the surrealistically romantic *My Own Private Idaho* (1991), in which a narcoleptic street kid unsuccessfully pursues a fellow hustler.

Although Van Sant is one of the few well-known openly gay film directors, he has consistently refused to identify himself as an activist or his work as part of the new "queer cinema." Critics have nevertheless noted a positive gay "sensibility" in his frequently homoerotic music videos; in his handling of lesbian characters in *Even Cowgirls Get the Blues* (1994); and in shorts such as *The Discipline of DE,* an early film (c. 1981) inspired by WILLIAM BURROUGHS (who also made cameo appearances in *Drugstore Cowboy* and *Even Cowgirls Get the Blues*).

Van Vechten, Carl

(1880–1964)

U.S. writer, critic, photographer, tastemaker. Van Vechten left his hometown, Cedar Rapids, Iowa, to study at the University of Chicago and, later, to pursue a career as a gossip columnist. In New York from 1906, he quickly established himself as one of the city's most influential critics and tastemakers, championing SERGEI DIAGHILEV's Ballets Russes and other forerunners of modernism in seven influential books on ART and MUSIC (and one about cats) as well as putting together the city's most talked-about salon for Mabel Dodge, the Greenwich Village hostess. He began to write fiction in the 1920s and published his first novel, *Peter Whiffle: His Life and Works,* in 1922. In *Peter Whiffle* and six later best-selling novels, many with interlocking characters and themes, Van Vechten wrote vividly and humorously about fictional types much like himself and his friends. Some, like the Duke of Middlebottom (*The Blind Bow-Boy,* 1923), whose motto was "A thing of beauty is a boy forever," were obviously gay. Other characters, like David Westlake, the drunken socialite who is the main character of *Parties* (1930), were more ambiguously drawn.

Van Vechten and his wife, the actress Fania Marinoff, both had lively and diverse social and sex lives and included most of the era's best-known bohemians among their friends. Interested from his childhood in AFRICAN-AMERICAN music and culture, Van Vechten publicized the HARLEM RENAISSANCE in the 1920s and made late-night trips to ill-reputed Harlem clubs fashionable for New York socialites and wealthy visitors from Europe. He told his friend LANGSTON HUGHES (whose poems he persuaded Alfred A. Knopf to publish) that "now is the psychological moment when everything chic is Negro." In 1926, he alienated many of his Harlem friends with his most controversial novel, *Nigger Heaven* (1926), which some Harlemites found offensive because of both its title (inspired by a slang term for the upper balcony of a theater) and its fairly unvarnished depiction of Harlem life.

In his private life as in his novels, Van Vechten linked the nascent gay and lesbian SUBCULTURES of Greenwich Village, Harlem, and Paris. Besides Hughes, he helped promote and publish RONALD FIRBANK and GERTRUDE STEIN in the U.S. Through the 1960s, he pursued a successful third career as a photographer. A flamboyant figure throughout his life, Van Vechten was famous for setting trends: for example, he was supposedly the first man in New York to wear a wristwatch.

✧ Carl Van Vechten, *Fragments from an Unwritten Autobiography* (2 vols., 1955).

Verlaine, Paul
(1844–1896), and
Rimbaud, [Jean Nicolas] Arthur
(1854–1891)

French poets. Verlaine, an established poet and a married man, and Rimbaud, an unconventional youth who sometimes prostituted himself with older men, met and fell in love in August 1871, after Rimbaud had sent Verlaine some poems. Soon, all Paris was gossiping about their scandalous relationship. Outcasts from society, even bohemian literary circles, they drank absinthe, fought, broke up, got back together, and fought again. Meanwhile, Rimbaud managed to find the time to complete masterpieces like *Une Saison en Enfer (A Season in Hell)* and *Illuminations,* challengingly evocative works that later established him as one of the greatest and most influential modern French poets.

Arthur Rimbaud.

During a drunken quarrel in July 1873, Verlaine shot Rimbaud in the arm, made up with him, then threatened to shoot him again. Terrified, Rimbaud called out to a passing policeman, and Verlaine was arrested and sentenced to two years in PRISON. A brief reunion in 1875 ended in more fighting and a permanent separation. Verlaine made an unsuccessful attempt to repair his relationship with his wife, then left to live on his own. Drunk and debauched, Verlaine's greatest achievement of his last two decades was publishing and critiquing the works of the "late Arthur Rimbaud." Rimbaud's work, which had been mostly ignored previously, now caused a literary sensation.

Away from France but still alive, Rimbaud had in the meantime forsaken writing to survive as an adventurer and gunrunner in Ethiopia and the Middle East. There he developed bone cancer and, after returning to France in 1891, died at the age of 37. Verlaine died less than five years later.

Only a few of either writer's poems deal openly with homoerotic themes, and none of these were widely published during their lifetimes. Many critics cite allusions to Rimbaud's troubled relationship with Verlaine in his *A Season in Hell,* but the main significance of the couple for critics who acknowledge their homosexuality has been as preeminent exemplars of the outcast status of gay love. As critic Paul Schmidt writes, "They were joined in the ultimate homosexual paradox, the problem of trying to establish a relationship beyond the patterns of kinship, and within a state that is defined precisely by the denial of bonds and ties: by separateness, apartness, in-betweenness, individualization and reflexivity."

✧ Paul Schmidt, "Visions of Violence: Rimbaud and Verlaine," in *Homosexualities and French Literature: Cultural Contexts/Critical Texts,* edited by George Stambolian and Elaine Marks.

Vice Versa

Believed to be the first lesbian periodical in the U.S. Subtitled "America's Gayest Magazine," *Vice Versa* was published in Los Angeles in nine issues dated June 1947 through February 1948 (the "Valentine issue"). The publication's name was meant to suggest the "vice" of homosexuality as well as the opposite—i.e., vice versa—of a conventional straight lifestyle.

Vice Versa was dedicated "in all seriousness to those of us who will never quite be able to adapt ourselves to the iron-bound rules of Convention."

Although no bylines appeared in the publication, *Vice Versa* was written and edited by Edith Eyde, who later wrote under the pseudonym LISA BEN (an anagram for lesbian). Eyde perfectly typed each nine- to twelve-page manuscript in justified columns, using carbon paper to create a total of twelve copies. At work, her big commercial typewriter could handle the job in two six-page (one original, five copies) typings. She mailed out the finished copies to friends until one of them warned her that she could be charged with using the U.S. mail to distribute "dirty" material. She then personally handed it to friends, who in turn passed it on to other "gay gals." Eyde never charged for the publication.

Vice Versa contained news commentary, creative writing, letters, a bibliography of books of interest to lesbians, and book, movie, and THEATER reviews, all written in a colloquial, upbeat style. Many of the articles published in *Vice Versa* were later reprinted in THE LADDER.

✧ Leland Moss, "Lisa Ben," *Gaysweek* (January 23, 1978).

✧ Jonathan Ned Katz, *Gay/Lesbian Almanac* (1983).

Rodger Streitmatter, *Unspeakable: The Rise of the Gay and Lesbian Press in America* (1995).

Vidal, Gore

Eugene Luther Gore Vidal Jr.; (1925–)

U.S. writer, critic, political activist. From a patrician background, Vidal became a highly successful writer and extremely visible public figure with no formal higher education. As early as his first published novel, *Williwaw*

(1946), his work included openly gay characters. His *The City and the Pillar,* published in 1948, was in fact the first widely read American novel with gay male characters. Ahead of his time, Vidal was forced by his publishers to make the ending tragic.

Sexually attracted to both men and women, Vidal has consistently rejected the very concept of homosexuality, believing terms like "heterosexual," "homosexual," and "gay" have no real meaning other than as descriptors of types of sex acts. Nevertheless, in public Vidal has always been a vociferous advocate of sexual change and openness. As early as 1967, two years before STONEWALL, he was one of the few positive voices on a 1967 *CBS Reports* program on "homosexuals."

A prolific author of witty and iconoclastic essays as well as fiction, much of Vidal's work is of particular interest to gay and lesbian readers. *Myra Breckinridge* (1968), one of his most famous books, is an outrageous account of a TRANSSEXUAL.

✧ Gore Vidal, *Palimpsest* (1995).

Video, see FILM AND VIDEO, GAY, LESBIAN, AND QUEER.

Vietnam, see SOUTHEAST ASIA.

Violence, see DOMESTIC VIOLENCE; HATE CRIME.

Violet Quill

Informal literary group formed by Christopher Cox, Robert Ferro, Michael Grumley, ANDREW HOLLERAN, FELICE PICANO, EDMUND WHITE, and George Whitmore in New York City. All seven writers had become acquainted with one another by the late 1970s and in March 1980 held their first informal gathering as the "Violet [or Lavender] Quill" club. Over the next year, they met seven more times in members' Manhattan apartments, reading from works in progress and sharing critiques, ideas, and gossip over dessert.

From diverse backgrounds, the men were united by the New York gay social scene as well as a desire to create a new LITERATURE unique to post-STONEWALL gay life. Although their writing styles and subjects varied widely, they published a body of fictional and nonfictional work before and after 1980 that has much in common. Violet Quill writing tended to exalt fleeting beauty, rarefied sensibilities, and the tribal rituals of the Manhattan and FIRE ISLAND scenes in works that were usually autobiographical, stylish, and redolent of the gay wit of the era. Promiscuity and the difficulty of finding true love are givens, as is the importance of friendship. Often, they evince a sense of impending loss that seems almost to prophesy the onset of AIDS.

Internecine clashes, particularly between Ferro and Whitmore, led to the dissolution of the group, but most of the men remained friends in the years that followed. Four of the seven men died of complications from AIDS.

✧ *The Violet Quill Reader: The Emergence of Gay Writing After Stonewall,* edited by David Bergman (1994).

Vivien, Renée

(Pauline Mary Tarn; 1877–1909)

English-born French-language writer. Born in London to an American heiress and an English dry-goods magnate, she lived in Paris with her family until she was nine. Her mother took her back to London after her father's death in 1886 and unsuccessfully attempted to have her declared insane to gain control of her inheritance. Eleven unhappy years later, she left London for Paris and began writing exclusively in French.

Renée Vivien painted by Alice Pike Barney, the mother of her lover.

In 1899, she met NATALIE BARNEY and they began a now legendary affair. Together the women championed a lesbian demimonde of writers and artists that was unprecedented as much for its brilliance as its disdain of convention. Marking her own reincarnation, Tarn changed her name to Renée ("reborn") Vivien (as in the exclamation *vive,* "long live").

For the first few years of her writing career, she signed herself "R." or "René Vivien," leading readers to believe that her love poems "to Lorely" were written to a woman by a man. Critics grew hostile when she switched from the male René to the female "Renée," but by that time she had already acquired a reputation as a leading Symbolist poet.

Along with lesbian love and heroic ANDROGYNY, death and destructive lust are major themes of much of her work. In her own life, Vivien grew despondent over the death in 1901 of Violet Shilleto, an adored childhood friend, as well as the conflicts in her tumultuous relationship with Barney, whom she (correctly) suspected of casual infidelities. After a suicide attempt, she left Barney in 1901 for the Baroness Hélène de Zuylen de Nyevelt (née Rothschild), who, according to COLETTE, was described as her "master." The baroness published two books of poetry and two novels with Paule Riversdale, probably a collaborative PSEUDONYM for herself and Vivien.

Vivien and Barney reunited briefly in 1904 and traveled to Mytilene on the Greek isle of Lesbos. Both wealthy, the two women dreamed of starting a lesbian artists' colony there and reviving the ancient traditions of SAPPHO. Vivien bought a villa, hung a sign reading "Paradise" in Greek over the garden gate, and visited once a year, but the Sapphic colony was never established.

Vivien and Barney nevertheless played a pivotal role in reclaiming Sappho as a lesbian poet. Both wrote verse inspired by Sappho, and Vivien translated her into French. Largely due to their influence, Sapphic themes (as well as AMAZON imagery and other classical allusions) became identified with lesbian writing.

Vivien wrote 13 books of poetry, 2 novellas, and 3 volumes of short fiction and prose poetry. In addition to classical imagery, her poetry draws on traditions of courtly love, mysticism, and religion. Women and feminine androgynes dominate her writing; male characters are negligible and mostly negative. She explained: "I neither love nor hate men, what I hold against them is the great wrong they have done to women. They are political adversaries whom I want to injure for the good of the cause."

Although RADCLYFFE HALL and UNA TROUBRIDGE so admired Vivien's melancholy yet passionate lesbian poems that they marked their seventh anniversary by reading some of them aloud, Vivien was forgotten by most readers until the 1970s. None of her books was available in English until JEANNETTE

HOWARD FOSTER's translation of her 1904 novel based on her affair with Barney was published as *A Woman Appeared to Me* in 1976.

Vivien died of alcoholism and anorexia at the age of 32. LILLIAN FADERMAN, Susan Gubar, and other critics have suggested that Vivien internalized and unwittingly fostered the 19th-century French literary vogue of portraying lesbians as enthrallingly decadent yet ultimately morbid monstrosities. Others, such as Elaine Marks, have called for a reappraisal of her writing in light of the transgressive tactics of lesbian writers like MONIQUE WITTIG. Still others, including literary critic Karla Jay, view her as an almost mythological figure whose life story was as much a legacy as her visionary, if flawed, creative product.

- ✧ *Homosexualities and French Literature: Cultural Contexts/Critical Texts,* edited by George Stambolian and Elaine Marks (1979).
- ✧ Karla Jay, *The Amazon and the Page: Natalie Clifford Barney and Renée Vivien* (1988).

Von Praunheim, Rosa

(Holger Mischwitzki; 1942–)

German filmmaker, activist. Born in Latvia to German parents he once called "nice Nazis," he jokingly exhibited paintings under the PSEUDONYM Rosa von Praunheim to suggest a glamorous older woman living in the Praunheim section of Frankfurt, where he studied ART in the early 1960s. He continued to use the name after he had come OUT as an openly gay and unabashedly political FILM director in Berlin in the late 1960s because of its associations with "pink" (*rosa* in German) ACTIVISM and resistance to the oppression symbolized by the PINK TRIANGLE.

Von Praunheim began to make gay political statements in his work for German TELEVISION as early as *Sisters of the Revolution* (1969), but it was *It's Not the Homosexual Who Is Perverse But the Society in Which He Lives,* his controversial 1970 film, that established him as a major gay filmmaker. A Godardian look at a Berliner's unhappy assimilation into gay life, this film was, despite its title, as much an attack on the mores of the stereotypical Berlin homosexual

Rosa von Praunheim (left) in A Virus Has No Morals.

as on "the Society in Which He Lives." Although the film portrayed Berlin's gay SUBCULTURE as squalid and vicious, it is credited with catalyzing the formation of GAY LIBERATION movements in many of the German cities in which it was shown.

Fascinated by the U.S. and the burgeoning American gay and lesbian subculture of the 1970s, von Praunheim interviewed a widely varied selection of activists, documented a San Francisco PRIDE CELEBRATION, and charted the rise of Anita Bryant's antigay and -lesbian crusade (see **1/18/1977**) in his 1978 documentary, *Army of Lovers or Revolt of the Perverts.* Like his earlier work on the German gay scene, *Army of Lovers* evinced as much anger at gay male sexual obsessiveness and American gay and lesbian ASSIMILATIONISM as at homophobic oppression. He later told interviewer Mark Nash that he believed "most gays are very conservative. To push gays into action you have to confront them."

Von Praunheim's *A Virus Has No Morals* (1986) was not only one of the first films to deal with the AIDS epidemic, it was also one of the very few to treat it with dark satire and gallows humor. *Film Comment* characterized it as having "the general air of a Lana Turner melodrama choreographed by JOHN WATERS." Other critics praised it for its provocative originality. Von Praunheim went on to make several other AIDS-themed films as well as two innovative screen bios: *Affengeil* (1991), about the actress Lotti Huber; and *I Am My Own Woman* (1992), featuring Charlotte von Mahlsdorf, one of GERMANY's best-known transvestites.

A prominent figure in Germany, von Praunheim caused controversy by OUTING politicians and actors in a television interview broadcast in 1992.

✧ Mark Nash, "Rosa von Praunheim," in *Monthly Film Bulletin* (September 1990).

✧ Jim Merrett, interview with Rosa von Praunheim in *The Guide* (February 1994).

✧ Rosa von Praunheim, *Fifty Years of Perversity* (1995).

W

Waddell, Tom

(Tom Fluabacher; 1937–1987)

U.S. doctor of internal medicine, athlete, activist, founding organizer of the GAY GAMES. Born in Paterson, New Jersey, Waddell studied dance as a child, then trained as an athlete. After his parents' divorce when he was 15, he lived with Hazel and Gene Waddell and was adopted by them six years later. He competed as a gymnast in college before entering medical school to become a specialist in infectious diseases. Although drafted into the U.S. Army and trained as a paratrooper, Waddell resisted being sent to Vietnam and was openly critical of U.S. involvement in the Vietnam War. At the 1968 Olympics, where he placed sixth in the decathlon, he supported the American sprinters John Carlos and Tommie Smith in the controversy that ensued after they gave Black Power salutes during their medal ceremony. Back in civilian life and practicing medicine in San Francisco, Waddell remained involved in a variety of political and athletic activities. From the 1970s, he was open about his gayness in press reports. In 1976, Waddell and then lover Charles Deaton were the first gay men to be featured in the "Couples" section of *People* magazine. Waddell fathered a daughter, Jessica, with lesbian Sara Lewinstein, a Gay Games administrator.

In 1980, Waddell and other Bay Area athletes, including his lover, Zohn Artman, formed San Francisco Arts and Athletics (SFAA) and began to organize a "Gay Olympics." As president of SFAA, Waddell was named in a suit brought by the U.S. Olympic Committee to prevent the organization from using the word "Olympics." Despite the stress and financial hardship of fighting the suit (which was settled in favor of the U.S. Olympic Committee in 1987) Waddell and his supporters persisted, staging two successful Gay Games in 1982 and 1986.

From the beginning, Waddell's vision of the games as a model of community inclusiveness and individual self-affirmation was the cornerstone of the event's philosophy. He wanted the games to cultivate gay and lesbian pride and unity while serving the Olympic ideal of "educating people through sport in a spirit of better understanding." At Gay Games II, held shortly after he had been diagnosed with an AIDS-related disease, Waddell was able to see his vision realized. He took pride in "the age-spread, with athletes ranging from 17 to 70," and in the games' celebration of togetherness: "The captain of one of the gay softball teams is straight, and black, and he felt like part of a family." That year, despite his recent bout with *Pneumocystis carinii* pneumonia, Waddell won a gold medal in the javelin competition. He died the following summer of AIDS-related complications at the age of 49.

✧ Roy M. Coe, *A Sense of Pride: The Story of Gay Games II* (1986).

✧ Tom Waddell and Dick Schaap, *Gay Olympian: The Life and Death of Dr. Tom Waddell* (1996).

Wald, Lillian D.

(1867–1940)

U.S. nurse, social reformer. The third of four children born to Central European Jewish immigrant parents, Wald grew up in Cincinnati, where her father, Max, ran a successful optical goods business. Her mother provided a warm, secure home Wald would later describe as indulgent and extremely happy. After completing nursing school, she began to organize home nursing classes for immigrant families on New York City's Lower East Side. Appalled by the misery she found there, she dropped out of medical school, moved into a tenement, and established the Henry Street Visiting Nurses Service (later the Henry Street Settlement). Staffed by women committed "to live in the neighborhood as nurses" and "contribute to it our citizenship," Wald's service was the first public health nursing system in the U.S.

The Henry Street Settlement grew into a network of seven houses offering educational and social as well as medical services. In 1909, Wald defied a New York City law prohibiting racially mixed assemblies to invite the National Negro Conference to Henry Street for a series of meetings, out of which grew the National Association for the Advancement of Colored People.

Wald also worked to reform child labor laws, established the first public-school nursing system (1902) and founded the group that later became the National Organization for Public Health Nursing (1912). Besides being active in the women's suffrage movement, she served as president of the American Union Against Militarism (1916), from which emerged the AMERICAN CIVIL LIBERTIES UNION.

Historian Blanche Wiesen Cook cites Wald as one of a number of highly influential turn-of-the-century women whose emotional needs were fulfilled almost exclusively by other women. Although their political philosophies differed, these women shared a commitment to breaking free of the constraints society placed on women, not only to advance women's rights but also to battle poverty, prejudice, and war. Wald, like her friend JANE ADDAMS, founded institutions in which she lived surrounded and supported by a tightly knit community of intimate women colleagues, some of whom—including Lavinia L. Dock, Mabel Hyde Kittredge, and Helen Arthur—she considered "special friends" or "crushes." As is typical of accounts of women of this era, contemporaries obscured or perhaps even destroyed records of these intimacies, but a surviving letter written to Wald by Arthur (who enjoyed CROSS-DRESSING) suggests that the passions of the Henry Street women were not entirely devoted to social reform: "If I had you, the real you instead of one ten thousandth part of you, I might shove the unworthy things way off—summertime has spoiled the Judge [Arthur's nickname] who longs to get back to your comfortable lap and the delights of kicking her pajamaed legs in peace and comfort instead of being solicitously hustled from your room at ten o'clock."

Wald published two anecdotal autobiographies, *The House on Henry Street* (1915) and *Windows on Henry Street* (1934).

✧ Blanche Wiesen Cook, *Women and Support Networks* (1979).

✧ *Lillian D. Wald,* edited by Clare Coss (1989).

Wales, see UNITED KINGDOM.

Warner, Sylvia Townsend
(1893–1978)

English writer, musicologist. Born in Harrow, Middlesex, Townsend Warner was educated by her French governess, her Anglo-Indian mother, and her father, a history master at Harrow School. She planned to study composition in Vienna with Arnold Schoenberg but instead worked in a munitions factory after WORLD WAR I broke out. She spent the decade after the war coediting the ten-volume *Tudor Church Music* (1922–1929) while beginning a literary career which would eventually include seven novels and eight collections of short stories in addition to poetry, essays, literary criticism, translations, and a biography of T. H. White.

Her successful novel *Lolly Willowes* (1926) was the first to be selected for promotion by the Book-of-the-Month Club. *Mr. Fortune's Maggot* (1927) inspired an opera by Paul Nordoff. She published 144 short stories in *The New Yorker* between the late 1930s and the 1970s, exploring, as she told her editor, William Maxwell, "my obsessive Innocent & the Guilty. Perhaps one day I shall be pure-minded enough to write a story where the innocent are charming and the guilty nauseating." Among her enduringly popular themes are class politics, repressed same-sex desire, and complex relationships between women.

Townsend Warner's lover for nearly forty years was the poet Valentine Ackland (1906–1969), who often wore men's clothes and was well-known for her fishing and shooting skills. Commemorating their January 12, 1931, "marriage," Townsend Warner wrote, "It was our most completed night, and after our love I slept unstirring in her arms, still covered with her love, till we woke and ate whatever meal it is lovers eat at five in the morning." Ackland later wrote that "never since then have we ceased to love each other." Both women joined the Communist Party in the mid-1930s and were active in the fight against fascism. They journeyed to Spain on two occasions during the Spanish Civil War, once to work with the Red Cross in Barcelona, and a second time to attend the Second International Congress of Writers in Defense of Culture. They lived openly as a couple in rural Dorset, England, from the 1930s until Ackland's death, their relationship surviving Ackland's affair with another woman. Ackland frankly described her troubles with her family and her struggles with alcoholism in a 1949 memoir, published posthumously as *For Sylvia: An Honest Account* in 1985. The two women collaborated on two volumes of poetry, *Whether a Dove or a Seagull* (1934) and *The Nature of the Moment* (1973).

In addition to a collection of letters (published posthumously with the stipulation that no love letters be included), Townsend Warner left 38 journal notebooks. The notebooks, the first of which were edited in 1996, reveal an unabashed sexuality and a profound devotion to Ackland.

✧ Wendy Mulford, *This Narrow Place: Sylvia Townsend Warner and Valentine Ackland: Life, Letters, and Politics, 1930–1951* (1988).

✧ *The Diaries of Sylvia Townsend Warner,* edited by Claire Harman (1996).

Warren, Patricia Nell
(1936–)

U.S. novelist, editor, artist. Born in Helena, Montana, and raised on her father's well-known Grant-Kohrs Ranch, Warren began writing at the age of ten and progressed to win the *Atlantic Monthly* college fiction award while a freshman in college. After graduating from Manhattanville College, she was married to George Tarnawsky from 1957 to 1973. Warren held several editorial positions at the

Reader's Digest, and in 1971 became a staff writer for *Runner's World.* Herself a long-distance runner, she joined with other women in the early 1970s to fight discriminatory track and field policies in the Amateur Athletic Union (AAU).

Warren brought many of her own experiences as an athlete and activist to *The Front Runner,* published in **April 1974**, the novel she calls her "coming out book." Dedicated to "all the athletes who have fought for human rights in sports," the novel is a first-person narrative account of a closeted 39-year-old track coach's love affair with a young track star who is also a gay activist. Originally banned in IRELAND and SOUTH AFRICA but a best-seller in much of the rest of the world, *The Front Runner* was one of the first widely read novels to feature gay male lovers who were both sympathetic and masculine. Many gay readers found the lovers so attractive and convincing that it was rumored the author was actually a gay man. The book also included the provocative claim (made by the coach/narrator) that "homosexuality is the great skeleton in the closet of American athletics." Warren published a sequel, *Harlan's Race,* in 1995 and plans a third book in the series to be entitled *Billy's Boy.*

Warren's other novels have addressed themes ranging from homosexuality in RELIGIOUS ORDERS (*The Fancy Dancer,* 1976) and the rise of homophobic crusaders (*The Beauty Queen,* 1978) to the lives of NATIVE AMERICAN and European women in the Old West (*One is the Sun*). A prolific writer, Warren has also published novels under the PSEUDONYM Patricia Kilina, and, with her ex-husband, published translations of Ukrainian poetry. Her awards include the 1978 Walt Whitman Award for Excellence in Gay Literature.

Deeply committed to providing lesbian, gay, bisexual, and transgendered YOUTH, whom she calls Generation D (for "dispossessed"), with "more respect in our own community," Warren has worked as a volunteer teacher at the EAGLES (Emphasizing Adolescent Gay and Lesbian Educational Services) Center in Los Angeles.

✧ Stuart Timmons, "Still a Front-Runner," *The Advocate* (June 7, 1988).

✧ Patricia Nell Warren, "Generation of the Dispossessed," *The Harvard Gay and Lesbian Review* (vol. 1, no. 4, Fall 1994).

Waters, Ethel

(1896–1977)

U.S. singer, actress. Waters grew up on the streets of Chester, Pennsylvania. "Tough, headstrong and resilient," as she would later describe herself, she ran with gangs, married briefly (the first of three times) at the age of 13, and survived by cleaning houses and stealing food. At 17, she escaped to Baltimore and started singing the blues as Sweet Mama Stringbean on the southern vaudeville circuit. In her 20s, she headlined in HARLEM RENAISSANCE era nightclubs and began a successful recording career on "race" labels. Her Broadway debut in *Africana* (1927) led to bigger THEATER and FILM roles, including Hagar in the play *Mamba's Daughters* (1939) and Berenice in CARSON MCCULLERS's *The Member of the Wedding* (1950) and in the film adaptation (1952). She was the first black woman to receive equal billing with white stars on Broadway and in HOLLYWOOD and the first to establish herself as a major American dramatic actress. She also became the first singer to confront racism in a popular song, "Supper Time" (1933). "Stormy Weather," which she introduced at the Cotton Club in 1933, became what she called "the theme song of my life."

In Harlem in the early 1920s, Waters was well-known for being "in the life" with dancer Ethel Williams. "The two Ethels" were friendly with CARL VAN VECHTEN but also included drag queens among their friends. Waters sometimes loaned them ball gowns and took pride when they won prizes at drag balls she attended. Her autobiography, *His Eye Is on the Sparrow* (with Charles Samuels, 1951), includes an account of a meeting around 1930 with RADCLYFFE HALL, which sparked rumors of an affair with the notorious writer.

✧ Donald Bogle, *Brown Sugar* (1980).

✧ Stephen Bourne, "Ethel Waters: Stormy Weather," *Capital Gay* (December 3, 1993).

Waters, John

(1946–)

U.S. filmmaker, writer. Waters grew up in an upper-middle-class Catholic family outside of Baltimore, Maryland. In love with FILM from his earliest youth, he began making 8-mm movies while still a teenager, and directed his first 16-mm film, *Eat Your Makeup,* in 1968. Waters later claimed to have been inspired by the films of Andy Warhol and RAINER WERNER FASSBINDER, but from the beginning his work provoked even stronger reactions than his controversial mentors had received. *Eat Your Makeup,* for example, included a humorous parody of the assassination of President John F. Kennedy—which, since it had occurred only five years before, was still a painfully fresh memory for most Americans.

John Waters.

By the time Waters achieved national prominence with *Pink Flamingos* (1972), produced on a budget of $10,000, he had already laid cinematic claim to a broad—and low—swath of American culture, making movies that, like *Pink Flamingos,* were proudly promoted as having "something to offend everyone." His stars included David Lochary, Edith Massey, Mary Vivian Pearce, Mink Stole, and, the most famous, DIVINE, who wowed audiences by being raped by a giant lobster (*Multiple Maniacs,* 1971), eating dog feces (*Pink Flamingos*), and going to the electric chair (*Female Trouble,* 1975). Divine was absent from *Desperate Living* (1977), the movie many consider Waters's queerest for its outrageous parodies of lesbian BUTCH/FEMME relationships and send-up of gay and lesbian "outlaw" culture.

Beginning with *Polyester* (1981), in which a Baltimore housewife (Divine) seeks respite from a host of life crises in the arms of heartthrob Tab Tomorrow (Tab Hunter), Waters's films were released nationally by New Line Cinema. *Hairspray* (1988), *Cry-Baby* (1990), and *Serial Mom* (1994) disseminated Waters's brand of CAMP humor to wider audiences, and helped establish him as a nationally recognized seer of bad taste. Although ever closer to the HOLLYWOOD mainstream, Waters maintains the provocative edge that has made his films cult classics with queer audiences around the world.

✧ John Waters, *Shock Value: A Tasteful Book About Bad Taste* (1995).

Well of Loneliness, The

Novel published in **July 1928** by RADCLYFFE HALL, which was banned in the UNITED KINGDOM and caused international controversy because of its frank descriptions and defense of lesbian desire. The first widely read novel written in English to address lesbianism, *The Well of Loneliness* continued to attract large numbers of lesbian readers through the 1950s and 1960s, when it was marketed in the U.S. by PULP FICTION publishers. It was finally printed in the U.K. in 1949 and had been translated into 14 languages by 1943, the year Hall died. It has never gone out of print.

Although some lesbian critics have deplored Hall's characterization of Stephen Gordon, the novel's main character, as a tortured "invert"—i.e., a man trapped in a woman's body—few would disagree with Bonnie Zimmerman, who acknowledged that "for over 40 years, *The Well of Loneliness* and Stephen Gordon virtually defined lesbianism."

The Well of Loneliness recounts 35 years in the life of Stephen Gordon, who is given a boy's name and upbringing to satisfy her aristocratic parents' longing for a son. As a young woman, Stephen finds herself irresistibly drawn to other women despite the condemnation of virtually everyone around her. During WORLD WAR I, she joins an ambulance brigade in FRANCE and meets Mary, the woman who is to become the major love of her life. The two women encounter other homoerotically inclined men and women, but Stephen becomes increasingly ridden with despair at the prospects for a satisfying life as a couple at the fringes of society. To "save" Mary, she feigns an affair to drive her into a heterosexual marriage.

As Hall made clear in a letter to literary historian Gorham Munson, she was well aware of impending notoriety, and conversely the price for remaining silent: ". . . I realise that it is the price I must pay for having intentionally come out into the open. . . ." And she describes the price each person pays: "Nothing is so spiritually degrading or so undermining of one's morale as living a lie, as keeping friends only by false pretences." Hall railed against the "conspiracy of silence" enforced on inverts by society's believing intelligent persons desire to "legalize their unions," mindful of the imperfections in society but unwilling to lapse into chaos without some social codes: "Preposterous, do you say? And yet it may come, though I may not be here to welcome its coming."

Her novel deliberately presented a character that wasn't already in a case study of unstable persons. Hers was an activist stance—to change condemning attitudes and hurtful actions directed toward inverts by their families, doctors, teachers, psychiatrists, and others.

Hall knew she was a pioneer. And although she disavowed the literalness of details and characters, to give the novel conviction she admitted drawing "ruthlessly upon myself."

American gay historian Jonathan Ned Katz views the book as a central lesbian political contribution to homosexual resistance. Its impact around the world is undeniable.

➤ Also see **November 1928**; **December 15, 1928**; **April 19, 1929**.

✧ Vera Brittain, *Radclyffe Hall: A Case of Obscenity?* (1968).

✧ Radclyffe Hall on *The Well of Loneliness* (1934 letter to Stuart Munson) 1996.

Publishing History, *The Well of Loneliness*

Legal Actions were against the publisher and bookseller, not the author, so the defendants were representatives of the publishing houses. The legal case in Britian rested on the Lord Campbell Obscene Publications Act of 1857, which gave magistrates the power to seize and destroy material they judged obscene in theme and intent. Since the lesbian theme was presented in an understanding, positive light, rather than being condemned, the court ruled the book obscene. The magistrates ruled that no "opinion" could constitute evidence and therefore dismissed the defense witnesses. The American court also judged the book obscene because it "idealized and extolled" perversion and would "debauch public morals."

1928

July: Hall receives her advance copies. Publication on July 27 by Jonathan Cape Ltd.
August: Second edition issued. Book is withdrawn soon after James Douglas, *Sunday Express* editor, appeals to the Home Secretary to ban the book. Cape cancels the forthcoming third edition under threat of obscenity proceeding.
September: Paris, France, publication by Pegasus Press. Cape subleases rights and flies type molds to Paris.
November: British case begins in Bow Street Magistrates Court. Novel ordered to be burned by Sir Charles Biron.
December: Appeal heard and dismissed at London Sessions. U.S. publication by Covici Friede of New York (Alfred A. Knopf withdraws).

1929

January: 800 copies seized in U.S. on complaint of John S. Sumner, secretary of the Society for the Suppression of Vice, on grounds of circulating indecent literature.
February: Sumner case begins in Manhattan Magistrates Court. Book ruled obscene. Ruling appealed.
March: French translation published by Gallimard.
April: New York Appeals Court Special Sessions overturns obscenity decision. Court decision concludes that although the book dealt with a delicate social problem, it was not written in an obscene manner.

1949

Falcon Press in England (later Hammond & Hammond) publishes novel without reaction.

1974

Broadcast in 17 episodes on the BBC's *Book at Bedtime.*

White, Edmund

(Edmund Valentine White III; 1940–)

U.S. writer, critic, teacher. Born in Ohio, White grew up in Chicago and Cincinnati and studied Chinese at the University of Michigan. In the 1960s, he moved to New York and worked in PUBLISHING, except for a year's sabbatical in Rome, until 1983. In the late 1970s, he was one of seven members of the VIOLET QUILL. Since 1983, he has lived mostly in Paris with extended stays in the U.S.

One of the most admired openly gay writers in the world, White's contributions to the building of a gay SUBCULTURE go far beyond his acclaimed fiction. In 1977, he and Dr. Charles Silverstein celebrated *The Joy of Gay Sex* in a best-seller he dedicated "to all my tricks, from Ed." Equally resonant of the promiscuity and abandon of the 1970s was his pioneering book of travel essays, *States of Desire* (1980). He has also compiled two major anthologies, written influential essays, and published a biography of JEAN GENET.

White's eloquent fiction has ranged from imaginatively cultured fantasies (*Forgetting Elena,* 1973; *Nocturnes for the King of Naples,* 1978; *Caracole,* 1985) to semiautobiographical novels (*A Boy's Own Story,* 1982; *The Beautiful Room Is Empty,* 1988) to works of era-evoking essays (*The Burning Library,* 1994) and short fiction (*Skinned Alive,* 1995). He is one of the creators of the world of gay LITERATURE he sought but failed to find in his youth, and his work epitomizes what he calls the "twin urges" of gay fiction: "the obligation to explain, and the ambition to excite."

White, Patrick

(1912–1990)

Australian writer. The scion of a wealthy and socially prominent Australian family, White was born in England while his parents were on a two-year stay there. He grew up on his parents' Hunter Valley estate and in Sydney until he was sent back to England to attend an elite public school, which he loathed, and, eventually, Cambridge University. During WORLD WAR II, while serving in North Africa and Greece as an intelligence officer with the Royal Air Force, he met Manoly Lascaris, the man who was to become his lifelong lover.

White wrote 12 novels, 9 plays, and several books of poetry and short fiction, earning international acclaim and the 1973 Nobel Prize for literature. Intensely private and noted for his ambivalence toward both AUSTRALIA and the subject of homosexuality, White was nonetheless relatively open in private about his sexuality. He broached the topic publicly in two of his last works, the novel *The Twyborn Affair* (1979), which featured a main character with three differently gendered personae—a man, a woman, and a transvestite male—and his autobiography, *Flaws in the Glass* (1981). By the end of his life, White had reconciled himself to the gay and lesbian SUBCULTURE at the same time he became a prominent activist in the aboriginal rights and environmental movements.

✧ David Marr, *Patrick White: A Life* (1991).

Whitman, Walt

(1819–1892)

U.S. poet. Born in West Hills, Long Island, Whitman moved with his family to Brooklyn when he was four, then back to the country as a teenager. He worked for several years as a schoolteacher and newspaper editor on Long Island and published his first short story, "Death in the Schoolroom," in 1841, the same year he abruptly abandoned teaching to pursue a career in Manhattan as a writer of newspaper and magazine articles as well as the sensationalistic, even grisly, "pamphlet novels" that were popular at the time.

Over the next decade Whitman turned to poetry, completing and publishing the first edition of *Leaves of Grass* in 1855. For the rest of his life, through service as a nurse in the Civil War and growing fame as one of America's most acclaimed poets, Whitman enlarged *Leaves of Grass* eight times.

Beginning with its first edition, *Leaves of Grass* "sang" the sensuality of the body, but it was with the version of the "Calamus" section in the 1860 edition that Whitman's poetry became associated with HOMOEROTICISM. "In paths untrodden," Whitman wrote, ". . . I proceed for all who are or have been young

Walt Whitman.

men, / To tell the secret of my nights and days, / To celebrate the need of comrades."

Although the Calamus poems strike modern readers—and struck many contemporaries such as EDWARD CARPENTER and JOHN ADDINGTON SYMONDS—as openly homoerotic, most of Whitman's early readers interpreted them as exalting (nonsexual) devotion and intimacy between men. Whitman himself linked them to a loosely defined concept he called "adhesiveness," a term derived from phrenology that, in Whitman's interpretation, denoted a capability for deep, lasting, and mutually supportive companionship. Contemporaries tended to find his intimations of *heterosexual* intimacy more disturbing and even, as some readers thought, obscene.

Whitman revised and added to *Leaves of Grass* for the rest of his life. As public awareness of homosexuality grew, he began to cross out "he" and "his" in some of the poems and substitute "she" and "her." He encouraged rumor that he had had secret women lovers, and, most unlikely, had fathered children, a myth he conveyed to Symonds in a letter written shortly before his death.

These revisions and fabrications made it possible for biographers and literary critics to deny his homosexuality for decades after his death. Only in recent decades have scholars given serious attention to his relationships with men such as Peter Doyle, a streetcar conductor, and the soldiers he tended while working as a nurse during the Civil War.

Biographer and historian David S. Reynolds has recently uncovered documents that offer new evidence of Whitman's homosexuality. According to papers found in a Long Island community where Whitman taught as a young man, he may have taken liberties with some of his male students. As a result, he was apparently denounced from the pulpit and then tarred and feathered by an angry mob, leaving him so injured it took a month to recover.

Whitman's work had an extraordinary influence on LITERATURE in virtually every language (as early as 1901, Japanese poets like Yone Noguchi were writing in a Whitmanesque style), but he has been an especially vital source of inspiration for gay and lesbian writers.

- ✧ *Complete Poetry and Selected Prose of Walt Whitman,* edited by James E. Miler Jr. (1959).
- ✧ Justin Kaplan, *Walt Whitman. A Life* (1980).
- ✧ Robert K. Martin, *The Continuing Presence of Walt Whitman: The Life After the Life* (1992).
- ✧ David S. Reynolds, *Walt Whitman: A Cultural Biography* (1995).

Wicca

Also called Wicce, Witchcraft, or "the Craft." Religion based on beliefs and rituals thought to predate CHRISTIANITY. Modern Wicca, which emerged after witchcraft was decriminalized in the UNITED KINGDOM in 1951, is today practiced in a variety of forms. One group of believers worship the Horned God and the Goddess. Others, adherents of Dianic Wicca, the form most common among lesbians, venerate a Great Goddess symbolized by Diana (Greek Artemis).

Dianic Wiccans have evolved a number of special rituals to mark important events in lesbian lives, such as "croning," which marks the passage of women at age 56 into the "sage age." Wiccan "thealogists" (from *thea,* the Greek word for "goddess") like Zzuzsanna Budapest and Starhawk have also inspired unique lesbian cosmologies. Some Dianic Wiccans believe, for example, that the universe was born out of lesbian desire: in the beginning, there was only the Goddess, who reached out to touch her own reflection in the mirrorlike void, kindling an explosion of energy that created the cosmos. In general, however, Wiccans are nondogmatic, celebrating instead the "Goddess" within each woman—whether she be "maiden," "mother," or "crone"—and her connection with the universal forces of nature.

✧ Cynthia Eller, *Living in the Lap of the Goddess* (1993).

Wicker, Randy

(pseudonym of Charles Hayden; aka Randolphe/Randolfe Wicker; 1938–)

U.S. activist, public relations pioneer, entrepreneur. A native of Plainfield, New Jersey, Wicker was raised Catholic by his grandmother in Florida and came to an early and unusually open acceptance of his gayness as a boy. He discovered ONE magazine and the *Mattachine Review* while still in college and arranged to spend a summer vacation at the One office in Los Angeles. In 1958 his summer destination was New York City so he could participate in New York MATTACHINE Society activities. Already a militant, he shocked discreet Mattachine members by printing and distributing posters to advertise a meeting, tripling attendance. In his last two years at the University of Texas at Austin, he became involved in the civil rights movement and was revealed to be gay while running for student body president. Although his prominence protected him, his lover was expelled. By 1961, when he moved to New York, he had reached the then controversial conclusions that gay people needed not only to emulate the ACTIVISM of the AFRICAN-AMERICAN civil rights movement but also to work to raise public awareness of gay and lesbian issues.

As Randy Wicker (his HOMOPHILE movement PSEUDONYM) and head of a group he called the Homosexual League of New York, he spearheaded an unprecedented media campaign. He successfully pressured newspapers into listing homophile meetings, became the first "acknowledged homosexual" to speak on radio (**7/15/1962**) and on national TELEVISION (**11/16/1964**) and gleaned generally favorable coverage in publications ranging from *Newsweek* to *The New York Times.* He was also among the first to picket for gay and lesbian rights (**9/19/1964**; **4/17–18/1965**) and was active in ECHO (East Coast Homophile Organizations).

Despite his successes in persuading American media to cover gay and lesbian issues, Wicker tired of movement activities in the late 1960s. As he wrote THE ADVOCATE, he "decided it was time to save" himself instead. He and lover Peter Ogren started a protest-button business and later used the proceeds to open an

Randy Wicker, 1963.

antique shop on Christopher Street in Greenwich Village. In 1972, however, he returned to gay and lesbian public relations to write, with KAY TOBIN, *The Gay Crusaders.*

In the mid-1990s, Wicker entered the cloning rights debate, heading the Cloning Rights United Front in New York.

Wilde, Dolly

(Dorothy Ierne Wilde; 1896–1941)

English writer. The only child of OSCAR WILDE's brother Willie, she fled England at the beginning of WORLD WAR I to drive an ambulance at the front, sending her mother a telegram that read, "Sailing!" In Paris in 1926, she began a ten-year love affair with NATALIE BARNEY that proved painful for both women: Wilde is rumored to have twice attempted suicide, and Barney commemorated her in her *In Memory of Dorothy Ierne Wilde* (1951) as "half androgyne and half goddess."

Wilde, who considered herself "more Oscar-like than he was like himself," once went to a masquerade party dressed as her uncle. JANET FLANNER reported that she looked "both important and earnest." Her personal magnetism also enthralled RADCLYFFE HALL and UNA TROUBRIDGE. "Wilde himself lives again," wrote Troubridge, describing his niece as "so like him in face that it is uncanny—and like him, of course, also in nature, but I think—as far as a superficial estimate can judge—the better man."

Wilde's literary talent, preserved in her letters to Barney, was apparently co-opted by her conversational skills. Flanner wrote, "For a brilliant talker, she had an amazing capacity for listening." Other friends, who included DJUNA BARNES, GERTRUDE STEIN, and VIRGINIA WOOLF, found her well read and exceptionally amusing, despite her often excessive drinking and cocaine consumption.

Wilde, suffering from an incurable cancer, died of an apparent drug overdose at the age of 45.

✧ Janet Flanner, "Oscar Wilde's Niece," *Prose* (no. 6, 1973).

Wilde, Oscar

(1854–1900)

Irish writer, critic. Born into a well-to-do Anglo-Irish family in Dublin, Wilde benefited from a brilliant education and a stimulating upbringing dominated by his eccentric and witty mother, a writer herself. By the age of 30, Wilde was famous in Europe and the U.S., acclaimed as much for his personal flamboyance and wit as for his literary output. When his sex life became a matter of court record, however, England was no longer amused.

Married at the age of 29 to Constance Lloyd and the father of two boys, Wilde first had sex with a man, a young Cambridge student, when he was 32. Although he remained on cordial terms with his wife, Wilde gradually withdrew from conjugal relations with her and seems to have been exclusively homosexual from the late 1880s on, except for one transaction with a female prostitute shortly before his death.

Years before his first sexual experience with a man, however, Wilde had created a public persona that the 20th century would come to consider uniquely gay. Wilde made the "art for art's sake" dictum of the aesthetic movement uniquely his own, embellishing its wan delicacies with a fierce yet stylish iconoclasm. He alternately delighted and infuriated contemporaries with proclamations such as "All art is quite useless," "Life is much too important a topic ever to talk seriously about," and "Wickedness is a myth invented by good people to account for the curious attractiveness of others."

This aesthetic was expressed first in essays, criticism, and lectures, then in Wilde's only novel, *The Picture of Dorian Gray* (1891), and finally in some of the wittiest plays ever written, including *Lady Windermere's Fan* (1892) and *The Importance of Being Earnest* (1895).

In private, Wilde was capable of generosity and warmth, as when he met WALT WHITMAN while on a lecture tour of the U.S. in 1882. Whitman described him as "so frank and outspoken and manly." Wilde in turn said the poet

Oscar Wilde (left) and Lord Alfred "Bosie" Douglas.

was "the grandest man I have ever seen" and later boasted of the farewell kiss Whitman had planted on his lips.

In 1892, Wilde fell in love with Lord Alfred "Bosie" Douglas, a beautiful ("quite like a narcissus—so white and gold," Wilde wrote), legendarily self-centered aristocrat who was 22 at the time. Bosie introduced Wilde to working-class male prostitutes with whom Wilde proceeded to have a series of affairs, scandalizing upper-class associates by dining with them in public and actually seeming to enjoy their company.

Meanwhile, Bosie's father, the Marquess of Queensberry, an eccentric and unpopular aristocrat best known for having codified the Queensberry rules of boxing, had decided that Wilde was responsible for corrupting Bosie. Taunted by his son, Queensberry began to insult and threaten Wilde. In February 1895, he sent a note to Wilde's club addressed "To Oscar Wilde posing Somdomite." (The Marquess's handwriting was apparently as unsteady as his spelling: it was not until late in this century that a handwriting expert deciphered the message. Until then, most people thought it read, inexplicably, "To Oscar Wilde posing as somdomite.") Wilde, against his solicitor's advice, brought a libel suit against Queensberry. After Wilde lost his suit, he was himself prosecuted twice for "gross indecency between males."

Wilde's first trial is remembered for his famous defense of the "love that dare not speak its name" (a quotation from a poem written by Douglas): "It is beautiful, it is fine, it is the noblest form of affection. There is nothing unnatural about it." After the jury failed to reach a verdict, he was brought to trial a second time, found guilty, and sentenced in **May 1895** to two years' hard labor.

Although in poor health, Wilde was forced to sleep on a plank bed and fed a diet that consisted mostly of gruel and suet. Held incommunicado for three months, he suffered from chronic diarrhea and insomnia and endured frequent punishments for not cleaning his cell properly or for trying to talk to the other prisoners. Conditions improved somewhat during his second year of imprisonment, and he was allowed to read more extensively and write—supposedly as a letter to Douglas—*De Profundis,* in which he both attacked Douglas and defended his own sexuality.

Wilde was released from prison in May 1897 and left immediately for FRANCE. Apart from writing the long poem *The Ballad of Reading Gaol* (1898), which included the line "each man kills the thing he loves," he accomplished little before dying on November 30, 1900.

The effect of the publicity surrounding Wilde and his trial on the development of a gay and lesbian consciousness is immeasurable. As Claude J. Summers has observed, Wilde became "Saint Oscar," a martyr who crystallized a particular image of the homosexual as aesthete at the same time that his fate had a paralyzing effect on generations of gay men and lesbians.

Ironically, for someone who once wrote "the one duty we owe to history is to rewrite it," his own story has been both twisted and bowdlerized by many writers. As late as 1994, a biographer would cast doubt on his gayness, saying he had no relationship with "the gays on Castro Street or Christopher Street," a statement millions of gay men and lesbians around the world would refute.

✧ Richard Ellmann, *Oscar Wilde* (1987).

✧ Claude J. Summers, *Gay Fictions: Wilde to Stonewall* (1990).

George Platt Lynes took this photograph of Tennessee Williams in the late 1940s.

Williams, Tennessee

(Thomas Lanier Williams; 1911–1983)

U.S. writer. A sensitive, sickly child, Williams grew up in Mississippi and Missouri, the son of an outgoing shoe salesman with whom he never got along (but much later thanked for giving him "the best of my work, as well as the impulse to work") and a genteel mother with whom he thought he had an "excessive attachment" (but whom he also later disparaged "for teaching me to expect more love from the world, more softness in it, than I could ever offer"). The other characters in the childhood dramas that came to shape his adult plays were his maternal grandparents, the Reverend Dakin and "Grand" Rose; and his sister Rose, a tempestuous young woman whom his mother had lobotomized after, Williams sometimes claimed, she had accused their father of sexually abusing her.

Although he began writing as a youth and published a short story in the magazine *Weird Tales* at the age of 17, he came into his own as a playwright only after moving to New Orleans in the 1940s. Around the same time, at the age of 29, he had his first sexual affair with another man, a dancer named Kip. Kip left him to get married and died, with Williams at his bedside, of a brain tumor in 1944.

Williams's first successfully produced play was *The Glass Menagerie* (1944), based in part on his troubled sister. In the late 1940s and 1950s, Williams was the most famous and critically acclaimed playwright in the U.S., with epochmaking achievements that included *A Streetcar Named Desire* (1947), *Summer and Smoke* (1948), *The Rose Tattoo* (1951), *Cat on a Hot Tin Roof* (1955), and *Sweet Bird of Youth* (1959). Offstage, from 1948 until the early 1960s, he had a passionate and often satisfying relationship with Frank Merlo, a working-class man who was Williams's main source of emotional support until Williams's ever more frequent bouts of depression, coupled with alcohol and drug abuse, drove them apart a little over a year before Merlo's death from cancer in 1963.

The 1960s, which Williams once said he "slept through," were years of emotional and professional deterioration for Williams, leading to a severe nervous breakdown in 1969. His last plays, which included *Small Craft Warnings* (1972) and *Vieux Carré* (1979), failed to attract the acclaim of his earlier work. Williams died at the age of 71, apparently from choking accidentally on a plastic bottle cap.

Although recognized as one of the greatest gay artists of the 20th century, Williams has received a mixed reception from gay critics, who have sometimes found his characterizations of gay men depressing and negative. Williams defended his negative depictions as honest accounts of gay life as he had experienced it. He characterized his approach to gayness as "Chekhovian," because, like the wistful characters in Chekhov's plays, gay people of his era "were living for a future that would happen after they were dead."

Some critics, straight and gay alike, have also

accused him of creating female characters, like the tragic Blanche in *A Streetcar Named Desire,* who were actually gay men in drag. Williams himself felt the idea was "a preposterous allegation and a very dangerous one," especially when voiced by other gay men, because it reflected the "chauvinistic attitudes" gay playwrights (such as EDWARD ALBEE) suffered from straight critics. Williams himself suffered dismissal from critics like Louis Kronenberger, who, writing in *Time,* the publication responsible for OUTING Williams in the 1950s, excoriated Williams's world as a "fetid swamp."

In addition to his more famous plays, Williams also published dozens of short stories, several books of poetry, and two novels, including *Moise and the World of Reason* (1975). In contrast to his work for the THEATER, a more restricted art form until after STONEWALL, his other writings abound in explicit gay references and characters. His friend GORE VIDAL praised his stories as "the true memoir of Tennessee Williams," a richer account of his artistic and emotional life than Williams's own explicitly confessional, tragically self-deprecating *Memoirs* (1975).

✧ George Whitmore, interview with Tennessee Williams in *Gay Sunshine Interviews,* edited by Winston Leyland (1978).

✧ Gore Vidal, introduction to *Tennessee Williams: Collected Stories* (1985).

✧ Donald Spoto, *The Kindness of Strangers: The Life of Tennessee Williams* (1985).

Willson, Mary Ann, and Miss Brundidge

(sometimes Wilson; no other name known for Brundidge, or Brundage; active c. 1800–c. 1850)

Willson, a painter, and Brundidge, a farmer, lived in Greenville, New York, in the 1820s. They were the inspiration for ALMA ROUTSONG's groundbreaking novel *A Place for Us* (later retitled *Patience and Sarah*).

In the 1940s, after the Harry Stone Gallery in New York City acquired 20 of her paintings, Willson was rediscovered and acclaimed by ART critics as one of the most original "primitive" American watercolorists. Accompanying the paintings was a four-page letter signed, "An Admirer of Art," detailing a visit to the artist around 1850. Her depictions of birds, flowers, and people and her biblical scenes feature rich unmixed colors extracted from berries, plants, and brick dust, applied to materials that range from candle wrapping paper to tea boxes. Although the images are crude, they are embellished with minuscule repetitive patterns that are so sophisticatedly abstract some critics mistakenly speculated that the paintings were modern forgeries designed to exploit the lucrative folk art market.

Sources from the 19th century document that Willson and Brundidge moved from Connecticut to upstate New York and acquired a log house on a small piece of land with a cow and a garden filled with ferns and wildflowers. Brundidge farmed while Willson painted and sold her watercolors to neighbors at a top price of 25 cents or bartered them with peddlers, who in turn sold them from CANADA to Mobile, Alabama. After Brundidge died, Willson was "inconsolable" and moved away.

One account describes them as having a "romantic attachment." Other neighbors believed that the "two old maids" had both suffered failed romances and together sought "peace and forgetfulness in the wilderness." Lesbian and gay historians consider their relationship an intriguing suggestion of ROMANTIC FRIENDSHIPS among women in premodern rural society.

✧ N. F. Karlins, "Mary Ann Willson," *Antiques* (vol. 10, no. 5, November 1976).

✧ *Heresies* (Fall 1977).

Wilson, Barbara

(1950–)

U.S. writer, translator, publisher. Born in Long Beach, California, Wilson has spent most of her adult life in Seattle, where she cofounded Seal Press in 1976 with Rachel da Silva. Now based in Oakland, she has also traveled widely and lived abroad for extended periods of time.

Wilson published a children's book, *The Geography Lesson* (1977), and two collections of short stories, *Talk and Contact* (1978) and *Thin Ice* (1981), before debuting her first novel, *Ambitious Women* (1982). In 1984, she launched a DETECTIVE FICTION series featuring Seattle print shop collective member Pam Nilsen. In 1991, she began a second mystery series, this time exploring exotic locales through the eyes of androgynous adventuress and translator Cassandra Reilly.

Although Wilson does not consider herself a mystery writer, preferring to think of her crime novels and short stories as experimental fiction, she has been one of the most influential innovators in the genre of lesbian detective fiction. Her Pam Nilsen series went beyond recounting Nilsen's coming OUT and problem-beset love life—staples of the genre—to take on issues of lesbian identity (*Murder in the Collective,* 1984), the complex ethics of prostitution (*Sisters of the Road,* 1986), and both sides of the lesbian SEX WARS (*The Dog Collar Murders,* 1989). The more offbeat Cassandra Reilly series (*Gaudí Afternoon,* 1990, and *Trouble in Transylvania,* 1993) has been acclaimed for its humor, unusual insights into unfamiliar cultures, and imaginative GENDER-bending. Lesbian and straight critics alike have praised Wilson for her ability to educate and provoke thought while still delivering satisfying doses of psychological suspense.

Wilson has also translated several books from Norwegian and written *Cows and Horses* (1989), a novel, which critic Bonnie Zimmerman calls an "antiromance," about a woman trying to survive a breakup with her lover. Reflecting Wilson's belief that her creative life is also shaped by work relationships, the novel also recounts the breakup of a retail business. *Gaudí Afternoon* won a Lambda Literary AWARD and the British Crime Writers' Association Award for best mystery set in Europe.

✧ Interview with Barbara Wilson by Barbara Findlen, *Ms.* (November/December 1991).

✧ Barbara Wilson, "My Work," in *Inversions: Writings by Dykes, Queers and Lesbians,* edited by Betsy Warland (1991).

Winant, Fran

(1943–)

U.S. artist, poet, activist. Born in New York City, Winant showed as much talent for writing as for drawing as a child, inventing a secret language for her diary and to keep friends from reading her poetry on the school bus. When, inspired by her beloved shepherd-greyhound Cindy, she began to paint seriously in the 1970s, this hieroglyphiclike language resurfaced in texts appearing around figures in paintings like *Cindy* (1976), *The Kiss* (1981), and *Dog with Private Language* (n.d.).

Winant was an early member of GAY LIBERATION FRONT (she can be seen in PETER HUJAR's exuberant poster announcing New York City's pioneering gay PRIDE CELEBRATION held on **6/28/1970**) and, later, RADICALESBIANS. She was a cofounder of the Lesbian Food Conspiracy (a Radicalesbian food co-op) and a founder of Violet Press, which published three books of her poetry—*Looking at Women* (1971), *Dyke Jacket* (1976), and *Goddess of Lesbian Dreams* (1980)—as well as *We Are All Lesbians* (1973), an early lesbian poetry anthology that Winant edited. Many of her poems continue to be reprinted in lesbian, gay, and mainstream anthologies.

Winant received a B.A. in studio art from Fordham University in 1975 and also attended the School of Visual Arts. In Winant's paintings, which she began exhibiting in 1976, "the traditional image of woman as object of desire," as she once told lesbian artist and critic Harmony Hammond, "was replaced by the image of my dog Cindy as a passionate presence surrounded by strong currents of love." One of the first and most influential OUT lesbian artists, Winant has also remarked: "What is queer about my art is my sensibility. That is, my ability to continually cross boundaries in experiencing and expressing love." In the 1980s, stimulated by her experiences of meditation, she began painting more abstract images that suggest crystal or plant forms.

✧ Jessica Falstein, Maxine Fine, Flavia Rando, Ellen Turner, and Fran Winant, "A New York City Collective," *Heresies* (no. 3, Fall 1977).

✧ Kay Larsen, "Lesbian Art: The Colonized Self," *Village Voice* (March 8, 1978).

✧ Emmanuel Cooper, *The Sexual Perspective: Homosexuality and Art in the Last 100 Years in the West* (1994).

Winckelmann, Johann Joachim
(1717–1768)

German art historian, archaeologist. The son of a Brandenburg shoemaker, Winckelmann educated himself out of poverty and worked as a pastor, tutor, and, later, librarian. In the course of mastering the classics, he became convinced that artistic greatness necessitated a thorough imitation of the ancient Greeks, including their idealization of the male nude. A brilliant 50-page pamphlet on Greek aesthetics—*Gedanken über die Nachahmung der Griechischen Werke* (1755, "Thoughts on the Imitation of Greek Works")—gained him wide renown, and in 1763 Pope Clement XIII appointed him Papal Antiquary, with duties that included superintending excavations at Pompeii. He is considered one of the founders of scientific archaeology and, thanks especially to his pioneering *Geschichte der Kunst des Altherthums* (1764, "History of the Art of Antiquity"), of modern art history.

Winckelmann had ROMANTIC FRIENDSHIPS with younger men throughout his life. His correspondence also hints at casual sexual liaisons with Italian youths, and a contemporary, the philandering memoirist Casanova, wrote that he once caught Winckelmann in flagrante delicto with a handsome young man. Mortified, Winckelmann denied being a "pederast": he had simply been attempting for the past "three or four years" to consummate the "inconceivable" act in order to deepen his understanding of the Greek and Roman intellectuals he so admired.

Johann Joachim Winckelmann.

In the spring of 1768, Winckelmann aborted, for reasons that remain unclear, a trip home to Germany and set back to Rome via Trieste, where he met and spent a week in the company of Francesco Arcangeli, a 31-year-old out-of-work cook. On May 8, Winckelmann was found in his hotel room dying from multiple knife wounds, and Arcangeli was arrested attempting to flee the hotel. Repeatedly interrogated and eventually sentenced to be broken on the wheel, Arcangeli confessed to the murder but never provided a credible motive. To this day, the circumstances of Winckelmann's death remain shrouded in mystery. French novelist Dominique Fernandez has suggested that Winckelmann was the earliest known example of a gay man killed for making a pass at "rough trade." Other gay writers, noting that Arcangeli was pockmarked and over 30, point out that he was far from Winckelmann's "type" of the beautiful Greek youth.

As critic and biographer Denis M. Sweet has documented, Winckelmann's legacy has mutated from country to country and era to era. For 19th-century Germans, he was a symbol of nationalistic pride, the first German writer to gain an international following. For Walter Pater and others associated with the English aesthetic movement, he was the almost mystically inspired link between modern times and the cultural values of the Greeks. For ADOLF BRAND and his followers, Winckelmann's genius helped legitimate their erotic attraction to handsome teenage boys. And, finally, for 20th-century gay men, he is not only, as his entry in *The Gay and Lesbian Literary Heritage* begins, "the first German to have been publicly acknowledged as a homosexual," but also the prototype of the now common conception of gay men as endowed with superior taste "by nature."

On another front, Winckelmann's writings, which include more than 1,000 highly confessional letters, offer something for virtually every shade of opinion in the CONSTRUCTIONISM VS. ESSENTIALISM debate. Those who believe that there is a gay essence that transcends time periods and cultures find similarities between him and modern gay men in his aestheticism and even in his admiration of muscular Italian fishermen. Those who maintain that sexualities are constructions largely shaped by the attitudes of the societies in which people live can point to his even greater enthusiasm for the androgynous beauty of eunuchs and castrati singers. For all historians, Winckelmann is a fascinating example of someone attracted to other men who managed to find success and acclaim during a century when at least 150 "sodomites" were burned, garroted, or hanged in Western Europe.

- Denis M. Sweet, "The Personal, the Political, and the Aesthetic: Johann Joachim Winckelmann's German Enlightenment Life," in *The Pursuit of Sodomy: Male Homosexuality in Renaissance and Enlightenment Europe,* edited by Kent Gerard and Gert Hekma (1989).
- Robert Aldrich, *The Seduction of the Mediterranean: Writing, Art and Homosexual Fantasy* (1993).
- Simon Richter, "Johann Joachim Winckelmann," in *The Gay and Lesbian Literary Heritage: A Reader's Companion to the Writers and Their Works, from Antiquity to the Present,* edited by Claude J. Summers (1995).

Winterson, Jeanette
(1959–)

English writer, editor. Adopted by stern Pentecostal evangelicals in Lancashire, Winterson began preaching as early as the age of 8 by some accounts and was preparing for a career as a missionary when her fellow church members discovered that she had fallen in love with another girl. After an unsuccessful "exorcism," Winterson, although only 15 at the time, ran away from home and supported herself with a variety of odd jobs while completing her studies and, eventually, attending Oxford University.

Winterson made these events the basis of her Whitbread Prize–winning first novel, *Oranges Are Not the Only Fruit* (1985), which in January 1990 became the first contemporary lesbian novel to be adapted for British TELEVISION. In subsequent novels—*The Passion* (1987), *Sexing the Cherry* (1989), *Written on the Body* (1992), and *Gut Symmetries* 1997)—Winterson has used unconventional narrative structures and playful magic realism to explore themes that include ANDROGYNY, blurred GENDER identities, and shifting sexual orientations, earning her a reputation, as *Newsweek* reported, as "Britain's most talked about feminist writer."

Winterson has also edited anthologies and written a woman's fitness guide.

✧ Hilary Hinds, "*Oranges Are Not the Only Fruit:* Reaching Audiences Other Lesbian Texts Cannot Reach," in *New Lesbian Criticism: Literary and Cultural Readings,* edited by Sally R. Munt (1992).

Witchcraft, see WICCA.

Wittig, Monique

(1935–)

French-born U.S. writer, theorist. The daughter of poet Henri Dubois, Wittig studied at the Sorbonne and won critical acclaim at the age of 28 as the author of *L'Opoponax* (1964; translated as *E*), an experimental work that used vivid present-tense sense descriptions to reproduce the unarbitrated immediacy of life as experienced by a child. With the publication of *Les Guérillères,* a series of prose poems about women world conquerors, in 1969, Wittig established herself as an influential GENDER theorist by her use of the French word *elles* ("they" feminine) in place of the conventional universal *ils* ("they" masculine, but used in conventional French as the plural third-person pronoun for all groups that include at least one man).

Challenging and provocative use of language also characterized her later books and essays, such as *Le Corps Lesbien* (1993, *The Lesbian Body*), *Brouillon pour un Dictionnaire des Amantes* (with Sande Zeig, 1976; translated as *Lesbian Peoples: Material for a Dictionary*), and "The Straight Mind" (1981). Wittig, who thinks of her fiction as a "war machine," works "to pulverize the old forms and formal conventions" in order to prove that they are constructed by culture rather than "natural."

In 1978, Wittig launched an attack on sexual politics with the now famous salvo: "I am a lesbian, not a woman." She later explained: "Lesbian is the only concept I know which is beyond the categories of sex (woman and man), because the designated subject (lesbian) is *not* a woman, either economically, or politically, or ideologically. For what makes a woman is a specific social relation to a man . . . a relation which implies personal and physical obligation as well as economic obligation." Lesbians, Wittig believes, "escape" these relations "by refusing to become or stay heterosexual."

Wittig teaches at the University of Arizona.

✧ Erika Ostrovsky, *A Continuous Journey: The Fiction of Monique Wittig* (1991).

✧ Monique Wittig, "One Is Not Born a Woman," in *The Lesbian and Gay Studies Reader,* edited by Henry Abelove, Michele Aina Barale, and David M. Halperin (1993).

Wittman, Carl

(1943–1986)

U.S. activist, writer. Born and raised in New Jersey, the child of leftist parents, Wittman got involved in the civil rights movement while attending Swarthmore College. He became one of the leaders of the radical left-wing Students for a Democratic Society (SDS) in 1963 and, together with SDS president Tom Hayden, developed new organizing strategies and theory for the group.

Although the leftist COUNTERCULTURE was notorious for its HOMOPHOBIA, Wittman came OUT in an antiwar publication after moving to San Francisco to work as a labor organizer in 1967. Shortly before the STONEWALL Uprising, he wrote *Refugees from Amerika: A Gay Manifesto.* Printed in San Francisco on **December 22, 1970**, and then reprinted and distributed across the U.S. in 1971, it became what movement historian Donn Teal called "the bible of gay liberation." The manifesto was both emblematic of its era and prophetic of the ways the gay SUBCULTURE was to evolve in the 1970s. It covered everything from the risks of ghettoization to sex, stressing self-liberation as the only possible means of achieving the aims of the movement.

In 1974, he and his lover, Allan Troxler, published the first issue of the magazine *RFD* while living on their commune in Wolf Creek, Oregon. He moved to Durham, North Carolina, in 1981 and worked as an environmental activist until his death of complications of AIDS. He was one of the founders of the Durham Gay and Lesbian Health Project.

✧ Donn Teal, *The Gay Militants: How Gay Liberation Began in America, 1969–1971* (1971).

Wockner, Rex

(1957–)

U.S. journalist. Wockner began having sex with other boys as a child growing up in Watseka, Illinois, but did not describe himself as "gay" until 1979, the year he graduated with a degree in journalism from Drake University. After college, he pursued graduate studies in Western philosophy, worked as a paralegal and a broadcast news reporter, and helped found the Gay Community AIDS Project in Cham-

Rex Wockner on assignment in Prague, 1990.

paign-Urbana, Illinois. He began writing for the gay and lesbian press in 1985 and has since published articles in almost 200 publications around the world.

By 1987, Wockner had come to the realization that, except for major events in media centers like New York, news of interest to lesbians and gay men seldom traveled beyond local publications. The next year, while working as the national and international news reporter for the Chicago publication *Outlines,* Wockner began selling as many as 25 articles a month to publications in the United States, Europe, and AUSTRALIA.

Now a kind of one-man gay Associated Press, Wockner travels widely to cover events in situ, besides drawing on several hundred news sources in dozens of countries. His "Wockner International News" reports, archived on the Internet from May 1994, serve as the chief world news source for lesbian and gay newspapers and magazines published in some 40 languages.

In addition to pioneering an unprecedentedly wide-reaching gay and lesbian news network, Wockner has earned a reputation for accuracy and objectivity, reporting not only the triumphs but also the faux pas of the international lesbian and gay rights movement. As a result, he is as apt to be quoted in Britain's *The Economist* as in Australia's *OutRage.* Though passionate in his beliefs—which include the conviction that, treated competently, AIDS is no longer a fatal disease—he avoids direct participation in gay and lesbian ACTIVISM in keeping with established standards of journalistic ethics. At the same time, he does not shun controversy: he appeared on several American TELEVISION talk shows after inadvertently OUTING actor Richard Chamberlain.

Wockner's news reports have documented the emergence of lesbian and gay organizations everywhere from Estonia to Sri Lanka. He maintains, however, that "the division of the population into 'gay' and 'straight' is a Western First World notion that has not been around very long and will not persist into the future."

Wockner's lover and officially registered domestic partner is Jesse Lynn Durfee, a teacher.

Wojnarowicz, David
(1954–1992)

U.S. artist, writer, activist. Abused as a child, Wojnarowicz ran away to New York City from his home in Red Bank, New Jersey, while still a teenager. He survived by hustling on the streets and eventually graduated from Manhattan's High School of Music and Art. By the early 1980s, his images of plummeting figures and burning buildings spray-stenciled on downtown walls had earned him a place among the rising stars of the antiestablishment art scene.

Wider fame came with his paintings, photographs, and installations, especially those that integrated his inflammatory texts. He used his personal history as well as provocative descriptions of the society around him in his work to combat HOMOPHOBIA and—especially after his lover PETER HUJAR died of HIV-related disease in 1987 and he himself was diagnosed with AIDS in 1988—to attack public prejudice and governmental apathy toward people with AIDS. *Close to the Knives: A Memoir of Disintegration* (1990) recalled public SEX scenes and evoked his anxiety as his friends succumbed one by one to AIDS: "I could do nothing more than wait for that moment where I'd hear the whistling sound and feel the presence of the bomb tracking me. I was diagnosed not long after that." It also included a controversial essay, "Postcards from America: X-Rays from Hell," which drew fire from Jesse Helms when it was used to introduce an AIDS art show catalog in 1989.

Wojnarowicz reached the height of his fame in 1990 and 1991, when he successfully brought suits against the right-wing American Family Association for unauthorized use of his art in the organization's virulently antigay mailings.

He was survived by his lover, Tom Rauffenbart. His *Memories That Smell Like Gasoline* (1992) was published posthumously.

✧ *David Wojnarowicz: Tongues of Fire,* edited by Barry Blinderman (1990).

Wolfenden Report

Popular name for *The Report of the Departmental Committee on Homosexual Offences and Prostitution,* presented to the British Parliament on September 3, 1957, and published the next day. This government document of almost 200 pages recommended that "male homosexual acts" between consenting adults in private be decriminalized. It thus sought the reversal of more than four centuries of British SODOMY legislation.

The report was the product of three years of research and public hearings carried out by a 15-member committee headed by Sir John Wolfenden, an English educator. The Home Secretary appointed the committee on **April 28, 1954**, in response to a growing outcry in the media and in Parliament over the large numbers of men prosecuted in the early 1950s for sodomy and "indecency" with other men, among whom were MPs, titled aristocrats, and celebrities like Sir John Gielgud. Jeffrey Weeks cites estimates that a full 4 percent of the men in British prisons at the time were incarcerated on same-sex charges.

The conclusions of the report were based on the belief that the purpose of LAW is not to promote morality but rather to safeguard public order and to protect the weaker members of society. Based on this thinking, the committee actually recommended harsher penalties for public manifestations of homosexuality such as soliciting. Behavior in private between adults that did not harm others was held to be outside the purview of criminal law.

The release of the report caused a sensation. Within hours, the first printing of 5,000 copies sold out and a second printing was ordered the next day. Nevertheless, it took ten years of public and parliamentary debate before legislation recommended by the report passed into British law. The Wolfenden Report also had an enormous impact on legislative thinking in CANADA, AUSTRALIA, and NEW ZEALAND. However, it had almost no effect on laws in dozens of other countries, including former British colonies in AFRICA, the CARIBBEAN, and SOUTH ASIA whose legal systems were also largely based on the British common law tradition. In the U.S., the report was noted in the HOMOPHILE press, but it was not until the parliamentary debates of the 1960s and the publication of an American edition of the report that it became widely known.

Although homophile activists welcomed the report and the later law reform based on its recommendations, neither the report nor the reforms went as far as they had hoped. For one thing, although the report fell short of characterizing homosexuality as a "sickness," most of the committee members persisted in the belief that homosexuality was a negative aberration. For another, the report specifically advised tolerance of *private* sex acts between *two* men *over 21.* Three-ways, group sex, and even public displays of affection between men remained "nuisances" that the law was "entitled to recognize and deal with," and young men 16 to 20 still merited "protection" from gay eroticism. All these aspects of the report had major repercussions on the British gay and lesbian rights movement in the 1980s and 1990s.

➤ Also see UNITED KINGDOM.

✧ Jeffrey Weeks, *Coming Out: Homosexual Politics in Britain from the Nineteenth Century to the Present* (1990).

✧ Stephen Jeffery-Poulter, *Peers, Queers and Commons: The Struggle for Gay Law Reform from 1950 to the Present* (1991).

"Woman-Identified Woman"

Influential radical lesbian position paper first distributed on **May 1, 1970**, at the LAVENDER MENACE action during the Second Congress to Unite Women in New York City. The outcome of a study group attended by Ellen Bedoz (Shumsky), RITA MAE BROWN, Cynthia Funk, Lois Hart, March Hoffman (later Artemis March), and "Barbara XX," the paper was edited by Hoffman and originally credited to all six women "and other Radical Lesbians."

From its opening definition of a lesbian as "the rage of all women condensed to the point of explosion," the paper advanced lesbianism as a sociopolitical stance, not a sexual alternative or a sexual category. And far from constituting a "lavender menace," lesbians were essential to the women's movement as the vanguard of women's liberation, the ultimate women-identified women free from female role, identity, and behavior as defined by a male-dominated society and free to assert the primacy of their own needs and work in solidarity with other women to fight male oppression. The fear of being labeled "lesbian," the statement charged, was a divisive sexist tactic to discourage independence and female bonding. Therefore, women who complied with lesbian-baiting were caught in the heterosexual cycle of seeking male approval and being a woman on male terms, revealing just how male-identified they were. "Woman-Identified Woman" had an immediate impact on the women's movement because it echoed radical feminist goals of equality, independence, self-actualization, and freedom from rigid sex roles.

After publication in the community papers *Rat* and *Come Out!*, the paper was widely reprinted, notably in *Notes from the Third Year: Women's Liberation* (1971) and most major collections of feminist documents since.

✧ Sidney Abbott and Barbara Love, *Sappho Was a Right-On Woman* (1972).

✧ Alice Echols, *Daring to Be Bad: Radical Feminism in America, 1967–1975* (1989).

✧ Dana R. Shugar, *Separatism and Women's Community* (1995).

Woodson, Jacqueline

(1963–)

U.S. writer. Born in Columbus, Ohio, Woodson grew up in South Carolina and Brooklyn, New York. She began writing at an early age and went to work as an editorial assistant for children's books after graduating from Adelphi University. The publication of *Last Summer with Maizon* (1990) established her as one of

Jacqueline Woodson.

the first persons of color to write lesbian- and gay-themed fiction for young adults.

"Ours is a society that disregards girls, that renders them invisible," Woodson asserts. "I want to write against this invisibility and explore social issues important to their existence." Those issues have included racism, classism, divorce, alcoholism, violence, mental illness, and AIDS, in addition to matters directly related to sexuality. In *From the Notebooks of Melanin Sun* (1995), for example, a 13-year-old boy respects and loves his mother despite problems with his friends over her lesbianism.

The recipient of numerous AWARDS, Woodson has published six books for young adults as well as a "mainstream" novel, *Autobiography of a Family Photo* (1995). Critics have acclaimed her writing for its poetic eloquence, and her characters for their strength and deep-felt sense of purpose. Currently on the faculty of the M.F.A. program at Goddard College, she advises her students to start their writing with memory "because we all have memory, those true, known places."

➤ Also see YOUTH, LESBIAN AND GAY.

✧ Catherine Saalfield, "Jacqueline Woodson," in *Contemporary Lesbian Writers of the United States,* edited by Sandra Pollack and Denise D. Knight (1993).

✧ Mary Quattlebaum, "Jacqueline Woodson's Books for Brave Girls," in *The Bookwoman* (Winter 1995/96).

Woolf, Virginia

(née Adeline Virginia Stephen; 1882–1941)

English writer. The product of an upper-middle-class Victorian upbringing that was both straitlaced and tumultuous, scarred by her mother's death and sexual abuse, she set up a household in London's Bloomsbury section with her older sister Vanessa and brothers Thoby and Adrian in 1904 and emerged as the creative leader of the literary and artistic movement that came to be called the BLOOMSBURY Group. She married the writer Leonard Woolf in 1912 and together with him founded the Hogarth Press in 1917. The same year, she began writing influential reviews for the *Times Literary Supplement.*

After publishing her first novel, *The Voyage Out* (1915), Woolf abandoned conventional narrative to author a series of experimental works of fiction—including *Jacob's Room* (1922), *Mrs. Dalloway* (1925), *To the Lighthouse* (1927), *Orlando: A Biography* (1928), *The Waves* (1931), and *Between the Acts* (1941)—that established her as one of the most important writers of the 20th century. In 1928, she delivered a series of lectures, collected the following year as *A Room of One's Own,* that are often cited, along with the essays in *Three Guineas* (1938), as the founding texts of feminist literary criticism.

Woolf had intellectual, platonic relationships with men, but, as she stated in a now famous line written to her friend ETHEL SMYTH (who was passionately in love with Woolf), "Women alone stir my imagination." Throughout her life, she drew support from ROMANTIC FRIENDSHIPS with older mother-figures, who included JOHN ADDINGTON SYMONDS's daughter Madge Vaughan and writer Violet Dickinson as well as Smyth; however, biographers believe her only physically consummated "Sapphist" affair was with VITA SACKVILLE-WEST, with whom she maintained a passionate though often long-distance relationship from 1925 until her death.

Despite the deep-felt devotion to women evident in her writing and her association with the free-thinking Bloomsbury set, Woolf was capable on occasion of expressing views that critics have found homophobic and even anti-Semitic (although Leonard Woolf was

Quentin Crisp (left, with Tilda Swinton) made an appearance as Elizabeth I in the film adaption of Virginia Woolf's Orlando.

Jewish). Alienated from both the promiscuous lesbianism of Sackville-West and the male identification of RADCLYFFE HALL (whom she nonetheless supported out of a belief in literary freedom), Woolf seems never to have found a model that would satisfactorily describe her sexual identity. Yet HOMOEROTICISM, lesbian relationships, and GENDER nonconformity are a feature of many of her works, most notably in *Mrs. Dalloway,* one of whose characters was modeled on Madge Vaughan, and *Orlando,* about which Woolf wrote Sackville-West: "It's all about you and the lure of your mind—heart you have none."

Woolf suffered through much of her life from debilitating bouts of depression, which began after her mother's death when she was 13. Shortly after completing her last novel, *Between the Acts,* she committed suicide by walking into the river Ouse near her country home.

✧ Quentin Bell, *Virginia Woolf: A Biography* (1972).

World War I

International conflict from 1914 to 1918, which furthered the development of gay and lesbian identities in several important ways. Although it did not have the impact of WORLD WAR II, World War I had the similar effect of giving thousands of previously isolated sexual misfits the chance to meet and bond with others who shared their desires. Gay historians like George Chauncey (*Gay New York,* 1994) have unearthed evidence that suggests that many early-20th-century urbanites were much more aware of the existence of same-sex eroticism than was commonly assumed by people, even historians, who had lived through the greater repression of the MCCARTHY ERA. Still, large pockets of ignorance remained: J. R. ACKERLEY, for example, had never heard the word "homo" before 1917, when a fellow prisoner of war asked him if he was one.

World War I was a liberating experience for many British and American lesbians. Obtaining jobs at home usually reserved for men afforded some an unprecedented degree of financial independence. In her short story "Miss Ogilvy Finds Herself," RADCLYFFE HALL described one of the many women who (like DOROTHY ARZNER and DOLLY WILDE) broke free from confining GENDER roles to drive ambulances at the front, only to have to return: "Poor all the Miss Ogilvies back from the War, with their tunics, their trenchcoats, and their childish illusions!" SYLVIA BEACH, GERTRUDE STEIN AND ALICE B. TOKLAS, and many others worked with the Red Cross.

Yet another incidental effect of World War I was the formation of the first known HOMOPHILE group in the U.S., HENRY GERBER's Society for Human Rights (see **12/10/1924**), which was inspired by Gerber's discovery of the German homophile movement while serving as part of the U.S. Army force that occupied part of GERMANY after the war.

The return of AFRICAN-AMERICAN soldiers from service in Europe is also viewed by historians as one of the factors that stimulated the HARLEM RENAISSANCE.

World War II

Global conflict from 1939 through 1945 that stimulated what gay historian JOHN D'EMILIO calls a "nationwide coming OUT experience." D'Emilio was among the first to cite the experiences of the hundreds of thousands of lesbians and gay Americans who served in the war as keys to the development of a gay and lesbian consciousness in the U.S.

According to D'Emilio and Allan Bérubé, who researched and wrote the definitive account of lesbians and gay men in World War II, the war experience furthered the GAY AND LESBIAN RIGHTS MOVEMENT in the U.S. in several important ways. The first war in which American MILITARY recruits were extensively tested for "homosexual tendencies"—and the first time large numbers of service personnel thought to be gay and lesbian were given so-called blue discharges—World War II had the unintended effect of forcing millions to consider and define their sexuality for the first time in their lives. Moreover, gay men and lesbians who escaped detection had more and better chances of meeting others who shared their sexual interests and of forming long-term friendships in the service than they would have had in their home towns. Many were also able to travel to cities like New York and San Francisco, where they came into contact with more experienced gay men and lesbians. And finally, after the war, thousands of gay and lesbian veterans settled in large coastal cities, leading to an unprecedented concentration of lesbians and gay men that would later permit activists like HARRY HAY, PHYLLIS LYON, and DEL MARTIN to recruit members for pioneering HOMOPHILE groups. The majority of early MATTACHINE members, for example, had served in World War II. Even away from the coasts, as Bérubé has observed, veterans who had discovered the pleasures of lesbian and gay life in the service were a ready clientele for the gay and lesbian BARS opened in medium-sized cities like Kansas City, Missouri.

Gay men as disparate as QUENTIN CRISP, TENNESSEE WILLIAMS, and TOM OF FINLAND lauded the seemingly limitless opportunites for sexual encounters with soldiers and sailors afforded by the war. Women like PAT BOND have also cited their wartime experiences as a time when they began to realize that other women were "that way."

On the other hand, perhaps partially as a result of the increase in awareness of homosexuality during wartime, investigations of gay and lesbian service members intensified after World War II. Bars and CRUISING areas were raided with increasing frequency, and workplace discrimination became much more severe during the MCCARTHY ERA.

✧ John D'Emilio, *Sexual Politics, Sexual Communities: The Making of a Homosexual Minority in the United States, 1940–1970* (1983).

✧ Allan Bérubé, *Coming Out Under Fire: The History of Gay Men and Women in World War II* (1990).

Y

Yourcenar, Marguerite

(Marguerite de Crayencour; 1903–1987)

Belgian-born French writer. Born in Brussels to an aristocratic French father and a Belgian mother who died soon after she was born, Yourcenar spent much of her youth in London and Paris. She had her first two books privately printed while still a teenager, using the anagram of her birth name that became her PSEUDONYM, before achieving fame with *Alexis* (1929), a novel in the form of a letter written by a man who has decided to leave his wife to pursue other men. She traveled widely until 1939, when she settled in the U.S. with Grace Frick, an American academic. From 1942 until her death, she and Frick (who died in 1979) spent most of their time at their house on Mount Desert Island off the coast of Maine. In 1981, Yourcenar became the first woman ever inducted into the prestigious Académie Française.

Yourcenar's best-known statement about her sexuality is one she gave *The New York Times:* "Because I lived with a woman for 40 years, people assumed that I was a lesbian." Throughout her life she tried to preserve her privacy, rarely giving out details about her personal life. She is known, however, to have had affairs with a number of women and was a friend and admirer of NATALIE BARNEY. She also had romantic but probably nonsexual friendships with several gay men. Most critics believe she rejected conventional notions of GENDER, identifying instead with a combination of masculinity and femininity she found in gay men.

Yourcenar's identification with gay men is reflected in her most acclaimed works. She portrayed love relationships between men both in antiquity (*Memoirs of Hadrian,* 1951; English translation, 1954) and in the 20th century (*Le Coup de Grâce,* 1939; English translation, 1957), and male same-sex eroticism in other works, such as *The Abyss* (in French as *L'Oeuvre au Noir,* 1968; English translation, 1976). She also translated and wrote about CONSTANTINE CAVAFY and published an influential essay on YUKIO MISHIMA.

✧ Josyane Savigneau, *Marguerite Yourcenar: Inventing a Life* (1992).

Youth, Lesbian and Gay

A high percentage of gay men and lesbians come to the realization that they are primarily attracted to members of their own sex at a very young age, some even before puberty. For many of them, this realization begins a process of coming OUT that can take years to complete to the individual's satisfaction. Almost everyone agrees that coming out—or even simply being perceived as gay or lesbian—is more stressful for younger people than for adults, who have greater freedom to express nonconformist identities and, usually, easier access to social contacts and community services. A 1989 U.S. Department of Health and Human Services task force on youth suicide found that gay and lesbian teens were two to three times more likely to commit suicide than their heterosexual peers. Although some experts have criticized this study, its findings were supported by another study conducted in Alberta, CANADA, which reported in 1996 that gay and bisexual men aged 18 to 27 were three times more likely to have attempted suicide than straight men.

Brett Barsky stars in Trevor, an Academy Award–winning short film about a young gay boy.

Social Services

The Hetrick-Martin Institute (founded by Emery S. Hetrick and Damien Martin in New York City in 1979 and originally called the Institute for the Protection of Lesbian and Gay Youth; renamed after its founders in 1987) was an international pioneer in offering social services to gay, lesbian, and bisexual youth. Hetrick, a psychiatrist and New York University Medical School professor, and Martin, a communications professor at New York University, decided to found the institute when they heard about a gay boy who had been expelled from a home for runaway teens after he had been gang-raped by other boys at the facility. Hetrick and Martin recognized that gay and lesbian teens were isolated not only by the tendency, as in this case, for schools and government agencies to blame them for the problems they faced but also by the reluctance of adult lesbians and gay men to offer support out of fear of being suspected of PEDOPHILIA. Believing that lesbians and gay men "would never have a healthy adult community" if they did nothing to help their younger peers, Hetrick and Martin began by offering counseling services for a small group of young people.

According to *You Are Not Alone,* a publication of the Hetrick-Martin Institute, more than 170 organizations across the U.S. provide at least some services for queer youth, ranging from hotlines and meeting facilities to full-fledged high schools in Los Angeles and New York.

Z

Zapata, Luis

(1951–)

Mexican writer. Zapata grew up in a comfortably well-to-do household in Chilpancingo de los Bravos, the capital of the state of Guerrero. Beginning with his first published novel, *Hasta en las Mejores Familias* ("Even in the Best Families," 1975), his work has been characterized by explicitly gay themes, in particular the conflict between gay male desire and the COMPULSORY HETEROSEXUALITY that pervades Mexican society. He was the first openly gay Mexican author to gain wide international readership and, with the publication of *Adonis García: A Picaresque Novel* by Gay Sunshine Press in 1981, the first to be translated into English. Other works include *En Jirones* ("In Shreds," 1985), a novel in diary form of a young man's obsession with another man who abandons him to get married; "My Deep Dark Pain Is Love," the title story of Gay Sunshine Press's 1983 collection of Latin American gay fiction; and *La Hermana Secreta de Angélica María* ("The Secret Sister of Angélica María," 1989), a novel about a movie buff who is also a hermaphrodite. Critics have praised Zapata's work for his entertaining use of CAMP and graphic eroticism.

✧ David William Foster, *Gay and Lesbian Themes in Latin American Writing* (1991).

✧ Maurice Westmoreland, "Luis Zapata," in *The Gay and Lesbian Literary Heritage: A Reader's Companion to the Writers and Their Works, from Antiquity to the Present,* edited by Claude J. Summers (1995).

Zaps

Disruptive, surprise protest tactics, including picketing, heckling, sit-ins, bombardment by phone, fax, or e-mail, and computer hacking.

Although many of the confrontational tactics that came to be described as "zapping" were foreshadowed by actions directed by FRANK KAMENY in Washington, D.C., beginning in the early 1960s, the term "zap" was borrowed from the COUNTERCULTURE to describe early GAY LIBERATION FRONT and, especially, GAY ACTIVIST ALLIANCE (GAA) activities. These include a GAA campaign against New York City mayor John V. Lindsay (**4/13/1970**); the LAVENDER MENACE action against Betty Friedan and other antilesbian leaders of the NATIONAL ORGANIZATION FOR WOMEN (**5/1/1970**); protests against the AMERICAN PSYCHIATRIC ASSOCIATION's position of considering (and aggressively treating) homosexuality as a disease (**5/14/1970**); and actions taken to fight HOMOPHOBIA in print (**10/27/1970**).

Although "zap" as a term is used less today, the confrontational approach it represents has been revived by ACT UP, QUEER NATION, and other self-described DIRECT ACTION groups beginning in the late 1980s.

✧ Donn Teal, *The Gay Militants: How Gay Liberation Began in America, 1969–1971* (1971).

✧ Dennis Altman, *Homosexual: Oppression & Liberation* (rev. ed., 1993).

Zimbabwe, see AFRICA, SUB-SAHARAN.

Zoology

The question of whether or not "homosexuality" exists in animals is as controversial as the issue of what difference it makes for human beings if it does. Since ancient times, some moralists have contended that same-sex eroticism does not occur among animals and so is "against nature." Others, since at least the time of Plato, have pointed out that by this criterion reading and writing are equally "unnatural." Still others have used animal lore, such as the false belief that hyenas regularly change their sex (see **c. 100**), to condemn and persecute same-sex eroticism among women and men as "bestial."

Modern zoology, a branch of BIOLOGY, has debunked traditional animal lore, but, according to a growing number of feminist critics of science like Donna Haraway, has not been immune to cultural and personal biases that can severely distort "scientific" interpretations. How animal sexual behavior and response is reported—even whether it is reported—often depends largely on the expectations of the observer. Just one example of this is the belief, almost universal among primatologists until the 1970s, that nonhuman female primates did not have orgasms. Influenced by 19th-century Western cultural expectations, scientists tended to describe primate sexuality in terms of male aggression, female passivity, and a mutual urge to procreate, virtually discounting the possibility that female as well as male monkeys might actually derive pleasure from sex.

Female bonding is common among primates.

One result of these biases is that *reliable* data on same-sex sexual behavior among animals are available for very few species. Observers of animal behavior have either ignored it or interpreted it variously as accidental, "practice," fulfilling some nonerotic function, or (influenced by Sigmund Freud) exemplifying "polymorphous perversity."

Nevertheless, same-sex mating behavior and affectional bonding have been observed in a wide variety of vertebrates. Female western gulls sometimes pair off for several years and mount each other while incubating eggs. Similar behaviors have been documented among female sage grouse, male mallard ducks, and female and male greylag geese and turkeys. Sexually indiscriminate mounting is so common among domestic animals like cows, pigs, and sheep that it has inspired techniques for obtaining sperm for artificial insemination. One study of pigs found boar "couples" who continued to mate with each other even when placed among sexually responsive sows. Among dogs, young male basenjis not uncommonly mount strange males to the point of ejaculation.

Primatology, although possibly the branch

of zoology most relevant to the study of human sexuality, has until recently lagged behind other areas of animal studies. In apes, for example, sexual behavior of any sort had rarely been observed in the wild until primatologists like Jane Goodall and Biruté Galdikas developed new observation techniques. Several researchers, however, have reported high rates of same-sex activity among female bonobos (a subspecies of chimpanzee). Some female bonobos, according to primatologist Linda M. Wolfe, remain "exclusively homosexual" their entire lives. Same-sex eroticism is also well documented for langurs and Japanese macaques.

➤ Also see GENDER; SOCIOBIOLOGY.

✧ Patrick A. Tyler "Homosexual Behaviour in Animals," in *The Psychology of Sexual Diversity* (1984).

✧ Donna Haraway, *Primate Visions: Gender, Race, and Nature in the World of Modern Science* (1989).

✧ Meredith F. Small, *Female Choices: Sexual Behavior of Female Primates* (1993).

✧ *Sex, Cells, and Same-Sex Desire: The Biology of Sexual Preference,* edited by John P. De Cecco and David Allen Parker (1995).

Chronology

c. 12,000 B.C.

Near the end of the Upper Paleolithic Era, human beings have left artifacts and works of art suggesting an appreciation of HOMOEROTICISM. Examples include a few cave paintings and hundreds of phallic "batons" among which is a graphically carved double dildo from Gorge d'Enfer (in present-day FRANCE) that seems to have been crafted for two women to use together.

c. 5000 B.C.

Examples of HOMOEROTICISM in European Mesolithic art include a rock engraving found in Addaura, Sicily, in which men and women dance around two cavorting male figures, both of whom have erections.

c. 2600 B.C.

In Fifth Dynasty Egypt, the tomb of two men who worked as manicurists and hairdressers for King Niuserre features a bas-relief of the two men embracing, a rare pose in Egyptian art even in depictions of male-female couples.

c. 2500 B.C.

In Sumer, in the Middle East, an unknown poet begins composing the Epic of GILGAMESH. The world's oldest surviving epic includes LITERATURE's first homoerotic love story, the death-defying friendship of the sexually insatiable Gilgamesh and the wild man Enkidu.

c. 2200 B.C.

In Sixth Dynasty Egypt, a chronicler suggests that King Neferkare and General Sisene, a high-ranking official, have had a secret affair.

Also in Egypt, a book about women's dreams includes references to two women having sex with each other.

c. 1750 B.C.

In Babylonia, the Code of Hammurabi mentions *girsequ,* male palace servants who provide sexual services for men in the ruling class.

In GREECE, the Middle East, and SOUTH ASIA, chroniclers and geographers leave accounts of battles with nations of AMAZONS, women warriors who live in matriarchal societies.

c. 700 B.C.

In CHINA, the *Shi Jing* ("Classic of Songs/Poetry"), the oldest surviving Chinese anthology, contains verse expressing admiration and affection for strong, handsome men. This and other sources suggest that Chinese traditions of HOMOEROTICISM go back at least as far as the Zhou (Chou) Dynasty (1122–256 B.C.)

c. 630 B.C.

In GREECE, the poet Alcman writes a hymn for a chorus of virgins in celebration of the marriage of two young women, Agido and Hagesichora. United in love, the couple become part of a community of young women called a *thiasos* (see **c. 600 B.C.**) and vow to remain impervious to the charms of the other desirable young women who surround them.

In Sparta, GREECE, men and women lead largely separate lives. Ruling-class women as well as men are expected to have romantic mentoring relationships with younger members of their own sex.

c. 600 B.C.

In GREECE, men leave inscriptions on a rock wall on the island of Thera recording the sex they have there with boys (*paides*), perhaps as part of an initiation ritual. One example: "Here Krimon and his boy, Bathykles' brother, had anal intercourse."

Also in GREECE, on the island of Lesbos, SAPPHO composes the most praised love poetry of the ancient world. The head of a *thiasos*—a community of women in which girls study music, dance, and other arts—Sappho immortalizes the desire and passion she and other women in the *thiasos* feel for one another.

594 B.C.

In Athens, GREECE, a law code attributed to Solon includes strict regulations meant to protect freeborn boys from the sexual advances of inappropriate—as opposed to appropriately aristocratic—male adults.

c. 570 B.C.

In GREECE, HOMOEROTICISM becomes one of the most popular themes for decorating vases and other pieces of pottery. Ranging from tender to grotesque, the painted scenes feature men, youths, boys, lusty satyrs, and an occasional god. One (or possibly two) shows seductive behavior between women.

c. 520 B.C.

In GREECE, a poem by the lyric poet Anacreon is the earliest recorded instance of a writer using "Lesbos" in a sense that may suggest sexual orientation: Anacreon addresses a "girl from Lesbos" who rejects the white-haired poet and "gapes at another girl" instead.

514 B.C.

In Athens, GREECE, Hipparchus, the ruling tyrant's brother, becomes jealous and insulting when a handsome young man named Harmodius rejects his advances. Harmodius and his lover Aristogiton kill him in revenge but fail in their attempt to assassinate his brother. Arrested and executed, the couple is immortalized by later generations of Greeks as heroes in the struggle for democracy and emblems of the positive potential power of love relationships between men.

c. 500 B.C.

In CHINA, Duke Ling of Wei lavishes attention on a male courtier named Mizi Xia, then spurns him when his looks fade. Mizi Xia remains loyal, however, and his name becomes part of the Chinese language: for more than 2,000 years a *"mizi xia"* will suggest a man who loves men.

c. 450 B.C.

In Palestine, the Holiness Code of Leviticus becomes part of the laws of JUDAISM. Leviticus 20:13 reads: "If a man also lie with mankind as he lieth with a woman, both of them have committed an abomination: they shall surely be put to death." BIBLE scholars and jurists will dispute the exact meaning of these words over the next 2,500 years; most, however, interpret the passage to mandate the death penalty for male-male sex acts.

c. 400 B.C.

In GREECE, on the island of Telos, a poet named Erinna writes a long poem lamenting the loss of her beloved Baucis to marriage and death. Erinna, who later dies at the age of 19, is one of several Greek women poets whose work, now mostly lost but widely acclaimed in ancient times, is thought to have included elements of HOMOEROTICISM.

387 B.C.

In Athens, GREECE, Plato's *Symposium* includes a speech by a man named Aristophanes, who suggests what is probably the world's first recorded theory of sexual orientation: All human beings were originally similar to Siamese twins. After the gods split them apart, each yearned for his or her "lost half." Those who had been male/female thus sought the opposite sex; those who had been male/male or female/female desired the same sex.

346 B.C.

In Athens, GREECE, a prominent citizen named Timarchus is successfully prosecuted and barred from politics, largely for having prostituted himself to men in his youth. The verdict is evidence of the Athenian bias against male citizens—as opposed to women, foreigners, and slaves—who allow themselves to be penetrated during sex.

338 B.C.

In GREECE, the MILITARY heroism and fighting spirit of the Sacred Band of Thebes, a corps of 150 male couples, impresses Philip of Macedon, the leader of the army that slaughters all 300 of the lovers.

c. 200 B.C.

In present-day Peru (see LATIN AMERICA), the Moche people achieve a standard of perfection in ceramic sculpture seldom equaled since. Many of their imaginative, often humorous creations are erotic, with depictions of female-female sexual activity alongside male-male and male-female figures. Same-sex eroticism remains common among many peoples in the region until the Inca era. Also see **c. 1475**.

In India (see SOUTH ASIA), the epic *Rāmāyana* includes a brief but evocative scene of female-female eroticism.

c. 185 B.C.

In India (see SOUTH ASIA), Brahman philosophers compile the highly influential Laws of Manu. Believing that all erotic thought and behavior weakens the mind and character, they prescribe ritual bathing to wash away the "pollution" of same-sex acts.

c. 55 B.C.

In ROME, Catullus writes poetry, much of which is inspired by his lively and varied sex life, that will be praised and imitated for generations to come. Besides describing an ill-fated affair with a woman he calls Lesbia, Catullus addresses eight poems to his young male lover Juventius.

c. 40 B.C.

The Greek geographer and historian Strabo writes of communities of Celtic women living in Gaul (in present-day FRANCE) and the sacred sexual rituals they perform with one another.

c. 30 B.C.

In ROME, the poets Virgil and Horace celebrate the amorous attractions of both young men and women. Virgil's second *Eclogue,* a monologue relating the shepherd Corydon's unrequited love for a slave boy called Alexis, becomes the most famous Roman homoerotic poem.

A.D. 1

In CHINA, Emperor Ai of the Han Dynasty attempts on his deathbed to name his lover Dong Xian as his successor. Other forces prevail, and Dong Xian is forced to commit suicide. As with Mizi Xia (see **c. 500 B.C.**), however, their relationship achieves a kind of immortality: the tale of the Emperor's cutting his sleeve off so as not to disturb Dong Xian, who had fallen asleep on it, inspires subsequent generations to call eroticism between men *duanxiu* ("cut sleeve") love.

c. 40

Philo, an influential Greco-Jewish philosopher who synthesizes elements of PLATO with JUDAISM, is among the first to condemn all forms of sex not leading to procreation, in particular same-sex eroticism.

41

In ROME, Claudius distinguishes himself by being the only emperor reigning in the first two centuries of the empire who is thought *not* to have sexual relationships with men.

c. 50

In the ROMAN EMPIRE, Dorotheos of Sidon is one of several writers on the science of ASTROLOGY who makes reference to birth charts that cause both men and women to experience sexual desire for members of their own sex.

c. 60

St. Paul writes "epistles" to communities of early Christians living in ROME and Corinth. Although the exact meaning of Paul's pronouncements will be disputed, Romans 1:26–27 and, to a lesser extent, 1 Corinthians 6:9 lay the New Testament foundation for condemning same-sex acts between women as well as men.

In ROME, Petronius Arbiter writes a comic novel called *The Satyricon* in which he evokes the attitudes, lifestyles, and BISEXUALITY of libertines of his day.

c. 85

Martial publishes the first of more than a dozen books of his scabrous but witty epigrams. Several hundred describe the love lives and sexual practices of people the poet knows in ROME, including men who make love to boys, men who make love to other men, and, in several poems, women who make love to other women.

91

Flavius Josephus, a Jewish historian writing for a broad Greco-Roman audience, helps popularize the idea that the sin for which SODOM AND GOMORRAH were destroyed was homosexuality, rather than simply unconscionable behavior toward strangers. Via his and other writings, the word "SODOMY" passes into Greek and Latin.

c. 100

Plutarch's highly influential biographies and essays written in Greek influence later attitudes toward same-sex eroticism through passages describing, among other relevant topics, man-boy and adult male-male love in the lives of famous men in GREECE and ROME, woman-girl love in Sparta, and the supposed "fact" that same-sex acts are unknown among animals.

On the other hand, the even more popular *Physiologus,* a "bestiary" recently translated from Greek into Latin (from which it will be translated and adapted over the next 1,200 years into all the European languages), explains that the hyena is despised because it spontaneously changes from male to female, not unlike some men "who are unchaste with other men."

c. 120

Juvenal's scathing satires target men in same-sex MARRIAGES, gigolos who pretend to be "effeminate" to gain access to their lovers' wives, upper-class women who shamelessly and semipublicly consort with each other, and a host of other types the poet finds all too common in ROME.

October 130

In ROME, Emperor HADRIAN mourns the drowning of his lover Antinous, founding a city and erecting temples and statues over the entire empire in his honor. Annual memorial games are celebrated for the next 200 years.

c. 160

Writing in Greek, the author Lucian provides a rare hint of the life- and love-styles considered typical for "tribades" (lesbians; see **c. 1600**) in ROME and elsewhere. In the fifth of his *Dialogues of the Courtesans,* a musician/courtesan tells how she was seduced by a wealthy female couple, who have what is perhaps the earliest example of a BUTCH-FEMME relationship. Lucian also makes reference to "masculine-looking" *hetairistriai* on the Isle of Lesbos who have sex only with other women.

193

In Palestine, Rabbi Judah the Prince compiles the Mishna, the codification of three centuries of rabbinical debates, including decisions that fix stoning to death as the penalty for male-male intercourse. As part of the Talmud (Learning), the Mishna becomes one of the fundamental texts of JUDAISM.

In CHINA, documents, including *Records of the Han,* allude to the existence of passionate relationships between women living in the Han Emperor's palace.

c. 200

In Upper Egypt, a spell cast to make a woman named Sarapias fall in love with another named Herais is one of several recorded on papyrus fragments. The spells are among the few surviving proofs of the existence of HOMOEROTICISM between women in the ROMAN EMPIRE.

249

Philip the Arab attempts to outlaw male prostitution in the ROMAN EMPIRE. The law is widely ignored: a special tax on male prostitutes continues to be collected in many parts of the empire for years to come.

c. 275

In CHINA, according to an official history, it is common for men at the Western Jin (Tsin) Dynasty court to be as attracted to each other as to women.

314

Drawing on teachings of the early Church fathers, the Council of Ancyra is the first to condemn SODOMY along with a host of other sex-related sins.

342

The Emperors Constans I and Constantius II promulgate what is probably the first law in the ROMAN EMPIRE directed against consensual sex acts between men. Reflecting the Roman abhorrence of adult citizens who allow themselves to be penetrated during sex, the edict specifies capital punishment for men who *nubit in feminam* ("mate as if a woman"). Also see **390**.

390

Lamenting the ineffectiveness of previous legislation (see **342**) and attacking the spread of male effeminacy in the ROMAN EMPIRE, the

Emperor Theodosius I issues a new edict prescribing public burning for offenders. Vaguely worded, the edict seems to apply mainly to transgender prostitutes. Also see **438**.

In Thessalonica, an outpost of the ROMAN EMPIRE, the commander of the local militia arrests a popular charioteer famous for his effeminacy on charges probably related to the edict described above. An uprising ensues, and the militia slaughters more than 3,000 people in seven hours.

c. 400

In India (see SOUTH ASIA), the *Kama Sutra* describes harem lesbianism.

438

Theodosius II amends the ROMAN EMPIRE laws regulating sex between men (see **390**) to specify burning at the stake for all men who make a practice of "condemning their male body" to be used "as a woman's."

533

In the Byzantine Empire, Justinian I blames men who lust after other men for natural disasters that threaten the state. He orders castration as punishment for SODOMY.

c. 650

In the territory that is to become PORTUGAL and SPAIN, the Visigothic Code is the first in post-Roman Western Europe to make sex between men a crime. Castration is the prescribed punishment.

651

The canonical text of the Koran, the foundation of ISLAM, is established, containing several negative references to sex between men as practiced by "the people of Lut [Lot]," the Sodomites and Gomorrhans of the Christian tradition. No punishment, however, is explicitly mandated.

700

"Penitentials," refined in Wales and IRELAND over the past two centuries, now become common throughout Western Europe. Containing lists of sins and recommended penances, penitentials are handy guides for priests, who have begun to hear private confessions. Sex between men is usually among the sins mentioned; starting about this year some penitentials also list sexual acts between women. In general, same-sex sin is not treated much more harshly than heterosexual adultery.

720

One of the first books written in JAPAN, the *Nihon Shoki* ("Japanese Chronicles"), includes an account of two male lovers who enraged the gods by sacrilegiously being buried in the same tomb. This is probably the earliest surviving mention of same-sex love in Japan. Also see **806**.

c. 800

Male homoerotic poetry in praise of beautiful youths becomes one of the major themes of Arabic poetry during the Abbāsid Caliphate (750–1258), typified by the brilliant, often obscene lyrics of ABŪ NUWĀS.

806

Kūkai (posthumously called Kōbō Daishi) returns to JAPAN from CHINA, bringing with him, according to Japanese tradition, the "Chinese custom" of male-male love along with *Shingon* ("true word") BUDDHISM. Also see **720**; **1254**.

829

The Synod of Paris blames Moorish and Hungarian invasions and Viking raids on same-sex eroticism, bestiality, and residual paganism.

866

In the Byzantine Empire, Michael III joins in a SAME-SEX UNION with Basil the Macedonian. The next year Basil murders Michael and usurps the throne.

914

In the Byzantine Empire, a commentator adds a marginal note to a text of the second-century Christian theologian Clement of Alexandria, explaining that by "women who act like men" Clement means those women who are "abominable tribades [see **c. 160**], *hetairistriai* [see **c. 160**], or *Lesbiai.*" This is the earliest recorded usage of "LESBIAN" in a context that clearly refers to same-sex acts.

960

In CHINA, the Song (Sung) Dynasty capital of Kaifeng is said to have thousands of male prostitutes. Also see **c. 1115**.

1051

Peter Damian writes *Liber Gomorrhianus,* urging Pope Leo IX to deal more harshly with sins against nature in the Church. The Pope, however, stresses the value of mercy in his reply.

1073

Pope Gregory VII orders SAPPHO's works, the world's oldest poetry of love between women (see **c. 600 B.C.**), destroyed in public bonfires in ROME and Constantinople.

c. 1115

In CHINA, the empire's first LAW forbidding male prostitution (see **960**) is promulgated. Part of a campaign to control both female and male prostitution, the law is never strenuously enforced and passes into oblivion with the end of the Song (Sung) Dynasty.

c. 1200

In southern FRANCE and northern SPAIN, troubadours travel from court to court, singing Provençal songs of courtly love that sometimes describe love between men and between women.

In Flanders, *The Life of Saint Godelive,* the story of a martyred 12th-century noblewoman who was later named patroness of the country, mentions in an aside that women are by nature prone to almost uncontrollable lusts and that they most frequently satisfy these lusts with one another, especially when sleeping together in the same bed. Also see **1212**.

1212

The Council of Paris, a local church body, forbids nuns from sleeping in the same bed and mandates that a lamp be left burning through the night in convent sleeping quarters.

c. 1250

The Norwegian LAW of the Gulathing is the first recorded legislation against male SODOMY in SCANDINAVIA. Men found guilty are to be banished from civilized communities as permanent "outlaws."

1252

Thomas Aquinas begins teaching at the University of Paris. One of the ROMAN CATHOLIC CHURCH's most influential theologians, he synthesizes 1,200 years of sex-negative Christian writings into one unified system of sexual morality, including same-sex eroticism among sexual acts that are "against nature."

1254

In JAPAN, Tachibana Narisue compiles the *Kokon Chomonju* ("Collection of Stories Heard from Writers Old and New"), which includes a number of romantic tales of the monk-boy love prevalent in Japanese BUDDHISM. Also see **806**.

1256

In SPAIN, Alfonso X of Castile issues *Las Siete Partidas,* one of the first civil LAW codes in Europe to make "sins against nature," including SODOMY, capital crimes. The punishment for sodomy is castration followed by stoning to death. Also see **1497**.

1260

In Orleans, FRANCE, a new LAW code mandates punishments for both men and women who commit same-sex acts: removal of the testicles or the clitoris, respectively, for a first offense; removal of the penis or breasts for a second offense; and burning at the stake for a third offense.

c. 1270

In FRANCE, new LAWS promulgated by St. Louis (Louis IX) make *bougerie* ("anal intercourse") a capital crime punishable by burning at the stake. Although civil authorities enforce the law, cases are still tried before a bishop.

September 28, 1292

In Ghent (in present-day BELGIUM), a knifemaker named John is sentenced to be burned at the stake for having sex with another man. This is the first documented execution for SODOMY in Western Europe.

1308

Philip IV of FRANCE orders the arrest of all Knights Templar on charges of heresy and SODOMY as a pretext for confiscating the knights' extensive wealth. The leaders of the religious order are burned at the stake in 1314.

1323

In FRANCE, a Franciscan subdeacon named Arnold of Verniolle is convicted of SODOMY and heresy. The court records provide an account of how someone like Arnold, who is attracted to young men, goes about finding sexual partners in rural France. Arnold is sentenced to live the remainder of his life imprisoned in chains and with nothing but bread and water for sustenance.

1327

In England (see UNITED KINGDOM), Edward II, known for his male lovers, loses out in a power struggle with his estranged wife and a cabal of the country's barons. His assassins, rumor has it, execute him by ramming a red-hot poker into his rectum.

1391

Two women and fifteen men are arrested and tried on charges of SODOMY in Mechelen (in present-day BELGIUM). Only one man, however, is executed.

April 9, 1424

In Florence, Bernardino of Siena (canonized in 1450) brings a three-day series of sermons against SODOMY and other forms of lust to a climax with a spectacular bonfire of "vanities"—cosmetics, wigs, and lewd attire. The preachings of Bernardino and others galvanize public opinion against same-sex relations and influence authorities to take more stringent action to suppress them. Also see **1432**.

1425

The Mexica Aztecs (in present-day MEXICO) establish dominion over surrounding peoples. Aztec law mandates marriage and punishes both male and female same-sex acts with death.

1432

Florence becomes the first European city to set up a special authority to prosecute crimes of SODOMY. Called the Uffiziali di Notte (Officers of the Night), this special court prosecutes more than 10,000 men and boys over the next 70 years. About 2,000 are believed to have been convicted. Most avoid further punishment by paying fines. Also see **April 9, 1424**.

1451

Pope Nicholas V authorizes the papal INQUISITION to prosecute male SODOMY.

c. 1475

In present-day Peru (see LATIN AMERICA), the Inca emperor Capac Yupanqui, according to word-of-mouth accounts chronicled a century later, energetically persecutes men who have sex with other men, burning them alive in public squares and destroying their homes. Most of those persecuted are members of recently subjugated peoples. Also see **c. 200 B.C.**

1476

LEONARDO DA VINCI is twice anonymously denounced to Florentine authorities (see **1432**) for alleged acts of SODOMY. He is acquitted of the charges for lack of witnesses.

November 1, 1494

In Florence, the fanatical monk Savonarola blasts citizens for their "abominable vice," commanding them to renounce their mistresses and "beardless youths." Also see **1497**.

1497

In Florence, Savonarola's campaign against vice, including SODOMY (see **11/1/1494**), is resisted by the Compagnacci, a group of young men, many of whose leaders have been convicted on sodomy charges. The youths jeer and harrass the preacher's followers in the streets and squares of the city.

In present-day SPAIN, King Ferdinand and Queen Isabella amend the SODOMY laws (see **1256**). Henceforth, those found guilty of the crime will be burned at the stake and have their property confiscated instead of being castrated and stoned to death.

1499

In SPAIN, Fernando de Rojas writes his tragicomic masterpiece in an attempt to fight the current craze for man-boy love. Before long, troupes of older males take their place.

1512

In Florence, a large group of young men converge on the government palace to protest the current crackdown on SODOMY and to demand the release of men recently arrested. Also see **1514**.

October 5, 1513

Spanish conquistador Vasco Núñez de Balboa discovers a community of CROSS-DRESSING males in present-day Panama and, according to eyewitnesses, feeds at least 40 of them to his dogs.

1514

Perhaps influenced by youth protests (see **1497** and **1512**), authorities in Florence decrease the fines for SODOMY convictions levied on men aged 18 through 25. Studies of contemporary municipal court and population records indicate that as many as one Florentine man in twelve would be charged with sodomy at some point in his youth.

1531

Martin Luther accuses Catholic clergy and monks of being sodomites in his *Warning to His Beloved Germans.*

1532

In the NETHERLANDS, new statutes make "unnatural vice" a capital crime.

Charles V promulgates a law as part of the *Constitutio* of the Holy Roman Empire that specifically forbids female same-sex relations as well as male.

1533

In England (see UNITED KINGDOM), Henry VIII's government transfers authority for prosecuting "buggery" from the Church to civil courts. The new law makes anal intercourse punishable by hanging.

1542

In JAPAN, Takeda Shingen, a 22-year-old *daimyo* (warlord), signs a contract with Kasuga Gensuke, his 16-year-old lover, vowing that he has never had—and has no intention of ever having—sex with a certain Yashichiro, and pledging his fidelity to Kasuga on penalty of divine retribution.

1549

Francis Xavier begins his mission in JAPAN. Writing to a Jesuit colleague, he reports that the Japanese have only one major fault: no one finds the "sin against nature . . . abnormal or abominable." Also see **1596**.

1551

Writing from BRAZIL, Portuguese missionary Father Pêro Correia asserts that same-sex eroticism among indigenous women is quite common, in fact as widespread as in AFRICA, where he was previously stationed. Native Brazilian women, he observes, carry weapons and even form same-sex MARRIAGES.

1555

In Calvinist Geneva, officials begin to pay closer attention to the sin of SODOMY, especially among the city's burgeoning foreign population. Records through 1670 list one beheading, one hanging, six drownings, six banishments, and four whippings, all for sodomy. Also see **1568**.

1566

Pope Pius IV begins a campaign in ROME to rid the city of "Sodomites."

1568

In Geneva, a woman charged with fornication with a man confesses that she also had sex with a woman four years ago. She is drowned.

1582

Oda Nobunaga, one of the most revered and feared warlords in the history of JAPAN, dies, ambushed by a confederate. At Nobunaga's side, faithful to the end, is his adolescent lover, Mori Ranmaru.

1593

Christopher Marlowe's tragedy *Edward II* (see **1327**) is probably the first play written in English to portray a male couple's love relationship sympathetically.

1596

Francis Cabral, a Catholic missionary, informs the Vatican in a letter that the casual attitude toward same-sex relations he sees everywhere in JAPAN is a major barrier to Japanese acceptance of CHRISTIANITY. Also see **1549**.

c. 1600

The word "tribade" (from a Greek root meaning "to rub") emerges in Western Europe as a term describing women who enjoy each other sexually. Also see **c. 160**.

1609

Matteo Ricci, Jesuit emissary to CHINA, is one of many Europeans who are shocked to find that "unnatural vice" is not only legal and widespread among the Chinese, it is even discussed in public.

May 24, 1610

The Virginia Colony passes the first anti-SODOMY law of the American colonial period. Also see **November 15, 1636**.

1623

MICHELANGELO's grandnephew publishes the first printed edition of the artist's poems, substituting female pronouns for male in the love verse. The originals are not made available in printed form until 1863.

November 30, 1624

In the Virginia Colony, Richard Cornish is hanged for allegedly making advances on a ship's steward. His conviction and execution, angrily contested by his brother and others, is the first to be recorded in the American colonies.

c. 1630

In CHINA, *The Classified Brief History of Love* contains a detailed chapter on *duanxiu* ("cut sleeve"—see **A.D. 1**) love, with anecdotes recounting two millennia of male-male relationships.

1631

In England (see UNITED KINGDOM), the Earl of Castlehaven is convicted on SODOMY charges brought by his son, who fears that the male servant his father favors may inherit part of the Earl's property. The Earl is beheaded.

November 11, 1634

In IRELAND, "An Act for the Punishment for the Vice of Buggery" is passed by the Irish House of Commons, making anal intercourse punishable by hanging. The primary advocate of the act is Anglican Bishop John Atherton. Also see **December 5, 1641**.

November 15, 1636

The Plymouth Colony (in present-day Massachusetts) issues the first complete legal code in the colonies. "SODOMY, rapes, buggery" constitute one of eight categories of crimes punishable by death.

1641

Thomas Bartholin's revision of his father's *Institutiones Anatomicae,* the most influential European anatomy text of the century, provides authoritative support for the theory that an enlarged clitoris is the cause of lesbian desire. Also see **1760**.

December 5, 1641

In an ironic twist, the second man to be hanged for the "vice of buggery" in IRELAND is Bishop John Atherton (see **11/11/1634**).

December 5, 1642

In the first documented example of legal prosecution in North America for same-sex relations between women, a Massachusetts Bay servant is sentenced to be whipped for "unseemly practices" with another woman.

1646

In BRAZIL, Portuguese colonial authorities extend LAWS forbidding same-sex relations to include women as well as men. The punishment is burning at the stake.

March 6, 1649

In Plymouth, Massachusetts, two married women are charged with "lewd behavior each with other upon a bed." Charges are dropped against Mary Hammon, at 15 the younger of the two, but the older woman, Sara Norman, is forced to confess her "unchaste behavior" in public.

c. 1650

In CHINA, novelist and short story writer Li Yu amuses readers with tall tales and adventure stories that include accounts of same-sex relations.

1652

In JAPAN, authorities declare a ban on all-boy troupes of kabuki actors in an attempt to fight the current craze for man-boy love. Before long, troupes of older males take their place.

1654

In PORTUGAL, Francisco Correa Netto, a cathedral sacristan, writes a series of love letters to a guitarist and musical instrument maker named Manuel Viegas. The oldest surviving openly homoerotic letters in a modern European language, Netto's writings tell a tale of seduction, passionate lovemaking, and, ultimately, betrayal: Viegas deserts Netto to marry a woman and turns the letters over to Church authorities for possible prosecution by the Portuguese INQUISITION.

March 1, 1656

In present-day Connecticut, the New Haven LAW code is the first in the American colonies to make same-sex acts between women punishable by the death penalty. The code quotes Romans 1:26 ("if any woman change the natural use into that which is against nature") as the basis for the law.

1686

In JAPAN, Ihara Saikaku's *Life of an Amorous Woman* includes a brief account of sex between the book's heroine and a female employer. Also see **1687**.

1687

In JAPAN, Ihara Saikaku publishes *The Great Mirror of Male Love,* 40 tales of love between older and younger men. Half the stories describe samurai affairs; the other half spotlight kabuki actors and their admirers.

1688

In England (see UNITED KINGDOM), APHRA BEHN, considered by many to be the first professional woman writer, writes "To the Fair Clarinda, Who Made Love to Me, Imagined More than Woman," in which she teasingly defends her sexual attraction to a young woman.

1697

In CHINA, Qing (Ch'ing) Dynasty Emperor Kangxi has three of his son's servants executed when he learns that they have been procuring male youths for themselves and his son. Also see **1740**.

1706

In RUSSIA, Peter the Great criminalizes sex between men in the MILITARY. Male-male sex remains legal and, according to contemporary accounts, widespread among civilians. Also see **1832**.

1725

Customers at a London "molly house" fight off a police raid in what is perhaps the first documented example of a gay male protest against LAW enforcement.

Paris is the home of some 20,000 "sodomites," according to police Lieutenant-General Lenoir. About 50 men are arrested each year for the crime. Although SODOMY remains a capital crime, most of those arrested are imprisoned, often for life.

1726

In Paris, Benjamin Deschauffours is burned at the stake in the Place de Greve. Although accused of other crimes including rape and murder, many contemporaries believe he has been unjustly punished for being guilty of SODOMY. One publishes an anonymous tract in protest.

1730

In the NETHERLANDS, an unprecedentedly severe campaign against SODOMY begins, focusing in some cities on orphanages and in others on public CRUISING areas. By 1731, courts throughout the country have found some 250 men and boys guilty of the crime. Approximately one tenth are strangled and burned at the stake. Most of the rest are whipped or banished. Also see **September 1731**.

September 1731

In Faan, a small village in northern Holland (see the NETHERLANDS), 22 young men are strangled and burned at the stake despite protests from relatives and neighbors. Most had confessed to engaging in mutual masturbation with each other.

1732

In IRELAND, William King publishes the first edition of *The Toast,* a vicious poetic satire on a group of women in Dublin. In one section, *The Toast* uses the term "lesbian loves," making it one of the earliest surviving examples in English of the word "LESBIAN" in a same-sex context.

1740

In CHINA, the Qing (Ch'ing) Dynasty enacts the first Chinese law forbidding consensual SODOMY between adult males. Offenders are to spend one month wearing a cangue around their neck and receive 100 blows. The statute, however, is rarely enforced. Also see **1697**.

July 1750

Two workers named Bruno Lenoir and Jean Diot are burned at the stake after being caught having sex on a Paris street. They are the last—and the first in 25 years—to be executed in FRANCE solely for the crime of SODOMY.

1760

Besides reminding the European reading public of the dangers of masturbation, Dr. Tissot's *Onanisme* lends additional support to a by now widespread belief (see **1641**): same-sex passions among women are caused by unusually large clitorides. Tissot considers this condition, akin to "hermaphroditism," disturbingly common. Over the next few decades, the Swiss physician's work is widely translated and republished.

1764

Typical of Enlightenment attitudes, Voltaire's *Dictionnaire Philosophique* includes an article on *"l'amour nommé socratique,"* complete with a listing of historical figures who were devotees of same-sex eroticism.

1770

In *Les Confessions,* Jean-Jacques Rousseau describes his terror and revulsion when a "self-styled African" attempted to seduce him, but then relates a friend's defense of the seduction attempt. This is perhaps the first plea for tolerance of same-sex love in modern European literature.

1778

Two Irish cousins, Lady Eleanor Butler and Sarah Ponsonby, elope to Wales to become the celebrated LADIES OF LLANGOLLEN. Their ROMANTIC FRIENDSHIP, almost certainly sexual, becomes one of the most talked-about relationships of the age.

February 23, 1778

Prussian MILITARY genius Baron Friedrich Wilhelm von Steuben arrives at Valley Forge,

Pennsylvania, in the company of a handsome 17-year-old secretary. Fearing prosecution for alleged indiscretions with young men back in Prussia, Steuben has signed on to train George Washington's ragtag Continental Army. Most historians consider his success at this task a major factor in the American victory.

March 11, 1778

At Valley Forge, Pennsylvania, Lieutenant Frederick Gotthold Enslin becomes the first American to be discharged from the MILITARY on an attempted SODOMY charge.

1782

Johann Friedel's *Letters on the Gallantries of Berlin* is the first book to describe male-male street CRUISING and prostitution in this German city.

1783

In FRANCE, Friar Pascal is the last person to be burned at the stake for SODOMY. The punishment is unusually harsh for Enlightenment France: Pascal had compounded his crime by murdering a boy he was trying to rape. All but eight of those convicted of sodomy since 1715 have been imprisoned rather than executed.

October 25, 1783

At West Point, New York, Deborah Sampson is honorably discharged from the Massachusetts Regiment. Wounded in one of several battles in which she fought, Sampson had escaped discovery for almost a year and a half until falling sick with a fever. One of the earliest American examples of a PASSING woman, Sampson formed several attachments with women while dressed as a man. She later marries and receives a MILITARY pension.

c. 1785

In JAPAN, popular prints by Kitagawa Utamaro and other artists depict erotic encounters between women and between men as well as heterosexual situations.

1788

In England (see UNITED KINGDOM), Mary Wollstonecraft publishes *Mary: A Fiction,* drawing on her own life to chronicle the devotion of one woman to another. The type of ROMANTIC FRIENDSHIP described in the novel will become a common theme of fiction as well as actual women's lives in the 19th century.

1790

In FRANCE, groups of militant "sodomite-citizens" demand freedom and recognition in petitions addressed to the National Assembly, the governing body of the French Revolution.

1791

In present-day GERMANY, the *Magazine of Experimental Psychical Studies* publishes what is considered the first attempt at a scientific article on gay men.

September 25, 1791

In FRANCE, the new LAW code, enacted as part of the French Revolution, effectively decriminalizes SODOMY by including no mention of sex between consenting adults. Also see **1810**.

1795

In FRANCE, the Marquis de Sade publishes *Philosophy in the Boudoir,* complete with almost every variety of sex imaginable. The book is suppressed two decades later, but remains widely available as an underground classic until it is openly republished in the 1960s.

1796

In FRANCE, encyclopedist Denis Diderot's posthumously published *La Religieuse* includes a decadent and libidinous Mother Superior who tries to seduce the young nun of the novel's title. His characterization of a woman attracted to other women as emotionally depraved will become common in 19th-century French novels. Also see **1835**.

1798

Médéric Louis-Elie Moreau de St. Méry, a French lawyer and politician, leaves Philadelphia, where he later writes that he was shocked to observe women enjoying "unnatural pleasures" with each other—even though, like most Americans, such women are, compared with the French, "not affectionate."

c. 1805

Halet Efendi, the Turkish ambassador to FRANCE, is shocked at the number and flagrancy of boy prostitutes working around the Palais Royal market. Europeans consider all Muslims sodomites, he writes, but no place in the Muslim world is as scandalous as Paris.

1807

In CHINA, scholar Shen Fu's autobiography hints at ways cloistered upper-class Chinese women may have arranged love relationships with other women. When his wife, Shen Yun, falls in love with a singing girl, she attempts to obtain the girl as Shen Fu's concubine. Thwarted by her husband's family, Shen Yun sickens and dies after the girl is forced to marry another man.

1810

In London, the police raid the White Swan pub on Vere Street. One of the first "gay bars," the White Swan is patronized by a variety of men, most of whom contemporaries describe as effeminate but also including "Fanny, an athletic bargeman," and "Lucy, a Herculean coal-heaver."

In FRANCE, the Napoleonic Code takes effect, leaving consensual sex between adults decriminalized. Many Western European countries conquered by Napoleon, as well as their colonies around the world, adopt this code.

1812

Responding to the previous year's controversial trial—and subsequent libel suit—of two Scottish schoolmistresses, Miss Pirie and Miss Woods, for "improper and criminal conduct" with each other and one of their pupils, British legal authorities engage in a debate over whether sex between two women is possible. The consensus: it is not. Also see **November 20, 1934**.

1813

In present-day GERMANY, jurist Anselm von Feuerbach helps persuade Bavarian lawmakers to follow the lead of the Napoleonic Code (see **1810**) and decriminalize sex acts between consenting adults.

1816

In London, four members of the crew of the *Africaine* are hanged. Their execution is part of an intensified English campaign to punish "buggery" in the navy.

1822

SPAIN's new criminal code includes no mention of SODOMY.

1832

RUSSIA criminalizes male-male "anal contact" among civilians for the first time (see **1706**). The penalty is four to five years' exile in Siberia.

August 1833

In London, Captain Nicholas Nicholls, 50, is sentenced to death on a charge of SODOMY. His sentence is protested by the anonymous poet who is writing *Don Leon,* purportedly an autobiographical poem by LORD BYRON but actually by some contemporary who is remarkably familiar with the late poet's love life. *Don Leon* is not only one of the earliest works of protest against the persecution of same-sex love; it is also cited as evidence of an emerging identity constructed around the "inborn passions" of men whose "predilection is for males":

Whence spring these inclinations, rank and strong?
And harming no one, wherefore call them wrong?

c. 1835

Although not technically a BERDACHE—she wears women's clothes and is considered attractive in a feminine way—the Crow known as Woman Chief takes a total of four wives as a sign of the elite status she has won by virtue of her bravery and skills in hunting and war.

1835

In FRANCE, two popular novels—Honoré de Balzac's *The Girl with the Golden Eyes* and Théophile Gautier's *Mademoiselle de Maupin* (whose eponymous heroine is among the first to refer to herself as a member of the "third sex")—introduce androgynously beautiful lesbian femmes fatales. These glamorously decadent heroines leave stereotypes that endure for more than one and a half centuries.

1836

In SWITZERLAND, HEINRICH HOESSLI publishes the first volume of *Eros: Die Männerliebe der Griechen* ("Eros: The Love Between Men of the Greeks"), a historical survey and defense of same-sex love and one of the first books to call for social tolerance of persons drawn to it.

1840

In present-day GERMANY, the state of Hanover decriminalizes same-sex relations.

In the UNITED KINGDOM, the last execution for SODOMY takes place. Capital punishment, however, remains possible until the legal reform of **1861**.

July 20, 1845

In Paris, a mob attacks a group of about 50 men arrested by police in a sweep of the Tuileries Gardens, a popular CRUISING area.

July 19, 1848

Elizabeth Cady Stanton and co-organizer Lucretia Mott invite several hundred women to Seneca Falls, New York, for the first Women's Rights Convention. About 100 sign a "Declaration of Sentiments" modeled on the Declaration of Independence. The document marks the beginning of organized feminism in the U.S.

1850

Yokel's Preceptor, a guide to London's unconventional attractions, lists Fleet Street and the Strand among places where one is almost certain to find men on the prowl for other men.

1851

In Prussia, the most powerful of the states that will later become GERMANY, the government enacts the forerunner of Paragraph 175 (see **1871**), penalizing male-male sex acts. Although less harsh than preceding legislation, the new law runs counter to a trend in other German states of decriminalizing consensual adult sex acts (see **1813**; **1840**).

1852

AUSTRIA makes sex between women illegal for the first time, while reducing the penalties for male-male relations.

Johann Ludwig Casper, a specialist in forensic medicine, is the first in GERMANY to state that the tendency to be attracted to members of one's own sex is inborn.

July 4, 1855

WALT WHITMAN publishes the first edition of his *Leaves of Grass.* Also see **1860**.

1857

In FRANCE, Dr. Ambroise Tardieu publishes a highly influential "medico-legal study" complete with a list of "symptoms" he believes are typical of a man prone to indulge in "practices against nature." These include a funnel-shaped rectum, deformed lips, and small teeth.

1860

WALT WHITMAN publishes the third edition of his *Leaves of Grass.* Announcing his new resolve to be "the poet of comrades," the book now includes the sex-positive "Children of Adam" and the homoerotic "Calamus" poems. Also see **1855**.

1861

The maximum sentence for SODOMY in England, IRELAND, and Wales (see UNITED KINGDOM) is reduced from hanging to life in PRISON.

1862

In GERMANY, KARL HEINRICH ULRICHS coins the term *"Urning"* (Uranian) based on a passage in Plato's *Symposium* (see **387 B.C.**). In Ulrichs's usage, Uranian refers to a member of what he considers the "third sex"—a person with "a feminine soul confined in a masculine body" or vice versa. The term and concept gain currency in Europe and North America over the next few decades. Also see **1864**; **August 19, 1867**; **May 6, 1868**.

1863

In the U.S., two PASSING women serving in the Union Army are discovered when they get drunk and nearly drown in a river in Tennessee. The two soldiers—one a teamster and the other serving as part of General Philip Sheridan's cavalry escort—had discovered each other after enlisting independently and formed, in Sheridan's words, an "intimacy." They are discharged from the MILITARY, given women's clothing, and sent away from the front.

1864

In GERMANY, KARL HEINRICH ULRICHS (see **1862**) publishes the first of 12 pamphlets of social and legal studies of "Uranian" love.

c. 1865

Able to support themselves by working in the booming silk-spinning industry, women in Guangtong, CHINA, begin a "marriage resistance movement," formalizing bonds with each other and living apart from their families. The movement, which lasts until the Japanese invasion of 1937, harbors more than 100,000 women at its peak. Many of them form long-term sexual relationships.

1866

Horatio Alger, minister at the Unitarian Church of Brewster, Massachusetts, is fired from his post for "deeds . . . too revolting to relate" with two boys. He flees Brewster for New York City and a career as a popular writer of inspirational novels for boys.

1867

Charles Baudelaire's *Les Fleurs du Mal* includes several poems that celebrate and exoticize lesbians, one of whom is SAPPHO. Baudelaire is one of the leaders of a mostly French trend portraying lesbianism as divinely evil decadence.

August 19, 1867

In Munich (in present-day GERMANY), KARL HEINRICH ULRICHS (see **1862**) is jeered when he attempts to persuade a conclave of jurists that same-sex love should be tolerated rather than persecuted. He is probably the first to come OUT publicly in defense of what he calls "Uranism" (homosexuality).

May 6, 1868

In a draft of a letter to KARL HEINRICH ULRICHS (see **1862**), KÁROLY MÁRIA KERTBENY, a Hungarian-German doctor who is an early sympathizer of Ulrichs, uses both *"homosexuel"* and *"heterosexuel,"* terms Kertbeny has recently coined.

1869

In an open letter to the Prussian minister of justice advocating the decriminalization of male-male sex relations, KÁROLY MÁRIA KERTBENY (see **5/6/1868**) uses the word *"homosexuel"* in a public forum for the first time.

German physician Dr. Karl Friedrich Otto von Westphal publishes an article in a scholarly journal that is one of the first works to look at homosexuality (which he calls "contrary sexual feeling") through the sights of the infant science of psychiatry. In terms that suggest homosexuality is a mental illness rather than a moral failing, he recommends that governments decriminalize same-sex acts so that homosexuals will be more likely to seek medical treatment.

c. 1870

In Rome, a group of American women Henry James called "the white, marmorean flock" create some of the most-praised sculptures of their time. This women-identified network, which revolves around the actress CHARLOTTE CUSHMAN, includes Emma Stebbins, Anne Whitney, and Mary Edmonia Lewis, several of whom are in BOSTON MARRIAGES.

1871

Despite protests (see **1869**), the new legal code for a unified GERMANY includes Paragraph 175, which makes sex acts between men punishable by a PRISON sentence of three to ten years. Also see **March 18, 1922**.

May 1873

In JAPAN, as part of a campaign of "modernization" and national revitalization, the Meiji government makes consensual sex between men illegal for the first time in Japanese history. The penalty is ninety days' imprisonment. Also see **1883**.

June 1, 1880

The United States Census finds 63 men in 22 states incarcerated for "crimes against nature."

1883

The government of JAPAN reverses itself (see **5/1873**) and decriminalizes consensual sex between men 16 or older.

1885

In England (see UNITED KINGDOM), the Labouchère Amendment is passed, reducing the maximum PRISON sentence for SODOMY from life to two years but also broadening the scope of the LAW to include any "gross indecency" between two men.

1886

In GERMANY, RICHARD VON KRAFFT-EBING publishes his enormously influential *Psychopathia Sexualis.* The book promotes a medical/psychiatric theory of homosexuality, which is described as a form of degeneracy. Also see **1901**.

1889

In Paris, the *Guide des Plaisirs* directs readers to a Montmartre restaurant frequented by lesbians.

The maximum sentence for SODOMY in Scotland (see UNITED KINGDOM) is reduced from hanging to a prison sentence.

ITALY decriminalizes consensual same-sex acts between adults.

1890

In London, newspapers accuse the government of a cover-up in a scandal that broke out the previous year involving a male brothel on Cleveland Street, telegraph messenger boys, and prominent aristocrats. Reaction to the scandal reflects growing awareness of London's gay male SUBCULTURE as well as an increase in social intolerance of homosexuality.

January 26, 1892

Newspapers across the U.S. report on the murder of 17-year-old Freda Ward by her lover, 19-year-old Alice Mitchell. Both members of upper-class Memphis society, the two women had vowed never to separate. When Ward's family refused to allow Mitchell to have contact with her, Mitchell waylaid Ward on a train and slashed her throat. Besides being one of the first times lesbianism is discussed in the nation's media, the Mitchell-Ward case becomes a frequently cited example of the dangerous "pathology" of same-sex love. Mitchell is later found insane and committed to an asylum.

1894

In FRANCE, Pierre Louÿs publishes *Les Chansons de Bilitis* (*The Songs of Bilitis*), including lesbian love poetry written in the voice of Bilitis, a fictitious character described as living on Lesbos at the time of SAPPHO (see **c. 600 B.C.**).

1895

In BRAZIL, Adolfo Caminha publishes *Bom-Crioulo,* a naturalistic novel about the sexual and romantic obsession of a virile black sailor for a 15-year-old cabin boy.

January 1895

In England (see UNITED KINGDOM), EDWARD CARPENTER quietly publishes a pamphlet entitled "Homogenic Love and Its Place in a Free Society," one of the first documents to assert that same-sex love and the men and women who practice it make a positive contribution to society.

May 25, 1895

In England (see UNITED KINGDOM), OSCAR WILDE is found guilty of gross obscenity and is sentenced to two years' hard labor. The international publicity given his trial brings awareness of the existence of homosexuality to a new high. Also see **May 19, 1897**.

1896

In GERMANY, the first successful gay periodical, ADOLF BRAND's *Der Eigene* ("One's Own" or "The Special"), makes its debut.

On Staten Island, New York, ALICE AUSTEN begins to create a photographic record of the lives of her small group of women friends and her lover, Gertrude Tate.

May 14, 1897

In GERMANY, MAGNUS HIRSCHFELD organizes the Scientific Humanitarian Committee, considered by many historians to be the first formal group to advocate civil rights for lesbians and gay men. The group launches a petition drive urging the repeal of Paragraph 175 (see **1871**). Also see **March 18, 1922**.

May 19, 1897

OSCAR WILDE is released from prison (see **5/25/1895**). A short time later, he leaves England to spend the remaining three years of his life in self-imposed exile in FRANCE and ITALY.

January 13, 1898

In GERMANY, the Reichstag debates a petition urging the revocation of Paragraph 175 (see **1871**). Promoted by MAGNUS HIRSCHFELD and signed by dozens of prominent German opinion leaders, the motion is supported by only one political party in the Reichstag, the Social Democratic Party led by August Bebel. The Reichstag votes against reform.

1899

In GERMANY, MAGNUS HIRSCHFELD publishes the first of 23 volumes of the *Jahrbuch für Sexuelle Zwischenstufen* ("Yearbook for Sexual Intermediate Types"), a compendium of scholarly articles and an annual comprehensive bibliography relating to the study of male and female homosexuality.

Arthur J. Cohen publishes *A Marriage Below Zero,* the first American novel to discuss sex between two men openly.

c. 1900

In the NETHERLANDS, the weekly newspaper *Pst-Pst* contains some of the earliest documented examples of lesbian PERSONAL ADS.

In GERMANY, Elisar von Kupffer publishes *Freundesliebe* ("Comrade Love") a groundbreaking anthology of writings about love between men gathered from around the world.

1901

In GERMANY, an article by RICHARD VON KRAFFT-EBING is published in MAGNUS HIRSCHFELD's *Jahrbuch für Sexuelle Zwischenstufen* (see **1899**) refuting the "degeneracy" theory of homosexuality Krafft-Ebing had espoused in his *Psychopathia Sexualis* (see **1886**). Some homosexuals, Krafft-Ebing writes, can be normal.

Austrian writer Aimée Duc (PSEUDONYM of Minna Wettstein-Adelt) publishes *Sind Es Frauen?* ("Are These Women?"), a novel about a group of independent women university students in Geneva, SWITZERLAND. *Sind Es Frauen?* is one of the first positive depictions of lesbian love in any language.

1902

In England (see UNITED KINGDOM), EDWARD CARPENTER publishes *Iolaus: An Anthology of Friendship,* the first English-language anthology of writings on same-sex love from "pagan" times to the present.

1903

In Berlin, MAGNUS HIRSCHFELD oversees the first large-scale survey of sexual preferences. Distributed to 6,611 students and workers, the survey finds that 2.2 percent of male respondents report having had sex with men.

In RUSSIA, the penalty for male SODOMY, which had been four to five years' exile in Siberia, is reduced to imprisonment for at least three months.

Influenced by MAGNUS HIRSCHFELD's work, Vladimir Nabokov, father of the famous writer, and other political reformers begin a campaign to decriminalize sex between men in RUSSIA.

February 21, 1903

In New York City, police conduct the first recorded raid on a gay BATHHOUSE, the Ariston on West 55th Street, arresting 26 of the 78 men caught in the raid. Twelve of those arrested are brought to trial on SODOMY charges, and 7 men receive sentences ranging from 4 to 20 years in PRISON.

October 8, 1904

In an address to the Scientific Humanitarian Committee (see **5/14/1897**) in Berlin, women's rights leader Anna Rueling urges feminists to unite with "Uranian" (see **1862**) women and men in the fight for social reform, citing concerns and goals common to both movements.

1905

Sigmund Freud writes extensively about homosexuality for the first time in *Three Essays on the Theory of Sexuality,* asserting that homosexuality is a form of arrested or deflected development while rejecting the idea, common in PSYCHOLOGY and medical writings at the time, that homosexuality is a symptom of degeneracy.

1906

In RUSSIA, MIKHAIL KUZMIN publishes *Wings,* the tale of a young man's coming to know and value his attraction to other men.

1907

In RUSSIA, bisexual intellectual Lidiya Zinovyeva-Annibal publishes *33 Abominations,* the first Russian novel to make explicit lesbianism its theme.

Sholem Asch's drama *Gott fun Nekoma* (*The God of Vengeance*) premieres in Berlin. The story of a Jewish girl whose father runs a brothel, the play includes two tender lesbian love scenes, among the first on the modern European stage. Also see **December 19, 1922**.

In New York City, Dr. Otto Spengler, representing MAGNUS HIRSCHFELD's Scientific Humanitarian Committee, delivers what is probably the first public address on homosexuality in the U.S.

1908

Edward Prime Stevenson, an American writer who has spent most of his adult life in Europe, publishes *The Intersexes: A History of Similisexualism as a Problem in Social Life* under a PSEUDONYM in ITALY. The book is the first detailed account of gay male SUBCULTURES in large American cities.

In GERMANY, a movement to make lesbian sex acts illegal falls short of the necessary support it needs to pass legislation in the Reichstag.

1911

In the NETHERLANDS, a conservative parliamentary coalition makes same-sex relations illegal between adults and minors under 21. Previously, the AGE OF CONSENT had been the same as for male-female relations, 16 years of age.

Also in the NETHERLANDS, Jacob Schorer founds Holland's Scientific Humanitarian Committee (its Dutch acronym is NWHK). Modeled after MAGNUS HIRSCHFELD's organization in GERMANY (see **5/14/1897**), the NWHK works to lower the AGE OF CONSENT (see above) and to win greater social tolerance for Dutch lesbians and gay men.

February 10, 1911

In GERMANY, the feminist League for the Protection of Mothers condemns Paragraph 175 (see **1871**) and voices its rejection of attempts to extend the law to cover women as well as men.

1912

In New York City, the women's group HETERODOXY is formed.

May 25, 1913

Colonel Alfred Redl, former chief of Austrian counterintelligence, commits suicide when it becomes known that he has been blackmailed, on account of his homosexuality, into working for the Russians for the past year. Later in the century, the Redl affair will be cited by U.S. senators as evidence of the security risk homosexuals pose. Also see **December 15, 1950**.

1915

On a speaking tour across the U.S., Emma Goldman defends homosexuality along with free love, birth control, and pacifism. Drawn by her outspoken advocacy, men and, especially, women seek her out to talk about the unhappy lives they lead having to hide their homosexuality.

February 4, 1915

In Chicago on a speaking tour, EDITH LEES ELLIS, openly lesbian wife of HAVELOCK ELLIS, exhorts women to begin "organizing a new love world."

March 1915

In her avant-garde *Little Review,* Chicago writer and editor MARGARET ANDERSON chides EDITH LEES ELLIS (see **2/4/1915**) for the timidity and vagueness of her prolesbian remarks. Her article is probably the first defense of same-sex love published by an American lesbian.

1916

In Alexandria, CONSTANTINE CAVAFY privately publishes his first manifestly homoerotic poems.

In Sydney, AUSTRALIA, Charles Webster Leadbeater founds the Liberal Catholic Church, the first religious group to minister openly to gay men and lesbians.

SOPHIA PARNOK publishes the first book of Russian poetry to contain poems written in an openly lesbian voice. Many of her love poems are addressed to legendary poet Marina Tsvetaeva, her lover of the past year.

December 21, 1917

In RUSSIA, the Bolsheviks abrogate the entire criminal code in favor of "revolutionary justice." Among the laws nullified are those relating to sex acts between men. Also see **January 1934**; **March 7, 1934**.

1918

CHARLES DEMUTH paints *Turkish Bath,* suggestively depicting men at what is probably the Lafayette Bathhouse. Since 1915, many of Demuth's paintings have been inspired by New York City's emerging gay male SUBCULTURE.

In GERMANY, Kurt Hiller, a socialist and gay rights activist, is the first to describe lesbians and gay men as a "minority" deserving of the same sort of protection as American President Woodrow Wilson has advocated for European ethnic minorities.

1919

In GERMANY, Anna E. Weirauch publishes the first of three volumes of her novel *The Scorpion.* Widely translated, it is one of the first widely disseminated books written by a woman to make lesbian lovemaking and relationships its theme. It is also notable for its lack of BUTCH/FEMME relationships.

May 24, 1919

Anders als die Andern ("Different from the Others"), the first progay FILM, premieres in Berlin. MAGNUS HIRSCHFELD is a producer and makes a cameo appearance. The movie stars Conrad Veidt.

July 1, 1919

In Berlin, MAGNUS HIRSCHFELD opens the Institute of Sexual Research. Also see **May 6, 1933**.

c. 1920

In New York City, lesbians and gay men open some 20 restaurants and "personality clubs" in Greenwich Village.

In Paris, ROMAINE BROOKS has begun to paint portraits of famous or soon-to-be-famous lesbians, including her lover, NATALIE BARNEY; UNA TROUBRIDGE; and herself.

1920

MAGNUS HIRSCHFELD's Scientific Humanitarian Committee (see **5/14/1897**) forms a coalition with two other German homosexual organizations, ADOLF BRAND's Gemeinschaft der Eigenen (Community of [Those Who Are] Their Own Persons) and the German Friendship Association, to revitalize the fight to decriminalize sex between adult males.

1921

In the UNITED KINGDOM, the House of Commons approves a clause making "gross indecency by females" subject to the same penalties as those between males (see **1885**). The House of Lords, however, rejects the clause on the grounds that it would simply publicize a vice that the overwhelming majority of British women know nothing about.

In Berlin, MAGNUS HIRSCHFELD sponsors the first conference of the World League for Sexual Reform.

April 30, 1921

In FRANCE, MARCEL PROUST publishes the first part of *Sodome et Gomorrhe (Cities of the Plain)*, part of his 16-volume opus *À la Recherche du Temps Perdu (Remembrance of Things Past)*. The themes of male and female same-sex passion interwoven into the previous volumes now come to the fore in an extended essay on the homosexual.

July 19, 1921

The U.S. Senate Naval Affairs Committee issues its "Report on Alleged Immoral Conditions and Practices at the Naval Training Station, Newport, R.I.," accusing officers under the command of Franklin D. Roosevelt, former assistant secretary of the U.S. Navy, of ordering enlisted men to engage in "immoral practices" in order to entrap "perverts" in the MILITARY and obtain evidence against them. The report is also one of the first to document gay male CRUISING areas, including Riverside Drive in New York City.

March 18, 1922

MAGNUS HIRSCHFELD's petition (see **5/14/1897**) for the repeal of Paragraph 175 (see **1871**) is presented to the Reichstag. Although 6,000 people have signed the petition, including Sigmund Freud, the late Leo Tolstoy, and Albert Einstein, it fails to persuade German lawmakers to decriminalize sex between men.

December 19, 1922

The God of Vengeance (see **1907**) opens at the Provincetown Playhouse. The drama, translated from Yiddish and performed in English for the first time, includes the first lesbian scenes on the American stage. Also see **March 6, 1923**.

February 4, 1923

Nazi thugs fire guns into a Vienna HOMOPHILE gathering attended by MAGNUS HIRSCHFELD and wound a number of people in the crowd.

March 6, 1923

Shortly after *The God of Vengeance* (see **12/19/1922**) moves to Broadway, the producer, the theater owner, and 12 cast members are arrested and charged with "presenting an obscene, indecent, immoral and impure theatrical production." The play had previously been performed successfully and without interference in nine countries in Europe. Although a jury rules against the play two months later, the verdict is later overturned on appeal.

December 1924

In Hanover, GERMANY, a gay man named Fritz Haarmann has confessed to more than 120 murders, mostly of young men. This month, he is tried and found guilty of 27 counts of murder. The publicity given the case results in a major setback for the German HOMOPHILE movement.

December 10, 1924

HENRY GERBER, a German-born immigrant and early activist, receives a charter from the state of Illinois for the Society for Human Rights, an organization intended to be an American equivalent of contemporary German emancipation groups such as MAGNUS HIRSCHFELD'S (see **5/14/1897**). Gerber is arrested soon after and the society falls apart.

May 1925

At the end of a year's worth of police raids on predominantly lesbian and gay restaurants and clubs in New York City's Greenwich Village, only three are left open.

Meanwhile, the HARLEM RENAISSANCE gives rise to the earliest documented AFRICAN-AMERICAN lesbian and gay SUBCULTURE. Also see **1926**.

1926

In FRANCE, ANDRÉ GIDE comes OUT in his autobiographical essay, *Si le Grain ne Meurt* (*If It Dies . . .*). He is believed to be the first public figure to do so.

Richard Bruce Nugent publishes his experimental short story "Smoke, Lilies, and Jade" in *Fire!,* a magazine anthology of HARLEM RENAISSANCE writers. Nugent's story contains what is probably the first fictional evocation of passion between black men written by an AFRICAN-AMERICAN.

The annual Hamilton Lodge Ball, another major feature of the HARLEM RENAISSANCE, attracts thousands of CROSS-DRESSING men and women.

September 29, 1926

The Captive, a melodrama about a young woman seduced by an older woman (her "shadow"), creates a sensation on Broadway.

June 1928

MA RAINEY records "Prove It on Me Blues," in which she sings of a night out on the town with friends:

> They must been womens
> Cause I don't like no mens.
> It's true I wear a collar and a tie . . .
> They say I do it.
> Ain't nobody caught me.
> You sure got to prove it on me.

July 1928

RADCLYFFE HALL'S THE WELL OF LONELINESS, the first major novel in English with an explicitly prolesbian theme, is published in Paris. Advertised extensively in England (see UNITED KINGDOM), the book proceeds into multiple printings. Also see **November 1928**.

November 1928

In the UNITED KINGDOM, a court action begins against RADCLYFFE HALL'S THE WELL OF LONELINESS (see **7/1928**). Despite protests from intellectuals including George Bernard Shaw and H. G. Wells, the book is declared obscene and sales are banned in England.

December 15, 1928

THE WELL OF LONELINESS (see **7/1928**) is published in the U.S. Americans buy more than 20,000 copies of the book in the next month, making it a best-seller. Also see **April 19, 1929**.

April 19, 1929

In New York City, an appellate court rules that, contrary to a verdict reached earlier in the year by a lower court, THE WELL OF LONELINESS (see **7/1928**; **11/1928**; **12/15/1928**) is not obscene. The decision clears the way for even wider distribution of the best-selling novel.

c. 1930

Mass-market publications like *Sexology,* sold in drugstores across the U.S., provide ordinary Americans with pop-psychological theories and commentary on homosexuality. For many young lesbians and gay men, these articles are the only indication that they are not alone.

In CHINA, American writer Agnes Smedley visits two women silk spinners who live and work together as lovers. "MARRIAGE" between women, she is told, is common in silk-producing areas of the country.

1930

Denmark (see SCANDINAVIA) decriminalizes consensual sex acts between men. (Sex between women has never been illegal under Danish LAW.) The Danish reform is one of the few successes of the early HOMOPHILE movement.

BESSIE SMITH records "It's Dirty but Good":

I know women that don't like men . . .
It's dirty but good, oh, yes, it's dirty but good.
There ain't much difference, it's just dirty but
good.

MAGNUS HIRSCHFELD visits the U.S. and delivers a series of lectures to medical groups in which he presents his case for the decriminalization of same-sex acts.

April 1, 1930

In HOLLYWOOD, the Motion Picture Producers and Distributors of America (MPPDA) introduces a self-regulatory code of movie ethics, discouraging filmmakers from including frank depictions of sex and sexuality. Nicknamed the Hays Code after the head of the MPPDA, former Republican National Committee chairman Will H. Hays, the regulations become mandatory on **July 1, 1934**.

1931

Strange Brother, Blair Niles's novel about bohemian life in the latter days of the HARLEM RENAISSANCE, is the first widely read American account of openly gay men, drag balls, and police raids.

1932

In FRANCE, COLETTE explores the world of lesbian passion in *Ces Plaisirs,* better known under its later title *Le Pur et l'Impur (The Pure and the Impure).*

Poland (see EASTERN EUROPE) decriminalizes consensual same-sex relations between adults.

1933

In SWITZERLAND, Karl Meier, a German-born refugee from NAZI PERSECUTION, founds the publication that evolves into *Der Kreis,* the leading international HOMOPHILE journal of the next three decades. The publication adds

Le Cercle, a French-language version, in 1943 and an English-language edition in 1952.

February 23–24, 1933

In GERMANY, Adolf Hitler's government launches the NAZI PERSECUTION of homosexuality with directives closing gay and lesbian clubs, banning PORNOGRAPHY and HOMOPHILE publications, and dissolving homosexual rights groups.

May 6, 1933

In Berlin, young Nazis attack and destroy the Institute of Sexual Research (see **7/1/1919**). A few days later, the institute's priceless collection of more than 20,000 publications and 5,000 photographs is burned in a public ceremony.

November 29, 1933

Close to bankruptcy after repeated Nazi raids and seizures of his publications and property, ADOLF BRAND (see **1896**) writes a letter to his followers announcing the end of the HOMOPHILE movement he has led.

1934

PAUL CADMUS's *The Fleet's In!,* painted as part of a Public Works of Art commission, is exhibited at the Corcoran Gallery in Washington, D.C. The controversy the painting ignites during its brief showing catapults the artist and his uniquely American brand of HOMOEROTICISM to instant fame.

January 1934

A purge of suspected homosexuals, including many artists, writers, and actors, begins in major cities in the Soviet Union (see RUSSIA). Most of those arrested are deported to prison camps despite the fact that same-sex relations have not been illegal since 1917. Also see **December 21, 1917**; **March 7, 1934.**

March 7, 1934

Article 121 makes SODOMY between men illegal in all the republics of the USSR (see RUSSIA). Maxim Gorky, a popular writer and the leading Soviet intellectual of the period, praises the "proletarian humanism" of the law, which punishes sex between consenting male adults with up to five years' "deprivation of freedom." Also see **December 21, 1917**; **January 1934**; **May 27, 1993**.

June 28, 1934

In GERMANY, some 300 Nazi Party members are arrested and murdered in a purge ordered by Adolf Hitler that comes to be known as the Night of the Long Knives. The most prominent victim of the purge is SA (Brown Shirts) chief Ernst Röhm, a gay man whom Hitler accuses of having formed a subversive "homosexual clique."

July 1, 1934

HOLLYWOOD makes adherence to the Hays Code (see **4/1/1930**) mandatory. Among its provisions: "Pictures shall not infer that low forms of sex relationships are the accepted or common thing," and "Sex perversion or any inference to it is forbidden on the screen." Also see **October 3, 1961**.

October 1934

In GERMANY, Nazi officials begin arresting large numbers of known and suspected homosexuals. The Gestapo orders local police forces to submit lists of "homosexually active persons."

November 20, 1934

Lillian Hellman's *The Children's Hour* opens on Broadway to rave reviews and sell-out audiences. A largely sympathetic account of two schoolteachers accused of lesbianism by one of their students, the play is loosely based on an actual case in 19th-century Scotland (see **1812**).

March 1935

BESSIE SMITH records the song "B-D Woman" in praise of "bulldaggers," perhaps the first popular release to pay tribute to BUTCH lesbians.

April 1935

In a reply to an American mother worried about her son's homosexuality, Sigmund Freud (see **1905**) expresses his view that "homosexuality is assuredly no advantage, but it is nothing to be ashamed of." Although the letter is not published until 1951 (and even then has little effect on the treatment of homosexuality by contemporary PSYCHOLOGY), the tolerant views expressed are representative of Freud in the last decades of his life.

June 28, 1935

In GERMANY, exactly a year after the murder of Ernst Röhm (see **6/28/1934**), the government enacts new, stricter legislation against male same-sex eroticism, partly formalizing the ongoing NAZI PERSECUTION of gay men.

September 6, 1935

New York University professor Dr. Louis W. Max tells a meeting of the American Psychological Association that he has successfully treated a "partially fetishistic" homosexual "neurosis" with electric shock therapy delivered at "intensities considerably higher than those usually employed on human subjects." Max's presentation is the first documented instance of aversion therapy used to "cure" homosexuality.

1936

Mona's, the first lesbian BAR in San Francisco, opens on Columbus Avenue. Also see **April 1966**.

January 1936

In the USSR (see RUSSIA), People's Commissar for Justice Nikolai Krylenko asserts that homosexuality is counterrevolutionary and cannot exist in a socialist state.

1939

In New York City, Mayor Fiorello La Guardia orders a citywide "cleanup" of gay and lesbian gathering places in preparation for the 1939 World's Fair, closing down most of the city's best-known gay BARS.

In the NETHERLANDS, a group of gay men parts ways with the reticent philosophy of the country's Scientific Humanitarian Commission (see **1911**) and form Levensrecht (Right to Live), one of the first organizations in the world to advocate and foster an open SUBCULTURE. They publish two issues of a magazine before being suppressed during the Nazi occupation (see **7/31/1940**). Also see **1946.**

Also in the NETHERLANDS, Benno Stokvis publishes *De Homosexuelen: 35 Autobiographieen* ("Homosexuals: 35 Autobiographies"), in which gay men and lesbians tell their life stories in the hope of promoting social tolerance.

1940

In New York City, a BAR called Gloria's goes to court to fight being closed down, citing recent scientific studies and arguing that "there is no rule or regulation" preventing a "sex variant" from being served at a bar. Courts reject the argument, however, allowing the State Liquor Authority to continue closing bars frequented by gay men and lesbians. Also see **April 22, 1966**.

July 31, 1940

The German Reich Commissar of the occupied NETHERLANDS territories makes all sexual activities between men illegal.

1941

The U.S. MILITARY orders the first "blue" discharges of gay and lesbian service people.

SWITZERLAND's new LAW code contains no mention of consensual same-sex relations between adults.

1942

In a letter published by *The Guardian,* J. R. ACKERLEY protests the trials of 20 men in Abergavenny, Wales, for SODOMY and "indecency." Three of the men, Ackerley writes, have attempted suicide, one successfully. The survivors receive PRISON sentences of between one and twelve years. The case is symptomatic of the escalation in prosecutions for same-sex acts in the UNITED KINGDOM in the 1940s and 1950s. Also see **1952**.

February 1, 1942

In GERMANY, a legal amendment formally extends the death penalty to men found guilty of having sex with another man.

August 6, 1942

In FRANCE, the Vichy government raises the AGE OF CONSENT for both male and female same-sex acts to 21 and prescribes penalties of between six months' and three years' imprisonment. Also see **February 8, 1945**; **August 4, 1982**.

November 14, 1942

In GERMANY, the SS (storm troops) informs concentration camp commandants that they are free to sterilize any of the prisoners under their control. The directive gives official approval to the practice, already instituted in some camps, of castrating males suspected of sexual attraction to other men.

1943

The U.S. MILITARY expands "blue" discharges (see **1941**) to cover "homosexuals" as a class. Sexual orientation, not conduct, is now the criterion.

JIM KEPNER begins the private collection that will grow to become the International Gay and Lesbian Archive in Los Angeles (see **1972**).

1944

Sweden (see SCANDINAVIA) decriminalizes consensual, private same-sex relations between adults.

August 1944

This month's issue of *Politics* carries poet ROBERT DUNCAN's precedent-setting manifesto "The Homosexual in Society."

1945

In New York City, the Quaker Emergency Committee meets to work for the establishment of a center where young people arrested on same-sex charges can go for assistance and counseling. The Readjustment Center that results from the QUAKERS' efforts is believed to be the first social welfare agency for gay men and lesbians in the U.S.

February 8, 1945

In liberated FRANCE, the administration of General Charles de Gaulle decides to maintain the Vichy government's decree (see **8/6/1942**) establishing a discriminatory AGE OF CONSENT for same-sex acts. Also see **August 4, 1982**.

December 1945

In Los Angeles, BOB MIZER and two partners establish the Athletic Model Guild. Mizer continues to develop the business after the departure of his partners. Also see **November 1951**.

1946

In the NETHERLANDS, members of Levensrecht (see **1939**) resurface and form a new organization called Cultuur- en Ontspannings-Centrum (COC, Culture and Recreation Center). COC quickly becomes the largest HOMOPHILE group in the world.

June 1947

In Los Angeles, LISA BEN (a PSEUDONYM that is an anagram for "lesbian") types and mails 12 copies of VICE VERSA—"America's Gayest Magazine." The first lesbian newsletter, *Vice Versa* includes book and movie reviews, poems, and upbeat essays encouraging lesbians to persevere in their quest for a more satisfying life.

January 1948

GORE VIDAL's *The City and the Pillar* is the first widely read American novel with gay male characters. Although the portrayals are generally positive, his publishers force him to make the ending an unhappy one.

January 3, 1948

The KINSEY REPORT on men is published, shocking the nation with its revelation of the high incidence of same-sex acts among American men.

March 8, 1948

In New York City, the Veterans Benevolent Association incorporates "to unite socially and fraternally, all veterans and their friends, of good and moral character." The group, which has about 100 members at its height, helps gay male veterans with legal and employment problems, besides holding social events attended by as many as 500. Also see **1954**; **December 1955**.

February 1, 1949

The Paris Prefect of Police issues a decree forbidding men from DANCING together in public.

July 1949

YUKIO MISHIMA publishes *Kamen no Kokuhaku* (*Confessions of a Mask*), JAPAN's first modern novel to deal openly with male homosexuality.

1950

The first paperback originals include lesbian-themed PULP FICTION, debuting with Tereska Torres's *Women's Barracks,* published by Fawcett Crest.

James Barr's *Quatrefoil,* the romantic tale of a young naval officer, is published. Although it has the tragic ending that remains mandatory for novels about gay men and lesbians, it is one of the first books to feature positive gay male characters who could conceivably be taken as role models.

In SCANDINAVIA, Allan Hellman founds Sweden's first gay and lesbian rights organization, which becomes the National Federation for Sexual Equality in 1952.

February 28, 1950

Testifying before the U.S. Senate Committee on Expenditures in the Executive Department (whose members include Joseph R. McCarthy), Undersecretary of State John Peurifroy reveals that the majority of dismissals of State Department employees are based on accusations of homosexuality. Over the next few months, McCarthy and other conservatives accuse the Truman administration of laxity in rooting out homosexuals in government, bringing the MCCARTHY ERA into high gear. Also see **April 1, 1950**; **June 14, 1950**.

April 1, 1950

Bowing to MCCARTHY ERA pressure from anti-Communist conservatives, the Civil Service Commission intensifies its efforts to locate and dismiss lesbians and gay men working in government. Over the next six months, 382 are fired, compared with 192 for the preceding two and a half years. Also see **February 28, 1950**; **June 14, 1950**; **December 15, 1950**.

June 1950

In Los Angeles, a group of black and white men and women, including Merton Bird and DORR LEGG, form Knights of the Clock, a support group for interracial gay, lesbian, and heterosexual couples.

June 14, 1950

After months of controversy (see **2/28/1950**), the U.S. Senate authorizes a wide-ranging investigation of homosexuals "and other moral perverts" working in national government. Also see **December 15, 1950**.

November 11, 1950

In Los Angeles, Chuck Rowland; HARRY HAY and his lover, Rudi Gernreich; Dale Jennings; and Bob Hull hold the first of a series of weekly gatherings leading to the formation of a HOMOPHILE organization the men will call the MATTACHINE Society.

December 15, 1950

A U.S. Senate committee makes public its report on "The Employment of Homosexuals and Other Sex Perverts" (see **6/14/1950**). Asserting that homosexuals are a security risk not simply because they are liable to blackmail (see **5/25/1913**) but also because homosexuality inevitably perverts "moral fibre," the report recommends stringent measures be taken to root all lesbians and gay men out of government. Also see **February 28, 1950**; **April 1, 1950**.

1951

In FRANCE, André Baudry founds Arcadie, a moderate HOMOPHILE organization that also produces a publication of the same name.

The California Supreme Court rules in favor of San Francisco's famed Black Cat Bar, finding that no state law prohibits gay men and lesbians from being served alcohol in a public establishment. Four years later, however, a LAW is passed allowing the state to deny liquor licences to any BAR that is a "resort for sexual perverts."

DONALD WEBSTER CORY (PSEUDONYM of Edward Sagarin) publishes *The Homosexual in America,* a plea for tolerance that includes the then revolutionary idea that there is "no homosexual problem except that created by the heterosexual society." Perhaps the first American writer to describe lesbians and gay men as a persecuted minority, Cory insists that the "homosexual" must "rise up and demand his rights."

LANGSTON HUGHES publishes *Montage of a Dream Deferred,* which includes "Café, 3 A.M.," a poem about a police raid on a gay BAR.

November 1951

In Los Angeles, BOB MIZER's Athletic Model Guild (see **12/1945**) capitalizes on a successful mailing venture by producing *Physique Pictorial,* the first PHYSIQUE MAGAZINE for gay men. Also see **October 1953**.

1952

In the UNITED KINGDOM, Gordon Westwood's *Society and the Homosexual* profiles British gay male life and describes the harmful effects of antigay laws.

Also in the UNITED KINGDOM, brilliant mathematician and computer pioneer ALAN TURING is one of 1,686 men charged this year with "gross indecency with males." He is sentenced to undergo a year of hormonal treatments that cause impotence and breast development. He commits suicide in 1954, at the age of 41.

In CANADA, as part of the MCCARTHY ERA campaign against leftists and "sex perverts," the Royal Canadian Mounted Police institutes A-3, a special unit whose mission is to root out lesbians and gay men in Canadian government jobs and, somewhat later, to delineate "homosexual networks" in Ottawa and other cities. A-3 compiles a list of suspected "perverts" that quickly grows to include about 3,000 names.

Also in CANADA, Parliament makes "homosexualism" an impediment to IMMIGRATION into the country.

Claire Morgan (PSEUDONYM of PATRICIA HIGHSMITH) publishes *The Price of Salt,* one of the first lesbian novels to offer a (relatively) happy ending.

The AMERICAN PSYCHIATRIC ASSOCIATION includes homosexuality as a "sociopathic personality disturbance" in its first official list of mental disorders. Also see **1968**.

February 1952

In Los Angeles, Dale Jennings, one of the original MATTACHINE members (see **11/11/1950**), is charged with "lewd and dissolute" behavior after being entrapped by a plainclothes officer. The Mattachine Society decides to form a special "Citizens Committee to Outlaw Entrapment" to help him fight the charges and mobilize the gay and lesbian community against police harassment. Also see **June 23, 1952**.

June 23, 1952

After an unprecedented campaign that includes the first use of fliers by a HOMOPHILE group and extensive fund-raising to pay legal fees, the Citizens Committee to Outlaw Entrapment (see **2/1952**) declares "a great victory": the case against Dale Jennings, who acknowledges his homosexuality but pleads innocent to charges of "lewd and dissolute behavior," is dropped when the jury fails to reach a verdict after 36 hours of deliberation.

June 27, 1952

In the U.S., the McCarran-Walter Immigration and Nationality Act bars immigrants "afflicted with psychopathic personality," a phrase that is interpreted to include all homosexuals. Also see **1967**.

July 1952

HARRY HAY and other members of the MATTACHINE Society set up a not-for-profit educational organization and apply for incorporation under California law as the Mattachine Foundation, Inc.

October 15, 1952

In Los Angeles, DORR LEGG and six friends, including Dale Jennings, all with ties to the MATTACHINE Society, discuss forming a group to promote education and research activities beneficial to gay men and lesbians. ONE, Inc., results from the meeting. Also see **January 1953**.

1953

Theodore Sturgeon publishes "The World Well Lost," which is considered the first SCIENCE FICTION story to treat homosexuality sympathetically.

In the UNITED KINGDOM, MARY RENAULT publishes *The Charioteer,* the story of a young soldier's passion for another man. Because of fears of prosecution for obscenity, it will be six years before the novel is issued in the U.S.

January 1953

In Los Angeles, ONE, Inc. (see **10/15/1952**), publishes the first issue of *One* magazine.

February 1953

The MATTACHINE Foundation issues a statement denying that the organization espouses any particular "ism," reflecting suspicions held by members and outsiders alike that the Mattachine is in danger of being commandeered by Marxists. Also see **April 11, 1953**.

March 29, 1953

The *Los Angeles Times* accuses the MATTACHINE Society of dangerously subversive activities.

April 1953

President Dwight D. Eisenhower signs Executive Order 10450, mandating the dismissal of all federal employees determined to be guilty of "sexual perversion." As a result, more than 640 federal employees lose their jobs over the next year and a half. Many more are allowed to resign quietly.

April 11, 1953

The MATTACHINE Society holds its first constitutional convention at a church in Los Angeles. The original founders (see **11/11/1950**) begin to lose control of the group to a moderate, anti-Communist contingent led by Kenneth Burns, Hal Call, and Marilyn Rieger. Also see **May 23–24, 1953**.

May 23–24, 1953

When the MATTACHINE Society reconvenes to approve a constitution (see **4/11/1953**), it refuses to seat delegates associated with the Communist Party, including Chuck Rowland, one of the original founders. For the remainder of the decade, the society pursues a low-profile, nonconfrontational approach to winning societal acceptance of lesbians and gay men. Also see **December 15, 1959**.

May 24, 1953

A MATTACHINE Foundation circular estimates total membership in the society at over 2,000. There are almost 100 different discussion groups meeting in California from San Diego to the Bay Area.

August 1953

The KINSEY REPORT on women is released.

October 1953

BOB MIZER's *Physique Pictorial* (see **11/1951**), the first nationally distributed magazine featuring erotic male photography and illustrations, makes its newsstand debut. The quarterly is sold all over the country, providing many men their first hint of the possibilities of gay male eroticism. Later, Mizer will also take political positions, telling readers to join HOMOPHILE organizations and the AMERICAN CIVIL LIBERTIES UNION, and, most important, to know their rights. Also see **Spring 1957**.

November 1953

In the UNITED KINGDOM, historian and philosopher Dr. Jacob Bronowski says "homosexual" on a British Broadcasting Company radio program, *Behind the News*. This is the earliest documented instance of the word's use in an English-language broadcast.

December 3, 1953

In the UNITED KINGDOM, alarmed by the rise in prosecutions for male-male sex (including several much publicized recent cases involving prominent Britons), two MPs first raise the issue of sex LAW reform in the House of Commons. Also see **April 28, 1954**.

1954

Estimating that there are more than 6,000 homosexuals in Miami, local police begin a concerted campaign against gay men in which hundreds are arrested on BEACHES and in BARS.

In New York City, the Veterans Benevolent Association (see **3/8/1948**) breaks up due to factionalism and disagreement among members over how active the organization should be in the fight for gay civil rights.

March 1954

In the UNITED KINGDOM, the Moral Welfare Council of the Church of England (see ANGLICAN COMMUNION) issues a report recommending that LAWS penalizing same-sex acts be revoked and that the AGE OF CONSENT be 17 for all sexual acts.

April 28, 1954

In the UNITED KINGDOM, the Home Office announces that a special committee (later called the Wolfenden Committee) will be formed to study the issue of sex LAW reform. Also see **September 4, 1957**.

May 1954

Addressing an American Psychological Association meeting in Chicago, psychologist Dr. EVELYN HOOKER presents the results of research done with Rorschach and other personality tests on 30 "male overt homosexuals" and 30 heterosexual men. Dr. Hooker challenges the medical model of homosexuality by demonstrating that the responses of gay and straight men to Rorschach ink blot tests are indistinguishable; gay men appear to be as well adjusted as straights. Also see **January 1955**.

October 1954

The Los Angeles postmaster refuses to accept the October 1954 edition of ONE magazine, calling it "obscene, lewd, lascivious and filthy." One, Inc., appeals the decision in court. Also see **January 13, 1958**.

January 1955

The MATTACHINE *Review* publishes its first issue. Contents include the results of Dr. EVELYN HOOKER's groundbreaking study (see **5/1954**).

September 21, 1955

In San Francisco, four lesbian couples, including PHYLLIS LYON and DEL MARTIN, found the DAUGHTERS OF BILITIS, the first HOMOPHILE organization exclusively for women. Also see **October 1956**.

October 1955

In San Francisco, ALLEN GINSBERG gives a riotous public reading of his poem *Howl,* a protest against conformity, a celebration of gay sex, and the manifesto of the BEAT GENERATION.

November 2, 1955

In Boise, Idaho, three men are accused of having sex with teenagers, setting off a politically motivated, 15-month investigation of local gay male networks. Some 1,400 people are questioned in the MCCARTHY ERA witch-hunt that results. Dozens are arrested, nine men are imprisoned for as long as 15 years, and an untold number of gay men flee the city.

November 24, 1955

In the wake of the murder of a Sioux City, Iowa, boy earlier this year, 29 men suspected of homosexuality have been committed to mental asylums as a preventive measure authorized by the state's "sexual psychopath" laws.

December 1955

Sam Morford, a psychologist, and Tony Segura, a Cuban-born research chemist, hold the first meeting of a New York City chapter of the MATTACHINE Society. Both men had been members of the League, an informal and clandestine discussion group that grew out of the Veterans Benevolent Association (see **3/8/1948**; **1954**). Also see **January 10, 1956**.

1956

JAMES BALDWIN publishes *Giovanni's Room,* his first novel depicting openly gay main characters. Also see **1962**.

JEANNETTE FOSTER publishes *Sex Variant Women in Literature,* a groundbreaking historical and bibliographical survey of lesbian and female "variant" themes in English, French, and German literature.

At a meeting of the Western Psychological Association, Dr. EVELYN HOOKER presents the results of her study (see **5/1954**), which shows that gay men are no more likely to have psychological problems than heterosexual men.

January 10, 1956

The MATTACHINE Society of New York holds its first public meeting. About 30 people attend the meeting, which is held at the Diplomat Hotel.

September 1956

In Los Angeles, ONE, Inc., members JIM KEPNER, DORR LEGG, Merritt Thompson, and Julian Underwood begin "U.S. Homophile Studies Classes," the earliest organized LESBIAN AND GAY STUDIES program in the U.S.

October 1956

The DAUGHTERS OF BILITIS publishes the first issue of THE LADDER, mailing 200 copies to lesbians and San Francisco community professionals.

1957

ANN BANNON publishes the paperback original *Odd Girl Out,* the first of four widely read PULP FICTION novels that depict lesbian life of the era as lived by the characters Beth, Laura, and, starting with the second book in the series, Beebo.

January 7, 1957

The board of directors of the AMERICAN CIVIL LIBERTIES UNION approves a national policy statement asserting that LAWS against SODOMY and federal restrictions on employment of lesbians and gay men are constitutional.

Spring 1957

BOB MIZER's *Physique Pictorial* (see **10/1953**) prints the first of TOM OF FINLAND's illustrations to appear in the U.S.

September 4, 1957

In the UNITED KINGDOM, the WOLFENDEN REPORT (see **4/28/1954**) is published. It recommends that private consensual sex acts between men aged 21 or older be decriminalized. Also see **May 1958**.

January 13, 1958

The U.S. Supreme Court unanimously reverses three lower court rulings that an issue of ONE magazine seized in Los Angeles (see **10/1954**) was obscene. The Court's affirmation of free speech for gay and lesbian writing opens the way for more widely distributed publications.

May 1958

In the UNITED KINGDOM, a distinguished group of (mostly heterosexual) men and women demonstrate their support for implementing the recommendations of the WOLFENDEN REPORT (see **9/4/1957**) by becoming founding members of the Homosexual Law Reform Society and its officially registered charity, the Albany Trust. Also see **July 27, 1967**.

September 20, 1958

In New York City, lesbians including BARBARA GITTINGS hold the first DAUGHTERS OF BILITIS—New York meeting at the offices of the MATTACHINE Society of New York. The chapter is the first lesbian organization on the East Coast.

December 1958

Joe Cino opens Caffé Cino at 31 Cornelia Street in Greenwich Village. The coffeehouse, which caters to a largely gay, bohemian clientele, provides a venue for several openly gay playwrights, including ROBERT PATRICK, Doric Wilson, and Lanford Wilson, and leads to the development of an alternative theatrical scene off-Broadway.

October 7, 1959

Russell Wolden, running for mayor of San Francisco as a Democrat, accuses the incumbent of welcoming and collaborating with the city's "sex deviates." His tactic backfires: the city's newspapers accuse him of irresponsible mudslinging, and he loses in the next month's elections.

December 15, 1959

Reflecting the cautious conservatism of the current HOMOPHILE movement, MATTACHINE officer Don Lucas writes Boston Mattachine founder Prescott Townsend (locally notorious Boston Brahmin–turned-activist) asking him *not* to begin a campaign for Massachusetts SODOMY law reform. Lucas believes the risk of a backlash is too great.

1960

In CUBA, the police begin Operación P, arresting prostitutes, pimps, and "pederasts" and herding them into concentration camps. Although same-sex relations are not illegal, large numbers of gay men and smaller numbers of lesbians are arrested as part of a wide-ranging campaign against people whom Fidel Castro's government believes are inimical to the revolution.

May 1960

In San Francisco, the DAUGHTERS OF BILITIS sponsors a national convention of lesbians, probably the first public gathering focused on the topic of lesbianism in the U.S.

May 12, 1960

In the UNITED KINGDOM, the first public meeting of the Homosexual Law Reform Society (see **5/1958**) is attended by more than 1,000 people.

July 30, 1960

In FRANCE, the National Assembly adds *homosexualité* to a list of *fléaux sociaux* ("social plagues") that the government is charged to combat.

October 3, 1961

In HOLLYWOOD, the Motion Picture Producers and Distributors of America (MPPDA) announces a revision of its production code (see **4/1/1930**; **7/1/1934**). "In keeping with the culture, the mores and the values of our time," the revision advises, "homosexuality and other sexual aberrations may now be treated with care, discretion and restraint." The new ruling paves the way for the release of films like *The Children's Hour* and *Advise and Consent,* but the MPPDA later amends the revision to specify that "sexual aberration" may be "suggested but not actually spelled out." Also see **December 1961**.

November 5, 1961

New York Times critic Howard Taubman launches an attack on "the increasing incidence of homosexuality on the New York stage" in an article headlined "Not What It

Seems: Homosexual Motif Gets Heterosexual Guise."

November 7, 1961

Legendary San Francisco drag queen José Sarria runs for city supervisor. The first openly gay person to run for public office in the U.S., Sarria receives almost 6,000 votes.

November 15, 1961

A Washington, D.C., chapter of the MATTACHINE Society is formed. Activist FRANK KAMENY is elected president.

December 1961

The release of the British movie *Victim* in the U.S. marks the first use of the word "HOMOSEXUAL" in a feature FILM. It is denied motion picture code seal of approval (see **10/3/1961**) as a result.

1962

JAMES BALDWIN publishes *Another Country,* a groundbreaking novel constructed around issues of race and sexual orientation.

In San Francisco, a group of gay BAR owners and employees forms the Tavern Guild, believed to be the first gay business association in the U.S.

January 1962

Illinois criminal code reform passed last year takes effect this month, making Illinois the first state in U.S. history in which consensual same-sex acts are legal between adults.

July 15, 1962

In New York City, RANDY WICKER talks listener-supported radio station WBAI into broadcasting a taped program in which seven gay people discuss homosexuality. Widely publicized in the local press, the program is probably the first favorable broadcast on the subject in the U.S.

1963

Five women found the Minorities Research Group in London, the first lesbian organization in the UNITED KINGDOM. Similar to the American DAUGHTERS OF BILITIS, the group aims to provide isolated lesbians with counseling, education, and opportunities for socializing. Some members of the organization go on to found KENRIC in 1965. Also see **1964**.

Also in the UNITED KINGDOM, the English Society of Friends publishes *Towards a Quaker View of Sex.* The QUAKERS are the first mainstream Christian church to issue a public statement expressing tolerance of same-sex relationships. Also see **1945**.

Grove Press publishes JOHN RECHY's *City of Night* to generally positive reviews, pioneering a new level of sexual explicitness both in the text and in the book's packaging: the cover features a photograph of Times Square male prostitutes.

January 1963

At FRANK KAMENY's suggestion, the New York and Washington, D.C., chapters of the MATTACHINE, the New York chapter of the DAUGHTERS OF BILITIS, and Philadelphia's Janus Society join to found the East Coast Homophile Organizations. Nicknamed ECHO, the association marks the beginning of a new era of ACTIVISM for the U.S. HOMOPHILE movement. Also see **May 29, 1965**; **October 23, 1965**; **August 12–17, 1968**.

1964

CANADA's first HOMOPHILE magazine, *Two* (inspired by ONE—see **1/1953**), is issued by Kamp Publishing Company in Toronto.

In Philadelphia, Clarke P. Polak begins publishing *Drum* magazine under the auspices of the city's Janus Society, a HOMOPHILE group founded in 1960. The first U.S. gay publication to combine serious news coverage with unabashedly erotic content, *Drum* reflects a growing spirit of ACTIVISM among American gay men.

In the UNITED KINGDOM, women associated with the Minorities Research Group (see **1963**) begin publishing *Arena Three,* the country's first lesbian magazine.

The national convention of the AMERICAN CIVIL LIBERTIES UNION modifies the organization's position on sexual rights. Henceforth, the organization opposes government interference in the private sex lives of consenting adults.

April 1964

The Association for Social Knowledge, CANADA's first HOMOPHILE organization, is founded in Vancouver. Also see **December 31, 1966**.

June 1964

Life magazine entitles a cover story "Homosexuality in America." The article, which features photographs taken at a leather BAR called the Tool Box in San Francisco, challenges the gay male "pansy" stereotype at the same time it helps build awareness of the emerging American gay and lesbian SUBCULTURE.

September 1964

In San Francisco, Bill Plath, William Beardemphl, Mark Forrester, JIM FOSTER, and others found the SOCIETY FOR INDIVIDUAL RIGHTS (SIR). In addition to activities in support of a gay man's "right to his own sexual orientation," SIR will become one of the first gay male groups to provide community support systems as well as a wide range of social and educational programs. Also see **April 1966**.

September 19, 1964

In New York City, RANDY WICKER, Renee Cafiero, other activists, and representatives of the New York League for Sexual Freedom picket the Whitehall Induction Center in protest of the MILITARY's antigay and -lesbian policies. Many consider this the first public gay and lesbian rights demonstration in the U.S.

November 16, 1964

RANDY WICKER is a guest on *The Les Crane Show,* becoming the first openly gay person to appear on national TELEVISION. Following the show, Wicker is barraged by hundreds of letters from isolated lesbians and gay men across the country.

December 1964

In San Francisco, after several months of talks and a tour of local gay and lesbian gathering spots, a group of Protestant ministers join with lesbian and gay male activists to form the Council on Religion and the Homosexual. Also see **December 31, 1964**.

December 31, 1964

San Francisco police attempt to intimidate some 600 guests attending a New Year's Ball sponsored by the Council on Religion and the Homosexual (see **12/1964**), photographing each of the guests as they arrive and demanding entry without a search warrant. The ball is the first time many liberal heterosexuals have witnessed police harassment of lesbians and gay men. Three lawyers and Nancy May, a straight volunteer, are arrested. Also see **January 2, 1965**.

1965

In Antwerp, BELGIUM, activists form the Belgische Vereiniging voor Sexuale Rechtvaardigheid COC, the country's first HO-

MOPHILE organization, on the model of the COC in the NETHERLANDS (see **1946**).

In the UNITED KINGDOM, Dr. J. C. Barker reports on the development of new aversion therapy methods to "treat" homosexuality in the *British Journal of Psychiatry.* Barker claims his method—injecting drugs every two hours for six days and nights to produce dizziness and nausea in the patient while he views pictures of nude males—is highly effective in helping gay men achieve "recovery."

In San Francisco, the SOCIETY FOR INDIVIDUAL RIGHTS (see **9/1964**) begins publishing *Vector,* a slick, lively, community-oriented publication sold on newsstands throughout the city.

January 2, 1965

In San Francisco, Council on Religion and the Homosexual (see **12/1964**) representatives, most of whom are heterosexual, hold a press conference to protest the police force's "deliberate harassment" of the group's New Year's Ball (see **12/31/1964**). Also see **February 11, 1965**.

February 11, 1965

At the San Francisco trial of the four people arrested at the Council on Religion and the Homosexual's New Year's Ball (see **12/31/1964**), the judge orders the jury to find the defendants not guilty. The decision is widely seen as a turning point in the HOMOPHILE movement's fight for gay and lesbian civil rights.

April 17–18, 1965

In New York City, Craig Rodwell, RANDY WICKER, and other activists protest discrimination in the U.S. and CUBA (see **1960**) against gay men and lesbians in small but visible demonstrations in front of the United Nations building.

May 29, 1965

The East Coast Homophile Organizations (ECHO; see **1/1963**) stages the first demonstration in front of the White House in protest of U.S. government discrimination against gay men and lesbians. Seven men, including Jack Nichols, and three women, including JUDY GRAHN, picket. ABC and wire services report on the event. Also see **October 23, 1965**.

July 4, 1965

A small group of conservatively dressed lesbians and gay men picket Independence Hall in Philadelphia in one of the first public demonstrations for gay rights. Among those marching is BARBARA GITTINGS.

July 31, 1965

Lesbian and gay demonstrators picket the Pentagon to protest discrimination in the MILITARY.

August 28, 1965

The State Department is picketed by gay and lesbian demonstrators for the first time.

October 23, 1965

The East Coast Homophile Organizations (ECHO; **1/1963**) stages a second demonstration at the White House. The FBI reports 35 picketers.

1966

The premiere of *The Group* marks the first time the word "LESBIAN" is used in a HOLLYWOOD movie.

March 1966

In Kansas City, Missouri, Drew Schafer and friends form the Phoenix Society for Individual Freedom, one of several dozen new HOMOPHILE groups that arise in medium-size cities across the U.S. in the three years prior to the STONEWALL Uprising.

April 1966

In San Francisco, the SOCIETY FOR INDIVIDUAL RIGHTS (see **9/1964**) opens the first gay COMMUNITY CENTER in the United States.

Also in San Francisco, RIKKI STREICHER opens Maud's Study, one of the longest-lasting lesbian BARS anywhere, in the city's Haight district.

April 22, 1966

In New York City, Dick Leitsch, John Timmins, RANDY WICKER, and Craig Rodwell challenge liquor commission policies that deny gay men and lesbians the right to be served alcoholic beverages at BARS by holding a "sip-in." Reporters watch them as they are refused service at Julius, a popular gay bar in Greenwich Village. Also see **1967**.

May 1966

In CHINA, Mao Zedong launches the Great Proletarian Cultural Revolution in an attempt to purge the Communist Party and Chinese society of all vestiges of bourgeois and revisionist thinking. Among its millions of victims are people from all walks of life suspected of being gay or lesbian. Over the next decade, thousands of lesbians and gay men are publicly humiliated, tortured, exiled to the countryside, driven to commit suicide, or, in many instances, executed.

Fall 1966

In New York City, Bob Martin and other Columbia University students form the Student Homophile League. The next spring, the organization becomes the first officially recognized gay or lesbian group at an American college.

December 31, 1966

In Vancouver, the Association for Social Knowledge (see **4/1964**) opens the first COMMUNITY CENTER "to serve the homosexual community" in CANADA.

1967

The New Jersey Supreme Court issues a precedent-setting decision asserting that the state liquor commission is no longer justified in forbidding BARS from serving gay men and lesbians.

Following New Jersey's lead (see above), the New York Supreme Court rules that BARS may now legally serve "known" homosexuals. Also see **April 22, 1966**.

The U.S. Supreme Court rules that a Canadian gay man may be deported under the terms of the McCarran-Walter Immigration and Nationality Act (see **6/27/1952**), which bars persons "afflicted with psychopathic personality" from immigrating or becoming citizens.

Isabel Miller (PSEUDONYM of ALMA ROUTSONG) publishes *A Place for Us* (later titled *Patience and Sarah*).

CBS Reports broadcasts the first nationally televised American program on gay men and lesbians. Although most of "The Homosexuals" focuses on arrests, "causes," and "treatments," an interview segment gives GORE VIDAL the chance to comment favorably on ANDRÉ GIDE's call for "floating sexuality."

January 1, 1967

In Los Angeles, police conduct brutal raids on several gay BARS. Enraged by the sight of a few men exchanging customary New Year's kisses at midnight at the Black Cat in Silver Lake, LAPD undercover agents attack patrons and employees, leaving several severely injured and arresting 16. Also see **January 5, 1967**.

January 5, 1967

PRIDE, a Los Angeles HOMOPHILE group, mobilizes a crowd of several hundred demonstrators on Sunset Boulevard to protest police raids on gay BARS (**1/1/1967**).

January 6, 1967

New York City's Civil Service Commission makes public its year-old policy of allowing city agencies to hire and employ lesbians and gay men. The new policy comes partly in response to MATTACHINE Society of New York lobbying efforts.

July 27, 1967

In the UNITED KINGDOM, almost ten years after the publication of the WOLFENDEN REPORT (see **9/4/1957**), the Sexual Offences Act takes effect, decriminalizing most private sex acts between men aged 21 or over in England and Wales. Also see **July 22, 1980**; **October 25, 1982**; **August 7, 1987**; **February 16, 1991**.

August 1967

The board of directors of the AMERICAN CIVIL LIBERTIES UNION passes a resolution urging the decriminalization of consensual sex between adults. Also see **January 7, 1957**; **1964**.

In Los Angeles, PRIDE members Dick Michaels, Bill Rand, and Sam Winston publish the first issue of the *Los Angeles Advocate,* the forerunner of THE ADVOCATE, in an edition of 500 copies.

November 24, 1967

In New York City, Craig Rodwell opens the first gay BOOKSTORE in the U.S., the Oscar Wilde Memorial Bookshop.

December 1967

Vector, the monthly magazine of the SOCIETY FOR INDIVIDUAL RIGHTS (SIR) (see **9/1964**; **4/1966**), reports that SIR now has almost 1,000 members, making it the largest HOMOPHILE organization in the U.S.

1968

In its official listing of mental disorders, the AMERICAN PSYCHIATRIC ASSOCIATION recategorizes homosexuality as a "sexual deviation" or "a non-psychotic mental disorder." Previously (see **1952**), the group has considered homosexuality a "sociopathic" disorder. Also see **December 15, 1973**.

February 1968

In New York City, Craig Rodwell begins editing a "gay lib" newsletter called *Hymnal.*

Spring 1968

In New York City, the first *Gay Scene Guide* is published, listing some 125 BARS and CRUISING venues in the metropolitan area.

May 1968

In FRANCE, massive student unrest brings the country to a standstill. Among the demonstrators is the country's first GAY LIBERATION group, Pédéraste. Also see **March 10, 1971**.

August 12–17, 1968

The North American Conference of Homophile Organizations, nicknamed NACHO, made up of delegates from 26 groups, convenes in Chicago to discuss goals and strategy. Although delegates fail to form a unified national organization, they pass a five-point "Homosexual Bill of Rights" and resolve to make "Gay Is Good" the slogan of the movement.

September 1968

In New York City, radio station WBAI begins weekly broadcasts of *The New Symposium,* featuring interviews of gay men and lesbians and news reports.

October 6, 1968

In Los Angeles, the Reverend Troy Perry holds the first METROPOLITAN COMMUNITY CHURCH service in the living room of his home. Also see **December 3, 1968**.

December 3, 1968

At the METROPOLITAN COMMUNITY CHURCH in Los Angeles, the Reverend Troy Perry officiates at what is probably the first public SAME-SEX UNION ceremony in the U.S.

March 28, 1969

In San Francisco, SOCIETY FOR INDIVIDUAL RIGHTS president Leo Laurence and his lover are featured in a photo-illustrated article in the *Berkeley Barb.* Calling for "the Homosexual Revolution of 1969," Laurence exhorts gay men and lesbians to join the Black Panthers and other left-wing groups and to "come OUT" en masse. Also see **May 1969**.

May 1969

In San Francisco, SOCIETY FOR INDIVIDUAL RIGHTS president Leo Laurence is expelled from the organization for characterizing members as "timid" and "middle-class, uptight, bitchy old queens." In response, Laurence founds a militant group, the Committee for Homosexual Freedom.

Also in San Francisco, CARL WITTMAN begins writing *Refugees from Amerika: A Gay Manifesto,* one of the most influential documents of the coming GAY LIBERATION era. Also see **December 22, 1970**.

May 15, 1969

In CANADA, the House of Commons votes to decriminalize private same-sex acts between consenting adults. The new law goes into effect in August.

June 28, 1969

In Greenwich Village, New York, police raid the STONEWALL Inn at 2:00 A.M. For once, patrons—and the crowd gathered outside—fight back. The American GAY LIBERATION movement begins.

June 29, 1969

In New York City, the MATTACHINE Action Committee issues a flier urging organized demonstrations in protest of the previous night's police raid on the STONEWALL Inn.

June 30, 1969

Footnote to history: In Kew Gardens, Queens, a vigilante group cuts down all the trees and bushes in part of a local park popular as a gay male CRUISING area. Lamenting the loss of greenery, *The New York Times* runs nine different articles on the ensuing controversy. The STONEWALL Uprising and the protests that follow are mentioned a total of three times. Also see **August 3, 1969**.

July 2, 1969

In New York City, 500 marchers confront police in the first "gay pride" demonstration, a march down Christopher Street.

July 4, 1969

DAUGHTERS OF BILITIS and MATTACHINE society members picket Independence Hall in Philadelphia for the fifth and last time (see **7/4/1965**).

July 9, 1969

The MATTACHINE Society of New York invites activists to gather in Greenwich Village for the first "gay power" meeting.

July 31, 1969

In New York City, militants separate from the more moderate HOMOPHILE movement to form a COUNTERCULTURE-inspired group they vote to call GAY LIBERATION FRONT.

August 3, 1969

In New York City, GAY LIBERATION FRONT (see **7/31/1969**) and the MATTACHINE Society of New York join forces to protest the Queens vigilante tree-cutting (see **6/30/1969**) and alleged police complicity.

September 1, 1969

West Germany rescinds its prohibitions against sex acts between consenting male adults. (Lesbian sex acts have never been against the law in GERMANY.)

September 3, 1969

The American Sociological Association condemns "oppressive actions against any persons for reasons of sexual preference." It is the first national professional organization to voice support of gay and lesbian civil rights.

September 15, 1969

Gay Power, "New York's First Homosexual Newspaper" and the first publication to emerge from the post-STONEWALL movement, publishes its premiere issue.

October 2, 1969

A National Institute of Mental Health study, chaired by Dr. EVELYN HOOKER, urges government bodies to decriminalize private sex acts between consenting adults.

October 31, 1969

Time magazine features a seven-page article entitled "The Homosexual: Newly Visible, Newly Understood." GAY LIBERATION FRONT activists demonstrate in front of Time, Inc., offices to protest the article's inclusion of negative comments by mental health experts.

In San Francisco, lesbians and gay men protest homophobic language in the *Examiner.* Newspaper employees respond by showering the demonstrators with purple ink. Violence ensues.

November 14, 1969

In New York City, GAY LIBERATION FRONT (see **7/31/1969**) launches the premiere issue of the newspaper *Come Out!,* "A Newspaper by and for the Gay Community."

November 15, 1969

In Washington, D.C., representatives of GAY LIBERATION FRONT (see **7/31/1969**) join hundreds of thousands of other demonstrators protesting the Vietnam War.

December 1969

In Chicago, Harry Wiemhoff places an ad in the University of Chicago student newspaper calling for the formation of a local GAY LIBERATION FRONT. By the following spring the movement is firmly established in the city.

December 21, 1969

In New York City, Jim Owles and MARTY ROBINSON leave GAY LIBERATION FRONT (see **7/31/1969**) to form a group exclusively dedicated to the pursuit of gay rights. The new organization is called GAY ACTIVISTS ALLIANCE.

December 28, 1969

In Berkeley, California, Don Jackson outlines a plan for a "gay colony" in California's Alpine County, whose current population is 450. Although his proposal attracts widespread media attention—and support from activists, including JIM KEPNER and Don Kilhefner—few gay men and lesbians are willing to make the move.

December 31, 1969

In San Francisco, the Cockettes, one of the first GENDER-bending performing groups, makes its debut.

January 1970

In AUSTRALIA, women in Melbourne found a local branch of the DAUGHTERS OF BILITIS. The group is the first HOMOPHILE organization in the country. Also see **July 1970**.

March 8, 1970

In New York City, police conduct an early-morning raid on the Snake Pit BAR and arrest 167 persons. Diego Vinales, afraid of being deported to his native ARGENTINA, leaps from a second-story police station window and impales himself on a wrought-iron fence. Later in the day, some 500 GAY LIBERATION FRONT activists and other supporters demonstrate in protest.

March 17, 1970

The FILM version of *The Boys in the Band,* the first major HOLLYWOOD look at gay life, premieres.

April 1970

Dissatisfied with the overwhelmingly male ambience of most movement activities, GAY LIBERATION FRONT lesbians organize the first "all-women's dances" in New York City.

April 13, 1970

In New York City, GAY ACTIVISTS ALLIANCE borrows a tactic of the New Left and unleashes the first gay ZAP, a surprise disruption of a public event to call attention to a political issue. Activists begin shouting "gay power" during a public appearance by Mayor John Lindsay, who has resisted meeting with activists. Also see **May 14, 1970**; **September 14, 1970**.

May 1, 1970

At the Second Congress to Unite Women in New York City, lesbian feminists stage the LAVENDER MENACE action in protest of lesbophobia in the women's movement and particularly in the NATIONAL ORGANIZATION FOR WOMEN. Also see **September 6, 1971**.

At the same congress, RADICALESBIANS distribute an epoch-defining manifesto entitled "WOMAN-IDENTIFIED WOMAN." The manifesto, which is also published in the June 1970 issue of *Come Out!,* is among the first to advocate lesbianism as a (feminist) political choice and solidarity with SEPARATISM.

May 14, 1970

In New York City, GAY LIBERATION FRONT activists ZAP a special session of the AMERICAN PSYCHIATRIC ASSOCIATION dealing with "sex problems." The activists protest an Australian doctor's paper on the use of electroshock aversion therapy to "treat" homosexuality.

May 21, 1970

Running for Congress, Bella Abzug openly seeks gay and lesbian support at a GAY ACTIVISTS ALLIANCE meeting in New York City. One of the first politicians to ally herself with the gay rights movement, she wins election in November.

June 24, 1970

In New York City, police arrest GAY ACTIVISTS ALLIANCE members Tom Doerr, Arthur Evans, Jim Owles, Phil Raia, and MARTY ROBINSON for staging a sit-in at the headquarters of the Republican State Committee. The men, who wanted to present their demands for "fair employment" practices to New York State Governor Nelson Rockefeller, become known as the Rockefeller Five. Also see **August 5, 1970**.

June 28, 1970

In New York City, the tradition of annually commemorating the anniversary of the STONEWALL Uprising begins with a "Christopher Street Liberation Day" march and a "gay-in" in Central Park. About 15,000 people participate, making it the largest gay and lesbian rally yet.

Los Angeles celebrates the STONEWALL anniversary with a march down Hollywood Boulevard that draws about 1,000 people.

Smaller marches take place in Chicago and San Francisco. The anniversary is also marked by special celebrations at gay BARS around the world, including clubs in Buenos Aires, ARGENTINA; Lima, Peru; and Managua, Nicaragua.

July 1970

AUSTRALIA's first lesbian or gay organization (see **1/1970**), Australian DAUGHTERS OF BILITIS, begins to hold public meetings in Melbourne. A straight woman acts as a spokesperson for the group.

July 2, 1970

The Fifth Biennial Convention of the LUTHERAN CHURCH in America expresses its opposition to discrimination and oppression of gay men and lesbians.

July 4, 1970

The General Assembly of the UNITARIAN UNIVERSALIST ASSOCIATION becomes the first mainstream religious group in the U.S. to recognize publicly the existence of gay, lesbian, and bisexual clergy and laity among its members and to demand "an end to all discrimination against homosexuals."

July 10–12, 1970

The national organization of DAUGHTERS OF BILITIS is disbanded. Local chapters are free to continue as independent entities.

July 25, 1970

The Vatican issues a statement reminding the faithful that the ROMAN CATHOLIC CHURCH considers homosexuality a moral aberration.

Late Summer 1970

Reflecting a strengthening feminist identity, women active in GAY LIBERATION FRONT form their own "Gay Women's Liberation Front" within the movement, then break away to start a completely independent organization called Gay Liberation Front Women.

August 1970

In New York City, police begin the traditional "election-year clean-up," repeatedly inspecting gay clubs and arresting more than 300 gay men and lesbians on charges of "loitering." Also see **August 29, 1970**; **September 14, 1970**.

August 5, 1970

In New York City, the Rockefeller Five (see **6/24/1970**) appear in court, but their trial is postponed (charges are later dismissed). DAUGHTERS OF BILITIS activist Isabel Miller (PSEUDONYM of ALMA ROUTSONG) is among the speakers at a rally held after their court appearance.

August 21, 1970

Huey Newton, leader of the Black Panthers, expresses his support of the GAY LIBERATION movement.

August 24, 1970

"Homosexuals in Revolt" is a front-page story in *The New York Times.* The article reports "a new mood now taking hold among the nation's homosexuals. In growing numbers they are publicly identifying themselves as homosexuals, taking a measure of pride in that identity and seeking militantly to end what they see as society's persecution of them."

August 29, 1970

In New York City, a peaceful demonstration against police harassment (see **8/1970**) is followed by an evening of rioting in Greenwich Village.

September 14, 1970

In New York City, GAY ACTIVISTS ALLIANCE stages the first of an orchestrated campaign of ZAPS in protest of continuing police harassment (see **8/1970**), heckling Mayor John Lindsay as he enters the Metropolitan Opera House for its opening night gala.

September 19, 1970

In Sydney, AUSTRALIA, John Ware and Christabel Poll, founders of the newly formed Campaign Against Moral Persecution, Inc. (CAMP, Inc.) become the first gay man and the first lesbian, respectively, to come OUT in the country's history when an interview featuring them is published in the newspaper *The Australian.* Also see **February 6, 1971**.

September 23, 1970

On the CBS TELEVISION series *Medical Center,* a medical researcher announces, "I am a homosexual." Although his "condition" is portrayed as unfortunate, the program is acclaimed as the first sympathetic treatment of a gay man in an American TV drama.

September 26, 1970

In Los Angeles, GAY LIBERATION FRONT demonstrators persuade BAR owners to allow gay patrons to hold hands.

September 27, 1970

Chicago Gay Alliance separates from the local GAY LIBERATION FRONT (GLF), declaring in a position statement that GLF's political agenda is too broad to be effective in the struggle for gay and lesbian civil rights.

October 8, 1970

In New York City, two policemen invade a private club to interrupt a DAUGHTERS OF BILITIS—New York business meeting. The blatantly harassing nature of the police action persuades many members of the hitherto low-profile group of the need for militancy.

October 9, 1970

In Minneapolis, FREE (GAY LIBERATION of Minnesota) opens the first "Regional Gay Convention" in the Midwest.

October 13, 1970

Bob Mellors and Aubrey Walter host the UNITED KINGDOM's first GAY LIBERATION FRONT meeting at the London School of Economics. Also see **November 27, 1970**.

October 27, 1970

To protest a September 1970 *Harper's* cover story entitled "The Struggle for Sexual Identity," in which editor Joseph Epstein had lamented homosexuals as "an affront to our rationality" and homosexuality as "anathema," Columbia graduate student Pete Fisher stages a sit-in at the magazine's Park Avenue offices with 40 other GAY ACTIVISTS ALLIANCE (GAA) members. Although the *Harper's* ZAP fails to elicit an official response from the magazine, it has an enormous impact on future media coverage of lesbian and gay issues, in addition to leading to GAA's national TELEVISION debut (see **11/27/1970**).

October 28, 1970

KATE MILLETT becomes one of the first leaders of the growing women's movement to acknowledge her lesbianism when she comes OUT as a bisexual at a DAUGHTERS OF BILITIS meeting in New York City. Also see **September 6, 1971**.

November 1970

CANADA's first GAY LIBERATION FRONT is formed in Vancouver.

November 27, 1970

GAY ACTIVISTS ALLIANCE representatives MARTY ROBINSON and Arthur Evans and MATTACHINE Society of New York president Dick Leitsch appear on Dick Cavett's TELEVISION talk show to explain the aims of the GAY LIBERATION movement. Also see **October 27, 1970**.

In London, the GAY LIBERATION FRONT (see **10/13/1970**) mounts its first public demonstration, a torch-lit protest march on Highbury Fields.

December 4, 1970

New York City's first gay COMMUNITY CENTER opens in Greenwich Village.

December 22, 1970

The *San Francisco Free Press* prints CARL WITTMAN's *Refugees from Amerika: A Gay Manifesto* (see **5/1969**). Reprinted and distributed all across the country in the next year, it quickly becomes the bible of GAY LIBERATION.

1971

In Berlin, GERMANY, the premiere of ROSA VON PRAUNHEIM's *It Is Not the Homosexual Who Is Perverse but the Society in Which He Lives* marks the beginning of the German GAY LIBERATION movement.

January 3, 1971

Ti-Grace Atkinson advocates political lesbianism—a total and exclusive commitment to women that may or may not include sex (see LESBIAN, POLITICAL)—at a DAUGHTERS OF BILITIS—New York meeting.

January 17, 1971

The New York Times Magazine includes a groundbreaking seven-page essay by writer MERLE MILLER entitled "What It Means to Be a Homosexual."

February 6, 1971

In Sydney, AUSTRALIA, CAMP (Campaign Against Moral Persecution—see **9/19/1970**) holds its first public meetings.

March 10, 1971

In FRANCE, GUY HOCQUENGHEM and other, mostly lesbian activists disrupt a Paris conference on the "problem" of homosexuality. The demonstration leads to the formation the following month of a GAY LIBERATION group, Front Homosexuel d'Action Révolutionnaire.

March 14, 1971

In Albany, New York, an estimated 2,000 people march on the state capitol in protest of antigay and antilesbian LAWS and policies.

April 1, 1971

In FRANCE, police confiscate copies of Jean-Paul Sartre's newspaper *Tout* when it publishes an editorial advocating social acceptance of homosexuality (which is not criminalized in France).

May 1971

In Ann Arbor, Michigan, the lesbian newspaper *Spectre* publishes one of the earliest position statements of lesbian SEPARATISM.

May 6, 1971

In New York City, GAY ACTIVISTS ALLIANCE opens the Firehouse, a COMMUNITY CENTER offering an alternative to BARS and BATHS.

July 1, 1971

In the UNITED KINGDOM, a court upholds a lower-court decision ruling that PERSONAL ADS for gay men and lesbians constitute "indecency" whether or not same-sex relations are legal. Also see **June 1972**.

In AUSTRIA, Parliament rescinds LAWS against sex between consenting adults but adds legislation penalizing individuals who make public statements or join organizations that favor homosexuality. Although the new legislation is used to harass lesbians and gay men and, later, to prevent the import of gay and lesbian PORNOGRAPHY, including SAFE(R) SEX literature, no individuals or organizations are successfully prosecuted under the laws.

September 1971

In the NETHERLANDS, lesbian SEPARATISM leads to the founding of the all-women's group Lavender September.

JAPAN's first magazine for gay men, *Barazoku* ("Rose Tribe"), makes its debut. A cover blurb, in English, reads, "For Young Men and Guys," followed by the lyrics, also in English, of the first verse of "Bridge over Troubled Waters."

September 6, 1971

The annual convention of the NATIONAL ORGANIZATION FOR WOMEN passes a resolution acknowledging "oppression of lesbians as a legitimate concern of feminism." Also see **May 1, 1970**; **February 1973**; **March 4, 1973**.

October 1, 1971

Connecticut is the second state (after Illinois—see **1/1962**) to decriminalize same-sex acts between consenting adults.

October 8, 1971

AUSTRALIA's first public gay and lesbian rights demonstration takes place in Sydney outside the headquarters of the Liberal Party. Gay writer and activist DENNIS ALTMAN is one of about 70 protesters.

October 10, 1971

Seven lesbians, including BARBARA GITTINGS, break new ground on U.S. TELEVISION when they appear on *The David Susskind Show.*

December 29, 1971

Wakefield Poole's trend-setting *Boys in the Sand* premieres, prompting *Variety* to remark, "There are no more closets." Shot on FIRE ISLAND, Poole's slickly produced FILM marks a dramatic departure from the low-budget PORNOGRAPHY previously available.

1972

In Hollywood, California, JIM KEPNER founds the International Gay and Lesbian Archive.

In AUSTRALIA, a breakthrough TELEVISION program called *Number 96* debuts with a sympathetically portrayed, openly gay main character and numerous gay and lesbian supporting cast members. Complete with nudity and interracial love stories, the show is top-rated on all five of the weeknights it is shown.

January 27, 1972

In New York City, a municipal rights ordinance for lesbians and gay men is defeated. The bill remains a hotly contested part of City Council politics for the next 14 years. Also see **March 20, 1986**.

March 1972

An American Bar Association committee recommends the decriminalization of consensual same-sex acts.

March 7, 1972

The first U.S. municipal rights ordinance forbidding hiring discrimination against lesbians and gay men is passed in East Lansing, Michigan.

June 1972

In the UNITED KINGDOM, the *International Times* is found guilty of a "conspiracy to corrupt public morals" for publishing "contact adverts" (PERSONAL ADS) for gay men.

June 25, 1972

The UNITED CHURCH OF CHRIST becomes the first mainstream U.S. denomination to ordain an openly gay man, William Johnson.

June 27, 1972

In the UNITED KINGDOM, the fortnightly *Gay News,* the first and best-known British gay newspaper, is founded.

July 1, 1972

The UNITED KINGDOM's first Gay Pride March draws about 2,000 gay men and lesbians to the center of London.

July 10, 1972

Ann Arbor, Michigan, passes the first comprehensive gay and lesbian municipal rights ordinance.

July 12, 1972

At the Democratic National Convention, MADELINE DAVIS, representing the MATTACHINE Society of the Niagara Frontier, and SOCIETY FOR INDIVIDUAL RIGHTS leader JIM FOSTER are the first speakers to advocate lesbian and gay rights at a national political convention.

August 9, 1972

The Ohio Secretary of State refuses to grant articles of incorporation to the Greater Cincinnati Gay Society. Two years later, the Ohio Supreme Court upholds the decision, stating that even though homosexual acts are now legal in Ohio, "the promotion of homosexuality as a valid life style is contrary to the public policy of the state."

November 1, 1972

Almost 20 million people watch the first positive treatment of gay characters on American TELEVISION: ABC's broadcast of *That Certain Summer,* a sympathetic but ultimately disheartening TV movie about a boy who finds out his father is gay.

January 18, 1973

Viewers of *An American Family,* 12-part TELEVISION documentary shown on PBS about the lives of an "average" American family, discover that son Lance is living as an openly gay man in New York City.

February 1973

The NATIONAL ORGANIZATION FOR WOMEN passes a resolution declaring lesbian and gay rights a "top priority." Also see **May 1, 1970**; **September 6, 1971**; **March 4, 1973**.

March 4, 1973

Betty Friedan, one of the founders of the NATIONAL ORGANIZATION FOR WOMEN, tells *The New York Times* that "man-hating" lesbians are seeking to take control of the organization. Also see **February 1973**.

May 1973

Dykes and Gorgons, a publication of the East Coast–based Gutter Dyke Collective, takes lesbian SEPARATISM to its most extreme position, angering many other lesbians with its call to "rid the world of men." The first step: "wimmin" must stop having male babies. The collective is also one of the first to declare that male-to-female TRANSSEXUALS cannot be lesbians, an issue that will remain controversial for decades to come.

July 4, 1973

In Seattle, the Lesbian Separatist Group (later the Gorgons) issues *The Amazon Analysis,* a manifesto and handbook of lesbian SEPARATISM. The paper's nearly 100 mimeographed pages are passed among lesbians across the country.

October 1, 1973

In Touch, the first glossy *Playboy*-style magazine for gay men, debuts with a blend of erotica, male nude PHOTOGRAPHY, and feature stories.

October 15, 1973

Dr. HOWARD BROWN announces the founding of the NATIONAL GAY (later: AND LESBIAN) TASK FORCE, considered the first gay or lesbian rights organization with a truly national scope. Dr. Bruce Voeller is named the first executive director.

November 5, 1973

The U.S. Supreme Court rules that Florida's anti-SODOMY laws are constitutional.

November 23, 1973

In New York City, 325 persons attend the first conference of the Gay Academic Union. The pioneering LESBIAN AND GAY STUDIES group, which was founded the previous March, includes MARTIN BAUML DUBERMAN, JOHN D'EMILIO, JONATHAN NED KATZ, and JOAN NESTLE among its members.

December 15, 1973

After years of controversy and often stormy debate, the Board of Trustees of the AMERICAN PSYCHIATRIC ASSOCIATION declares that "by itself, homosexuality does not meet the criteria for being a psychiatric disorder."

1974

The NETHERLANDS ends discrimination against lesbians and gay men in the country's MILITARY services.

RITA MAE BROWN publishes her largely autobiographical *Rubyfruit Jungle,* the most widely read lesbian novel of the post-STONEWALL era.

February 1974

The Australian and New Zealand College of Psychiatrists becomes one of the first such groups in the world to eliminate homosexuality from its official listing of mental disorders. Also see **December 15, 1973**.

March 2, 1974

Five activists discuss gay and lesbian issues on a nationally televised forum, *The David Susskind Show.*

April 1974

The Front Runner, PATRICIA NELL WARREN's romantic gay male love story, goes on sale.

The national board of Alcoholics Anonymous (AA) permits gay and lesbian AA meetings to be listed in the group's directory for the first time.

April 1, 1974

In Michigan, Kathy Kozachenko wins a seat on the Ann Arbor City Council. She is the first openly lesbian or gay person elected to public office in the U.S.

April 4, 1974

In New York City, more than 1,000 people gather in Greenwich Village to demonstrate support for a gay and lesbian municipal rights ordinance currently under debate in the City Council. The bill has been strongly opposed by, among others, the Roman Catholic Archdiocese of New York and the Uniformed Fire Officers Association.

April 10, 1974

The GAY ACTIVISTS ALLIANCE publication *Out—The Gay Perspective* debuts, with Ernest Peter Cohen as editor in chief.

May 1974
In Chile (see LATIN AMERICA), where a military junta led by Augusto Pinochet seized power last year, the regime begins arresting gay and lesbian activists as part of its campaign against leftists.

May 1, 1974
In Oporto, PORTUGAL, activists organize the country's first public demonstrations in favor of gay and lesbian rights a week after the overthrow of the long installed Salazar regime.

May 14, 1974
In the U.S. Congress, New York Democratic Representatives Bella Abzug and Edward I. Koch introduce the first bill proposing to broaden the 1964 Civil Rights Act to include protection against discrimination based on "sexual orientation, sex or marital status."

May 24, 1974
From the USSR (see RUSSIA) comes a rare public acknowledgment of the country's repressive policies against gay men and lesbians. American news services report that noted FILM director Sergei Paradzhanov has been given six years' hard labor for crimes including "partial homosexuality" and "incitement to suicide." He is one of an estimated 1,000 persons arrested each year on charges related to homosexuality.

August 1974
AT&T is the first major American corporation to agree to an equal opportunity policy for lesbians and gay men.

Fall 1974
The scholarly quarterly *Journal of Homosexuality* makes its debut.

September 27, 1974
The NATIONAL GAY [later: AND LESBIAN] TASK FORCE and other lesbian and gay activists persuade major consumer advertisers to withdraw commercials from a *Marcus Welby, M.D.*, episode about a high school boy who is raped by a male teacher. Their achievement is hailed as the first successful protest against alleged defamation of gay men on American TELEVISION. Also see **November 24, 1974**.

November 5, 1974
ELAINE NOBLE becomes the first openly lesbian or gay politician to be elected to state office when a Boston district chooses her as its representative to the Massachusetts legislature. Also see **April 1, 1974**; **December 9, 1974**.

November 18, 1974
The New Yorker publishes Allan Gurganus's short story "Minor Heroism," the first piece of fiction with an openly gay theme in the magazine's history.

November 24, 1974
The NATIONAL GAY [later: AND LESBIAN] TASK FORCE protests an episode of NBC's *Police Woman* (aired on November 8) that featured lesbian murderers in a home for aged women. The network agrees not to rerun the episode, but MCA-TV producer David Gerber keeps it in syndication release. Also see **September 27, 1974**.

December 9, 1974
Minnesota State Senator Allan Spear becomes the first gay male state officeholder to come OUT. Also see **April 1, 1974**; **November 5, 1974**.

January 31, 1975
The American Association for the Advancement of Science approves a resolution de-

nouncing discrimination against lesbians and gay men.

May 12, 1975

California becomes the 11th state to decriminalize same-sex acts.

June 1, 1975

The national debut of *Drummer* magazine spotlights the rise of open S/M and leather sub-subcultures within the gay male SUBCULTURE.

June 19, 1975

The American Medical Association approves a resolution recommending the repeal of state laws against consensual same-sex acts between adults.

July 1975

In San Francisco, Randy Burns, Barbara Cameron, and ten other NATIVE AMERICANS organize Gay American Indians, the first group of its kind in the U.S. Within a year, members from more than 20 different Native American tribes join the organization.

July 1, 1975

In MEXICO, lesbian activists at the first United Nations World Conference on Women come to the attention of the world press, when Pedro Gringoire attacks their efforts to make lesbian rights part of the conference agenda in an essay published in *Excelsior,* the country's leading newspaper. Gringoire calls lesbianism a "pathological irregularity," a "sexual aberration," and a "severe illness." Lesbian activists score gains in visibility as a result, but fail to elicit an official response to their demands at the conference.

July 3, 1975

The U.S. Civil Service Commission decides to consider applications by lesbians and gay men on a case-by-case basis. Previously, homosexuality was grounds for automatic disqualification. Also see **February 7, 1977**; **August 4, 1995**.

July 15, 1975

Santa Cruz County, California, is the first U.S. county to make job discrimination against gay men and lesbians illegal.

July 23, 1975

World-famous evangelist Billy Graham states that he is in favor of gay men being ordained as ministers.

August 13, 1975

THE ADVOCATE calls 1975 the Year of the Disco (see DANCING, SOCIAL). Across the U.S. and around the world, discos have changed the face of the gay and lesbian SUBCULTURE.

December 9, 1975

Reporter Lynn Rosellini kicks off a series of articles in the *Washington Star* about homosexuality and SPORTS, revealing that "some of the biggest names in football . . . are homosexual or bisexual." Also see **December 11, 1975**.

December 11, 1975

DAVID KOPAY, a former Washington Redskins linebacker, is featured in the *Washington Star*'s series of articles on homosexuality and SPORTS (see **12/9/1975**), becoming the first major professional athlete to come OUT voluntarily.

1976

In AFRICA, Mozambique's Marxist government begins to incarcerate lesbians and gay men in "reeducation camps."

In FRANCE, MICHEL FOUCAULT publishes *La*

Volonté de Savoir, the first volume of what is to become his three-volume *The History of Sexuality.* Foucault's work later becomes one of the most important texts in the CONSTRUCTIONISM VS. ESSENTIALISM controversy.

The San Francisco Police Department becomes the first American LAW ENFORCEMENT agency to institute a policy of encouraging officers to come OUT.

Also in San Francisco, Rudi Cox applies for a position as a sheriff's deputy, becoming the first openly gay LAW ENFORCEMENT officer in the U.S.

The General Convention of the American EPISCOPAL CHURCH passes a resolution calling homosexuals "children of God" and urging acceptance and respect on the part of the Church.

January 15, 1976

The ROMAN CATHOLIC CHURCH reaffirms its opposition to same-sex eroticism, calling it "a serious depravity" in the Vatican document "Declaration on Certain Questions Concerning Sexual Ethics."

January 19, 1976

Campaigning for the Democratic presidential nomination, former Vice President Hubert Humphrey becomes one of the first nationally known politicians to endorse gay and lesbian rights.

February 10, 1976

Garry Trudeau's *Doonesbury* is the first mainstream COMIC STRIP to feature a gay male character.

March 12, 1976

In Los Angeles, Jimmy Carter, campaigning for the Democratic presidential nomination, expresses support for gay and lesbian rights and says he would be willing to sign an executive order banning discrimination against lesbians and gay men in the MILITARY. Also see **May 21, 1976**.

March 24, 1976

In ARGENTINA, a military coup leads to seven years of brutal dictatorship, during which gay and lesbian meeting places are frequently raided, and some 400 gay men are "disappeared"—kidnapped, tortured, and killed—by military commandos.

March 29, 1976

The U.S. Supreme Court rules that Virginia's anti-SODOMY laws are constitutional.

April 4, 1976

Pope Paul VI publicly denies press reports that he has had affairs with men.

May 1976

Publisher Charles Ortleb debuts *Christopher Street,* the first nationally distributed gay and lesbian literary magazine.

May 14, 1976

In CANADA, Montreal police launch a campaign of raids on lesbian and gay BARS and BATHHOUSES.

May 21, 1976

Jimmy Carter, campaigning for the Democratic presidential nomination, expresses support for a federal gay and lesbian civil rights bill. Also see **March 12, 1976**.

May 24, 1976

The *San Francisco Chronicle* begins running ARMISTEAD MAUPIN's *Tales of the City.* The serial, which is later published in book form (and, still later, televised), includes a number of gay, lesbian, bisexual, and transsexual characters.

November 10, 1976

Lynn Ransom of Oakland, California, is one of the first openly lesbian mothers to win custody of her CHILDREN in court.

January 10, 1977

The EPISCOPAL CHURCH ordains Ellen Marie Barrett. She is the first openly lesbian cleric of any major religious organization in the U.S.

January 12, 1977

An article in THE ADVOCATE reports that the CIA has files on about 300,000 people who have been arrested on charges relating to homosexuality.

January 18, 1977

In Miami, Florida, Anita Bryant, a former beauty queen, launches a nationwide crusade against gay and lesbian rights in response to Dade County's new municipal rights ordinance forbidding housing and employment discrimination against lesbians and gay men. Accusing lesbians and gay men of corrupting the nation's youth, Bryant dubs her crusade the "Save Our Children" campaign. Also see **March 20, 1977**; **June 7, 1977**.

February 7, 1977

The U.S. State Department announces it will begin considering job applications from lesbians and gay men for employment in the foreign service and other international agencies. Also see **July 3, 1975**; **August 4, 1995**.

February 9, 1977

In San Francisco, the world's first lesbian and gay FILM festival draws an audience of about 200 people.

March 1, 1977

In New York City, *Blueboy Forum* debuts on a cable network. The show is probably the first regularly scheduled gay-themed TELEVISION program in the U.S.

March 17, 1977

The Arkansas legislature recriminalizes same-sex acts between consenting adults. The new law, approved two years after Arkansas had repealed its anti-SODOMY laws, is the first of a series of setbacks for gay and lesbian civil rights that evidence the rise of a conservative backlash in the U.S. Also see **March 20, 1977**.

March 20, 1977

The Arkansas State House of Representatives unanimously passes a resolution in praise of Anita Bryant (see **1/18/1977**; **6/7/1977**) and her antigay and -lesbian rights campaign.

May 25, 1977

In a unanimous vote, the San Francisco school board decides to make information on lesbian and gay sexuality a part of the city schools' sex education programs.

March 26, 1977

Officers of the NATIONAL GAY [later: AND LESBIAN] TASK FORCE Bruce Voeller and Jean O'Leary and other leaders—including Pokey Anderson, Charles Brydon, CHARLOTTE BUNCH, FRANK KAMENY, Cookie Lutkefedder, Mary Mendola, ELAINE NOBLE, Rev. Troy Perry, Betty Powell, George Raya, Myra Riddell, and Charlotte Spitzer—meet with White House aide Midge Costanza. The meeting marks the first official discussion of gay and lesbian rights in the White House.

June 7, 1977

Dade County, Florida, residents vote two to one in favor of repealing the county's gay and lesbian municipal rights ordinance (see **1/18/1977**).

Also in Florida, Governor Reubin Askew

signs a law prohibiting gay men and lesbians from adopting CHILDREN.

June 26, 1977

Gay PRIDE CELEBRATIONS across the country, including the original STONEWALL-inspired New York City march, held today, attract record numbers of participants. The heavy turnout is judged a response to the backlash against gay and lesbian rights inspired by Anita Bryant's campaign (see **1/18/1977**; **6/7/1977**).

July 12, 1977

Denis Lemon, the editor of *Gay News,* is the first person to be convicted of "blasphemy" in the UNITED KINGDOM in 55 years. Lemon had printed James Kirkup's homoerotic poem about Christ, "The Love That Dares to Speak Its Name."

October 19, 1977

In the UNITED KINGDOM, Rev. Ian Paisley fights progay LAW reform in Northern IRELAND by declaring a "Save Ulster from Sodomy" campaign.

October 23, 1977

In Montreal, CANADA, more than 1,000 demonstrators protest antigay and -lesbian police actions.

November 2, 1977

Senior Action in a Gay Environment (SAGE) is founded in New York City as a support group for AGING lesbians and gay men.

November 8, 1977

HARVEY MILK is elected to the San Francisco Board of Supervisors. He is the first openly gay elected official of a large U.S. city. Also see **November 27, 1978**.

December 15, 1977

In CANADA, Quebec is the first province to make rights protection for lesbians and gay men an explicit part of its Charter for Human Rights.

December 30, 1977

In CANADA, Toronto police take action against *The Body Politic,* the country's leading gay and lesbian newspaper, seizing materials and charging the publication with "using the mails to distribute immoral, indecent, and scurrilous material." Also see **May 12, 1982**.

1978

In Iceland, activists form Samtökin '78. With its founding, every country in SCANDINAVIA now has an open gay and lesbian rights organization.

The National Coalition of Black Gays—later the National Coalition of Black Lesbians and Gays—is founded in New York City to help unite lesbians and gay AFRICAN-AMERICANS across the country and to support local organizing efforts.

April 1978

BRAZIL's first gay publication, *Lampião,* makes its debut. Also see **August 1978**.

June 25, 1978

San Francisco artist Gilbert Baker debuts the first RAINBOW FLAG design. Thirty volunteers have dyed and sewn two gigantic banners featuring his design for the city's annual Gay Freedom Day Parade, which this year draws a record 350,000 participants.

July 1978

In AUSTRALIA, police arrest lesbian and gay merrymakers at Sydney's first Mardi Gras, sparking angry protest marches all over the country until all those arrested are released without charge. Considered by some to be Australia's "STONEWALL," the protests revitalize the Australian gay and lesbian movement.

August 1978

São Paulo and Rio de Janeiro police begin a yearlong investigation of BRAZIL's only gay and lesbian publication, *Lampião* (see **4/1978**), on charges of offending public morality. With the support of the Brazilian Journalists Union, activists fight the charges, and the case is dropped for lack of evidence.

August 8, 1978

Representatives of 17 gay, predominantly male and European organizations found the INTERNATIONAL [as of 1986: LESBIAN AND] GAY ASSOCIATION at a meeting hosted by the English Campaign for Homosexual Equality in Coventry, England.

November 7, 1978

California voters decisively reject Proposition 6, an initiative launched by state senator John Briggs that would have made it illegal for lesbians and gay men or "anyone advocating a homosexual lifestyle" to teach in the state's schools.

November 27, 1978

In San Francisco, Dan White shoots and kills Mayor George Moscone and Supervisor HARVEY MILK (see **11/8/1977**; **5/21/1979**).

1979

LARRY KRAMER publishes *Faggots,* a scathing satire of fast-lane gay male life in New York City.

February 1979

In FRANCE, *Gai Pied* makes its debut. The magazine, which becomes the best-selling gay or lesbian publication in Europe, is considered by many to be the main focus of the French gay male movement for the next decade.

In BRAZIL, a public debate held at the University of São Paulo leads to the formation of Brazil's first gay and lesbian organization, Somos (We Are).

May 20, 1979

In Chicago, David Kloss wins the first Mr. International Leather Contest.

May 21, 1979

In San Francisco, a jury finds Dan White guilty of manslaughter rather than murder in the shooting deaths of HARVEY MILK and Mayor George Moscone (see **11/27/1978**). Several thousand demonstrators protest the verdict in a march on City Hall. A night of rioting ensues, during which dozens of demonstrators and police officers are injured.

June 10, 1979

In SPAIN, a policeman shoots and kills a gay man in a bar in Rentería, near the Basque city of San Sebastian. Basque nationalist groups join forces with EHGAM, a Basque GAY LIBERATION organization, and stage a series of protest rallies and a general strike, culminating in a demonstration in which 2,000 lesbian and gay EHGAM supporters march through San Sebastian.

August 1979

In Los Angeles, a collective comprising Bia Lowe, Louise Moore, Jody Palmer, Barbara Stopha, Tyaga, and Terry Wolverton launch "The Great American Lesbian Art Show," the first national assembly of its kind in the U.S. TEE CORINNE, Harmony Hammond, and KATE MILLETT are among the exhibitors.

August 31, 1979

RADICAL FAERIES stage their first major gathering.

September 17, 1979

In California, Governor Jerry Brown appoints Stephen M. Lachs to the Los Angeles Superior Court. He is the first openly gay judge in the U.S. Also see **August 26, 1981**.

October 12, 1979

The first National Third World Lesbian and Gay Conference opens in Washington, D.C., in preparation for the upcoming March on Washington (see **10/14/1979**).

October 14, 1979

An estimated 100,000 people, with delegations representing every state and ten foreign countries, participate in the first-ever March on Washington for Lesbian and Gay Rights.

1980

PAT CALIFIA begins to muster the pro-erotica combatants of the lesbian SEX WARS, publishing "Among Us, Against Us: Right Wing Feminism" in THE ADVOCATE and, later in the year, including a section on lesbian S/M in the landmark Naiad Press anthology *Sapphistry: The Book of Lesbian Sexuality.*

Denise Kreps wins a court battle in Contra Costa County, California, to become the first openly lesbian LAW ENFORCEMENT officer in the U.S.

January 10, 1980

Sisters of Perpetual Indulgence, a gay male RELIGIOUS ORDER whose motto is "Give Up the Guilt," founds a San Francisco convent following a successful mission in Iowa the previous year. Originally a form of CAMP street THEATER, the controversial nuns later become highly visible promoters of SAFE(R) SEX.

April 14, 1980

In Havana, CUBA, thousands of citizens invade the Peruvian embassy to try to obtain permission to leave the country. Over the next few months, Fidel Castro lets more than 100,000 people leave from the port of Mariel on leaky boats and makeshift rafts. Among the refugees, many of whom have been released from prisons and mental institutions, are an estimated 25,000 gay men seeking asylum from persecution (see **1960**).

May 30, 1980

In Rhode Island, after winning a suit against his high school, Aaron Fricke takes Paul Guilbert to his senior prom.

June 20, 1980

In San Francisco, the Sisters of Perpetual Indulgence (see **1/10/1980**) make their debut in the city's annual Gay Freedom Day Parade.

July 22, 1980

In the UNITED KINGDOM, the House of Commons extends the Sexual Offences Act (see **7/27/1967**) to cover Scotland, decriminalizing most private consensual sex acts between men.

August 14, 1980

The 75 openly lesbian and gay delegates and alternates at the Democratic National Convention in New York City join to nominate Washington, D.C., GAY ACTIVISTS ALLIANCE president Mel Boozer for vice president of the U.S. Boozer tells the convention that "bigotry is bigotry" and that HOMOPHOBIA "dishonors our way of life just as much" as racism, before withdrawing his nomination in favor of Walter Mondale.

September 1980

JOHN BOSWELL publishes *Christianity, Social Intolerance, and Homosexuality,* arguing that CHRISTIANITY did not become severely hostile to same-sex relations until the second half of the 12th century. The controversial book becomes one of the opening salvos in the great CONSTRUCTIONISM VS. ESSENTIALISM debate.

September 20, 1980

Bruce Mailman opens the Saint disco (see DANCING, SOCIAL) in New York City, heralding what many gay New Yorkers will remember as the zenith of the CLONE era.

November 18, 1980

In New York City, a former policeman fires a submachine gun into two Greenwich Village gay BARS, killing two men and wounding six others.

February 5, 1981

In CANADA, Toronto police stage a brutal raid on four BATHHOUSES and arrest 20 men as "keepers of a bawdy house" and 286 men as "found-ins." Soon dubbed Canada's "STONEWALL," the raid sets a North American record for the number of gay men arrested in a single police campaign. Also see **February 6, 1981**.

February 6, 1981

In CANADA, more than 3,000 people brave the winter cold to protest the previous night's raid (see **2/5/1981**) in a demonstration in downtown Toronto.

July 2, 1981

"Rare Cancer Seen in Homosexuals" is the first story in *The New York Times* about the mysterious disease that will later be named AIDS (see **7/27/1982**).

August 7, 1981

Black and White Men Together members begin weekly demonstrations outside the Ice Palace, a popular disco in New York City, in protest of the club's allegedly racist door policies.

August 26, 1981

In California, Governor Jerry Brown appoints Mary Morgan to the San Francisco Municipal Court. She is the first openly lesbian judge in the U.S. Also see **September 17, 1979**.

October 22, 1981

In a case brought to the court by Northern Ireland Gay Rights Association member Jeff Dudgeon, the European Court of Human Rights rules that Northern Ireland (see UNITED KINGDOM) violates basic human rights by criminalizing gay male sex. Also see **October 25, 1982**.

January 12, 1982

In New York City, gay men gather at LARRY KRAMER's apartment and agree to form Gay Men's Health Crisis in response to the escalating epidemic of fatal illnesses in their community.

February 12, 1982

The FILM *Making Love,* one of the first positive HOLLYWOOD depictions of BISEXUALITY and gay male romance, opens in theaters across the U.S.

February 25, 1982

Wisconsin becomes the first state to approve civil rights protection for lesbians and gay men.

April 13, 1982

In Los Angeles, U.S. Congress representatives open the first committee hearings on the disease that will come to be known as AIDS (see **7/27/1982**).

May 12, 1982

In CANADA, police once again (see **12/30/1977**) raid *The Body Politic,* the country's leading gay and lesbian newspaper, on charges of publishing an allegedly obscene article.

July 12, 1982

In FRANCE, the Ministry of Health removes homosexuality from its official list of "mental illnesses." Also see **August 4, 1982**.

July 27, 1982

Representatives of various gay, government, and health organizations decide on the term "acquired immune deficiency syndrome," or AIDS, at a Centers for Disease Control meeting convened in Washington, D.C. The mysterious syndrome is now reaching epidemic proportions among gay men in the U.S.

August 3, 1982

In Atlanta, Georgia, a police officer enters Michael Hardwick's home to serve him with a warrant for a traffic violation and discovers him having oral sex with another man. Hardwick is arrested, held in jail for 12 hours, and charged with SODOMY. Although the state later drops the charge, the case goes to the U.S. Supreme Court as *Bowers v. Hardwick*. Also see **June 30, 1986**.

August 4, 1982

In FRANCE, the AGE OF CONSENT for same-sex acts is lowered from 21 to 15, the same as for heterosexual acts. Also see **August 6, 1942**; **February 8, 1945**.

August 25, 1982

Iran (see CENTRAL ASIA) reinstitutes *shari'a,* the holy law of ISLAM, proscribing all same-sex acts. Punishments include 100 lashes of the whip, beheading, and stoning to death. Also see **January 1, 1990**.

August 28–September 5, 1982

In San Francisco, almost 50,000 people attend the first GAY GAMES.

October 1, 1982

Former Los Angeles Dodgers outfielder GLENN BURKE becomes the first professional baseball player to come OUT.

October 25, 1982

In the UNITED KINGDOM, the House of Commons extends the Sexual Offences Act (see **7/27/1967**) to cover Northern Ireland. Also see **October 22, 1981**.

December 1982

San Francisco mayor Dianne Feinstein enrages the gay and lesbian community when she vetoes a bill authorizing DOMESTIC PARTNERSHIP benefits for city employees. Activists begin a "Dump Dianne" campaign in response.

December 18, 1982

In CANADA, the Quebec parliament becomes the first North American legislative body to authorize DOMESTIC PARTNERSHIP benefits for same-sex couples.

June 1983

In the U.S., a Church of the Brethren position paper is published, stating that "a person's sexual orientation is not a moral issue, but that sexual behavior does have moral significance." The statement adds that "sexual orientation should not be grounds for denying the request for ordination" to the ministry of the church.

Although generally approved by the Protestant church's 1.75 million members, a group of conservatives issue a strongly worded protest.

June 27, 1983

Parades and rallies in cities across the U.S. are dedicated to people suffering from AIDS. In Chicago, former mayor Jane S. Byrne leads the city's 14th annual Gay and Lesbian Parade, attended by about 30,000 people. The Centers for Disease Control reports 1,641 AIDS cases and 644 deaths. An estimated 70 percent of AIDS sufferers are gay.

July 18, 1983

Responding to House Ethics Committee charges, Representative GERRY E. STUDDS (D-Mass.) acknowledges his homosexuality to the House and admits to having had a sexual relationship with a 17-year-old male page in 1973. The same week, Representative Daniel B. Crane (R-Ill.) confesses to similar charges involving a 17-year-old female page in 1980. Also see **July 20, 1983**.

July 20, 1983

The House votes to censure Representatives GERRY E. STUDDS (D-Mass.) and Daniel B. Crane (R-Ill.) for sexual misconduct with House pages (see **7/18/1983**). Studds later reads reporters a statement saying that the censure was not warranted: his affair with the page was private and mutually voluntary. He adds that he hopes "to emerge from the present situation a wiser, a more tolerant and a more complete human being." Also see **August 15, 1983**.

August 15, 1983

Returning to his district for the first time since his House censure (see **7/20/1983**), Representative GERRY E. STUDDS (D-Mass.) receives three standing ovations from supporters.

August 21, 1983

La Cage aux Folles opens on Broadway to rave reviews and $4 million in advance ticket sales. With a book written by HARVEY FIERSTEIN, *La Cage* is a romantic musical comedy based on a popular French FILM about two male lovers, the manager and the leading star of a nightclub featuring female impersonators.

August 22, 1983

Organizers of a Washington march marking the 20th anniversary of Dr. Martin Luther King Jr.'s "I Have a Dream" speech announce that no representatives from gay or lesbian rights groups will be allowed to speak. A group of lesbians and gay men stage a sit-in at the organizers' office in response.

September 1983

The Alliance for Gay Artists honors NBC's *Cheers* and *Gimme a Break* and ABC's *Dynasty* for positive, realistic depictions of gay men on TELEVISION. Awards are also given to *Donahue* for giving gay and lesbian guests a public forum and for *The Fifth of July,* a PBS and Showtime production of the Lanford Wilson play, which featured Richard Thomas as a gay handicapped man and Jeff Daniels as his lover.

September 8, 1983

In San Francisco, the Ninth U.S. Circuit Court of Appeals rules that federal IMMIGRATION authorities cannot prevent lesbians and gay men from entering the country purely on the basis of their sexuality. Also see **October 27, 1990**.

October 15, 1983

A Washington, D.C., Superior Court judge dismisses a lawsuit brought by gay students against Georgetown University three years ago, ruling that the students cannot force the university to grant their organization recognition, because the federal government does not have an official national policy on homosexual rights. Also see **March 29, 1988**.

October 21, 1983

Through a spokesperson, the ORTHODOX EASTERN CHURCHES in the United States threaten to withdraw from the National Council of Churches if the predominantly gay and lesbian METROPOLITAN COMMUNITY CHURCH is allowed to join. In response, the council decides to table the group's application for membership.

1984

In Leningrad, RUSSIA, Alexander Zaremba organizes one of the first gay and lesbian groups in the USSR. The KGB subsequently forces many of those active in the group to emigrate.

March 12, 1984

The European Parliament approves its first resolution in support of lesbian and gay rights. The resolution is based on a report previously accepted by the Parliament from Italian member Vera Squarcialupi.

April 9, 1984

In San Francisco, the Department of Public Health closes the city's BATHHOUSES in the belief that they contribute to the spread of AIDS. The decision comes after a heated, divisive debate between gay men who believe the baths can be used as a forum for SAFE(R) SEX education and those who see them as contributing to the spread of the epidemic.

July 1984

The U.S. Conference of Mayors overwhelmingly approves a resolution advocating gay and lesbian rights protection at all levels of government. The resolution, which the NATIONAL GAY [later: AND LESBIAN] TASK FORCE helped draft, is the first to be passed by a national organization of elected officials.

July 13, 1984

Brothers, the first American TELEVISION show with an openly gay lead character (brother Donald), premiers on the Showtime cable network.

November 10, 1984

In the UNITED KINGDOM, Labour MP Chris Smith becomes the first member of the House of Commons to come OUT voluntarily.

December 5, 1984

Berkeley, California, becomes the first city in the U.S. to extend spousal benefits to the domestic partners of city employees.

March 25, 1985

Pivotal year for Oscars: Vanessa Redgrave is the first woman to be nominated for Best Actress playing a lesbian role (*The Bostonians*); *The Times of Harvey Milk* wins Best Documentary (first documentary on a gay subject to do so), so an estimated 1 billion viewers hear its director, Robert Epstein, express his thanks to "my partner in life, John Wright."

April 1, 1985

In New York City, the Hetrick-Martin Institute opens the Harvey Milk School for 20 openly lesbian and gay teenagers in the basement of a Greenwich Village church. The city-funded high school provides a place of refuge for the students, many of whom have dropped out of other schools to escape repeated abuse and harassment.

July 25, 1985

In Paris, a spokesperson for ROCK HUDSON acknowledges that the actor is suffering from AIDS. Later, media reports openly discuss his homosexuality for the first time. The publicity given his illness marks a turning point in building public awareness of the threat of

AIDS and in galvanizing support for efforts to fight the disease.

Also in Paris, the French Parliament amends the penal code to prohibit discrimination based on "moral habits," one of which is homosexuality. FRANCE is the first country to legislate gay and lesbian rights.

October 4, 1985

In the UNITED KINGDOM, the Labour Party Annual Conference approves a resolution calling for the end of all legal discrimination against lesbians and gay men.

November 1985

In New York City, city officials use a "nuisance abatement" statute to close down gay male sex clubs and BATHHOUSES, including the Mineshaft and the New St. Mark's Baths, in the belief that these establishments contribute to the spread of AIDS.

November 13, 1985

In the UNITED KINGDOM, Manchester gay rights advocate and politician Margaret Roff becomes the country's first openly lesbian (or gay) mayor.

November 17, 1985

In New York City, more than 700 people concerned about negative publicity surrounding AIDS, BATHHOUSES, and gay promiscuity attend a town meeting that leads to the founding of the GAY AND LESBIAN ALLIANCE AGAINST DEFAMATION.

November 27, 1985

Activist CLEVE JONES conceives THE NAMES PROJECT quilt at an AIDS candlelight vigil in San Francisco. Also see **October 11, 1987**.

March 20, 1986

After 14 years of debate and controversy (see **1/27/1972**), the New York City Council passes a municipal rights ordinance for the city's gay men and lesbians.

March 24, 1986

William Hurt wins an Academy Award for Best Actor for his portrayal of an imprisoned South American hairdresser in *Kiss of the Spider Woman*. It is the first time an actor playing a gay character has received an Oscar.

April 1986

Donna Deitch's *Desert Hearts* premieres in New York City. Based on JANE RULE's novel *Desert of the Heart,* the FILM is the first lesbian-produced feature about lesbians to be released commercially in the U.S.

May 7, 1986

In RUSSIA, a former Soviet deputy health minister tells readers of *Literaturnaya Gazeta,* a popular weekly newspaper, that AIDS is not a concern in the USSR because homosexuality and drug use are both illegal.

June 30, 1986

In *Bowers v. Hardwick* (see **8/3/1982**) the U.S. Supreme Court rules that the U.S. Constitution—as well as the precedence of Judeo-Christian prohibitions and Anglo-American SODOMY laws—gives states the right to regulate and proscribe same-sex relations.

July 9, 1986

In NEW ZEALAND, Parliament passes the Homosexual Law Reform Act, decriminalizing sex between men and establishing the same legal provisions for all sexual relations. Also see **July 28, 1993**.

August 9–17, 1986

In San Francisco, the second GAY GAMES attracts twice as many participants as the first: 3,482 athletes from 16 countries participate in 17 different events.

August 26, 1986

Jerry Smith, former Washington Redskins tight end, is the first celebrity to acknowledge voluntarily that he has AIDS. He dies of the disease seven weeks after his announcement.

October 1, 1986

The ROMAN CATHOLIC CHURCH issues Joseph Cardinal Ratzinger's "Letter to the Bishops of the Catholic Church on the Pastoral Care of Homosexual Persons." In the document, Ratzinger clarifies the Church's condemnation of the "homosexual inclination" as a "tendency toward an intrinsic moral evil" and an "objective disorder," and criticizes Catholics who have been guilty of "an overly benign interpretation of the homosexual condition."

October 30, 1986

In Lima, Peru (see LATIN AMERICA), police raid a lesbian bar and arrest about 70 women. Television reporters, who have been previously notified by police, are present to film the women for local news reports. As a result, many of the women lose their jobs; some are beaten by their families; at least two are raped on their way home from the police station.

1987

Hungary's first gay rights organization, Homeros, is founded in Budapest.

March 14, 1987

In New York City, the AIDS Coalition to Unleash Power (ACT UP) is formed as a DIRECT ACTION group by LARRY KRAMER and some 300 other activists.

March 24, 1987

In New York City, ACT UP launches its first public action, a clamorous sit-in at the corner of Broadway and Wall Street in protest of government delays in approving possible AIDS treatments. Seventeen people are arrested.

May 1987

Canadian filmmaker Patricia Rozema's romantic lesbian comedy *I've Heard the Mermaid Singing* wins the Prix de la Jeunesse at the Cannes Film Festival.

May 27, 1987

Lambda Book Report, the first periodical devoted exclusively to lesbian and gay literature, makes its debut.

May 30, 1987

A *Boston Globe* headline reads, "Frank Discusses Being Gay." Asked if he is gay, Representative BARNEY FRANK (D-Mass.) replies, "Yes, so what?" He is the second U.S. congressman to come OUT (see **7/18/1983**).

June 15, 1987

The New York Times decides to allow its writers to use the word "GAY" as an adjectival synonym for "HOMOSEXUAL."

August 7, 1987

In London, more than 100 lesbians and gay men stage a kiss-in at Piccadilly Circus in defiance of the Sexual Offences Act (see **7/27, 1967**), which decriminalized private sex acts between consenting adults but left public displays of same-sex affection a misdemeanor.

October 1987

In Mexico City, the first-ever Latin American Lesbian Conference draws about 250 participants from countries in both North and South America.

October 11, 1987

In Washington, D.C., the largest lesbian and gay rights rally to date convenes. According to organizers, more than half a million people participate in the second March on Washington.

THE NAMES PROJECT AIDS Memorial Quilt (see **11/27/1985**) is shown publicly for the first time as part of the March on Washington. Stretched out over two city blocks, the Quilt integrates 1,920 panels, commemorating more than 2,000 persons who have died of AIDS. Also see **October 1992**.

October 13, 1987

Over 600 lesbians, gay men, and supporters are arrested on the steps of the U.S. Supreme Court in the largest civil disobedience protest in the history of the gay and lesbian rights movement.

December 8, 1987

In the UNITED KINGDOM, Conservative MP David Wilshire introduces Clause 28 as an amendment to the Local Government Bill. The proposed amendment makes it illegal for local authorities to "promote homosexuality or . . . promote the teaching in any maintained school of the acceptability of homosexuality." Also see **January 9, 1988**.

December 15–18, 1988

In the NETHERLANDS, the Free University of Amsterdam convenes the International Scientific Conference on Gay and Lesbian Studies. The highlight of the session is a heated debate inspired by the CONSTRUCTIONISM VS. ESSENTIALISM controversy, entitled "Homosexuality, Which Homosexuality?"

January 1988

In Hungary, Homeros Lambda becomes the first gay and lesbian rights group in EASTERN EUROPE to obtain official recognition.

January 5, 1988

Raleigh, North Carolina, enacts a gay rights ordinance. Raleigh is the hometown of the famous homophobe Jesse Helms.

January 9, 1988

In the UNITED KINGDOM, more than 10,000 lesbians and gay men demonstrate their opposition to Clause 28 (see **12/8/1987**) in a march through central London. Also see **February 2, 1988**; **February 20, 1988**; **March 9, 1988**.

February 2, 1988

In the UNITED KINGDOM, three women protest Clause 28 (see **12/8/1987**) by swinging on ropes off the public gallery into the chamber of the House of Lords. Their shouts of "Lesbians are angry!" and "It's our lives you're dealing with" distill the current mood of British lesbian and gay activists, galvanized as never before in opposition to the bill. Also see **January 9, 1988**; **February 20, 1988**; **March 9, 1988**.

February 5, 1988

Arizona Governor Evan Mecham, who at the beginning of his administration tried to purge lesbians and gay men from state government, is impeached by the Arizona House of Representatives.

February 20, 1988

In the UNITED KINGDOM, between 15,000 and 20,000 demonstrators take part in a march in Manchester to protest Clause 28 (see **12/8/1987**). Also see **March 9, 1988**; **April 30, 1988**; **May 24, 1988**.

February 29, 1988

In CANADA, Vancouver MP Svend J. Robinson comes OUT—in French as well as in English—on national TELEVISION. He is the country's first openly gay or lesbian member of Parliament. Also see **September 27, 1994**.

March 9, 1988

In the UNITED KINGDOM, Clause 28 of the Local Government Bill (see **12/8/1987**) is approved by the House of Commons and becomes Section 28 of the Local Government Act. Also see **April 30, 1988**; **May 24, 1988**.

March 23, 1988

ISRAEL decriminalizes same-sex acts between consenting adults.

March 29, 1988

After eight years in court (see **10/15/1983**), Georgetown University loses its fight to keep lesbian and gay groups off campus. The university argued against the groups on freedom of religion grounds, based on its status as an institution of the ROMAN CATHOLIC CHURCH.

April 30, 1988

In the UNITED KINGDOM, some 30,000 demonstrators, including rock stars and other celebrities, march in London to protest the passage of Clause 28 (see **3/9/1988**). This is the largest lesbian and gay rally in the history of the U.K. Also see **May 24, 1988**.

May 7, 1988

In Sacramento, California, 8,000 activists mark the National Day of Protest with the largest gay and lesbian rights rally in the state's history.

In New York City, some 500 ACT UP activists protest the nation's lethargic response to the AIDS crisis by blocking traffic in the financial district.

May 24, 1988

In the UNITED KINGDOM, Clause 28 of the Local Government Act (see **3/9/1988**) takes effect, prohibiting government from providing support to prolesbian and -gay organizations.

June 16, 1988

In San Antonio, the Southern BAPTIST Convention passes a resolution calling homosexuality "an abomination" and blaming AIDS on gay men.

June 26, 1988

Art Agnos is the first San Francisco mayor to ride in a gay PRIDE CELEBRATION parade.

October 11, 1988

Urging thousands of lesbians and gay men across the country to be open about their sexuality with friends, families, and coworkers, Robert H. Eichberg, a psychologist and activist, and Jean O'Leary, executive director of National Gay Rights Advocates, launch the first National Coming Out Day.

In Maryland, more than 1,000 demonstrators, led by ACT UP activists, invade the grounds of the Federal Food and Drug Administration to focus attention on the AIDS crisis and to protest the agency's slow drug approval process. About 150 demonstrators are arrested.

October 26, 1988

The European Court of Human Rights rules that LAWS in IRELAND criminalizing sex between men are in violation of the Charter of Human Rights. The court was petitioned by David Norris, an MP in the Dail of Ireland.

November 28, 1988

A Dallas judge sentences the killer of two gay men to 30 years in PRISON instead of a life sentence because, as he later tells the *Dallas Times Herald,* "I don't much care for queers cruising the streets." The Dallas Gay Alliance joins political leaders across the country in protesting the judge's decision.

December 21, 1988

The Chicago City Council votes 28–17 to approve a bill banning discrimination on the basis of sexual orientation.

January 1989

In the UNITED KINGDOM, AIDS activists meeting in London hold the first meeting of British ACT UP.

January 31, 1989

In San Francisco, AIDS activists stage a protest on the Golden Gate Bridge, bringing morning rush-hour traffic to a standstill. Twenty-nine demonstrators are arrested.

February 6, 1989

By a vote of 251–121, the American Bar Association's House of Delegates approves a referendum in favor of federal rights legislation for lesbians and gay men.

April 30, 1989

In Austin, Texas, more than 20,000 people march on the state capital in the largest gay and lesbian rights demonstration in the state's history.

May 1989

In the UNITED KINGDOM, IAN MCKELLEN, fellow ACTOR Michael Cashman, and dozens of other gay men and lesbians found the Stonewall Group to monitor legislation in Parliament and lobby for equal rights for lesbians and gay men.

June 2, 1989

Lambda Book Report presents the first Lambda Literary AWARDS as part of the American Booksellers Association convention in Washington, D.C. ARMISTEAD MAUPIN emcees; "Lammy" winners include DOROTHY ALLISON, PAUL MONETTE, Michael Nava, KAREN THOMPSON, and EDMUND WHITE.

June 12, 1989

In Washington, D.C., Corcoran Gallery of Art director Christina Orr-Cahill announces the cancellation of "The Perfect Moment," a show of 150 photos and objects by ROBERT MAPPLETHORPE that includes 13 S/M images. The museum is afraid of losing National Endowment for the Arts funding.

June 25, 1989

The U.S. Postal Service becomes the first federal agency to extend official recognition of the GAY AND LESBIAN RIGHTS MOVEMENT by issuing a "Lesbian and Gay Pride" stamp in commemoration of the 20th anniversary of the STONEWALL Uprising.

October 1, 1989

Denmark (see SCANDINAVIA) authorizes "registered partnerships" for lesbian and gay couples. The partnerships are considered similar to MARRIAGE, although they do not include rights to adoption, artificial insemination, or religious wedding ceremonies in state LUTHERAN CHURCHES.

November 1989

An episode of the U.S. TELEVISION program *Thirtysomething* features two men in bed. Network executives later estimate that the episode cost them about $500,000 in ADVERTISING from sponsors fearful of a backlash from conservative customers.

November 16, 1989

GERMANY's first public office devoted to lesbian and gay concerns is established in Berlin.

Called the Referat für Gleichgeschlectliche Lebensweisen (Center for Homosexual Lifestyles), the state-level office works to eliminate discrimination and promote understanding of gay men and lesbians.

December 10, 1989

In New York City, ACT UP gathers about 5,000 demonstrators in front of St. Patrick's Cathedral to protest the ROMAN CATHOLIC CHURCH's opposition to SAFE SEX education and the promotion of condom use.

January 1, 1990

In Iran (see CENTRAL ASIA), short-wave radio broadcasts report that three gay men have just been beheaded and two lesbians stoned to death as part of an intensified campaign against "vice."

February 1990

In Prague, Czechoslovakia (see EASTERN EUROPE), activists organize the country's first public gay and lesbian rights demonstrations. Also see **June 23, 1990**.

February 23, 1990

In Taiwan (see CHINA), a group of women form Women Chih Chian (Women Among Us), the first lesbian organization for Chinese-speaking women in Asia.

April 23, 1990

The HATE CRIME STATISTICS ACT, passed by the 101st Congress, is signed into law by President George Bush. The act requires the Department of Justice to collect and publish statistics for five years on HATE CRIME motivated by prejudice based on race, religion, sexual orientation, or ethnic origin. It is the first LAW to extend federal recognition to gay men and lesbians.

April 28, 1990

In New York City, QUEER NATION stages its first public action. Almost 500 members of the recently formed organization march in Greenwich Village in protest of a pipe bomb attack on a local gay bar.

May 10, 1990

In the UNITED KINGDOM, gay and lesbian activists found the DIRECT ACTION group OUTRAGE!, vowing to begin a campaign of civil disobedience unprecedented in the U.K.

May 28–30, 1990

In Tallinn, Estonia (see EASTERN EUROPE), the Estonian Academy of Sciences History Institute sponsors the first international conference on homosexuality and other sexual minorities to be held in the USSR. British historian Jeffrey Weeks and Dutch sociologist Gert Hekma are among the attendees.

June 23, 1990

In Prague, Czechoslavakia (see EASTERN EUROPE), activists organize SOHO, the country's first national network of lesbian and gay organizations.

June 24, 1990

Activists associated with QUEER NATION (see **4/28/1990**) distribute a manifesto emblazoned with the words "Queers Read This" at New York City's annual PRIDE CELEBRATION march. Headlined "I Hate Straights" and signed "Anonymous Queers," the broadsheet is a harbinger of revitalized militancy among lesbian and gay activists.

October 1990

SOUTH AFRICA has its first lesbian and gay pride march. The event, held in Johannesburg, draws about 800 men and women, both black and white.

October 27, 1990

U.S. restrictions against IMMIGRATION of lesbians and gay men are rescinded. Also see **June 27, 1952**.

December 1990

A reunited GERMANY abolishes Paragraph 175 (see **1871**).

January 9, 1991

In the UNITED KINGDOM, an unprecedented number of prominent gay and lesbian artists come OUT in a public forum. Wishing to "respectfully distance" themselves from DEREK JARMAN's criticism of IAN MCKELLEN's acceptance of a knighthood from the Conservative government of Margaret Thatcher, they publish a widely discussed statement in support of McKellen in the *Guardian*. The signees are Simon Callow, Michael Cashman, Nancy Diuguid, Simon Fanshawe, Stephen Fry, Philip Hedley, Bryony Lavery, Michael Leonard, David Lun, Tim Luscombe, Alec McCowen, Cameron Mackintosh, Pam St. Clement, John Schlesinger, Antony Sher, Martin Sherman, Ned Sherrin, and Nick Wright.

February 7, 1991

In an interview reported in the popular press, the president of the USSR Academy of Medical Sciences asserts that homosexuality is a disease that must be fought by all legal means.

February 16, 1991

In London, the DIRECT ACTION group OUTRAGE! (see **5/10/1990**) organizes a gay and lesbian kiss-in at Piccadilly Circus in protest of a section of the Sexual Offences Act (see **7/27/1967**) that makes public displays of affection between men illegal. Also this day in London, 7,000 demonstrators march to protest the recent arrest of gay male S/M devotees and other antigay and -lesbian initiatives.

June, 1991

The first Black Lesbian and Gay Pride celebration is held in Washington, D.C.

September 1991

At a worldwide conference held in Yokohama, JAPAN, AMNESTY INTERNATIONAL resolves to work to help persons imprisoned for consensual same-sex acts between adults or simply on account of their sexual orientation.

September 29, 1991

California Governor Pete Wilson vetoes AB 101 a gay and lesbian employment rights bill, inciting what some call Stonewall II, a month of marches and angry protests across the state.

October 19, 1991

At least nine lesbian and gay employees of Cracker Barrel Old Country Stores have been fired as a result of the company's policy of supporting "heterosexual values." QUEER NATION, among other activist groups, mounts a series of protests.

December 1991

In Minnesota, KAREN THOMPSON is named SHARON KOWALSKI's legal guardian. The decision, which comes eight years after a car accident left Kowalski paralyzed and speech-impaired, is seen as a precedent-setting victory for the DISABLED as well as lesbian and gay couples.

February 1992

Levi Strauss & Co. makes domestic partners of gay and lesbian employees eligible for health insurance coverage. With 23,000 employees, Levi Strauss is the largest company in the U.S. to do so to date.

February 27, 1992

CANADA's Supreme Court resolves *Butler v. Her Majesty the Queen* by redefining "obscenity" as material that violates the civil rights of women. The decision, which reflects theories espoused by American anti-PORNOGRAPHY activist ANDREA DWORKIN, results in the banning of a variety of lesbian and gay literature and films, including most literary and graphic depictions of S/M and anal eroticism.

April 1992

In CHINA, the Ministry of Public Security orders the release of two lesbians who have been imprisoned for two weeks on charges of "unruly behavior"—i.e., living together. The ministry announces that there is no legal basis for forbidding lesbians from cohabiting. Also see **November 1992**.

May 17, 1992

In SWITZERLAND, voters approve a wide-ranging reform of the country's LAWS, including the deletion of all discriminatory language related to homosexuality, with 73 percent voting in favor.

June 1992

The government of Nicaragua (see LATIN AMERICA) criminalizes same-sex acts for the first time in its history. Persons who "promote" same-sex acts "in scandalous form" as well as actual practitioners are liable to sentences of one to three years' imprisonment.

June 16, 1992

Popular singer K. D. LANG comes OUT in a cover story published in THE ADVOCATE, setting off a year of U.S. media reports on "lesbian chic."

July 3, 1992

In Buenos Aires, an estimated 300 lesbians and gay men march in ARGENTINA's first-ever PRIDE CELEBRATION.

July 7, 1992

In New York City, some 50 activists attend the first public meeting of the LESBIAN AVENGERS, a DIRECT ACTION group conceptualized the previous spring. Also see **April 24, 1993**.

August 19, 1992

In GERMANY, some 250 lesbian and gay couples all over the country try to register for MARRIAGE. The demonstration, organized by the Schwulerverband in Deutschland (Gay League of Germany), receives widespread media attention.

September 24, 1992

The Kentucky Supreme Court rules that the state's anti-SODOMY laws violate the rights to privacy and equal protection as guaranteed by the state constitution.

September 26, 1992

Amid a bitterly contested campaign in Oregon for and against Measure 9, an antigay rights initiative (see **11/3/1992**), a lesbian and a gay man are killed when local skinheads throw a Molotov cocktail into their apartment in Salem.

October 1992

THE NAMES PROJECT AIDS Memorial Quilt (see **11/27/1985**) is displayed in Washington, D.C., for the fourth time. More than 400,000 people come to the Washington Monument grounds to view the Quilt's 20,000-plus panels, which extend over more than 13 acres. Also see **October 11, 1987**.

November 1992

In CHINA, the national government reports that same-sex acts are no longer considered an offense against "social order." Also see **April 1992**.

November 3, 1992

In Colorado, 53 percent of voters approve Amendment 2, an initiative banning state and municipal rights ordinances for lesbians and gay men. "Family values" organizations in more than 35 states begin campaigning for similar propositions.

In Oregon, voters reject Measure 9, an initiative similar to Amendment 2 (see above). Also see **September 26, 1992**.

November 23, 1992

In AUSTRALIA, Prime Minister Paul Keating revokes the country's restrictions on gay men and lesbians in the MILITARY.

1993

Two years after his death, Yevgeny Kharitonov's openly homoerotic poetry and prose are published for the first time in RUSSIA. Previously distributed via underground *samizdat,* Kharitonov achieved a reputation as the first major gay male writer in Russia since MIKHAIL KUZMIN, who died in 1936.

In the NETHERLANDS, the government begins using ADVERTISING brochures to encourage lesbians and gay men in the country's navy to come OUT and be open about their sexuality.

January 1993

Representative Steve Gunderson (R-Wisc.), the third U.S. congressman to come OUT, resigns the position of deputy whip in protest over intolerant statements made at last year's Republican National Convention.

January 1, 1993

The World Health Organization officially deletes "homosexuality" from its list of "diseases."

February 1993

In the NETHERLANDS, the Second House of Parliament adopts the Equal Treatment Act, which forbids all discrimination based "on the sole ground" of homosexuality.

March 14, 1993

In BRAZIL, armed men abduct, torture, and behead Renildo José dos Santos, an openly bisexual local city councilor in the state of Alagoas. Santos, who had been under attack from the local mayor and the mayor's allies, had repeatedly been denied police protection, despite a previous attempt on his life.

March 22, 1993

Lawrence Poirier comes OUT to his best friend Michael in cartoonist Lynn Johnston's popular COMIC STRIP *For Better or for Worse.* Some 40 newspapers in the U.S. and CANADA refuse to run the four-week story; thousands cancel subscriptions to papers that do; in the end, however, 70 percent of the more than 2,500 letters Johnston receives about the series are positive.

April 24, 1993

In Washington, D.C., the third gay and lesbian March on Washington (see **4/25/1993**) is prefaced by a mass wedding ceremony held outside the Internal Revenue Service building. METROPOLITAN COMMUNITY CHURCH founder Reverend Troy Perry conducts the service, joining 1,500 lesbian and gay couples in MARRIAGE.

Just before midnight, LESBIAN AVENGERS march on the White House in what organizers claim is the largest lesbian demonstration ever.

April 25, 1993

The third gay and lesbian March on Washington draws more than 1 million participants, according to organizers. Extensive TELEVISION and newspaper coverage makes it the most widely publicized march yet.

May 7, 1993

The Hawaii Supreme Court rules that the state must prove a "compelling interest" for denying same-sex partners a MARRIAGE license. Also see **April 12, 1994**.

May 27, 1993

In RUSSIA, President Boris Yeltsin publishes a decree decriminalizing consensual adult male SODOMY. Also see **March 7, 1934**.

June 30, 1993

IRELAND decriminalizes same-sex relations for consenting adults and sets the AGE OF CONSENT at 17 for all sexual activities.

July 1993

The United Nations grants the INTERNATIONAL LESBIAN AND GAY ASSOCIATION (ILGA) observer status. ILGA is the first gay or lesbian organization to be recognized by the U.N. Also see **September 16, 1994**.

In the U.S., the Clinton administration institutes new guidelines on homosexuality in the MILITARY. Dubbed "don't ask, don't tell," the policy in most instances prohibits military officials from investigating instances of homosexuality without prior cause while forbidding service members from expressing their sexuality openly.

July 28, 1993

NEW ZEALAND becomes the seventh country in the world to outlaw discrimination based on sexual orientation.

September 21, 1993

Amanda Bearse talks about being a lesbian in an ADVOCATE interview. She is the first prime-time TELEVISION star to come OUT.

November 18, 1993

In Romania, Marius Aitai, Ovidiu Chetea, and Cosmin Hutanu are sentenced to up to 2½ years in PRISON for same-sex acts in private. AMNESTY INTERNATIONAL calls for their immediate release and protests the imprisonment of 54 other people on similar charges, as well as the reportedly widespread torture and sexual abuse of persons arrested on suspicion of homosexuality.

December 6, 1993

The Massachusetts state senate approves the first state LAW to protect lesbian and gay public school students against discrimination.

December 7, 1993

In Texas, Williamson County commissioners reverse last week's decision to deny Apple Computer tax breaks for a new facility in the county because of its policy of extending benefits to employees' same-sex domestic partners. Several of the commissioners, however, continue to express condemnation of "the gay lifestyle."

February 1994

In Ovett, Mississippi, lovers Brenda and Wanda Henson draw national attention to a campaign of harassment and threats launched by local residents in protest of their 120-acre Camp Sister Spirit. Although the Hensons deny that their project, which they call a "feminist retreat," is part of the LESBIAN LAND movement, local residents call it a "lesbian colony" because about 70 percent of the membership of the nonprofit organization that supports the camp is lesbian. U.S. Attorney General Janet Reno later dispatches two Justice Department representatives to investigate charges that the Hensons' civil rights are being violated.

February 8, 1994

The European Parliament, meeting in Strasbourg, FRANCE, approves a resolution initiated by Claudia Roth, representing GERMANY's Green Party, that affirms a broadly defined gay and lesbian rights agenda, including the right to marry. Also see **February 9, 1994**.

February 9, 1994

Pope John Paul II attacks the European Parliament resolution in favor of lesbian and gay rights (see **2/8/1994**) as "immoral."

April 12, 1994

In response to a Hawaii Supreme court decision questioning the state's right to bar same-sex MARRIAGE (see **5/7/1993**), the state senate passes a bill declaring that the need to "foster and protect the propagation of the human race" is justification for the ban. Also see **September 20, 1996**.

April 24, 1994

In RUSSIA, Yaroslav Mogutin, the country's most visible openly gay journalist, makes headlines when he attempts to register his marriage to American artist Robert Filippini. The head of Moscow's Wedding Palace No. 4 politely refuses his application.

June 27, 1994

Deborah Batts becomes the first openly lesbian or gay U.S. federal judge.

August 1994

In JAPAN, more than 1,200 lesbians, gay men, and supporters gather on the streets of Tokyo for the country's first open lesbian and gay PRIDE CELEBRATION.

August 23, 1994

In AUSTRALIA, the federal government acts to overturn Tasmania's anti-SODOMY law. Tasmania is the last Australian state to penalize same-sex relations.

September 16, 1994

At the insistence of the U.S., the United Nations suspends the INTERNATIONAL LESBIAN AND GAY ASSOCIATION (ILGA) from observer status because of allegations that ILGA's members include groups that promote PEDOPHILIA.

September 27, 1994

In CANADA, Real Menard, a Montreal representative of the Bloc Quebecois, becomes the second MP to come OUT when he tells reporters that he is "speaking for the community" to which he belongs when he protests the televised statements of another member of Parliament, Roseanne Skoke of Nova Scotia, among which is the claim that "this [gay and lesbian] love, this compassion, based on an inhuman act, defiles humanity, destroys family . . . and is annihilating mankind."

November 8, 1994

The Republican right sweeps elections across the U.S., but there are some gay and lesbian gains, including new state legislature representatives and senators in Arizona, California, and Rhode Island, and one reelected in Texas. An antigay and -lesbian rights initiative, Proposition 1, is defeated in Idaho.

December 6, 1994

Delegates of the American Medical Association declare their opposition to medical treatments administered to "cure" lesbians or gay men, urging "nonjudgmental recognition of sexual orientation."

December 23, 1994

In a much publicized adoption (see CHILDREN) case in Seattle, Washington, Ross and Luis Lopton win permanent custody of their four-year-old foster son, Gailen. The child's birth mother had challenged the men's right to adopt him.

December 28, 1994

About 70 men from Bangladesh, India, Nepal, Pakistan, and Sri Lanka attend the first regional conference for gay rights in SOUTH ASIA, a five-day event organized in New Delhi by activist Ashok Row Kawi.

January 27, 1995

At a press conference in Washington, D.C., the House majority whip, Dick Armey (R-Tex.), refers to Representative BARNEY FRANK (D-Mass.) as "Barney Fag." He later apologizes, insisting it was a slip of the tongue.

March 18, 1995

The Archbishop of Canterbury, the chief primate of the ANGLICAN COMMUNION tells the press: "We reject HOMOPHOBIA in any form." He and the other 35 Anglican primates call for a Church-wide debate on issues of sexuality "at variance with the received Christian moral tradition."

March 22, 1995

The Montana state senate amends a bill mandating registration of persons previously convicted of "violent" crimes to include "deviate sexual conduct." The bill would require anyone convicted of oral or anal sex with a member of his or her own sex to register with the local LAW ENFORCEMENT authority. Also see **March 23, 1995**.

March 23, 1995

Threatened with an economic boycott and facing strong opposition from state and national lesbian and gay activists, the Montana Senate unanimously votes to delete same-sex acts from a list of crimes for which convicts have to register with local authorities. Also see **March 22, 1995**.

April 15, 1995

In ARGENTINA, Buenos Aires police raid Boicot, a lesbian disco, and arrest 10 women ostensibly to check their police records. Lesbian activist Monica Santino obtains their release after three hours, during which time the women are subjected to verbal abuse and threats.

June 13, 1995

Following Attorney General Janet Reno's decision not to file a brief in the Colorado constitutional amendment case (see **11/3/1992**) and protests over a meeting with elected lesbian and gay officials for which security guards wore rubber gloves out of fear of HIV infection, the Clinton administration attempts to smooth relations with activists by naming the first-ever White House liaison to the gay and lesbian communities

August 1, 1995

After refusing to allow the Gay and Lesbian Association of Zimbabwe to exhibit at a human rights book fair, President Robert Mugabe opens the fair with an attack on lesbians and gay men, saying they are alien to African traditions and that he doesn't believe "they have any rights at all." Also see **August 1, 1996**.

August 4, 1995

U.S. President Bill Clinton signs an executive order forbidding the federal government from denying security clearances on the basis of a person's sexual orientation. Administration spokespersons advise reporters, however, that individuals might still be denied clearance if they were in the CLOSET and feared exposure to family or friends. Also see **July 3, 1975**; **February 7, 1977**.

August 11, 1995

South KOREA marks its first PRIDE CELEBRATION with a march and other events in Seoul.

August 26, 1995

Spokespersons for Republican presidential candidate Robert Dole announce that his campaign is returning a $1,000 donation from the LOG CABIN FEDERATION, saying the gay and lesbian Republican organization has "a specific political agenda that's fundamentally at odds" with the senator's.

October 16, 1995

In Washington, D.C., NATION OF ISLAM leader Louis Farrakhan's Million Man March divides AFRICAN-AMERICAN gay men: some, disturbed by Nation of Islam HOMOPHOBIA, decide to stay home; others, viewing the march as an affirmation of the need for black unity, attend. No openly gay speaker is permitted to speak at the rally that follows the march.

October 17, 1995

For the first time in its history, the United Nations considers lesbian and gay rights abuses at its International Tribunal on Human Rights Violations Against Sexual Minorities. Following testimony from a number of women and men who have suffered abuse ranging from torture to forced institutionalization, the tribunal recommends that the U.N. document sexual orientation and GENDER identity issues around the world and integrate them into the organization's human rights agenda.

November 7, 1995

Maine voters reject the "Act to Limit Protected Classes," which would have outlawed antidiscrimination ordinances for lesbians and gay men and nullified Portland's 1992 gay and lesbian rights ordinance.

November 30, 1995

The first U.S. government-sponsored ADVERTISING targeting gay men debuts on the eve of World AIDS Day when the Centers for Disease Control and Prevention releases a public service TELEVISION announcement cautioning men to have "smart sex."

May 15, 1996

A U.S. EPISCOPAL CHURCH court rules that there is no "core doctrine" against ordaining a gay man as a deacon, the clergy rank below that of priest.

May 20, 1996

Ruling that "A State cannot so deem a class of person a stranger to its laws," the U.S. Supreme Court declares Colorado's Amendment 2 (see **11/3/1992**) unconstitutional.

June 1996

In CANADA, a legislative measure guaranteeing civil rights protection for lesbians and gay men becomes LAW.

August 1, 1996

Representative Jim Kolbe of Arizona becomes the fourth congressman—and second Republican—to come OUT after an e-mail campaign launched by San Francisco activist Michael Petrelis and others protests his support of the Defense of Marriage Act (see **9/20/1996**).

In Harare, Zimbabwe, gay and lesbian organizations succeed in opening a booth at AFRICA's largest annual human rights book fair, thanks to a favorable court ruling obtained after being barred from last year's fair (see **8/1/1995**). Since the Attorney General of Zimbabwe has appealed the decision to the country's Supreme Court, participants are careful to restrict their display to flowers, but they attract larger crowds than any of the other 300 booths at the fair.

September 13, 1996

In the U.S. Congress, a bill that would ban employment discrimination against lesbians and gay men is defeated by one vote.

September 15, 1996

The European Parliament approves a resolution calling for an end to "all discrimination and/or inequality of treatment concerning homosexuals" in every country of the European Union.

September 20, 1996

President Bill Clinton signs the Defense of Marriage Act, which bars same-sex partners from receiving federal spousal benefits MARRIAGE (see **4/12/1994**).

In Saudi Arabia (see ARAB WORLD), 24 Filipino workers receive the first 50 lashes of their 200-lash sentence for alleged "homosexual behavior." Despite protests from AMNESTY INTERNATIONAL, the government goes ahead with the sentence and later deports the workers.

October 1996

In Washington, D.C., 1.2 million people view THE NAMES PROJECT AIDS Memorial Quilt. Also see **November 27, 1985**; **October 11, 1987**; **October 1992**.

October 1, 1996

In ARGENTINA, Buenos Aires police begin a campaign of raids on gay and lesbian clubs and arrests of CROSS-DRESSING patrons and TRANSSEXUALS in an apparent protest against impending gay and lesbian rights measures. Also see **October 10, 1996**.

October 10, 1996

In ARGENTINA, the city of Buenos Aires enacts legislation banning discrimination based on sexual orientation and repealing laws that allowed police to arrest lesbians and gay men and hold them without charge for 24 hours.

November 1996

San Francisco Mayor Willie Brown signs a bill that requires all companies doing business with the city to offer gay and lesbian employees DOMESTIC PARTNERSHIP benefits.

INDEX

Page numbers in *italics* indicate major discussion.